DOCUMENTS IN INTERNATIONAL ENVIRONMENTAL LAW

Documents in International Environmental Law, second edition, is the companion volume to the second edition of Philippe Sands' *Principles of International Environmental Law*. It comprises a representative selection of international environmental treaties and documents which are essential for anyone interested in international law in the field of environmental protection. This edition represents an up-to-date collection of the most important documents and aims to make the text and the key information on the legal status of the various acts, including its parties where a treaty is concerned, easily accessible to students, academics and practitioners. Each document is introduced with a short Editorial Note, summarising the main provisions of the instrument and places it in its wider context. Editorial notes are followed by information on the date of adoption/signature of the document, its entry into force and a list of the parties (if a treaty).

PHILIPPE SANDS QC is Professor of Laws and Director of the Centre for International Courts and Tribunals at University College London, and a barrister at Matrix Chambers, Gray's Inn. He was co-founder of FIELD (Foundation for International Environmental Law and Development), and as Legal Director established its programmes on Climate Change and Sustainable Development.

PAOLO GALIZZI is Lecturer in Environmental Law at Imperial College London. He is also a Fellow in International and European Environmental Law at the British Institute of International and Comparative Law, London. He is an Associate Editor of the *Yearbook of International Environmental Law* and has published extensively on international and European environmental law.

DOCUMENTS IN INTERNATIONAL ENVIRONMENTAL LAW

PHILIPPE SANDS AND PAOLO GALIZZI

CAMBRIDGE
UNIVERSITY PRESS

PUBLISHED BY THE PRESS SYNDICATE OF THE UNIVERSITY OF CAMBRIDGE
The Pitt Building, Trumpington Street, Cambridge, United Kingdom

CAMBRIDGE UNIVERSITY PRESS
The Edinburgh Building, Cambridge, CB2 2RU, UK
40 West 20th Street, New York, NY 10011–4211, USA
477 Williamstown Road, Port Melbourne, VIC 3207, Australia
Ruiz de Alarcón 13, 28014 Madrid, Spain
Dock House, The Waterfront, Cape Town 8001, South Africa

http://www.cambridge.org

First edition first published by Manchester University Press 1994
Second edition first published by Cambridge University Press 2004

Printed in the United Kingdom at the University Press, Cambridge

Typeface Minion 10/12 pt.   *System* LaTeX 2_ε [TB]

A catalogue record for this book is available from the British Library

Library of Congress Cataloguing in Publication data
Documents in international environmental law / [edited by] Philippe Sands and
Paolo Galizzi. – 2nd ed.
p.   cm.
Includes bibliographical references and index.
ISBN 0 521 83266 7 (hc) – ISBN 0 521 54030 5 (pb)
1. Environmental law, International – Sources.   I. Sands, Philippe, 1960–   II. Galizzi, Paolo.
K3583.D63   2004
344.04′6 – dc22   2003061117

ISBN 0 521 83266 7 hardback
ISBN 0 521 54030 5 paperback

The publisher has used its best endeavours to ensure that the URLs for external websites referred
to in this book are correct and active at the time of going to press. However, the publisher has no
responsibility for the websites and can make no guarantee that a site will remain live or that the
content is or will remain appropriate.

To all our students
PG and PS

CONTENTS

Preface   *page* xv

PART I   **General instruments**

1   Stockholm Declaration of the United Nations Conference
    on the Human Environment, 16 June 1972   3

2   UN General Assembly Resolution 37/7 on a World
    Charter for Nature, 28 October 1982   11

3   Rio Declaration on Environment and Development,
    16 June 1992   17

4   Draft Articles on Prevention of Transboundary Harm
    from Hazardous Activities, 2001   24

PART II   **Atmosphere**

5   Convention on Long-Range Transboundary Air Pollution,
    13 November 1979   33

5A Protocol to the 1979 Convention on Long-Range
    Transboundary Air Pollution on Further Reduction of
    Sulphur Emissions, 14 June 1994   44

5B Non-Compliance Procedure   59

6   Convention for the Protection of the Ozone Layer,
    22 March 1985   63

6A Montreal Protocol on Substances that Deplete the Ozone
    Layer, 16 September 1987   82

6B Non-Compliance Procedure   125

7   United Nations Framework Convention on Climate
    Change, 9 May 1992   128

7A   Kyoto Protocol to the United Nations Framework
      Convention on Climate Change, 11 December
      1997   153

7B   Marrakech Accords (extracts)   179
      (i)   Guidelines for the Implementation of Article 6 of
             the Kyoto Protocol   181
      (ii)   Modalities and Procedures for a Clean Development
             Mechanism   193
      (iii) Modalities, Rules and Guidelines for Emissions Trading
             under Article 17 of the Kyoto Protocol   217
      (iv)   Procedures and Mechanisms Relating to Compliance
             under the Kyoto Protocol   220

PART IIIA   **Oceans: global**

8   London Convention on the Prevention of Marine
      Pollution by Dumping of Wastes and Other Matter,
      29 December 1972   237

8A   Protocol to the Convention on the Prevention of Marine
      Pollution by Dumping of Wastes and Other Matter,
      7 November 1996   252

9   International Convention for the Prevention of Pollution
      from Ships, 2 November 1973   275

9A   Protocol of 1978 Relating to the International Convention
      for the Prevention of Pollution from Ships 1973,
      17 February 1978   289

10   United Nations Convention on the Law of the Sea,
      10 December 1982 (extracts)   294

11   Agreement for the Implementation of the Provisions
      of UNCLOS Relating to the Conservation and
      Management of Straddling Fish Stocks and Highly
      Migratory Fish Stocks, 4 December 1995   336

PART IIIB   **Oceans: regional**

12   Convention for the Protection of the Marine Environment
      and the Coastal Region of the Mediterranean, 16 February
      1976, as revised in Barcelona, 10 June 1995   375

12A   Protocol for the Prevention and Elimination of Pollution
      of the Mediterranean Sea by Dumping from Ships and
      Aircraft or Incineration at Sea, 16 February 1976, as
      revised on 10 June 1995   394

12B Protocol Concerning Co-operation in Preventing
Pollution from Ships and, in Cases of Emergency,
Combating Pollution of the Mediterranean Sea,
25 January 2002   403

12C Protocol for the Protection of the Mediterranean Sea
against Pollution from Land-Based Sources and Activities,
17 May 1980, as amended on 7 March 1996   417

12D Protocol Concerning Specially Protected Areas
and Biological Diversity in the Mediterranean,
10 June 1995, and including Annexes adopted on
24 November 1996   434

12E Protocol for the Protection of the Mediterranean Sea
against Pollution Resulting from Exploration and
Exploitation of the Continental Shelf and the Seabed and
its Subsoil, 14 October 1994   459

12F Protocol on the Prevention of Pollution of the
Mediterranean Sea by Transboundary Movements
of Hazardous Wastes and their Disposal,
1 October 1996   486

13 Convention for the Protection of the Marine Environment
of the North-East Atlantic, 22 September 1992   505

PART IV   **Freshwater resources**

14 Convention on the Protection and Use of Transboundary
Watercourses and International Lakes, 17 March
1992   539

14A Protocol on Water and Health to the 1992 Convention on
the Protection and Use of Transboundary Watercourses
and International Lakes, 17 June 1999   558

15 United Nations Convention on the Law of the
Non-Navigational Uses of International Watercourses,
21 May 1997   579

PART V   **Biodiversity**

16 International Convention for the Regulation of Whaling,
2 December 1946   601

17 Convention on Wetlands of International Importance
Especially as Waterfowl Habitat, 2 February 1971   636

18   Convention Concerning the Protection of the World
      Cultural and Natural Heritage, 16 November
      1972   644

19   Convention on International Trade in Endangered Species
      of Wild Fauna and Flora, 3 March 1973   661

20   Convention on the Conservation of Migratory Species of
      Wild Animals, 23 June 1979   681

21   Convention on Biological Diversity, 5 June 1992   696

21A   Cartagena Protocol on Biosafety to the Convention on
      Biological Diversity, 29 January 2000   725

22   Non-Legally Binding Authoritative Statement of
      Principles for a Global Consensus on the Management,
      Conservation and Sustainable Development of All Types
      of Forests, 13 June 1992   751

23   United Nations Convention to Combat Desertification in
      Countries Experiencing Serious Drought and/or
      Desertification, Particularly in Africa, 17 June
      1994   759

PART VIA   **Hazardous substances and activities: nuclear**

24   Treaty Banning Nuclear Weapon Tests in the Atmosphere,
      in Outer Space and Under Water, 5 August 1963   793

25   Convention on Nuclear Safety, 20 September
      1994   797

PART VIB   **Hazardous substances and activities: pesticides**

26   Convention on the Prior Informed Consent Procedure for
      Certain Hazardous Chemicals and Pesticides in
      International Trade, 10 September 1998   813

27   Convention on Persistent Organic Pollutants,
      22 May 2001   838

PART VIC   **Hazardous substances and activities: waste**

28   Convention on the Control of Transboundary Movements
      of Hazardous Wastes and Their Disposal, 22 March
      1989   879

28A Decision III/1 of the Conference of the Parties (Amendment to the Basel Convention), 22 September 1995 (the 'Basel Ban') 915

28B Protocol on Liability and Compensation for Damage Resulting from Transboundary Movements of Hazardous Wastes and Their Disposal, 10 December 1999 918

29 Convention on the Ban of the Import into Africa and the Control of Transboundary Movement and Management of Hazardous Wastes within Africa, 29 January 1991 936

30 Code of Practice on the International Transboundary Movement of Radioactive Waste, 21 September 1990 968

PART VII **Human rights and the environment**

Introduction 975

31 European Convention on Human Rights and Fundamental Freedoms, 4 November 1950 (extract) 977

32 African Charter on Human and Peoples' Rights, 27 June 1981 (extract) 978

33 Additional Protocol to the American Convention on Human Rights in the Area of Economic, Social and Cultural Rights (the 'Protocol of San Salvador'), 17 November 1988 (extract) 979

PART VIII **War and the environment**

34 Convention on the Prohibition of Military or Any Other Hostile Use of Environmental Modification Techniques, 18 May 1977 983

35 Protocol I Additional to the Geneva Convention of 12 August 1949, and Relating to the Protection of Victims of International Armed Conflicts, 8 June 1977 (extracts) 989

36 United Nations Security Council Resolution 687, 3 April 1991 (extract) 998

PART IX   **Trade and the environment**

37   Agreement Establishing the World Trade Organization,
      15 April 1994 (extracts)   1001

37A   General Agreement on Tariffs and Trade, 1947/1994
      (extracts)   1006

37B   Agreement on Technical Barriers to Trade
      (extracts)   1012

37C   Agreement on the Application of Sanitary and
      Phythosanitary Measures (extracts)   1015

37D   Agreement on Trade Related Aspects of Intellectual
      Property Rights (extracts)   1020

PART X   **Environmental impact assessment and access
           to information**

38   Convention on Environmental Impact Assessment in a
      Transboundary Context, 25 February 1991   1023

38A   Protocol on Strategic Environmental Assessment,
      21 May 2003   1042

39   Convention on the Transboundary Effects of Industrial
      Accidents, 17 March 1992   1063

40   World Bank Operational Policy 4.01 on Environmental
      Assessment, January 1999   1097

41   Convention on Access to Information, Public
      Participation in Decision-Making and Access to Justice in
      Environmental Matters, 25 June 1998   1109

41A   Compliance Committee and Procedures for the Review
      of Compliance   1136

41B   Protocol on Pollutant Release and Transfer Registers,
      21 May 2003   1143

PART XI   **Liability for environmental damage and breaches of
           environmental obligations**

42   International Convention on Civil Liability for Oil
      Pollution Damage, 27 November 1992   1181

43 International Convention on the Establishment of an
International Fund for Compensation for Oil Pollution
Damage, 27 November 1992   1198

44 Articles on the Responsibility of States for Internationally
Wrongful Acts, adopted by the International Law
Commission at its fifty-third session, 2001   1224

45 Convention on Civil Liability for Damage Resulting
from Activities Dangerous to the Environment,
21 June 1993   1240

46 International Convention on Liability and Compensation
for Damage in Connection with the Carriage of Hazardous
and Noxious Substances by Sea, 3 May 1996   1263

PART XII   **The Antarctic**

47 Antarctic Treaty, 1 December 1959   1305

47A Protocol on Environmental Protection to the Antarctic
Treaty, 4 October 1991   1313

48 Convention for the Conservation of Antarctic Seals,
1 June 1972   1357

49 Convention on the Conservation of Antarctic Marine
Living Resources, 20 May 1980   1365

PREFACE

Documents in International Environmental Law is the companion volume to the second edition of Philippe Sands' *Principles of International Environmental Law*. It comprises a representative (and non-exhaustive) selection of international environmental treaties and documents which are essential for anyone interested in international law in the field of environmental protection.

This volume builds on the two volumes "*Documents in international law*" published by Manchester University Press in 1994 and edited by Philippe Sands, Richard Tarasofsky and Mary Weiss. Since 1994 several important new treaties have been adopted, and several existing treaties have been amended. This volume represents an up-to-date collection of the most important such documents and like its predecessor aims to make easily accessible to students, academics and practitioners the text and the key information on the legal status of the various acts, including its parties, where a treaty is concerned. At a time when almost all the documents here published are accessible on the web, we nevertheless consider that advantages may be obtained in reproducing them in a single volume. Books can follow us around. Over time we can highlight key provisions, insert notes, and compare texts wherever we are and as much as we like.

Each document is presented according to the same format. It is introduced with a short Editorial Note, which summarises the main provisions of the instrument and places it in its wider context. Editorial notes are followed by information on the date of adoption/signature of the document, its entry into force and a list of the parties (if a treaty). The status of treaties is generally as of 1 June 2003. Declarations and reservations to the treaties have not been reproduced. For up-to-date information on the status and other information for each document, readers are advised to consult the relevant website (usually indicated) or the depositary.[1]

Most of the documents have been reproduced in their entirety. In some cases, however, we have only included extracts relating to environmental matters (e.g.

---

[1] The lists of Parties are reproduced as provided by the depositaries. Some of the tables therefore refer to certain States which may no longer exist or which have modified their legal status and denomination. The reader will therefore need to obtain information directly from the depositary as to the legal status of the treaty for such countries and for any successor State.

the 1977 Additional Protocol I to the Geneva Conventions of 12 August 1949),
or we have omitted annexes or appendices which include detailed technical arrangements of less interest to the general reader or which do not relate expressly
to environmental matters (and which are easily available on the web).

   This collection does not purport to be comprehensive. It comprises some
70 treaties and other documents, which have been chosen by reference to academic and practical requirements. The instruments included regulate each of
the main environmental media and sector, and they represent a broad spec-
trum of approaches taken in developing principles and rules of international
environmental law. Space limitations did not allow us to include selected judicial decisions, which can however be found in other publications.[2] For these
reasons also we excluded certain other documents which we originally planned
to include. The success of this volume may well lead to an expansion of the
documents included in a future edition.

Paolo Galizzi
Imperial College London

Philippe Sands
Faculty of Laws
University College London

1 June 2003

---

[2] For example, "*International Environmental Law Reports*", edited by Cairo Robb and published by CUP.

PART I

General instruments

Stockholm Declaration of the United Nations Conference on the Human Environment, 16 June 1972

Editorial note

The UN Conference on the Human Environment was held at Stockholm from 5 to 16 June 1972. It was convened pursuant to UN General Assembly Resolution 2398 (XXIII) of 3 December 1968 (*Ybk UN* 1968, pp. 476–7), on a proposal from Sweden. Delegates from 113 States attended the Conference, representing most of the UN membership with the exception of the USSR, Cuba and a number of other socialist countries who refused to attend on the ground that the criteria for invitations to the Conference had effectively excluded certain States, notably the German Democratic Republic.

The Conference adopted a Declaration of Principles for the Preservation and Enhancement of the Human Environment and an Action Plan consisting of 109 Recommendations for environmental action at the international level (Report of the UN Conference on the Human Environment, *UN Doc.* A/CONF.48/14 at 2–65 and Corr. 1 (1972)).

The Declaration of Principles is based on a draft Declaration prepared by the Preparatory Committee for the Conference (*UN Doc.* A/CONF.48/PC.17). It reflects the compromise that was eventually reached between, on the one hand, those delegates who believed it should serve principally to stimulate public awareness of, and concern over, environmental issues and, on the other hand, those delegates who insisted that it should provide specific guidelines to future governmental and intergovernmental action.

In the context of transfrontier pollution the most significant of the 26 Principles are Principles 21 and 22. Principle 21 affirms the responsibility of States to ensure that activities within their jurisdiction do not cause damage in another State or beyond national jurisdiction, such as in outer space or on the high seas. This responsibility is said to extend also to activities under a State's 'control', such as those carried out by its nationals or by or on ships registered in its territory.

Principle 22 requires States to co-operate in developing international environmental law. It is a substantially weakened version of an earlier proposal to include a provision requiring States to pay compensation for all environmental damage caused by activities carried on within their territory.

The draft Declaration prepared by the Preparatory Committee also contained a third relevant principle, 'Principle 20'. This provided:

> Relevant information must be supplied by States on activities or developments within their jurisdiction or under their control whenever they believe, or have reason to believe, that such information is needed to avoid the risk of significant adverse effects on the environment in areas beyond their national jurisdiction (*UN Doc.* A/CONF.48/4 Annex para. 20 at 4 (1972)).

This Principle was not agreed at the Conference following the objections of a number of developing States, which maintained that the obligation to consult might be abused by developed States to impede development projects.

The Report of the Conference was considered by the UN General Assembly at its 27th session. On 15 December 1972 eleven resolutions concerning the environment were passed. Resolution 2994 (XXVII) (*Ybk UN* 1972, p. 330) notes with satisfaction the Conference Report. Resolution 2995 (XXVII) (*Ybk UN* 1972, pp. 330–1) was a partial revival of the Preparatory Committee's Principle 20. It provides that technical information on proposed works should be supplied to other States where there is a risk of significant transboundary environmental harm, but that this information should be received in good faith and not used to delay or impede development of natural resources. Resolution 2996 (XXVII) (*Ybk UN* 1972, p. 331) affirms that Resolution 2995 is not to be construed as limiting Principles 21 and 22 of the Stockholm Declaration. Resolutions 2997 to 3004 (XXVII) (*Ybk UN* 1972, pp. 331–7) concern institutional and financial arrangements for international environmental co-operation, and in particular the establishment of the UN Environmental Programme, to be based at Nairobi, Kenya.

Stockholm Declaration of the United Nations Conference on the Human Environment

The United Nations Conference on the Human Environment,
   Having met at Stockholm from 5 to 16 June 1972,
   Having considered the need for a common outlook and for common principles to inspire and guide the peoples of the world in the preservation and enhancement of the human environment,

I

Proclaims that:
   1. Man is both creature and moulder of his environment, which gives him physical sustenance and affords him the opportunity for intellectual, moral, social and spiritual growth. In the long and tortuous evolution of the human

race on this planet a stage has been reached when, through the rapid accelera-
tion of science and technology, man has acquired the power to transform his
environment in countless ways and on an unprecedented scale. Both aspects of
man's environment, the natural and the man-made, are essential to his well-
being and to the enjoyment of basic human rights – even the right to life itself.

2. The protection and improvement of the human environment is a major issue, which affects the well-being of peoples and economic development
throughout the world; it is the urgent desire of the peoples of the whole world
and the duty of all Governments.

3. Man has constantly to sum up experience and go on discovering, invent-
ing, creating and advancing. In our time, man's capability to transform his
surroundings, if used wisely, can bring to all peoples the benefits of development and the opportunity to enhance the quality of life. Wrongly or heedlessly
applied, the same power can do incalculable harm to human beings and the
human environment. We see around us growing evidence of man-made harm
in many regions of the earth: dangerous levels of pollution in water, air, earth
and living beings; major and undesirable disturbances to the ecological balance
of the biosphere; destruction and depletion of irreplaceable resources; and gross
deficiencies, harmful to the physical, mental and social health of man, in the
man-made environment, particularly in the living and working environment.

4. In the developing countries most of the environmental problems are
caused by under-development. Millions continue to live far below the minimum levels required for a decent human existence, deprived of adequate
food and clothing, shelter and education, health and sanitation. Therefore,
the developing countries must direct their efforts to development, bearing in
mind their priorities and the need to safeguard and improve the environment.
For the same purpose, the industrialized countries should make efforts to reduce
the gap between themselves and the developing countries. In the industrialized
countries, environmental problems are generally related to industrialization
and technological development.

5. The natural growth of population continuously presents problems for the
preservation of the environment, and adequate policies and measures should
be adopted, as appropriate, to face these problems. Of all things in the world,
people are the most precious. It is the people that propel social progress, create
social wealth, develop science and technology and, through their hard work,
continuously transform the human environment. Along with social progress
and the advance of production, science and technology, the capability of man
to improve the environment increases with each passing day.

6. A point has been reached in history when we must shape our actions
throughout the world with a more prudent care for their environmental consequences. Through ignorance or indifference we can do massive and irreversible
harm to the earthly environment on which our life and well being depend. Conversely, through fuller knowledge and wiser action, we can achieve for ourselves

and our posterity a better life in an environment more in keeping with human needs and hopes. There are broad vistas for the enhancement of environmental quality and the creation of a good life. What is needed is an enthusiastic but calm state of mind and intense but orderly work. For the purpose of attaining freedom in the world of nature, man must use knowledge to build, in collaboration with nature, a better environment. To defend and improve the human environment for present and future generations has become an imperative goal for mankind-a goal to be pursued together with, and in harmony with, the established and fundamental goals of peace and of worldwide economic and social development.

7. To achieve this environmental goal will demand the acceptance of responsibility by citizens and communities and by enterprises and institutions at every level, all sharing equitably in common efforts. Individuals in all walks of life as well as organizations in many fields, by their values and the sum of their actions, will shape the world environment of the future. Local and national governments will bear the greatest burden for large-scale environmental policy and action within their jurisdictions. International cooperation is also needed in order to raise resources to support the developing countries in carrying out their responsibilities in this field. A growing class of environmental problems, because they are regional or global in extent or because they affect the common international realm, will require extensive cooperation among nations and action by international organizations in the common interest. The Conference calls upon Governments and peoples to exert common efforts for the preservation and improvement of the human environment, for the benefit of all the people and for their posterity.

II
Principles

States the common conviction that:

Principle 1

Man has the fundamental right to freedom, equality and adequate conditions of life, in an environment of a quality that permits a life of dignity and well-being, and he bears a solemn responsibility to protect and improve the environment for present and future generations. In this respect, policies promoting or perpetuating apartheid, racial segregation, discrimination, colonial and other forms of oppression and foreign domination stand condemned and must be eliminated.

Principle 2

The natural resources of the earth, including the air, water, land, flora and fauna and especially representative samples of natural ecosystems, must be safeguarded for the benefit of present and future generations through careful planning or management, as appropriate.

Principle 3

The capacity of the earth to produce vital renewable resources must be maintained and, wherever practicable, restored or improved.

Principle 4

Man has a special responsibility to safeguard and wisely manage the heritage of wildlife and its habitat, which are now gravely imperilled by a combination of adverse factors. Nature conservation, including wildlife, must therefore receive importance in planning for economic development.

Principle 5

The non-renewable resources of the earth must be employed in such a way as to guard against the danger of their future exhaustion and to ensure that benefits from such employment are shared by all mankind.

Principle 6

The discharge of toxic substances or of other substances and the release of heat, in such quantities or concentrations as to exceed the capacity of the environment to render them harmless, must be halted in order to ensure that serious or irreversible damage is not inflicted upon ecosystems. The just struggle of the peoples of ill countries against pollution should be supported.

Principle 7

States shall take all possible steps to prevent pollution of the seas by substances that are liable to create hazards to human health, to harm living resources and marine life, to damage amenities or to interfere with other legitimate uses of the sea.

Principle 8

Economic and social development is essential for ensuring a favorable living and working environment for man and for creating conditions on earth that are necessary for the improvement of the quality of life.

Principle 9

Environmental deficiencies generated by the conditions of underdevelopment and natural disasters pose grave problems and can best be remedied by accelerated development through the transfer of substantial quantities of financial and technological assistance as a supplement to the domestic effort of the developing countries and such timely assistance as may be required.

Principle 10

For the developing countries, stability of prices and adequate earnings for primary commodities and raw materials are essential to environmental management, since economic factors as well as ecological processes must be taken into account.

Principle 11

The environmental policies of all States should enhance and not adversely affect the present or future development potential of developing countries, nor should they hamper the attainment of better living conditions for all, and appropriate steps should be taken by States and international organizations with a view to reaching agreement on meeting the possible national and international economic consequences resulting from the application of environmental measures.

Principle 12

Resources should be made available to preserve and improve the environment, taking into account the circumstances and particular requirements of developing countries and any costs which may emanate from their incorporating environmental safeguards into their development planning and the need for making available to them, upon their request, additional international technical and financial assistance for this purpose.

Principle 13

In order to achieve a more rational management of resources and thus to improve the environment, States should adopt an integrated and coordinated approach to their development planning so as to ensure that development is compatible with the need to protect and improve environment for the benefit of their population.

Principle 14

Rational planning constitutes an essential tool for reconciling any conflict between the needs of development and the need to protect and improve the environment.

Principle 15

Planning must be applied to human settlements and urbanization with a view to avoiding adverse effects on the environment and obtaining maximum social, economic and environmental benefits for all. In this respect projects which are designed for colonialist and racist domination must be abandoned.

Principle 16

Demographic policies which are without prejudice to basic human rights and which are deemed appropriate by Governments concerned should be applied in those regions where the rate of population growth or excessive population concentrations are likely to have adverse effects on the environment or development, or where low population density may prevent improvement of the human environment and impede development.

Principle 17

Appropriate national institutions must be entrusted with the task of planning, managing or controlling the environmental resources of States with a view to enhancing environmental quality.

Principle 18

Science and technology, as part of their contribution to economic and social development, must be applied to the identification, avoidance and control of environmental risks and the solution of environmental problems and for the common good of mankind.

Principle 19

Education in environmental matters, for the younger generation as well as adults, giving due consideration to the underprivileged, is essential in order to broaden the basis for an enlightened opinion and responsible conduct by individuals, enterprises and communities in protecting and improving the environment in its full human dimension. It is also essential that mass media of communications avoid contributing to the deterioration of the environment, but, on the contrary, disseminate information of an educational nature on the need to protect and improve the environment in order to enable man to develop in every respect.

Principle 20

Scientific research and development in the context of environmental problems, both national and multinational, must be promoted in all countries, especially the developing countries. In this connection, the free flow of up-to-date scientific information and transfer of experience must be supported and assisted, to facilitate the solution of environmental problems; environmental technologies should be made available to developing countries on terms which would encourage their wide dissemination without constituting an economic burden on the developing countries.

Principle 21

States have, in accordance with the Charter of the United Nations and the principles of international law, the sovereign right to exploit their own resources

pursuant to their own environmental policies, and the responsibility to ensure that activities within their jurisdiction or control do not cause damage
to the environment of other States or of areas beyond the limits of national
jurisdiction.

Principle 22

States shall cooperate to develop further the international law regarding liability
and compensation for the victims of pollution and other environmental damage
caused by activities within the jurisdiction or control of such States to areas
beyond their jurisdiction.

Principle 23

Without prejudice to such criteria as may be agreed upon by the international
community, or to standards which will have to be determined nationally, it
will be essential in all cases to consider the systems of values prevailing in each
country, and the extent of the applicability of standards which are valid for the
most advanced countries but which may be inappropriate and of unwarranted
social cost for the developing countries.

Principle 24

International matters concerning the protection and improvement of the environment should be handled in a cooperative spirit by all countries, big or
small, on an equal footing. Co-operation through multilateral or bilateral
arrangements or other appropriate means is essential to effectively control,
prevent, reduce and eliminate adverse environmental effects resulting from
activities conducted in all spheres, in such a way that due account is taken of
the sovereignty and interests of all States.

Principle 25

States shall ensure that international organizations play a coordinated, efficient
and dynamic role for the protection and improvement of the environment.

Principle 26

Man and his environment must be spared the effects of nuclear weapons and
all other means of mass destruction. States must strive to reach prompt agreement, in the relevant international organs, on the elimination and complete
destruction of such weapons.

UN General Assembly Resolution 37/7 on a World Charter for Nature, 28 October 1982

Editorial Note

The World Charter for Nature (adopted by a vote of 111 in favour, 1 against (USA) and 18 abstentions) seeks to have its guiding principles given effect through national legislation and international practice (Articles 14 and 22). These principles include: respect for nature (Article 1); safeguarding of habitats necessary to maintain sufficient population levels for the survival of all life forms (Article 2); protection of unique areas, representative samples of all ecosystems, and of habitats of rare or endangered species (Article 3); and the utilisation of man's environment so as to maintain 'optimal sustainable productivity' while maintaining the integrity of all ecosystems and species (Article 4).

In order to realise these principles, the Charter sets out several specific require-ments, including, taking into account the effects of economic development on natural resources and the environment (Article 6–9); not wasting natural resources (Article 10); controlling activities which risk harming nature by using 'best available technologies', avoiding high risk activity, and restoring degraded areas (Article 11); and avoiding discharging pollutants (Article 12). To further implement the Charter's objectives, States are also required to take the following action: disseminate information on nature (Article 15); encourage public consultation and participation in all planning decisions (Article 16); provide funding for the conservation of nature (Article 17); and make available remedies for harm to a person's environment (Article 23).

Website: www.un.org/documents/ga/res/37/a37r007.htm

World Charter for Nature

The General Assembly,

   Having considered the report of the Secretary-General on the revised draft World Charter for Nature,

   Recalling that, in its resolution 35/7 of 30 October 1980, it expressed its conviction that the benefits which could be obtained from nature depended on the maintenance of natural processes and on the diversity of life forms and that those benefits were jeopardized by the excessive exploitation and the destruction of natural habitats,

Further recalling that, in the same resolution, it recognized the need for appropriate measures at the national and international levels to protect nature and promote international co-operation in that field,

Recalling that, in its resolution 36/6 of 27 October 1981, it again expressed its awareness of the crucial importance attached by the international community to the promotion and development of co-operation aimed at protecting and safeguarding the balance and quality of nature and invited the Secretary-General to transmit to Member States the text of the revised version of the draft World Charter for Nature contained in the report of the *Ad Hoc* Group of Experts on the draft World Charter for Nature, as well as any further observations by States, with a view to appropriate consideration by the General Assembly at its thirty-seventh session,

Conscious of the spirit and terms of its resolutions 35/7 and 36/6, in which it solemnly invited Member States, in the exercise of their permanent sovereignty over their natural resources, to conduct their activities in recognition of the supreme importance of protecting natural systems, maintaining the balance and quality of nature and conserving natural resources, in the interests of present and future generations,

Having considered the supplementary report of the Secretary-General,

Expressing its gratitude to the *Ad Hoc* Group of Experts which, through its work, has assembled the necessary elements for the General Assembly to be able to complete the consideration of and adopt the revised draft World Charter for Nature at its thirty-seventh session, as it had previously recommended,

Adopts and solemnly proclaims the World Charter for Nature contained in the annex to the present resolution.

Annex
*World Charter for Nature**

The General Assembly,

Reaffirming the fundamental purposes of the United Nations, in particular the maintenance of international peace and security, the development of friendly relations among nations and the achievement of international co-operation in solving international problems of an economic, social, cultural, technical, intellectual or humanitarian character,

Aware that:

(a) Mankind is a part of nature, and life depends on the uninterrupted functioning of natural systems which ensure the supply of energy and nutrients,

(b) Civilization is rooted in nature, which has shaped human culture and influenced all artistic and scientific achievement, and living in harmony with

* Footnotes omitted.

nature gives man the best opportunities for the development of his creativity, and for rest and recreation,

Convinced that:

(a) Every form of life is unique, warranting respect regardless of its worth to
    man, and, to accord other organisms such recognition, man must be guided
    by a moral code of action,
(b) Man can alter nature and exhaust natural resources by his action or its con-
    sequences and, therefore, must fully recognize the urgency of maintaining
    the stability and quality of nature and of conserving natural resources.

Persuaded that:

(a) Lasting benefits from nature depend upon the maintenance of essential
    ecological processes and life support systems, and upon the diversity of life
    forms, which are jeopardized through excessive exploitation and habitat
    destruction by man,
(b) The degradation of natural systems owing to excessive consumption and
    misuse of natural resources, as well as to failure to establish an appropriate
    economic order among peoples and among States, leads to the breakdown
    of the economic, social and political framework of civilization,
(c) Competition for scarce resources creates conflicts, whereas the conserva-
    tion of nature and natural resources contributes to justice and the main-
    tenance of peace and cannot be achieved until mankind learns to live in
    peace and to forsake war and armaments,

Reaffirming that man must acquire the knowledge to maintain and enhance
his ability to use natural resources in a manner which ensures the preservation
of the species and ecosystems for the benefit of present and future generations,

Firmly convinced of the need for appropriate measures, at the national and
international, individual and collective, and private and public levels, to protect
nature and promote international co-operation in this field,

Adopts, to these ends, the present World Charter for Nature, which proclaims
the following principles of conservation by which all human conduct affecting
nature is to be guided and judged.

I. General principles

1. Nature shall be respected and its essential processes shall not be impaired.

2. The genetic viability on the earth shall not be compromised; the population
levels of all life forms, wild and domesticated, must be at least sufficient for
their survival, and to this end necessary habitats shall be safeguarded.

3. All areas of the earth, both land and sea, shall be subject to these principles of conservation; special protection shall be given to unique areas, to

representative samples of all the different types of ecosystems and to the habi-tats of rare or endangered species.

4. Ecosystems and organisms, as well as the land, marine and atmospheric resources that are utilized by man, shall be managed to achieve and maintain optimum sustainable productivity, but not in such a way as to endanger the integrity of those other ecosystems or species with which they coexist.

5. Nature shall be secured against degradation caused by warfare or other hostile activities.

II. Functions

6. In the decision-making process it shall be recognized that man's needs can be met only by ensuring the proper functioning of natural systems and by respecting the principles set forth in the present Charter.

7. In the planning and implementation of social and economic development activities, due account shall be taken of the fact that the conservation of nature is an integral part of those activities.

8. In formulating long-term plans for economic development, population growth and the improvement of standards of living, due account shall be taken of the long-term capacity of natural systems to ensure the subsistence and settlement of the populations concerned, recognizing that this capacity may be enhanced through science and technology.

9. The allocation of areas of the earth to various uses shall be planned, and due account shall be taken of the physical constraints, the biological productivity and diversity and the natural beauty of the areas concerned.

10. Natural resources shall not be wasted, but used with a restraint appro-priate to the principles set forth in the present Charter, in accordance with the following rules:

(a) Living resources shall not be utilized in excess of their natural capacity for regeneration;
(b) The productivity of soils shall be maintained or enhanced through mea-sures which safeguard their long-term fertility and the process of organic decomposition, and prevent erosion and all other forms of degradation;
(c) Resources, including water, which are not consumed as they are used shall be reused or recycled;
(d) Non-renewable resources which are consumed as they are used shall be exploited with restraint, taking into account their abundance, the rational possibilities of converting them for consumption, and the compatibility of their exploitation with the functioning of natural systems.

11. Activities which might have an impact on nature shall be controlled, and the best available technologies that minimize significant risks to nature or other adverse effects shall be used; in particular:

(a) Activities which are likely to cause irreversible damage to nature shall be avoided;

(b) Activities which are likely to pose a significant risk to nature shall be pre-ceded by an exhaustive examination; their proponents shall demonstrate that expected benefits outweigh potential damage to nature, and where potential adverse effects are not fully understood, the activities should not proceed;

(c) Activities which may disturb nature shall be preceded by assessment of their consequences, and environmental impact studies of development projects shall be conducted sufficiently in advance, and if they are to be undertaken, such activities shall be planned and carried out so as to minimize potential adverse effects;

(d) Agriculture, grazing, forestry and fisheries practices shall be adapted to the natural characteristics and constraints of given areas;

(e) Areas degraded by human activities shall be rehabilitated for purposes in accord with their natural potential and compatible with the well-being of affected populations.

12. Discharge of pollutants into natural systems shall be avoided and:

(a) Where this is not feasible, such pollutants shall be treated at the source, using the best practicable means available;

(b) Special precautions shall be taken to prevent discharge of radioactive or toxic wastes.

13. Measures intended to prevent, control or limit natural disasters, infesta-tions and diseases shall be specifically directed to the causes of these scourges and shall avoid adverse side-effects on nature.

III. Implementation

14. The principles set forth in the present Charter shall be reflected in the law and practice of each State, as well as at the international level.

15. Knowledge of nature shall be broadly disseminated by all possible means, particularly by ecological education as an integral part of general education.

16. All planning shall include, among its essential elements, the formulation of strategies for the conservation of nature, the establishment of inventories of ecosystems and assessments of the effects on nature of proposed policies and activities; all of these elements shall be disclosed to the public by appropriate means in time to permit effective consultation and participation.

17. Funds, programmes and administrative structures necessary to achieve the objective of the conservation of nature shall be provided.

18. Constant efforts shall be made to increase knowledge of nature by scientific research and to disseminate such knowledge unimpeded by restrictions of any kind.

19. The status of natural processes, ecosystems and species shall be closely monitored to enable early detection of degradation or threat, ensure timely intervention and facilitate the evaluation of conservation policies and methods.

20. Military activities damaging to nature shall be avoided.

21. States and, to the extent they are able, other public authorities, international organizations, individuals, groups and corporations shall:

(a) Co-operate in the task of conserving nature through common activities and other relevant actions, including information exchange and consultations;

(b) Establish standards for products and manufacturing processes that may have adverse effects on nature, as well as agreed methodologies for assessing these effects;

(c) Implement the applicable international legal provisions for the conservation of nature and the protection of the environment;

(d) Ensure that activities within their jurisdictions or control do not cause damage to the natural systems located within other States or in the areas beyond the limits of national jurisdiction;

(e) Safeguard and conserve nature in areas beyond national jurisdiction.

22. Taking fully into account the sovereignty of States over their natural resources, each State shall give effect to the provisions of the present Charter through its competent organs and in co-operation with other States.

23. All persons, in accordance with their national legislation, shall have the opportunity to participate, individually or with others, in the formulation of decisions of direct concern to their environment, and shall have access to means of redress when their environment has suffered damage or degradation.

24. Each person has a duty to act in accordance with the provisions of the present Charter; acting individually, in association with others or through participation in the political process, each person shall strive to ensure that the objectives and requirements of the present Charter are met.

Rio Declaration on Environment and Development, 16 June 1992

Editorial note

The Rio Declaration on Environment and Development, adopted at the 1992 UN Conference on Environment and Development (UNCED), is intended to develop the principles adopted in the 1972 Stockholm Declaration.

The Rio Declaration comprises twenty-seven principles which set out the basis upon which states and people are to co-operate and further develop 'international law in the field of sustainable development' (Principle 27).

Although it is non-binding some provisions reflect rules of customary law, others reflect emerging rules, and yet others provide guidance as to future legal developments.

Principle 1 of the Rio Declaration reflects a shift towards an anthropocentric approach to environmental and developmental issues, declaring that human beings are 'at the centre of concerns for sustainable development', and that they are 'entitled to a healthy and productive life in harmony with nature'; this falls short of recognising a right to a clean and healthy environment. The all-important Principle 21 of Stockholm has been transposed into Principle 2 of the Rio Declaration, the only change being the addition of the words 'and developmental' in relation to matters within national sovereignty. Also, Stockholm's Principle 22, which urged the formation of liability rules, has been repeated in slightly amended language in Principle 13 of the Rio Declaration.

The heart of the Rio Declaration is found in Principles 3 and 4, which should be read together to understand the political context in which they were negotiated and the trade-off they represent: a right to development (Principle 3) is tempered by the integration of environmental protection into the development process (Principle 4).

The Rio Declaration recognises a principle of 'common but differentiated responsibility' (Principle 7) noting the different contribution of countries to regional and global environmental degradation. Principle 11 of the Rio Declaration commits all states to enact 'effective environmental legislation', although the standards, objectives and priorities 'should reflect the environmental and developmental context to which they apply'. Principle 11 also recognises that standards applied by some countries 'may be inappropriate and of unwarranted economic and social cost to other countries, in particular developing countries'. The Rio Declaration, like the Stockholm Declaration, recognises and expands upon the relationship between the international economic order and environmental degradation. Recognition is given to the special needs of developing countries, which shall be given priority, although the countries' interests should be addressed by international efforts in matters concerning environment and development (Principle 6). The Declaration encourages an open international economic system where trade restrictions for environmental purposes do not constitute 'a means of arbitrary or unjustifiable discrimination or a disguised restriction on international trade' (Principle 12).

The Declaration establishes a number of procedural requirements, including public participation in environmental decision-making, adequate public access to information, and access to any relevant judicial proceedings (Principle 10). States are also required to develop national and international law in respect of liability and compensation for environmental damage (Principle 13). The Declaration requires States to adopt a 'precautionary approach' towards environmental protection, such that where a risk exists of serious or irreversible damage, lack of full scientific certainty should not postpone 'cost effective' environmental protection measures (Principle 15). Internalisation of environmental costs and economic instruments should be promoted in a manner that takes into account that the polluter should bear the cost of pollution (Principle 16).

As a package the Rio Declaration includes provisions which are more specific than those adopted in the Stockholm Declaration. It provides a framework for the development of environmental law at the national and international level which will serve as an important point of reference to guide decision-making. Its contribution to the development of rules of customary law has become clearer over time, although many of its provisions were already found in treaties and other international acts and reflected in the domestic practice of many states.

Website: www.unep.org/unep/rio.htm

Rio de Janeiro Declaration on Environment and Development

Preamble

The United Nations Conference on Environment and Development,
    Having met at Rio de Janeiro from 3 to 14 June 1992,
    Reaffirming the Declaration of the United Nations Conference on the Human Environment, adopted at Stockholm on 16 June 1972, and seeking to build upon it, with the goal of establishing a new and equitable global partnership through the creation of new levels of cooperation among States, key sectors of societies and people,

Working towards international agreements which respect the interests of all and protect the integrity of the global environmental and developmental system,

Recognizing the integral and interdependent nature of the Earth, our home,

Proclaims that:

Principle 1

Human beings are at the centre of concerns for sustainable development. They are entitled to a healthy and productive life in harmony with nature.

Principle 2

States have, in accordance with the Charter of the United Nations and the principles of international law, the sovereign right to exploit their own resources pursuant to their own environmental and developmental policies, and the responsibility to ensure that activities within their jurisdiction or control do not cause damage to the environment of other States or of areas beyond the limits of national jurisdiction.

Principle 3

The right to development must be fulfilled so as to equitably meet developmental and environmental needs of present and future generations.

Principle 4

In order to achieve sustainable development, environmental protection shall constitute an integral part of the development process and cannot be considered in isolation from it.

Principle 5

All States and all people shall cooperate in the essential task of eradicating poverty as an indispensable requirement for sustainable development, in order to decrease the disparities in standards of living and better meet the needs of the majority of the people of the world.

Principle 6

The special situation and needs of developing countries, particularly the least developed and those most environmentally vulnerable, shall be given special priority. International actions in the field of environment and development should also address the interests and needs of all countries.

Principle 7

States shall cooperate in a spirit of global partnership to conserve, protect and restore the health and integrity of the Earth's ecosystem. In view of the different contributions to global environmental degradation, States have common but differentiated responsibilities. The developed countries acknowledge the responsibility that they bear in the international pursuit to sustainable development in view of the pressures their societies place on the global environment and of the technologies and financial resources they command.

Principle 8

To achieve sustainable development and a higher quality of life for all people, States should reduce and eliminate unsustainable patterns of production and consumption and promote appropriate demographic policies.

Principle 9

States should cooperate to strengthen endogenous capacity-building for sustainable development by improving scientific understanding through exchanges of scientific and technological knowledge, and by enhancing the development, adaptation, diffusion and transfer of technologies, including new and innovative technologies.

Principle 10

Environmental issues are best handled with the participation of all concerned citizens, at the relevant level. At the national level, each individual shall have appropriate access to information concerning the environment that is held by public authorities, including information on hazardous materials and activities in their communities, and the opportunity to participate in decision-making processes. States shall facilitate and encourage public awareness and participation by making information widely available. Effective access to judicial and administrative proceedings, including redress and remedy, shall be provided.

Principle 11

States shall enact effective environmental legislation. Environmental standards, management objectives and priorities should reflect the environmental and development context to which they apply. Standards applied by some countries may be inappropriate and of unwarranted economic and social cost to other countries, in particular developing countries.

Principle 12

States should cooperate to promote a supportive and open international economic system that would lead to economic growth and sustainable development in all countries, to better address the problems of environmental degradation. Trade policy measures for environmental purposes should not constitute a means of arbitrary or unjustifiable discrimination or a disguised restriction on international trade. Unilateral actions to deal with environmental challenges outside the jurisdiction of the importing country should be avoided. Environmental measures addressing transboundary or global environmental problems should, as far as possible, be based on an international consensus.

Principle 13

States shall develop national law regarding liability and compensation for the victims of pollution and other environmental damage. States shall also co-operate in an expeditious and more determined manner to develop further international law regarding liability and compensation for adverse effects of environmental damage caused by activities within their jurisdiction or control to areas beyond their jurisdiction.

Principle 14

States should effectively cooperate to discourage or prevent the relocation and transfer to other States of any activities and substances that cause severe environmental degradation or are found to be harmful to human health.

Principle 15

In order to protect the environment, the precautionary approach shall be widely applied by States according to their capabilities. Where there are threats of serious or irreversible damage, lack of full scientific certainty shall not be used as a reason for postponing cost-effective measures to prevent environmental degradation.

Principle 16

National authorities should endeavour to promote the internalization of environmental costs and the use of economic instruments, taking into account the approach that the polluter should, in principle, bear the cost of pollution, with due regard to the public interest and without distorting international trade and investment.

Principle 17

Environmental impact assessment, as a national instrument, shall be undertaken for proposed activities that are likely to have a significant adverse impact on the environment and are subject to a decision of a competent national authority.

Principle 18

States shall immediately notify other States of any natural disasters or other emergencies that are likely to produce sudden harmful effects on the environment of those States. Every effort shall be made by the international community to help States so afflicted.

Principle 19

States shall provide prior and timely notification and relevant information to potentially affected States on activities that may have a significant adverse transboundary environmental effect and shall consult with those States at an early stage and in good faith.

Principle 20

Women have a vital role in environmental management and development. Their full participation is therefore essential to achieve sustainable development.

Principle 21

The creativity, ideals and courage of the youth of the world should be mobilized to forge a global partnership in order to achieve sustainable development and ensure a better future for all.

Principle 22

Indigenous people and their communities and other local communities have a vital role in environmental management and development because of their knowledge and traditional practices. States should recognize and duly support their identity, culture and interests and enable their effective participation in the achievement of sustainable development.

Principle 23

The environment and natural resources of people under oppression, domination and occupation shall be protected.

Principle 24

Warfare is inherently destructive of sustainable development. States shall therefore respect international law providing protection for the environment in times of armed conflict and cooperate in its further development, as necessary.

Principle 25

Peace, development and environmental protection are interdependent and indivisible.

Principle 26

States shall resolve all their environmental disputes peacefully and by appropriate means in accordance with the Charter of the United Nations.

Principle 27

States and people shall cooperate in good faith and in a spirit of partnership in the fulfilment of the principles embodied in this Declaration and in the further development of international law in the field of sustainable development.

Draft Articles on Prevention of Transboundary Harm from Hazardous Activities, 2001

Editorial note

The Draft Articles on Prevention of Transboundary Harm from Hazardous Activities were adopted at the 53rd session of the International Law Commission (2001) and deal with prevention in the context of authorisation and regulation of hazardous activities which may pose a significant risk of transboundary harm.

Article 1 limits the scope of the articles to activities not prohibited by international law and which involve a risk of causing significant transboundary harm through their physical consequences. Article 2 defines the terms used by the Draft Articles and in particular 'harm' includes harm caused to persons, property or the environment (Article 2(b)). The State of origin of the activities likely to cause significant transboundary harm shall take appropriate measures to prevent or minimise the harm and risk related to such activities (Article 3). States shall co-operate in good faith (Article 4) and adopt the necessary internal measures to implement the provisions of the Draft Articles (Article 5). The State of origin shall require prior authorisation for activities covered by the Draft Articles to be carried out on its territory or under its jurisdiction or control (Article 6). Decisions on the authorisation required by the State of origin shall be based on an assessment of the possible transboundary harm caused by a given activity (Article 7). The State of origin, in case of risk of significant transboundary harm, shall provide the State likely to be affected with timely notification and transmit the available technical and other relevant information (Article 8). States concerned by activities shall enter into consultation with a view of achieving solutions on an equitable balance of interests (Article 9). Factors to be involved in reaching an equitable solution are listed in Article 10. If the State of origin has failed to notify activities planned or carried out and a State has reasonable grounds to believe that an activity planned or carried out in the State of origin may involve a risk of significant transboundary harm, the latter has the right to request notification and information from the State of origin (Article 11). Exchange of information is to continue until considered appropriate by the States concerned (Article 12). The States concerned shall inform the public and ascertain their views (Article 13). Information and data may be withheld, in good faith, for reasons of national security and for the protection of industrial secrets (Article 14). States concerned are required not to discriminate on the grounds of nationality or residence or place where the injury might occur in granting access to judicial or other procedures to seek protection or redress (Article 15). The State of origin shall develop contingency plans for emergency situations and shall notify of an emergency without delay (Articles 16 and 17). The Draft Articles are without prejudice to other rules under treaty or customary law (Article 18). Provisions for the settlement of disputes are contained in Article 19.

Website: www.un.org/law/ilc/texts/prevention/preventionfra.htm

Draft Articles on Prevention of Transboundary Harm from Hazardous Activities

Adopted by the International Law Commission at its fifty-third session (2001)

The States Parties,

Having in mind Article 13, paragraph 1 (a) of the Charter of the United Nations, which provides that the General Assembly shall initiate studies and make recommendations for the purpose of encouraging the progressive development of international law and its codification,

Bearing in mind the principle of permanent sovereignty of States over the natural resources within their territory or otherwise under their jurisdiction or control,

Bearing also in mind that the freedom of States to carry on or permit activities in their territory or otherwise under their jurisdiction or control is not unlimited,

Recalling the Rio Declaration on Environment and Development of 13 June 1992,

Recognizing the importance of promoting international cooperation,

Have agreed as follows:

Article 1
Scope

The present articles apply to activities not prohibited by international law which involve a risk of causing significant transboundary harm through their physical consequences.

Article 2
Use of terms

For the purposes of the present articles:

(a) *Risk of causing significant transboundary harm* includes risks taking the form of a high probability of causing significant transboundary harm and a low probability of causing disastrous transboundary harm;

(b) *Harm* means harm caused to persons, property or the environment;
(c) *Transboundary harm* means harm caused in the territory of or in other places under the jurisdiction or control of a State other than the State of origin, whether or not the States concerned share a common border;
(d) *State of origin* means the State in the territory or otherwise under the jurisdiction or control of which the activities referred to in article 1 are planned or are carried out;
(e) *State likely to be affected* means the State or States in the territory of which there is the risk of significant transboundary harm or which have jurisdiction or control over any other place where there is such a risk;
(f) *States concerned* means the State of origin and the State likely to be affected.

Article 3
Prevention

The State of origin shall take all appropriate measures to prevent significant transboundary harm or at any event to minimize the risk thereof.

Article 4
Cooperation

States concerned shall cooperate in good faith and, as necessary, seek the assistance of one or more competent international organizations in preventing significant transboundary harm or at any event in minimizing the risk thereof.

Article 5
Implementation

States concerned shall take the necessary legislative, administrative or other action including the establishment of suitable monitoring mechanisms to implement the provisions of the present articles.

Article 6
Authorization

1. The State of origin shall require its prior authorization for:

(a) Any activity within the scope of the present articles carried out in its territory or otherwise under its jurisdiction or control;
(b) Any major change in an activity referred to in subparagraph (a);
(c) Any plan to change an activity which may transform it into one falling within the scope of the present articles.

2. The requirement of authorization established by a State shall be made applicable in respect of all pre-existing activities within the scope of the present articles.
Authorizations already issued by the State for pre-existing activities shall be reviewed in order to comply with the present articles.

3. In case of a failure to conform to the terms of the authorization, the State of origin shall take such actions as appropriate, including where necessary terminating the authorization.

Article 7
Assessment of risk

Any decision in respect of the authorization of an activity within the scope of the present articles shall, in particular, be based on an assessment of the possible transboundary harm caused by that activity, including any environmental impact assessment.

Article 8
Notification and information

1. If the assessment referred to in article 7 indicates a risk of causing significant transboundary harm, the State of origin shall provide the State likely to be affected with timely notification of the risk and the assessment and shall transmit to it the available technical and all other relevant information on which the assessment is based.

2. The State of origin shall not take any decision on authorization of the activity pending the receipt, within a period not exceeding six months, of the response from the State likely to be affected.

Article 9
Consultations on preventive measures

1. The States concerned shall enter into consultations, at the request of any of them, with a view to achieving acceptable solutions regarding measures to be adopted in order to prevent significant transboundary harm or at any event to minimize the risk thereof. The States concerned shall agree, at the commencement of such consultations, on a reasonable time-frame for the consultations.

2. The States concerned shall seek solutions based on an equitable balance of interests in the light of article 10.

3. If the consultations referred to in paragraph 1 fail to produce an agreed solution, the State of origin shall nevertheless take into account the interests of the State likely to be affected in case it decides to authorize the activity to be pursued, without prejudice to the rights of any State likely to be affected.

Article 10
Factors involved in an equitable balance of interests

In order to achieve an equitable balance of interests as referred to in paragraph 2 of article 9, the States concerned shall take into account all relevant factors and circumstances, including:

(a) The degree of risk of significant transboundary harm and of the availability of means of preventing such harm, or minimizing the risk thereof or repairing the harm;
(b) The importance of the activity, taking into account its overall advantages of a social, economic and technical character for the State of origin in relation to the potential harm for the State likely to be affected;
(c) The risk of significant harm to the environment and the availability of means of preventing such harm, or minimizing the risk thereof or restoring the environment;
(d) The degree to which the State of origin and, as appropriate, the State likely to be affected are prepared to contribute to the costs of prevention;
(e) The economic viability of the activity in relation to the costs of prevention and to the possibility of carrying out the activity elsewhere or by other means or replacing it with an alternative activity;
(f) The standards of prevention which the State likely to be affected applies to the same or comparable activities and the standards applied in comparable regional or international practice.

Article 11
Procedures in the absence of notification

1. If a State has reasonable grounds to believe that an activity planned or carried out in the State of origin may involve a risk of causing significant transboundary harm to it, it may request the State of origin to apply the provision of article 8. The request shall be accompanied by a documented explanation setting forth its grounds.

2. In the event that the State of origin nevertheless finds that it is not under an obligation to provide a notification under article 8, it shall so inform the requesting State within a reasonable time, providing a documented explanation setting forth the reasons for such finding. If this finding does not satisfy that State, at its request, the two States shall promptly enter into consultations in the manner indicated in article 9.

3. During the course of the consultations, the State of origin shall, if so requested by the other State, arrange to introduce appropriate and feasible measures to minimize the risk and, where appropriate, to suspend the activity in question for a reasonable period.

Article 12
Exchange of information

While the activity is being carried out, the States concerned shall exchange in a timely manner all available information concerning that activity relevant to preventing significant transboundary harm or at any event minimizing the risk thereof. Such an exchange of information shall continue until such time as the States concerned consider it appropriate even after the activity is terminated.

Article 13
Information to the public

States concerned shall, by such means as are appropriate, provide the public likely to be affected by an activity within the scope of the present articles with relevant information relating to that activity, the risk involved and the harm which might result and ascertain their views.

Article 14
National security and industrial secrets

Data and information vital to the national security of the State of origin or to the protection of industrial secrets or concerning intellectual property may be withheld, but the State of origin shall cooperate in good faith with the State likely to be affected in providing as much information as possible under the circumstances.

Article 15
Non-discrimination

Unless the States concerned have agreed otherwise for the protection of the interests of persons, natural or juridical, who may be or are exposed to the risk of significant transboundary harm as a result of an activity within the scope of the present articles, a State shall not discriminate on the basis of nationality or residence or place where the injury might occur, in granting to such persons, in accordance with its legal system, access to judicial or other procedures to seek protection or other appropriate redress.

Article 16
Emergency preparedness

The State of origin shall develop contingency plans for responding to emergencies, in cooperation, where appropriate, with the State likely to be affected and competent international organizations.

Article 17
Notification of an emergency

The State of origin shall, without delay and by the most expeditious means, at its disposal, notify the State likely to be affected of an emergency concerning an activity within the scope of the present articles and provide it with all relevant and available information.

Article 18
Relationship to other rules of international law

The present articles are without prejudice to any obligation incurred by States under relevant treaties or rules of customary international law.

Article 19
Settlement of disputes

1. Any dispute concerning the interpretation or application of the present articles shall be settled expeditiously through peaceful means of settlement chosen by mutual agreement of the parties to the dispute, including negotiations, mediation, conciliation, arbitration or judicial settlement.

2. Failing an agreement on the means for the peaceful settlement of the dispute within a period of six months, the parties to the dispute shall, at the request of any of them, have recourse to the establishment of an impartial fact-finding commission.

3. The Fact-finding Commission shall be composed of one member nominated by each party to the dispute and in addition a member not having the nationality of any of the parties to the dispute chosen by the nominated members who shall serve as Chairperson.

4. If more than one State is involved on one side of the dispute and those States do not agree on a common member of the Commission and each of them nominates a member, the other party to the dispute has the right to nominate an equal number of members of the Commission.

5. If the members nominated by the parties to the dispute are unable to agree on a Chairperson within three months of the request for the establishment of the Commission, any party to the dispute may request the Secretary-General of the United Nations to appoint the Chairperson who shall not have the nationality of any of the parties to the dispute. If one of the parties to the dispute fails to nominate a member within three months of the initial request pursuant to paragraph 2, any other party to the dispute may request the Secretary-General of the United Nations to appoint a person who shall not have the nationality of any of the parties to the dispute. The person so appointed shall constitute a single-member Commission.

6. The Commission shall adopt its report by a majority vote, unless it is a single-member Commission, and shall submit that report to the parties to the dispute setting forth its findings and recommendations, which the parties to the dispute shall consider in good faith.

PART II

Atmosphere

Convention on Long-Range Transboundary Air Pollution, 13 November 1979

Editorial note

The Geneva Convention was negotiated within the UN Economic Commission for Europe on the initiative of Scandinavian countries which had long been concerned about the problem of acid precipitation. The definition of 'air pollution' in Article 1(a) is clearly wide enough to bring many substances within the scope of the Convention. This was the first multilateral Convention relating to the protection of the environment which involved almost all nations of Eastern and Western Europe, and its parties included the USA and the then USSR. It was also the first to deal specifically with the problem of long-range transboundary air pollution where it is not possible to distinguish the contribution of individual emission sources (Article 1(b)). The politically varied and regionally comprehensive adherence to the Convention might be a result of the 'soft' nature of the obligations it establishes. In particular it is clear from a solitary footnote that the question of State liability for damage from transboundary air pollution is beyond its scope. Article 2, which sets out the general obligation to limit, reduce and prevent air pollution, is hedged with qualifications. The 'best available technology' requirement in Article 6 is limited to that which is 'economically feasible'.

The Convention obliges States to exchange information, consult and undertake research. Article 8 sets out in detail the type of information to be exchanged. Article 5 imposes an obligation to consult 'upon request' the Parties to the consultation being, on the one hand, States 'which are actually affected by or exposed to a significant risk of long-range transboundary air pollution' and, on the other hand, States 'within which and subject to whose jurisdiction a significant contribution to long-range transboundary air pollution originates, or could originate'. While provision is made in Article 7 for multilateral research and development the form this is to take is unclear.

Article 9 provides for further development of the 'Co-operative programme for the monitoring and evaluation of the long-range transmission of air pollutants in Europe' (EMEP). EMEP has established stations to monitor the flows of sulphur dioxide across national borders.

Since its entry into force in 1983, the Convention has been extended by eight Protocols which identify specific obligations or measures to be taken by Parties.

The eight Protocols adopted so far include:

- the 1984 Geneva Protocol on Long-term Financing of the Cooperative Programme for Monitoring and Evaluation of the Long-range Transmission of Air Pollutants in Europe (EMEP);
- the 1985 Helsinki Protocol on the Reduction of Sulphur Emissions or their Transboundary Fluxes by at least 30 percent;
- the 1988 Sofia Protocol concerning the Control of Emissions of Nitrogen Oxides or their Transboundary Fluxes;
- the 1991 Geneva Protocol concerning the Control of Emissions of Volatile Organic Compounds or their Transboundary Fluxes;
- the 1994 Oslo Protocol on Further Reduction of Sulphur Emissions;
- the 1998 Aarhus Protocol on Heavy Metals (not yet in force);
- the 1998 Aarhus Protocol on Persistent Organic Pollutants (POPs) (not yet in force);
- the 1999 Gothenburg Protocol to Abate Acidification, Eutrophication and Ground-level Ozone (not yet in force).

The 1984 EMEP Protocol seeks to ensure the availability of adequate financial resources to implement EMEP beyond the amounts provided by UNEP and voluntary contributions. The 1984 Protocol provides for financing the costs of the international centres co-operating within EMEP on the basis of mandatory contributions covering the annual costs of the EMEP work programme, supplemented by voluntary contributions. The basis of annual contributions is set out in an Annex.

The 1985 Sulphur Protocol was adopted in response to evidence of widespread damage in parts of Europe and North America to natural resources, and to historical monuments and human health, caused by acidification of the environment from sulphur dioxides, nitrogen oxides and other pollutants from the combustion of fossil fuels. The 1985 Protocol establishes a 'Thirty Per Cent Club' by committing all parties to reduce their national annual sulphur emissions or their transboundary fluxes by at least 30 percent as soon as possible and at the latest by 1993, using 1980 levels as the basis for calculation of reductions. This inflexible approach to standard-setting has not been adopted in the subsequent Protocols to the 1979 LRTAP Convention because it fails to take account of current and historic emissions and other differentials existing between states. The 1985 Sulphur Protocol envisages further reductions, and revisions were adopted in the 1994 Protocol on Further Reduction of Sulphur Emissions (which is reproduced below).

The third Protocol to the LRTAP Convention concerns the Control of Emissions of Nitrogen Oxides or Their Transboundary Fluxes (1988 NOx Protocol). It is more comprehensive and flexible than the 1985 Sulphur Protocol. It requires the reduction of 'total annual emissions', introducing into international law the concepts of 'national emission standards' and an approach based on 'critical loads aimed at the establishment of an effect-oriented scientific basis'. It also recognises the need to 'create more favourable conditions for exchange of technology'.

The fourth Protocol addresses the 'Control of Emissions of Volatile Organic Compounds and Their Transboundary Fluxes' (1991 VOC Protocol). Unlike the earlier LRTAP Protocols the parties have a choice of at least three ways to meet this requirement, to be specified upon signature. This reflects the need to adopt differentiated commitments based upon a party's emissions and particular geographic and demographic circumstances.

Negotiations under the auspices of the 1985 Sulphur Protocol resulted in the conclusion of the 1994 Oslo Protocol on Further Reduction of Sulphur Emissions, which is reproduced below at document 5A. All the above-mentioned Protocols are in force.

The three latest Protocols adopted under the 1979 Geneva Convention have not yet entered into force.

The 1998 Heavy Metals Protocol was adopted in Aarhus on 24 June 1998. It targets three particularly harmful heavy metals – lead, cadmium and mercury – requiring parties to reduce their emissions of these metals below the levels in a selected reference year (between 1985 and 1995). The Protocol aims to reduce emissions of heavy metals from industrial sources, combustion processes and waste incineration. Parties are required to implement emission standards for these pollutants for stationary sources, based on best available technologies suggested in the Protocol. In addition, parties undertake to phase out the use of leaded petrol and to introduce measures designed to lower heavy metal emissions from other products. A number of other product management measures are proposed for mercury containing products. Parties are to develop strategies, policies and programmes, without undue delay, to discharge their obligations under the Protocol.

The Protocol on Persistent Organic Pollutants (POPs) was adopted by the Executive Body at the same time as the Heavy Metals Protocol. Its ultimate objective is to eliminate discharges, emissions and losses of POPs to the atmosphere. The Protocol focuses on a list of sixteen substances (including pesticides, industrial chemicals and contaminants) singled out according to agreed risk criteria. Parties to the Protocol undertake to eliminate the production and use of certain POPs listed in Annex I and to restrict the use of other substances listed in Annex II. For a third group of POPs listed in Annex III, parties are required to reduce their emissions of these substances from the level of emissions in a given reference year (between 1985 and 1995). For emissions of dioxins and furans, parties are required to apply emissions limits, based on best available technologies, for new and existing stationary sources, and must take effective measures to control emissions of POPs from mobile sources. The Protocol includes provisions dealing with the disposal of wastes containing or generated from listed substances.

The most recent Protocol to the LRTAP Convention is the 1999 Gothenburg Protocol to Abate Acidification, Eutrophication and Ground-Level Ozone, adopted by the Executive Body on 30 November 1999. The Protocol's objective is to control and reduce anthropogenic emissions of four pollutants – sulphur, NOx, ammonia and VOCs, which are likely to cause adverse effects on human health, natural ecosystems, materials and crops due to acidification, eutrophication or ground-level ozone.

Date of signature: 13 November 1979

Entry into force: 16 March 1983

Depositary: Secretary-General of the United Nations

Contracting Parties: Armenia, Austria, Azerbaijan, Belarus, Belgium, Bosnia and Herzegovina, Bulgaria, Canada, Croatia, Cyprus, Czech Republic, Denmark, Estonia, Finland, France, Georgia, Germany, Greece, Hungary, Iceland, Ireland, Italy, Kazakhstan, Kyrgyzstan, Latvia, Liechtenstein, Lithuania, Luxembourg, Malta, Monaco, Netherlands, Norway, Poland, Portugal, Republic of Moldova, Romania, Russian Federation, Slovakia, Slovenia, Spain, Sweden, Switzerland, The Former Yugoslav Republic of Macedonia, Turkey, Ukraine, United Kingdom, United States, Yugoslavia, European Community.

Website: www.unece.org/env/lrtap/

Geneva Convention on Long-Range Transboundary Air Pollution

The Parties to the present Convention,

Determined to promote relations and cooperation in the field of environmental protection,

Aware of the significance of the activities of the United Nations Economic Commission for Europe in strengthening such relations and cooperation, particularly in the field of air pollution including long-range transport of air pollutants,

Recognizing the contribution of the Economic Commission for Europe to the multilateral implementation of the pertinent provisions of the Final Act of the Conference on Security and Cooperation in Europe,

Cognizant of the references in the chapter on environment of the Final Act of the Conference on Security and Cooperation in Europe calling for cooperation to control air pollution and its effects, including long-range transport of air pollutants, and to the development through international cooperation of an extensive programme for the monitoring and evaluation of long-range transport of air pollutants, starting with sulphur dioxide and with possible extension to other pollutants,

Considering the pertinent provisions of the Declaration of the United Nations Conference on the Human Environment, and in particular principle 21, which expresses the common conviction that States have, in accordance with the Charter of the United Nations and the principles of international law, the sovereign right to exploit their own resources pursuant to their own environmental policies, and the responsibility to ensure that activities within their jurisdiction or control do not cause damage to the environment of other States or of areas beyond the limits of national jurisdiction,

Recognizing the existence of possible adverse effects, in the short and long term, of air pollution including transboundary air pollution,

Concerned that a rise in the level of emissions of air pollutants within the region as forecast may increase such adverse effects,

Recognizing the need to study the implications of the long-range transport of air pollutants and the need to seek solutions for the problems identified,

Affirming their willingness to reinforce active international cooperation to develop appropriate national policies and by means of exchange of information, consultation, research and monitoring to coordinate national action for combating air pollution including long-range transboundary air pollution,

Have agreed as follows:

Definitions

Article 1

For the purposes of the present Convention:

(a) 'Air pollution' means the introduction by man, directly or indirectly, of substances or energy into the air resulting in deleterious effects of such a nature as to endanger human health, harm living resources and ecosystems and material property and impair or interfere with amenities and other legitimate uses of the environment, and 'air pollutants' shall be construed accordingly;

(b) 'Long-range transboundary air pollution' means air pollution whose physical origin is situated wholly or in part within the area under the national jurisdiction of one State and which has adverse effects in the area under the jurisdiction of another State at such a distance that it is not generally possible to distinguish the contribution of individual emission sources or groups of sources.

Fundamental Principles

Article 2

The Contracting Parties, taking due account of the facts and problems involved, are determined to protect man and his environment against air pollution and shall endeavour to limit and, as far as possible, gradually reduce and prevent air pollution including long-range transboundary air pollution.

Article 3

The Contracting Parties, within the framework of the present Convention, shall by means of exchanges of information, consultation, research and monitoring, develop without undue delay policies and strategies which shall serve as a means of combating the discharge of air pollutants, taking into account efforts already made at national and international levels.

Article 4

The Contracting Parties shall exchange information on and review their policies, scientific activities and technical measures aimed at combating, as far as possible, the discharge of air pollutants which may have adverse effects, thereby contributing to the reduction of air pollution including long-range transboundary air pollution.

Article 5

Consultations shall be held, upon request, at an early stage between, on the one hand, Contracting Parties which are actually affected by or exposed to a significant risk of long-range transboundary air pollution and, on the other hand, Contracting Parties within which and subject to whose jurisdiction a significant contribution to long-range transboundary air pollution originates, or could originate, in connection with activities carried on or contemplated therein.

Air quality management

Article 6

Taking into account articles 2 to 5, the ongoing research, exchange of information and monitoring and the results thereof, the cost and effectiveness of local and other remedies and, in order to combat air pollution, in particular that originating from new or rebuilt installations, each Contracting Party undertakes to develop the best policies and strategies including air quality management systems and, as part of them, control measures compatible with balanced development, in particular by using the best available technology which is economically feasible and low- and non-waste technology.

Research and development

Article 7

The Contracting Parties, as appropriate to their needs, shall initiate and cooperate in the conduct of research into and/or development of:

(a) Existing and proposed technologies for reducing emissions of sulphur com-pounds and other major air pollutants, including technical and economic feasibility, and environmental consequences;

(b) Instrumentation and other techniques for monitoring and measuring emis-sion rates and ambient concentrations of air pollutants;

(c) Improved models for a better understanding of the transmission of long-range transboundary air pollutants;

(d) The effects of sulphur compounds and other major air pollutants on human health and the environment, including agriculture, forestry, materials, aquatic and other natural ecosystems and visibility, with a view to establishing a scientific basis for dose/effect relationships designed to protect the environment;

(e) The economic, social and environmental assessment of alternative mea-sures for attaining environmental objectives including the reduction of long-range transboundary air pollution;

(f) Education and training programmes related to the environmental aspects of pollution by sulphur compounds and other major air pollutants.

Exchange of information

Article 8

The Contracting Parties, within the framework of the Executive Body referred to in article 10 and bilaterally, shall, in their common interests, exchange available information on:

(a) Data on emissions at periods of time to be agreed upon, of agreed air pollutants, starting with sulphur dioxide, coming from grid-units of agreed size; or on the fluxes of agreed air pollutants, starting with sulphur dioxide, across national borders, at distances and at periods of time to be agreed upon;

(b) Major changes in national policies and in general industrial development, and their potential impact, which would be likely to cause significant changes in long-range transboundary air pollution;

(c) Control technologies for reducing air pollution relevant to long-range transboundary air pollution;

(d) The projected cost of the emission control of sulphur compounds and other major air pollutants on a national scale;

(e) Meteorological and physico-chemical data relating to the processes during transmission;

(f) Physico-chemical and biological data relating to the effects of long-range transboundary air pollution and the extent of the damage* which these data indicate can be attributed to long-range transboundary air pollution;

---

* The present Convention does not contain a rule on State liability as to damage.

(g) National, subregional and regional policies and strategies for the control of sulphur compounds and other major air pollutants.

Implementation and further development of the cooperative programme for the monitoring and evaluation of the long-range transmission of air pollutants in Europe

Article 9

The Contracting Parties stress the need for the implementation of the existing 'Cooperative programme for the monitoring and evaluation of the long-range transmission of air pollutants in Europe' (hereinafter referred to as EMEP) and, with regard to the further development of this programme, agree to emphasize:

(a) The desirability of Contracting Parties joining in and fully implementing EMEP which, as a first step, is based on the monitoring of sulphur dioxide and related substances;

(b) The need to use comparable or standardized procedures for monitoring whenever possible;

(c) The desirability of basing the monitoring programme on the framework of both national and international programmes. The establishment of monitoring stations and the collection of data shall be carried out under the national jurisdiction of the country in which the monitoring stations are located;

(d) The desirability of establishing a framework for a cooperative environmental monitoring programme, based on and taking into account present and future national, subregional, regional and other international programmes;

(e) The need to exchange data on emissions at periods of time to be agreed upon, of agreed air pollutants, starting with sulphur dioxide, coming from grid-units of agreed size; or on the fluxes of agreed air pollutants, starting with sulphur dioxide, across national borders, at distances and at periods of time to be agreed upon. The method, including the model, used to determine the fluxes, as well as the method, including the model used to determine the transmission of air pollutants based on the emissions per grid-unit, shall be made available and periodically reviewed, in order to improve the methods and the models;

(f) Their willingness to continue the exchange and periodic updating of national data on total emissions of agreed air pollutants, starting with sulphur dioxide;

(g) The need to provide meteorological and physico-chemical data relating to processes during transmission;

(h) The need to monitor chemical components in other media such as water, soil and vegetation, as well as a similar monitoring programme to record effects on health and environment;

(i) The desirability of extending the national EMEP networks to make them operational for control and surveillance purposes.

Executive Body

Article 10

1. The representatives of the Contracting Parties shall, within the framework of the Senior Advisers to ECE Governments on Environmental Problems, constitute the Executive Body of the present Convention, and shall meet at least annually in that capacity.

2. The Executive Body shall:

(a) Review the implementation of the present Convention;
(b) Establish, as appropriate, working groups to consider matters related to the implementation and development of the present Convention and to this end to prepare appropriate studies and other documentation and to submit recommendations to be considered by the Executive Body;
(c) Fulfil such other functions as may be appropriate under the provisions of the present Convention.

3. The Executive Body shall utilize the Steering Body for the EMEP to play an integral part in the operation of the present Convention, in particular with regard to data collection and scientific cooperation.

4. The Executive Body, in discharging its functions, shall, when it deems appropriate, also make use of information from other relevant international organizations.

Secretariat

Article 11

The Executive Secretary of the Economic Commission for Europe shall carry out, for the Executive Body, the following secretariat functions:

(a) To convene and prepare the meetings of the Executive Body;
(b) To transmit to the Contracting Parties reports and other information received in accordance with the provisions of the present Convention;
(c) To discharge the functions assigned by the Executive Body.

Amendments to the Convention

Article 12

1. Any Contracting Party may propose amendments to the present Convention.

2. The text of proposed amendments shall be submitted in writing to the Executive Secretary of the Economic Commission for Europe, who shall communicate them to all Contracting Parties. The Executive Body shall discuss proposed amendments at its next annual meeting provided that such proposals have been circulated by the Executive Secretary of the Economic Commission for Europe to the Contracting Parties at least ninety days in advance.

3. An amendment to the present Convention shall be adopted by consensus of the representatives of the Contracting Parties, and shall enter into force for the Contracting Parties which have accepted it on the ninetieth day after the date on which two-thirds of the Contracting Parties have deposited their instruments of acceptance with the depositary. Thereafter, the amendment shall enter into force for any other Contracting Party on the ninetieth day after the date on which that Contracting Party deposits its instrument of acceptance of the amendment.

Settlement of disputes

Article 13

If a dispute arises between two or more Contracting Parties to the present Convention as to the interpretation or application of the Convention, they shall seek a solution by negotiation or by any other method of dispute settlement acceptable to the parties to the dispute.

Signature

Article 14

1. The present Convention shall be open for signature at the United Nations Office at Geneva from 13 to 16 November 1979 on the occasion of the High-level Meeting within the framework of the Economic Commission for Europe on the Protection of the Environment, by the member States of the Economic Commission for Europe as well as States having consultative status with the Economic Commission for Europe, pursuant to paragraph 8 of Economic and Social Council resolution 36 (IV) of 28 March 1947, and by regional economic integration organizations, constituted by sovereign States members of the Economic Commission for Europe, which have competence in respect of the negotiation, conclusion and application of international agreements in matters covered by the present Convention.

2. In matters within their competence, such regional economic integration organizations shall, on their own behalf, exercise the rights and fulfil the responsibilities which the present Convention attributes to their member States. In such cases, the member States of these organizations shall not be entitled to exercise such rights individually.

Ratification, acceptance, approval and accession

Article 15

1. The present Convention shall be subject to ratification, acceptance or approval.

2. The present Convention shall be open for accession as from 17 November 1979 by the States and organizations referred to in article 14, paragraph 1.

3. The instruments of ratification, acceptance, approval or accession shall be deposited with the Secretary-General of the United Nations, who will perform the functions of the depositary.

Entry into force

Article 16

1. The present Convention shall enter into force on the ninetieth day after the date of deposit of the twenty-fourth instrument of ratification, acceptance, approval or accession.

2. For each Contracting Party which ratifies, accepts or approves the present Convention or accedes thereto after the deposit of the twenty-fourth instrument of ratification, acceptance, approval or accession, the Convention shall enter into force on the ninetieth day after the date of deposit by such Contracting Party of its instrument of ratification, acceptance, approval or accession.

Withdrawal

Article 17

At any time after five years from the date on which the present Convention has come into force with respect to a Contracting Party, that Contracting Party may withdraw from the Convention by giving written notification to the depositary. Any such withdrawal shall take effect on the ninetieth day after the date of its receipt by the depositary.

Authentic texts

Article 18

The original of the present Convention, of which the English, French and Russian texts are equally authentic, shall be deposited with the Secretary-General of the United Nations.

IN WITNESS WHEREOF the undersigned, being duly authorized thereto, have signed the present Convention.

DONE at Geneva, this thirteenth day of November, one thousand nine hundred and seventy-nine.

5A

Protocol to the 1979 Convention on Long-Range Transboundary Air Pollution on Further Reduction of Sulphur Emissions, 14 June 1994

Editorial note

Negotiations under the auspices of the 1985 Sulphur Protocol resulted in the conclusion of the 1994 Oslo Protocol on Further Reduction of Sulphur Emissions, which entered into force on 5 August 1998. Like its predecessor, the 1994 Protocol contemplates future negotiations on further obligations to reduce sulphur emissions. The 1994 Protocol applies and develops the concepts of 'critical loads' and the 'effects-based approach' introduced in the 1988 NOx Protocol. The basic obligation to which the Parties commit is to 'control and reduce their sulphur emissions in order to protect human health and the environment from adverse effects, in particular acidifying effects, and to ensure, as far as possible, without entailing excessive costs, that depositions of oxidised sulphur compounds in the long term do not exceed critical loads for sulphur given, in annex I, as critical sulphur depositions, in accordance with present scientific knowledge' (Article 2(1)).

As a first step, parties are required to meet the targets and timetable for reductions of sulphur emissions specified in Annex II (Article 2(2) and (3)). The Protocol requires the parties to make use of the 'most effective measures for the reduction of sulphur emissions' from new and existing sources, including controlling the sulphur content of fuel, energy efficient measures, promotion of renewable energy and the application of best available control technologies using the guidance provided in Annex IV of the Protocol (Article 2(4)). The Protocol also permits the parties to apply economic instruments to encourage the adoption of cost-effective approaches to the reduction of sulphur emissions, and to enter into agreements for the joint implementation of the Protocol with other parties (Article 2(6) and (7)).

All parties (other than the United States and Canada) must apply national emissions limits to major new stationary sources, and introduce pollution control measures for major existing stationary sources by 1 July 2004 (Article 2(5)(a) and (b); emission limits are specified in Annex V). Parties were also required to apply national standards for the sulphur content of gas oil no later than two years after the Protocol entered into force (Article 2(5)(c)).

Parties are required to implement their basic obligations under Article 2 through the adoption of national strategies, policies and programmes and by taking and applying national measures to control and reduce sulphur emissions (Article 4(1)). Each Party must collect and maintain information on actual levels of sulphur emissions, and of ambient concentrations and depositions of oxidised sulphur and other acidifying compounds; and the effects of depositions of oxidised sulphur and other acidifying compounds (Article 4(2)). The Protocol requires periodic reporting to the Executive Body on national implementation measures and the levels of national annual sulphur emissions (Article 5).

The Protocol requires parties to facilitate the exchange of technologies and techniques for reducing sulphur emissions and encourages research, development, monitoring and co-operation in respect of various matters relating to the harmonisation of methods for the establishment of critical loads; the improvement of monitoring techniques and modelling systems; the development of strategies for the further reduction of sulphur emissions; the understanding of the wider effects of sulphur emissions on human health and the environment; emission abatement and energy efficiency technologies; and the economic evaluation of benefits for the environment and human health resulting from the reduction of sulphur emissions (Articles 3 and 6).

Like the other Protocols, the 1994 Protocol makes use of the institutions established under the 1979 LRTAP Convention. Article 7 contemplates the establishment of a new body, an Implementation Committee, to oversee compliance. In 1998, the parties to the 1994 Protocol decided that the structure, functions and procedures of the Implementation Committee should be those set out in decision 1997/2 of the Executive Body (Decision 1998/6). The Implementation Committee now oversees compliance with all of the Protocols to the LRTAP Convention. The compliance procedure is reproduced below after the text of the 1994 Sulphur Protocol (Document 5B).

Date of signature: 14 June 1994

Entry into force: 5 August 1998

Depositary: Secretary-General of the United Nations

Contracting Parties: Austria, Belgium, Canada, Croatia, Czech Republic, Denmark, Finland, France, Germany, Greece, Hungary, Ireland, Italy, Liechtenstein, Luxembourg, Monaco, Netherlands, Norway, Slovakia, Slovenia, Spain, Sweden, Switzerland, United Kingdom, European Community.

Website: www.unece.org/env/lrtap/

Protocol to the 1979 Convention on Long-Range Transboundary Air Pollution on Further Reduction of Sulphur Emissions

The Parties,

Determined to implement the Convention on Long-range Transboundary Air Pollution,

Concerned that emissions of sulphur and other air pollutants continue to be transported across international boundaries and, in exposed parts of Europe and North America, are causing widespread damage to natural resources of vital environmental and economic importance, such as forests, soils and waters, and to materials, including historic monuments, and, under certain circumstances, have harmful effects on human health,

Resolved to take precautionary measures to anticipate, prevent or minimize emissions of air pollutants and mitigate their adverse effects,

Convinced that where there are threats of serious or irreversible damage, lack of full scientific certainty should not be used as a reason for postponing such measures, taking into account that such precautionary measures to deal with emissions of air pollutants should be cost-effective,

Mindful that measures to control emissions of sulphur and other air pollutants would also contribute to the protection of the sensitive Arctic environment,

Considering that the predominant sources of air pollution contributing to the acidification of the environment are the combustion of fossil fuels for energy production, and the main technological processes in various industrial sectors, as well as transport, which lead to emissions of sulphur, nitrogen oxides, and other pollutants,

Conscious of the need for a cost-effective regional approach to combating air pollution that takes account of the variations in effects and abatement costs between countries,

Desiring to take further and more effective action to control and reduce sulphur emissions,

Cognizant that any sulphur control policy, however cost-effective it may be at the regional level, will result in a relatively heavy economic burden on countries with economies that are in transition to a market economy,

Bearing in mind that measures taken to reduce sulphur emissions should not constitute a means of arbitrary or unjustifiable discrimination or a disguised restriction on international competition and trade,

Taking into consideration existing scientific and technical data on emissions, atmospheric processes and effects on the environment of sulphur oxides, as well as on abatement costs,

Aware that, in addition to emissions of sulphur, emissions of nitrogen oxides and of ammonia are also causing acidification of the environment,

Noting that under the United Nations Framework Convention on Climate Change, adopted in New York on 9 May 1992, there is agreement to establish national policies and take corresponding measures to combat climate change, which can be expected to lead to reductions of sulphur emissions,

Affirming the need to ensure environmentally sound and sustainable development,

Recognizing the need to continue scientific and technical cooperation to elaborate further the approach based on critical loads and critical levels, including efforts to assess several air pollutants and various effects on the environment, materials and human health,

Underlining that scientific and technical knowledge is developing and that it will be necessary to take such developments into account when reviewing the adequacy of the obligations entered into under the present Protocol and deciding on further action,

Acknowledging the Protocol on the Reduction of Sulphur Emissions or Their Transboundary Fluxes by at least 30 per cent, adopted in Helsinki on 8 July 1985, and the measures already taken by many countries which have had the effect of reducing sulphur emissions,

Have agreed as follows:

Article 1
Definitions

For the purposes of the present Protocol,

1. 'Convention' means the Convention on Long-range Transboundary Air Pollution, adopted in Geneva on 13 November 1979;
2. 'EMEP' means the Cooperative Programme for Monitoring and Evaluation of the Long-range Transmission of Air Pollutants in Europe;
3. 'Executive Body' means the Executive Body for the Convention constituted under article 10, paragraph 1, of the Convention;
4. 'Commission' means the United Nations Economic Commission for Europe;
5. 'Parties' means, unless the context otherwise requires, the Parties to the present Protocol;
6. 'Geographical scope of EMEP' means the area defined in article 1, paragraph 4, of the Protocol to the 1979 Convention on Long-range Transboundary Air Pollution on Long-term Financing of the Cooperative Programme for Monitoring and Evaluation of the Long-range Transmission of Air Pollutants in Europe (EMEP), adopted in Geneva on 28 September 1984;
7. 'SOMA' means a sulphur oxides management area designated in annex III under the conditions laid down in article 2, paragraph 3;

8. 'Critical load' means a quantitative estimate of an exposure to one or more pollutants below which significant harmful effects on specified sensitive elements of the environment do not occur, according to present knowledge;

9. 'Critical levels' means the concentration of pollutants in the atmosphere above which direct adverse effects on receptors, such as human beings, plants, ecosystems or materials, may occur, according to present knowledge;

10. 'Critical sulphur deposition' means a quantitative estimate of the exposure to oxidized sulphur compounds, taking into account the effects of base cation uptake and base cation deposition, below which significant harmful effects on specified sensitive elements of the environment do not occur, according to present knowledge;

11. 'Emission' means the discharge of substances into the atmosphere;

12. 'Sulphur emissions' means all emissions of sulphur compounds expressed as kilotonnes of sulphur dioxide (kt SO_2) to the atmosphere originating from anthropogenic sources excluding from ships in international traffic outside territorial waters;

13. 'Fuel' means any solid, liquid or gaseous combustible material with the exception of domestic refuse and toxic or dangerous waste;

14. 'Stationary combustion source' means any technical apparatus or group of technical apparatus that is co-located on a common site and is or could be discharging waste gases through a common stack, in which fuels are oxidized in order to use the heat generated;

15. 'Major new stationary combustion source' means any stationary combustion source the construction or substantial modification of which is authorized after 31 December 1995 and the thermal input of which, when operating at rated capacity, is at least 50 MW_{th}. It is a matter for the competent national authorities to decide whether a modification is substantial or not, taking into account such factors as the environmental benefits of the modification;

16. 'Major existing stationary combustion source' means any existing stationary combustion source the thermal input of which, when operating at rated capacity, is at least 50 MW_{th};

17. 'Gas oil' means any petroleum product within HS 2710, or any petroleum product which, by reason of its distillation limits, falls within the category of middle distillates intended for use as fuel and of which at least 85 per cent by volume, including distillation losses, distils at 350° C;

18. 'Emission limit value' means the permissible concentration of sulphur compounds expressed as sulphur dioxide in the waste gases from a stationary combustion source expressed in terms of mass per volume of the waste gases expressed in mg SO_2/Nm_3, assuming an oxygen content by volume in the waste gas of 3 per cent in the case of liquid and gaseous fuels and 6 per cent in the case of solid fuels;

19. 'Emission limitation' means the permissible total quantity of sulphur compounds expressed as sulphur dioxide discharged from a combustion source
or group of combustion sources located either on a common site or within
a defined geographical area, expressed in kilotonnes per year;

20. 'Desulphurization rate' means the ratio of the quantity of sulphur which is
separated at the combustion source site over a given period to the quantity
of sulphur contained in the fuel which is introduced into the combustion
source facilities and which is used over the same period;

21. 'Sulphur budget' means a matrix of calculated contributions to the deposition of oxidized sulphur compounds in receiving areas, originating from
the emissions from specified areas.

Article 2
Basic obligations

1. The Parties shall control and reduce their sulphur emissions in order to
protect human health and the environment from adverse effects, in particular
acidifying effects, and to ensure, as far as possible, without entailing excessive
costs, that depositions of oxidized sulphur compounds in the long term do not
exceed critical loads for sulphur given, in annex I, as critical sulphur depositions,
in accordance with present scientific knowledge.

2. As a first step, the Parties shall, as a minimum, reduce and maintain their
annual sulphur emissions in accordance with the timing and levels specified in
annex II.

3. In addition, any Party:

(a) Whose total land area is greater than 2 million square kilometres;
(b) Which has committed itself under paragraph 2 above to a national sulphur
emission ceiling no greater than the lesser of its 1990 emissions or its obligation in the 1985 Helsinki Protocol on the Reduction of Sulphur Emissions
or Their Transboundary Fluxes by at least 30 per cent, as indicated in
annex II;
(c) Whose annual sulphur emissions that contribute to acidification in areas
under the jurisdiction of one or more other Parties originate only from
within areas under its jurisdiction that are listed as SOMAs in annex III,
and has presented documentation to this effect; and
(d) Which has specified upon signature of, or accession to, the present Protocol
its intention to act in accordance with this paragraph, shall, as a minimum,
reduce and maintain its annual sulphur emissions in the area so listed in
accordance with the timing and levels specified in annex II.

4. Furthermore, the Parties shall make use of the most effective measures
for the reduction of sulphur emissions, appropriate in their particular circumstances, for new and existing sources, which include, *inter alia*:

- Measures to increase energy efficiency;
- Measures to increase the use of renewable energy;
- Measures to reduce the sulphur content of particular fuels and to encourage the use of fuel with a low sulphur content, including the combined use of high-sulphur with low-sulphur or sulphur-free fuel;
- Measures to apply best available control technologies not entailing excessive cost, using the guidance in annex IV.

5. Each Party, except those Parties subject to the United States/Canada Air Quality Agreement of 1991, shall as a minimum:

(a) Apply emission limit values at least as stringent as those specified in annex V to all major new stationary combustion sources;

(b) No later than 1 July 2004 apply, as far as possible without entailing excessive costs, emission limit values at least as stringent as those specified in annex V to those major existing stationary combustion sources the thermal input of which is above 500 MW_{th} taking into account the remaining lifetime of a plant, calculated from the date of entry into force of the present Protocol, or apply equivalent emission limitations or other appropriate provisions, provided that these achieve the sulphur emission ceilings specified in annex II and, subsequently, further approach the critical loads as given in annex I; and no later than 1 July 2004 apply emission limit values or emission limitations to those major existing stationary combustion sources the thermal input of which is between 50 and 500 MW_{th} using annex V as guidance;

(c) No later than two years after the date of entry into force of the present Protocol apply national standards for the sulphur content of gas oil at least as stringent as those specified in annex V. In cases where the supply of gas oil cannot otherwise be ensured, a State may extend the time period given in this subparagraph to a period of up to ten years. In this case it shall specify, in a declaration to be deposited together with the instrument of ratification, acceptance, approval or accession, its intention to extend the time period.

6. The Parties may, in addition, apply economic instruments to encourage the adoption of cost-effective approaches to the reduction of sulphur emissions.

7. The Parties to this Protocol may, at a session of the Executive Body, in accordance with rules and conditions which the Executive Body shall elaborate and adopt, decide whether two or more Parties may jointly implement the obligations set out in annex II. These rules and conditions shall ensure the fulfilment of the obligations set out in paragraph 2 above and also promote the achievement of the environmental objectives set out in paragraph 1 above.

8. The Parties shall, subject to the outcome of the first review provided for under article 8 and no later than one year after the completion of that review, commence negotiations on further obligations to reduce emissions.

Article 3
Exchange of technology

1. The Parties shall, consistent with their national laws, regulations and practices, facilitate the exchange of technologies and techniques, including those that increase energy efficiency, the use of renewable energy and the processing of low-sulphur fuels, to reduce sulphur emissions, particularly through the promotion of:

(a) The commercial exchange of available technology;
(b) Direct industrial contacts and cooperation, including joint ventures;
(c) The exchange of information and experience;
(d) The provision of technical assistance.

2. In promoting the activities specified in paragraph 1 above, the Parties shall create favourable conditions by facilitating contacts and cooperation among appropriate organizations and individuals in the private and public sectors that are capable of providing technology, design and engineering services, equipment or finance.

3. The Parties shall, no later than six months after the date of entry into force of the present Protocol, commence consideration of procedures to create more favourable conditions for the exchange of technology to reduce sulphur emissions.

Article 4
National strategies, policies, programmes, measures and information

1. Each Party shall, in order to implement its obligations under article 2:

(a) Adopt national strategies, policies and programmes, no later than six months after the present Protocol enters into force for it; and
(b) Take and apply national measures to control and reduce its sulphur emissions.

2. Each Party shall collect and maintain information on:

(a) Actual levels of sulphur emissions, and of ambient concentrations and depositions of oxidized sulphur and other acidifying compounds, taking into account, for those Parties within the geographical scope of EMEP, the work plan of EMEP; and
(b) The effects of depositions of oxidized sulphur and other acidifying compounds.

Article 5
Reporting

1. Each Party shall report, through the Executive Secretary of the Commission, to the Executive Body, on a periodic basis as determined by the Executive Body, information on:

(a) The implementation of national strategies, policies, programmes and measures referred to in article 4, paragraph 1;
(b) The levels of national annual sulphur emissions, in accordance with guidelines adopted by the Executive Body, containing emission data for all relevant source categories; and
(c) The implementation of other obligations that it has entered into under the present Protocol, in conformity with a decision regarding format and content to be adopted by the Parties at a session of the Executive Body. The terms of this decision shall be reviewed as necessary to identify any additional elements regarding the format and/or content of the information that are to be included in the reports.

2. Each Party within the geographical scope of EMEP shall report, through the Executive Secretary of the Commission, to EMEP, on a periodic basis to be determined by the Steering Body of EMEP and approved by the Parties at a session of the Executive Body, information on the levels of sulphur emissions with temporal and spatial resolution as specified by the Steering Body of EMEP.

3. In good time before each annual session of the Executive Body, EMEP shall provide information on:

(a) Ambient concentrations and deposition of oxidized sulphur compounds; and
(b) Calculations of sulphur budgets.

Parties in areas outside the geographical scope of EMEP shall make available similar information if requested to do so by the Executive Body.

4. The Executive Body shall, in accordance with article 10, paragraph 2 (*b*), of the Convention, arrange for the preparation of information on the effects of depositions of oxidized sulphur and other acidifying compounds.

5. The Parties shall, at sessions of the Executive Body, arrange for the preparation, at regular intervals, of revised information on calculated and internationally optimized allocations of emission reductions for the States within the geographical scope of EMEP, with integrated assessment models, with a view to reducing further, for the purposes of article 2, paragraph 1, of the present Protocol, the difference between actual depositions of oxidized sulphur compounds and critical load values.

Article 6
Research, development and monitoring

The Parties shall encourage research, development, monitoring and cooperation related to:

(a) The international harmonization of methods for the establishment of critical loads and critical levels and the elaboration of procedures for such harmonization;

(b) The improvement of monitoring techniques and systems and of the modelling of transport, concentrations and deposition of sulphur compounds;

(c) Strategies for the further reduction of sulphur emissions based on critical loads and critical levels as well as on technical developments, and the improvement of integrated assessment modelling to calculate internationally optimized allocations of emission reductions taking into account an equitable distribution of abatement costs;

(d) The understanding of the wider effects of sulphur emissions on human health, the environment, in particular acidification, and materials, including historic and cultural monuments, taking into account the relationship between sulphur oxides, nitrogen oxides, ammonia, volatile organic compounds and tropospheric ozone;

(e) Emission abatement technologies, and technologies and techniques to enhance energy efficiency, energy conservation and the use of renewable energy;

(f) The economic evaluation of benefits for the environment and human health resulting from the reduction of sulphur emissions.

Article 7
Compliance

1. An Implementation Committee is hereby established to review the implementation of the present Protocol and compliance by the Parties with their obligations. It shall report to the Parties at sessions of the Executive Body and may make such recommendations to them as it considers appropriate.

2. Upon consideration of a report, and any recommendations, of the Implementation Committee, the Parties, taking into account the circumstances of a matter and in accordance with Convention practice, may decide upon and call for action to bring about full compliance with the present Protocol, including measures to assist a Party's compliance with the Protocol, and to further the objectives of the Protocol.

3. The Parties shall, at the first session of the Executive Body after the entry into force of the present Protocol, adopt a decision that sets out the structure and functions of the Implementation Committee as well as procedures for its review of compliance.

4. The application of the compliance procedure shall be without prejudice
to the provisions of article 9 of the present Protocol.

Article 8
Reviews by the Parties at sessions of the Executive Body

1. The Parties shall, at sessions of the Executive Body, pursuant to article
10, paragraph 2 (*a*), of the Convention, review the information supplied by
the Parties and EMEP, the data on the effects of depositions of sulphur and
other acidifying compounds and the reports of the Implementation Committee
referred to in article 7, paragraph 1, of the present Protocol.
  2.

(a) The Parties shall, at sessions of the Executive Body, keep under review the
    obligations set out in the present Protocol, including:
    (i) Their obligations in relation to their calculated and internationally
        optimized allocations of emission reductions referred to in article 5,
        paragraph 5; and
    (ii) The adequacy of the obligations and the progress made towards the
        achievement of the objectives of the present Protocol;
(b) Reviews shall take into account the best available scientific information on
    acidification, including assessments of critical loads, technological develop-
    ments, changing economic conditions and the fulfilment of the obligations
    on emission levels;
(c) In the context of such reviews, any Party whose obligations on sulphur
    emission ceilings under annex II hereto do not conform to the calculated
    and internationally optimized allocations of emission reductions for that
    Party, required to reduce the difference between depositions of sulphur
    in 1990 and critical sulphur depositions within the geographical scope of
    EMEP by at least 60 per cent, shall make every effort to undertake revised
    obligations;
(d) The procedures, methods and timing for such reviews shall be specified by
    the Parties at a session of the Executive Body. The first such review shall be
    completed in 1997.

Article 9
Settlement of disputes

1. In the event of a dispute between any two or more Parties concerning
the interpretation or application of the present Protocol, the Parties concerned
shall seek a settlement of the dispute through negotiation or any other peaceful
means of their own choice. The Parties to the dispute shall inform the Executive
Body of their dispute.

2. When ratifying, accepting, approving or acceding to the present Protocol, or at any time thereafter, a Party which is not a regional economic integration organization may declare in a written instrument submitted to the Depositary that, in respect of any dispute concerning the interpretation or application of the Protocol, it recognizes one or both of the following means of dispute settlement as compulsory *ipso facto* and without agreement, in relation to any Party accepting the same obligation:

(a) Submission of the dispute to the International Court of Justice;
(b) Arbitration in accordance with procedures to be adopted by the Parties at a session of the Executive Body as soon as practicable, in an annex on arbitration.

A Party which is a regional economic integration organization may make a declaration with like effect in relation to arbitration in accordance with the procedures referred to in subparagraph (b) above.

3. A declaration made under paragraph 2 above shall remain in force until it expires in accordance with its terms or until three months after written notice of its revocation has been deposited with the Depositary.

4. A new declaration, a notice of revocation or the expiry of a declaration shall not in any way affect proceedings pending before the International Court of Justice or the arbitral tribunal, unless the Parties to the dispute agree otherwise.

5. Except in a case where the Parties to a dispute have accepted the same means of dispute settlement under paragraph 2, if after twelve months following notification by one Party to another that a dispute exists between them, the Parties concerned have not been able to settle their dispute through the means mentioned in paragraph 1 above, the dispute shall be submitted, at the request of any of the Parties to the dispute, to conciliation.

6. For the purpose of paragraph 5, a conciliation commission shall be created. The commission shall be composed of an equal number of members appointed by each Party concerned or, where Parties in conciliation share the same interest, by the group sharing that interest, and a chairman chosen jointly by the members so appointed. The commission shall render a recommendatory award, which the Parties shall consider in good faith.

Article 10
Annexes

The annexes to the present Protocol shall form an integral part of the Protocol. Annexes I and IV are recommendatory in character.

Critical sulphur deposition
Sulphur emission ceilings and percentage emission reductions

Designation of sulphur oxides management areas (SOMAs)
Control technologies for sulphur emissions from stationary sources
Emission and sulphur content limit values

Article 11
Amendments and adjustments

1. Any Party may propose amendments to the present Protocol. Any Party to the Convention may propose an adjustment to annex II to the present Protocol to add to it its name, together with emission levels, sulphur emission ceilings and percentage emission reductions.

2. Such proposed amendments and adjustments shall be submitted in writing to the Executive Secretary of the Commission, who shall communicate them to all Parties. The Parties shall discuss the proposed amendments and adjustments at the next session of the Executive Body, provided that those proposals have been circulated by the Executive Secretary to the Parties at least ninety days in advance.

3. Amendments to the present Protocol and to its annexes II, III and V shall be adopted by consensus of the Parties present at a session of the Executive Body, and shall enter into force for the Parties which have accepted them on the ninetieth day after the date on which two thirds of the Parties have deposited with the Depositary their instruments of acceptance thereof. Amendments shall enter into force for any other Party on the ninetieth day after the date on which that Party has deposited its instrument of acceptance thereof.

4. Amendments to the annexes to the present Protocol, other than to the annexes referred to in paragraph 3 above, shall be adopted by consensus of the Parties present at a session of the Executive Body. On the expiry of ninety days from the date of its communication by the Executive Secretary of the Commission, an amendment to any such annex shall become effective for those Parties which have not submitted to the Depositary a notification in accordance with the provisions of paragraph 5 below, provided that at least sixteen Parties have not submitted such a notification.

5. Any Party that is unable to approve an amendment to an annex, other than to an annex referred to in paragraph 3 above, shall so notify the Depositary in writing within ninety days from the date of the communication of its adoption. The Depositary shall without delay notify all Parties of any such notification received. A Party may at any time substitute an acceptance for its previous notification and, upon deposit of an instrument of acceptance with the Depositary, the amendment to such an annex shall become effective for that Party.

6. Adjustments to annex II shall be adopted by consensus of the Parties present at a session of the Executive Body and shall become effective for all Parties to the present Protocol on the ninetieth day following the date on which

the Executive Secretary of the Commission notifies those Parties in writing of
the adoption of the adjustment.

Article 12
Signature

1. The present Protocol shall be open for signature at Oslo on 14 June 1994,
then at United Nations Headquarters in New York until 12 December 1994 by
States members of the Commission as well as States having consultative status
with the Commission, pursuant to paragraph 8 of Economic and Social Council resolution 36 (IV) of 28 March 1947, and by regional economic integration
organizations, constituted by sovereign States members of the Commission,
which have competence in respect of the negotiation, conclusion and application of international agreements in matters covered by the Protocol, provided
that the States and organizations concerned are Parties to the Convention and
are listed in Annex II.

2. In matters within their competence, such regional economic integration
organizations shall, on their own behalf, exercise the rights and fulfil the responsibilities which the present Protocol attributes to their member States. In
such cases, the member States of these organizations shall not be entitled to
exercise such rights individually.

Article 13
Ratification, acceptance, approval and accession

1. The present Protocol shall be subject to ratification, acceptance or approval
by Signatories.

2. The present Protocol shall be open for accession as from 12 December
1994 by the States and organizations that meet the requirements of article 12,
paragraph 1.

Article 14
Depositary

The instruments of ratification, acceptance, approval or accession shall be deposited with the Secretary-General of the United Nations, who will perform
the functions of Depositary.

Article 15
Entry into force

1. The present Protocol shall enter into force on the ninetieth day following
the date on which the sixteenth instrument of ratification, acceptance, approval
or accession has been deposited with the Depositary.

2. For each State and organization referred to in article 12, paragraph 1,
which ratifies, accepts or approves the present Protocol or accedes thereto after
the deposit of the sixteenth instrument of ratification, acceptance, approval or

accession, the Protocol shall enter into force on the ninetieth day following the date of deposit by such Party of its instrument of ratification, acceptance, approval or accession.

Article 16
Withdrawal

At any time after five years from the date on which the present Protocol has come into force with respect to a Party, that Party may withdraw from it by giving written notification to the Depositary. Any such withdrawal shall take effect on the ninetieth day following the date of its receipt by the Depositary, or on such later date as may be specified in the notification of the withdrawal.

Article 17
Authentic texts

The original of the present Protocol, of which the English, French and Russian texts are equally authentic, shall be deposited with the Secretary-General of the United Nations.

IN WITNESS WHEREOF the undersigned, being duly authorized thereto, have signed the present Protocol.

DONE at Oslo, this fourteenth day of June one thousand nine hundred and ninety-four.

[Annexes omitted]

5B

Non-Compliance Procedure

Decision 1997/2 Concerning the Implementation Committee, its Structure and Functions and Procedures for Review of Compliance

The Executive Body,

Determined to promote and improve compliance with the existing protocols to the 1979 Convention on Long-range Transboundary Air Pollution,

Recalling article 10, paragraph 2, of the Convention, as well as article 7 of the 1994 Protocol on Further Reduction of Sulphur Emissions and article 3, paragraph 3, of the 1991 Protocol concerning the Control of Emissions of Volatile Organic Compounds or their Transboundary Fluxes,

1. *Establishes* the Implementation Committee for the review of compliance by the Parties with their obligations under the protocols to the Convention;
2. *Decides* that the structure and functions of the Implementation Committee and the procedures for review of compliance shall be those set out in the annex to this decision;
3. *Urges* the Parties to the 1994 Protocol on Further Reduction of Sulphur Emissions to decide that the structure, functions and procedures set out in the annex to this decision shall apply for the review of compliance with article 7, paragraph 3, of that Protocol, in place of the regime adopted at the special session of the Executive Body in Oslo on 14 June 1994;
4. *Urges* the Parties to the 1991 Protocol concerning the Control of Emissions of Volatile Organic Compounds or their Transboundary Fluxes to decide to use the Implementation Committee established by this decision for the purposes of article 3, paragraph 3, of that Protocol and to apply the structure, functions and procedures set out in the annex to this decision to monitor compliance with that Protocol;
5. *Resolves* that the Implementation Committee as well as the structure, functions and procedures set out in the annex to this decision shall be available for the review of compliance with future protocols in accordance with the terms of such protocols and of any decisions of the Parties thereto.

Annex
Structure and functions of the Implementation Committee and procedures for review of compliance

Structure

1. The Committee shall consist of eight Parties to the Convention; each member of the Committee shall be a Party to at least one protocol. The Parties, meeting within the Executive Body, shall, as soon as practicable, elect four Parties to the Committee for a term of two years and four Parties for a term of one year. At each session thereafter, the Executive Body shall elect four new Parties for a term of two years. Outgoing Parties may be re-elected for one consecutive term, unless in a given case the Executive Body decides otherwise. The Committee shall elect its own Chairman and Vice-Chairman.

Meetings

2. The Committee shall, unless it decides otherwise, meet twice a year. The secretariat shall arrange for and service its meetings.

Functions of the Committee

3. The Committee shall:

(a) Review periodically compliance by the Parties with the reporting requirements of the protocols;
(b) Consider any submission or referral made in accordance with paragraphs 4 and 5 below with a view to securing a constructive solution;
(c) Be satisfied, before considering such a submission or referral, that the quality of data reported by a Party has been evaluated by a relevant technical body under the Executive Body and/or, where appropriate, by an expert nominated by the Bureau of the Executive Body; and
(d) Prepare, at the request of the Executive Body, and based on any relevant experience acquired in the performance of its functions under subparagraphs (a), (b) and (c) above, a report on compliance with or implementation of specified obligations in an individual protocol.

Submissions by Parties

4. A submission may be brought before the Committee by:

(a) One or more Parties to a protocol that have reservations about another Party's compliance with its obligations under that instrument. Such a submission shall be addressed in writing to the secretariat and supported by corroborating information. The secretariat shall, within two weeks of receiving a submission, send a copy of it to the Party whose compliance is at issue. Any reply and information in support thereof shall be submitted to the secretariat and to the Parties involved within three months or such longer period as the circumstances of a particular case may require. The secretariat shall transmit the submission and the reply, as well as all corroborating and supporting information, to the Committee, which shall consider the matter as soon as practicable; or

(b) A Party that concludes that, despite its best endeavours, it is or will be unable to comply fully with its obligations under a protocol. Such a submission shall be addressed in writing to the secretariat and explain, in particular, the specific circumstances that the Party considers to be the cause of its non-compliance. The secretariat shall transmit the submission to the Committee, which shall consider it as soon as practicable.

Referrals by the secretariat

5. Where the secretariat, in particular upon reviewing the reports submitted in accordance with a protocol's reporting requirements, becomes aware of possible non-compliance by a Party with its obligations, it may request the Party concerned to furnish necessary information about the matter. If there is no response or the matter is not resolved within three months or such longer period as the circumstances of the matter may require, the secretariat shall bring the matter to the attention of the Committee.

Information gathering

6. To assist the performance of its functions under paragraph 3 above, the Committee may:

(a) Request further information on matters under its consideration, through the secretariat;

(b) Undertake, at the invitation of the Party concerned, information gathering in the territory of that Party; and

(c) Consider any information forwarded by the secretariat concerning compliance with the protocols.

7. The Committee shall ensure the confidentiality of any information that has been provided to it in confidence.

Entitlement to participate

8. A Party in respect of which a submission or referral is made shall be entitled to participate in the consideration by the Committee of that submission or referral, but shall not take part in the preparation and adoption of any report or recommendations of the Committee in accordance with paragraph 9 below.

Committee report to the Executive Body

9. The Committee shall report at least once a year on its activities to the Executive Body and make such recommendations as it considers appropriate,

taking into account the circumstances of the matter, regarding compliance with the protocols. Each report shall be finalized by the Committee no later than ten weeks in advance of the session of the Executive Body at which it is to be considered.

Competence of Committee members

10. Only those Committee members that are Parties to the protocol in respect of which compliance procedures in accordance with paragraphs 3, 6, 7 and 9 above are being undertaken may participate in those procedures. If as a result of the operation of this paragraph the size of the Committee is reduced to five members or less, the Committee shall forthwith refer the matter in question to the Executive Body.

Consideration by the Executive Body

11. The Parties to the protocol concerned, meeting within the Executive Body, may, upon consideration of a report and any recommendations of the Committee, decide upon measures of a non-discriminatory nature to bring about full compliance with the protocol in question, including measures to assist a Party's compliance. Any such decision shall be taken by consensus.

Relationship to settlement of disputes

12. Application of the present compliance procedures shall be without prejudice to the settlement of disputes provisions of the protocols.

Convention for the Protection of the Ozone Layer, 22 March 1985

Editorial note

The Vienna Convention for the Protection of the Ozone Layer, negotiated under the auspices of UNEP, is intended to protect humans and the environment from the harmful effects of activities which modify the ozone layer (Article 2(1)). To achieve this end, the Convention requires Parties to co-operate, according to their means, in research and legislative measures (Article 2(2)(a) and (b)) and to formulate agreed standards, procedures and measures in the form of Protocols and Annexes (Article 2(2)(c)). Parties are also required to facilitate the exchange of relevant 'scientific, technical, socio-economic commercial and legal' information (Article 4(1)), as set out in Annex II. A further obligation is to facilitate exchange of technology, subject to relevant national law (Article 4(2)). Parties are required to report on the measures taken to implement the Convention and Protocols (Article 5).

The Convention establishes a Conference of the Parties which meets on a regular basis to review the Convention (Article 6). UNEP provides Secretariat functions, including the co-ordination of meetings and reports to the Conference of the Parties (Article 7). If a dispute arises between the Parties, the Convention provides several methods of dispute resolution, including: (a) mediation at the request of the Parties involved (Article 11(2)); (b) voluntary submission to arbitration and/or to the ICJ (Article 11(3)); (c) the submission of the dispute to a conciliation body (Article 11(4)). Adoption of amendments to the Convention requires a three-fourths majority of all the Parties present and voting at a meeting of the Conference of the Parties (Article 9(3)). Protocols are also to be adopted at Conferences of the Parties (Article 8). To date, the only Protocol adopted is the 1987 Montreal Protocol on Substances that Deplete the Ozone Layer. Amending a Protocol requires adoption by a two-thirds majority of the Parties present and voting (Article 9(4)). Amendments to the Convention enter into force for those accepting them after acceptance by three-fourths of the Parties, while amendments to a Protocol enter into force for those accepting them upon acceptance by two-thirds of the Parties (Article 9(5)). Amending Annexes of the Convention or a Protocol follow the same procedure as amending the Convention or a Protocol (Article 10(3)). No reservations are permitted to the Convention.

Date of signature: 22 March 1985

Entry into force: 22 September 1989

Depositary: Secretary-General of the United Nations

Contracting Parties: Albania, Algeria, Angola, Antigua and Barbuda, Argentina, Armenia, Australia, Austria, Azerbaijan, Bahamas, Bahrain, Bangladesh, Barbados, Belarus, Belgium, Belize, Benin, Bolivia, Bosnia and Herzegovina, Botswana, Brazil, Brunei Darussalam, Bulgaria, Burkina Faso, Burundi, Cambodia, Cameroon, Canada, Cape Verde, Central African Republic, Chad, Chile, China, Colombia, Comoros, Congo, Congo (Democratic Republic of), Costa Rica, Cote d'Ivoire, Croatia, Cuba, Cyprus, Czech Republic, Denmark, Djibouti, Dominica, Dominican Republic, Ecuador, Egypt, El Salvador, Equatorial Guinea, Estonia, Ethiopia, European Community, Federated States of Micronesia, Fiji, Finland, France, Gabon, Gambia, Georgia, Germany, Ghana, Greece, Grenada, Guatemala, Guinea, Guinea Bissau, Guyana, Haiti, Honduras, Hungary, Iceland, India, Indonesia, Iran (Islamic Republic of), Ireland, Israel, Italy, Jamaica, Japan, Jordan, Kazakhstan, Kenya, Kiribati, Korea (Democratic People's Republic of), Korea (Republic of), Kuwait, Kyrgyzstan, Lao People's Democratic Republic, Latvia, Lebanon, Lesotho, Liberia, Libyan Arab Jamahiriya, Liechtenstein, Lithuania, Luxembourg, Madagascar, Malawi, Malaysia, Maldives, Mali, Malta, Marshall Islands, Mauritania, Mauritius, Mexico, Moldova, Monaco, Mongolia, Morocco, Mozambique, Myanmar, Namibia, Nauru, Nepal, Netherlands, New Zealand, Nicaragua, Niger, Nigeria, Norway, Oman, Pakistan, Palau, Panama, Papua New Guinea, Paraguay, Peru, Philippines, Poland, Portugal, Qatar, Romania, Russian Federation, Rwanda, Saint Kitts and Nevis, Saint Lucia, Saint Vincent and the Grenadines, São Tomé and Príncipe, Samoa, Saudi Arabia, Senegal, Seychelles, Sierra Leone, Singapore, Slovakia, Slovenia, Solomon

Islands, Somalia, South Africa, Spain, Sri Lanka, Sudan, Suriname, Swaziland, Sweden, Switzerland, Syrian Arab Republic, Tajikistan, Tanzania (United Republic of), Thailand, The Former Yugoslav Republic of Macedonia, Togo, Tonga, Trinidad and Tobago, Tunisia, Turkey, Turkmenistan, Tuvalu, Uganda, Ukraine, United Arab Emirates, United Kingdom, United States of America, Uruguay, Uzbekistan, Vanuatu, Venezuela, Vietnam, Yemen, Yugoslavia, Zambia, Zimbabwe.

Website: www.unep.org/ozone

The Vienna Convention for the Protection of the Ozone Layer

Preamble

The Parties to this Convention,

Aware of the potentially harmful impact on human health and the environment through modification of the ozone layer,

Recalling the pertinent provisions of the Declaration of the United Nations Conference on the Human Environment, and in particular principle 21, which provides that 'States have, in accordance with the Charter of the United Nations and the principles of international law, the sovereign right to exploit their own resources pursuant to their own environmental policies, and the responsibility to ensure that activities within their jurisdiction or control do not cause damage to the environment of other States or of areas beyond the limits of national jurisdiction',

Taking into account the circumstances and particular requirements of developing countries,

Mindful of the work and studies proceeding within both international and national organizations and, in particular, of the World Plan of Action on the Ozone Layer of the United Nations Environment Programme,

Mindful also of the precautionary measures for the protection of the ozone layer which have already been taken at the national and international levels,

Aware that measures to protect the ozone layer from modifications due to human activities require international co-operation and action, and should be based on relevant scientific and technical considerations,

Aware also of the need for further research and systematic observations to further develop scientific knowledge of the ozone layer and possible adverse effects resulting from its modification,

Determined to protect human health and the environment against adverse effects resulting from modifications of the ozone layer,

Have agreed as follows:

Article 1
Definitions

For the purposes of this Convention:

1. 'The ozone layer' means the layer of atmospheric ozone above the planetary boundary layer.
2. 'Adverse effects' means changes in the physical environment or biota, including changes in climate, which have significant deleterious effects on human health or on the composition, resilience and productivity of natural and managed ecosystems, or on materials useful to mankind.
3. 'Alternative technologies or equipment' means technologies or equipment the use of which makes it possible to reduce or effectively eliminate emissions of substances which have or are likely to have adverse effects on the ozone layer.
4. 'Alternative substances' means substances which reduce, eliminate or avoid adverse effects on the ozone layer.
5. 'Parties' means, unless the text otherwise indicates, Parties to this Convention.
6. 'Regional economic integration organization' means an organization constituted by sovereign States of a given region which has competence in respect of matters governed by this Convention or its protocols and has been duly authorized, in accordance with its internal procedures, to sign, ratify, accept, approve or accede to the instruments concerned.
7. 'Protocols' means protocols to this Convention.

Article 2
General obligations

1. The Parties shall take appropriate measures in accordance with the provisions of this Convention and of those protocols in force to which they are party to protect human health and the environment against adverse effects resulting or likely to result from human activities which modify or are likely to modify the ozone layer.

2. To this end the Parties shall, in accordance with the means at their disposal and their capabilities:

(a) Co-operate by means of systematic observations, research and information exchange in order to better understand and assess the effects of human activities on the ozone layer and the effects on human health and the environment from modification of the ozone layer;
(b) Adopt appropriate legislative or administrative measures and co-operate in harmonizing appropriate policies to control, limit, reduce or prevent human activities under their jurisdiction or control should it be found that these activities have or are likely to have adverse effects resulting from modification or likely modification of the ozone layer;

(c) Co-operate in the formulation of agreed measures, procedures and standards for the implementation of this Convention, with a view to the adoption of protocols and annexes;

(d) Co-operate with competent international bodies to implement effectively this Convention and protocols to which they are party.

3. The provisions of this Convention shall in no way affect the right of Parties to adopt, in accordance with international law, domestic measures additional to those referred to in paragraphs 1 and 2 above, nor shall they affect additional domestic measures already taken by a Party, provided that these measures are not incompatible with their obligations under this Convention.

4. The application of this article shall be based on relevant scientific and technical considerations.

Article 3
Research and systematic observations

1. The Parties undertake, as appropriate, to initiate and co-operate in, directly or through competent international bodies, the conduct of research and scientific assessments on:

(a) The physical and chemical processes that may affect the ozone layer;

(b) The human health and other biological effects deriving from any modifications of the ozone layer, particularly those resulting from changes in ultra-violet solar radiation having biological effects (UV-B);

(c) Climatic effects deriving from any modifications of the ozone layer;

(d) Effects deriving from any modifications of the ozone layer and any consequent change in UV-B radiation on natural and synthetic materials useful to mankind;

(e) Substances, practices, processes and activities that may affect the ozone layer, and their cumulative effects;

(f) Alternative substances and technologies;

(g) Related socio-economic matters; and as further elaborated in annexes I and II.

2. The Parties undertake to promote or establish, as appropriate, directly or through competent international bodies and taking fully into account national legislation and relevant ongoing activities at both the national and international levels, joint or complementary programmes for systematic observation of the state of the ozone layer and other relevant parameters, as elaborated in annex I.

3. The Parties undertake to co-operate, directly or through competent international bodies, in ensuring the collection, validation and transmission of research and observational data through appropriate world data centres in a regular and timely fashion.

Article 4
Co-operation in the legal, scientific and technical fields

1. The Parties shall facilitate and encourage the exchange of scientific, technical, socio-economic, commercial and legal information relevant to this Convention as further elaborated in annex II. Such information shall be supplied to bodies agreed upon by the Parties. Any such body receiving information regarded as confidential by the supplying Party shall ensure that such information is not disclosed and shall aggregate it to protect its confidentiality before it is made available to all Parties.

2. The Parties shall co-operate, consistent with their national laws, regulations and practices and taking into account in particular the needs of the developing countries, in promoting, directly or through competent international bodies, the development and transfer of technology and knowledge. Such co-operation shall be carried out particularly through:

(a) Facilitation of the acquisition of alternative technologies by other Parties;
(b) Provision of information on alternative technologies and equipment, and supply of special manuals or guides to them;
(c) The supply of necessary equipment and facilities for research and systematic observations;
(d) Appropriate training of scientific and technical personnel.

Article 5
Transmission of information

The Parties shall transmit, through the secretariat, to the Conference of the Parties established under article 6 information on the measures adopted by them in implementation of this Convention and of protocols to which they are party in such form and at such intervals as the meetings of the parties to the relevant instruments may determine.

Article 6
Conference of the Parties

1. A Conference of the Parties is hereby established. The first meeting of the Conference of the Parties shall be convened by the secretariat designated on an interim basis under article 7 not later than one year after entry into force of this Convention. Thereafter, ordinary meetings of the Conference of the Parties shall be held at regular intervals to be determined by the Conference at its first meeting.

2. Extraordinary meetings of the Conference of the Parties shall be held at such other times as may be deemed necessary by the Conference, or at the written request of any Party, provided that, within six months of the request being communicated to them by the secretariat, it is supported by at least one third of the Parties.

3. The Conference of the Parties shall by consensus agree upon and adopt rules of procedure and financial rules for itself and for any subsidiary bodies it may establish, as well as financial provisions governing the functioning of the secretariat.

4. The Conference of the Parties shall keep under continuous review the implementation of this Convention, and, in addition, shall:

(a) Establish the form and the intervals for transmitting the information to be submitted in accordance with article 5 and consider such information as well as reports submitted by any subsidiary body;

(b) Review the scientific information on the ozone layer, on its possible modification and on possible effects of any such modification;

(c) Promote, in accordance with article 2, the harmonization of appropriate policies, strategies and measures for minimizing the release of substances causing or likely to cause modification of the ozone layer, and make recommendations on any other measures relating to this Convention;

(d) Adopt, in accordance with articles 3 and 4, programmes for research, systematic observations, scientific and technological co-operation, the exchange of information and the transfer of technology and knowledge;

(e) Consider and adopt, as required, in accordance with articles 9 and 10, amendments to this Convention and its annexes;

(f) Consider amendments to any protocol, as well as to any annexes thereto, and, if so decided, recommend their adoption to the parties to the protocol concerned;

(g) Consider and adopt, as required, in accordance with article 10, additional annexes to this Convention;

(h) Consider and adopt, as required, protocols in accordance with article 8;

(i) Establish such subsidiary bodies as are deemed necessary for the implementation of this Convention;

(j) Seek, where appropriate, the services of competent international bodies and scientific committees, in particular the World Meteorological Organization and the World Health Organization as well as the Co-ordinating Committee on the Ozone Layer, in scientific research, systematic observations and other activities pertinent to the objectives of this Convention, and make use as appropriate of information from these bodies and committees;

(k) Consider and undertake any additional action that may be required for the achievement of the purposes of this Convention.

5. The United Nations, its specialized agencies and the International Atomic Energy Agency, as well as any State not party to this Convention, may be represented at meetings of the Conference of the Parties by observers. Any body or agency, whether national or international, governmental or non-governmental, qualified in fields relating to the protection of the ozone layer which has informed the secretariat of its wish to be represented at a meeting of the

Conference of the Parties as an observer may be admitted unless at least one-third of the Parties present object. The admission and participation of observers shall be subject to the rules of procedure adopted by the Conference of the Parties.

Article 7
Secretariat

1. The functions of the secretariat shall be:

(a) To arrange for and service meetings provided for in articles 6, 8, 9 and 10;
(b) To prepare and transmit reports based upon information received in accordance with articles 4 and 5, as well as upon information derived from meetings of subsidiary bodies established under article 6;
(c) To perform the functions assigned to it by any protocol;
(d) To prepare reports on its activities carried out in implementation of its functions under this Convention and present them to the Conference of the Parties;
(e) To ensure the necessary co-ordination with other relevant international bodies, and in particular to enter into such administrative and contractual arrangements as may be required for the effective discharge of its functions;
(f) To perform such other functions as may be determined by the Conference of the Parties.

2. The secretariat functions will be carried out on an interim basis by the United Nations Environment Programme until the completion of the first ordinary meeting of the Conference of the Parties held pursuant to article 6. At its first ordinary meeting, the Conference of the Parties shall designate the secretariat from amongst those existing competent international organizations which have signified their willingness to carry out the secretariat functions under this Convention.

Article 8
Adoption of protocols

1. The Conference of the Parties may at a meeting adopt protocols pursuant to article 2.
2. The text of any proposed protocol shall be communicated to the Parties by the secretariat at least six months before such a meeting.

Article 9
Amendment of the Convention or protocols

1. Any Party may propose amendments to this Convention or to any protocol. Such amendments shall take due account, *inter alia*, of relevant scientific and technical considerations.

2. Amendments to this Convention shall be adopted at a meeting of the Conference of the Parties. Amendments to any protocol shall be adopted at a meeting of the Parties to the protocol in question. The text of any proposed amendment to this Convention or to any protocol, except as may otherwise be provided in such protocol, shall be communicated to the Parties by the secretariat at least six months before the meeting at which it is proposed for adoption. The secretariat shall also communicate proposed amendments to the signatories to this Convention for information.

3. The Parties shall make every effort to reach agreement on any proposed amendment to this Convention by consensus. If all efforts at consensus have been exhausted, and no agreement reached, the amendment shall as a last resort be adopted by a three-fourths majority vote of the Parties present and voting at the meeting, and shall be submitted by the Depositary to all Parties for ratification, approval or acceptance.

4. The procedure mentioned in paragraph 3 above shall apply to amendments to any protocol, except that a two-thirds majority of the parties to that protocol present and voting at the meeting shall suffice for their adoption.

5. Ratification, approval or acceptance of amendments shall be notified to the Depositary in writing. Amendments adopted in accordance with paragraphs 3 or 4 above shall enter into force between parties having accepted them on the ninetieth day after the receipt by the Depositary of notification of their ratification, approval or acceptance by at least three-fourths of the Parties to this Convention or by at least two-thirds of the parties to the protocol concerned, except as may otherwise be provided in such protocol. Thereafter the amendments shall enter into force for any other Party on the ninetieth day after that Party deposits its instrument of ratification, approval or acceptance of the amendments.

6. For the purposes of this article, 'Parties present and voting' means Parties present and casting an affirmative or negative vote.

Article 10
Adoption and amendment of annexes

1. The annexes to this Convention or to any protocol shall form an integral part of this Convention or of such protocol, as the case may be, and, unless expressly provided otherwise, a reference to this Convention or its protocols constitutes at the same time a reference to any annexes thereto. Such annexes shall be restricted to scientific, technical and administrative matters.

2. Except as may be otherwise provided in any protocol with respect to its annexes, the following procedure shall apply to the proposal, adoption and entry into force of additional annexes to this Convention or of annexes to a protocol:

(a) Annexes to this Convention shall be proposed and adopted according to the procedure laid down in article 9, paragraphs 2 and 3, while annexes to any protocol shall be proposed and adopted according to the procedure laid down in article 9, paragraphs 2 and 4;

(b) Any party that is unable to approve an additional annex to this Convention or annex to any protocol to which it is party shall so notify the Depositary, in writing, within six months from the date of the communication of the adoption by the Depositary. The Depositary shall without delay notify all Parties of any such notification received. A Party may at any time substitute an acceptance for a previous declaration of objection and the annexes shall thereupon enter into force for that Party;

(c) On the expiry of six months from the date of the circulation of the communication by the Depositary, the annex shall become effective for all Parties to this Convention or to any protocol concerned which have not submitted a notification in accordance with the provision of subparagraph (b) above.

3. The proposal, adoption and entry into force of amendments to annexes to this Convention or to any protocol shall be subject to the same procedure as for the proposal, adoption and entry into force of annexes to the Convention or annexes to a protocol. Annexes and amendments thereto shall take due account, *inter alia*, of relevant scientific and technical considerations.

4. If an additional annex or an amendment to an annex involves an amendment to this Convention or to any protocol, the additional annex or amended annex shall not enter into force until such time as the amendment to this Convention or to the protocol concerned enters into force.

Article 11
Settlement of disputes

1. In the event of a dispute between Parties concerning the interpretation or application of this Convention, the parties concerned shall seek solution by negotiation.

2. If the parties concerned cannot reach agreement by negotiation, they may jointly seek the good offices of, or request mediation by, a third party.

3. When ratifying, accepting, approving or acceding to this Convention, or at any time thereafter, a State or regional economic integration organization may declare in writing to the Depositary that for a dispute not resolved in accordance with paragraph 1 or paragraph 2 above, it accepts one or both of the following means of dispute settlement as compulsory:

(a) Arbitration in accordance with procedures to be adopted by the Conference of the Parties at its first ordinary meeting;

(b) Submission of the dispute to the International Court of Justice.

4. If the parties have not, in accordance with paragraph 3 above, accepted the same or any procedure, the dispute shall be submitted to conciliation in accordance with paragraph 5 below unless the parties otherwise agree.

5. A conciliation commission shall be created upon the request of one of the parties to the dispute. The commission shall be composed of an equal number of members appointed by each party concerned and a chairman chosen jointly by the members appointed by each party. The commission shall render a final and recommendatory award, which the parties shall consider in good faith.

6. The provisions of this Article shall apply with respect to any protocol except as provided in the protocol concerned.

Article 12
Signature

This Convention shall be open for signature by States and by regional economic integration organizations at the Federal Ministry for Foreign Affairs of the Republic of Austria in Vienna from 22 March 1985 to 21 September 1985, and at United Nations Headquarters in New York from 22 September 1985 to 21 March 1986.

Article 13
Ratification, acceptance or approval

1. This Convention and any protocol shall be subject to ratification, acceptance or approval by States and by regional economic integration organizations. Instruments of ratification, acceptance or approval shall be deposited with the Depositary.

2. Any organization referred to in paragraph 1 above which becomes a Party to this Convention or any protocol without any of its member States being a Party shall be bound by all the obligations under the Convention or the protocol, as the case may be. In the case of such organizations, one or more of whose member States is a Party to the Convention or relevant protocol, the organization and its member States shall decide on their respective responsibilities for the performance of their obligation under the Convention or protocol, as the case may be. In such cases, the organization and the member States shall not be entitled to exercise rights under the Convention or relevant protocol concurrently.

3. In their instruments of ratification, acceptance or approval, the organizations referred to in paragraph 1 above shall declare the extent of their competence with respect to the matters governed by the Convention or the relevant protocol. These organizations shall also inform the Depositary of any substantial modification in the extent of their competence.

Article 14
Accession

1. This Convention and any protocol shall be open for accession by States and by regional economic integration organizations from the date on which the Convention or the protocol concerned is closed for signature. The instruments of accession shall be deposited with the Depositary.

2. In their instruments of accession, the organizations referred to in paragraph 1 above shall declare the extent of their competence with respect to the matters governed by the Convention or the relevant protocol. These organizations shall also inform the Depositary of any substantial modification in the extent of their competence.

3. The provisions of article 13, paragraph 2, shall apply to regional economic integration organizations which accede to this Convention or any protocol.

Article 15
Right to vote

1. Each Party to this Convention or to any protocol shall have one vote.

2. Except as provided for in paragraph 1 above, regional economic integration organizations, in matters within their competence, shall exercise their right to vote with a number of votes equal to the number of their member States which are Parties to the Convention or the relevant protocol. Such organizations shall not exercise their right to vote if their member States exercise theirs, and vice versa.

Article 16
Relationship between the Convention and its protocols

1. A State or a regional economic integration organization may not become a party to a protocol unless it is, or becomes at the same time, a Party to the Convention.

2. Decisions concerning any protocol shall be taken only by the parties to the protocol concerned.

Article 17
Entry into force

1. This Convention shall enter into force on the ninetieth day after the date of deposit of the twentieth instrument of ratification, acceptance, approval or accession.

2. Any protocol, except as otherwise provided in such protocol, shall enter into force on the ninetieth day after the date of deposit of the eleventh instrument of ratification, acceptance or approval of such protocol or accession thereto.

3. For each Party which ratifies, accepts or approves this Convention or accedes thereto after the deposit of the twentieth instrument of ratification,

acceptance, approval or accession, it shall enter into force on the ninetieth day after the date of deposit by such Party of its instrument of ratification, acceptance, approval or accession.

4. Any protocol, except as otherwise provided in such protocol, shall enter into force for a party that ratifies, accepts or approves that protocol or accedes thereto after its entry into force pursuant to paragraph 2 above, on the ninetieth day after the date on which that party deposits its instrument of ratification, acceptance, approval or accession, or on the date which the Convention enters into force for that Party, whichever shall be the later.

5. For the purposes of paragraphs 1 and 2 above, any instrument deposited by a regional economic integration organization shall not be counted as additional to those deposited by member States of such organization.

Article 18
Reservations

No reservations may be made to this Convention.

Article 19
Withdrawal

1. At any time after four years from the date on which this Convention has entered into force for a Party, that Party may withdraw from the Convention by giving written notification to the Depositary.

2. Except as may be provided in any protocol, at any time after four years from the date on which such protocol has entered into force for a party, that party may withdraw from the protocol by giving written notification to the Depositary.

3. Any such withdrawal shall take effect upon expiry of one year after the date of its receipt by the Depositary, or on such later date as may be specified in the notification of the withdrawal.

4. Any Party which withdraws from this Convention shall be considered as also having withdrawn from any protocol to which it is party.

Article 20
Depositary

1. The Secretary-General of the United Nations shall assume the functions of depositary of this Convention and any protocols.

2. The Depositary shall inform the Parties, in particular, of:

(a) The signature of this Convention and of any protocol, and the deposit of instruments of ratification, acceptance, approval or accession in accordance with articles 13 and 14;
(b) The date on which the Convention and any protocol will come into force in accordance with article 17;
(c) Notifications of withdrawal made in accordance with article 19;

(d) Amendments adopted with respect to the Convention and any protocol, their acceptance by the parties and their date of entry into force in accordance with article 9;

(e) All communications relating to the adoption and approval of annexes and to the amendment of annexes in accordance with article 10;

(f) Notifications by regional economic integration organizations of the extent of their competence with respect to matters governed by this Convention and any protocols, and of any modifications thereof.

(g) Declarations made in accordance with article 11, paragraph 3.

Article 21
Authentic texts

The original of this Convention, of which the Arabic, Chinese, English, French, Russian and Spanish texts are equally authentic, shall be deposited with the Secretary-General of the United Nations.

IN WITNESS WHEREOF the undersigned, being duly authorized to that effect, have signed this Convention.

DONE AT VIENNA ON THE 22ND DAY OF MARCH 1985

Annex I
Research and systematic observations

1. The Parties to the Convention recognize that the major scientific issues are:

(a) Modification of the ozone layer which would result in a change in the amount of solar ultra-violet radiation having biological effects (UV-B) that reaches the Earth's surface and the potential consequences for human health, for organisms, ecosystems and materials useful to mankind;

(b) Modification of the vertical distribution of ozone, which could change the temperature structure of the atmosphere and the potential consequences for weather and climate.

2. The Parties to the Convention, in accordance with article 3, shall cooperate in conducting research and systematic observations and in formulating recommendations for future research and observation in such areas as:

(a) Research into the physics and chemistry of the atmosphere
    (i) Comprehensive theoretical models: further development of models which consider the interaction between radiative, dynamic and chemical processes; studies of the simultaneous effects of various man-made and naturally occurring species upon atmospheric ozone; interpretation of satellite and non-satellite measurement data sets;

evaluation of trends in atmospheric and geophysical parameters, and the development of methods for attributing changes in these parameters to specific causes;

(ii) Laboratory studies of: rate coefficients, absorption cross sections and mechanisms of tropospheric and stratospheric chemical and photochemical processes; spectroscopic data to support field measurements in all relevant spectral regions;

(iii) Field measurements: the concentration and fluxes of key source gases of both natural and anthropogenic origin; atmospheric dynamics studies; simultaneous measurements of photochemically-related species down to the planetary boundary layer, using *in situ* and remote sensing instruments; intercomparison of different sensors, including co-ordinated correlative measures for satellite instrumentation; three-dimensional fields of key atmospheric trace constituents, solar spectral flux and meteorological parameters;

(iv) Instrument development, including satellite and nonsatellite sensors for atmospheric trace constituents, solar flux and meteorological parameters;

(b) Research into health, biological and photodegradation effects

(i) The relationship between human exposure to visible and ultra-violet solar radiation and (a) the development of both non-melanoma and melanoma skin cancer and (b) the effects on the immunological system;

(ii) Effects of UV-B radiation, including the wavelength dependence, upon (a) agricultural crops, forests and other terrestrial ecosystems and (b) the aquatic food web and fisheries, as well as possible inhibition of oxygen production by marine phytoplankton;

(iii) The mechanisms by which UV-B radiation acts on biological materials, species and ecosystems, including: the relationship between dose, dose rate, and response; photorepair, adaptation, and protection;

(iv) Studies of biological action spectra and the spectral response using polychromatic radiation in order to include possible interactions of the various wavelength regions;

(v) The influence of UV-B radiation on: the sensitivities and activities of biological species important to the biospheric balance; primary processes such as photosynthesis and biosynthesis;

(vi) The influence of UV-B radiation on the photodegradation of pollutants, agricultural chemicals and other materials;

(c) Research on effects on climate

(i) Theoretical and observational studies of the radiative effects of ozone and other trace species and the impact on climate parameters, such as land and ocean surface temperatures, precipitation patterns, the exchange between the troposphere and stratosphere;

   (ii) The investigation of the effects of such climate impacts on various aspects of human activity;

(b) Systematic observation on:

   (i) The status of the ozone layer (i.e. the spatial and temporal variability of the total column content and vertical distribution) by making the Global Ozone Observing System, based on the integration of satellite and groundbased systems, fully operational;

   (ii) The tropospheric and stratospheric concentrations of source gases for the HO_x, NO_x, ClO_x and carbon families;

   (iii) The temperature from the ground to the mesosphere, utilizing both ground-based and satellite systems;

   (iv) Wavelength-resolved solar flux reaching, and thermal radiation leaving, the Earth's atmosphere, utilizing satellite measurements;

   (v) Wavelength-resolved solar flux reaching the Earth's surface in the ultra-violet range having biological effects (UV-B);

   (vi) Aerosol properties and distribution from the ground to the mesosphere, utilizing ground-based, airborne and satellite systems;

   (vii) Climatically important variables by the maintenance of programmes of high-quality meteorological surface measurements;

   (viii) Trace species, temperatures, solar flux and aerosols utilizing improved methods for analyzing global data.

3. The Parties to the Convention shall co-operate, taking into account the particular needs of the developing countries, in promoting the appropriate scientific and technical training required to participate in the research and systematic observations outlined in this annex. Particular emphasis should be given to the intercalibration of observational instrumentation and methods with a view to generating comparable or standardized scientific data sets.

4. The following chemical substances of natural and anthropogenic origin, not listed in order of priority, are thought to have the potential to modify the chemical and physical properties of the ozone layer.

(a) Carbon substances

   (i) *Carbon monoxide* (CO) Carbon monoxide has significant natural and anthropogenic sources, and is thought to play a major direct role in tropospheric photochemistry, and an indirect role in stratospheric photochemistry.

   (ii) *Carbon dioxide* (CO_2) Carbon dioxide has significant natural and anthropogenic sources, and affects stratospheric ozone by influencing the thermal structure of the atmosphere.

   (iii) *Methane* (CH_4) Methane has both natural and anthropogenic sources, and affects both tropospheric and stratospheric ozone.

    (iv) *Non-methane hydrocarbon species* Non-methane hydrocarbon species, which consist of a large number of chemical substances, have both natural and anthropogenic sources, and play a direct role in tropospheric photochemistry and an indirect role in stratospheric photochemistry.

(b) Nitrogen substances

    (i) *Nitrous oxide* (N_2O) The dominant sources of N_2O are natural, but anthropogenic contributions are becoming increasingly important. Nitrous oxide is the primary source of stratospheric NO_X, which play a vital role in controlling the abundance of stratospheric ozone.

    (ii) *Nitrogen oxides* (NO_X) Ground-level sources of NO_X play a major direct role only in tropospheric photochemical processes and an indirect role in stratosphere photochemistry, whereas injection of NO_X close to the tropopause may lead directly to a change in upper tropospheric and stratospheric ozone.

(c) Chlorine substances

    (i) *Fully halogenated alkanes*, e.g. CCl_4, $CFCl_3$ (CFC-11), CF_2Cl_2 (CFC-12), $C_2F_3Cl_3$ (CFC-113), $C_2F_4Cl_2$ (CFC-114) Fully halogenated alkanes are anthropogenic and act as a source of ClO_X which plays a vital role in ozone photochemistry, especially in the 30–50 km altitude region.

    (ii) *Partially halogenated alkanes*, e.g. CH_3Cl, CHF_2Cl (CFC-22), CH_3CCl_3, $CHFCl_2$ (CFC-21) The sources of CH_3Cl are natural, whereas the other partially halogenated alkanes mentioned above are anthropogenic in origin. These gases also act as a source of stratospheric ClO_X.

(d) Bromine substances

    Fully halogenated alkanes, e.g. CF_3Br These gases are anthropogenic and act as a source of BrO_X, which behaves in a manner similar to ClO_X.

(e) Hydrogen substances

    (i) *Hydrogen* (H_2) Hydrogen, the source of which is natural and anthropogenic, plays a minor role in stratospheric photochemistry.

    (ii) *Water* (H_2O) Water, the source of which is natural, plays a vital role in both tropospheric and stratospheric photochemistry. Local sources of water vapor in the stratosphere include the oxidation of methane and, to a lesser extent, of hydrogen.

Annex II
Information exchange

1. The Parties to the Convention recognize that the collection and sharing of information is an important means of implementing the objectives of this

Convention and of assuring that any actions that may be taken are appropriate and equitable. Therefore, Parties shall exchange scientific, technical, socio-economic, business, commercial and legal information.

2. The Parties to the Convention, in deciding what information is to be collected and exchanged, should take into account the usefulness of the information and the costs of obtaining it. The Parties further recognize that co-operation under this annex has to be consistent with national laws, regulations and practices regarding patents, trade secrets, and protection of confidential and proprietary information.

3. *Scientific information*
This includes information on:

(a) Planned and ongoing research, both governmental and private, to facilitate the co-ordination of research programmes so as to make the most effective use of available national and international resources;
(b) The emission data needed for research;
(c) Scientific results published in peer-reviewed literature on the understanding of the physics and chemistry of the Earth's atmosphere and of its susceptibility to change, in particular on the state of the ozone layer and effects on human health, environment and climate which would result from changes on all time-scales in either the total column content or the vertical distribution of ozone;
(d) The assessment of research results and the recommendation for future research.

4. *Technical information*
This includes information on:

(a) The availability and cost of chemical substitutes and of alternative technologies to reduce the emissions of ozone modifying substances and related planned and ongoing research;
(b) The limitations and any risks involved in using chemical or other substitutes and alternative technologies.

5. *Socio-economic and commercial information on the substances referred to in annex I*
This includes information on:

(a) Production and production capacity;
(b) Use and use patterns;
(c) Imports/exports;
(d) The costs, risks and benefits of human activities which may indirectly modify the ozone layer and of the impacts of regulatory actions taken or being considered to control these activities.

6. *Legal information*

This includes information on:

(a) National laws, administrative measures and legal research relevant to the protection of the ozone layer;
(b) International agreements, including bilateral agreements, relevant to the protection of the ozone layer;
(c) Methods and terms of licensing and availability of patents relevant to the protection of the ozone layer.

Montreal Protocol on Substances that Deplete the Ozone Layer, 16 September 1987, as either adjusted and/or amended in London 1990, Copenhagen 1992, Vienna 1995, Montreal 1997 and Beijing 1999 (consolidated version)

Editorial note

The 1987 Montreal Protocol to the Vienna Convention is the only Protocol to date adopted under the ozone layer treaty regime.

The Montreal Protocol sets forth specific legal obligations, including limitations and reductions on the calculated levels of consumption and production of certain controlled ozone-depleting substances. Its negotiation and conclusion, shortly after the 1985 Vienna Convention, were prompted by new scientific evidence indicating that emissions of certain substances were significantly depleting and modifying the ozone layer and would have potential climatic effects (Preamble). The absence of scientific evidence that actual harm was occurring required the international community to take 'precautionary measures to control equitably total global emissions' of substances that deplete the ozone layer (Preamble).

The original text of the Montreal Protocol was adopted in 1987 and has been subsequently modified on several occasions. In 1990 the Second Meeting of the Parties to the Montreal Protocol adopted the first Adjustment and Amendments to the Montreal Protocol (London Adjustment and Amendment). The 1990 Montreal Protocol Amendments introduced important changes. The Preamble was amended to include reference to the need to take into account the 'developmental needs of developing countries', the provision of 'additional financial resources and access to relevant technologies', and the 'transfer of alternative technologies'. The definition of 'controlled substances' and 'production' was amended (Article 1(4) and (5)), and a definition of 'transitional substances' was introduced (Article 1(9)). The amended definition of 'production' excludes 'recycled' and 'reused' amounts (Article 1(5)). Article 2(5) was amended to establish new rules concerning transfers of calculated levels of production between parties and changes were introduced to all the important operational provisions, particularly those requiring the reduction and, ultimately, prohibition of the use of controlled substances which were subject to control measures relating to consumption, production and trade. New rules were also adopted relating to financial arrangements and technology transfer.

In 1992 the Fourth Meeting of the Parties to the Montreal Protocol adopted a second round of Adjustment and Amendments (Copenhagen Adjustment and Amendment). The 1992 Adjustments introduced changes to the timetable for phasing out substances under Articles 2A to 2E of the amended 1987 Montreal Protocol; listed three new controlled substances and further trade restrictions; adopted new reporting requirements, enlarged the Implementation Committee, and adopted an indicative list of measures to be taken against parties which were not in compliance; it also established the Multilateral Fund on a permanent basis. Since 1992, there have been three further rounds of adjustments in 1995, 1997 and 1999 and two amendments have been adopted, the first at the Ninth Meeting of the Parties in 1997 (Montreal Amendment) and the second at the Eleventh Meeting of the Parties in 1999 (Beijing Amendment). The 1997 Montreal Amendment established a new timetable for phasing out the use of methyl bromide and adopted a new licensing system for controlling trade based on licences issued by the Parties for each export and import of controlled substances. The licensing system will enable customs and police officials to track trade in CFCs and to detect unlicensed trade. The 1999 Beijing Amendment provides for new production controls on Group I, Annex C substances, lists bromochloromethane as a controlled substance and institutes new reporting obligations for quarantine and pre-shipment uses of methyl bromide.

The text of the Montreal Protocol reproduced in this volume is the consolidated version of the original text adopted in 1987 as modified by the various adjustments and amendments identified above.

Articles 2A to 2I regulate the production and consumption of the substances covered by the provisions of the Protocol: *CFCs* (Article 2A), *Halons* (Article 2B), *Additional CFCs* (Article 2C), *Carbon tetrachloride* (Article 2D), *Methylchloroform* (Article 2E), *Hydrofluorocarbons* (Article 2F), *Hydrobromofluorocarbons* (Article 2G), *Methyl bromide* (Article 2H) and *Bromochloromethane* (Article 2I). Articles 2A to 2I provide for specific targets and timetables for the production and consumption of the regulated substances. For example, Article 2A as adjusted and amended, requires each party to limit its calculated level of consumption of Annex A Group I substances to 1986 levels within nineteen months of the entry into force of the Protocol. Thereafter annual consumption is to be reduced to 25 percent of 1986 levels by 1 June 1994, with a complete phase-out by 1 January 1996. Each party is also to reduce calculated levels of production of Annex A substances by the same amounts and by the same dates, except that for each amount the level may be increased by up to 10 percent based on the 1986 level provided that such increase is only to satisfy the 'basic domestic needs' of developing country parties operating under Article 5. The 1999 limit of production may be increased, in the same circumstances, by a quantity equal to the annual average of production for basic domestic needs for the period 1995–1997 unless the parties decide otherwise. The 1999 Beijing Adjustments introduced new reductions for production for basic domestic needs by Article 5 parties. These parties are required to phase out production of Group I Annex A CFCs by 1 January 2010, with intermediate reductions of 20% by 2003, 50% by 2005 and 85% by 2007 based on their annual averages of production for basic domestic needs for the period 1995–1997.

Article 2 deals with transfer of production and rules regarding facilities under construction. For the purpose of industrial rationalisation, Article 2(5) sets out the conditions under which parties whose 1986 production level of Annex A Group I substances was less than twenty-five kilotonnes could transfer to or receive from any other party production which exceeded the limits in Article 2(1), (3) and (4). The 1992 Amendment introduced a new Article 2(5)bis allowing any party not operating under Article 5(1) to transfer to another such party any portion of its calculated level of consumption set out in Article 2F provided that certain conditions are fulfilled. Article 2(6) allows a party not operating under Article 5 to complete facilities for production under construction or contracted for prior to 16 September 1987, provided that facilities are completed by 31 December 1990 and the party's level of consumption remains below 0.5 kilograms per capita. By Article 2(8) of the 1987 Montreal Protocol, parties which are member states of a regional economic integration organisation (such as the EC) may 'jointly fulfil' their obligations provided that their total combined level of consumption does not exceed levels set by the Protocol, and that certain procedural obligations are fulfilled (the parties to any such agreement must inform the Secretariat and all member states of the regional organisation, and the organisation itself).

Article 4 establishes innovative trade provisions to achieve its environmental objectives. These measures address trade in controlled substances by parties with states which are not parties to the Protocol, trade in products containing controlled substances, and trade in products produced with but not containing controlled substances.

The Protocol includes special provisions to take account of the special needs of developing countries (Article 5). Article 5(1), for example, allowed developing country parties whose calculated level of consumption was less than 0.3 kilograms *per capita* a grace period of ten years beyond the dates set for phase-out in paragraphs 1 to 4 of Article 2 of the Protocol (1987 version).

The original provisions of the Montreal Protocol were insufficiently attractive to encourage the participation of many developing countries, and further incentives were adopted by the 1990 Amendments. These developed the rules concerning the special situation of developing countries by replacing Article 5 in full and establishing, under a new Article 10, a mechanism to provide financial resources. The amended Article 5 created an incentive for developing countries to become parties to the Protocol before 1 January 1999 by fixing that date as the final point at which states will be able to benefit from the commencement of the ten year period of delay for compliance with the control measures in Articles 2A to 2E as amended (Article 5(1)). Significantly, Article 5(5) as amended by the 1990 Amendment recognised that the capacity of developing country parties to fulfil their obligations and their implementation would depend upon 'the effective implementation of the financial co-operation as provided by Article 10 and transfer of technology as provided by Article 10A'. Other changes provided by the new Article 5 include limiting parties operating under Article 5(1) to annual levels of consumption of 0.2 kilograms per capita of Annex B substances and providing for the situation in which a party operating under Article 5(1) finds itself unable to obtain an adequate supply of controlled substances or is unable to implement any or all of its obligations in Articles 2A or 2E due to the inadequate implementation of the new provisions on financial co-operation and transfer of technology. The really significant change, however, was the amendment to Article 10, which set a precedent followed in subsequent agreements addressing global environmental problems.

The original Article 10 of the Montreal Protocol contained rather innocuous and traditional environmental treaty provisions on technical assistance, particularly for developing countries, to facilitate participation in and implementation of the Protocol, including through the preparation of work plans. The 1990 Amendments introduced financial incentives, almost of a compensatory nature, to entice hesitant developing countries to join the Montreal Protocol regime. The new Article 10 established a 'Financial Mechanism' to provide financial and technical co-operation, including the transfer of technologies, to parties operating under Article 5(1) of the Protocol to enable their compliance with Articles 2A to 2E of the amended Protocol. The mechanism, which is to meet 'all agreed incremental costs' of such parties, includes a Multilateral Fund to meet, on a grant or concessional basis, the agreed incremental costs; to finance certain clearing house functions related to, *inter alia*, identifying needs for and facilitating co-operation; and to finance secretarial services of the Fund. The Fund operates under the authority of the parties, who decide on its overall policies, and is operated by an Executive Committee which discharges its tasks and responsibilities with the co-operation of the World Bank, UNEP, UNDP and (more recently) UNIDO. The Multilateral Fund is financed by contributions from parties not operating under Article 5(1) on the basis of the UN scale of assessments, in convertible currency, in kind, and/or in national currencies.

The Protocol as amended in 1990 also allows bilateral and regional co-operation in financing in certain specified circumstances. Resources are to be disbursed with the concurrence of the beneficiary party. Under Article 10(A), introduced by the 1990 Amendments, each party agrees to take every practicable step to ensure that the best available, environmentally safe substitutes and technologies are expeditiously transferred, under fair and most favourable conditions, to parties operating under Article 5(1).

The principal technique for ensuring compliance with the Protocol and its amendments, apart from the non-compliance procedure and trade sanctions, are the reporting requirements, which are more detailed than most environmental treaties (Article 7). Article 9 provides for research, development, public awareness and exchange of information.

The Protocol is operated under the auspices of regular meetings of the parties (Article 11) whose functions include reviewing implementation of the Protocol; deciding on any adjustments or reductions under Article 2(9) and on the addition or removal of substances from any Annex under Article 2(10); assessing the Article 2 control measures; and considering and adopting proposals for amendment of the Protocol or any Annex and for any new Annex. Fourteen meetings of the parties have been held to date. At their first meeting the parties approved procedures and mechanisms for determining non-compliance in accordance with Article 8 of the Protocol and the consequences thereof. The Protocol also establishes specific tasks for the Secretariat, which is provided by UNEP (Article 12).

Date of signature:	Montreal Protocol – 16 September 1987
Date of adoption of amendments:	London Amendment – 2nd Meeting of the Parties – 27–29 June 1990
	Copenhagen Amendment – 4th Meeting of the Parties – 23–25 November 1992
	Montreal Amendment – 9th Meeting of the Parties – 15–17 September 1997
	Beijing Amendment – 11th Meeting of the Parties – 27 November – 3 December 1999
Entry into force:	Montreal Protocol – 1 January 1989
	London Amendment – 10 August 1992
	Copenhagen Amendment – 14 June 1994
	Montreal Amendment – 10 November 1999
	Beijing Amendment – 25 February 2002
Depositary:	Secretary-General of the United Nations

Contracting Parties: Albania, Algeria, Angola, Antigua and Barbuda, Argentina, Armenia, Australia, Austria, Azerbaijan, Bahamas, Bahrain, Bangladesh, Barbados, Belarus, Belgium, Belize, Benin, Bolivia, Bosnia and Herzegovina, Botswana, Brazil, Brunei Darussalam, Bulgaria, Burkina Faso, Burundi, Cambodia, Cameroon, Canada, Cape Verde, Central African Republic, Chad, Chile, China, Colombia, Comoros, Congo, Congo (Democratic Republic of), Costa Rica, Cote d'Ivoire, Croatia, Cuba, Cyprus, Czech Republic, Denmark, Djibouti, Dominica, Dominican Republic, Ecuador, Egypt, El Salvador, Estonia, Ethiopia, European Community, Federated States of Micronesia, Fiji, Finland, France, Gabon, Gambia, Georgia, Germany, Ghana, Greece, Grenada, Guatemala, Guinea, Guinea Bissau, Guyana, Haiti, Honduras, Hungary, Iceland, India, Indonesia, Iran (Islamic Republic of), Ireland, Israel, Italy, Jamaica, Japan, Jordan, Kazakhstan, Kenya, Kiribati, Korea (Democratic People's Republic of), Korea (Republic of), Kuwait, Kyrgyzstan, Lao People's Democratic Republic, Latvia, Lebanon, Lesotho, Liberia, Libyan Arab Jamahiriya, Liechtenstein, Lithuania, Luxembourg, Madagascar, Malawi, Malaysia, Maldives, Mali, Malta, Marshall Islands, Mauritania, Mauritius, Mexico, Moldova, Monaco, Mongolia, Morocco, Mozambique, Myanmar, Namibia, Nauru, Nepal, Netherlands, New Zealand, Nicaragua, Niger, Nigeria, Norway, Oman, Pakistan, Palau, Panama, Papua New Guinea, Paraguay, Peru, Philippines, Poland, Portugal, Qatar, Romania, Russian Federation, Rwanda, Saint Kitts and Nevis, Saint Lucia, Saint Vincent and the Grenadines, São Tomé and Príncipe, Samoa, Saudi Arabia, Senegal, Seychelles, Sierra Leone, Singapore, Slovakia, Slovenia, Solomon Islands, Somalia, South Africa, Spain, Sri Lanka, Sudan, Suriname, Swaziland, Sweden, Switzerland, Syrian Arab Republic, Tajikistan, Tanzania (United Republic of), Thailand, The Former Yugoslav Republic of Macedonia, Togo, Tonga, Trinidad and Tobago, Tunisia, Turkey, Turkmenistan, Tuvalu, Uganda, Ukraine, United Arab Emirates, United Kingdom, United States of America, Uruguay, Uzbekistan, Vanuatu, Venezuela, Vietnam, Yemen, Yugoslavia, Zambia, Zimbabwe.

Contracting Parties
(London Amendment):

Algeria, Antigua and Barbuda, Argentina, Australia, Austria, Azerbaijan, Bahamas, Bahrain, Bangladesh, Barbados, Belarus, Belgium, Belize, Benin, Bolivia, Botswana, Brazil, Bulgaria, Burkina Faso, Burundi, Cameroon, Canada, Cape Verde, Chad, Chile, China, Colombia, Comoros, Congo, Congo (Democratic Republic of), Costa Rica, Cote d'Ivoire, Croatia, Cuba, Cyprus, Czech Republic, Denmark, Djibouti, Dominica, Dominican Republic, Ecuador, Egypt, El Salvador, Estonia, European Community, Federated States of Micronesia, Fiji, Finland, France, Gabon, Gambia, Georgia, Germany, Ghana, Greece, Grenada, Guatemala, Guinea, Guinea Bissau, Guyana, Haiti, Honduras, Hungary, Iceland, India, Indonesia, Iran (Islamic Republic of), Ireland, Israel, Italy, Jamaica, Japan, Jordan, Kazakhstan, Kenya, Korea (Democratic People's Republic of), Korea (Republic of), Kuwait, Latvia, Lebanon, Liberia, Libyan Arab Jamahiriya, Liechtenstein, Lithuania, Luxembourg, Madagascar, Malawi, Malaysia, Maldives, Mali, Malta, Marshall Islands, Mauritius, Mexico, Moldova, Monaco, Mongolia, Morocco, Mozambique, Myanmar, Namibia, Nepal, Netherlands, New Zealand, Nicaragua, Niger, Nigeria, Norway, Oman, Pakistan, Palau, Panama, Papua New Guinea, Paraguay, Peru, Philippines, Poland, Portugal, Qatar, Romania, Russian Federation, Saint Kitts and Nevis, Saint Lucia, Saint Vincent and the Grenadines, São Tomé and Príncipe, Samoa, Saudi Arabia, Senegal, Seychelles, Sierra Leone, Singapore, Slovakia, Slovenia,

Solomon Islands, Somalia, South Africa, Spain, Sri Lanka, Sudan, Sweden, Switzerland, Syrian Arab Republic, Tajikistan, Tanzania (United Republic of), Thailand, The Former Yugoslav Republic of Macedonia, Togo, Trinidad and Tobago, Tunisia, Turkey, Turkmenistan, Tuvalu, Uganda, Ukraine, United Kingdom, United States of America, Uruguay, Uzbekistan, Vanuatu, Venezuela, Vietnam, Yemen, Zambia, Zimbabwe.

Contracting Parties
(Copenhagen Amendment)   Algeria, Antigua and Barbuda, Argentina, Australia, Austria, Azerbaijan, Bahamas, Bahrain, Bangladesh, Barbados, Belgium, Belize, Benin, Bolivia, Botswana, Brazil, Bulgaria, Burkina Faso, Burundi, Cameroon, Canada, Cape Verde, Chad, Chile, Colombia, Comoros, Congo, Congo (Democratic Republic of), Costa Rica, Croatia, Cuba, Czech Republic, Denmark, Djibouti, Dominican Republic, Ecuador, Egypt, El Salvador, Estonia, European Community, Federated States of Micronesia, Fiji, Finland, France, Gabon, Georgia, Germany, Ghana, Greece, Grenada, Guatemala, Guinea Bissau, Guyana, Haiti, Honduras, Hungary, Iceland, Indonesia, Iran (Islamic Republic of), Ireland, Israel, Italy, Jamaica, Japan, Jordan, Kenya, Korea (Democratic People's Republic of), Korea (Republic of), Kuwait, Latvia, Lebanon, Liberia, Liechtenstein, Lithuania, Luxembourg, Madagascar, Malawi, Malaysia, Maldives, Marshall Islands, Mauritius, Mexico, Moldova, Monaco, Mongolia, Morocco, Mozambique, Netherlands, New Zealand, Nicaragua, Niger, Nigeria, Norway, Oman, Pakistan, Palau, Panama, Paraguay, Peru, Philippines, Poland, Portugal, Qatar, Romania, Saint Kitts and Nevis, Saint Lucia, Saint Vincent and the Grenadines, São Tomé and Príncipe, Samoa, Saudi Arabia, Senegal, Seychelles, Sierra Leone, Singapore, Slovakia, Slovenia, Solomon Islands, Somalia, South Africa, Spain, Sri Lanka, Sudan, Sweden, Switzerland, Syrian Arab

Republic, Tanzania (United Republic of), Thailand, The Former Yugoslav Republic of Macedonia, Togo, Trinidad and Tobago, Tunisia, Turkey, Tuvalu, Uganda, Ukraine, United Kingdom, United States of America, Uruguay, Uzbekistan, Vanuatu, Venezuela, Vietnam, Yemen, Zimbabwe.

Contracting Parties
(Montreal Amendment)

Antigua and Barbuda, Argentina, Australia, Austria, Azerbaijan, Bahrain, Bangladesh, Barbados, Bolivia, Bulgaria, Burkina Faso, Burundi, Canada, Cape Verde, Chad, Chile, Comoros, Congo, Croatia, Czech Republic, Djibouti, Egypt, El Salvador, European Community, Federated States of Micronesia, Finland, Gabon, Georgia, Germany, Grenada, Guatemala, Guinea Bissau, Guyana, Haiti, Hungary, Iceland, Iran (Islamic Republic of), Italy, Japan, Jordan, Kenya, Korea (Democratic People's Republic of), Korea (Republic of), Latvia, Lebanon, Luxembourg, Madagascar, Malaysia, Maldives, Marshall Islands, Monaco, Mongolia, Netherlands, New Zealand, Niger, Nigeria, Norway, Palau, Panama, Paraguay, Poland, Romania, Saint Kitts and Nevis, Saint Lucia, São Tomé and Príncipe, Samoa, Senegal, Seychelles, Sierra Leone, Singapore, Slovakia, Slovenia, Solomon Islands, Somalia, Spain, Sri Lanka, Sweden, Switzerland, Syrian Arab Republic, Tanzania (United Republic of), The Former Yugoslav Republic of Macedonia, Togo, Trinidad and Tobago, Tunisia, Tuvalu, Uganda, United Kingdom, Uruguay, Venezuela, Yemen.

Contracting Parties
(Beijing Amendment)

Barbados, Bulgaria, Burkina Faso, Burundi, Canada, Chile, Comoros, Congo, Croatia, Czech Republic, European Community, Federated States of Micronesia, Finland, Gabon, Germany, Guatemala, Guinea Bissau, Hungary, Japan, Jordan, Korea (Democratic People's Republic of), Luxembourg, Madagascar, Malaysia,

Maldives, Netherlands, New Zealand, Norway, Palau, Panama, Saint Lucia, São Tomé and Príncipe, Samoa, Seychelles, Sierra Leone, Slovakia, Slovenia, Somalia, Spain, Sri Lanka, Sweden, Switzerland, Tanzania (United Republic of), The Former Yugoslav Republic of Macedonia, Togo, United Kingdom.

Website: www.unep.org/ozone/

Montreal Protocol on Substances that Deplete the Ozone Layer (consolidated version)

Preamble

The Parties to this Protocol,

Being Parties to the Vienna Convention for the Protection of the Ozone Layer,

Mindful of their obligation under that Convention to take appropriate measures to protect human health and the environment against adverse effects resulting or likely to result from human activities which modify or are likely to modify the ozone layer,

Recognizing that world-wide emissions of certain substances can significantly deplete and otherwise modify the ozone layer in a manner that is likely to result in adverse effects on human health and the environment,

Conscious of the potential climatic effects of emissions of these substances,

Aware that measures taken to protect the ozone layer from depletion should be based on relevant scientific knowledge, taking into account technical and economic considerations,

Determined to protect the ozone layer by taking precautionary measures to control equitably total global emissions of substances that deplete it, with the ultimate objective of their elimination on the basis of developments in scientific knowledge, taking into account technical and economic considerations and bearing in mind the developmental needs of developing countries,

Acknowledging that special provision is required to meet the needs of developing countries, including the provision of additional financial resources and access to relevant technologies, bearing in mind that the magnitude of funds necessary is predictable, and the funds can be expected to make a substantial difference in the world's ability to address the scientifically established problem of ozone depletion and its harmful effects,

Noting the precautionary measures for controlling emissions of certain chlorofluorocarbons that have already been taken at national and regional levels,

Considering the importance of promoting international co-operation in the research, development and transfer of alternative technologies relating to the control and reduction of emissions of substances that deplete the ozone layer, bearing in mind in particular the needs of developing countries,

Have agreed as follows:

Article 1
Definitions

For the purposes of this Protocol:

1. 'Convention' means the Vienna Convention for the Protection of the Ozone Layer, adopted on 22 March 1985.
2. 'Parties' means, unless the text otherwise indicates, Parties to this Protocol.
3. 'Secretariat' means the Secretariat of the Convention.
4. 'Controlled substance' means a substance in Annex A, Annex B, Annex C or Annex E to this Protocol, whether existing alone or in a mixture. It includes the isomers of any such substance, except as specified in the relevant Annex, but excludes any controlled substance or mixture which is in a manufactured product other than a container used for the transportation or storage of that substance.
5. 'Production' means the amount of controlled substances produced, minus the amount destroyed by technologies to be approved by the Parties and minus the amount entirely used as feedstock in the manufacture of other chemicals. The amount recycled and reused is not to be considered as 'production'.
6. 'Consumption' means production plus imports minus exports of controlled substances.
7. 'Calculated levels' of production, imports, exports and consumption means levels determined in accordance with Article 3.
8. 'Industrial rationalization' means the transfer of all or a portion of the calculated level of production of one Party to another, for the purpose of achieving economic efficiencies or responding to anticipated shortfalls in supply as a result of plant closures.

Article 2
Control measures

1. Incorporated in Article 2A.

2. Replaced by Article 2B.

3. Replaced by Article 2A.

4. Replaced by Article 2A.

5. Any Party may, for one or more control periods, transfer to another Party any portion of its calculated level of production set out in Articles 2A to 2F, and Article 2H, provided that the total combined calculated levels of production of the Parties concerned for any group of controlled substances do not exceed the production limits set out in those Articles for that group. Such transfer of

production shall be notified to the Secretariat by each of the Parties concerned, stating the terms of such transfer and the period for which it is to apply.

5 *bis*. Any Party not operating under paragraph 1 of Article 5 may, for one or more control periods, transfer to another such Party any portion of its calculated level of consumption set out in Article 2F, provided that the calculated level of consumption of controlled substances in Group I of Annex A of the Party transferring the portion of its calculated level of consumption did not exceed 0.25 kilograms per capita in 1989 and that the total combined calculated levels of consumption of the Parties concerned do not exceed the consumption limits set out in Article 2F. Such transfer of consumption shall be notified to the Secretariat by each of the Parties concerned, stating the terms of such transfer and the period for which it is to apply.

6. Any Party not operating under Article 5, that has facilities for the production of Annex A or Annex B controlled substances under construction, or contracted for, prior to 16 September 1987, and provided for in national legislation prior to 1 January 1987, may add the production from such facilities to its 1986 production of such substances for the purposes of determining its calculated level of production for 1986, provided that such facilities are completed by 31 December 1990 and that such production does not raise that Party's annual calculated level of consumption of the controlled substances above 0.5 kilograms per capita.

7. Any transfer of production pursuant to paragraph 5 or any addition of production pursuant to paragraph 6 shall be notified to the Secretariat, no later than the time of the transfer or addition.

8.

(a) Any Parties which are Member States of a regional economic integration organization as defined in Article 1(6) of the Convention may agree that they shall jointly fulfil their obligations respecting consumption under this Article and Articles 2A to 2I provided that their total combined calculated level of consumption does not exceed the levels required by this Article and Articles 2A to 2I.

(b) The Parties to any such agreement shall inform the Secretariat of the terms of the agreement before the date of the reduction in consumption with which the agreement is concerned.

(c) Such agreement will become operative only if all Member States of the regional economic integration organization and the organization concerned are Parties to the Protocol and have notified the Secretariat of their manner of implementation.

9.

(a) Based on the assessments made pursuant to Article 6, the Parties may decide whether:

(i) Adjustments to the ozone depleting potentials specified in Annex A, Annex B, Annex C and/or Annex E should be made and, if so, what the adjustments should be; and

(ii) Further adjustments and reductions of production or consumption of the controlled substances should be undertaken and, if so, what the scope, amount and timing of any such adjustments and reductions should be;

(b) Proposals for such adjustments shall be communicated to the Parties by the Secretariat at least six months before the meeting of the Parties at which they are proposed for adoption;

(c) In taking such decisions, the Parties shall make every effort to reach agreement by consensus. If all efforts at consensus have been exhausted, and no agreement reached, such decisions shall, as a last resort, be adopted by a two-thirds majority vote of the Parties present and voting representing a majority of the Parties operating under Paragraph 1 of Article 5 present and voting and a majority of the Parties not so operating present and voting;

(d) The decisions, which shall be binding on all Parties, shall forthwith be communicated to the Parties by the Depositary. Unless otherwise provided in the decisions, they shall enter into force on the expiry of six months from the date of the circulation of the communication by the Depositary.

10. Based on the assessments made pursuant to Article 6 of this Protocol and in accordance with the procedure set out in Article 9 of the Convention, the Parties may decide:

(a) whether any substances, and if so which, should be added to or removed from any annex to this Protocol, and

(b) the mechanism, scope and timing of the control measures that should apply to those substances.

11. Notwithstanding the provisions contained in this Article and Articles 2A to 2I Parties may take more stringent measures than those required by this Article and Articles 2A to 2I.

Article 2A
CFCs

1. Each Party shall ensure that for the twelve-month period commencing on the first day of the seventh month following the date of entry into force of this Protocol, and in each twelve-month period thereafter, its calculated level of consumption of the controlled substances in Group I of Annex A does not exceed its calculated level of consumption in 1986.

By the end of the same period, each Party producing one or more of these substances shall ensure that its calculated level of production of the substances does not exceed its calculated level of production in 1986, except that such level may have increased by no more than ten per cent based on the 1986 level. Such increase shall be permitted only so as to satisfy the basic domestic needs of the Parties operating under Article 5 and for the purposes of industrial rationalization between Parties.

2. Each Party shall ensure that for the period from 1 July 1991 to 31 December 1992 its calculated levels of consumption and production of the controlled substances in Group I of Annex A do not exceed 150 per cent of its calculated levels of production and consumption of those substances in 1986; with effect from 1 January 1993, the twelve-month control period for these controlled substances shall run from 1 January to 31 December each year.

3. Each Party shall ensure that for the twelve-month period commencing on 1 January 1994, and in each twelve-month period thereafter, its calculated level of consumption of the controlled substances in Group I of Annex A does not exceed, annually, twenty-five per cent of its calculated level of consumption in 1986. Each Party producing one or more of these substances shall, for the same periods, ensure that its calculated level of production of the substances does not exceed, annually, twenty-five per cent of its calculated level of production in 1986. However, in order to satisfy the basic domestic needs of the Parties operating under paragraph 1 of Article 5, its calculated level of production may exceed that limit by up to ten per cent of its calculated level of production in 1986.

4. Each Party shall ensure that for the twelve-month period commencing on 1 January 1996, and in each twelve-month period thereafter, its calculated level of consumption of the controlled substances in Group I of Annex A does not exceed zero. Each Party producing one or more of these substances shall, for the same periods, ensure that its calculated level of production of the substances does not exceed zero. However, in order to satisfy the basic domestic needs of the Parties operating under paragraph 1 of Article 5, its calculated level of production may exceed that limit by a quantity equal to the annual average of its production of the controlled substances in Group I of Annex A for basic domestic needs for the period 1995 to 1997 inclusive. This paragraph will apply save to the extent that the Parties decide to permit the level of production or consumption that is necessary to satisfy uses agreed by them to be essential.

5. Each Party shall ensure that for the twelve-month period commencing on 1 January 2003 and in each twelve-month period thereafter, its calculated level of production of the controlled substances in Group I of Annex A for the basic domestic needs of the Parties operating under paragraph 1 of Article 5 does not exceed eighty per cent of the annual average of its production of those substances for basic domestic needs for the period 1995 to 1997 inclusive.

6. Each Party shall ensure that for the twelve-month period commencing on 1 January 2005 and in each twelve-month period thereafter, its calculated level of production of the controlled substances in Group I of Annex A for the basic domestic needs of the Parties operating under paragraph 1 of

Article 5 does not exceed fifty per cent of the annual average of its production of those substances for basic domestic needs for the period 1995 to 1997
inclusive.

7. Each Party shall ensure that for the twelve-month period commencing
on 1 January 2007 and in each twelve-month period thereafter, its calculated level of production of the controlled substances in Group I of Annex
A for the basic domestic needs of the Parties operating under paragraph 1 of
Article 5 does not exceed fifteen per cent of the annual average of its production of those substances for basic domestic needs for the period 1995 to 1997
inclusive.

8. Each Party shall ensure that for the twelve-month period commencing on
1 January 2010 and in each twelve-month period thereafter, its calculated level
of production of the controlled substances in Group I of Annex A for the basic
domestic needs of the Parties operating under paragraph 1 of Article 5 does
not exceed zero.

9. For the purposes of calculating basic domestic needs under paragraphs
4 to 8 of this Article, the calculation of the annual average of production by a
Party includes any production entitlements that it has transferred in accordance
with paragraph 5 of Article 2, and excludes any production entitlements that it
has acquired in accordance with paragraph 5 of Article 2.

Article 2B
Halons

1. Each Party shall ensure that for the twelve-month period commencing
on 1 January 1992, and in each twelve-month period thereafter, its calculated
level of consumption of the controlled substances in Group II of Annex A
does not exceed, annually, its calculated level of consumption in 1986. Each
Party producing one or more of these substances shall, for the same periods,
ensure that its calculated level of production of the substances does not exceed,
annually, its calculated level of production in 1986. However, in order to satisfy
the basic domestic needs of the Parties operating under paragraph 1 of Article
5, its calculated level of production may exceed that limit by up to ten per cent
of its calculated level of production in 1986.

2. Each Party shall ensure that for the twelve-month period commencing on
1 January 1994, and in each twelve-month period thereafter, its calculated level
of consumption of the controlled substances in Group II of Annex A does not
exceed zero. Each Party producing one or more of these substances shall, for the
same periods, ensure that its calculated level of production of the substances
does not exceed zero. However, in order to satisfy the basic domestic needs
of the Parties operating under paragraph 1 of Article 5, its calculated level of
production may, until 1 January 2002 exceed that limit by up to fifteen per cent
of its calculated level of production in 1986; thereafter, it may exceed that limit

by a quantity equal to the annual average of its production of the controlled substances in Group II of Annex A for basic domestic needs for the period 1995 to 1997 inclusive. This paragraph will apply save to the extent that the Parties decide to permit the level of production or consumption that is necessary to satisfy uses agreed by them to be essential.

3. Each Party shall ensure that for the twelve-month period commencing on 1 January 2005 and in each twelve-month period thereafter, its calculated level of production of the controlled substances in Group II of Annex A for the basic domestic needs of the Parties operating under paragraph 1 of Article 5 does not exceed fifty per cent of the annual average of its production of those substances for basic domestic needs for the period 1995 to 1997 inclusive.

4. Each Party shall ensure that for the twelve-month period commencing on 1 January 2010 and in each twelve-month period thereafter, its calculated level of production of the controlled substances in Group II of Annex A for the basic domestic needs of the Parties operating under paragraph 1 of Article 5 does not exceed zero.

Article 2C
Other fully halogenated CFCs

1. Each Party shall ensure that for the twelve-month period commencing on 1 January 1993, its calculated level of consumption of the controlled substances in Group I of Annex B does not exceed, annually, eighty per cent of its calculated level of consumption in 1989. Each Party producing one or more of these substances shall, for the same period, ensure that its calculated level of production of the substances does not exceed, annually, eighty per cent of its calculated level of production in 1989. However, in order to satisfy the basic domestic needs of the Parties operating under paragraph 1 of Article 5, its calculated level of production may exceed that limit by up to ten per cent of its calculated level of production in 1989.

2. Each Party shall ensure that for the twelve-month period commencing on 1 January 1994, and in each twelve-month period thereafter, its calculated level of consumption of the controlled substances in Group I of Annex B does not exceed, annually, twenty-five per cent of its calculated level of consumption in 1989. Each Party producing one or more of these substances shall, for the same periods, ensure that its calculated level of production of the substances does not exceed, annually, twenty-five per cent of its calculated level of production in 1989. However, in order to satisfy the basic domestic needs of the Parties operating under paragraph 1 of Article 5, its calculated level of production may exceed that limit by up to ten per cent of its calculated level of production in 1989.

3. Each Party shall ensure that for the twelve-month period commencing on 1 January 1996, and in each twelve-month period thereafter, its calculated level

of consumption of the controlled substances in Group I of Annex B does not exceed zero. Each Party producing one or more of these substances shall, for the same periods, ensure that its calculated level of production of the substances does not exceed zero. However, in order to satisfy the basic domestic needs of the Parties operating under paragraph 1 of Article 5, its calculated level of production may, until 1 January 2003 exceed that limit by up to fifteen per cent of its calculated level of production in 1989; thereafter, it may exceed that limit by a quantity equal to eighty per cent of the annual average of its production of the controlled substances in Group I of Annex B for basic domestic needs for the period 1998 to 2000 inclusive. This paragraph will apply save to the extent that the Parties decide to permit the level of production or consumption that is necessary to satisfy uses agreed by them to be essential.

4. Each Party shall ensure that for the twelve-month period commencing on 1 January 2007 and in each twelve-month period thereafter, its calculated level of production of the controlled substances in Group I of Annex B for the basic domestic needs of the Parties operating under paragraph 1 of Article 5 does not exceed fifteen per cent of the annual average of its production of those substances for basic domestic needs for the period 1998 to 2000 inclusive.

5. Each Party shall ensure that for the twelve-month period commencing on 1 January 2010 and in each twelve-month period thereafter, its calculated level of production of the controlled substances in Group I of Annex B for the basic domestic needs of the Parties operating under paragraph 1 of Article 5 does not exceed zero.

Article 2D
Carbon tetrachloride

1. Each Party shall ensure that for the twelve-month period commencing on 1 January 1995, its calculated level of consumption of the controlled substance in Group II of Annex B does not exceed, annually, fifteen per cent of its calculated level of consumption in 1989. Each Party producing the substance shall, for the same period, ensure that its calculated level of production of the substance does not exceed, annually, fifteen per cent of its calculated level of production in 1989. However, in order to satisfy the basic domestic needs of the Parties operating under paragraph 1 of Article 5, its calculated level of production may exceed that limit by up to ten per cent of its calculated level of production in 1989.

2. Each Party shall ensure that for the twelve-month period commencing on 1 January 1996, and in each twelve-month period thereafter, its calculated level of consumption of the controlled substance in Group II of Annex B does not exceed zero. Each Party producing the substance shall, for the same periods, ensure that its calculated level of production of the substance does not exceed zero. However, in order to satisfy the basic domestic needs of the Parties

operating under paragraph 1 of Article 5, its calculated level of production may exceed that limit by up to fifteen per cent of its calculated level of production in 1989. This paragraph will apply save to the extent that the Parties decide to permit the level of production or consumption that is necessary to satisfy uses agreed by them to be essential.

Article 2E
1,1,1-trichloroethane (methyl chloroform)

1. Each Party shall ensure that for the twelve-month period commencing on 1 January 1993, its calculated level of consumption of the controlled substance in Group III of Annex B does not exceed, annually, its calculated level of consumption in 1989. Each Party producing the substance shall, for the same period, ensure that its calculated level of production of the substance does not exceed, annually, its calculated level of production in 1989. However, in order to satisfy the basic domestic needs of the Parties operating under paragraph 1 of Article 5, its calculated level of production may exceed that limit by up to ten per cent of its calculated level of production in 1989.

2. Each Party shall ensure that for the twelve-month period commencing on 1 January 1994, and in each twelve-month period thereafter, its calculated level of consumption of the controlled substance in Group III of Annex B does not exceed, annually, fifty per cent of its calculated level of consumption in 1989. Each Party producing the substance shall, for the same periods, ensure that its calculated level of production of the substance does not exceed, annually, fifty per cent of its calculated level of production in 1989. However, in order to satisfy the basic domestic needs of the Parties operating under paragraph 1 of Article 5, its calculated level of production may exceed that limit by up to ten per cent of its calculated level of production in 1989.

3. Each Party shall ensure that for the twelve-month period commencing on 1 January 1996, and in each twelve-month period thereafter, its calculated level of consumption of the controlled substance in Group III of Annex B does not exceed zero. Each Party producing the substance shall, for the same periods, ensure that its calculated level of production of the substance does not exceed zero. However, in order to satisfy the basic domestic needs of the Parties operating under paragraph 1 of Article 5, its calculated level of production may exceed that limit by up to fifteen per cent of its calculated level of production for 1989. This paragraph will apply save to the extent that the Parties decide to permit the level of production or consumption that is necessary to satisfy uses agreed by them to be essential.

Article 2F
Hydrochlorofluorocarbons

1. Each Party shall ensure that for the twelve-month period commencing on 1 January 1996, and in each twelve-month period thereafter, its calculated level

of consumption of the controlled substances in Group I of Annex C does not
exceed, annually, the sum of:

(a) Two point eight per cent of its calculated level of consumption in 1989 of
    the controlled substances in Group I of Annex A; and
(b) Its calculated level of consumption in 1989 of the controlled substances in
    Group I of Annex C.

  2. Each Party shall ensure that for the twelve-month period commencing
on 1 January 2004, and in each twelve-month period thereafter, its calculated
level of consumption of the controlled substances in Group I of Annex C does
not exceed, annually, sixty-five per cent of the sum referred to in paragraph 1
of this Article.
  3. Each Party shall ensure that for the twelve-month period commencing on
1 January 2010, and in each twelve-month period thereafter, its calculated level
of consumption of the controlled substances in Group I of Annex C does not
exceed, annually, thirty-five per cent of the sum referred to in paragraph 1 of
this Article.
  4. Each Party shall ensure that for the twelve-month period commencing
on 1 January 2015, and in each twelve-month period thereafter, its calculated
level of consumption of the controlled substances in Group I of Annex C does
not exceed, annually, ten per cent of the sum referred to in paragraph 1 of this
Article.
  5. Each Party shall ensure that for the twelve-month period commencing
on 1 January 2020, and in each twelve-month period thereafter, its calculated
level of consumption of the controlled substances in Group I of Annex C
does not exceed, annually, zero point five per cent of the sum referred to in
paragraph 1 of this Article. Such consumption shall, however, be restricted to
the servicing of refrigeration and air conditioning equipment existing at that
date.
  6. Each Party shall ensure that for the twelve-month period commencing on
1 January 2030, and in each twelve-month period thereafter, its calculated level
of consumption of the controlled substances in Group I of Annex C does not
exceed zero.
  7. As of 1 January 1996, each Party shall endeavour to ensure that:

(a) The use of controlled substances in Group I of Annex C is limited to
    those applications where other more environmentally suitable alternative
    substances or technologies are not available;
(b) The use of controlled substances in Group I of Annex C is not outside the
    areas of application currently met by controlled substances in Annexes A,
    B and C, except in rare cases for the protection of human life or human
    health; and

(c) Controlled substances in Group I of Annex C are selected for use in a manner that minimizes ozone depletion, in addition to meeting other environmental, safety and economic considerations.

8. Each Party producing one or more of these substances shall ensure that for the twelve-month period commencing on 1 January 2004, and in each twelve-month period thereafter, its calculated level of production of the controlled substances in Group I of Annex C does not exceed, annually, the average of:

(a) The sum of its calculated level of consumption in 1989 of the controlled substances in Group I of Annex C and two point eight per cent of its calculated level of consumption in 1989 of the controlled substances in Group I of Annex A; and

(b) The sum of its calculated level of production in 1989 of the controlled substances in Group I of Annex C and two point eight per cent of its calculated level of production in 1989 of the controlled substances in Group I of Annex A. However, in order to satisfy the basic domestic needs of the Parties operating under paragraph 1 of Article 5, its calculated level of production may exceed that limit by up to fifteen per cent of its calculated level of production of the controlled substances in Group I of Annex C as defined above.

Article 2G
Hydrobromofluorocarbons

Each Party shall ensure that for the twelve-month period commencing on 1 January 1996, and in each twelve-month period thereafter, its calculated level of consumption of the controlled substances in Group II of Annex C does not exceed zero. Each Party producing the substances shall, for the same periods, ensure that its calculated level of production of the substances does not exceed zero.

This paragraph will apply save to the extent that the Parties decide to permit the level of production or consumption that is necessary to satisfy uses agreed by them to be essential.

Article 2H
Methyl bromide

1. Each Party shall ensure that for the twelve-month period commencing on 1 January 1995, and in each twelve-month period thereafter, its calculated level of consumption of the controlled substance in Annex E does not exceed, annually, its calculated level of consumption in 1991. Each Party producing the substance shall, for the same period, ensure that its calculated level of production of the substance does not exceed, annually, its calculated level of production in 1991. However, in order to satisfy the basic domestic needs of the Parties operating under paragraph 1 of Article 5, its calculated level of

production may exceed that limit by up to ten per cent of its calculated level of production in 1991.

2. Each Party shall ensure that for the twelve-month period commencing on 1 January 1999, and in the twelve-month period thereafter, its calculated level of consumption of the controlled substance in Annex E does not exceed, annually, seventy-five per cent of its calculated level of consumption in 1991. Each Party producing the substance shall, for the same periods, ensure that its calculated level of production of the substance does not exceed, annually, seventy-five per cent of its calculated level of production in 1991. However, in order to satisfy the basic domestic needs of the Parties operating under paragraph 1 of Article 5, its calculated level of production may exceed that limit by up to ten per cent of its calculated level of production in 1991.

3. Each Party shall ensure that for the twelve-month period commencing on 1 January 2001, and in the twelve-month period thereafter, its calculated level of consumption of the controlled substance in Annex E does not exceed, annually, fifty per cent of its calculated level of consumption in 1991. Each Party producing the substance shall, for the same periods, ensure that its calculated level of production of the substance does not exceed, annually, fifty per cent of its calculated level of production in 1991. However, in order to satisfy the basic domestic needs of the Parties operating under paragraph 1 of Article 5, its calculated level of production may exceed that limit by up to ten per cent of its calculated level of production in 1991.

4. Each Party shall ensure that for the twelve-month period commencing on 1 January 2003, and in the twelve-month period thereafter, its calculated level of consumption of the controlled substance in Annex E does not exceed, annually, thirty per cent of its calculated level of consumption in 1991. Each Party producing the substance shall, for the same periods, ensure that its calculated level of production of the substance does not exceed, annually, thirty per cent of its calculated level of production in 1991. However, in order to satisfy the basic domestic needs of the Parties operating under paragraph 1 of Article 5, its calculated level of production may exceed that limit by up to ten per cent of its calculated level of production in 1991.

5. Each Party shall ensure that for the twelve-month period commencing on 1 January 2005, and in each twelve-month period thereafter, its calculated level of consumption of the controlled substance in Annex E does not exceed zero. Each Party producing the substance shall, for the same periods, ensure that its calculated level of production of the substance does not exceed zero. However, in order to satisfy the basic domestic needs of the Parties operating under paragraph 1 of Article 5, its calculated level of production may, until 1 January 2002 exceed that limit by up to fifteen per cent of its calculated level of production in 1991; thereafter, it may exceed that limit by a quantity equal to the annual average of its production of the controlled substance in Annex E for basic domestic needs for the period 1995 to 1998 inclusive. This paragraph will apply

save to the extent that the Parties decide to permit the level of production or consumption that is necessary to satisfy uses agreed by them to be critical uses.

5 *bis*. Each Party shall ensure that for the twelve-month period commencing on 1 January 2005 and in each twelve-month period thereafter, its calculated level of production of the controlled substance in Annex E for the basic domestic needs of the Parties operating under paragraph 1 of Article 5 does not exceed eighty per cent of the annual average of its production of the substance for basic domestic needs for the period 1995 to 1998 inclusive.

5 *ter*. Each Party shall ensure that for the twelve-month period commencing on 1 January 2015 and in each twelve-month period thereafter, its calculated level of production of the controlled substance in Annex E for the basic domestic needs of the Parties operating under paragraph 1 of Article 5 does not exceed zero.

6. The calculated levels of consumption and production under this Article shall not include the amounts used by the Party for quarantine and pre-shipment applications.

Article 2I
Bromochloromethane

Each Party shall ensure that for the twelve-month period commencing on 1 January 2002, and in each twelve-month period thereafter, its calculated level of consumption and production of the controlled substance in Group III of Annex C does not exceed zero. This paragraph will apply save to the extent that the Parties decide to permit the level of production or consumption that is necessary to satisfy uses agreed by them to be essential.

Article 3
Calculation of control levels

For the purposes of Articles 2, 2A to 2I and 5, each Party shall, for each group of substances in Annex A, Annex B, Annex C or Annex E determine its calculated levels of:

(a) Production by:
    (i) multiplying its annual production of each controlled substance by the ozone depleting potential specified in respect of it in Annex A, Annex B, Annex C or Annex E;
    (ii) adding together, for each such Group, the resulting figures;
(b) Imports and exports, respectively, by following, *mutatis mutandis*, the procedure set out in subparagraph (a); and
(c) Consumption by adding together its calculated levels of production and imports and subtracting its calculated level of exports as determined in accordance with subparagraphs (a) and (b). However, beginning on

1 January 1993, any export of controlled substances to non-Parties shall not be subtracted in calculating the consumption level of the exporting Party.

Article 4
Control of trade with non-Parties

1. As of 1 January 1990, each party shall ban the import of the controlled substances in Annex A from any State not party to this Protocol.

1 *bis.* Within one year of the date of the entry into force of this paragraph, each Party shall ban the import of the controlled substances in Annex B from any State not party to this Protocol.

1 *ter.* Within one year of the date of entry into force of this paragraph, each Party shall ban the import of any controlled substances in Group II of Annex C from any State not party to this Protocol.

1 *qua.* Within one year of the date of entry into force of this paragraph, each Party shall ban the import of the controlled substance in Annex E from any State not party to this Protocol.

1 *quin.* As of 1 January 2004, each Party shall ban the import of the controlled substances in Group I of Annex C from any State not party to this Protocol.

1 *sex.* Within one year of the date of entry into force of this paragraph, each Party shall ban the import of the controlled substance in Group III of Annex C from any State not party to this Protocol.

2. As of 1 January 1993, each Party shall ban the export of any controlled substances in Annex A to any State not party to this Protocol.

2 *bis.* Commencing one year after the date of entry into force of this paragraph, each Party shall ban the export of any controlled substances in Annex B to any State not party to this Protocol.

2 *ter.* Commencing one year after the date of entry into force of this paragraph, each Party shall ban the export of any controlled substances in Group II of Annex C to any State not party to this Protocol.

2 *qua.* Commencing one year of the date of entry into force of this paragraph, each Party shall ban the export of the controlled substance in Annex E to any State not party to this Protocol.

2 *quin.* As of 1 January 2004, each Party shall ban the export of the controlled substances in Group I of Annex C to any State not party to this Protocol.

2 *sex.* Within one year of the date of entry into force of this paragraph, each Party shall ban the export of the controlled substance in Group III of Annex C to any State not party to this Protocol.

3. By 1 January 1992, the Parties shall, following the procedures in Article 10 of the Convention, elaborate in an annex a list of products containing controlled substances in Annex A. Parties that have not objected to the annex in accordance with those procedures shall ban, within one year of the annex having

become effective, the import of those products from any State not party to this Protocol.

3 *bis*. Within three years of the date of the entry into force of this paragraph, the Parties shall, following the procedures in Article 10 of the Convention, elaborate in an annex a list of products containing controlled substances in Annex B. Parties that have not objected to the annex in accordance with those procedures shall ban, within one year of the annex having become effective, the import of those products from any State not party to this Protocol.

3 *ter*. Within three years of the date of entry into force of this paragraph, the Parties shall, following the procedures in Article 10 of the Convention, elaborate in an annex a list of products containing controlled substances in Group II of Annex C. Parties that have not objected to the annex in accordance with those procedures shall ban, within one year of the annex having become effective, the import of those products from any State not party to this Protocol.

4. By 1 January 1994, the Parties shall determine the feasibility of banning or restricting, from States not party to this Protocol, the import of products produced with, but not containing, controlled substances in Annex A. If determined feasible, the Parties shall, following the procedures in Article 10 of the Convention, elaborate in an annex a list of such products. Parties that have not objected to the annex in accordance with those procedures shall ban, within one year of the annex having become effective, the import of those products from any State not party to this Protocol.

4 *bis*. Within five years of the date of the entry into force of this paragraph, the Parties shall determine the feasibility of banning or restricting, from States not party to this Protocol, the import of products produced with, but not containing, controlled substances in Annex B. If determined feasible, the Parties shall, following the procedures in Article 10 of the Convention, elaborate in an annex a list of such products. Parties that have not objected to the annex in accordance with those procedures shall ban or restrict, within one year of the annex having become effective, the import of those products from any State not party to this Protocol.

4 *ter*. Within five years of the date of entry into force of this paragraph, the Parties shall determine the feasibility of banning or restricting, from States not party to this Protocol, the import of products produced with, but not containing, controlled substances in Group II of Annex C. If determined feasible, the Parties shall, following the procedures in Article 10 of the Convention, elaborate in an annex a list of such products. Parties that have not objected to the annex in accordance with those procedures shall ban or restrict, within one year of the annex having become effective, the import of those products from any State not party to this Protocol.

5. Each Party undertakes to the fullest practicable extent to discourage the export to any State not party to this Protocol of technology for producing and for utilizing controlled substances in Annexes A, B, C and E.

6. Each Party shall refrain from providing new subsidies, aid, credits, guarantees or insurance programmes for the export to States not party to this Protocol of products, equipment, plants or technology that would facilitate the production of controlled substances in Annexes A, B, C and E.

7. Paragraphs 5 and 6 shall not apply to products, equipment, plants or technology that improve the containment, recovery, recycling or destruction of controlled substances, promote the development of alternative substances, or otherwise contribute to the reduction of emissions of controlled substances in Annexes A, B, C and E.

8. Notwithstanding the provisions of this Article, imports and exports referred to in paragraphs 1 to 4 *ter* of this Article may be permitted from, or to, any State not party to this Protocol, if that State is determined, by a meeting of the Parties, to be in full compliance with Article 2, Articles 2A to 2I and this Article, and have submitted data to that effect as specified in Article 7.

9. For the purposes of this Article, the term 'State not party to this Protocol' shall include, with respect to a particular controlled substance, a State or regional economic integration organization that has not agreed to be bound by the control measures in effect for that substance.

10. By 1 January 1996, the Parties shall consider whether to amend this Protocol in order to extend the measures in this Article to trade in controlled substances in Group I of Annex C and in Annex E with States not party to the Protocol.

Article 4A
Control of trade with Parties

1. Where, after the phase-out date applicable to it for a controlled substance, a Party is unable, despite having taken all practicable steps to comply with its obligation under the Protocol, to cease production of that substance for domestic consumption, other than for uses agreed by the Parties to be essential, it shall ban the export of used, recycled and reclaimed quantities of that substance, other than for the purpose of destruction.

2. Paragraph 1 of this Article shall apply without prejudice to the operation of Article 11 of the Convention and the non-compliance procedure developed under Article 8 of the Protocol.

Article 4B
Licensing

1. Each Party shall, by 1 January 2000 or within three months of the date of entry into force of this Article for it, whichever is the later, establish and implement a system for licensing the import and export of new, used, recycled and reclaimed controlled substances in Annexes A, B, C and E.

2. Notwithstanding paragraph 1 of this Article, any Party operating under paragraph 1 of Article 5 which decides it is not in a position to establish and implement a system for licensing the import and export of controlled substances in Annexes C and E, may delay taking those actions until 1 January 2005 and 1 January 2002, respectively.

3. Each Party shall, within three months of the date of introducing its licensing system, report to the Secretariat on the establishment and operation of that system.

4. The Secretariat shall periodically prepare and circulate to all Parties a list of the Parties that have reported to it on their licensing systems and shall forward this information to the Implementation Committee for consideration and appropriate recommendations to the Parties.

Article 5
Special situation of developing countries

1. Any Party that is a developing country and whose annual calculated level of consumption of the controlled substances in Annex A is less than 0.3 kilograms per capita on the date of the entry into force of the Protocol for it, or any time thereafter until 1 January 1999, shall, in order to meet its basic domestic needs, be entitled to delay for ten years its compliance with the control measures set out in Articles 2A to 2E, provided that any further amendments to the adjustments or Amendment adopted at the Second Meeting of the Parties in London, 29 June 1990, shall apply to the Parties operating under this paragraph after the review provided for in paragraph 8 of this Article has taken place and shall be based on the conclusions of that review.

1 *bis.* The Parties shall, taking into account the review referred to in paragraph 8 of this Article, the assessments made pursuant to Article 6 and any other relevant information, decide by 1 January 1996, through the procedure set forth in paragraph 9 of Article 2:

(a) With respect to paragraphs 1 to 6 of Article 2F, what base year, initial levels, control schedules and phase-out date for consumption of the controlled substances in Group I of Annex C will apply to Parties operating under paragraph 1 of this Article;

(b) With respect to Article 2G, what phase-out date for production and consumption of the controlled substances in Group II of Annex C will apply to Parties operating under paragraph 1 of this Article; and

(c) With respect to Article 2H, what base year, initial levels and control schedules for consumption and production of the controlled substance in Annex E will apply to Parties operating under paragraph 1 of this Article.

2. However, any Party operating under paragraph 1 of this Article shall exceed neither an annual calculated level of consumption of the controlled substances in Annex A of 0.3 kilograms per capita nor an annual calculated

level of consumption of controlled substances of Annex B of 0.2 kilograms per capita.

3. When implementing the control measures set out in Articles 2A to 2E, any Party operating under paragraph 1 of this Article shall be entitled to use:

(a) For controlled substances under Annex A, either the average of its annual calculated level of consumption for the period 1995 to 1997 inclusive or a calculated level of consumption of 0.3 kilograms per capita, whichever is the lower, as the basis for determining its compliance with the control measures relating to consumption.

(b) For controlled substances under Annex B, the average of its annual calculated level of consumption for the period 1998 to 2000 inclusive or a calculated level of consumption of 0.2 kilograms per capita, whichever is the lower, as the basis for determining its compliance with the control measures relating to consumption.

(c) For controlled substances under Annex A, either the average of its annual calculated level of production for the period 1995 to 1997 inclusive or a calculated level of production of 0.3 kilograms per capita, whichever is the lower, as the basis for determining its compliance with the control measures relating to production.

(d) For controlled substances under Annex B, either the average of its annual calculated level of production for the period 1998 to 2000 inclusive or a calculated level of production of 0.2 kilograms per capita, whichever is the lower, as the basis for determining its compliance with the control measures relating to production.

4. If a Party operating under paragraph 1 of this Article, at any time before the control measures obligations in Articles 2A to 2I become applicable to it, finds itself unable to obtain an adequate supply of controlled substances, it may notify this to the Secretariat. The Secretariat shall forthwith transmit a copy of such notification to the Parties, which shall consider the matter at their next Meeting, and decide upon appropriate action to be taken.

5. Developing the capacity to fulfil the obligations of the Parties operating under paragraph 1 of this Article to comply with the control measures set out in Articles 2A to 2E and Article 2I, and any control measures in Articles 2F to 2H that are decided pursuant to paragraph 1 *bis* of this Article, and their implementation by those same Parties will depend upon the effective implementation of the financial co-operation as provided by Article 10 and the transfer of technology as provided by Article 10A.

6. Any Party operating under paragraph 1 of this Article may, at any time, notify the Secretariat in writing that, having taken all practicable steps it is unable to implement any or all of the obligations laid down in Articles 2A to 2E and Article 2I, or any or all obligations in Articles 2F to 2H that are

decided pursuant to paragraph 1 *bis* of this Article, due to the inadequate implementation of Articles 10 and 10A. The Secretariat shall forthwith transmit a copy of the notification to the Parties, which shall consider the matter at their next Meeting, giving due recognition to paragraph 5 of this Article and shall decide upon appropriate action to be taken.

7. During the period between notification and the Meeting of the Parties at which the appropriate action referred to in paragraph 6 above is to be decided, or for a further period if the Meeting of the Parties so decides, the non-compliance procedures referred to in Article 8 shall not be invoked against the notifying Party.

8. A Meeting of the Parties shall review, not later than 1995, the situation of the Parties operating under paragraph 1 of this Article, including the effective implementation of financial co-operation and transfer of technology to them, and adopt such revisions that may be deemed necessary regarding the schedule of control measures applicable to those Parties.

8 *bis*. Based on the conclusions of the review referred to in paragraph 8 above:

(a) With respect to the controlled substances in Annex A, a Party operating under paragraph 1 of this Article shall, in order to meet its basic domestic needs, be entitled to delay for ten years its compliance with the control measures adopted by the Second Meeting of the Parties in London, 29 June 1990, and reference by the Protocol to Articles 2A and 2B shall be read accordingly;

(b) With respect to the controlled substances in Annex B, a Party operating under paragraph 1 of this Article shall, in order to meet its basic domestic needs, be entitled to delay for ten years its compliance with the control measures adopted by the Second Meeting of the Parties in London, 29 June 1990, and reference by the Protocol to Articles 2C to 2E shall be read accordingly.

8 *ter*. Pursuant to paragraph 1 *bis* above:

(a) Each Party operating under paragraph 1 of this Article shall ensure that for the twelve-month period commencing on 1 January 2016, and in each twelve-month period thereafter, its calculated level of consumption of the controlled substances in Group I of Annex C does not exceed, annually, its calculated level of consumption in 2015. As of 1 January 2016 each Party operating under paragraph 1 of this Article shall comply with the control measures set out in paragraph 8 of Article 2F and, as the basis for its compliance with these control measures, it shall use the average of its calculated levels of production and consumption in 2015;

(b) Each Party operating under paragraph 1 of this Article shall ensure that for the twelve-month period commencing on 1 January 2040, and in each twelve-month period thereafter, its calculated level of consumption of the controlled substances in Group I of Annex C does not exceed zero;

(c) Each Party operating under paragraph 1 of this Article shall comply with Article 2G;

(d) With regard to the controlled substance contained in Annex E:

(i) As of 1 January 2002 each Party operating under paragraph 1 of this Article shall comply with the control measures set out in paragraph 1 of Article 2H and, as the basis for its compliance with these control measures, it shall use the average of its annual calculated level of consumption and production, respectively, for the period of 1995 to 1998 inclusive;

(ii) Each Party operating under paragraph 1 of this Article shall ensure that for the twelve-month period commencing on 1 January 2005, and in each twelve-month period thereafter, its calculated levels of consumption and production of the controlled substance in Annex E do not exceed, annually, eighty per cent of the average of its annual calculated levels of consumption and production, respectively, for the period of 1995 to 1998 inclusive;

(iii) Each Party operating under paragraph 1 of this Article shall ensure that for the twelve-month period commencing on 1 January 2015 and in each twelve-month period thereafter, its calculated levels of consumption and production of the controlled substance in Annex E do not exceed zero. This paragraph will apply save to the extent that the Parties decide to permit the level of production or consumption that is necessary to satisfy uses agreed by them to be critical uses;

(iv) The calculated levels of consumption and production under this subparagraph shall not include the amounts used by the Party for quarantine and pre-shipment applications.

9. Decisions of the Parties referred to in paragraph 4, 6 and 7 of this Article shall be taken according to the same procedure applied to decision-making under Article 10.

Article 6
Assessment and review of control measures

Beginning in 1990, and at least every four years thereafter, the Parties shall assess the control measures provided for in Article 2 and Articles 2A to 2I on the basis of available scientific, environmental, technical and economic information. At least one year before each assessment, the Parties shall convene appropriate panels of experts qualified in the fields mentioned and determine the composition and terms of reference of any such panels. Within one year of being convened, the panels will report their conclusions, through the Secretariat, to the Parties.

Article 7
Reporting of data

1. Each Party shall provide to the Secretariat, within three months of becoming a Party, statistical data on its production, imports and exports of each of the controlled substances in Annex A for the year 1986, or the best possible estimates of such data where actual data are not available.

2. Each Party shall provide to the Secretariat statistical data on its production, imports and exports of each of the controlled substances

– in Annex B and Annexes I and II of Group C for the year 1989;
– in Annex E, for the year 1991,

or the best possible estimates of such data where actual data are not available, not later than three months after the date when the provisions set out in the Protocol with regard to the substances in Annexes B, C and E respectively enter into force for that Party.

3. Each Party shall provide to the Secretariat statistical data on its annual production (as defined in paragraph 5 of Article 1) of each of the controlled substances listed in Annexes A, B, C and E and, separately, for each substance,

– Amounts used for feedstocks,
– Amounts destroyed by technologies approved by the Parties, and
– Imports from and exports to Parties and non-Parties respectively,

for the year during which provisions concerning the substances in Annexes A, B, C and E respectively entered into force for that Party and for each year thereafter. Each Party shall provide to the Secretariat statistical data on the annual amount of the controlled substance listed in Annex E used for quarantine and pre-shipment applications. Data shall be forwarded not later than nine months after the end of the year to which the data relate.

3 *bis*. Each Party shall provide to the Secretariat separate statistical data of its annual imports and exports of each of the controlled substances listed in Group II of Annex A and Group I of Annex C that have been recycled.

4. For Parties operating under the provisions of paragraph 8 (a) of Article 2, the requirements in paragraphs 1, 2, 3 and 3 *bis* of this Article in respect of statistical data on imports and exports shall be satisfied if the regional economic integration organization concerned provides data on imports and exports between the organization and States that are not members of that organization.

Article 8
Non-compliance

The Parties, at their first meeting, shall consider and approve procedures and institutional mechanisms for determining non-compliance with the provisions of this Protocol and for treatment of Parties found to be in non-compliance.

Article 9
Research, development, public awareness and exchange of information

1. The Parties shall co-operate, consistent with their national laws, regulations and practices and taking into account in particular the needs of developing countries, in promoting, directly or through competent international bodies, research, development and exchange of information on:

(a) best technologies for improving the containment, recovery, recycling, or destruction of controlled substances or otherwise reducing their emissions;
(b) possible alternatives to controlled substances, to products containing such substances, and to products manufactured with them; and
(c) costs and benefits of relevant control strategies.

2. The Parties, individually, jointly or through competent international bodies, shall co-operate in promoting public awareness of the environmental effects of the emissions of controlled substances and other substances that deplete the ozone layer.

3. Within two years of the entry into force of this Protocol and every two years thereafter, each Party shall submit to the Secretariat a summary of the activities it has conducted pursuant to this Article.

Article 10
Financial mechanism

1. The Parties shall establish a mechanism for the purposes of providing financial and technical co-operation, including the transfer of technologies, to Parties operating under paragraph 1 of Article 5 of this Protocol to enable their compliance with the control measures set out in Articles 2A to 2E and Article 2I, and any control measures in Articles 2F to 2H that are decided pursuant to paragraph 1 *bis* of Article 5 of the Protocol. The mechanism, contributions to which shall be additional to other financial transfers to Parties operating under that paragraph, shall meet all agreed incremental costs of such Parties in order to enable their compliance with the control measures of the Protocol. An indicative list of the categories of incremental costs shall be decided by the meeting of the Parties.

2. The mechanism established under paragraph 1 shall include a Multilateral Fund. It may also include other means of multilateral, regional and bilateral co-operation.

3. The Multilateral Fund shall:

(a) Meet, on a grant or concessional basis as appropriate, and according to criteria to be decided upon by the Parties, the agreed incremental costs;
(b) Finance clearing-house functions to:

    (i) Assist Parties operating under paragraph 1 of Article 5, through coun-
try specific studies and other technical co-operation, to identify their
needs for co-operation;

    (ii) Facilitate technical co-operation to meet these identified needs;

    (iii) Distribute, as provided for in Article 9, information and relevant
materials, and hold workshops, training sessions, and other related
activities, for the benefit of Parties that are developing countries; and

    (iv) Facilitate and monitor other multilateral, regional and bilateral
co-operation available to Parties that are developing countries;

(c) Finance the secretarial services of the Multilateral Fund and related support
costs.

4. The Multilateral Fund shall operate under the authority of the Parties who
shall decide on its overall policies.

5. The Parties shall establish an Executive Committee to develop and monitor
the implementation of specific operational policies, guidelines and administrative arrangements, including the disbursement of resources, for the purpose
of achieving the objectives of the Multilateral Fund. The Executive Committee shall discharge its tasks and responsibilities, specified in its terms of reference as agreed by the Parties, with the co-operation and assistance of the
International Bank for Reconstruction and Development (World Bank), the
United Nations Environment Programme, the United Nations Development
Programme or other appropriate agencies depending on their respective areas
of expertise. The members of the Executive Committee, which shall be selected
on the basis of a balanced representation of the Parties operating under paragraph 1 of Article 5 and of the Parties not so operating, shall be endorsed by the
Parties.

6. The Multilateral Fund shall be financed by contributions from Parties
not operating under paragraph 1 of Article 5 in convertible currency or, in
certain circumstances, in kind and/or in national currency, on the basis of the
United Nations scale of assessments. Contributions by other Parties shall be
encouraged. Bilateral and, in particular cases agreed by a decision of the Parties,
regional co-operation may, up to a percentage and consistent with any criteria
to be specified by decision of the Parties, be considered as a contribution to the
Multilateral Fund, provided that such co-operation, as a minimum:

(a) Strictly relates to compliance with the provisions of this Protocol;

(b) Provides additional resources; and

(c) Meets agreed incremental costs.

7. The Parties shall decide upon the programme budget of the Multilateral
Fund for each fiscal period and upon the percentage of contributions of the
individual Parties thereto.

8. Resources under the Multilateral Fund shall be disbursed with the concurrence of the beneficiary Party.

9. Decisions by the Parties under this Article shall be taken by consensus whenever possible. If all efforts at consensus have been exhausted and no agreement reached, decisions shall be adopted by a two-thirds majority vote of the Parties present and voting, representing a majority of the Parties operating under paragraph 1 of Article 5 present and voting and a majority of the Parties not so operating present and voting.

10. The financial mechanism set out in this Article is without prejudice to any future arrangements that may be developed with respect to other environmental issues.

Article 10A
Transfer of technology

Each Party shall take every practicable step, consistent with the programmes supported by the financial mechanism, to ensure:

(a) that the best available, environmentally safe substitutes and related technologies are expeditiously transferred to Parties operating under paragraph 1 of Article 5; and

(b) that the transfers referred to in subparagraph (a) occur under fair and most favourable conditions.

Article 11
Meetings of the parties

1. The Parties shall hold meetings at regular intervals. The Secretariat shall convene the first meeting of the Parties not later than one year after the date of the entry into force of this Protocol and in conjunction with a meeting of the Conference of the Parties to the Convention, if a meeting of the latter is scheduled within that period.

2. Subsequent ordinary meetings of the parties shall be held, unless the Parties otherwise decide, in conjunction with meetings of the Conference of the Parties to the Convention. Extraordinary meetings of the Parties shall be held at such other times as may be deemed necessary by a meeting of the Parties, or at the written request of any Party, provided that within six months of such a request being communicated to them by the Secretariat, it is supported by at least one third of the Parties.

3. The Parties, at their first meeting, shall:

(a) adopt by consensus rules of procedure for their meetings;
(b) adopt by consensus the financial rules referred to in paragraph 2 of Article 13;
(c) establish the panels and determine the terms of reference referred to in Article 6;

(d) consider and approve the procedures and institutional mechanisms speci-
    fied in Article 8; and

(e) begin preparation of workplans pursuant to paragraph 3 of Article 10.

4. The functions of the meetings of the Parties shall be to:

(a) review the implementation of this Protocol;

(b) decide on any adjustments or reductions referred to in paragraph 9 of
    Article 2;

(c) decide on any addition to, insertion in or removal from any annex of
    substances and on related control measures in accordance with paragraph
    10 of Article 2;

(d) establish, where necessary, guidelines or procedures for reporting of infor-
    mation as provided for in Article 7 and paragraph 3 of Article 9;

(e) review requests for technical assistance submitted pursuant to paragraph
    2 of Article 10;

(f) review reports prepared by the secretariat pursuant to subparagraph (c) of
    Article 12;

(g) assess, in accordance with Article 6, the control measures;

(h) consider and adopt, as required, proposals for amendment of this Protocol
    or any annex and for any new annex;

(i) consider and adopt the budget for implementing this Protocol; and

(j) consider and undertake any additional action that may be required for the
    achievement of the purposes of this Protocol.

5. The United Nations, its specialized agencies and the International Atomic
Energy Agency, as well as any State not party to this Protocol, may be represented
at meetings of the Parties as observers. Any body or agency, whether national or
international, governmental or non-governmental, qualified in fields relating
to the protection of the ozone layer which has informed the secretariat of
its wish to be represented at a meeting of the Parties as an observer may be
admitted unless at least one third of the Parties present object. The admission
and participation of observers shall be subject to the rules of procedure adopted
by the Parties.

Article 12
Secretariat

For the purposes of this Protocol, the Secretariat shall:

(a) arrange for and service meetings of the Parties as provided for in
    Article 11;

(b) receive and make available, upon request by a Party, data provided pursuant
    to Article 7;

(c) prepare and distribute regularly to the Parties reports based on information
    received pursuant to Articles 7 and 9;

(d) notify the Parties of any request for technical assistance received pursuant to Article 10 so as to facilitate the provision of such assistance;

(e) encourage non-Parties to attend the meetings of the Parties as observers and to act in accordance with the provisions of this Protocol;

(f) provide, as appropriate, the information and requests referred to in sub-paragraphs (c) and (d) to such non-party observers; and

(g) perform such other functions for the achievement of the purposes of this Protocol as may be assigned to it by the Parties.

Article 13
Financial provisions

1. The funds required for the operation of this Protocol, including those for the functioning of the Secretariat related to this Protocol, shall be charged exclusively against contributions from the Parties.

2. The Parties, at their first meeting, shall adopt by consensus financial rules for the operation of this Protocol.

Article 14
Relationship of this Protocol to the Convention

Except as otherwise provided in this Protocol, the provisions of the Convention relating to its protocols shall apply to this Protocol.

Article 15
Signature

This Protocol shall be open for signature by States and by regional economic integration organizations in Montreal on 16 September 1987, in Ottawa from 17 September 1987 to 16 January 1988, and at United Nations Headquarters in New York from 17 January 1988 to 15 September 1988.

Article 16
Entry into force

1. This Protocol shall enter into force on 1 January 1989, provided that at least eleven instruments of ratification, acceptance, approval of the Protocol or accession thereto have been deposited by States or regional economic integration organizations representing at least two-thirds of 1986 estimated global consumption of the controlled substances, and the provisions of paragraph 1 of Article 17 of the Convention have been fulfilled. In the event that these conditions have not been fulfilled by that date, the Protocol shall enter into force on the ninetieth day following the date on which the conditions have been fulfilled.

2. For the purposes of paragraph 1, any such instrument deposited by a regional economic integration organization shall not be counted as additional to those deposited by member States of such organization.

3. After the entry into force of this Protocol, any State or regional economic integration organization shall become a Party to it on the ninetieth day following the date of deposit of its instrument of ratification, acceptance, approval or accession.

Article 17
Parties joining after entry into force

Subject to Article 5, any State or regional economic integration organization which becomes a Party to this Protocol after the date of its entry into force, shall fulfil forthwith the sum of the obligations under Article 2, as well as under Articles 2A to 2I and Article 4, that apply at that date to the States and regional economic integration organizations that became Parties on the date the Protocol entered into force.

Article 18
Reservations

No reservations may be made to this Protocol.

Article 19
Withdrawal

Any Party may withdraw from this Protocol by giving written notification to the Depositary at any time after four years of assuming the obligations specified in paragraph 1 of Article 2A. Any such withdrawal shall take effect upon expiry of one year after the date of its receipt by the Depositary, or on such later date as may be specified in the notification of the withdrawal.

Article 20
Authentic texts

The original of this Protocol, of which the Arabic, Chinese, English, French, Russian and Spanish texts are equally authentic, shall be deposited with the Secretary-General of the United Nations.

IN WITNESS WHEREOF the undersigned, being duly authorized to that effect, have signed this Protocol.

DONE at Montreal this sixteenth day of September, one thousand nine hundred and eighty seven.

Annex A
Controlled substances

Group	Substance	Ozone-depleting potential*
Group I		
$CFCl_3$	(CFC-11)	1.0
CF_2Cl_2	(CFC-12)	1.0
$C_2F_3Cl_3$	(CFC-113)	0.8
$C_2F_4Cl_2$	(CFC-114)	1.0
C_2F_5Cl	(CFC-115)	0.6
Group II		
CF_2BrCl	(halon-1211)	3.0
CF_3Br	(halon-1301)	10.0
$C_2F_4Br_2$	(halon-2402)	6.0

* These ozone depleting potentials are estimates based on existing knowledge and will be reviewed and revised periodically.

Annex B
Controlled substances

Group	Substance	Ozone-depleting potential
Group I		
CF_3Cl	(CFC-13)	1.0
C_2FCl_5	(CFC-111)	1.0
$C_2F_2Cl_4$	(CFC-112)	1.0
C_3FCl_7	(CFC-211)	1.0
$C_3F_2Cl_6$	(CFC-212)	1.0
$C_3F_3Cl_5$	(CFC-213)	1.0
$C_3F_4Cl_4$	(CFC-214)	1.0
$C_3F_5Cl_3$	(CFC-215)	1.0
$C_3F_6Cl_2$	(CFC-216)	1.0
C_3F_7Cl	(CFC-217)	1.0
Group II		
CCl_4	carbon tetrachloride	1.1
Group III		
$C_2H_3Cl_3$*	1,1,1-trichloroethane* (methyl chloroform)	0.1

* This formula does not refer to 1,1,2-trichloroethane.

Annex C
Controlled substances

Group	Substance	Number of isomers	Ozone-depleting potential*
Group I			
$CHFCl_2$	(HCFC-21)**	1	0.04
CHF_2Cl	(HCFC-22)**	1	0.055
CH_2FCl	(HCFC-31)	1	0.02
C_2HFCl_4	(HCFC-121)	2	0.01–0.04
$C_2HF_2Cl_3$	(HCFC-122)	3	0.02–0.08
$C_2HF_3Cl_2$	(HCFC-123)	3	0.02–0.06
$CHCl_2CF_3$	(HCFC-123)**	–	0.02
C_2HF_4Cl	(HCFC-124)	2	0.02–0.04
$CHFClCF_3$	(HCFC-124)**	–	0.022
$C_2H_2FCl_3$	(HCFC-131)	3	0.007–0.05
$C_2H_2F_2Cl_2$	(HCFC-132)	4	0.008–0.05
$C_2H_2F_3Cl$	(HCFC-133)	3	0.02–0.06
$C_2H_3FCl_2$	(HCFC-141)	3	0.005–0.07
CH_3CFCl_2	(HCFC-141b)**	–	0.11
$C_2H_3F_2Cl$	(HCFC-142)	3	0.008–0.07
CH_3CF_2Cl	(HCFC-142b)**	–	0.065
C_2H_4FCl	(HCFC-151)	2	0.003–0.005
C_3HFCl_6	(HCFC-221)	5	0.015–0.07
$C_3HF_2Cl_5$	(HCFC-222)	9	0.01–0.09
$C_3HF_3Cl_4$	(HCFC-223)	12	0.01–0.08
$C_3HF_4Cl_3$	(HCFC-224)	12	0.01–0.09
$C_3HF_5Cl_2$	(HCFC-225)	9	0.02–0.07
$CF_3CF_2CHCl_2$	(HCFC-225ca)**	–	0.025
CF_2ClCF_2CHClF	(HCFC-225cb)**	–	0.033
C_3HF_6Cl	(HCFC-226)	5	0.02–0.10
$C_3H_2FCl_5$	(HCFC-231)	9	0.05–0.09
$C_3H_2F_2Cl_4$	(HCFC-232)	16	0.008–0.10
$C_3H_2F_3Cl_3$	(HCFC-233)	18	0.007–0.23
$C_3H_2F_4Cl_2$	(HCFC-234)	16	0.01–0.28
$C_3H_2F_5Cl$	(HCFC-235)	9	0.03–0.52
$C_3H_3FCl_4$	(HCFC-241)	12	0.004–0.09
$C_3H_3F_2Cl_3$	(HCFC-242)	18	0.005–0.13
$C_3H_3F_3Cl_2$	(HCFC-243)	18	0.007–0.12
$C_3H_3F_4Cl$	(HCFC-244)	12	0.009–0.14

(*cont.*)

Group	Substance	Number of isomers	Ozone-depleting potential*
$C_3H_4FCl_3$	(HCFC-251)	12	0.001–0.01
$C_3H_4F_2Cl_2$	(HCFC-252)	16	0.005–0.04
$C_3H_4F_3Cl$	(HCFC-253)	12	0.003–0.03
$C_3H_5FCl_2$	(HCFC-261)	9	0.002–0.02
$C_3H_5F_2Cl$	(HCFC-262)	9	0.002–0.02
C_3H_6FCl	(HCFC-271)	5	0.001–0.03
Group II			
$CHFBr_2$		1	1.00
CHF_2Br	(HBFC-22B1)	1	0.74
CH_2FBr		1	0.73
C_2HFBr_4		2	0.3–0.8
$C_2HF_2Br_3$		3	0.5–1.8
$C_2HF_3Br_2$		3	0.4–1.6
C_2HF_4Br		2	0.7–1.2
$C_2H_2FBr_3$		3	0.1–1.1
$C_2H_2F_2Br_2$		4	0.2–1.5
$C_2H_2F_3Br$		3	0.7–1.6
$C_2H_3FBr_2$		3	0.1–1.7
$C_2H_3F_2Br$		3	0.2–1.1
C_2H_4FBr		2	0.07–0.1
C_3HFBr_6		5	0.3–1.5
$C_3HF_2Br_5$		9	0.2–1.9
$C_3HF_3Br_4$		12	0.3–1.8
$C_3HF_4Br_3$		12	0.5–2.2
$C_3HF_5Br_2$		9	0.9–2.0
C_3HF_6Br		5	0.7–3.3
$C_3H_2FBr_5$		9	0.1–1.9
$C_3H_2F_2Br_4$		16	0.2–2.1
$C_3H_2F_3Br_3$		18	0.2–5.6
$C_3H_2F_4Br_2$		16	0.3–7.5
$C_3H_2F_5Br$		8	0.9–14.0
$C_3H_3FBr_4$		12	0.08–1.9
$C_3H_3F_2Br_3$		18	0.1–3.1
$C_3H_3F_3Br_2$		18	0.1–2.5
$C_3H_3F_4Br$		12	0.3–4.4
$C_3H_4FBr_3$		12	0.03–0.3
$C_3H_4F_2Br_2$		16	0.1–1.0
$C_3H_4F_3Br$		12	0.07–0.8

(*cont.*)

Group	Substance	Number of isomers	Ozone-depleting potential
$C_3H_5FBr_2$		9	0.04–0.4
$C_3H_5F_2Br$		9	0.07–0.8
C_3H_6FBr		5	0.02–0.7
Group III			
CH_2BrCl	bromochloromethane	1	0.12

* Where a range of ODPs is indicated, the highest value in that range shall be used for the purposes of the Protocol. The ODPs listed as a single value have been determined from calculations based on laboratory measurements. Those listed as a range are based on estimates and are less certain. The range pertains to an isomeric group. The upper value is the estimate of the ODP of the isomer with the highest ODP, and the lower value is the estimate of the ODP of the isomer with the lowest ODP.

** Identifies the most commercially viable substances with ODP values listed against them to be used for the purposes of the Protocol.

Annex D*
A list of products** containing controlled substances specified in Annex A

	Products	Customs code number
1.	Automobile and truck air conditioning units (whether incorporated in vehicles or not)	. . . .
2.	Domestic and commercial refrigeration and air conditioning/heat pump equipment***	. . . .
	e.g. Refrigerators	. . . .
	Freezers	. . . .
	Dehumidifiers	. . . .
	Water coolers	. . . .
	Ice machines	. . . .
	Air conditioning and heat pump units	. . . .
3.	Aerosol products, except medical aerosols	. . . .
4.	Portable fire extinguisher	. . . .
5.	Insulation boards, panels and pipe covers	. . . .
6.	Pre-polymers	. . . .

* This Annex was adopted by the Third Meeting of the Parties in Nairobi, 21 June 1991 as required by paragraph 3 of Article 4 of the Protocol.

** Though not when transported in consignments of personal or household effects or in similar non-commercial situations normally exempted from customs attention.

*** When containing controlled substances in Annex A as a refrigerant and/or in insulating material of the product.

Annex E
Controlled substance

Group	Substance	Ozone-depleting potential
Group I		
CH_3Br	methyl bromide	0.6

6B

Non-Compliance Procedure[1]

The following procedure[1] has been formulated pursuant to Article 8 of the Montreal Protocol. It shall apply without prejudice to the operation of the settlement of disputes procedure laid down in Article 11 of the Vienna Convention.

1. If one or more Parties have reservations regarding another Party's implementation of its obligations under the Protocol, those concerns may be addressed in writing to the Secretariat. Such a submission shall be supported by corroborating information.

2. The Secretariat shall, within two weeks of its receiving a submission, send a copy of that submission to the Party whose implementation of a particular provision of the Protocol is at issue. Any reply and information in support thereof are to be submitted to the Secretariat and to the Parties involved within three months of the date of the despatch or such longer period as the circumstances of any particular case may require. If the Secretariat has not received a reply from the Party three months after sending it the original submission, the Secretariat shall send a reminder to the Party that it has yet to provide its reply. The Secretariat shall, as soon as the reply and information from the Party are available, but not later than six months after receiving the submission, transmit the submission, the reply and the information, if any, provided by the Parties to the Implementation Committee referred to in paragraph 5, which shall consider the matter as soon as practicable.

3. Where the Secretariat, during the course of preparing its report, becomes aware of possible non-compliance by any Party with its obligations under the Protocol, it may request the Party concerned to furnish necessary information about the matter. If there is not response from the Party concerned within three months or such longer period as the circumstances of the matter may require or the matter is not resolved through administrative action or through diplomatic contacts, the Secretariat shall include the matter in its report to the Meeting of the Parties pursuant to Article 12 (c) of the Protocol and inform the Implementation Committee, which shall consider the matter as soon as practicable.

---

[1] Adopted by Decision IV/5 (4th Meeting of the Parties) and revised by Decision X/10 (10th Meeting of the Parties).

4. Where a Party concludes that, despite having made its best, bona fide efforts, it is unable to comply fully with its obligations under the Protocol, it may address to the Secretariat a submission in writing, explaining, in particular, the specific circumstances that it considers to be the cause of its non-compliance. The Secretariat shall transmit such submission to the Implementation Committee which shall consider it as soon as practicable.

5. An Implementation Committee is hereby established. It shall consist of 10 Parties elected by the Meeting of the Parties for two years, based on equitable geographical distribution. Each Party so elected to the Committee shall be requested to notify the Secretariat, within two months of its election, of the name of the individual who is to represent it and shall endeavour to ensure that the same individual remains its representative throughout the entire term of office. Outgoing Parties may be re-elected for one immediate consecutive term. A Party that has completed a second consecutive two-year term as a Committee member shall be eligible for election again only after an absence of one year from the Committee. The Committee shall elect its own President and Vice-President. Each shall serve for one year at a time. The Vice-President shall, in addition, serve as the rapporteur of the Committee.

6. The Implementation Committee shall, unless it decides otherwise, meet twice a year. The Secretariat shall arrange for and service its meetings.

7. The functions of the Implementation Committee shall be:

(a) To receive, consider and report on any submission in accordance with paragraphs 1, 2 and 4;
(b) To receive, consider and report on any information or observations forwarded by the Secretariat in connection with the preparation of the reports referred to in Article 12 (c) of the Protocol and on any other information received and forwarded by the Secretariat concerning compliance with the provisions of the Protocol;
(c) To request, where it considers necessary, through the Secretariat, further information on matters under its consideration;
(d) To identify the facts and possible causes relating to individual cases of non-compliance referred to the Committee and make appropriate recommendations to the Meeting of the Parties;
(e) To undertake, upon the invitation of the Party concerned, information-gathering in the territory of that Party for fulfilling the functions of the Committee;
(f) To maintain, in particular for the purposes of drawing up its recommendations, an exchange of information with the Executive Committee of the Multilateral Fund related to the provision of financial and technical cooperation, including the transfer of technologies to Parties operating under Article 5, paragraph 1, of the Protocol.

8. The Implementation Committee shall consider the submissions, information and observations referred to in paragraph 7 with a view to securing an amicable solution of the matter on the basis of respect for the provisions of the Protocol.

9. The Implementation Committee shall report to the Meeting of the Parties, including any recommendations it considers appropriate. The report shall be made available to the Parties not later than six weeks before their meeting. After receiving a report by the Committee the Parties may, taking into consideration the circumstances of the matter, decide upon and call for steps to bring about full compliance with the Protocol, including measures to assist the Parties' compliance with the Protocol, and to further the Protocol's objectives.

10. Where a Party that is not a member of the Implementation Committee is identified in a submission under paragraph 1, or itself makes such a submission, it shall be entitled to participate in the consideration by the Committee of that submission.

11. No Party, whether or not a member of the Implementation Committee, involved in a matter under consideration by the Implementation Committee, shall take part in the elaboration and adoption of recommendations on that matter to be included in the report of the Committee.

12. The Parties involved in a matter referred to in paragraphs 1, 3 or 4 shall inform, through the Secretariat, the Meeting of the Parties of the results of proceedings taken under Article 11 of the Convention regarding possible non-compliance, about implementation of those results and about implementation of any decision of the Parties pursuant to paragraph 9.

13. The Meeting of the Parties may, pending completion of proceedings initiated under Article 11 of the Convention, issue an interim call and/or recommendations.

14. The Meeting of the Parties may request the Implementation Committee to make recommendations to assist the Meeting's consideration of matters of possible non-compliance.

15. The members of the Implementation Committee and any Party involved in its deliberations shall protect the confidentiality of information they receive in confidence.

16. The report, which shall not contain any information received in confidence, shall be made available to any person upon request. All information exchanged by or with the Committee that is related to any recommendation by the Committee to the Meeting of the Parties shall be made available by the Secretariat to any Party upon its request; that Party shall ensure the confidentiality of the information it has received in confidence.

United Nations Framework Convention on Climate Change, 9 May 1992

Editorial note

The ultimate objective of the UN Framework Convention on Climate Change is the 'stabilisation of greenhouse gas concentrations in the atmosphere at a level that would prevent dangerous anthropogenic interference with the climate system' (Article 2). The Convention requires all Parties, in accordance with their differentiated responsibilities and capabilities, to *inter alia*: formulate and implement programmes which mitigate the adverse effects of climate change and facilitate adaptation to it; promote and co-operate in developing, applying and transferring technology that reduces or prevents emissions of greenhouse gases;* promote 'sustainable management' and conservation of sinks and reservoirs of all greenhouse gases;* and take account of climate change in social, economic and environmental programmes (Article 4(1)).

Specifically, developed country Parties and countries of Central and Eastern Europe (listed in Annex I) are required to take measures to limit their greenhouse gas emissions,* 'with the aim of returning individually or jointly to their 1990 levels' by the end of the decade (2000), and enhance their sinks and reservoirs (Articles 4(2)(a) and 4(2)(b)). The Conference of the Parties (described below) reviewed the adequacy of this requirement at its first session with a view to amending it as appropriate (Article 4(2)(d)). Developed country Parties (not including Parties from Central and Eastern Europe) are required to transfer 'new and additional' financial resources to assist developing country Parties in meeting the compliance costs of the requirements of the Convention (Article 4(3)). These developed country Parties are also required to assist developing country Parties which are particularly vulnerable to the adverse effects of climate change in meeting the adaptation costs to those circumstances (Article 4(4)). These Parties are further required to 'take all practical steps' to transfer 'environmentally sound' technology to developing country Parties (Article 4(5)).

In fulfilling their obligations, Parties from Central and Eastern Europe are granted flexibility (Article 4(6)) and the Convention states that developing

---

* Which are not controlled by the Montreal Protocol on substances that Deplete the Ozone Layer.

country Parties will implement their obligations in accordance with the extent to which developed country Parties have fulfilled their commitments to transfer financial resources and technology (Article 4(7)).

The Convention establishes several institutions including a Conference of the Parties, which is to be the governing body (Article 7), a Secretariat (Article 8), and subsidiary bodies which provide advice on scientific and technical matters (Article 9) and on effective implementation of the Convention (Article 10). In addition, a financial mechanism is created for the provision of financial resources and the transfer of technology which is required to have an equitable and balanced representation with a 'transparent systems of governance' (Article 11). The Global Environmental Facility (GEF) has been restructured to fulfil these requirements (Article 21) and has been designated as the financial mechanism of the Convention ad interim.

Upon ratification or anytime afterward, Parties can agree to the submission of disputes to the compulsory jurisdiction of the ICJ and/or to arbitration as provided for by the Conference of the Parties (Article 14(2)(a)). If a dispute remains unsettled after twelve months and is not pending before the ICJ or an arbitration panel, compulsory conciliation is provided for at the request of an involved Party (Article 14(5)). Amendments are adopted on the basis of a three-quarters majority of the Parties present and voting at the Conference of the Parties (Article 15(3)), and the Conference of the Parties may adopt Protocols (Article 17). To date, the only Protocol adopted is the 1997 Kyoto Protocol. The Convention does not allow for reservations (Article 24).

Date of signature:	9 May 1992
Entry into force:	21 March 1994
Depositary:	Secretary-General of the United Nations
Contracting Parties:	Afghanistan, Albania, Algeria, Angola, Antigua and Barbuda, Argentina, Armenia, Australia, Austria, Azerbaijan, Bahamas, Bahrain, Bangladesh, Barbados, Belarus, Belgium, Belize, Benin, Bhutan, Bolivia, Bosnia and Herzegovina, Botswana, Brazil, Bulgaria, Burkina Faso, Burundi, Cambodia, Cameroon, Canada, Cape Verde, Central African Republic, Chad, Chile, China, Colombia, Comoros, Congo, Congo (Democratic Republic of), Cook Islands, Costa Rica, Cote d'Ivoire, Croatia, Cuba, Cyprus, Czech Republic, Denmark, Djibouti, Dominica, Dominican Republic, Ecuador, Egypt, El Salvador, Equatorial Guinea, Eritrea, Estonia, Ethiopia, European Community, Fiji, Finland, France, Gabon,

Gambia, Georgia, Germany, Ghana, Greece, Grenada, Guatemala, Guinea, Guinea Bissau, Guyana, Haiti, Honduras, Hungary, Iceland, India, Indonesia, Iran (Islamic Republic of), Ireland, Israel, Italy, Jamaica, Japan, Jordan, Kazakhstan, Kenya, Kiribati, Korea (Democratic People's Republic of), Korea (Republic of), Kuwait, Kyrgyzstan, Lao People's Democratic Republic, Latvia, Lebanon, Lesotho, Liberia, Libyan Arab Jamahiriya, Liechtenstein, Lithuania, Luxembourg, Madagascar, Malawi, Malaysia, Maldives, Mali, Malta, Marshall Islands, Mauritania, Mauritius, Mexico, Micronesia (Federated States of), Moldova, Monaco, Mongolia, Morocco, Mozambique, Myanmar, Namibia, Nauru, Nepal, Netherlands, New Zealand, Nicaragua, Niger, Nigeria, Niue, Norway, Oman, Pakistan, Palau, Panama, Papua New Guinea, Paraguay, Peru, Philippines, Poland, Portugal, Qatar, Romania, Russian Federation, Rwanda, Saint Kitts and Nevis, Saint Lucia, Saint Vincent and the Grenadines, Samoa, San Marino, São Tomé and Príncipe, Saudi Arabia, Senegal, Serbia and Montenegro, Seychelles, Sierra Leone, Singapore, Slovakia, Slovenia, Solomon Islands, South Africa, Spain, Sri Lanka, Sudan, Suriname, Swaziland, Sweden, Switzerland, Syrian Arab Republic, Tajikistan, Tanzania (United Republic of), Thailand, The Former Yugoslav Republic of Macedonia, Togo, Tonga, Trinidad and Tobago, Tunisia, Turkmenistan, Tuvalu, Uganda, Ukraine, United Arab Emirates, United Kingdom, United States of America, Uruguay, Uzbekistan, Vanuatu, Venezuela, Vietnam, Yemen, Zambia, Zimbabwe.

Website: www.unfccc.int

United Nations Framework Convention on Climate Change

The Parties to this Convention,

   Acknowledging that change in the Earth's climate and its adverse effects are a common concern of humankind,

   Concerned that human activities have been substantially increasing the atmospheric concentrations of greenhouse gases, that these increases enhance the natural greenhouse effect, and that this will result on average in an additional warming of the Earth's surface and atmosphere and may adversely affect natural ecosystems and humankind,

Noting that the largest share of historical and current global emissions of greenhouse gases has originated in developed countries, that per capita emissions in developing countries are still relatively low and that the share of global emissions originating in developing countries will grow to meet their social and development needs,

Aware of the role and importance in terrestrial and marine ecosystems of sinks and reservoirs of greenhouse gases,

Noting that there are many uncertainties in predictions of climate change, particularly with regard to the timing, magnitude and regional patterns thereof,

Acknowledging that the global nature of climate change calls for the widest possible cooperation by all countries and their participation in an effective and appropriate international response, in accordance with their common but differentiated responsibilities and respective capabilities and their social and economic conditions,

Recalling the pertinent provisions of the Declaration of the United Nations Conference on the Human Environment, adopted at Stockholm on 16 June 1972,

Recalling also that States have, in accordance with the Charter of the United Nations and the principles of international law, the sovereign right to exploit their own resources pursuant to their own environmental and developmental policies, and the responsibility to ensure that activities within their jurisdiction or control do not cause damage to the environment of other States or of areas beyond the limits of national jurisdiction,

Reaffirming the principle of sovereignty of States in international cooperation to address climate change,

Recognizing that States should enact effective environmental legislation, that environmental standards, management objectives and priorities should reflect the environmental and developmental context to which they apply, and that standards applied by some countries may be inappropriate and of unwarranted economic and social cost to other countries, in particular developing countries,

Recalling the provisions of General Assembly resolution 44/228 of 22 December 1989 on the United Nations Conference on Environment and Development, and resolutions 43/53 of 6 December 1988, 44/207 of 22 December 1989, 45/212 of 21 December 1990 and 46/169 of 19 December 1991 on protection of global climate for present and future generations of mankind,

Recalling also the provisions of General Assembly resolution 44/206 of 22 December 1989 on the possible adverse effects of sea-level rise on islands and coastal areas, particularly low-lying coastal areas and the pertinent provisions of General Assembly resolution 44/172 of 19 December 1989 on the implementation of the Plan of Action to Combat Desertification,

Recalling further the Vienna Convention for the Protection of the Ozone Layer, 1985, and the Montreal Protocol on Substances that Deplete the Ozone Layer, 1987, as adjusted and amended on 29 June 1990,

Noting the Ministerial Declaration of the Second World Climate Conference adopted on 7 November 1990,

Conscious of the valuable analytical work being conducted by many States on climate change and of the important contributions of the World Meteorological Organization, the United Nations Environment Programme and other organs, organizations and bodies of the United Nations system, as well as other international and intergovernmental bodies, to the exchange of results of scientific research and the coordination of research,

Recognizing that steps required to understand and address climate change will be environmentally, socially and economically most effective if they are based on relevant scientific, technical and economic considerations and continually re-evaluated in the light of new findings in these areas,

Recognizing that various actions to address climate change can be justified economically in their own right and can also help in solving other environmental problems,

Recognizing also the need for developed countries to take immediate action in a flexible manner on the basis of clear priorities, as a first step towards comprehensive response strategies at the global, national and, where agreed, regional levels that take into account all greenhouse gases, with due consideration of their relative contributions to the enhancement of the greenhouse effect,

Recognizing further that low-lying and other small island countries, countries with low-lying coastal, arid and semiarid areas or areas liable to floods, drought and desertification, and developing countries with fragile mountainous ecosystems are particularly vulnerable to the adverse effects of climate change,

Recognizing the special difficulties of those countries, especially developing countries, whose economies are particularly dependent on fossil fuel production, use and exportation, as a consequence of action taken on limiting greenhouse gas emissions,

Affirming that responses to climate change should be coordinated with social and economic development in an integrated manner with a view to avoiding adverse impacts on the latter, taking into full account the legitimate priority needs of developing countries for the achievement of sustained economic growth and the eradication of poverty,

Recognizing that all countries, especially developing countries, need access to resources required to achieve sustainable social and economic development and that, in order for developing countries to progress towards that goal, their energy consumption will need to grow taking into account the possibilities for achieving greater energy efficiency and for controlling greenhouse gas emissions in general, including through the application of new technologies on terms which make such an application economically and socially beneficial,

Determined to protect the climate system for present and future generations,
Have agreed as follows:

Article 1
Definitions*

For the purposes of this Convention:

1. 'Adverse effects of climate change' means changes in the physical environment or biota resulting from climate change which have significant deleterious effects on the composition, resilience or productivity of natural and managed ecosystems or on the operation of socio-economic systems or on human health and welfare.
2. 'Climate change' means a change of climate which is attributed directly or indirectly to human activity that alters the composition of the global atmosphere and which is in addition to natural climate variability observed over comparable time periods.
3. 'Climate system' means the totality of the atmosphere, hydrosphere, biosphere and geosphere and their interactions.
4. 'Emissions' means the release of greenhouse gases and/or their precursors into the atmosphere over a specified area and period of time.
5. 'Greenhouse gases' means those gaseous constituents of the atmosphere, both natural and anthropogenic, that absorb and re-emit infrared radiation.
6. 'Regional economic integration organization' means an organization constituted by sovereign States of a given region which has competence in respect of matters governed by this Convention or its protocols and has been duly authorized, in accordance with its internal procedures, to sign, ratify, accept, approve or accede to the instruments concerned.
7. 'Reservoir' means a component or components of the climate system where a greenhouse gas or a precursor of a greenhouse gas is stored.
8. 'Sink' means any process, activity or mechanism which removes a greenhouse gas, an aerosol or a precursor of a greenhouse gas from the atmosphere.
9. 'Source' means any process or activity which releases a greenhouse gas, an aerosol or a precursor of a greenhouse gas into the atmosphere.

Article 2
Objective

The ultimate objective of this Convention and any related legal instruments that the Conference of the Parties may adopt is to achieve, in accordance with the relevant provisions of the Convention, stabilization of greenhouse gas concentrations in the atmosphere at a level that would prevent dangerous

* Titles of articles are included solely to assist the reader.

anthropogenic interference with the climate system. Such a level should be achieved within a time-frame sufficient to allow ecosystems to adapt naturally to climate change, to ensure that food production is not threatened and to enable economic development to proceed in a sustainable manner.

Article 3
Principles

In their actions to achieve the objective of the Convention and to implement its provisions, the Parties shall be guided, *inter alia*, by the following:

1. The Parties should protect the climate system for the benefit of present and future generations of humankind, on the basis of equity and in accordance with their common but differentiated responsibilities and respective capabilities. Accordingly, the developed country Parties should take the lead in combating climate change and the adverse effects thereof.

2. The specific needs and special circumstances of developing country Parties, especially those that are particularly vulnerable to the adverse effects of climate change, and of those Parties, especially developing country Parties, that would have to bear a disproportionate or abnormal burden under the Convention, should be given full consideration.

3. The Parties should take precautionary measures to anticipate, prevent or minimize the causes of climate change and mitigate its adverse effects. Where there are threats of serious or irreversible damage, lack of full scientific certainty should not be used as a reason for postponing such measures, taking into account that policies and measures to deal with climate change should be cost-effective so as to ensure global benefits at the lowest possible cost. To achieve this, such policies and measures should take into account different socio-economic contexts, be comprehensive, cover all relevant sources, sinks and reservoirs of greenhouse gases and adaptation, and comprise all economic sectors. Efforts to address climate change may be carried out cooperatively by interested Parties.

4. The Parties have a right to, and should, promote sustainable development. Policies and measures to protect the climate system against human-induced change should be appropriate for the specific conditions of each Party and should be integrated with national development programmes, taking into account that economic development is essential for adopting measures to address climate change.

5. The Parties should cooperate to promote a supportive and open international economic system that would lead to sustainable economic growth and development in all Parties, particularly developing country Parties, thus enabling them better to address the problems of climate change. Measures taken to combat climate change, including unilateral ones, should not constitute a means of arbitrary or unjustifiable discrimination or a disguised restriction on international trade.

Article 4
Commitments

1. All Parties, taking into account their common but differentiated responsibilities and their specific national and regional development priorities, objectives and circumstances, shall:

(a) Develop, periodically update, publish and make available to the Conference of the Parties, in accordance with Article 12, national inventories of anthropogenic emissions by sources and removals by sinks of all greenhouse gases not controlled by the Montreal Protocol, using comparable methodologies to be agreed upon by the Conference of the Parties;

(b) Formulate, implement, publish and regularly update national and, where appropriate, regional programmes containing measures to mitigate climate change by addressing anthropogenic emissions by sources and removals by sinks of all greenhouse gases not controlled by the Montreal Protocol, and measures to facilitate adequate adaptation to climate change;

(c) Promote and cooperate in the development, application and diffusion, including transfer, of technologies, practices and processes that control, reduce or prevent anthropogenic emissions of greenhouse gases not controlled by the Montreal Protocol in all relevant sectors, including the energy, transport, industry, agriculture, forestry and waste management sectors;

(d) Promote sustainable management, and promote and cooperate in the conservation and enhancement, as appropriate, of sinks and reservoirs of all greenhouse gases not controlled by the Montreal Protocol, including biomass, forests and oceans as well as other terrestrial, coastal and marine ecosystems;

(e) Cooperate in preparing for adaptation to the impacts of climate change; develop and elaborate appropriate and integrated plans for coastal zone management, water resources and agriculture, and for the protection and rehabilitation of areas, particularly in Africa, affected by drought and desertification, as well as floods;

(f) Take climate change considerations into account, to the extent feasible, in their relevant social, economic and environmental policies and actions, and employ appropriate methods, for example impact assessments, formulated and determined nationally, with a view to minimizing adverse effects on the economy, on public health and on the quality of the environment, of projects or measures undertaken by them to mitigate or adapt to climate change;

(g) Promote and cooperate in scientific, technological, technical, socio-economic and other research, systematic observation and development of data archives related to the climate system and intended to further the understanding and to reduce or eliminate the remaining uncertainties regarding the causes, effects, magnitude and timing of climate change and the economic and social consequences of various response strategies;

(h) Promote and cooperate in the full, open and prompt exchange of relevant scientific, technological, technical, socio-economic and legal information related to the climate system and climate change, and to the economic and social consequences of various response strategies;

(i) Promote and cooperate in education, training and public awareness related to climate change and encourage the widest participation in this process, including that of non-governmental organizations; and

(j) Communicate to the Conference of the Parties information related to implementation, in accordance with Article 12.

2. The developed country Parties and other Parties included in Annex I commit themselves specifically as provided for in the following:

(a) Each of these Parties shall adopt national[1] policies and take corresponding measures on the mitigation of climate change, by limiting its anthropogenic emissions of greenhouse gases and protecting and enhancing its greenhouse gas sinks and reservoirs. These policies and measures will demonstrate that developed countries are taking the lead in modifying longer-term trends in anthropogenic emissions consistent with the objective of the Convention, recognizing that the return by the end of the present decade to earlier levels of anthropogenic emissions of carbon dioxide and other greenhouse gases not controlled by the Montreal Protocol would contribute to such modification, and taking into account the differences in these Parties' starting points and approaches, economic structures and resource bases, the need to maintain strong and sustainable economic growth, available technologies and other individual circumstances, as well as the need for equitable and appropriate contributions by each of these Parties to the global effort regarding that objective. These Parties may implement such policies and measures jointly with other Parties and may assist other Parties in contributing to the achievement of the objective of the Convention and, in particular, that of this subparagraph;

(b) In order to promote progress to this end, each of these Parties shall communicate, within six months of the entry into force of the Convention for it and periodically thereafter, and in accordance with Article 12, detailed information on its policies and measures referred to in subparagraph (a) above, as well as on its resulting projected anthropogenic emissions by sources and removals by sinks of greenhouse gases not controlled by the Montreal Protocol for the period referred to in subparagraph (a), with

---

[1] This includes policies and measures adopted by regional economic integration organizations.

the aim of returning individually or jointly to their 1990 levels these anthropogenic emissions of carbon dioxide and other greenhouse gases not controlled by the Montreal Protocol. This information will be reviewed by the Conference of the Parties, at its first session and periodically thereafter, in accordance with Article 7;

(c) Calculations of emissions by sources and removals by sinks of greenhouse gases for the purposes of subparagraph (b) above should take into account the best available scientific knowledge, including of the effective capacity of sinks and the respective contributions of such gases to climate change. The Conference of the Parties shall consider and agree on methodologies for these calculations at its first session and review them regularly thereafter;

(d) The Conference of the Parties shall, at its first session, review the adequacy of subparagraphs (a) and (b) above. Such review shall be carried out in the light of the best available scientific information and assessment on climate change and its impacts, as well as relevant technical, social and economic information. Based on this review, the Conference of the Parties shall take appropriate action, which may include the adoption of amendments to the commitments in subparagraphs (a) and (b) above. The Conference of the Parties, at its first session, shall also take decisions regarding criteria for joint implementation as indicated in subparagraph (a) above. A second review of subparagraphs (a) and (b) shall take place not later than 31 December 1998, and thereafter at regular intervals determined by the Conference of the Parties, until the objective of the Convention is met;

(e) Each of these Parties shall:
  (i) Coordinate as appropriate with other such Parties, relevant economic and administrative instruments developed to achieve the objective of the Convention; and
  (ii) Identify and periodically review its own policies and practices which encourage activities that lead to greater levels of anthropogenic emissions of greenhouse gases not controlled by the Montreal Protocol than would otherwise occur;

(f) The Conference of the Parties shall review, not later than 31 December 1998, available information with a view to taking decisions regarding such amendments to the lists in Annexes I and II as may be appropriate, with the approval of the Party concerned;

(g) Any Party not included in Annex I may, in its instrument of ratification, acceptance, approval or accession, or at any time thereafter, notify the Depositary that it intends to be bound by subparagraphs (a) and (b) above. The Depositary shall inform the other signatories and Parties of any such notification.

3. The developed country Parties and other developed Parties included in Annex II shall provide new and additional financial resources to meet the agreed full costs incurred by developing country Parties in complying with their obligations under Article 12, paragraph 1. They shall also provide such financial resources, including for the transfer of technology, needed by the developing country Parties to meet the agreed full incremental costs of implementing measures that are covered by paragraph 1 of this Article and that are agreed between a developing country Party and the international entity or entities referred to in Article 11, in accordance with that Article. The implementation of these commitments shall take into account the need for adequacy and predictability in the flow of funds and the importance of appropriate burden sharing among the developed country Parties.

4. The developed country Parties and other developed Parties included in Annex II shall also assist the developing country Parties that are particularly vulnerable to the adverse effects of climate change in meeting costs of adaptation to those adverse effects.

5. The developed country Parties and other developed Parties included in Annex II shall take all practicable steps to promote, facilitate and finance, as appropriate, the transfer of, or access to, environmentally sound technologies and knowhow to other Parties, particularly developing country Parties, to enable them to implement the provisions of the Convention. In this process, the developed country Parties shall support the development and enhancement of endogenous capacities and technologies of developing country Parties. Other Parties and organizations in a position to do so may also assist in facilitating the transfer of such technologies.

6. In the implementation of their commitments under paragraph 2 above, a certain degree of flexibility shall be allowed by the Conference of the Parties to the Parties included in Annex I undergoing the process of transition to a market economy, in order to enhance the ability of these Parties to address climate change, including with regard to the historical level of anthropogenic emissions of greenhouse gases not controlled by the Montreal Protocol chosen as a reference.

7. The extent to which developing country Parties will effectively implement their commitments under the Convention will depend on the effective implementation by developed country Parties of their commitments under the Convention related to financial resources and transfer of technology and will take fully into account that economic and social development and poverty eradication are the first and overriding priorities of the developing country Parties.

8. In the implementation of the commitments in this Article, the Parties shall give full consideration to what actions are necessary under the Convention, including actions related to funding, insurance and the transfer of technology, to

meet the specific needs and concerns of developing country Parties arising from the adverse effects of climate change and/or the impact of the implementation of response measures, especially on:

(a) Small island countries;
(b) Countries with low-lying coastal areas;
(c) Countries with arid and semi-arid areas, forested areas and areas liable to forest decay;
(d) Countries with areas prone to natural disasters;
(e) Countries with areas liable to drought and desertification;
(f) Countries with areas of high urban atmospheric pollution;
(g) Countries with areas with fragile ecosystems, including mountainous ecosystems;
(h) Countries whose economies are highly dependent on income generated from the production, processing and export, and/or on consumption of fossil fuels and associated energy-intensive products; and
(i) Land-locked and transit countries.

Further, the Conference of the Parties may take actions, as appropriate, with respect to this paragraph.

9. The Parties shall take full account of the specific needs and special situations of the least developed countries in their actions with regard to funding and transfer of technology.

10. The Parties shall, in accordance with Article 10, take into consideration in the implementation of the commitments of the Convention the situation of Parties, particularly developing country Parties, with economies that are vulnerable to the adverse effects of the implementation of measures to respond to climate change. This applies notably to Parties with economies that are highly dependent on income generated from the production, processing and export, and/or consumption of fossil fuels and associated energy-intensive products and/or the use of fossil fuels for which such Parties have serious difficulties in switching to alternatives.

Article 5
Research and systematic observation

In carrying out their commitments under Article 4, paragraph 1(g), the Parties shall:

(a) Support and further develop, as appropriate, international and intergovernmental programmes and networks or organizations aimed at defining, conducting, assessing and financing research, data collection and systematic observation, taking into account the need to minimize duplication of effort;

(b) Support international and intergovernmental efforts to strengthen systematic observation and national scientific and technical research capacities and capabilities, particularly in developing countries, and to promote access to, and the exchange of, data and analyses thereof obtained from areas beyond national jurisdiction; and

(c) Take into account the particular concerns and needs of developing countries and cooperate in improving their endogenous capacities and capabilities to participate in the efforts referred to in subparagraphs (a) and (b) above.

Article 6
Education, training and public awareness

In carrying out their commitments under Article 4, paragraph 1(i), the Parties shall:

(a) Promote and facilitate at the national and, as appropriate, subregional and regional levels, and in accordance with national laws and regulations, and within their respective capacities:

   (i) The development and implementation of educational and public awareness programmes on climate change and its effects;

   (ii) Public access to information on climate change and its effects;

   (iii) Public participation in addressing climate change and its effects and developing adequate responses; and

   (iv) Training of scientific, technical and managerial personnel.

(b) Cooperate in and promote, at the international level, and, where appropriate, using existing bodies:

   (i) The development and exchange of educational and public awareness material on climate change and its effects; and

   (ii) The development and implementation of education and training programmes, including the strengthening of national institutions and the exchange or secondment of personnel to train experts in this field, in particular for developing countries.

Article 7
Conference of the Parties

1. A Conference of the Parties is hereby established.

2. The Conference of the Parties, as the supreme body of this Convention, shall keep under regular review the implementation of the Convention and any related legal instruments that the Conference of the Parties may adopt, and shall make, within its mandate, the decisions necessary to promote the effective implementation of the Convention. To this end, it shall:

(a) Periodically examine the obligations of the Parties and the institutional arrangements under the Convention, in the light of the objective of the

Convention, the experience gained in its implementation and the evolution of scientific and technological knowledge;

(b) Promote and facilitate the exchange of information on measures adopted by the Parties to address climate change and its effects, taking into account the differing circumstances, responsibilities and capabilities of the Parties and their respective commitments under the Convention;

(c) Facilitate, at the request of two or more Parties, the coordination of measures adopted by them to address climate change and its effects, taking into account the differing circumstances, responsibilities and capabilities of the Parties and their respective commitments under the Convention;

(d) Promote and guide, in accordance with the objective and provisions of the Convention, the development and periodic refinement of comparable methodologies, to be agreed on by the Conference of the Parties, *inter alia*, for preparing inventories of greenhouse gas emissions by sources and removals by sinks, and for evaluating the effectiveness of measures to limit the emissions and enhance the removals of these gases;

(e) Assess, on the basis of all information made available to it in accordance with the provisions of the Convention, the implementation of the Convention by the Parties, the overall effects of the measures taken pursuant to the Convention, in particular environmental, economic and social effects as well as their cumulative impacts and the extent to which progress towards the objective of the Convention is being achieved;

(f) Consider and adopt regular reports on the implementation of the Convention and ensure their publication;

(g) Make recommendations on any matters necessary for the implementation of the Convention;

(h) Seek to mobilize financial resources in accordance with Article 4, paragraphs 3, 4 and 5, and Article 11;

(i) Establish such subsidiary bodies as are deemed necessary for the implementation of the Convention;

(j) Review reports submitted by its subsidiary bodies and provide guidance to them;

(k) Agree upon and adopt, by consensus, rules of procedure and financial rules for itself and for any subsidiary bodies;

(l) Seek and utilize, where appropriate, the services and cooperation of, and information provided by, competent international organizations and intergovernmental and non-governmental bodies; and

(m) Exercise such other functions as are required for the achievement of the objective of the Convention as well as all other functions assigned to it under the Convention.

3. The Conference of the Parties shall, at its first session, adopt its own rules of procedure as well as those of the subsidiary bodies established by the

Convention, which shall include decision-making procedures for matters not already covered by decision-making procedures stipulated in the Convention. Such procedures may include specified majorities required for the adoption of particular decisions.

4. The first session of the Conference of the Parties shall be convened by the interim secretariat referred to in Article 21 and shall take place not later than one year after the date of entry into force of the Convention. Thereafter, ordinary sessions of the Conference of the Parties shall be held every year unless otherwise decided by the Conference of the Parties.

5. Extraordinary sessions of the Conference of the Parties shall be held at such other times as may be deemed necessary by the Conference, or at the written request of any Party, provided that, within six months of the request being communicated to the Parties by the secretariat, it is supported by at least one third of the Parties.

6. The United Nations, its specialized agencies and the International Atomic Energy Agency, as well as any State member thereof or observers thereto not Party to the Convention, may be represented at sessions of the Conference of the Parties as observers. Any body or agency, whether national or international, governmental or non-governmental, which is qualified in matters covered by the Convention, and which has informed the secretariat of its wish to be represented at a session of the Conference of the Parties as an observer, may be so admitted unless at least one third of the Parties present object. The admission and participation of observers shall be subject to the rules of procedure adopted by the Conference of the Parties.

Article 8
Secretariat

1. A secretariat is hereby established.
2. The functions of the secretariat shall be:

(a) To make arrangements for sessions of the Conference of the Parties and its subsidiary bodies established under the Convention and to provide them with services as required;
(b) To compile and transmit reports submitted to it;
(c) To facilitate assistance to the Parties, particularly developing country Parties, on request, in the compilation and communication of information required in accordance with the provisions of the Convention;
(d) To prepare reports on its activities and present them to the Conference of the Parties;
(e) To ensure the necessary coordination with the secretariats of other relevant international bodies;

(f) To enter, under the overall guidance of the Conference of the Parties, into such administrative and contractual arrangements as may be required for the effective discharge of its functions; and

(g) To perform the other secretariat functions specified in the Convention and in any of its protocols and such other functions as may be determined by the Conference of the Parties.

3. The Conference of the Parties, at its first session, shall designate a permanent secretariat and make arrangements for its functioning.

Article 9
Subsidiary body for scientific and technological advice

1. A subsidiary body for scientific and technological advice is hereby established to provide the Conference of the Parties and, as appropriate, its other subsidiary bodies with timely information and advice on scientific and technological matters relating to the Convention. This body shall be open to participation by all Parties and shall be multidisciplinary. It shall comprise government representatives competent in the relevant field of expertise. It shall report regularly to the Conference of the Parties on all aspects of its work.

2. Under the guidance of the Conference of the Parties, and drawing upon existing competent international bodies, this body shall:

(a) Provide assessments of the state of scientific knowledge relating to climate change and its effects;

(b) Prepare scientific assessments on the effects of measures taken in the implementation of the Convention;

(c) Identify innovative, efficient and state-of-the-art technologies and know-how and advise on the ways and means of promoting development and/or transferring such technologies;

(d) Provide advice on scientific programmes, international cooperation in research and development related to climate change, as well as on ways and means of supporting endogenous capacity building in developing countries; and

(e) Respond to scientific, technological and methodological questions that the Conference of the Parties and its subsidiary bodies may put to the body.

3. The functions and terms of reference of this body may be further elaborated by the Conference of the Parties.

Article 10
Subsidiary body for implementation

1. A subsidiary body for implementation is hereby established to assist the Conference of the Parties in the assessment and review of the effective

implementation of the Convention. This body shall be open to participation by all Parties and comprise government representatives who are experts on matters related to climate change. It shall report regularly to the Conference of the Parties on all aspects of its work.

2. Under the guidance of the Conference of the Parties, this body shall:

(a) Consider the information communicated in accordance with Article 12, paragraph 1, to assess the overall aggregated effect of the steps taken by the Parties in the light of the latest scientific assessments concerning climate change;

(b) Consider the information communicated in accordance with Article 12, paragraph 2, in order to assist the Conference of the Parties in carrying out the reviews required by Article 4, paragraph 2(d); and

(c) Assist the Conference of the Parties, as appropriate, in the preparation and implementation of its decisions.

Article 11
Financial mechanism

1. A mechanism for the provision of financial resources on a grant or concessional basis, including for the transfer of technology, is hereby defined. It shall function under the guidance of and be accountable to the Conference of the Parties, which shall decide on its policies, programme priorities and eligibility criteria related to this Convention. Its operation shall be entrusted to one or more existing international entities.

2. The financial mechanism shall have an equitable and balanced representation of all Parties within a transparent system of governance.

3. The Conference of the Parties and the entity or entities entrusted with the operation of the financial mechanism shall agree upon arrangements to give effect to the above paragraphs, which shall include the following:

(a) Modalities to ensure that the funded projects to address climate change are in conformity with the policies, programme priorities and eligibility criteria established by the Conference of the Parties;

(b) Modalities by which a particular funding decision may be reconsidered in light of these policies, programme priorities and eligibility criteria;

(c) Provision by the entity or entities of regular reports to the Conference of the Parties on its funding operations, which is consistent with the requirement for accountability set out in paragraph 1 above; and

(d) Determination in a predictable and identifiable manner of the amount of funding necessary and available for the implementation of this Convention and the conditions under which that amount shall be periodically reviewed.

4. The Conference of the Parties shall make arrangements to implement the above-mentioned provisions at its first session, reviewing and taking into

account the interim arrangements referred to in Article 21, paragraph 3, and shall decide whether these interim arrangements shall be maintained. Within four years thereafter, the Conference of the Parties shall review the financial mechanism and take appropriate measures.

5. The developed country Parties may also provide and developing country Parties avail themselves of, financial resources related to the implementation of the Convention through bilateral, regional and other multilateral channels.

Article 12
Communication of information related to implementation

1. In accordance with Article 4, paragraph 1, each Party shall communicate to the Conference of the Parties, through the secretariat, the following elements of information:

(a) A national inventory of anthropogenic emissions by sources and removals by sinks of all greenhouse gases not controlled by the Montreal Protocol, to the extent its capacities permit, using comparable methodologies to be promoted and agreed upon by the Conference of the Parties;

(b) A general description of steps taken or envisaged by the Party to implement the Convention; and

(c) Any other information that the Party considers relevant to the achievement of the objective of the Convention and suitable for inclusion in its communication, including, if feasible, material relevant for calculations of global emission trends.

2. Each developed country Party and each other Party included in Annex I shall incorporate in its communication the following elements of information:

(a) A detailed description of the policies and measures that it has adopted to implement its commitment under Article 4, paragraphs 2(a) and 2(b); and

(b) A specific estimate of the effects that the policies and measures referred to in subparagraph (a) immediately above will have on anthropogenic emissions by its sources and removals by its sinks of greenhouse gases during the period referred to in Article 4, paragraph 2(a).

3. In addition, each developed country Party and each other developed Party included in Annex II shall incorporate details of measures taken in accordance with Article 4, paragraphs 3, 4 and 5.

4. Developing country Parties may, on a voluntary basis, propose projects for financing, including specific technologies, materials, equipment, techniques or practices that would be needed to implement such projects, along with, if possible, an estimate of all incremental costs, of the reductions of emissions and increments of removals of greenhouse gases, as well as an estimate of the consequent benefits.

5. Each developed country Party and each other Party included in Annex I shall make its initial communication within six months of the entry into force of the Convention for that Party. Each Party not so listed shall make its initial communication within three years of the entry into force of the Convention for that Party, or of the availability of financial resources in accordance with Article 4, paragraph 3. Parties that are least developed countries may make their initial communication at their discretion. The frequency of subsequent communications by all Parties shall be determined by the Conference of the Parties, taking into account the differentiated timetable set by this paragraph.

6. Information communicated by Parties under this Article shall be transmitted by the secretariat as soon as possible to the Conference of the Parties and to any subsidiary bodies concerned. If necessary, the procedures for the communication of information may be further considered by the Conference of the Parties.

7. From its first session, the Conference of the Parties shall arrange for the provision to developing country Parties of technical and financial support, on request, in compiling and communicating information under this Article, as well as in identifying the technical and financial needs associated with proposed projects and response measures under Article 4. Such support may be provided by other Parties, by competent international organizations and by the secretariat, as appropriate.

8. Any group of Parties may, subject to guidelines adopted by the Conference of the Parties, and to prior notification to the Conference of the Parties, make a joint communication in fulfilment of their obligations under this Article, provided that such a communication includes information on the fulfilment by each of these Parties of its individual obligations under the Convention.

9. Information received by the secretariat that is designated by a Party as confidential, in accordance with criteria to be established by the Conference of the Parties, shall be aggregated by the secretariat to protect its confidentiality before being made available to any of the bodies involved in the communication and review of information.

10. Subject to paragraph 9 above, and without prejudice to the ability of any Party to make public its communication at any time, the secretariat shall make communications by Parties under this Article publicly available at the time they are submitted to the Conference of the Parties.

Article 13
Resolution of questions regarding implementation

The Conference of the Parties shall, at its first session, consider the establishment of a multilateral consultative process, available to Parties on their request, for the resolution of questions regarding the implementation of the Convention.

Article 14
Settlement of disputes

1. In the event of a dispute between any two or more Parties concerning the interpretation or application of the Convention, the Parties concerned shall seek a settlement of the dispute through negotiation or any other peaceful means of their own choice.

2. When ratifying, accepting, approving or acceding to the Convention, or at any time thereafter, a Party which is not a regional economic integration organization may declare in a written instrument submitted to the Depositary that, in respect of any dispute concerning the interpretation or application of the Convention, it recognizes as compulsory *ipso facto* and without special agreement, in relation to any Party accepting the same obligation:

(a) Submission of the dispute to the International Court of Justice, and/or
(b) Arbitration in accordance with procedures to be adopted by the Conference of the Parties as soon as practicable, in an annex on arbitration.

A Party which is a regional economic integration organization, may make a declaration with like effect in relation to arbitration in accordance with the procedures referred to in subparagraph (b) above.

3. A declaration made under paragraph 2 above shall remain in force until it expires in accordance with its terms or until three months after written notice of its revocation has been deposited with the Depositary.

4. A new declaration, a notice of revocation or the expiry of a declaration shall not in any way affect proceedings pending before the International Court of Justice or the arbitral tribunal, unless the parties to the dispute otherwise agree.

5. Subject to the operation of paragraph 2 above, if after twelve months following notification by one Party to another that a dispute exists between them, the Parties concerned have not been able to settle their dispute through the means mentioned in paragraph 1 above, the dispute shall be submitted, at the request of any of the parties to the dispute, to conciliation.

6. A conciliation commission shall be created upon the request of one of the parties to the dispute. The commission shall be composed of an equal number of members appointed by each party concerned and a chairman chosen jointly by the members appointed by each party. The commission shall render a recommendatory award, which the parties shall consider in good faith.

7. Additional procedures relating to conciliation shall be adopted by the Conference of the Parties, as soon as practicable, in an annex on conciliation.

8. The provisions of this Article shall apply to any related legal instrument which the Conference of the Parties may adopt, unless the instrument provides otherwise.

Article 15
Amendments to the Convention

1. Any Party may propose amendments to the Convention.

2. Amendments to the Convention shall be adopted at an ordinary session of the Conference of the Parties. The text of any proposed amendment to the Convention shall be communicated to the Parties by the secretariat at least six months before the meeting at which it is proposed for adoption. The secretariat shall also communicate proposed amendments to the signatories to the Convention and, for information, to the Depositary.

3. The Parties shall make every effort to reach agreement on any proposed amendment to the Convention by consensus. If all efforts at consensus have been exhausted, and no agreement reached, the amendment shall as a last resort be adopted by a three-fourths majority vote of the Parties present and voting at the meeting. The adopted amendment shall be communicated by the secretariat to the Depositary, who shall circulate it to all Parties for their acceptance.

4. Instruments of acceptance in respect of an amendment shall be deposited with the Depositary. An amendment adopted in accordance with paragraph 3 above shall enter into force for those Parties having accepted it on the ninetieth day after the date of receipt by the Depositary of an instrument of acceptance by at least three fourths of the Parties to the Convention.

5. The amendment shall enter into force for any other Party on the ninetieth day after the date on which that Party deposits with the Depositary its instrument of acceptance of the said amendment.

6. For the purposes of this Article, 'Parties present and voting' means Parties present and casting an affirmative or negative vote.

Article 16
Adoption and amendment of annexes to the Convention

1. Annexes to the Convention shall form an integral part thereof and, unless otherwise expressly provided, a reference to the Convention constitutes at the same time a reference to any annexes thereto. Without prejudice to the provisions of Article 14, paragraphs 2(b) and 7, such annexes shall be restricted to lists, forms and any other material of a descriptive nature that is of a scientific, technical, procedural or administrative character.

2. Annexes to the Convention shall be proposed and adopted in accordance with the procedure set forth in Article 15, paragraphs 2, 3 and 4.

3. An annex that has been adopted in accordance with paragraph 2 above shall enter into force for all Parties to the Convention six months after the date of the communication by the Depositary to such Parties of the adoption of the annex, except for those Parties that have notified the Depositary, in writing, within that period of their non-acceptance of the annex. The annex shall enter into force for Parties which withdraw their notification of non-acceptance on

the ninetieth day after the date on which withdrawal of such notification has been received by the Depositary.

4. The proposal, adoption and entry into force of amendments to annexes to the Convention shall be subject to the same procedure as that for the proposal, adoption and entry into force of annexes to the Convention in accordance with paragraphs 2 and 3 above.

5. If the adoption of an annex or an amendment to an annex involves an amendment to the Convention, that annex or amendment to an annex shall not enter into force until such time as the amendment to the Convention enters into force.

Article 17
Protocols

1. The Conference of the Parties may, at any ordinary session, adopt protocols to the Convention.

2. The text of any proposed protocol shall be communicated to the Parties by the secretariat at least six months before such a session.

3. The requirements for the entry into force of any protocol shall be established by that instrument.

4. Only Parties to the Convention may be Parties to a protocol.

5. Decisions under any protocol shall be taken only by the Parties to the protocol concerned.

Article 18
Right to vote

1. Each Party to the Convention shall have one vote, except as provided for in paragraph 2 below.

2. Regional economic integration organizations, in matters within their competence, shall exercise their right to vote with a number of votes equal to the number of their member States that are Parties to the Convention. Such an organization shall not exercise its right to vote if any of its member States exercises its right, and vice versa.

Article 19
Depositary

The Secretary-General of the United Nations shall be the Depositary of the Convention and of protocols adopted in accordance with Article 17.

Article 20
Signature

This Convention shall be open for signature by States Members of the United Nations or of any of its specialized agencies or that are Parties to the Statute of the International Court of Justice and by regional economic integration organizations at Rio de Janeiro, during the United Nations Conference on Environment and Development, and thereafter at United Nations Headquarters in New York from 20 June 1992 to 19 June 1993.

Article 21
Interim arrangements

1. The secretariat functions referred to in Article 8 will be carried out on an interim basis by the secretariat established by the General Assembly of the United Nations in its resolution 45/212 of 21 December 1990, until the completion of the first session of the Conference of the Parties.

2. The head of the interim secretariat referred to in paragraph 1 above will cooperate closely with the Intergovernmental Panel on Climate Change to ensure that the Panel can respond to the need for objective scientific and technical advice. Other relevant scientific bodies could also be consulted.

3. The Global Environment Facility of the United Nations Development Programme, the United Nations Environment Programme and the International Bank for Reconstruction and Development shall be the international entity entrusted with the operation of the financial mechanism referred to in Article 11 on an interim basis. In this connection, the Global Environment Facility should be appropriately restructured and its membership made universal to enable it to fulfil the requirements of Article 11.

Article 22
Ratification, acceptance, approval or accession

1. The Convention shall be subject to ratification, acceptance, approval or accession by States and by regional economic integration organizations. It shall be open for accession from the day after the date on which the Convention is closed for signature. Instruments of ratification, acceptance, approval or accession shall be deposited with the Depositary.

2. Any regional economic integration organization which becomes a Party to the Convention without any of its member States being a Party shall be bound by all the obligations under the Convention. In the case of such organizations, one or more of whose member States is a Party to the Convention, the organization and its member States shall decide on their respective responsibilities for the performance of their obligations under the Convention. In such cases, the organization and the member States shall not be entitled to exercise rights under the Convention concurrently.

3. In their instruments of ratification, acceptance, approval or accession, regional economic integration organizations shall declare the extent of their competence with respect to the matters governed by the Convention. These organizations shall also inform the Depositary, who shall in turn inform the Parties, of any substantial modification in the extent of their competence.

Article 23
Entry into force

1. The Convention shall enter into force on the ninetieth day after the date of deposit of the fiftieth instrument of ratification, acceptance, approval or accession.

2. For each State or regional economic integration organization that ratifies, accepts or approves the Convention or accedes thereto after the deposit of the fiftieth instrument of ratification, acceptance, approval or accession, the Convention shall enter into force on the ninetieth day after the date of deposit by such State or regional economic integration organization of its instrument of ratification, acceptance, approval or accession.

3. For the purposes of paragraphs 1 and 2 above, any instrument deposited by a regional economic integration organization shall not be counted as additional to those deposited by States members of the organization.

Article 24
Reservations

No reservations may be made to the Convention.

Article 25
Withdrawal

1. At any time after three years from the date on which the Convention has entered into force for a Party, that Party may withdraw from the Convention by giving written notification to the Depositary.

2. Any such withdrawal shall take effect upon expiry of one year from the date of receipt by the Depositary of the notification of withdrawal, or on such later date as may be specified in the notification of withdrawal.

3. Any Party that withdraws from the Convention shall be considered as also having withdrawn from any protocol to which it is a Party.

Article 26
Authentic texts

The original of this Convention, of which the Arabic, Chinese, English, French, Russian and Spanish texts are equally authentic, shall be deposited with the Secretary-General of the United Nations.

IN WITNESS WHEREOF the undersigned, being duly authorized to that effect, have signed this Convention.

DONE at New York this ninth day of May one thousand nine hundred and ninety-two.

Annex I

Australia	Japan
Austria	Latvia*
Belarus*	Lithuania*
Belgium	Luxembourg
Bulgaria*	Netherlands
Canada	New Zealand
Czechoslovakia*	Norway
Denmark	Poland*
European Community	Portugal
Estonia*	Romania*
Finland	Russian Federation*
France	Spain
Germany	Sweden
Greece	Switzerland
Hungary*	Turkey
Iceland	Ukraine*
Ireland	United Kingdom
Italy	United States of America

*Countries that are undergoing the process of transition to a market economy.

Annex II

Australia	Japan
Austria	Luxembourg
Belgium	Netherlands
Canada	New Zealand
Denmark	Norway
European Community	Portugal
Finland	Spain
France	Sweden
Germany	Switzerland
Greece	Turkey
Iceland	United Kingdom
Ireland	United States of America
Italy	

Kyoto Protocol to the United Nations Framework Convention on Climate Change, 11 December 1997

Editorial note

The Kyoto Protocol to the Framework Convention on Climate Change was adopted by the third conference of the parties in December 1997. Negotiations for a protocol to the Convention commenced in 1995 after the first conference of the parties, meeting in Berlin, determined that the commitments provided for in Article 4(2)(a) and (b) of the Convention were 'not adequate' and decided to launch a process to strengthen the commitments of Annex I parties through the adoption of a protocol or another legal instrument. Negotiations were to be conducted as a matter of urgency with a view to adopting the results at the Third conference of the parties in 1997. The Kyoto Protocol was adopted at the Third conference of the parties and opened for signature on 16 March 1998.

The Kyoto Protocol commits Annex I parties to quantified emissions reductions and a timetable for their achievement. The basic obligation accepted by the Annex I parties is set out in Article 3(1). It provides that Annex I parties 'shall, individually or jointly, ensure that their aggregate anthropogenic carbon dioxide equivalent emissions of the greenhouse gases listed in Annex A do not exceed their assigned amounts'. The 'assigned amounts' are calculated pursuant to each party's quantified emission limitation and reduction commitment inscribed in Annex B. Annex I parties must implement their obligation under Article 3(1) 'with a view to reducing their overall emissions of [Annex A] gases by at least 5 per cent below 1990 levels in the commitment period 2008 to 2012'. A timetable for emissions reductions is set by Articles 3(1), 3(2) and 3(7). In the pre-commitment period up until 2005, each Annex I party is required to 'have made demonstrable progress in achieving its commitments under [the] Protocol'. The first commitment period commences in 2008 and continues until 2012. During this period the 'assigned amount' for each Annex I Party is 'equal to the percentage inscribed for it in Annex B of its aggregate anthropogenic carbon dioxide equivalent emissions of the listed greenhouse gases in 1990 . . . multiplied by five'. However, Annex I parties with economies in transition need not use 1990 as their base year, but rather can use a different base year, calculated in accordance with Article 3(5). Commitments for subsequent periods will be established by amendments to Annex B adopted in accordance with the provisions of Article 21(7). The Meeting of the Parties to the Protocol is required to initiate reconsideration of the commitments in Annex B at least seven years before the end of the first commitment period. Banking of assigned amounts for future commitment periods is permitted as any Annex I party with emissions in a commitment period which are less than its assigned amount can request the difference be added to its assigned amount for subsequent commitment periods (Article 13(3)).

Annex B lists differentiated targets for individual countries and regional economic organisations. For example, the European Community and its member states agreed to an emissions limitation of 92% of the 1990 base year, or an 8% reduction in the first commitment period of 2008–2012. The United States agreed to a 7% reduction. Japan and Canada each accepted a 6% reduction, while Australia and Iceland were permitted to make increases of respectively 8% and 10%. Russia, the largest emitter of the Eastern bloc countries, agreed to stabilise its emissions at 100% of 1990 levels.

Six gases are covered by the emissions reduction commitments of the Annex I parties: carbon dioxide, methane, nitrous oxide, hydrofluorocarbons, perfluorocarbons and sulphur hexafluoride (Annex A).

Article 2 of the Protocol contains a list of policies and measures which Parties may implement in order to achieve their quantified limitation and emission reduction targets. Article 2 provides that each Annex I Party, in achieving its emission limitation and reduction commitments under Article 3, shall implement policies and measures 'in accordance with its national circumstances'. A list of indicative measures follows, which includes enhancement of energy efficiency, the protection and enhancement of sinks, the promotion of sustainable forms of agriculture, increased research on and use of new and renewable forms of energy, measures to limit or reduce emissions in the transport sector and the limitation or reduction of methane emissions. Parties are required to cooperate 'to enhance the individual and combined effectiveness of their policies and measures' through taking steps to share relevant experience and information, including developing ways of improving the compatibility, transparency and effectiveness of policies and measures (Article 2(1)(b)).

Parties are allowed to meet their targets by using so called flexible mechanisms provided by Article 6 (joint implementation), Article 12 (Clean Development Mechanism) and Article 17 (emission trading) of the Protocol.

Article 6 provides that for the purpose of meeting its commitments under Article 3 any Annex I party may transfer to, or acquire from, any other Annex I party 'emission reduction credits resulting from projects aimed at reducing anthropogenic emissions by sources or enhancing anthropogenic removals by sinks of greenhouse gases in any sector of the economy' (Article 6(1)).

The Clean Development Mechanism allows Annex I parties to carry out emissions reductions projects in non-Annex I parties and use the certified emission reductions (CERs) accruing from such project activities 'to contribute to compliance with part of their quantified emission limitation and reduction commitments under Article 3' (Article 12(3)(b)). Certified emissions reductions obtained between 2000 and 2005 can be used to assist in achieving compliance in the first commitment period (Article 12(10)). A share of the proceeds from certified project activities must be used to cover administrative expenses 'as well as to assist developing country Parties that are particularly vulnerable to the adverse effects of climate change to meet the costs of adaptation' (Article 12(8)).

Article 17 allows Annex B parties to 'participate in emissions trading for the purposes of fulfilling their commitments under Article 3' but provides that any such trading must be 'supplemental' to domestic actions taken to achieve emissions reductions. Article 17 left to the Conference of the Parties the task of defining 'relevant principles, modalities, rules and guidelines, in particular for verification, reporting and accountability for emissions trading'.

Article 3(3) allows for commitments to be met by 'net changes in greenhouse gas emissions by sources and removals by sinks resulting from direct human-induced land-use change and forestry activities, limited to afforestation, reforestation and deforestation since 1990, measured as verifiable changes in carbon stocks in each commitment period'. Article 3(4) provides that the conference of the parties serving as the meeting of the parties to the Protocol shall at its first session or as soon as practicable thereafter 'decide upon modalities, rules and guidelines as to how, and which, additional human-induced activities related to changes in greenhouse gas emissions by sources and removals by sinks in the agricultural soils and land-use change and forestry categories shall be added to, or subtracted from, the assigned amounts for parties included in Annex I'. Any such decision would apply in the second and subsequent commitment periods, although a party may choose to have it apply for the first commitment period, provided that the 'additional human-induced activities' have taken place since 1990.

Article 10 deals with the advancement of the implementation of commitments by all parties, including developing country parties. The preamble to Article 10 affirms that the provision is not 'introducing any new commitments for Parties not included in Annex I' but is merely reaffirming existing commitments under Article 4(1) of the Convention, and 'continuing to advance the implementation of these commitments in order to achieve sustainable development'. A number of measures are listed in Article 10 which cover areas such as the formulation of 'cost-effective national, and where appropriate regional programmes to improve the quality of local emission factors, activity data and/or models which reflect the socioeconomic conditions of each Party for the preparation and periodic updating of national inventories' of emissions of greenhouse gases and the formulation, implementation, publication and updating of 'national and, where appropriate, regional programmes containing measures to mitigate climate change and measures to facilitate adequate

adaptation to climate change'. Other measures include the provision of information on programmes which contain measures addressing climate change and
its adverse impacts, and the promotion of effective modalities relating to the
transfer of environmentally sound technologies pertinent to climate change.
Detailed reporting obligations are established by Articles 5, 7 and 8 of the
Protocol.

Apart from the review of information submitted by Parties, the Protocol contemplates a further mechanism for ensuring compliance with commitments
under the Protocol. Article 18 provides that the Meeting of the Parties at its
first session shall 'approve appropriate and effective procedures and mechanisms to determine and to address cases of non-compliance with the provisions of this Protocol, including through the development of an indicative list
of consequences, taking into account the cause, type, degree and frequency
of non-compliance'. Any such procedures and mechanisms entailing 'binding consequences' would, however, require an amendment to the Protocol. An
amendment to the Protocol can be adopted by a three-fourths majority vote
of the Parties present and voting at the meeting at which it is proposed for
adoption, followed by its ratification or acceptance by at least three-fourths of
the Parties to the Protocol (Article 20).

In order to enter into force the Protocol requires the ratification, acceptance,
approval or accession of at least fifty-five Parties to the Convention, which must
incorporate Annex I parties which accounted for at least 55 percent of the total
carbon dioxide emissions of Annex I parties in 1990 (Article 25).

Date of signature: 11 December 1997

Entry into force: Not yet in force

Depositary: Secretary-General of the United Nations

Contracting Parties: Antigua and Barbuda, Argentina, Armenia, Austria,
                       Azerbaijan, Bahamas, Bangladesh, Barbados, Belgium,
                       Benin, Bhutan, Bolivia, Brazil, Bulgaria, Burundi,
                       Cambodia, Cameroon, Canada, Chile, China, Colom-
                       bia, Cook Islands, Costa Rica, Cuba, Cyprus, Czech
                       Republic, Denmark, Djibouti, Dominican Republic,
                       Ecuador, El Salvador, Equatorial Guinea, Estonia,
                       European Community, Fiji, Finland, France, Gambia,
                       Georgia, Germany, Greece, Grenada, Guatemala,
                       Guinea, Honduras, Hungary, Iceland, India, Ireland,
                       Italy, Jamaica, Japan, Jordan, Kiribati, Korea (Republic
                       of), Lao Democratic People's Republic, Latvia, Lesotho,
                       Liberia, Lithuania, Luxembourg, Malawi, Malaysia,

Maldives, Mali, Malta, Mauritius, Mexico, Micronesia (Federated States of), Moldova (Republic of), Mongolia, Morocco, Nauru, Netherlands, New Zealand, Nicaragua, Niue, Norway, Palau, Panama, Papua New Guinea, Paraguay, Peru, Poland, Portugal, Romania, Samoa, Senegal, Seychelles, Slovakia, Slovenia, Solomon Islands, South Africa, Spain, Sri Lanka, Sweden, Tanzania (United Republic of), Thailand, Trinidad and Tobago, Tunisia, Turkmenistan, Tuvalu, Uganda, United Kingdom, Uruguay, Uzbekistan, Vanuatu, Vietnam.

Website: www.unfccc.int

Kyoto Protocol to the United Nations Framework Convention on Climate Change

The Parties to this Protocol,

Being Parties to the United Nations Framework Convention on Climate Change, hereinafter referred to as 'the Convention',

In pursuit of the ultimate objective of the Convention as stated in its Article 2,

Recalling the provisions of the Convention,

Being guided by Article 3 of the Convention,

Pursuant to the Berlin Mandate adopted by decision 1/CP.1 of the Conference of the Parties to the Convention at its first session,

Have agreed as follows:

Article 1

For the purposes of this Protocol, the definitions contained in Article 1 of the Convention shall apply. In addition:

1. 'Conference of the Parties' means the Conference of the Parties to the Convention.
2. 'Convention' means the United Nations Framework Convention on Climate Change, adopted in New York on 9 May 1992.
3. 'Intergovernmental Panel on Climate Change' means the Intergovernmental Panel on Climate Change established in 1988 jointly by the World Meteorological Organization and the United Nations Environment Programme.
4. 'Montreal Protocol' means the Montreal Protocol on Substances that Deplete the Ozone Layer, adopted in Montreal on 16 September 1987 and as subsequently adjusted and amended.
5. 'Parties present and voting' means Parties present and casting an affirmative or negative vote.

6. 'Party' means, unless the context otherwise indicates, a Party to this Protocol.

7. 'Party included in Annex I' means a Party included in Annex I to the Convention, as may be amended, or a Party which has made a notification under Article 4, paragraph 2(g), of the Convention.

Article 2

1. Each Party included in Annex I, in achieving its quantified emission limitation and reduction commitments under Article 3, in order to promote sustainable development, shall:

(a) Implement and/or further elaborate policies and measures in accordance with its national circumstances, such as:
   (i) Enhancement of energy efficiency in relevant sectors of the national economy;
   (ii) Protection and enhancement of sinks and reservoirs of greenhouse gases not controlled by the Montreal Protocol, taking into account its commitments under relevant international environmental agreements; promotion of sustainable forest management practices, afforestation and reforestation;
   (iii) Promotion of sustainable forms of agriculture in light of climate change considerations;
   (iv) Research on, and promotion, development and increased use of, new and renewable forms of energy, of carbon dioxide sequestration technologies and of advanced and innovative environmentally sound technologies;
   (v) Progressive reduction or phasing out of market imperfections, fiscal incentives, tax and duty exemptions and subsidies in all greenhouse gas emitting sectors that run counter to the objective of the Convention and application of market instruments;
   (vi) Encouragement of appropriate reforms in relevant sectors aimed at promoting policies and measures which limit or reduce emissions of greenhouse gases not controlled by the Montreal Protocol;
   (vii) Measures to limit and/or reduce emissions of greenhouse gases not controlled by the Montreal Protocol in the transport sector;
   (viii) Limitation and/or reduction of methane emissions through recovery and use in waste management, as well as in the production, transport and distribution of energy;

(b) Cooperate with other such Parties to enhance the individual and combined effectiveness of their policies and measures adopted under this Article, pursuant to Article 4, paragraph 2(e)(i), of the Convention. To this end, these Parties shall take steps to share their experience and exchange information on such policies and measures, including developing ways of improving their comparability, transparency and effectiveness. The Conference of the Parties serving as the meeting of the Parties to this Protocol shall, at its first session or as soon as practicable thereafter, consider ways to facilitate such cooperation, taking into account all relevant information.

2. The Parties included in Annex I shall pursue limitation or reduction of emissions of greenhouse gases not controlled by the Montreal Protocol from aviation and marine bunker fuels, working through the International Civil Aviation Organization and the International Maritime Organization, respectively.

3. The Parties included in Annex I shall strive to implement policies and measures under this Article in such a way as to minimize adverse effects, including the adverse effects of climate change, effects on international trade, and social, environmental and economic impacts on other Parties, especially developing country Parties and in particular those identified in Article 4, paragraphs 8 and 9, of the Convention, taking into account Article 3 of the Convention. The Conference of the Parties serving as the meeting of the Parties to this Protocol may take further action, as appropriate, to promote the implementation of the provisions of this paragraph.

4. The Conference of the Parties serving as the meeting of the Parties to this Protocol, if it decides that it would be beneficial to coordinate any of the policies and measures in paragraph 1(a) above, taking into account different national circumstances and potential effects, shall consider ways and means to elaborate the coordination of such policies and measures.

Article 3

1. The Parties included in Annex I shall, individually or jointly, ensure that their aggregate anthropogenic carbon dioxide equivalent emissions of the greenhouse gases listed in Annex A do not exceed their assigned amounts, calculated pursuant to their quantified emission limitation and reduction commitments inscribed in Annex B and in accordance with the provisions of this Article, with a view to reducing their overall emissions of such gases by at least 5 per cent below 1990 levels in the commitment period 2008 to 2012.

2. Each Party included in Annex I shall, by 2005, have made demonstrable progress in achieving its commitments under this Protocol.

3. The net changes in greenhouse gas emissions by sources and removals by sinks resulting from direct human-induced land-use change and forestry activities, limited to afforestation, reforestation and deforestation since 1990, measured as verifiable changes in carbon stocks in each commitment period, shall be used to meet the commitments under this Article of each Party included in Annex I. The greenhouse gas emissions by sources and removals by sinks associated with those activities shall be reported in a transparent and verifiable manner and reviewed in accordance with Articles 7 and 8.

4. Prior to the first session of the Conference of the Parties serving as the meeting of the Parties to this Protocol, each Party included in Annex I shall provide, for consideration by the Subsidiary Body for Scientific and Technological Advice, data to establish its level of carbon stocks in 1990 and to enable an estimate to be made of its changes in carbon stocks in subsequent years. The Conference of the Parties serving as the meeting of the Parties to this Protocol shall, at its first session or as soon as practicable thereafter, decide upon modalities, rules and guidelines as to how, and which, additional human-induced activities related to changes in greenhouse gas emissions by sources and removals by sinks in the agricultural soils and the land-use change and forestry categories shall be added to, or subtracted from, the assigned amounts for Parties included in Annex I, taking into account uncertainties, transparency in reporting, verifiability, the methodological work of the Intergovernmental Panel on Climate Change, the advice provided by the Subsidiary Body for Scientific and Technological Advice in accordance with Article 5 and the decisions of the Conference of the Parties. Such a decision shall apply in the second and subsequent commitment periods. A Party may choose to apply such a decision on these additional human-induced activities for its first commitment period, provided that these activities have taken place since 1990.

5. The Parties included in Annex I undergoing the process of transition to a market economy whose base year or period was established pursuant to decision 9/CP.2 of the Conference of the Parties at its second session shall use that base year or period for the implementation of their commitments under this Article. Any other Party included in Annex I undergoing the process of transition to a market economy which has not yet submitted its first national communication under Article 12 of the Convention may also notify the Conference of the Parties serving as the meeting of the Parties to this Protocol that it intends to use an historical base year or period other than 1990 for the implementation of its commitments under this Article. The Conference of the Parties serving as the meeting of the Parties to this Protocol shall decide on the acceptance of such notification.

6. Taking into account Article 4, paragraph 6, of the Convention, in the implementation of their commitments under this Protocol other than those under this Article, a certain degree of flexibility shall be allowed by the Conference of the Parties serving as the meeting of the Parties to this Protocol to the Parties included in Annex I undergoing the process of transition to a market economy.

7. In the first quantified emission limitation and reduction commitment period, from 2008 to 2012, the assigned amount for each Party included in Annex I shall be equal to the percentage inscribed for it in Annex B of its aggregate anthropogenic carbon dioxide equivalent emissions of the greenhouse gases listed in Annex A in 1990, or the base year or period determined in accordance with paragraph 5 above, multiplied by five. Those Parties included in Annex I for whom land-use change and forestry constituted a net source of greenhouse

gas emissions in 1990 shall include in their 1990 emissions base year or period the aggregate anthropogenic carbon dioxide equivalent emissions by sources minus removals by sinks in 1990 from land-use change for the purposes of calculating their assigned amount.

8. Any Party included in Annex I may use 1995 as its base year for hydrofluorocarbons, perfluorocarbons and sulphur hexafluoride, for the purposes of the calculation referred to in paragraph 7 above.

9. Commitments for subsequent periods for Parties included in Annex I shall be established in amendments to Annex B to this Protocol, which shall be adopted in accordance with the provisions of Article 21, paragraph 7. The Conference of the Parties serving as the meeting of the Parties to this Protocol shall initiate the consideration of such commitments at least seven years before the end of the first commitment period referred to in paragraph 1 above.

10. Any emission reduction units, or any part of an assigned amount, which a Party acquires from another Party in accordance with the provisions of Article 6 or of Article 17 shall be added to the assigned amount for the acquiring Party.

11. Any emission reduction units, or any part of an assigned amount, which a Party transfers to another Party in accordance with the provisions of Article 6 or of Article 17 shall be subtracted from the assigned amount for the transferring Party.

12. Any certified emission reductions which a Party acquires from another Party in accordance with the provisions of Article 12 shall be added to the assigned amount for the acquiring Party.

13. If the emissions of a Party included in Annex I in a commitment period are less than its assigned amount under this Article, this difference shall, on request of that Party, be added to the assigned amount for that Party for subsequent commitment periods.

14. Each Party included in Annex I shall strive to implement the commitments mentioned in paragraph 1 above in such a way as to minimize adverse social, environmental and economic impacts on developing country Parties, particularly those identified in Article 4, paragraphs 8 and 9, of the Convention. In line with relevant decisions of the Conference of the Parties on the implementation of those paragraphs, the Conference of the Parties serving as the meeting of the Parties to this Protocol shall, at its first session, consider what actions are necessary to minimize the adverse effects of climate change and/or the impacts of response measures on Parties referred to in those paragraphs. Among the issues to be considered shall be the establishment of funding, insurance and transfer of technology.

Article 4

1. Any Parties included in Annex I that have reached an agreement to fulfil their commitments under Article 3 jointly, shall be deemed to have met those commitments provided that their total combined aggregate anthropogenic

carbon dioxide equivalent emissions of the greenhouse gases listed in Annex A do not exceed their assigned amounts calculated pursuant to their quantified emission limitation and reduction commitments inscribed in Annex B and in accordance with the provisions of Article 3. The respective emission level allocated to each of the Parties to the agreement shall be set out in that agreement.

2. The Parties to any such agreement shall notify the secretariat of the terms of the agreement on the date of deposit of their instruments of ratification, acceptance or approval of this Protocol, or accession thereto. The secretariat shall in turn inform the Parties and signatories to the Convention of the terms of the agreement.

3. Any such agreement shall remain in operation for the duration of the commitment period specified in Article 3, paragraph 7.

4. If Parties acting jointly do so in the framework of, and together with, a regional economic integration organization, any alteration in the composition of the organization after adoption of this Protocol shall not affect existing commitments under this Protocol. Any alteration in the composition of the organization shall only apply for the purposes of those commitments under Article 3 that are adopted subsequent to that alteration.

5. In the event of failure by the Parties to such an agreement to achieve their total combined level of emission reductions, each Party to that agreement shall be responsible for its own level of emissions set out in the agreement.

6. If Parties acting jointly do so in the framework of, and together with, a regional economic integration organization which is itself a Party to this Protocol, each member State of that regional economic integration organization individually, and together with the regional economic integration organization acting in accordance with Article 24, shall, in the event of failure to achieve the total combined level of emission reductions, be responsible for its level of emissions as notified in accordance with this Article.

Article 5

1. Each Party included in Annex I shall have in place, no later than one year prior to the start of the first commitment period, a national system for the estimation of anthropogenic emissions by sources and removals by sinks of all greenhouse gases not controlled by the Montreal Protocol. Guidelines for such national systems, which shall incorporate the methodologies specified in paragraph 2 below, shall be decided upon by the Conference of the Parties serving as the meeting of the Parties to this Protocol at its first session.

2. Methodologies for estimating anthropogenic emissions by sources and removals by sinks of all greenhouse gases not controlled by the Montreal Protocol shall be those accepted by the Intergovernmental Panel on Climate Change and agreed upon by the Conference of the Parties at its third session. Where such methodologies are not used, appropriate adjustments shall be applied according to methodologies agreed upon by the Conference of the Parties serving

as the meeting of the Parties to this Protocol at its first session. Based on the work of, *inter alia*, the Intergovernmental Panel on Climate Change and advice provided by the Subsidiary Body for Scientific and Technological Advice, the Conference of the Parties serving as the meeting of the Parties to this Protocol shall regularly review and, as appropriate, revise such methodologies and adjustments, taking fully into account any relevant decisions by the Conference of the Parties. Any revision to methodologies or adjustments shall be used only for the purposes of ascertaining compliance with commitments under Article 3 in respect of any commitment period adopted subsequent to that revision.

3. The global warming potentials used to calculate the carbon dioxide equivalence of anthropogenic emissions by sources and removals by sinks of greenhouse gases listed in Annex A shall be those accepted by the Intergovernmental Panel on Climate Change and agreed upon by the Conference of the Parties at its third session. Based on the work of, *inter alia*, the Intergovernmental Panel on Climate Change and advice provided by the Subsidiary Body for Scientific and Technological Advice, the Conference of the Parties serving as the meeting of the Parties to this Protocol shall regularly review and, as appropriate, revise the global warming potential of each such greenhouse gas, taking fully into account any relevant decisions by the Conference of the Parties. Any revision to a global warming potential shall apply only to commitments under Article 3 in respect of any commitment period adopted subsequent to that revision.

Article 6

1. For the purpose of meeting its commitments under Article 3, any Party included in Annex I may transfer to, or acquire from, any other such Party emission reduction units resulting from projects aimed at reducing anthropogenic emissions by sources or enhancing anthropogenic removals by sinks of greenhouse gases in any sector of the economy, provided that:

(a) Any such project has the approval of the Parties involved;
(b) Any such project provides a reduction in emissions by sources, or an enhancement of removals by sinks, that is additional to any that would otherwise occur;
(c) It does not acquire any emission reduction units if it is not in compliance with its obligations under Articles 5 and 7; and
(d) The acquisition of emission reduction units shall be supplemental to domestic actions for the purposes of meeting commitments under Article 3.

2. The Conference of the Parties serving as the meeting of the Parties to this Protocol may, at its first session or as soon as practicable thereafter, further elaborate guidelines for the implementation of this Article, including for verification and reporting.

3. A Party included in Annex I may authorize legal entities to participate, under its responsibility, in actions leading to the generation, transfer or acquisition under this Article of emission reduction units.

4. If a question of implementation by a Party included in Annex I of the requirements referred to in this Article is identified in accordance with the relevant provisions of Article 8, transfers and acquisitions of emission reduction units may continue to be made after the question has been identified, provided that any such units may not be used by a Party to meet its commitments under Article 3 until any issue of compliance is resolved.

Article 7

1. Each Party included in Annex I shall incorporate in its annual inventory of anthropogenic emissions by sources and removals by sinks of greenhouse gases not controlled by the Montreal Protocol, submitted in accordance with the relevant decisions of the Conference of the Parties, the necessary supplementary information for the purposes of ensuring compliance with Article 3, to be determined in accordance with paragraph 4 below.

2. Each Party included in Annex I shall incorporate in its national communication, submitted under Article 12 of the Convention, the supplementary information necessary to demonstrate compliance with its commitments under this Protocol, to be determined in accordance with paragraph 4 below.

3. Each Party included in Annex I shall submit the information required under paragraph 1 above annually, beginning with the first inventory due under the Convention for the first year of the commitment period after this Protocol has entered into force for that Party. Each such Party shall submit the information required under paragraph 2 above as part of the first national communication due under the Convention after this Protocol has entered into force for it and after the adoption of guidelines as provided for in paragraph 4 below. The frequency of subsequent submission of information required under this Article shall be determined by the Conference of the Parties serving as the meeting of the Parties to this Protocol, taking into account any timetable for the submission of national communications decided upon by the Conference of the Parties.

4. The Conference of the Parties serving as the meeting of the Parties to this Protocol shall adopt at its first session, and review periodically thereafter, guidelines for the preparation of the information required under this Article, taking into account guidelines for the preparation of national communications by Parties included in Annex I adopted by the Conference of the Parties. The Conference of the Parties serving as the meeting of the Parties to this Protocol shall also, prior to the first commitment period, decide upon modalities for the accounting of assigned amounts.

Article 8

1. The information submitted under Article 7 by each Party included in Annex I shall be reviewed by expert review teams pursuant to the relevant decisions of the Conference of the Parties and in accordance with guidelines adopted for this purpose by the Conference of the Parties serving as the meeting of the Parties to this Protocol under paragraph 4 below. The information submitted under Article 7, paragraph 1, by each Party included in Annex I shall be reviewed as part of the annual compilation and accounting of emissions inventories and assigned amounts. Additionally, the information submitted under Article 7, paragraph 2, by each Party included in Annex I shall be reviewed as part of the review of communications.

2. Expert review teams shall be coordinated by the secretariat and shall be composed of experts selected from those nominated by Parties to the Convention and, as appropriate, by intergovernmental organizations, in accordance with guidance provided for this purpose by the Conference of the Parties.

3. The review process shall provide a thorough and comprehensive technical assessment of all aspects of the implementation by a Party of this Protocol. The expert review teams shall prepare a report to the Conference of the Parties serving as the meeting of the Parties to this Protocol, assessing the implementation of the commitments of the Party and identifying any potential problems in, and factors influencing, the fulfilment of commitments. Such reports shall be circulated by the secretariat to all Parties to the Convention. The secretariat shall list those questions of implementation indicated in such reports for further consideration by the Conference of the Parties serving as the meeting of the Parties to this Protocol.

4. The Conference of the Parties serving as the meeting of the Parties to this Protocol shall adopt at its first session, and review periodically thereafter, guidelines for the review of implementation of this Protocol by expert review teams taking into account the relevant decisions of the Conference of the Parties.

5. The Conference of the Parties serving as the meeting of the Parties to this Protocol shall, with the assistance of the Subsidiary Body for Implementation and, as appropriate, the Subsidiary Body for Scientific and Technological Advice, consider:

(a) The information submitted by Parties under Article 7 and the reports of the expert reviews thereon conducted under this Article; and
(b) Those questions of implementation listed by the secretariat under paragraph 3 above, as well as any questions raised by Parties.

6. Pursuant to its consideration of the information referred to in paragraph 5 above, the Conference of the Parties serving as the meeting of the Parties to this Protocol shall take decisions on any matter required for the implementation of this Protocol.

Article 9

1. The Conference of the Parties serving as the meeting of the Parties to this Protocol shall periodically review this Protocol in the light of the best available scientific information and assessments on climate change and its impacts, as well as relevant technical, social and economic information. Such reviews shall be coordinated with pertinent reviews under the Convention, in particular those required by Article 4, paragraph 2(d), and Article 7, paragraph 2(a), of the Convention. Based on these reviews, the Conference of the Parties serving as the meeting of the Parties to this Protocol shall take appropriate action.

2. The first review shall take place at the second session of the Conference of the Parties serving as the meeting of the Parties to this Protocol. Further reviews shall take place at regular intervals and in a timely manner.

Article 10

All Parties, taking into account their common but differentiated responsibilities and their specific national and regional development priorities, objectives and circumstances, without introducing any new commitments for Parties not included in Annex I, but reaffirming existing commitments under Article 4, paragraph 1, of the Convention, and continuing to advance the implementation of these commitments in order to achieve sustainable development, taking into account Article 4, paragraphs 3, 5 and 7, of the Convention, shall:

(a) Formulate, where relevant and to the extent possible, cost-effective national and, where appropriate, regional programmes to improve the quality of local emission factors, activity data and/or models which reflect the socio-economic conditions of each Party for the preparation and periodic updating of national inventories of anthropogenic emissions by sources and removals by sinks of all greenhouse gases not controlled by the Montreal Protocol, using comparable methodologies to be agreed upon by the Conference of the Parties, and consistent with the guidelines for the preparation of national communications adopted by the Conference of the Parties;

(b) Formulate, implement, publish and regularly update national and, where appropriate, regional programmes containing measures to mitigate climate change and measures to facilitate adequate adaptation to climate change:

  (i) Such programmes would, *inter alia*, concern the energy, transport and industry sectors as well as agriculture, forestry and waste management. Furthermore, adaptation technologies and methods for improving spatial planning would improve adaptation to climate change; and

  (ii) Parties included in Annex I shall submit information on action under this Protocol, including national programmes, in accordance with Article 7; and other Parties shall seek to include in their national communications, as appropriate, information on programmes which contain measures that the Party believes contribute to addressing climate change and its adverse impacts, including the abatement of increases in greenhouse gas emissions, and enhancement of and removals by sinks, capacity building and adaptation measures;

(c) Cooperate in the promotion of effective modalities for the development, application and diffusion of, and take all practicable steps to promote, facilitate and finance, as appropriate, the transfer of, or access to, environmentally sound technologies, know-how, practices and processes pertinent to climate change, in particular to developing countries, including the formulation of policies and programmes for the effective transfer of environmentally sound technologies that are publicly owned or in the public domain and the creation of an enabling environment for the private sector, to promote and enhance the transfer of, and access to, environmentally sound technologies;

(d) Cooperate in scientific and technical research and promote the maintenance and the development of systematic observation systems and development of data archives to reduce uncertainties related to the climate system, the adverse impacts of climate change and the economic and social consequences of various response strategies, and promote the development and strengthening of endogenous capacities and capabilities to participate in international and intergovernmental efforts, programmes and networks on research and systematic observation, taking into account Article 5 of the Convention;

(e) Cooperate in and promote at the international level, and, where appropriate, using existing bodies, the development and implementation of education and training programmes, including the strengthening of national capacity building, in particular human and institutional capacities and the exchange or secondment of personnel to train experts in this field, in particular for developing countries, and facilitate at the national level public awareness of, and public access to information on, climate change. Suitable modalities should be developed to implement these activities through the relevant bodies of the Convention, taking into account Article 6 of the Convention;

(f) Include in their national communications information on programmes and activities undertaken pursuant to this Article in accordance with relevant decisions of the Conference of the Parties; and

(g) Give full consideration, in implementing the commitments under this Article, to Article 4, paragraph 8, of the Convention.

Article 11

1. In the implementation of Article 10, Parties shall take into account the provisions of Article 4, paragraphs 4, 5, 7, 8 and 9, of the Convention.

2. In the context of the implementation of Article 4, paragraph 1, of the Convention, in accordance with the provisions of Article 4, paragraph 3, and

Article 11 of the Convention, and through the entity or entities entrusted with the operation of the financial mechanism of the Convention, the developed country Parties and other developed Parties included in Annex II to the Convention shall:

(a) Provide new and additional financial resources to meet the agreed full costs incurred by developing country Parties in advancing the implementation of existing commitments under Article 4, paragraph 1(a), of the Convention that are covered in Article 10, subparagraph (a); and

(b) Also provide such financial resources, including for the transfer of technology, needed by the developing country Parties to meet the agreed full incremental costs of advancing the implementation of existing commitments under Article 4, paragraph 1, of the Convention that are covered by Article 10 and that are agreed between a developing country Party and the international entity or entities referred to in Article 11 of the Convention, in accordance with that Article.

The implementation of these existing commitments shall take into account the need for adequacy and predictability in the flow of funds and the importance of appropriate burden sharing among developed country Parties. The guidance to the entity or entities entrusted with the operation of the financial mechanism of the Convention in relevant decisions of the Conference of the Parties, including those agreed before the adoption of this Protocol, shall apply *mutatis mutandis* to the provisions of this paragraph.

3. The developed country Parties and other developed Parties in Annex II to the Convention may also provide, and developing country Parties avail themselves of, financial resources for the implementation of Article 10, through bilateral, regional and other multilateral channels.

Article 12

1. A clean development mechanism is hereby defined.

2. The purpose of the clean development mechanism shall be to assist Parties not included in Annex I in achieving sustainable development and in contributing to the ultimate objective of the Convention, and to assist Parties included in Annex I in achieving compliance with their quantified emission limitation and reduction commitments under Article 3.

3. Under the clean development mechanism:

(a) Parties not included in Annex I will benefit from project activities resulting in certified emission reductions; and

(b) Parties included in Annex I may use the certified emission reductions accruing from such project activities to contribute to compliance with part of their quantified emission limitation and reduction commitments under Article 3, as determined by the Conference of the Parties serving as the meeting of the Parties to this Protocol.

4. The clean development mechanism shall be subject to the authority and guidance of the Conference of the Parties serving as the meeting of the Parties to this Protocol and be supervised by an executive board of the clean development mechanism.

5. Emission reductions resulting from each project activity shall be certified by operational entities to be designated by the Conference of the Parties serving as the meeting of the Parties to this Protocol, on the basis of:

(a) Voluntary participation approved by each Party involved;
(b) Real, measurable, and long-term benefits related to the mitigation of climate change; and
(c) Reductions in emissions that are additional to any that would occur in the absence of the certified project activity.

6. The clean development mechanism shall assist in arranging funding of certified project activities as necessary.

7. The Conference of the Parties serving as the meeting of the Parties to this Protocol shall, at its first session, elaborate modalities and procedures with the objective of ensuring transparency, efficiency and accountability through independent auditing and verification of project activities.

8. The Conference of the Parties serving as the meeting of the Parties to this Protocol shall ensure that a share of the proceeds from certified project activities is used to cover administrative expenses as well as to assist developing country Parties that are particularly vulnerable to the adverse effects of climate change to meet the costs of adaptation.

9. Participation under the clean development mechanism, including in activities mentioned in paragraph 3(a) above and in the acquisition of certified emission reductions, may involve private and/or public entities, and is to be subject to whatever guidance may be provided by the executive board of the clean development mechanism.

10. Certified emission reductions obtained during the period from the year 2000 up to the beginning of the first commitment period can be used to assist in achieving compliance in the first commitment period.

Article 13

1. The Conference of the Parties, the supreme body of the Convention, shall serve as the meeting of the Parties to this Protocol.

2. Parties to the Convention that are not Parties to this Protocol may participate as observers in the proceedings of any session of the Conference of the Parties serving as the meeting of the Parties to this Protocol. When the Conference of the Parties serves as the meeting of the Parties to this Protocol, decisions under this Protocol shall be taken only by those that are Parties to this Protocol.

3. When the Conference of the Parties serves as the meeting of the Parties to this Protocol, any member of the Bureau of the Conference of the Parties

representing a Party to the Convention but, at that time, not a Party to this Protocol, shall be replaced by an additional member to be elected by and from amongst the Parties to this Protocol.

4. The Conference of the Parties serving as the meeting of the Parties to this Protocol shall keep under regular review the implementation of this Protocol and shall make, within its mandate, the decisions necessary to promote its effective implementation. It shall perform the functions assigned to it by this Protocol and shall:

(a) Assess, on the basis of all information made available to it in accordance with the provisions of this Protocol, the implementation of this Protocol by the Parties, the overall effects of the measures taken pursuant to this Protocol, in particular environmental, economic and social effects as well as their cumulative impacts and the extent to which progress towards the objective of the Convention is being achieved;

(b) Periodically examine the obligations of the Parties under this Protocol, giving due consideration to any reviews required by Article 4, paragraph 2(d), and Article 7, paragraph 2, of the Convention, in the light of the objective of the Convention, the experience gained in its implementation and the evolution of scientific and technological knowledge, and in this respect consider and adopt regular reports on the implementation of this Protocol;

(c) Promote and facilitate the exchange of information on measures adopted by the Parties to address climate change and its effects, taking into account the differing circumstances, responsibilities and capabilities of the Parties and their respective commitments under this Protocol;

(d) Facilitate, at the request of two or more Parties, the coordination of measures adopted by them to address climate change and its effects, taking into account the differing circumstances, responsibilities and capabilities of the Parties and their respective commitments under this Protocol;

(e) Promote and guide, in accordance with the objective of the Convention and the provisions of this Protocol, and taking fully into account the relevant decisions by the Conference of the Parties, the development and periodic refinement of comparable methodologies for the effective implementation of this Protocol, to be agreed on by the Conference of the Parties serving as the meeting of the Parties to this Protocol;

(f) Make recommendations on any matters necessary for the implementation of this Protocol;

(g) Seek to mobilize additional financial resources in accordance with Article 11, paragraph 2;

(h) Establish such subsidiary bodies as are deemed necessary for the implementation of this Protocol;

(i) Seek and utilize, where appropriate, the services and cooperation of, and information provided by, competent international organizations and intergovernmental and non-governmental bodies; and

(j) Exercise such other functions as may be required for the implementation of this Protocol, and consider any assignment resulting from a decision by the Conference of the Parties.

5. The rules of procedure of the Conference of the Parties and financial procedures applied under the Convention shall be applied *mutatis mutandis* under this Protocol, except as may be otherwise decided by consensus by the Conference of the Parties serving as the meeting of the Parties to this Protocol.

6. The first session of the Conference of the Parties serving as the meeting of the Parties to this Protocol shall be convened by the secretariat in conjunction with the first session of the Conference of the Parties that is scheduled after the date of the entry into force of this Protocol. Subsequent ordinary sessions of the Conference of the Parties serving as the meeting of the Parties to this Protocol shall be held every year and in conjunction with ordinary sessions of the Conference of the Parties, unless otherwise decided by the Conference of the Parties serving as the meeting of the Parties to this Protocol.

7. Extraordinary sessions of the Conference of the Parties serving as the meeting of the Parties to this Protocol shall be held at such other times as may be deemed necessary by the Conference of the Parties serving as the meeting of the Parties to this Protocol, or at the written request of any Party, provided that, within six months of the request being communicated to the Parties by the secretariat, it is supported by at least one third of the Parties.

8. The United Nations, its specialized agencies and the International Atomic Energy Agency, as well as any State member thereof or observers thereto not party to the Convention, may be represented at sessions of the Conference of the Parties serving as the meeting of the Parties to this Protocol as observers. Any body or agency, whether national or international, governmental or non-governmental, which is qualified in matters covered by this Protocol and which has informed the secretariat of its wish to be represented at a session of the Conference of the Parties serving as the meeting of the Parties to this Protocol as an observer, may be so admitted unless at least one third of the Parties present object. The admission and participation of observers shall be subject to the rules of procedure, as referred to in paragraph 5 above.

Article 14

1. The secretariat established by Article 8 of the Convention shall serve as the secretariat of this Protocol.

2. Article 8, paragraph 2, of the Convention on the functions of the secretariat, and Article 8, paragraph 3, of the Convention on arrangements made for the functioning of the secretariat, shall apply *mutatis mutandis* to this Protocol.

The secretariat shall, in addition, exercise the functions assigned to it under this Protocol.

Article 15

1. The Subsidiary Body for Scientific and Technological Advice and the Subsidiary Body for Implementation established by Articles 9 and 10 of the Convention shall serve as, respectively, the Subsidiary Body for Scientific and Technological Advice and the Subsidiary Body for Implementation of this Protocol. The provisions relating to the functioning of these two bodies under the Convention shall apply *mutatis mutandis* to this Protocol. Sessions of the meetings of the Subsidiary Body for Scientific and Technological Advice and the Subsidiary Body for Implementation of this Protocol shall be held in conjunction with the meetings of, respectively, the Subsidiary Body for Scientific and Technological Advice and the Subsidiary Body for Implementation of the Convention.

2. Parties to the Convention that are not Parties to this Protocol may participate as observers in the proceedings of any session of the subsidiary bodies. When the subsidiary bodies serve as the subsidiary bodies of this Protocol, decisions under this Protocol shall be taken only by those that are Parties to this Protocol.

3. When the subsidiary bodies established by Articles 9 and 10 of the Convention exercise their functions with regard to matters concerning this Protocol, any member of the Bureaux of those subsidiary bodies representing a Party to the Convention but, at that time, not a party to this Protocol, shall be replaced by an additional member to be elected by and from amongst the Parties to this Protocol.

Article 16

The Conference of the Parties serving as the meeting of the Parties to this Protocol shall, as soon as practicable, consider the application to this Protocol of, and modify as appropriate, the multilateral consultative process referred to in Article 13 of the Convention, in the light of any relevant decisions that may be taken by the Conference of the Parties. Any multilateral consultative process that may be applied to this Protocol shall operate without prejudice to the procedures and mechanisms established in accordance with Article 18.

Article 17

The Conference of the Parties shall define the relevant principles, modalities, rules and guidelines, in particular for verification, reporting and accountability for emissions trading. The Parties included in Annex B may participate in emissions trading for the purposes of fulfilling their commitments under Article 3. Any such trading shall be supplemental to domestic actions for the purpose of meeting quantified emission limitation and reduction commitments under that Article.

Article 18

The Conference of the Parties serving as the meeting of the Parties to this Protocol shall, at its first session, approve appropriate and effective procedures and mechanisms to determine and to address cases of non-compliance with the provisions of this Protocol, including through the development of an indicative list of consequences, taking into account the cause, type, degree and frequency of non-compliance. Any procedures and mechanisms under this Article entailing binding consequences shall be adopted by means of an amendment to this Protocol.

Article 19

The provisions of Article 14 of the Convention on settlement of disputes shall apply *mutatis mutandis* to this Protocol.

Article 20

1. Any Party may propose amendments to this Protocol.

2. Amendments to this Protocol shall be adopted at an ordinary session of the Conference of the Parties serving as the meeting of the Parties to this Protocol. The text of any proposed amendment to this Protocol shall be communicated to the Parties by the secretariat at least six months before the meeting at which it is proposed for adoption. The secretariat shall also communicate the text of any proposed amendments to the Parties and signatories to the Convention and, for information, to the Depositary.

3. The Parties shall make every effort to reach agreement on any proposed amendment to this Protocol by consensus. If all efforts at consensus have been exhausted, and no agreement reached, the amendment shall as a last resort be adopted by a three-fourths majority vote of the Parties present and voting at the meeting. The adopted amendment shall be communicated by the secretariat to the Depositary, who shall circulate it to all Parties for their acceptance.

4. Instruments of acceptance in respect of an amendment shall be deposited with the Depositary. An amendment adopted in accordance with paragraph 3 above shall enter into force for those Parties having accepted it on the ninetieth day after the date of receipt by the Depositary of an instrument of acceptance by at least three fourths of the Parties to this Protocol.

5. The amendment shall enter into force for any other Party on the ninetieth day after the date on which that Party deposits with the Depositary its instrument of acceptance of the said amendment.

Article 21

1. Annexes to this Protocol shall form an integral part thereof and, unless otherwise expressly provided, a reference to this Protocol constitutes at the same time a reference to any annexes thereto. Any annexes adopted after the entry into force of this Protocol shall be restricted to lists, forms and any other

material of a descriptive nature that is of a scientific, technical, procedural or administrative character.

2. Any Party may make proposals for an annex to this Protocol and may propose amendments to annexes to this Protocol.

3. Annexes to this Protocol and amendments to annexes to this Protocol shall be adopted at an ordinary session of the Conference of the Parties serving as the meeting of the Parties to this Protocol. The text of any proposed annex or amendment to an annex shall be communicated to the Parties by the secretariat at least six months before the meeting at which it is proposed for adoption. The secretariat shall also communicate the text of any proposed annex or amendment to an annex to the Parties and signatories to the Convention and, for information, to the Depositary.

4. The Parties shall make every effort to reach agreement on any proposed annex or amendment to an annex by consensus. If all efforts at consensus have been exhausted, and no agreement reached, the annex or amendment to an annex shall as a last resort be adopted by a three-fourths majority vote of the Parties present and voting at the meeting. The adopted annex or amendment to an annex shall be communicated by the secretariat to the Depositary, who shall circulate it to all Parties for their acceptance.

5. An annex, or amendment to an annex other than Annex A or B, that has been adopted in accordance with paragraphs 3 and 4 above shall enter into force for all Parties to this Protocol six months after the date of the communication by the Depositary to such Parties of the adoption of the annex or adoption of the amendment to the annex, except for those Parties that have notified the Depositary, in writing, within that period of their non-acceptance of the annex or amendment to the annex. The annex or amendment to an annex shall enter into force for Parties which withdraw their notification of non-acceptance on the ninetieth day after the date on which withdrawal of such notification has been received by the Depositary.

6. If the adoption of an annex or an amendment to an annex involves an amendment to this Protocol, that annex or amendment to an annex shall not enter into force until such time as the amendment to this Protocol enters into force.

7. Amendments to Annexes A and B to this Protocol shall be adopted and enter into force in accordance with the procedure set out in Article 20, provided that any amendment to Annex B shall be adopted only with the written consent of the Party concerned.

Article 22

1. Each Party shall have one vote, except as provided for in paragraph 2 below.

2. Regional economic integration organizations, in matters within their competence, shall exercise their right to vote with a number of votes equal to the

number of their member States that are Parties to this Protocol. Such an organization shall not exercise its right to vote if any of its member States exercises
its right, and vice versa.

Article 23

The Secretary-General of the United Nations shall be the Depositary of this
Protocol.

Article 24

1. This Protocol shall be open for signature and subject to ratification, acceptance or approval by States and regional economic integration organizations
which are Parties to the Convention. It shall be open for signature at United
Nations Headquarters in New York from 16 March 1998 to 15 March 1999.
This Protocol shall be open for accession from the day after the date on which
it is closed for signature. Instruments of ratification, acceptance, approval or
accession shall be deposited with the Depositary.

2. Any regional economic integration organization which becomes a Party
to this Protocol without any of its member States being a Party shall be bound
by all the obligations under this Protocol. In the case of such organizations, one
or more of whose member States is a Party to this Protocol, the organization
and its member States shall decide on their respective responsibilities for the
performance of their obligations under this Protocol. In such cases, the organization and the member States shall not be entitled to exercise rights under
this Protocol concurrently.

3. In their instruments of ratification, acceptance, approval or accession,
regional economic integration organizations shall declare the extent of their
competence with respect to the matters governed by this Protocol. These organizations shall also inform the Depositary, who shall in turn inform the Parties,
of any substantial modification in the extent of their competence.

Article 25

1. This Protocol shall enter into force on the ninetieth day after the date on
which not less than 55 Parties to the Convention, incorporating Parties included
in Annex I which accounted in total for at least 55 per cent of the total carbon
dioxide emissions for 1990 of the Parties included in Annex I, have deposited
their instruments of ratification, acceptance, approval or accession.

2. For the purposes of this Article, 'the total carbon dioxide emissions for
1990 of the Parties included in Annex I' means the amount communicated on
or before the date of adoption of this Protocol by the Parties included in Annex
I in their first national communications submitted in accordance with Article
12 of the Convention.

3. For each State or regional economic integration organization that ratifies,
accepts or approves this Protocol or accedes thereto after the conditions set

out in paragraph 1 above for entry into force have been fulfilled, this Protocol shall enter into force on the ninetieth day following the date of deposit of its instrument of ratification, acceptance, approval or accession.

4. For the purposes of this Article, any instrument deposited by a regional economic integration organization shall not be counted as additional to those deposited by States members of the organization.

Article 26

No reservations may be made to this Protocol.

Article 27

1. At any time after three years from the date on which this Protocol has entered into force for a Party, that Party may withdraw from this Protocol by giving written notification to the Depositary.

2. Any such withdrawal shall take effect upon expiry of one year from the date of receipt by the Depositary of the notification of withdrawal, or on such later date as may be specified in the notification of withdrawal.

3. Any Party that withdraws from the Convention shall be considered as also having withdrawn from this Protocol.

Article 28

The original of this Protocol, of which the Arabic, Chinese, English, French, Russian and Spanish texts are equally authentic, shall be deposited with the Secretary-General of the United Nations.

DONE at Kyoto this eleventh day of December one thousand nine hundred and ninety-seven.

IN WITNESS WHEREOF the undersigned, being duly authorized to that effect, have affixed their signatures to this Protocol on the dates indicated.

Annex A

Greenhouse gases

Carbon dioxide (CO_2)
Methane (CH_4)
Nitrous oxide (N_2O)
Hydrofluorocarbons (HFCs)
Perfluorocarbons (PFCs)
Sulphur hexafluoride (SF_6)

Sectors/source categories

Energy
   Fuel combustion
      Energy industries
      Manufacturing industries and construction
      Transport
      Other sectors
      Other
   Fugitive emissions from fuels
      Solid fuels
      Oil and natural gas
      Other

Industrial processes
   Mineral products
   Chemical industry
   Metal production
   Other production
   Production of halocarbons and sulphur hexafluoride
   Consumption of halocarbons and sulphur hexafluoride
   Other

Solvent and other product use

Agriculture
   Enteric fermentation
   Manure management
   Rice cultivation
   Agricultural soils
   Prescribed burning of savannas
   Field burning of agricultural residues
   Other

Waste
   Solid waste disposal on land
   Wastewater handling
   Waste incineration
   Other

Annex B

Party	Quantified emission limitation or reduction commitment (percentage of base year or period)
Australia	108
Austria	92
Belgium	92
Bulgaria*	92
Canada	94
Croatia*	95
Czech Republic*	92
Denmark	92
Estonia*	92
European Community	92
Finland	92
France	92
Germany	92
Greece	92
Hungary*	94
Iceland	110
Ireland	92
Italy	92
Japan	94
Latvia*	92
Liechtenstein	92
Lithuania*	92
Luxembourg	92
Monaco	92
Netherlands	92
New Zealand	100
Norway	101
Poland*	94
Portugal	92
Romania*	92
Russian Federation*	100
Slovakia*	92
Slovenia*	92
Spain	92
Sweden	92
Switzerland	92
Ukraine*	100
United Kingdom	92
United States of America	93

*Countries that are undergoing the process of transition to a market economy.

Marrakech Accords (extracts)

Editorial note

Following the adoption of the Protocol negotiations on the subsidiary rules, guidelines, and methodologies called for by the Protocol text continued. A number of issues reflected divisions between states. In particular, matters relating to carbon sinks, rules for emissions trading and penalties for non-compliance with commitments under the Protocol proved difficult for negotiators. These are addressed in the 'Marrakesh Accords' agreed at the Seventh Conference of the Parties in November 2001. The Marrakesh Accords' 218 pages translate the Bonn Agreement into legal text of some complexity, suggesting more possibilities for hidden meanings, ambiguities and 'agreements to disagree' than the almost 30 pages of the Kyoto Protocol. The Accords make a notable contribution to the proliferation of acronyms in international environmental law.

The Marrakech Accords will be presented to the first meeting of the Conference of the Parties serving as the Meeting of the Parties to the Protocol (COP/MOP) for adoption.

The following decisions were adopted at Marrakech:

- Decision 2/CP.7: Capacity Building in developing countries (non-Annex I Parties)
- Decision 3/CP.7: Capacity Building in countries with economies in transition
- Decision 4/CP.7: Development and transfer of technologies (decisions 4/CP.4 and 9/CP.5)
- Decision 5/CP.7: Implementation of Article 4, paragraph 8 and 9, of the Convention (decision 3/CP.3 and Article 2, paragraph 3, and Article 3, paragraph 14, of the Kyoto Protocol)
- Decision 6/CP.7: Additional guidance to an operating entity of the financial mechanism
- Decision 7/CP.7: Funding under the Convention
- Decision 8/CP.7: Activities implemented jointly under the pilot phase (decisions 6/CP.4 and 13/CP.5)
- Decision 9/CP.7: Matters relating to Article 3, paragraph 14, of the Kyoto Protocol
- Decision 10/CP.7: Funding under the Kyoto Protocol

- Decision 11/CP.7: Land use, land-use change and forestry
- Decision 12/CP.7: Forest management activities under Article 3, paragraph 4, of the Kyoto Protocol: the Russian Federation
- Decision 13/CP.7: 'Good practices' in policies and measures among Parties included in Annex I to the Convention
- Decision 14/CP.7: Impact of single projects on emissions in the commitment period
- Decision 15/CP.7: Principles, nature and scope of the mechanisms pursuant to Articles 6, 12 and 17 of the Kyoto Protocol
- Decision 16/CP.7: Guidelines for the implementation of Article 6 of the Kyoto Protocol
- Decision 17/CP.7: Modalities and procedures for a clean development mechanism, as defined in Article 12 of the Kyoto Protocol
- Decision 18/CP.7: Modalities, rules and guidelines for emissions trading under Article 17 of the Kyoto Protocol
- Decision 19/CP.7: Modalities for accounting of assigned amounts under Article 7, paragraph 4, of the Kyoto Protocol
- Decision 20/CP.7: Guidelines for national systems under Article 5, paragraph 1, of the Kyoto Protocol
- Decision 21/CP.7: Good practice guidance and adjustments under Article 5, paragraph 2, of the Kyoto Protocol
- Decision 22/CP.7: Guidance for the preparation of the information required under Article 7 of the Kyoto Protocol
- Decision 23/CP.7: Guidelines for review under Article 8 of the Kyoto Protocol
- Decision 24/CP.7: Procedures and mechanisms relating to compliance under the Kyoto Protocol
- Decision 25/CP.7: Third Assessment Report of the Intergovernmental Panel, on Climate Change
- Decision 26/CP.7: Amendment to the list in Annex II to the Convention
- Decision 27/CP.7: Guidance to an entity entrusted with the operation of the financial mechanism of the Convention, for the operation of the least developed countries fund
- Decision 28/CP.7: Guidelines for the preparation of national adaptation programmes of action
- Decision 29/CP.7: Establishment of a least developed countries expert group
- Decision 30/CP.7: Third compilation and synthesis of initial national communications from Parties not included in Annex I to the Convention
- Decision 31/CP.7: Consultative Group of Experts on National Communications from non-Annex I Parties
- Decision 32/CP.7: Other matters relating to communications from Parties not included in Annex I to the Convention
- Decision 33/CP.7: National communications from Parties included in Annex I to the Convention

- Decision 34/CP.7: Revision of the guidelines for the preparation of national communications by Parties included in Annex I to the Convention, Part I: UNFCCC reporting guidelines on annual inventories, and the guidelines for the technical review of greenhouse gas inventories from Parties included in Annex I to the Convention
- Decision 35/CP.7: Request from a group of countries of Central Asia, Caucasus, Albania and Moldova countries on their status under the Convention
- Decision 36/CP.7: Improving the participation of women in the representation of Parties in bodies established under the United Nations Framework Convention on Climate Change and the Kyoto Protocol of the Parties
- Decision 38/CP.7: Programme budget for the biennium 2002–2003
- Decision 39/CP.7: Income and budget performance in the biennium 2000–2001 and arrangements for administrative support to the Convention

The principal decisions of the Marrakech Accords relate to the rules for implementation of the Kyoto Protocol's 'flexibility mechanisms' and the establishment of a compliance mechanism. The text of the Annexes to the decisions on joint implementation (Article 6), clean development mechanism (Article 12), emission trading (Article 17) and compliance (Article 18) are reproduced below.

7B(i)
Guidelines for the Implementation of Article 6 of the Kyoto Protocol*

A. Definitions

1. For the purpose of the present annex the definitions contained in Article 1[1] and the provisions of Article 14 shall apply. Furthermore:

(a) An 'emission reduction unit' or 'ERU' is a unit issued pursuant to the relevant provisions in the annex to decision -/CMP.1 (*Modalities for the accounting of assigned amounts*) and is equal to one metric tonne of carbon dioxide equivalent, calculated using global warming potentials defined by decision 2/CP.3 or as subsequently revised in accordance with Article 5;

(b) A 'certified emission reduction' or 'CER' is a unit issued pursuant to Article 12 and requirements thereunder, as well as the relevant provisions in the annex to decision -/CMP.1 (*Article 12*), and is equal to one metric tonne of carbon dioxide equivalent, calculated using global warming potentials defined by decision 2/CP.3 or as subsequently revised in accordance with Article 5;

---

* Annex to Decision 16/CP.7 – Draft Decision -/CMP.1 (*Article 6*)

[1] In the context of this annex, 'Article' refers to an Article of the Kyoto Protocol, unless otherwise specified.

(c) An 'assigned amount unit' or 'AAU' is a unit issued pursuant to the relevant provisions in the annex to decision -/CMP.1 (*Modalities for the accounting of assigned amounts*) and is equal to one metric tonne of carbon dioxide equivalent, calculated using global warming potentials defined by decision 2/CP.3 or as subsequently revised in accordance with Article 5;

(d) A 'removal unit' or 'RMU' is a unit issued pursuant to the relevant provisions in the annex to decision -/CMP.1 (*Modalities for the accounting of assigned amounts*) and is equal to one metric tonne of carbon dioxide equivalent, calculated using global warming potentials defined by decision 2/CP.3 or as subsequently revised in accordance with Article 5;

(e) 'Stakeholders' means the public, including individuals, groups or communities affected, or likely to be affected, by the project.

B. Role of the Conference of the Parties serving as the meeting of the Parties to the Kyoto Protocol

2. The Conference of the Parties serving as the meeting of the Parties to the Kyoto Protocol (COP/MOP) shall provide guidance regarding the implementation of Article 6 and exercise authority over the Article 6 supervisory committee.

C. Article 6 supervisory committee

3. The Article 6 supervisory committee shall supervise, *inter alia*, the verification of ERUs generated by Article 6 project activities, referred to in section E below, and be responsible for:

(a) Reporting on its activities to each session of the COP/MOP;

(b) The accreditation of independent entities in accordance with standards and procedures contained in Appendix A below;

(c) The review of standards and procedures for the accreditation of independent entities in Appendix A below, giving consideration to relevant work of the executive board of the clean development mechanism (CDM) and, as appropriate, making recommendations to the COP/MOP on revisions to these standards and procedures;

(d) The review and revision of reporting guidelines and criteria for baselines and monitoring in Appendix B below, for consideration by the COP/MOP, giving consideration to relevant work of the executive board of the CDM, as appropriate;

(e) The elaboration of the Article 6 project design document, for consideration by the COP/MOP, taking into consideration Appendix B of the Annex on modalities and procedures for a clean development mechanism and giving consideration to relevant work of the executive board of the CDM, as appropriate;

(f) The review procedures set out in paragraphs 35 and 39 below;

(g) The elaboration of any rules of procedure additional to those contained in the present annex, for consideration by the COP/MOP.

4. The Article 6 supervisory committee shall comprise ten members from Parties to the Kyoto Protocol, as follows:

(a) Three members from Parties[2] included in Annex I that are undergoing the process of transition to a market economy;
(b) Three members from Parties included in Annex I not referred to in subparagraph (a) above;
(c) Three members from Parties not included in Annex I;
(d) One member from the small island developing States.

5. Members, including alternate members, of the Article 6 supervisory committee shall be nominated by the relevant constituencies referred to in paragraph 4 above and be elected by the COP/MOP. The COP/MOP shall elect to the Article 6 supervisory committee five members and five alternate members for a term of two years and five members and five alternate members for a term of three years. Thereafter, the COP/MOP shall elect, every year, five new members and five alternate members for a term of two years. Appointment pursuant to paragraph 12 below shall count as one term. The members and alternate members shall remain in office until their successors are elected.

6. Members of the Article 6 supervisory committee may be eligible to serve a maximum of two consecutive terms. Terms as alternate members do not count.

7. The Article 6 supervisory committee shall elect annually a chairperson and vicechairperson from among its members, with one being from a Party included in Annex I and the other being from a Party not included in Annex I. The positions of chairperson and vice-chairperson shall alternate annually between a member from a Party included in Annex I and a member from a Party not included in Annex I.

8. The COP/MOP shall elect an alternate member for each member of the Article 6 supervisory committee based on the criteria in paragraphs 4, 5 and 6 above. The nomination by a constituency of a candidate member shall be accompanied by a nomination of a candidate alternate member from the same constituency.

9. The Article 6 supervisory committee shall meet at least two times each year, whenever possible in conjunction with the meetings of the subsidiary bodies, unless decided otherwise. All documentation for the Article 6 supervisory committee meetings shall be made available to alternate members.

10. Members, including alternate members, of the Article 6 supervisory committee shall:

---

[2] In the context of this annex, 'Party' refers to a Party to the Kyoto Protocol, unless otherwise specified.

(a) Serve in their personal capacities and shall have recognized competence relating to climate change issues and in relevant technical and policy fields. The cost of participation of members and of alternate members from developing country Parties and other Parties eligible under UNFCCC practice shall be covered by the budget for the Article 6 supervisory committee;

(b) Have no pecuniary or financial interest in any aspect of an Article 6 project;

(c) Subject to their responsibility to the Article 6 supervisory committee, not disclose any confidential or proprietary information coming to their knowledge by reason of their duties for the Article 6 supervisory committee. The duty of a member, including an alternate member, not to disclose confidential information constitutes an obligation in respect to that member, including an alternate member, and shall remain an obligation after the expiration or termination of that member's, including an alternate member's, function for the Article 6 supervisory committee;

(d) Be bound by the rules of procedure of the Article 6 supervisory committee;

(e) Take a written oath of service witnessed by the Executive Secretary of the UNFCCC or his/her authorized representative before assuming his or her duties.

11. The Article 6 supervisory committee may suspend and recommend to the COP/MOP the termination of the membership of a particular member, including an alternate member, for cause including, *inter alia*, breach of the conflict of interest provisions, breach of the confidentiality provisions, or failure to attend two consecutive meetings of the Article 6 supervisory committee without proper justification.

12. If a member, or an alternate member, of the Article 6 supervisory committee resigns or is otherwise unable to complete the assigned term of office or to perform the functions of that office, the Article 6 supervisory committee may decide, bearing in mind the proximity of the next session of the COP/MOP, to appoint another member, or an alternate member, from the same constituency to replace the said member for the remainder of that member's mandate. In such a case, the Article 6 supervisory committee shall take into account any views expressed by the group that had nominated the member.

13. The Article 6 supervisory committee shall draw on the expertise necessary to perform its functions, in particular taking into account national accreditation procedures.

14. At least two thirds of the members of the Article 6 supervisory committee, representing a majority of members from Parties included in Annex I and a majority of members from Parties not included in Annex I, must be present to constitute a quorum.

15. Decisions by the Article 6 supervisory committee shall be taken by consensus, whenever possible. If all efforts at reaching a consensus have been exhausted and no agreement has been reached, decisions shall as a last resort be

adopted by a three-fourths majority vote of the members present and voting at the meeting. Members abstaining from voting shall be considered as not voting.

16. The full text of all decisions of the Article 6 supervisory committee shall be made publicly available. Decisions shall be made available in all six official languages of the United Nations.

17. The working language of the Article 6 supervisory committee shall be English.

18. Meetings of the Article 6 supervisory committee shall be open to attendance, as observers, by all Parties and by all UNFCCC accredited observers and stakeholders, except where otherwise decided by the Article 6 supervisory committee.

19. The secretariat shall service the Article 6 supervisory committee.

D. Participation requirements

20. A Party involved in an Article 6 project shall inform the secretariat of:

(a) Its designated focal point for approving projects pursuant to Article 6, paragraph 1(a);
(b) Its national guidelines and procedures for approving Article 6 projects, including the consideration of stakeholders' comments, as well as monitoring and verification.

21. Subject to the provisions of paragraph 22 below, a Party included in Annex I with a commitment inscribed in Annex B is eligible to transfer and/or acquire ERUs issued in accordance with the relevant provisions, if it is in compliance with the following eligibility requirements:

(a) It is a Party to the Kyoto Protocol;
(b) Its assigned amount pursuant to Article 3, paragraphs 7 and 8, has been calculated and recorded in accordance with decision -/CMP.1 (*Modalities for the accounting of assigned amounts*);
(c) It has in place a national system for the estimation of anthropogenic emissions by sources and anthropogenic removals by sinks of all greenhouse gases not controlled by the Montreal Protocol, in accordance with Article 5, paragraph 1, and the requirements in the guidelines decided thereunder;
(d) It has in place a national registry in accordance with Article 7, paragraph 4, and the requirements in the guidelines decided thereunder;
(e) It has submitted annually the most recent required inventory, in accordance with Article 5, paragraph 2, and Article 7, paragraph 1, and the requirements in the guidelines decided thereunder, including the national inventory report and the common reporting format. For the first commitment period, the quality assessment needed for the purpose of determining

eligibility to use the mechanisms shall be limited to the parts of the inventory pertaining to emissions of greenhouse gases from sources/sector
categories from Annex A to the Kyoto Protocol and the submission of the
annual inventory on sinks;

(f) It submits the supplementary information on assigned amount in accordance with Article 7, paragraph 1, and the requirements in the guidelines
decided thereunder and makes any additions to, and subtractions from, assigned amount pursuant to Article 3, paragraphs 7 and 8, including for the
activities under Article 3, paragraphs 3 and 4, in accordance with Article 7,
paragraph 4, and the requirements in the guidelines decided thereunder.

22. A Party included in Annex I with a commitment inscribed in Annex B
shall be considered:

(a) To meet the eligibility requirements referred to in paragraph 21 above after
16 months have elapsed since the submission of its report to facilitate the
calculation of its assigned amount pursuant to Article 3, paragraphs 7 and
8, and to demonstrate its capacity to account for its emissions and assigned
amount, in accordance with the modalities adopted for the accounting
of assigned amount under Article 7, paragraph 4, unless the enforcement
branch of the compliance committee finds in accordance with decision
24/CP.7 that the Party does not meet these requirements, or, at an earlier
date, if the enforcement branch of the compliance committee has decided
that it is not proceeding with any questions of implementation relating to
these requirements indicated in reports of the expert review teams under
Article 8 of the Kyoto Protocol, and has transmitted this information to
the secretariat;

(b) To continue to meet the eligibility requirements referred to in paragraph
21 above unless and until the enforcement branch of the compliance committee decides that the Party does not meet one or more of the eligibility
requirements, has suspended the Party's eligibility, and has transmitted this
information to the secretariat.

23. Where it is considered to meet the eligibility requirements set out in
paragraph 21 above, a host Party may verify reductions in anthropogenic emissions by sources or enhancements of anthropogenic removals by sinks from
an Article 6 project as being additional to any that would otherwise occur, in
accordance with Article 6, paragraph 1 (b). Upon such verification, the host
Party may issue the appropriate quantity of ERUs in accordance with the relevant provisions of decision -/CMP.1 (*Modalities for the accounting of assigned
amounts*).

24. Where a host Party does not meet the eligibility requirements set out
in paragraph 21 above, the verification of reductions in anthropogenic emissions by sources or enhancements of anthropogenic removals by sinks from

an Article 6 project as being additional to any that would otherwise occur, in accordance with Article 6, paragraph 1(b), shall occur through the verification procedure under the Article 6 supervisory committee, as set out in section E below. The host Party may however only issue and transfer ERUs upon meeting the requirements in paragraphs 21 (a), (b) and (d) above.

25. A host Party which meets the requirements in paragraph 21 above may at any time elect to use the verification procedure under the Article 6 supervisory committee.

26. The provisions in Article 6, paragraph 4, shall pertain, *inter alia*, to the requirements of paragraph 21 above.

27. The secretariat shall maintain a publicly accessible list of Parties that meet the eligibility requirements and that have been suspended in accordance with relevant provisions contained in decision 24/CP.7.

28. A Party hosting an Article 6 project shall make publicly available, directly or through the secretariat, information on the project in accordance with the reporting guidelines set out in Appendix B below and the requirements contained in decision -/CMP.1 (*Modalities for the accounting of assigned amounts*).

29. A Party that authorizes legal entities to participate in Article 6 projects shall remain responsible for the fulfilment of its obligations under the Kyoto Protocol and shall ensure that such participation is consistent with the present annex. Legal entities may only transfer or acquire ERUs if the authorizing Party is eligible to do so at that time.

E. Verification procedure under the Article 6 supervisory committee

30. The verification procedure under the Article 6 supervisory committee is the determination by an independent entity, accredited pursuant to Appendix A below, of whether a project and the ensuing reductions of anthropogenic emissions by sources or enhancements of anthropogenic removals by sinks meet the relevant requirements of Article 6 and these guidelines.

31. Project participants shall submit to an accredited independent entity a project design document that contains all information needed for the determination of whether the project:

(a) Has been approved by the Parties involved;
(b) Would result in a reduction of anthropogenic emissions by sources or an enhancement of anthropogenic removals by sinks that is additional to any that would otherwise occur;
(c) Has an appropriate baseline and monitoring plan in accordance with the criteria set out in Appendix B below.

32. The accredited independent entity shall make the project design document publicly available through the secretariat, subject to confidentiality provisions set out in paragraph 40 below, and receive comments from Parties, stakeholders and UNFCCC accredited observers on the project design

document and any supporting information for 30 days from the date the project design document is made publicly available.

33. The accredited independent entity shall determine whether:

(a) The project has been approved by the Parties involved;
(b) The project would result in a reduction of anthropogenic emissions by sources or an enhancement of anthropogenic removals by sinks that is additional to any that would otherwise occur;
(c) The project has an appropriate baseline and monitoring plan in accordance with the criteria set out in Appendix B below;
(d) Project participants have submitted to the accredited independent entity documentation on the analysis of the environmental impacts of the project activity, including transboundary impacts, in accordance with procedures as determined by the host Party, and, if those impacts are considered significant by the project participants or the host Party, have undertaken an environmental impact assessment in accordance with procedures as required by the host Party.

34. The accredited independent entity shall make its determination publicly available through the secretariat, together with an explanation of its reasons, including a summary of comments received and a report of how due account was taken of these.

35. The determination regarding a project design document shall be deemed final 45 days after the date on which the determination is made public, unless a Party involved in the project or three of the members of the Article 6 supervisory committee request a review by the Article 6 supervisory committee. If such a review is requested, the Article 6 supervisory committee shall finalize the review as soon as possible, but no later than six months or at the second meeting following the request for review. The Article 6 supervisory committee shall communicate its decision on the determination and the reasons for it to the project participants and the public. Its decision shall be final.

36. Project participants shall submit to an accredited independent entity a report in accordance with the monitoring plan on reductions in anthropogenic emissions by sources or enhancements of anthropogenic removals by sinks that have already occurred. The report shall be made publicly available.

37. The accredited independent entity shall, upon receipt of a report referred to under paragraph 36 above, make a determination of the reductions in anthropogenic emissions by sources or enhancements of anthropogenic removals by sinks reported by project participants in accordance with Appendix B below, provided that they were monitored and calculated in accordance with paragraph 33 above.

38. The accredited independent entity shall make its determination under paragraph 37 above publicly available through the secretariat, together with an explanation of its reasons.

39. The determination regarding reported reductions in anthropogenic emissions by sources or enhancements of anthropogenic removals by sinks shall be deemed final 15 days after the date on which it is made public, unless a Party involved in the project or three of the members of the Article 6 supervisory committee request a review by the Article 6 supervisory committee. If such a review is requested, the Article 6 supervisory committee shall:

(a) At its next meeting or no later than 30 days after the formal request for the review decide on its course of action. If it decides that the request has merit, it shall perform a review;

(b) Complete its review within 30 days following its decision to perform the review;

(c) Inform the project participants of the outcome of the review, and make public its decision and the reasons for it.

40. Information obtained from project participants marked as proprietary or confidential shall not be disclosed without the written consent of the provider of the information, except as required by applicable national law of the host Party. Information used to determine whether reductions in anthropogenic emissions by sources or enhancements of anthropogenic removals by sinks are additional, to describe the baseline methodology and its application, and to support an environmental impact assessment referred to in paragraph 33(d) above, shall not be considered as proprietary or confidential.

41. Any provisions relating to the commitment period reserve or other limitations to transfers under Article 17 shall not apply to transfers by a Party of ERUs issued into its national registry that were verified in accordance with the verification procedure under the Article 6 supervisory committee.

42. The Article 6 supervisory committee shall suspend or withdraw the accreditation of an independent entity if it has carried out a review and found that the entity no longer meets the accreditation standards laid down in Appendix A. The Article 6 supervisory committee may suspend or withdraw accreditation only after the accredited independent entity has had the opportunity of a hearing and depending on the outcome of the hearing. The suspension or withdrawal is with immediate effect. The affected entity shall be notified, immediately and in writing, once the Article 6 supervisory committee has decided upon its suspension or withdrawal. The decision by the Article 6 supervisory committee on such a case shall be made public.

43. Verified projects shall not be affected by the suspension or withdrawal of the accreditation of an accredited independent entity unless significant deficiencies are identified in the determination referred to in paragraphs 33 or 37 above for which the entity was responsible. In this case, the Article 6 supervisory committee shall decide whether a different accredited independent entity shall be appointed to assess and, where appropriate, correct such deficiencies.

If such an assessment reveals that excess ERUs have been transferred as a result of the deficiencies identified in the determination referred to in paragraphs 33 or 37 above, the independent entity whose accreditation has been withdrawn or suspended shall acquire an equivalent amount of AAUs and ERUs and place them in the holding account of the Party hosting the project within 30 days from the assessment mentioned above.

44. Any suspension or withdrawal of an accredited independent entity that adversely affects verified projects shall be decided on by the Article 6 supervisory committee only after the affected project participants have had the opportunity of a hearing.

45. Any costs related to the assessment referred to in paragraph 44 above shall be borne by the accredited independent entity whose accreditation has been withdrawn or suspended.

Appendix A
Standards and procedures for the accreditation of independent entities

1. An independent entity shall:

(a) Be a legal entity (either a domestic legal entity or an international organization) and provide documentation of this status;

(b) Employ a sufficient number of persons having the necessary competence to perform all necessary functions relevant to the verification of ERUs generated by Article 6 projects relating to the type, range and volume of work performed, under a responsible senior executive;

(c) Have the financial stability, insurance coverage and resources required for its activities;

(d) Have sufficient arrangements to cover legal and financial liabilities arising from its activities;

(e) Have documented internal procedures for carrying out its functions including, *inter alia*, procedures for the allocation of responsibilities within the organization and for handling complaints. These procedures shall be made publicly available;

(f) Have the necessary expertise to carry out the functions specified in this and relevant decisions by the COP/MOP, and, in particular, have sufficient knowledge and understanding of:

  (i) The guidelines for the implementation of Article 6 of the Kyoto Protocol, relevant decisions of the COP/MOP and of the Article 6 supervisory committee;

  (ii) Environmental issues relevant to the verification of Article 6 projects;

  (iii) The technical aspects of Article 6 activities relevant to environmental issues, including expertise in the setting of baselines and monitoring of emissions and other environmental impacts;

(iv) Relevant environmental auditing requirements and methodologies;

(v) Methodologies for the accounting of anthropogenic emissions by sources and/or anthropogenic removals by sinks;

(g) Have a management structure that has overall responsibility for performance and implementation of the entity's functions, including quality assurance procedures, and all relevant decisions relating to verification. The applicant independent entity shall make available:

(i) The names, qualifications, experience and terms of reference of the senior executive, board members, senior officers and other relevant personnel;

(ii) An organizational chart showing lines of authority, responsibility and allocation of functions stemming from the senior executive;

(iii) Its quality assurance policy and procedures;

(iv) Administrative procedures, including document control;

(v) Its policy and procedures for the recruitment and training of independent entity personnel, for ensuring their competence for all necessary functions and for monitoring their performance;

(vi) Its procedures for handling complaints, appeals and disputes;

(h) Not have pending any judicial process for malpractice, fraud and/or other activity incompatible with its functions as an accredited independent entity.

2. An applicant independent entity shall meet the following operational requirements:

(a) Work in a credible, independent, non-discriminatory and transparent manner, complying with applicable national law and meeting, in particular, the following requirements:

(i) An applicant independent entity shall have a documented structure, which safeguards impartiality, including provisions to ensure the impartiality of its operations;

(ii) If it is part of a larger organization, and where parts of that organization are, or may become, involved in the identification, development or financing of any Article 6 project, the applicant independent entity shall:

- Make a declaration of all the organization's actual and potential Article 6 activities;

- Clearly define the links with other parts of the organization, demonstrating that no conflicts of interest exist;

- Demonstrate that no actual or potential conflict of interest exists between its functions as an accredited independent entity and any other functions that it may have, and demonstrate how business is managed to minimize any identified risk to impartiality. The demonstration shall cover all potential sources of conflict of

interest, whether they arise from within the applicant independent
entity or from the activities of related bodies;

- Demonstrate that it, together with its senior executive and staff, is
not involved in any commercial, financial or other processes which
might influence its judgement or endanger trust in its independence
of judgement and integrity in relation to its activities, and that it
complies with any rules applicable in this respect;

(b) Have adequate arrangements to safeguard confidentiality of the information obtained from Article 6 project participants in accordance with provisions contained in the annex on guidelines for the implementation of
Article 6.

Appendix B
Criteria for baseline setting and monitoring

Criteria for baseline setting

1. The baseline for an Article 6 project is the scenario that reasonably represents the anthropogenic emissions by sources or anthropogenic removals by
sinks of greenhouse gases that would occur in the absence of the proposed
project. A baseline shall cover emissions from all gases, sectors and source categories listed in Annex A, and anthropogenic removals by sinks, within the
project boundary.

2. A baseline shall be established:

(a) On a project-specific basis and/or using a multi-project emission factor;
(b) In a transparent manner with regard to the choice of approaches, assumptions, methodologies, parameters, data sources and key factors;
(c) Taking into account relevant national and/or sectoral policies and circumstances, such as sectoral reform initiatives, local fuel availability, power
sector expansion plans, and the economic situation in the project sector;
(d) In such a way that ERUs cannot be earned for decreases in activity levels
outside the project activity or due to *force majeure*;
(e) Taking account of uncertainties and using conservative assumptions.

3. Project participants shall justify their choice of baseline.

Monitoring

4. Project participants shall include, as part of the project design document,
a monitoring plan that provides for:

(a) The collection and archiving of all relevant data necessary for estimating or
measuring anthropogenic emissions by sources and/or anthropogenic removals by sinks of greenhouse gases occurring within the project boundary
during the crediting period;

(b) The collection and archiving of all relevant data necessary for determining the baseline of anthropogenic emissions by sources and/or anthropogenic removals by sinks of greenhouse gases within the project boundary during the crediting period;

(c) The identification of all potential sources of, and the collection and archiving of data on increased anthropogenic emissions by sources and/or reduced anthropogenic removals by sinks of greenhouse gases outside the project boundary that are significant and reasonably attributable to the project during the crediting period. The project boundary shall encompass all anthropogenic emissions by sources and/or removals by sinks of greenhouse gases under the control of the project participants that are significant and reasonably attributable to the Article 6 project;

(d) The collection and archiving of information on environmental impacts, in accordance with procedures as required by the host Party, where applicable;

(e) Quality assurance and control procedures for the monitoring process;

(f) Procedures for the periodic calculation of the reductions of anthropogenic emissions by sources and/or enhancements of anthropogenic removals by sinks by the proposed Article 6 project, and for leakage effects, if any. Leakage is defined as the net change of anthropogenic emissions by sources and/or removals by sinks of greenhouse gases which occurs outside the project boundary, and that is measurable and attributable to the Article 6 project;

(g) Documentation of all steps involved in the calculations referred to in subparagraphs (b) and (f) above.

5. Revisions, if any, to the monitoring plan to improve its accuracy and/or completeness of information shall be justified by project participants and shall be submitted for the determination referred to in paragraph 37 of the annex on guidelines for the implementation of Article 6 of the Kyoto Protocol by the accredited independent entity.

6. The implementation of the monitoring plan and its revisions, as applicable, shall be a condition for verification.

7B(ii)
Modalities and Procedures for a Clean Development Mechanism*

A. Definitions

1. For the purposes of the present annex the definitions contained in Article 1[1] and the provisions of Article 14 shall apply. Furthermore:

---

* Annex to Decision 17/CP.7 – Draft Decision -/CMP.1 (*Article 12*)

[1] In the context of this annex, 'Article' refers to an Article of the Kyoto Protocol, unless otherwise specified.

(a) An 'emission reduction unit' or 'ERU' is a unit issued pursuant to the relevant provisions in the annex to decision -/CMP.1 (*Modalities for the accounting of assigned amounts*) and is equal to one metric tonne of carbon dioxide equivalent, calculated using global warming potentials defined by decision 2/CP.3 or as subsequently revised in accordance with Article 5;

(b) A 'certified emission reduction' or 'CER' is a unit issued pursuant to Article 12 and requirements thereunder, as well as the relevant provisions in these modalities and procedures, and is equal to one metric tonne of carbon dioxide equivalent, calculated using global warming potentials defined by decision 2/CP.3 or as subsequently revised in accordance with Article 5;

(c) An 'assigned amount unit' or 'AAU' is a unit issued pursuant to the relevant provisions in the annex to decision -/CMP.1 (*Modalities for the accounting of assigned amounts*) and is equal to one metric tonne of carbon dioxide equivalent, calculated using global warming potentials defined by decision 2/CP.3 or as subsequently revised in accordance with Article 5;

(d) A 'removal unit' or 'RMU' is a unit issued pursuant to the relevant provisions in the annex to decision -/CMP.1 (*Modalities for the accounting of assigned amounts*) and is equal to one metric tonne of carbon dioxide equivalent, calculated using global warming potentials defined by decision 2/CP.3 or as subsequently revised in accordance with Article 5;

(e) 'Stakeholders' means the public, including individuals, groups or communities affected, or likely to be affected, by the proposed clean development mechanism project activity.

B. Role of the Conference of the Parties serving as the meeting of the Parties to the Kyoto Protocol

2. The Conference of the Parties serving as the meeting of the Parties to the Kyoto Protocol (COP/MOP) shall have authority over and provide guidance to the clean development mechanism (CDM).

3. The COP/MOP shall provide guidance to the executive board by taking decisions on:

(a) The recommendations made by the executive board on its rules of procedure;

(b) The recommendations made by the executive board, in accordance with provisions of decision 17/CP.7, the present annex and relevant decisions of the COP/MOP;

(c) The designation of operational entities accredited by the executive board in accordance with Article 12, paragraph 5, and accreditation standards contained in Appendix A below.

4. The COP/MOP shall further:

(a) Review annual reports of the executive board;
(b) Review the regional and subregional distribution of designated operational entities and take appropriate decisions to promote accreditation of such entities from developing country Parties.[2]
(c) Review the regional and subregional distribution of CDM project activities with a view to identifying systematic or systemic barriers to their equitable distribution and take appropriate decisions, based, *inter alia*, on a report by the executive board;
(d) Assist in arranging funding of CDM project activities, as necessary.

C. Executive board

5. The executive board shall supervise the CDM, under the authority and guidance of the COP/MOP, and be fully accountable to the COP/MOP. In this context, the executive board shall:

(a) Make recommendations to the COP/MOP on further modalities and procedures for the CDM, as appropriate;
(b) Make recommendations to the COP/MOP on any amendments or additions to rules of procedure for the executive board contained in the present annex, as appropriate;
(c) Report on its activities to each session of the COP/MOP;
(d) Approve new methodologies related to, *inter alia*, baselines, monitoring plans and project boundaries in accordance with the provisions of Appendix C below;
(e) Review provisions with regard to simplified modalities, procedures and the definitions of small scale project activities and make recommendations to the COP/MOP;
(f) Be responsible for the accreditation of operational entities, in accordance with accreditation standards contained in Appendix A below, and make recommendations to the COP/MOP for the designation of operational entities, in accordance with Article 12, paragraph 5.
    This responsibility includes:
    (i) Decisions on re-accreditation, suspension and withdrawal of accreditation;
    (ii) Operationalization of accreditation procedures and standards;
(g) Review the accreditation standards in Appendix A below and make recommendations to the COP/MOP for consideration, as appropriate;

---

[2] In the context of this annex, 'Party' refers to a Party to the Kyoto Protocol, unless otherwise specified.

(h) Report to the COP/MOP on the regional and subregional distribution of CDM project activities with a view to identifying systematic or systemic barriers to their equitable distribution;

(i) Make publicly available relevant information, submitted to it for this purpose, on proposed CDM project activities in need of funding and on investors seeking opportunities, in order to assist in arranging funding of CDM project activities, as necessary;

(j) Make any technical reports commissioned available to the public and provide a period of at least eight weeks for public comments on draft methodologies and guidance before documents are finalized and any recommendations are submitted to the COP/MOP for their consideration;

(k) Develop, maintain and make publicly available a repository of approved rules, procedures, methodologies and standards;

(l) Develop and maintain the CDM registry as defined in Appendix D below;

(m) Develop and maintain a publicly available database of CDM project activities containing information on registered project design documents, comments received, verification reports, its decisions as well as information on all CERs issued;

(n) Address issues relating to observance of modalities and procedures for the CDM by project participants and/or operational entities, and report on them to the COP/MOP;

(o) Elaborate and recommend to the COP/MOP for adoption at its next session procedures for conducting the reviews referred to in paragraphs 41 and 65 below including, *inter alia*, procedures to facilitate consideration of information from Parties, stakeholders and UNFCCC accredited observers. Until their adoption by the COP/MOP, the procedures shall be applied provisionally;

(p) Carry out any other functions ascribed to it in decision 17/CP.7, the present annex and relevant decisions of the COP/MOP.

6. Information obtained from CDM project participants marked as proprietary or confidential shall not be disclosed without the written consent of the provider of the information, except as required by national law. Information used to determine additionality as defined in paragraph 43 below, to describe the baseline methodology and its application, and to support an environmental impact assessment referred to in paragraph 37(c) below, shall not be considered as proprietary or confidential.

7. The executive board shall comprise ten members from Parties to the Kyoto Protocol, as follows: one member from each of the five United Nations regional groups, two other members from the Parties included in Annex I, two other members from the Parties not included in Annex I, and one representative of the small island developing States, taking into account the current practice in the Bureau of the Conference of the Parties.

8. Members, including alternate members, of the executive board shall:

(a) Be nominated by the relevant constituencies referred to in paragraph 7 above and be elected by the COP/MOP. Vacancies shall be filled in the same way;

(b) Be elected for a period of two years and be eligible to serve a maximum of two consecutive terms. Terms as alternate members do not count. Five members and five alternate members shall be elected initially for a term of three years and five members and five alternate members for a term of two years. Thereafter, the COP/MOP shall elect, every year, five new members, and five new alternate members, for a term of two years. Appointment pursuant to paragraph 11 below shall count as one term. The members, and alternate members, shall remain in office until their successors are elected;

(c) Possess appropriate technical and/or policy expertise and shall act in their personal capacity. The cost of participation of members, and of alternate members, from developing country Parties and other Parties eligible under UNFCCC practice shall be covered by the budget for the executive board;

(d) Be bound by the rules of procedure of the executive board;

(e) Take a written oath of service witnessed by the Executive Secretary of the UNFCCC or his/her authorized representative before assuming his or her duties;

(f) Have no pecuniary or financial interest in any aspect of a CDM project activity or any designated operational entity;

(g) Subject to their responsibilities to the executive board, not disclose any confidential or proprietary information coming to their knowledge by reason of their duties for the executive board. The duty of the member, including alternate member, not to disclose confidential information constitutes an obligation in respect of that member, and alternate member, and shall remain an obligation after the expiration or termination of that member's function for the executive board.

9. The COP/MOP shall elect an alternate for each member of the executive board based on the criteria in paragraphs 7 and 8 above. The nomination by a constituency of a candidate member shall be accompanied by a nomination for a candidate alternate member from the same constituency.

10. The executive board may suspend and recommend to the COP/MOP the termination of the membership of a particular member, including an alternate member, for cause including, *inter alia*, breach of the conflict of interest provisions, breach of the confidentiality provisions, or failure to attend two consecutive meetings of the executive board without proper justification.

11. If a member, or an alternate member, of the executive board resigns or is otherwise unable to complete the assigned term of office or to perform the functions of that office, the executive board may decide, bearing in mind the

proximity of the next session of the COP/MOP, to appoint another member, or an alternate member, from the same constituency to replace the said member for the remainder of that member's mandate.

12. The executive board shall elect its own chairperson and vice-chairperson, with one being a member from a Party included in Annex I and the other being from a Party not included in Annex I. The positions of chairperson and vice-chairperson shall alternate annually between a member from a Party included in Annex I and a member from a Party not included in Annex I.

13. The executive board shall meet as necessary but no less than three times a year, bearing in mind the provisions of paragraph 41 below. All documentation for executive board meetings shall be made available to alternate members.

14. At least two thirds of the members of the executive board, representing a majority of members from Parties included in Annex I and a majority of members from Parties not included in Annex I, must be present to constitute a quorum.

15. Decisions by the executive board shall be taken by consensus, whenever possible. If all efforts at reaching a consensus have been exhausted and no agreement has been reached, decisions shall be taken by a three-fourths majority of the members present and voting at the meeting. Members abstaining from voting shall be considered as not voting.

16. Meetings of the executive board shall be open to attendance, as observers, by all Parties and by all UNFCCC accredited observers and stakeholders, except where otherwise decided by the executive board.

17. The full text of all decisions of the executive board shall be made publicly available. The working language of the executive board shall be English. Decisions shall be made available in all six official languages of the United Nations.

18. The executive board may establish committees, panels or working groups to assist it in the performance of its functions. The executive board shall draw on the expertise necessary to perform its functions, including from the UNFCCC roster of experts. In this context, it shall take fully into account the consideration of regional balance.

19. The secretariat shall service the executive board.

D. Accreditation and designation of operational entities

20. The executive board shall:

(a) Accredit operational entities which meet the accreditation standards contained in Appendix A below;
(b) Recommend the designation of operational entities to the COP/MOP;
(c) Maintain a publicly available list of all designated operational entities;
(d) Review whether each designated operational entity continues to comply with the accreditation standards contained in Appendix A below and on

this basis confirm whether to reaccredit each operational entity every three years;

(e) Conduct spot-checking at any time and, on the basis of the results, decide to conduct the above-mentioned review, if warranted.

21. The executive board may recommend to the COP/MOP to suspend or withdraw the designation of a designated operational entity if it has carried out a review and found that the entity no longer meets the accreditation standards or applicable provisions in decisions of the COP/MOP. The executive board may recommend the suspension or withdrawal of designation only after the designated operational entity has had the possibility of a hearing. The suspension or withdrawal is with immediate effect, on a provisional basis, once the executive board has made a recommendation, and remains in effect pending a final decision by the COP/MOP. The affected entity shall be notified, immediately and in writing, once the executive board has recommended its suspension or withdrawal. The recommendation by the executive board and the decision by the COP/MOP on such a case shall be made public.

22. Registered project activities shall not be affected by the suspension or withdrawal of designation of a designated operational entity unless significant deficiencies are identified in the relevant validation, verification or certification report for which the entity was responsible. In this case, the executive board shall decide whether a different designated operational entity shall be appointed to review, and where appropriate correct, such deficiencies. If such a review reveals that excess CERs were issued, the designated operational entity whose accreditation has been withdrawn or suspended shall acquire and transfer, within 30 days of the end of review, an amount of reduced tonnes of carbon dioxide equivalent equal to the excess CERs issued, as determined by the executive board, to a cancellation account maintained in the CDM registry by the executive board.

23. Any suspension or withdrawal of a designated operational entity that adversely affects registered project activities shall be recommended by the executive board only after the affected project participants have had the possibility of a hearing.

24. Any costs related to the review referred to in paragraph 22 above shall be borne by the designated operational entity whose designation has been withdrawn or suspended.

25. The executive board may seek assistance in performing the functions in paragraph 20 above, in accordance with the provisions of paragraph 18 above.

E. Designated operational entities

26. Designated operational entities shall be accountable to the COP/MOP through the executive board and shall comply with the modalities and

procedures in decision 17/CP.7, the present annex and relevant decisions of the COP/MOP and the executive board.

27. A designated operational entity shall:

(a) Validate proposed CDM project activities;
(b) Verify and certify reductions in anthropogenic emissions by sources of greenhouse gases;
(c) Comply with applicable laws of the Parties hosting CDM project activities when carrying out its functions referred to in subparagraph (e) below;
(d) Demonstrate that it, and its subcontractors, have no real or potential conflict of interest with the participants in the CDM project activities for which it has been selected to carry out validation or verification and certification functions;
(e) Perform one of the following functions related to a given CDM project activity: validation or verification and certification. Upon request, the executive board may, however, allow a single designated operational entity to perform all these functions within a single CDM project activity;
(f) Maintain a publicly available list of all CDM project activities for which it has carried out validation, verification and certification;
(g) Submit an annual activity report to the executive board;
(h) Make information obtained from CDM project participants publicly available, as required by the executive board. Information marked as proprietary or confidential shall not be disclosed without the written consent of the provider of the information, except as required by national law. Information used to determine additionality as defined in paragraph 43 below, to describe the baseline methodology and its application, and to support an environmental impact assessment referred to in paragraph 37(c) below, shall not be considered as proprietary or confidential.

F. Participation requirements

28. Participation in a CDM project activity is voluntary.

29. Parties participating in the CDM shall designate a national authority for the CDM.

30. A Party not included in Annex I may participate in a CDM project activity if it is a Party to the Kyoto Protocol.

31. Subject to the provisions of paragraph 32 below, a Party included in Annex I with a commitment inscribed in Annex B is eligible to use CERs, issued in accordance with the relevant provisions, to contribute to compliance with part of its commitment under Article 3, paragraph 1, if it is in compliance with the following eligibility requirements:

(a) It is a Party to the Kyoto Protocol;

(b) Its assigned amount pursuant to Article 3, paragraphs 7 and 8, has been calculated and recorded in accordance with decision -/CMP.1 (*Modalities for the accounting of assigned amounts*);

(c) It has in place a national system for the estimation of anthropogenic emissions by sources and anthropogenic removals by sinks of all greenhouse gases not controlled by the Montreal Protocol, in accordance with Article 5, paragraph 1, and the requirements in the guidelines decided thereunder;

(d) It has in place a national registry in accordance with Article 7, paragraph 4, and the requirements in the guidelines decided thereunder;

(e) It has submitted annually the most recent required inventory, in accordance with Article 5, paragraph 2, and Article 7, paragraph 1, and the requirements in the guidelines decided thereunder, including the national inventory report and the common reporting format. For the first commitment period, the quality assessment needed for the purpose of determining eligibility to use the mechanisms shall be limited to the parts of the inventory pertaining to emissions of greenhouse gases from sources/sector categories from Annex A to the Kyoto Protocol and the submission of the annual inventory on sinks;

(f) It submits the supplementary information on assigned amount in accordance with Article 7, paragraph 1, and the requirements in the guidelines decided thereunder and makes any additions to, and subtractions from, assigned amount pursuant to Article 3, paragraphs 7 and 8, including for the activities under Article 3, paragraphs 3 and 4, in accordance with Article 7, paragraph 4, and the requirements in the guidelines decided thereunder.

32. A Party included in Annex I with a commitment inscribed in Annex B shall be considered:

(a) To meet the eligibility requirements referred to in paragraph 31 above after 16 months have elapsed since the submission of its report to facilitate the calculation of its assigned amount pursuant to Article 3, paragraphs 7 and 8, and to demonstrate its capacity to account for its emissions and assigned amount, in accordance with the modalities adopted for the accounting of assigned amount under Article 7, paragraph 4, unless the enforcement branch of the compliance committee finds in accordance with decision 24/CP.7 that the Party does not meet these requirements, or, at an earlier date, if the enforcement branch of the compliance committee has decided that it is not proceeding with any questions of implementation relating to these requirements indicated in reports of the expert review teams under Article 8 of the Kyoto Protocol, and has transmitted this information to the secretariat;

(b) To continue to meet the eligibility requirements referred to in paragraph 31 above unless and until the enforcement branch of the compliance committee decides that the Party does not meet one or more of the eligibility requirements, has suspended the Party's eligibility, and has transmitted this information to the secretariat.

33. A Party that authorizes private and/or public entities to participate in Article 12 project activities shall remain responsible for the fulfilment of its obligations under the Kyoto Protocol and shall ensure that such participation is consistent with the present annex. Private and/or public entities may only transfer and acquire CERs if the authorizing Party is eligible to do so at that time.

34. The secretariat shall maintain publicly accessible lists of:

(a) Parties not included in Annex I which are Parties to the Kyoto Protocol;
(b) Parties included in Annex I that do not meet the requirements in paragraph 31 above or have been suspended.

G. Validation and registration

35. Validation is the process of independent evaluation of a project activity by a designated operational entity against the requirements of the CDM as set out in decision 17/CP.7, the present annex and relevant decisions of the COP/MOP, on the basis of the project design document, as outlined in Appendix B below.

36. Registration is the formal acceptance by the executive board of a validated project as a CDM project activity. Registration is the prerequisite for the verification, certification and issuance of CERs related to that project activity.

37. The designated operational entity selected by project participants to validate a project activity, being under a contractual arrangement with them, shall review the project design document and any supporting documentation to confirm that the following requirements have been met:

(a) The participation requirements as set out in paragraphs 28 to 30 above are satisfied;
(b) Comments by local stakeholders have been invited, a summary of the comments received has been provided, and a report to the designated operational entity on how due account was taken of any comments has been received;
(c) Project participants have submitted to the designated operational entity documentation on the analysis of the environmental impacts of the project activity, including transboundary impacts and, if those impacts are considered significant by the project participants or the host Party, have undertaken an environmental impact assessment in accordance with procedures as required by the host Party;

(d) The project activity is expected to result in a reduction in anthropogenic emissions by sources of greenhouse gases that are additional to any that would occur in the absence of the proposed project activity, in accordance with paragraphs 43 to 52 below;

(e) The baseline and monitoring methodologies comply with requirements pertaining to:
  (i) Methodologies previously approved by the executive board; or
  (ii) Modalities and procedures for establishing a new methodology, as set out in paragraph 38 below;

(f) Provisions for monitoring, verification and reporting are in accordance with decision 17/CP.7, the present annex and relevant decisions of the COP/MOP;

(g) The project activity conforms to all other requirements for CDM project activities in decision 17/CP.7, the present annex and relevant decisions by the COP/MOP and the executive board.

38. If the designated operational entity determines that the project activity intends to use a new baseline or monitoring methodology, as referred to in paragraph 37(e) (ii) above, it shall, prior to a submission for registration of this project activity, forward the proposed methodology, together with the draft project design document, including a description of the project and identification of the project participants, to the executive board for review. The executive board shall expeditiously, if possible at its next meeting but not later than four months, review the proposed new methodology in accordance with the modalities and procedures of the present annex. Once approved by the executive board it shall make the approved methodology publicly available along with any relevant guidance and the designated operational entity may proceed with the validation of the project activity and submit the project design document for registration. In the event that the COP/MOP requests the revision of an approved methodology, no CDM project activity may use this methodology. The project participants shall revise the methodology, as appropriate, taking into consideration any guidance received.

39. A revision of a methodology shall be carried out in accordance with the modalities and procedures for establishing new methodologies as set out in paragraph 38 above. Any revision to an approved methodology shall only be applicable to project activities registered subsequent to the date of revision and shall not affect existing registered project activities during their crediting periods.

40. The designated operational entity shall:

(a) Prior to the submission of the validation report to the executive board, have received from the project participants written approval of voluntary participation from the designated national authority of each Party involved, including confirmation by the host Party that the project activity assists it in achieving sustainable development;

(b) In accordance with provisions on confidentiality contained in paragraph 27(h) above, make publicly available the project design document;

(c) Receive, within 30 days, comments on the validation requirements from Parties, stakeholders and UNFCCC accredited non-governmental organizations and make them publicly available;

(d) After the deadline for receipt of comments, make a determination as to whether, on the basis of the information provided and taking into account the comments received, the project activity should be validated;

(e) Inform project participants of its determination on the validation of the project activity. Notification to the project participants will include:

　(i) Confirmation of validation and date of submission of the validation report to the executive board; or

　(ii) An explanation of reasons for non-acceptance if the project activity, as documented, is judged not to fulfil the requirements for validation;

(f) Submit to the executive board, if it determines the proposed project activity to be valid, a request for registration in the form of a validation report including the project design document, the written approval of the host Party as referred to in subparagraph (a) above, and an explanation of how it has taken due account of comments received;

(g) Make this validation report publicly available upon transmission to the executive board.

41. The registration by the executive board shall be deemed final eight weeks after the date of receipt by the executive board of the request for registration, unless a Party involved in the project activity or at least three members of the executive board request a review of the proposed CDM project activity. The review by the executive board shall be made in accordance with the following provisions:

(a) It shall be related to issues associated with the validation requirements;

(b) It shall be finalized no later than at the second meeting following the request for review, with the decision and the reasons for it being communicated to the project participants and the public.

42. A proposed project activity that is not accepted may be reconsidered for validation and subsequent registration, after appropriate revisions, provided that it follows the procedures and meets the requirements for validation and registration, including those related to public comments.

43. A CDM project activity is additional if anthropogenic emissions of greenhouse gases by sources are reduced below those that would have occurred in the absence of the registered CDM project activity.

44. The baseline for a CDM project activity is the scenario that reasonably represents the anthropogenic emissions by sources of greenhouse gases that would occur in the absence of the proposed project activity. A baseline shall cover emissions from all gases, sectors and source categories listed in Annex A within the project boundary. A baseline shall be deemed to reasonably represent the anthropogenic emissions by sources that would occur in the absence of the proposed project activity if it is derived using a baseline methodology referred to in paragraphs 37 and 38 above.

45. A baseline shall be established:

(a) By project participants in accordance with provisions for the use of approved and new methodologies, contained in decision 17/CP.7, the present annex and relevant decisions of the COP/MOP;

(b) In a transparent and conservative manner regarding the choice of approaches, assumptions, methodologies, parameters, data sources, key factors and additionality, and taking into account uncertainty;

(c) On a project-specific basis;

(d) In the case of small-scale CDM project activities which meet the criteria specified in decision 17/CP.7 and relevant decisions by the COP/MOP, in accordance with simplified procedures developed for such activities;

(e) Taking into account relevant national and/or sectoral policies and circumstances, such as sectoral reform initiatives, local fuel availability, power sector expansion plans, and the economic situation in the project sector.

46. The baseline may include a scenario where future anthropogenic emissions by sources are projected to rise above current levels, due to the specific circumstances of the host Party.

47. The baseline shall be defined in a way that CERs cannot be earned for decreases in activity levels outside the project activity or due to *force majeure*.

48. In choosing a baseline methodology for a project activity, project participants shall select from among the following approaches the one deemed most appropriate for the project activity, taking into account any guidance by the executive board, and justify the appropriateness of their choice:

(a) Existing actual or historical emissions, as applicable; or

(b) Emissions from a technology that represents an economically attractive course of action, taking into account barriers to investment; or

(c) The average emissions of similar project activities undertaken in the previous five years, in similar social, economic, environmental and technological circumstances, and whose performance is among the top 20 per cent of their category.

49. Project participants shall select a crediting period for a proposed project activity from one of the following alternative approaches:

(a) A maximum of seven years which may be renewed at most two times, provided that, for each renewal, a designated operational entity determines and informs the executive board that the original project baseline is still valid or has been updated taking account of new data where applicable; or

(b) A maximum of ten years with no option of renewal.

50. Reductions in anthropogenic emissions by sources shall be adjusted for leakage in accordance with the monitoring and verification provisions in paragraphs 59 and 62(f) below, respectively.

51. Leakage is defined as the net change of anthropogenic emissions by sources of greenhouse gases which occurs outside the project boundary, and which is measurable and attributable to the CDM project activity.

52. The project boundary shall encompass all anthropogenic emissions by sources of greenhouse gases under the control of the project participants that are significant and reasonably attributable to the CDM project activity.

H. Monitoring

53. Project participants shall include, as part of the project design document, a monitoring plan that provides for:

(a) The collection and archiving of all relevant data necessary for estimating or measuring anthropogenic emissions by sources of greenhouse gases occurring within the project boundary during the crediting period;

(b) The collection and archiving of all relevant data necessary for determining the baseline of anthropogenic emissions by sources of greenhouse gases within the project boundary during the crediting period;

(c) The identification of all potential sources of, and the collection and archiving of data on, increased anthropogenic emissions by sources of greenhouse gases outside the project boundary that are significant and reasonably attributable to the project activity during the crediting period;

(d) The collection and archiving of information relevant to the provisions in paragraph 37(c) above;

(e) Quality assurance and control procedures for the monitoring process;

(f) Procedures for the periodic calculation of the reductions of anthropogenic emissions by sources by the proposed CDM project activity, and for leakage effects;

(g) Documentation of all steps involved in the calculations referred to in paragraph 53(c) and (f) above.

54. A monitoring plan for a proposed project activity shall be based on a previously approved monitoring methodology or a new methodology, in accordance with paragraphs 37 and 38 above, that:

(a) Is determined by the designated operational entity as appropriate to the circumstances of the proposed project activity and has been successfully applied elsewhere;

(b) Reflects good monitoring practice appropriate to the type of project activity.

55. For small-scale CDM project activities meeting the criteria specified in decision 17/CP.7 and relevant decisions by the COP/MOP, project participants may use simplified modalities and procedures for small-scale projects.

56. Project participants shall implement the monitoring plan contained in the registered project design document.

57. Revisions, if any, to the monitoring plan to improve its accuracy and/or completeness of information shall be justified by project participants and shall be submitted for validation to a designated operational entity.

58. The implementation of the registered monitoring plan and its revisions, as applicable, shall be a condition for verification, certification and the issuance of CERs.

59. Subsequent to the monitoring and reporting of reductions in anthropogenic emissions, CERs resulting from a CDM project activity during a specified time period shall be calculated, applying the registered methodology, by subtracting the actual anthropogenic emissions by sources from baseline emissions and adjusting for leakage.

60. The project participants shall provide to the designated operational entity, contracted by the project participants to perform the verification, a monitoring report in accordance with the registered monitoring plan set out in paragraph 53 above for the purpose of verification and certification.

I. Verification and certification

61. Verification is the periodic independent review and *ex post* determination by the designated operational entity of the monitored reductions in anthropogenic emissions by sources of greenhouse gases that have occurred as a result of a registered CDM project activity during the verification period. Certification is the written assurance by the designated operational entity that, during a specified time period, a project activity achieved the reductions in anthropogenic emissions by sources of greenhouse gases as verified.

62. In accordance with the provisions on confidentiality in paragraph 27(h) above, the designated operational entity contracted by the project participants to perform the verification shall make the monitoring report publicly available, and shall:

(a) Determine whether the project documentation provided is in accordance with the requirements of the registered project design document and relevant provisions of decision 17/CP.7, the present annex and relevant decisions of the COP/MOP;

(b) Conduct on-site inspections, as appropriate, that may comprise, *inter alia*, a review of performance records, interviews with project participants and local stakeholders, collection of measurements, observation of established practices and testing of the accuracy of monitoring equipment;

(c) If appropriate, use additional data from other sources;

(d) Review monitoring results and verify that the monitoring methodologies for the estimation of reductions in anthropogenic emissions by sources have been applied correctly and their documentation is complete and transparent;

(e) Recommend to the project participants appropriate changes to the monitoring methodology for any future crediting period, if necessary;

(f) Determine the reductions in anthropogenic emissions by sources of greenhouse gases that would not have occurred in the absence of the CDM project activity, based on the data and information derived under subparagraph (a) above and obtained under subparagraph (b) and/or (c) above, as appropriate, using calculation procedures consistent with those contained in the registered project design document and in the monitoring plan;

(g) Identify and inform the project participants of any concerns related to the conformity of the actual project activity and its operation with the registered project design document. Project participants shall address the concerns and supply relevant additional information;

(h) Provide a verification report to the project participants, the Parties involved and the executive board. The report shall be made publicly available.

63. The designated operational entity shall, based on its verification report, certify in writing that, during the specified time period, the project activity achieved the verified amount of reductions in anthropogenic emissions by sources of greenhouse gases that would not have occurred in the absence of the CDM project activity. It shall inform the project participants, Parties involved and the executive board of its certification decision in writing immediately upon completion of the certification process and make the certification report publicly available.

J. Issuance of certified emission reductions

64. The certification report shall constitute a request for issuance to the executive board of CERs equal to the verified amount of reductions of anthropogenic emissions by sources of greenhouse gases.

65. The issuance shall be considered final 15 days after the date of receipt of the request for issuance, unless a Party involved in the project activity or at least three members of the executive board request a review of the proposed issuance of CERs. Such a review shall be limited to issues of fraud, malfeasance or incompetence of the designated operational entities and be conducted as follows:

(a) Upon receipt of a request for such a review, the executive board, at its next meeting, shall decide on its course of action. If it decides that the request has merit it shall perform a review and decide whether the proposed issuance of CERs should be approved;
(b) The executive board shall complete its review within 30 days following its decision to perform the review;
(c) The executive board shall inform the project participants of the outcome of the review, and make public its decision regarding the approval of the proposed issuance of CERs and the reasons for it.

66. Upon being instructed by the executive board to issue CERs for a CDM project activity, the CDM registry administrator, working under the authority of the executive board, shall, promptly, issue the specified quantity of CERs into the pending account of the executive board in the CDM registry, in accordance with Appendix D below. Upon such issuance, the CDM registry administrator shall promptly:

(a) Forward the quantity of CERs corresponding to the share of proceeds to cover administrative expenses and to assist in meeting costs of adaptation, respectively, in accordance with Article 12, paragraph 8, to the appropriate accounts in the CDM registry for the management of the share of proceeds;
(b) Forward the remaining CERs to the registry accounts of Parties and project participants involved, in accordance with their request.

Appendix A
Standards for the accreditation of operational entities

1. An operational entity shall:

(a) Be a legal entity (either a domestic legal entity or an international organization) and provide documentation of this status;
(b) Employ a sufficient number of persons having the necessary competence to perform validation, verification and certification functions relating to the type, range and volume of work performed, under a responsible senior executive;
(c) Have the financial stability, insurance coverage and resources required for its activities;
(d) Have sufficient arrangements to cover legal and financial liabilities arising from its activities;
(e) Have documented internal procedures for carrying out its functions including, among others, procedures for the allocation of responsibility within the organization and for handling complaints. These procedures shall be made publicly available;

(f) Have, or have access to, the necessary expertise to carry out the functions specified in modalities and procedures of the CDM and relevant decisions by the COP/MOP, in particular knowledge and understanding of:

   (i) The modalities and procedures and guidelines for the operation of the CDM, relevant decisions of the COP/MOP and of the executive board;

   (ii) Issues, in particular environmental, relevant to validation, verification and certification of CDM project activities, as appropriate;

   (iii) The technical aspects of CDM project activities relevant to environmental issues, including expertise in the setting of baselines and monitoring of emissions;

   (iv) Relevant environmental auditing requirements and methodologies;

   (v) Methodologies for accounting of anthropogenic emissions by sources;

   (vi) Regional and sectoral aspects;

(g) Have a management structure that has overall responsibility for performance and implementation of the entity's functions, including quality assurance procedures, and all relevant decisions relating to validation, verification and certification. The applicant operational entity shall make available:

   (i) The names, qualifications, experience and terms of reference of senior management personnel such as the senior executive, board members, senior officers and other relevant personnel;

   (ii) An organizational chart showing lines of authority, responsibility and allocation of functions stemming from senior management;

   (iii) Its quality assurance policy and procedures;

   (iv) Administrative procedures, including document control;

   (v) Its policy and procedures for the recruitment and training of operational entity personnel, for ensuring their competence for all necessary functions for validation, verification and certification functions, and for monitoring their performance;

   (vi) Its procedures for handling complaints, appeals and disputes;

(h) Not have pending any judicial process for malpractice, fraud and/or other activity incompatible with its functions as a designated operational entity.

2. An applicant operational entity shall meet the following operational requirements:

(a) Work in a credible, independent, non-discriminatory and transparent manner, complying with applicable national law and meeting, in particular, the following requirements:

   (i) An applicant operational entity shall have a documented structure, which safeguards impartiality, including provisions to ensure impartiality of its operations;

(ii) If it is part of a larger organization, and where parts of that organization
are, or may become, involved in the identification, development or
financing of any CDM project activity, the applicant operational entity
shall:

- Make a declaration of all the organization's actual and planned involvement in CDM project activities, if any, indicating which part of
  the organization is involved and in which particular CDM project
  activities;
- Clearly define the links with other parts of the organization, demonstrating that no conflicts of interest exist;
- Demonstrate that no conflict of interest exists between its functions
  as an operational entity and any other functions that it may have, and
  demonstrate how business is managed to minimize any identified
  risk to impartiality. The demonstration shall cover all sources of
  conflict of interest, whether they arise from within the applicant
  operational entity or from the activities of related bodies;
- Demonstrate that it, together with its senior management and staff,
  is not involved in any commercial, financial or other processes which
  might influence its judgement or endanger trust in its independence
  of judgement and integrity in relation to its activities, and that it
  complies with any rules applicable in this respect;

(b) Have adequate arrangements to safeguard confidentiality of the information obtained from CDM project participants in accordance with provisions contained in the present annex.

Appendix B
Project design document

1. The provisions of this appendix shall be interpreted in accordance with
the annex above on modalities and procedures for a CDM.

2. The purpose of this appendix is to outline the information required in the
project design document. A project activity shall be described in detail taking
into account the provisions of the annex on modalities and procedures for a
CDM, in particular, section G on validation and registration and section H on
monitoring, in a project design document which shall include the following:

(a) A description of the project comprising the project purpose, a technical
description of the project, including how technology will be transferred, if
any, and a description and justification of the project boundary;

(b) A proposed baseline methodology in accordance with the annex on modalities and procedures for a CDM including, in the case of the:

(i) Application of an approved methodology:

- Statement of which approved methodology has been selected;

- Description of how the approved methodology will be applied in the context of the project;

(ii) Application of a new methodology:
- Description of the baseline methodology and justification of choice, including an assessment of strengths and weaknesses of the methodology;
- Description of key parameters, data sources and assumptions used in the baseline estimate, and assessment of uncertainties;
- Projections of baseline emissions;
- Description of how the baseline methodology addresses potential leakage;

(iii) Other considerations, such as a description of how national and/or sectoral policies and circumstances have been taken into account and an explanation of how the baseline was established in a transparent and conservative manner;

(c) Statement of the estimated operational lifetime of the project and which crediting period was selected;

(d) Description of how the anthropogenic emissions of GHG by sources are reduced below those that would have occurred in the absence of the registered CDM project activity;

(e) Environmental impacts:
  (i) Documentation on the analysis of the environmental impacts, including transboundary impacts;
  (ii) If impacts are considered significant by the project participants or the host Party: conclusions and all references to support documentation of an environmental impact assessment that has been undertaken in accordance with the procedures as required by the host Party;

(f) Information on sources of public funding for the project activity from Parties included in Annex I which shall provide an affirmation that such funding does not result in a diversion of official development assistance and is separate from and is not counted towards the financial obligations of those Parties;

(g) Stakeholder comments, including a brief description of the process, a summary of the comments received, and a report on how due account was taken of any comments received;

(h) Monitoring plan:
  (i) Identification of data needs and data quality with regard to accuracy, comparability, completeness and validity;
  (ii) Methodologies to be used for data collection and monitoring including quality assurance and quality control provisions for monitoring, collecting and reporting;
  (iii) In the case of a new monitoring methodology, provide a description of the methodology, including an assessment of strengths and weaknesses

of the methodology and whether or not it has been applied successfully elsewhere;

(i) Calculations:

   (i) Description of formulae used to calculate and estimate anthropogenic emissions by sources of greenhouse gases of the CDM project activity within the project boundary;

   (ii) Description of formulae used to calculate and to project leakage, defined as: the net change of anthropogenic emissions by sources of greenhouse gases which occurs outside the CDM project activity boundary, and that is measurable and attributable to the CDM project activity;

   (iii) The sum of (i) and (ii) above representing the CDM project activity emissions;

   (iv) Description of formulae used to calculate and to project the anthropogenic emissions by sources of greenhouse gases of the baseline;

   (v) Description of formulae used to calculate and to project leakage;

   (vi) The sum of (iv) and (v) above representing the baseline emissions;

   (vii) Difference between (vi) and (iii) above representing the emission reductions of the CDM project activity;

(j) References to support the above, if any.

Appendix C
Terms of reference for establishing guidelines on baselines and monitoring methodologies

The executive board, drawing on experts in accordance with the modalities and procedures for a CDM, shall develop and recommend to the COP/MOP, *inter alia*:

(a) General guidance on methodologies relating to baselines and monitoring consistent with the principles set out in those modalities and procedures in order to:

   (i) Elaborate the provisions relating to baseline and monitoring methodologies contained in decision 17/CP.7, the annex above and relevant decisions of the COP/MOP;

   (ii) Promote consistency, transparency and predictability;

   (iii) Provide rigour to ensure that net reductions in anthropogenic emissions are real and measurable, and an accurate reflection of what has occurred within the project boundary;

   (iv) Ensure applicability in different geographical regions and to those project categories which are eligible in accordance with decision 17/CP.7 and relevant decisions of the COP/MOP;

   (v) Address the additionality requirement of Article 12, paragraph 5(c), and paragraph 43 of the above annex;

(b) Specific guidance in the following areas:
   (i) Definition of project categories (e.g. based on sector, subsector, project type, technology, geographic area) that show common methodological characteristics for baseline setting, and/or monitoring, including guidance on the level of geographic aggregation, taking into account data availability;
   (ii) Baseline methodologies deemed to reasonably represent what would have occurred in the absence of a project activity;
   (iii) Monitoring methodologies that provide an accurate measure of actual reductions in anthropogenic emissions as a result of the project activity, taking into account the need for consistency and cost-effectiveness;
   (iv) Decision trees and other methodological tools, where appropriate, to guide choices in order to ensure that the most appropriate methodologies are selected, taking into account relevant circumstances;
   (v) The appropriate level of standardization of methodologies to allow a reasonable estimation of what would have occurred in the absence of a project activity wherever possible and appropriate. Standardization should be conservative in order to prevent any overestimation of reductions in anthropogenic emissions;
   (vi) Determination of project boundaries including accounting for all greenhouse gases that should be included as a part of the baseline, and monitoring. Relevance of leakage and recommendations for establishing appropriate project boundaries and methods for the *ex post* evaluation of the level of leakage;
   (vii) Accounting for applicable national policies and specific national or regional circumstances, such as sectoral reform initiatives, local fuel availability, power sector expansion plans, and the economic situation in the sector relevant to the project activity;
   (viii) The breadth of the baseline, e.g. how the baseline makes comparisons between the technology/fuel used and other technologies/fuels in the sector;
(c) In developing the guidance in (a) and (b) above, the executive board shall take into account:
   (i) Current practices in the host country or an appropriate region, and observed trends;
   (ii) Least cost technology for the activity or project category.

Appendix D
Clean development mechanism registry requirements

1. The executive board shall establish and maintain a CDM registry to ensure the accurate accounting of the issuance, holding, transfer and acquisition of CERs by Parties not included in Annex I. The executive board shall identify a registry administrator to maintain the registry under its authority.

2. The CDM registry shall be in the form of a standardized electronic database which contains, *inter alia*, common data elements relevant to the issuance, holding, transfer and acquisition of CERs. The structure and data formats of the CDM registry shall conform to technical standards to be adopted by the COP/MOP for the purpose of ensuring the accurate, transparent and efficient exchange of data between national registries, the CDM registry and the independent transaction log.

3. The CDM registry shall have the following accounts:

(a) One pending account for the executive board, into which CERs are issued before being transferred to other accounts;

(b) At least one holding account for each Party not included in Annex I hosting a CDM project activity or requesting an account;

(c) At least one account for the purpose of cancelling ERUs, CERs, AAUs and RMUs equal to excess CERs issued, as determined by the executive board, where the accreditation of designated operational entity has been withdrawn or suspended;

(d) At least one account for the purpose of holding and transferring CERs corresponding to the share of proceeds to cover administrative expenses and to assist in meeting costs of adaptation in accordance with Article 12, paragraph 8. Such an account may not otherwise acquire CERs.

4. Each CER shall be held in only one account in one registry at a given time.

5. Each account within the CDM registry shall have a unique account number comprising the following elements:

(a) Party/organization identifier: the Party for which the account is maintained, using the two-letter country code defined by the International Organization for Standardization (ISO 3166), or, in the cases of the pending account and an account for managing the CERs corresponding to the share of proceeds, the executive board or another appropriate organization;

(b) A unique number: a number unique to that account for the Party or organization for which the account is maintained.

6. Upon being instructed by the executive board to issue CERs for a CDM project activity, the registry administrator shall, in accordance with the transaction procedures set out in decision -/CMP.1 (*Modalities for the accounting of assigned amounts*):

(a) Issue the specified quantity of CERs into a pending account of the executive board;

(b) Forward the quantity of CERs corresponding to the share of proceeds to cover administrative expenses and to assist in meeting costs of adaptation, in accordance with Article 12, paragraph 8, to the appropriate accounts in the CDM registry for holding and transferring such CERs;

(c) Forward the remaining CERs to the registry accounts of project participants and Parties involved, in accordance with their request.

7. Each CER shall have a unique serial number comprising the following elements:

(a) Commitment period: the commitment period for which the CER is issued;
(b) Party of origin: the Party which hosted the CDM project activity, using the twoletter country code defined by ISO 3166;
(c) Type: this shall identify the unit as a CER;
(d) Unit: a number unique to the CER for the identified commitment period and Party of origin;
(e) Project identifier: a number unique to the CDM project activity for the Party of origin.

8. Where the accreditation of a designated operational entity has been withdrawn or suspended, ERUs, CERs, AAUs and/or RMUs equal to the excess CERs issued, as determined by the executive board, shall be transferred to a cancellation account in the CDM registry. Such ERUs, CERs, AAUs and RMUs may not be further transferred or used for the purpose of demonstrating the compliance of a Party with its commitment under Article 3, paragraph 1.

9. The CDM registry shall make non-confidential information publicly available and provide a publicly accessible user interface through the Internet that allows interested persons to query and view it.

10. The information referred to in paragraph 9 above shall include up-to-date information, for each account number in the registry, on the following:

(a) Account name: the holder of the account;
(b) Representative identifier: the representative of the account holder, using the Party/organization identifier (the two-letter country code defined by ISO 3166) and a number unique to that representative for that Party or organization;
(c) Representative name and contact information: the full name, mailing address, telephone number, facsimile number and e-mail address of the representative of the account holder.

11. The information referred to in paragraph 9 above shall include the following CDM project activity information, for each project identifier against which the CERs have been issued:

(a) Project name: a unique name for the CDM project activity;
(b) Project location: the Party and town or region in which the CDM project activity is located;
(c) Years of CER issuance: the years in which CERs have been issued as a result of the CDM project activity;

(d) Operational entities: the operational entities involved in the validation, verification and certification of the CDM project activity;

(e) Reports: downloadable electronic versions of documentation to be made publicly available in accordance with the provisions of the present annex.

12. The information referred to in paragraph 9 above shall include the following holding and transaction information relevant to the CDM registry, by serial number, for each calendar year (defined according to Greenwich Mean Time):

(a) The total quantity of CERs in each account at the beginning of the year;

(b) The total quantity of CERs issued;

(c) The total quantity of CERs transferred and the identity of the acquiring accounts and registries;

(d) The total quantity of ERUs, CERs, AAUs and RMUs cancelled in accordance with paragraph 8 above;

(e) Current holdings of CERs in each account.

7B(iii)
Modalities, Rules and Guidelines for Emissions Trading under Article 17 of the Kyoto Protocol*[1]

1. For the purpose of the present annex the definitions contained in Article 1[2] and the provisions of Article 14 shall apply. Furthermore:

(a) An 'emission reduction unit' or 'ERU' is a unit issued pursuant to the relevant provisions in the annex to decision -/CMP.1 (*Modalities for the accounting of assigned amounts*) and is equal to one metric tonne of carbon dioxide equivalent, calculated using global warming potentials defined by decision 2/CP.3 or as subsequently revised in accordance with Article 5;

(b) A 'certified emission reduction' or 'CER' is a unit issued pursuant to Article 12 and requirements thereunder, as well as the relevant provisions in the annex to decision -/CMP.1 (*Article 12*), and is equal to one metric tonne of carbon dioxide equivalent, calculated using global warming potentials defined by decision 2/CP.3 or as subsequently revised in accordance with Article 5;

(c) An 'assigned amount unit' or 'AAU' is a unit issued pursuant to the relevant provisions in the annex to decision -/CMP.1 (*Modalities for the accounting*

---

* Annex to Decision 18/CP.7 – Draft Decision -/CMP.1 (*Article 17*)

[1] The annex to decision -/CMP.1 (*Modalities for the accounting of assigned amounts*) contains operational provisions and procedures relevant to this annex.

[2] In the context of this annex, 'Article' refers to an Article of the Kyoto Protocol, unless otherwise specified.

of assigned amounts) and is equal to one metric tonne of carbon dioxide equivalent, calculated using global warming potentials defined by decision 2/CP.3 or as subsequently revised in accordance with Article 5;

(d) A 'removal unit' or 'RMU' is a unit issued pursuant to the relevant provisions in the annex to decision -/CMP.1 (*Modalities for the accounting of assigned amounts*) and is equal to one metric tonne of carbon dioxide equivalent, calculated using global warming potentials defined by decision 2/CP.3 or as subsequently revised in accordance with Article 5.

2. Subject to the provisions of paragraph 3 below, a Party[3] included in Annex I with a commitment inscribed in Annex B is eligible to transfer and/or acquire ERUs, CERs, AAUs, or RMUs issued in accordance with the relevant provisions, if it is in compliance with the following eligibility requirements:

(a) It is a Party to the Kyoto Protocol;
(b) Its assigned amount pursuant to Article 3, paragraphs 7 and 8, has been calculated and recorded in accordance with decision -/CMP.1 (*Modalities for the accounting of assigned amounts*);
(c) It has in place a national system for the estimation of anthropogenic emissions by sources and anthropogenic removals by sinks of all greenhouse gases not controlled by the Montreal Protocol, in accordance with Article 5, paragraph 1, and the requirements in the guidelines decided thereunder;
(d) It has in place a national registry in accordance with Article 7, paragraph 4, and the requirements in the guidelines decided thereunder;
(e) It has submitted annually the most recent required inventory, in accordance with Article 5, paragraph 2, and Article 7, paragraph 1, and the requirements in the guidelines decided thereunder, including the national inventory report and the common reporting format. For the first commitment period, the quality assessment needed for the purpose of determining eligibility to use the mechanisms shall be limited to the parts of the inventory pertaining to emissions of greenhouse gases from sources/sector categories from Annex A to the Kyoto Protocol and the submission of the annual inventory on sinks;
(f) It submits the supplementary information on assigned amount in accordance with Article 7, paragraph 1, and the requirements in the guidelines decided thereunder and makes any additions to, and subtractions from, assigned amount pursuant to Article 3, paragraphs 7 and 8, including for the activities under Article 3, paragraphs 3 and 4, in accordance with Article 7, paragraph 4, and the requirements in the guidelines decided thereunder;

3. A Party included in Annex I with a commitment inscribed in Annex B shall be considered:

---

[3] In the context of this annex, 'Party' refers to a Party to the Kyoto Protocol, unless otherwise specified.

(a) To meet the eligibility requirements referred to in paragraph 2 above after 16 months have elapsed since the submission of its report to facilitate the calculation of its assigned amount pursuant to Article 3, paragraphs 7 and 8, and to demonstrate its capacity to account for its emissions and assigned amount, in accordance with the modalities adopted for the accounting of assigned amount under Article 7, paragraph 4, unless the enforcement branch of the compliance committee finds in accordance with decision 24/CP.7 that the Party does not meet these requirements, or, at an earlier date, if the enforcement branch of the compliance committee has decided that it is not proceeding with any questions of implementation relating to these requirements indicated in reports of the expert review teams under Article 8 of the Kyoto Protocol, and has transmitted this information to the secretariat;

(b) To continue to meet the eligibility requirements referred to in paragraph 2 above unless and until the enforcement branch of the compliance committee decides that the Party does not meet one or more of the eligibility requirements, has suspended the Party's eligibility and has transmitted this information to the secretariat.

4. The secretariat shall maintain a publicly accessible list of Parties that meet the eligibility requirements and of Parties that have been suspended.

5. Transfers and acquisitions between national registries shall be made under the responsibility of the Parties concerned in accordance with the provisions in decision – CMP.1 (*Modalities for the accounting of assigned amounts*). A Party that authorizes legal entities to transfer and/or acquire under Article 17 shall remain responsible for the fulfilment of its obligations under the Kyoto Protocol and shall ensure that such participation is consistent with the present annex. The Party shall maintain an up-to-date list of such entities and make it available to the secretariat and the public through its national registry. Legal entities may not transfer and/or acquire under Article 17 during any period of time in which the authorizing Party does not meet the eligibility requirements or has been suspended.

6. Each Party included in Annex I shall maintain, in its national registry, a commitment period reserve which should not drop below 90 per cent of the Party's assigned amount calculated pursuant to Article 3, paragraphs 7 and 8, of the Kyoto Protocol, or 100 per cent of five times its most recently reviewed inventory, whichever is lowest.

7. The commitment period reserve shall consist of holdings of ERUs, CERs, AAUs and/or RMUs for the relevant commitment period which have not been cancelled in accordance with decision -/CMP.1 (*Modalities for the accounting of assigned amounts*).

8. Upon establishment of its assigned amount pursuant to Article 3, paragraphs 7 and 8, and until expiration of the additional period for fulfilling

commitments, a Party shall not make a transfer which would result in these holdings being below the required level of the commitment period reserve.

9. If calculations under paragraph 6 above, or cancellations of ERUs, CERs, AAUs and/or RMUs raise the required level of the commitment period reserve above the Party's holdings of ERUs, CERs, AAUs and/or RMUs valid for the relevant commitment period, which have not been cancelled, the Party shall be notified by the secretariat and, within 30 days of this notification, shall bring its holdings to the required level.

10. Any provisions relating to the commitment period reserve or other limitations to transfers under Article 17 shall not apply to transfers by a Party of ERUs issued into its national registry which were verified in accordance with the verification procedure under the Article 6 supervisory committee.

11. The secretariat shall perform functions as requested.

7B(iv)
Procedures and Mechanisms Relating to Compliance under the Kyoto Protocol*

In pursuit of the ultimate objective of the United Nations Framework Convention on Climate Change, hereinafter referred to as 'the Convention', as stated in its Article 2,

Recalling the provisions of the United Nations Framework Convention on Climate Change, and the Kyoto Protocol to the Convention, herein after referred to as 'the Protocol',

Being guided by Article 3 of the Convention,

Pursuant to the mandate adopted in decision 8/CP.4 by the Conference of the Parties at its fourth session,

The following procedures and mechanisms *have been adopted*:

I. Objective

The objective of these procedures and mechanisms is to facilitate, promote and enforce compliance with the commitments under the Protocol.

II. Compliance committee

1. A compliance committee, hereinafter referred to as 'the Committee', is hereby established.

2. The Committee shall function through a plenary, a bureau and two branches, namely, the facilitative branch and the enforcement branch.

3. The Committee shall consist of twenty members elected by the Conference of the Parties serving as the meeting of the Parties to the Protocol, ten of whom

* Annex to Decision 24/CP.7.

are to be elected to serve in the facilitative branch and ten to be elected to serve in the enforcement branch.

4. Each branch shall elect, from among its members and for a term of two years, a chairperson and a vice-chairperson, one of whom shall be from a Party included in Annex I and one from a Party not included in Annex I. These persons shall constitute the bureau of the Committee. The chairing of each branch shall rotate between Parties included in Annex and Parties not included in Annex I in such a manner that at any time one chairperson shall be from among the Parties included in Annex I and the other chairperson shall be from among the Parties not included in Annex I.

5. For each member of the Committee, the Conference of the Parties serving as the meeting of the Parties to the Protocol shall elect an alternate member.

6. Members of the Committee and their alternates shall serve in their individual capacities. They shall have recognized competence relating to climate change and in relevant fields such as the scientific, technical, socio-economic or legal fields.

7. The facilitative branch and the enforcement branch shall interact and cooperate in their functioning and, as necessary, on a case-by-case basis, the bureau of the Committee may designate one or more members of one branch to contribute to the work of the other branch on a non-voting basis.

8. The adoption of decisions by the Committee shall require a quorum of at least three fourths of the members to be present.

9. The Committee shall make every effort to reach agreement on any decisions by consensus. If all efforts at reaching consensus have been exhausted, the decisions shall as a last resort be adopted by a majority of at least three fourths of the members present and voting. In addition, the adoption of decisions by the enforcement branch shall require a majority of members from Parties included in Annex I present and voting, as well as a majority of members from Parties not included in Annex I present and voting. 'Members present and voting' means members present and casting an affirmative or a negative vote.

10. The Committee shall, unless it decides otherwise, meet at least twice each year, taking into account the desirability of holding such meetings in conjunction with the meetings of the subsidiary bodies under the Convention.

11. The Committee shall take into account any degree of flexibility allowed by the Conference of the Parties serving as the meeting of the Parties to the Protocol, pursuant to Article 3, paragraph 6, of the Protocol and taking into account Article 4, paragraph 6, of the Convention, to the Parties included in Annex I undergoing the process of transition to a market economy.

III. Plenary of the committee

1. The plenary shall consist of the members of the facilitative branch and the enforcement branch. The chairpersons of the two branches shall be the co-chairpersons of the plenary.

2. The functions of the plenary shall be:

(a) To report on the activities of the Committee, including a list of decisions taken by the branches, to each ordinary session of the Conference of the Parties serving as the meeting of the Parties to the Protocol;

(b) To apply the general policy guidance referred to in section XII(c) below, received from the Conference of the Parties serving as the meeting of the Parties to the Protocol;

(c) To submit proposals on administrative and budgetary matters to the Conference of the Parties serving as the meeting of the Parties to the Protocol for the effective functioning of the Committee;

(d) To develop any further rules of procedure that may be needed, including rules on confidentiality, conflict of interest, submission of information by intergovernmental and nongovernmental organizations, and translation, for adoption by the Conference of the Parties serving as the meeting of the Parties to the Protocol by consensus; and

(e) To perform such other functions as may be requested by the Conference of the Parties serving as the meeting of the Parties to the Protocol for the effective functioning of the Committee.

IV. Facilitative branch

1. The facilitative branch shall be composed of:

(a) One member from each of the five regional groups of the United Nations and one member from the small island developing States, taking into account the interest groups as reflected by the current practice in the Bureau of the Conference of the Parties;

(b) Two members from Parties included in Annex I; and

(c) Two members from Parties not included in Annex I.

2. The Conference of the Parties serving as the meeting of the Parties to the Protocol shall elect five members for a term of two years and five members for a term of four years. Each time thereafter, the Conference of the Parties serving as the meeting of the Parties to the Protocol shall elect five new members for a term of four years. Members shall not serve for more than two consecutive terms.

3. In electing the members of the facilitative branch, the Conference of the Parties serving as the meeting of the Parties to the Protocol shall seek to reflect competences in a balanced manner in the fields referred to in section II, paragraph 6, above.

4. The facilitative branch shall be responsible for providing advice and facilitation to Parties in implementing the Protocol, and for promoting compliance by Parties with their commitments under the Protocol, taking into account the principle of common but differentiated responsibilities and

respective capabilities as contained in Article 3, paragraph 1, of the Convention. It shall also take into account the circumstances pertaining to the questions before it.

5. Within its overall mandate, as specified in paragraph 4 above, and falling outside the mandate of the enforcement branch, as specified in section V, paragraph 4, below, the facilitative branch shall be responsible for addressing questions of implementation:

(a) Relating to Article 3, paragraph 14, of the Protocol, including questions of implementation arising from the consideration of information on how a Party included in Annex I is striving to implement Article 3, paragraph 14, of the Protocol; and

(b) With respect to the provision of information on the use by a Party included in Annex I of Articles 6, 12 and 17 of the Protocol as supplemental to its domestic action, taking into account any reporting under Article 3, paragraph 2, of the Protocol.

6. With the aim of promoting compliance and providing for early warning of potential noncompliance, the facilitative branch shall be further responsible for providing advice and facilitation for compliance with:

(a) Commitments under Article 3, paragraph 1, of the Protocol, prior to the beginning of the relevant commitment period and during that commitment period;

(b) Commitments under Article 5, paragraphs 1 and 2, of the Protocol, prior to the beginning of the first commitment period; and

(c) Commitments under Article 7, paragraphs 1 and 4, of the Protocol prior to the beginning of the first commitment period.

7. The facilitative branch shall be responsible for applying the consequences set out in section XIV below.

V. Enforcement branch

1. The enforcement branch shall be composed of:

(a) One member from each of the five regional groups of the United Nations and one member from the small island developing States, taking into account the interest groups as reflected by the current practice in the Bureau of the Conference of the Parties;

(b) Two members from Parties included in Annex I; and

(c) Two members from Parties not included in Annex I.

2. The Conference of the Parties serving as the meeting of the Parties to the Protocol shall elect five members for a term of two years and five members for a term of four years. Each time thereafter, the Conference of the Parties serving as the meeting of the Parties to the Protocol shall elect five new members for

a term of four years. Members shall not serve for more than two consecutive terms.

3. In electing the members of the enforcement branch, the Conference of the Parties serving as the meeting of the Parties to the Protocol shall be satisfied that the members have legal experience.

4. The enforcement branch shall be responsible for determining whether a Party included in Annex I is not in compliance with:

(a) Its quantified emission limitation or reduction commitment under Article 3, paragraph 1, of the Protocol;
(b) The methodological and reporting requirements under Article 5, paragraphs 1 and 2, and Article 7, paragraphs 1 and 4, of the Protocol; and
(c) The eligibility requirements under Articles 6, 12 and 17 of the Protocol.

5. The enforcement branch shall also determine whether to apply:

(a) Adjustments to inventories under Article 5, paragraph 2, of the Protocol, in the event of a disagreement between an expert review team under Article 8 of the Protocol and the Party involved; and
(b) A correction to the compilation and accounting database for the accounting of assigned amounts under Article 7, paragraph 4, of the Protocol, in the event of a disagreement between an expert review team under Article 8 of the Protocol and the Party involved concerning the validity of a transaction or such Party's failure to take corrective action.

6. The enforcement branch shall be responsible for applying the consequences set out in section XV below for the cases of non-compliance mentioned in paragraph 4 above. The consequences of non-compliance with Article 3, paragraph 1, of the Protocol to be applied by the enforcement branch shall be aimed at the restoration of compliance to ensure environmental integrity, and shall provide for an incentive to comply.

VI. Submissions

1. The Committee shall receive, through the secretariat, questions of implementation indicated in reports of expert review teams under Article 8 of the Protocol, together with any written comments by the Party which is subject to the report, or questions of implementation submitted by:

(a) Any Party with respect to itself; or
(b) Any Party with respect to another Party, supported by corroborating information.

2. The secretariat shall forthwith make available to the Party in respect of which the question of implementation is raised, hereinafter referred to as 'the

Party concerned', any question of implementation submitted under paragraph 1 above.

3. In addition to the reports referred to in paragraph 1 above, the Committee shall also receive, through the secretariat, other final reports of expert review teams.

VII. Allocation and preliminary examination

1. The bureau of the Committee shall allocate questions of implementation to the appropriate branch in accordance with the mandates of each branch set out in section IV, paragraphs 4–7, and Section V, paragraphs 4–6.

2. The relevant branch shall undertake a preliminary examination of questions of implementation to ensure that, except in the case of a question raised by a Party with respect to itself, the question before it:

(a) Is supported by sufficient information;
(b) Is not *de minimis* or ill-founded; and
(c) Is based on the requirements of the Protocol.

3. The preliminary examination of questions of implementation shall be completed within three weeks from the date of receipt of these questions by the relevant branch.

4. After the preliminary examination of questions of implementation, the Party concerned shall, through the secretariat, be notified in writing of the decision and, in the event of a decision to proceed, be provided with a statement identifying the question of implementation, the information on which the question is based and the branch that will consider the question.

5. In the event of the review of eligibility requirements for a Party included in Annex I under Articles 6, 12 and 17 of the Protocol, the enforcement branch shall also, through the secretariat, notify forthwith the Party concerned, in writing, of the decision not to proceed with questions of implementation relating to eligibility requirements under those articles.

6. Any decision not to proceed shall be made available by the secretariat to other Parties and to the public.

7. The Party concerned shall be given an opportunity to comment in writing on all information relevant to the question of implementation and the decision to proceed.

VIII. General procedures

1. Following the preliminary examination of questions of implementation, the procedures set out in this section shall apply to the Committee, except where otherwise provided in these procedures and mechanisms.

2. The Party concerned shall be entitled to designate one or more persons to represent it during the consideration of the question of implementation by

the relevant branch. This Party shall not be present during the elaboration and adoption of a decision of the branch.

3. Each branch shall base its deliberations on any relevant information provided by:

(a) Reports of the expert review teams under Article 8 of the Protocol;
(b) The Party concerned;
(c) The Party that has submitted a question of implementation with respect to another Party;
(d) Reports of the Conference of the Parties, the Conference of the Parties serving as the meeting of the Parties to the Protocol, and the subsidiary bodies under the Convention and the Protocol; and
(e) The other branch.

4. Competent intergovernmental and non-governmental organizations may submit relevant factual and technical information to the relevant branch.

5. Each branch may seek expert advice.

6. Any information considered by the relevant branch shall be made available to the Party concerned. The branch shall indicate to the Party concerned which parts of this information it has considered. The Party concerned shall be given an opportunity to comment in writing on such information. Subject to any rules relating to confidentiality, the information considered by the branch shall also be made available to the public, unless the branch decides, of its own accord or at the request of the Party concerned, that information provided by the Party concerned shall not be made available to the public until its decision has become final.

7. Decisions shall include conclusions and reasons. The relevant branch shall forthwith, through the secretariat, notify the Party concerned in writing of its decision, including conclusions and reasons therefor. The secretariat shall make final decisions available to other Parties and to the public.

8. The Party concerned shall be given an opportunity to comment in writing on any decision of the relevant branch.

9. If the Party concerned so requests, any question of implementation submitted under section VI, paragraph 1; any notification under section VII, paragraph 4; any information under paragraph 3 above; and any decision of the relevant branch, including conclusions and reasons therefor, shall be translated into one of the six official languages of the United Nations.

IX. Procedures for the enforcement branch

1. Within ten weeks from the date of receipt of the notification under section VII, paragraph 4, the Party concerned may make a written submission to the enforcement branch, including rebuttal of information submitted to the branch.

2. If so requested in writing by the Party concerned within ten weeks from the date of receipt of the notification under section VII, paragraph 4, the enforcement branch shall hold a hearing at which the Party concerned shall have the opportunity to present its views. The hearing shall take place within four weeks from the date of receipt of the request or of the written submission under paragraph 1 above, whichever is the later. The Party concerned may present expert testimony or opinion at the hearing. Such a hearing shall be held in public, unless the enforcement branch decides, of its own accord or at the request of the Party concerned, that part or all of the hearing shall take place in private.

3. The enforcement branch may put questions to and seek clarification from the Party concerned, either in the course of such a hearing or at any time in writing, and the Party concerned shall provide a response within six weeks thereafter.

4. Within four weeks from the date of receipt of the written submission of the Party concerned under paragraph 1 above, or within four weeks from the date of any hearing pursuant to paragraph 2 above, or within fourteen weeks from the notification under section VII, paragraph 4, if the Party has not provided a written submission, whichever is the latest, the enforcement branch shall:

(a) Adopt a preliminary finding that the Party concerned is not in compliance with commitments under one or more of the articles of the Protocol referred to in section V, paragraph 4; or

(b) Otherwise determine not to proceed further with the question.

5. The preliminary finding, or the decision not to proceed, shall include conclusions and reasons therefor.

6. The enforcement branch shall forthwith, through the secretariat, notify the Party concerned in writing of its preliminary finding or decision not to proceed. The secretariat shall make the decision not to proceed available to the other Parties and to the public.

7. Within ten weeks from the date of receipt of the notification of the preliminary finding, the Party concerned may provide a further written submission to the enforcement branch. If the Party concerned does not do so within that period of time, the enforcement branch shall forthwith adopt a final decision confirming its preliminary finding.

8. If the Party concerned provides a further written submission, the enforcement branch shall, within four weeks from the date it received the further submission, consider it and adopt a final decision, indicating whether the preliminary finding, as a whole or any part of it to be specified, is confirmed.

9. The final decision shall include conclusions and reasons therefor.

10. The enforcement branch shall forthwith, through the secretariat, notify the Party concerned in writing of its final decision. The secretariat shall make the final decision available to the other Parties and to the public.

11. The enforcement branch, when the circumstances of an individual case so warrant, may extend any time frames provided for in this section.

12. Where appropriate, the enforcement branch may, at any time, refer a question of implementation to the facilitative branch for consideration.

X. Expedited procedures for the enforcement branch

1. Where a question of implementation relates to eligibility requirements under Articles 6, 12 and 17 of the Protocol, sections VII to IX shall apply, except that:

(a) The preliminary examination referred to in section VII, paragraph 2, shall be completed within two weeks from the date of receipt of the question of implementation by the enforcement branch;

(b) The Party concerned may make a written submission within four weeks from the date of receipt of the notification under section VII, paragraph 4;

(c) If so requested in writing by the Party concerned within two weeks from the date of receipt of the notification under section VII, paragraph 4, the enforcement branch shall hold a hearing as referred to in section IX, paragraph 2, that shall take place within two weeks from the date of receipt of the request or of the written submission under subparagraph (b) above, whichever is the later;

(d) The enforcement branch shall adopt its preliminary finding or a decision not to proceed within six weeks of the notification under section VII, paragraph 4, or within two weeks of a hearing under section IX, paragraph 2, whichever is the shorter;

(e) The Party concerned may make a further written submission within four weeks from the date of receipt of the notification referred to in section IX, paragraph 6;

(f) The enforcement branch shall adopt its final decision within two weeks from the date of receipt of any further written submission referred to in section IX, paragraph 7; and

(g) The periods of time stipulated in section IX shall apply only if, in the opinion of the enforcement branch, they do not interfere with the adoption of decisions in accordance with subparagraphs (d) and (f) above.

2. Where the eligibility of a Party included in Annex I under Articles 6, 12 and 17 of the Protocol has been suspended under section XV, paragraph 4, the Party concerned may submit a request to reinstate its eligibility, either through an expert review team or directly to the enforcement branch. If the enforcement branch receives a report from the expert review team indicating that there is no longer a question of implementation with respect to the eligibility of the

Party concerned, it shall reinstate that Party's eligibility, unless the enforcement branch considers that there continues to be such a question of implementation, in which case the procedure referred to in paragraph 1 above shall apply. In response to a request submitted to it directly by the Party concerned, the enforcement branch shall decide as soon as possible, either that there no longer continues to be a question of implementation with respect to that Party's eligibility in which case it shall reinstate that Party's eligibility, or that the procedure referred to in paragraph 1 above shall apply.

3. Where the eligibility of a Party to make transfers under Article 17 of the Protocol has been suspended under section XV, paragraph 5 (c), the Party may request the enforcement branch to reinstate that eligibility. On the basis of the compliance action plan submitted by the Party in accordance with section XV, paragraph 6, and any progress reports submitted by the Party including information on its emissions trends, the enforcement branch shall reinstate that eligibility, unless it determines that the Party has not demonstrated that it will meet its quantified emission limitation or reduction commitment in the commitment period subsequent to the one for which the Party was determined to be in non-compliance, hereinafter referred to as 'the subsequent commitment period'. The enforcement branch shall apply the procedure referred to in paragraph 1 above, adapted insofar as necessary for the purposes of the procedure in the present paragraph.

4. Where the eligibility of a Party to make transfers under Article 17 of the Protocol has been suspended under section XV, paragraph 5 (c), the enforcement branch shall reinstate that eligibility forthwith if the Party demonstrates that it has met its quantified emission limitation or reduction commitment in the subsequent commitment period, either through the report of the expert review team under Article 8 of the Protocol for the final year of the subsequent commitment period or through a decision of the enforcement branch.

5. In the event of a disagreement whether to apply adjustments to inventories under Article 5, paragraph 2, of the Protocol, or whether to apply a correction to the compilation and accounting database for the accounting of assigned amounts under Article 7, paragraph 4, of the Protocol, the enforcement branch shall decide on the matter within twelve weeks of being informed in writing of such disagreement. In doing so, the enforcement branch may seek expert advice.

XI. Appeals

1. The Party in respect of which a final decision has been taken may appeal to the Conference of the Parties serving as the meeting of the Parties to the Protocol against a decision of the enforcement branch relating to Article 3, paragraph 1, of the Protocol if that Party believes it has been denied due process.

2. The appeal shall be lodged with the secretariat within 45 days after the Party has been informed of the decision of the enforcement branch. The Conference

of the Parties serving as the meeting of the Parties to the Protocol shall consider the appeal at its first session after the lodging of the appeal.

3. The Conference of the Parties serving as the meeting of the Parties to the Protocol may agree by a three-fourths majority vote of the Parties present and voting at the meeting to override the decision of the enforcement branch, in which event the Conference of the Parties serving as the meeting of the Parties to the Protocol shall refer the matter of the appeal back to the enforcement branch.

4. The decision of the enforcement branch shall stand pending the decision on appeal. It shall become definitive if, after 45 days, no appeal has been made against it.

XII. Relationship with the Conference of the Parties serving as the meeting of the Parties to the Protocol

The Conference of the Parties serving as the meeting of the Parties to the Protocol shall:

(a) In considering the reports of the expert review teams in accordance with Article 8, paragraphs 5 and 6 of the Protocol, identify any general problems that should be addressed in the general policy guidance referred to in subparagraph (c) below;

(b) Consider the reports of the plenary on the progress of its work;

(c) Provide general policy guidance, including on any issues regarding implementation that may have implications for the work of the subsidiary bodies under the Protocol;

(d) Adopt decisions on proposals on administrative and budgetary matters; and

(e) Consider and decide appeals in accordance with section XI.

XIII. Additional period for fulfilling commitments

For the purpose of fulfilling commitments under Article 3, paragraph 1, of the Protocol, a Party may, until the hundredth day after the date set by the Conference of the Parties serving as the meeting of the Parties to the Protocol for the completion of the expert review process under Article 8 of the Protocol for the last year of the commitment period, continue to acquire, and other Parties may transfer to such Party, emission reduction units, certified emission reductions, assigned amount units and removal units under Articles 6, 12 and 17 of the Protocol, from the preceding commitment period, provided the eligibility of any such Party has not been suspended in accordance with section XV, paragraph 4.

XIV. Consequences applied by the facilitative branch

The facilitative branch, taking into account the principle of common but differentiated responsibilities and respective capabilities, shall decide on the application of one or more of the following consequences:

(a) Provision of advice and facilitation of assistance to individual Parties regarding the implementation of the Protocol;
(b) Facilitation of financial and technical assistance to any Party concerned, including technology transfer and capacity building from sources other than those established under the Convention and the Protocol for the developing countries;
(c) Facilitation of financial and technical assistance, including technology transfer and capacity building, taking into account Article 4, paragraphs 3, 4 and 5, of the Convention; and
(d) Formulation of recommendations to the Party concerned, taking into account Article 4, paragraph 7, of the Convention.

XV. Consequences applied by the enforcement branch

1. Where the enforcement branch has determined that a Party is not in compliance with Article 5, paragraph 1 or paragraph 2, or Article 7, paragraph 1 or paragraph 4, of the Protocol, it shall apply the following consequences, taking into account the cause, type, degree and frequency of the non-compliance of that Party:

(a) Declaration of non-compliance; and
(b) Development of a plan in accordance with paragraphs 2 and 3 below.

2. The Party not in compliance under paragraph 1 above, shall, within three months after the determination of non-compliance, or such longer period that the enforcement branch considers appropriate, submit to the enforcement branch for review and assessment a plan that includes:

(a) An analysis of the causes of non-compliance of the Party;
(b) Measures that the Party intends to implement in order to remedy the non-compliance; and
(c) A timetable for implementing such measures within a time frame not exceeding twelve months which enables the assessment of progress in the implementation.

3. The Party not in compliance under paragraph 1 above shall submit to the enforcement branch progress reports on the implementation of the plan on a regular basis.

4. Where the enforcement branch has determined that a Party included in Annex I does not meet one or more of the eligibility requirements under Articles 6, 12 and 17 of the Protocol, it shall suspend the eligibility of that Party in accordance with relevant provisions under those articles. At the request of the Party concerned, eligibility may be reinstated in accordance with the procedure in section X, paragraph 2.

5. Where the enforcement branch has determined that the emissions of a Party have exceeded its assigned amount, calculated pursuant to its quantified emission limitation or reduction commitment inscribed in Annex B to the Protocol and in accordance with the provisions of Article 3 of the Protocol as well as the modalities for the accounting of assigned amounts under Article 7, paragraph 4, of the Protocol, taking into account emission reduction units, certified emission reductions, assigned amount units and removal units the Party has acquired in accordance with section XIII, it shall declare that that Party is not in compliance with its commitments under Article 3, paragraph 1, of the Protocol, and shall apply the following consequences:

(a) Deduction from the Party's assigned amount for the second commitment period of a number of tonnes equal to 1.3 times the amount in tonnes of excess emissions;
(b) Development of a compliance action plan in accordance with paragraphs 6 and 7 below; and
(c) Suspension of the eligibility to make transfers under Article 17 of the Protocol until the Party is reinstated in accordance with section X, paragraph 3 or paragraph 4.

6. The Party not in compliance under paragraph 5 above shall, within three months after the determination of non-compliance or, where the circumstances of an individual case so warrant, such longer period that the enforcement branch considers appropriate, submit to the enforcement branch for review and assessment a compliance action plan that includes:

(a) An analysis of the causes of the non-compliance of the Party;
(b) Action that the Party intends to implement in order to meet its quantified emission limitation or reduction commitment in the subsequent commitment period, giving priority to domestic policies and measures; and
(c) A timetable for implementing such action, which enables the assessment of annual progress in the implementation, within a time frame that does not exceed three years or up to the end of the subsequent commitment period, whichever occurs sooner. At the request of the Party, the enforcement branch may, where the circumstances of an individual case so warrant, extend the time for implementing such action for a period which shall not exceed the maximum period of three years mentioned above.

7. The Party not in compliance under paragraph 5 above shall submit to the enforcement branch a progress report on the implementation of the compliance action plan on an annual basis.

8. For subsequent commitment periods, the rate referred to in paragraph 5 (a) above shall be determined by an amendment.

XVI. Relationship with Articles 16 and 19 of the Protocol

The procedures and mechanisms relating to compliance shall operate without prejudice to Articles 16 and 19 of the Protocol.

XVII. Secretariat

The secretariat referred to in Article 14 of the Protocol shall serve as the secretariat of the Committee.

PART IIIA

Oceans: global

London Convention on the Prevention of Marine Pollution by Dumping of Wastes and Other Matter, 29 December 1972

Editorial note

The London Convention on the Prevention of Marine Pollution by Dumping of Wastes and Other Matter prohibits the dumping of 'wastes and other matter' listed in Annex I, requires a specific permit to be granted for dumping 'wastes and other matter' listed in Annex II, and requires a general permit to be granted for dumping 'wastes and other matter' listed in Annex III (Article IV(1)). 'Wastes and other matter' is defined broadly as any type of material or substance (Article III(4)). The rules do not restrict a Party from prohibiting dumping of any matter not included in Annex I (Article IV(3)). Permits are subject to grants by national authorities in respect of all matter intended to be dumped that is loaded in a Party's territory and, if loaded in the territory of a non-Party, in respect of vessels flying its flag (Article VI). Parties are required to take measures to prevent and punish breaches of the Convention (Article VII). Parties also undertake to develop rules governing liability and dispute settlement (Article X). Exceptions to the Convention's obligations are permitted for dumping in cases of extreme risk to human life, ships or aircraft and where no alternative to dumping is apparent (Article V). In addition, the Convention does not apply to disposal of material in the normal operation of aircrafts, ships or other man-made structures or to materials disposed of in the course of exploiting the sea-bed resources (Articles III(1)(b) and III(1)(c)).

The Parties review the Convention at special and annual consultative meetings (Article XIV). Amendments to the Convention and the Annexes require adoption by two-thirds of the Parties in attendance at these meetings (Articles XV(1) and XV(2)). If the amendment is to the Convention, it enters into force for those Parties accepting it after two-thirds of the Parties accept it (Article XV(1)). If the amendment is to an Annex, it enters into force for those Parties accepting it upon adoption (Article XV(2)).

The Convention will be replaced entirely by a new Protocol adopted in 1996, which is not yet in force (see below).

Date of signature: 29 December 1972

Entry into force: 30 August 1975

Depositary: Mexico, USSR, United Kingdom and USA

Contracting Parties: Afghanistan, Angola, Antigua and Barbuda, Argentina, Australia, Azerbaijan, Barbados, Belarus, Belgium, Brazil, Canada, Cape Verde, Chile, China, Costa Rica, Congo (Democratic Republic of), Cote d'Ivoire, Croatia, Cuba, Cyprus, Denmark, Dominican Republic, Egypt, Finland, France, Gabon, Germany, Greece, Guatemala, Haiti, Honduras, Hungary, Iceland, Iran (Islamic Republic of), Ireland, Italy, Jamaica, Japan, Jordan, Kenya, Kiribati, Korea (Republic of), Libyan Arab Jamahiriya, Luxembourg, Malta, Mexico, Monaco, Morocco, Nauru, Netherlands, New Zealand, Nigeria, Norway, Oman, Pakistan, Panama, Papua New Guinea, Philippines, Poland, Portugal, Russian Federation, Saint Lucia, Seychelles, Slovenia, Solomon Islands, South Africa, Spain, Suriname, Sweden, Switzerland, Tonga, Tunisia, Ukraine, United Arab Emirates, United Kingdom, United States of America, Vanuatu, Yugoslavia, Hong Kong – China (Associate Member).

Website: www.londonconvention.org

Convention on the Prevention of Marine Pollution by Dumping of Wastes and Other Matter

The Contracting Parties to this Convention,

   Recognizing that the marine environment and the living organisms which it supports are of vital importance to humanity, and all people have an interest in assuring that it is so managed that its quality and resources are not impaired;

   Recognizing that the capacity of the sea to assimilate wastes and render them harmless, and its ability to regenerate natural resources, is not unlimited;

   Recognizing that States have, in accordance with the Charter of the United Nations and the principles of international law, the sovereign right to exploit their own resources pursuant to their own environmental policies, and the responsibility to ensure that activities within their jurisdiction or control do not cause damage to the environment of other States or of areas beyond the limits of national jurisdiction;

   Recalling resolution 2749(XXV) of the General Assembly of the United Nations on the principles governing the sea-bed and the ocean floor and the subsoil thereof, beyond the limits of national jurisdiction;

   Noting that marine pollution originates in many sources, such as dumping and discharges through the atmosphere, rivers, estuaries, outfalls and pipelines, and that it is important that States use the best practicable means to prevent such pollution and develop products and processes which will reduce the amount of harmful wastes to be disposed of;

Being convinced that international action to control the pollution of the sea by dumping can and must be taken without delay but that this action should not preclude discussion of measures to control other sources of marine pollution as soon as possible; and

Wishing to improve protection of the marine environment by encouraging States with a common interest in particular geographical areas to enter into appropriate agreements supplementary to this Convention;

Have agreed as follows:

Article I

Contracting Parties shall individually and collectively promote the effective control of all sources of pollution of the marine environment, and pledge themselves especially to take all practicable steps to prevent the pollution of the sea by the dumping of waste and other matter that is liable to create hazards to human health, to harm living resources and marine life, to damage amenities or to interfere with other legitimate uses of the sea.

Article II

Contracting Parties shall, as provided for in the following articles, take effective measures individually, according to their scientific, technical and economic capabilities, and collectively, to prevent marine pollution caused by dumping and shall harmonize their policies in this regard.

Article III

For the purposes of this Convention:

1.

(a) 'Dumping' means:
   (i) any deliberate disposal at sea of wastes or other matter from vessels, aircraft, platforms or other man-made structures at sea;
   (ii) any deliberate disposal at sea of vessels, aircraft, platforms or other man-made structures at sea.
(b) 'Dumping' does not include:
   (i) the disposal at sea of wastes or other matter incidental to, or derived from the normal operations of vessels, aircraft, platforms or other man-made structures at sea and their equipment, other than wastes or other matter transported by or to vessels, aircraft, platforms or other man-made structures at sea, operating for the purpose of disposal of such matter or derived from the treatment of such wastes or other matter on such vessels, aircraft, platforms or structures;

(ii) placement of matter for a purpose other than the mere disposal thereof, provided that such placement is not contrary to the aims of this Convention.

(c) The disposal of wastes or other matter directly arising from, or related to the exploration, exploitation and associated off-shore processing of sea-bed mineral resources will not be covered by the provisions of this Convention.

2. 'Vessels and aircraft' means waterborne or airborne craft of any type whatsoever. This expression includes air cushioned craft and floating craft, whether self-propelled or not.

3. 'Sea' means all marine waters other than the internal waters of States.

4. 'Wastes or other matter' means material and substance of any kind, form or description.

5. 'Special permit' means permission granted specifically on application in advance and in accordance with Annex II and Annex III.

6. 'General permit' means permission granted in advance and in accordance with Annex III.

7. 'The Organization' means the Organization designated by the Contracting Parties in accordance with article XIV(2).

Article IV

1. In accordance with the provisions of this Convention Contracting Parties shall prohibit the dumping of any wastes or other matter in whatever form or condition except as otherwise specified below:

(a) the dumping of wastes or other matter listed in Annex I is prohibited;
(b) the dumping of wastes or other matter listed in Annex II requires a prior special permit;
(c) the dumping of all other wastes or matter requires a prior general permit.

2. Any permit shall be issued only after careful consideration of all the factors set forth in Annex III, including prior studies of the characteristics of the dumping site, as set forth in sections B and C of that Annex.

3. No provision of this Convention is to be interpreted as preventing a Contracting Party from prohibiting, insofar as that Party is concerned, the dumping of wastes or other matter not mentioned in Annex I. That Party shall notify such measures to the Organization.

Article V

1. The provisions of article IV shall not apply when it is necessary to secure the safety of human life or of vessels, aircraft, platforms or other man-made structures at sea in cases of *force majeure* caused by stress of weather, or in any case which constitutes a danger to human life or a real threat to vessels, aircraft, platforms or other man-made structures at sea, if dumping appears to be the

only way of averting the threat and if there is every probability that the damage consequent upon such dumping will be less than would otherwise occur. Such dumping shall be so conducted as to minimize the likelihood of damage to human or marine life and shall be reported forthwith to the Organization.

2. A Contracting Party may issue a special permit as an exception to article IV(1)(a), in emergencies, posing unacceptable risk relating to human health and admitting no other feasible solution. Before doing so the Party shall consult any other country or countries that are likely to be affected and the Organization which, after consulting other Parties, and international organizations as appropriate, shall, in accordance with article XIV promptly recommend to the Party the most appropriate procedures to adopt. The Party shall follow these recommendations to the maximum extent feasible consistent with the time within which action must be taken and with the general obligation to avoid damage to the marine environment and shall inform the Organization of the action it takes. The Parties pledge themselves to assist one another in such situations.

3. Any Contracting Party may waive its rights under paragraph (2) at the time of, or subsequent to ratification of, or accession to this Convention.

Article VI

1. Each Contracting Party shall designate an appropriate authority or authorities to:

(a) issue special permits which shall be required prior to, and for, the dumping of matter listed in Annex II and in the circumstances provided for in article V(2);
(b) issue general permits which shall be required prior to, and for, the dumping of all other matter;
(c) keep records of the nature and quantities of all matter permitted to be dumped and the location, time and method of dumping;
(d) monitor individually, or in collaboration with other Parties and competent international organizations, the condition of the seas for the purposes of this Convention.

2. The appropriate authority or authorities of a contracting Party shall issue prior special or general permits in accordance with paragraph (1) in respect of matter intended for dumping:

(a) loaded in its territory;
(b) loaded by a vessel or aircraft registered in its territory or flying its flag, when the loading occurs in the territory of a State not party to this Convention.

3. In issuing permits under sub-paragraphs (1)(a) and (b) above, the appropriate authority or authorities shall comply with Annex III, together with such additional criteria, measures and requirements as they may consider relevant.

4. Each Contracting Party, directly or through a Secretariat established under a regional agreement, shall report to the Organization, and where appropriate to other Parties, the information specified in sub-paragraphs(c) and (d) of paragraph (1) above, and the criteria, measures and requirements it adopts in accordance with paragraph (3) above. The procedure to be followed and the nature of such reports shall be agreed by the Parties in consultation.

Article VII

1. Each Contracting Party shall apply the measures required to implement the present Convention to all:

(a) vessels and aircraft registered in its territory or flying its flag;
(b) vessels and aircraft loading in its territory or territorial seas matter which is to be dumped;
(c) vessels and aircraft and fixed or floating platforms under its jurisdiction believed to be engaged in dumping.

2. Each Party shall take in its territory appropriate measures to prevent and punish conduct in contravention of the provisions of this Convention.
3. The Parties agree to co-operate in the development of procedures for the effective application of this Convention particularly on the high seas, including procedures for the reporting of vessels and aircraft observed dumping in contravention of the Convention.
4. This Convention shall not apply to those vessels and aircraft entitled to sovereign immunity under international law. However, each Party shall ensure by the adoption of appropriate measures that such vessels and aircraft owned or operated by it act in a manner consistent with the object and purpose of this Convention, and shall inform the Organization accordingly.
5. Nothing in this Convention shall affect the right of each Party to adopt other measures, in accordance with the principles of international law, to prevent dumping at sea.

Article VIII

In order to further the objectives of this Convention, the Contracting Parties with common interests to protect the marine environment in a given geographical area shall endeavour, taking into account characteristic regional features, to enter into regional agreements consistent with this Convention for the prevention of pollution, especially by dumping. The Contracting Parties to the present Convention shall endeavour to act consistently with the objectives and provisions of such regional agreements, which shall be notified to them by the Organization. Contracting Parties shall seek to co-operate with the Parties to regional agreements in order to develop harmonized procedures to be followed by Contracting Parties to the different conventions concerned. Special attention shall be given to co-operation in the field of monitoring and scientific research.

Article IX

The Contracting Parties shall promote, through collaboration within the Organization and other international bodies, support for those Parties which request it for:

(a) the training of scientific and technical personnel;
(b) the supply of necessary equipment and facilities for research and monitoring;
(c) the disposal and treatment of waste and other measures to prevent or mitigate pollution caused by dumping;

preferably within the countries concerned, so furthering the aims and purposes of this Convention.

Article X

In accordance with the principles of international law regarding State responsibility for damage to the environment of other States or to any other area of the environment, caused by dumping of wastes and other matter of all kinds, the Contracting Parties undertake to develop procedures for the assessment of liability and the settlement of disputes regarding dumping.

Article XI

The Contracting Parties shall at their first consultative meeting consider procedures for the settlement of disputes concerning the interpretation and application of this Convention.

Article XII

The Contracting Parties pledge themselves to promote, within the competent specialized agencies and other international bodies, measures to protect the marine environment against pollution caused by:

(a) hydrocarbons, including oil and their wastes;
(b) other noxious or hazardous matter transported by vessels for purposes other than dumping;
(c) wastes generated in the course of operation of vessels, aircraft, platforms and other man-made structures at sea;
(d) radio-active pollutants from all sources, including vessels;
(e) agents of chemical and biological warfare;
(f) wastes or other matter directly arising from, or related to the exploration, exploitation and associated off-shore processing of sea-bed mineral resources.

The Parties will also promote, within the appropriate international organization, the codification of signals to be used by vessels engaged in dumping.

Article XIII

Nothing in this Convention shall prejudice the codification and development of the law of the sea by the United Nations Conference on the Law of the Sea convened pursuant to resolution 2750 C (XXV) of the General Assembly of the United Nations nor the present or future claims and legal views of any State concerning the law of the sea and the nature and extent of coastal and flag State jurisdiction. The Contracting Parties agree to consult at a meeting to be convened by the Organization after the Law of the Sea Conference, and in any case not later than 1976, with a view to defining the nature and extent of the right and the responsibility of a coastal State to apply the Convention in a zone adjacent to its coast.

Article XIV

1. The Government of the United Kingdom of Great Britain and Northern Ireland as a depositary shall call a meeting of the Contracting Parties not later than three months after the entry into force of this Convention to decide on organizational matters.

2. The Contracting Parties shall designate a competent Organization existing at the time of that meeting to be responsible for secretariat duties in relation to this Convention. Any Party to this Convention not being a member of this Organization shall make an appropriate contribution to the expenses incurred by the Organization in performing these duties.

3. The Secretariat duties of the Organization shall include:

(a) the convening of consultative meetings of the Contracting Parties not less frequently than once every two years and of special meetings of the Parties at any time on the request of two thirds of the Parties;

(b) preparing and assisting, in consultation with the Contracting Parties and appropriate International Organizations, in the development and implementation of procedures referred to in sub-paragraph (4)(e) of this article;

(c) considering enquiries by, and information from the Contracting Parties, consulting with them and with the appropriate International Organizations, and providing recommendations to the Parties on questions related to, but not specifically covered by the Convention;

(d) conveying to the Parties concerned all notifications received by the Organization in accordance with articles IV(3), V(1) and (2), VI(4), XV, XX and XXI.

Prior to the designation of the Organization these functions shall, as necessary, be performed by the depositary, who for this purpose shall be the Government of the United Kingdom of Great Britain and Northern Ireland.

4. Consultative or special meetings of the Contracting Parties shall keep under continuing review the implementation of this Convention and may, *inter alia*:

(a) review and adopt amendments to this Convention and its Annexes in accordance with article XV;

(b) invite the appropriate scientific body or bodies to collaborate with and to advise the Parties or the Organization on any scientific or technical aspect relevant to this Convention, including particularly the content of the Annexes;

(c) receive and consider reports made pursuant to article VI(4);

(d) promote co-operation with and between regional organizations concerned with the prevention of marine pollution;

(e) develop or adopt, in consultation with appropriate International Organizations, procedures referred to in article V(2), including basic criteria for determining exceptional and emergency situations, and procedures for consultative advice and the safe disposal of matter in such circumstances, including the designation of appropriate dumping areas, and recommend accordingly;

(f) consider any additional action that may be required.

5. The Contracting Parties at their first consultative meeting shall establish rules of procedure as necessary.

Article XV

1.

(a) At meetings of the Contracting Parties called in accordance with article XIV amendments to this Convention may be adopted by a two-thirds majority of those present. An amendment shall enter into force for the Parties which have accepted it on the sixtieth day after two thirds of the Parties shall have deposited an instrument of acceptance of the amendment with the Organization. Thereafter the amendment shall enter into force for any other Party 30 days after that Party deposits its instrument of acceptance of the amendment.

(b) The Organization shall inform all Contracting Parties of any request made for a special meeting under article XIV and of any amendments adopted at meetings of the Parties and of the date on which each such amendment enters into force for each Party.

2. Amendments to the Annexes will be based on scientific or technical considerations. Amendments to the annexes approved by a two-thirds majority of
those present at a meeting called in accordance with article XIV shall enter into
force for each Contracting Party immediately on notification of its acceptance
to the Organization and 100 days after approval by the meeting for all other
Parties except for those which before the end of the 100 days make a declaration that they are not able to accept the amendment at that time. Parties should
endeavour to signify their acceptance of an amendment to the Organization as
soon as possible after approval at a meeting. A Party may at any time substitute an acceptance for a previous declaration of objection and the amendment
previously objected to shall thereupon enter into force for that Party.

3. An acceptance or declaration of objection under this article shall be made
by the deposit of an instrument with the Organization. The Organization shall
notify all Contracting Parties of the receipt of such instruments.

4. Prior to the designation of the Organization, the Secretarial functions
herein attributed to it shall be performed temporarily by the Government of
the United Kingdom of Great Britain and Northern Ireland, as one of the
depositaries of this Convention.

Article XVI

This Convention shall be open for signature by any State at London, Mexico
City, Moscow and Washington from 29 December 1972 until 31 December
1973.

Article XVII

This Convention shall be subject to ratification. The instruments of ratification
shall be deposited with the Governments of Mexico, the Union of Soviet Socialist
Republics, the United Kingdom of Great Britain and Northern Ireland, and the
United States of America.

Article XVIII

After 31 December 1973, this Convention shall be open for accession by any
State. The instruments of accession shall be deposited with the Governments of
Mexico, the Union of Soviet Socialist Republics, the United Kingdom of Great
Britain and Northern Ireland, and the United States of America.

Article XIX

1. This Convention shall enter into force on the thirtieth day following the
date of deposit of the fifteenth instrument of ratification or accession.

2. For each Contracting Party ratifying or acceding to the Convention after
the deposit of the fifteenth instrument of ratification or accession, the Convention shall enter into force on the thirtieth day after deposit by such Party of its
instrument of ratification or accession.

Article XX

The depositaries shall inform Contracting Parties:

(a) of signatures to this Convention and of the deposit of instruments of ratification, accession or withdrawal, in accordance with articles XVI, XVII, XVIII and XXI, and
(b) of the date on which this Convention will enter into force, in accordance with article XIX.

Article XXI

Any Contracting Party may withdraw from this Convention by giving six months' notice in writing to a depositary, which shall promptly inform all Parties of such notice.

Article XXII

The original of this Convention of which the English, French, Russian and Spanish texts are equally authentic, shall be deposited with the Governments of Mexico, the Union of Soviet Socialist Republics, the United Kingdom of Great Britain and Northern Ireland and the United States of America who shall send certified copies thereof to all States.

IN WITNESS WHEREOF the undersigned Plenipotentiaries, being duly authorized thereto by their respective Governments, have signed the present Convention.

DONE in quadruplicate at London, Mexico City, Moscow and Washington, this twenty-ninth day of December, 1972.

Annex I
[Substances which are prohibited from ocean disposal]

1. Organohalogen compounds.
2. Mercury and mercury compounds.
3. Cadmium and cadmium compounds.
4. Persistent plastics and other persistent synthetic materials, for example, netting and ropes, which may float or may remain in suspension in the sea in such a manner as to interfere materially with fishing, navigation or other legitimate uses of the sea.
5. Crude oil and its wastes, refined petroleum products, petroleum, distillate residues, and any mixtures containing any of these, taken on board for the purpose of dumping.
6. Radioactive wastes or other radioactive matter.

7. Materials in whatever form (e.g. solids, liquids, semi-liquids, gases or in a living state) produced for biological and chemical warfare.

8. With the exception of paragraph 6 above, the preceding paragraphs of this Annex do not apply to substances which are rapidly rendered harmless by physical, chemical or biological processes in the sea provided they do not:

(i) make edible marine organisms unpalatable, or

(ii) endanger human health or that of domestic animals.

The consultative procedure provided for under Article XIV should be followed by a Party if there is doubt about the harmlessness of the substance.

9. Except for industrial waste as defined in paragraph 11 below, this Annex does not apply to wastes or other materials (e.g. sewage sludge and dredged material) containing the matters referred to in paragraphs 1–5 above as trace contaminants. Such wastes shall be subject to the provisions of Annexes II and III as appropriate.

Paragraph 6 does not apply to wastes or other materials (e.g. sewage sludge and dredged material) containing de minimis (exempt) levels of radioactivity as defined by the IAEA and adopted by the Contracting Parties. Unless otherwise prohibited by Annex I, such wastes shall be subject to the provisions of Annexes II and III as appropriate.

10.

(a) Incineration at sea of industrial waste, as defined in paragraph 11 below, and sewage sludge is prohibited.

(b) The incineration at sea of any other wastes or other matter requires the issue of a special permit.

(c) In the issue of special permits for incineration at sea Contracting Parties shall apply regulations as are developed under this Convention.

(d) For the purpose of this Annex:

(i) 'Marine incineration facility' means a vessel, platform, or other man-made structure operating for the purpose of incineration at sea.

(ii) 'Incineration at sea' means the deliberate combustion of wastes or other matter on marine incineration facilities for the purpose of their thermal destruction. Activities incidental to the normal operation of vessels, platforms or other man-made structures are excluded from the scope of this definition.

11. Industrial waste as from 1 January 1996.

For the purposes of this Annex:

'Industrial waste' means waste materials generated by manufacturing or processing operations and does not apply to:

(a) dredged material;

(b) sewage sludge;

(c) fish waste, or organic materials resulting from industrial fish processing operations;

(d) vessels and platforms or other man-made structures at sea, provided that material capable of creating floating debris or otherwise contributing to pollution of the marine environment has been removed to the maximum extent;

(e) uncontaminated inert geological materials the chemical constituents of which are unlikely to be released into the marine environment;

(f) uncontaminated organic materials of natural origin.

Dumping of wastes and other matter specified in subparagraphs (a) – (f) above shall be subject to all other provisions of Annex I, and to the provisions of Annexes II and III.

This paragraph shall not apply to the radioactive wastes or any other radioactive matter referred to in paragraph 6 of this Annex.

12. Within 25 years from the date on which the amendment to paragraph 6 enters into force and at each 25 year interval thereafter, the Contracting Parties shall complete a scientific study relating to all radioactive wastes and other radioactive matter other than high level wastes or matter, taking into account such other factors as the Contracting Parties consider appropriate, and shall review the position of such substances on Annex I in accordance with the procedures set forth in Article XV.

(Addendum to Annex I – Regulations for the control of incineration of wastes and other matter at sea – omissis)

Annex II

The following substances and materials requiring special care are listed for the purposes of Article VI(1)(a).

A. Wastes containing significant amounts of the matters listed below:

arsenic   )
beryllium   )
chromium   )
copper   )   and their compounds
lead   )
nickel   )
vanadium   )
zinc   )
organosilicon compounds
cyanides
fluorides
pesticides and their by-products not covered in Annex I.

B. Containers, scrap metal and other bulky wastes liable to sink to the sea bottom which may present a serious obstacle to fishing or navigation.

C. In the issue of special permits for the incineration of substances and materials listed in this Annex, the Contracting Parties shall apply the Regulations for the Control of Incineration of Wastes and Other Matter at Sea set forth in the Addendum to Annex I and take full account of the Technical Guidelines on the Control of Incineration of Wastes and Other Matter at Sea adopted by the Contracting Parties in consultation, to the extent specified in these Regulations and Guidelines.

D. Materials which, though of a non-toxic nature, may become harmful due to the quantities in which they are dumped, or which are liable to seriously reduce amenities.

Annex III

Provisions to be considered in establishing criteria governing the issue of permits for the dumping of matter at sea, taking into account article IV(2), include:

A – Characteristics and composition of the matter

1. Total amount and average composition of matter dumped (e.g. per year).
2. Form, e.g. solid, sludge, liquid, or gaseous.
3. Properties: physical (e.g. solubility and density), chemical and biochemical (e.g. oxygen demand, nutrients) and biological (e.g. presence of viruses, bacteria, yeasts, parasites).
4. Toxicity.
5. Persistence: physical, chemical and biological.
6. Accumulation and biotransformation in biological materials or sediments.
7. Susceptibility to physical, chemical and biochemical changes and interaction in the aquatic environment with other dissolved organic and inorganic materials.
8. Probability of production of taints or other changes reducing marketability of resources (fish, shellfish, etc.).
9. In issuing a permit for dumping, Contracting Parties should consider whether an adequate scientific basis exists concerning characteristics and composition of the matter to be dumped to assess the impact of the matter on marine life and on human health.

B – Characteristics of dumping site and method of deposit

1. Location (e.g. co-ordinates of the dumping area, depth and distance from the coast), location in relation to other areas (e.g. amenity areas, spawning, nursery and fishing areas and exploitable resources).
2. Rate of disposal per specific period (e.g. quantity per day, per week, per month).

3. Methods of packaging and containment, if any.
4. Initial dilution achieved by proposed method of release.
5. Dispersal characteristics (e.g. effects of currents, tides and wind on horizontal transport and vertical mixing).
6. Water characteristics (e.g. temperature, pH, salinity, stratification, oxygen indices of pollution-dissolved oxygen (DO), chemical oxygen demand (COD), biochemical oxygen demand (BOD) – nitrogen present in organic and mineral form including ammonia, suspended matter, other nutrients and productivity).
7. Bottom characteristics (e.g. topography, geochemical and geological characteristics and biological productivity).
8. Existence and effects of other dumpings which have been made in the dumping area (e.g. heavy metal background reading and organic carbon content).
9. In issuing a permit for dumping, Contracting Parties should consider whether an adequate scientific basis exists for assessing the consequences of such dumping, as outlined in this Annex, taking into account seasonal variations.

C – General considerations and conditions

1. Possible effects on amenities (e.g. presence of floating or stranded material, turbidity, objectionable odour, discolouration and foaming).
2. Possible effects on marine life, fish and shellfish culture, fish stocks and fisheries, seaweed harvesting and culture.
3. Possible effects on other uses of the sea (e.g. impairment of water quality for industrial use, underwater corrosion of structures, interference with ship operations from floating materials, interference with fishing or navigation through deposit of waste or solid objects on the sea floor and protection of areas of special importance for scientific or conservation purposes).
4. The practical availability of alternative land-based methods of treatment, disposal or elimination, or of treatment to render the matter less harmful for dumping at sea.

Protocol to the Convention on the Prevention of Marine Pollution by Dumping of Wastes and Other Matter, 7 November 1996

Editorial note

The 1996 Protocol will replace the 1972 London Convention once in force. Twenty-six ratifications or other expressions of consent by States are required before the Protocol will enter into force; and at least 15 of these must come from Contracting Parties to the Convention (Article 25(1)). The objective of the 1996 Protocol is to 'protect and preserve the marine environment from all sources of pollution' and, to this end, Contracting Parties are required to take effective measures to prevent, reduce and where practicable eliminate marine pollution caused by dumping or incineration at sea (Article 2). In respect of internal waters, each Contracting Party has a discretion either to apply the provisions of the Protocol or to adopt 'other effective permitting and regulatory measures to control the deliberate disposal of wastes or other matter' where such disposal would be 'dumping' or 'incineration at sea' within the meaning of the Protocol (Article 7(2)). The purpose of the Protocol is similar to that of the 1972 London Convention, but the Protocol is more restrictive: application of a 'precautionary approach' to environmental protection from dumping of wastes or other matter is included as a general obligation (Article 3(1)); a 'reverse list' approach is adopted whereby Contracting Parties are required to prohibit the dumping of 'any wastes or other matter' with the exception of those listed in Annex 1, which require a permit; (Article 4(1) and 4(2)) incineration of wastes at sea is prohibited (Article 5); and the export of wastes or other matter to other countries for dumping or incineration at sea is banned (Article 6). The Protocol includes extended technical co-operation and assistance provisions, (Article 13) as well as a commitment to develop procedures for assessing and promoting compliance with the Protocol within two years of its entry into force (Article 11). Article 26 of the Protocol makes provision for a transitional period to allow new Contracting Parties to phase in compliance with the Protocol over a period of five years, provided certain conditions are met.

Date of signature: 7 November 1996

Entry into force: Not yet in force.

Depositary: Secretary-General IMO

Contracting Parties: Angola, Australia, Canada, Denmark, Georgia,
                       Germany, Ireland, New Zealand, Norway, South Africa,
                       Spain, Sweden, Switzerland, Trinidad and Tobago,
                       United Kingdom, Vanuatu.

Websites: www.londonconvention.org
                       www.imo.org

1996 Protocol to the Convention on the Prevention of Marine Pollution by Dumping of Wastes and Other Matter

The Contracting Parties to this Protocol,

Stressing the need to protect the marine environment and to promote the sustainable use and conservation of marine resources,

Noting in this regard the achievements within the framework of the Convention on the Prevention of Marine Pollution by Dumping of Wastes and Other Matter, 1972 and especially the evolution towards approaches based on precaution and prevention,

Noting further the contribution in this regard by complementary regional and national instruments which aim to protect the marine environment and which take account of specific circumstances and needs of those regions and States,

Reaffirming the value of a global approach to these matters and in particular the importance of continuing co-operation and collaboration between Contracting Parties in implementing the Convention and the Protocol,

Recognizing that it may be desirable to adopt, on a national or regional level, more stringent measures with respect to prevention and elimination of pollution of the marine environment from dumping at sea than are provided for in international conventions or other types of agreements with a global scope,

Taking into account relevant international agreements and actions, especially the United Nations Convention on the Law of the Sea, 1982, the Rio Declaration on Environment and Development and Agenda 21,

Recognizing also the interests and capacities of developing States and in particular small island developing States,

Being convinced that further international action to prevent, reduce and where practicable eliminate pollution of the sea caused by dumping can and must be taken without delay to protect and preserve the marine environment and to manage human activities in such a manner that the marine ecosystem will continue to sustain the legitimate uses of the sea and will continue to meet the needs of present and future generations,

   Have agreed as follows:

Article 1
Definitions

   For the purposes of this Protocol:

1. 'Convention' means the Convention on the Prevention of Marine Pollution by Dumping of Wastes and Other Matter, 1972, as amended.
2. 'Organization' means the International Maritime Organization.
3. 'Secretary-General' means the Secretary-General of the Organization.
4.1 'Dumping' means:
   .1 any deliberate disposal into the sea of wastes or other matter from vessels, aircraft, platforms or other man-made structures at sea;
   .2 any deliberate disposal into the sea of vessels, aircraft, platforms or other man-made structures at sea;
   .3 any storage of wastes or other matter in the seabed and the subsoil thereof from vessels, aircraft, platforms or other man-made structures at sea; and
   .4 any abandonment or toppling at site of platforms or other man-made structures at sea, for the sole purpose of deliberate disposal.
  .2 'Dumping' does not include:
   .1 the disposal into the sea of wastes or other matter incidental to, or derived from the normal operations of vessels, aircraft, platforms or other man-made structures at sea and their equipment, other than wastes or other matter transported by or to vessels, aircraft, platforms or other man-made structures at sea, operating for the purpose of disposal of such matter or derived from the treatment of such wastes or other matter on such vessels, aircraft, platforms or other man-made structures;
   .2 placement of matter for a purpose other than the mere disposal thereof, provided that such placement is not contrary to the aims of this Protocol; and
   .3 notwithstanding paragraph 4.1.4, abandonment in the sea of matter (e.g., cables, pipelines and marine research devices) placed for a purpose other than the mere disposal thereof.
  .3 The disposal or storage of wastes or other matter directly arising from, or related to the exploration, exploitation and associated off-shore processing of seabed mineral resources is not covered by the provisions of this Protocol.
5.1 'Incineration at sea' means the combustion on board a vessel, platform or other man-made structure at sea of wastes or other matter for the purpose of their deliberate disposal by thermal destruction.

.2 'Incineration at sea' does not include the incineration of wastes or other matter on board a vessel, platform, or other man-made structure at sea if such wastes or other matter were generated during the normal operation of that vessel, platform or other man-made structure at sea.

6. 'Vessels and aircraft' means waterborne or airborne craft of any type whatsoever. This expression includes sair-cushioned craft and floating craft, whether self-propelled or not.

7. 'Sea' means all marine waters other than the internal waters of States, as well as the seabed and the subsoil thereof; it does not include sub-seabed repositories accessed only from land.

8. 'Wastes or other matter' means material and substance of any kind, form or description.

9. 'Permit' means permission granted in advance and in accordance with relevant measures adopted pursuant to article 4.1.2 or 8.2.

10. 'Pollution' means the introduction, directly or indirectly, by human activity, of wastes or other matter into the sea which results or is likely to result in such deleterious effects as harm to living resources and marine ecosystems, hazards to human health, hindrance to marine activities, including fishing and other legitimate uses of the sea, impairment of quality for use of sea water and reduction of amenities.

Article 2
Objectives

Contracting Parties shall individually and collectively protect and preserve the marine environment from all sources of pollution and take effective measures, according to their scientific, technical and economic capabilities, to prevent, reduce and where practicable eliminate pollution caused by dumping or incineration at sea of wastes or other matter. Where appropriate, they shall harmonize their policies in this regard.

Article 3
General obligations

1. In implementing this Protocol, Contracting Parties shall apply a precautionary approach to environmental protection from dumping of wastes or other matter whereby appropriate preventative measures are taken when there is reason to believe that wastes or other matter introduced into the marine environment are likely to cause harm even when there is no conclusive evidence to prove a causal relation between inputs and their effects.

2. Taking into account the approach that the polluter should, in principle, bear the cost of pollution, each Contracting Party shall endeavour to promote practices whereby those it has authorized to engage in dumping or incineration at sea bear the cost of meeting the pollution prevention and control

requirements for the authorized activities, having due regard to the public interest.

3. In implementing the provisions of this Protocol, Contracting Parties shall act so as not to transfer, directly or indirectly, damage or likelihood of damage from one part of the environment to another or transform one type of pollution into another.

4. No provision of this Protocol shall be interpreted as preventing Contracting Parties from taking, individually or jointly, more stringent measures in accordance with international law with respect to the prevention, reduction and where practicable elimination of pollution.

Article 4
Dumping of wastes or other matter

1.1 Contracting Parties shall prohibit the dumping of any wastes or other matter with the exception of those listed in Annex 1.

.2 The dumping of wastes or other matter listed in Annex 1 shall require a permit. Contracting Parties shall adopt administrative or legislative measures to ensure that issuance of permits and permit conditions comply with provisions of Annex 2. Particular attention shall be paid to opportunities to avoid dumping in favour of environmentally preferable alternatives.

2. No provision of this Protocol shall be interpreted as preventing a Contracting Party from prohibiting, insofar as that Contracting Party is concerned, the dumping of wastes or other matter mentioned in Annex 1. That Contracting Party shall notify the Organization of such measures.

Article 5
Incineration at sea

Contracting Parties shall prohibit incineration at sea of wastes or other matter.

Article 6
Export of wastes or other matter

Contracting Parties shall not allow the export of wastes or other matter to other countries for dumping or incineration at sea.

Article 7
Internal waters

1. Notwithstanding any other provision of this Protocol, this Protocol shall relate to internal waters only to the extent provided for in paragraphs 2 and 3.

2. Each Contracting Party shall at its discretion either apply the provisions of this Protocol or adopt other effective permitting and regulatory measures to control the deliberate disposal of wastes or other matter in marine internal

waters where such disposal would be 'dumping' or 'incineration at sea' within the meaning of article 1, if conducted at sea.

3. Each Contracting Party should provide the Organization with information on legislation and institutional mechanisms regarding implementation, compliance and enforcement in marine internal waters. Contracting Parties should also use their best efforts to provide on a voluntary basis summary reports on the type and nature of the materials dumped in marine internal waters.

Article 8
Exceptions

1. The provisions of articles 4.1 and 5 shall not apply when it is necessary to secure the safety of human life or of vessels, aircraft, platforms or other man-made structures at sea in cases of *force majeure* caused by stress of weather, or in any case which constitutes a danger to human life or a real threat to vessels, aircraft, platforms or other man-made structures at sea, if dumping or incineration at sea appears to be the only way of averting the threat and if there is every probability that the damage consequent upon such dumping or incineration at sea will be less than would otherwise occur. Such dumping or incineration at sea shall be conducted so as to minimize the likelihood of damage to human or marine life and shall be reported forthwith to the Organization.

2. A Contracting Party may issue a permit as an exception to articles 4.1 and 5, in emergencies posing an unacceptable threat to human health, safety, or the marine environment and admitting of no other feasible solution. Before doing so the Contracting Party shall consult any other country or countries that are likely to be affected and the Organization which, after consulting other Contracting Parties, and competent international organizations as appropriate, shall, in accordance with article 18.6 promptly recommend to the Contracting Party the most appropriate procedures to adopt. The Contracting Party shall follow these recommendations to the maximum extent feasible consistent with the time within which action must be taken and with the general obligation to avoid damage to the marine environment and shall inform the Organization of the action it takes. The Contracting Parties pledge themselves to assist one another in such situations.

3. Any Contracting Party may waive its rights under paragraph 2 at the time of, or subsequent to ratification of, or accession to this Protocol.

Article 9
Issuance of permits and reporting

1. Each Contracting Party shall designate an appropriate authority or authorities to:

.1 issue permits in accordance with this Protocol;

.2 keep records of the nature and quantities of all wastes or other matter for which dumping permits have been issued and where practicable the quantities actually dumped and the location, time and method of dumping; and

.3 monitor individually, or in collaboration with other Contracting Parties and competent international organizations, the condition of the sea for the purposes of this Protocol.

2. The appropriate authority or authorities of a Contracting Party shall issue permits in accordance with this Protocol in respect of wastes or other matter intended for dumping or, as provided for in article 8.2, incineration at sea:

.1 loaded in its territory; and

.2 loaded onto a vessel or aircraft registered in its territory or flying its flag, when the loading occurs in the territory of a State not a Contracting Party to this Protocol.

3. In issuing permits, the appropriate authority or authorities shall comply with the requirements of article 4, together with such additional criteria, measures and requirements as they may consider relevant.

4. Each Contracting Party, directly or through a secretariat established under a regional agreement, shall report to the Organization and where appropriate to other Contracting Parties:

.1 the information specified in paragraphs 1.2 and 1.3;

.2 the administrative and legislative measures taken to implement the provisions of this Protocol, including a summary of enforcement measures; and

.3 the effectiveness of the measures referred to in paragraph 4.2 and any problems encountered in their application.

The information referred to in paragraphs 1.2 and 1.3 shall be submitted on an annual basis. The information referred to in paragraphs 4.2 and 4.3 shall be submitted on a regular basis.

5. Reports submitted under paragraphs 4.2 and 4.3 shall be evaluated by an appropriate subsidiary body as determined by the Meeting of Contracting Parties. This body will report its conclusions to an appropriate Meeting or Special Meeting of Contracting Parties.

Article 10
Application and enforcement

1. Each Contracting Party shall apply the measures required to implement this Protocol to all:

.1 vessels and aircraft registered in its territory or flying its flag;

.2 vessels and aircraft loading in its territory the wastes or other matter which are to be dumped or incinerated at sea; and

.3 vessels, aircraft and platforms or other man-made structures believed to be engaged in dumping or incineration at sea in areas within which it is entitled to exercise jurisdiction in accordance with international law.

2. Each Contracting Party shall take appropriate measures in accordance with international law to prevent and if necessary punish acts contrary to the provisions of this Protocol.

3. Contracting Parties agree to co-operate in the development of procedures for the effective application of this Protocol in areas beyond the jurisdiction of any State, including procedures for the reporting of vessels and aircraft observed dumping or incinerating at sea in contravention of this Protocol.

4. This Protocol shall not apply to those vessels and aircraft entitled to sovereign immunity under international law. However, each Contracting Party shall ensure by the adoption of appropriate measures that such vessels and aircraft owned or operated by it act in a manner consistent with the object and purpose of this Protocol and shall inform the Organization accordingly.

5. A State may, at the time it expresses its consent to be bound by this Protocol, or at any time thereafter, declare that it shall apply the provisions of this Protocol to its vessels and aircraft referred to in paragraph 4, recognising that only that State may enforce those provisions against such vessels and aircraft.

Article 11
Compliance procedures

1. No later than two years after the entry into force of this Protocol, the Meeting of Contracting Parties shall establish those procedures and mechanisms necessary to assess and promote compliance with this Protocol. Such procedures and mechanisms shall be developed with a view to allowing for the full and open exchange of information, in a constructive manner.

2. After full consideration of any information submitted pursuant to this Protocol and any recommendations made through procedures or mechanisms established under paragraph 1, the Meeting of Contracting Parties may offer advice, assistance or co-operation to Contracting Parties and non-Contracting Parties.

Article 12
Regional co-operation

In order to further the objectives of this Protocol, Contracting Parties with common interests to protect the marine environment in a given geographical area shall endeavour, taking into account characteristic regional features, to enhance regional co-operation including the conclusion of regional agreements consistent with this Protocol for the prevention, reduction and where practicable elimination of pollution caused by dumping or incineration at sea of wastes or other matter. Contracting Parties shall seek to co-operate with the parties to regional agreements in order to develop harmonized procedures to be followed by Contracting Parties to the different conventions concerned.

Article 13
Technical co-operation and assistance

1. Contracting Parties shall, through collaboration within the Organization and in co-ordination with other competent international organizations, promote bilateral and multilateral support for the prevention, reduction and where practicable elimination of pollution caused by dumping as provided for in this Protocol to those Contracting Parties that request it for:

   .1 training of scientific and technical personnel for research, monitoring and enforcement, including as appropriate the supply of necessary equipment and facilities, with a view to strengthening national capabilities;

   .2 advice on implementation of this Protocol;

   .3 information and technical co-operation relating to waste minimization and clean production processes;

   .4 information and technical co-operation relating to the disposal and treatment of waste and other measures to prevent, reduce and where practicable eliminate pollution caused by dumping; and

   .5 access to and transfer of environmentally sound technologies and corresponding know-how, in particular to developing countries and countries in transition to market economies, on favourable terms, including on concessional and preferential terms, as mutually agreed, taking into account the need to protect intellectual property rights as well as the special needs of developing countries and countries in transition to market economies.

2. The Organization shall perform the following functions:

   .1 forward requests from Contracting Parties for technical co-operation to other Contracting Parties, taking into account such factors as technical capabilities;

   .2 co-ordinate requests for assistance with other competent international organizations, as appropriate; and

   .3 subject to the availability of adequate resources, assist developing countries and those in transition to market economies, which have declared their intention to become Contracting Parties to this Protocol, to examine the means necessary to achieve full implementation.

Article 14
Scientific and technical research

1. Contracting Parties shall take appropriate measures to promote and facilitate scientific and technical research on the prevention, reduction and where practicable elimination of pollution by dumping and other sources of

marine pollution relevant to this Protocol. In particular, such research should include observation, measurement, evaluation and analysis of pollution by scientific methods.

2. Contracting Parties shall, to achieve the objectives of this Protocol, promote the availability of relevant information to other Contracting Parties who request it on:

   .1 scientific and technical activities and measures undertaken in accordance with this Protocol;

   .2 marine scientific and technological programmes and their objectives; and

   .3 the impacts observed from the monitoring and assessment conducted pursuant to article 9.1.3.

Article 15
Responsibility and liability

In accordance with the principles of international law regarding State responsibility for damage to the environment of other States or to any other area of the environment, the Contracting Parties undertake to develop procedures regarding liability arising from the dumping or incineration at sea of wastes or other matter.

Article 16
Settlement of disputes

1. Any disputes regarding the interpretation or application of this Protocol shall be resolved in the first instance through negotiation, mediation or conciliation, or other peaceful means chosen by parties to the dispute.

2. If no resolution is possible within twelve months after one Contracting Party has notified another that a dispute exists between them, the dispute shall be settled, at the request of a party to the dispute, by means of the Arbitral Procedure set forth in Annex 3, unless the parties to the dispute agree to use one of the procedures listed in paragraph 1 of Article 287 of the 1982 United Nations Convention on the Law of the Sea. The parties to the dispute may so agree, whether or not they are also States Parties to the 1982 United Nations Convention on the Law of the Sea.

3. In the event an agreement to use one of the procedures listed in paragraph 1 of Article 287 of the 1982 United Nations Convention on the Law of the Sea is reached, the provisions set forth in Part XV of that Convention that are related to the chosen procedure would also apply, *mutatis mutandis*.

4. The twelve month period referred to in paragraph 2 may be extended for another twelve months by mutual consent of the parties concerned.

5. Notwithstanding paragraph 2, any State may, at the time it expresses its consent to be bound by this Protocol, notify the Secretary-General that, when it is a party to a dispute about the interpretation or application of

article 3.1 or 3.2, its consent will be required before the dispute may be settled by means of the Arbitral Procedure set forth in Annex 3.

Article 17
International co-operation

Contracting Parties shall promote the objectives of this Protocol within the competent international organizations.

Article 18
Meetings of Contracting Parties

1. Meetings of Contracting Parties or Special Meetings of Contracting Parties shall keep under continuing review the implementation of this Protocol and evaluate its effectiveness with a view to identifying means of strengthening action, where necessary, to prevent, reduce and where practicable eliminate pollution caused by dumping and incineration at sea of wastes or other matter. To these ends, Meetings of Contracting Parties or Special Meetings of Contracting Parties may:
   .1 review and adopt amendments to this Protocol in accordance with articles 21 and 22;
   .2 establish subsidiary bodies, as required, to consider any matter with a view to facilitating the effective implementation of this Protocol;
   .3 invite appropriate expert bodies to advise the Contracting Parties or the Organization on matters relevant to this Protocol;
   .4 promote co-operation with competent international organizations concerned with the prevention and control of pollution;
   .5 consider the information made available pursuant to article 9.4;
   .6 develop or adopt, in consultation with competent international organizations, procedures referred to in article 8.2, including basic criteria for determining exceptional and emergency situations, and procedures for consultative advice and the safe disposal of matter at sea in such circumstances;
   .7 consider and adopt resolutions; and
   .8 consider any additional action that may be required.
2. The Contracting Parties at their first Meeting shall establish rules of procedure as necessary.

Article 19
Duties of the organization

1. The Organization shall be responsible for Secretariat duties in relation to this Protocol. Any Contracting Party to this Protocol not being a member of this Organization shall make an appropriate contribution to the expenses incurred by the Organization in performing these duties.
2. Secretariat duties necessary for the administration of this Protocol include:

.1 convening Meetings of Contracting Parties once per year, unless otherwise decided by Contracting Parties, and Special Meetings of Contracting Parties at any time on the request of two-thirds of the Contracting Parties;

.2 providing advice on request on the implementation of this Protocol and on guidance and procedures developed thereunder;

.3 considering enquiries by, and information from Contracting Parties, consulting with them and with the competent international organizations, and providing recommendations to Contracting Parties on questions related to, but not specifically covered by, this Protocol;

.4 preparing and assisting, in consultation with Contracting Parties and the competent international organizations, in the development and implementation of procedures referred to in article 18.6.;

.5 conveying to the Contracting Parties concerned all notifications received by the Organization in accordance with this Protocol; and

.6 preparing, every two years, a budget and a financial account for the administration of this Protocol which shall be distributed to all Contracting Parties.

3. The Organization shall, subject to the availability of adequate resources, in addition to the requirements set out in article 13.2.3.

.1 collaborate in assessments of the state of the marine environment; and

.2 co-operate with competent international organizations concerned with the prevention and control of pollution.

Article 20
Annexes

Annexes to this Protocol form an integral part of this Protocol.

Article 21
Amendment of the Protocol

1. Any Contracting Party may propose amendments to the articles of this Protocol. The text of a proposed amendment shall be communicated to Contracting Parties by the Organization at least six months prior to its consideration at a Meeting of Contracting Parties or a Special Meeting of Contracting Parties.

2. Amendments to the articles of this Protocol shall be adopted by a two-thirds majority vote of the Contracting Parties which are present and voting at the Meeting of Contracting Parties or Special Meeting of Contracting Parties designated for this purpose.

3. An amendment shall enter into force for the Contracting Parties which have accepted it on the sixtieth day after two-thirds of the Contracting Parties shall have deposited an instrument of acceptance of the amendment with the Organization. Thereafter the amendment shall enter into force for any other

Contracting Party on the sixtieth day after the date on which that Contracting Party has deposited its instrument of acceptance of the amendment.

4. The Secretary-General shall inform Contracting Parties of any amendments adopted at Meetings of Contracting Parties and of the date on which such amendments enter into force generally and for each Contracting Party.

5. After entry into force of an amendment to this Protocol, any State that becomes a Contracting Party to this Protocol shall become a Contracting Party to this Protocol as amended, unless two-thirds of the Contracting Parties present and voting at the Meeting or Special Meeting of Contracting Parties adopting the amendment agree otherwise.

Article 22
Amendment of the Annexes

1. Any Contracting Party may propose amendments to the Annexes to this Protocol. The text of a proposed amendment shall be communicated to Contracting Parties by the Organization at least six months prior to its consideration by a Meeting of Contracting Parties or Special Meeting of Contracting Parties.

2. Amendments to the Annexes other than Annex 3 will be based on scientific or technical considerations and may take into account legal, social and economic factors as appropriate. Such amendments shall be adopted by a two-thirds majority vote of the Contracting Parties present and voting at a Meeting of Contracting Parties or Special Meeting of Contracting Parties designated for this purpose.

3. The Organization shall without delay communicate to Contracting Parties amendments to the Annexes that have been adopted at a Meeting of Contracting Parties or Special Meeting of Contracting Parties.

4. Except as provided in paragraph 7, amendments to the Annexes shall enter into force for each Contracting Party immediately on notification of its acceptance to the Organization or 100 days after the date of their adoption at a Meeting of Contracting Parties, if that is later, except for those Contracting Parties which before the end of the 100 days make a declaration that they are not able to accept the amendment at that time. A Contracting Party may at any time substitute an acceptance for a previous declaration of objection and the amendment previously objected to shall thereupon enter into force for that Contracting Party.

5. The Secretary-General shall without delay notify Contracting Parties of instruments of acceptance or objection deposited with the Organization.

6. A new Annex or an amendment to an Annex which is related to an amendment to the articles of this Protocol shall not enter into force until such time as the amendment to the articles of this Protocol enters into force.

7. With regard to amendments to Annex 3 concerning the Arbitral Procedure and with regard to the adoption and entry into force of new Annexes the procedures on amendments to the articles of this Protocol shall apply.

Article 23
Relationship between the Protocol and the Convention

This Protocol will supersede the Convention as between Contracting Parties to this Protocol which are also Parties to the Convention.

Article 24
Signature, ratification, acceptance, approval and accession

1. This Protocol shall be open for signature by any State at the Headquarters of the Organization from 1 April 1997 to 31 March 1998 and shall thereafter remain open for accession by any State.
2. States may become Contracting Parties to this Protocol by:
    .1 signature not subject to ratification, acceptance or approval; or
    .2 signature subject to ratification, acceptance or approval, followed by ratification, acceptance or approval; or
    .3 accession.
3. Ratification, acceptance, approval or accession shall be effected by the deposit of an instrument to that effect with the Secretary-General.

Article 25
Entry into force

1. This Protocol shall enter into force on the thirtieth day following the date on which:
    .1 at least 26 States have expressed their consent to be bound by this Protocol in accordance with article 24; and
    .2 at least 15 Contracting Parties to the Convention are included in the number of States referred to in paragraph 1.1.
2. For each State that has expressed its consent to be bound by this Protocol in accordance with article 24 following the date referred to in paragraph 1, this Protocol shall enter into force on the thirtieth day after the date on which such State expressed its consent.

Article 26
Transitional period

1. Any State that was not a Contracting Party to the Convention before 31 December 1996 and that expresses its consent to be bound by this Protocol prior to its entry into force or within five years after its entry into force may, at the time it expresses its consent, notify the Secretary-General that, for reasons described in the notification, it will not be able to comply with specific provisions of this Protocol other than those provided in

paragraph 2, for a transitional period that shall not exceed that described in paragraph 4.

2. No notification made under paragraph 1 shall affect the obligations of a Contracting Party to this Protocol with respect to incineration at sea or the dumping of radioactive wastes or other radioactive matter.

3. Any Contracting Party to this Protocol that has notified the Secretary-General under paragraph 1 that, for the specified transitional period, it will not be able to comply, in part or in whole, with article 4.1 or article 9 shall nonetheless during that period prohibit the dumping of wastes or other matter for which it has not issued a permit, use its best efforts to adopt administrative or legislative measures to ensure that issuance of permits and permit conditions comply with the provisions of Annex 2, and notify the Secretary-General of any permits issued.

4. Any transitional period specified in a notification made under paragraph 1 shall not extend beyond five years after such notification is submitted.

5. Contracting Parties that have made a notification under paragraph 1 shall submit to the first Meeting of Contracting Parties occurring after deposit of their instrument of ratification, acceptance, approval or accession a programme and timetable to achieve full compliance with this Protocol, together with any requests for relevant technical co-operation and assistance in accordance with article 13 of this Protocol.

6. Contracting Parties that have made a notification under paragraph 1 shall establish procedures and mechanisms for the transitional period to implement and monitor submitted programmes designed to achieve full compliance with this Protocol. A report on progress toward compliance shall be submitted by such Contracting Parties to each Meeting of Contracting Parties held during their transitional period for appropriate action.

Article 27
Withdrawal

1. Any Contracting Party may withdraw from this Protocol at any time after the expiry of two years from the date on which this Protocol enters into force for that Contracting Party.

2. Withdrawal shall be effected by the deposit of an instrument of withdrawal with the Secretary-General.

3. A withdrawal shall take effect one year after receipt by the Secretary-General of the instrument of withdrawal or such longer period as may be specified in that instrument.

Article 28
Depositary

1. This Protocol shall be deposited with the Secretary-General.

2. In addition to the functions specified in articles 10.5, 16.5, 21.4, 22.5 and 26.5, the Secretary-General shall:

   .1 inform all States which have signed this Protocol or acceded thereto of:
- .1 each new signature or deposit of an instrument of ratification, acceptance, approval or accession, together with the date thereof;
- .2 the date of entry into force of this Protocol; and
- .3 the deposit of any instrument of withdrawal from this Protocol together with the date on which it was received and the date on which the withdrawal takes effect.

   .2 transmit certified copies of this Protocol to all States which have signed this Protocol or acceded thereto.

3. As soon as this Protocol enters into force, a certified true copy thereof shall be transmitted by the Secretary-General to the Secretariat of the United Nations for registration and publication in accordance with Article 102 of the Charter of the United Nations.

Article 29
Authentic texts

This Protocol is established in a single original in the Arabic, Chinese, English, French, Russian and Spanish languages, each text being equally authentic.

IN WITNESS WHEREOF the undersigned being duly authorized by their respective Governments for that purpose have signed this Protocol.

DONE AT LONDON, this seventh day of November, one thousand nine hundred and ninety-six.

Annex 1
Wastes or other matter that may be considered for dumping

1. The following wastes or other matter are those that may be considered for dumping being mindful of the Objectives and General Obligations of this Protocol set out in articles 2 and 3:
   - .1 dredged material;
   - .2 sewage sludge;
   - .3 fish waste, or material resulting from industrial fish processing operations;
   - .4 vessels and platforms or other man-made structures at sea;
   - .5 inert, inorganic geological material;
   - .6 organic material of natural origin; and
   - .7 bulky items primarily comprising iron, steel, concrete and similarly unharmful materials for which the concern is physical impact, and limited to those circumstances where such wastes are generated at locations, such as small islands with isolated communities, having no practicable access to disposal options other than dumping.

2. The wastes or other matter listed in paragraphs 1.4 and 1.7 may be considered for dumping, provided that material capable of creating floating debris or

otherwise contributing to pollution of the marine environment has been
removed to the maximum extent and provided that the material dumped
poses no serious obstacle to fishing or navigation.

3. Notwithstanding the above, materials listed in paragraphs 1.1 to 1.7 containing levels of radioactivity greater than *de minimis* (exempt) concentrations
   as defined by the IAEA and adopted by Contracting Parties, shall not be
   considered eligible for dumping; provided further that within 25 years of
   20 February 1994, and at each 25 year interval thereafter, Contracting Parties shall complete a scientific study relating to all radioactive wastes and
   other radioactive matter other than high level wastes or matter, taking into
   account such other factors as Contracting Parties consider appropriate and
   shall review the prohibition on dumping of such substances in accordance
   with the procedures set forth in article 22.

Annex 2
Assessment of wastes or other matter that may be considered for dumping

General

1. The acceptance of dumping under certain circumstances shall not remove
   the obligations under this Annex to make further attempts to reduce the
   necessity for dumping.

Waste prevention audit

2. The initial stages in assessing alternatives to dumping should, as appropriate,
   include an evaluation of:
   .1 types, amounts and relative hazard of wastes generated;
   .2 details of the production process and the sources of wastes within that
      process; and
   .3 feasibility of the following waste reduction/prevention techniques:
      .1 product reformulation;
      .2 clean production technologies;
      .3 process modification;
      .4 input substitution; and
      .5 on-site, closed-loop recycling.

3. In general terms, if the required audit reveals that opportunities exist for
   waste prevention at source, an applicant is expected to formulate and implement a waste prevention strategy, in collaboration with relevant local
   and national agencies, which includes specific waste reduction targets and
   provision for further waste prevention audits to ensure that these targets
   are being met. Permit issuance or renewal decisions shall assure compliance
   with any resulting waste reduction and prevention requirements.

4. For dredged material and sewage sludge, the goal of waste management should be to identify and control the sources of contamination. This should be achieved through implementation of waste prevention strategies and requires collaboration between the relevant local and national agencies involved with the control of point and non-point sources of pollution. Until this objective is met, the problems of contaminated dredged material may be addressed by using disposal management techniques at sea or on land.

Consideration of waste management options

5. Applications to dump wastes or other matter shall demonstrate that appropriate consideration has been given to the following hierarchy of waste management options, which implies an order of increasing environmental impact:
   .1 re-use;
   .2 off-site recycling;
   .3 destruction of hazardous constituents;
   .4 treatment to reduce or remove the hazardous constituents; and
   .5 disposal on land, into air and in water.
6. A permit to dump wastes or other matter shall be refused if the permitting authority determines that appropriate opportunities exist to re-use, recycle or treat the waste without undue risks to human health or the environment or disproportionate costs. The practical availability of other means of disposal should be considered in the light of a comparative risk assessment involving both dumping and the alternatives.

Chemical, physical and biological properties

7. A detailed description and characterization of the waste is an essential precondition for the consideration of alternatives and the basis for a decision as to whether a waste may be dumped. If a waste is so poorly characterized that proper assessment cannot be made of its potential impacts on human health and the environment, that waste shall not be dumped.
8. Characterization of the wastes and their constituents shall take into account:
   .1 origin, total amount, form and average composition;
   .2 properties: physical, chemical, biochemical and biological;
   .3 toxicity;
   .4 persistence: physical, chemical and biological; and
   .5 accumulation and biotransformation in biological materials or sediments.

Action list

9. Each Contracting Party shall develop a national Action List to provide a mechanism for screening candidate wastes and their constituents on the basis of their potential effects on human health and the marine environment. In selecting substances for consideration in an Action List, priority

shall be given to toxic, persistent and bioaccumulative substances from anthropogenic sources (e.g., cadmium, mercury, organohalogens, petroleum hydrocarbons, and, whenever relevant, arsenic, lead, copper, zinc, beryllium, chromium, nickel and vanadium, organosilicon compounds, cyanides, fluorides and pesticides or their by-products other than organohalogens). An Action List can also be used as a trigger mechanism for further waste prevention considerations.

10. An Action List shall specify an upper level and may also specify a lower level. The upper level should be set so as to avoid acute or chronic effects on human health or on sensitive marine organisms representative of the marine ecosystem. Application of an Action List will result in three possible categories of waste:

  .1 wastes which contain specified substances, or which cause biological responses, exceeding the relevant upper level shall not be dumped, unless made acceptable for dumping through the use of management techniques or processes;

  .2 wastes which contain specified substances, or which cause biological responses, below the relevant lower levels should be considered to be of little environmental concern in relation to dumping; and

  .3 wastes which contain specified substances, or which cause biological responses, below the upper level but above the lower level require more detailed assessment before their suitability for dumping can be determined.

Dump-site selection

11. Information required to select a dump-site shall include:

  .1 physical, chemical and biological characteristics of the water-column and the seabed;

  .2 location of amenities, values and other uses of the sea in the area under consideration;

  .3 assessment of the constituent fluxes associated with dumping in relation to existing fluxes of substances in the marine environment; and

  .4 economic and operational feasibility.

Assessment of potential effects

12. Assessment of potential effects should lead to a concise statement of the expected consequences of the sea or land disposal options, i.e., the 'Impact Hypothesis'. It provides a basis for deciding whether to approve or reject the proposed disposal option and for defining environmental monitoring requirements.

13. The assessment for dumping should integrate information on waste characteristics, conditions at the proposed dump-site(s), fluxes, and proposed disposal techniques and specify the potential effects on human health, living resources, amenities and other legitimate uses of the sea. It should define the nature, temporal and spatial scales and duration of expected impacts based on reasonably conservative assumptions.

14. An analysis of each disposal option should be considered in the light of a comparative assessment of the following concerns: human health risks, environmental costs, hazards, (including accidents), economics and exclusion of future uses. If this assessment reveals that adequate information is not available to determine the likely effects of the proposed disposal option then this option should not be considered further. In addition, if the interpretation of the comparative assessment shows the dumping option to be less preferable, a permit for dumping should not be given.

15. Each assessment should conclude with a statement supporting a decision to issue or refuse a permit for dumping.

Monitoring

16. Monitoring is used to verify that permit conditions are met – compliance monitoring – and that the assumptions made during the permit review and site selection process were correct and sufficient to protect the environment and human health – field monitoring. It is essential that such monitoring programmes have clearly defined objectives.

Permit and permit conditions

17. A decision to issue a permit should only be made if all impact evaluations are completed and the monitoring requirements are determined. The provisions of the permit shall ensure, as far as practicable, that environmental disturbance and detriment are minimized and the benefits maximized. Any permit issued shall contain data and information specifying:
    .1 the types and sources of materials to be dumped;
    .2 the location of the dump-site(s);
    .3 the method of dumping; and
    .4 monitoring and reporting requirements.

18. Permits should be reviewed at regular intervals, taking into account the results of monitoring and the objectives of monitoring programmes. Review of monitoring results will indicate whether field programmes need to be continued, revised or terminated and will contribute to informed decisions regarding the continuance, modification or revocation of permits. This provides an important feedback mechanism for the protection of human health and the marine environment.

Annex 3
Arbitral procedure

Article 1

1. An Arbitral Tribunal (hereinafter referred to as the 'Tribunal') shall be established upon the request of a Contracting Party addressed to another Contracting Party in application of article 16 of this Protocol. The request for arbitration shall consist of a statement of the case together with any supporting documents.
2. The requesting Contracting Party shall inform the Secretary-General of:
   .1 its request for arbitration; and
   .2 the provisions of this Protocol the interpretation or application of which is, in its opinion, the subject of disagreement.
3. The Secretary-General shall transmit this information to all Contracting States.

Article 2

1. The Tribunal shall consist of a single arbitrator if so agreed between the parties to the dispute within 30 days from the date of receipt of the request for arbitration.
2. In the case of the death, disability or default of the arbitrator, the parties to a dispute may agree upon a replacement within 30 days of such death, disability or default.

Article 3

1. Where the parties to a dispute do not agree upon a Tribunal in accordance with article 2 of this Annex, the Tribunal shall consist of three members:
   .1 one arbitrator nominated by each party to the dispute; and
   .2 a third arbitrator who shall be nominated by agreement between the two first named and who shall act as its Chairman.
2. If the Chairman of a Tribunal is not nominated within 30 days of nomination of the second arbitrator, the parties to a dispute shall, upon the request of one party, submit to the Secretary-General within a further period of 30 days an agreed list of qualified persons. The Secretary-General shall select the Chairman from such list as soon as possible. He shall not select a Chairman who is or has been a national of one party to the dispute except with the consent of the other party to the dispute.
3. If one party to a dispute fails to nominate an arbitrator as provided in paragraph 1.1 within 60 days from the date of receipt of the request for arbitration, the other party may request the submission to the Secretary-General within a period of 30 days of an agreed list of qualified persons. The Secretary-General shall select the Chairman of the Tribunal from such list

as soon as possible. The Chairman shall then request the party which has not nominated an arbitrator to do so. If this party does not nominate an arbitrator within 15 days of such request, the Secretary-General shall, upon request of the Chairman, nominate the arbitrator from the agreed list of qualified persons.

4. In the case of the death, disability or default of an arbitrator, the party to the dispute who nominated him shall nominate a replacement within 30 days of such death, disability or default. If the party does not nominate a replacement, the arbitration shall proceed with the remaining arbitrators. In the case of the death, disability or default of the Chairman, a replacement shall be nominated in accordance with the provision of paragraphs 1.2 and 2 within 90 days of such death, disability or default.

5. A list of arbitrators shall be maintained by the Secretary-General and composed of qualified persons nominated by the Contracting Parties. Each Contracting Party may designate for inclusion in the list four persons who shall not necessarily be its nationals. If the parties to the dispute have failed within the specified time limits to submit to the Secretary-General an agreed list of qualified persons as provided for in paragraphs 2, 3 and 4, the Secretary-General shall select from the list maintained by him the arbitrator or arbitrators not yet nominated.

Article 4

The Tribunal may hear and determine counter-claims arising directly out of the subject matter of the dispute.

Article 5

Each party to the dispute shall be responsible for the costs entailed by the preparation of its own case. The remuneration of the members of the Tribunal and of all general expenses incurred by the arbitration shall be borne equally by the parties to the dispute. The Tribunal shall keep a record of all its expenses and shall furnish a final statement thereof to the parties.

Article 6

Any Contracting Party which has an interest of a legal nature which may be affected by the decision in the case may, after giving written notice to the parties to the dispute which have originally initiated the procedure, intervene in the arbitration procedure with the consent of the Tribunal and at its own expense. Any such intervenor shall have the right to present evidence, briefs and oral argument on the matters giving rise to its intervention, in accordance with procedures established pursuant to article 7 of this Annex, but shall have no rights with respect to the composition of the Tribunal.

Article 7

A Tribunal established under the provisions of this Annex shall decide its own rules of procedure.

Article 8

1. Unless a Tribunal consists of a single arbitrator, decisions of the Tribunal as to its procedure, its place of meeting, and any question related to the dispute laid before it, shall be taken by majority vote of its members. However, the absence or abstention of any member of the Tribunal who was nominated by a party to the dispute shall not constitute an impediment to the Tribunal reaching a decision. In case of equal voting, the vote of the Chairman shall be decisive.
2. The parties to the dispute shall facilitate the work of the Tribunal and in particular shall, in accordance with their legislation and using all means at their disposal:
   .1 provide the Tribunal with all necessary documents and information; and
   .2 enable the Tribunal to enter their territory, to hear witnesses or experts, and to visit the scene.
3. The failure of a party to the dispute to comply with the provisions of paragraph 2 shall not preclude the Tribunal from reaching a decision and rendering an award.

Article 9

The Tribunal shall render its award within five months from the time it is established unless it finds it necessary to extend that time limit for a period not to exceed five months. The award of the Tribunal shall be accompanied by a statement of reasons for the decision. It shall be final and without appeal and shall be communicated to the Secretary-General who shall inform the Contracting Parties. The parties to the dispute shall immediately comply with the award.

International Convention for the Prevention of Pollution from Ships, 2 November 1973

Editorial note

The International Convention for the Prevention of Pollution From Ships, adopted under the auspices of the IMCO (now the IMO), covers all technical aspects of pollution from ships save for waste disposal by dumping at sea. The Convention attempts to control discharges of harmful substances into the sea from vessels by establishing a certification system for ships and by requiring comprehensive enforcement of its obligations. Certificates are to be granted by each Party's national authorities in accordance with the 'Regulations' set out in the Convention's five Annexes, which address, respectively, oil pollution (entered into force on 2 October 1983), pollution by noxious liquid substances (entered into force on 6 April 1987), pollution by harmful substances in packaged form (entered into force on 1 July 1992), pollution by sewage from ships (entered into force on 27 September 2003), pollution by garbage from ships (entered into force on 31 December 1988). Annexes I and II are binding upon the Convention's entry into force for a Party, while Annexes III, IV, and V are binding at the option of each Party (Article 14(1)). Annex VI (not yet in force) was adopted in 1997 with the aim of preventing air pollution from ships. The Convention applies to ships flying the flag of a Party or operating within a Party's jurisdiction, but sovereign immunity applies to warships or ships in non-commercial governmental service (Article 3). In the event of a casualty involving a ship subject to the Regulations which has caused a 'major deleterious effect' to the environment, the flag State is to conduct an investigation of the casualty and report to the IMO any findings which may assist in revising the Convention (Article 12).

The Convention sets forth extensive provisions for its enforcement. Violations of the Convention are to be punished either by the flag State or by a Party in whose jurisdiction the violation has occurred (Article 4). Under the Convention, Parties may inspect ships in their ports or offshore installations for the purpose of verifying the validity of a certificate or, if there are reasonable grounds for doing so, for verifying the correspondence of the ship's actual conditions to the provisions of the certificate (Article 5). A ship may also be subject to inspection to determine whether a discharge in violation of the Regulations has occurred, in which case the relevant information is to be transmitted to the flag State so that proceedings can be taken by the flag State (Article 6).

The IMO provides institutional support for the Convention. If negotiation fails to resolve a dispute, the Convention provides for compulsory arbitration, at the request of any involved Party, in accordance with the procedure set forth in Protocol II to the Convention (Article 10). The Convention sets out a detailed procedure for amendments (Article 16), which has been used on numerous occasions to amend the Convention's Annexes. Protocol I of the Convention outlines Parties' requirements on reporting incidents involving harmful substances and was amended in 1985 so as to include discharges into the sea of harmful substances in packaged form.

The Convention was to have entered into force following ratification by fifteen States, whose combined gross tonnage is at least 50 percent of the world commercial fleet (Article 15). Once in force, the Convention would have superseded the 1954 International Convention for the Prevention of Pollution of the Sea by Oil (Article 9). Although the Convention has not entered into force *per se*, it has been brought into effect in accordance with the 1978 Protocol (see below at document 9A).

Date of signature: 2 November 1973

Entry into force: Not yet in force *per se*

Depositary: Secretary-General of the IMO

Contracting Parties: See below under document 9A

Website: www.imo.org

International Convention for the Prevention of Pollution from Ships

The Parties to the Convention,

Being conscious of the need to preserve the human environment in general and the marine environment in particular,

Recognizing that deliberate, negligent or accidental release of oil and other harmful substances from ships constitutes a serious source of pollution,

Recognizing also the importance of the International Convention for the Prevention of Pollution of the Sea by Oil, 1954, as being the first multilateral instrument to be concluded with the prime objective of protecting the environment, and appreciating the significant contribution which that Convention has made in preserving the seas and coastal environment from pollution,

Desiring to achieve the complete elimination of intentional pollution of the marine environment by oil and other harmful substances and the minimization of accidental discharge of such substances,

Considering that this object may best be achieved by establishing rules not limited to oil pollution having a universal purport,

Have agreed as follows:

Article 1
General obligations under the Convention

1. The Parties to the Convention undertake to give effect to the provisions of the present Convention and those Annexes thereto by which they are bound, in order to prevent the pollution of the marine environment by the discharge of harmful substances or effluents containing such substances in contravention of the Convention.

2. Unless expressly provided otherwise, a reference to the present Convention constitutes at the same time a reference to its Protocol and to the Annexes.

Article 2
Definitions

For the purposes of the present Convention, unless expressly provided otherwise:

1. 'Regulations' means the Regulations contained in the Annexes to the present Convention.

2. 'Harmful substance' means any substance which, if introduced into the sea, is liable to create hazards to human health, to harm living resources and marine life, to damage amenities or to interfere with other legitimate uses of the sea, and includes any substance subject to control by the present Convention.

3.

a) 'Discharge', in relation to harmful substances or effluents containing such substances, means any release howsoever caused from a ship and includes any escape, disposal, spilling, leaking, pumping, emitting or emptying;

b) 'Discharge' does not include:

    (i) dumping within the meaning of the Convention on the Prevention of Marine Pollution by Dumping of Wastes and Other Matter, done at London on 13 November 1972; or

    (ii) release of harmful substances directly arising from the exploration, exploitation and associated off-shore processing of sea-bed mineral resources; or

    (iii) release of harmful substances for purpose of legitimate scientific research into pollution abatement or control.

4. 'Ship' means a vessel of any type whatsoever operating in the marine environment and includes hydrofoil boats, air-cushion vehicles, submersibles, floating craft and fixed or floating platforms.

5. 'Administration' means the Government of the State under whose authority the ship is operating. With respect to a ship entitled to fly a flag of any State, the Administration is the Government of that State. With respect to fixed or floating platforms engaged in exploration and exploitation of the sea-bed and subsoil thereof adjacent to the coast over which the coastal State exercises sovereign rights for the purposes of exploration and exploitation of their natural resources, the Administration is the Government of the coastal State concerned.

6. 'Incident' means an event involving the actual or probable discharge into the sea of a harmful substance, or effluents containing such a substance.

7. 'Organization' means the Inter-Governmental Maritime Consultative Organization.

Article 3
Application

1. The present Convention shall apply to:

a) ships entitled to fly the flag of a Party to the Convention; and
b) ships not entitled to fly the flag of a Party but which operate under the authority of a Party.

2. Nothing in the present Article shall be construed as derogating from or extending the sovereign rights of the Parties under international law over the sea-bed and subsoil thereof adjacent to their coasts for the purposes of exploration and exploitation of their natural resources.

3. The present Convention shall not apply to any warship, naval auxiliary or other ship owned or operated by a State and used, for the time being only on government non-commercial service. However, each Party shall ensure by the adoption of appropriate measures not impairing the operations or operational capabilities of such ships owned or operated by it, that such ships act in a manner consistent, so far as is reasonable and practicable, with the present Convention.

Article 4
Violation

1. Any violation of the requirements of the present Convention shall be prohibited and sanctions shall be established therefor under the law of the Administration of the ship concerned wherever the violation occurs. If the Administration is informed of such a violation and is satisfied that sufficient evidence is available to enable proceedings to be brought in respect of the

alleged violation, it shall cause such proceedings to be taken as soon as possible, in accordance with its law.

2. Any violation of the requirements of the present Convention within the jurisdiction of any Party to the Convention shall be prohibited and sanctions shall be established therefor under the law of that Party. Whenever such a violation occurs, the Party shall either:

a) cause proceedings to be taken in accordance with its law; or
b) furnish to the Administration of the ship such information and evidence as may be in its possession that a violation has occurred.

3. Where information or evidence with respect to any violation of the present Convention by a ship is furnished to the Administration of that ship, the Administration shall promptly inform the Party which has furnished the information or evidence and the Organization, of the action taken.

4. The penalties specified under the law of a Party pursuant to the present Article shall be adequate in severity to discharge violations of the present Convention and shall be equally severe irrespective of where the violations occur.

Article 5
Certificates and special rules on inspection of ships

1. Subject to the provisions of paragraph (2) of the present Article a certificate issued under the authority of a Party to the Convention in accordance with the provisions of the Regulations shall be accepted by the other Parties and regarded for all purposes covered by the present Convention as having the same validity as a certificate issued by them.

2. A ship required to hold a certificate in accordance with the provisions of the Regulations is subject, while in the ports or off-shore terminals under the jurisdiction of a Party, to inspection by officers duly authorized by that Party. Any such inspection shall be limited to verifying that there is on board a valid certificate, unless there are clear grounds for believing that the condition of the ship or its equipment does not correspond substantially with the particulars of that certificate. In that case, or if the ship does not carry a valid certificate the Party carrying out the inspection shall take such steps as will ensure that the ship shall not sail until it can proceed to sea without presenting an unreasonable threat of harm to the marine environment. That Party may, however, grant such a ship permission to leave the port or off-shore terminal for the purpose of proceedings to the nearest appropriate repair yard available.

3. If a Party denies a foreign ship entry to the ports or off-shore terminals under its jurisdiction or takes any action against such a ship for the reason that the ship does not comply with the provisions of the present Convention, the Party

shall immediately inform the consul or diplomatic representative of the Party whose flag the ship is entitled to fly, or if this is not possible, the Administration of the ship concerned. Before denying entry or taking such action the Party may request consultation with the Administration of the ship concerned. Information shall also be given to the Administration when a ship does not carry a valid certificate in accordance with the provisions of the Regulations.

4. With respect to the ships of non-Parties to the Convention, Parties shall apply the requirements of the present Convention as may be necessary to ensure that no more favourable treatment is given to such ships.

Article 6
Detection of violations and enforcement of the Convention

1. Parties to the Convention shall co-operate in the detection of violations and the enforcement of the provisions of the present Convention, using all appropriate and practicable measures of detection and environmental monitoring, adequate procedures for reporting and accumulation of evidence.

2. A ship to which the present Convention applies may, in any port or off-shore terminal of a Party, be subject to inspection by officers appointed or authorized by that Party for the purpose of verifying whether the ship has discharged any harmful substances in violation of the provisions of the Regulations. If an inspection indicates a violation of the Convention, a report shall be forwarded to the Administration for any appropriate action.

3. Any Party shall furnish to the Administration evidence, if any, that the ship has discharged harmful substances or effluents containing such substances in violation of the provisions of the Regulations. If it is practicable to do so, the competent authority of the former Party shall notify the Master of the ship of the alleged violation.

4. Upon receiving such evidence, the Administration so informed shall investigate the matter, and may request the other Party to furnish further or better evidence of the alleged contravention. If the Administration is satisfied that sufficient evidence is available to enable proceedings to be brought in respect of the alleged violation, it shall cause such proceedings to be taken in accordance with its law as soon as possible. The Administration shall promptly inform the Party which has reported the alleged violation, as well as the Organization, of the action taken.

5. A Party may also inspect a ship to which the present Convention applies when it enters the ports or off-shore terminals under its jurisdiction, if a request for an investigation is received from any Party together with sufficient evidence that the ship has discharged harmful substances or effluents containing such substances in any place. The report of such investigation shall be sent to the Party requesting it and to the Administration so that the appropriate action may be taken under the present Convention.

Article 7
Undue delay to ships

1. All possible efforts shall be made to avoid a ship being unduly detained or delayed under Article 4, 5, and 6 of the present Convention.

2. When a ship is unduly detained or delayed under Article 4, 5, and 6 of the present Convention, it shall be entitled to compensation for any loss or damage suffered.

Article 8
Reports on incidents involving harmful substances

1. A report of an incident shall be made without delay to the fullest extent possible in accordance with the provisions of Protocol I to the present Convention.

2. Each Party to the Convention shall:

a) make all arrangements necessary for an appropriate officer or agency to receive and process all reports on incidents; and
b) notify the Organization with complete details of such arrangements for circulation to other Parties and Member States of the Organization.

3. Whenever a Party receives a report under the provisions of the present Article, the Party shall relay the report without delay to:

a) the Administration of the ship involved; and
b) any other State which may be affected.

4. Each Party to the Convention undertakes to issue instructions to its maritime inspection vessels and aircraft and to other appropriate services to report to its authorities any incident referred to in Protocol I to the present Convention. That Party shall, if it considers it appropriate, report accordingly to the Organization and to any other party concerned.

Article 9
Other treaties and interpretation

1. Upon its entry into force, the present Convention supersedes the International Convention for the Prevention of Pollution of the Sea by Oil, 1954, as amended, as between Parties to that Convention.

2. Nothing in the present Convention shall prejudice the codification and development of the law of the sea by the United Nations Conference on the Law of the Sea convened pursuant to Resolution 2750 C (XXV) of the General Assembly of the United Nations nor the present or future claims and legal views of any State concerning the law of the sea and the nature and extent of coastal and flag State jurisdiction.

3. The term 'jurisdiction' in the present Convention shall be construed in the light of international law in force at the time of application or interpretation of the present Convention.

Article 10
Settlement of disputes

Any dispute between two or more Parties to the Convention concerning the interpretation or application of the present Convention shall, if settlement by negotiation between the Parties involved has not been possible, and if these Parties do not otherwise agree, be submitted upon request of any of them to arbitration as set out in Protocol II to the present Convention.

Article 11
Communication of information

1. The Parties to the Convention undertake to communicate to the Organization:

a) the text of laws, orders, decrees and regulations and other instruments which have been promulgated on the various matters within the scope of the present Convention;

b) a list of non-governmental agencies which are authorized to act on their behalf in matters relating to the design, construction and equipment of ships carrying harmful substances in accordance with the provisions of the Regulations;

c) a sufficient number of specimens of their certificates issued under the provisions of the Regulations;

d) a list of reception facilities including their location, capacity and available facilities and other characteristics;

e) official reports or summaries of official reports in so far as they show the results of the application of the present Convention; and

f) an annual statistical report, in a form standardized by the Organization, of penalties actually imposed for infringement of the present Convention.

2. The Organization shall notify Parties of the receipt of any communications under the present Article and circulate to all Parties any information communicated to it under sub-paragraphs (1) (b) to (f) of the present Article.

Article 12
Casualties to ships

1. Each Administration undertakes to conduct an investigation of any casualty occurring to any of its ships subject to the provisions of the Regulations if such casualty has produced a major deleterious effect upon the marine environment.

2. Each Party to the Convention undertakes to supply the Organization with information concerning the findings of such investigation, when it judges that such information may assist in determining what changes in the present Convention might be desirable.

Article 13
Signature, ratification, acceptance, approval and accession

1. The present Convention shall remain open for signature at the Headquarters of the Organization from 15 January 1974 until 31 December 1974 and shall thereafter remain open for accession. States may become Parties to the present Convention by:

a) signature without reservation as to ratification, acceptance or approval; or
b) signature subject to ratification, acceptance or approval, followed by ratification, acceptance or approval; or
c) accession.

2. Ratification, acceptance, approval or accession shall be effected by the deposit of an instrument to that effect with the Secretary-General of the Organization.

3. The Secretary-General of the Organization shall inform all States which have signed the present Convention or acceded to it of any signature or of the deposit of any new instrument of ratification, acceptance, approval or accession and the date of its deposit.

Article 14
Optional Annexes

1. A State may at the time of signing, ratifying, accepting, approving or acceding to the present Convention declare that it does not accept any one or all of Annexes III, IV, and V (hereinafter referred to as 'Optional Annexes') of the present Convention. Subject to the above, Parties to the Convention shall be bound by any Annex in its entirety.

2. A State which has declared that it is not bound by an Optional Annex may at any time accept such Annex by depositing with the Organization an instrument of the kind referred to in Article 13 (2).

3. A State which makes a declaration under paragraph (1) of the present Article in respect of an Optional Annex and which has not subsequently accepted that Annex in accordance with paragraph (2) of the present Article shall not be under any obligation nor entitled to claim any privileges under the present Convention in respect of matters related to such Annex and all reference to Parties in the present Convention shall not include that State in so far as matters related to such Annex are concerned.

4. The Organization shall inform the States which have signed or acceded to the present Convention of any declaration under the present Article as well as

the receipt of any instrument deposited in accordance with the provisions of paragraph (2) of the present Article.

Article 15
Entry into force

1. The Convention shall enter into force twelve months after the date on which not less than 15 States, the combined merchant fleets of which constitute not less than fifty per cent of the gross tonnage of the world's merchant shipping, have become parties to it in accordance with Article 13.

2. An Optional Annex shall enter into force twelve months after the date on which the conditions stipulated in paragraph (1) of the present Article have been satisfied in relation to that Annex.

3. The Organization shall inform the States which have signed the present Convention or acceded to it of the date on which it enters into force and of the date on which an Optional Annex enters into force in accordance with paragraph (2) of the present Article.

4. For States which have deposited an instrument of ratification, acceptance, approval or accession in respect of the present Convention or any Optional Annex after the requirements for entry into force thereof have been met but prior to the date of entry into force, the ratification, acceptance, approval or accession shall take effect on the date of entry into force of the Convention or such Annex or three months after the date of deposit of the instrument whichever is the later date.

5. For States which have deposited an instrument of ratification, acceptance, approval or accession after the date on which the Convention or an Optional Annex entered into force, the Convention or the Optional Annex shall become effective three months after the date of deposit of the instrument.

6. After the date on which all the conditions required under Article 16 to bring an amendment to the present Convention or an Optional Annex into force have been fulfilled, any instrument of ratification, acceptance, approval or accession deposited shall apply to the Convention or Annex as amended.

Article 16
Amendments

1. The present Convention may be amended by any of the procedures specified in the following paragraphs.

2. Amendments after consideration by the Organization:

a) any amendment proposed by a Party to the Convention shall be submitted to the Organization and circulated by its Secretary-General to all Members of the Organization and all Parties at least six months prior to its consideration;

b) any amendment proposed and circulated as above shall be submitted to an appropriate body by the Organization for consideration;

c) Parties to the Convention, whether or not Members of the Organization, shall be entitled to participate in the proceedings of the appropriate body;

d) amendments shall be adopted by a two-thirds majority of only the Parties to the Convention present and voting;

e) if adopted in accordance with sub-paragraph d) above, amendments shall be communicated by the Secretary-General of the Organization to all the Parties to the Convention for acceptance;

f) an amendment shall be deemed to have been accepted in the following circumstances:

(i) an amendment to an Article of the Convention shall be deemed to have been accepted on the date on which it is accepted by two-thirds of the Parties, the combined merchant fleets of which constitute not less than fifty per cent of the gross tonnage of the world's merchant fleet;

(ii) an amendment to an Annex to the Convention shall be deemed to have been accepted in accordance with the procedure specified in subparagraph (f) (iii) unless the appropriate body, at the time of its adoption, determines that the amendment shall be deemed to have been accepted on the date on which it is accepted by two-thirds of the Parties, the combined merchant fleets of which constitute not less than fifty per cent of the gross tonnage of the world's merchant fleet. Nevertheless, at any time before the entry into force of an amendment to an Annex to the Convention, a Party may notify the Secretary-General of the Organization that its express approval will be necessary before the amendment enters into force for it. The latter shall bring such notification and the date of its receipt to the notice of Parties.

(iii) an amendment to an Appendix to an Annex to the Convention shall be deemed to have been accepted at the end of a period to be determined by the appropriate body at the time of its adoption, which period shall be not less than ten months, unless within that period an objection is communicated to the Organization by not less than one-third of the Parties or by the Parties the combined merchant fleets of which constitute not less than fifty per cent of the gross tonnage of the world's merchant fleet whichever condition is fulfilled;

(iv) an amendment to Protocol I to the Convention shall be subject to the same procedures as for the amendments to the Annexes to the Convention, as provided for in sub-paragraphs (f) (ii) or (f) (iii), above;

(v) an amendment to Protocol II to the Convention shall be subject to the same procedures as for the amendments to an Article of the Convention, as provided for in sub-paragraph (f) (i) above;

g) the amendment shall enter into force under the following conditions:

(i) in the case of an amendment to an Article of the Convention, to Protocol II, or to Protocol I or to an Annex to the Convention not under the procedure specified in sub-paragraph (f) (iii), the amendment accepted in conformity with the foregoing provisions shall enter into force six months after the date of its acceptance with respect to the Parties which have declared that they have accepted it;

(ii) in the case of an amendment to Protocol I, to an Appendix to an Annex or to an Annex to the Convention under the procedure specified in subparagraph (f) (iii), the amendment deemed to have been accepted in accordance with the foregoing conditions shall enter into force six months after its acceptance for all the Parties with the exception of those which, before that date, have made a declaration that they do not accept it or a declaration under sub-paragraph (f) (ii), that their express approval is necessary.

3. Amendment by a Conference:

a) Upon the request of a Party, concurred in by at least one-third of the Parties, the Organization shall convene a Conference of Parties to the Convention to consider amendments to the present Convention.

b) Every amendment adopted by such a Conference by a two-thirds majority of those present and voting of the Parties shall be communicated by the Secretary-General of the Organization to all Contracting Parties for their acceptance.

c) Unless the Conference decides otherwise, the amendment shall be deemed to have been accepted and to have entered into force in accordance with the procedures specified for that purpose in paragraph (2) (f) and (g) above.

4.

a) In the case of an amendment to an Optional Annex, a reference in the present Article to a 'Party to the Convention' shall be deemed to mean a reference to a Party bound by that Annex.

b) Any Party which has declined to accept an amendment to an Annex shall be treated as a non-Party only for the purpose of application of that Amendment.

5. The adoption and entry into force of a new Annex shall be subject to the same procedures as for the adoption and entry into force of an Article of the Convention.

6. Unless expressly provided otherwise, any amendment to the present Convention made under this Article, which relates to the structure of a ship, shall apply only to ships for which the building contract is placed, or in the absence of a building contract, the keel of which is laid, on or after the date on which the amendment comes into force.

7. Any amendment to a Protocol or to an Annex shall relate to the substance of that Protocol or Annex and shall be consistent with the Articles of the present Convention.

8. The Secretary-General of the Organization shall inform all Parties of any amendments which enter into force under the present Article, together with the date on which each such amendment enters into force.

9. Any declaration of acceptance or of objection to an amendment under the present Article shall be notified in writing to the Secretary-General of the Organization. The latter shall bring such notification and the date of its receipt to the notice of the Parties to the Convention.

Article 17
Promotion of technical co-operation

The Parties to the Convention shall promote in consultation with the Organization and other international bodies, with assistance and coordination by the Executive Director of the United Nations Environment Programme, support for those Parties which request technical assistance for:

a) the training of scientific and technical personnel;
b) the supply of necessary equipment and facilities for reception and monitoring;
c) the facilitation of other measures and arrangements to prevent or mitigate pollution of the marine environment by ships; and
d) the encouragement of research;

preferably within the countries concerned, so furthering the aims and purposes of the present Convention.

Article 18
Denunciation

1. The present Convention or any Optional Annex may be denounced by any Party to the Convention at any time after the expiry of five years from the date on which the Convention or such Annex enters into force for that Party.

2. Denunciation shall be effected by notification in writing to the Secretary-General of the Organization who shall inform all the other Parties of any such notification received and of the date of its receipt as well as the date on which such denunciation takes effect.

3. A denunciation shall take effect twelve months after receipt of the notification of denunciation by the Secretary-General of the Organization or after the expiry of any other longer period which may be indicated in the notification.

Article 19
Deposit and registration

1. The present Convention shall be deposited with the Secretary-General of the Organization who shall transmit certified true copies thereof to all States which have signed the present Convention or acceded to it.

2. As soon as the present Convention enters into force, the text shall be transmitted by the Secretary-General of the Organization to the Secretary-General of the United Nations for registration and publication, in accordance with Article 102 of the Charter of the United Nations.

Article 20
Languages

The present Convention is established in a single copy in the English, French, Russian and Spanish languages, each text being equally authentic. Official translations in the Arabic, German, Italian and Japanese languages shall be prepared and deposited with the signed original.

IN WITNESS WHEREOF the undersigned being duly authorized by their respective Governments for that purpose have signed the present Convention.

DONE at London this second day of November, one thousand nine hundred and seventy-three.

[*Annexes and Protocols omitted*]

9A

Protocol of 1978 Relating to the International Convention for the Prevention of Pollution from Ships 1973, 17 February 1978

Editorial note

The Protocol of 1978 relating to the International Convention for the Prevention of Pollution from Ships, 1973, was adopted largely in response to the 1973 Convention not yet entering into force. It was perceived that many States were reluctant to join because of the requirements of Annex II. Accordingly, the Protocol incorporates the 1973 Convention by reference, but limits its scope so as to relieve the Parties of their obligations under Annex II for at least three years (Article II), by which time it was expected that the technical problems associated with Annex II would be resolved. The Protocol has modified the requirements of Annex I to account for new innovations in the manner in which oil is transported.

Date of signature: 12 February 1978

Entry into force: 2 October 1983

Depositary: Secretary-General of the IMO

Contracting Parties: Algeria, Angola, Antigua and Barbuda, Argentina, Australia, Austria, Bahamas, Bangladesh, Barbados, Belarus, Belgium, Belize, Benin, Bolivia, Brazil, Brunei Darussalem, Bulgaria, Cambodia, Canada, Chile, China, Colombia, Comoros, Cote d'Ivoire, Croatia, Cuba, Cyprus, Czech Republic, Democratic People's Republic of Korea, Denmark, Djibouti, Dominica, Dominican Republic, Ecuador, Egypt, Equatorial Guinea, Estonia, Finland, France, Gabon, Gambia, Georgia, Germany, Ghana, Greece, Guatemala, Guinea, Guyana, Honduras, Hungary, Iceland, India, Indonesia, Iran, Ireland, Israel, Italy, Jamaica, Japan, Kazakhstan, Kenya, Latvia, Lebanon, Liberia, Lithuania, Luxembourg, Malawi, Malaysia, Malta, Marshall Islands, Mauritania, Mauritius, Mexico, Monaco, Morocco, Myanmar,

289

Namibia, Netherlands, New Zealand, Nicaragua, Nigeria, Norway, Oman, Pakistan, Panama, Papua New Guinea, Peru, Philippines, Poland, Portugal, Republic of Korea, Romania, Russian Federation, Saint Kitts and Nevis, Saint Lucia, Saint Vincent and Grenadines, Samoa, São Tomé and Príncipe, Senegal, Seychelles, Sierra Leone, Singapore, Slovakia, Slovenia, South Africa, Spain, Sri Lanka, Suriname, Sweden, Switzerland, Syrian Arab Republic, Togo, Tonga, Trinidad and Tobago, Tunisia, Turkey, Tuvalu, Ukraine, United Kingdom, United States of America, Uruguay, Vanuatu, Venezuela, Vietnam, Yugoslavia, Hong Kong-China (Associate Member).

Website: www.imo.org

Protocol of 1978 Relating to the International Convention for the Prevention of Pollution from Ships 1973

The Parties to the present Protocol,

Recognizing the significant contribution which can be made by the International Convention for the Prevention of Pollution from Ships, 1973, to the protection of the marine environment from pollution from ships,

Recognizing also the need to improve further the prevention and control of marine pollution from ships, particularly oil tankers,

Recognizing further the need for implementing the Regulations for the Prevention of Pollution by Oil contained in Annex I of that Convention as early and as widely as possible,

Acknowledging however the need to defer the application of Annex II of that Convention until certain technical problems have been satisfactorily resolved.

Considering that these objections may best be achieved by the conclusion of a Protocol relating to the International Convention for the Prevention of Pollution from Ships, 1973,

Have agreed as follows:

Article I
General obligations

1. The Parties to the present Protocol undertake to give effect to the provisions of:

a) the present Protocol and the Annex hereto which shall constitute an integral part of the present Protocol; and

b) the International Convention for the Prevention of Pollution from Ships, 1973 (hereinafter referred to as 'the Convention'), subject to the modifications and additions set out in the present Protocol.

2. The provisions of the Convention and the present Protocol shall be read and interpreted together as one single instrument.

3. Every reference to the present Protocol constitutes at the same time a reference to the Annex hereto.

Article II
Implementation of Annex II of the Convention

1. Notwithstanding the provisions of Article 14(1) of the Convention, the Parties to the present Protocol agree that they shall not be bound by the provisions of Annex II of the Convention for a period of three years from the date of entry into force of the present Protocol or for such longer period as may be decided by a two-thirds majority of the Parties to the present Protocol in the Marine Environment Protection Committee (hereinafter referred to as 'the Committee') of the Inter-Governmental Maritime Consultative Organization (hereinafter referred to as 'the Organization').

2. During the period specified in paragraph 1 of this Article, the Parties to the present Protocol shall not be under any obligations nor entitled to claim any privileges under the Convention in respect of matters relating to Annex II of the Convention and all reference to Parties in the Convention shall not include the Parties to the present Protocol in so far as matters relating to that Annex are concerned.

Article III
Communication of information

The text of Article 11(1)(b) of the Convention is replaced by the following:

'a list of nominated surveyors or recognized organizations which are authorized to act on their behalf in the administration of matters relating to the design, construction, equipment and operation of ships carrying harmful substances in accordance with the provisions of the Regulations for circulation to the Parties for information of their officers. The Administration shall therefore notify the Organization of the specific responsibilities and conditions of the authority delegated to nominated surveyors or recognized organizations.'

Article IV
Signature, ratification, acceptance, approval and accession

1. The present Protocol shall be open for signature at the Headquarters of the Organization from 1 June 1978 to 31 May 1979 and shall thereafter remain open for accession. States may become Parties to the present Protocol by:

a) signature without reservation as to ratification, acceptance or approval; or
b) signature, subject to ratification, acceptance or approval, followed by ratification, acceptance or approval; or
c) accession.

2. Ratification, acceptance, approval or accession shall be effected by the deposit of an instrument to that effect with the Secretary-General of the Organization.

Article V
Entry into force

1. The present Protocol shall enter into force twelve months after the date on which not less than fifteen States, the combined merchant fleets of which constitute not less than fifty per cent of the gross tonnage of the world's merchant shipping, have become Parties to it in accordance with Article IV of the present Protocol.

2. Any instrument of ratification, acceptance, approval or accession deposited after the date on which the present Protocol enters into force shall take effect three months after the date of deposit.

3. After the date on which an amendment to the present Protocol is deemed to have been accepted in accordance with Article 16 of the Convention, any instrument of ratification, acceptance, approval or accession deposited shall apply to the present Protocol as amended.

Article VI
Amendments

The procedures set out in Article 16 of the Convention in respect of amendments to the Articles, an Annex and an Appendix to an Annex of the Convention shall apply respectively to amendments to the Articles, the Annex and an Appendix to the Annex of the present Protocol.

Article VII
Denunciation

1. The present Protocol may be denounced by any Party to the present Protocol at any time after the expiry of five years from the date on which the Protocol enters into force for that Party.

2. Denunciation shall be effected by the deposit of an instrument of denunciation with the Secretary-General of the Organization.

3. A denunciation shall take effect twelve months after receipt of the notification by the Secretary-General of the Organization or after the expiry of any other longer period which may be indicated in the notification.

Article VIII
Depositary

1. The present Protocol shall be deposited with the Secretary-General of the Organization (hereinafter referred to as 'the Depositary').

2. The Depositary shall:

a) inform all States which have signed the present Protocol or acceded thereto of:
   (i) each new signature or deposit of an instrument of ratification, acceptance, approval or accession, together with the date thereof;
   (ii) the date of entry into force of the present Protocol;
   (iii) the deposit of any instrument of denunciation of the present Protocol together with the date on which it is received and the date on which the denunciation takes effect;
   (iv) any decision made in accordance with Article II(1) of the present Protocol;
b) transmit certified true copies of the present Protocol to all States which have signed the present Protocol or acceded thereto.

3. As soon as the present Protocol enters into force, a certified true copy thereof shall be transmitted by the Depositary to the Secretariat of the United Nations for registration and publication in accordance with Article 102 of the Charter of the United Nations.

Article IX
Languages

The present Protocol is established in a single original in the English, French, Russian and Spanish language, each text being equally authentic. Official translations in the Arabic, German, Italian and Japanese languages shall be prepared and deposited with the signed original.

IN WITNESS WHEREOF the undersigned being duly authorized by their respective Governments for that purpose have signed the present Protocol.

DONE at London this seventeenth day of February one thousand nine hundred and seventy-eight.

[Annexes omitted]

10

United Nations Convention on the Law of the Sea, 10 December 1982 (extracts)

Editorial note

The 1982 UN Convention on the Law of the Sea (UNCLOS), negotiated under the auspices of the Third United Nations Conference on the Law of the Sea, aims to establish a comprehensive legal regime to govern activities in and in relation to the world's seas and oceans. The selected Articles reproduced below are directly concerned with natural resources and the marine environment. Much of the Convention is considered to be declaratory of customary international law. The Convention's comprehensive definition of pollution of the marine environment (Article 1) has been used or relied on in subsequent agreements for the protection of the marine environment.

The Convention affirms the right of innocent passage in territorial waters, subject to certain limitations: passage loses its innocence if a foreign vessel engages in an act of wilful and serious pollution contrary to the Convention (Article 19(2)(h)), and coastal States are entitled to adopt the necessary laws relating to innocent passage for the purpose of, *inter alia*, the conservation of marine living resources and the protection of the marine environment (Article 21(1)). The Convention further provides that ships in passage must comply with international regulations for control of pollution (Article 39). The Convention permits States bordering straits and archipelagic sea lanes to make laws to protect, *inter alia*, the environment against pollution (Articles 42, 43 and 54).

The Convention establishes a regime of access to natural resources depending on where the activity takes place: within a State's exclusive economic zone (EEZ) or on the high seas. In so doing, the Convention confers rights and duties upon States which reflect a balance between the interests of coastal States and others, including flag States, land-locked States and developing States.

EEZs are areas of up to two hundred nautical miles from a State's shore (Article 57) in which States are given the sovereign right to explore, exploit, conserve and manage all natural resources as well as the exclusive right to determine the total allowable catch (TAC) of living resources (Article 61). If a State is unable to harvest its TAC, other States are to be granted access by agreement to those resources, subject to the conservation measures enacted by the coastal State (Article 62). If a stock occurs within the EEZ of two States or within the EEZ and areas beyond, then the coastal and fishing States are required to agree on the necessary conservation and developmental measures (Article 63). In the case of highly migratory species listed in Annex I, the coastal and fishing States are to co-operate on measures to achieve their 'optimum utilization' (Article 64). With respect to marine mammals, coastal States are permitted to regulate their exploitation more strictly than required under the Convention (Articles 65 and 120). The Convention gives coastal States the responsibility for the conservation of anadromous species in whose waters they originate (Article 67) and for the management of catadromous species which spend the greater part of their cycle in their waters (Article 67). Land-locked and 'geographically disadvantaged' States are granted rights of access to the surplus within an EEZ on an equitable basis through bilateral or multilateral agreements (Articles 69 and 70), except where a coastal State's economy is 'overwhelmingly' dependent upon the exploitation of the resources (Article 71). Coastal States are empowered to enforce compliance of its rules enacted in conformity with the Convention by inspection, arrest and judicial proceedings against vessels and their crews (Article 73).

On the high seas, the Convention entitles all States to fish subject to treaty obligations and certain rights, duties and interests of coastal States (Article 116), but also places on all States a duty to conserve living resources (Article 117). The Convention requires all Parties to co-operate in conservation and management measures of living resources on the high seas, and fishing States, in particular, are required to enter into negotiations on these measures (Article 118). The Convention outlines the measures States are required to take in determining the allowable catch and establishing other conservation measures for living resources on the high seas (Article 119).

States bordering a semi-enclosed sea are encouraged to co-operate by co-ordinating their management, conservation, exploration and exploitation of living resources, their protection and preservation of the marine environment, and their pursuit of scientific research policies (Article 123).

The Convention created a regime regulating the exploitation of the sea-bed and ocean floor beyond the limits of national jurisdiction (the 'Area'). The original provisions of the Convention were to be found in Part XI. Industrialised countries objected to several provisions in Part XI and to address those criticisms the Secretary-General of the UN convened a series of informal consultations which led to the adoption, on 28 July 1994, of the Agreement relating to the implementation of Part XI of the United Nations Convention on the Law of the Sea of 10 December 1982. The Agreement entered into force on 28 July 1996.

Part XII of the Convention provides for the protection and preservation of the marine environment. States are required to protect and preserve the marine environment (Article 192) and the right to exploit their natural resources must be exercised in accordance with this obligation (Article 193). States are required to take measures to prevent, reduce and control pollution of the marine environment (Article 194(1)) and must ensure that activities under their jurisdiction or control do not cause pollution in areas outside where they exercise sovereign rights (Article 194(2)).

When a State becomes aware of imminent danger to the environment, it is required to promptly notify any other State which it considers may be affected and any competent international organisation (Article 198). The Convention also requires States to carry out environmental monitoring (Article 204) and assessment (Article 206).

States are required to promote and provide scientific and technical assistance to developing States in respect of environmental matters (Article 202). Developing States are also to benefit from preferences by international organisations for funds and services for the purpose of prevention, reduction and control of pollution (Article 203).

The Convention requires States to adopt laws and regulations to prevent, reduce and control pollution from the following sources: land-based sources (Article 207); sea-bed activities (Article 208); activities in the Area (Article 209); dumping (Article 210); vessels (Article 211); and from or through the atmosphere (Article 212). The Convention's specific requirements differ according to the source of pollution, with some involving individual State action and others involving international co-ordination, with some calling for compliance with existing international standards and others requiring those standards only to be taken into account.

In addition, the Convention requires enforcement of the laws and regulations adopted by the Parties in relation to pollution from land-based sources (Article 213); sea-bed activities (Article 214); activities in the Area (Article 215); dumping (Article 216); and from or through the atmosphere (Article 222). Detailed rules are provided for the institution of proceedings by flag States (Article 217); port States (Article 218); and coastal States (Article 220). The Convention also provides safeguards against abuses of State enforcement powers (Articles 223–233).

The Convention requires States to co-operate in the implementation of existing law and the development of further law in relation to responsibility for non-fulfilment of international obligations and liability for damage, with a view to assuring 'prompt and adequate compensation' (Article 235). Sovereign immunity is provided for, but States are to ensure that such vessels encompassed under it comply as far as is reasonable and practical with the requirements of the Convention (Article 236). Part XII of the Convention is to apply without any prejudice to any obligations Parties may have under specific conventions relating to the protection of the marine environment, and such obligations are to be carried out in a manner consistent with the general principles and obligations of the Convention (Article 237).

The Convention provides for compulsory dispute settlement with one of the following bodies: the International Tribunal for the Law of the Sea (Annex VI); the International Court of Justice; the arbitral tribunal (Annex VII); or the special arbitral tribunal (Annex VII), which can hear disputes concerning fisheries and the protection of the marine environment (Article 287). Disputes exempt from compulsory dispute settlement include those involving the exercise of sovereign or discretionary powers by coastal States over living resources in their EEZ (Article 297(3)(a)). Notwithstanding this exemption, compulsory conciliation under Annex V is provided for in some instances of coastal State action (Article 297(3)(b)). The Convention provides two procedures for its amendment (Articles 312–316). Reservations are not permitted except where expressly provided for (Article 309) and denunciation of the Convention is permitted (Article 317).

Date of signature: 10 December 1982

Entry into force: 16 November 1994

Depositary: Secretary-General of the United Nations

Contracting Parties: Algeria, Angola, Antigua and Barbuda, Argentina, Armenia, Australia, Austria, Bahamas, Bahrain, Bangladesh, Barbados, Belgium, Belize, Benin, Bolivia, Bosnia and Herzegovina, Botswana, Brazil, Brunei Darussalam, Bulgaria, Cameroon, Cape Verde, Chile, China, Comoros, Cook Islands, Costa Rica, Cote d'Ivoire, Croatia, Cuba, Cyprus, Czech Republic, Democratic Republic of the Congo, Djibouti, Dominica, Egypt, Equatorial Guinea, European Community, Fiji, Finland, France, Gabon, Gambia, Georgia, Germany, Ghana, Greece, Grenada, Guatemala, Guinea, Guinea Bissau, Guyana, Haiti, Honduras, Hungary, Iceland, India, Indonesia, Iraq, Ireland, Italy, Jamaica, Japan, Jordan, Kenya, Kuwait, Lao People's Democratic Republic, Lebanon, Luxembourg, Madagascar, Malaysia, Maldives, Mali, Malta, Marshall Islands, Mauritania, Mauritius, Mexico, Micronesia (Federated States of), Monaco, Mongolia, Mozambique, Myanmar, Namibia, Nauru, Nepal, Netherlands, New Zealand, Nicaragua, Nigeria, Norway, Oman, Pakistan, Palau, Panama, Papua New Guinea, Paraguay, Philippines, Poland, Portugal, Qatar, Republic of Korea, Romania, Russian Federation, Saint Kitts and Nevis, Saint Lucia, Saint Vincent and Grenadines, Samoa, São Tomé and

Príncipe, Saudi Arabia, Senegal, Serbia and Montenegro, Seychelles, Sierra Leone, Singapore, Slovakia, Slovenia, Solomon Islands, Somalia, South Africa, Spain, Sri Lanka, Sudan, Suriname, Sweden, Tanzania (United Republic of), The Former Yugoslav Republic of Macedonia, Togo, Tonga, Trinidad and Tobago, Tunisia, Tuvalu, Uganda, Ukraine, United Kingdom, Uruguay, Vanuatu, Vietnam, Yemen, Zambia, Zimbabwe.

Website: ww.un.org/Depts/los/index.htm

United Nations Convention on the Law of the Sea (extracts)

[. . .]

Part I
Introduction

Article 1
Use of terms and scope

1. For the purposes of this Convention:

(1) 'Area' means the seabed and ocean floor and subsoil thereof, beyond the limits of national jurisdiction;
(2) 'Authority' means the International Seabed Authority;
(3) 'activities in the Area' means all activities of exploration for, and exploitation of, the resources of the Area;
(4) 'pollution of the marine environment' means the introduction by man, directly or indirectly, of substances or energy into the marine environment, including estuaries, which results or is likely to result in such deleterious effects as harm to living resources and marine life, hazards to human health, hindrance to marine activities, including fishing and other legitimate uses of the sea, impairment of quality for use of sea water and reduction of amenities;
(5)

   (a) 'dumping' means:
      (i) any deliberate disposal of wastes or other matter from vessels, aircraft, platforms or other man-made structures at sea;
      (ii) any deliberate disposal of vessels, aircraft, platforms or other man-made structures at sea;
   (b) 'dumping' does not include:
      (i) the disposal of wastes or other matter incidental to, or derived from the normal operations of vessels, aircraft, platforms or other

man-made structures at sea and their equipment, other than wastes or other matter transported by or to vessels, aircraft, platforms or other man-made structures at sea, operating for the purpose of disposal of such matter or derived from the treatment of such wastes or other matter on such vessels, aircraft, platforms or structures;

(ii) placement of matter for a purpose other than the mere disposal thereof, provided that such placement is not contrary to the aims of this Convention.

2.

(1) 'States Parties' means States which have consented to be bound by this Convention and for which this Convention is in force.

(2) This Convention applies *mutatis mutandis* to the entities referred to in article 305, paragraph l(b), (c), (d), (e) and (f), which become Parties to this Convention in accordance with the conditions relevant to each, and to that extent 'States Parties' refers to those entities.

[. . .]

Section 3
Innocent passage in the territorial sea

Subsection A
Rules applicable to all ships

Article 19
Meaning of innocent passage

1. Passage is innocent so long as it is not prejudicial to the peace, good order or security of the coastal State. Such passage shall take place in conformity with this Convention and with other rules of international law.

2. Passage of a foreign ship shall be considered to be prejudicial to the peace, good order or security of the coastal State if in the territorial sea it engages in any of the following activities:
[. . .]

(h) any act of wilful and serious pollution contrary to this Convention;
 (i) any fishing activities;

[. . .]

Article 21
Laws and regulations of the coastal State relating to innocent passage

1. The coastal State may adopt laws and regulations, in conformity with the provisions of this Convention and other rules of international law, relating

to innocent passage through the territorial sea, in respect of all or any of the
following:

(a) the safety of navigation and the regulation of maritime traffic;

[. . .]

(d) the conservation of the living resources of the sea;
(e) the prevention of infringement of the fisheries laws and regulations of the
    coastal State;
(f) the preservation of the environment of the coastal State and the prevention,
    reduction and control of pollution thereof.

2. Such laws and regulations shall not apply to the design, construction,
manning or equipment of foreign ships unless they are giving effect to generally
accepted international rules or standards.
3. The coastal State shall give due publicity to all such laws and regulations.
4. Foreign ships exercising the right of innocent passage through the territorial sea shall comply with all such laws and regulations and all generally accepted international regulations relating to the prevention of collisions at sea.
[. . .]

Article 23
Foreign nuclear-powered ships and ships carrying nuclear or other inherently dangerous or noxious substances

Foreign nuclear-powered ships and ships carrying nuclear or other inherently
dangerous or noxious substances shall, when exercising the right of innocent
passage through the territorial sea, carry documents and observe special precautionary measures established for such ships by international agreements.
[. . .]

Part III
Straits used for international navigation

Section 2
Transit passage

Article 39
Duties of ships and aircraft during transit passage

[. . .]
2. Ships in transit passage shall:
[. . .]

(b) comply with generally accepted international regulations, procedures and
    practices for the prevention, reduction and control of pollution from ships.

[. . .]

Article 42
Laws and regulations of States bordering straits relating to transit passage

1. Subject to the provisions of this section, States bordering straits may adopt laws and regulations relating to transit passage through straits, in respect of all or any of the following:

[. . .]

(b) the prevention, reduction and control of pollution, by giving effect to applicable international regulations regarding the discharge of oil, oily wastes and other noxious substances in the strait;
(c) with respect to fishing vessels, the prevention of fishing, including the stowage of fishing gear;

[. . .]

Article 43
Navigational and safety aids and other improvements and the prevention, reduction and control of pollution

User States and States bordering a strait should by agreement cooperate:

[. . .]

(b) for the prevention, reduction and control of pollution from ships.

[. . .]

Part IV
Archipelagic states

Article 54
Duties of ships and aircraft during their passage, research and survey activities, duties of the archipelagic State and laws and regulations of the archipelagic State relating to archipelagic sea lanes passage

Articles 39, 40, 42 and 44 apply *mutatis mutandis* to archipelagic sea lanes passage.

Part V
Exclusive economic zone

Article 55
Specific legal regime of the exclusive economic zone

The exclusive economic zone is an area beyond and adjacent to the territorial sea, subject to the specific legal regime established in this Part, under which the rights and jurisdiction of the coastal State and the rights and freedoms of other States are governed by the relevant provisions of this Convention.

Article 56
Rights, jurisdiction and duties of the coastal State in the exclusive economic zone

1. In the exclusive economic zone, the coastal State has:

(a) sovereign rights for the purpose of exploring and exploiting, conserving and managing the natural resources, whether living or non-living, of the waters superjacent to the seabed and of the seabed and its subsoil, and with regard to other activities for the economic exploitation and exploration of the zone, such as the production of energy from the water, currents and winds;

(b) jurisdiction as provided for in the relevant provisions of this Convention with regard to:
   (i) the establishment and use of artificial islands, installations and structures;
   (ii) marine scientific research;
   (iii) the protection and preservation of the marine environment;

(c) other rights and duties provided for in this Convention.

2. In exercising its rights and performing its duties under this Convention in the exclusive economic zone, the coastal State shall have due regard to the rights and duties of other States and shall act in a manner compatible with the provisions of this Convention.

3. The rights set out in this article with respect to the seabed and subsoil shall be exercised in accordance with Part VI.

Article 57
Breadth of the exclusive economic zone

The exclusive economic zone shall not extend beyond 200 nautical miles from the baselines from which the breadth of the territorial sea is measured.

Article 58
Rights and duties of other States in the exclusive economic zone

1. In the exclusive economic zone, all States, whether coastal or land-locked, enjoy, subject to the relevant provisions of this Convention, the freedoms referred to in article 87 of navigation and overflight and of the laying of submarine cables and pipelines, and other internationally lawful uses of the sea related to these freedoms, such as those associated with the operation of ships, aircraft and submarine cables and pipelines, and compatible with the other provisions of this Convention.

2. Articles 88 to 115 and other pertinent rules of international law apply to the exclusive economic zone in so far as they are not incompatible with this Part.

3. In exercising their rights and performing their duties under this Convention in the exclusive economic zone, States shall have due regard to the rights and duties of the coastal State and shall comply with the laws and regulations adopted by the coastal State in accordance with the provisions of this Convention and other rules of international law in so far as they are not incompatible with this Part.

Article 59
Basis for the resolution of conflicts regarding the attribution of rights and jurisdiction in the exclusive economic zone

In cases where this Convention does not attribute rights or jurisdiction to the coastal State or to other States within the exclusive economic zone, and a conflict arises between the interests of the coastal State and any other State or States, the conflict should be resolved on the basis of equity and in the light of all the relevant circumstances, taking into account the respective importance of the interests involved to the parties as well as to the international community as a whole.

Article 60
Artificial islands, installations and structures in the exclusive economic zone

1. In the exclusive economic zone, the coastal State shall have the exclusive right to construct and to authorize and regulate the construction, operation and use of:

(a) artificial islands;
(b) installations and structures for the purposes provided for in article 56 and other economic purposes;
(c) installations and structures which may interfere with the exercise of the rights of the coastal State in the zone.

2. The coastal State shall have exclusive jurisdiction over such artificial islands, installations and structures, including jurisdiction with regard to customs, fiscal, health, safety and immigration laws and regulations.

3. Due notice must be given of the construction of such artificial islands, installations or structures, and permanent means for giving warning of their presence must be maintained. Any installations or structures which are abandoned or disused shall be removed to ensure safety of navigation, taking into account any generally accepted international standards established in this regard by the competent international organization. Such removal shall also have due regard to fishing, the protection of the marine environment and the rights and duties of other States. Appropriate publicity shall be given to the depth, position and dimensions of any installations or structures not entirely removed.

4. The coastal State may, where necessary, establish reasonable safety zones around such artificial islands, installations and structures in which it may take appropriate measures to ensure the safety both of navigation and of the artificial islands, installations and structures.

5. The breadth of the safety zones shall be determined by the coastal State, taking into account applicable international standards. Such zones shall be designed to ensure that they are reasonably related to the nature and function of the artificial islands, installations or structures, and shall not exceed a distance of 500 metres around them, measured from each point of their outer edge, except as authorized by generally accepted international standards or as recommended by the competent international organization. Due notice shall be given of the extent of safety zones.

6. All ships must respect these safety zones and shall comply with generally accepted international standards regarding navigation in the vicinity of artificial islands, installations, structures and safety zones.

7. Artificial islands, installations and structures and the safety zones around them may not be established where interference may be caused to the use of recognized sea lanes essential to international navigation.

8. Artificial islands, installations and structures do not possess the status of islands. They have no territorial sea of their own, and their presence does not affect the delimitation of the territorial sea, the exclusive economic zone or the continental shelf.

Article 61
Conservation of the living resources

1. The coastal State shall determine the allowable catch of the living resources in its exclusive economic zone.

2. The coastal State, taking into account the best scientific evidence available to it, shall ensure through proper conservation and management measures that the maintenance of the living resources in the exclusive economic zone is not endangered by over-exploitation. As appropriate, the coastal State and competent international organizations, whether subregional, regional or global, shall cooperate to this end.

3. Such measures shall also be designed to maintain or restore populations of harvested species at levels which can produce the maximum sustainable yield, as qualified by relevant environmental and economic factors, including the economic needs of coastal fishing communities and the special requirements of developing States, and taking into account fishing patterns, the interdependence of stocks and any generally recommended international minimum standards, whether subregional, regional or global.

4. In taking such measures the coastal State shall take into consideration the effects on species associated with or dependent upon harvested species with a view to maintaining or restoring populations of such associated or dependent

species above levels at which their reproduction may become seriously threatened.

5. Available scientific information, catch and fishing effort statistics, and other data relevant to the conservation of fish stocks shall be contributed and exchanged on a regular basis through competent international organizations, whether subregional, regional or global, where appropriate and with participation by all States concerned, including States whose nationals are allowed to fish in the exclusive economic zone.

Article 62
Utilization of the living resources

1. The coastal State shall promote the objective of optimum utilization of the living resources in the exclusive economic zone without prejudice to article 61.

2. The coastal State shall determine its capacity to harvest the living resources of the exclusive economic zone. Where the coastal State does not have the capacity to harvest the entire allowable catch, it shall, through agreements or other arrangements and pursuant to the terms, conditions, laws and regulations referred to in paragraph 4, give other States access to the surplus of the allowable catch, having particular regard to the provisions of articles 69 and 70, especially in relation to the developing States mentioned therein.

3. In giving access to other States to its exclusive economic zone under this article, the coastal State shall take into account all relevant factors, including, *inter alia*, the significance of the living resources of the area to the economy of the coastal State concerned and its other national interests, the provisions of articles 69 and 70, the requirements of developing States in the subregion or region in harvesting part of the surplus and the need to minimize economic dislocation in States whose nationals have habitually fished in the zone or which have made substantial efforts in research and identification of stocks.

4. Nationals of other States fishing in the exclusive economic zone shall comply with the conservation measures and with the other terms and conditions established in the laws and regulations of the coastal State. These laws and regulations shall be consistent with this Convention and may relate, *inter alia*, to the following:

(a) licensing of fishermen, fishing vessels and equipment, including payment of fees and other forms of remuneration, which, in the case of developing coastal States, may consist of adequate compensation in the field of financing, equipment and technology relating to the fishing industry;

(b) determining the species which may be caught, and fixing quotas of catch, whether in relation to particular stocks or groups of stocks or catch per vessel over a period of time or to the catch by nationals of any State during a specified period;

(c) regulating seasons and areas of fishing, the types, sizes and amount of gear, and the types, sizes and number of fishing vessels that may be used;

(d) fixing the age and size of fish and other species that may be caught;

(e) specifying information required of fishing vessels, including catch and effort statistics and vessel position reports;

(f) requiring, under the authorization and control of the coastal State, the conduct of specified fisheries research programmes and regulating the conduct of such research, including the sampling of catches, disposition of samples and reporting of associated scientific data;

(g) the placing of observers or trainees on board such vessels by the coastal State;

(h) the landing of all or any part of the catch by such vessels in the ports of the coastal State;

(i) terms and conditions relating to joint ventures or other cooperative arrangements;

(j) requirements for the training of personnel and the transfer of fisheries technology, including enhancement of the coastal State's capability of undertaking fisheries research;

(k) enforcement procedures.

5. Coastal States shall give due notice of conservation and management laws and regulations.

Article 63
Stocks occurring within the exclusive economic zones of two or more coastal States or both within the exclusive economic zone and in an area beyond and adjacent to it

1. Where the same stock or stocks of associated species occur within the exclusive economic zones of two or more coastal States, these States shall seek, either directly or through appropriate subregional or regional organizations, to agree upon the measures necessary to coordinate and ensure the conservation and development of such stocks without prejudice to the other provisions of this Part.

2. Where the same stock or stocks of associated species occur both within the exclusive economic zone and in an area beyond and adjacent to the zone, the coastal State and the States fishing for such stocks in the adjacent area shall seek, either directly or through appropriate subregional or regional organizations, to agree upon the measures necessary for the conservation of these stocks in the adjacent area.

Article 64
Highly migratory species

1. The coastal State and other States whose nationals fish in the region for the highly migratory species listed in Annex I shall cooperate directly or through

appropriate international organizations with a view to ensuring conservation and promoting the objective of optimum utilization of such species throughout the region, both within and beyond the exclusive economic zone. In regions for which no appropriate international organization exists, the coastal State and other States whose nationals harvest these species in the region shall cooperate to establish such an organization and participate in its work.

2. The provisions of paragraph 1 apply in addition to the other provisions of this Part.

Article 65
Marine mammals

Nothing in this Part restricts the right of a coastal State or the competence of an international organization, as appropriate, to prohibit, limit or regulate the exploitation of marine mammals more strictly than provided for in this Part. States shall cooperate with a view to the conservation of marine mammals and in the case of cetaceans shall in particular work through the appropriate international organizations for their conservation, management and study.

Article 66
Anadromous stocks

1. States in whose rivers anadromous stocks originate shall have the primary interest in and responsibility for such stocks.

2. The State of origin of anadromous stocks shall ensure their conservation by the establishment of appropriate regulatory measures for fishing in all waters landward of the outer limits of its exclusive economic zone and for fishing provided for in paragraph 3(b). The State of origin may, after consultations with the other States referred to in paragraphs 3 and 4 fishing these stocks, establish total allowable catches for stocks originating in its rivers.

3.

(a) Fisheries for anadromous stocks shall be conducted only in waters landward of the outer limits of exclusive economic zones, except in cases where this provision would result in economic dislocation for a State other than the State of origin. With respect to such fishing beyond the outer limits of the exclusive economic zone, States concerned shall maintain consultations with a view to achieving agreement on terms and conditions of such fishing giving due regard to the conservation requirements and the needs of the State of origin in respect of these stocks.

(b) The State of origin shall cooperate in minimizing economic dislocation in such other States fishing these stocks, taking into account the normal catch and the mode of operations of such States, and all the areas in which such fishing has occurred.

(c) States referred to in subparagraph (b), participating by agreement with the State of origin in measures to renew anadromous stocks, particularly by expenditures for that purpose, shall be given special consideration by the State of origin in the harvesting of stocks originating in its rivers.

(d) Enforcement of regulations regarding anadromous stocks beyond the exclusive economic zone shall be by agreement between the State of origin and the other States concerned.

4. In cases where anadromous stocks migrate into or through the waters landward of the outer limits of the exclusive economic zone of a State other than the State of origin, such State shall cooperate with the State of origin with regard to the conservation and management of such stocks.

5. The State of origin of anadromous stocks and other States fishing these stocks shall make arrangements for the implementation of the provisions of this article, where appropriate, through regional organizations.

Article 67
Catadromous species

1. A coastal State in whose waters catadromous species spend the greater part of their life cycle shall have responsibility for the management of these species and shall ensure the ingress and egress of migrating fish.

2. Harvesting of catadromous species shall be conducted only in waters landward of the outer limits of exclusive economic zones. When conducted in exclusive economic zones, harvesting shall be subject to this article and the other provisions of this Convention concerning fishing in these zones.

3. In cases where catadromous fish migrate through the exclusive economic zone of another State, whether as juvenile or maturing fish, the management, including harvesting, of such fish shall be regulated by agreement between the State mentioned in paragraph 1 and the other State concerned. Such agreement shall ensure the rational management of the species and take into account the responsibilities of the State mentioned in paragraph 1 for the maintenance of these species.

Article 68
Sedentary species

This Part does not apply to sedentary species as defined in article 77, paragraph 4.

Article 69
Right of land-locked States

1. Land-locked States shall have the right to participate, on an equitable basis, in the exploitation of an appropriate part of the surplus of the living resources of the exclusive economic zones of coastal States of the same subregion or region,

taking into account the relevant economic and geographical circumstances of all the States concerned and in conformity with the provisions of this article and of articles 61 and 62.

2. The terms and modalities of such participation shall be established by the States concerned through bilateral, subregional or regional agreements taking into account, *inter alia*:

(a) the need to avoid effects detrimental to fishing communities or fishing industries of the coastal State;
(b) the extent to which the land-locked State, in accordance with the provisions of this article, is participating or is entitled to participate under existing bilateral, subregional or regional agreements in the exploitation of living resources of the exclusive economic zones of other coastal States;
(c) the extent to which other land-locked States and geographically disadvantaged States are participating in the exploitation of the living resources of the exclusive economic zone of the coastal State and the consequent need to avoid a particular burden for any single coastal State or a part of it;
(d) the nutritional needs of the populations of the respective States.

3. When the harvesting capacity of a coastal State approaches a point which would enable it to harvest the entire allowable catch of the living resources in its exclusive economic zone, the coastal State and other States concerned shall cooperate in the establishment of equitable arrangements on a bilateral, subregional or regional basis to allow for participation of developing land-locked States of the same subregion or region in the exploitation of the living resources of the exclusive economic zones of coastal States of the subregion or region, as may be appropriate in the circumstances and on terms satisfactory to all parties. In the implementation of this provision the factors mentioned in paragraph 2 shall also be taken into account.

4. Developed land-locked States shall, under the provisions of this article, be entitled to participate in the exploitation of living resources only in the exclusive economic zones of developed coastal States of the same subregion or region having regard to the extent to which the coastal State, in giving access to other States to the living resources of its exclusive economic zone, has taken into account the need to minimize detrimental effects on fishing communities and economic dislocation in States whose nationals have habitually fished in the zone.

5. The above provisions are without prejudice to arrangements agreed upon in subregions or regions where the coastal States may grant to land-locked States of the same subregion or region equal or preferential rights for the exploitation of the living resources in the exclusive economic zones.

Article 70
Right of geographically disadvantaged States

1. Geographically disadvantaged States shall have the right to participate, on an equitable basis, in the exploitation of an appropriate part of the surplus of the living resources of the exclusive economic zones of coastal States of the same subregion or region, taking into account the relevant economic and geographical circumstances of all the States concerned and in conformity with the provisions of this article and of articles 61 and 62.

2. For the purposes of this Part, 'geographically disadvantaged States' means coastal States, including States bordering enclosed or semi-enclosed seas, whose geographical situation makes them dependent upon the exploitation of the living resources of the exclusive economic zones of other States in the subregion or region for adequate supplies of fish for the nutritional purposes of their populations or parts thereof, and coastal States which can claim no exclusive economic zones of their own.

3. The terms and modalities of such participation shall be established by the States concerned through bilateral, subregional or regional agreements taking into account, *inter alia*:

(a) the need to avoid effects detrimental to fishing communities or fishing industries of the coastal State;
(b) the extent to which the geographically disadvantaged State, in accordance with the provisions of this article, is participating or is entitled to participate under existing bilateral, subregional or regional agreements in the exploitation of living resources of the exclusive economic zones of other coastal States;
(c) the extent to which other geographically disadvantaged States and land-locked States are participating in the exploitation of the living resources of the exclusive economic zone of the coastal State and the consequent need to avoid a particular burden for any single coastal State or a part of it;
(d) the nutritional needs of the populations of the respective States.

4. When the harvesting capacity of a coastal State approaches a point which would enable it to harvest the entire allowable catch of the living resources in its exclusive economic zone, the coastal State and other States concerned shall cooperate in the establishment of equitable arrangements on a bilateral, subregional or regional basis to allow for participation of developing geographically disadvantaged States of the same subregion or region in the exploitation of the living resources of the exclusive economic zones of coastal States of the subregion or region, as may be appropriate in the circumstances and on terms satisfactory to all parties. In the implementation of this provision the factors mentioned in paragraph 3 shall also be taken into account.

5. Developed geographically disadvantaged States shall, under the provisions of this article, be entitled to participate in the exploitation of living resources only in the exclusive economic zones of developed coastal States of the same subregion or region having regard to the extent to which the coastal State, in giving access to other States to the living resources of its exclusive economic zone, has taken into account the need to minimize detrimental effects on fishing communities and economic dislocation in States whose nationals have habitually fished in the zone.

6. The above provisions are without prejudice to arrangements agreed upon in subregions or regions where the coastal States may grant to geographically disadvantaged States of the same subregion or region equal or preferential rights for the exploitation of the living resources in the exclusive economic zones.

Article 71
Non-applicability of articles 69 and 70

The provisions of articles 69 and 70 do not apply in the case of a coastal State whose economy is overwhelmingly dependent on the exploitation of the living resources of its exclusive economic zone.

Article 72
Restrictions on transfer of rights

1. Rights provided under articles 69 and 70 to exploit living resources shall not be directly or indirectly transferred to third States or their nationals by lease or licence, by establishing joint ventures or in any other manner which has the effect of such transfer unless otherwise agreed by the States concerned.

2. The foregoing provision does not preclude the States concerned from obtaining technical or financial assistance from third States or international organizations in order to facilitate the exercise of the rights pursuant to articles 69 and 70, provided that it does not have the effect referred to in paragraph 1.

Article 73
Enforcement of laws and regulations of the coastal State

1. The coastal State may, in the exercise of its sovereign rights to explore, exploit, conserve and manage the living resources in the exclusive economic zone, take such measures, including boarding, inspection, arrest and judicial proceedings, as may be necessary to ensure compliance with the laws and regulations adopted by it in conformity with this Convention.

2. Arrested vessels and their crews shall be promptly released upon the posting of reasonable bond or other security.

3. Coastal State penalties for violations of fisheries laws and regulations in the exclusive economic zone may not include imprisonment, in the absence of agreements to the contrary by the States concerned, or any other form of corporal punishment.

4. In cases of arrest or detention of foreign vessels the coastal State shall promptly notify the flag State, through appropriate channels, of the action taken and of any penalties subsequently imposed.
[...]

Part VI
Continental shelf

Article 79
Submarine cables and pipelines on the continental shelf

1. All States are entitled to lay submarine cables and pipelines on the continental shelf, in accordance with the provisions of this article.

2. Subject to its right to take reasonable measures for the exploration of the continental shelf, the exploitation of its natural resources and the prevention, reduction and control of pollution from pipelines, the coastal State may not impede the laying or maintenance of such cables or pipelines.

3. The delineation of the course for the laying of such pipelines on the continental shelf is subject to the consent of the coastal State.

4. Nothing in this Part affects the right of the coastal State to establish conditions for cables or pipelines entering its territory or territorial sea, or its jurisdiction over cables and pipelines constructed or used in connection with the exploration of its continental shelf or exploitation of its resources or the operations of artificial islands, installations and structures under its jurisdiction.

5. When laying submarine cables or pipelines, States shall have due regard to cables or pipelines already in position. In particular, possibilities of repairing existing cables or pipelines shall not be prejudiced.

Article 80
Artificial islands, installations and structures on the continental shelf

Article 60 applies *mutatis mutandis* to artificial islands, installations and structures on the continental shelf.
[...]

Part VII
High seas

Article 94
Duties of the flag State

1. Every State shall effectively exercise its jurisdiction and control in administrative, technical and social matters over ships flying its flag.

2. In particular every State shall:

(a) maintain a register of ships containing the names and particulars of ships flying its flag, except those which are excluded from generally accepted international regulations on account of their small size; and

(b) assume jurisdiction under its internal law over each ship flying its flag and its master, officers and crew in respect of administrative, technical and social matters concerning the ship.

3. Every State shall take such measures for ships flying its flag as are necessary to ensure safety at sea with regard, *inter alia*, to:

(a) the construction, equipment and seaworthiness of ships;
(b) the manning of ships, labour conditions and the training of crews, taking into account the applicable international instruments;
(c) the use of signals, the maintenance of communications and the prevention of collisions.

4. Such measures shall include those necessary to ensure:

(a) that each ship, before registration and thereafter at appropriate intervals, is surveyed by a qualified surveyor of ships, and has on board such charts, nautical publications and navigational equipment and instruments as are appropriate for the safe navigation of the ship;
(b) that each ship is in the charge of a master and officers who possess appropriate qualifications, in particular in seamanship, navigation, communications and marine engineering, and that the crew is appropriate in qualification and numbers for the type, size, machinery and equipment of the ship;
(c) that the master, officers and, to the extent appropriate, the crew are fully conversant with and required to observe the applicable international regulations concerning the safety of life at sea, the prevention of collisions, the prevention, reduction and control of marine pollution, and the maintenance of communications by radio.

5. In taking the measures called for in paragraphs 3 and 4 each State is required to conform to generally accepted international regulations, procedures and practices and to take any steps which may be necessary to secure their observance.

6. A State which has clear grounds to believe that proper jurisdiction and control with respect to a ship have not been exercised may report the facts to the flag State. Upon receiving such a report, the flag State shall investigate the matter and, if appropriate, take any action necessary to remedy the situation.

7. Each State shall cause an inquiry to be held by or before a suitably qualified person or persons into every marine casualty or incident of navigation on the high seas involving a ship flying its flag and causing loss of life or serious injury to nationals of another State or serious damage to ships or installations of another State or to the marine environment. The flag State and the other State shall cooperate in the conduct of any inquiry held by that other State into any such marine casualty or incident of navigation.

Article 95
Immunity of warships on the high seas

Warships on the high seas have complete immunity from the jurisdiction of any State other than the flag State.

Article 96
Immunity of ships used only on government non-commercial service

Ships owned or operated by a State and used only on government non-commercial service shall, on the high seas, have complete immunity from the jurisdiction of any State other than the flag State.
[. . .]

Section 2
Conservation and management of the living resources of the high seas

Article 116
Right to fish on the high seas

All States have the right for their nationals to engage in fishing on the high seas subject to:

(a) their treaty obligations;
(b) the rights and duties as well as the interests of coastal States provided for, *inter alia*, in article 63, paragraph 2, and articles 64 to 67; and
(c) the provisions of this section.

Article 117
Duty of States to adopt with respect to their nationals measures for the conservation of the living resources of the high seas

All States have the duty to take, or to cooperate with other States in taking, such measures for their respective nationals as may be necessary for the conservation of the living resources of the high seas.

Article 118
Cooperation of States in the conservation and management of living resources

States shall cooperate with each other in the conservation and management of living resources in the areas of the high seas. States whose nationals exploit identical living resources, or different living resources in the same area, shall enter into negotiations with a view to taking the measures necessary for the conservation of the living resources concerned. They shall, as appropriate, cooperate to establish subregional or regional fisheries organizations to this end.

Article 119
Conservation of the living resources of the high seas

1. In determining the allowable catch and establishing other conservation measures for the living resources in the high seas, States shall:

(a) take measures which are designed, on the best scientific evidence available to the States concerned, to maintain or restore populations of harvested species at levels which can produce the maximum sustainable yield, as qualified by relevant environmental and economic factors, including the special requirements of developing States, and taking into account fishing patterns, the interdependence of stocks and any generally recommended international minimum standards, whether subregional, regional or global;

(b) take into consideration the effects on species associated with or dependent upon harvested species with a view to maintaining or restoring populations of such associated or dependent species above levels at which their reproduction may become seriously threatened.

2. Available scientific information, catch and fishing effort statistics, and other data relevant to the conservation of fish stocks shall be contributed and exchanged on a regular basis through competent international organizations, whether subregional, regional or global, where appropriate and with participation by all States concerned.

3. States concerned shall ensure that conservation measures and their implementation do not discriminate in form or in fact against the fishermen of any State.

Article 120
Marine mammals

Article 65 also applies to the conservation and management of marine mammals in the high seas.

Part VIII
Regime of islands

Article 121
Regime of islands

1. An island is a naturally formed area of land, surrounded by water, which is above water at high tide.

2. Except as provided for in paragraph 3, the territorial sea, the contiguous zone, the exclusive economic zone and the continental shelf of an island are determined in accordance with the provisions of this Convention applicable to other land territory.

3. Rocks which cannot sustain human habitation or economic life of their own shall have no exclusive economic zone or continental shelf.

[...]

Part IX
Enclosed or semi-enclosed seas

Article 123
Cooperation of States bordering enclosed or semi-enclosed seas

States bordering an enclosed or semi-enclosed sea should cooperate with each other in the exercise of their rights and in the performance of their duties under this Convention. To this end they shall endeavour, directly or through an appropriate regional organization:

(a) to coordinate the management, conservation, exploration and exploitation of the living resources of the sea;
(b) to coordinate the implementation of their rights and duties with respect to the protection and preservation of the marine environment;
(c) to coordinate their scientific research policies and undertake where appropriate joint programmes of scientific research in the area;
(d) to invite, as appropriate, other interested States or international organizations to cooperate with them in furtherance of the provisions of this article.

[...]

Part XII
Protection and preservation of the marine environment

Section 1
General provisions

Article 192
General obligation

States have the obligation to protect and preserve the marine environment.

Article 193
Sovereign right of States to exploit their natural resources

States have the sovereign right to exploit their natural resources pursuant to their environmental policies and in accordance with their duty to protect and preserve the marine environment.

Article 194
Measures to prevent, reduce and control pollution of
the marine environment

1. States shall take, individually or jointly as appropriate, all measures consistent with this Convention that are necessary to prevent, reduce and control pollution of the marine environment from any source, using for this purpose

the best practicable means at their disposal and in accordance with their capabilities, and they shall endeavour to harmonize their policies in this connection.

2. States shall take all measures necessary to ensure that activities under their jurisdiction or control are so conducted as not to cause damage by pollution to other States and their environment, and that pollution arising from incidents or activities under their jurisdiction or control does not spread beyond the areas where they exercise sovereign rights in accordance with this Convention.

3. The measures taken pursuant to this Part shall deal with all sources of pollution of the marine environment. These measures shall include, *inter alia*, those designed to minimize to the fullest possible extent:

(a) the release of toxic, harmful or noxious substances, especially those which are persistent, from land-based sources, from or through the atmosphere or by dumping;

(b) pollution from vessels, in particular measures for preventing accidents and dealing with emergencies, ensuring the safety of operations at sea, preventing intentional and unintentional discharges, and regulating the design, construction, equipment, operation and manning of vessels;

(c) pollution from installations and devices used in exploration or exploitation of the natural resources of the seabed and subsoil, in particular measures for preventing accidents and dealing with emergencies, ensuring the safety of operations at sea, and regulating the design, construction, equipment, operation and manning of such installations or devices;

(d) pollution from other installations and devices operating in the marine environment, in particular measures for preventing accidents and dealing with emergencies, ensuring the safety of operations at sea, and regulating the design, construction, equipment, operation and manning of such installations or devices.

4. In taking measures to prevent, reduce or control pollution of the marine environment, States shall refrain from unjustifiable interference with activities carried out by other States in the exercise of their rights and in pursuance of their duties in conformity with this Convention.

5. The measures taken in accordance with this Part shall include those necessary to protect and preserve rare or fragile ecosystems as well as the habitat of depleted, threatened or endangered species and other forms of marine life.

Article 195
Duty not to transfer damage or hazards or transform one type of pollution into another

In taking measures to prevent, reduce and control pollution of the marine environment, States shall act so as not to transfer, directly or indirectly, damage or hazards from one area to another or transform one type of pollution into another.

Article 196
Use of technologies or introduction of alien or new species

1. States shall take all measures necessary to prevent, reduce and control pollution of the marine environment resulting from the use of technologies under their jurisdiction or control, or the intentional or accidental introduction of species, alien or new, to a particular part of the marine environment, which may cause significant and harmful changes thereto.

2. This article does not affect the application of this Convention regarding the prevention, reduction and control of pollution of the marine environment.

Section 2
Global and regional cooperation

Article 197
Cooperation on a global or regional basis

States shall cooperate on a global basis and, as appropriate, on a regional basis, directly or through competent international organizations, in formulating and elaborating international rules, standards and recommended practices and procedures consistent with this Convention, for the protection and preservation of the marine environment, taking into account characteristic regional features.

Article 198
Notification of imminent or actual damage

When a State becomes aware of cases in which the marine environment is in imminent danger of being damaged or has been damaged by pollution, it shall immediately notify other States it deems likely to be affected by such damage, as well as the competent international organizations.

Article 199
Contingency plans against pollution

In the cases referred to in article 198, States in the area affected, in accordance with their capabilities, and the competent international organizations shall cooperate, to the extent possible, in eliminating the effects of pollution and preventing or minimizing the damage. To this end, States shall jointly develop and promote contingency plans for responding to pollution incidents in the marine environment.

Article 200
Studies, research programmes and exchange of information and data

States shall cooperate, directly or through competent international organizations, for the purpose of promoting studies, undertaking programmes of scientific research and encouraging the exchange of information and data acquired about pollution of the marine environment. They shall endeavour to participate actively in regional and global programmes to acquire knowledge for the assessment of the nature and extent of pollution, exposure to it, and its pathways, risks and remedies.

Article 201
Scientific criteria for regulations

In the light of the information and data acquired pursuant to article 200, States shall cooperate, directly or through competent international organizations, in establishing appropriate scientific criteria for the formulation and elaboration of rules, standards and recommended practices and procedures for the prevention, reduction and control of pollution of the marine environment.

Section 3
Technical assistance

Article 202
Scientific and technical assistance to developing States

States shall, directly or through competent international organizations:

(a) promote programmes of scientific, educational, technical and other assistance to developing States for the protection and preservation of the marine environment and the prevention, reduction and control of marine pollution. Such assistance shall include, *inter alia*:
  (i) training of their scientific and technical personnel;
  (ii) facilitating their participation in relevant international programmes;
  (iii) supplying them with necessary equipment and facilities;
  (iv) enhancing their capacity to manufacture such equipment;
  (v) advice on and developing facilities for research, monitoring, educational and other programmes;
(b) provide appropriate assistance, especially to developing States, for the minimization of the effects of major incidents which may cause serious pollution of the marine environment;
(c) provide appropriate assistance, especially to developing States, concerning the preparation of environmental assessments.

Article 203
Preferential treatment for developing States

Developing States shall, for the purposes of prevention, reduction and control of pollution of the marine environment or minimization of its effects, be granted preference by international organizations in:

(a) the allocation of appropriate funds and technical assistance; and
(b) the utilization of their specialized services.

Section 4
Monitoring and environmental assessment

Article 204
Monitoring of the risks or effects of pollution

1. States shall, consistent with the rights of other States, endeavour, as far as practicable, directly or through the competent international organizations, to observe, measure, evaluate and analyse, by recognized scientific methods, the risks or effects of pollution of the marine environment.

2. In particular, States shall keep under surveillance the effects of any activities which they permit or in which they engage in order to determine whether these activities are likely to pollute the marine environment.

Article 205
Publication of reports

States shall publish reports of the results obtained pursuant to article 204 or provide such reports at appropriate intervals to the competent international organizations, which should make them available to all States.

Article 206
Assessment of potential effects of activities

When States have reasonable grounds for believing that planned activities under their jurisdiction or control may cause substantial pollution of or significant and harmful changes to the marine environment, they shall, as far as practicable, assess the potential effects of such activities on the marine environment and shall communicate reports of the results of such assessments in the manner provided in article 205.

Section 5
International rules and national legislation to prevent, reduce and control pollution of the marine environment

Article 207
Pollution from land-based sources

1. States shall adopt laws and regulations to prevent, reduce and control pollution of the marine environment from land-based sources, including rivers, estuaries, pipelines and outfall structures, taking into account internationally agreed rules, standards and recommended practices and procedures.

2. States shall take other measures as may be necessary to prevent, reduce and control such pollution.

3. States shall endeavour to harmonize their policies in this connection at the appropriate regional level.

4. States, acting especially through competent international organizations or diplomatic conference, shall endeavour to establish global and regional rules, standards and recommended practices and procedures to prevent, reduce and control pollution of the marine environment from land-based sources, taking into account characteristic regional features, the economic capacity of developing States and their need for economic development. Such rules, standards and recommended practices and procedures shall be re-examined from time to time as necessary.

5. Laws, regulations, measures, rules, standards and recommended practices and procedures referred to in paragraphs 1, 2 and 4 shall include those designed to minimize, to the fullest extent possible, the release of toxic, harmful or noxious substances, especially those which are persistent, into the marine environment.

Article 208
Pollution from seabed activities subject to national jurisdiction

1. Coastal States shall adopt laws and regulations to prevent, reduce and control pollution of the marine environment arising from or in connection with seabed activities subject to their jurisdiction and from artificial islands, installations and structures under their jurisdiction, pursuant to articles 60 and 80.

2. States shall take other measures as may be necessary to prevent, reduce and control such pollution.

3. Such laws, regulations and measures shall be no less effective than international rules, standards and recommended practices and procedures.

4. States shall endeavour to harmonize their policies in this connection at the appropriate regional level.

5. States, acting especially through competent international organizations or diplomatic conference, shall establish global and regional rules, standards and recommended practices and procedures to prevent, reduce and control pollution of the marine environment referred to in paragraph l. Such rules, standards and recommended practices and procedures shall be re-examined from time to time as necessary.

Article 209
Pollution from activities in the Area

1. International rules, regulations and procedures shall be established in accordance with Part XI to prevent, reduce and control pollution of the marine environment from activities in the Area. Such rules, regulations and procedures shall be re-examined from time to time as necessary.

2. Subject to the relevant provisions of this section, States shall adopt laws and regulations to prevent, reduce and control pollution of the marine environment from activities in the Area undertaken by vessels, installations, structures and other devices flying their flag or of their registry or operating under their

authority, as the case may be. The requirements of such laws and regulations shall be no less effective than the international rules, regulations and procedures referred to in paragraph 1.

Article 210
Pollution by dumping

1. States shall adopt laws and regulations to prevent, reduce and control pollution of the marine environment by dumping.

2. States shall take other measures as may be necessary to prevent, reduce and control such pollution.

3. Such laws, regulations and measures shall ensure that dumping is not carried out without the permission of the competent authorities of States.

4. States, acting especially through competent international organizations or diplomatic conference, shall endeavour to establish global and regional rules, standards and recommended practices and procedures to prevent, reduce and control such pollution. Such rules, standards and recommended practices and procedures shall be re-examined from time to time as necessary.

5. Dumping within the territorial sea and the exclusive economic zone or onto the continental shelf shall not be carried out without the express prior approval of the coastal State, which has the right to permit, regulate and control such dumping after due consideration of the matter with other States which by reason of their geographical situation may be adversely affected thereby.

6. National laws, regulations and measures shall be no less effective in preventing, reducing and controlling such pollution than the global rules and standards.

Article 211
Pollution from vessels

1. States, acting through the competent international organization or general diplomatic conference, shall establish international rules and standards to prevent, reduce and control pollution of the marine environment from vessels and promote the adoption, in the same manner, wherever appropriate, of routeing systems designed to minimize the threat of accidents which might cause pollution of the marine environment, including the coastline, and pollution damage to the related interests of coastal States. Such rules and standards shall, in the same manner, be re-examined from time to time as necessary.

2. States shall adopt laws and regulations for the prevention, reduction and control of pollution of the marine environment from vessels flying their flag or of their registry. Such laws and regulations shall at least have the same effect as that of generally accepted international rules and standards established through the competent international organization or general diplomatic conference.

3. States which establish particular requirements for the prevention, reduction and control of pollution of the marine environment as a condition for the entry of foreign vessels into their ports or internal waters or for a call at their

off-shore terminals shall give due publicity to such requirements and shall communicate them to the competent international organization. Whenever such
requirements are established in identical form by two or more coastal States
in an endeavour to harmonize policy, the communication shall indicate which
States are participating in such cooperative arrangements. Every State shall require the master of a vessel flying its flag or of its registry, when navigating
within the territorial sea of a State participating in such cooperative arrangements, to furnish, upon the request of that State, information as to whether it
is proceeding to a State of the same region participating in such cooperative
arrangements and, if so, to indicate whether it complies with the port entry
requirements of that State. This article is without prejudice to the continued
exercise by a vessel of its right of innocent passage or to the application of
article 25, paragraph 2.

    4. Coastal States may, in the exercise of their sovereignty within their terri-
torial sea, adopt laws and regulations for the prevention, reduction and control of marine pollution from foreign vessels, including vessels exercising the
right of innocent passage. Such laws and regulations shall, in accordance with
Part II, section 3, not hamper innocent passage of foreign vessels.

    5. Coastal States, for the purpose of enforcement as provided for in section 6,
may in respect of their exclusive economic zones adopt laws and regulations for
the prevention, reduction and control of pollution from vessels conforming to
and giving effect to generally accepted international rules and standards established through the competent international organization or general diplomatic
conference.

    6.

(a) Where the international rules and standards referred to in paragraph 1
    are inadequate to meet special circumstances and coastal States have rea-
    sonable grounds for believing that a particular, clearly defined area of their
    respective exclusive economic zones is an area where the adoption of special
    mandatory measures for the prevention of pollution from vessels is required
    for recognized technical reasons in relation to its oceanographical and eco-
    logical conditions, as well as its utilization or the protection of its resources
    and the particular character of its traffic, the coastal States, after appropri-
    ate consultations through the competent international organization with
    any other States concerned, may, for that area, direct a communication to
    that organization, submitting scientific and technical evidence in support
    and information on necessary reception facilities. Within 12 months after
    receiving such a communication, the organization shall determine whether
    the conditions in that area correspond to the requirements set out above.
    If the organization so determines, the coastal States may, for that area,
    adopt laws and regulations for the prevention, reduction and control of
    pollution from vessels implementing such international rules and standards
    or navigational practices as are made applicable, through the organization,

for special areas. These laws and regulations shall not become applicable to foreign vessels until 15 months after the submission of the communication to the organization.

(b) The coastal States shall publish the limits of any such particular, clearly defined area.

(c) If the coastal States intend to adopt additional laws and regulations for the same area for the prevention, reduction and control of pollution from vessels, they shall, when submitting the aforesaid communication, at the same time notify the organization thereof. Such additional laws and regulations may relate to discharges or navigational practices but shall not require foreign vessels to observe design, construction, manning or equipment standards other than generally accepted international rules and standards; they shall become applicable to foreign vessels 15 months after the submission of the communication to the organization, provided that the organization agrees within 12 months after the submission of the communication.

7. The international rules and standards referred to in this article should include *inter alia* those relating to prompt notification to coastal States, whose coastline or related interests may be affected by incidents, including maritime casualties, which involve discharges or probability of discharges.

Article 212
Pollution from or through the atmosphere

1. States shall adopt laws and regulations to prevent, reduce and control pollution of the marine environment from or through the atmosphere, applicable to the air space under their sovereignty and to vessels flying their flag or vessels or aircraft of their registry, taking into account internationally agreed rules, standards and recommended practices and procedures and the safety of air navigation.

2. States shall take other measures as may be necessary to prevent, reduce and control such pollution.

3. States, acting especially through competent international organizations or diplomatic conference, shall endeavour to establish global and regional rules, standards and recommended practices and procedures to prevent, reduce and control such pollution.

Section 6
Enforcement

Article 213
Enforcement with respect to pollution from land-based sources

States shall enforce their laws and regulations adopted in accordance with article 207 and shall adopt laws and regulations and take other measures necessary to implement applicable international rules and standards established through competent international organizations or diplomatic conference to prevent, reduce and control pollution of the marine environment from land-based sources.

Article 214
Enforcement with respect to pollution from seabed activities

States shall enforce their laws and regulations adopted in accordance with article 208 and shall adopt laws and regulations and take other measures necessary to implement applicable international rules and standards established through competent international organizations or diplomatic conference to prevent, reduce and control pollution of the marine environment arising from or in connection with seabed activities subject to their jurisdiction and from artificial islands, installations and structures under their jurisdiction, pursuant to articles 60 and 80.

Article 215
Enforcement with respect to pollution from activities in the Area

Enforcement of international rules, regulations and procedures established in accordance with Part XI to prevent, reduce and control pollution of the marine environment from activities in the Area shall be governed by that Part.

Article 216
Enforcement with respect to pollution by dumping

1. Laws and regulations adopted in accordance with this Convention and applicable international rules and standards established through competent international organizations or diplomatic conference for the prevention, reduction and control of pollution of the marine environment by dumping shall be enforced:

(a) by the coastal State with regard to dumping within its territorial sea or its exclusive economic zone or onto its continental shelf;
(b) by the flag State with regard to vessels flying its flag or vessels or aircraft of its registry;
(c) by any State with regard to acts of loading of wastes or other matter occurring within its territory or at its off-shore terminals.

2. No State shall be obliged by virtue of this article to institute proceedings when another State has already instituted proceedings in accordance with this article.

Article 217
Enforcement by flag States

1. States shall ensure compliance by vessels flying their flag or of their registry with applicable international rules and standards, established through the

competent international organization or general diplomatic conference, and with their laws and regulations adopted in accordance with this Convention for the prevention, reduction and control of pollution of the marine environment from vessels and shall accordingly adopt laws and regulations and take other measures necessary for their implementation. Flag States shall provide for the effective enforcement of such rules, standards, laws and regulations, irrespective of where a violation occurs.

2. States shall, in particular, take appropriate measures in order to ensure that vessels flying their flag or of their registry are prohibited from sailing, until they can proceed to sea in compliance with the requirements of the international rules and standards referred to in paragraph 1, including requirements in respect of design, construction, equipment and manning of vessels.

3. States shall ensure that vessels flying their flag or of their registry carry on board certificates required by and issued pursuant to international rules and standards referred to in paragraph 1. States shall ensure that vessels flying their flag are periodically inspected in order to verify that such certificates are in conformity with the actual condition of the vessels. These certificates shall be accepted by other States as evidence of the condition of the vessels and shall be regarded as having the same force as certificates issued by them, unless there are clear grounds for believing that the condition of the vessel does not correspond substantially with the particulars of the certificates.

4. If a vessel commits a violation of rules and standards established through the competent international organization or general diplomatic conference, the flag State, without prejudice to articles 218, 220 and 228, shall provide for immediate investigation and where appropriate institute proceedings in respect of the alleged violation irrespective of where the violation occurred or where the pollution caused by such violation has occurred or has been spotted.

5. Flag States conducting an investigation of the violation may request the assistance of any other State whose cooperation could be useful in clarifying the circumstances of the case. States shall endeavour to meet appropriate requests of flag States.

6. States shall, at the written request of any State, investigate any violation alleged to have been committed by vessels flying their flag. If satisfied that sufficient evidence is available to enable proceedings to be brought in respect of the alleged violation, flag States shall without delay institute such proceedings in accordance with their laws.

7. Flag States shall promptly inform the requesting State and the competent international organization of the action taken and its outcome. Such information shall be available to all States.

8. Penalties provided for by the laws and regulations of States for vessels flying their flag shall be adequate in severity to discourage violations wherever they occur.

Article 218
Enforcement by port States

1. When a vessel is voluntarily within a port or at an off-shore terminal of a State, that State may undertake investigations and, where the evidence so warrants, institute proceedings in respect of any discharge from that vessel outside the internal waters, territorial sea or exclusive economic zone of that State in violation of applicable international rules and standards established through the competent international organization or general diplomatic conference.

2. No proceedings pursuant to paragraph 1 shall be instituted in respect of a discharge violation in the internal waters, territorial sea or exclusive economic zone of another State unless requested by that State, the flag State, or a State damaged or threatened by the discharge violation, or unless the violation has caused or is likely to cause pollution in the internal waters, territorial sea or exclusive economic zone of the State instituting the proceedings.

3. When a vessel is voluntarily within a port or at an off-shore terminal of a State, that State shall, as far as practicable, comply with requests from any State for investigation of a discharge violation referred to in paragraph 1, believed to have occurred in, caused, or threatened damage to the internal waters, territorial sea or exclusive economic zone of the requesting State. It shall likewise, as far as practicable, comply with requests from the flag State for investigation of such a violation, irrespective of where the violation occurred.

4. The records of the investigation carried out by a port State pursuant to this article shall be transmitted upon request to the flag State or to the coastal State. Any proceedings instituted by the port State on the basis of such an investigation may, subject to section 7, be suspended at the request of the coastal State when the violation has occurred within its internal waters, territorial sea or exclusive economic zone. The evidence and records of the case, together with any bond or other financial security posted with the authorities of the port State, shall in that event be transmitted to the coastal State. Such transmittal shall preclude the continuation of proceedings in the port State.

Article 219
Measures relating to seaworthiness of vessels to avoid pollution

Subject to section 7, States which, upon request or on their own initiative, have ascertained that a vessel within one of their ports or at one of their off-shore terminals is in violation of applicable international rules and standards relating to seaworthiness of vessels and thereby threatens damage to the marine environment shall, as far as practicable, take administrative measures to prevent the vessel from sailing. Such States may permit the vessel to proceed only to the nearest appropriate repair yard and, upon removal of the causes of the violation, shall permit the vessel to continue immediately.

Article 220
Enforcement by coastal States

1. When a vessel is voluntarily within a port or at an off-shore terminal of a State, that State may, subject to section 7, institute proceedings in respect of any violation of its laws and regulations adopted in accordance with this Convention or applicable international rules and standards for the prevention, reduction and control of pollution from vessels when the violation has occurred within the territorial sea or the exclusive economic zone of that State.

2. Where there are clear grounds for believing that a vessel navigating in the territorial sea of a State has, during its passage therein, violated laws and regulations of that State adopted in accordance with this Convention or applicable international rules and standards for the prevention, reduction and control of pollution from vessels, that State, without prejudice to the application of the relevant provisions of Part II, section 3, may undertake physical inspection of the vessel relating to the violation and may, where the evidence so warrants, institute proceedings, including detention of the vessel, in accordance with its laws, subject to the provisions of section 7.

3. Where there are clear grounds for believing that a vessel navigating in the exclusive economic zone or the territorial sea of a State has, in the exclusive economic zone, committed a violation of applicable international rules and standards for the prevention, reduction and control of pollution from vessels or laws and regulations of that State conforming and giving effect to such rules and standards, that State may require the vessel to give information regarding its identity and port of registry, its last and its next port of call and other relevant information required to establish whether a violation has occurred.

4. States shall adopt laws and regulations and take other measures so that vessels flying their flag comply with requests for information pursuant to paragraph 3.

5. Where there are clear grounds for believing that a vessel navigating in the exclusive economic zone or the territorial sea of a State has, in the exclusive economic zone, committed a violation referred to in paragraph 3 resulting in a substantial discharge causing or threatening significant pollution of the marine environment, that State may undertake physical inspection of the vessel for matters relating to the violation if the vessel has refused to give information or if the information supplied by the vessel is manifestly at variance with the evident factual situation and if the circumstances of the case justify such inspection.

6. Where there is clear objective evidence that a vessel navigating in the exclusive economic zone or the territorial sea of a State has, in the exclusive economic zone, committed a violation referred to in paragraph 3 resulting in a discharge causing major damage or threat of major damage to the coastline or related interests of the coastal State, or to any resources of its territorial sea or exclusive economic zone, that State may, subject to section 7, provided that the evidence so warrants, institute proceedings, including detention of the vessel, in accordance with its laws.

7. Notwithstanding the provisions of paragraph 6, whenever appropriate procedures have been established, either through the competent international organization or as otherwise agreed, whereby compliance with require-ments for bonding or other appropriate financial security has been assured, the coastal State if bound by such procedures shall allow the vessel to proceed.

8. The provisions of paragraphs 3, 4, 5, 6 and 7 also apply in respect of national laws and regulations adopted pursuant to article 211, paragraph 6.

Article 221
Measures to avoid pollution arising from maritime casualties

1. Nothing in this Part shall prejudice the right of States, pursuant to inter-national law, both customary and conventional, to take and enforce measures beyond the territorial sea proportionate to the actual or threatened damage to protect their coastline or related interests, including fishing, from pollution or threat of pollution following upon a maritime casualty or acts relating to such a casualty, which may reasonably be expected to result in major harmful consequences.

2. For the purposes of this article, 'maritime casualty' means a collision of vessels, stranding or other incident of navigation, or other occurrence on board a vessel or external to it resulting in material damage or imminent threat of material damage to a vessel or cargo.

Article 222
Enforcement with respect to pollution from or through the atmosphere

States shall enforce, within the air space under their sovereignty or with re-gard to vessels flying their flag or vessels or aircraft of their registry, their laws and regulations adopted in accordance with article 212, paragraph 1, and with other provisions of this Convention and shall adopt laws and regula-tions and take other measures necessary to implement applicable international rules and standards established through competent international organiza-tions or diplomatic conference to prevent, reduce and control pollution of the marine environment from or through the atmosphere, in conformity with

all relevant international rules and standards concerning the safety of air
navigation.

Section 7
Safeguards

Article 223
Measures to facilitate proceedings

In proceedings instituted pursuant to this Part, States shall take measures to
facilitate the hearing of witnesses and the admission of evidence submitted by
authorities of another State, or by the competent international organization,
and shall facilitate the attendance at such proceedings of official representatives
of the competent international organization, the flag State and any State affected
by pollution arising out of any violation. The official representatives attending
such proceedings shall have such rights and duties as may be provided under
national laws and regulations or international law.

Article 224
Exercise of powers of enforcement

The powers of enforcement against foreign vessels under this Part may only be
exercised by officials or by warships, military aircraft, or other ships or aircraft
clearly marked and identifiable as being on government service and authorized
to that effect.

Article 225
Duty to avoid adverse consequences in the exercise of
the powers of enforcement

In the exercise under this Convention of their powers of enforcement against
foreign vessels, States shall not endanger the safety of navigation or otherwise
create any hazard to a vessel, or bring it to an unsafe port or anchorage, or
expose the marine environment to an unreasonable risk.

Article 226
Investigation of foreign vessels

1.

(a) States shall not delay a foreign vessel longer than is essential for purposes
of the investigations provided for in articles 216, 218 and 220. Any physical inspection of a foreign vessel shall be limited to an examination of
such certificates, records or other documents as the vessel is required to
carry by generally accepted international rules and standards or of any

similar documents which it is carrying; further physical inspection of the vessel may be undertaken only after such an examination and only when:

   (i) there are clear grounds for believing that the condition of the vessel or its equipment does not correspond substantially with the particulars of those documents;

   (ii) the contents of such documents are not sufficient to confirm or verify a suspected violation; or

   (iii) the vessel is not carrying valid certificates and records.

(b) If the investigation indicates a violation of applicable laws and regulations or international rules and standards for the protection and preservation of the marine environment, release shall be made promptly subject to reasonable procedures such as bonding or other appropriate financial security.

(c) Without prejudice to applicable international rules and standards relating to the seaworthiness of vessels, the release of a vessel may, whenever it would present an unreasonable threat of damage to the marine environment, be refused or made conditional upon proceeding to the nearest appropriate repair yard. Where release has been refused or made conditional, the flag State of the vessel must be promptly notified, and may seek release of the vessel in accordance with Part XV.

2. States shall cooperate to develop procedures for the avoidance of unnecessary physical inspection of vessels at sea.

Article 227
Non-discrimination with respect to foreign vessels

In exercising their rights and performing their duties under this Part, States shall not discriminate in form or in fact against vessels of any other State.

Article 228
Suspension and restrictions on institution of proceedings

1. Proceedings to impose penalties in respect of any violation of applicable laws and regulations or international rules and standards relating to the prevention, reduction and control of pollution from vessels committed by a foreign vessel beyond the territorial sea of the State instituting proceedings shall be suspended upon the taking of proceedings to impose penalties in respect of corresponding charges by the flag State within six months of the date on which proceedings were first instituted, unless those proceedings relate to a case of major damage to the coastal State or the flag State in question has repeatedly disregarded its obligation to enforce effectively the applicable international rules and standards in respect of violations committed by its vessels. The flag

State shall in due course make available to the State previously instituting proceedings a full dossier of the case and the records of the proceedings, whenever the flag State has requested the suspension of proceedings in accordance with this article. When proceedings instituted by the flag State have been brought to a conclusion, the suspended proceedings shall be terminated. Upon payment of costs incurred in respect of such proceedings, any bond posted or other financial security provided in connection with the suspended proceedings shall be released by the coastal State.

2. Proceedings to impose penalties on foreign vessels shall not be instituted after the expiry of three years from the date on which the violation was committed, and shall not be taken by any State in the event of proceedings having been instituted by another State subject to the provisions set out in paragraph 1.

3. The provisions of this article are without prejudice to the right of the flag State to take any measures, including proceedings to impose penalties, according to its laws irrespective of prior proceedings by another State.

Article 229
Institution of civil proceedings

Nothing in this Convention affects the institution of civil proceedings in respect of any claim for loss or damage resulting from pollution of the marine environment.

Article 230
Monetary penalties and the observance of recognized rights of the accused

1. Monetary penalties only may be imposed with respect to violations of national laws and regulations or applicable international rules and standards for the prevention, reduction and control of pollution of the marine environment, committed by foreign vessels beyond the territorial sea.

2. Monetary penalties only may be imposed with respect to violations of national laws and regulations or applicable international rules and standards for the prevention, reduction and control of pollution of the marine environment, committed by foreign vessels in the territorial sea, except in the case of a wilful and serious act of pollution in the territorial sea.

3. In the conduct of proceedings in respect of such violations committed by a foreign vessel which may result in the imposition of penalties, recognized rights of the accused shall be observed.

Article 231
Notification to the flag State and other States concerned

States shall promptly notify the flag State and any other State concerned of any measures taken pursuant to section 6 against foreign vessels, and shall submit to the flag State all official reports concerning such measures. However, with respect to violations committed in the territorial sea, the foregoing obligations of the coastal State apply only to such measures as are taken in proceedings. The diplomatic agents or consular officers and where possible the maritime authority of the flag State, shall be immediately informed of any such measures taken pursuant to section 6 against foreign vessels.

Article 232
Liability of States arising from enforcement measures

States shall be liable for damage or loss attributable to them arising from measures taken pursuant to section 6 when such measures are unlawful or exceed those reasonably required in the light of available information. States shall provide for recourse in their courts for actions in respect of such damage or loss.

Article 233
Safeguards with respect to straits used for international navigation

Nothing in sections 5, 6 and 7 affects the legal regime of straits used for international navigation. However, if a foreign ship other than those referred to in section 10 has committed a violation of the laws and regulations referred to in article 42, paragraph 1(a) and (b), causing or threatening major damage to the marine environment of the straits, the States bordering the straits may take appropriate enforcement measures and if so shall respect *mutatis mutandis* the provisions of this section.

Section 8
Ice-covered areas

Article 234
Ice-covered areas

Coastal States have the right to adopt and enforce non-discriminatory laws and regulations for the prevention, reduction and control of marine pollution from vessels in ice-covered areas within the limits of the exclusive economic zone, where particularly severe climatic conditions and the presence of ice covering such areas for most of the year create obstructions or exceptional hazards to navigation, and pollution of the marine environment could cause major harm to or irreversible disturbance of the ecological balance. Such laws and regulations shall have due regard to navigation and the protection and preservation of the marine environment based on the best available scientific evidence.

Section 9
Responsibility and liability

Article 235
Responsibility and liability

1. States are responsible for the fulfilment of their international obligations concerning the protection and preservation of the marine environment. They shall be liable in accordance with international law.

2. States shall ensure that recourse is available in accordance with their legal systems for prompt and adequate compensation or other relief in respect of damage caused by pollution of the marine environment by natural or juridical persons under their jurisdiction.

3. With the objective of assuring prompt and adequate compensation in respect of all damage caused by pollution of the marine environment, States shall cooperate in the implementation of existing international law and the further development of international law relating to responsibility and liability for the assessment of and compensation for damage and the settlement of related disputes, as well as, where appropriate, development of criteria and procedures for payment of adequate compensation, such as compulsory insurance or compensation funds.

Section 10
Sovereign immunity

Article 236
Sovereign immunity

The provisions of this Convention regarding the protection and preservation of the marine environment do not apply to any warship, naval auxiliary, other vessels or aircraft owned or operated by a State and used, for the time being, only on government non-commercial service. However, each State shall ensure, by the adoption of appropriate measures not impairing operations or operational capabilities of such vessels or aircraft owned or operated by it, that such vessels or aircraft act in a manner consistent, so far as is reasonable and practicable, with this Convention.

Section 11
Obligations under other conventions on the protection and
preservation of the marine environment

Article 237
Obligations under other conventions on the protection and
preservation of the marine environment

1. The provisions of this Part are without prejudice to the specific obligations assumed by States under special conventions and agreements concluded

previously which relate to the protection and preservation of the marine environment and to agreements which may be concluded in furtherance of the general principles set forth in this Convention.

2. Specific obligations assumed by States under special conventions, with respect to the protection and preservation of the marine environment, should be carried out in a manner consistent with the general principles and objectives of this Convention.

[...]

Agreement for the Implementation of the Provisions of UNCLOS Relating to the Conservation and Management of Straddling Fish Stocks and Highly Migratory Fish Stocks, 4 December 1995

Editorial note

The Straddling Stocks Agreement sets out specific principles to guide the development of conservation and management measures for straddling and highly migratory fish stocks, with a view to addressing the problems identified in Chapter 17 of Agenda 21. By Article 2 the object of the Agreement is 'to ensure the long-term conservation and sustainable use of straddling fish stocks and highly migratory fish stocks through effective implementation of the relevant provisions of the Convention'. The Agreement applies to the conservation and management of straddling fish stocks and highly migratory fish stocks beyond areas under national jurisdiction, except that its Articles 6 and 7 apply also to the conservation and management of such stocks within areas under national jurisdiction, and coastal states must apply the general principles enumerated in Article 5 to stocks within areas under national jurisdiction (Article 3(1) and (2)). No reservations are permitted (Article 42). Part II addresses management and conservation. Article 5 commits coastal states and states fishing on the high seas to adopt a broad range of measures 'to ensure long-term sustainability of straddling fish stocks and highly migratory fish stocks and promote the objective of their optimum utilization' (Article 5(a)). Contracting Parties must ensure that 'such measures are based on the best scientific evidence available and are designed to maintain or restore stocks at levels capable of producing maximum sustainable yield, as qualified by relevant environmental and economic factors, including the special requirements of developing States, and taking into account fishing patterns, the interdependence of stocks and any generally recommended international minimum standards, whether subregional, regional or global' (Article 5(b)). Parties are to 'assess the impacts of fishing, other human activities and environmental factors on target stocks and species belonging to the same ecosystem or associated with or dependent upon the target stocks' (Article 5(d)). They shall 'adopt, where necessary, conservation and management measures for species belonging to the same ecosystem or associated with or dependent upon the target stocks, with a view to maintaining or restoring populations of such species above levels at which their reproduction

may become seriously threatened (Article 5(e)). They shall also 'minimize pollution, waste, discards, catch by lost or abandoned gear, catch of non-target
species, both fish and non-fish species, (hereinafter referred to as non-target
species) and impacts on associated or dependent species, in particular endangered species, through measures including, to the extent practicable, the
development and use of selective, environmentally safe and cost-effective fishing gear and techniques' and 'protect biodiversity in the marine environment'
(Article 5(f) and (g)). Furthermore, Parties shall 'take measures to prevent or
eliminate overfishing and excess fishing capacity and to ensure that levels
of fishing effort do not exceed those commensurate with the sustainable use
of fishery resources' (Article 5(h)). Parties are also required to share data concerning fishing activities and promote scientific research to support fishery conservation and management (Article 5(j) and (k)). Finally, Contracting Parties
shall 'implement and enforce conservation and management measures through
effective monitoring, control and surveillance' (Article 5(l)). In adopting the
measures mentioned above, Parties are to apply the precautionary approach
(Article 5(c)) in accordance with Article 6 and Annex II. Coastal states and
states fishing in adjacent high seas areas are required to co-operate in devis-
ing conservation and management measures for straddling and highly migratory stocks to ensure the compatibility of national and high seas measures
(Article 7). Part III of the 1995 Agreement addresses mechanisms for international co-operation, and envisages a significant role for subregional and regional
fisheries organisations and arrangements in facilitating co-operation by states
in the development and enforcement of conservation and management measures for straddling and migratory stocks (Articles 8–10). Part III also provides
for the conditions for new membership or participation of organizations, transparency in their activities and decision-making and strengthening of existing
organizations (Articles 11–13), as well as rules on enclosed and semi-enclosed
seas and certain high seas areas (Articles 15 and 16). Part V governs the duties
of the flag state, including the obligation to take such measures as may be necessary to ensure that vessels flying its flag comply with regional and subregional
conservation and management measures. Part VI addresses compliance and
enforcement, and Part VII provides for the dispute settlement provisions of the
1982 Convention to apply also to the 1995 Agreement.

Date of signature: 4 December 1995

Entry into force: 11 November 2001

Depositary: Secretary-General of the United Nations

Contracting Parties: Australia, Bahamas, Barbados, Brazil, Canada, Cook
                      Islands, Costa Rica, Cyprus, Fiji, Iceland, Iran, Maldives,

Malta, Mauritius, Micronesia (Federated States of), Monaco, Namibia, Nauru, New Zealand, Norway, Papua New Guinea, Russian Federation, Saint Lucia, Samoa, Senegal, Seychelles, Solomon Islands, Sri Lanka, Tonga, United Kingdom, United States of America, Uruguay.

Website: www.un.org/Depts/los/index.htm

Agreement for the Implementation of the Provisions of UNCLOS Relating to the Conservation and Management of Straddling Fish Stocks and Highly Migratory Fish Stocks

The States Parties to this Agreement,

Recalling the relevant provisions of the United Nations Convention on the Law of the Sea of 10 December 1982,

Determined to ensure the long-term conservation and sustainable use of straddling fish stocks and highly migratory fish stocks,

Resolved to improve cooperation between States to that end,

Calling for more effective enforcement by flag States, port States and coastal States of the conservation and management measures adopted for such stocks,

Seeking to address in particular the problems identified in chapter 17, programme area C, of Agenda 21 adopted by the United Nations Conference on Environment and Development, namely, that the management of high seas fisheries is inadequate in many areas and that some resources are overutilized;

Noting that there are problems of unregulated fishing, over-capitalization, excessive fleet size, vessel reflagging to escape controls, insufficiently selective gear, unreliable databases and lack of sufficient cooperation between States,

Committing themselves to responsible fisheries,

Conscious of the need to avoid adverse impacts on the marine environment, preserve biodiversity, maintain the integrity of marine ecosystems and minimize the risk of long-term or irreversible effects of fishing operations,

Recognizing the need for specific assistance, including financial, scientific and technological assistance, in order that developing States can participate effectively in the conservation, management and sustainable use of straddling fish stocks and highly migratory fish stocks,

Convinced that an agreement for the implementation of the relevant provisions of the Convention would best serve these purposes and contribute to the maintenance of international peace and security,

Affirming that matters not regulated by the Convention or by this Agreement continue to be governed by the rules and principles of general international law,

Have agreed as follows:

Part I
General provisions

Article 1
Use of terms and scope

1. For the purposes of this Agreement:

(a) 'Convention' means the United Nations Convention on the Law of the Sea of 10 December 1982;
(b) 'conservation and management measures' means measures to conserve and manage one or more species of living marine resources that are adopted and applied consistent with the relevant rules of international law as reflected in the Convention and this Agreement;
(c) 'fish' includes molluscs and crustaceans except those belonging to sedentary species as defined in article 77 of the Convention; and
(d) 'arrangement' means a cooperative mechanism established in accordance with the Convention and this Agreement by two or more States for the purpose, *inter alia*, of establishing conservation and management measures in a subregion or region for one or more straddling fish stocks or highly migratory fish stocks.

2.

(a) 'States Parties' means States which have consented to be bound by this Agreement and for which the Agreement is in force.
(b) This Agreement applies *mutatis mutandis*:
  (i) to any entity referred to in article 305, paragraph 1 (c), (d) and (e), of the Convention and
  (ii) subject to article 47, to any entity referred to as an 'international organization' in Annex IX, article 1, of the Convention which becomes a Party to this Agreement, and to that extent 'States Parties' refers to those entities.

3. This Agreement applies *mutatis mutandis* to other fishing entities whose vessels fish on the high seas.

Article 2
Objective

The objective of this Agreement is to ensure the long-term conservation and sustainable use of straddling fish stocks and highly migratory fish stocks through effective implementation of the relevant provisions of the Convention.

Article 3
Application

1. Unless otherwise provided, this Agreement applies to the conservation and management of straddling fish stocks and highly migratory fish stocks beyond areas under national jurisdiction, except that articles 6 and 7 apply also to the conservation and management of such stocks within areas under national jurisdiction, subject to the different legal regimes that apply within areas under national jurisdiction and in areas beyond national jurisdiction as provided for in the Convention.

2. In the exercise of its sovereign rights for the purpose of exploring and exploiting, conserving and managing straddling fish stocks and highly migratory fish stocks within areas under national jurisdiction, the coastal State shall apply *mutatis mutandis* the general principles enumerated in article 5.

3. States shall give due consideration to the respective capacities of developing States to apply articles 5, 6 and 7 within areas under national jurisdiction and their need for assistance as provided for in this Agreement.

To this end, Part VII applies *mutatis mutandis* in respect of areas under national jurisdiction.

Article 4
Relationship between this Agreement and the Convention

Nothing in this Agreement shall prejudice the rights, jurisdiction and duties of States under the Convention. This Agreement shall be interpreted and applied in the context of and in a manner consistent with the Convention.

Part II
Conservation and management of straddling fish stocks and highly migratory fish stocks

Article 5
General principles

In order to conserve and manage straddling fish stocks and highly migratory fish stocks, coastal States and States fishing on the high seas shall, in giving effect to their duty to cooperate in accordance with the Convention:

(a) adopt measures to ensure long-term sustainability of straddling fish stocks and highly migratory fish stocks and promote the objective of their optimum utilization;

(b) ensure that such measures are based on the best scientific evidence available and are designed to maintain or restore stocks at levels capable of producing maximum sustainable yield, as qualified by relevant environmental and economic factors, including the special requirements of developing States, and taking into account fishing patterns, the interdependence of stocks and any generally recommended international minimum standards, whether subregional, regional or global;

(c) apply the precautionary approach in accordance with article 6;

(d) assess the impacts of fishing, other human activities and environmental factors on target stocks and species belonging to the same ecosystem or associated with or dependent upon the target stocks;

(e) adopt, where necessary, conservation and management measures for species belonging to the same ecosystem or associated with or dependent upon the target stocks, with a view to maintaining or restoring populations of such species above levels at which their reproduction may become seriously threatened;

(f) minimize pollution, waste, discards, catch by lost or abandoned gear, catch of non-target species, both fish and non-fish species, (hereinafter referred to as non-target species) and impacts on associated or dependent species, in particular endangered species, through measures including, to the extent practicable, the development and use of selective, environmentally safe and cost-effective fishing gear and techniques;

(g) protect biodiversity in the marine environment;

(h) take measures to prevent or eliminate overfishing and excess fishing capacity and to ensure that levels of fishing effort do not exceed those commensurate with the sustainable use of fishery resources;

(i) take into account the interests of artisanal and subsistence fishers;

(j) collect and share, in a timely manner, complete and accurate data concerning fishing activities on, *inter alia*, vessel position, catch of target and non-target species and fishing effort, as set out in Annex I, as well as information from national and international research programmes;

(k) promote and conduct scientific research and develop appropriate technologies in support of fishery conservation and management; and

(l) implement and enforce conservation and management measures through effective monitoring, control and surveillance.

Article 6
Application of the precautionary approach

1. States shall apply the precautionary approach widely to conservation, management and exploitation of straddling fish stocks and highly migratory fish stocks in order to protect the living marine resources and preserve the marine environment.

2. States shall be more cautious when information is uncertain, unreliable or inadequate. The absence of adequate scientific information shall not be used as a reason for postponing or failing to take conservation and management measures.

3. In implementing the precautionary approach, States shall:

(a) improve decision-making for fishery resource conservation and management by obtaining and sharing the best scientific information available and implementing improved techniques for dealing with risk and uncertainty;

(b) apply the guidelines set out in Annex II and determine, on the basis of the best scientific information available, stock-specific reference points and the action to be taken if they are exceeded;

(c) take into account, *inter alia,* uncertainties relating to the size and productivity of the stocks, reference points, stock condition in relation to such reference points, levels and distribution of fishing mortality and the impact of fishing activities on non-target and associated or dependent species, as well as existing and predicted oceanic, environmental and socio-economic conditions; and

(d) develop data collection and research programmes to assess the impact of fishing on non-target and associated or dependent species and their environment, and adopt plans which are necessary to ensure the conservation of such species and to protect habitats of special concern.

4. States shall take measures to ensure that, when reference points are approached, they will not be exceeded. In the event that they are exceeded, States shall, without delay, take the action determined under paragraph 3 (b) to restore the stocks.

5. Where the status of target stocks or non-target or associated or dependent species is of concern, States shall subject such stocks and species to enhanced monitoring in order to review their status and the efficacy of conservation and management measures. They shall revise those measures regularly in the light of new information.

6. For new or exploratory fisheries, States shall adopt as soon as possible cautious conservation and management measures, including, *inter alia,* catch limits and effort limits. Such measures shall remain in force until there are sufficient data to allow assessment of the impact of the fisheries on the long-term sustainability of the stocks, whereupon conservation and management measures based on that assessment shall be implemented. The latter measures shall, if appropriate, allow for the gradual development of the fisheries.

7. If a natural phenomenon has a significant adverse impact on the status of straddling fish stocks or highly migratory fish stocks, States shall adopt conservation and management measures on an emergency basis to ensure that fishing activity does not exacerbate such adverse impact. States shall also adopt such measures on an emergency basis where fishing activity presents a serious threat to the sustainability of such stocks. Measures taken on an emergency basis shall be temporary and shall be based on the best scientific evidence available.

Article 7
Compatibility of conservation and management measures

1. Without prejudice to the sovereign rights of coastal States for the purpose of exploring and exploiting, conserving and managing the living marine resources within areas under national jurisdiction as provided for in the Convention, and the right of all States for their nationals to engage in fishing on the high seas in accordance with the Convention:

(a) with respect to straddling fish stocks, the relevant coastal States and the States whose nationals fish for such stocks in the adjacent high seas area shall seek, either directly or through the appropriate mechanisms for cooperation provided for in Part III, to agree upon the measures necessary for the conservation of these stocks in the adjacent high seas area;

(b) with respect to highly migratory fish stocks, the relevant coastal States and other States whose nationals fish for such stocks in the region shall cooperate, either directly or through the appropriate mechanisms for cooperation provided for in Part III, with a view to ensuring conservation and promoting the objective of optimum utilization of such stocks throughout the region, both within and beyond the areas under national jurisdiction.

2. Conservation and management measures established for the high seas and those adopted for areas under national jurisdiction shall be compatible in order to ensure conservation and management of the straddling fish stocks and highly migratory fish stocks in their entirety. To this end, coastal States and States fishing on the high seas have a duty to cooperate for the purpose of achieving compatible measures in respect of such stocks. In determining compatible conservation and management measures, States shall:

(a) take into account the conservation and management measures adopted and applied in accordance with article 61 of the Convention in respect of the same stocks by coastal States within areas under national jurisdiction and ensure that measures established in respect of such stocks for the high seas do not undermine the effectiveness of such measures;

(b) take into account previously agreed measures established and applied for the high seas in accordance with the Convention in respect of the same stocks by relevant coastal States and States fishing on the high seas;

(c) take into account previously agreed measures established and applied in accordance with the Convention in respect of the same stocks by a subregional or regional fisheries management organization or arrangement;

(d) take into account the biological unity and other biological characteristics of the stocks and the relationships between the distribution of the stocks, the fisheries and the geographical particularities of the region concerned, including the extent to which the stocks occur and are fished in areas under national jurisdiction;

(e) take into account the respective dependence of the coastal States and the States fishing on the high seas on the stocks concerned; and

(f) ensure that such measures do not result in harmful impact on the living marine resources as a whole.

3. In giving effect to their duty to cooperate, States shall make every effort to agree on compatible conservation and management measures within a reasonable period of time.

4. If no agreement can be reached within a reasonable period of time, any of the States concerned may invoke the procedures for the settlement of disputes provided for in Part VIII.

5. Pending agreement on compatible conservation and management measures, the States concerned, in a spirit of understanding and cooperation, shall make every effort to enter into provisional arrangements of a practical nature. In the event that they are unable to agree on such arrangements, any of the States concerned may, for the purpose of obtaining provisional measures, submit the dispute to a court or tribunal in accordance with the procedures for the settlement of disputes provided for in Part VIII.

6. Provisional arrangements or measures entered into or prescribed pursuant to paragraph 5 shall take into account the provisions of this Part, shall have due regard to the rights and obligations of all States concerned, shall not jeopardize or hamper the reaching of final agreement on compatible conservation and management measures and shall be without prejudice to the final outcome of any dispute settlement procedure.

7. Coastal States shall regularly inform States fishing on the high seas in the subregion or region, either directly or through appropriate subregional or regional fisheries management organizations or arrangements, or through other appropriate means, of the measures they have adopted for straddling fish stocks and highly migratory fish stocks within areas under their national jurisdiction.

8. States fishing on the high seas shall regularly inform other interested States, either directly or through appropriate subregional or regional fisheries management organizations or arrangements, or through other appropriate means, of the measures they have adopted for regulating the activities of vessels flying their flag which fish for such stocks on the high seas.

Part III
Mechanisms for international cooperation concerning straddling fish stocks and highly migratory fish stocks

Article 8
Cooperation for conservation and management

1. Coastal States and States fishing on the high seas shall, in accordance with the Convention, pursue cooperation in relation to straddling fish stocks and

highly migratory fish stocks either directly or through appropriate subregional or regional fisheries management organizations or arrangements, taking into account the specific characteristics of the subregion or region, to ensure effective conservation and management of such stocks.

2. States shall enter into consultations in good faith and without delay, particularly where there is evidence that the straddling fish stocks and highly migratory fish stocks concerned may be under threat of over-exploitation or where a new fishery is being developed for such stocks. To this end, consultations may be initiated at the request of any interested State with a view to establishing appropriate arrangements to ensure conservation and management of the stocks. Pending agreement on such arrangements, States shall observe the provisions of this Agreement and shall act in good faith and with due regard to the rights, interests and duties of other States.

3. Where a subregional or regional fisheries management organization or arrangement has the competence to establish conservation and management measures for particular straddling fish stocks or highly migratory fish stocks, States fishing for the stocks on the high seas and relevant coastal States shall give effect to their duty to cooperate by becoming members of such organization or participants in such arrangement, or by agreeing to apply the conservation and management measures established by such organization or arrangement. States having a real interest in the fisheries concerned may become members of such organization or participants in such arrangement. The terms of participation in such organization or arrangement shall not preclude such States from membership or participation; nor shall they be applied in a manner which discriminates against any State or group of States having a real interest in the fisheries concerned.

4. Only those States which are members of such an organization or participants in such an arrangement, or which agree to apply the conservation and management measures established by such organization or arrangement, shall have access to the fishery resources to which those measures apply.

5. Where there is no subregional or regional fisheries management organization or arrangement to establish conservation and management measures for a particular straddling fish stock or highly migratory fish stock, relevant coastal States and States fishing on the high seas for such stock in the subregion or region shall cooperate to establish such an organization or enter into other appropriate arrangements to ensure conservation and management of such stock and shall participate in the work of the organization or arrangement.

6. Any State intending to propose that action be taken by an intergovernmental organization having competence with respect to living resources should, where such action would have a significant effect on conservation and management measures already established by a competent subregional or regional fisheries management organization or arrangement, consult through that organization or arrangement with its members or participants. To the extent

practicable, such consultation should take place prior to the submission of the proposal to the intergovernmental organization.

Article 9
Subregional and regional fisheries management organizations and arrangements

1. In establishing subregional or regional fisheries management organizations or in entering into subregional or regional fisheries management arrangements for straddling fish stocks and highly migratory fish stocks, States shall agree, *inter alia*, on:

(a) the stocks to which conservation and management measures apply, taking into account the biological characteristics of the stocks concerned and the nature of the fisheries involved;
(b) the area of application, taking into account article 7, paragraph 1, and the characteristics of the subregion or region, including socio-economic, geographical and environmental factors;
(c) the relationship between the work of the new organization or arrangement and the role, objectives and operations of any relevant existing fisheries management organizations or arrangements; and
(d) the mechanisms by which the organization or arrangement will obtain scientific advice and review the status of the stocks, including, where appropriate, the establishment of a scientific advisory body.

2. States cooperating in the formation of a subregional or regional fisheries management organization or arrangement shall inform other States which they are aware have a real interest in the work of the proposed organization or arrangement of such cooperation.

Article 10
Functions of subregional and regional fisheries management organizations and arrangements

In fulfilling their obligation to cooperate through subregional or regional fisheries management organizations or arrangements, States shall:

(a) agree on and comply with conservation and management measures to ensure the long-term sustainability of straddling fish stocks and highly migratory fish stocks;
(b) agree, as appropriate, on participatory rights such as allocations of allowable catch or levels of fishing effort;
(c) adopt and apply any generally recommended international minimum standards for the responsible conduct of fishing operations;

(d) obtain and evaluate scientific advice, review the status of the stocks and assess the impact of fishing on non-target and associated or dependent species;

(e) agree on standards for collection, reporting, verification and exchange of data on fisheries for the stocks;

(f) compile and disseminate accurate and complete statistical data, as described in Annex I, to ensure that the best scientific evidence is available, while maintaining confidentiality where appropriate;

(g) promote and conduct scientific assessments of the stocks and relevant research and disseminate the results thereof;

(h) establish appropriate cooperative mechanisms for effective monitoring, control, surveillance and enforcement;

(i) agree on means by which the fishing interests of new members of the organization or new participants in the arrangement will be accommodated;

(j) agree on decision-making procedures which facilitate the adoption of conservation and management measures in a timely and effective manner;

(k) promote the peaceful settlement of disputes in accordance with Part VIII;

(l) ensure the full cooperation of their relevant national agencies and industries in implementing the recommendations and decisions of the organization or arrangement; and

(m) give due publicity to the conservation and management measures established by the organization or arrangement.

Article 11
New members or participants

In determining the nature and extent of participatory rights for new members of a subregional or regional fisheries management organization, or for new participants in a subregional or regional fisheries management arrangement, States shall take into account, *inter alia*:

(a) the status of the straddling fish stocks and highly migratory fish stocks and the existing level of fishing effort in the fishery;

(b) the respective interests, fishing patterns and fishing practices of new and existing members or participants;

(c) the respective contributions of new and existing members or participants to conservation and management of the stocks, to the collection and provision of accurate data and to the conduct of scientific research on the stocks;

(d) the needs of coastal fishing communities which are dependent mainly on fishing for the stocks;

(e) the needs of coastal States whose economies are overwhelmingly dependent on the exploitation of living marine resources; and

(f) the interests of developing States from the subregion or region in whose areas of national jurisdiction the stocks also occur.

Article 12
Transparency in activities of subregional and regional fisheries management organizations and arrangements

1. States shall provide for transparency in the decision-making process and other activities of subregional and regional fisheries management organizations and arrangements.

2. Representatives from other intergovernmental organizations and representatives from non-governmental organizations concerned with straddling fish stocks and highly migratory fish stocks shall be afforded the opportunity to take part in meetings of subregional and regional fisheries management organizations and arrangements as observers or otherwise, as appropriate, in accordance with the procedures of the organization or arrangement concerned. Such procedures shall not be unduly restrictive in this respect. Such intergovernmental organizations and non-governmental organizations shall have timely access to the records and reports of such organizations and arrangements, subject to the procedural rules on access to them.

Article 13
Strengthening of existing organizations and arrangements

States shall cooperate to strengthen existing subregional and regional fisheries management organizations and arrangements in order to improve their effectiveness in establishing and implementing conservation and management measures for straddling fish stocks and highly migratory fish stocks.

Article 14
Collection and provision of information and cooperation in scientific research

1. States shall ensure that fishing vessels flying their flag provide such information as may be necessary in order to fulfil their obligations under this Agreement. To this end, States shall in accordance with Annex I:

(a) collect and exchange scientific, technical and statistical data with respect to fisheries for straddling fish stocks and highly migratory fish stocks;
(b) ensure that data are collected in sufficient detail to facilitate effective stock assessment and are provided in a timely manner to fulfil the requirements of subregional or regional fisheries management organizations or arrangements; and
(c) take appropriate measures to verify the accuracy of such data.

2. States shall cooperate, either directly or through subregional or regional fisheries management organizations or arrangements:

(a) to agree on the specification of data and the format in which they are to be provided to such organizations or arrangements, taking into account the nature of the stocks and the fisheries for those stocks; and

(b) to develop and share analytical techniques and stock assessment methodologies to improve measures for the conservation and management of straddling fish stocks and highly migratory fish stocks.

3. Consistent with Part XIII of the Convention, States shall cooperate, either directly or through competent international organizations, to strengthen scientific research capacity in the field of fisheries and promote scientific research related to the conservation and management of straddling fish stocks and highly migratory fish stocks for the benefit of all. To this end, a State or the competent international organization conducting such research beyond areas under national jurisdiction shall actively promote the publication and dissemination to any interested States of the results of that research and information relating to its objectives and methods and, to the extent practicable, shall facilitate the participation of scientists from those States in such research.

Article 15
Enclosed and semi-enclosed seas

In implementing this Agreement in an enclosed or semi-enclosed sea, States shall take into account the natural characteristics of that sea and shall also act in a manner consistent with Part IX of the Convention and other relevant provisions thereof.

Article 16
Areas of high seas surrounded entirely by an area under the national jurisdiction of a single State

1. States fishing for straddling fish stocks and highly migratory fish stocks in an area of the high seas surrounded entirely by an area under the national jurisdiction of a single State and the latter State shall cooperate to establish conservation and management measures in respect of those stocks in the high seas area. Having regard to the natural characteristics of the area, States shall pay special attention to the establishment of compatible conservation and management measures for such stocks pursuant to article 7. Measures taken in respect of the high seas shall take into account the rights, duties and interests of the coastal State under the Convention, shall be based on the best scientific evidence available and shall also take into account any conservation and management measures adopted and applied in respect of the same stocks in accordance with article 61 of the Convention by the coastal State in the area under national jurisdiction. States shall also agree on measures for monitoring, control, surveillance and enforcement to ensure compliance with the conservation and management measures in respect of the high seas.

2. Pursuant to article 8, States shall act in good faith and make every effort to agree without delay on conservation and management measures to be applied in the carrying out of fishing operations in the area referred to in paragraph 1. If, within a reasonable period of time, the fishing States concerned and the coastal State are unable to agree on such measures, they shall, having regard to paragraph 1, apply article 7, paragraphs 4, 5 and 6, relating to provisional arrangements or measures. Pending the establishment of such provisional arrangements or measures, the States concerned shall take measures in respect of vessels flying their flag in order that they not engage in fisheries which could undermine the stocks concerned.

Part IV
Non-members and non-participants

Article 17
Non-members of organizations and non-participants in arrangements

1. A State which is not a member of a subregional or regional fisheries management organization or is not a participant in a subregional or regional fisheries management arrangement, and which does not otherwise agree to apply the conservation and management measures established by such organization or arrangement, is not discharged from the obligation to cooperate, in accordance with the Convention and this Agreement, in the conservation and management of the relevant straddling fish stocks and highly migratory fish stocks.

2. Such State shall not authorize vessels flying its flag to engage in fishing operations for the straddling fish stocks or highly migratory fish stocks which are subject to the conservation and management measures established by such organization or arrangement.

3. States which are members of a subregional or regional fisheries management organization or participants in a subregional or regional fisheries management arrangement shall, individually or jointly, request the fishing entities referred to in article 1, paragraph 3, which have fishing vessels in the relevant area to cooperate fully with such organization or arrangement in implementing the conservation and management measures it has established, with a view to having such measures applied de facto as extensively as possible to fishing activities in the relevant area. Such fishing entities shall enjoy benefits from participation in the fishery commensurate with their commitment to comply with conservation and management measures in respect of the stocks.

4. States which are members of such organization or participants in such arrangement shall exchange information with respect to the activities of fishing vessels flying the flags of States which are neither members of the organization nor participants in the arrangement and which are engaged in fishing operations

for the relevant stocks. They shall take measures consistent with this Agreement and international law to deter activities of such vessels which undermine the effectiveness of subregional or regional conservation and management measures.

Part V
Duties of the flag State

Article 18
Duties of the flag State

1. A State whose vessels fish on the high seas shall take such measures as may be necessary to ensure that vessels flying its flag comply with subregional and regional conservation and management measures and that such vessels do not engage in any activity which undermines the effectiveness of such measures.

2. A State shall authorize the use of vessels flying its flag for fishing on the high seas only where it is able to exercise effectively its responsibilities in respect of such vessels under the Convention and this Agreement.

3. Measures to be taken by a State in respect of vessels flying its flag shall include:

(a) control of such vessels on the high seas by means of fishing licences, authorizations or permits, in accordance with any applicable procedures agreed at the subregional, regional or global level;

(b) establishment of regulations:
  (i) to apply terms and conditions to the licence, authorization or permit sufficient to fulfil any subregional, regional or global obligations of the flag State;
  (ii) to prohibit fishing on the high seas by vessels which are not duly licensed or authorized to fish, or fishing on the high seas by vessels otherwise than in accordance with the terms and conditions of a licence, authorization or permit;
  (iii) to require vessels fishing on the high seas to carry the licence, authorization or permit on board at all times and to produce it on demand for inspection by a duly authorized person; and
  (iv) to ensure that vessels flying its flag do not conduct unauthorized fishing within areas under the national jurisdiction of other States;

(c) establishment of a national record of fishing vessels authorized to fish on the high seas and provision of access to the information contained in that record on request by directly interested States, taking into account any national laws of the flag State regarding the release of such information;

(d) requirements for marking of fishing vessels and fishing gear for identification in accordance with uniform and internationally recognizable vessel and gear marking systems, such as the Food and Agriculture Organization of the United Nations Standard Specifications for the Marking and Identification of Fishing Vessels;

(e) requirements for recording and timely reporting of vessel position, catch of target and non-target species, fishing effort and other relevant fisheries data in accordance with subregional, regional and global standards for collection of such data;

(f) requirements for verifying the catch of target and non-target species through such means as observer programmes, inspection schemes, unloading reports, supervision of transshipment and monitoring of landed catches and market statistics;

(g) monitoring, control and surveillance of such vessels, their fishing operations and related activities by, *inter alia*:

   (i) the implementation of national inspection schemes and subregional and regional schemes for cooperation in enforcement pursuant to articles 21 and 22, including requirements for such vessels to permit access by duly authorized inspectors from other States;

  (ii) the implementation of national observer programmes and subregional and regional observer programmes in which the flag State is a participant, including requirements for such vessels to permit access by observers from other States to carry out the functions agreed under the programmes; and

(iii) the development and implementation of vessel monitoring systems, including, as appropriate, satellite transmitter systems, in accordance with any national programmes and those which have been subregionally, regionally or globally agreed among the States concerned;

(h) regulation of transshipment on the high seas to ensure that the effectiveness of conservation and management measures is not undermined; and

(i) regulation of fishing activities to ensure compliance with subregional, regional or global measures, including those aimed at minimizing catches of non-target species.

4. Where there is a subregionally, regionally or globally agreed system of monitoring, control and surveillance in effect, States shall ensure that the measures they impose on vessels flying their flag are compatible with that system.

Part VI
Compliance and enforcement

Article 19
Compliance and enforcement by the flag State

1. A State shall ensure compliance by vessels flying its flag with subregional and regional conservation and management measures for straddling fish stocks and highly migratory fish stocks. To this end, that State shall:

(a) enforce such measures irrespective of where violations occur;
(b) investigate immediately and fully any alleged violation of subregional or regional conservation and management measures, which may include the physical inspection of the vessels concerned, and report promptly to the State alleging the violation and the relevant subregional or regional organization or arrangement on the progress and outcome of the investigation;
(c) require any vessel flying its flag to give information to the investigating authority regarding vessel position, catches, fishing gear, fishing operations and related activities in the area of an alleged violation;
(d) if satisfied that sufficient evidence is available in respect of an alleged violation, refer the case to its authorities with a view to instituting proceedings without delay in accordance with its laws and, where appropriate, detain the vessel concerned; and
(e) ensure that, where it has been established, in accordance with its laws, a vessel has been involved in the commission of a serious violation of such measures, the vessel does not engage in fishing operations on the high seas until such time as all outstanding sanctions imposed by the flag State in respect of the violation have been complied with.

2. All investigations and judicial proceedings shall be carried out expeditiously. Sanctions applicable in respect of violations shall be adequate in severity to be effective in securing compliance and to discourage violations wherever they occur and shall deprive offenders of the benefits accruing from their illegal activities. Measures applicable in respect of masters and other officers of fishing vessels shall include provisions which may permit, *inter alia*, refusal, withdrawal or suspension of authorizations to serve as masters or officers on such vessels.

Article 20
International cooperation in enforcement

1. States shall cooperate, either directly or through subregional or regional fisheries management organizations or arrangements, to ensure compliance with and enforcement of subregional and regional conservation and management measures for straddling fish stocks and highly migratory fish stocks.

2. A flag State conducting an investigation of an alleged violation of conservation and management measures for straddling fish stocks or highly migratory fish stocks may request the assistance of any other State whose cooperation may be useful in the conduct of that investigation. All States shall endeavour to meet reasonable requests made by a flag State in connection with such investigations.

3. A flag State may undertake such investigations directly, in cooperation with other interested States or through the relevant subregional or regional fisheries management organization or arrangement. Information on the progress and

outcome of the investigations shall be provided to all States having an interest in, or affected by, the alleged violation.

4. States shall assist each other in identifying vessels reported to have engaged in activities undermining the effectiveness of subregional, regional or global conservation and management measures.

5. States shall, to the extent permitted by national laws and regulations, establish arrangements for making available to prosecuting authorities in other States evidence relating to alleged violations of such measures.

6. Where there are reasonable grounds for believing that a vessel on the high seas has been engaged in unauthorized fishing within an area under the jurisdiction of a coastal State, the flag State of that vessel, at the request of the coastal State concerned, shall immediately and fully investigate the matter. The flag State shall cooperate with the coastal State in taking appropriate enforcement action in such cases and may authorize the relevant authorities of the coastal State to board and inspect the vessel on the high seas. This paragraph is without prejudice to article 111 of the Convention.

7. States Parties which are members of a subregional or regional fisheries management organization or participants in a subregional or regional fisheries management arrangement may take action in accordance with international law, including through recourse to subregional or regional procedures established for this purpose, to deter vessels which have engaged in activities which undermine the effectiveness of or otherwise violate the conservation and management measures established by that organization or arrangement from fishing on the high seas in the subregion or region until such time as appropriate action is taken by the flag State.

Article 21
Subregional and regional cooperation in enforcement

1. In any high seas area covered by a subregional or regional fisheries management organization or arrangement, a State Party which is a member of such organization or a participant in such arrangement may, through its duly authorized inspectors, board and inspect, in accordance with paragraph 2, fishing vessels flying the flag of another State Party to this Agreement, whether or not such State Party is also a member of the organization or a participant in the arrangement, for the purpose of ensuring compliance with conservation and management measures for straddling fish stocks and highly migratory fish stocks established by that organization or arrangement.

2. States shall establish, through subregional or regional fisheries management organizations or arrangements, procedures for boarding and inspection pursuant to paragraph 1, as well as procedures to implement other provisions of this article. Such procedures shall be consistent with this article and the basic procedures set out in article 22 and shall not discriminate against non-members

of the organization or non-participants in the arrangement. Boarding and inspection as well as any subsequent enforcement action shall be conducted in accordance with such procedures. States shall give due publicity to procedures established pursuant to this paragraph.

3. If, within two years of the adoption of this Agreement, any organization or arrangement has not established such procedures, boarding and inspection pursuant to paragraph 1, as well as any subsequent enforcement action, shall, pending the establishment of such procedures, be conducted in accordance with this article and the basic procedures set out in article 22.

4. Prior to taking action under this article, inspecting States shall, either directly or through the relevant subregional or regional fisheries management organization or arrangement, inform all States whose vessels fish on the high seas in the subregion or region of the form of identification issued to their duly authorized inspectors. The vessels used for boarding and inspection shall be clearly marked and identifiable as being on government service. At the time of becoming a Party to this Agreement, a State shall designate an appropriate authority to receive notifications pursuant to this article and shall give due publicity of such designation through the relevant subregional or regional fisheries management organization or arrangement.

5. Where, following a boarding and inspection, there are clear grounds for believing that a vessel has engaged in any activity contrary to the conservation and management measures referred to in paragraph 1, the inspecting State shall, where appropriate, secure evidence and shall promptly notify the flag State of the alleged violation.

6. The flag State shall respond to the notification referred to in paragraph 5 within three working days of its receipt, or such other period as may be prescribed in procedures established in accordance with paragraph 2, and shall either:

(a) fulfil, without delay, its obligations under article 19 to investigate and, if evidence so warrants, take enforcement action with respect to the vessel, in which case it shall promptly inform the inspecting State of the results of the investigation and of any enforcement action taken; or
(b) authorize the inspecting State to investigate.

7. Where the flag State authorizes the inspecting State to investigate an alleged violation, the inspecting State shall, without delay, communicate the results of that investigation to the flag State. The flag State shall, if evidence so warrants, fulfil its obligations to take enforcement action with respect to the vessel. Alternatively, the flag State may authorize the inspecting State to take such enforcement action as the flag State may specify with respect to the vessel, consistent with the rights and obligations of the flag State under this Agreement.

8. Where, following boarding and inspection, there are clear grounds for believing that a vessel has committed a serious violation, and the flag State has either failed to respond or failed to take action as required under paragraphs 6 or 7, the inspectors may remain on board and secure evidence and may require the master to assist in further investigation including, where appropriate, by bringing the vessel without delay to the nearest appropriate port, or to such other port as may be specified in procedures established in accordance with paragraph 2. The inspecting State shall immediately inform the flag State of the name of the port to which the vessel is to proceed. The inspecting State and the flag State and, as appropriate, the port State shall take all necessary steps to ensure the well-being of the crew regardless of their nationality.

9. The inspecting State shall inform the flag State and the relevant organization or the participants in the relevant arrangement of the results of any further investigation.

10. The inspecting State shall require its inspectors to observe generally accepted international regulations, procedures and practices relating to the safety of the vessel and the crew, minimize interference with fishing operations and, to the extent practicable, avoid action which would adversely affect the quality of the catch on board. The inspecting State shall ensure that boarding and inspection is not conducted in a manner that would constitute harassment of any fishing vessel.

11. For the purposes of this article, a serious violation means:

(a) fishing without a valid licence, authorization or permit issued by the flag State in accordance with article 18, paragraph 3 (a);
(b) failing to maintain accurate records of catch and catch-related data, as required by the relevant subregional or regional fisheries management organization or arrangement, or serious misreporting of catch, contrary to the catch reporting requirements of such organization or arrangement;
(c) fishing in a closed area, fishing during a closed season or fishing without, or after attainment of, a quota established by the relevant subregional or regional fisheries management organization or arrangement;
(d) directed fishing for a stock which is subject to a moratorium or for which fishing is prohibited;
(e) using prohibited fishing gear;
(f) falsifying or concealing the markings, identity or registration of a fishing vessel;
(g) concealing, tampering with or disposing of evidence relating to an investigation;
(h) multiple violations which together constitute a serious disregard of conservation and management measures; or

(i) such other violations as may be specified in procedures established by the relevant subregional or regional fisheries management organization or arrangement.

12. Notwithstanding the other provisions of this article, the flag State may, at any time, take action to fulfil its obligations under article 19 with respect to an alleged violation. Where the vessel is under the direction of the inspecting State, the inspecting State shall, at the request of the flag State, release the vessel to the flag State along with full information on the progress and outcome of its investigation.

13. This article is without prejudice to the right of the flag State to take any measures, including proceedings to impose penalties, according to its laws.

14. This article applies *mutatis mutandis* to boarding and inspection by a State Party which is a member of a subregional or regional fisheries management organization or a participant in a subregional or regional fisheries management arrangement and which has clear grounds for believing that a fishing vessel flying the flag of another State Party has engaged in any activity contrary to relevant conservation and management measures referred to in paragraph 1 in the high seas area covered by such organization or arrangement, and such vessel has subsequently, during the same fishing trip, entered into an area under the national jurisdiction of the inspecting State.

15. Where a subregional or regional fisheries management organization or arrangement has established an alternative mechanism which effectively discharges the obligation under this Agreement of its members or participants to ensure compliance with the conservation and management measures established by the organization or arrangement, members of such organization or participants in such arrangement may agree to limit the application of paragraph 1 as between themselves in respect of the conservation and management measures which have been established in the relevant high seas area.

16. Action taken by States other than the flag State in respect of vessels having engaged in activities contrary to subregional or regional conservation and management measures shall be proportionate to the seriousness of the violation.

17. Where there are reasonable grounds for suspecting that a fishing vessel on the high seas is without nationality, a State may board and inspect the vessel. Where evidence so warrants, the State may take such action as may be appropriate in accordance with international law.

18. States shall be liable for damage or loss attributable to them arising from action taken pursuant to this article when such action is unlawful or exceeds that reasonably required in the light of available information to implement the provisions of this article.

Article 22
Basic procedures for boarding and inspection pursuant to article 21

1. The inspecting State shall ensure that its duly authorized inspectors:

(a) present credentials to the master of the vessel and produce a copy of the text of the relevant conservation and management measures or rules and regulations in force in the high seas area in question pursuant to those measures;

(b) initiate notice to the flag State at the time of the boarding and inspection;

(c) do not interfere with the master's ability to communicate with the authorities of the flag State during the boarding and inspection;

(d) provide a copy of a report on the boarding and inspection to the master and to the authorities of the flag State, noting therein any objection or statement which the master wishes to have included in the report;

(e) promptly leave the vessel following completion of the inspection if they find no evidence of a serious violation; and

(f) avoid the use of force except when and to the degree necessary to ensure the safety of the inspectors and where the inspectors are obstructed in the execution of their duties. The degree of force used shall not exceed that reasonably required in the circumstances.

2. The duly authorized inspectors of an inspecting State shall have the authority to inspect the vessel, its licence, gear, equipment, records, facilities, fish and fish products and any relevant documents necessary to verify compliance with the relevant conservation and management measures.

3. The flag State shall ensure that vessel masters:

(a) accept and facilitate prompt and safe boarding by the inspectors;

(b) cooperate with and assist in the inspection of the vessel conducted pursuant to these procedures;

(c) do not obstruct, intimidate or interfere with the inspectors in the performance of their duties;

(d) allow the inspectors to communicate with the authorities of the flag State and the inspecting State during the boarding and inspection;

(e) provide reasonable facilities, including, where appropriate, food and accommodation, to the inspectors; and

(f) facilitate safe disembarkation by the inspectors.

4. In the event that the master of a vessel refuses to accept boarding and inspection in accordance with this article and article 21, the flag State shall, except in circumstances where, in accordance with generally accepted international regulations, procedures and practices relating to safety at sea, it is necessary to delay the boarding and inspection, direct the master of the vessel

to submit immediately to boarding and inspection and, if the master does not comply with such direction, shall suspend the vessel's authorization to fish and order the vessel to return immediately to port. The flag State shall advise the inspecting State of the action it has taken when the circumstances referred to in this paragraph arise.

Article 23
Measures taken by a port State

1. A port State has the right and the duty to take measures, in accordance with international law, to promote the effectiveness of subregional, regional and global conservation and management measures. When taking such measures a port State shall not discriminate in form or in fact against the vessels of any State.

2. A port State may, *inter alia*, inspect documents, fishing gear and catch on board fishing vessels, when such vessels are voluntarily in its ports or at its offshore terminals.

3. States may adopt regulations empowering the relevant national authorities to prohibit landings and transshipments where it has been established that the catch has been taken in a manner which undermines the effectiveness of subregional, regional or global conservation and management measures on the high seas.

4. Nothing in this article affects the exercise by States of their sovereignty over ports in their territory in accordance with international law.

Part VII
Requirements of developing States

Article 24
Recognition of the special requirements of developing States

1. States shall give full recognition to the special requirements of developing States in relation to conservation and management of straddling fish stocks and highly migratory fish stocks and development of fisheries for such stocks. To this end, States shall, either directly or through the United Nations Development Programme, the Food and Agriculture Organization of the United Nations and other specialized agencies, the Global Environment Facility, the Commission on Sustainable Development and other appropriate international and regional organizations and bodies, provide assistance to developing States.

2. In giving effect to the duty to cooperate in the establishment of conservation and management measures for straddling fish stocks and highly migratory fish stocks, States shall take into account the special requirements of developing States, in particular:

(a) the vulnerability of developing States which are dependent on the exploitation of living marine resources, including for meeting the nutritional requirements of their populations or parts thereof;

(b) the need to avoid adverse impacts on, and ensure access to fisheries by, subsistence, small-scale and artisanal fishers and women fishworkers, as well as indigenous people in developing States, particularly small island developing States; and

(c) the need to ensure that such measures do not result in transferring, directly or indirectly, a disproportionate burden of conservation action onto developing States.

Article 25
Forms of cooperation with developing States

1. States shall cooperate, either directly or through subregional, regional or global organizations:

(a) to enhance the ability of developing States, in particular the least-developed among them and small island developing States, to conserve and manage straddling fish stocks and highly migratory fish stocks and to develop their own fisheries for such stocks;

(b) to assist developing States, in particular the least-developed among them and small island developing States, to enable them to participate in high seas fisheries for such stocks, including facilitating access to such fisheries subject to articles 5 and 11; and

(c) to facilitate the participation of developing States in subregional and regional fisheries management organizations and arrangements.

2. Cooperation with developing States for the purposes set out in this article shall include the provision of financial assistance, assistance relating to human resources development, technical assistance, transfer of technology, including through joint venture arrangements, and advisory and consultative services.

3. Such assistance shall, *inter alia*, be directed specifically towards:

(a) improved conservation and management of straddling fish stocks and highly migratory fish stocks through collection, reporting, verification, exchange and analysis of fisheries data and related information;

(b) stock assessment and scientific research; and

(c) monitoring, control, surveillance, compliance and enforcement, including training and capacity-building at the local level, development and funding of national and regional observer programmes and access to technology and equipment.

Article 26
Special assistance in the implementation of this Agreement

1. States shall cooperate to establish special funds to assist developing States in the implementation of this Agreement, including assisting developing States to meet the costs involved in any proceedings for the settlement of disputes to which they may be parties.

2. States and international organizations should assist developing States in establishing new subregional or regional fisheries management organizations or arrangements, or in strengthening existing organizations or arrangements, for the conservation and management of straddling fish stocks and highly migratory fish stocks.

Part VIII
Peaceful settlement of disputes

Article 27
Obligation to settle disputes by peaceful means

States have the obligation to settle their disputes by negotiation, inquiry, mediation, conciliation, arbitration, judicial settlement, resort to regional agencies or arrangements, or other peaceful means of their own choice.

Article 28
Prevention of disputes

States shall cooperate in order to prevent disputes. To this end, States shall agree on efficient and expeditious decision-making procedures within subregional and regional fisheries management organizations and arrangements and shall strengthen existing decision-making procedures as necessary.

Article 29
Disputes of a technical nature

Where a dispute concerns a matter of a technical nature, the States concerned may refer the dispute to an ad hoc expert panel established by them. The panel shall confer with the States concerned and shall endeavour to resolve the dispute expeditiously without recourse to binding procedures for the settlement of disputes.

Article 30
Procedures for the settlement of disputes

1. The provisions relating to the settlement of disputes set out in Part XV of the Convention apply *mutatis mutandis* to any dispute between States Parties to this Agreement concerning the interpretation or application of this Agreement, whether or not they are also Parties to the Convention.

2. The provisions relating to the settlement of disputes set out in Part XV of the Convention apply *mutatis mutandis* to any dispute between States Parties to this Agreement concerning the interpretation or application of a subregional, regional or global fisheries agreement relating to straddling fish stocks or highly migratory fish stocks to which they are parties, including any dispute concerning the conservation and management of such stocks, whether or not they are also Parties to the Convention.

3. Any procedure accepted by a State Party to this Agreement and the Convention pursuant to article 287 of the Convention shall apply to the settlement of disputes under this Part, unless that State Party, when signing, ratifying or acceding to this Agreement, or at any time thereafter, has accepted another procedure pursuant to article 287 for the settlement of disputes under this Part.

4. A State Party to this Agreement which is not a Party to the Convention, when signing, ratifying or acceding to this Agreement, or at any time thereafter, shall be free to choose, by means of a written declaration, one or more of the means set out in article 287, paragraph 1, of the Convention for the settlement of disputes under this Part. Article 287 shall apply to such a declaration, as well as to any dispute to which such State is a party which is not covered by a declaration in force. For the purposes of conciliation and arbitration in accordance with Annexes V, VII and VIII to the Convention, such State shall be entitled to nominate conciliators, arbitrators and experts to be included in the lists referred to in Annex V, article 2, Annex VII, article 2, and Annex VIII, article 2, for the settlement of disputes under this Part.

5. Any court or tribunal to which a dispute has been submitted under this Part shall apply the relevant provisions of the Convention, of this Agreement and of any relevant subregional, regional or global fisheries agreement, as well as generally accepted standards for the conservation and management of living marine resources and other rules of international law not incompatible with the Convention, with a view to ensuring the conservation of the straddling fish stocks and highly migratory fish stocks concerned.

Article 31
Provisional measures

1. Pending the settlement of a dispute in accordance with this Part, the parties to the dispute shall make every effort to enter into provisional arrangements of a practical nature.

2. Without prejudice to article 290 of the Convention, the court or tribunal to which the dispute has been submitted under this Part may prescribe any provisional measures which it considers appropriate under the circumstances to preserve the respective rights of the parties to the dispute or to prevent damage to the stocks in question, as well as in the circumstances referred to in article 7, paragraph 5, and article 16, paragraph 2.

3. A State Party to this Agreement which is not a Party to the Convention may declare that, notwithstanding article 290, paragraph 5, of the Convention, the

International Tribunal for the Law of the Sea shall not be entitled to prescribe, modify or revoke provisional measures without the agreement of such State.

Article 32
Limitations on applicability of procedures for the settlement of disputes

Article 297, paragraph 3, of the Convention applies also to this Agreement.

Part IX
Non-parties to this Agreement

Article 33
Non-parties to this Agreement

1. States Parties shall encourage non-parties to this Agreement to become parties thereto and to adopt laws and regulations consistent with its provisions.

2. States Parties shall take measures consistent with this Agreement and international law to deter the activities of vessels flying the flag of non-parties which undermine the effective implementation of this Agreement.

Part X
Good faith and abuse of rights

Article 34
Good faith and abuse of rights

States Parties shall fulfil in good faith the obligations assumed under this Agreement and shall exercise the rights recognized in this Agreement in a manner which would not constitute an abuse of right.

Part XI
Responsibility and liability

Article 35
Responsibility and liability

States Parties are liable in accordance with international law for damage or loss attributable to them in regard to this Agreement.

Part XII
Review conference

Article 36
Review conference

1. Four years after the date of entry into force of this Agreement, the Secretary-General of the United Nations shall convene a conference with a

view to assessing the effectiveness of this Agreement in securing the conservation and management of straddling fish stocks and highly migratory fish stocks.
The Secretary-General shall invite to the conference all States Parties and those
States and entities which are entitled to become parties to this Agreement as
well as those intergovernmental and non-governmental organizations entitled
to participate as observers.

2. The conference shall review and assess the adequacy of the provisions of
this Agreement and, if necessary, propose means of strengthening the substance
and methods of implementation of those provisions in order better to address
any continuing problems in the conservation and management of straddling
fish stocks and highly migratory fish stocks.

Part XIII
Final provisions

Article 37
Signature

This Agreement shall be open for signature by all States and the other entities
referred to in article 1, paragraph 2(b), and shall remain open for signature at
United Nations Headquarters for twelve months from the fourth of December
1995.

Article 38
Ratification

This Agreement is subject to ratification by States and the other entities referred
to in article 1, paragraph 2(b). The instruments of ratification shall be deposited
with the Secretary-General of the United Nations.

Article 39
Accession

This Agreement shall remain open for accession by States and the other entities
referred to in article 1, paragraph 2(b). The instruments of accession shall be
deposited with the Secretary-General of the United Nations.

Article 40
Entry into force

1. This Agreement shall enter into force 30 days after the date of deposit of
the thirtieth instrument of ratification or accession.

2. For each State or entity which ratifies the Agreement or accedes thereto
after the deposit of the thirtieth instrument of ratification or accession, this
Agreement shall enter into force on the thirtieth day following the deposit of
its instrument of ratification or accession.

Article 41
Provisional application

1. This Agreement shall be applied provisionally by a State or entity which consents to its provisional application by so notifying the depositary in writing. Such provisional application shall become effective from the date of receipt of the notification.

2. Provisional application by a State or entity shall terminate upon the entry into force of this Agreement for that State or entity or upon notification by that State or entity to the depositary in writing of its intention to terminate provisional application.

Article 42
Reservations and exceptions

No reservations or exceptions may be made to this Agreement.

Article 43
Declarations and statements

Article 42 does not preclude a State or entity, when signing, ratifying or acceding to this Agreement, from making declarations or statements, however phrased or named, with a view, *inter alia*, to the harmonization of its laws and regulations with the provisions of this Agreement, provided that such declarations or statements do not purport to exclude or to modify the legal effect of the provisions of this Agreement in their application to that State or entity.

Article 44
Relation to other agreements

1. This Agreement shall not alter the rights and obligations of States Parties which arise from other agreements compatible with this Agreement and which do not affect the enjoyment by other States Parties of their rights or the performance of their obligations under this Agreement.

2. Two or more States Parties may conclude agreements modifying or suspending the operation of provisions of this Agreement, applicable solely to the relations between them, provided that such agreements do not relate to a provision derogation from which is incompatible with the effective execution of the object and purpose of this Agreement, and provided further that such agreements shall not affect the application of the basic principles embodied herein, and that the provisions of such agreements do not affect the enjoyment by other States Parties of their rights or the performance of their obligations under this Agreement.

3. States Parties intending to conclude an agreement referred to in paragraph 2 shall notify the other States Parties through the depositary of this Agreement of their intention to conclude the agreement and of the modification or suspension for which it provides.

Article 45
Amendment

1. A State Party may, by written communication addressed to the Secretary-General of the United Nations, propose amendments to this Agreement and request the convening of a conference to consider such proposed amendments.

The Secretary-General shall circulate such communication to all States Parties. If, within six months from the date of the circulation of the communication, not less than one half of the States Parties reply favourably to the request, the Secretary-General shall convene the conference.

2. The decision-making procedure applicable at the amendment conference convened pursuant to paragraph 1 shall be the same as that applicable at the United Nations Conference on Straddling Fish Stocks and Highly Migratory Fish Stocks, unless otherwise decided by the conference. The conference should make every effort to reach agreement on any amendments by way of consensus and there should be no voting on them until all efforts at consensus have been exhausted.

3. Once adopted, amendments to this Agreement shall be open for signature at United Nations Headquarters by States Parties for twelve months from the date of adoption, unless otherwise provided in the amendment itself.

4. Articles 38, 39, 47 and 50 apply to all amendments to this Agreement.

5. Amendments to this Agreement shall enter into force for the States Parties ratifying or acceding to them on the thirtieth day following the deposit of instruments of ratification or accession by two thirds of the States Parties. Thereafter, for each State Party ratifying or acceding to an amendment after the deposit of the required number of such instruments, the amendment shall enter into force on the thirtieth day following the deposit of its instrument of ratification or accession.

6. An amendment may provide that a smaller or a larger number of ratifications or accessions shall be required for its entry into force than are required by this article.

7. A State which becomes a Party to this Agreement after the entry into force of amendments in accordance with paragraph 5 shall, failing an expression of a different intention by that State:

(a) be considered as a Party to this Agreement as so amended; and
(b) be considered as a Party to the unamended Agreement in relation to any State Party not bound by the amendment.

Article 46
Denunciation

1. A State Party may, by written notification addressed to the Secretary-General of the United Nations, denounce this Agreement and may indicate its reasons. Failure to indicate reasons shall not affect the validity of the

denunciation. The denunciation shall take effect one year after the date of receipt of the notification, unless the notification specifies a later date.

2. The denunciation shall not in any way affect the duty of any State Party to fulfil any obligation embodied in this Agreement to which it would be subject under international law independently of this Agreement.

Article 47
Participation by international organizations

1. In cases where an international organization referred to in Annex IX, article 1, of the Convention does not have competence over all the matters governed by this Agreement, Annex IX to the Convention shall apply *mutatis mutandis* to participation by such international organization in this Agreement, except that the following provisions of that Annex shall not apply:

(a) article 2, first sentence; and
(b) article 3, paragraph 1.

2. In cases where an international organization referred to in Annex IX, article 1, of the Convention has competence over all the matters governed by this Agreement, the following provisions shall apply to participation by such international organization in this Agreement:

(a) at the time of signature or accession, such international organization shall make a declaration stating:
 (i) that it has competence over all the matters governed by this Agreement;
 (ii) that, for this reason, its member States shall not become States Parties, except in respect of their territories for which the international organization has no responsibility; and
 (iii) that it accepts the rights and obligations of States under this Agreement;
(b) participation of such an international organization shall in no case confer any rights under this Agreement on member States of the international organization;
(c) in the event of a conflict between the obligations of an international organization under this Agreement and its obligations under the agreement establishing the international organization or any acts relating to it, the obligations under this Agreement shall prevail.

Article 48
Annexes

1. The Annexes form an integral part of this Agreement and, unless expressly provided otherwise, a reference to this Agreement or to one of its Parts includes a reference to the Annexes relating thereto.

2. The Annexes may be revised from time to time by States Parties. Such revisions shall be based on scientific and technical considerations. Notwithstanding

the provisions of article 45, if a revision to an Annex is adopted by consensus at a meeting of States Parties, it shall be incorporated in this Agreement and shall take effect from the date of its adoption or from such other date as may be specified in the revision. If a revision to an Annex is not adopted by consensus at such a meeting, the amendment procedures set out in article 45 shall apply.

Article 49
Depositary

The Secretary-General of the United Nations shall be the depositary of this Agreement and any amendments or revisions thereto.

Article 50
Authentic texts

The Arabic, Chinese, English, French, Russian and Spanish texts of this Agreement are equally authentic.

IN WITNESS WHEREOF, the undersigned Plenipotentiaries, being duly authorized thereto, have signed this Agreement.

OPENED FOR SIGNATURE at New York, this fourth day of December, one thousand nine hundred and ninety-five, in a single original, in the Arabic, Chinese, English, French, Russian and Spanish languages.

Annex I
Standard requirements for the collection and sharing of data

Article 1
General principles

1. The timely collection, compilation and analysis of data are fundamental to the effective conservation and management of straddling fish stocks and highly migratory fish stocks. To this end, data from fisheries for these stocks on the high seas and those in areas under national jurisdiction are required and should be collected and compiled in such a way as to enable statistically meaningful analysis for the purposes of fishery resource conservation and management. These data include catch and fishing effort statistics and other fishery-related information, such as vessel-related and other data for standardizing fishing effort. Data collected should also include information on non-target and associated or dependent species. All data should be verified to ensure accuracy. Confidentiality of non-aggregated data shall be maintained. The dissemination of such data shall be subject to the terms on which they have been provided.

2. Assistance, including training as well as financial and technical assistance, shall be provided to developing States in order to build capacity in the field of conservation and management of living marine resources. Assistance should focus on enhancing capacity to implement data collection and verification,

observer programmes, data analysis and research projects supporting stock assessments. The fullest possible involvement of developing State scientists and managers in conservation and management of straddling fish stocks and highly migratory fish stocks should be promoted.

Article 2
Principles of data collection, compilation and exchange

The following general principles should be considered in defining the parameters for collection, compilation and exchange of data from fishing operations for straddling fish stocks and highly migratory fish stocks:

(a) States should ensure that data are collected from vessels flying their flag on fishing activities according to the operational characteristics of each fishing method (e.g., each individual tow for trawl, each set for long-line and purse-seine, each school fished for pole-and-line and each day fished for troll) and in sufficient detail to facilitate effective stock assessment;

(b) States should ensure that fishery data are verified through an appropriate system;

(c) States should compile fishery-related and other supporting scientific data and provide them in an agreed format and in a timely manner to the relevant subregional or regional fisheries management organization or arrangement where one exists. Otherwise, States should cooperate to exchange data either directly or through such other cooperative mechanisms as may be agreed among them;

(d) States should agree, within the framework of subregional or regional fisheries management organizations or arrangements, or otherwise, on the specification of data and the format in which they are to be provided, in accordance with this Annex and taking into account the nature of the stocks and the fisheries for those stocks in the region. Such organizations or arrangements should request non-members or non-participants to provide data concerning relevant fishing activities by vessels flying their flag;

(e) such organizations or arrangements shall compile data and make them available in a timely manner and in an agreed format to all interested States under the terms and conditions established by the organization or arrangement; and

(f) scientists of the flag State and from the relevant subregional or regional fisheries management organization or arrangement should analyse the data separately or jointly, as appropriate.

Article 3
Basic fishery data

1. States shall collect and make available to the relevant subregional or regional fisheries management organization or arrangement the following types

of data in sufficient detail to facilitate effective stock assessment in accordance with agreed procedures:

(a) time series of catch and effort statistics by fishery and fleet;
(b) total catch in number, nominal weight, or both, by species (both target and non-target) as is appropriate to each fishery. [Nominal weight is defined by the Food and Agriculture Organization of the United Nations as the live-weight equivalent of the landings];
(c) discard statistics, including estimates where necessary, reported as number or nominal weight by species, as is appropriate to each fishery;
(d) effort statistics appropriate to each fishing method; and
(e) fishing location, date and time fished and other statistics on fishing operations as appropriate.

2. States shall also collect where appropriate and provide to the relevant subregional or regional fisheries management organization or arrangement information to support stock assessment, including:

(a) composition of the catch according to length, weight and sex;
(b) other biological information supporting stock assessments, such as information on age, growth, recruitment, distribution and stock identity; and
(c) other relevant research, including surveys of abundance, biomass surveys, hydro-acoustic surveys, research on environmental factors affecting stock abundance, and oceanographic and ecological studies.

Article 4
Vessel data and information

1. States should collect the following types of vessel-related data for standardizing fleet composition and vessel fishing power and for converting between different measures of effort in the analysis of catch and effort data:

(a) vessel identification, flag and port of registry;
(b) vessel type;
(c) vessel specifications (e.g., material of construction, date built, registered length, gross registered tonnage, power of main engines, hold capacity and catch storage methods); and
(d) fishing gear description (e.g., types, gear specifications and quantity).

2. The flag State will collect the following information:

(a) navigation and position fixing aids;
(b) communication equipment and international radio call sign; and
(c) crew size.

Article 5
Reporting

A State shall ensure that vessels flying its flag send to its national fisheries administration and, where agreed, to the relevant subregional or regional fisheries management organization or arrangement, logbook data on catch and effort, including data on fishing operations on the high seas, at sufficiently frequent intervals to meet national requirements and regional and international obligations. Such data shall be transmitted, where necessary, by radio, telex, facsimile or satellite transmission or by other means.

Article 6
Data verification

States or, as appropriate, subregional or regional fisheries management organizations or arrangements should establish mechanisms for verifying fishery data, such as:

(a) position verification through vessel monitoring systems;
(b) scientific observer programmes to monitor catch, effort, catch composition (target and non-target) and other details of fishing operations;
(c) vessel trip, landing and transshipment reports; and
(d) port sampling.

Article 7
Data exchange

1. Data collected by flag States must be shared with other flag States and relevant coastal States through appropriate subregional or regional fisheries management organizations or arrangements. Such organizations or arrangements shall compile data and make them available in a timely manner and in an agreed format to all interested States under the terms and conditions established by the organization or arrangement, while maintaining confidentiality of non-aggregated data, and should, to the extent feasible, develop database systems which provide efficient access to data.

2. At the global level, collection and dissemination of data should be effected through the Food and Agriculture Organization of the United Nations. Where a subregional or regional fisheries management organization or arrangement does not exist, that organization may also do the same at the subregional or regional level by arrangement with the States concerned.

Annex II
Guidelines for the application of precautionary reference points in conservation and management of straddling fish stocks and highly migratory fish stocks

1. A precautionary reference point is an estimated value derived through an agreed scientific procedure, which corresponds to the state of the

resource and of the fishery, and which can be used as a guide for fisheries management.

2. Two types of precautionary reference points should be used: conservation, or limit, reference points and management, or target, reference points. Limit reference points set boundaries which are intended to constrain harvesting within safe biological limits within which the stocks can produce maximum sustainable yield. Target reference points are intended to meet management objectives.

3. Precautionary reference points should be stock-specific to account, *inter alia*, for the reproductive capacity, the resilience of each stock and the characteristics of fisheries exploiting the stock, as well as other sources of mortality and major sources of uncertainty.

4. Management strategies shall seek to maintain or restore populations of harvested stocks, and where necessary associated or dependent species, at levels consistent with previously agreed precautionary reference points. Such reference points shall be used to trigger pre-agreed conservation and management action. Management strategies shall include measures which can be implemented when precautionary reference points are approached.

5. Fishery management strategies shall ensure that the risk of exceeding limit reference points is very low. If a stock falls below a limit reference point or is at risk of falling below such a reference point, conservation and management action should be initiated to facilitate stock recovery. Fishery management strategies shall ensure that target reference points are not exceeded on average.

6. When information for determining reference points for a fishery is poor or absent, provisional reference points shall be set. Provisional reference points may be established by analogy to similar and better-known stocks. In such situations, the fishery shall be subject to enhanced monitoring so as to enable revision of provisional reference points as improved information becomes available.

7. The fishing mortality rate which generates maximum sustainable yield should be regarded as a minimum standard for limit reference points. For stocks which are not overfished, fishery management strategies shall ensure that fishing mortality does not exceed that which corresponds to maximum sustainable yield, and that the biomass does not fall below a predefined threshold. For overfished stocks, the biomass which would produce maximum sustainable yield can serve as a rebuilding target.

PART IIIB

Oceans: regional

Convention for the Protection of the Marine Environment and the Coastal Region of the Mediterranean, 16 February 1976, as revised in Barcelona, 10 June 1995

Editorial note

The Convention for the Protection of the Mediterranean Sea Against Pollution was the first framework convention negotiated under the auspices of the UNEP Regional Seas Programme. The 1976 Barcelona Convention was revised in 1995. The revised convention, which has not yet entered into force, will be known as the Convention for the Protection of the Marine Environment and the Coastal Region of the Mediterranean. The text reproduced in this volume is the text of the 1976 Convention as revised in 1995.

The Convention encourages Parties to enter into agreements with each other for the promotion of sustainable development, the protection of the environment, the conservation and preservation of natural resources in the Mediterranean (Article 3(2)). The Parties shall individually or jointly take all appropriate measures to prevent, abate, combat and to the fullest extent possible eliminate pollution of the Mediterranean to contribute to its sustainable development (Article 4(1)). The Parties agree to take appropriate measures to pursue the protection of the marine environment and natural resources as an integral part of the development process, meeting the needs of present and future generations (Article 4(2)). In order to protect the environment and contribute to the sustainable development of the Mediterranean, the Parties shall, *inter alia*, apply the precautionary principle (Article 4(3)(a)), the polluter pays principle (Article 4(3)(b)), and undertake environmental impact assessment for proposed activities likely to cause significant harm (Article 4(3)(c)). Parties shall implement the Convention by adopting programmes and measures and by utilising the best available techniques and best environmental practices (Article 4(4)(a) and (b)). More specifically, Parties are required to take measures to reduce pollution caused by dumping (Article 5), from ships (Article 6), from exploitation and exploration of the continental shelf and seabed and its subsoil (Article 7), and from land-based sources (Article 8). Parties are required to co-operate during pollution emergencies (Article 9). Contracting Parties shall take measures for the conservation of biological diversity (Article 10) and for the prevention of pollution resulting from the transboundary movement of hazardous wastes and their disposal (Article 11). Parties shall endeavour to establish a system of pollution monitoring in the Mediterranean (Article 12). Parties undertake, as far as possible, to co-operate in the fields of science and technology, to promote research, exchange information and transfer of environmentally sound technology (Article 13). Parties shall ensure that the public is given access to information and the opportunity to participate in decision-making processes relevant to the field of application of the Convention (Article 15). Parties undertake to develop rules on liability and compensation for damage (Article 16).

Secretariat functions are performed by UNEP (Article 17) and the Parties are to meet every two years to review the implementation of the Convention (Article 18).

Additional Protocols to the Convention may be adopted (Article 21). Six Protocols have been adopted under the 1976 Convention: the 1976 Barcelona Dumping Protocol (amended in 1995), the 1976 Barcelona Emergency Protocol (new Protocol adopted in 2002), the 1980 Athens Protocol for the Protection of the Mediterranean Sea against Pollution from Land-Based Sources (amended in 1996), the 1982 Geneva Protocol concerning Mediterranean Specially Protected Areas (replaced in 1995), the 1994 Protocol for the Protection of the Mediterranean Sea against Pollution Resulting from Exploration and Exploitation of the Continental Shelf and the Seabed and its Subsoil, and the 1996 Protocol on the Prevention of Pollution of the Mediterranean Sea by Transboundary Movements of Hazardous Wastes and their Disposal (the texts of the revised protocols are reproduced below (see Documents 12A–F)). Every Party to the Convention must become a Party to at least one of its Protocols and no State may become a Party to a Protocol without being a Party to the Convention (Article 29).

Amendments to the Convention and Protocols require a three-fourths majority vote of the Parties present at the meeting (Article 22). In the event of a dispute between Parties which cannot be settled by methods of their choice, those Parties shall, by common agreement, submit the matter to arbitration as provided by Annex A (Article 28).

Date of signature: 16 February 1976 (Amended on 10 June 1995)

Entry into force: 12 February 1978 (1995 Amendments not yet in force)

Depositary: Government of Spain

Contracting Parties
(1976 Convention):   Albania, Algeria, Bosnia and Herzegovina, Croatia, Cyprus, European Community, Egypt, France, Greece, Israel, Italy, Lebanon, Libya, Malta, Monaco, Morocco, Slovenia, Spain, Syria, Tunisia, Turkey, Yugoslavia.

Acceptance of 1995
Amendment: Albania, Croatia, Cyprus, European Community, Egypt,
                        France, Italy, Malta, Monaco, Spain, Tunisia, Turkey.

Websites: www.unepmap.org
                        www.unep.ch/seas/

Convention for the Protection of the Marine Environment and the Coastal Region of the Mediterranean, as revised in Barcelona in 1995

The Contracting Parties,

Conscious of the economic, social, health and cultural value of the marine environment of the Mediterranean Sea Area,

Fully aware of their responsibility to preserve and sustainably develop this common heritage for the benefit and enjoyment of present and future generations,

Recognizing the threat posed by pollution to the marine environment, its ecological equilibrium, resources and legitimate uses,

Mindful of the special hydrographic and ecological characteristics of the Mediterranean Sea Area and its particular vulnerability to pollution,

Noting that existing international conventions on the subject do not cover, in spite of the progress achieved, all aspects and sources of marine pollution and do not entirely meet the special requirements of the Mediterranean Sea Area,

Realizing fully the need for close cooperation among the States and international organizations concerned in a coordinated and comprehensive regional approach for the protection and enhancement of the marine environment in the Mediterranean Sea Area,

Fully aware that the Mediterranean Action Plan, since its adoption in 1975 and through its evolution, has contributed to the process of sustainable development in the Mediterranean region and has represented a substantive and dynamic tool for the implementation of the activities related to the Convention and its Protocols by the Contracting Parties,

Taking into account the results of the United Nations Conference on Environment and Development, held in Rio de Janeiro from 4 to 14 June 1992,

Also taking into account the Declaration of Genoa of 1985, the Charter of Nicosia of 1990, the Declaration of Cairo of 1992 on Euro-Mediterranean Co-operation on the Environment within the Mediterranean Basin, the recommendations of the Conference of Casablanca of 1993, and the Declaration of Tunis of 1994 on the Sustainable Development of the Mediterranean,

Bearing in mind the relevant provisions of the United Nations Convention on the Law of the Sea, done at Montego Bay on 10 December 1982 and signed by many Contracting Parties,

Have agreed as follows:

Article 1
Geographical coverage

1. For the purposes of this Convention, the Mediterranean Sea Area shall mean the maritime waters of the Mediterranean Sea proper, including its gulfs and seas, bounded to the west by the meridian passing through Cape Spartel lighthouse, at the entrance of the Straits of Gibraltar, and to the east by the southern limits of the Straits of the Dardanelles between Mehmetcik and Kumkale lighthouses.

2. The application of the Convention may be extended to coastal areas as defined by each Contracting Party within its own territory.

3. Any Protocol to this Convention may extend the geographical coverage to which that particular Protocol applies.

Article 2
Definitions

For the purposes of this Convention:

(a) 'Pollution' means the introduction by man, directly or indirectly, of substances or energy into the marine environment, including estuaries, which results, or is likely to result, in such deleterious effects as harm to living resources and marine life, hazards to human health, hindrance to marine activities, including fishing and other legitimate uses of the sea, impairment of quality for use of seawater and reduction of amenities.

(b) 'Organization' means the body designated as responsible for carrying out secretariat functions pursuant to article 17 of this Convention.

Article 3
General provisions

1. The Contracting Parties, when applying this Convention and its related Protocols, shall act in conformity with international law.

2. The Contracting Parties may enter into bilateral or multilateral agreements, including regional or sub-regional agreements for the promotion of sustainable development, the protection of the environment, the conservation and preservation of natural resources in the Mediterranean Sea Area, provided that such agreements are consistent with this Convention and the Protocols and conform to international law. Copies of such agreements shall be communicated to the Organization. As appropriate, Contracting Parties should make use

of existing organizations, agreements or arrangements in the Mediterranean Sea Area.

3. Nothing in this Convention and its Protocols shall prejudice the rights and positions of any State concerning the United Nations Convention on the Law of the Sea of 1982.

4. The Contracting Parties shall take individual or joint initiatives compatible with international law through the relevant international organizations to encourage the implementation of the provisions of this Convention and its Protocols by all the non-party States.

5. Nothing in this Convention and its Protocols shall affect the sovereign immunity of warships or other ships owned or operated by a State while engaged in government non-commercial service. However, each Contracting Party shall ensure that its vessels and aircraft, entitled to sovereign immunity under international law, act in a manner consistent with this Protocol.

Article 4
General obligations

1. The Contracting Parties shall individually or jointly take all appropriate measures in accordance with the provisions of this Convention and those Protocols in force to which they are party to prevent, abate, combat and to the fullest possible extent eliminate pollution of the Mediterranean Sea Area and to protect and enhance the marine environment in that Area so as to contribute towards its sustainable development.

2. The Contracting Parties pledge themselves to take appropriate measures to implement the Mediterranean Action Plan and, further, to pursue the protection of the marine environment and the natural resources of the Mediterranean Sea Area as an integral part of the development process, meeting the needs of present and future generations in an equitable manner. For the purpose of implementing the objectives of sustainable development the Contracting Parties shall take fully into account the recommendations of the Mediterranean Commission on Sustainable Development established within the framework of the Mediterranean Action Plan.

3. In order to protect the environment and contribute to the sustainable development of the Mediterranean Sea Area, the Contracting Parties shall:

(a) apply, in accordance with their capabilities, the precautionary principle, by virtue of which where there are threats of serious or irreversible damage, lack of full scientific certainty shall not be used as a reason for postponing cost-effective measures to prevent environmental degradation;

(b) apply the polluter pays principle, by virtue of which the costs of pollution prevention, control and reduction measures are to be borne by the polluter, with due regard to the public interest;

(c) undertake environmental impact assessment for proposed activities that are likely to cause a significant adverse impact on the marine environment and are subject to an authorization by competent national authorities;
(d) promote cooperation between and among States in environmental impact assessment procedures related to activities under their jurisdiction or control which are likely to have a significant adverse effect on the marine environment of other States or areas beyond the limits of national jurisdiction, on the basis of notification, exchange of information and consultation;
(e) commit themselves to promote the integrated management of the coastal zones, taking into account the protection of areas of ecological and landscape interest and the rational use of natural resources.

4. In implementing the Convention and the related Protocols, the Contracting Parties shall:

(a) adopt programmes and measures which contain, where appropriate, time limits for their completion;
(b) utilize the best available techniques and the best environmental practices and promote the application of, access to and transfer of environmentally sound technology, including clean production technologies, taking into account the social, economic and technological conditions.

5. The Contracting Parties shall cooperate in the formulation and adoption of Protocols, prescribing agreed measures, procedures and standards for the implementation of this Convention.

6. The Contracting Parties further pledge themselves to promote, within the international bodies considered to be competent by the Contracting Parties, measures concerning the implementation of programmes of sustainable development, the protection, conservation and rehabilitation of the environment and of the natural resources in the Mediterranean Sea Area.

Article 5
Pollution caused by dumping from ships and aircraft or incineration at sea

The Contracting Parties shall take all appropriate measures to prevent, abate and to the fullest possible extent eliminate pollution of the Mediterranean Sea Area caused by dumping from ships and aircraft or incineration at sea.

Article 6
Pollution from ships

The Contracting Parties shall take all measures in conformity with international law to prevent, abate, combat and to the fullest possible extent eliminate pollution of the Mediterranean Sea Area caused by discharges from ships and to ensure the effective implementation in that Area of the rules which are generally recognized at the international level relating to the control of this type of pollution.

Article 7
Pollution resulting from exploration and exploitation of the continental shelf and the seabed and its subsoil

The Contracting Parties shall take all appropriate measures to prevent, abate, combat and to the fullest possible extent eliminate pollution of the Mediterranean Sea Area resulting from exploration and exploitation of the continental shelf and the seabed and its subsoil.

Article 8
Pollution from land-based sources

The Contracting Parties shall take all appropriate measures to prevent, abate, combat and to the fullest possible extent eliminate pollution of the Mediterranean Sea Area and to draw up and implement plans for the reduction and phasing out of substances that are toxic, persistent and liable to bioaccumulate arising from land-based sources. These measures shall apply:

(a) to pollution from land-based sources originating within the territories of the Parties, and reaching the sea:
  - directly from outfalls discharging into the sea or through coastal disposal;
  - indirectly through rivers, canals or other watercourses, including underground watercourses, or through run-off;
(b) to pollution from land-based sources transported by the atmosphere.

Article 9
Cooperation in dealing with pollution emergencies

1. The Contracting Parties shall cooperate in taking the necessary measures for dealing with pollution emergencies in the Mediterranean Sea Area, whatever the causes of such emergencies, and reducing or eliminating damage resulting therefrom.

2. Any Contracting Party which becomes aware of any pollution emergency in the Mediterranean Sea Area shall without delay notify the Organization and, either through the Organization or directly, any Contracting Party likely to be affected by such emergency.

Article 10
Conservation of biological diversity

The Contracting Parties shall, individually or jointly, take all appropriate measures to protect and preserve biological diversity, rare or fragile ecosystems, as well as species of wild fauna and flora which are rare, depleted, threatened or endangered and their habitats, in the area to which this Convention applies.

Article 11
Pollution resulting from the transboundary movements of hazardous wastes and their disposal

The Contracting Parties shall take all appropriate measures to prevent, abate and to the fullest possible extent eliminate pollution of the environment which can be caused by transboundary movements and disposal of hazardous wastes, and to reduce to a minimum, and if possible eliminate, such transboundary movements.

Article 12
Monitoring

1. The Contracting Parties shall endeavour to establish, in close cooperation with the international bodies which they consider competent, complementary or joint programmes, including, as appropriate, programmes at the bilateral or multilateral levels, for pollution monitoring in the Mediterranean Sea Area and shall endeavour to establish a pollution monitoring system for that Area.

2. For this purpose, the Contracting Parties shall designate the competent authorities responsible for pollution monitoring within areas under their national jurisdiction and shall participate as far as practicable in international arrangements for pollution monitoring in areas beyond national jurisdiction.

3. The Contracting Parties undertake to cooperate in the formulation, adoption and implementation of such annexes to this Convention as may be required to prescribe common procedures and standards for pollution monitoring.

Article 13
Scientific and technological cooperation

1. The Contracting Parties undertake as far as possible to cooperate directly, or when appropriate through competent regional or other international organizations, in the fields of science and technology and to exchange data as well as other scientific information for the purpose of this Convention.

2. The Contracting Parties undertake to promote the research on, access to and transfer of environmentally sound technology, including clean production technologies, and to cooperate in the formulation, establishment and implementation of clean production processes.

3. The Contracting Parties undertake to cooperate in the provision of technical and other possible assistance in fields relating to marine pollution, with priority to be given to the special needs of developing countries in the Mediterranean region.

Article 14
Environmental legislation

1. The Contracting Parties shall adopt legislation implementing the Convention and the Protocols.

2. The Secretariat may, upon request from a Contracting Party, assist that Party in the drafting of environmental legislation in compliance with the Convention and the Protocols.

Article 15
Public information and participation

1. The Contracting Parties shall ensure that their competent authorities shall give to the public appropriate access to information on the environmental state in the field of application of the Convention and the Protocols, on activities or measures adversely affecting or likely to affect it and on activities carried out or measures taken in accordance with the Convention and the Protocols.

2. The Contracting Parties shall ensure that the opportunity is given to the public to participate in decision-making processes relevant to the field of application of the Convention and the Protocols, as appropriate.

3. The provision of paragraph 1 of this Article shall not prejudice the right of Contracting Parties to refuse, in accordance with their legal systems and applicable international regulations, to provide access to such information on the ground of confidentiality, public security or investigation proceedings, stating the reasons for such a refusal.

Article 16
Liability and compensation

The Contracting Parties undertake to cooperate in the formulation and adoption of appropriate rules and procedures for the determination of liability and compensation for damage resulting from pollution of the marine environment in the Mediterranean Sea Area.

Article 17
Institutional arrangements

The Contracting Parties designate the United Nations Environment Programme as responsible for carrying out the following secretariat functions:

   (i) To convene and prepare the meetings of Contracting Parties and conferences provided for in articles 18, 21 and 22;
  (ii) To transmit to the Contracting Parties notifications, reports and other information received in accordance with articles 3, 9 and 26;
 (iii) To receive, consider and reply to enquiries and information from the Contracting Parties;

(iv) To receive, consider and reply to enquiries and information from non-governmental organizations and the public when they relate to subjects of common interest or to activities carried out at the regional level; in this case, the Contracting Parties concerned shall be informed;

(v) To perform the functions assigned to it by the protocols to this Convention;

(vi) To regularly report to the Contracting Parties on the implementation of the Convention and of the Protocols;

(vii) To perform such other functions as may be assigned to it by the Contracting Parties;

(viii) To ensure the necessary coordination with other international bodies which the Contracting Parties consider competent, and in particular, to enter into such administrative arrangements as may be required for the effective discharge of the secretariat functions.

Article 18
Meetings of the Contracting Parties

1. The Contracting Parties shall hold ordinary meetings once every two years and extraordinary meetings at any other time deemed necessary, upon the request of the Organization or at the request of any Contracting Party, provided that such requests are supported by at least two Contracting Parties.

2. It shall be the function of the meetings of the Contracting Parties to keep under review the implementation of this Convention and the protocols and, in particular:

(i) To review generally the inventories carried out by Contracting Parties and competent international organizations on the state of marine pollution and its effects in the Mediterranean Sea Area;

(ii) To consider reports submitted by the Contracting Parties under article 26;

(iii) To adopt, review and amend as required the annexes to this Convention and to the protocols, in accordance with the procedure established in article 23;

(iv) To make recommendations regarding the adoption of any additional protocols or any amendments to this Convention or the protocols in accordance with the provisions of articles 21 and 22;

(v) To establish working groups as required to consider any matters related to this Convention and the protocols and annexes;

(vi) To consider and undertake any additional action that may be required for the achievement of the purposes of this Convention and the protocols;

(vii) To approve the Programme Budget.

Article 19
Bureau

1. The Bureau of the Contracting Parties shall be composed of representatives of the Contracting Parties elected by the Meetings of the Contracting Parties. In electing the members of the Bureau, the Meetings of the Contracting Parties shall observe the principle of equitable geographical distribution.

2. The functions of the Bureau and the terms and conditions upon which it shall operate shall be set in the Rules of Procedure adopted by the Meetings of the Contracting Parties.

Article 20
Observers

1. The Contracting Parties may decide to admit as observers at their meetings and conferences:

(a) any State which is not a Contracting Party to the Convention;
(b) any international governmental organization or any non-governmental organization the activities of which are related to the Convention.

2. Such observers may participate in meetings without the right to vote and may present any information or report relevant to the objectives of the Convention.

3. The conditions for the admission and participation of observers shall be established in the Rules of Procedure adopted by the Contracting Parties.

Article 21
Adoption of additional protocols

1. The Contracting Parties, at a diplomatic conference, may adopt additional protocols to this Convention pursuant to paragraph 5 of article 4.

2. A diplomatic conference for the purpose of adopting additional protocols shall be convened by the Organization at the request of two thirds of the Contracting Parties.

Article 22
Amendment of the Convention or Protocols

1. Any Contracting Party to this Convention may propose amendments to the Convention. Amendments shall be adopted by a diplomatic conference which shall be convened by the Organization at the request of two thirds of the Contracting Parties.

2. Any Contracting Party to this Convention may propose amendments to any protocol. Such amendments shall be adopted by a diplomatic conference which shall be convened by the Organization at the request of two thirds of the Contracting Parties to the protocol concerned.

3. Amendments to this Convention shall be adopted by a three-fourths majority vote of the Contracting Parties to the Convention which are represented at the diplomatic conference and shall be submitted by the Depositary for acceptance by all Contracting Parties to the Convention. Amendments to any protocol shall be adopted by a three-fourths majority vote of the Contracting Parties to such protocol which are represented at the diplomatic conference and shall be submitted by the Depositary for acceptance by all Contracting Parties to such protocol.

4. Acceptance of amendments shall be notified to the Depositary in writing. Amendments adopted in accordance with paragraph 3 of this article shall enter into force between Contracting Parties having accepted such amendments on the thirtieth day following the receipt by the Depositary of notification of their acceptance by at least three fourths of the Contracting Parties to this Convention or to the protocol concerned, as the case may be.

5. After the entry into force of an amendment to this Convention or to a protocol, any new Contracting Party to this Convention or such protocol shall become a Contracting Party to the instrument as amended.

Article 23
Annexes and amendments to annexes

1. Annexes to this Convention or to any protocol shall form an integral part of the Convention or such protocol, as the case may be.

2. Except as may be otherwise provided in any protocol, the following procedure shall apply to the adoption and entry into force of any amendments to annexes to this Convention or to any protocol, with the exception of amendments to the annex on arbitration:

(i) Any Contracting Party may propose amendments to the annexes to this Convention or to any protocol at the meetings referred to in article 18;

(ii) Such amendments shall be adopted by a three-fourths majority vote of the Contracting Parties to the instrument in question;

(iii) The Depositary shall without delay communicate the amendments so adopted to all Contracting Parties;

(iv) Any Contracting Party that is unable to approve an amendment to the annexes to this Convention or to any protocol shall so notify in writing the Depositary within a period determined by the Contracting Parties concerned when adopting the amendment;

(v) The Depositary shall without delay notify all Contracting Parties of any notification received pursuant to the preceding sub-paragraph;

(vi) On expiry of the period referred to in sub-paragraph (iv) above, the amendment to the annex shall become effective for all Contracting Parties to this Convention or to the protocol concerned which have not submitted a notification in accordance with the provisions of that sub-paragraph.

3. The adoption and entry into force of a new annex to this Convention or to any protocol shall be subject to the same procedure as for the adoption and entry into force of an amendment to an annex in accordance with the provisions of paragraph 2 of this article, provided that, if any amendment to the Convention or the protocol concerned is involved, the new annex shall not enter into force until such time as the amendment to the Convention or the protocol concerned enters into force.

4. Amendments to the annex on arbitration shall be considered to be amendments to this Convention and shall be proposed and adopted in accordance with the procedures set out in article 22 above.

Article 24
Rules of procedure and financial rules

1. The Contracting Parties shall adopt rules of procedure for their meetings and conferences envisaged in articles 18, 21 and 22 above.

2. The Contracting Parties shall adopt financial rules, prepared in consultation with the Organization, to determine, in particular, their financial participation in the Trust Fund.

Article 25
Special exercise of voting right

Within the areas of their competence, the European Economic Community and any regional economic grouping referred to in article 30 of this Convention shall exercise their right to vote with a number of votes equal to the number of their member States which are Contracting Parties to this Convention and to one or more protocols; the European Economic Community and any grouping as referred to above shall not exercise their right to vote in cases where the member States concerned exercise theirs, and conversely.

Article 26
Reports

1. The Contracting Parties shall transmit to the Organization reports on:

(a) the legal, administrative or other measures taken by them for the implementation of this Convention, the Protocols and of the recommendations adopted by their meetings;
(b) the effectiveness of the measures referred to in subparagraph (a) and problems encountered in the implementation of the instruments as mentioned above.

2. The reports shall be submitted in such form and at such intervals as the Meetings of Contracting Parties may determine.

Article 27
Compliance control

The meetings of the Contracting Parties shall, on the basis of periodical reports referred to in Article 26 and any other report submitted by the Contracting Parties, assess the compliance with the Convention and the Protocols as well as the measures and recommendations. They shall recommend, when appropriate, the necessary steps to bring about full compliance with the Convention and the Protocols and promote the implementation of the decisions and recommendations.

Article 28
Settlements of disputes

1. In case of a dispute between Contracting Parties as to the interpretation or application of this Convention or the protocols, they shall seek a settlement of the dispute through negotiation or any other peaceful means of their own choice.

2. If the Parties concerned cannot settle their dispute through the means mentioned in the preceding paragraph, the dispute shall upon common agreement be submitted to arbitration under the conditions laid down in annex A to this Convention.

3. Nevertheless, the Contracting Parties may at any time declare that they recognize as compulsory *ipso facto* and without special agreement, in relation to any other Party accepting the same obligation, the application of the arbitration procedure in conformity with the provisions of annex A. Such declaration shall be notified in writing to the Depositary, who shall communicate it to the other Parties.

Article 29
Relationship between the Convention and Protocols

1. No one may become a Contracting Party to this Convention unless it becomes at the same time a Contracting Party to at least one of the protocols. No one may become a Contracting Party to a protocol unless it is, or becomes at the same time, a Contracting Party to this Convention.

2. Any protocol to this Convention shall be binding only on the Contracting Parties to the protocol in question.

3. Decisions concerning any protocol pursuant to articles 18, 22 and 23 of this Convention shall be taken only by the Parties to the protocol concerned.

Article 30
Signature

This Convention, the Protocol for the Prevention of Pollution of the Mediterranean Sea by Dumping from Ships and Aircraft and the Protocol concerning cooperation in Combating Pollution of the Mediterranean Sea by Oil and Other Harmful Substances in Cases of Emergency shall be open for signature in Barcelona on 16 February 1976 and in Madrid from 17 February 1976 to 16 February 1977 by any State invited as a participant in the Conference of Plenipotentiaries of the Coastal States of the Mediterranean Region on the Protection of the Mediterranean Sea, held in Barcelona from 2 to 16 February 1976, and by any State entitled to sign any protocol in accordance with the provisions of such protocol. They shall also be open until the same date for signature by the European Economic Community and by any similar regional economic grouping at least one member of which is a coastal State of the Mediterranean Sea Area and which exercise competence in fields covered by this Convention, as well as by any protocol affecting them.

Article 31
Ratification, acceptance or approval

This Convention and any protocol thereto shall be subject to ratification, acceptance, or approval. Instruments of ratification, acceptance or approval shall be deposited with the Government of Spain, which will assume the functions of Depositary.

Article 32
Accession

1. As from 17 February 1977, the present Convention, the Protocol for the Prevention of Pollution of the Mediterranean Sea by Dumping from Ships and Aircraft, and the Protocol concerning Cooperation in Combating Pollution of the Mediterranean Sea by Oil and other Harmful Substances in Cases of Emergency shall be open for accession by the States, by the European Economic Community and by any grouping as referred to in article 30.

2. After the entry into force of the Convention and of any protocol, any State not referred to in article 30 may accede to this Convention and to any protocol, subject to prior approval by three fourths of the Contracting Parties to the protocol concerned.

3. Instruments of accession shall be deposited with the Depositary.

Article 33
Entry into force

1. This Convention shall enter into force on the same date as the protocol first entering into force.

2. The Convention shall also enter into force with regard to the States, the European Economic Community and any regional economic grouping referred to in article 30 if they have complied with the formal requirements for becoming Contracting Parties to any other protocol not yet entered into force.

3. Any protocol to this Convention, except as otherwise provided in such protocol, shall enter into force on the thirtieth day following the date of deposit of at least six instruments of ratification, acceptance, or approval of, or accession to such protocol by the Parties referred to in article 30.

4. Thereafter, this Convention and any protocol shall enter into force with respect to any State, the European Economic Community and any regional economic grouping referred to in article 30 on the thirtieth day following the date of deposit of the instruments of ratification, acceptance, approval or accession.

Article 34
Withdrawal

1. At any time after three years from the date of entry into force of this Convention, any Contracting Party may withdraw from this Convention by giving written notification of withdrawal.

2. Except as may be otherwise provided in any protocol to this Convention, any Contracting Party may, at any time after three years from the date of entry into force of such protocol, withdraw from such protocol by giving written notification of withdrawal.

3. Withdrawal shall take effect 90 days after the date on which notification of withdrawal is received by the Depositary.

4. Any Contracting Party which withdraws from this Convention shall be considered as also having withdrawn from any protocol to which it was a Party.

5. Any Contracting Party which, upon its withdrawal from a protocol, is no longer a Party to any protocol to this Convention, shall be considered as also having withdrawn from this Convention.

Article 35
Responsibilities of the Depositary

1. The Depositary shall inform the Contracting Parties, any other Party referred to in article 30, and the Organization:

 (i) Of the signature of this Convention and of any protocol thereto, and of the deposit of instruments of ratification, acceptance, approval or accession in accordance with articles 30, 31 and 32;
 (ii) Of the date on which the Convention and any protocol will come into force in accordance with the provisions of article 33;
(iii) Of notifications of withdrawal made in accordance with article 34;
(iv) Of the amendments adopted with respect to the Convention and to any protocol, their acceptance by the Contracting Parties and the date of entry into force of those amendments in accordance with the provisions of article 22;

(v) Of the adoption of new annexes and of the amendment of any annex in accordance with article 23;

(vi) Of declarations recognizing as compulsory the application of the arbitration procedure mentioned in paragraph 3 of article 28.

2. The original of this Convention and of any protocol thereto shall be deposited with the Depositary, the Government of Spain, which shall send certified copies thereof to the Contracting Parties, to the Organization, and to the Secretary-General of the United Nations for registration and publication in accordance with Article 102 of the United Nations Charter.

IN WITNESS THEREOF the undersigned, being duly authorized by their respective Governments, have signed this Convention.

DONE at Barcelona on 16 February 1976 in a single copy in the Arabic, English, French and Spanish languages, the four texts being equally authoritative.

Annex A
Arbitration

Article 1

Unless the Parties to the dispute otherwise agree, the arbitration procedure shall be conducted in accordance with the provisions of this annex.

Article 2

1. At the request addressed by one Contracting Party to another Contracting Party in accordance with the provisions of paragraph 2 or paragraph 3 of article 28 of the Convention, an arbitral tribunal shall be constituted. The request for arbitration shall state the subject matter of the application including, in particular, the articles of the Convention or the protocol, the interpretation or application of which is in dispute.

2. The claimant party shall inform the Organization that it has requested the setting up of an arbitral tribunal, stating the name of the other Party to the dispute and articles of the Convention or the protocols the interpretation or application of which is in its opinion in dispute. The Organization shall forward the information thus received to all Contracting Parties to the Convention.

Article 3

The arbitral tribunal shall consist of three members: each of the Parties to the dispute shall appoint an arbitrator; the two arbitrators so appointed shall designate by common agreement the third arbitrator who shall be the chairman of the tribunal. The latter shall not be a national of one of the Parties to the dispute, nor have his usual place of residence in the territory of one of these

Parties, nor be employed by any of them, nor have dealt with the case in any other capacity.

Article 4

1. If the chairman of the arbitral tribunal has not been designated within two months of the appointment of the second arbitrator, the Secretary-General of the United Nations shall, at the request of the more diligent Party, designate him within a further two months' period.

2. If one of the Parties to the dispute does not appoint an arbitrator within two months of receipt of the request, the other Party may inform the Secretary-General of the United Nations who shall designate the chairman of the arbitral tribunal within a further two months' period. Upon designation, the chairman of the arbitral tribunal shall request the Party which has not appointed an arbitrator to do so within two months. After such period, he shall inform the Secretary-General of the United Nations, who shall make this appointment within a further two months' period.

Article 5

1. The arbitral tribunal shall decide according to the rules of international law and, in particular, those of this Convention and the protocols concerned.

2. Any arbitral tribunal constituted under the provisions of this annex shall draw up its own rules of procedure.

Article 6

1. The decisions of the arbitral tribunal, both on procedure and on substance, shall be taken by majority vote of its members.

2. The tribunal may take all appropriate measures in order to establish the facts. It may, at the request of one of the Parties, recommend essential interim measures of protection.

3. If two or more arbitral tribunals constituted under the provisions of this annex are seized of requests with identical or similar subjects, they may inform themselves of the procedures for establishing the facts and take them into account as far as possible.

4. The Parties to the dispute shall provide all facilities necessary for the effective conduct of the proceedings.

5. The absence or default of a Party to the dispute shall not constitute an impediment to the proceedings.

Article 7

1. The award of the arbitral tribunal shall be accompanied by a statement of reasons. It shall be final and binding upon the Parties to the dispute.

2. Any dispute which may arise between the Parties concerning the interpretation or execution of the award may be submitted by the more diligent Party

to the arbitral tribunal which made the award or, if the latter cannot be seized thereof, to another arbitral tribunal constituted for this purpose in the same manner as the first.

Article 8

The European Economic Community and any regional economic grouping referred to in article 30 of the Convention, like any Contracting Party to the Convention, are empowered to appear as complainants or as respondents before the arbitral tribunal.

12A

Protocol for the Prevention and Elimination of Pollution of the Mediterranean Sea by Dumping from Ships and Aircraft or Incineration at Sea, 16 February 1976, as revised on 10 June 1995

Editorial note

The Protocol for the Prevention and Elimination of Pollution of the Mediter-ranean Sea by Dumping from Ships and Aircraft or Incineration at Sea was adopted in 1976 and has been revised in 1995. The text reproduced in this volume is the Protocol as revised in 1995, although the 1995 amendments have not yet entered into force.

Dumping is defined as including any deliberate disposal of wastes or other matter from ships or aircraft, any deliberate disposal at sea of ships and aircraft and any deliberate disposal and burial of wastes or other matter on the seabed or in the marine subsoil from ships or aircraft (Article 3(2)). Dumping does not include the disposal at sea of waste if disposal is incidental to the normal operation by vessels or aircraft (Article 3(2)). The dumping of wastes or other matter is prohibited with the exception of those listed in Article 4 paragraph 2 (Article 4(1)): dredged material, fish waste or organic materials resulting from the processing of fish and other marine organisms, vessels (until 31 December 2000), platforms and other man-made structures at sea (provided that material capable of creating floating debris or otherwise contributing to pollution of the marine environment has been removed to the maximum extent), inert uncontaminated geological materials the chemical constituents of which are unlikely to be released into the marine environment (Article 4(2)(a) to (e)).

The dumping of the wastes and other matters mentioned above requires a special prior permit (Article 5). Such permit shall be issued only after careful consideration of the factors set forth in the Annex to the Protocol (characteris-tics and composition of the matter, characteristics of dumping site and method of deposit, general considerations and conditions).

Incineration at sea is prohibited (Article 7).

Exceptions to the prohibitions of dumping and incineration at sea are provided in case of *force majeure* or any other cause when human life or the safety of a ship or aircraft is threatened (Article 8). If a Party in a critical situation of an exceptional nature considers that wastes or other matter not listed in Article 4(2) of the Protocol cannot be disposed of on land without unacceptable danger or damage, the Party concerned shall forthwith consult with UNEP (Secretariat of the Convention). The Organization shall recommend methods of storage or the most satisfactory means of destruction or disposal under the prevailing circumstances (Article 9).

Each Party shall designate competent authorities for issuing permits for authorised dumping and keep records of the nature, quantity, location, date and method of authorised dumping (Article 10). The requirements of the Protocol shall be applied by each Party to ships and aircraft registered in the territory or flying its flag; ships and aircraft loading in its territory wastes or other matters which are to be dumped; ships and aircraft believed to be engaged in dumping in areas under its jurisdiction (Article 11). Parties must report incidents which give rise to suspicions of violation of the Protocol (Article 12).

Nothing in the Protocol affects the rights of each Party to adopt other measures to prevent pollution by dumping, subject to being in accordance with international law (Article 13). The Protocol requires Parties to meet in ordinary sessions to, *inter alia*, review the implementation of the Protocol (Article 14). Such meetings are to be held in conjunction with ordinary meetings of the Parties to the Barcelona Convention, although Parties may hold extraordinary meetings in addition (Article 14).

Date of signature: 16 February 1976 (amended on 10 June 1995)

Entry into force: 12 February 1978 (1995 Amendment not yet in force)

Depositary: Government of Spain

Contracting Parties

(1976 Dumping Protocol): Albania, Algeria, Bosnia and Herzegovina, Croatia, Cyprus, European Community, Egypt, France, Greece, Israel, Italy, Lebanon, Libya, Malta, Monaco, Morocco, Slovenia, Spain, Syria, Tunisia, Turkey, Yugoslavia.

Acceptance of 1995

Amendment: Albania, Croatia, European Community, Egypt, France, Italy, Malta, Monaco, Morocco, Spain, Tunisia, Turkey.

Websites: www.unemap.org
www.unep.ch/seas/

Protocol for the Prevention and Elimination of Pollution of the Mediterranean Sea by Dumping from Ships and Aircraft or Incineration at Sea[1]

The Contracting Parties to the present Protocol,

Being Parties to the Convention for the protection of the Mediterranean Sea against pollution,

Recognizing the danger posed to the marine environment by the dumping or incineration of wastes or other matter,

Considering that the coastal States of the Mediterranean Sea have a common interest in protecting the marine environment from this danger,

Bearing in mind that Chapter 17 of Agenda 21 of UNCED calls on the Contracting Parties to the Convention on the Prevention of Marine Pollution by Dumping of Wastes and other Matter (London, 1972) to take the necessary measures to end dumping in the ocean and the incineration of hazardous substances,

Taking into account Resolutions LC 49(16) and LC 50(16), approved by the 16th Consultative Meeting of the 1972 London Convention, which prohibit the dumping and incineration of industrial wastes at sea,

Have agreed as follows:

Article 1

The Contracting Parties to this Protocol (hereinafter referred to as 'the Parties') shall take all appropriate measures to prevent, abate and eliminate to the fullest extent possible pollution of the Mediterranean Sea caused by dumping from ships and aircraft or incineration at sea.

Article 2

The area to which this Protocol applies shall be the Mediterranean Sea Area as defined in Article 1 of the Convention for the Protection of the Marine Environment and the Coastal Region of the Mediterranean (hereinafter referred to as 'the Convention').

---

[1] The Protocol for the Prevention of Pollution of the Mediterranean Sea by Dumping from Ships and Aircraft (the Dumping Protocol) was adopted on 16 February 1976 by the Conference of Plenipotentiaries of the Coastal States of the Mediterranean Region for the Protection of the Mediterranean Sea, held in Barcelona. The Protocol entered into force on 12 February 1978.

   The original Protocol was modified by amendments adopted on 10 June 1995 by the Conference of Plenipotentiaries on the Convention for the Protection of the Mediter-ranean Sea against Pollution and its Protocols, held in Barcelona on 9 and 10 June 1995 (UNEP(OCA)/MED IG.6/7). The amended Protocol, recorded as "Protocol for the Pre-vention and Elimination of Pollution of the Mediterranean Sea by Dumping from Ships and Aircraft or Incineration at Sea", has not yet entered into force.

Article 3

For the purposes of this Protocol:

1. 'Ships and aircraft' means waterborne or airborne craft of any type whatsoever. This expression includes air-cushioned craft and floating craft, whether self-propelled or not, and platforms and other man-made structures at sea and their equipment.
2. 'Wastes or other matter' means material and substances of any kind, form or description.
3. 'Dumping' means:
   (a) Any deliberate disposal at sea of wastes or other matter from ships or aircraft;
   (b) Any deliberate disposal at sea of ships or aircraft.
   (c) Any deliberate disposal or storage and burial of wastes or other matter on the seabed or in the marine subsoil from ships or aircraft.
4. 'Dumping' does not include:
   (a) The disposal at sea of wastes or other matter incidental to, or derived from, the normal operations of vessels or aircraft and their equipment, other than wastes or other matter transported by or to vessels or aircraft, operating for the purpose of disposal of such matter, or derived from the treatment of such wastes or other matter on such vessels or aircraft;
   (b) Placement of matter for a purpose other than the mere disposal thereof, provided that such placement is not contrary to the aims of this Protocol.
5. 'Incineration at sea' means the deliberate combustion of wastes or other matter in the maritime waters of the Mediterranean Sea, with the aim of thermal destruction and does not include activities incidental to the normal operations of ships or aircraft.
6. 'Organization' means the body referred to in Article 17 of the Convention.

Article 4

1. The dumping of wastes or other matter, with the exception of those listed in paragraph 2 of this Article, is prohibited.
2. The following is the list referred to in the preceding paragraph:
   (a) dredged material;
   (b) fish waste or organic materials resulting from the processing of fish and other marine organisms;
   (c) vessels, until 31 December 2000;
   (d) platforms and other man-made structures at sea, provided that material capable of creating floating debris or otherwise contributing to pollution of the marine environment has been removed to the

maximum extent, without prejudice to the provisions of the Protocol concerning Pollution Resulting from Exploration and Exploitation of the Continental Shelf, the Seabed and its Subsoil;

(e) inert uncontaminated geological materials the chemical constituents of which are unlikely to be released into the marine environment.

Article 5

The dumping of the wastes or other matter listed in Article 4.2 requires a prior special permit from the competent national authorities.

Article 6

1. The permit referred to in Article 5 shall be issued only after careful consideration of the factors set forth in the Annex to this Protocol or the criteria, guidelines and relevant procedures adopted by the meeting of the Contracting Parties pursuant to paragraph 2 below:

2. The Contracting Parties shall draw up and adopt criteria, guidelines and procedures for the dumping of wastes or other matter listed in Article 4.2 so as to prevent, abate and eliminate pollution.

Article 7

Incineration at sea is prohibited.

Article 8

The provisions of articles 4, 5 and 6 shall not apply in case of *force majeure* due to stress of weather or any other cause when human life or the safety of a ship or aircraft is threatened. Such dumpings shall immediately be reported to the Organization and, either through the Organization or directly, to any Party or Parties likely to be affected, together with full details of the circumstances and of the nature and quantities of the wastes or other matter dumped.

Article 9

If a Party in a critical situation of an exceptional nature considers that wastes or other matter not listed in Article 4.2 of this Protocol cannot be disposed of on land without unacceptable danger or damage, above all for the safety of human life, the Party concerned shall forthwith consult the Organization. The Organization, after consulting the Parties to this Protocol, shall recommend methods of storage or the most satisfactory means of destruction or disposal under the prevailing circumstances. The Party shall inform the Organization of the steps adopted in pursuance of these recommendations. The Parties pledge themselves to assist one another in such situations.

Article 10

1. Each Party shall designate one or more competent authorities to:

(a) Issue the permits provided for in Article 5;
(b) Keep records of the nature and quantities of the wastes or other matter permitted to be dumped and of the location, date and method of dumping.

2. The competent authorities of each Party shall issue the permits provided for in Articles 5 in respect of the wastes or other matter intended for dumping:

(a) Loaded in its territory;
(b) Loaded by a ship or aircraft registered in its territory or flying its flag, when the loading occurs in the territory of a State not Party to this Protocol.

Article 11

1. Each Party shall apply the measures required to implement this Protocol to all:

(a) Ships and aircraft registered in its territory or flying its flag;
(b) Ships and aircraft loading in its territory wastes or other matter which are to be dumped;
(c) Ships and aircraft believed to be engaged in dumping in areas under its jurisdiction in this matter.

Article 12

Each Party undertakes to issue instructions to its maritime inspection ships and aircraft and to other appropriate services to report to its authorities any incidents or conditions in the Mediterranean Sea area which give rise to suspicions that dumping in contravention of the provisions of this Protocol has occurred or is about to occur. That Party shall, if it considers it appropriate, report accordingly to any other Party concerned.

Article 13

Nothing in this Protocol shall affect the right of each Party to adopt other measures, in accordance with international law, to prevent pollution due to dumping.

Article 14

1. Ordinary meetings of the Parties to this Protocol shall be held in conjunction with ordinary meetings of the Contracting Parties to the Convention held pursuant to article 18 of the Convention. The Parties to this Protocol may also hold extraordinary meetings in conformity with article 18 of the Convention.

2. It shall be the function of the meetings of the Parties to this Protocol:

(a) To keep under review the implementation of this Protocol, and to consider the efficacy of the measures adopted and the need for any other measures, in particular in the form of annexes;
(b) To study and consider the records of the permits issued in accordance with articles 5, 6 and 7 and of the dumping which has taken place;
(c) To review and amend as required any annex to this Protocol;
(d) To discharge such other functions as may be appropriate for the implementation of this Protocol.

3. The adoption of amendments to the Annex to this Protocol pursuant to Article 23 of the Convention shall require a three-fourths majority vote of the Parties.

Article 15

1. The provisions of the Convention relating to any Protocol shall apply with respect to the present Protocol.

2. The rules of procedure and the financial rules adopted pursuant to article 24 of the Convention shall apply with respect to this Protocol, unless the Parties to this Protocol agree otherwise.

IN WITNESS WHEREOF the undersigned, being duly authorized by their respective Governments, have signed this Protocol.

DONE at Barcelona on 16 February 1976 in a single copy in the Arabic, English, French and Spanish languages, the four texts being equally authoritative.

ANNEX

The factors to be considered in establishing criteria governing the issue of permits for the dumping of matter at sea taking into account Article 6 include:

A. CHARACTERISTICS AND COMPOSITION OF THE MATTER

1. Total amount and average compositions of matter dumped (e.g. per year).
2. Form (e.g. solid, sludge, liquid or gaseous).
3. Properties: physical (e.g. solubility and density), chemical and biochemical (e.g. oxygen demand, nutrients) and biological (e.g. presence of viruses, bacteria, yeasts, parasites).
4. Toxicity.
5. Persistence: physical, chemical and biological.

6. Accumulation and biotransformation in biological materials or sediments.
7. Susceptibility to physical, chemical and biochemical changes and interaction in the aquatic environment with other dissolved organic and inorganic materials.
8. Probability of production of taints or other changes reducing marketability of resources (fish, shellfish, etc.).

B. CHARACTERISTICS OF DUMPING SITE AND METHOD OF DEPOSIT

1. Location (e.g. co-ordinates of the dumping area, depth and distance from the coast), location in relation to other areas (e.g. amenity areas, spawning, nursery and fishing areas and exploitable resources).
2. Rate of disposal per specific period (e.g. quantity per day, per week, per month).
3. Methods of packaging and containment, if any.
4. Initial dilution achieved by proposed method of release, particularly the speed of the ship.
5. Dispersal characteristics (e.g. effects of currents, tides and wind on horizontal transport and vertical mixing).
6. Water characteristics (e.g. temperature, pH, salinity, stratification, oxygen indices of pollution-dissolved oxygen (DO), chemical oxygen demand (C.O.D.), biochemical oxygen demand (BOD), nitrogen present in organic and mineral form, including ammonia, suspended matter, other nutrients and productivity).
7. Bottom characteristics (e.g. topography, geochemical and geological characteristics and biological productivity).
8. Existence and effects of other dumpings which have been made in the dumping area (e.g. heavy metal background reading and organic carbon content).
9. When issuing a permit for dumping, the Contracting Parties shall endeavour to determine whether an adequate scientific basis exists for assessing the consequences of such dumping in the area concerned, in accordance with the foregoing provisions and taking into account seasonal variations.

C. GENERAL CONSIDERATIONS AND CONDITIONS

1. Possible effects on amenities (e.g. presence of floating or stranded material, turbidity, objectionable odour, discolouration and foaming).
2. Possible effects on marine life, fish and shellfish culture, fish stocks and fisheries, seaweed harvesting and culture.

3. Possible effects on other uses of the sea (e.g. impairment of water quality for industrial use, underwater corrosion of structures, interference with ship operations from floating materials, interference with fishing or navigation through deposit of waste or solid objects on the sea floor and protection of areas of special importance for scientific or conservation purposes).
4. The practical availability of alternative land-based methods of treatment, disposal or elimination or of treatment to render the matter less harmful for sea dumping.

Protocol Concerning Co-operation in Preventing Pollution from Ships and, in Cases of Emergency, Combating Pollution of the Mediterranean Sea, 25 January 2002

Editorial note

The Protocol Concerning Co-operation in Preventing Pollution from Ships and, in Cases of Emergency, Combating Pollution of the Mediterranean Sea adopted on 25 January 2002 has not yet entered into force. The Protocol will replace an earlier 1976 Protocol, which is currently in force. The text of the 2002 Protocol is reproduced below.

The Protocol requires Parties to co-operate to implement international regulations to prevent, reduce and control pollution of the marine environment from ships (Article 3(1)(a)) and to take all necessary measures in cases of pollution incidents (Article 3(1)(b)). Parties, in co-operating, should take into account as appropriate the participation of local authorities, non-governmental organisations and socio-economic actors (Article 3(2)).

Parties are required to endeavour to maintain and promote contingency plans and other means of preventing and combating pollution incidents (Article 4(1)). Parties shall also take measures to ensure the effective implementation in the Mediterranean Sea Area of the relevant international conventions in their capacity as flag State, port State and coastal State to prevent the pollution from ships (Article 4(2)). Parties must develop and apply monitoring activities in this regard (Article 5) and co-operate, as far as practicable, in the salvage and recovery of harmful substances released in specific forms of packaging (Article 6).

The Protocol requires Parties to disseminate and exchange information relating to marine pollution from harmful substances (Article 7(1)). Such information must be transmitted to the 'regional centre', which will communicate it to other Parties and, on the basis of reciprocity, to non-Party coastal States (Article 7(2)). Parties undertake to co-ordinate their communications (Article 8). Parties are required to issue instructions to masters or other persons having charge of ships flying their flag and to the pilots of aircraft registered in their territory to report by the most rapid and adequate channels all incidents which result or may result in a discharge of oil or hazardous and noxious substances and the presence of spillages likely to cause pollution (Article 9).

Any Party faced with a pollution incident shall make the necessary assessment of, *inter alia*, the nature, extent and possible consequence of the incident (Article 10(1)(a)) and take measures to prevent, reduce and eliminate the effects of the incident (Article 10(1)(b)). Each Party must also immediately inform all Parties likely to be affected and continue to observe the situation for as long as possible (Article 10(1)(c) and (d)). Where action is taken to combat pollution from ships, all possible measures shall be taken to safeguard human lives and the ship itself (Article 10(2)).

Each Party shall take the necessary steps to ensure that ships flying its flag have on board a pollution emergency plan. Emergency plans are also required for authorities or operators in charge of sea ports and offshore installations (Article 11).

In case of a pollution incident, any Party may call for assistance from other Parties. Parties shall use their best endeavours to render assistance (Article 12). Parties shall bear the costs of their respective action for providing assistance, unless otherwise agreed (Article 13).

Parties shall take all necessary steps to ensure that reception facilities meeting the needs of ships are available at their ports and terminals (Article 14). Parties shall take the necessary steps to assess the environmental risks of the recognised routes used in maritime traffic and shall take appropriate measures aimed at reducing the risk of accidents or the environmental consequences thereof (Article 15). They are also to define national, subregional or regional strategies concerning reception in places of refuge of ships in distress presenting a threat to the marine environment (Article 16).

The Protocol establishes meetings of the Parties which shall review its implementation and are to be held in conjunction with the Conference of the Parties of the Barcelona Convention (Article 18).

The Protocol shall enter into force on the thirtieth day following deposit of the sixth instrument of ratification, acceptance, approval or accession (Article 25(1)). From the date of its entry into force, it shall replace the 1976 Emergency Protocol (Article 25(2)).

Date of signature:	16 February 1976 (replaced by Protocol signed on 25 January 2002)
Entry into force:	12 February 1976 (2002 Protocol not yet in force)
Depositary:	Government of Spain
Contracting Parties (1976 Emergency Protocol):	Albania, Algeria, Bosnia and Herzegovina, Croatia, Cyprus, European Community, Egypt,

France, Greece, Israel, Italy, Lebanon, Libya, Malta, Monaco, Morocco, Slovenia, Spain, Syria, Tunisia, Turkey.

Contracting Parties
(2002 Emergency Protocol):   Monaco

Websites: www.unepmap.org
                              www.unep.ch/seas

Protocol Concerning Co-operation in Preventing Pollution from Ships and, in Cases of Emergency, Combating Pollution of the Mediterranean Sea

The Contracting Parties to the present Protocol,

Being Parties to the Convention for the Protection of the Mediterranean Sea against Pollution, adopted at Barcelona on 16 February 1976 and amended on 10 June 1995,

Desirous of implementing Articles 6 and 9 of the said Convention,

Recognizing that grave pollution of the sea by oil and hazardous and noxious substances or a threat thereof in the Mediterranean Sea Area involves a danger for the coastal States and the marine environment,

Considering that the cooperation of all the coastal States of the Mediterranean Sea is called for to prevent pollution from ships and to respond to pollution incidents, irrespective of their origin,

Acknowledging the role of the International Maritime Organization and the importance of cooperating within the framework of this Organization, in particular in promoting the adoption and the development of international rules and standards to prevent, reduce and control pollution of the marine environment from ships,

Emphasizing the efforts made by the Mediterranean coastal States for the implementation of these international rules and standards,

Acknowledging also the contribution of the European Community to the implementation of international standards as regards maritime safety and the prevention of pollution from ships,

Recognizing also the importance of cooperation in the Mediterranean Sea Area in promoting the effective implementation of international regulations to prevent, reduce and control pollution of the marine environment from ships,

Recognizing further the importance of prompt and effective action at the national, subregional and regional levels in taking emergency measures to deal with pollution of the marine environment or a threat thereof,

Applying the precautionary principle, the polluter pays principle and the method of environmental impact assessment, and utilizing the best available techniques and the best environmental practices, as provided for in Article 4 of the Convention,

Bearing in mind the relevant provisions of the United Nations Convention on the Law of the Sea, done at Montego Bay on 10 December 1982, which is in force and to which many Mediterranean coastal States and the European Community are Parties,

Taking into account the international conventions dealing in particular with maritime safety, the prevention of pollution from ships, preparedness for and response to pollution incidents, and liability and compensation for pollution damage,

Wishing to further develop mutual assistance and cooperation in preventing and combating pollution,

Have agreed as follows:

Article 1
Definitions

For the purpose of this Protocol:

(a) 'Convention' means the Convention for the Protection of the Mediterranean Sea against Pollution, adopted at Barcelona on 16 February 1976 and amended on 10 June 1995;

(b) 'Pollution incident' means an occurrence or series of occurrences having the same origin, which results or may result in a discharge of oil and/or hazardous and noxious substances and which poses or may pose a threat to the marine environment, or to the coastline or related interests of one or more States, and which requires emergency action or other immediate response;

(c) 'Hazardous and noxious substances' means any substance other than oil which, if introduced into the marine environment, is likely to create hazards to human health, to harm living resources and marine life, to damage amenities or to interfere with other legitimate uses of the sea;

(d) 'Related interests' means the interests of a coastal State directly affected or threatened and concerning, among others:
  (i) maritime activities in coastal areas, in ports or estuaries, including fishing activities;
  (ii) the historical and tourist appeal of the area in question, including water sports and recreation;
  (iii) the health of the coastal population;
  (iv) the cultural, aesthetic, scientific and educational value of the area;
  (v) the conservation of biological diversity and the sustainable use of marine and coastal biological resources;

(e) 'International regulations' means regulations aimed at preventing, reducing and controlling pollution of the marine environment from ships as adopted, at the global level and in conformity with international law, under the aegis of United Nations specialized agencies, and in particular of the International Maritime Organization;

(f) 'Regional Centre' means the 'Regional Marine Pollution Emergency Response Centre for the Mediterranean Sea' (REMPEC), established by Resolution 7 adopted by the Conference of Plenipotentiaries of the Coastal States of the Mediterranean Region on the Protection of the Mediterranean Sea at Barcelona on 9 February 1976, which is administered by the International Maritime Organization and the United Nations Environment Programme, and the objectives and functions of which are defined by the Contracting Parties to the Convention.

Article 2
Protocol area

The area to which the Protocol applies shall be the Mediterranean Sea Area as defined in Article 1 of the Convention.

Article 3
General provisions

1. The Parties shall cooperate:

(a) to implement international regulations to prevent, reduce and control pollution of the marine environment from ships; and

(b) to take all necessary measures in cases of pollution incidents.

2. In cooperating, the Parties should take into account as appropriate the participation of local authorities, non-governmental organizations and socioeconomic actors.

3. Party shall apply this Protocol without prejudice to the sovereignty or the jurisdiction of other Parties or other States. Any measures taken by a Party to apply this Protocol shall be in accordance with international law.

Article 4
Contingency plans and other means of preventing and combating pollution incidents

1. The Parties shall endeavour to maintain and promote, either individually or through bilateral or multilateral cooperation, contingency plans and other means of preventing and combating pollution incidents. These means shall include, in particular, equipment, ships, aircraft and personnel prepared for operations in cases of emergency, the enactment, as appropriate, of relevant legislation, the development or strengthening of the capability to respond to a pollution incident and the designation of a national authority or authorities responsible for the implementation of this Protocol.

2. The Parties shall also take measures in conformity with international law to prevent the pollution of the Mediterranean Sea Area from ships in order to ensure the effective implementation in that Area of the relevant international conventions in their capacity as flag State, port State and coastal State, and their applicable legislation. They shall develop their national capacity as regards the implementation of those international conventions and may cooperate for their effective implementation through bilateral or multilateral agreements.

3. The Parties shall inform the Regional Centre every two years of the measures taken for the implementation of this Article. The Regional Centre shall present a report to the Parties on the basis of the information received.

Article 5
Monitoring

The Parties shall develop and apply, either individually or through bilateral or multilateral cooperation, monitoring activities covering the Mediterranean Sea Area in order to prevent, detect and combat pollution, and to ensure compliance with the applicable international regulations.

Article 6
Cooperation in recovery operations

In case of release or loss overboard of hazardous and noxious substances in packaged form, including those in freight containers, portable tanks, road and rail vehicles and shipborne barges, the Parties shall cooperate as far as practicable in the salvage of these packages and the recovery of such substances so as to prevent or reduce the danger to the marine and coastal environment.

Article 7
Dissemination and exchange of information

1. Each Party undertakes to disseminate to the other Parties information concerning:

(a) the competent national organization or authorities responsible for combating pollution of the sea by oil and hazardous and noxious substances;
(b) the competent national authorities responsible for receiving reports of pollution of the sea by oil and hazardous and noxious substances and for dealing with matters concerning measures of assistance between Parties;
(c) the national authorities entitled to act on behalf of the State in regard to measures of mutual assistance and cooperation between Parties;
(d) the national organization or authorities responsible for the implementation of paragraph 2 of Article 4, in particular those responsible for the implementation of the international conventions concerned and other relevant applicable regulations, those responsible for port reception facilities

and those responsible for the monitoring of discharges which are illegal under MARPOL 73/78;

(e) its regulations and other matters which have a direct bearing on preparedness for and response to pollution of the sea by oil and hazardous and noxious substances;

(f) new ways in which pollution of the sea by oil and hazardous and noxious substances may be avoided, new measures for combating pollution, new developments in the technology of conducting monitoring and the development of research programmes.

2. The Parties which have agreed to exchange information directly shall communicate such information to the Regional Centre. The latter shall communicate this information to the other Parties and, on a basis of reciprocity, to coastal States of the Mediterranean Sea Area which are not Parties to this Protocol.

3. Parties concluding bilateral or multilateral agreements within the framework of this Protocol shall inform the Regional Centre of such agreements, which shall communicate them to the other Parties.

Article 8
Communication of information and reports concerning pollution incidents

The Parties undertake to coordinate the utilization of the means of communication at their disposal in order to ensure, with the necessary speed and reliability, the reception, transmission and dissemination of all reports and urgent information concerning pollution incidents. The Regional Centre shall have the necessary means of communication to enable it to participate in this coordinated effort and, in particular, to fulfil the functions assigned to it by paragraph 2 of Article 12.

Article 9
Reporting procedure

1. Each Party shall issue instructions to masters or other persons having charge of ships flying its flag and to the pilots of aircraft registered in its territory to report by the most rapid and adequate channels in the circumstances, following reporting procedures to the extent required by, and in accordance with, the applicable provisions of the relevant international agreements, to the nearest coastal State and to this Party:

(a) all incidents which result or may result in a discharge of oil or hazardous and noxious substances;

(b) the presence, characteristics and extent of spillages of oil or hazardous and noxious substances, including hazardous and noxious substances in packaged form, observed at sea which pose or are likely to pose a threat to the marine environment or to the coast or related interests of one or more of the Parties.

2. Without prejudice to the provisions of Article 20 of the Protocol, each Party shall take appropriate measures with a view to ensuring that the master of every ship sailing in its territorial waters complies with the obligations under (a) and (b) of paragraph 1 and may request assistance from the Regional Centre in this respect. It shall inform the International Maritime Organization of the measures taken.

3. Each Party shall also issue instructions to persons having charge of sea ports or handling facilities under its jurisdiction to report to it, in accordance with applicable laws, all incidents which result or may result in a discharge of oil or hazardous and noxious substances.

4. In accordance with the relevant provisions of the Protocol for the Protection of the Mediterranean Sea against Pollution Resulting from Exploration and Exploitation of the Continental Shelf and the Seabed and its Subsoil, each Party shall issue instructions to persons having charge of offshore units under its jurisdiction to report to it by the most rapid and adequate channels in the circumstances, following reporting procedures it has prescribed, all incidents which result or may result in a discharge of oil or hazardous and noxious substances.

5. In paragraphs 1, 3 and 4 of this Article, the term 'incident' means an incident meeting the conditions described therein, whether or not it is a pollution incident.

6. The information collected in accordance with paragraphs 1, 3 and 4 shall be communicated to the Regional Centre in the case of a pollution incident.

7. The information collected in accordance with paragraphs 1, 3 and 4 shall be immediately communicated to the other Parties likely to be affected by a pollution incident:

(a) by the Party which has received the information, preferably directly or through the Regional Centre; or
(b) by the Regional Centre.
    In case of direct communication between Parties, these shall inform the Regional Centre of the measures taken, and the Centre shall communicate them to the other Parties.

8. The Parties shall use a mutually agreed standard form proposed by the Regional Centre for the reporting of pollution incidents as required under paragraphs 6 and 7 of this Article.

9. In consequence of the application of the provisions of paragraph 7, the Parties are not bound by the obligation laid down in Article 9, paragraph 2, of the Convention.

Article 10
Operational measures

1. Any Party faced with a pollution incident shall:

(a) make the necessary assessments of the nature, extent and possible consequences of the pollution incident or, as the case may be, the type and
approximate quantity of oil or hazardous and noxious substances and the
direction and speed of drift of the spillage;
(b) take every practicable measure to prevent, reduce and, to the fullest possible
extent, eliminate the effects of the pollution incident;
(c) immediately inform all Parties likely to be affected by the pollution incident
of these assessments and of any action which it has taken or intends to take,
and simultaneously provide the same information to the Regional Centre,
which shall communicate it to all other Parties;
(d) continue to observe the situation for as long as possible and report thereon
in accordance with Article 9.

2. Where action is taken to combat pollution originating from a ship, all
possible measures shall be taken to safeguard:

(a) human lives;
(b) the ship itself, in doing so, damage to the environment in general shall be
prevented or minimized.

Any Party which takes such action shall inform the International Maritime
Organization either directly or through the Regional Centre.

Article 11
Emergency measures on board ships, on offshore
installations and in ports

1. Each Party shall take the necessary steps to ensure that ships flying its flag
have on board a pollution emergency plan as required by, and in accordance
with, the relevant international regulations.

2. Each Party shall require masters of ships flying its flag, in case of a pollution
incident, to follow the procedures described in the shipboard emergency plan
and in particular to provide the proper authorities, at their request, with such
detailed information about the ship and its cargo as is relevant to actions taken
in pursuance of Article 9, and to cooperate with these authorities.

3. Without prejudice to the provisions of Article 20 of the Protocol, each
Party shall take appropriate measures with a view to ensuring that the master
of every ship sailing in its territorial waters complies with the obligation under
paragraph 2 and may request assistance from the Regional Centre in this respect. It shall inform the International Maritime Organization of the measures
taken.

4. Each Party shall require that authorities or operators in charge of sea ports and handling facilities under its jurisdiction as it deems appropriate have pollution emergency plans or similar arrangements that are coordinated with the national system established in accordance with Article 4 and approved in accordance with procedures established by the competent national authority.

5. Each Party shall require operators in charge of offshore installations under its jurisdiction to have a contingency plan to combat any pollution incident, which is coordinated with the national system established in accordance with Article 4 and in accordance with the procedures established by the competent national authority.

Article 12
Assistance

1. Any Party requiring assistance to deal with a pollution incident may call for assistance from other Parties, either directly or through the Regional Centre, starting with the Parties which appear likely to be affected by the pollution. This assistance may comprise, in particular, expert advice and the supply to or placing at the disposal of the Party concerned of the required specialized personnel, products, equipment and nautical facilities. Parties so requested shall use their best endeavours to render this assistance.

2. Where the Parties engaged in an operation to combat pollution cannot agree on the organization of the operation, the Regional Centre may, with the approval of all the Parties involved, coordinate the activity of the facilities put into operation by these Parties.

3. In accordance with applicable international agreements, each Party shall take the necessary legal and administrative measures to facilitate:

(a) the arrival and utilization in and departure from its territory of ships, aircraft and other modes of transport engaged in responding to a pollution incident or transporting personnel, cargoes, materials and equipment required to deal with such an incident; and

(b) the expeditious movement into, through and out of its territory of the personnel, cargoes, materials and equipment referred to in subparagraph (a).

Article 13
Reimbursement of costs of assistance

1. Unless an agreement concerning the financial arrangements governing actions of Parties to deal with pollution incidents has been concluded on a bilateral or multilateral basis prior to the pollution incident, Parties shall bear the costs of their respective action in dealing with pollution in accordance with paragraph 2.

2.

(a) If the action was taken by one Party at the express request of another Party, the requesting Party shall reimburse to the assisting Party the costs of its action. If the request is cancelled, the requesting Party shall bear the costs already incurred or committed by the assisting Party;

(b) if the action was taken by a Party on its own initiative, that Party shall bear the cost of its action;

(c) the principles laid down in subparagraphs (a) and (b) above shall apply unless the Parties concerned otherwise agree in any individual case.

3. Unless otherwise agreed, the costs of the action taken by a Party at the request of another Party shall be fairly calculated according to the law and current practice of the assisting Party concerning the reimbursement of such costs.

4. The Party requesting assistance and the assisting Party shall, where appropriate, cooperate in concluding any action in response to a compensation claim. To that end, they shall give due consideration to existing legal regimes.

Where the action thus concluded does not permit full compensation for expenses incurred in the assistance operation, the Party requesting assistance may ask the assisting Party to waive reimbursement of the expenses exceeding the sums compensated or to reduce the costs which have been calculated in accordance with paragraph 3. It may also request a postponement of the reimbursement of such costs. In considering such a request, assisting Parties shall give due consideration to the needs of developing countries.

5. The provisions of this Article shall not be interpreted as in any way prejudicing the rights of Parties to recover from third parties the costs of actions taken to deal with pollution incidents under other applicable provisions and rules of national and international law applicable to one or to the other Party involved in the assistance.

Article 14
Port reception facilities

1. The Parties shall individually, bilaterally or multilaterally take all necessary steps to ensure that reception facilities meeting the needs of ships are available in their ports and terminals. They shall ensure that these facilities are used efficiently without causing undue delay to ships. The Parties are invited to explore ways and means to charge reasonable costs for the use of these facilities.

2. The Parties shall also ensure the provision of adequate reception facilities for pleasure craft.

3. The Parties shall take all the necessary steps to ensure that reception facilities operate efficiently to limit any impact of their discharges to the marine environment.

4. The Parties shall take the necessary steps to provide ships using their ports with updated information relevant to the obligations arising from MARPOL 73/78 and from their legislation applicable in this field.

Article 15
Environmental risks of maritime traffic

In conformity with generally accepted international rules and standards and the global mandate of the International Maritime Organization, the Parties shall individually, bilaterally or multilaterally take the necessary steps to assess the environmental risks of the recognized routes used in maritime traffic and shall take the appropriate measures aimed at reducing the risks of accidents or the environmental consequences thereof.

Article 16
Reception of ships in distress in ports and places of refuge

The Parties shall define national, subregional or regional strategies concerning reception in places of refuge, including ports, of ships in distress presenting a threat to the marine environment. They shall cooperate to this end and inform the Regional Centre of the measures they have adopted.

Article 17
Subregional agreements

The Parties may negotiate, develop and maintain appropriate bilateral or multilateral subregional agreements in order to facilitate the implementation of this Protocol, or part of it. Upon request of the interested Parties, the Regional Centre shall assist them, within the framework of its functions, in the process of developing and implementing these subregional agreements.

Article 18
Meetings

1. Ordinary meetings of the Parties to this Protocol shall be held in conjunction with ordinary meetings of the Contracting Parties to the Convention, held pursuant to Article 18 of the Convention. The Parties to this Protocol may also hold extraordinary meetings as provided in Article 18 of the Convention.

2. It shall be the function of the meetings of the Parties to this Protocol, in particular:

(a) to examine and discuss reports from the Regional Centre on the implementation of this Protocol, and particularly of its Articles 4, 7 and 16;
(b) to formulate and adopt strategies, action plans and programmes for the implementation of this Protocol;

(c) to keep under review and consider the efficacy of these strategies, action plans and programmes, and the need to adopt any new strategies, action plans and programmes and to develop measures to that effect;

(d) to discharge such other functions as may be appropriate for the implementation of this Protocol.

Article 19
Relationship with the Convention

1. The provisions of the Convention relating to any protocol shall apply with respect to the present Protocol.

2. The rules of procedure and the financial rules adopted pursuant to Article 24 of the Convention shall apply with respect to this Protocol, unless the Parties agree otherwise.

Final provisions

Article 20
Effect of the Protocol on domestic legislation

In implementing the provisions of this Protocol, the right of Parties to adopt relevant stricter domestic measures or other measures in conformity with international law, in the matters covered by this Protocol, shall not be affected.

Article 21
Relations with third parties

The Parties shall, where appropriate, invite States that are not Parties to the Protocol and international organizations to cooperate in the implementation of the Protocol.

Article 22
Signature

This Protocol shall be open for signature at Valletta, Malta, on 25 January 2002 and in Madrid from 26 January 2002 to 25 January 2003 by any Contracting Party to the Convention.

Article 23
Ratification, acceptance or approval

This Protocol shall be subject to ratification, acceptance or approval. The instruments of ratification, acceptance or approval shall be deposited with the Government of Spain, which will assume the functions of Depositary.

Article 24
Accession

As from 26 January 2003, this Protocol shall be open for accession by any Party to the Convention.

Article 25
Entry into force

1. This Protocol shall enter into force on the thirtieth day following the deposit of the sixth instrument of ratification, acceptance, approval or accession.

2. From the date of its entry into force, this Protocol shall replace the Protocol concerning Cooperation in Combating Pollution of the Mediterranean Sea by Oil and other Harmful Substances in Cases of Emergency of 1976 in the relations between the Parties to both instruments.

IN WITNESS WHEREOF, the undersigned, being duly authorized thereto, have signed this Protocol.

DONE at Valletta, Malta, on 25 January 2002, in a single copy in the Arabic, English, French and Spanish languages, the four texts being equally authentic.

12C

Protocol for the Protection of the Mediterranean Sea against Pollution from Land-Based Sources and Activities, 17 May 1980, as amended on 7 March 1996

Editorial note

The Protocol for the Protection of the Mediterranean Sea against Pollution from Land-Based Sources, adopted under the Barcelona Convention, was adopted on 17 May 1980. The Protocol was modified by amendments adopted on 7 March 1996, which have not yet entered into force. The text of the Protocol reproduced below is the consolidated version of the 1980 Protocol as modified in 1996.

The Protocol aims to reduce pollution from land-based sources and activities. Pollution from land-based sources includes discharge from rivers, coastal establishments or outfalls or emanating from any other land-based sources and activities (Article 1).

The Protocol applies to discharges originating from land-based point and diffuse sources and activities within the territory of the Contracting States that may affect directly or indirectly the Mediterranean Sea Area (Article 4(1)(a)) and to inputs of polluting substances transported by atmosphere (Article 4(1)(b)). It also applies to discharges from fixed man-made offshore structures (Article 4(2)).

Parties undertake to eliminate discharges of substances listed in Annex I according to agreed standards and timetables (Article 5). Discharges of substances listed in Annex II are to be strictly limited and subject to authorisation by national authorities (Article 6). Parties are required to progressively formulate and adopt common guidelines or standards or criteria to address, *inter alia*, the quality of water used for specific purposes necessary to protect human health, living resources and ecosystems; control progressive replacement of products and processes which cause significant pollution (Article 7(1)). Such common guidelines, standards or criteria shall take into account local ecological, geographical and physical characteristics, the economic capacity of the Parties and their need for development, the level of existing pollution and the real absorptive capacity of the marine environment (Article 7(2)).

Parties shall carry out monitoring activities and make the findings accessible to the public (Article 8). The Protocol requires the Parties to co-operate in the scientific and technological fields related to pollution from land-based

417

sources and activities and to promote access to sound technology, including clean technology (Article 9). The Protocol further requires Parties to provide technical assistance to developing countries to prevent pollution from land-based sources (Article 10). In case of transboundary pollution likely to cause pollution to the marine environment, Parties must co-operate to ensure the full application of the Protocol (Article 11). In the event that a discharge from one Party risks adversely affecting the interests of other Parties, the Parties concerned, at the request of one of them, shall consult to find a satisfactory solution (Article 12).

Parties are generally required to submit reports every two years of measures, results and difficulties arising in the application of the Protocol (Article 13). Meetings of the Parties shall be held in conjunction with ordinary meetings of the Contracting Parties to the Barcelona Convention (Article 14). Programmes to implement measures and timetables regarding the substances listed in the Annexes shall be adopted by a two-thirds majority at the meeting of the Parties and are binding on those Parties accepting them (Article 15).

Date of signature: 17 May 1980 (amended on 7 March 1996)

Entry into force: 17 June 1983 (1996 amendments not yet in force)

Depositary: Government of Spain

Contracting Parties
(1976 Land-Based
Sources Protocol):   Albania, Algeria, Bosnia and Herzegovina, Croatia, Cyprus, European Community, Egypt, France, Greece, Israel, Italy, Lebanon, Libya, Malta, Monaco, Morocco, Slovenia, Spain, Syria, Tunisia, Turkey, Yugoslavia.

Acceptance of 1996
Amendment: Albania, Cyprus, European Community, France, Italy, Malta, Monaco, Morocco, Spain, Tunisia, Turkey.

Websites: www.unepmap.org
www.unep.ch/seas/

Protocol for the Protection of the Mediterranean Sea against Pollution from Land-Based Sources and Activities, as amended in 1996

The Contracting Parties to the present Protocol,

Being Parties to the Convention for the Protection of the Mediterranean Sea against Pollution, adopted at Barcelona on 16 February 1976 and amended on 10 June 1995,

Desirous of implementing article 4, paragraph 5, and articles 8 and 21 of the said Convention,

Noting the increasing environmental pressures resulting from human activities in the Mediterranean Sea Area, particularly in the fields of industrialization and urbanization, as well as the seasonal increase in the coastal population due to tourism,

Recognizing the danger posed to the marine environment, living resources and human health by pollution from land-based sources and activities and the serious problems resulting therefrom in many coastal waters and river estuaries of the Mediterranean Sea, primarily due to the release of untreated, insufficiently treated or inadequately disposed of domestic or industrial discharges containing substances that are toxic, persistent and liable to bioaccumulate,

Applying the precautionary principle and the polluter pays principle, undertaking environmental impact assessment and utilizing the best available techniques and the best environmental practice, including clean production technologies, as provided for in article 4 of the Convention,

Recognizing the difference in levels of development between the coastal States, and taking account of the economic and social imperatives of the developing countries,

Determined to take, in close cooperation, the necessary measures to protect the Mediterranean Sea against pollution from land-based sources and activities,

Taking into consideration the Global Programme of Action for the Protection of the Marine Environment from Land-Based Activities, adopted in Washington, D.C., on 3 November 1995,

Have agreed as follows:

Article 1
General provision

The Contracting Parties to this Protocol (hereinafter referred to as 'the Parties') shall take all appropriate measures to prevent, abate, combat and eliminate to the fullest possible extent pollution of the Mediterranean Sea Area caused by discharges from rivers, coastal establishments or outfalls, or emanating from any other land-based sources and activities within their territories, giving priority to the phasing out of inputs of substances that are toxic, persistent and liable to bioaccumulate.

Article 2
Definitions

For the purposes of this Protocol:

(a) 'The Convention' means the Convention for the Protection of the Mediterranean Sea against Pollution, adopted at Barcelona on 16 February 1976 and amended on 10 June 1995;

(b) 'Organization' means the body referred to in article 17 of the Convention;

(c) 'Freshwater limit' means the place in watercourses where, at low tides and in a period of low freshwater flow, there is an appreciable increase in salinity due to the presence of sea-water;

(d) The 'Hydrologic Basin' means the entire watershed area within the territories of the Contracting Parties, draining into the Mediterranean Sea Area as defined in article 1 of the Convention.

Article 3
Protocol area

The area to which this Protocol applies (hereinafter referred to as the 'Protocol Area') shall be:

(a) The Mediterranean Sea Area as defined in article 1 of the Convention;

(b) The hydrologic basin of the Mediterranean Sea Area;

(c) Waters on the landward side of the baselines from which the breadth of the territorial sea is measured and extending, in the case of watercourses, up to the freshwater limit;

(d) Brackish waters, coastal salt waters including marshes and coastal lagoons, and ground waters communicating with the Mediterranean Sea.

Article 4
Protocol application

1. This Protocol shall apply:

(a) To discharges originating from land-based point and diffuse sources and activities within the territories of the Contracting Parties that may affect directly or indirectly the Mediterranean Sea Area. These discharges shall include those which reach the Mediterranean Area, as defined in article 3(a), (c) and (d) of this Protocol, through coastal disposals, rivers, outfalls, canals, or other watercourses, including ground water flow, or through run-off and disposal under the seabed with access from land;

(b) To inputs of polluting substances transported by the atmosphere to the Mediterranean Sea Area from land-based sources or activities within the territories of the Contracting Parties under the conditions defined in annex III to this Protocol.

2. This Protocol shall also apply to polluting discharges from fixed man-made offshore structures which are under the jurisdiction of a Party and which serve purposes other than exploration and exploitation of mineral resources of the continental shelf and the sea-bed and its subsoil.

3. The Parties shall invite States that are not parties to the Protocol and have in their territories parts of the hydrologic basin of the Mediterranean Area to cooperate in the implementation of the Protocol.

Article 5
General obligations

1. The Parties undertake to eliminate pollution deriving from land-based sources and activities, in particular to phase out inputs of the substances that are toxic, persistent and liable to bioaccumulate listed in annex I.

2. To this end, they shall elaborate and implement, individually or jointly, as appropriate, national and regional action plans and programmes, containing measures and timetables for their implementation.

3. The priorities and timetables for implementing the action plans, programmes and measures shall be adopted by the Parties taking into account the elements set out in annex I and shall be periodically reviewed.

4. When adopting action plans, programmes and measures, the Parties shall take into account, either individually or jointly, the best available techniques and the best environmental practice including, where appropriate, clean production technologies, taking into account the criteria set forth in annex IV.

5. The Parties shall take preventive measures to reduce to the minimum the risk of pollution caused by accidents.

Article 6
Authorization or regulation system

1. Point source discharges into the Protocol Area, and releases into water or air that reach and may affect the Mediterranean Area, as defined in article 3(a), (c) and (d) of this Protocol, shall be strictly subject to authorization or regulation by the competent authorities of the Parties, taking due account of the provisions of this Protocol and annex II thereto, as well as the relevant decisions or recommendations of the meetings of the Contracting Parties.

2. To this end, the Parties shall provide for systems of inspection by their competent authorities to assess compliance with authorizations and regulations.

3. The Parties may be assisted by the Organization, upon request, in establishing new, or strengthening existing, competent structures for inspection of compliance with authorizations and regulations. Such assistance shall include special training of personnel.

4. The Parties establish appropriate sanctions in case of non-compliance with the authorizations and regulations and ensure their application.

Article 7
Common guidelines, standards and criteria

1. The Parties shall progressively formulate and adopt, in cooperation with the competent international organizations, common guidelines and, as appropriate, standards or criteria dealing in particular with:

(a) The length, depth and position of pipelines for coastal outfalls, taking into account, in particular, the methods used for pretreatment of effluents;
(b) Special requirements for effluents necessitating separate treatment;
(c) The quality of sea-water used for specific purposes that is necessary for the protection of human health, living resources and ecosystems;
(d) The control and progressive replacement of products, installations and industrial and other processes causing significant pollution of the marine environment;
(e) Specific requirements concerning the quantities of the substances discharged (listed in annex I), their concentration in effluents and methods of discharging them.

2. Without prejudice to the provisions of article 5 of this Protocol, such common guidelines, standards or criteria shall take into account local ecological, geographical and physical characteristics, the economic capacity of the Parties and their need for development, the level of existing pollution and the real absorptive capacity of the marine environment.

3. The action plans, programmes and measures referred to in articles 5 and 15 of this Protocol shall be adopted by taking into account, for their progressive implementation, the capacity to adapt and reconvert existing installations, the economic capacity of the Parties and their need for development.

Article 8
Monitoring

Within the framework of the provisions of, and the monitoring programmes provided for in article 12 of the Convention, and if necessary in cooperation with the competent international organizations, the Parties shall carry out at the earliest possible date monitoring activities and make access to the public of the findings in order:

(a) Systematically to assess, as far as possible, the levels of pollution along their coasts, in particular with regard to the sectors of activity and categories of substances listed in annex I, and periodically to provide information in this respect;
(b) To evaluate the effectiveness of action plans, programmes and measures implemented under this Protocol to eliminate to the fullest possible extent pollution of the marine environment.

Article 9
Scientific and technical cooperation

In conformity with article 13 of the Convention, the Parties shall cooperate in scientific and technological fields related to pollution from land-based sources and activities, particularly research on inputs, pathways and effects of pollutants and on the development of new methods for their treatment, reduction or elimination, as well as the development of clean production processes to this effect. To this end, the Parties shall, in particular, endeavour to:

(a) Exchange scientific and technical information;
(b) Coordinate their research programmes;
(c) Promote access to, and transfer of, environmentally sound technology including clean production technology.

Article 10
Technical assistance

1. The Parties shall, directly or with the assistance of competent regional or other international organizations, bilaterally or multilaterally, cooperate with a view to formulating and, as far as possible, implementing programmes of assistance to developing countries, particularly in the fields of science, education and technology, with a view to preventing, reducing or, as appropriate, phasing out inputs of pollutants from land-based sources and activities and their harmful effects in the marine environment.

2. Technical assistance would include, in particular, the training of scientific and technical personnel, as well as the acquisition, utilization and production by those countries of appropriate equipment and, as appropriate, clean production technologies, on advantageous terms to be agreed upon among the Parties concerned.

Article 11
Transboundary pollution

1. If discharges from a watercourse which flows through the territories of two or more Parties or forms a boundary between them are likely to cause pollution of the marine environment of the Protocol Area, the Parties in question, respecting the provisions of this Protocol in so far as each of them is concerned, are called upon to cooperate with a view to ensuring its full application.

2. A Party shall not be responsible for any pollution originating on the territory of a non-contracting State. However, the said Party shall endeavour to cooperate with the said State so as to make possible full application of the Protocol.

Article 12
Settlement of disputes

1. Taking into account article 28, paragraph 1, of the Convention, when land-based pollution originating from the territory of one Party is likely to prejudice directly the interests of one or more of the other Parties, the Parties concerned shall, at the request of one or more of them, undertake to enter into consultation with a view to seeking a satisfactory solution.

2. At the request of any Party concerned, the matter shall be placed on the agenda of the next meeting of the Parties held in accordance with article 14 of this Protocol; the meeting may make recommendations with a view to reaching a satisfactory solution.

Article 13
Reports

1. The Parties shall submit reports every two years, unless decided otherwise by the Meeting of the Contracting Parties, to the meetings of the Contracting Parties, through the Organization, of measures taken, results achieved and, if the case arises, of difficulties encountered in the application of this Protocol. Procedures for the submission of such reports shall be determined at the meetings of the Parties.

2. Such reports shall include, *inter alia*:

(a) Statistical data on the authorizations granted in accordance with article 6 of this Protocol;
(b) Data resulting from monitoring as provided for in article 8 of this Protocol;
(c) Quantities of pollutants discharged from their territories;
(d) Action plans, programmes and measures implemented in accordance with articles 5, 7 and 15 of this Protocol.

Article 14
Meetings

1. Ordinary meetings of the Parties shall take place in conjunction with ordinary meetings of the Contracting Parties to the Convention held pursuant to article 18 of the Convention. The Parties may also hold extraordinary meetings in accordance with article 18 of the Convention.

2. The functions of the meetings of the Parties to this Protocol shall be, *inter alia*:

(a) To keep under review the implementation of this Protocol and to consider the efficacy of the action plans, programmes and measures adopted;
(b) To revise and amend any annex to this Protocol, as appropriate;
(c) To formulate and adopt action plans, programmes and measures in accordance with articles 5, 7 and 15 of this Protocol;
(d) To adopt, in accordance with article 7 of this Protocol, common guidelines, standards or criteria, in any form decided upon by the Parties;
(e) To make recommendations in accordance with article 12, paragraph 2, of this Protocol;
(f) To consider the reports submitted by the Parties under article 13 of this Protocol;
(g) To discharge such other functions as may be appropriate for the application of this Protocol.

Article 15
Adoption of action plans, programmes and measures

1. The meeting of the Parties shall adopt, by a two-thirds majority, the short-term and medium-term regional action plans and programmes containing measures and timetables for their implementation provided for in article 5 of this Protocol.

2. Regional action plans and programmes as referred to in paragraph 1 shall be formulated by the Organization and considered and approved by the relevant technical body of the Contracting Parties within one year at the latest of the entry into force of the amendments to this Protocol. Such regional action plans and programmes shall be put on the agenda for the subsequent meeting of the Parties for adoption. The same procedure shall be followed for any additional action plans and programmes.

3. The measures and timetables adopted in accordance with paragraph 1 of this article shall be notified by the Secretariat to all the Parties. Such measures and timetables become binding on the one hundred and eightieth day following the day of notification for the Parties which have not notified the Secretariat of an objection within one hundred and seventy-nine days from the date of notification.

4. The Parties which have notified an objection in accordance with the preceding paragraph shall inform the meeting of the Parties of the provisions they intend to take, it being understood that these Parties may at any time give their consent to these measures or timetables.

Article 16
Final provisions

1. The provisions of the Convention relating to any Protocol shall apply with respect to this Protocol.

2. The rules of procedure and the financial rules adopted pursuant to article 24 of the Convention shall apply with respect to this Protocol, unless the Parties to this Protocol agree otherwise.

3. This Protocol shall be open for signature, at Athens from 17 May 1980 to 16 June 1980, and at Madrid from 17 June 1980 to 16 May 1981, by any State invited to the Conference of Plenipotentiaries of the Coastal States of the Mediterranean Region for the Protection of the Mediterranean Sea against Pollution from Land-Based Sources held at Athens from 12 May to 17 May 1980. It shall also be open until the same dates for signature by the European Economic Community and by any similar regional economic grouping of which at least one member is a coastal State of the Mediterranean Sea Area and which exercises competence in fields covered by this Protocol.

4. This Protocol shall be subject to ratification, acceptance or approval. Instruments of ratification, acceptance or approval shall be deposited with the Government of Spain, which will assume the functions of Depositary.

5. As from 17 May 1981, this Protocol shall be open for accession by the States referred to in paragraph 3 above, by the European Economic Community and by any grouping referred to in that paragraph.

6. This Protocol shall enter into force on the thirtieth day following the deposit of at least six instruments of ratification, acceptance or approval of, or accession to, the Protocol by the Parties referred to in paragraph 3 of this article.

IN WITNESS WHEREOF the undersigned, being duly authorized by their respective Governments, have signed this Protocol.

DONE at Athens on 17 May 1980 and amended at Syracuse on 7 March 1996 in a single copy in the Arabic, English, French and Spanish languages, the four texts being equally authoritative.

Annex I
Elements to be taken into account in the preparation of action plans, programmes and measures for the elimination of pollution from land-based sources and activities

This annex contains elements which will be taken into account in the preparation of action plans, programmes and measures for the elimination of pollution from land-based sources and activities referred to in articles 5, 7 and 15 of this Protocol.

Such action plans, programmes and measures will aim to cover the sectors of activity listed in section A and also cover the groups of substances enumerated in section C, selected on the basis of the characteristics listed in section B of the present annex.

Priorities for action should be established by the Parties, on the basis of the relative importance of their impact on public health, the environment and socio-economic and cultural conditions. Such programmes should cover point sources, diffuse sources and atmospheric deposition.

In preparing action plans, programmes and measures, the Parties, in conformity with the Global Programme of Action for the Protection of the Marine Environment from Land-based Activities, adopted in Washington, D.C. in 1995, will give priority to substances that are toxic, persistent and liable to bioaccumulate, in particular to persistent organic pollutants (POPs), as well as to wastewater treatment and management.

A. Sectors of activity

The following sectors of activity (not listed in order of priority) will be primarily considered when setting priorities for the preparation of action plans, programmes and measures for the elimination of the pollution from land-based sources and activities:

1. Energy production;
2. Fertilizer production;
3. Production and formulation of biocides;
4. The pharmaceutical industry;
5. Petroleum refining;
6. The paper and paper-pulp industry;
7. Cement production;
8. The tanning industry;
9. The metal industry;
10. Mining;
11. The shipbuilding and repairing industry;
12. Harbour operations;
13. The textile industry;
14. The electronic industry;
15. The recycling industry;
16. Other sectors of the organic chemical industry;
17. Other sectors of the inorganic chemical industry;
18. Tourism;
19. Agriculture;
20. Animal husbandry;
21. Food processing;
22. Aquaculture;
23. Treatment and disposal of hazardous wastes;
24. Treatment and disposal of domestic waste water;
25. Management of municipal solid waste;
26. Disposal of sewage sludge;
27. The waste management industry;
28. Incineration of waste and management of its residues;
29. Works which cause physical alteration of the natural state of the coastline;
30. Transport.

B. Characteristics of substances in the environment

For the preparation of action plans, programmes and measures, the Parties should take into account the characteristics listed below:

1. Persistence;
2. Toxicity or other noxious properties (e.g. carcinogenicity, mutagenicity, teratogenicity);
3. Bioaccumulation;
4. Radioactivity;

5. The ratio between observed concentrations and no observed effect concentrations (NOEC);
6. The risk of eutrophication of anthropogenic origin;
7. Health effects and risks;
8. Transboundary significance;
9. The risk of undesirable changes in the marine ecosystem and irreversibility or durability of effects;
10. Interference with the sustainable exploitation of living resources or with other legitimate uses of the sea;
11. Effects on the taste and/or smell of marine products for human consumption;
12. Effects on the smell, colour, transparency or other characteristics of seawater;
13. Distribution pattern (i.e. quantities involved, use patterns and probability of reaching the marine environment).

C. Categories of substances

The following categories of substances and sources of pollution will serve as guidance in the preparation of action plans, programmes and measures:

1. Organohalogen compounds and substances which may form such compounds in the marine environment. Priority will be given to Aldrin, Chlordane, DDT, Dieldrin, Dioxins and Furans, Endrin, Heptachlor, Hexachlorobenzene, Mirex, PCBs and Toxaphene;
2. Organophosphorus compounds and substances which may form such compounds in the marine environment;
3. Organotin compounds and substances which may form such compounds in the marine environment;
4. Polycyclic aromatic hydrocarbons;
5. Heavy metals and their compounds;
6. Used lubricating oils;
7. Radioactive substances, including their wastes, when their discharges do not comply with the principles of radiation protection as defined by the competent international organizations, taking into account the protection of the marine environment;
8. Biocides and their derivatives;
9. Pathogenic microorganisms;
10. Crude oils and hydrocarbons of petroleum origin;
11. Cyanides and fluorides;
12. Non-biodegradable detergents and other non-biodegradable surface-active substances;
13. Compounds of nitrogen and phosphorus and other substances which may cause eutrophication;

14. Litter (any persistent manufactured or processed solid material which is discarded, disposed of, or abandoned in the marine and coastal environment);
15. Thermal discharges;
16. Acid or alkaline compounds which may impair the quality of water;
17. Non-toxic substances that have an adverse effect on the oxygen content of the marine environment;
18. Non-toxic substances that may interfere with any legitimate use of the sea;
19. Non-toxic substances that may have adverse effects on the physical or chemical characteristics of seawater.

Annex II
Elements to be taken into account in the issue of the authorizations for discharges of wastes

With a view to the issue of an authorization for the discharges of wastes containing substances referred to in article 6 to this Protocol, particular account will be taken, as the case may be, of the following factors:

A. Characteristics and composition of the discharges

1. Type and size of point or diffuse source (e.g. industrial process).
2. Type of discharges (e.g. origin, average composition).
3. State of waste (e.g. solid, liquid, sludge, slurry).
4. Total amount (volume discharged, e.g. per year).
5. Discharge pattern (continuous, intermittent, seasonally variable, etc.).
6. Concentrations with respect to relevant constituents of substances listed in annex I and of other substances as appropriate.
7. Physical, chemical and biochemical properties of the waste discharges.

B. Characteristics of discharge constituents with respect to their harmfulness

1. Persistence (physical, chemical, biological) in the marine environment.
2. Toxicity and other harmful effects.
3. Accumulation in biological materials or sediments.
4. Biochemical transformation producing harmful compounds.
5. Adverse effects on the oxygen content and balance.
6. Susceptibility to physical, chemical and biochemical changes and interaction in the aquatic environment with other sea-water constituents which may produce harmful biological or other effects on any of the uses listed in section E below.
7. All other characteristics as listed in annex I, section B.

C. Characteristics of discharge site and receiving environment

1. Hydrographic, meteorological, geological and topographical characteristics of the coastal area.
2. Location and type of the discharge (outfall, canal outlet, etc.) and its relation to other areas (such as amenity areas, spawning, nursery, and fishing areas, shellfish grounds) and other discharges.
3. Initial dilution achieved at the point of discharge into the receiving environment.
4. Dispersion characteristics such as effects of currents, tides and wind on horizontal transport and vertical mixing.
5. Receiving water characteristics with respect to physical, chemical, biological and ecological conditions in the discharge area.
6. Capacity of the receiving marine environment to receive waste discharges without undesirable effects.

D. Availability of waste technologies

The methods of waste reduction and discharge for industrial effluents as well as domestic sewage should be selected taking into account the availability and feasibility of:

(a) Alternative treatment processes;
(b) Re-use or elimination methods;
(c) On-land disposal alternatives;
(d) Appropriate low-waste technologies.

E. Potential impairment of marine ecosystems and sea-water uses

1. Effects on human health through pollution impact on:
   (a) Edible marine organisms;
   (b) Bathing waters;
   (c) Aesthetics.
2. Effects on marine ecosystems, in particular living resources, endangered species and critical habitats.
3. Effects on other legitimate uses of the sea.

Annex III
Conditions of application to pollution transported through the atmosphere

This annex defines the conditions of application of this Protocol to pollution from land-based sources transported by the atmosphere in terms of Article 4.1(b) are the following:

1. This Protocol shall apply to polluting discharges into the atmosphere under the following conditions:

(a) the discharged substance is or could be transported to the Mediterranean Sea Area under prevailing meteorological conditions;
(b) the input of the substance into the Mediterranean Sea Area is hazardous for the environment in relation to the quantities of the same substance reaching the Area by other means.

2. This Protocol shall also apply to polluting discharges into the atmosphere affecting the Mediterranean Sea Area from land-based sources within the territories of the Parties and from fixed man-made offshore structures, subject to the provisions of article 4.2 of this Protocol.

3. In the case of pollution of the Mediterranean Sea Area from land-based sources through the atmosphere, the provisions of articles 5 and 6 of this Protocol shall apply progressively to appropriate substances and sources listed in annex I to this Protocol as will be agreed by the Parties.

4. Subject to the conditions specified in paragraph 1 of this annex, the provisions of Article 7.1 of this Protocol shall also apply to:

(a) discharges – quantity and rate – of substances emitted to the atmosphere, on the basis of the information available to the Contracting Parties concerning the location and distribution of air pollution sources;
(b) the content of hazardous substances in fuel and raw materials;
(c) the efficiency of air pollution control technologies and more efficient manufacturing and fuel burning processes;
(d) the application of hazardous substances in agriculture and forestry.

5. The provisions of annex II to this Protocol shall apply to pollution through the atmosphere whenever appropriate. Air pollution monitoring and modelling using acceptable common emission factors and methodologies shall be carried out in the assessment of atmospheric deposition of substances, as well as in the compilation of inventories of quantities and rates of pollutant emissions into the atmosphere from land-based sources.

6. All Articles, including parts thereof to this Protocol not mentioned in paragraphs 1 to 5 above shall apply equally to pollution from land-based sources transported by the atmosphere wherever applicable and subject to the conditions specified in paragraph 1 of this Annex.

Annex IV
Criteria for the definition of best available techniques and best environmental practice

A. Best available techniques

1. The use of the best available techniques shall emphasize the use of non-waste technology, if available.

2. The term 'best available techniques' means the latest stage of development (state of the art) of processes, of facilities or of methods of operation which indicate the practical suitability of a particular measure for limiting discharges, emissions and waste. In determining whether a set of processes, facilities and methods of operation constitute the best available techniques in general or individual cases, special consideration shall be given to:

(a) comparable processes, facilities or methods of operation which have recently been successfully tried out;
(b) technological advances and changes in scientific knowledge and understanding;
(c) the economic feasibility of such techniques;
(d) time limits for installation in both new and existing plants;
(e) the nature and volume of the discharges and emissions concerned.

3. It therefore follows that what is 'best available techniques' for a particular process will change with time in the light of technological advances, economic and social factors, as well as changes in scientific knowledge and understanding.

4. If the reduction of discharges and emissions resulting from the use of best available techniques does not lead to environmentally acceptable results, additional measures have to be applied.

5. 'Techniques' include both the technology used and the way in which the installation is designed, built, maintained, operated and dismantled.

B. Best environmental practice

6. The term 'best environmental practice' means the application of the most appropriate combination of environmental control measures and strategies. In making a selection for individual cases, at least the following graduated range of measures should be considered:

(a) the provision of information and education to the public and to users about the environmental consequences of choice of particular activities and choice of products, their use and ultimate disposal;
(b) the development and application of codes of good environmental practice which cover all aspects of the activity in the product's life;
(c) the mandatory application of labels informing users of environmental risks related to a product, its use and ultimate disposal;
(d) saving resources, including energy;
(e) making collection and disposal systems available to the public;
(f) avoiding the use of hazardous substances or products and the generation of hazardous waste;
(g) recycling, recovery and re-use;

(h) the application of economic instruments to activities, products or groups of products;

(i) establishing a system of licensing, involving a range of restrictions or a ban.

7. In determining what combination of measures constitute best environmental practice, in general or individual cases, particular consideration should be given to:

(a) the environmental hazard of the product and its production, use and ultimate disposal;

(b) the substitution by less polluting activities or substances;

(c) the scale of use;

(d) the potential environmental benefit or penalty of substitute materials or activities;

(e) advances and changes in scientific knowledge and understanding;

(f) time limits for implementation;

(g) social and economic implications.

8. It therefore follows that best environmental practice for a particular source will change with time in the light of technological advances, economic and social factors, as well as changes in scientific knowledge and understanding.

9. If the reduction of inputs resulting from the use of best environmental practice does not lead to environmentally acceptable results, additional measures have to be applied and best environmental practice redefined.

12D

Protocol Concerning Specially Protected Areas and Biological Diversity in the Mediterranean, 10 June 1995, and including Annexes adopted on 24 November 1996

Editorial note

The Protocol Concerning Specially Protected Areas and Biological Diversity in the Mediterranean was adopted on 10 June 1995 and entered into force on 12 December 1999. The Protocol replaces the 1982 Protocol Concerning Mediterranean Specially Protected Areas in the relationship among the Parties to both instruments (Article 32). The text of the 1995 Protocol is reproduced below.

The Protocol aims to protect, preserve and manage in a sustainable and environmentally sound way areas of particular natural or cultural value by the establishment of specially protected areas (Article 3(1)(a)). It also aims at protecting, preserving and managing threatened or endangered species of flora and fauna (Article 3(1)(b)). The Parties, furthermore, shall co-operate in the conservation and sustainable use of biological diversity (Article 3(2)). The objective of specially protected areas is to safeguard representative types of coastal and marine ecosystems, habitats which are in danger of disappearing, habitats critical to the survival, reproduction and recovery of endangered, threatened or endemic species of flora and fauna and sites of particular importance because of their scientific, aesthetic, cultural or educational interest (Article 4).

Central to the Protocol is the obligation of the Parties to establish specially protected areas in the marine and coastal zones subject to their jurisdiction (Article 5(1)). The Protocol provides suggestions for measures which Parties may take to protect the marine environment (Article 6). Parties shall adopt planning, management, supervision and monitoring measures for the specially protected areas (Article 7).

The Parties shall draw up a 'List of Specially Protected Areas of Mediterranean Importance' (SPAMI List) (Article 8(1) and (2)). The procedure for the establishment and listing of SPAMIs is described in Article 9.

The Protocol requires Parties to manage species of flora and fauna with the aim of maintaining them in a favourable state of conservation (Article 11(1)). Parties shall: identify and compile lists of the endangered species of flora and fauna in areas subject to their jurisdiction and accord such species protected status (Article 11(2)); control and prohibit the taking, possession or killing, the commercial trade, transport and the exhibition for commercial purposes of endangered species of fauna, their eggs, parts or products (Article 11(3)(a)); take measures to avoid, to the extent possible, disturbance of wild fauna (Article 11(3)(b)); co-operate and co-ordinate their efforts for the protection and recovery of migratory species (Article 11(4)); regulate and where appropriate prohibit destruction or disturbance of protected flora (Article 11(5)).

Parties shall co-operate in the adoption of measures to ensure the protection and conservation of the flora and fauna listed in the Annexes to the Protocol (Article 12). Parties shall take all appropriate measures to regulate the intentional or accidental introduction of non-indigenous or genetically modified species and prohibit those that may have harmful impacts on the environment (Article 13).

Each Party shall compile comprehensive inventories of areas under their jurisdiction that contain rare or fragile ecosystems, that are reservoirs of biological diversity, and that are important for threatened or endangered species, and of species of fauna and flora that are endangered or threatened (Article 15). Parties shall evaluate in the planning process decisions on industrial and other projects and activities that could significantly affect protected areas and their habitats and take into consideration the effects of the proposed projects and activities (Article 17).

Parties shall take into account the traditional subsistence and cultural activities of their local populations when formulating protective measures and may grant exceptions, although no exceptions can be made that will endanger the maintenance of an ecosystem protected under the Protocol or cause extinction or substantial reduction of populations of flora and fauna (Article 18).

The Parties shall give appropriate publicity to the established specially protected areas and endeavour to inform the public of their interest and value (Article 19) and shall encourage and develop scientific, technical and management research relating to the aims of the Protocol (Article 20). They shall establish co-operation programmes and exchange information on the experience acquired and the problems encountered (Article 20) and co-operate in mutual assistance and assistance with developing countries in implementing the Protocol (Article 21). Parties are to submit regular reports to ordinary meetings of the Parties on the implementation of the Protocol (Article 23). Each Party shall designate a National Focal Point to serve as liaison with the Regional Activity Centre for Specially Protected Areas (Article 24).

Date of signature: 3 April 1982 (new Protocol: 10 June 1995)

Entry into force: 23 March 1986 (new Protocol: 12 December 1999)

Depositary: Government of Spain

Contracting Parties
(1982 Protocol):   Albania, Algeria, Bosnia and Herzegovina, Croatia,
                        Cyprus, European Community, Egypt, France, Greece,
                        Israel, Italy, Lebanon, Libya, Malta, Monaco, Morocco,
                        Slovenia, Spain, Syria, Tunisia, Turkey, Yugoslavia.

Contracting Parties
(1995 Protocol):   Albania, Cyprus, European Community, Egypt, France,
                        Italy, Malta, Monaco, Spain, Tunisia, Turkey.

Websites: www.unepmap.org
                        www.unep.ch/seas/

Protocol concerning Specially Protected Areas and Biological Diversity in the Mediterranean

The Contracting Parties to the present Protocol,
   Being Parties to the Convention for the Protection of the Mediterranean Sea against Pollution, adopted at Barcelona on 16 February 1976,
   Conscious of the profound impact of human activities on the state of the marine environment and the littoral and more generally on the ecosystems of areas having prevailing Mediterranean features,
   Stressing the importance of protecting and, as appropriate, improving the state of the Mediterranean natural and cultural heritage, in particular through the establishment of specially protected areas and also by the protection and conservation of threatened species,
   Considering the instruments adopted by the United Nations Conference on Environment and Development and particularly the Convention on Biological Diversity (Rio de Janeiro, 1992),
   Conscious that when there is a threat of significant reduction or loss of biological diversity, lack of full scientific certainty should not be invoked as a reason for postponing measures to avoid or minimize such a threat,
   Considering that all the Contracting Parties should cooperate to conserve, protect and restore the health and integrity of ecosystems and that they have, in this respect, common but differentiated responsibilities,
   Have agreed as follows:

Part I
General provisions

Article 1
Definitions

For the purposes of this Protocol:

(a) 'Convention' means the Convention for the Protection of the Mediterranean Sea against Pollution, adopted at Barcelona on 16 February 1976 and amended at Barcelona in 1995;

(b) 'Biological diversity' means the variability among living organisms from all sources including, *inter alia*, terrestrial, marine and other aquatic ecosystems and the ecological complexes of which they are part; this includes diversity within species, between species and of ecosystems;

(c) 'Endangered species' means any species that is in danger of extinction throughout all or part of its range;

(d) 'Endemic species' means any species whose range is restricted to a limited geographical area;

(e) 'Threatened species' means any species that is likely to become extinct within the foreseeable future throughout all or part of its range and whose survival is unlikely if the factors causing numerical decline or habitat degradation continue to operate;

(f) 'Conservation status of a species' means the sum of the influences acting on the species that may affect its long-term distribution and abundance;

(g) 'Parties' means the Contracting Parties to this Protocol;

(h) 'Organization' means the organization referred to in Article 2 of the Convention;

(i) 'Centre' means the Regional Activity Centre for Specially Protected Areas.

Article 2
Geographical coverage

1. The area to which this Protocol applies shall be the area of the Mediterranean Sea as delimited in Article 1 of the Convention. It also includes:

- the seabed and its subsoil;
- the waters, the seabed and its subsoil on the landward side of the baseline from which the breadth of the territorial sea is measured and extending, in the case of watercourses, up to the freshwater limit;
- the terrestrial coastal areas designated by each of the Parties, including wetlands.

2. Nothing in this Protocol nor any act adopted on the basis of this Protocol shall prejudice the rights, the present and future claims or legal views of any State relating to the law of the sea, in particular, the nature and the extent of marine areas, the delimitation of marine areas between States with opposite or adjacent coasts, freedom of navigation on the high seas, the right and the modalities of passage through straits used for international navigation and the right of innocent passage in territorial seas, as well as the nature and extent of the jurisdiction of the coastal State, the flag State and the port State.

3. No act or activity undertaken on the basis of this Protocol shall constitute grounds for claiming, contending or disputing any claim to national sovereignty or jurisdiction.

Article 3
General obligations

1. Each Party shall take the necessary measures to:

(a) protect, preserve and manage in a sustainable and environmentally sound way areas of particular natural or cultural value, notably by the establishment of specially protected areas;

(b) protect, preserve and manage threatened or endangered species of flora and fauna.

2. The Parties shall cooperate, directly or through the competent international organizations, in the conservation and sustainable use of biological diversity in the area to which this Protocol applies.

3. The Parties shall identify and compile inventories of the components of biological diversity important for its conservation and sustainable use.

4. The Parties shall adopt strategies, plans and programmes for the conservation of biological diversity and the sustainable use of marine and coastal biological resources and shall integrate them into their relevant sectoral and intersectoral policies.

5. The Parties shall monitor the components of biological diversity referred to in paragraph 3 of this Article and shall identify processes and categories of activities which have or are likely to have a significant adverse impact on the conservation and sustainable use of biological diversity, and monitor their effects.

6. Each Party shall apply the measures provided for in this Protocol without prejudice to the sovereignty or the jurisdiction of other Parties or other States. Any measures taken by a Party to enforce these measures shall be in accordance with international law.

Part II
Protection of areas

Section one
Specially Protected Areas

Article 4
Objectives

The objective of specially protected areas is to safeguard:

(a) representative types of coastal and marine ecosystems of adequate size to ensure their long-term viability and to maintain their biological diversity;

(b) habitats which are in danger of disappearing in their natural area of distribution in the Mediterranean or which have a reduced natural area of distribution as a consequence of their regression or on account of their intrinsically restricted area;

(c) habitats critical to the survival, reproduction and recovery of endangered, threatened or endemic species of flora or fauna;

(d) sites of particular importance because of their scientific, aesthetic, cultural or educational interest.

Article 5
Establishment of Specially Protected Areas

1. Each Party may establish specially protected areas in the marine and coastal zones subject to its sovereignty or jurisdiction.

2. If a Party intends to establish, in an area subject to its sovereignty or national jurisdiction, a specially protected area contiguous to the frontier and to the limits of a zone subject to the sovereignty or national jurisdiction of another Party, the competent authorities of the two Parties shall endeavour to cooperate, with a view to reaching agreement on the measures to be taken and shall, *inter alia*, examine the possibility of the other Party establishing a corresponding specially protected area or adopting any other appropriate measures.

3. If a Party intends to establish, in an area subject to its sovereignty or national jurisdiction, a specially protected area contiguous to the frontier and to the limits of a zone subject to the sovereignty or national jurisdiction of a State that is not a Party to this Protocol, the Party shall endeavour to cooperate with that State as referred to in the previous paragraph.

4. If a State which is not party to this Protocol intends to establish a specially protected area contiguous to the frontier and to the limits of a zone subject to the sovereignty or national jurisdiction of a Party to this Protocol, the latter shall endeavour to cooperate with that State as referred to in paragraph 2.

Article 6
Protection measures

The Parties, in conformity with international law and taking into account the characteristics of each specially protected area, shall take the protection measures required, in particular:

(a) the strengthening of the application of the other Protocols to the Convention and of other relevant treaties to which they are Parties;

(b) the prohibition of the dumping or discharge of wastes and other substances likely directly or indirectly to impair the integrity of the specially protected area;

(c) the regulation of the passage of ships and any stopping or anchoring;

(d) the regulation of the introduction of any species not indigenous to the specially protected area in question, or of genetically modified species, as well as the introduction or reintroduction of species which are or have been present in the specially protected area;

(e) the regulation or prohibition of any activity involving the exploration or modification of the soil or the exploitation of the subsoil of the land part, the seabed or its subsoil;

(f) the regulation of any scientific research activity;

(g) the regulation or prohibition of fishing, hunting, taking of animals and harvesting of plants or their destruction, as well as trade in animals, parts of animals, plants, parts of plants, which originate in specially protected areas;

(h) the regulation and if necessary the prohibition of any other activity or act likely to harm or disturb the species or that might endanger the state of conservation of the ecosystems or species or might impair the natural or cultural characteristics of the specially protected area;

(i) any other measure aimed at safeguarding ecological and biological processes and the landscape.

Article 7
Planning and management

1. The Parties shall, in accordance with the rules of international law, adopt planning, management, supervision and monitoring measures for the specially protected areas.

2. Such measures should include for each specially protected area:

(a) the development and adoption of a management plan that specifies the legal and institutional framework and the management and protection measures applicable;

(b) the continuous monitoring of ecological processes, habitats, population dynamics, landscapes, as well as the impact of human activities;

(c) the active involvement of local communities and populations, as appropriate, in the management of specially protected areas, including assistance to local inhabitants who might be affected by the establishment of such areas;

(d) the adoption of mechanisms for financing the promotion and management of specially protected areas, as well as the development of activities which ensure that management is compatible with the objectives of such areas;

(e) the regulation of activities compatible with the objectives for which the specially protected area was established and the terms of the related permits;

(f) the training of managers and qualified technical personnel, as well as the development of an appropriate infrastructure.

3. The Parties shall ensure that national contingency plans incorporate measures for responding to incidents that could cause damage or constitute a threat to the specially protected areas.

4. When specially protected areas covering both land and marine areas have been established, the Parties shall endeavour to ensure the coordination of the administration and management of the specially protected area as a whole.

Section two
Specially Protected Areas of Mediterranean Importance

Article 8
Establishment of the list of Specially Protected Areas of Mediterranean Importance

1. In order to promote cooperation in the management and conservation of natural areas, as well as in the protection of threatened species and their habitats, the Parties shall draw up a 'List of Specially Protected Areas of Mediterranean Importance', hereinafter referred to as the 'SPAMI List'.

2. The SPAMI List may include sites which:

- are of importance for conserving the components of biological diversity in the Mediterranean;
- contain ecosystems specific to the Mediterranean area or the habitats of endangered species;
- are of special interest at the scientific, aesthetic, cultural or educational levels.

3. The Parties agree:

(a) to recognize the particular importance of these areas for the Mediterranean;
(b) to comply with the measures applicable to the SPAMIs and not to authorize nor undertake any activities that might be contrary to the objectives for which the SPAMIs were established.

Article 9
Procedure for the establishment and listing of SPAMIs

1. SPAMIs may be established, following the procedure provided for in paragraph 2 to 4 of this Article, in:

(a) the marine and coastal zones subject to the sovereignty or jurisdiction of the Parties;
(b) zones partly or wholly on the high seas.

2. Proposals for inclusion in the List may be submitted:

(a) by the Party concerned, if the area is situated in a zone already delimited, over which it exercises sovereignty or jurisdiction;
(b) by two or more neighbouring Parties concerned if the area is situated, partly or wholly, on the high sea;
(c) by the neighbouring Parties concerned in areas where the limits of national sovereignty or jurisdiction have not yet been defined.

3. Parties making proposals for inclusion in the SPAMI List shall provide the Centre with an introductory report containing information on the area's

geographical location, its physical and ecological characteristics, its legal status, its management plans and the means for their implementation, as well as a statement justifying its Mediterranean importance;

(a) where a proposal is formulated under subparagraphs 2 (b) and 2 (c) of this Article, the neighbouring Parties concerned shall consult each other with a view to ensuring the consistency of the proposed protection and management measures, as well as the means for their implementation;

(b) proposals made under paragraph 2 of this Article shall indicate the protection and management measures applicable to the area as well as the means of their implementation.

4. The procedure for inclusion of the proposed area in the List is the following:

(a) for each area, the proposal shall be submitted to the National Focal Points, which shall examine its conformity with the common guidelines and criteria adopted pursuant to Article 16;

(b) if a proposal made in accordance with subparagraph 2 (a) of this Article is consistent with the guidelines and common criteria, after assessment, the Organization shall inform the meeting of the Parties, which shall decide to include the area in the SPAMI List;

(c) if a proposal made in accordance with subparagraphs 2 (b) and 2 (c) of this Article is consistent with the guidelines and common criteria, the Centre shall transmit it to the Organization, which shall inform the meeting of the Parties. The decision to include the area in the SPAMI list shall be taken by consensus by the Contracting Parties, which shall also approve the management measures applicable to the area.

5. The Parties which proposed the inclusion of the area in the List shall implement the protection and conservation measures specified in their proposals in accordance with paragraph 3 of this Article. The Contracting Parties undertake to observe the rules thus laid down. The Centre shall inform the competent international organizations of the List and of the measures taken in the SPAMIs.

6. The Parties may revise the SPAMI List. To this end, the Centre shall prepare a report.

Article 10
Changes in the status of SPAMIs

Changes in the delimitation or legal status of a SPAMI or the suppression of all or part of such an area shall not be decided upon unless there are important reasons for doing so, taking into account the need to safeguard the environment and comply with the obligations laid down in this Protocol and a procedure similar to that followed for the creation of the SPAMI and its inclusion in the List shall be observed.

Part III
Protection and conservation of species

Article 11
National measures for the protection and conservation of species

1. The Parties shall manage species of flora and fauna with the aim of maintaining them in a favourable state of conservation.

2. The Parties shall, in the zones subject to their sovereignty or national jurisdiction, identify and compile lists of the endangered or threatened species of flora and fauna and accord protected status to such species. The Parties shall regulate and, where appropriate, prohibit activities having adverse effects on such species or their habitats, and carry out management, planning and other measures to ensure a favourable state of conservation of such species.

3. With respect to protected species of fauna, the Parties shall control and, where appropriate, prohibit:

(a) the taking, possession or killing (including, to the extent possible, the incidental taking, possession or killing), the commercial trade, the transport and the exhibition for commercial purposes of these species, their eggs, parts or products;

(b) to the extent possible, the disturbance of wild fauna, particularly during the period of breeding, incubation, hibernation or migration, as well as other periods of biological stress.

4. In addition to the measures specified in the previous paragraph, the Parties shall coordinate their efforts, through bilateral or multilateral action, including if necessary, agreements for the protection and recovery of migratory species whose range extends into the area to which this Protocol applies.

5. With respect to protected species of flora and their parts and products, the Parties shall regulate, and where appropriate, prohibit all forms of destruction and disturbance, including the picking, collecting, cutting, uprooting, possession of, commercial trade in, or transport and exhibition for commercial purposes of such species.

6. The Parties shall formulate and adopt measures and plans with regard to ex situ reproduction, in particular captive breeding, of protected fauna and propagation of protected flora.

7. The Parties shall endeavour, directly or through the Centre, to consult with range States that are not Parties to this Protocol, with a view to coordinating their efforts to manage and protect endangered or threatened species.

8. The Parties shall make provision, where possible, for the return of protected species exported or held illegally. Efforts should be made by Parties to reintroduce such specimens to their natural habitat.

Article 12
Cooperative measures for the protection and conservation of species

1. The Parties shall adopt cooperative measures to ensure the protection and conservation of the flora and fauna listed in the Annexes to this Protocol relating to the List of Endangered or Threatened Species and the List of Species whose Exploitation is Regulated.

2. The Parties shall ensure the maximum possible protection and recovery of the species of fauna and flora listed in the Annex relating to the List of Endangered or Threatened Species by adopting at the national level the measures provided for in paragraphs 3 and 5 of Article 11 of this Protocol.

3. The Parties shall prohibit the destruction of and damage to the habitat of species listed in the Annex relating to the List of Endangered or Threatened Species and shall formulate and implement action plans for their conservation or recovery. They shall continue to cooperate in implementing the relevant action plans already adopted.

4. The Parties, in cooperation with competent international organizations, shall take all appropriate measures to ensure the conservation of the species listed in the Annex relating to the List of Species whose Exploitation is Regulated while at the same time authorizing and regulating the exploitation of these species so as to ensure and maintain their favourable state of conservation.

5. When the range area of a threatened or endangered species extends to both sides of a national frontier or of the limit that separates the territories or the areas subject to the sovereignty or the national jurisdiction of two Parties to this Protocol, these Parties shall cooperate with a view to ensuring the protection and conservation and, if necessary, the recovery of such species.

6. Provided that no other satisfactory solutions are available and that the exemption does not harm the survival of the population or of any other species, the Parties may grant exemptions to the prohibitions prescribed for the protection of the species listed in the Annexes to this Protocol for scientific, educational or management purposes necessary to ensure the survival of the species or to prevent significant damage. Such exemptions shall be notified to the Contracting Parties.

Article 13
Introduction of non-indigenous or genetically modified species

1. The Parties shall take all appropriate measures to regulate the intentional or accidental introduction of non-indigenous or genetically modified species to the wild and prohibit those that may have harmful impacts on the ecosystems, habitats or species in the area to which this Protocol applies.

2. The Parties shall endeavour to implement all possible measures to eradicate species that have already been introduced when, after scientific assessment, it appears that such species cause or are likely to cause damage to ecosystems, habitats or species in the area to which this Protocol applies.

Part IV
Provisions common to protected areas and species

Article 14
Amendments to Annexes

1. The procedures for amendments to Annexes to this Protocol shall be those set forth in Article 23 of the Convention.

2. All proposed amendments submitted to the meeting of Contracting Parties shall have been the subject of prior evaluation by the meeting of National Focal Points.

Article 15
Inventories

Each Party shall compile comprehensive inventories of:

(a) areas over which they exercise sovereignty or jurisdiction that contain rare or fragile ecosystems, that are reservoirs of biological diversity, that are important for threatened or endangered species;
(b) species of fauna or flora that are endangered or threatened.

Article 16
Guidelines and common criteria

The Parties shall adopt:

(a) common criteria for the choice of protected marine and coastal areas that could be included in the SPAMI List which shall be annexed to the Protocol;
(b) common criteria for the inclusion of additional species in the Annexes;
(c) guidelines for the establishment and management of specially protected areas.

The criteria and guidelines referred to in paragraphs (b) and (c) may be amended by the meeting of the Parties on the basis of a proposal made by one or more Parties.

Article 17
Environmental impact assessment

In the planning process leading to decisions on industrial and other projects and activities that could significantly affect protected areas and species and their habitats, the Parties shall evaluate and take into consideration the possible direct or indirect, immediate or long-term, impact, including the cumulative impact of the projects and activities being contemplated.

Article 18
Integration of traditional activities

1. In formulating protective measures, the Parties shall take into account the traditional subsistence and cultural activities of their local populations. They

shall grant exemptions, as necessary, to meet such needs. No exemption which is allowed for this reason shall:

(a) endanger either the maintenance of ecosystems protected under this Protocol or the biological processes contributing to the maintenance of those ecosystems;

(b) cause either the extinction of, or a substantial reduction in, the number of individuals making up the populations or species of flora and fauna, in particular endangered, threatened, migratory or endemic species.

2. Parties which grant exemptions from the protection measures shall inform the Contracting Parties accordingly.

Article 19
Publicity, information, public awareness and education

1. The Parties shall give appropriate publicity to the establishment of specially protected areas, their boundaries, applicable regulations, and to the designation of protected species, their habitats and applicable regulations.

2. The Parties shall endeavour to inform the public of the interest and value of specially protected areas and species, and of the scientific knowledge which may be gained from the point of view of nature conservation and other points of view. Such information should have an appropriate place in education programmes. The Parties shall also endeavour to promote the participation of their public and their conservation organizations in measures that are necessary for the protection of the areas and species concerned, including environmental impact assessments.

Article 20
Scientific, technical and management research

1. The Parties shall encourage and develop scientific and technical research relating to the aims of this Protocol. They shall also encourage and develop research into the sustainable use of specially protected areas and the management of protected species.

2. The Parties shall consult, when necessary, among themselves and with competent international organizations with a view to identifying, planning and undertaking scientific and technical research and monitoring programmes necessary for the identification and monitoring of protected areas and species and assessing the effectiveness of measures taken to implement management and recovery plans.

3. The Parties shall exchange, directly or through the Centre, scientific and technical information concerning current and planned research and monitoring programmes and the results thereof. They shall, to the fullest extent possible, coordinate their research and monitoring programmes, and endeavour jointly to define or standardize their procedures.

4. In technical and scientific research, the Parties shall give priority to SPAMIs and species appearing in the Annexes to this Protocol.

Article 21
Mutual cooperation

1. The Parties shall, directly or with the assistance of the Centre or international organizations concerned, establish cooperation programmes to coordinate the establishment, conservation, planning and management of specially protected areas, as well as the selection, management and conservation of protected species. There shall be regular exchanges of information concerning the characteristics of protected areas and species, the experience acquired and the problems encountered.

2. The Parties shall, at the earliest opportunity, communicate any situation that might endanger the ecosystems of specially protected areas or the survival of protected species of flora and fauna to the other Parties, to the States that might be affected and to the Centre.

Article 22
Mutual assistance

1. The Parties shall cooperate, directly or with the assistance of the Centre or the international organizations concerned, in formulating, financing and implementing programmes of mutual assistance and assistance to developing countries that express a need for it with a view to implementing this Protocol.

2. These programmes shall include public environmental education, the training of scientific, technical and management personnel, scientific research, the acquisition, utilization, design and development of appropriate equipment, and transfer of technology on advantageous terms to be agreed among the Parties concerned.

3. The Parties shall, in matters of mutual assistance, give priority to the SPAMIs and species appearing in the Annexes to this Protocol.

Article 23
Reports of the Parties

The Parties shall submit to ordinary meetings of the Parties a report on the implementation of this Protocol, in particular on:

(a) the status and the state of the areas included in the SPAMI List;
(b) any changes in the delimitation or legal status of the SPAMIs and protected species;
(c) possible exemptions allowed pursuant to Articles 12 and 18 of this Protocol.

Part V
Institutional provisions

Article 24
National focal points

Each Party shall designate a National Focal Point to serve as liaison with the Centre on the technical and scientific aspects of the implementation of this Protocol. The National Focal Points shall meet periodically to carry out the functions deriving from this Protocol.

Article 25
Coordination

1. The Organization shall be responsible for coordinating the implementation of this Protocol. For this purpose, it shall receive the support of the Centre, to which it may entrust the following functions:

(a) assisting the Parties, in cooperation with the competent international, intergovernmental and non-governmental organizations, in:
  • establishing and managing specially protected areas in the area to which this Protocol applies;
  • conducting programmes of technical and scientific research as provided for in Article 20 of this Protocol;
  • conducting the exchange of scientific and technical information among the Parties as provided for in Article 20 of this Protocol;
  • preparing management plans for specially protected areas and species;
  • developing cooperative programmes pursuant to Article 21 of this Protocol;
  • preparing educational materials designed for various groups;
(b) convening and organizing the meetings of the National Focal Points and providing them with secretariat services;
(c) formulating recommendations on guidelines and common criteria pursuant to Article 16 of this Protocol;
(d) creating and updating databases of specially protected areas, protected species and other matters relevant to this Protocol;
(e) preparing reports and technical studies that may be required for the implementation of this Protocol;
(f) elaborating and implementing the training programmes mentioned in Article 22, paragraph 2;
(g) cooperating with regional and international governmental and non-governmental organizations concerned with the protection of areas and species, provided that the specificity of each organization and the need to avoid the duplication of activities are respected;

(h) carrying out the functions assigned to it in the action plans adopted in the framework of this Protocol;

(i) carrying out any other function assigned to it by the Parties.

Article 26
Meetings of the Parties

1. The ordinary meetings of the Parties to this Protocol shall be held in conjunction with the ordinary meetings of the Contracting Parties to the Convention held pursuant to Article 18 of the Convention. The Parties may also hold extraordinary meetings in conformity with that Article.

2. The meetings of the Parties to this Protocol are particularly aimed at:

(a) keeping under review the implementation of this Protocol;

(b) overseeing the work of the Organization and of the Centre relating to the implementation of this Protocol and providing policy guidance for their activities;

(c) considering the efficacy of the measures adopted for the management and protection of areas and species, and examining the need for other measures, in particular in the form of Annexes and amendments to this Protocol or to its Annexes;

(d) adopting the guidelines and common criteria provided for in Article 16 of this Protocol;

(e) considering reports transmitted by the Parties under Article 23 of this Protocol, as well as any other pertinent information which the Parties transmit through the Centre;

(f) making recommendations to the Parties on the measures to be adopted for the implementation of this Protocol;

(g) examining the recommendations of the meetings of the National Focal Points pursuant to Article 24 of this Protocol;

(h) deciding on the inclusion of an area in the SPAMI List in conformity with Article 9, paragraph 4, of this Protocol;

(i) examining any other matter relevant to this Protocol, as appropriate;

(j) discussing and evaluating the exemptions allowed by the Parties in conformity with Articles 12 and 18 of this Protocol.

Part VI
Final provisions

Article 27
Effect of the Protocol on domestic legislation

The provisions of this Protocol shall not affect the right of Parties to adopt relevant stricter domestic measures for the implementation of this Protocol.

Article 28
Relationship with third parties

1. The Parties shall invite States that are not Parties to the Protocol and international organizations to cooperate in the implementation of this Protocol.

2. The Parties undertake to adopt appropriate measures, consistent with international law, to ensure that no one engages in any activity contrary to the principles or purposes of this Protocol.

Article 29
Signature

This Protocol shall be open for signature in Barcelona on 10 June 1995 and in Madrid from 11 June 1995 to 10 June 1996 by any Contracting Party to the Convention.

Article 30
Ratification, acceptance or approval

This Protocol shall be subject to ratification, acceptance or approval. Instruments of ratification, acceptance or approval shall be deposited with the Government of Spain, which will assume the functions of Depositary.

Article 31
Accession

As from 10 June 1996, this Protocol shall be open for accession by any State and regional economic grouping which is Party to the Convention.

Article 32
Entry into force

1. This Protocol shall enter into force on the thirtieth day following the deposit of the sixth instrument of ratification, acceptance or approval of, or accession to, the Protocol.

2. From the date of its entry into force, this Protocol shall replace the Protocol Concerning Mediterranean Specially Protected Areas of 1982, in the relationship among the Parties to both instruments.

IN WITNESS WHEREOF, the undersigned, being duly authorized, have signed this Protocol.

DONE at Barcelona, on 10 June 1995, in a single copy in the Arabic, English, French and Spanish languages, the four texts being equally authoritative, for signature by any Party to the Convention.

Annex I
Common criteria for the choice of protected marine and coastal areas that could be included in the SPAMI List

A. General principles

The Contracting Parties agree that the following general principles will guide their work in establishing the SPAMI List:

a) The conservation of the natural heritage is the basic aim that must characterize a SPAMI. The pursuit of other aims such as the conservation of the cultural heritage, and the promotion of scientific research, education, participation, collaboration, is highly desirable in SPAMIs and constitutes a factor in favour of a site being included on the List, to the extent in which it remains compatible with the aims of conservation.

b) No limit is imposed on the total number of areas included in the List or on the number of areas any individual Party can propose for inscription. Nevertheless, the Parties agree that sites will be selected on a scientific basis and included in the List according to their qualities; they will have therefore to fulfil the requirements set out by the Protocol and the present criteria.

c) The listed SPAMI and their geographical distribution will have to be representative of the Mediterranean region and its biodiversity. To this end the List will have to represent the highest number possible of types of habitats and ecosystems.

d) The SPAMIs will have to constitute the core of a network aiming at the effective conservation of the Mediterranean heritage. To attain this objective, the Parties will develop their cooperation on bilateral and multilateral bases in the field of conservation and management of natural sites and notably through the establishment of transboundary SPAMIs.

e) The sites included in the SPAMI List are intended to have a value of example and model for the protection of the natural heritage of the region. To this end, the Parties ensure that sites included in the List are provided with adequate legal status, protection measures and management methods and means.

B. General features of the areas that could be included in the SPAMI List

1. To be eligible for inclusion in the SPAMI List, an area must fulfil at least one of the general criteria set in Article 8 paragraph 2 of the Protocol. Several of these general criteria can in certain cases be fulfilled by the same area, and such a circumstance cannot but strengthen the case for the inclusion of the area in the List.

2. The regional value is a basic requirement of an area for being included in the SPAMI List. The following criteria should be used in evaluating the Mediterranean interest of an area:

a) Uniqueness
The area contains unique or rare ecosystems, or rare or endemic species.
b) Natural representativeness
The area has highly representative ecological processes, or community or habitat types or other natural characteristics. Representativeness is the degree to which an area represents a habitat type, ecological process, biological community, physiographic feature or other natural characteristic.
c) Diversity
The area has a high diversity of species, communities, habitats or ecosystems.
d) Naturalness
The area has a high degree of naturalness as a result of the lack or low level of human-induced disturbance and degradation.
e) Presence of habitats that are critical to endangered, threatened or endemic species.
f) Cultural representativeness
The area has a high representative value with respect to the cultural heritage, due to the existence of environmentally sound traditional activities integrated with nature which support the well-being of local populations.

3. To be included in the SPAMI List, an area having scientific, educational or aesthetic interest must, respectively, present a particular value for research in the field of natural sciences or for activities of environmental education or awareness or contain outstanding natural features, landscapes or seascapes.

4. Besides the fundamental criteria specified in article 8, paragraph 2, of the Protocol, a certain number of other characteristics and factors should be considered as favourable for the inclusion of the site in the List. These include:

a) the existence of threats likely to impair the ecological, biological, aesthetic or cultural value of the area;
b) the involvement and active participation of the public in general, and particularly of local communities, in the process of planning and management of the area;
c) the existence of a body representing the public, professional, non-governmental sectors and the scientific community involved in the area;
d) the existence in the area of opportunities for sustainable development;
e) the existence of an integrated coastal management plan within the meaning of Article 4 paragraph 3 (e) of the Convention.

C. Legal status

1. All areas eligible for inclusion in the SPAMI List must be awarded a legal status guaranteeing their effective long-term protection.

2. To be included in the SPAMI List, an area situated in a zone already delimited over which a Party exercises sovereignty or jurisdiction must have a protected status recognized by the Party concerned.

3. In the case of areas situated, partly or wholly, on the high sea or in a zone where the limits of national sovereignty or jurisdiction have not yet been defined, the legal status, the management plan, the applicable measures and the other elements provided for in Article 9, paragraph 3, of the Protocol will be provided by the neighbouring Parties concerned in the proposal for inclusion in the SPAMI List.

D. Protection, planning and management measures

1. Conservation and management objectives must be clearly defined in the texts relating to each site, and will constitute the basis for assessment of the adequacy of the adopted measures and the effectiveness of their implementation at the revisions of the SPAMI List.

2. Protection, planning and management measures applicable to each area must be adequate for the achievement of the conservation and management objectives set for the site in the short and long term, and take in particular into account the threats upon it.

3. Protection, planning and management measures must be based on an adequate knowledge of the elements of the natural environment and of socio-economic and cultural factors that characterize each area. In case of shortcomings in basic knowledge, an area proposed for inclusion in the SPAMI List must have a programme for the collection of the unavailable data and information.

4. The competence and responsibility with regard to administration and implementation of conservation measures for areas proposed for inclusion in the SPAMI List must be clearly defined in the texts governing each area.

5. In the respect of the specificity characterizing each protected site, the protection measures for a SPAMI must take account of the following basic aspects:

a) the strengthening of the regulation of the release or dumping of wastes and other substances likely directly or indirectly to impair the integrity of the area;

b) the strengthening of the regulation of the introduction or reintroduction of any species into the area;

c) the regulation of any activity or act likely to harm or disturb the species, or that might endanger the conservation status of the ecosystems or species or might impair the natural, cultural or aesthetic characteristics of the area;

d) the regulation applicable to the zones surrounding the area in question.

6. To be included in the SPAMI List, a protected area must have a management body, endowed with sufficient powers as well as means and human resources to prevent and/or control activities likely to be contrary to the aims of the protected area.

7. To be included in the SPAMI List an area will have to be endowed with a management plan. The main rules of this management plan are to be laid down as from the time of inclusion and implemented immediately. A detailed management plan must be presented within three years of the time of inclusion. Failure to respect this obligation entails the removal of the site from the List.

8. To be included in the SPAMI List, an area will have to be endowed with a monitoring programme. This programme should include the identification and monitoring of a certain number of significant parameters for the area in question, in order to allow the assessment of the state and evolution of the area, as well as the effectiveness of protection and management measures implemented, so that they may be adapted if need be. To this end further necessary studies are to be commissioned.

Annex II
List of endangered or threatened species

Magnoliophyta

Posidonia oceanica
Zostera marina
Zostera noltii

Chlorphyta

Caulerpa ollivieri

Phaeophyta

Cystoseira amentacea (including var. stricta and var. spicata)
Cystoseira mediterranea
Cystoseira sedoides
Cystoseira spinosa (including C. adriatica)
Cystoseira zosteroides
Laminaria rodriguezii

Rhodophyta

Goniolithon byssoides
Lithophyllum lichenoides
Ptilophora mediterranea
Schimmelmannia schousboei

Porifera

Asbestopluma hypogea
Aplysina sp. plur.
Axinella cannabina
Axinella polypoides
Geodia cydonium
Ircinia foetida
Ircinia pipette
Petrobiona massiliana
Tethya sp. plur

Cnicaria

Astroides calycularis
Errina aspera
Gerardia savaglia

Echinodermata

Asterina pancerii
Centrostephanus longispinus
Ophidiaster ophidianus

Bryozoa

Hornera lichenoides

Mollusca

Ranella olearia (= Argobuccinum olearium = A. giganteum)
Charonia lampas (= Ch. rubicunda = Ch. nodifera)
Charonia tritonis (= Ch. seguenziae)
Dendropoma petraeum
Erosaria spurca
Gibbula nivosa
Lithophaga lithophaga
Luria lurida (= Cypraea lurida)
Mitra zonata
Patella ferruginea
Patella nigra
Pholas dactylus
Pinna nobilis
Pinna rudis (= P. pernula)
Schilderia achatidea
Tonna galea
Zonaria pyrum

Crustacea

Ocypode cursor
Pachylasma giganteum

Pisces

Acipenser naccarii
Acipenser sturio
Aphanius fasciatus
Aphanius iberus
Cetorhinus maximus
Carcharodon carcharias
Hippocampus ramulosus
Hippocampus hippocampus
Huso huso
Lethenteron zanandreai
Mobula mobular
Pomatoschistus canestrinii
Pomatoschistus tortonesei
Valencia hispanica
Valencia letourneuxi

Reptiles

Caretta caretta
Chelonia mydas
Dermochelys coriacea
Eretmochelys imbricate
Lepidochelys kempii
Trionyx triunguis

Aves

Pandion haliaetus
Calonectris diomedea
Falco eleonorae
Hydrobates pelagicus
Larus audouinii
Numenius tenuirostris
Phalacrocorax aristotelis
Phalacrocorax pygmaeus
Pelecanus onocrotalus
Pelecanus crispus
Phoenicopterus rubber

Puffinus yelkouan
Sterna albifrons
Sterna bengalensis
Sterna sandvicensis

Mammalia

Balaenoptera acutorostrata
Balaenoptera borealis
Balaenoptera physalus
Delphinus delphis
Eubalaena glacialis
Globicephala melas
Grampus griseus
Kogia simus
Megaptera novaeangliae
Mesoplodon densirostris
Monachus monachus
Orcinus orca
Phocoena phocoena
Physeter macrocephalus
Pseudorca crassidens
Stenella coeruleoalba
Steno bredanensis
Tursiops truncates
Ziphius cavirostris

Annex III
List of species whose exploitation is regulated

Porifera

Hippospongia communis
Spongia agaricina
Spongia officinalis
Spongia zimocca

Cnidaria

Antipathes sp. plur.
Corallium rubrum

Echinodermata

Paracentrotus lividus

Crustacea

Homarus gammarus
Maja squinado
Palinurus elephas
Scyllarides latus
Scyllarus pigmaeus
Scyllarus arctus

Pisces

Alosa alosa
Alosa fallax
Anguilla anguilla
Epinephelus marginatus
Isurus oxyrinchus
Lamna nasus
Lampetra fluviatilis
Petromyzon marinus
Prionace glauca
Raja alba
Sciaena umbra
Squatina squatina
Thunnus thynnus
Umbrina cirrosa
Xiphias gladius

Protocol for the Protection of the Mediterranean Sea against Pollution Resulting from Exploration and Exploitation of the Continental Shelf and the Seabed and its Subsoil, 14 October 1994

Editorial note

The Protocol for the Protection of the Mediterranean Sea against Pollution Resulting from Exploration and Exploitation of the Continental Shelf and the Seabed and its Subsoil aims at preventing, abating, combating and controlling pollution resulting from activities concerning the exploration and/or exploitation of the resources in the Mediterranean Sea Area by ensuring, *inter alia*, that the best available techniques, environmentally effective and economically appropriate, are used for this purpose (Article 3). For this purpose, the Protocol requires that all activities in the Protocol Area shall be subject to the prior written authorisation for the exploration and exploitation from the competent authority. Before granting an authorisation, the competent authority shall be satisfied that the installation complies with international standards and practice (Article 4). Parties shall prescribe that applications for authorisation, or application for renewals of an authorisation, are subject to submission by the candidate operator of a request to the competent authority. The application must contain, *inter alia*, a survey concerning the effects of the proposed activity; the precise definition of the area involved; particulars of the professional qualifications of the candidate; safety measures; a contingency plan; monitoring procedures; plans for removal of installations; precautions for specially protected areas; insurance to cover liability (Article 5).

The competent authority shall grant the authorisation only after examination of the requirements listed in Article 5 and in Annex IV. The authorisation shall specify the activities and the period of validity and may impose conditions (Article 6). Parties shall prescribe sanctions for violations of obligations arising out of the Protocol (Article 7).

Operators must use the best available, environmentally effective and economically appropriate techniques and observe internationally accepted standards regarding wastes, as well as the use, storage and discharge of harmful or noxious substances and materials, with a view to minimising the risk of pollution (Article 8). Specific provisions are set out for harmful or noxious substances and materials (Article 9), oil and oily mixture and drilling fluids and cutting

(Article 10), sewage (Article 11), garbage (Article 12). Operators must dispose satisfactorily of all wastes and harmful substances in designated onshore facilities (Article 13). Exceptions are allowed in case of *force majeure* (Article 14).

Safety measures shall be taken with regard to the design, construction, placement, equipment, making, operation and maintenance of installations (Article 15). Operators of installations are required to have a contingency plan to combat accidental pollution (Article 16) and to report to the competent authority without delay any event on their installation likely to cause pollution and any observed event at sea causing or likely to cause pollution (Article 17). Operators are also required to monitor the effects of their activities on the environment (Article 19) and to remove any installation which is abandoned or disused (Article 20).

Parties shall, where appropriate, co-operate in scientific and technological research (Article 22) and for the formulation and adoption of international rules, standards and recommended practices and procedures for achieving the goals of the Protocol (Article 23).

Parties shall take all measures to avoid transboundary pollution and shall immediately notify other Parties in case of damage (Article 26). As soon as possible, Parties shall formulate and adopt rules on liability and compensation for damage from activities regulated by the Protocol (Article 27(1)). Pending development of such rules, Parties shall take measures to ensure that liability for damage caused by activities is imposed on operators (Article 27(2)).

Date of signature:	14 October 1994
Entry into force:	Not yet in force
Depositary:	Government of Spain
Contracting Parties:	Albania, Cyprus, Morocco, Tunisia
Websites:	www.unepmap.org
	www.unep.ch/seas/

Protocol for the Protection of the Mediterranean Sea against Pollution Resulting from Exploration and Exploitation of the Continental Shelf and the Seabed and its Subsoil

The Contracting Parties to the present Protocol,

   Being Parties to the Convention for the Protection of the Mediterranean Sea against Pollution, adopted at Barcelona on 16 February 1976,

   Bearing in mind Article 7 of the said Convention,

   Bearing in mind the increase in the activities concerning exploration and exploitation of the Mediterranean seabed and its subsoil,

Recognizing that the pollution which may result therefrom represents a serious danger to the environment and to human beings,

Desirous of protecting and preserving the Mediterranean Sea from pollution resulting from exploration and exploitation activities,

Taking into account the Protocols related to the Convention for the Protection of the Mediterranean Sea against Pollution and, in particular, the Protocol concerning Cooperation in Combating Pollution of the Mediterranean Sea by Oil and Other Harmful Substances in Cases of Emergency, adopted at Barcelona on 16 February 1976, and the Protocol Concerning Mediterranean Specially Protected Areas, adopted at Geneva on 3 April 1982,

Bearing in mind the relevant provisions of the United Nations Convention on the Law of the Sea, done at Montego Bay on 10 December 1982 and signed by many Contracting Parties,

Recognizing the differences in levels of development among the coastal States, and taking account of the economic and social imperatives of the developing countries,

Have agreed as follows:

Section I
General provisions

Article 1
Definitions

For the purposes of this Protocol:

(a) 'Convention' means the Convention for the Protection of the Mediterranean Sea against Pollution, adopted at Barcelona on 16 February 1976;
(b) 'Organization' means the body referred to in Article 17 of the Convention;
(c) 'Resources' means all mineral resources, whether solid, liquid or gaseous;
(d) 'Activities concerning exploration and/or exploitation of the resources in the Protocol Area' (hereinafter referred to as 'activities') means:
   (i) Activities of scientific research concerning the resources of the seabed and its subsoil;
   (ii) Exploration activities:
      • Seismological activities; surveys of the seabed and its subsoil; sample taking;
      • Exploration drilling;
   (iii) Exploitation activities:
      • Establishment of an installation for the purpose of recovering resources, and activities connected therewith;
      • Development drilling;
      • Recovery, treatment and storage;
      • Transportation to shore by pipeline and loading of ships;
      • Maintenance, repair and other ancillary operations;

(e) 'Pollution' is defined as in Article 2, paragraph (a), of the Convention;
(f) 'Installation' means any fixed or floating structure, and any integral part thereof, that is engaged in activities, including, in particular:
   (i) Fixed or mobile offshore drilling units;
   (ii) Fixed or floating production units including dynamically-positioned units;
   (iii) Offshore storage facilities including ships used for this purpose;
   (iv) Offshore loading terminals and transport systems for the extracted products, such as submarine pipelines;
   (v) Apparatus attached to it and equipment for the reloading, processing, storage and disposal of substances removed from the seabed or its subsoil;
(g) 'Operator' means:
   (i) Any natural or juridical person who is authorized by the Party exercising jurisdiction over the area where the activities are undertaken (hereinafter referred to as the 'Contracting Party') in accordance with this Protocol to carry out activities and/or who carries out such activities; or
   (ii) Any person who does not hold an authorization within the meaning of this Protocol but is *de facto* in control of such activities;
(h) 'Safety zone' means a zone established around installations in conformity with the provisions of general international law and technical requirements, with appropriate markings to ensure the safety of both navigation and the installations;
(i) 'Wastes' means substances and materials of any kind, form or description resulting from activities covered by this Protocol which are disposed of or are intended for disposal or are required to be disposed of;
(j) 'Harmful or noxious substances and materials' means substances and materials of any kind, form or description, which might cause pollution, if introduced into the Protocol Area;
(k) 'Chemical Use Plan' means a plan drawn up by the operator of any offshore installation which shows:
   (i) The chemicals which the operator intends to use in the operations;
   (ii) The purpose or purposes for which the operator intends to use the chemicals;
   (iii) The maximum concentrations of the chemicals which the operator intends to use within any other substances, and maximum amounts intended to be used in any specified period;
   (iv) The area within which the chemical may escape into the marine environment;
(l) 'Oil' means petroleum in any form including crude oil, fuel oil, oily sludge, oil refuse and refined products and, without limiting the generality of the foregoing, includes the substances listed in the Appendix to this Protocol;

(m) 'Oily mixture' means a mixture with any oil content;
(n) 'Sewage' means:
    (i) Drainage and other wastes from any form of toilets, urinals and watercloset scuppers;
    (ii) Drainage from medical premises (dispensary, sick bay, etc.) via wash basins, wash tubs and scuppers located in such premises;
    (iii) Other waste waters when mixed with the drainages defined above;
(o) 'Garbage' means all kinds of food, domestic and operational waste generated during the normal operation of the installation and liable to be disposed of continuously or periodically, except those substances which are defined or listed elsewhere in this Protocol;
(p) 'Freshwater limit' means the place in water courses where, at low tides and in a period of low freshwater flow, there is an appreciable increase in salinity due to the presence of sea water.

Article 2
Geographical coverage

1. The area to which this Protocol applies (referred to in this Protocol as the 'Protocol Area') shall be:

(a) The Mediterranean Sea Area as defined in Article 1 of the Convention, including the continental shelf and the seabed and its subsoil;
(b) Waters, including the seabed and its subsoil, on the landward side of the baselines from which the breadth of the territorial sea is measured and extending, in the case of watercourses, up to the freshwater limit.

2. Any of the Contracting Parties to this Protocol (referred to in this Protocol as 'the Parties') may also include in the Protocol area wetlands or coastal areas of their territory.

3. Nothing in this Protocol, nor any act adopted on the basis of this Protocol, shall prejudice the rights of any State concerning the delimitation of the continental shelf.

Article 3
General undertakings

1. The Parties shall take, individually or through bilateral or multilateral cooperation, all appropriate measures to prevent, abate, combat and control pollution in the Protocol Area resulting from activities, *inter alia* by ensuring that the best available techniques, environmentally effective and economically appropriate, are used for this purpose.

2. The Parties shall ensure that all necessary measures are taken so that activities do not cause pollution.

Section II
Authorization system

Article 4
General principles

1. All activities in the Protocol Area, including erection on site of installations, shall be subject to the prior written authorization for exploration or exploitation from the competent authority. Such authority, before granting the authorization, shall be satisfied that the installation has been constructed according to international standards and practice and that the operator has the technical competence and the financial capacity to carry out the activities. Such authorization shall be granted in accordance with the appropriate procedure, as defined by the competent authority.

2. Authorization shall be refused if there are indications that the proposed activities are likely to cause significant adverse effects on the environment that could not be avoided by compliance with the conditions laid down in the authorization and referred to in Article 6, paragraph 3, of this Protocol.

3. When considering approval of the siting of an installation, the Contracting Party shall ensure that no detrimental effects will be caused to existing facilities by such siting, in particular, to pipelines and cables.

Article 5
Requirements for authorizations

1. The Contracting Party shall prescribe that any application for authorization or for the renewal of an authorization is subject to the submission of the project by the candidate operator to the competent authority and that any such application must include, in particular, the following:

(a) A survey concerning the effects of the proposed activities on the environment; the competent authority may, in the light of the nature, scope, duration and technical methods employed in the activities and of the characteristics of the area, require that an environmental impact assessment be prepared in accordance with Annex IV to this Protocol;
(b) The precise definition of the geographical areas where the activity is envisaged, including safety zones;
(c) Particulars of the professional and technical qualifications of the candidate operator and personnel on the installation, as well as of the composition of the crew;
(d) The safety measures as specified in Article 15;
(e) The operator's contingency plan as specified in Article 16;
(f) The monitoring procedures as specified in Article 19;
(g) The plans for removal of installations as specified in Article 20;
(h) Precautions for specially protected areas as specified in Article 21;

(i) The insurance or other financial security to cover liability as prescribed in Article 27, paragraph 2 (b).

2. The competent authority may decide, for scientific research and exploration activities, to limit the scope of the requirements laid down in paragraph 1 of this Article, in the light of the nature, scope, duration and technical methods employed in the activities and of the characteristics of the area.

Article 6
Granting of authorizations

1. The authorizations referred to in Article 4 shall be granted only after examination by the competent authority of the requirements listed in Article 5 and Annex IV.

2. Each authorization shall specify the activities and the period of validity of the authorization, establish the geographical limits of the area subject to the authorization and specify the technical requirements and the authorized installations. The necessary safety zones shall be established at a later appropriate stage.

3. The authorization may impose conditions regarding measures, techniques or methods designed to reduce to the minimum risks of and damage due to pollution resulting from the activities.

4. The Parties shall notify the Organization as soon as possible of authorizations granted or renewed. The Organization shall keep a register of all the authorized installations in the Protocol Area.

Article 7
Sanctions

Each Party shall prescribe sanctions to be imposed for breach of obligations arising out of this Protocol, or for non-observance of the national laws or regulations implementing this Protocol, or for non-fulfilment of the specific conditions attached to the authorization.

Section III
Wastes and harmful or noxious substances and materials

Article 8
General obligation

Without prejudice to other standards or obligations referred to in this Section, the Parties shall impose a general obligation upon operators to use the best available, environmentally effective and economically appropriate techniques and to observe internationally accepted standards regarding wastes, as well as the use, storage and discharge of harmful or noxious substances and materials, with a view to minimizing the risk of pollution.

Article 9
Harmful or noxious substances and materials

1. The use and storage of chemicals for the activities shall be approved by the competent authority, on the basis of the Chemical Use Plan.

2. The Contracting Party may regulate, limit or prohibit the use of chemicals for the activities in accordance with guidelines to be adopted by the Contracting Parties.

3. For the purpose of protecting the environment, the Parties shall ensure that each substance and material used for activities is accompanied by a compound description provided by the entity producing such substance or material.

4. The disposal into the Protocol Area of harmful or noxious substances and materials resulting from the activities covered by this Protocol and listed in Annex I to this Protocol is prohibited.

5. The disposal into the Protocol Area of harmful or noxious substances and materials resulting from the activities covered by this Protocol and listed in Annex II to this Protocol requires, in each case, a prior special permit from the competent authority.

6. The disposal into the Protocol Area of all other harmful or noxious substances and materials resulting from the activities covered by this Protocol and which might cause pollution requires a prior general permit from the competent authority.

7. The permits referred to in paragraphs 5 and 6 above shall be issued only after careful consideration of all the factors set forth in Annex III to this Protocol.

Article 10
Oil and oily mixtures and drilling fluids and cuttings

1. The Parties shall formulate and adopt common standards for the disposal of oil and oily mixtures from installations into the Protocol Area:

(a) Such common standards shall be formulated in accordance with the provisions of Annex V, A;
(b) Such common standards shall not be less restrictive than the following, in particular:
  (i) For machinery space drainage, a maximum oil content of 15 mg per litre whilst undiluted;
  (ii) For production water, a maximum oil content of 40 mg per litre as an average in any calendar month; the content shall not at any time exceed 100 mg per litre;
(c) The Parties shall determine by common agreement which method will be used to analyze the oil content.

2. The Parties shall formulate and adopt common standards for the use and disposal of drilling fluids and drill cuttings into the Protocol Area. Such

common standards shall be formulated in accordance with the provisions of Annex V, B.

3. Each Party shall take appropriate measures to enforce the common standards adopted pursuant to this Article or to enforce more restrictive standards that it may have adopted.

Article 11
Sewage

1. The Contracting Party shall prohibit the discharge of sewage from installations permanently manned by 10 or more persons into the Protocol Area except in cases where:

(a) The installation is discharging sewage after treatment as approved by the competent authority at a distance of at least four nautical miles from the nearest land or fixed fisheries installation, leaving the Contracting Party to decide on a case by case basis; or

(b) The sewage is not treated, but the discharge is carried out in accordance with international rules and standards; or

(c) The sewage has passed through an approved sewage treatment plant certified by the competent authority.

2. The Contracting Party shall impose stricter provisions, as appropriate, where deemed necessary, *inter alia* because of the regime of the currents in the area or proximity to any area referred to in Article 21.

3. The exceptions referred to in paragraph 1 shall not apply if the discharge produces visible floating solids or produces colouration, discolouration or opacity of the surrounding water.

4. If the sewage is mixed with wastes and harmful or noxious substances and materials having different disposal requirements, the more stringent requirements shall apply.

Article 12
Garbage

1. The Contracting Party shall prohibit the disposal into the Protocol Area of the following products and materials:

(a) All plastics, including but not limited to synthetic ropes, synthetic fishing nets and plastic garbage bags;

(b) All other non-biodegradable garbage, including paper products, rags, glass, metal, bottles, crockery, dunnage, lining and packing materials.

2. Disposal into the Protocol Area of food wastes shall take place as far away as possible from land, in accordance with international rules and standards.

3. If garbage is mixed with other discharges having different disposal or discharge requirements, the more stringent requirements shall apply.

Article 13
Reception facilities, instructions and sanctions

The Parties shall ensure that:

(a) Operators dispose satisfactorily of all wastes and harmful or noxious substances and materials in designated onshore reception facilities, except as otherwise authorized by the Protocol;

(b) Instructions are given to all personnel concerning proper means of disposal;

(c) Sanctions are imposed in respect of illegal disposals.

Article 14
Exceptions

1. The provisions of this Section shall not apply in case of:

(a) *Force majeure* and in particular for disposals:
   - to save human life,
   - to ensure the safety of installations,
   - in case of damage to the installation or its equipment,
   on condition that all reasonable precautions have been taken after the damage is discovered or after the disposal has been performed to reduce the negative effects.

(b) The discharge into the sea of substances containing oil or harmful or noxious substances or materials which, subject to the prior approval of the competent authority, are being used for the purpose of combating specific pollution incidents in order to minimize the damage due to the pollution.

2. However, the provisions of this Section shall apply in any case where the operator acted with the intent to cause damage or recklessly and with knowledge that damage will probably result.

3. Disposals carried out in the circumstances referred to in paragraph 1 of this Article shall be reported immediately to the Organization and, either through the Organization or directly, to any Party or Parties likely to be affected, together with full details of the circumstances and of the nature and quantities of wastes or harmful or noxious substances or materials discharged.

Section IV
Safeguards

Article 15
Safety measures

1. The Contracting Party within whose jurisdiction activities are envisaged or are being carried out shall ensure that safety measures are taken with regard to the design, construction, placement, equipment, marking, operation and maintenance of installations.

2. The Contracting Party shall ensure that at all times the operator has on the installations adequate equipment and devices, maintained in good working order, for protecting human life, preventing and combating accidental pollution and facilitating prompt response to an emergency, in accordance with the best available environmentally effective and economically appropriate techniques and the provisions of the operator's contingency plan referred to in Article 16.

3. The competent authority shall require a certificate of safety and fitness for the purpose (hereinafter referred to as 'certificate') issued by a recognized body to be submitted in respect of production platforms, mobile offshore drilling units, offshore storage facilities, offshore loading systems and pipelines and in respect of such other installations as may be specified by the Contracting Party.

4. The Parties shall ensure through inspection that the activities are conducted by the operators in accordance with this Article.

Article 16
Contingency planning

1. In cases of emergency the Contracting Parties shall implement *mutatis mutandis* the provisions of the Protocol concerning Cooperation in Combating Pollution of the Mediterranean Sea by Oil and Other Harmful Substances in Cases of Emergency.

2. Each Party shall require operators in charge of installations under its jurisdiction to have a contingency plan to combat accidental pollution, co-ordinated with the contingency plan of the Contracting Party established in accordance with the Protocol concerning Cooperation in Combating Pollution of the Mediterranean Sea by Oil and Other Harmful Substances in Cases of Emergency and approved in conformity with the procedures established by the competent authorities.

3. Each Contracting Party shall establish coordination for the development and implementation of contingency plans. Such plans shall be established in accordance with guidelines adopted by the competent international organization. They shall, in particular, be in accordance with the provisions of Annex VII to this Protocol.

Article 17
Notification

Each Party shall require operators in charge of installations under its jurisdiction to report without delay to the competent authority:

(a) Any event on their installation causing or likely to cause pollution in the Protocol Area;
(b) Any observed event at sea causing or likely to cause pollution in the Protocol Area.

Article 18
Mutual assistance in cases of emergency

In cases of emergency, a Party requiring assistance in order to prevent, abate or combat pollution resulting from activities may request help from the other Parties, either directly or through the Regional Marine Pollution Emergency Response Centre for the Mediterranean Sea (REMPEC), which shall do their utmost to provide the assistance requested. For this purpose, a Party which is also a Party to the Protocol concerning Cooperation in Combating Pollution of the Mediterranean Sea by Oil and Other Harmful Substances in Cases of Emergency shall apply the pertinent provisions of the said Protocol.

Article 19
Monitoring

1. The operator shall be required to measure, or to have measured by a qualified entity, expert in the matter, the effects of the activities on the environment in the light of the nature, scope, duration and technical methods employed in the activities and of the characteristics of the area and to report on them periodically or upon request by the competent authority for the purpose of an evaluation by such competent authority according to a procedure established by the competent authority in its authorization system.

2. The competent authority shall establish, where appropriate, a national monitoring system in order to be in a position to monitor regularly the installations and the impact of the activities on the environment, so as to ensure that the conditions attached to the grant of the authorization are being fulfilled.

Article 20
Removal of installations

1. The operator shall be required by the competent authority to remove any installation which is abandoned or disused, in order to ensure safety of navigation, taking into account the guidelines and standards adopted by the competent international organization. Such removal shall also have due regard to other legitimate uses of the sea, in particular fishing, the protection of the marine environment and the rights and duties of other Contracting Parties. Prior to such removal, the operator under its responsibility shall take all necessary measures to prevent spillage or leakage from the site of the activities.

2. The competent authority shall require the operator to remove abandoned or disused pipelines in accordance with paragraph 1 of this Article or to clean them inside and abandon them or to clean them inside and bury them so that they neither cause pollution, endanger navigation, hinder fishing, threaten the marine environment, nor interfere with other legitimate uses of the sea or with the rights and duties of other Contracting Parties. The competent authority shall ensure that appropriate publicity is given to the depth, position and dimensions of any buried pipeline and that such information is indicated

on charts and notified to the Organization and other competent international organizations and the Parties.

3. The provisions of this Article apply also to installations disused or abandoned by any operator whose authorization may have been withdrawn or suspended in compliance with Article 7.

4. The competent authority may indicate eventual modifications to be made to the level of activities and to the measures for the protection of the marine environment which had initially been provided for.

5. The competent authority may regulate the cession or transfer of authorized activities to other persons.

6. Where the operator fails to comply with the provisions of this Article, the competent authority shall undertake, at the operator's expense, such action or actions as may be necessary to remedy the operator's failure to act.

Article 21
Specially protected areas

For the protection of the areas defined in the Protocol concerning Mediterranean Specially Protected Areas and any other area established by a Party and in furtherance of the goals stated therein, the Parties shall take special measures in conformity with international law, either individually or through multilateral or bilateral cooperation, to prevent, abate, combat and control pollution arising from activities in these areas.

In addition to the measures referred to in the Protocol concerning Mediterranean Specially Protected Areas for the granting of authorization, such measures may include, *inter alia*:

(a) Special restrictions or conditions when granting authorizations for such areas:
   (i) The preparation and evaluation of environmental impact assessments;
   (ii) The elaboration of special provisions in such areas concerning monitoring, removal of installations and prohibition of any discharge.
(b) Intensified exchange of information among operators, the competent authorities, Parties and the Organization regarding matters which may affect such areas.

Section V
Cooperation

Article 22
Studies and research programmes

In conformity with Article 13 of the Convention, the Parties shall, where appropriate, cooperate in promoting studies and undertaking programmes of scientific and technological research for the purpose of developing new methods of:

(a) Carrying out activities in a way that minimizes the risk of pollution;
(b) Preventing, abating, combating and controlling pollution, especially in cases of emergency.

Article 23
International rules, standards and recommended practices and procedures

1. The Parties shall cooperate, either directly or through the Organization or other competent international organizations, in order to:

(a) Establish appropriate scientific criteria for the formulation and elaboration of international rules, standards and recommended practices and procedures for achieving the aims of this Protocol;
(b) Formulate and elaborate such international rules, standards and recommended practices and procedures;
(c) Formulate and adopt guidelines in accordance with international practices and procedures to ensure observance of the provisions of Annex VI.

2. The Parties shall, as soon as possible, endeavour to harmonize their laws and regulations with the international rules, standards and recommended practices and procedures referred to in paragraph 1 of this Article.

3. The Parties shall endeavour, as far as possible, to exchange information relevant to their domestic policies, laws and regulations and the harmonization referred to in paragraph 2 of this Article.

Article 24
Scientific and technical assistance to developing countries

1. The Parties shall, directly or with the assistance of competent regional or other international organizations, cooperate with a view to formulating and, as far as possible, implementing programmes of assistance to developing countries, particularly in the fields of science, law, education and technology, in order to prevent, abate, combat and control pollution due to activities in the Protocol Area.

2. Technical assistance shall include, in particular, the training of scientific, legal and technical personnel, as well as the acquisition, utilization and production by those countries of appropriate equipment on advantageous terms to be agreed upon among the Parties concerned.

Article 25
Mutual information

The Parties shall inform one another directly or through the Organization of measures taken, of results achieved and, if the case arises, of difficulties encountered in the application of this Protocol. Procedures for the collection and submission of such information shall be determined at the meetings of the Parties.

Article 26
Transboundary pollution

1. Each Party shall take all measures necessary to ensure that activities under its jurisdiction are so conducted as not to cause pollution beyond the limits of its jurisdiction.

2. A Party within whose jurisdiction activities are being envisaged or carried out shall take into account any adverse environmental effects, without discrimination as to whether such effects are likely to occur within the limits of its jurisdiction or beyond such limits.

3. If a Party becomes aware of cases in which the marine environment is in imminent danger of being damaged, or has been damaged, by pollution, it shall immediately notify other Parties which in its opinion are likely to be affected by such damage, as well as the Regional Marine Pollution Emergency Response Centre for the Mediterranean Sea (REMPEC), and provide them with timely information that would enable them, where necessary, to take appropriate measures. REMPEC shall distribute the information immediately to all relevant Parties.

4. The Parties shall endeavour, in accordance with their legal systems and, where appropriate, on the basis of an agreement, to grant equal access to and treatment in administrative proceedings to persons in other States who may be affected by pollution or other adverse effects resulting from proposed or existing operations.

5. Where pollution originates in the territory of a State which is not a Contracting Party to this Protocol, any Contracting Party affected shall endeavour to cooperate with the said State so as to make possible the application of the Protocol.

Article 27
Liability and compensation

1. The Parties undertake to cooperate as soon as possible in formulating and adopting appropriate rules and procedures for the determination of liability and compensation for damage resulting from the activities dealt with in this Protocol, in conformity with Article 16 of the Convention.

2. Pending development of such procedures, each Party:

(a) Shall take all measures necessary to ensure that liability for damage caused by activities is imposed on operators, and they shall be required to pay prompt and adequate compensation;

(b) Shall take all measures necessary to ensure that operators shall have and maintain insurance cover or other financial security of such type and under such terms as the Contracting Party shall specify in order to ensure compensation for damages caused by the activities covered by this Protocol.

Section VI
Final provisions

Article 28
Appointment of competent authorities

Each Contracting Party shall appoint one or more competent authorities to:

(a) Grant, renew and register the authorizations provided for in Section II of this Protocol;
(b) Issue and register the special and general permits referred to in Article 9 of this Protocol;
(c) Issue the permits referred to in Annex V to this Protocol;
(d) Approve the treatment system and certify the sewage treatment plant referred to in Article 11, paragraph 1, of this Protocol;
(e) Give the prior approval for exceptional discharges referred to in Article 14, paragraph 1 (b), of this Protocol;
(f) Carry out the duties regarding safety measures referred to in Article 15, paragraphs 3 and 4, of this Protocol;
(g) Perform the functions relating to contingency planning described in Article 16 and Annex VII to this Protocol;
(h) Establish monitoring procedures as provided in Article 19 of this Protocol;
(i) Supervise the removal operations of the installations as provided in Article 20 of this Protocol.

Article 29
Transitional measures

Each Party shall elaborate procedures and regulations regarding activities, whether authorized or not, initiated before the entry into force of this Protocol, to ensure their conformity, as far as practicable, with the provisions of this Protocol.

Article 30
Meetings

1. Ordinary meetings of the Parties shall take place in conjunction with ordinary meetings of the Contracting Parties to the Convention held pursuant to Article 18 of the Convention. The Parties may also hold extraordinary meetings in accordance with Article 18 of the Convention.

2. The functions of the meetings of the Parties to this Protocol shall be, *inter alia*:

(a) To keep under review the implementation of this Protocol and to consider the efficacy of the measures adopted and the advisability of any other measures, in particular in the form of annexes and appendices;

(b) To revise and amend any annex or appendix to this Protocol;

(c) To consider the information concerning authorizations granted or renewed in accordance with Section II of this Protocol;

(d) To consider the information concerning the permits issued and approvals given in accordance with Section III of this Protocol;

(e) To adopt the guidelines referred to in Article 9, paragraph 2, and Article 23, paragraph 1 (c), of this Protocol;

(f) To consider the records of the contingency plans and means of intervention in emergencies adopted in accordance with Article 16 of this Protocol;

(g) To establish criteria and formulate international rules, standards and recommended practices and procedures in accordance with Article 23, paragraph 1, of this Protocol, in whatever form the Parties may agree;

(h) To facilitate the implementation of the policies and the achievement of the objectives referred to in Section V, in particular the harmonization of national and European Community legislation in accordance with Article 23, paragraph 2, of this Protocol;

(i) To review progress made in the implementation of Article 27 of this Protocol;

(j) To discharge such other functions as may be appropriate for the application of this Protocol.

Article 31
Relations with the convention

1. The provisions of the Convention relating to any Protocol shall apply with respect to this Protocol.

2. The rules of procedure and the financial rules adopted pursuant to Article 24 of the Convention shall apply with respect to this Protocol, unless the Parties to this Protocol agree otherwise.

Article 32
Final clause

1. This Protocol shall be open for signature at Madrid from 14 October 1994 to 14 October 1995, by any State Party to the Convention invited to the Conference of Plenipotentiaries of the Coastal States of the Mediterranean Region on the Protocol for the Protection of the Mediterranean Sea against Pollution resulting from Exploration and Exploitation of the Seabed and its Subsoil, held at Madrid on 13 and 14 October 1994. It shall also be open until the same dates for signature by the European Community and by any similar regional economic grouping of which at least one member is a coastal State of the Protocol Area and which exercises competence in fields covered by this Protocol in conformity with Article 30 of the Convention.

2. This Protocol shall be subject to ratification, acceptance or approval. Instruments of ratification, acceptance or approval shall be deposited with the Government of Spain, which will assume the functions of Depositary.

3. As from 15 October 1995, this Protocol shall be open for accession by the States referred to in paragraph 1 above, by the European Community and by any grouping referred to in that paragraph.

4. This Protocol shall enter into force on the thirtieth day following the date of deposit of at least six instruments of ratification, acceptance or approval of, or accession to, the Protocol by the Parties referred to in paragraph 1 of this Article.

IN WITNESS WHEREOF the undersigned, being duly authorized, have signed this Protocol.

DONE in Madrid on 14 October 1994.

Annex I
Harmful or noxious substances and materials the disposal of which in the Protocol area is prohibited

A. The following substances and materials and compounds thereof are listed for the purposes of Article 9, paragraph 4, of the Protocol. They have been selected mainly on the basis of their toxicity, persistence and bioaccumulation:

1. Mercury and mercury compounds
2. Cadmium and cadmium compounds
3. Organotin compounds and substances which may form such compounds in the marine environment [1]
4. Organophosphorus compounds and substances which may form such compounds in the marine environment[1]
5. Organohalogen compounds and substances which may form such compounds in the marine environment[1]
6. Crude oil, fuel oil, oily sludge, used lubricating oils and refined products
7. Persistent synthetic materials which may float, sink or remain in suspension and which may interfere with any legitimate use of the sea
8. Substances having proven carcinogenic, teratogenic or mutagenic properties in or through the marine environment
9. Radioactive substances, including their wastes, if their discharges do not comply with the principles of radiation protection as defined by the competent international organizations, taking into account the protection of the marine environment

[1] With the exception of those which are biologically harmless or which are rapidly converted into biologically harmless substances.

B. The present Annex does not apply to discharges which contain substances listed in section A that are below the limits defined jointly by the Parties and, in relation to oil, below the limits defined in Article 10 of this Protocol.

Annex II
Harmful or noxious substances and materials the disposal of which in the Protocol area is subject to a special permit

A. The following substances and materials and compounds thereof have been selected for the purpose of Article 9, paragraph 5, of the Protocol.

1. Arsenic
2. Lead
3. Copper
4. Zinc
5. Beryllium
6. Nickel
7. Vanadium
8. Chromium
9. Biocides and their derivatives not covered in Annex I
10. Selenium
11. Antimony
12. Molybdenum
13. Titanium
14. Tin
15. Barium (other than barium sulphate)
16. Boron
17. Uranium
18. Cobalt
19. Thallium
20. Tellurium
21. Silver
22. Cyanides

B. The control and strict limitation of the discharge of substances referred to in section A must be implemented in accordance with Annex III.

Annex III
Factors to be considered for the issue of the permits

For the purpose of the issue of a permit required under Article 9, paragraph 7, particular account will be taken, as the case may be, of the following factors:

A. Characteristics and composition of the waste

1. Type and size of waste source (e.g. industrial process);
2. Type of waste (origin, average composition);
3. Form of waste (solid, liquid, sludge, slurry, gaseous);
4. Total amount (volume discharged, e.g. per year);
5. Discharge pattern (continuous, intermittent, seasonally variable, etc.);
6. Concentrations with respect to major constituents, substances listed in Annex I, substances listed in Annex II, and other substances as appropriate;
7. Physical, chemical and biochemical properties of the waste.

B. Characteristics of waste constituents with respect to their harmfulness

1. Persistence (physical, chemical, biological) in the marine environment;
2. Toxicity and other harmful effects;
3. Accumulation in biological materials or sediments;
4. Biochemical transformation producing harmful compounds;
5. Adverse effects on the oxygen content and balance;
6. Susceptibility to physical, chemical and biochemical changes and interaction in the aquatic environment with other sea-water constituents which may produce harmful biological or other effects on any of the uses listed in Section E below.

C. Characteristics of discharge site and receiving marine environment

1. Hydrographic, meteorological, geological and topographical characteristics of the area;
2. Location and type of the discharge (outfall, canal, outlet, etc.) and its relation to other areas (such as amenity areas, spawning, nursery and fishing areas, shellfish grounds) and other discharges;
3. Initial dilution achieved at the point of discharge into the receiving marine environment;
4. Dispersion characteristics such as effects of currents, tides and wind on horizontal transport and vertical mixing;
5. Receiving water characteristics with respect to physical, chemical, biological and ecological conditions in the discharge area;
6. Capacity of the receiving marine environment to receive waste discharges without undesirable effects.

D. Availability of waste technologies

The methods of waste reduction and discharge for industrial effluents as well as domestic sewage should be selected taking into account the availability and feasibility of:

(a) Alternative treatment processes;
(b) Reuse or elimination methods;
(c) On-land disposal alternatives;
(d) Appropriate low-waste technologies.

E. Potential impairment of marine ecosystem and sea-water uses

1. Effects on human life through pollution impact on:

(a) Edible marine organisms;
(b) Bathing waters;
(c) Aesthetics.

2. Effects on marine ecosystems, in particular living resources, endangered species and critical habitats.
3. Effects on other legitimate uses of the sea in conformity with international law.

Annex IV
Environmental impact assessment

1. Each Party shall require that the environmental impact assessment contains at least the following:

(a) A description of the geographical boundaries of the area within which the activities are to be carried out, including safety zones where applicable;
(b) A description of the initial state of the environment of the area;
(c) An indication of the nature, aims, scope and duration of the proposed activities;
(d) A description of the methods, installations and other means to be used, possible alternatives to such methods and means;
(e) A description of the foreseeable direct or indirect short and long-term effects of the proposed activities on the environment, including fauna, flora and the ecological balance;
(f) A statement setting out the measures proposed for reducing to the minimum the risk of damage to the environment as a result of carrying out the proposed activities, including possible alternatives to such measures;
(g) An indication of the measures to be taken for the protection of the environment from pollution and other adverse effects during and after the proposed activities;
(h) A reference to the methodology used for the environmental impact assessment;
(i) An indication of whether the environment of any other State is likely to be affected by the proposed activities.

2. Each Party shall promulgate standards taking into account the international rules, standards and recommended practices and procedures, adopted

in accordance with Article 23 of the Protocol, by which environmental impact assessments are to be evaluated.

Annex V
Oil and oily mixtures and drilling fluids and cuttings

The following provisions shall be prescribed by the Parties in accordance with Article 10:

A. Oil and oily mixtures

1. Spills of high oil content in processing drainage and platform drainage shall be contained, diverted and then treated as part of the product, but the remainder shall be treated to an acceptable level before discharge, in accordance with good oilfield practice;

2. Oily waste and sludges from separation processes shall be transported to shore;

3. All the necessary precautions shall be taken to minimize losses of oil into the sea from oil collected or flared from well testing;

4. All the necessary precautions shall be taken to ensure that any gas resulting from oil activities should be flared or used in an appropriate manner.

B. Drilling fluids and drill cuttings

1. Water-based drilling fluids and drill cuttings shall be subject to the following requirements:

(a) The use and disposal of such drilling fluids shall be subject to the Chemical Use Plan and the provisions of Article 9 of this Protocol;
(b) The disposal of the drill cuttings shall either be made on land or into the sea in an appropriate site or area as specified by the competent authority.

2. Oil-based drilling fluids and drill cuttings are subject to the following requirements:

(a) Such fluids shall only be used if they are of a sufficiently low toxicity and only after the operator has been issued a permit by the competent authority when it has verified such low toxicity;
(b) The disposal into the sea of such drilling fluids is prohibited;
(c) The disposal of the drill cuttings into the sea is only permitted on condition that efficient solids control equipment is installed and properly operated, that the discharge point is well below the surface of the water, and that the oil content is less than 100 grams of oil per kilogram dry cuttings;
(d) The disposal of such drill cuttings in specially protected areas is prohibited;

(e) In case of production and development drilling, a programme of seabed sampling and analysis relating to the zone of contamination must be undertaken.

   3. Diesel-based drilling fluids:
The use of diesel-based drilling fluids is prohibited. Diesel oil may exceptionally be added to drilling fluids in such circumstances as the Parties may specify.

Annex VI
Safety measures

The following provisions shall be prescribed by the Parties in accordance with Article 15:

(a) That the installation must be safe and fit for the purpose for which it is to be used, in particular, that it must be designed and constructed so as to withstand, together with its maximum load, any natural condition, including, more specifically, maximum wind and wave conditions as established by historical weather patterns, earthquake possibilities, seabed conditions and stability, and water depth;

(b) That all phases of the activities, including storage and transport of recovered resources, must be properly prepared, that the whole activity must be open to control for safety reasons and must be conducted in the safest possible way, and that the operator must apply a monitoring system for all activities;

(c) That the most advanced safety systems must be used and periodically tested in order to minimize the dangers of leakages, spillages, accidental discharges, fire, explosions, blow-outs or any other threat to human safety or the environment, that a trained specialized crew to operate and maintain these systems must be present and that this crew must undertake periodic exercises. In the case of authorized not permanently manned installations, the permanent availability of a specialized crew shall be ensured;

(d) That the installation and, where necessary, the established safety zone, must be marked in accordance with international recommendations so as to give adequate warning of its presence and sufficient details for its identification;

(e) That in accordance with international maritime practice, the installations must be indicated on charts and notified to those concerned;

(f) That, in order to secure observance of the foregoing provisions, the person and/or persons having the responsibility for the installation and/or the activities, including the person responsible for the blow-out preventer, must have the qualifications required by the competent authority, and that sufficient qualified staff must be permanently available. Such qualifications shall include, in particular, training, on a continuing basis, in safety and environmental matters.

Annex VII
Contingency plan

A. The operator's contingency plan

1. Operators are obliged to ensure:

(a) That the most appropriate alarm system and communication system are available at the installation and they are in good working order;

(b) That the alarm is immediately raised on the occurrence of an emergency and that any emergency is immediately communicated to the competent authority;

(c) That, in coordination with the competent authority, transmission of the alarm and appropriate assistance and coordination of assistance can be organized and supervised without delay;

(d) That immediate information about the nature and extent of the emergency is given to the crew on the installation and to the competent authority;

(e) That the competent authority is constantly informed about the progress of combating the emergency;

(f) That at all times sufficient and most appropriate materials and equipment, including stand-by boats and aircraft, are available to put into effect the emergency plan;

(g) That the most appropriate methods and techniques are known to the specialized crew referred to in Annex VI, paragraph (c), in order to combat leakages, spillages, accidental discharges, fire, explosions, blow-outs and any other threat to human life or the environment;

(h) That the most appropriate methods and techniques are known to the specialized crew responsible for reducing and preventing long-term adverse effects on the environment;

(i) That the crew is thoroughly familiar with the operator's contingency plan, that periodic emergency exercises are held so that the crew has a thorough working knowledge of the equipment and procedures and that each individual knows exactly his role within the plan.

2. The operator shall cooperate, on an institutional basis, with other operators or entities capable of rendering necessary assistance, so as to ensure that, in cases where the magnitude or nature of an emergency creates a risk for which assistance is or might be required, such assistance can be rendered.

B. National coordination and direction

The competent authority for emergencies of a Contracting Party shall ensure:

(a) The coordination of the national contingency plan and/or procedures and the operator's contingency plan and control of the conduct of actions, especially in case of significant adverse effects of the emergency;

(b) Direction to the operator to take any action it may specify in the course of preventing, abating or combating pollution or in the preparation of further action for that purpose, including placing an order for a relief drilling rig, or to prevent the operator from taking any specified action;

(c) The coordination of actions in the course of preventing, abating or combating pollution or in preparation for further action for that purpose within the national jurisdiction with such actions undertaken within the jurisdiction of other States or by international organizations;

(d) Collection and ready availability of all necessary information concerning the existing activities;

(e) The provision of an up-to-date list of the persons and entities to be alerted and informed about an emergency, its development and the measures taken;

(f) The collection of all necessary information concerning the extent and means of combating contingencies, and the dissemination of this information to interested Parties;

(g) The coordination and supervision of the assistance referred to in Part A above, in cooperation with the operator;

(h) The organization and if necessary, the coordination of specified actions, including intervention by technical experts and trained personnel with the necessary equipment and materials;

(i) Immediate communication to the competent authorities of other Parties which might be affected by a contingency to enable them to take appropriate measures where necessary;

(j) The provision of technical assistance to other Parties, if necessary;

(k) Immediate communication to the competent international organizations with a view to avoiding danger to shipping and other interests.

Appendix
List of oils*

Asphalt solutions

Blending Stocks
Roofers Flux
Straight Run Residue

Oils

Clarified
Crude Oil

* The list of oils should not necessarily be considered as exhaustive.

Mixtures containing crude oil
Diesel Oil
Fuel Oil No. 4
Fuel Oil No. 5
Fuel Oil No. 6
Residual Fuel Oil
Road Oil
Transformer Oil
Aromatic Oil (excluding vegetable oil)
Lubricating Oils and Blending Stocks
Mineral Oil
Motor Oil
Penetrating Oil
Spindle Oil
Turbine Oil

Distillates

Straight Run
Flashed Feed Stocks

Gas oil

Cracked

Jet fuels

JP-1 (Kerosene)
JP-3
JP-4
JP-5 (Kerosene, Heavy)
Turbo Fuel
Kerosene
Mineral Spirit

Naphtha

Solvent
Petroleum
Heartcut Distillate Oil

Gasoline blending stocks

Alkylates – fuel
Reformates
Polymer – fuel

Gasolines

Casinghead (natural)
Automotive
Aviation
Straight Run
Fuel Oil No. 1 (Kerosene)
Fuel Oil No. 1-D
Fuel Oil No. 2
Fuel Oil No. 2-D

Protocol on the Prevention of Pollution of the Mediterranean Sea by Transboundary Movements of Hazardous Wastes and their Disposal, 1 October 1996

Editorial note

The Protocol on the Prevention of Pollution of the Mediterranean Sea by Transboundary Movements of Hazardous Wastes and their Disposal aims to prevent, abate and eliminate pollution in the Mediterranean Sea Area caused by transboundary movements and disposal of hazardous wastes (Article 5). Hazardous wastes are defined as wastes that belong to any category in Annex I to the Protocol; wastes defined or considered to be hazardous by the domestic legislation of the State of export, import or transit; wastes that possess the characteristics contained in Annex II to the Protocol; hazardous substances that have been banned or expired or whose registration has been cancelled or refused or voluntarily withdrawn or omitted (Article 3). The generator, the exporter or the importer, depending on the circumstances, shall bear the responsibility for checking with the competent authorities of the State of export, import or transit that a particular waste, prior to its transboundary movement, is not subject to the Protocol (Article 3(3)).

Parties shall take all appropriate measures to reduce to a minimum, and where possible to eliminate, the generation of hazardous waste (Article 5(2)). They shall also take all appropriate measures to reduce to a minimum the transboundary movement of hazardous waste in the Mediterranean, and if possible eliminate such movement (Article 5(3)). To achieve this goal, Parties have a right to ban the import of hazardous wastes (Article 5(3)). The export or transit of hazardous wastes to developing countries must be prohibited (Article 5(4)). In exceptional cases, when the hazardous wastes cannot be disposed of in an environmentally sound manner in the country in which they originated, transboundary movement can be allowed (Article 6). In the exceptional cases in which transboundary movement of hazardous wastes is permitted, adequate information must be made available to the public, which must have an opportunity to participate in relevant procedures, whenever possible and appropriate (Article 12).

Parties shall co-operate as far as possible in scientific and technological fields related to the application of the Protocol and in taking measures to implement the precautionary approach (Article 8).

Any transboundary movement of hazardous wastes in contravention of the Protocol or of other rules of international law shall be considered illegal and each Party shall introduce legislation to prevent and punish illegal traffic of hazardous waste (Article 9). In case of illegal traffic, the State of export shall ensure that the waste is taken back by the generator or exporter, if the illegal traffic is due to their conduct, or, if necessary, by the State of export itself (Article 9(3)). If the illegal traffic is due to the conduct of the importer or disposer, the State of import shall ensure that the waste in question is eliminated according to environmentally sound methods (Article 9(4)). If the responsibility for the illegal traffic cannot be assigned, the Parties concerned shall ensure environmentally sound disposal through co-operation (Article 9(5)).

Parties shall co-operate with a view to formulate and implement programmes of assistance for developing countries (Article 10) and shall exchange information on their experience in the application of the Protocol (Article 11). Any Party which has reason to believe that another Party is acting or has acted in breach of the Protocol informs UNEP and the Party against whom the allegations are made. UNEP shall carry out a verification of the allegation and submit a report to the Parties (Article 13). The Parties shall co-operate to set out, as soon as possible, appropriate guidelines for the evaluation of the damage, as well as rules in the field of liability and compensation for damage (Article 14).

Date of signature:	1 October 1996
Entry into force:	Not yet in force
Depositary:	Government of Spain
Contracting Parties:	Albania, Malta, Morocco, Tunisia
Websites:	www.unepmap.org
	www.unep.ch/seas/

Protocol on the Prevention of Pollution of the Mediterranean Sea by Transboundary Movements of Hazardous Wastes and their Disposal

The Contracting Parties to the present Protocol,

Being Parties to the Convention for the Protection of the Mediterranean Sea against Pollution, adopted at Barcelona on 16 February 1976 and amended on 10 June 1995,

Conscious of the danger threatening the environment of the Mediterranean Sea caused by the transboundary movements and disposal of hazardous wastes,

Convinced that the most effective way of protecting human health and the marine environment from the dangers posed by hazardous wastes is the reduction and elimination of their generation, for example through substitution and other clean production methods,

Recognizing the increased will for the prohibition of transboundary movements of hazardous wastes and their disposal in other States, especially in developing countries,

Taking into account the 1992 Rio Declaration on Environment and Development and especially Principle 14 which declares that States 'should effectively cooperate to discourage or prevent the relocation and transfer to other States of any activities or substances that cause severe environmental degradation or are found to be harmful to human health',

Aware of the growing international concern regarding the need to ensure that pollution originating in one State is not transferred to other States and, consistent with this objective, of the need to reduce transboundary movements of hazardous wastes to a minimum as far as possible, with the ultimate aim of phasing out such movements,

Recognizing also that any State has the sovereign right to ban the entry, transit or disposal of hazardous wastes in its territory,

Bearing in mind the relevant provisions of the United Nations Convention on the Law of the Sea of 1982,

Taking into account also the Basel Convention on the Control of Transboundary Movements of Hazardous Wastes and their Disposal, adopted on 22 March 1989, in particular Article 11, and decisions I/22, II/12 and III/1 adopted by the First, Second and Third Meetings respectively of the Conference of the Parties to the Basel Convention,

Taking into account further that many States, among them Contracting Parties to the Barcelona Convention, have taken legal measures and entered into international agreements consistent with the Basel Convention to ban transboundary movements of hazardous wastes, for example, the IVth ACP/EEC Convention signed in Lomé on 15 December 1989 by the European Economic Community and the African, Caribbean and Pacific Group of States, and the Bamako Convention on the Ban of the Import into Africa and the Control of Transboundary Movement and Management of Hazardous Wastes within Africa, adopted under the auspices of the Organization of African Unity on 30 January 1991,

Recognizing further the differences in levels of economic and legislative development among the various Mediterranean coastal States, and realizing that hazardous waste should not be allowed to be transported in order to take advantage of such economic or legislative disparities to the detriment of the environment and of the social well-being of developing countries,

Bearing in mind also the fact that the most effective way of dealing with the threats represented by wastes for human health and the environment consists in decreasing or even prohibiting the transfer of activities which generate hazardous wastes,

Have agreed as follows:

Article 1
Definitions

For the purposes of this Protocol:

(a) 'Convention' means the Convention for the Protection of the Mediterranean Sea against Pollution, adopted at Barcelona on 16 February 1976
and amended on 10 June 1995;

(b) A 'Party' means a Contracting Party to this Protocol in accordance with
Article 29, paragraph 1, of the Convention;

(c) 'Wastes' means substances or objects which are disposed of or are intended
to be disposed of or are required to be disposed of by the provisions of
national law;

(d) 'Hazardous wastes' means wastes or categories of substances as specified
in Article 3 of this Protocol;

(e) 'Disposal' means any operation specified in Annex III to this Protocol;

(f) 'Transboundary movement' means any movement of hazardous wastes
from an area under the national jurisdiction of one State to or through an
area under the national jurisdiction of another State or to or through an
area not under the national jurisdiction of any State, provided at least two
States are involved in the movement;

(g) 'Approved site or facility' means a site or facility for the disposal of hazardous wastes which is authorized or permitted to operate for this purpose
by a relevant authority of the State where the site or facility is located;

(h) 'Competent authority' means one governmental authority designated by
a Party to be responsible, within such geographical areas as the Party may
think fit, for receiving the notification of a transboundary movement of
hazardous waste, and any information related to it, and for responding to
such a notification;

(i) 'Clean production methods' means those which reduce or avoid the generation of hazardous wastes in conformity with Articles 5 and 8 of this
Protocol;

(j) 'Environmentally sound management' of hazardous wastes means taking
all practicable steps to ensure that hazardous wastes are collected, transported and disposed of (including after-care of disposal sites) in a manner
which will protect human health and the environment against the adverse
effects which may result from such wastes;

(k) 'Area under the national jurisdiction of a State' means any land, marine area
or airspace within which a State exercises administrative and regulatory
responsibilities in accordance with international law in regard to the protection of human health or the environment;

(l) 'State of export' means a Party from which a transboundary movement of
hazardous wastes is planned to be initiated or is initiated;

(m) 'State of import' means a Party to which a transboundary movement of
hazardous wastes is planned or takes place for the purpose of disposal

therein or for the purpose of loading prior to disposal in an area not under the national jurisdiction of any State;

(n) 'State of transit' means any State, other than the State of export or import, through which a movement of hazardous wastes is planned or takes place;

(o) 'Exporter' means any person under the jurisdiction of the State of export who arranges for hazardous wastes to be exported;

(p) 'Importer' means any person under the jurisdiction of the State of import who arranges for hazardous wastes to be imported;

(q) 'Generator' means any person whose activity produces hazardous wastes or, if that person is not known, the person who is in possession and/or control of those wastes;

(r) 'Disposer' means any person to whom hazardous wastes are shipped and who carries out the disposal of such wastes;

(s) 'Illegal traffic' means any transboundary movement of hazardous wastes as specified in Article 9;

(t) 'Person' means any natural or legal person;

(u) 'Developing countries' means those countries which are not Member States of the Organization for Economic Co-operation and Development (OECD);

(v) 'Developed countries' means those countries which are Member States of the Organization for Economic Co-operation and Development (OECD);[1]

(w) 'Organization' means the body referred to in Article 2 (b) of the Convention.

Article 2
Protocol area

The Protocol area as referred to in this Protocol shall mean the area as defined in Article 1 of the Convention.

Article 3
Scope of the protocol

1. This Protocol shall apply to:

(a) Wastes that belong to any category in Annex I to this Protocol;

(b) Wastes that are not covered under paragraph (a) above but are defined as, or are considered to be, hazardous wastes by the domestic legislation of the State of export, import or transit;

(c) Wastes that possess any of the characteristics contained in Annex II to this Protocol;

(d) Hazardous substances that have been banned or are expired, or whose registration has been cancelled or refused through government regulatory

---

[1] For the purposes of this Protocol, Monaco shall have the same rights and obligations as Member States of the OECD.

action in the country of manufacture or export for human health or environmental reasons, or have been voluntarily withdrawn or omitted from the government registration required for use in the country of manufacture or export.

2. Wastes which derive from the normal operations of ships, the discharge of which is covered by another international instrument, are excluded from the scope of this Protocol.

3. The generator, the exporter or the importer, depending on the circumstances, shall bear the responsibility for checking with the competent authorities of the State of export, import or transit that a particular waste, prior to its transboundary movement, is not subject to this Protocol.

Article 4
National definitions of hazardous wastes

1. Each Party to the Convention shall, within six months of becoming a Party, inform the Organization of the wastes, other than those listed in Annex I to this Protocol, considered or defined as hazardous wastes under its national legislation, and of any requirements concerning transboundary movement procedures applicable to such wastes.

2. Each Party shall subsequently inform the Organization of any significant changes in information it has provided pursuant to paragraph 1 of this Article.

3. The Organization shall inform all Parties of the information it has received pursuant to paragraphs 1 and 2 of this Article.

4. The Parties shall be responsible for making the information transmitted to them by the Organization under paragraph 3 of this Article available to their exporters.

Article 5
General obligations

1. The Parties shall take all appropriate measures to prevent, abate and eliminate pollution of the Protocol area which can be caused by transboundary movements and disposal of hazardous wastes.

2. The Parties shall take all appropriate measures to reduce to a minimum, and where possible eliminate, the generation of hazardous wastes.

3. The Parties shall also take all appropriate measures to reduce to a minimum the transboundary movement of hazardous wastes, and if possible to eliminate such movement in the Mediterranean. To achieve this goal, Parties have the right individually or collectively to ban the import of hazardous wastes. Other Parties shall respect this sovereign decision and not permit the export of hazardous wastes to States which have prohibited their import.

4. Subject to the specific provisions relating to the transboundary movement of hazardous wastes through the territorial sea of a State of transit, referred to in

Article 6.4 of this Protocol, all Parties shall take appropriate legal, administrative and other measures within the area under their jurisdiction to prohibit the export and transit of hazardous wastes to developing countries, and Parties which are not Member States of the European Community[1] shall prohibit all imports and transit of hazardous wastes.

5. The Parties shall cooperate with other United Nations agencies, relevant international and regional organizations in order to prevent illegal traffic, and shall take appropriate measures to achieve this goal, including criminal punishment measures in accordance with their national legislation.

Article 6
Transboundary movement and notification procedures

In exceptional cases, unless otherwise prohibited, when hazardous wastes cannot be disposed of in an environmentally sound manner in the country in which they originated, transboundary movements of such wastes can be allowed if:

1. The special situation of the Mediterranean developing countries which do not have the technical capabilities nor the disposal facilities for the environmentally sound management of hazardous wastes is taken into consideration.

2. The competent authority of the State of import ensures that the hazardous waste is disposed of in an approved site or facility with the technical capacity for its environmentally sound disposal.

3. The transboundary movement of hazardous wastes only takes place with the prior written notification of the State of export as specified in Annex IV to this Protocol, and the prior written consent of the State(s) of import and the State(s) of transit. This paragraph does not apply to conditions of passage through the territorial sea, which are governed by paragraph 4 of this Article.

4. The transboundary movement of hazardous wastes through the territorial sea of a State of transit only takes place with the prior notification by the State of export to the State of transit, as specified in Annex IV to this Protocol. After reception of the notification, the State of transit brings to the attention of the State of export all the obligations relating to passage through its territorial sea in application of international law and the relevant provisions of its domestic legislation adopted in compliance with international law to protect the marine environment. Where necessary, the State of transit may take appropriate measures in accordance with international law. This procedure must be complied with within the delays provided for by the Basel Convention.

5. Every State involved in a transboundary movement ensures that such movement is consistent with international safety standards and financial guarantees, in particular the procedures and standards set out in the Basel Convention.

---

[1] For the purposes of this Protocol, Monaco shall have the same rights and obligations as Member States of the European Community.

Article 7
Duty to reimport

The State of export shall reimport the hazardous wastes if the transboundary movement cannot be completed by reason of impossibility of performance of the contracts relating to the movement and disposal of the wastes. To this end, any State of transit shall not oppose, hinder or prevent the return of those wastes to the State of export after being properly informed by the State of export.

Article 8
Regional cooperation

1. In conformity with Article 13 of the Convention, the Parties shall cooperate as far as possible in scientific and technological fields related to pollution from hazardous wastes, particularly in the implementation and development of new methods for reducing and eliminating hazardous waste generated through clean production methods.

2. To this end, the Parties shall submit annual reports to the Organization regarding the hazardous wastes they generate and transfer within the Protocol area in order to enable the Organization to produce a hazardous waste audit.

3. The Parties shall cooperate in taking appropriate measures to implement the precautionary approach based on prevention of pollution problems arising from hazardous wastes and their transboundary movement and disposal. To this end, the Parties shall ensure that clean production methods are applied to production processes.

Article 9
Illegal traffic

1. For the purpose of this Protocol, any transboundary movement of hazardous wastes in contravention of this Protocol or of other rules of international law shall be deemed to be illegal traffic.

2. Each Party shall introduce appropriate national legislation to prevent and punish illegal traffic, including criminal penalties on all persons involved in such illegal activities.

3. In the case of illegal traffic due to the conduct of the generator or the exporter, the State of export shall ensure that the wastes in question are taken back by the exporter or the generator or, if necessary, by itself, into the State of export within 30 days from the time the illegal traffic has come to its attention and that appropriate legal action is taken against the contravenor(s).

4. In the case of illegal traffic due to the conduct of the importer or disposer, the State of import shall ensure that the wastes in question are eliminated according to environmentally sound methods by the importer within 30 days from the time the illegal traffic has come to the attention of the State of import; if not possible, the State of export shall ensure that the wastes are taken

back by the exporter, the generator or, if necessary, by itself into the State of export. The competent authorities of the importing or exporting States shall ensure that legal proceedings according to this Protocol are taken against the contravenor(s).

5. In cases where the responsibility for the illegal traffic cannot be assigned either to the exporter or generator or to the importer or disposer, the Parties concerned or other Parties, as appropriate, shall ensure, through cooperation that the wastes in question are disposed of as soon as possible in an environmentally sound manner either in the State of export or the State of import or elsewhere as appropriate.

6. The Parties shall forward, as soon as possible, all information relating to illegal traffic to the Organization, which shall distribute the information to all Contracting Parties.

7. The Parties shall cooperate to ensure that no illegal traffic takes place. Upon request, the Organization shall assist Parties in their identification of cases of illegal traffic and shall circulate immediately to the Parties concerned any information it has received regarding illegal traffic.

8. The Organization shall undertake the necessary coordination with the Secretariat of the Basel Convention in relation to the effective prevention and monitoring of illegal traffic in hazardous wastes. Such coordination shall be mainly based on:

(a) Exchange of information on cases or alleged cases of illegal traffic in the Mediterranean and coordination of action to remedy such cases;
(b) Providing assistance in the field of capacity-building, including development of national legislation and of appropriate infrastructure in the Mediterranean States with a view to the prevention and penalization of illegal traffic in hazardous wastes;
(c) The establishment of a mechanism to prevent and monitor illegal traffic in hazardous wastes in the Mediterranean.

Article 10
Assistance to developing countries

The Parties shall, directly or with the assistance of competent or other international organizations or bilaterally, cooperate with a view to formulating and implementing programmes of financial and technical assistance to developing countries for the implementation of this Protocol.

Article 11
Transmission of information

The Parties shall inform one another through the Organization of measures taken, of results achieved and, if the case arises, of difficulties encountered in the application of this Protocol. Procedures for the collection and distribution of such information shall be determined at the meetings of the Parties.

Article 12
Information to and participation of the public

1. In the exceptional cases in which transboundary movement of hazardous wastes is permitted under Article 6 of this Protocol, the Parties shall ensure that adequate information is made available to the public, transmitted through such channels as the Parties deem appropriate.

2. The State of export and the State of import shall, in accordance with the provisions of this Protocol and whenever possible and appropriate, give the public an opportunity to participate in relevant procedures with the aim of making known its views and concerns.

Article 13
Verification

1. Any Party which has reason to believe that another Party is acting or has acted in breach of its obligations under this Protocol informs the Organization thereof, and, in such an event, simultaneously and immediately informs, directly or through the Organization, the Party against whom the allegations are made.

2. The Organization shall carry out a verification of the substance of the allegation through consultation with the Parties concerned and submit a report thereon to the Parties.

Article 14
Liability and compensation

The Parties shall cooperate with a view to setting out, as soon as possible, appropriate guidelines for the evaluation of the damage, as well as rules and procedures in the field of liability and compensation for damage resulting from the transboundary movement and disposal of hazardous wastes.

Article 15
Meetings

1. Ordinary meetings of the Parties shall take place in conjunction with ordinary meetings of the Contracting Parties to the Convention held pursuant to Article 18 of the Convention. The Parties to this Protocol may also hold extraordinary meetings in conformity with Article 18 of the Convention.

2. The functions of the meetings of the Parties shall be, *inter alia*:

(a) To keep under review the implementation of this Protocol, and consider any additional measures, including in the form of annexes;
(b) To revise and amend this Protocol and any annex thereto, as appropriate;
(c) To formulate and adopt programmes, methods and measures in accordance with the relevant Articles of this Protocol;

(d) To consider any information submitted by the Parties to the Organization or to the meetings of the Parties in accordance with the relevant Articles of this Protocol;

(e) To perform such other functions as may be appropriate for the application of this Protocol.

Article 16
Adoption of additional programmes and measures

The meeting of the Parties shall adopt, by a two-thirds (2/3) majority, any additional programmes and measures for the prevention and elimination of pollution from transboundary movements of hazardous wastes and their disposal.

Article 17
Final clauses

1. The provisions of the Convention relating to any Protocol shall apply with respect to this Protocol.

2. The rules of procedure and the financial rules adopted pursuant to Article 24 of the Convention shall apply with respect to this Protocol, unless the Parties to this Protocol agree otherwise.

3. This Protocol shall be open for signature at Izmir on 1 October 1996, and at Madrid from 2 October 1996 to 1 October 1997 by any State Party to the Convention. It shall also be open on the same dates for signature by the European Community and by any similar regional economic grouping of which at least one member is a coastal State of the Protocol area and which exercises competence in the fields covered by this Protocol.

4. This Protocol shall be subject to ratification, acceptance or approval. Instruments of ratification, acceptance or approval shall be deposited with the Government of Spain, which will assume the functions of Depositary.

5. As from 2 October 1997, this Protocol shall be open for accession by the States referred to in paragraph 3 above, by the European Community and by any grouping referred to in that paragraph.

6. This Protocol shall enter into force on the thirtieth (30) day following the deposit of at least six (6) instruments of ratification, acceptance or approval of, or accession to, the Protocol by the Parties referred to in paragraph 3 of this Article.

IN WITNESS WHEREOF, the undersigned, being duly authorized by their respective Governments, have signed this Protocol.

DONE at Izmir on this first day of October 1996 in a single copy in the Arabic, English, French, and Spanish languages, the four texts being equally authoritative.

Annex I
Categories of wastes subject to this Protocol

A. Hazardous wastes

Y0 All wastes containing or contaminated by radionuclides, the radionuclide concentration or properties of which result from human activity

Y1 Clinical wastes from medical care in hospitals, medical centres and clinics

Y2 Wastes from the production and preparation of pharmaceutical products

Y3 Waste pharmaceuticals, drugs and medicines

Y4 Wastes from the production, formulation and use of biocides and phytopharmaceuticals

Y5 Wastes from manufacturing, formulation and use of wood preserving chemicals

Y6 Wastes from the production, formulation and use of organic solvents

Y7 Wastes from heat treatment and tempering operations containing cyanides

Y8 Waste mineral oils unfit for their originally intended use

Y9 Waste oils/water, hydrocarbons/water mixtures, emulsions

Y10 Waste substances and articles containing or contaminated with polychlorinated biphenyls (PCBs) and/or polychlorinated terphenyls (PCTs) and/or polybrominated biphenyls (PBBs)

Y11 Waste tarry residues arising from refining, distillation and any pyrolytic treatment

Y12 Wastes from production, formulation and use of inks, dyes, pigments, paints, lacquers, varnishes

Y13 Wastes from production, formulation and use of resins, latex, plasticizers, glues/adhesives

Y14 Waste chemical substances arising from research and development or teaching activities which are not identified and/or are new and whose effects on man and/or the environment are not known

Y15 Wastes of an explosive nature not subject to other legislation

Y16 Wastes from production, formulation and use of photographic chemicals and processing materials

Y17 Wastes resulting from surface treatment of metals and plastics

Y18 Residues arising from industrial waste disposal operations

Wastes having as constituents:

Y19 Metal carbonyls

Y20 Beryllium; beryllium compounds

Y21 Hexavalent chromium compounds

Y22 Copper compounds

Y23 Zinc compounds

Y24 Arsenic; arsenic compounds

Y25 Selenium; selenium compounds

Y26 Cadmium; cadmium compounds

Y27 Antimony; antimony compounds
Y28 Tellurium; tellurium compounds
Y29 Mercury; mercury compounds
Y30 Thallium; thallium compounds
Y31 Lead; lead compounds
Y32 Inorganic fluorine compounds excluding calcium fluoride
Y33 Inorganic cyanides
Y34 Acidic solutions or acids in solid form
Y35 Basic solutions or bases in solid form
Y36 Asbestos (dust and fibres)
Y37 Organic phosphorus compounds
Y38 Organic cyanides
Y39 Phenols; phenolic compounds including chlorophenols
Y40 Ethers
Y41 Halogenated organic solvents
Y42 Organic solvents excluding halogenated solvents
Y43 Any congener of polychlorinated dibenzo-furan
Y44 Any congener of polychlorinated dibenzo-p-dioxin
Y45 Organohalogen compounds other than substances referred to in this Annex
     (e.g. Y39, Y41, Y42, Y43, Y44)

B. Household wastes

Y46 Wastes collected from households, including sewage and sewage sludges
Y47 Residues arising from the incineration of household wastes

Annex II
List of hazardous characteristics

UN Class*	Code	Characteristics
1	H1	Explosives An explosive substance or waste is a solid or liquid substance or waste (or mixture of substances or wastes) which is in itself capable by chemical reaction of producing gas at such a temperature and pressure and at such a speed as to cause damage to the surroundings.
3	H3	Flammable liquids The word 'flammable' has the same meaning as 'inflammable'. Flammable liquids are liquids, or mixtures of liquids, or liquids containing solids in solution or suspension (for example paints, varnishes, lacquers, etc., but not including substances or wastes otherwise classified on account of their

UN Class*	Code	Characteristics
		dangerous characteristics) which give off a flammable vapour at temperatures of not more than 60.5 degrees C, closed-cup test, or not more than 65.6 degrees C, open-cup test. (Since the results of open-cup tests and of closed-cup tests are not strictly comparable and even individual results by the same test are often variable, regulations varying from the above figures to make allowance for such difference would be within the spirit of this definition).
4.1	H4.1	Flammable solids Solids, or waste solids, other than those classed as explosives, which under conditions encountered in transport are readily combustible, or may cause or contribute to fire through friction.
4.2	H4.2	Substances or wastes liable to spontaneous combustion Substances or wastes which are liable to spontaneous heating under normal conditions encountered in transport, or in heating up on contact with air, and being liable to catch fire.
4.3	H4.3	Substances or wastes which, in contact with water, emit flammable gases Substances or wastes which, by interaction with water, are liable to become spontaneously flammable or to give off flammable gases in dangerous quantities.
5.1	H5.1	Oxidizing Substances or wastes which, while in themselves not necessarily combustible, may generally by yielding oxygen, cause or contribute to the combustion of other materials.
5.2	H5.2	Organic peroxides Organic substances or wastes which contain the bivalent-O-O-structure are thermally unstable substances which may undergo exothermic self-accelerating decomposition.
6.1	H6.1	Poisonous (Acute) Substances or wastes liable either to cause death or serious injury or to harm human health if swallowed or inhaled or by skin contact.
6.2	H6.2	Infectious substances Substances or wastes containing viable microorganisms or their toxins which are known or suspected to cause disease in animals or humans.

UN Class*	Code	Characteristics
8	H8	Corrosives Substances or wastes which, by chemical action, will cause severe damage when in contact with living tissue, or in the case of leakage, will materially damage, or even destroy, other goods or the means of transport; they may also cause other hazards.
9	H10	Liberation of toxic gases in contact with air or water Substances or wastes which, by interaction with air or water, are liable to give off toxic gases in dangerous quantities.
9	H11	Toxic (Delayed or chronic) Substances or wastes which, if they are inhaled or ingested or if they penetrate the skin, may involve delayed or chronic effects, including carcinogenicity.
9	H12	Ecotoxic Substances or wastes which if released present or may present immediate or delayed adverse impacts on the environment by means of bioaccumulation and/or toxic effects upon biotic systems.
9	H13	Capable, by any means, after disposal, of yielding another material, e.g. leachate, which possesses any of the characteristics listed above.

*Corresponds to the Hazardous classification system included in the United Nations Recommendations on the Transport of Dangerous Goods (ST/SG/AC.10/1/Rev.5, United Nations, New York, 1988).

Annex III
Disposal operations

The list of disposal operations contained in this Annex reflects those which occur or have occurred in practice. It does not necessarily reflect a list of acceptable disposal operations. Pursuant to Articles 5 and 6 of this Protocol, hazardous wastes must in any event be managed in an environmentally sound manner.

A. Operations which do not lead to the possibility of resource recovery, recycling, reclamation, direct reuse or alternative uses

Section A encompasses all such disposal operations which occur in practice.

D1 Deposit into or onto land (e.g. landfill, etc.)
D2 Land treatment (e.g. biodegradation of liquid or sludgy discards in soils, etc.)

D3 Deep injection (e.g. injection of pumpable discards into wells, salt domes or naturally occurring repositories, etc.)

D4 Surface impoundment (e.g. placement of liquid or sludge discards into pits, ponds, lagoons, etc.)

D5 Specially engineered landfill (e.g. placement into lined discrete cells which are capped and isolated from one another and the environment, etc.)

D6 Release into a water body except seas/oceans

D7 Release into seas/oceans including sea-bed insertion

D8 Biological treatment not specified elsewhere in this Annex which results in final compounds or mixtures which are discarded by means of any of the operations in Section A

D9 Physico-chemical treatment not specified elsewhere in this Annex which results in final compounds or mixtures which are discarded by means of any of the operations in Section A (e.g. evaporation, drying, calcination, neutralization, precipitation, etc.)

D10 Incineration on land

D11 Incineration at sea

D12 Permanent storage (e.g. emplacement of containers in mines, etc.)

D13 Blending or mixing prior to submission to any of the operations in Section A

D14 Repackaging prior to submission to any of the operations in Section A

D15 Storage pending any of the operations in Section A

B. Operations which may lead to resource recovery, recycling, reclamation, direct reuse or alternative uses

Section B encompasses all such operations with respect to materials legally defined as or considered to be hazardous wastes and which otherwise would have been destined for operations included in Section A.

R1 Use as a fuel (other than in direct incineration) or other means to generate energy

R2 Solvent reclamation/regeneration

R3 Recycling/reclamation of organic substances which are not used as solvents

R4 Recycling/reclamation of metals and metal compounds

R5 Recycling/reclamation of other inorganic materials

R6 Regeneration of acids or bases

R7 Recovery of components used for pollution abatement

R8 Recovery of components from catalysts

R9 Used oil re-refining or other reuses of previously used oil

R10 Land treatment resulting in benefit to agriculture or ecological improvement

R11 Uses of residual materials obtained from any of the operations numbered R1–R10

R12 Exchange of wastes for submission to any of the operations numbered R1–R11

R13 Accumulation of material intended for any operation in Section B

Annex IV (A)
Information to be provided on notification

1. Reason for waste export;
2. Exporter of the waste (1);
3. Generator(s) of the waste and site of generation (1);
4. Importer and disposer of the waste and actual site of disposal (1);
5. Intended carrier(s) of the waste or their agents, if known (1);
6. Country of export of the waste Competent authority (2);
7. Expected countries of transit Competent authority (2);
8. Country of import of the waste Competent authority (2);
9. Projected date(s) of shipment(s) and period of time over which waste is to be exported and proposed itinerary (including point of entry and exit) (3);
10. Means of transport envisaged (road, rail, sea, air, inland waters);
11. Information relating to insurance (4);
12. Designation and physical description of the waste including Y number and UN number and its composition (5) and information on any special handling requirements including emergency provisions in case of accidents;
13. Type of packaging envisaged (e.g. bulk, drums, tanker);
14. Estimated quantity in weight/volume (6);
15. Process by which the waste is generated (7);
16. Code according to ANNEX I, classifications according to ANNEX II, H number, and UN class;
17. Method of disposal as per ANNEX III;
18. Declaration by the generator and exporter that the information is correct;
19. Information transmitted (including technical description of the plant) to the exporter or generator from the disposer of the waste upon which the latter has based his assessment that there is no reason to believe that the waste will not be managed in an environmentally sound manner in accordance with the laws and regulations of the country of import;
20. Information concerning the contract between the exporter and the disposer.

Notes

The Organization should make use of a Notification Form and accompanying documents such as those developed within the framework of the Basel Convention, the OECD and the European Community.

(1) Full name and address, telephone, telex or telefax number and the name, address, telephone, telex or telefax number of the person to be contacted.

(2) Full name and address, telephone, telex or telefax number.

(3) In the case of a general notification covering several shipments, either the expected dates of each shipment or, if this is not known, the expected frequency of the shipments will be required.

(4) Information to be provided on relevant insurance requirements and how they are met by exporter, carrier and disposer.

(5) The nature and the concentration of the most hazardous components, in terms of toxicity and other dangers presented by the waste both in handling and in relation to the proposed disposal method.

(6) In the case of a general notification covering several shipments, both the estimated total quantity and the estimated quantities for each individual shipment will be required.

(7) Insofar as this is necessary to assess the hazard and determine the appropriateness of the proposed disposal operation.

Annex IV (B)
Information to be provided on the movement document

1. Exporter of the waste (1);
2. Generator(s) of the waste and site of generation (1);
3. Disposer of the waste and actual site of disposal (1);
4. Carrier(s) of the waste (1) or his agent(s);
5. The date the transboundary movement started and date(s) and signature on receipt by each person who takes charge of the waste;
6. Means of transport (road, rail, inland waterway, sea, air) including countries of export, transit and import, also point of entry and exit where these have been designated;
7. General description of the waste (physical state, proper UN shipping name and class, UN number, Y number and H number as applicable);
8. Information on special handling requirements including emergency provision in case of accidents;
9. Type and number of packages;
10. Quantity in weight/volume;
11. Declaration by the generator or exporter that the information is correct;
12. Declaration by the generator or exporter indicating no objection from the competent authorities of all States concerned which are Parties;
13. Certification by disposer of receipt at designated disposal facility and indication of method of disposal and of the approximate date of disposal.
14. The insurance documents, bond or other guarantee as may be required by the Parties, as provided in Article 6, paragraph 5.

Notes

The Organization should make use of a Movement Document and accompanying documents such as those developed within the framework of the Basel Convention, the OECD and the European Community.

The information required on the Movement Document shall where possible be integrated in one document with that required under transport rules. Where this is not possible, the information should complement rather than duplicate that required under the transport rules. The Movement Document shall carry instructions as to who is to provide information and fill out any form.

(1) Full name and address, telephone, telex or telefax number and the name, address, telephone, telex or telefax number of the person to be contacted in case of emergency.

Convention for the Protection of the Marine Environment of the North-East Atlantic, 22 September 1992

Editorial note

The Convention for the Protection of the Marine Environment of the North-East Atlantic, adopted under the auspices of the Paris and Oslo Commissions, has replaced the Oslo Convention for the Prevention of Marine Pollution by Dumping from Ships and Aircraft, 1972 and the Paris Convention for the Prevention of Marine Pollution by Land-Based Sources, 1974. Its central obligation requires Parties to adopt programmes and measures to 'prevent and eliminate pollution' of the maritime area (Article 2(1)). To that end, the Convention requires the Parties to apply: (a) the precautionary principle, whereby preventive measures to forestall risks to human health, the environment or legitimate uses of the sea are taken 'even where there is no conclusive evidence of a causal relationship between the inputs and the effects' (Article 2(2)(a)); and (b) the polluter pays principle, whereby the polluter bears the costs of pollution prevention, control and reduction (Article 2(2)(b)). In implementing the Convention, Parties are required to take into account the criteria in Appendix I to apply 'best available techniques' and 'best environmental practice', including, where appropriate, 'clean technology'. The Convention does not prevent the Parties from taking more stringent provisions than those set out in the Convention (Article 2(5)).

The Annexes to the Convention provide specific regulation on the prevention and elimination of pollution from: land-based sources (Article 3, Annex I); dumping or incineration (Article 4, Annex II); and offshore sources (Article 5, Annex III). Annex III provides an explicit exception to France and the United Kingdom from the prohibition on dumping low and intermediate radioactive substances, effective fifteen years from 1 January 1993. Parties are required to co-operate in the adoption of further Annexes to combat pollution from other sources (Article 7). Subject to specific grounds of confidentiality, the Convention requires Parties to make available to the public information on the state of the maritime area, activities affecting or likely to affect it, and measures taken in accordance with the Convention (Article 9). The Convention requires

Parties to enter into consultations, at the request of any Party, with a view to agreeing on an arrangement in response to prejudicial transboundary pollution (Article 21).

The Convention establishes a Commission made up of representatives of the Parties to meet at 'regular intervals' in order to supervise the Convention's implementation and to draw up programmes and measures in accordance with the Convention's obligations (Article 10). The Commission is empowered to adopt decisions and recommendations by a three-quarters majority vote of the Parties (Article 13(1)). Decisions bind Parties which accept them so long as three-quarters of the Parties accept them after two hundred days (Article 13(2)). Parties are required to report on the measures taken to implement the Convention and their effectiveness (Article 22). On the basis of these reports, the Commission is to assess compliance with the Convention and take decisions to effect compliance and assist Parties in meeting their obligations (Article 23). The Convention also creates a permanent Secretariat to administer the Convention and the Commission (Article 12). The Convention provides for compulsory dispute settlement, at the request of an involved Party, by means of binding arbitration (Article 32). Amendments of the Convention must be adopted by a unanimous vote of Parties at the Commission and enter into force for those accepting them after ratification, acceptance or approval by seven Parties (Article 15). Amending Annexes follows the same procedure except that they can be adopted by the Commission with only a three-quarters majority vote of Parties bound by that Annex (Article 17). Appendices can be amended by a three-quarters majority vote at the Commission of Parties bound by that Appendix and such amendments enter into force so long as three-quarters of those Parties continue to accept them after two hundred days (Article 19). Reservations to the Convention are not permitted (Article 28).

Date of signature: 22 September 1992

Entry into force: 25 March 1998

Depositary: Government of France

Contracting Parties: Belgium, Denmark, European Community, Finland, France, Germany, Iceland, Ireland, Luxembourg, Netherlands, Norway, Portugal, Spain, Sweden, Switzerland, United Kingdom

Website: www.ospar.org

Convention for the Protection of the Marine Environment of the North-East Atlantic

The Contracting Parties,

Recognising that the marine environment and the fauna and flora which it supports are of vital importance to all nations;

Recognising the inherent worth of the marine environment of the North-East Atlantic and the necessity for providing coordinated protection for it;

Recognising that concerted action at national, regional and global levels is essential to prevent and eliminate marine pollution and to achieve sustainable management of the maritime area, that is, the management of human activities in such a manner that the marine ecosystem will continue to sustain the legitimate uses of the sea and will continue to meet the needs of present and future generations;

Mindful that the ecological equilibrium and the legitimate uses of the sea are threatened by pollution;

Considering the recommendations of the United Nations Conference on the Human Environment, held in Stockholm in June 1972;

Considering also the results of the United Nations Conference on the Environment and Development held in Rio de Janeiro in June 1992;

Recalling the relevant provisions of customary international law reflected in Part XII of the United Nations Law of the Sea Convention and, in particular, Article 197 on global and regional cooperation for the protection and preservation of the marine environment;

Considering that the common interests of States concerned with the same marine area should induce them to cooperate at regional or sub-regional levels;

Recalling the positive results obtained within the context of the Convention for the prevention of marine pollution by dumping from ships and aircraft signed in Oslo on 15th February 1972, as amended by the protocols of 2nd March 1983 and 5th December 1989, and the Convention for the prevention of marine pollution from land-based sources signed in Paris on 4th June 1974, as amended by the protocol of 26th March 1986;

Convinced that further international action to prevent and eliminate pollution of the sea should be taken without delay, as part of progressive and coherent measures to protect the marine environment;

Recognising that it may be desirable to adopt, on the regional level, more stringent measures with respect to the prevention and elimination of pollution of the marine environment or with respect to the protection of the marine environment against the adverse effects of human activities than are provided for in international conventions or agreements with a global scope;

Recognising that questions relating to the management of fisheries are appropriately regulated under international and regional agreements dealing specifically with such questions;

Considering that the present Oslo and Paris Conventions do not adequately control some of the many sources of pollution, and that it is therefore justifiable to replace them with the present Convention, which addresses all sources of pollution of the marine environment and the adverse effects of human activities upon it, takes into account the precautionary principle and strengthens regional cooperation;

Have agreed as follows:

Article 1
Definitions

For the purposes of the Convention:

(a) 'Maritime area' means the internal waters and the territorial seas of the Contracting Parties, the sea beyond and adjacent to the territorial sea under the jurisdiction of the coastal state to the extent recognised by international law, and the high seas, including the bed of all those waters and its sub-soil, situated within the following limits:

  (i) those parts of the Atlantic and Arctic Oceans and their dependent seas which lie north of 36° north latitude and between 42° west longitude and 51° east longitude, but excluding:

    (1) the Baltic Sea and the Belts lying to the south and east of lines drawn from Hasenore Head to Gniben Point, from Korshage to Spodsbjerg and from Gilbjerg Head to Kullen,

    (2) the Mediterranean Sea and its dependent seas as far as the point of intersection of the parallel of 36° north latitude and the meridian of 5° 36′ west longitude;

  (ii) that part of the Atlantic Ocean north of 59° north latitude and between 44° west longitude and 42° west longitude.

(b) 'Internal waters' means the waters on the landward side of the baselines from which the breadth of the territorial sea is measured, extending in the case of watercourses up to the freshwater limit.

(c) 'Freshwater limit' means the place in a watercourse where, at low tide and in a period of low freshwater flow, there is an appreciable increase in salinity due to the presence of seawater.

(d) 'Pollution' means the introduction by man, directly or indirectly, of substances or energy into the maritime area which results, or is likely to result, in hazards to human health, harm to living resources and marine ecosystems, damage to amenities or interference with other legitimate uses of the sea.

(e) 'Land-based sources' means point and diffuse sources on land from which substances or energy reach the maritime area by water, through the air, or directly from the coast. It includes sources associated with any deliberate disposal under the sea-bed made accessible from land by tunnel, pipeline or other means and sources associated with man-made structures placed, in the maritime area under the jurisdiction of a Contracting Party, other than for the purpose of offshore activities.

(f) 'Dumping' means
   (i) any deliberate disposal in the maritime area of wastes or other matter
      (1) from vessels or aircraft;
      (2) from offshore installations;
   (ii) any deliberate disposal in the maritime area of
      (1) vessels or aircraft;
      (2) offshore installations and offshore pipelines.

(g) 'Dumping' does not include:
   (i) the disposal in accordance with the International Convention for the Prevention of Pollution from Ships, 1973, as modified by the Protocol of 1978 relating thereto, or other applicable international law, of wastes or other matter incidental to, or derived from, the normal operations of vessels or aircraft or offshore installations other than wastes or other matter transported by or to vessels or aircraft or offshore installations for the purpose of disposal of such wastes or other matter or derived from the treatment of such wastes or other matter on such vessels or aircraft or offshore installations;
   (ii) placement of matter for a purpose other than the mere disposal thereof, provided that, if the placement is for a purpose other than that for which the matter was originally designed or constructed, it is in accordance with the relevant provisions of the Convention; and
   (iii) for the purposes of Annex III, the leaving wholly or partly in place of a disused offshore installation or disused offshore pipeline, provided that any such operation takes place in accordance with any relevant provision of the Convention and with other relevant international law.

(h) 'Incineration' means any deliberate combustion of wastes or other matter in the maritime area for the purpose of their thermal destruction.

(i) 'Incineration' does not include the thermal destruction of wastes or other matter in accordance with applicable international law incidental to, or derived from the normal operation of vessels or aircraft, or offshore in-stallations other than the thermal destruction of wastes or other matter on vessels or aircraft or offshore installations operating for the purpose of such thermal destruction.

(j) 'Offshore activities' means activities carried out in the maritime area for the purposes of the exploration, appraisal or exploitation of liquid and gaseous hydrocarbons.

(k) 'Offshore sources' means offshore installations and offshore pipelines from which substances or energy reach the maritime area.

(l) 'Offshore installation' means any man-made structure, plant or vessel or parts thereof, whether floating or fixed to the seabed, placed within the maritime area for the purpose of offshore activities.

(m) 'Offshore pipeline' means any pipeline which has been placed in the maritime area for the purpose of offshore activities.

(n) 'Vessels or aircraft' means waterborne or airborne craft of any type whatsoever, their parts and other fittings. This expression includes air-cushion craft, floating craft whether self-propelled or not, and other man-made structures in the maritime area and their equipment, but excludes offshore installations and offshore pipelines.

(o) 'Wastes or other matter' does not include:
   (i) human remains;
   (ii) offshore installations;
   (iii) offshore pipelines;
   (iv) unprocessed fish and fish offal discarded from fishing vessels.

(p) 'Convention' means, unless the text otherwise indicates, the Convention for the Protection of the Marine Environment of the North-East Atlantic, its Annexes and Appendices.

(q) 'Oslo Convention' means the Convention for the Prevention of Marine Pollution by Dumping from Ships and Aircraft signed in Oslo on 15th February 1972, as amended by the protocols of 2nd March 1983 and 5th December 1989.

(r) 'Paris Convention' means the Convention for the Prevention of Marine Pollution from Land-based Sources, signed in Paris on 4th June 1974, as amended by the protocol of 26th March 1986.

(s) 'Regional economic integration organisation' means an organisation constituted by sovereign States of a given region which has competence in respect of matters governed by the Convention and has been duly authorised, in accordance with its internal procedures, to sign, ratify, accept, approve or accede to the Convention.

Article 2
General obligations

1.

(a) The Contracting Parties shall, in accordance with the provisions of the Convention, take all possible steps to prevent and eliminate pollution and shall take the necessary measures to protect the maritime area against the adverse effects of human activities so as to safeguard human health and to conserve marine ecosystems and, when practicable, restore marine areas which have been adversely affected.

(b) To this end Contracting Parties shall, individually and jointly, adopt programmes and measures and shall harmonise their policies and strategies.

2. The Contracting Parties shall apply:

(a) the precautionary principle, by virtue of which preventive measures are to be taken when there are reasonable grounds for concern that substances or energy introduced, directly or indirectly, into the marine environment may bring about hazards to human health, harm living resources and marine ecosystems, damage amenities or interfere with other legitimate uses of the sea, even when there is no conclusive evidence of a causal relationship between the inputs and the effects;

(b) the polluter pays principle, by virtue of which the costs of pollution prevention, control and reduction measures are to be borne by the polluter.

3.

(a) In implementing the Convention, Contracting Parties shall adopt programmes and measures which contain, where appropriate, time-limits for their completion and which take full account of the use of the latest technological developments and practices designed to prevent and eliminate pollution fully.

(b) To this end they shall:
   (i) taking into account the criteria set forth in Appendix 1, define with respect to programmes and measures the application of, *inter alia*,
      – best available techniques
      – best environmental practice including, where appropriate, clean technology;
   (ii) in carrying out such programmes and measures, ensure the application of best available techniques and best environmental practice as so defined, including, where appropriate, clean technology.

4. The Contracting Parties shall apply the measures they adopt in such a way as to prevent an increase in pollution of the sea outside the maritime area or in other parts of the environment.

5. No provision of the Convention shall be interpreted as preventing the Contracting Parties from taking, individually or jointly, more stringent measures with respect to the prevention and elimination of pollution of the maritime area or with respect to the protection of the maritime area against the adverse effects of human activities.

Article 3
Pollution from land-based sources

The Contracting Parties shall take, individually and jointly, all possible steps to prevent and eliminate pollution from land-based sources in accordance with the provisions of the Convention, in particular as provided for in Annex I.

Article 4
Pollution by dumping or incineration

The Contracting Parties shall take, individually and jointly, all possible steps to prevent and eliminate pollution by dumping or incineration of wastes or other matter in accordance with the provisions of the Convention, in particular as provided for in Annex II.

Article 5
Pollution from offshore sources

The Contracting Parties shall take, individually and jointly, all possible steps to prevent and eliminate pollution from offshore sources in accordance with the provisions of the Convention, in particular as provided for in Annex III.

Article 6
Assessment of the quality of the marine environment

The Contracting Parties shall, in accordance with the provisions of the Convention, in particular as provided for in Annex IV:

(a) undertake and publish at regular intervals joint assessments of the quality status of the marine environment and of its development, for the maritime area or for regions or sub-regions thereof;
(b) include in such assessments both an evaluation of the effectiveness of the measures taken and planned for the protection of the marine environment and the identification of priorities for action.

Article 7
Pollution from other sources

The Contracting Parties shall cooperate with a view to adopting Annexes, in addition to the Annexes mentioned in Articles 3, 4, 5 and 6 above, prescribing measures, procedures and standards to protect the maritime area against pollution from other sources, to the extent that such pollution is not already the subject of effective measures agreed by other international organisations or prescribed by other international conventions.

Article 8
Scientific and technical research

1. To further the aims of the Convention, the Contracting Parties shall establish complementary or joint programmes of scientific or technical research and, in accordance with a standard procedure, to transmit to the Commission:

(a) the results of such complementary, joint or other relevant research;
(b) details of other relevant programmes of scientific and technical research.

2. In so doing, the Contracting Parties shall have regard to the work carried out, in these fields, by the appropriate international organisations and agencies.

Article 9
Access to information

1. The Contracting Parties shall ensure that their competent authorities are required to make available the information described in paragraph 2 of this Article to any natural or legal person, in response to any reasonable request, without that person's having to prove an interest, without unreasonable charges, as soon as possible and at the latest within two months.

2. The information referred to in paragraph 1 of this Article is any available information in written, visual, aural or data-base form on the state of the maritime area, on activities or measures adversely affecting or likely to affect it and on activities or measures introduced in accordance with the Convention.

3. The provisions of this Article shall not affect the right of Contracting Parties, in accordance with their national legal systems and applicable international regulations, to provide for a request for such information to be refused where it affects:

(a) the confidentiality of the proceedings of public authorities, international relations and national defence;
(b) public security;
(c) matters which are, or have been, *sub judice*, or under enquiry (including disciplinary enquiries), or which are the subject of preliminary investigation proceedings;
(d) commercial and industrial confidentiality, including intellectual property;
(e) the confidentiality of personal data and/or files;
(f) material supplied by a third party without that party being under a legal obligation to do so;
(g) material, the disclosure of which would make it more likely that the environment to which such material related would be damaged.

4. The reasons for a refusal to provide the information requested must be given.

Article 10
Commission

1. A Commission, made up of representatives of each of the Contracting Parties, is hereby established. The Commission shall meet at regular intervals and at any time when, due to special circumstances, it is so decided in accordance with the Rules of Procedure.

2. It shall be the duty of the Commission:

(a) to supervise the implementation of the Convention;
(b) generally to review the condition of the maritime area, the effectiveness of the measures being adopted, the priorities and the need for any additional or different measures;
(c) to draw up, in accordance with the General Obligations of the Convention, programmes and measures for the prevention and elimination of pollution and for the control of activities which may, directly or indirectly, adversely affect the maritime area; such programmes and measure may, when appropriate, include economic instruments;
(d) to establish at regular intervals its programme of work;
(e) to set up such subsidiary bodies as it considers necessary and to define their terms of reference;
(f) to consider and, where appropriate, adopt proposals for the amendment of the Convention in accordance with Articles 15, 16, 17, 18, 19 and 27;
(g) to discharge the functions conferred by Articles 21 and 23 and such other functions as may be appropriate under the terms of the Convention;

3. To these ends the Commission may, *inter alia,*adopt decisions and recommendations in accordance with Article 13.

4. The Commission shall draw up its Rules of Procedure which shall be adopted by unanimous vote of the Contracting Parties.

5. The Commission shall draw up its Financial Regulations which shall be adopted by unanimous vote of the Contracting Parties.

Article 11
Observers

1. The Commission may, by unanimous vote of the Contracting Parties, decide to admit as an observer:

(a) any State which is not a Contracting Party to the Convention;
(b) any international governmental or any non-governmental organisation the activities of which are related to the Convention.

2. Such observers may participate in meetings of the Commission but without the right to vote and may present to the Commission any information or reports relevant to the objectives of the Convention.

3. The conditions for the admission and the participation of observers shall be set in the Rules of Procedure of the Commission.

Article 12
Secretariat

1. A permanent Secretariat is hereby established.

2. The Commission shall appoint an Executive Secretary and determine the duties of that post and the terms and conditions upon which it is to be held.

3. The Executive Secretary shall perform the functions that are necessary for the administration of the Convention and for the work of the Commission as well as the other tasks entrusted to the Executive Secretary by the Commission in accordance with its Rules of Procedure and its Financial Regulations.

Article 13
Decisions and recommendations

1. Decisions and recommendations shall be adopted by unanimous vote of the Contracting Parties. Should unanimity not be attainable, and unless otherwise provided in the Convention, the Commission may nonetheless adopt decisions or recommendations by a three-quarters majority vote of the Contracting Parties.

2. A decision shall be binding on the expiry of a period of two hundred days after its adoption for those Contracting Parties that voted for it and have not within that period notified the Executive Secretary in writing that they are unable to accept the decision, provided that at the expiry of that period three-quarters of the Contracting Parties have either voted for the decision and not withdrawn their acceptance or notified the Executive Secretary in writing that they are able to accept the decision. Such a decision shall become binding on any other Contracting Party which has notified the Executive Secretary in writing that it is able to accept the decision from the moment of that notification or after the expiry of a period of two hundred days after the adoption of the decision, whichever is later.

3. A notification under paragraph 2 of this Article to the Executive Secretary may indicate that a Contracting Party is unable to accept a decision insofar as it relates to one or more of its dependent or autonomous territories to which the Convention applies.

4. All decisions adopted by the Commission shall, where appropriate, contain provisions specifying the timetable by which the decision shall be implemented.

5. Recommendations shall have no binding force.

6. Decisions concerning any Annex or Appendix shall be taken only by the Contracting Parties bound by the Annex or Appendix concerned.

Article 14
Status of Annexes and Appendices

1. The Annexes and Appendices form an integral part of the Convention.
2. The Appendices shall be of a scientific, technical or administrative nature.

Article 15
Amendment of the Convention

1. Without prejudice to the provisions of paragraph 2 of Article 27 and to specific provisions applicable to the adoption or amendment of Annexes or Appendices, an amendment to the Convention shall be governed by the present Article.

2. Any Contracting Party may propose an amendment to the Convention. The text of the proposed amendment shall be communicated to the Contracting Parties by the Executive Secretary of the Commission at least six months before the meeting of the Commission at which it is proposed for adoption. The Executive Secretary shall also communicate the proposed amendment to the signatories to the Convention for information.

3. The Commission shall adopt the amendment by unanimous vote of the Contracting Parties.

4. The adopted amendment shall be submitted by the Depositary Government to the Contracting Parties for ratification, acceptance or approval. Ratification, acceptance or approval of the amendment shall be notified to the Depositary Government in writing.

5. The amendment shall enter into force for those Contracting Parties which have ratified, accepted or approved it on the thirtieth day after receipt by the Depositary Government of notification of its ratification, acceptance or approval by at least seven Contracting Parties. Thereafter the amendment shall enter into force for any other Contracting Party on the thirtieth day after that Contracting Party has deposited its instrument of ratification, acceptance or approval of the amendment.

Article 16
Adoption of Annexes

The provisions of Article 15 relating to the amendment of the Convention shall also apply to the proposal, adoption and entry into force of an Annex to the Convention, except that the Commission shall adopt any Annex referred to in Article 7 by a three-quarters majority vote of the Contracting Parties.

Article 17
Amendment of Annexes

1. The provisions of Article 15 relating to the amendment of the Convention shall also apply to an amendment to an Annex to the Convention, except that the Commission shall adopt amendments to any Annex referred to in Articles 3, 4, 5, 6 or 7 by a three-quarters majority vote of the Contracting Parties bound by that Annex.

2. If the amendment of an Annex is related to an amendment to the Convention, the amendment of the Annex shall be governed by the same provisions as apply to the amendment to the Convention.

Article 18
Adoption of Appendices

1. If a proposed Appendix is related to an amendment to the Convention or an Annex, proposed for adoption in accordance with Article 15 or Article 17, the proposal, adoption and entry into force of that Appendix shall be governed

by the same provisions as apply to the proposal, adoption and entry into force of that amendment.

2. If a proposed Appendix is related to an Annex to the Convention, proposed for adoption in accordance with Article 16, the proposal, adoption and entry into force of that Appendix shall be governed by the same provisions as apply to the proposal, adoption and entry into force of that Annex.

Article 19
Amendment of Appendices

1. Any Contracting Party bound by an Appendix may propose an amendment to that Appendix. The text of the proposed amendment shall be communicated to all Contracting Parties to the Convention by the Executive Secretary of the Commission as provided for in paragraph 2 of Article 15.

2. The Commission shall adopt the amendment to an Appendix by a three-quarters majority vote of the Contracting Parties bound by that Appendix.

3. An amendment to an Appendix shall enter into force on the expiry of a period of two hundred days after its adoption for those Contracting Parties which are bound by that Appendix and have not within that period notified the Depositary Government in writing that they are unable to accept that amendment, provided that at the expiry of that period three-quarters of the Contracting Parties bound by that Appendix have either voted for the amendment and not withdrawn their acceptance or have notified the Depositary Government in writing that they are able to accept the amendment.

4. A notification under paragraph 3 of this Article to the Depositary Government may indicate that a Contracting Party is unable to accept the amendment insofar as it relates to one or more of its dependent or autonomous territories to which the Convention applies.

5. An amendment to an Appendix shall become binding on any other Contracting Party bound by the Appendix which has notified the Depositary Government in writing that it is able to accept the amendment from the moment of that notification or after the expiry of a period of two hundred days after the adoption of the amendment, whichever is later.

6. The Depositary Government shall without delay notify all Contracting Parties of any such notification received.

7. If the amendment of an Appendix is related to an amendment to the Convention or an Annex, the amendment of the Appendix shall be governed by the same provisions as apply to the amendment to the Convention or that Annex.

Article 20
Right to vote

1. Each Contracting Party shall have one vote in the Commission.

2. Notwithstanding the provisions of paragraph 1 of this Article, the European Economic Community and other regional economic integration

organisations, within the areas of their competence, are entitled to a number of votes equal to the number of their Member States which are Contracting Parties to the Convention. Those organisations shall not exercise their right to vote in cases where their Member States exercise theirs and conversely.

Article 21
Transboundary pollution

1. When pollution originating from a Contracting Party is likely to prejudice the interests of one or more of the other Contracting Parties to the Convention, the Contracting Parties concerned shall enter into consultation, at the request of any one of them, with a view to negotiating a cooperation agreement.

2. At the request of any Contracting Party concerned, the Commission shall consider the question and may make recommendations with a view to reaching a satisfactory solution.

3. An agreement referred to in paragraph 1 of this Article may, *inter alia*, define the areas to which it shall apply, the quality objectives to be achieved and the methods for achieving these objectives, including methods for the application of appropriate standards and the scientific and technical information to be collected.

4. The Contracting Parties signatory to such an agreement shall, through the medium of the Commission, inform the other Contracting Parties of its purport and of the progress made in putting it into effect.

Article 22
Reporting to the Commission

The Contracting Parties shall report to the Commission at regular intervals on:

(a) the legal, regulatory, or other measures taken by them for the implementation of the provisions of the Convention and of decisions and recommendations adopted thereunder, including in particular measures taken to prevent and punish conduct in contravention of those provisions;

(b) the effectiveness of the measures referred to in subparagraph (a) of this Article;

(c) problems encountered in the implementation of the provisions referred to in subparagraph (a) of this Article.

Article 23
Compliance

The Commission shall:

(a) on the basis of the periodical reports referred to in Article 22 and any other report submitted by the Contracting Parties, assess their compliance with the Convention and the decisions and recommendations adopted thereunder;

(b) when appropriate, decide upon and call for steps to bring about full compliance with the Convention, and decisions adopted thereunder, and promote the implementation of recommendations, including measures to assist a Contracting Party to carry out its obligations.

Article 24
Regionalisation

The Commission may decide that any decision or recommendation adopted by it shall apply to all, or a specified part, of the maritime area and may provide for different timetables to be applied, having regard to the differences between ecological and economic conditions in the various regions and sub-regions covered by the Convention.

Article 25
Signature

The Convention shall be open for signature at Paris from 22nd September 1992 to 30th June 1993 by:

(a) the Contracting Parties to the Oslo Convention or the Paris Convention;
(b) any other coastal State bordering the maritime area;
(c) any State located upstream on watercourses reaching the maritime area;
(d) any regional economic integration organisation having as a member at least one State to which any of the subparagraphs (a) to (c) of this Article applies.

Article 26
Ratification, acceptance or approval

The Convention shall be subject to ratification, acceptance or approval. The instruments of ratification, acceptance or approval shall be deposited with the Government of the French Republic.

Article 27
Accessions

1. After 30th June 1993, the Convention shall be open for accession by the States and regional economic integration organisations referred to in Article 25.

2. The Contracting Parties may unanimously invite States or regional economic integration organisations not referred to in Article 25 to accede to the Convention. In the case of such an accession, the definition of the maritime area shall, if necessary, be amended by a decision of the Commission adopted by unanimous vote of the Contracting Parties. Any such amendment shall enter into force after unanimous approval of all the Contracting Parties on the thirtieth day after the receipt of the last notification by the Depositary Government.

3. Any such accession shall relate to the Convention including any Annex and any Appendix that have been adopted at the date of such accession, except when the instrument of accession contains an express declaration of non-acceptance of one or several Annexes other than Annexes I, II, III and IV.

4. The instruments of accession shall be deposited with the Government of the French Republic.

Article 28
Reservations

No reservation to the Convention may be made.

Article 29
Entry into force

1. The Convention shall enter into force on the thirtieth day following the date on which all Contracting Parties to the Oslo Convention and all Contracting Parties to the Paris Convention have deposited their instrument of ratification, acceptance, approval or accession.

2. For any State or regional economic integration organisation not referred to in paragraph 1 of this Article, the Convention shall enter into force in accordance with paragraph 1 of this Article, or on the thirtieth day following the date of the deposit of the instrument of ratification, acceptance, approval or accession by that State or regional economic integration organisations, whichever is later.

Article 30
Withdrawal

1. At any time after the expiry of two years from the date of entry into force of the Convention for a Contracting Party, that Contracting Party may withdraw from the Convention by notification in writing to the Depositary Government.

2. Except as may be otherwise provided in an Annex other than Annexes I to IV to the Convention, any Contracting Party may at any time after the expiry of two years from the date of entry into force of such Annex for that Contracting Party withdraw from such Annex by notification in writing to the Depositary Government.

3. Any withdrawal referred to in paragraphs 1 and 2 of this Article shall take effect one year after the date on which the notification of that withdrawal is received by the Depositary Government.

Article 31
Replacement of the Oslo and Paris Conventions

1. Upon its entry into force, the Convention shall replace the Oslo and Paris Conventions as between the Contracting Parties.

2. Notwithstanding paragraph 1 of this Article, decisions, recommendations and all other agreements adopted under the Oslo Convention or the Paris Convention shall continue to be applicable, unaltered in their legal nature, to

the extent that they are compatible with, or not explicitly terminated by, the Convention, any decisions or, in the case of existing recommendations, any recommendations adopted thereunder.

Article 32
Settlement of disputes

1. Any disputes between Contracting Parties relating to the interpretation or application of the Convention, which cannot be settled otherwise by the Contracting Parties concerned, for instance by means of inquiry or conciliation within the Commission, shall at the request of any of those Contracting Parties, be submitted to arbitration under the conditions laid down in this Article.

2. Unless the parties to the dispute decide otherwise, the procedure of the arbitration referred to in paragraph 1 of this Article shall be in accordance with paragraphs 3 to 10 of this Article.

3.

(a) At the request addressed by one Contracting Party to another Contracting Party in accordance with paragraph 1 of this Article, an arbitral tribunal shall be constituted. The request for arbitration shall state the subject matter of the application including in particular the Articles of the Convention, the interpretation or application of which is in dispute.

(b) The applicant party shall inform the Commission that it has requested the setting up of an arbitral tribunal, stating the name of the other party to the dispute and the Articles of the Convention the interpretation or application of which, in its opinion, is in dispute. The Commission shall forward the information thus received to all Contracting Parties to the Convention.

4. The arbitral tribunal shall consist of three members: each of the parties to the dispute shall appoint an arbitrator; the two arbitrators so appointed shall designate by common agreement the third arbitrator who shall be the chairman of the tribunal. The latter shall not be a national of one of the parties to the dispute, nor have his usual place of residence in the territory of one of these parties, nor be employed by any of them, nor have dealt with the case in any other capacity.

5.

(a) If the chairman of the arbitral tribunal has not been designated within two months of the appointment of the second arbitrator, the President of the International Court of Justice shall, at the request of either party, designate him within a further two months' period.

(b) If one of the parties to the dispute does not appoint an arbitrator within two months of receipt of the request, the other party may inform the President of the International Court of Justice who shall designate the chairman of the arbitral tribunal within a further two months' period. Upon designation, the chairman of the arbitral tribunal shall request the party which has not appointed an arbitrator to do so within two months. After such period, he shall inform the President of the International Court of Justice who shall make this appointment within a further two months' period.

6.

(a) The arbitral tribunal shall decide according to the rules of international law and, in particular, those of the Convention.
(b) Any arbitral tribunal constituted under the provisions of this Article shall draw up its own rules of procedure.
(c) In the event of a dispute as to whether the arbitral tribunal has jurisdiction, the matter shall be decided by the decision of the arbitral tribunal.

7.

(a) The decisions of the arbitral tribunal, both on procedure and on substance, shall be taken by majority voting of its members.
(b) The arbitral tribunal may take all appropriate measures in order to establish the facts. It may, at the request of one of the parties, recommend essential interim measures of protection.
(c) If two or more arbitral tribunals constituted under the provisions of this Article are seized of requests with identical or similar subjects, they may inform themselves of the procedures for establishing the facts and take them into account as far as possible.
(d) The parties to the dispute shall provide all facilities necessary for the effective conduct of the proceedings.
(e) The absence or default of a party to the dispute shall not constitute an impediment to the proceedings.

8. Unless the arbitral tribunal determines otherwise because of the particular circumstances of the case, the expenses of the tribunal, including the remuneration of its members, shall be borne by the parties to the dispute in equal shares. The tribunal shall keep a record of all its expenses, and shall furnish a final statement thereof to the parties.

9. Any Contracting Party that has an interest of a legal nature in the subject matter of the dispute which may be affected by the decision in the case, may intervene in the proceedings with the consent of the tribunal.

10.

(a) The award of the arbitral tribunal shall be accompanied by a statement of reasons. It shall be final and binding upon the parties to the dispute.
(b) Any dispute which may arise between the parties concerning the interpretation or execution of the award may be submitted by either party to the arbitral tribunal which made the award or, if the latter cannot be seized thereof, to another arbitral tribunal constituted for this purpose in the same manner as the first.

Article 33
Duties of the Depositary Government

The Depositary Government shall inform the Contracting Parties and the signatories to the Convention:

(a) of the deposit of instruments of ratification, acceptance, approval or accession, of declarations of non-acceptance and of notifications of withdrawal in accordance with Articles 26, 27 and 30;
(b) of the date on which the Convention comes into force in accordance with Article 29;
(c) of the receipt of notifications of acceptance, of the deposit of instruments of ratification, acceptance, approval or accession and of the entry into force of amendments to the Convention and of the adoption and amendment of Annexes or Appendices, in accordance with Articles 15, 16, 17, 18 and 19.

Article 34
Original text

The original of the Convention, of which the French and English texts shall be equally authentic, shall be deposited with the Government of the French Republic which shall send certified copies thereof to the Contracting Parties and the signatories to the Convention and shall deposit a certified copy with the Secretary General of the United Nations for registration and publication in accordance with Article 102 of the United Nations Charter.

IN WITNESS WHEREOF, the undersigned, being duly authorised by their respective Governments, have signed this Convention.

DONE at Paris, on the twenty-second day of September 1992

Annex I
On the prevention and elimination of pollution from land-based sources

Article 1

1. When adopting programmes and measures for the purpose of this Annex, the Contracting Parties shall require, either individually or jointly, the use of

– best available techniques for point sources
– best environmental practice for point and diffuse sources including, where appropriate, clean technology.

2. When setting priorities and in assessing the nature and extent of the programmes and measures and their time scales, the Contracting Parties shall use the criteria given in Appendix 2.

3. The Contracting Parties shall take preventive measures to minimise the risk of pollution caused by accidents.

4. When adopting programmes and measures in relation to radioactive substances, including waste, the Contracting Parties shall also take account of:

(a) the recommendations of the other appropriate international organisations and agencies;
(b) the monitoring procedures recommended by these international organisations and agencies.

Article 2

1. Point source discharges to the maritime area, and releases into water or air which reach and may affect the maritime area, shall be strictly subject to authorisation or regulation by the competent authorities of the Contracting Parties. Such authorisation or regulation shall, in particular, implement relevant decisions of the Commission which bind the relevant Contracting Party.

2. The Contracting Parties shall provide for a system of regular monitoring and inspection by their competent authorities to assess compliance with authorisations and regulations of releases into water or air.

Article 3

For the purposes of this Annex, it shall, *inter alia,* be the duty of the Commission to draw up:

(a) plans for the reduction and phasing out of substances that are toxic, persistent and liable to bioaccumulate arising from land-based sources;
(b) when appropriate, programmes and measures for the reduction of inputs of nutrients from urban, municipal, industrial, agricultural and other sources.

Annex II
On the prevention and elimination of pollution by dumping or incineration

Article 1

This Annex shall not apply to any deliberate disposal in the maritime area of:

(a) wastes or other matter from offshore installations;
(b) offshore installations and offshore pipelines.

Article 2

Incineration is prohibited.

Article 3

1. The dumping of all wastes or other matter is prohibited, except for those wastes or other matter listed in paragraphs 2 and 3 of this Article.

2. The list referred to in paragraph 1 of this Article is as follows:

(a) dredged material;
(b) inert materials of natural origin, that is solid, chemically unprocessed geological material the chemical constituents of which are unlikely to be released into the marine environment;
(c) sewage sludge until 31st December 1998;
(d) fish waste from industrial fish processing operations;
(e) vessels or aircraft until, at the latest, 31st December 2004.

3.

(a) The dumping of low and intermediate level radioactive substances, including wastes, is prohibited.
(b) [1] As an exception to subparagraph 3(a) of this Article, those Contracting Parties, the United Kingdom and France, who wish to retain the option of an exception to subparagraph 3(a) in any case not before the expiry of a period of 15 years from 1st January 1993, shall report to the meeting of the Commission at Ministerial level in 1997 on the steps taken to explore alternative land-based options.
(c) Unless, at or before the expiry of this period of 15 years, the Commission decides by a unanimous vote not to continue the exception provided in subparagraph 3(b), it shall take a decision pursuant to Article 13 of the Convention on the prolongation for a period of 10 years after 1st January 2008 of the prohibition, after which another meeting of the Commission at Ministerial level shall be held. Those Contracting Parties mentioned in subparagraph 3(b) of this Article still wishing to retain the option mentioned in subparagraph 3(b) shall report to the Commission meetings to be held at Ministerial level at two yearly intervals from 1999 onwards about the progress in establishing alternative land-based options and on the results of scientific studies which show that any potential dumping operations would not result in hazards to human health, harm to living resources or marine ecosystems, damage to amenities or interference with other legitimate uses of the sea.

---

[1] After the entry into force of OSPAR Decision 98/2 on Dumping of Radioactive Waste on 9 February 1999, subparagraphs (b) and (c) of this paragraph ceased to have effect.

Article 4

1. The Contracting Parties shall ensure that:

(a) no wastes or other matter listed in paragraph 2 of Article 3 of this Annex shall be dumped without authorisation by their competent authorities, or regulation;
(b) such authorisation or regulation is in accordance with the relevant applicable criteria, guidelines and procedures adopted by the Commission in accordance with Article 6 of this Annex;
(c) with the aim of avoiding situations in which the same dumping operation is authorised or regulated by more than one Contracting Party, their competent authorities shall, as appropriate, consult before granting an authorisation or applying regulation.

2. Any authorisation or regulation under paragraph 1 of this Article shall not permit the dumping of vessels or aircraft containing substances which result or are likely to result in hazards to human health, harm to living resources and marine ecosystems, damage to amenities or interference with other legitimate uses of the sea.

3. Each Contracting Party shall keep, and report to the Commission records of the nature and the quantities of wastes or other matter dumped in accordance with paragraph 1 of this Article, and of the dates, places and methods of dumping.

Article 5

No placement of matter in the maritime area for a purpose other than that for which it was originally designed or constructed shall take place without authorisation or regulation by the competent authority of the relevant Contracting Party. Such authorisation or regulation shall be in accordance with the relevant applicable criteria, guidelines and procedures adopted by the Commission in accordance with Article 6 of this Annex. This provision shall not be taken to permit the dumping of wastes or other matter otherwise prohibited under this Annex.

Article 6

For the purposes of this Annex, it shall, *inter alia*, be the duty of the Commission to draw up and adopt criteria, guidelines and procedures relating to the dumping of wastes or other matter listed in paragraph 2 of Article 3, and to the placement of matter referred to in Article 5, of this Annex, with a view to preventing and eliminating pollution.

Article 7

The provisions of this Annex concerning dumping shall not apply in case of *force majeure,* due to stress of weather or any other cause, when the safety of human life or of a vessel or aircraft is threatened. Such dumping shall be so conducted as to minimise the likelihood of damage to human or marine life and shall immediately be reported to the Commission, together with full details of the circumstances and of the nature and quantities of the wastes or other matter dumped.

Article 8

The Contracting Parties shall take appropriate measures, both individually and within relevant international organisations, to prevent and eliminate pollution resulting from the abandonment of vessels or aircraft in the maritime area caused by accidents. In the absence of relevant guidance from such international organisations, the measures taken by individual Contracting Parties should be based on such guidelines as the Commission may adopt.

Article 9

In an emergency, if a Contracting Party considers that wastes or other matter the dumping of which is prohibited under this Annex cannot be disposed of on land without unacceptable danger or damage, it shall forthwith consult other Contracting Parties with a view to finding the most satisfactory methods of storage or the most satisfactory means of destruction or disposal under the prevailing circumstances. The Contracting Party shall inform the Commission of the steps adopted following this consultation. The Contracting Parties pledge themselves to assist one another in such situations.

Article 10

1. Each Contracting Party shall ensure compliance with the provisions of this Annex:

(a) by vessels or aircraft registered in its territory;
(b) by vessels or aircraft loading in its territory the wastes or other matter which are to be dumped or incinerated;
(c) by vessels or aircraft believed to be engaged in dumping or incineration within its internal waters or within its territorial sea or within that part of the sea beyond and adjacent to the territorial sea under the jurisdiction of the coastal state to the extent recognised by international law.

2. Each Contracting Party shall issue instructions to its maritime inspection vessels and aircraft and to other appropriate services to report to its authorities any incidents or conditions in the maritime area which give rise to suspicions that dumping in contravention of the provisions of the present Annex has occurred or is about to occur. Any Contracting Party whose authorities receive such a report shall, if it considers it appropriate, accordingly inform any other Contracting Party concerned.

3. Nothing in this Annex shall abridge the sovereign immunity to which certain vessels are entitled under international law.

Annex III
On the prevention and elimination of pollution from offshore sources

Article 1

This Annex shall not apply to any deliberate disposal in the maritime area of:

(a) wastes or other matter from vessels or aircraft;
(b) vessels or aircraft.

Article 2

1. When adopting programmes and measures for the purpose of this Annex, the Contracting Parties shall require, either individually or jointly, the use of:

(a) best available techniques
(b) best environmental practice including, where appropriate, clean technology.

2. When setting priorities and in assessing the nature and extent of the programmes and measures and their time scales, the Contracting Parties shall use the criteria given in Appendix 2.

Article 3

1. Any dumping of wastes or other matter from offshore installations is prohibited.
2. This prohibition does not relate to discharges or emissions from offshore sources.

Article 4

1. The use on, or the discharge or emission from, offshore sources of substances which may reach and affect the maritime area shall be strictly subject to authorisation or regulation by the competent authorities of the Contracting Parties. Such authorisation or regulation shall, in particular, implement the relevant applicable decisions, recommendations and all other agreements adopted under the Convention.
2. The competent authorities of the Contracting Parties shall provide for a system of monitoring and inspection to assess compliance with authorisation or regulation as provided for in paragraph 1 of Article 4 of this Annex.

Article 5

1. No disused offshore installation or disused offshore pipeline shall be dumped and no disused offshore installation shall be left wholly or partly in

place in the maritime area without a permit issued by the competent authority of the relevant Contracting Party on a case-by-case basis. The Contracting Parties shall ensure that their authorities, when granting such permits, shall implement the relevant applicable decisions, recommendations and all other agreements adopted under the Convention.

2. No such permit shall be issued if the disused offshore installation or disused offshore pipeline contains substances which result or are likely to result in hazards to human health, harm to living resources and marine ecosystems, damage to amenities or interference with other legitimate uses of the sea.

3. Any Contracting Party which intends to take the decision to issue a permit for the dumping of a disused offshore installation or a disused offshore pipeline placed in the maritime area after 1st January 1998 shall, through the medium of the Commission, inform the other Contracting Parties of its reasons for accepting such dumping, in order to make consultation possible.

4. Each Contracting Party shall keep, and report to the Commission, records of the disused offshore installations and disused offshore pipelines dumped and of the disused offshore installations left in place in accordance with the provisions of this Article, and of the dates, places and methods of dumping.

Article 6

Articles 3 and 5 of this Annex shall not apply in case of *force majeure,* due to stress of weather or any other cause, when the safety of human life or of an offshore installation is threatened. Such dumping shall be so conducted as to minimise the likelihood of damage to human or marine life and shall immediately be reported to the Commission, together with full details of the circumstances and of the nature and quantities of the matter dumped.

Article 7

The Contracting Parties shall take appropriate measures, both individually and within relevant international organisations, to prevent and eliminate pollution resulting from the abandonment of offshore installations in the maritime area caused by accidents. In the absence of relevant guidance from such international organisations, the measures taken by individual Contracting Parties should be based on such guidelines as the Commission may adopt.

Article 8

No placement of a disused offshore installation or a disused offshore pipeline in the maritime area for a purpose other than that for which it was originally designed or constructed shall take place without authorisation or regulation by the competent authority of the relevant Contracting Party. Such authorisation or regulation shall be in accordance with the relevant applicable criteria, guidelines and procedures adopted by the Commission in accordance with subparagraph (d) of Article 10 of this Annex. This provision shall not be taken to permit the dumping of disused offshore installations or disused offshore pipelines in contravention of the provisions of this Annex.

Article 9

1. Each Contracting Party shall issue instructions to its maritime inspection vessels and aircraft and to other appropriate services to report to its authorities any incidents or conditions in the maritime area which give rise to suspicions that a contravention of the provisions of the present Annex has occurred or is about to occur. Any Contracting Party whose authorities receive such a report shall, if it considers it appropriate, accordingly inform any other Contracting Party concerned.

2. Nothing in this Annex shall abridge the sovereign immunity to which certain vessels are entitled under international law.

Article 10

For the purposes of this Annex, it shall, *inter alia,* be the duty of the Commission:

(a) to collect information about substances which are used in offshore activities and, on the basis of that information, to agree lists of substances for the purposes of paragraph 1 of Article 4 of this Annex;
(b) to list substances which are toxic, persistent and liable to bioaccumulate and to draw up plans for the reduction and phasing out of their use on, or discharge from, offshore sources;
(c) to draw up criteria, guidelines and procedures for the prevention of pollution from dumping of disused offshore installations and of disused offshore pipelines, and the leaving in place of offshore installations, in the maritime area;
(d) to draw up criteria, guidelines and procedures relating to the placement of disused offshore installations and disused offshore pipelines referred to in Article 8 of this Annex, with a view to preventing and eliminating pollution.

Annex IV
On the assessment of the quality of the marine environment

Article 1

1. For the purposes of this Annex 'monitoring' means the repeated measurement of:

(a) the quality of the marine environment and each of its compartments, that is, water, sediments and biota;
(b) activities or natural and anthropogenic inputs which may affect the quality of the marine environment;
(c) the effects of such activities and inputs.

2. Monitoring may be undertaken either for the purposes of ensuring compliance with the Convention, with the objective of identifying patterns and trends or for research purposes.

Article 2

For the purposes of this Annex, the Contracting Parties shall:

(a) cooperate in carrying out monitoring programmes and submit the resulting data to the Commission;

(b) comply with quality assurance prescriptions and participate in intercalibration exercises;

(c) use and develop, individually or preferably jointly, other duly validated scientific assessment tools, such as modelling, remote sensing and progressive risk assessment strategies;

(d) carry out, individually or preferably jointly, research which is considered necessary to assess the quality of the marine environment, and to increase knowledge and scientific understanding of the marine environment and, in particular, of the relationship between inputs, concentration and effects;

(e) take into account scientific progress which is considered to be useful for such assessment purposes and which has been made elsewhere either on the initiative of individual researchers and research institutions, or through other national and international research programmes or under the auspices of the European Economic Community or other regional economic integration organisations.

Article 3

For the purposes of this Annex, it shall, *inter alia*, be the duty of the Commission:

(a) to define and implement programmes of collaborative monitoring and assessment-related research, to draw up codes of practice for the guidance of participants in carrying out these monitoring programmes and to approve the presentation and interpretation of their results;

(b) to carry out assessments taking into account the results of relevant monitoring and research and the data relating to inputs of substances or energy into the maritime area which are provided by virtue of other Annexes to the Convention, as well as other relevant information;

(c) to seek, where appropriate, the advice or services of competent regional organisations and other competent international organisations and competent bodies with a view to incorporating the latest results of scientific research;

(d) to cooperate with competent regional organisations and other competent international organisations in carrying out quality status assessments.

Annex V
On the protection and conservation of the ecosystems and biological diversity of the maritime area[1]

Article 1

For the purposes of this Annex and of Appendix 3 the definitions of 'biological diversity', 'ecosystem' and 'habitat' are those contained in the Convention on Biological Diversity of 5 June 1992.

Article 2

In fulfilling their obligation under the Convention to take, individually and jointly, the necessary measures to protect the maritime area against the adverse effects of human activities so as to safeguard human health and to conserve marine ecosystems and, when practicable, restore marine areas which have been adversely affected, as well as their obligation under the Convention on Biological Diversity of 5 June 1992 to develop strategies, plans or programmes for the conservation and sustainable use of biological diversity, Contracting Parties shall:

(a) take the necessary measures to protect and conserve the ecosystems and the biological diversity of the maritime area, and to restore, where practicable, marine areas which have been adversely affected; and

(b) cooperate in adopting programmes and measures for those purposes for the control of the human activities identified by the application of the criteria in Appendix 3.

Article 3

1. For the purposes of this Annex, it shall *inter alia* be the duty of the Commission:

(a) to draw up programmes and measures for the control of the human activities identified by the application of the criteria in Appendix 3;

(b) in doing so:

(i) to collect and review information on such activities and their effects on ecosystems and biological diversity;

---

[1] In accordance with Article 15.5 of the Convention, Annex V has entered into force:

- on 30 August 2000 for Finland, Spain, Switzerland, Luxembourg, European Community, United Kingdom and Denmark;
- on 5 October 2000 for Sweden;
- on 18 July 2001 for Iceland; on 22 July 2001 for Norway and on 24 August 2001 for the Netherlands;
- on 13 January 2002 for Germany.

Annex V will enter into force for any other Contracting Party on the thirtieth day after that Contracting Party has deposited its instrument of ratification, acceptance or approval.

(ii) to develop means, consistent with international law, for instituting protective, conservation, restorative or precautionary measures related to specific areas or sites or related to particular species or habitats;

(iii) subject to Article 4 of this Annex, to consider aspects of national strategies and guidelines on the sustainable use of components of biological diversity of the maritime area as they affect the various regions and sub-regions of that area;

(iv) subject to Article 4 of this Annex, to aim for the application of an integrated ecosystem approach.

(c) also in doing so, to take account of programmes and measures adopted by Contracting Parties for the protection and conservation of ecosystems within waters under their sovereignty or jurisdiction.

2. In the adoption of such programmes and measures, due consideration shall be given to the question whether any particular programme or measure should apply to all, or a specified part, of the maritime area.

Article 4

1. In accordance with the penultimate recital of the Convention, no programme or measure concerning a question relating to the management of fisheries shall be adopted under this Annex. However where the Commission considers that action is desirable in relation to such a question, it shall draw that question to the attention of the authority or international body competent for that question. Where action within the competence of the Commission is desirable to complement or support action by those authorities or bodies, the Commission shall endeavour to cooperate with them.

2. Where the Commission considers that action under this Annex is desirable in relation to a question concerning maritime transport, it shall draw that question to the attention of the International Maritime Organisation. The Contracting Parties who are members of the International Maritime Organisation shall endeavour to cooperate within that Organisation in order to achieve an appropriate response, including in relevant cases that Organisation's agreement to regional or local action, taking account of any guidelines developed by that Organisation on the designation of special areas, the identification of particularly sensitive areas or other matters.

Appendix 1
Criteria for the definition of practices and techniques mentioned in paragraph 3(b)(i) of Article 2 of the Convention

Best available techniques

1. The use of the best available techniques shall emphasise the use of non-waste technology, if available.

2. The term 'best available techniques' means the latest stage of development (state of the art) of processes, of facilities or of methods of operation which indicate the practical suitability of a particular measure for limiting discharges, emissions and waste. In determining whether a set of processes, facilities and methods of operation constitute the best available techniques in general or individual cases, special consideration shall be given to:

(a) comparable processes, facilities or methods of operation which have recently been successfully tried out;
(b) technological advances and changes in scientific knowledge and understanding;
(c) the economic feasibility of such techniques;
(d) time limits for installation in both new and existing plants;
(e) the nature and volume of the discharges and emissions concerned.

3. It therefore follows that what is 'best available techniques' for a particular process will change with time in the light of technological advances, economic and social factors, as well as changes in scientific knowledge and understanding.

4. If the reduction of discharges and emissions resulting from the use of best available techniques does not lead to environmentally acceptable results, additional measures have to be applied.

5. 'Techniques' include both the technology used and the way in which the installation is designed, built, maintained, operated and dismantled.

Best environmental practice

6. The term 'best environmental practice' means the application of the most appropriate combination of environmental control measures and strategies. In making a selection for individual cases, at least the following graduated range of measures should be considered:

(a) the provision of information and education to the public and to users about the environmental consequences of choice of particular activities and choice of products, their use and ultimate disposal;
(b) the development and application of codes of good environmental practice which covers all aspect of the activity in the product's life;
(c) the mandatory application of labels informing users of environmental risks related to a product, its use and ultimate disposal;
(d) saving resources, including energy;
(e) making collection and disposal systems available to the public;
(f) avoiding the use of hazardous substances or products and the generation of hazardous waste;
(g) recycling, recovery and re-use;
(h) the application of economic instruments to activities, products or groups of products;
(i) establishing a system of licensing, involving a range of restrictions or a ban.

7. In determining what combination of measures constitute best environmental practice, in general or individual cases, particular consideration should
be given to:

(a) the environmental hazard of the product and its production, use and ulti-
    mate disposal;
(b) the substitution by less polluting activities or substances;
(c) the scale of use;
(d) the potential environmental benefit or penalty of substitute materials or
    activities;
(e) advances and changes in scientific knowledge and understanding;
(f) time limits for implementation;
(g) social and economic implications.

8. It therefore follows that best environmental practice for a particular source
will change with time in the light of technological advances, economic and social
factors, as well as changes in scientific knowledge and understanding.

9. If the reduction of inputs resulting from the use of best environmental
practice does not lead to environmentally acceptable results, additional measures have to be applied and best environmental practice redefined.

Appendix 2
Criteria mentioned in paragraph 2 of Article 1 of Annex I and in paragraph 2 of Article 2 of Annex III

1. When setting priorities and in assessing the nature and extent of the
programmes and measures and their time scales, the Contracting Parties shall
use the criteria given below:

(a) persistency;
(b) toxicity or other noxious properties;
(c) tendency to bioaccumulation;
(d) radioactivity;
(e) the ratio between observed or (where the results of observations are not yet
    available) predicted concentrations and no observed effect concentrations;
(f) anthropogenically caused risk of eutrophication;
(g) transboundary significance;
(h) risk of undesirable changes in the marine ecosystem and irreversibility or
    durability of effects;
(i) interference with harvesting of sea-foods or with other legitimate uses of
    the sea;
(j) effects on the taste and/or smell of products for human consumption from
    the sea, or effects on smell, colour, transparency or other characteristics of
    the water in the marine environment;

(k) distribution pattern (i.e., quantities involved, use pattern and liability to reach the marine environment);

(l) non-fulfilment of environmental quality objectives.

2. These criteria are not necessarily of equal importance for the consideration of a particular substance or group of substances.

3. The above criteria indicate that substances which shall be subject to programmes and measures include:

(a) heavy metals and their compounds;

(b) organohalogen compounds (and substances which may form such compounds in the marine environment);

(c) organic compounds of phosphorus and silicon;

(d) biocides such as pesticides, fungicides, herbicides, insecticides, slimicides and chemicals used, *inter alia*, for the preservation of wood, timber, wood pulp, cellulose, paper, hides and textiles;

(e) oils and hydrocarbons of petroleum origin;

(f) nitrogen and phosphorus compounds;

(g) radioactive substances, including wastes;

(h) persistent synthetic materials which may float, remain in suspension or sink.

Appendix 3
Criteria for identifying human activities for the purpose of Annex V

1. The criteria to be used, taking into account regional differences, for identifying human activities for the purposes of Annex V are:

(a) the extent, intensity and duration of the human activity under consideration;

(b) actual and potential adverse effects of the human activity on specific species, communities and habitats;

(c) actual and potential adverse effects of the human activity on specific ecological processes;

(d) irreversibility or durability of these effects.

2. These criteria are not necessarily exhaustive or of equal importance for the consideration of a particular activity.

PART IV

Freshwater resources

14

Convention on the Protection and Use of Transboundary Watercourses and International Lakes, 17 March 1992

Editorial note

The object of the Convention on the Protection and Use of Transboundary Watercourses and International Lakes, adopted under the auspices of the UNECE, is to protect the environment from adverse effects of human use of transboundary water. The basic obligations are to 'take all appropriate measures' to achieve the following objectives: prevention, reduction and control of pollution; use of transboundary waters in a manner which conforms with 'ecologically sound and rational water management'; use of transboundary waters that is 'reasonable and equitable'; and conservation and restoration of ecosystems (Article 2(2)). Pollution prevention, reduction and control measures should be taken at source (Article 2(3)) and should not result in the transfer of pollution to other sectors of the environment (Article 2(4)). The guiding principles underlying the chosen measures are the 'precautionary principle', the 'polluter-pays principle' and the interests of future generations (Article 2(5)). Parties are specifically entitled to take measures stricter than those required by this Convention (Article 2(8)).

In particular, the Convention outlines several means by which its objectives can be met, including the following: application of 'non-waste technology'; licensing and control of waste water discharges based on 'best available technology'; biological treatment of municipal waste water, or an equivalent substitute; application of 'best available technology' and 'best environmental practices' for land-based sources of pollution; environmental impact assessment; and minimisation of risk of accidental pollution (Article 3(1)). 'Best available technology' is defined in Annex I to the Convention and guidelines on 'best environmental practices' are set out in Annex II. The Convention requires Parties to co-operate in research and development (Article 5) as well as in the exchange of relevant information (Article 6).

Riparian States are required to conclude agreements or other arrangements that establish joint bodies in order to reduce, prevent and control adverse effects on the environment (Article 9). The Convention requires Riparian States to consult with each other at the request of one of them in respect of any matter covered by the Convention (Article 10). Co-operation between Riparian States is required in monitoring the transboundary waters and in assessing the effectiveness of environmental protection measures (Article 11). Further co-operation is required in research and development (Article 12); exchange of information (Article 13); warning systems (Article 14); and mutual assistance (Article 15). The Convention also requires Parties to make available to the public information on the conditions of watercourses, the measures taken to control environmental harm, and the effectiveness of those measures (Article 16).

The Convention provides for regular meetings of the Parties to review the Convention and consider amendments or any other appropriate action (Article 17). Secretariat services are to be provided by the UNECE (Article 19). In addition to any means chosen by the Parties, the Convention provides two optional dispute resolution venues: arbitration in accordance with the provisions of Annex IV and submission to the ICJ, with preference given to the ICJ unless the Parties agree otherwise (Article 22). Amendments require adoption by a consensus of the Parties present at a meeting of the Parties and enter into force for those that accept them upon ratification of two-thirds of Parties (Article 21).

On 17 June 1999 the Parties to the Convention adopted the Protocol on Water and Health (reproduced below). A second Protocol on civil liability for transboundary damage caused by hazardous activities has been adopted in May 2003 by the Parties to the Convention jointly with the Parties to the Industrial Accidents Convention.

Date of signature: 17 March 1992

Entry into force: 6 October 1996

Depositary: Secretary-General of the United Nations

Contracting Parties: Albania, Austria, Azerbaijan, Belgium, Croatia, Czech Republic, Denmark, Estonia, Finland, France, Germany, Greece, Hungary, Italy, Kazakhstan, Latvia, Liechtenstein, Lithuania, Luxembourg, Netherlands, Norway, Poland, Portugal, Republic of Moldova, Romania, Russian Federation, Slovakia, Slovenia, Spain, Sweden, Switzerland, European Community.

Website: www.unece.org/env/water/

Convention on the Protection and Use of Transboundary Watercourses and International Lakes

Preamble

The Parties to this Convention,

Mindful that the protection and use of transboundary watercourses and international lakes are important and urgent tasks, the effective accomplishment of which can only be ensured by enhanced cooperation,

Concerned over the existence and threats of adverse effects, in the short or long term, of changes in the conditions of transboundary watercourses and international lakes on the environment, economies and well-being of the member countries of the Economic Commission for Europe (ECE),

Emphasizing the need for strengthened national and international measures to prevent, control and reduce the release of hazardous substances into the aquatic environment and to abate eutrophication and acidification, as well as pollution of the marine environment, in particular coastal areas, from land-based sources,

Commending the efforts already undertaken by the ECE Governments to strengthen cooperation, on bilateral and multilateral levels, for the prevention, control and reduction of transboundary pollution, sustainable water management, conservation of water resources and environmental protection,

Recalling the pertinent provisions and principles of the Declaration of the Stockholm Conference on the Human Environment, the Final Act of the Conference on Security and Cooperation in Europe (CSCE), the Concluding Documents of the Madrid and Vienna Meetings of Representatives of the Participating States of the CSCE, and the Regional Strategy for Environmental Protection and Rational Use of Natural Resources in ECE Member Countries covering the Period up to the Year 2000 and Beyond,

Conscious of the role of the United Nations Economic Commission for Europe in promoting international cooperation for the prevention, control and reduction of transboundary water pollution and sustainable use of transboundary waters, and in this regard recalling the ECE Declaration of Policy on Prevention and Control of Water Pollution, including Transboundary Pollution; the ECE Declaration of Policy on the Rational Use of Water; the ECE Principles Regarding Cooperation in the Field of Transboundary Waters; the ECE Charter on Groundwater Management; and the Code of Conduct on Accidental Pollution of Transboundary Inland Waters,

Referring to decisions I (42) and I (44) adopted by the Economic Commission for Europe at its forty-second and forty-fourth sessions, respectively, and the outcome of the CSCE Meeting on the Protection of the Environment (Sofia, Bulgaria, 16 October – 3 November 1989),

Emphasizing that cooperation between member countries in regard to the protection and use of transboundary waters shall be implemented primarily through the elaboration of agreements between countries bordering the same waters, especially where no such agreements have yet been reached,

Have agreed as follows:

Article 1
Definitions

For the purposes of this Convention,

1. 'Transboundary waters' means any surface or ground waters which mark, cross or are located on boundaries between two or more States; wherever transboundary waters flow directly into the sea, these transboundary waters end at a straight line across their respective mouths between points on the low-water line of their banks;

2. 'Transboundary impact' means any significant adverse effect on the environment resulting from a change in the conditions of transboundary waters caused by a human activity, the physical origin of which is situated wholly or in part within an area under the jurisdiction of a Party, within an area under the jurisdiction of another Party. Such effects on the environment include effects on human health and safety, flora, fauna, soil, air, water, climate, landscape and historical monuments or other physical structures or the interaction among these factors; they also include effects on the cultural heritage or socio-economic conditions resulting from alterations to those factors;

3. 'Party' means, unless the text otherwise indicates, a Contracting Party to this Convention;

4. 'Riparian Parties' means the Parties bordering the same transboundary waters;

5. 'Joint body' means any bilateral or multilateral commission or other appropriate institutional arrangements for cooperation between the Riparian Parties;

6. 'Hazardous substances' means substances which are toxic, carcinogenic, mutagenic, teratogenic or bio-accumulative, especially when they are persistent;

7. 'Best available technology' (the definition is contained in annex I to this Convention).

Part I
Provisions relating to all Parties

Article 2
General provisions

1. The Parties shall take all appropriate measures to prevent, control and reduce any transboundary impact.

2. The Parties shall, in particular, take all appropriate measures:

(a) To prevent, control and reduce pollution of waters causing or likely to cause transboundary impact;
(b) To ensure that transboundary waters are used with the aim of ecologically sound and rational water management, conservation of water resources and environmental protection;
(c) To ensure that transboundary waters are used in a reasonable and equitable way, taking into particular account their transboundary character, in the case of activities which cause or are likely to cause transboundary impact;
(d) To ensure conservation and, where necessary, restoration of ecosystems.

3. Measures for the prevention, control and reduction of water pollution shall be taken, where possible, at source.

4. These measures shall not directly or indirectly result in a transfer of pollution to other parts of the environment.

5. In taking the measures referred to in paragraphs 1 and 2 of this article, the Parties shall be guided by the following principles:

(a) The precautionary principle, by virtue of which action to avoid the potential transboundary impact of the release of hazardous substances shall not be postponed on the ground that scientific research has not fully proved a causal link between those substances, on the one hand, and the potential transboundary impact, on the other hand;
(b) The polluter-pays principle, by virtue of which costs of pollution prevention, control and reduction measures shall be borne by the polluter;
(c) Water resources shall be managed so that the needs of the present generation are met without compromising the ability of future generations to meet their own needs.

6. The Riparian Parties shall cooperate on the basis of equality and reciprocity, in particular through bilateral and multilateral agreements, in order to develop harmonized policies, programmes and strategies covering the relevant catchment areas, or parts thereof, aimed at the prevention, control and reduction of transboundary impact and aimed at the protection of the environment of transboundary waters or the environment influenced by such waters, including the marine environment.

7. The application of this Convention shall not lead to the deterioration of environmental conditions nor lead to increased transboundary impact.

8. The provisions of this Convention shall not affect the right of Parties individually or jointly to adopt and implement more stringent measures than those set down in this Convention.

Article 3
Prevention, control and reduction

1. To prevent, control and reduce transboundary impact, the Parties shall develop, adopt, implement and, as far as possible, render compatible relevant legal, administrative, economic, financial and technical measures, in order to ensure, *inter alia*, that:

(a) The emission of pollutants is prevented, controlled and reduced at source through the application of, *inter alia*, low- and non-waste technology;

(b) Transboundary waters are protected against pollution from point sources through the prior licensing of waste-water discharges by the competent national authorities, and that the authorized discharges are monitored and controlled;

(c) Limits for waste-water discharges stated in permits are based on the best available technology for discharges of hazardous substances;

(d) Stricter requirements, even leading to prohibition in individual cases, are imposed when the quality of the receiving water or the ecosystem so requires;

(e) At least biological treatment or equivalent processes are applied to municipal waste water, where necessary in a step-by-step approach;

(f) Appropriate measures are taken, such as the application of the best available technology, in order to reduce nutrient inputs from industrial and municipal sources;

(g) Appropriate measures and best environmental practices are developed and implemented for the reduction of inputs of nutrients and hazardous substances from diffuse sources, especially where the main sources are from agriculture (guidelines for developing best environmental practices are given in annex II to this Convention);

(h) Environmental impact assessment and other means of assessment are applied;

(i) Sustainable water-resources management, including the application of the ecosystems approach, is promoted;

(j) Contingency planning is developed;

(k) Additional specific measures are taken to prevent the pollution of groundwaters;

(l) The risk of accidental pollution is minimized.

2. To this end, each Party shall set emission limits for discharges from point sources into surface waters based on the best available technology, which are specifically applicable to individual industrial sectors or industries from which hazardous substances derive. The appropriate measures mentioned in paragraph 1 of this article to prevent, control and reduce the input of hazardous substances from point and diffuse sources into waters,

may, *inter alia*, include total or partial prohibition of the production or use of such substances. Existing lists of such industrial sectors or industries and of such hazardous substances in international conventions or regulations, which are applicable in the area covered by this Convention, shall be taken into account.

3. In addition, each Party shall define, where appropriate, water-quality objectives and adopt water-quality criteria for the purpose of preventing, controlling and reducing transboundary impact. General guidance for developing such objectives and criteria is given in annex III to this Convention. When necessary, the Parties shall endeavour to update this annex.

Article 4
Monitoring

The Parties shall establish programmes for monitoring the conditions of transboundary waters.

Article 5
Research and development

The Parties shall cooperate in the conduct of research into and development of effective techniques for the prevention, control and reduction of transboundary impact. To this effect, the Parties shall, on a bilateral and/or multilateral basis, taking into account research activities pursued in relevant international forums, endeavour to initiate or intensify specific research programmes, where necessary, aimed, *inter alia*, at:

(a) Methods for the assessment of the toxicity of hazardous substances and the noxiousness of pollutants;
(b) Improved knowledge on the occurrence, distribution and environmental effects of pollutants and the processes involved;
(c) The development and application of environmentally sound technologies, production and consumption patterns;
(d) The phasing out and/or substitution of substances likely to have transboundary impact;
(e) Environmentally sound methods of disposal of hazardous substances;
(f) Special methods for improving the conditions of transboundary waters;
(g) The development of environmentally sound water-construction works and water-regulation techniques;
(h) The physical and financial assessment of damage resulting from transboundary impact.

The results of these research programmes shall be exchanged among the Parties in accordance with article 6 of this Convention.

Article 6
Exchange of information

The Parties shall provide for the widest exchange of information, as early as possible, on issues covered by the provisions of this Convention.

Article 7
Responsibility and liability

The Parties shall support appropriate international efforts to elaborate rules, criteria and procedures in the field of responsibility and liability.

Article 8
Protection of information

The provisions of this Convention shall not affect the rights or the obligations of Parties in accordance with their national legal systems and applicable supranational regulations to protect information related to industrial and commercial secrecy, including intellectual property, or national security.

Part II
Provisions relating to Riparian Parties

Article 9
Bilateral and multilateral cooperation

1. The Riparian Parties shall on the basis of equality and reciprocity enter into bilateral or multilateral agreements or other arrangements, where these do not yet exist, or adapt existing ones, where necessary to eliminate the contradictions with the basic principles of this Convention, in order to define their mutual relations and conduct regarding the prevention, control and reduction of transboundary impact. The Riparian Parties shall specify the catchment area, or part(s) thereof, subject to cooperation. These agreements or arrangements shall embrace relevant issues covered by this Convention, as well as any other issues on which the Riparian Parties may deem it necessary to cooperate.

2. The agreements or arrangements mentioned in paragraph 1 of this article shall provide for the establishment of joint bodies. The tasks of these joint bodies shall be, *inter alia*, and without prejudice to relevant existing agreements or arrangements, the following:

(a) To collect, compile and evaluate data in order to identify pollution sources likely to cause transboundary impact;
(b) To elaborate joint monitoring programmes concerning water quality and quantity;
(c) To draw up inventories and exchange information on the pollution sources mentioned in paragraph 2 (a) of this article;
(d) To elaborate emission limits for waste water and evaluate the effectiveness of control programmes;

(e) To elaborate joint water-quality objectives and criteria having regard to the provisions of article 3, paragraph 3 of this Convention, and to propose relevant measures for maintaining and, where necessary, improving the existing water quality;

(f) To develop concerted action programmes for the reduction of pollution loads from both point sources (e.g. municipal and industrial sources) and diffuse sources (particularly from agriculture);

(g) To establish warning and alarm procedures;

(h) To serve as a forum for the exchange of information on existing and planned uses of water and related installations that are likely to cause transboundary impact;

(i) To promote cooperation and exchange of information on the best available technology in accordance with the provisions of article 13 of this Convention, as well as to encourage cooperation in scientific research programmes;

(j) To participate in the implementation of environmental impact assessments relating to transboundary waters, in accordance with appropriate international regulations.

3. In cases where a coastal State, being Party to this Convention, is directly and significantly affected by transboundary impact, the Riparian Parties can, if they all so agree, invite that coastal State to be involved in an appropriate manner in the activities of multilateral joint bodies established by Parties riparian to such transboundary waters.

4. Joint bodies according to this Convention shall invite joint bodies, established by coastal States for the protection of the marine environment directly affected by transboundary impact, to cooperate in order to harmonize their work and to prevent, control and reduce the transboundary impact.

5. Where two or more joint bodies exist in the same catchment area, they shall endeavour to coordinate their activities in order to strengthen the prevention, control and reduction of transboundary impact within that catchment area.

Article 10
Consultations

Consultations shall be held between the Riparian Parties on the basis of reciprocity, good faith and good-neighbourliness, at the request of any such Party. Such consultations shall aim at cooperation regarding the issues covered by the provisions of this Convention. Any such consultations shall be conducted through a joint body established under article 9 of this Convention, where one exists.

Article 11
Joint monitoring and assessment

1. In the framework of general cooperation mentioned in article 9 of this Convention, or specific arrangements, the Riparian Parties shall establish and

implement joint programmes for monitoring the conditions of transboundary waters, including floods and ice drifts, as well as transboundary impact.

2. The Riparian Parties shall agree upon pollution parameters and pollutants whose discharges and concentration in transboundary waters shall be regularly monitored.

3. The Riparian Parties shall, at regular intervals, carry out joint or coordinated assessments of the conditions of transboundary waters and the effectiveness of measures taken for the prevention, control and reduction of transboundary impact. The results of these assessments shall be made available to the public in accordance with the provisions set out in article 16 of this Convention.

4. For these purposes, the Riparian Parties shall harmonize rules for the setting up and operation of monitoring programmes, measurement systems, devices, analytical techniques, data processing and evaluation procedures, and methods for the registration of pollutants discharged.

Article 12
Common research and development

In the framework of general cooperation mentioned in article 9 of this Convention, or specific arrangements, the Riparian Parties shall undertake specific research and development activities in support of achieving and maintaining the water-quality objectives and criteria which they have agreed to set and adopt.

Article 13
Exchange of information between Riparian Parties

1. The Riparian Parties shall, within the framework of relevant agreements or other arrangements according to article 9 of this Convention, exchange reasonably available data, *inter alia*, on:

(a) Environmental conditions of transboundary waters;
(b) Experience gained in the application and operation of best available technology and results of research and development;
(c) Emission and monitoring data;
(d) Measures taken and planned to be taken to prevent, control and reduce transboundary impact;
(e) Permits or regulations for waste-water discharges issued by the competent authority or appropriate body.

2. In order to harmonize emission limits, the Riparian Parties shall undertake the exchange of information on their national regulations.

3. If a Riparian Party is requested by another Riparian Party to provide data or information that is not available, the former shall endeavour to comply with the request but may condition its compliance upon the payment, by the

requesting Party, of reasonable charges for collecting and, where appropriate, processing such data or information.

4. For the purposes of the implementation of this Convention, the Riparian Parties shall facilitate the exchange of best available technology, particularly through the promotion of: the commercial exchange of available technology; direct industrial contacts and cooperation, including joint ventures; the exchange of information and experience; and the provision of technical assistance. The Riparian Parties shall also undertake joint training programmes and the organization of relevant seminars and meetings.

Article 14
Warning and alarm systems

The Riparian Parties shall without delay inform each other about any critical situation that may have transboundary impact. The Riparian Parties shall set up, where appropriate, and operate coordinated or joint communication, warning and alarm systems with the aim of obtaining and transmitting information. These systems shall operate on the basis of compatible data transmission and treatment procedures and facilities to be agreed upon by the Riparian Parties. The Riparian Parties shall inform each other about competent authorities or points of contact designated for this purpose.

Article 15
Mutual assistance

1. If a critical situation should arise, the Riparian Parties shall provide mutual assistance upon request, following procedures to be established in accordance with paragraph 2 of this article.

2. The Riparian Parties shall elaborate and agree upon procedures for mutual assistance addressing, *inter alia*, the following issues:

(a) The direction, control, coordination and supervision of assistance;
(b) Local facilities and services to be rendered by the Party requesting assistance, including, where necessary, the facilitation of border-crossing formalities;
(c) Arrangements for holding harmless, indemnifying and/or compensating the assisting Party and/or its personnel, as well as for transit through territories of third Parties, where necessary;
(d) Methods of reimbursing assistance services.

Article 16
Public information

1. The Riparian Parties shall ensure that information on the conditions of transboundary waters, measures taken or planned to be taken to prevent,

control and reduce transboundary impact, and the effectiveness of those measures, is made available to the public. For this purpose, the Riparian Parties shall ensure that the following information is made available to the public:

(a) Water-quality objectives;
(b) Permits issued and the conditions required to be met;
(c) Results of water and effluent sampling carried out for the purposes of monitoring and assessment, as well as results of checking compliance with the water-quality objectives or the permit conditions.

2. The Riparian Parties shall ensure that this information shall be available to the public at all reasonable times for inspection free of charge, and shall provide members of the public with reasonable facilities for obtaining from the Riparian Parties, on payment of reasonable charges, copies of such information.

Part III
Institutional and final provisions

Article 17
Meeting of Parties

1. The first meeting of the Parties shall be convened no later than one year after the date of the entry into force of this Convention. Thereafter, ordinary meetings shall be held every three years, or at shorter intervals as laid down in the rules of procedure. The Parties shall hold an extraordinary meeting if they so decide in the course of an ordinary meeting or at the written request of any Party, provided that, within six months of it being communicated to all Parties, the said request is supported by at least one third of the Parties.

2. At their meetings, the Parties shall keep under continuous review the implementation of this Convention, and, with this purpose in mind, shall:

(a) Review the policies for and methodological approaches to the protection and use of transboundary waters of the Parties with a view to further improving the protection and use of transboundary waters;
(b) Exchange information regarding experience gained in concluding and implementing bilateral and multilateral agreements or other arrangements regarding the protection and use of transboundary waters to which one or more of the Parties are party;
(c) Seek, where appropriate, the services of relevant ECE bodies as well as other competent international bodies and specific committees in all aspects pertinent to the achievement of the purposes of this Convention;
(d) At their first meeting, consider and by consensus adopt rules of procedure for their meetings;
(e) Consider and adopt proposals for amendments to this Convention;

(f) Consider and undertake any additional action that may be required for the achievement of the purposes of this Convention.

Article 18
Right to vote

1. Except as provided for in paragraph 2 of this article, each Party to this Convention shall have one vote.

2. Regional economic integration organizations, in matters within their competence, shall exercise their right to vote with a number of votes equal to the number of their member States which are Parties to this Convention. Such organizations shall not exercise their right to vote if their member States exercise theirs, and vice versa.

Article 19
Secretariat

The Executive Secretary of the Economic Commission for Europe shall carry out the following secretariat functions:

(a) The convening and preparing of meetings of the Parties;
(b) The transmission to the Parties of reports and other information received in accordance with the provisions of this Convention;
(c) The performance of such other functions as may be determined by the Parties.

Article 20
Annexes

Annexes to this Convention shall constitute an integral part thereof.

Article 21
Amendments to the Convention

1. Any Party may propose amendments to this Convention.

2. Proposals for amendments to this Convention shall be considered at a meeting of the Parties.

3. The text of any proposed amendment to this Convention shall be submitted in writing to the Executive Secretary of the Economic Commission for Europe, who shall communicate it to all Parties at least ninety days before the meeting at which it is proposed for adoption.

4. An amendment to the present Convention shall be adopted by consensus of the representatives of the Parties to this Convention present at a meeting of the Parties, and shall enter into force for the Parties to the Convention which have accepted it on the ninetieth day after the date on which two thirds of those Parties have deposited with the Depositary their instruments of acceptance of the amendment. The amendment shall enter into force for any other Party on

the ninetieth day after the date on which that Party deposits its instrument of acceptance of the amendment.

Article 22
Settlement of disputes

1. If a dispute arises between two or more Parties about the interpretation or application of this Convention, they shall seek a solution by negotiation or by any other means of dispute settlement acceptable to the parties to the dispute.

2. When signing, ratifying, accepting, approving or acceding to this Convention, or at any time thereafter, a Party may declare in writing to the Depositary that, for a dispute not resolved in accordance with paragraph 1 of this article, it accepts one or both of the following means of dispute settlement as compulsory in relation to any Party accepting the same obligation:

(a) Submission of the dispute to the International Court of Justice;
(b) Arbitration in accordance with the procedure set out in annex IV.

3. If the parties to the dispute have accepted both means of dispute settlement referred to in paragraph 2 of this article, the dispute may be submitted only to the International Court of Justice, unless the parties agree otherwise.

Article 23
Signature

This Convention shall be open for signature at Helsinki from 17 to 18 March 1992 inclusive, and thereafter at United Nations Headquarters in New York until 18 September 1992, by States members of the Economic Commission for Europe as well as States having consultative status with the Economic Commission for Europe pursuant to paragraph 8 of Economic and Social Council resolution 36 (IV) of 28 March 1947, and by regional economic integration organizations constituted by sovereign States members of the Economic Commission for Europe to which their member States have transferred competence over matters governed by this Convention, including the competence to enter into treaties in respect of these matters.

Article 24
Depositary

The Secretary-General of the United Nations shall act as the Depositary of this Convention.

Article 25
Ratification, acceptance, approval and accession

1. This Convention shall be subject to ratification, acceptance or approval by signatory States and regional economic integration organizations.

2. This Convention shall be open for accession by the States and organizations referred to in article 23.

3. Any organization referred to in article 23 which becomes a Party to this Convention without any of its member States being a Party shall be bound by all the obligations under this Convention. In the case of such organizations, one or more of whose member States is a Party to this Convention, the organization and its member States shall decide on their respective responsibilities for the performance of their obligations under this Convention. In such cases, the organization and the member States shall not be entitled to exercise rights under this Convention concurrently.

4. In their instruments of ratification, acceptance, approval or accession, the regional economic integration organizations referred to in article 23 shall declare the extent of their competence with respect to the matters governed by this Convention. These organizations shall also inform the Depositary of any substantial modification to the extent of their competence.

Article 26
Entry into force

1. This Convention shall enter into force on the ninetieth day after the date of deposit of the sixteenth instrument of ratification, acceptance, approval or accession.

2. For the purposes of paragraph 1 of this article, any instrument deposited by a regional economic integration organization shall not be counted as additional to those deposited by States members of such an organization.

3. For each State or organization referred to in article 23 which ratifies, accepts or approves this Convention or accedes thereto after the deposit of the sixteenth instrument of ratification, acceptance, approval or accession, the Convention shall enter into force on the ninetieth day after the date of deposit by such State or organization of its instrument of ratification, acceptance, approval or accession.

Article 27
Withdrawal

At any time after three years from the date on which this Convention has come into force with respect to a Party, that Party may withdraw from the Convention by giving written notification to the Depositary. Any such withdrawal shall take effect on the ninetieth day after the date of its receipt by the Depositary.

Article 28
Authentic texts

The original of this Convention, of which the English, French and Russian texts are equally authentic, shall be deposited with the Secretary-General of the United Nations.

IN WITNESS WHEREOF the undersigned, being duly authorized thereto, have signed this Convention.

DONE at Helsinki, this seventeenth day of March one thousand nine hundred and ninety-two.

Annex I
Definition of the term 'best available technology'

1. The term 'best available technology' is taken to mean the latest stage of development of processes, facilities or methods of operation which indicate the practical suitability of a particular measure for limiting discharges, emissions and waste. In determining whether a set of processes, facilities and methods of operation constitute the best available technology in general or individual cases, special consideration is given to:

(a) Comparable processes, facilities or methods of operation which have recently been successfully tried out;
(b) Technological advances and changes in scientific knowledge and understanding;
(c) The economic feasibility of such technology;
(d) Time limits for installation in both new and existing plants;
(e) The nature and volume of the discharges and effluents concerned;
(f) Low- and non-waste technology.

2. It therefore follows that what is 'best available technology' for a particular process will change with time in the light of technological advances, economic and social factors, as well as in the light of changes in scientific knowledge and understanding.

Annex II
Guidelines for developing best environmental practices

1. In selecting for individual cases the most appropriate combination of measures which may constitute the best environmental practice, the following graduated range of measures should be considered:

(a) Provision of information and education to the public and to users about the environmental consequences of the choice of particular activities and products, their use and ultimate disposal;
(b) The development and application of codes of good environmental practice which cover all aspects of the product's life;
(c) Labels informing users of environmental risks related to a product, its use and ultimate disposal;

(d) Collection and disposal systems available to the public;
(e) Recycling, recovery and reuse;
(f) Application of economic instruments to activities, products or groups of products;
(g) A system of licensing, which involves a range of restrictions or a ban.

2. In determining what combination of measures constitute best environmental practices, in general or in individual cases, particular consideration should be given to:

(a) The environmental hazard of:
    (i) The product;
    (ii) The product's production;
    (iii) The product's use;
    (iv) The product's ultimate disposal;
(b) Substitution by less polluting processes or substances;
(c) Scale of use;
(d) Potential environmental benefit or penalty of substitute materials or activities;
(e) Advances and changes in scientific knowledge and understanding;
(f) Time limits for implementation;
(g) Social and economic implications.

3. It therefore follows that best environmental practices for a particular source will change with time in the light of technological advances, economic and social factors, as well as in the light of changes in scientific knowledge and understanding.

Annex III
Guidelines for developing water-quality objectives and criteria

Water-quality objectives and criteria shall:

(a) Take into account the aim of maintaining and, where necessary, improving the existing water quality;
(b) Aim at the reduction of average pollution loads (in particular hazardous substances) to a certain degree within a certain period of time;
(c) Take into account specific water-quality requirements (raw water for drinking-water purposes, irrigation, etc.);
(d) Take into account specific requirements regarding sensitive and specially protected waters and their environment, e.g. lakes and groundwater resources;
(e) Be based on the application of ecological classification methods and chemical indices for the medium- and long-term review of water-quality maintenance and improvement;

(f) Take into account the degree to which objectives are reached and the additional protective measures, based on emission limits, which may be required in individual cases.

Annex IV
Arbitration

1. In the event of a dispute being submitted for arbitration pursuant to article 22, paragraph 2 of this Convention, a party or parties shall notify the secretariat of the subject-matter of arbitration and indicate, in particular, the articles of this Convention whose interpretation or application is at issue. The secretariat shall forward the information received to all Parties to this Convention.

2. The arbitral tribunal shall consist of three members. Both the claimant party or parties and the other party or parties to the dispute shall appoint an arbitrator, and the two arbitrators so appointed shall designate by common agreement the third arbitrator, who shall be the president of the arbitral tribunal. The latter shall not be a national of one of the parties to the dispute, nor have his or her usual place of residence in the territory of one of these parties, nor be employed by any of them, nor have dealt with the case in any other capacity.

3. If the president of the arbitral tribunal has not been designated within two months of the appointment of the second arbitrator, the Executive Secretary of the Economic Commission for Europe shall, at the request of either party to the dispute, designate the president within a further two-month period.

4. If one of the parties to the dispute does not appoint an arbitrator within two months of the receipt of the request, the other party may so inform the Executive Secretary of the Economic Commission for Europe, who shall designate the president of the arbitral tribunal within a further two-month period. Upon designation, the president of the arbitral tribunal shall request the party which has not appointed an arbitrator to do so within two months. If it fails to do so within that period, the president shall so inform the Executive Secretary of the Economic Commission for Europe, who shall make this appointment within a further two-month period.

5. The arbitral tribunal shall render its decision in accordance with international law and the provisions of this Convention.

6. Any arbitral tribunal constituted under the provisions set out in this annex shall draw up its own rules of procedure.

7. The decisions of the arbitral tribunal, both on procedure and on substance, shall be taken by majority vote of its members.

8. The tribunal may take all appropriate measures to establish the facts.

9. The parties to the dispute shall facilitate the work of the arbitral tribunal and, in particular, using all means at their disposal, shall:

(a) Provide it with all relevant documents, facilities and information;
(b) Enable it, where necessary, to call witnesses or experts and receive their evidence.

10. The parties and the arbitrators shall protect the confidentiality of any information they receive in confidence during the proceedings of the arbitral tribunal.

11. The arbitral tribunal may, at the request of one of the parties, recommend interim measures of protection.

12. If one of the parties to the dispute does not appear before the arbitral tribunal or fails to defend its case, the other party may request the tribunal to continue the proceedings and to render its final decision. Absence of a party or failure of a party to defend its case shall not constitute a bar to the proceedings.

13. The arbitral tribunal may hear and determine counter-claims arising directly out of the subject-matter of the dispute.

14. Unless the arbitral tribunal determines otherwise because of the particular circumstances of the case, the expenses of the tribunal, including the remuneration of its members, shall be borne by the parties to the dispute in equal shares. The tribunal shall keep a record of all its expenses, and shall furnish a final statement thereof to the parties.

15. Any Party to this Convention which has an interest of a legal nature in the subject-matter of the dispute, and which may be affected by a decision in the case, may intervene in the proceedings with the consent of the tribunal.

16. The arbitral tribunal shall render its award within five months of the date on which it is established, unless it finds it necessary to extend the time limit for a period which should not exceed five months.

17. The award of the arbitral tribunal shall be accompanied by a statement of reasons. It shall be final and binding upon all parties to the dispute. The award will be transmitted by the arbitral tribunal to the parties to the dispute and to the secretariat. The secretariat will forward the information received to all Parties to this Convention.

18. Any dispute which may arise between the parties concerning the interpretation or execution of the award may be submitted by either party to the arbitral tribunal which made the award or, if the latter cannot be seized thereof, to another tribunal constituted for this purpose in the same manner as the first.

Protocol on Water and Health to the 1992 Convention on the Protection and Use of Transboundary Watercourses and International Lakes, 17 June 1999

Editorial note

The Protocol on Water and Health aims to promote the protection of human health and well-being by improving water management, including protection of water ecosystems (Article 1). The Protocol commits parties to ensure adequate supplies of wholesome drinking water, adequate sanitation (thorough collective systems), effective protection of drinking water supplies, safeguards for human health against water-related diseases, and effective monitoring (Article 2(2)). These measures are to be based on an assessment of any proposed measure in respect of all its implications for human health, water resources and sustainable development, and are to be guided by the precautionary and polluter pays principles (Articles 4(4) and (5)(a) and (b)). In taking their actions parties are also to be guided by other principles and approaches, including the need to take preventive action, intergenerational equity, to adopt actions at the lowest appropriate administrative level, to make use of economic instruments, to ensure access to information and public participation, and to manage water resources in an integrated manner (Article 5). The Protocol also requires each party to establish and publish national and/or local targets to achieve or maintain a high level of protection against water–related diseases, and to that end to establish appropriate legal and institutional frameworks. Targets are to include *inter alia* quality of drinking water supplied, reduction of diseases, areas to be covered by collective systems, the occurrence of discharges of untreated waters, and the disposal or reuse of sludge (Article 6). The Protocol includes provisions on review and assessment of progress, response systems and public awareness and information (Articles 7–10), and provisions on international co-operation (including on transboundary waters) and joint and co-ordinated international action (Articles 11–13). Provision is also made for reviewing compliance by means of 'non-confrontational, non-judicial and consultative' means (Article 15). Meetings of the Parties shall be held in conjunction with meetings of the Parties to the Convention (Article 16). Disputes shall be settled by negotiation or by any other means of dispute settlement acceptable to the parties to the dispute (Article 20). The Protocol will enter into force ninety days after the deposit of the sixteenth instrument of ratification, acceptance, approval or accession (Article 23).

Date of signature: 17 June 1999

Entry into force: Not yet in force

Depositary: Secretary-General of the United Nations

Contracting Parties: Albania, Azerbaijan, Czech Republic, Hungary, Luxembourg, Romania, Russian Federation, Slovakia.

Website: www.unece.org/env/water/

Protocol on Water and Health to the 1992 Convention on the Protection and Use of Transboundary Watercourses and International Lakes

Preamble

The Parties to this Protocol,

   Mindful that water is essential to sustain life and that the availability of water in quantities, and of a quality, sufficient to meet basic human needs is a prerequisite both for improved health and for sustainable development,

   Acknowledging the benefits to human health and well-being that accrue from wholesome and clean water and a harmonious and properly functioning water environment,

   Aware that surface waters and groundwater are renewable resources with a limited capacity to recover from adverse impacts from human activities on their quantity and quality, that any failure to respect those limits may result in adverse effects, in both the short and long terms, on the health and well-being of those who rely on those resources and their quality, and that in consequence sustainable management of the hydrological cycle is essential for both meeting human needs and protecting the environment,

   Aware also of the consequences for public health of shortfalls of water in the quantities, and of the quality, sufficient to meet basic human needs, and of the serious effects of such shortfalls, in particular on the vulnerable, the disadvantaged and the socially excluded,

   Conscious that the prevention, control and reduction of water-related disease are important and urgent tasks which can only be satisfactorily discharged by enhanced cooperation at all levels and among all sectors, both within countries and between States,

   Conscious also that surveillance of water-related disease and the establishment of early-warning systems and response systems are important aspects of the prevention, control and reduction of water-related disease,

Basing themselves upon the conclusions of the United Nations Conference on Environment and Development (Rio de Janeiro, 1992), in particular the Rio Declaration on Environment and Development and Agenda 21, as well as upon the programme for the further implementation of Agenda 21 (New York, 1997) and the consequent decision of the Commission on Sustainable Development on the sustainable management of freshwater (New York, 1998),

Deriving inspiration from the relevant provisions of the 1992 Convention on the Protection and Use of Transboundary Watercourses and International Lakes and emphasizing the need both to encourage more widespread application of those provisions and to complement that Convention with further measures to strengthen the protection of public health,

Taking note of the 1991 Convention on Environmental Impact Assessment in a Transboundary Context, the 1992 Convention on the Transboundary Effects of Industrial Accidents, the 1997 United Nations Convention on the Law of the Non-Navigational Uses of International Watercourses and the 1998 Convention on Access to Information, Public Participation in Decision-making and Access to Justice in Environmental Matters,

Further taking note of the pertinent principles, targets and recommendations of the 1989 European Charter on Environment and Health, the 1994 Helsinki Declaration on Environment and Health, and the Ministerial declarations, recommendations and resolutions of the 'Environment for Europe' process,

Recognizing the sound basis and relevance of other environmental initiatives, instruments and processes in Europe, as well as the preparation and implementation of National Environment and Health Action Plans and of National Environment Action Plans,

Commending the efforts already undertaken by the United Nations Economic Commission for Europe and the Regional Office for Europe of the World Health Organization to strengthen bilateral and multilateral cooperation for the prevention, control and reduction of water-related disease,

Encouraged by the many examples of positive achievements by the States members of the United Nations Economic Commission for Europe and the States members of the Regional Committee for Europe of the World Health Organization in abating pollution and in maintaining and restoring water environments capable of supporting human health and well-being,

Have agreed as follows:

Article 1
Objective

The objective of this Protocol is to promote at all appropriate levels, nationally as well as in transboundary and international contexts, the protection of human health and well-being, both individual and collective, within a framework of sustainable development, through improving water management, including the protection of water ecosystems, and through preventing, controlling and reducing water-related disease.

Article 2
Definitions

For the purposes of this Protocol,

1. 'Water-related disease' means any significant adverse effects on human health, such as death, disability, illness or disorders, caused directly or indirectly by the condition, or changes in the quantity or quality, of any waters;

2. 'Drinking water' means water which is used, or intended to be available for use, by humans for drinking, cooking, food preparation, personal hygiene or similar purposes;

3. 'Groundwater' means all water which is below the surface of the ground in the saturation zone and in direct contact with the ground or subsoil;

4. 'Enclosed waters' means artificially created water bodies separated from surface freshwater or coastal water, whether within or outside a building;

5. 'Transboundary waters' means any surface or ground waters which mark, cross or are located on boundaries between two or more States; wherever transboundary waters flow directly into the sea, these transboundary waters end at a straight line across their respective mouths between points on the low-water line of their banks;

6. 'Transboundary effects of water-related disease' means any significant adverse effects on human health, such as death, disability, illness or disorders, in an area under the jurisdiction of one Party, caused directly or indirectly by the condition, or changes in the quantity or quality, of waters in an area under the jurisdiction of another Party, whether or not such effects constitute a transboundary impact;

7. 'Transboundary impact' means any significant adverse effect on the environment resulting from a change in the conditions of transboundary waters caused by a human activity, the physical origin of which is situated wholly or in part within an area under the jurisdiction of a Party to the Convention, within an area under the jurisdiction of another Party to the Convention. Such effects on the environment include effects on human health and safety, flora, fauna, soil, air, water, climate, landscape, and historical monuments or other physical structures or the interaction among these factors; they also include effects on the cultural heritage or socio-economic conditions resulting from alterations to those factors;

8. 'Sanitation' means the collection, transport, treatment and disposal or reuse of human excreta or domestic waste water, whether through collective systems or by installations serving a single household or undertaking;

9. 'Collective system' means:

(a) A system for the supply of drinking water to a number of households or undertakings; and/or

(b) A system for the provision of sanitation which serves a number of households or undertakings and, where appropriate, also provides for the collection, transport, treatment and disposal or reuse of industrial waste water,
whether provided by a body in the public sector, an undertaking in the
private sector or by a partnership between the two sectors;

10. 'Water-management plan' means a plan for the development, management, protection and/or use of the water within a territorial area or groundwater
aquifer, including the protection of the associated ecosystems;

11. 'The public' means one or more natural or legal persons, and, in accordance with national legislation or practice, their associations, organizations or
groups;

12. 'Public authority' means:

(a) Government at national, regional and other levels;
(b) Natural or legal persons performing public administrative functions under
national law, including specific duties, activities or services in relation to the
environment, public health, sanitation, water management or water supply;
(c) Any other natural or legal persons having public responsibilities or functions, or providing public services, under the control of a body or person
falling within subparagraphs (a) or (b) above;
(d) The institutions of any regional economic integration organization referred
to in article 21 which is a Party.

This definition does not include bodies or institutions acting in a judicial or
legislative capacity;

13. 'Local' refers to all relevant levels of territorial unit below the level of the
State;

14. 'Convention' means the Convention on the Protection and Use of
Transboundary Watercourses and International Lakes, done at Helsinki on
17 March 1992;

15. 'Meeting of the Parties to the Convention' means the body established
by the Parties to the Convention in accordance with its article 17;

16. 'Party' means, unless the text otherwise indicates, a State or a regional
economic integration organization referred to in article 21 which has consented
to be bound by this Protocol and for which this Protocol is in force;

17. 'Meeting of the Parties' means the body established by the Parties in
accordance with article 16.

Article 3
Scope

The provisions of this Protocol shall apply to:

(a) Surface freshwater;
(b) Groundwater;

(c) Estuaries;
(d) Coastal waters which are used for recreation or for the production of fish by aquaculture or for the production or harvesting of shellfish;
(e) Enclosed waters generally available for bathing;
(f) Water in the course of abstraction, transport, treatment or supply;
(g) Waste water throughout the course of collection, transport, treatment and discharge or reuse.

Article 4
General provisions

1. The Parties shall take all appropriate measures to prevent, control and reduce water-related disease within a framework of integrated water-management systems aimed at sustainable use of water resources, ambient water quality which does not endanger human health, and protection of water ecosystems.

2. The Parties shall, in particular, take all appropriate measures for the purpose of ensuring:

(a) Adequate supplies of wholesome drinking water which is free from any micro-organisms, parasites and substances which, owing to their numbers or concentration, constitute a potential danger to human health. This shall include the protection of water resources which are used as sources of drinking water, treatment of water and the establishment, improvement and maintenance of collective systems;
(b) Adequate sanitation of a standard which sufficiently protects human health and the environment. This shall in particular be done through the establishment, improvement and maintenance of collective systems;
(c) Effective protection of water resources used as sources of drinking water, and their related water ecosystems, from pollution from other causes, including agriculture, industry and other discharges and emissions of hazardous substances. This shall aim at the effective reduction and elimination of discharges and emissions of substances judged to be hazardous to human health and water ecosystems;
(d) Sufficient safeguards for human health against water-related disease arising from the use of water for recreational purposes, from the use of water for aquaculture, from the water in which shellfish are produced or from which they are harvested, from the use of waste water for irrigation or from the use of sewage sludge in agriculture or aquaculture;
(e) Effective systems for monitoring situations likely to result in outbreaks or incidents of water-related disease and for responding to such outbreaks and incidents and to the risk of them.

3. Subsequent references in this Protocol to 'drinking water' and 'sanitation' are to drinking water and sanitation that are required to meet the requirements of paragraph 2 of this article.

4. The Parties shall base all such measures upon an assessment of any proposed measure in respect of all its implications, including the benefits, disadvantages and costs, for:

(a) Human health;
(b) Water resources; and
(c) Sustainable development,

which takes account of the differing new impacts of any proposed measure on the different environmental mediums.

5. The Parties shall take all appropriate action to create legal, administrative and economic frameworks which are stable and enabling and within which the public, private and voluntary sectors can each make its contribution to improving water management for the purpose of preventing, controlling and reducing water-related disease.

6. The Parties shall require public authorities which are considering taking action, or approving the taking by others of action, that may have a significant impact on the environment of any waters within the scope of this Protocol to take due account of any potential impact of that action on public health.

7. Where a Party is a Party to the Convention on Environmental Impact Assessment in a Transboundary Context, compliance by public authorities of that Party with the requirements of that Convention in relation to a proposed action shall satisfy the requirement under paragraph 6 of this article in respect of that action.

8. The provisions of this Protocol shall not affect the rights of Parties to maintain, adopt or implement more stringent measures than those set down in this Protocol.

9. The provisions of this Protocol shall not affect the rights and obligations of any Party to this Protocol deriving from the Convention or any other existing international agreement, except where the requirements under this Protocol are more stringent than the corresponding requirements under the Convention or that other existing international agreement.

Article 5
Principles and approaches

In taking measures to implement this Protocol, the Parties shall be guided in particular by the following principles and approaches:

(a) The precautionary principle, by virtue of which action to prevent, control or reduce water-related disease shall not be postponed on the ground that scientific research has not fully proved a causal link between the factor at which such action is aimed, on the one hand, and the potential contribution of that factor to the prevalence of water-related disease and/or transboundary impacts, on the other hand;

(b) The polluter-pays principle, by virtue of which costs of pollution prevention, control and reduction shall be borne by the polluter;

(c) States have, in accordance with the Charter of the United Nations and
the principles of international law, the sovereign right to exploit their own
resources pursuant to their own environmental and developmental policies,
and the responsibility to ensure that activities within their jurisdiction or
control do not cause damage to the environment of other States or of areas
beyond the limits of national jurisdiction;

(d) Water resources shall be managed so that the needs of the present generation
are met without compromising the ability of future generations to meet
their own needs;

(e) Preventive action should be taken to avoid outbreaks and incidents of water-
related disease and to protect water resources used as sources of drinking
water because such action addresses the harm more efficiently and can be
more cost-effective than remedial action;

(f) Action to manage water resources should be taken at the lowest appropriate
administrative level;

(g) Water has social, economic and environmental values and should therefore
be managed so as to realize the most acceptable and sustainable combination of those values;

(h) Efficient use of water should be promoted through economic instruments
and awareness-building;

(i) Access to information and public participation in decision-making concerning water and health are needed, *inter alia*, in order to enhance the
quality and the implementation of the decisions, to build public awareness
of issues, to give the public the opportunity to express its concerns and to
enable public authorities to take due account of such concerns. Such access
and participation should be supplemented by appropriate access to judicial
and administrative review of relevant decisions;

(j) Water resources should, as far as possible, be managed in an integrated
manner on the basis of catchment areas, with the aims of linking social
and economic development to the protection of natural ecosystems and
of relating water-resource management to regulatory measures concerning other environmental mediums. Such an integrated approach should
apply across the whole of a catchment area, whether transboundary or
not, including its associated coastal waters, the whole of a groundwater
aquifer or the relevant parts of such a catchment area or groundwater
aquifer;

(k) Special consideration should be given to the protection of people who are
particularly vulnerable to water-related disease;

(l) Equitable access to water, adequate in terms both of quantity and of quality,
should be provided for all members of the population, especially those who
suffer a disadvantage or social exclusion;

(m) As a counterpart to their rights and entitlements to water under private law and public law, natural and legal persons and institutions, whether in the public sector or the private sector, should contribute to the protection of the water environment and the conservation of water resources; and

(n) In implementing this Protocol, due account should be given to local problems, needs and knowledge.

Article 6
Targets and target dates

1. In order to achieve the objective of this Protocol, the Parties shall pursue the aims of:

(a) Access to drinking water for everyone;

(b) Provision of sanitation for everyone within a framework of integrated water-management systems aimed at sustainable use of water resources, ambient water quality which does not endanger human health, and protection of water ecosystems.

2. For these purposes, the Parties shall each establish and publish national and/or local targets for the standards and levels of performance that need to be achieved or maintained for a high level of protection against water-related disease. These targets shall be periodically revised. In doing all this, they shall make appropriate practical and/or other provisions for public participation, within a transparent and fair framework, and shall ensure that due account is taken of the outcome of the public participation. Except where national or local circumstances make them irrelevant for preventing, controlling and reducing water-related disease, the targets shall cover, *inter alia*:

(a) The quality of the drinking water supplied, taking into account the Guidelines for drinking-water quality of the World Health Organization;

(b) The reduction of the scale of outbreaks and incidents of water-related disease;

(c) The area of territory, or the population sizes or proportions, which should be served by collective systems for the supply of drinking water or where the supply of drinking water by other means should be improved;

(d) The area of territory, or the population sizes or proportions, which should be served by collective systems of sanitation or where sanitation by other means should be improved;

(e) The levels of performance to be achieved by such collective systems and by such other means of water supply and sanitation respectively;

(f) The application of recognized good practice to the management of water supply and sanitation, including the protection of waters used as sources for drinking water;

(g) The occurrence of discharges of:

    (i) Untreated waste water; and

    (ii) Untreated storm water overflows from waste-water collection systems
       to waters within the scope of this Protocol;

(h) The quality of discharges of waste water from waste-water treatment
    installations to waters within the scope of this Protocol;

(i) The disposal or reuse of sewage sludge from collective systems of sanitation
    or other sanitation installations and the quality of waste water used for
    irrigation purposes, taking into account the Guidelines for the safe use
    of waste water and excreta in agriculture and aquaculture of the World
    Health Organization and the United Nations Environment Programme;

(j) The quality of waters which are used as sources for drinking water, which
    are generally used for bathing or which are used for aquaculture or for the
    production or harvesting of shellfish;

(k) The application of recognized good practice to the management of
    enclosed waters generally available for bathing;

(l) The identification and remediation of particularly contaminated sites
    which adversely affect waters within the scope of this Protocol or are likely
    to do so and which thus threaten to give rise to water-related disease;

(m) The effectiveness of systems for the management, development, protection
    and use of water resources, including the application of recognized good
    practice to the control of pollution from sources of all kinds;

(n) The frequency of the publication of information on the quality of the
    drinking water supplied and of other waters relevant to the targets in this
    paragraph in the intervals between the publication of information under
    article 7, paragraph 2.

3. Within two years of becoming a Party, each Party shall establish and
publish targets referred to in paragraph 2 of this article, and target dates for
achieving them.

4. Where a long process of implementation is foreseen for the achievement
of a target, intermediate or phased targets shall be set.

5. In order to promote the achievement of the targets referred to in paragraph
2 of this article, the Parties shall each:

(a) Establish national or local arrangements for coordination between their
    competent authorities;

(b) Develop water-management plans in transboundary, national and/or local
    contexts, preferably on the basis of catchment areas or groundwater
    aquifers. In doing so, they shall make appropriate practical and/or other
    provisions for public participation, within a transparent and fair frame-
    work, and shall ensure that due account is taken of the outcome of the
    public participation. Such plans may be incorporated in other relevant
    plans, programmes or documents which are being drawn up for other pur-
    poses, provided that they enable the public to see clearly the proposals for

achieving the targets referred to in this article and the respective target dates;

(c) Establish and maintain a legal and institutional framework for monitoring and enforcing standards for the quality of drinking water;

(d) Establish and maintain arrangements, including, where appropriate, legal and institutional arrangements, for monitoring, promoting the achievement of and, where necessary, enforcing the other standards and levels of performance for which targets referred to in paragraph 2 of this article are set.

Article 7
Review and assessment of progress

1. The Parties shall each collect and evaluate data on:

(a) Their progress towards the achievement of the targets referred to in article 6, paragraph 2;

(b) Indicators that are designed to show how far that progress has contributed towards preventing, controlling or reducing water-related disease.

2. The Parties shall each publish periodically the results of this collection and evaluation of data. The frequency of such publication shall be established by the Meeting of the Parties.

3. The Parties shall each ensure that the results of water and effluent sampling carried out for the purpose of this collection of data are available to the public.

4. On the basis of this collection and evaluation of data, each Party shall review periodically the progress made in achieving the targets referred to in article 6, paragraph 2, and publish an assessment of that progress. The frequency of such reviews shall be established by the Meeting of the Parties. Without prejudice to the possibility of more frequent reviews under article 6, paragraph 2, reviews under this paragraph shall include a review of the targets referred to in article 6, paragraph 2, with a view to improving the targets in the light of scientific and technical knowledge.

5. Each Party shall provide to the secretariat referred to in article 17, for circulation to the other Parties, a summary report of the data collected and evaluated and the assessment of the progress achieved. Such reports shall be in accordance with guidelines established by the Meeting of the Parties. These guidelines shall provide that the Parties can use for this purpose reports covering the relevant information produced for other international forums.

6. The Meeting of the Parties shall evaluate progress in implementing this Protocol on the basis of such summary reports.

Article 8
Response systems

1. The Parties shall each, as appropriate, ensure that:

(a) Comprehensive national and/or local surveillance and early-warning systems are established, improved or maintained which will:
- (i) Identify outbreaks or incidents of water-related disease or significant threats of such outbreaks or incidents, including those resulting from water-pollution incidents or extreme weather events;
- (ii) Give prompt and clear notification to the relevant public authorities about such outbreaks, incidents or threats;
- (iii) In the event of any imminent threat to public health from water-related disease, disseminate to members of the public who may be affected all information that is held by a public authority and that could help the public to prevent or mitigate harm;
- (iv) Make recommendations to the relevant public authorities and, where appropriate, to the public about preventive and remedial actions;

(b) Comprehensive national and local contingency plans for responses to such outbreaks, incidents and risks are properly prepared in due time;

(c) The relevant public authorities have the necessary capacity to respond to such outbreaks, incidents or risks in accordance with the relevant contingency plan.

2. Surveillance and early-warning systems, contingency plans and response capacities in relation to water-related disease may be combined with those in relation to other matters.

3. Within three years of becoming a Party, each Party shall have established the surveillance and early-warning systems, contingency plans and response capacities referred to in paragraph 1 of this article.

Article 9
Public awareness, education, training, research and development and information

1. The Parties shall take steps designed to enhance the awareness of all sectors of the public regarding:

(a) The importance of, and the relationship between, water management and public health;

(b) The rights and entitlements to water and corresponding obligations under private and public law of natural and legal persons and institutions, whether in the public sector or the private sector, as well as their moral obligations to contribute to the protection of the water environment and the conservation of water resources.

2. The Parties shall promote:

(a) Understanding of the public-health aspects of their work by those responsible for water management, water supply and sanitation; and

(b) Understanding of the basic principles of water management, water supply
and sanitation by those responsible for public health.

3. The Parties shall encourage the education and training of the professional
and technical staff who are needed for managing water resources and for operating systems of water supply and sanitation, and encourage the updating and
improvement of their knowledge and skills. This education and training shall
include relevant aspects of public health.

4. The Parties shall encourage:

(a) Research into, and development of, cost-effective means and techniques
for the prevention, control and reduction of water-related disease;
(b) Development of integrated information systems to handle information
about long-term trends, current concerns and past problems and successful
solutions to them in the field of water and health, and provision of such
information to competent authorities.

Article 10
Public information

1. As a complement to the requirements of this Protocol for Parties to publish
specific information or documents, each Party shall take steps within the framework of its legislation to make available to the public such information as is
held by public authorities and is reasonably needed to inform public discussion
of:

(a) The establishment of targets and of target dates for their achievement
and the development of water-management plans in accordance with
article 6;
(b) The establishment, improvement or maintenance of surveillance and early-
warning systems and contingency plans in accordance with article 8;
(c) The promotion of public awareness, education, training, research, development and information in accordance with article 9.

2. Each Party shall ensure that public authorities, in response to a request
for other information relevant to the implementation of this Protocol, make
such information available within a reasonable time to the public, within the
framework of national legislation.

3. The Parties shall ensure that information referred to in article 7, paragraph
4, and paragraph 1 of this article shall be available to the public at all reasonable
times for inspection free of charge, and shall provide members of the public with
reasonable facilities for obtaining from the Parties, on payment of reasonable
charges, copies of such information.

4. Nothing in this Protocol shall require a public authority to publish information or make information available to the public if:

(a) The public authority does not hold the information;
(b) The request for the information is manifestly unreasonable or formulated in too general a manner; or
(c) The information concerns material in the course of completion or concerns internal communications of public authorities where such an exemption is provided for in national law or customary practice, taking into account the public interest served by disclosure.

5. Nothing in this Protocol shall require a public authority to publish information or make information available to the public if disclosure of the information would adversely affect:

(a) The confidentiality of the proceedings of public authorities, where such confidentiality is provided for under national law;
(b) International relations, national defence or public security;
(c) The course of justice, the ability of a person to receive a fair trial or the ability of a public authority to conduct an enquiry of a criminal or disciplinary nature;
(d) The confidentiality of commercial or industrial information, where such confidentiality is protected by law in order to protect a legitimate economic interest. Within this framework, information on emissions and discharges which are relevant for the protection of the environment shall be disclosed;
(e) Intellectual property rights;
(f) The confidentiality of personal data and/or files relating to a natural person where that person has not consented to the disclosure of the information to the public, where such confidentiality is provided for in national law;
(g) The interests of a third party which has supplied the information requested without that party being under, or being capable of being put under, a legal obligation to do so, and where that party does not consent to the release of the material; or
(h) The environment to which the information relates, such as the breeding sites of rare species.

These grounds for not disclosing information shall be interpreted in a restrictive way, taking into account the public interest served by disclosure and taking into account whether the information relates to emissions and discharges into the environment.

Article 11
International cooperation

The Parties shall cooperate and, as appropriate, assist each other:

(a) In international actions in support of the objectives of this Protocol;
(b) On request, in implementing national and local plans in pursuance of this Protocol.

Article 12
Joint and coordinated international action

In pursuance of article 11, subparagraph (a), the Parties shall promote cooperation in international action relating to:

(a) The development of commonly agreed targets for matters referred to in
    article 6, paragraph 2;
(b) The development of indicators for the purposes of article 7, paragraph 1
    (b), to show how far action on water-related disease has been successful in
    preventing, controlling and reducing such disease;
(c) The establishment of joint or coordinated systems for surveillance and
    early-warning systems, contingency plans and response capacities as part
    of, or to complement, the national systems maintained in accordance with
    article 8 for the purpose of responding to outbreaks and incidents of water-
    related disease and significant threats of such outbreaks and incidents,
    especially from water-pollution incidents or extreme weather events;
(d) Mutual assistance in responding to outbreaks and incidents of water-related
    disease and significant threats of such outbreaks and incidents, especially
    from water-pollution incidents or extreme weather events;
(e) The development of integrated information systems and databases, ex-
    change of information and sharing of technical and legal knowledge and
    experience;
(f) The prompt and clear notification by the competent authorities of one Party
    to the corresponding authorities of other Parties which may be affected of:
    (i) Outbreaks and incidents of water-related disease, and
    (ii) Significant threats of such outbreaks and incidents which have been
         identified;
(g) The exchange of information on effective means of disseminating to the
    public information about water-related disease.

Article 13
Cooperation in relation to transboundary waters

1. Where any Parties border the same transboundary waters, as a complement
to their other obligations under articles 11 and 12, they shall cooperate and,
as appropriate, assist each other to prevent, control and reduce transboundary
effects of water-related disease. In particular, they shall:

(a) Exchange information and share knowledge about the transboundary
    waters and the problems and risks which they present with the other Parties
    bordering the same waters;
(b) Endeavour to establish with the other Parties bordering the same trans-
    boundary waters joint or coordinated water-management plans in accor-
    dance with article 6, paragraph 5 (b), and surveillance and early-warning

systems and contingency plans in accordance with article 8, paragraph 1, for the purpose of responding to outbreaks and incidents of water-related disease and significant threats of such outbreaks and incidents, especially from water-pollution incidents or extreme weather events;

(c) On the basis of equality and reciprocity, adapt their agreements and other arrangements regarding their transboundary waters in order to eliminate any contradictions with the basic principles of this Protocol and to define their mutual relations and conduct regarding the aims of this Protocol;

(d) Consult each other, at the request of any one of them, on the significance of any adverse effect on human health which may constitute a water-related disease.

2. Where the Parties concerned are Parties to the Convention, the cooperation and assistance in respect of any transboundary effects of water-related disease which are transboundary impacts shall take place in accordance with the provisions of the Convention.

Article 14
International support for national action

When cooperating and assisting each other in the implementation of national and local plans in pursuance of article 11, subparagraph (b), the Parties shall, in particular, consider how they can best help to promote:

(a) Preparation of water-management plans in transboundary, national and/or local contexts and of schemes for improving water supply and sanitation;

(b) Improved formulation of projects, especially infrastructure projects, in pursuance of such plans and schemes, in order to facilitate access to sources of finance;

(c) Effective execution of such projects;

(d) Establishment of systems for surveillance and early-warning systems, contingency plans and response capacities in relation to water-related disease;

(e) Preparation of legislation needed to support the implementation of this Protocol;

(f) Education and training of key professional and technical staff;

(g) Research into, and development of, cost-effective means and techniques for preventing, controlling and reducing water-related disease;

(h) Operation of effective networks to monitor and assess the provision and quality of water-related services, and development of integrated information systems and databases;

(i) Achievement of quality assurance for monitoring activities, including interlaboratory comparability.

Article 15
Review of compliance

The Parties shall review the compliance of the Parties with the provisions of this Protocol on the basis of the reviews and assessments referred to in article 7. Multilateral arrangements of a non-confrontational, non-judicial and consultative nature for reviewing compliance shall be established by the Parties at their first meeting. These arrangements shall allow for appropriate public involvement.

Article 16
Meeting of the Parties

1. The first meeting of the Parties shall be convened no later than eighteen months after the date of the entry into force of this Protocol. Thereafter, ordinary meetings shall be held at regular intervals to be determined by the Parties, but at least every three years, except in so far as other arrangements are necessary to achieve the aims of paragraph 2 of this article. The Parties shall hold an extraordinary meeting if they so decide in the course of an ordinary meeting or at the written request of any Party, provided that, within six months of it being communicated to all Parties, the said request is supported by at least one third of the Parties.

2. Where possible, ordinary meetings of the Parties shall be held in conjunction with the meetings of the Parties to the Convention.

3. At their meetings, the Parties shall keep under continuous review the implementation of this Protocol, and, with this purpose in mind, shall:

(a) Review the policies for and methodological approaches to the prevention, control and reduction of water-related disease, promote their convergence, and strengthen transboundary and international cooperation in accordance with articles 11, 12, 13 and 14;

(b) Evaluate progress in implementing this Protocol on the basis of information provided by the Parties in accordance with guidelines established by the Meeting of the Parties. Such guidelines shall avoid duplication of effort in reporting requirements;

(c) Be kept informed on progress made in the implementation of the Convention;

(d) Exchange information with the Meeting of the Parties to the Convention, and consider the possibilities for joint action with it;

(e) Seek, where appropriate, the services of relevant bodies of the Economic Commission for Europe and of the Regional Committee for Europe of the World Health Organization;

(f) Establish the modalities for the participation of other competent international governmental and non-governmental bodies in all meetings and other activities pertinent to the achievement of the purposes of this Protocol;

(g) Consider the need for further provisions on access to information, public participation in decision-making and public access to judicial and administrative review of decisions within the scope of this Protocol, in the light of experience gained on these matters in other international forums;

(h) Establish a programme of work, including projects to be carried out jointly under this Protocol and the Convention, and set up any bodies needed to implement this programme of work;

(i) Consider and adopt guidelines and recommendations which promote the implementation of the provisions of this Protocol;

(j) At the first meeting, consider and by consensus adopt rules of procedure for their meetings. These rules of procedure shall contain provision to promote harmonious cooperation with the Meeting of the Parties to the Convention;

(k) Consider and adopt proposals for amendments to this Protocol;

(l) Consider and undertake any additional action that may be required for the achievement of the purposes of this Protocol.

Article 17
Secretariat

1. The Executive Secretary of the Economic Commission for Europe and the Regional Director of the Regional Office for Europe of the World Health Organization shall carry out the following secretariat functions for this Protocol:

(a) The convening and preparing of meetings of the Parties;

(b) The transmission to the Parties of reports and other information received in accordance with the provisions of this Protocol;

(c) The performance of such other functions as may be determined by the Meeting of the Parties on the basis of available resources.

2. The Executive Secretary of the Economic Commission for Europe and the Regional Director of the Regional Office for Europe of the World Health Organization shall:

(a) Set out details of their work-sharing arrangements in a Memorandum of Understanding, and inform the Meeting of the Parties accordingly;

(b) Report to the Parties on the elements of, and the modalities for carrying out, the programme of work referred to in article 16, paragraph 3.

Article 18
Amendments to the Protocol

1. Any Party may propose amendments to this Protocol.

2. Proposals for amendments to this Protocol shall be considered at a meeting of the Parties.

3. The text of any proposed amendment to this Protocol shall be submitted in writing to the secretariat, which shall communicate it to all Parties at least ninety days before the meeting at which it is proposed for adoption.

4. An amendment to this Protocol shall be adopted by consensus of the representatives of the Parties present at the meeting. The adopted amendment shall be communicated by the secretariat to the Depositary, who shall circulate it to all Parties for their acceptance. The amendment shall enter into force for the Parties which have accepted it on the ninetieth day after the date on which two thirds of those Parties have deposited with the Depositary their instruments of acceptance of the amendment. The amendment shall enter into force for any other Party on the ninetieth day after the date on which that Party deposits its instrument of acceptance of the amendment.

Article 19
Right to vote

1. Except as provided for in paragraph 2 of this article, each Party shall have one vote.

2. Regional economic integration organizations, in matters within their competence, shall exercise their right to vote with a number of votes equal to the number of their member States which are Parties. Such organizations shall not exercise their right to vote if their member States exercise theirs, and vice versa.

Article 20
Settlement of disputes

1. If a dispute arises between two or more Parties about the interpretation or application of this Protocol, they shall seek a solution by negotiation or by any other means of dispute settlement acceptable to the parties to the dispute.

2. When signing, ratifying, accepting, approving or acceding to this Protocol, or at any time thereafter, a Party may declare in writing to the Depositary that for a dispute not resolved in accordance with paragraph 1 of this article, it accepts one of the following means of dispute settlement as compulsory in relation to any Party accepting the same obligation:

(a) Where the Parties are Parties to the Convention, and have accepted as compulsory in relation to each other one or both of the means of dispute settlement provided in the Convention, the settlement of the dispute in accordance with the provisions of the Convention for the settlement of disputes arising in connection with the Convention;

(b) In any other case, the submission of the dispute to the International Court of Justice, unless the Parties agree to arbitration or some other form of dispute resolution.

Article 21
Signature

This Protocol shall be open for signature in London on 17 and 18 June 1999 on the occasion of the Third Ministerial Conference on Environment and Health, and thereafter at United Nations Headquarters in New York until 18 June 2000, by States members of the Economic Commission for Europe, by States members of the Regional Committee for Europe of the World Health Organization, by States having consultative status with the Economic Commission for Europe pursuant to paragraph 8 of Economic and Social Council resolution 36 (IV) of 28 March 1947, and by regional economic integration organizations constituted by sovereign States members of the Economic Commission for Europe or members of the Regional Committee for Europe of the World Health Organization to which their member States have transferred competence over matters governed by this Protocol, including the competence to enter into treaties in respect of these matters.

Article 22
Ratification, acceptance, approval and accession

1. This Protocol shall be subject to ratification, acceptance or approval by signatory States and regional economic integration organizations.

2. This Protocol shall be open for accession by the States and organizations referred to in article 21.

3. Any organization referred to in article 21 which becomes a Party without any of its member States being a Party shall be bound by all the obligations under this Protocol. In the case of such organizations, one or more of whose member States is a Party, the organization and its member States shall decide on their respective responsibilities for the performance of their obligations under this Protocol. In such cases, the organization and the member States shall not be entitled to exercise rights under this Protocol concurrently.

4. In their instruments of ratification, acceptance, approval or accession, the regional economic integration organizations referred to in article 21 shall declare the extent of their competence with respect to the matters governed by this Protocol. These organizations shall also inform the Depositary of any substantial modification to the extent of their competence.

5. The instruments of ratification, acceptance, approval or accession shall be deposited with the Secretary-General of the United Nations.

Article 23
Entry into force

1. This Protocol shall enter into force on the ninetieth day after the date of deposit of the sixteenth instrument of ratification, acceptance, approval or accession.

2. For the purposes of paragraph 1 of this article, any instrument deposited by a regional economic integration organization shall not be counted as additional to those deposited by States members of such an organization.

3. For each State or organization referred to in article 21 which ratifies, accepts or approves this Protocol or accedes thereto after the deposit of the sixteenth instrument of ratification, acceptance, approval or accession, the Protocol shall enter into force on the ninetieth day after the date of deposit by such State or organization of its instrument of ratification, acceptance, approval or accession.

Article 24
Withdrawal

At any time after three years from the date on which this Protocol has come into force with respect to a Party, that Party may withdraw from the Protocol by giving written notification to the Depositary. Any such withdrawal shall take effect on the ninetieth day after the date of its receipt by the Depositary.

Article 25
Depositary

The Secretary-General of the United Nations shall act as the Depositary of this Protocol

Article 26
Authentic texts

The original of this Protocol, of which the English, French, German and Russian texts are equally authentic, shall be deposited with the Secretary-General of the United Nations.

IN WITNESS WHEREOF the undersigned, being duly authorized thereto, have signed this Protocol.

DONE in London, this seventeenth day of June one thousand nine hundred and ninety-nine.

United Nations Convention on the Law of the Non-Navigational Uses of International Watercourses, 21 May 1997

Editorial note

The 1997 United Nations Convention on the Law of the Non-navigational Uses of International Watercourses (Watercourses Convention) was based on the codification efforts of the International Law Commission (ILC) as reflected in draft Articles on the Law of Non-Navigational Uses of International Watercourses.

The ILC's work began in 1971, following a request from the UN General Assembly. A first reading of a full set of draft Articles was adopted at the ILC's forty-third session in 1991, and a revised set of draft articles was adopted in 1994. The tension between the interests of upstream and downstream states was tangible during the course of the ILC's efforts, and in the diplomatic negotiations leading to the adoption of the 1997 Convention.

The Watercourses Convention applies to uses of international watercourses and their waters for purposes other than navigation and encourages watercourse states to enter into watercourse agreements (Articles 1(1), 3 and 4).

The Convention comprises an introductory section (Part I) and five operational parts. The Convention is without prejudice to rights and obligations arising from agreements already in force (Article 3(1)), and permits states to enter into new agreements which 'apply and adjust' its provisions 'to the characteristics and uses of a particular international watercourse' (Article 3(3)).

Part II contains general principles. Article 5 of the Convention is of central importance: it provides that watercourse states 'shall . . . utilise an international watercourse in an equitable and reasonable manner', which requires the optimal and sustainable utilisation of the watercourse and its benefits 'consistent with adequate protection of the watercourse'. Article 6 identifies a non-exhaustive list of factors and circumstances which are to be taken into account to ensure an equitable and reasonable utilisation, including: (a) geographic and other factors of a natural character; (b) social and economic needs; (c) population; (d) effects on uses in another watercourse state; (e) existing and potential uses; (f) conservation of water resources; and (g) availability of alternatives. The right to equitable utilisation is balanced by the requirement of Article 7 (together with the obligation to prevent pollution, as required by Article 21), which commits watercourse states to 'take all appropriate measures to prevent the causing of significant harm to other watercourse States'. Where significant harm is nevertheless caused, the responsible state must take all appropriate measures, in consultation with the affected state, to eliminate or mitigate the harm and 'where appropriate, to discuss the question of compensation' (Article 7(1) and (2)).

Other principles require states to co-operate and regularly exchange data and information (Article 9) and deal with the relationship between different kinds of uses of a watercourse (Article 10). Part III is concerned with planned measures that may have an effect on an international watercourse. It establishes a phased procedure comprising information exchange and consultation, notification, and a waiting period of six months to allow for a reply to the notification, during which time the notifying state 'shall not implement or permit the implementation of the planned measures without the consent of the notified state' (Articles 11 to 14). The Convention envisages a reply to notification, consultations and negotiations, and procedures to be followed in the absence of a notification or a reply, or where urgent implementation of a particular measure is required (Articles 15 to 19).

Part IV deals specifically with protection, preservation and management of ecosystems, which watercourse states are under an obligation to jointly or individually protect and preserve (Article 20). Article 21 provides that pollution which may cause 'significant' harm to other watercourse states or their environment is to be prevented, reduced and controlled, and states should consult between themselves to establish lists of substances which should be prohibited, limited, investigated or monitored (Article 21(2) and (3)). 'Pollution' is defined broadly as 'any detrimental alteration in the composition or quality of the waters of an international watercourse which results directly or indirectly from human conduct' (Article 21(1)). New or alien species which may have detrimental effects to the ecosystem resulting in significant harm to other watercourse states should not be introduced (Article 22), and watercourse states are required to take all measures necessary to protect and preserve the marine environment, taking into account generally accepted international rules and standards (Article 23). Watercourse states are required, at the request of any of them, to enter into consultations concerning the management of an international watercourse, which may include the establishment of a joint management mechanism (Article 24). They must also co-operate, where appropriate, to 'respond to needs or opportunities for regulation of the flow of the waters of an international watercourse' through use of hydraulic works, and, within their own territories, must employ their best efforts to maintain and protect installations, facilities and other works related to an international watercourse (Articles 25 and 26).

Part V deals with harmful conditions and emergency situations (Articles 27 and 28), and Part VI establishes miscellaneous provisions on, *inter alia*, armed conflict, indirect contacts between watercourse states, confidentiality of certain data, and non-discrimination (Articles 29 to 32). Part VI also contains a dispute settlement provision which directs parties to seek settlement of any dispute concerning the Convention initially by way of negotiation, mediation, conciliation or submission of the dispute to arbitration or to the International Court with the agreement of both parties (Article 33(2)). Under Article 33(10), parties may elect, when ratifying, accepting, approving or acceding to the Convention, or at any time thereafter, to submit a written declaration recognising the jurisdiction of the International Court or an arbitral tribunal constituted in accordance with the Convention's Annex as 'compulsory *ipso facto* and without special agreement in relation to any party accepting the same obligation'. Alternatively, if the conditions in paragraph 10 are not met and the dispute is not resolved within six months of the initial request for negotiations, the dispute can be submitted, at the option of either of the parties, to an impartial fact-finding commission (Article 33(4) to (6)). The parties are to provide the Commission with such information as it may require and must permit Commissioners to have access to the state's territory for the purpose of inspecting facilities, plant or equipment, construction or any natural feature relevant for the purpose of the inquiry (Article 33(7)). The Commission reports back to the parties and may make recommendations designed to secure 'an equitable solution of the dispute', which the parties are required to consider in good faith (33(8)). The Convention will enter into force ninety days after the date of deposit of the thirty-fifth instrument of ratification, accession, approval or accession with the Secretary-General of the United Nations (Article 36).

Date of signature:	21 May 1997
Entry into force:	Not yet in force
Depositary:	Secretary-General of the United Nations
Contracting Parties:	Cote d'Ivoire, Finland, Germany, Hungary, Iraq, Jordan, Lebanon, Luxembourg, Namibia, Netherlands, Norway, Paraguay, Portugal, Qatar, South Africa, Sweden, Syrian Arab Republic, Tunisia, Venezuela, Yemen
Websites:	www.un.org/law/ilc/texts/nnavfra.htm www.internationalwaterlaw.org

United Nations Convention on the Law of the Non-Navigational Uses of International Watercourses

The Parties to the present Convention,

Conscious of the importance of international watercourses and the non-navigational uses thereof in many regions of the world,

Having in mind Article 13, paragraph 1 (a), of the Charter of the United Nations, which provides that the General Assembly shall initiate studies and make recommendations for the purpose of encouraging the progressive development of international law and its codification,

Considering that successful codification and progressive development of rules of international law regarding non-navigational uses of international watercourses would assist in promoting and implementing the purposes and principles set forth in Articles 1 and 2 of the Charter of the United Nations,

Taking into account the problems affecting many international watercourses resulting from, among other things, increasing demands and pollution,

Expressing the conviction that a framework convention will ensure the utilization, development, conservation, management and protection of international watercourses and the promotion of the optimal and sustainable utilization thereof for present and future generations,

Affirming the importance of international cooperation and good neighbourliness in this field,

Aware of the special situation and needs of developing countries,

Recalling the principles and recommendations adopted by the United Nations Conference on Environment and Development of 1992 in the Rio Declaration and Agenda 21,

Recalling also the existing bilateral and multilateral agreements regarding the non-navigational uses of international watercourses,

Mindful of the valuable contribution of international organizations, both governmental and non-governmental, to the codification and progressive development of international law in this field,

Appreciative of the work carried out by the International Law Commission on the law of the non-navigational uses of international watercourses,

Bearing in mind United Nations General Assembly resolution 49/52 of 9 December 1994,

Have agreed as follows:

Part I
Introduction

Article 1
Scope of the present Convention

1. The present Convention applies to uses of international watercourses and of their waters for purposes other than navigation and to measures of protection, preservation and management related to the uses of those watercourses and their waters.

2. The uses of international watercourses for navigation is not within the scope of the present Convention except insofar as other uses affect navigation or are affected by navigation.

Article 2
Use of terms

1. For the purposes of the present Convention:

(a) 'Watercourse' means a system of surface waters and groundwaters constituting by virtue of their physical relationship a unitary whole and normally
flowing into a common terminus;

(b) 'International watercourse' means a watercourse, parts of which are situated
in different States;

(c) 'Watercourse State' means a State Party to the present Convention in whose
territory part of an international watercourse is situated, or a Party that
is a regional economic integration organization, in the territory of one
or more of whose Member States part of an international watercourse is
situated;

(d) 'Regional economic integration organization' means an organization
constituted by sovereign States of a given region, to which its member
States have transferred competence in respect of matters governed by this
Convention and which has been duly authorized in accordance with its
internal procedures, to sign, ratify, accept, approve or accede to it.

Article 3
Watercourse agreements

1. In the absence of an agreement to the contrary, nothing in the present
Convention shall affect the rights or obligations of a watercourse State arising
from agreements in force for it on the date on which it became a party to the
present Convention.

2. Notwithstanding the provisions of paragraph 1, parties to agreements
referred to in paragraph 1 may, where necessary, consider harmonizing such
agreements with the basic principles of the present Convention.

3. Watercourse States may enter into one or more agreements, hereinafter
referred to as 'watercourse agreements', which apply and adjust the provisions
of the present Convention to the characteristics and uses of a particular international watercourse or part thereof.

4. Where a watercourse agreement is concluded between two or more watercourse States, it shall define the waters to which it applies. Such an agreement
may be entered into with respect to an entire international watercourse or any
part thereof or a particular project programme or use except insofar as the
agreement adversely affects, to a significant extent, the use by one or more
other watercourse States of the waters of the watercourse, without their express
consent.

5. Where a watercourse State considers that adjustment and application of the
provisions of the present Convention is required because of the characteristics
and uses of a particular international watercourse, watercourse States shall

consult with a view to negotiating in good faith for the purpose of concluding a watercourse agreement or agreements.

6. Where some but not all watercourse States to a particular international watercourse are parties to an agreement, nothing in such agreement shall affect the rights or obligations under the present Convention of watercourse States that are not parties to such an agreement.

Article 4
Parties to watercourse agreements

1. Every watercourse State is entitled to participate in the negotiation of and to become a party to any watercourse agreement that applies to the entire international watercourse, as well as to participate in any relevant consultations.

2. A watercourse State whose use of an international watercourse may be affected to a significant extent by the implementation of a proposed watercourse agreement that applies only to a part of the watercourse or to a particular project, programme or use is entitled to participate in consultations on such an agreement and, where appropriate, in the negotiation thereof in good faith with a view to becoming a party thereto, to the extent that its use is thereby affected.

Part II
General principles

Article 5
Equitable and reasonable utilization and participation

1. Watercourse States shall in their respective territories utilize an international watercourse in an equitable and reasonable manner. In particular, an international watercourse shall be used and developed by watercourse States with a view to attaining optimal and sustainable utilization thereof and benefits therefrom, taking into account the interests of the watercourse States concerned, consistent with adequate protection of the watercourse.

2. Watercourse States shall participate in the use, development and protection of an international watercourse in an equitable and reasonable manner. Such participation includes both the right to utilize the watercourse and the duty to cooperate in the protection and development thereof, as provided in the present Convention.

Article 6
Factors relevant to equitable and reasonable utilization

1. Utilization of an international watercourse in an equitable and reasonable manner within the meaning of article 5 requires taking into account all relevant factors and circumstances, including:

(a) Geographic, hydrographic, hydrological, climatic, ecological and other factors of a natural character;
(b) The social and economic needs of the watercourse States concerned;
(c) The population dependent on the watercourse in each watercourse State;
(d) The effects of the use or uses of the watercourses in one watercourse State on other watercourse States;
(e) Existing and potential uses of the watercourse;
(f) Conservation, protection, development and economy of use of the water resources of the watercourse and the costs of measures taken to that effect;
(g) The availability of alternatives, of comparable value, to a particular planned or existing use.

2. In the application of article 5 or paragraph 1 of this article, watercourse States concerned shall, when the need arises, enter into consultations in a spirit of cooperation.

3. The weight to be given to each factor is to be determined by its importance in comparison with that of other relevant factors. In determining what is a reasonable and equitable use, all relevant factors are to be considered together and a conclusion reached on the basis of the whole.

Article 7
Obligation not to cause significant harm

1. Watercourse States shall, in utilizing an international watercourse in their territories, take all appropriate measures to prevent the causing of significant harm to other watercourse States.

2. Where significant harm nevertheless is caused to another watercourse State, the States whose use causes such harm shall, in the absence of agreement to such use, take all appropriate measures, having due regard for the provisions of articles 5 and 6, in consultation with the affected State, to eliminate or mitigate such harm and, where appropriate, to discuss the question of compensation.

Article 8
General obligation to cooperate

1. Watercourse States shall cooperate on the basis of sovereign equality, territorial integrity, mutual benefit and good faith in order to attain optimal utilization and adequate protection of an international watercourse.

2. In determining the manner of such cooperation, watercourse States may consider the establishment of joint mechanisms or commissions, as deemed necessary by them, to facilitate cooperation on relevant measures and procedures in the light of experience gained through cooperation in existing joint mechanisms and commissions in various regions.

Article 9
Regular exchange of data and information

1. Pursuant to article 8, watercourse States shall on a regular basis exchange readily available data and information on the condition of the watercourse, in particular that of a hydrological, meteorological, hydrogeological and ecological nature and related to the water quality as well as related forecasts.

2. If a watercourse State is requested by another watercourse State to provide data or information that is not readily available, it shall employ its best efforts to comply with the request but may condition its compliance upon payment by the requesting State of the reasonable costs of collecting and, where appropriate, processing such data or information.

3. Watercourse States shall employ their best efforts to collect and, where appropriate, to process data and information in a manner which facilitates its utilization by the other watercourse States to which it is communicated.

Article 10
Relationship between different kinds of uses

1. In the absence of agreement or custom to the contrary, no use of an international watercourse enjoys inherent priority over other uses.

2. In the event of a conflict between uses of an international watercourse, it shall be resolved with reference to articles 5 to 7, with special regard being given to the requirements of vital human needs.

Part III
Planned measures

Article 11
Information concerning planned measures

Watercourse States shall exchange information and consult each other and, if necessary, negotiate on the possible effects of planned measures on the condition of an international watercourse.

Article 12
Notification concerning planned measures with possible adverse effects

Before a watercourse State implements or permits the implementation of planned measures which may have a significant adverse effect upon other watercourse States, it shall provide those States with timely notification thereof. Such notification shall be accompanied by available technical data and information, including the results of any environmental impact assessment, in order to enable the notified States to evaluate the possible effects of the planned measures.

Article 13
Period for reply to notification

Unless otherwise agreed:

(a) A watercourse State providing a notification under article 12 shall allow the notified States a period of six months within which to study and evaluate the possible effects of the planned measures and to communicate the findings to it;

(b) This period shall, at the request of a notified State for which the evaluation of the planned measures poses special difficulty, be extended for a period of six months.

Article 14
Obligations of the notifying State during the period for reply

During the period referred to in article 13, the notifying State:

(a) Shall cooperate with the notified States by providing them, on request, with any additional data and information that is available and necessary for an accurate evaluation; and

(b) Shall not implement or permit the implementation of the planned measures without the consent of the notified States.

Article 15
Reply to notification

The notified States shall communicate their findings to the notifying State as early as possible within the period applicable pursuant to article 13. If a notified State finds that implementation of the planned measures would be inconsistent with the provisions of articles 5 or 7, it shall attach to its finding a documented explanation setting forth the reasons for the finding.

Article 16
Absence of reply to notification

1. If, within the period applicable pursuant to article 13, the notifying State receives no communication under article 15, it may, subject to its obligations under articles 5 and 7, proceed with the implementation of the planned measures, in accordance with the notification and any other data and information provided to the notified States.

2. Any claim to compensation by a notified State which has failed to reply within the period applicable pursuant to article 13 may be offset by the costs incurred by the notifying State for action undertaken after the expiration of the time for a reply which would not have been undertaken if the notified State had objected within that period.

Article 17
Consultations and negotiations concerning planned measures

1. If a communication is made under article 15 that implementation of the planned measures would be inconsistent with the provisions of articles 5 or 7, the notifying State and the State making the communication shall enter into consultations and, if necessary, negotiations with a view to arriving at an equitable resolution of the situation.

2. The consultations and negotiations shall be conducted on the basis that each State must in good faith pay reasonable regard to the rights and legitimate interests of the other State.

3. During the course of the consultations and negotiations, the notifying State shall, if so requested by the notified State at the time it makes the communication, refrain from implementing or permitting the implementation of the planned measures for a period of six months unless otherwise agreed.

Article 18
Procedures in the absence of notification

1. If a watercourse State has reasonable grounds to believe that another watercourse State is planning measures that may have a significant adverse effect upon it, the former State may request the latter to apply the provisions of article 12. The request shall be accompanied by a documented explanation setting forth its grounds.

2. In the event that the State planning the measures nevertheless finds that it is not under an obligation to provide a notification under article 12, it shall so inform the other State, providing a documented explanation setting forth the reasons for such finding. If this finding does not satisfy the other State, the two States shall, at the request of that other State, promptly enter into consultations and negotiations in the manner indicated in paragraphs 1 and 2 of article 17.

3. During the course of the consultations and negotiations, the State planning the measures shall, if so requested by the other State at the time it requests the initiation of consultations and negotiations, refrain from implementing or permitting the implementation of those measures for a period of six months unless otherwise agreed.

Article 19
Urgent implementation of planned measures

1. In the event that the implementation of planned measures is of the utmost urgency in order to protect public health, public safety or other equally important interests, the State planning the measures may, subject to articles 5 and 7, immediately proceed to implementation, notwithstanding the provisions of article 14 and paragraph 3 of article 17.

2. In such case, a formal declaration of the urgency of the measures shall be communicated without delay to the other watercourse States referred to in article 12 together with the relevant data and information.

3. The State planning the measures shall, at the request of any of the States referred to in paragraph 2, promptly enter into consultations and negotiations with it in the manner indicated in paragraphs 1 and 2 of article 17.

Part IV
Protection, preservation and management

Article 20
Protection and preservation of ecosystems

Watercourse States shall, individually and, where appropriate, jointly, protect and preserve the ecosystems of international watercourses.

Article 21
Prevention, reduction and control of pollution

1. For the purpose of this article, 'pollution of an international watercourse' means any detrimental alteration in the composition or quality of the waters of an international watercourse which results directly or indirectly from human conduct.

2. Watercourse States shall, individually and, where appropriate, jointly, prevent, reduce and control the pollution of an international watercourse that may cause significant harm to other watercourse States or to their environment, including harm to human health or safety, to the use of the waters for any beneficial purpose or to the living resources of the watercourse. Watercourse States shall take steps to harmonize their policies in this connection.

3. Watercourse States shall, at the request of any of them, consult with a view to arriving at mutually agreeable measures and methods to prevent, reduce and control pollution of an international watercourse, such as:

(a) Setting joint water quality objectives and criteria;
(b) Establishing techniques and practices to address pollution from point and non-point sources;
(c) Establishing lists of substances the introduction of which into the waters of an international watercourse is to be prohibited, limited, investigated or monitored.

Article 22
Introduction of alien or new species

Watercourse States shall take all measures necessary to prevent the introduction of species, alien or new, into an international watercourse which may have effects detrimental to the ecosystem of the watercourse resulting in significant harm to other watercourse States.

Article 23
Protection and preservation of the marine environment

Watercourse States shall, individually and, where appropriate, in cooperation with other States, take all measures with respect to an international watercourse that are necessary to protect and preserve the marine environment, including estuaries, taking into account generally accepted international rules and standards.

Article 24
Management

1. Watercourse States shall, at the request of any of them, enter into consultations concerning the management of an international watercourse, which may include the establishment of a joint management mechanism.

2. For the purposes of this article, 'management' refers, in particular, to:

(a) Planning the sustainable development of an international watercourse and providing for the implementation of any plans adopted; and
(b) Otherwise promoting the rational and optimal utilization, protection and control of the watercourse.

Article 25
Regulation

1. Watercourse States shall cooperate, where appropriate, to respond to needs or opportunities for regulation of the flow of the waters of an international watercourse.

2. Unless otherwise agreed, watercourse States shall participate on an equitable basis in the construction and maintenance or defrayal of the costs of such regulation works as they may have agreed to undertake.

3. For the purposes of this article, 'regulation' means the use of hydraulic works or any other continuing measure to alter, vary or otherwise control the flow of the waters of an international watercourse.

Article 26
Installations

1. Watercourse States shall, within their respective territories, employ their best efforts to maintain and protect installations, facilities and other works related to an international watercourse.

2. Watercourse States shall, at the request of any of them which has reasonable grounds to believe that it may suffer significant adverse effects, enter into consultations with regard to:

(a) The safe operation and maintenance of installations, facilities or other works related to an international watercourse; and

(b) The protection of installations, facilities or other works from wilful or negligent acts or the forces of nature.

Part V
Harmful conditions and emergency situations
Article 27
Prevention and mitigation of harmful conditions

Watercourse States shall, individually and, where appropriate, jointly, take all appropriate measures to prevent or mitigate conditions related to an international watercourse that may be harmful to other watercourse States, whether resulting from natural causes or human conduct, such as flood or ice conditions, water-borne diseases, siltation, erosion, salt-water intrusion, drought or desertification.

Article 28
Emergency situations

1. For the purposes of this article, 'emergency' means a situation that causes, or poses an imminent threat of causing, serious harm to watercourse States or other States and that results suddenly from natural causes, such as floods, the breaking up of ice, landslides or earthquakes, or from human conduct, such as industrial accidents.

2. A watercourse State shall, without delay and by the most expeditious means available, notify other potentially affected States and competent international organizations of any emergency originating within its territory.

3. A watercourse State within whose territory an emergency originates shall, in cooperation with potentially affected States and, where appropriate, competent international organizations, immediately take all practicable measures necessitated by the circumstances to prevent, mitigate and eliminate harmful effects of the emergency.

4. When necessary, watercourse States shall jointly develop contingency plans for responding to emergencies, in cooperation, where appropriate, with other potentially affected States and competent international organizations.

Part VI
Miscellaneous provisions
Article 29
International watercourses and installations in time of armed conflict

International watercourses and related installations, facilities and other works shall enjoy the protection accorded by the principles and rules of international law applicable in international and non-international armed conflict and shall not be used in violation of those principles and rules.

Article 30
Indirect procedures

In cases where there are serious obstacles to direct contacts between watercourse States, the States concerned shall fulfil their obligations of cooperation provided for in the present Convention, including exchange of data and information, notification, communication, consultations and negotiations, through any indirect procedure accepted by them.

Article 31
Data and information vital to national defense or security

Nothing in the present Convention obliges a watercourse State to provide data or information vital to its national defence or security. Nevertheless, that State shall cooperate in good faith with the other watercourse States with a view to providing as much information as possible under the circumstances.

Article 32
Non-discrimination

Unless the watercourse States concerned have agreed otherwise for the protection of the interests of persons, natural or juridical, who have suffered or are under a serious threat of suffering significant transboundary harm as a result of activities related to an international watercourse, a watercourse State shall not discriminate on the basis of nationality or residence or place where the injury occurred, in granting to such persons, in accordance with its legal system, access to judicial or other procedures, or a right to claim compensation or other relief in respect of significant harm caused by such activities carried on in its territory.

Article 33
Settlement of disputes

1. In the event of a dispute between two or more Parties concerning the interpretation or application of the present Convention, the Parties concerned shall, in the absence of an applicable agreement between them, seek a settlement of the dispute by peaceful means in accordance with the following provisions.

2. If the Parties concerned cannot reach agreement by negotiation requested by one of them, they may jointly seek the good offices of, or request mediation or conciliation by, a third party, or make use, as appropriate, of any joint watercourse institutions that may have been established by them or agree to submit the dispute to arbitration or to the International Court of Justice.

3. Subject to the operation of paragraph 10, if after six months from the time of the request for negotiations referred to in paragraph 2, the Parties

concerned have not been able to settle their dispute through negotiation or any other means referred to in paragraph 2, the dispute shall be submitted, at the request of any of the parties to the dispute, to impartial fact-finding in accordance with paragraphs 4 to 9, unless the Parties otherwise agree.

4. A Fact-finding Commission shall be established, composed of one member nominated by each Party concerned and in addition a member not having the nationality of any of the Parties concerned chosen by the nominated members who shall serve as Chairman.

5. If the members nominated by the Parties are unable to agree on a Chairman within three months of the request for the establishment of the Commission, any Party concerned may request the Secretary-General of the United Nations to appoint the Chairman who shall not have the nationality of any of the parties to the dispute or of any riparian State of the watercourse concerned. If one of the Parties fails to nominate a member within three months of the initial request pursuant to paragraph 3, any other Party concerned may request the Secretary-General of the United Nations to appoint a person who shall not have the nationality of any of the parties to the dispute or of any riparian State of the watercourse concerned. The person so appointed shall constitute a single-member Commission.

6. The Commission shall determine its own procedure.

7. The Parties concerned have the obligation to provide the Commission with such information as it may require and, on request, to permit the Commission to have access to their respective territory and to inspect any facilities, plant, equipment, construction or natural feature relevant for the purpose of its inquiry.

8. The Commission shall adopt its report by a majority vote, unless it is a single-member Commission, and shall submit that report to the Parties concerned setting forth its findings and the reasons therefor and such recommendations as it deems appropriate for an equitable solution of the dispute, which the Parties concerned shall consider in good faith.

9. The expenses of the Commission shall be borne equally by the Parties concerned.

10. When ratifying, accepting, approving or acceding to the present Convention, or at any time thereafter, a Party which is not a regional economic integration organization may declare in a written instrument submitted to the Depositary that, in respect of any dispute not resolved in accordance with paragraph 2, it recognizes as compulsory *ipso facto* and without special agreement in relation to any Party accepting the same obligation:

(a) Submission of the dispute to the International Court of Justice; and/or
(b) Arbitration by an arbitral tribunal established and operating, unless the parties to the dispute otherwise agreed, in accordance with the procedure laid down in the annex to the present Convention.

A Party which is a regional economic integration organization may make a declaration with like effect in relation to arbitration in accordance with sub-paragraph (b).

Part VII
Final clauses

Article 34
Signature

The present Convention shall be open for signature by all States and by regional economic integration organizations from 21 May 1997until 21 May 2000 at United Nations Headquarters in New York.

Article 35
Ratification, acceptance, approval or accession

1. The present Convention is subject to ratification, acceptance, approval or accession by States and by regional economic integration organizations. The instruments of ratification, acceptance, approval or accession shall be deposited with the Secretary-General of the United Nations.

2. Any regional economic integration organization which becomes a Party to this Convention without any of its member States being a Party shall be bound by all the obligations under the Convention. In the case of such organizations, one or more of whose member States is a Party to this Convention, the organization and its member States shall decide on their respective responsibilities for the performance of their obligations under the Convention. In such cases, the organization and the member States shall not be entitled to exercise rights under the Convention concurrently.

3. In their instruments of ratification, acceptance, approval or accession, the regional economic integration organizations shall declare the extent of their competence with respect to the matters governed by the Convention. These organizations shall also inform the Secretary-General of the United Nations of any substantial modification in the extent of their competence.

Article 36
Entry into force

1. The present Convention shall enter into force on the ninetieth day following the date of deposit of the thirty-fifth instrument of ratification, acceptance, approval or accession with the Secretary-General of the United Nations.

2. For each State or regional economic integration organization that ratifies, accepts or approves the Convention or accedes thereto after the deposit of the thirty-fifth instrument of ratification, acceptance, approval or accession, the Convention shall enter into force on the ninetieth day after the deposit by

such State or regional economic integration organization of its instrument of ratification, acceptance, approval or accession.

3. For the purposes of paragraphs 1 and 2, any instrument deposited by a regional economic integration organization shall not be counted as additional to those deposited by States.

Article 37
Authentic texts

The original of the present Convention, of which the Arabic, Chinese, English, French, Russian and Spanish texts are equally authentic, shall be deposited with the Secretary-General of the United Nations.

IN WITNESS WHEREOF the undersigned plenipotentiaries, being duly authorized thereto, have signed this Convention.

DONE at New York, this 21 day of May one thousand nine hundred and ninety-seven.

Annex
Arbitration

Article 1

Unless the parties to the dispute otherwise agree, the arbitration pursuant to article 33 of the Convention shall take place in accordance with articles 2 to 14 of the present annex.

Article 2

The claimant party shall notify the respondent party that it is referring a dispute to arbitration pursuant to article 33 of the Convention. The notification shall state the subject matter of arbitration and include, in particular, the articles of the Convention, the interpretation or application of which are at issue. If the parties do not agree on the subject matter of the dispute, the arbitral tribunal shall determine the subject matter.

Article 3

1. In disputes between two parties, the arbitral tribunal shall consist of three members. Each of the parties to the dispute shall appoint an arbitrator and the two arbitrators so appointed shall designate by common agreement the third arbitrator, who shall be the Chairman of the tribunal. The latter shall not be a national of one of the parties to the dispute or of any riparian State of the watercourse concerned, nor have his or her usual place of residence in the territory of one of these parties or such riparian State, nor have dealt with the case in any other capacity.

2. In disputes between more than two parties, parties in the same interest shall appoint one arbitrator jointly by agreement.

3. Any vacancy shall be filled in the manner prescribed for the initial appointment.

Article 4

1. If the Chairman of the arbitral tribunal has not been designated within two months of the appointment of the second arbitrator, the President of the International Court of Justice shall, at the request of a party, designate the Chairman within a further two-month period.

2. If one of the parties to the dispute does not appoint an arbitrator within two months of receipt of the request, the other party may inform the President of the International Court of Justice, who shall make the designation within a further two-month period.

Article 5

The arbitral tribunal shall render its decisions in accordance with the provisions of this Convention and international law.

Article 6

Unless the parties to the dispute otherwise agree, the arbitral tribunal shall determine its own rules of procedure.

Article 7

The arbitral tribunal may, at the request of one of the Parties, recommend essential interim measures of protection.

Article 8

1. The parties to the dispute shall facilitate the work of the arbitral tribunal and, in particular, using all means at their disposal, shall:

(a) Provide it with all relevant documents, information and facilities; and
(b) Enable it, when necessary, to call witnesses or experts and receive their evidence.

2. The parties and the arbitrators are under an obligation to protect the confidentiality of any information they receive in confidence during the proceedings of the arbitral tribunal.

Article 9

Unless the arbitral tribunal determines otherwise because of the particular circumstances of the case, the costs of the tribunal shall be borne by the parties to the dispute in equal shares. The tribunal shall keep a record of all its costs, and shall furnish a final statement thereof to the parties.

Article 10

Any Party that has an interest of a legal nature in the subject matter of the dispute which may be affected by the decision in the case, may intervene in the proceedings with the consent of the tribunal.

Article 11

The tribunal may hear and determine counterclaims arising directly out of the subject matter of the dispute.

Article 12

Decisions both on procedure and substance of the arbitral tribunal shall be taken by a majority vote of its members.

Article 13

If one of the parties to the dispute does not appear before the arbitral tribunal or fails to defend its case, the other party may request the tribunal to continue the proceedings and to make its award. Absence of a party or a failure of a party to defend its case shall not constitute a bar to the proceedings. Before rendering its final decision, the arbitral tribunal must satisfy itself that the claim is well founded in fact and law.

Article 14

1. The tribunal shall render its final decision within five months of the date on which it is fully constituted unless it finds it necessary to extend the time limit for a period which should not exceed five more months.

2. The final decision of the arbitral tribunal shall be confined to the subject matter of the dispute and shall state the reasons on which it is based. It shall contain the names of the members who have participated and the date of the final decision. Any member of the tribunal may attach a separate or dissenting opinion to the final decision.

3. The award shall be binding on the parties to the dispute. It shall be without appeal unless the parties to the dispute have agreed in advance to an appellate procedure.

4. Any controversy which may arise between the parties to the dispute as regards the interpretation or manner of implementation of the final decision may be submitted by either party for decision to the arbitral tribunal which rendered it.

PART V

Biodiversity

International Convention for the Regulation of Whaling, 2 December 1946

Editorial note

The aims of the International Convention for the Regulation of Whaling are the 'proper conservation of whale stocks' and the 'orderly development of the whaling industry' (Preamble). The specific requirements to achieve these ends are set out in the Schedule attached to the Convention, which is amended on a regular basis. Exempted from the Convention's requirements are the killing, taking and treating of whales for scientific purposes in amounts determined by each Party (Article VIII).

Parties are required to apply the Convention to factory ships, land stations and whale catchers under their jurisdiction and to all waters where such entities perform whaling (Article I(2)). Parties must take appropriate measures to apply the Convention and punish the violators of it (Article IX(1)), but the prosecution of any violations is limited to the Party having jurisdiction over the offence (Article IX(2)).

The Convention establishes the International Whaling Commission (IWC) composed of representatives of the Parties (Article III(1)). The IWC is empowered, *inter alia*, to amend the provisions of the Schedule by adopting regulations relating to the 'conservation and utilization of whale resources' (Article V(1)). Such amendments must be taken by a three-fourths majority of members voting (Article III(2)). The Convention requires these amendments to: (a) be necessary for the attainment of the Convention's object and purposes and must provide for the 'conservation, development, and optimal utilization of whale resources'; (b) be based on scientific findings; (c) neither impose restrictions on numbers or nationality of factory ships or landing stations nor impose quotas on specific factory ships or landing stations; and (d) take into account the interests of whaling consumers and industry (Article V(2)). Amendments enter into force for all Parties, save those that have registered objections in accordance with the Convention (Article V(3)). In 1957, an amending Protocol (338 *UNTS* 366)[1] was adopted which added helicopters and other aircraft to the definition of whale catcher (amending Article II(3)) and allowed the

---

[1] Entered into force on 4 May 1959.

IWC to adopt amendments which relate to methods of inspection (amending Article V(1)).

Date of signature: 2 December 1946

Entry into force: 10 November 1948

Depositary: Government of the USA

Contracting Parties: Antigua and Barbuda, Argentina, Australia, Austria, Benin, Brazil, Chile, China, Costa Rica, Denmark, Dominica, Finland, France, Gabon, Germany, Grenada, Guinea, Iceland, India, Ireland, Italy, Japan, Kenya, Korea, Mexico, Monaco, Mongolia, Morocco, Netherlands, New Zealand, Norway, Oman, Palau, Panama, Peru, Portugal, Russian Federation, Saint Kitts and Nevis, Saint Vincent and The Grenadines, San Marino, Senegal, Solomon Islands, South Africa, Spain, Sweden, Switzerland, United Kingdom, United States of America.

Website: www.iwcoffice.org

International Convention for the Regulation of Whaling

The Governments whose duly authorized representatives have subscribed hereto,

Recognizing the interest of the nations of the world in safeguarding for future generations the great natural resources represented by the whale stocks;

Considering that the history of whaling has seen over-fishing of one area after another and of one species of whale after another to such a degree that it is essential to protect all species of whales from further over-fishing;

Recognizing that the whale stocks are susceptible of natural increases if whaling is properly regulated, and that increases in the size of whale stocks will permit increases in the numbers of whales which may be captured without endangering these natural resources;

Recognizing that it is in the common interest to achieve the optimum level of whale stocks as rapidly as possible without causing widespread economic and nutritional distress;

Recognizing that in the course of achieving these objectives, whaling operations should be confined to those species best able to sustain exploitation in order to give an interval for recovery to certain species of whales now depleted in numbers;

Desiring to establish a system of international regulation for the whale fisheries to ensure proper and effective conservation and development of whale stocks on the basis of the principles embodied in the provisions of the International Agreement for the Regulation of Whaling signed in London on 8 June 1937, and the protocols to that Agreement signed in London on 24 June 1938, and 26 November 1945; and

Having decided to conclude a convention to provide for the proper conservation of whale stocks and thus make possible the orderly development of the whaling industry;

Have agreed as follows:

Article I

1. This Convention includes the Schedule attached thereto which forms an integral part thereof. All references to 'Convention' shall be understood as including the said Schedule either in its present terms or as amended in accordance with the provisions of Article V.

2. This Convention applies to factory ships, land stations, and whale catchers under the jurisdiction of the Contracting Governments, and to all waters in which whaling is prosecuted by such factory ships, land stations, and whale catchers.

Article II

As used in this Convention:

1. 'factory ship' means a ship in which or on which whales are treated whether wholly or in part;
2. 'land station' means a factory on the land at which whales are treated whether wholly or in part;
3. 'whale catcher' means a ship used for the purpose of hunting, taking, towing, holding on to, or scouting for whales;[1]
4. 'Contracting Government' means any Government which has deposited an instrument of ratification or has given notice of adherence to this Convention.

Article III

1. The Contracting Governments agree to establish an International Whaling Commission, hereinafter referred to as the Commission, to be composed of one member from each Contracting Government. Each member shall have one vote and may be accompanied by one or more experts and advisers.

2. The Commission shall elect from its own members a Chairman and Vice-Chairman and shall determine its own Rules of Procedure. Decisions of the Commission shall be taken by a simple majority of those members voting

---

[1] Article II(3) was amended by Article I of the 1956 Protocol and shall be amended to read as follows: '3. "whale catcher" means a helicopter, or other aircraft, or a ship, used for the purpose of hunting, taking, killing, towing, holding on to, or scouting for whales.'

except that a three-fourths majority of those members voting shall be required for action in pursuance of Article V. The Rules of Procedure may provide for decisions otherwise than at meetings of the Commission.

3. The Commission may appoint its own Secretary and staff.

4. The Commission may set up, from among its own members and experts or advisers, such committees as it considers desirable to perform such functions as it may authorize.

5. The expenses of each member of the Commission and of his experts and advisers shall be determined and paid by his own Government.

6. Recognizing that specialized agencies related to the United Nations will be concerned with the conservation and development of whale fisheries and the products arising there from and desiring to avoid duplication of functions, the Contracting Governments will consult among themselves within two years after the coming into force of this Convention to decide whether the Commission shall be brought within the framework of a specialized agency related to the United Nations.

7. In the meantime the Government of the United Kingdom of Great Britain and Northern Ireland shall arrange, in consultation with the other Contracting Governments, to convene the first meeting of the Commission, and shall initiate the consultation referred to in paragraph 6 above.

8. Subsequent meetings of the Commission shall be convened as the Commission may determine.

Article IV

1. The Commission may either in collaboration with or through independent agencies of the Contracting Governments or other public or private agencies, establishments, or organizations, or independently

(a) encourage, recommend, or if necessary, organize studies and investigations relating to whales and whaling;
(b) collect and analyze statistical information concerning the current condition and trend of the whale stocks and the effects of whaling activities thereon;
(c) study, appraise, and disseminate information concerning methods of maintaining and increasing the populations of whale stocks.

2. The Commission shall arrange for the publication of reports of its activities, and it may publish independently or in collaboration with the International Bureau for Whaling Statistics at Sandefjord in Norway and other organizations and agencies such reports as it deems appropriate, as well as statistical, scientific, and other pertinent information relating to whales and whaling.

Article V

1. The Commission may amend from time to time the provisions of the Schedule by adopting regulations with respect to the conservation and

utilization of whale resources, fixing (a) protected and unprotected species; (b) open and closed seasons; (c) open and closed waters, including the designation of sanctuary areas; (d) size limits for each species; (e) time, methods, and intensity of whaling (including the maximum catch of whales to be taken in any one season); (f) types and specifications of gear and apparatus and appliances which may be used; (g) methods of measurement; and (h) catch returns and other statistical and biological records.[1]

2. These amendments of the Schedule (a) shall be such as are necessary to carry out the objectives and purposes of this Convention and to provide for the conservation, development, and optimum utilization of the whale resources; (b) shall be based on scientific findings; (c) shall not involve restrictions on the number or nationality of factory ships or land stations, nor allocate specific quotas to any factory ship or land station or to any group of factory ships or land stations; and (d) shall take into consideration the interests of the consumers of whale products and the whaling industry.

3. Each of such amendments shall become effective with respect to the Contracting Governments ninety days following notification of the amendment by the Commission to each of the Contracting Governments, except that (a) if any Government presents to the Commission objection to any amendment prior to the expiration of this ninety-day period, the amendment shall not become effective with respect to any of the Governments for an additional ninety days; (b) thereupon, any other Contracting Government may present objection to the amendment at any time prior to the expiration of the additional ninety-day period, or before the expiration of thirty days from the date of receipt of the last objection received during such additional ninety-day period, whichever date shall be the later; and (c) thereafter, the amendment shall become effective with respect to all Contracting Governments which have not presented objection but shall not become effective with respect to any Government which has so objected until such date as the objection is withdrawn. The Commission shall notify each Contracting Government immediately upon receipt of each objection and withdrawal and each Contracting Government shall acknowledge receipt of all notifications of amendments, objections, and withdrawals.

4. No amendments shall become effective before 1 July 1949.

Article VI

The Commission may from time to time make recommendations to any or all Contracting Governments on any matters which relate to whales or whaling and to the objectives and purposes of this Convention.

---

[1] Paragraph 1 of Article V of the 1946 Whaling Convention shall be amended by deleting the word 'and' preceding clause (h), substituting a semicolon for the period at the end of the paragraph, and adding the following language: 'and (i) methods of inspection'.

Article VII

The Contracting Governments shall ensure prompt transmission to the International Bureau of Whaling Statistics at Sandefjord in Norway, or to such other body as the Commission may designate, of notifications and statistical and other information required by this Convention in such form and manner as may be prescribed by the Commission.

Article VIII

1. Notwithstanding anything contained in this Convention, any Contracting Government may grant to any of its nationals a special permit authorizing that national to kill, take, and treat whales for purposes of scientific research subject to such restrictions as to number and subject to such other conditions as the Contracting Government thinks fit, and the killing, taking, and treating of whales in accordance with the provisions of this Article shall be exempt from the operation of this Convention. Each Contracting Government shall report at once to the Commission all such authorizations which it has granted. Each Contracting Government may at any time revoke any such special permit which it has granted.

2. Any whales taken under these special permits shall so far as practicable be processed and the proceeds shall be dealt with in accordance with directions issued by the Government by which the permit was granted.

3. Each Contracting Government shall transmit to such body as may be designated by the Commission, in so far as practicable, and at intervals of not more than one year, scientific information available to that Government with respect to whales and whaling, including the results of research conducted pursuant to paragraph 1 of this Article and to Article IV.

4. Recognizing that continuous collection and analysis of biological data in connection with the operations of factory ships and land stations are indispensable to sound and constructive management of the whale fisheries, the Contracting Governments will take all practicable measures to obtain such data.

Article IX

1. Each Contracting Government shall take appropriate measures to ensure the application of the provisions of this Convention and the punishment of infractions against the said provisions in operations carried out by persons or by vessels under its jurisdiction.

2. No bonus or other remuneration calculated with relation to the results of their work shall be paid to the gunners and crews of whale catchers in respect of any whales the taking of which is forbidden by this Convention.

3. Prosecution for infractions against or contraventions of this Convention shall be instituted by the Government having jurisdiction over the offence.

4. Each Contracting Government shall transmit to the Commission full details of each infraction of the provisions of this Convention by persons or vessels under the jurisdiction of that Government as reported by its inspectors. This information shall include a statement of measures taken for dealing with the infraction and of penalties imposed.

Article X

1. This Convention shall be ratified and the instruments of ratification shall be deposited with the Government of the United States of America.

2. Any Government which has not signed this Convention may adhere thereto after it enters into force by a notification in writing to the Government of the United States of America.

3. The Government of the United States of America shall inform all other signatory Governments and all adhering Governments of all ratifications deposited and adherences received.

4. This Convention shall, when instruments of ratification have been deposited by at least six signatory Governments, which shall include the Governments of the Netherlands, Norway, the Union of Soviet Socialist Republics, the United Kingdom of Great Britain and Northern Ireland, and the United States of America, enter into force with respect to those Governments and shall enter into force with respect to each Government which subsequently ratifies or adheres on the date of the deposit of its instrument of ratification or the receipt of its notification of adherence.

5. The provisions of the Schedule shall not apply prior to 1 July 1948. Amendments to the Schedule adopted pursuant to Article V shall not apply prior to 1 July 1949.

Article XI

Any Contracting Government may withdraw from this Convention on June thirtieth of any year by giving notice on or before January first of the same year to the depositary Government, which upon receipt of such a notice shall at once communicate it to the other Contracting Governments. Any other Contracting Government may, in like manner, within one month of the receipt of a copy of such a notice from the depositary Government, give notice of withdrawal, so that the Convention shall cease to be in force on June thirtieth of the same year with respect to the Government giving such notice of withdrawal.

This Convention shall bear the date on which it is opened for signature and shall remain open for signature for a period of fourteen days thereafter.

IN WITNESS WHEREOF the undersigned, being duly authorized, have signed this Convention.

DONE in Washington this second day of December 1946, in the English language, the original of which shall be deposited in the archives of the Government of the United States of America. The Government of the United States of America shall transmit certified copies thereof to all the other signatory and adhering Governments.

Schedule
As amended by the Commission at the Special Meeting, Cambridge, UK, 14 October 2002*

Explanatory notes

The Schedule printed on the following pages contains the amendments made by the Commission at its Special Meeting in October 2002 and at its 54th Annual Meeting in May 2002.

The amendments made at the Special Meeting are shown in **bold underlined type** and came into effect on 19 January 2003. The amendments made by the Commission at its 54th Annual Meeting are shown in ***italic bold type***.

In Tables 1, 2 and 3 unclassified stocks are indicated by a dash. Other positions in the Tables have been filled with a dot to aid legibility.

Numbered footnotes are integral parts of the Schedule formally adopted by the Commission. Other footnotes are editorial.

The Commission was informed in June 1992 by the ambassador in London that the membership of the Union of Soviet Socialist Republics in the International Convention for the Regulation of Whaling from 1948 is continued by the Russian Federation.

The Commission recorded at its 39th (1987) meeting the fact that references to names of native inhabitants in Schedule paragraph 13(b)(4) would be for geographical purposes alone, so as not to be in contravention of Article V.2(c) of the Convention (*Rep. int. Whal. Commn* 38:21).

I. Interpretation

1. The following expressions have the meanings respectively assigned to them, that is to say:

A. Baleen whales

'baleen whale' means any whale which has baleen or whale bone in the mouth, i.e. any whale other than a toothed whale.

'blue whale' (*Balaenoptera musculus*) means any whale known as blue whale, Sibbald's rorqual, or sulphur bottom, and including pygmy blue whale.

'bowhead whale' (*Balaena mysticetus*) means any whale known as bowhead, Arctic right whale, great polar whale, Greenland right whale, Greenland whale.

---

* Text provided by the IWC.

'Bryde's whale' (*Balaenoptera edeni, B. brydei*) means any whale known as Bryde's whale.

'fin whale' (*Balaenoptera physalus*) means any whale known as common finback, common rorqual, fin whale,herring whale, or true fin whale.

'gray whale' (*Eschrichtius robustus*) means any whale known as gray whale, California gray, devil fish, hard head, mussel digger, gray back, or rip sack.

'humpback whale' (*Megaptera novaeangliae*) means any whale known as bunch, humpback, humpback whale, humpbacked whale, hump whale or hunch-backed whale.

'minke whale' (*Balaenoptera acutorostrata, B. bonaerensis*) means any whale known as lesser rorqual, little piked whale, minke whale, pike-headed whale or sharp headed finner.

'pygmy right whale' (*Caperea marginata*) means any whale known as southern pygmy right whale or pygmy right whale.

'right whale' (*Eubalaena glacialis, E. australis*) means any whale known as Atlantic right whale, Arctic right whale, Biscayan right whale, Nordkaper, North Atlantic right whale, North Cape whale, Pacific right whale, or southern right whale.

'sei whale' (*Balaenoptera borealis*) means any whale known as sei whale, Rudolphi's rorqual, pollack whale, or coalfish whale.

B. Toothed whales

'toothed whale' means any whale which has teeth in the jaws.

'beaked whale' means any whale belonging to the genus *Mesoplodon*, or any whale known as Cuvier's beaked whale (*Ziphius cavirostris*), or Shepherd's beaked whale (*Tasmacetus shepherdi*).

'bottlenose whale' means any whale known as Baird's beaked whale (*Berardius bairdii*), Arnoux's whale (*Berardius arnuxii*), southern bottlenose whale (*Hyperoodon planifrons*), or northern bottlenose whale (*Hyperoodon ampullatus*).

'killer whale' (*Orcinus orca*) means any whale known as killer whale or orca.

'pilot whale' means any whale known as long-finned pilot whale (*Globicephala melaena*) or short-finned pilot whale (*G. macrorhynchus*).

'sperm whale' (*Physeter macrocephalus*) means any whale known as sperm whale, spermacet whale, cachalot or pot whale.

C. General

'strike' means to penetrate with a weapon used for whaling.

'land' means to retrieve to a factory ship, land station, or other place where a whale can be treated.

'take' means to flag, buoy or make fast to a whale catcher.

'lose' means to either strike or take but not to land.

'dauhval' means any unclaimed dead whale found floating.

'lactating whale' means (a) with respect to baleen whales – a female which has any milk present in a mammary gland, (b) with respect to sperm whales – a female which has milk present in a mammary gland the maximum thickness (depth) of which is 10cm or more. This measurement shall be at the mid ventral point of the mammary gland perpendicular to the body axis, and shall be logged to the nearest centimetre; that is to say, any gland between 9.5cm and 10.5cm shall be logged as 10cm. The measurement of any gland which falls on an exact 0.5 centimetre shall be logged at the next 0.5 centimetre, e.g. 10.5cm shall be logged as 11.0cm. However, notwithstanding these criteria, a whale shall not be considered a lactating whale if scientific (histological or other biological) evidence is presented to the appropriate national authority establishing that the whale could not at that point in its physical cycle have had a calf dependent on it for milk.

'small-type whaling' means catching operations using powered vessels with mounted harpoon guns hunting exclusively for minke, bottlenose, beaked, pilot or killer whales.

II. Seasons

Factory ship operations

2.

(a) It is forbidden to use a factory ship or whale catcher attached thereto for the purpose of taking or treating baleen whales except minke whales, in any waters south of 40° South Latitude except during the period from 12th December to 7th April following, both days inclusive.

(b) It is forbidden to use a factory ship or whale catcher attached thereto for the purpose of taking or treating sperm or minke whales, except as permitted by the Contracting Governments in accordance with sub-paragraphs (c) and (d) of this paragraph, and paragraph 5.

(c) Each Contracting Government shall declare for all factory ships and whale catchers attached thereto under its jurisdiction, an open season or seasons not to exceed eight months out of any period of twelve months during which the taking or killing of sperm whales by whale catchers may be permitted; provided that a separate open season may be declared for each factory ship and the whale catchers attached thereto.

(d) Each Contracting Government shall declare for all factory ships and whale catchers attached thereto under its jurisdiction one continuous open season not to exceed six months out of any period of twelve months during which the taking or killing of minke whales by the whale catchers may be permitted provided that:

   (1) a separate open season may be declared for each factory ship and the whale catchers attached thereto;

(2) the open season need not necessarily include the whole or any part of the period declared for other baleen whales pursuant to sub-paragraph (a) of this paragraph.

3. It is forbidden to use a factory ship which has been used during a season in any waters south of 40° South Latitude for the purpose of treating baleen whales, except minke whales, in any other area except the North Pacific Ocean and its dependent waters north of the Equator for the same purpose within a period of one year from the termination of that season; provided that catch limits in the North Pacific Ocean and dependent waters are established as provided in paragraphs 12 and 16 of this Schedule and provided that this paragraph shall not apply to a ship which has been used during the season solely for freezing or salting the meat and entrails of whales intended for human food or feeding animals.

Land station operations

4.

(a) It is forbidden to use a whale catcher attached to a land station for the purpose of killing or attempting to kill baleen and sperm whales except as permitted by the Contracting Government in accordance with subparagraphs (b), (c) and (d) of this paragraph.

(b) Each Contracting Government shall declare for all land stations under its jurisdiction, and whale catchers attached to such land stations, one open season during which the taking or killing of baleen whales, except minke whales, by the whale catchers shall be permitted. Such open season shall be for a period of not more than six consecutive months in any period of twelve months and shall apply to all land stations under the jurisdiction of the Contracting Government: provided that a separate open season may be declared for any land station used for the taking or treating of baleen whales, except minke whales, which is more than 1,000 miles from the nearest land station used for the taking or treating of baleen whales, except minke whales, under the jurisdiction of the same Contracting Government.

(c) Each Contracting Government shall declare for all land stations under its jurisdiction and for whale catchers attached to such land stations, one open season not to exceed eight continuous months in any one period of twelve months, during which the taking or killing of sperm whales by the whale catchers shall be permitted, provided that a separate open season may be declared for any land station used for the taking or treating of sperm whales which is more than 1,000 miles from the nearest land station used for the taking or treating of sperm whales under the jurisdiction of the same Contracting Government.

(d) Each Contracting Government shall declare for all land stations under its jurisdiction and for whale catchers attached to such land stations one open season not to exceed six continuous months in any period of twelve months during which the taking or killing of minke whales by the whale catchers shall be permitted (such period not being necessarily concurrent with the period declared for other baleen whales, as provided for in subparagraph (b) of this paragraph); provided that a separate open season may be declared for any land station used for the taking or treating of minke whales which is more than 1,000 miles from the nearest land station used for the taking or treating of minke whales under the jurisdiction of the same Contracting Government.

Except that a separate open season may be declared for any land station used for the taking or treating of minke whales which is located in an area having oceanographic conditions clearly distinguishable from those of the area in which are located the other land stations used for the taking or treating of minke whales under the jurisdiction of the same Contracting Government; but the declaration of a separate open season by virtue of the provisions of this sub-paragraph shall not cause thereby the period of time covering the open seasons declared by the same Contracting Government to exceed nine continuous months of any twelve months.

(e) The prohibitions contained in this paragraph shall apply to all land stations as defined in Article II of the Whaling Convention of 1946.

Other operations

5. Each Contracting Government shall declare for all whale catchers under its jurisdiction not operating in conjunction with a factory ship or land station one continuous open season not to exceed six months out of any period of twelve months during which the taking or killing of minke whales by such whale catchers may be permitted. Notwithstanding this paragraph one continuous open season not to exceed nine months may be implemented so far as Greenland is concerned.

III. Capture

6. The killing for commercial purposes of whales, except minke whales using the cold grenade harpoon shall be forbidden from the beginning of the 1980/81 pelagic and 1981 coastal seasons. The killing for commercial purposes of minke whales using the cold grenade harpoon shall be forbidden from the beginning of the 1982/83 pelagic and the 1983 coastal seasons.*

---

* The Governments of Brazil, Iceland, Japan, Norway and the Union of Soviet Socialist Republics lodged objections to the second sentence of paragraph 6 within the prescribed period. For all other Contracting Governments this sentence came into force on 8 March 1982.

Norway withdrew its objection on 9 July 1985 and Brazil on 8 January 1992.

Iceland withdrew from the Convention with effect from 30 June 1992.

The objections of Japan and the Russian Federation not having been withdrawn, this sentence is not binding upon these governments.

7.

(a) In accordance with Article V(1)(c) of the Convention, commercial whaling, whether by pelagic operations or from land stations, is prohibited in a region designated as the Indian Ocean Sanctuary. This comprises the waters of the Northern Hemisphere from the coast of Africa to 100°E, including the Red and Arabian Seas and the Gulf of Oman; and the waters of the Southern Hemisphere in the sector from 20°E to 130°E, with the Southern boundary set at 55°S. This prohibition applies irrespective of such catch limits for baleen or toothed whales as may from time to time be determined by the Commission. This prohibition shall be reviewed by the Commission at its Annual Meeting in 2002.*

(b) In accordance with Article V(1)(c) of the Convention, commercial whaling, whether by pelagic operations or from land stations, is prohibited in a region designated as the Southern Ocean Sanctuary. This Sanctuary comprises the waters of the Southern Hemisphere southwards of the following line: starting from 40 degrees S, 50 degrees W; thence due east to 20 degrees E; thence due south to 55 degrees S; thence due east to 130 degrees E; thence due north to 40 degrees S; thence due east to 130 degrees W; thence due south to 60 degrees S; thence due east to 50 degrees W; thence due north to the point of beginning. This prohibition applies irrespective of the conservation status of baleen and toothed whale stocks in this Sanctuary, as may from time to time be determined by the Commission. However, this prohibition shall be reviewed ten years after its initial adoption and at succeeding ten year intervals, and could be revised at such times by the Commission. Nothing in this subparagraph is intended to prejudice the special legal and political status of Antarctica.** +

Area limits for factory ships

8. It is forbidden to use a factory ship or whale catcher attached thereto, for the purpose of taking or treating baleen whales, except minke whales, in any of the following areas:

---

*   *At its 54th Annual Meeting in 2002, the Commission agreed to continue this prohibition but did not discuss whether or not it should set a time when it should be reviewed again.*

** The Government of Japan lodged an objection within the prescribed period to paragraph 7(b) to the extent that it applies to the Antarctic minke whale stocks.

The Government of the Russian Federation also lodged an objection to paragraph 7(b) within the prescribed period but withdrew it on 26 October 1994.

For all Contracting Governments except Japan paragraph 7(b) came into force on 6 December 1994.

+ Paragraph 7(b) contains a provision for review of the Southern Ocean Sanctuary 'ten years after its initial adoption'. Paragraph 7(b) was adopted at the 46th (1994) Annual Meeting. Therefore, the first review is due in 2004.

(a) in the waters north of 66°N, except that from 150°E eastwards as far as 140°W, the taking or killing of baleen whales by a factory ship or whale catcher shall be permitted between 66°N and 72°N;

(b) in the Atlantic Ocean and its dependent waters north of 40°S;

(c) in the Pacific Ocean and its dependent waters east of 150°W between 40°S and 35°N;

(d) in the Pacific Ocean and its dependent waters west of 150°W between 40°S and 20°N;

(e) in the Indian Ocean and its dependent waters north of 40°S.

Classification of areas and divisions

9.

(a) Classification of Areas Areas relating to Southern Hemisphere baleen whales except Bryde's whales are those waters between the ice-edge and the Equator and between the meridians of longitude listed in Table 1.

(b) Classification of Divisions Divisions relating to Southern Hemisphere sperm whales are those waters between the ice-edge and the Equator and between the meridians of longitude listed in Table 3.

(c) Geographical boundaries in the North Atlantic The geographical boundaries for the fin, minke and sei whale stocks in the North Atlantic are:

FIN WHALE STOCKS

NOVA SCOTIA
South and West of a line through:
47°N 54°W, 46°N 54°30'W,
46°N 42°W, 20°N 42°W.

NEWFOUNDLAND-LABRADOR
West of a line through:
75°N 73°30'W, 69°N 59°W, 61°N 59°W
52°20'N 42°W, 46°N 42°W and
North of a line through:
46°N 42°W, 46°N 54°30'W, 47°N 54°W.

WEST GREENLAND
East of a line through:
75°N 73°30'W, 69°N 59°W,
61°N 59°W, 52°20'N 42°W,

and West of a line through
52°20′N 42°W, 59°N 42°W,
59°N 44°W, Kap Farvel.

EAST GREENLAND-ICELAND
East of a line through:
Kap Farvel (South Greenland),
59°N 44°W, 59°N 42°W, 20°N 42°W
and West of a line through:
20°N 18°W, 60°N 18°W, 68°N 3°E,
74°N 3°E, and South of 74°N.

NORTH NORWAY
North and East of a line through:
74°N 22°W, 74°N 3°E, 68°N 3°E,
67°N 0°, 67°N 14°E.

WEST NORWAY-FAROE ISLANDS
South of a line through:
67°N 14°E, 67°N 0°, 60°N 18°W, and
North of a line through:
61°N 16°W, 61°N 0°, Thyborøn (Western entrance to Limfjorden,
   Denmark).

SPAIN-PORTUGAL-BRITISH ISLES
South of a line through:
Thyborøn (Denmark), 61°N 0°, 61°N 16°W,
and East of a line through:
63°N 11°W, 60°N 18°W, 22°N 18°W.

MINKE WHALE STOCKS

CANADIAN EAST COAST
West of a line through:
75°N 73°30′W, 69°N 59°W, 61°N 59°W,
52°20′N 42°W, 20°N 42°W.

CENTRAL
East of a line through:
Kap Farvel (South Greenland),
59°N 44°W, 59°N 42°W, 20°N 42°W,
and West of a line through:
20°N 18°W, 60°N 18°W, 68°N 3°E,
74°N 3°E, and South of 74°N.

WEST GREENLAND
East of a line through:
75°N 73°30'W, 69°N 59°W, 61°N 59°W
52°20'N 42°W, and
West of a line through:
52°20'N 42°W, 59°N 42°W,
59°N 44°W, Kap Farvel.

NORTHEASTERN
East of a line through:
20°N 18°W, 60°N 18°W, 68°N 3°E, 74°N 3°E,
and North of a line through:
74°N 3°E, 74°N 22°W.

SEI WHALE STOCKS

NOVA SCOTIA
South and West of a line through:
47°N 54°W, 46°N 54°30'W, 46°N 42°W,
20°N 42°W.

ICELAND-DENMARK STRAIT
East of a line through:
Kap Farvel (South Greenland),
59°N 44°W, 59°N 42°W, 20°N 42°W,
and West of a line through:
20°N 18°W, 60°N 18°W, 68°N 3°E,
74°N 3°E, and South of 74°N.

EASTERN
East of a line through:
20°N 18°W, 60°N 18°W, 68°N 3°E, 74°N 3°E,
and North of a line through:
74°N 3°E, 74°N 22°W.

(d) Geographical boundaries in the North Pacific   The geographical boundaries for the sperm, Bryde's and minke whale stocks in the North Pacific are:

SPERM WHALE STOCKS

WESTERN DIVISION
West of a line from the ice-edge south along the 180° meridian of longitude
to 180°, 50°N, then east along the 50°N parallel of latitude to 160°W, 50°N,
then south along the 160°W meridian of longitude to 160°W, 40°N, then

east along the 40°N parallel of latitude to 150°W, 40°N, then south along the 150°W meridian of longitude to the Equator.

EASTERN DIVISION
East of the line described above.

BRYDE'S WHALE STOCKS

EAST CHINA SEA
West of the Ryukyu Island chain.

EASTERN
East of 160°W (excluding the Peruvian stock area).

WESTERN
West of 160°W (excluding the East China Sea stock area).

MINKE WHALE STOCKS

SEA OF JAPAN-YELLOW SEA- EAST CHINA SEA
West of a line through the Philippine Islands, Taiwan, Ryukyu Islands, Kyushu, Honshu, Hokkaido and Sakhalin Island, north of the Equator.

OKHOTSK SEA-WEST PACIFIC
East of the Sea of Japan-Yellow Sea-East China Sea stock and west of 180°, north of the Equator.

REMAINDER
East of the Okhotsk Sea-West Pacific stock, north of the Equator.

(e) Geographical boundaries for Bryde's whale stocks in the Southern Hemisphere
SOUTHERN INDIAN OCEAN
20°E to 130°E,
South of the Equator.

SOLOMON ISLANDS
150°E to 170°E,
20°S to the Equator.

PERUVIAN
110°W to the South American coast,
10°S to 10°N.

EASTERN SOUTH PACIFIC
150°W to 70°W,
South of the Equator (excluding the Peruvian stock area),

WESTERN SOUTH PACIFIC
130°E to 150°W,
South of the Equator (excluding the Solomon Islands stock area).

SOUTH ATLANTIC
70°W to 20°E,
South of the Equator (excluding the South African inshore stock area).

SOUTH AFRICAN INSHORE
South African coast west of 27°E and out to the 200 metre isobath.

Classification of stocks

10. All stocks of whales shall be classified in one of three categories according to the advice of the Scientific Committee as follows:

(a) A Sustained Management Stock (SMS) is a stock which is not more than 10 per cent of Maximum Sustainable Yield (hereinafter referred to as MSY) stock level below MSY stock level, and not more than 20 per cent above that level; MSY being determined on the basis of the number of whales.

When a stock has remained at a stable level for a considerable period under a regime of approximately constant catches, it shall be classified as a Sustained Management Stock in the absence of any positive evidence that it should be otherwise classified.

Commercial whaling shall be permitted on Sustained Management Stocks according to the advice of the Scientific Committee. These stocks are listed in Tables 1, 2 and 3 of this Schedule.

For stocks at or above the MSY stock level, the permitted catch shall not exceed 90 per cent of the MSY. For stocks between the MSY stock level and 10 per cent below that level, the permitted catch shall not exceed the number of whales obtained by taking 90 per cent of the MSY and reducing that number by 10 per cent for every 1 per cent by which the stock falls short of the MSY stock level.

(b) An Initial Management Stock (IMS) is a stock more than 20 per cent of MSY stock level above MSY stock level. Commercial whaling shall be permitted on Initial Management Stocks according to the advice of the Scientific Committee as to measures necessary to bring the stocks to the MSY stock level and then optimum level in an efficient manner and without risk of reducing them below this level. The permitted catch for such stocks will not be more than 90 per cent of MSY as far as this is known, or, where it will be more appropriate, catching effort shall be limited to that which will take 90 per cent of MSY in a stock at MSY stock level.

In the absence of any positive evidence that a continuing higher percentage will not reduce the stock below the MSY stock level no more than 5 per cent of the estimated initial exploitable stock shall be taken in any one year. Exploitation should not commence until an estimate of stock size has been obtained which is satisfactory in the view of the Scientific Committee. Stocks classified as Initial Management Stock are listed in Tables 1, 2 and 3 of this Schedule.

(c) A Protection Stock (PS) is a stock which is below 10 per cent of MSY stock level below MSY stock level.

There shall be no commercial whaling on Protection Stocks. Stocks so classified are listed in Tables 1, 2 and 3 of this Schedule.

(d) Notwithstanding the other provisions of paragraph 10 there shall be a moratorium on the taking, killing or treating of whales, except minke whales, by factory ships or whale catchers attached to factory ships. This moratorium applies to sperm whales, killer whales and baleen whales, except minke whales.

(e) Notwithstanding the other provisions of paragraph 10, catch limits for the killing for commercial purposes of whales from all stocks for the 1986 coastal and the 1985/86 pelagic seasons and thereafter shall be zero. This provision will be kept under review, based upon the best scientific advice, and by 1990 at the latest the Commission will undertake a comprehensive assessment of the effects of this decision on whale stocks and consider modification of this provision and the establishment of other catch limits.*

Baleen whale catch limits

11. The number of baleen whales taken in the Southern Hemisphere in the *2002/2003* pelagic season and the *2003* coastal season shall not exceed the limits shown in Tables 1 and 2.

---

* The Governments of Japan, Norway, Peru and the Union of Soviet Socialist Republics lodged objection to paragraph 10(e) within the prescribed period. For all other Contracting Governments this paragraph came into force on 3 February 1983. Peru withdrew its objection on 22 July 1983.

The Government of Japan withdrew its objections with effect from 1 May 1987 with respect to commercial pelagic whaling; from 1 October 1987 with respect to commercial coastal whaling for minke and Bryde's whales; and from 1 April 1988 with respect to commercial coastal sperm whaling.

The objections of Norway and the Russian Federation not having been withdrawn, the paragraph is not binding upon these Governments.

12. The number of baleen whales taken in the North Pacific Ocean and dependent waters in *2003* and in the North Atlantic Ocean in *2003* shall not exceed the limits shown in Tables 1 and 2.

13.

(a) Notwithstanding the provisions of paragraph 10, catch limits for aboriginal subsistence whaling to satisfy aboriginal subsistence need for the 1984 whaling season and each whaling season thereafter shall be established in accordance with the following principles:

   (1) For stocks at or above MSY level, aboriginal subsistence catches shall be permitted so long as total removals do not exceed 90 per cent of MSY.

   (2) For stocks below the MSY level but above a certain minimum level, aboriginal subsistence catches shall be permitted so long as they are set at levels which will allow whale stocks to move to the MSY level.[1]

   (3) The above provisions will be kept under review, based upon the best scientific advice, and by 1990 at the latest the Commission will undertake a comprehensive assessment of the effects of these provisions on whale stocks and consider modification.

(b) Catch limits for aboriginal subsistence whaling are as follows:

   (1) The taking of bowhead whales from the Bering-Chukchi-Beaufort Seas stock by aborigines is permitted, but only when the meat and products of such whales are to be used exclusively for local consumption by the aborigines and further provided that:

      (i) **For the years 2003, 2004, 2005, 2006 and 2007, the number of bowhead whales landed shall not exceed 280. For each of these years the number of bowhead whales struck shall not exceed 67, except that any unused portion of a strike quota from any year (including 15 unused strikes from the 1998–2002 quota) shall be carried forward and added to the strike quotas of any subsequent years, provided that no more than 15 strikes shall be added to the strike quota for any one year.**

      (ii) It is forbidden to strike, take or kill calves or any bowhead whale accompanied by a calf.

      (iii) **This provision shall be reviewed annually by the Commission in light of the advice of the Scientific Committee.**

---

[1] The Commission, on advice of the Scientific Committee, shall establish as far as possible (a) a minimum stock level for each stock below which whales shall not be taken, and (b) a rate of increase towards the MSY level for each stock. The Scientific Committee shall advise on a minimum stock level and on a range of rates of increase towards the MSY level under different catch regimes.

(iv) **The findings and recommendations of the Scientific Committee's in-depth assessment for 2004 shall be binding on the parties involved and they shall modify the hunt accordingly.**

(2) The taking of gray whales from the Eastern stock in the North Pacific is permitted, but only by aborigines or a Contracting Government on behalf of aborigines, and then only when the meat and products of such whales are to be used exclusively for local consumption by the aborigines whose traditional aboriginal subsistence and cultural needs have been recognised.

 (i) For the years *2003, 2004, 2005, 2006 and 2007*, the number of gray whales taken in accordance with this sub-paragraph shall not exceed 620, provided that the number of gray whales taken in any one of the years *2003, 2004, 2005, 2006 and 2007* shall not exceed 140.

 (ii) It is forbidden to strike, take or kill calves or any gray whale accompanied by a calf.

 (iii) This provision shall be reviewed annually by the Commission in light of the advice of the Scientific Committee

(3) The taking by aborigines of minke whales from the West Greenland and Central stocks and fin whales from the West Greenland stock is permitted and then only when the meat and products are to be used exclusively for local consumption.

 (i) The number of fin whales from the West Greenland stock taken in accordance with this subparagraph shall not exceed the limits shown in Table 1.

 (ii) The number of minke whales from the Central stock taken in accordance with this sub-paragraph shall not exceed 12 in each of the years *2003, 2004, 2005, 2006 and 2007*, except that any unused portion of the quota for each year shall be carried forward from that year and added to the quota of any subsequent years, provided that no more than 3 shall be added to the quota for any one year.

 (iii) The number of minke whales struck from the West Greenland stock shall not exceed 175 in each of the years *2003, 2004, 2005, 2006 and 2007*, except that any unused portion of the strike quota for each year shall be carried forward from that year and added to the strike quota of any subsequent years, provided that no more than 15 strikes shall be added to the strike quota for any one year. This provision will be reviewed if new scientific data become available within the 5 year period and if necessary amended on the basis of the advice of the Scientific Committee.

(4) *For the seasons 2003–2007 the number of humpback whales to be taken by the Bequians of St. Vincent and The Grenadines shall not exceed 20.[1] The meat and products of such whales are to be used exclusively for local consumption in St. Vincent and The Grenadines. Such whaling must be conducted under formal legislation that accords with the submission of the Government of St. Vincent and The Grenadines (IWC/54/AS8 rev2). The quota for the seasons 2006 and 2007 shall only become operative after the Commission has received advice from the Scientific Committee that the take of 4 humpback whales for each season is unlikely to endanger the stock.*

14. It is forbidden to take or kill suckling calves or female whales accompanied by calves.

Baleen whale size limits

15.

(a) It is forbidden to take or kill any sei or Bryde's whales below 40 feet (12.2 metres) in length except that sei and Bryde's whales of not less than 35 feet (10.7 metres) may be taken for delivery to land stations, provided that the meat of such whales is to be used for local consumption as human or animal food.

(b) It is forbidden to take or kill any fin whales below 57 feet (17.4 metres) in length in the Southern Hemisphere, and it is forbidden to take or kill fin whales below 55 feet (16.8 metres) in the Northern Hemisphere; except that fin whales of not less than 55 feet (16.8 metres) may be taken in the Southern Hemisphere for delivery to land stations and fin whales of not less than 50 feet (15.2 metres) may be taken in the Northern Hemisphere for delivery to land stations, provided that, in each case the meat of such whales is to be used for local consumption as human or animal food.

Sperm whale catch limits

16. Catch limits for sperm whales of both sexes shall be set at zero in the Southern Hemisphere for the 1981/82 pelagic season and 1982 coastal seasons and following seasons, and at zero in the Northern Hemisphere for the 1982 and following coastal seasons; except that the catch limits for the 1982 coastal season and following seasons in the Western Division of the North Pacific shall remain undetermined and subject to decision by the Commission following special or annual meetings of the Scientific Committee. These limits shall remain in force until such time as the Commission, on the basis of the scientific information which will be reviewed annually, decides otherwise in accordance with the procedures followed at that time by the Commission.

---

[1] Each year this figure will be reviewed and if necessary amended on the basis of the advice of the Scientific Committee.

17. It is forbidden to take or kill suckling calves or female whales accompanied by calves.

Sperm whale size limits

18.

(a) It is forbidden to take or kill any sperm whales below 30 feet (9.2 metres) in length except in the North Atlantic Ocean where it is forbidden to take or kill any sperm whales below 35 feet (10.7 metres).

(b) It is forbidden to take or kill any sperm whale over 45 feet (13.7 metres) in length in the Southern Hemisphere north of 40° South Latitude during the months of October to January inclusive.

(c) It is forbidden to take or kill any sperm whale over 45 feet (13.7 metres) in length in the North Pacific Ocean and dependent water south of 40° North Latitude during the months of March to June inclusive.

IV. Treatment

19.

(a) It is forbidden to use a factory ship or a land station for the purpose of treating any whales which are classified as Protection Stocks in paragraph 10 or are taken in contravention of paragraphs 2, 3, 4, 5, 6, 7, 8, 11, 12, 14, 16 and 17 of this Schedule, whether or not taken by whale catchers under the jurisdiction of a Contracting Government.

(b) All other whales taken, except minke whales, shall be delivered to the factory ship or land station and all parts of such whales shall be processed by boiling or otherwise, except the internal organs, whale bone and flippers of all whales, the meat of sperm whales and parts of whales intended for human food or feeding animals. A Contracting Government may in less developed regions exceptionally permit treating of whales without use of land stations, provided that such whales are fully utilised in accordance with this paragraph.

(c) Complete treatment of the carcases of 'dauhval' and of whales used as fenders will not be required in cases where the meat or bone of such whales is in bad condition.

20.

(a) The taking of whales for treatment by a factory ship shall be so regulated or restricted by the master or person in charge of the factory ship that no whale carcase (except of a whale used as a fender, which shall be processed as soon as is reasonably practicable) shall remain in the sea for a longer period than thirty-three hours from the time of killing to the time when it is hauled up for treatment.

(b) Whales taken by all whale catchers, whether for factory ships or land stations, shall be clearly marked so as to identify the catcher and to indicate
the order of catching.

V. Supervision and control

21.

(a) There shall be maintained on each factory ship at least two inspectors
of whaling for the purpose of maintaining twenty-four hour inspection
provided that at least one such inspector shall be maintained on each
catcher functioning as a factory ship. These inspectors shall be appointed
and paid by the Government having jurisdiction over the factory ship;
provided that inspectors need not be appointed to ships which, apart from
the storage of products, are used during the season solely for freezing or
salting the meat and entrails of whales intended for human food or feeding
animals.

(b) Adequate inspection shall be maintained at each land station. The inspectors serving at each land station shall be appointed and paid by the
Government having jurisdiction over the land station.

(c) There shall be received such observers as the member countries may arrange
to place on factory ships and land stations or groups of land stations of
other member countries. The observers shall be appointed by the Commission acting through its Secretary and paid by the Government nominating
them.

22. Gunners and crews of factory ships, land stations, and whale catchers,
shall be engaged on such terms that their remuneration shall depend to a
considerable extent upon such factors as the species, size and yield of whales
and not merely upon the number of the whales taken. No bonus or other
remuneration shall be paid to the gunners or crews of whale catchers in respect
of the taking of lactating whales.

23. Whales must be measured when at rest on deck or platform after the
hauling out wire and grasping device have been released, by means of a tapemeasure made of a non-stretching material. The zero end of the tapemeasure
shall be attached to a spike or stable device to be positioned on the deck or
platform abreast of one end of the whale. Alternatively the spike may be stuck
into the tail fluke abreast of the apex of the notch. The tapemeasure shall be
held taut in a straight line parallel to the deck and the whale's body, and other
than in exceptional circumstances along the whale's back, and read abreast of
the other end of the whale. The ends of the whale for measurement purposes
shall be the tip of the upper jaw, or in sperm whales the most forward part of
the head, and the apex of the notch between the tail flukes.

Measurements shall be logged to the nearest foot or 0.1 metre. That is to say, any whale between 75 feet 6 inches and 76 feet 6 inches shall be logged as 76 feet, and any whale between 76 feet 6 inches and 77 feet 6 inches shall be logged as 77 feet. Similarly, any whale between 10.15 metres and 10.25 metres shall be logged as 10.2 metres, and any whale between 10.25 metres and 10.35 metres shall be logged as 10.3 metres. The measurement of any whale which falls on an exact half foot or 0.05 metre shall be logged at the next half foot or 0.05 metre, e.g. 76 feet 6 inches precisely shall be logged as 77 feet and 10.25 metres precisely shall be logged as 10.3 metres.

VI. Information required

24.

(a) All whale catchers operating in conjunction with a factory ship shall report by radio to the factory ship:
    (1) the time when each whale is taken
    (2) its species, and
    (3) its marking effected pursuant to paragraph 20(b).
(b) The information specified in sub-paragraph (a) of this paragraph shall be entered immediately by a factory ship in a permanent record which shall be available at all times for examination by the whaling inspectors; and in addition there shall be entered in such permanent record the following information as soon as it becomes available:
    (1) time of hauling up for treatment
    (2) length, measured pursuant to paragraph 23
    (3) sex
    (4) if female, whether lactating
    (5) length and sex of foetus, if present, and
    (6) a full explanation of each infraction.
(c) A record similar to that described in sub-paragraph (b) of this paragraph shall be maintained by land stations, and all of the information mentioned in the said sub-paragraph shall be entered therein as soon as available.
(d) A record similar to that described in sub-paragraph (b) of this paragraph shall be maintained by 'smalltype whaling' operations conducted from shore or by pelagic fleets, and all of this information mentioned in the said sub-paragraph shall be entered therein as soon as available.

25.

(a) All Contracting Governments shall report to the Commission for all whale catchers operating in conjunction with factory ships and land stations the following information:

(1) methods used to kill each whale, other than a harpoon, and in particular compressed air

(2) number of whales struck but lost.

(b) A record similar to that described in sub-paragraph (a) of this paragraph shall be maintained by vessels engaged in 'small-type whaling' operations and by native peoples taking species listed in paragraph 1, and all the information mentioned in the said sub-paragraph shall be entered therein as soon as available, and forwarded by Contracting Governments to the Commission.

26.

(a) Notification shall be given in accordance with the provisions of Article VII of the Convention, within two days after the end of each calendar week, of data on the number of baleen whales by species taken in any waters south of 40° South Latitude by all factory ships or whale catchers attached thereto under the jurisdiction of each Contracting Government, provided that when the number of each of these species taken is deemed by the Secretary to the International Whaling Commission to have reached 85 per cent of whatever total catch limit is imposed by the Commission notification shall be given as aforesaid at the end of each day of data on the number of each of these species taken.

(b) If it appears that the maximum catches of whales permitted by paragraph 11 may be reached before 7 April of any year, the Secretary to the International Whaling Commission shall determine, on the basis of the data provided, the date on which the maximum catch of each of these species shall be deemed to have been reached and shall notify the master of each factory ship and each Contracting Government of that date not less than four days in advance thereof. The taking or attempting to take baleen whales, so notified, by factory ships or whale catchers attached thereto shall be illegal in any waters south of 40° South Latitude after midnight of the date so determined.

(c) Notification shall be given in accordance with the provisions of Article VII of the Convention of each factory ship intending to engage in whaling operations in any waters south of 40° South Latitude.

27. Notification shall be given in accordance with the provisions of Article VII of the Convention with regard to all factory ships and catcher ships of the following statistical information:

(a) concerning the number of whales of each species taken, the number thereof lost, and the number treated at each factory ship or land station, and

(b) as to the aggregate amounts of oil of each grade and quantities of meal, fertiliser (guano), and other products derived from them, together with

(c) particulars with respect to each whale treated in the factory ship, land station or 'small-type whaling' operations as to the date and approximate latitude and longitude of taking, the species and sex of the whale, its length and, if it contains a foetus, the length and sex, if ascertainable, of the foetus.

The data referred to in (a) and (c) above shall be verified at the time of the tally and there shall also be notification to the Commission of any information which may be collected or obtained concerning the calving grounds and migration of whales.

28.

(a) Notification shall be given in accordance with the provisions of Article VII of the Convention with regard to all factory ships and catcher ships of the following statistical information:
  (1) the name and gross tonnage of each factory ship,
  (2) for each catcher ship attached to a factory ship or land station:
      (i) the dates on which each is commissioned and ceases whaling for the season,
      (ii) the number of days on which each is at sea on the whaling grounds each season,
      (iii) the gross tonnage, horsepower, length and other characteristics of each; vessels used only as tow boats should be specified.
  (3) A list of the land stations which were in operation during the period concerned, and the number of miles searched per day by aircraft, if any.
(b) The information required under paragraph (a)(2)(iii) should also be recorded together with the following information, in the log book format shown in Appendix A, and forwarded to the Commission:
  (1) where possible the time spent each day on different components of the catching operation,
  (2) any modifications of the measures in paragraphs (a)(2)(i)–(iii) or (b)(1) or data from other suitable indicators of fishing effort for 'small-type whaling' operations.

29.

(a) Where possible all factory ships and land stations shall collect from each whale taken and report on:
  (1) both ovaries or the combined weight of both testes,
  (2) at least one ear plug, or one tooth (preferably first mandibular).
(b) Where possible similar collections to those described in sub-paragraph (a) of this paragraph shall be undertaken and reported by 'small-type whaling' operations conducted from shore or by pelagic fleets.

(c) All specimens collected under sub-paragraphs (a) and (b) shall be properly labelled with platform or other identification number of the whale and be appropriately preserved.

(d) Contracting Governments shall arrange for the analysis as soon as possible of the tissue samples and specimens collected under sub-paragraphs (a) and (b) and report to the Commission on the results of such analyses.

30. A Contracting Government shall provide the Secretary to the International Whaling Commission with proposed scientific permits before they are issued and in sufficient time to allow the Scientific Committee to review and comment on them. The proposed permits should specify:

(a) objectives of the research;

(b) number, sex, size and stock of the animals to be taken;

(c) opportunities for participation in the research by scientists of other nations; and

(d) possible effect on conservation of stock.

Proposed permits shall be reviewed and commented on by the Scientific Committee at Annual Meetings when possible. When permits would be granted prior to the next Annual Meeting, the Secretary shall send the proposed permits to members of the Scientific Committee by mail for their comment and review. Preliminary results of any research resulting from the permits should be made available at the next Annual Meeting of the Scientific Committee.

31. A Contracting Government shall transmit to the Commission copies of all its official laws and regulations relating to whales and whaling and changes in such laws and regulations.

INTERNATIONAL CONVENTION FOR THE REGULATION OF WHALING, 1946, SCHEDULE APPENDIX A
TITLE PAGE
(one logbook per catcher per season)

Catcher name . . . .   Year built . . . .

Attached to expedition/land station . . . .

Season . . . .

Overall length . . . .   Wooden/steel hull . . . .

Gross tonnage . . . .

Type of engine . . . .   H.P . . . .

Maximum speed . . . .   Average searching speed . . . .

Asdic set, make and model no ....
Date of installation ....
Make and size of cannon ....
Type of first harpoon used ....   explosive/electric/non-explosive ....
Type of killer harpoon used ....
Length and type of forerunner ....
Type of whaleline ....
Height of barrel above sea level ....
Speedboat used,   Yes   No
Name of Captain ....
Number of years experience ....
Name of gunner ....
Number of years experience ....
Number of crew ....

DAILY RECORD SHEET TABLE 1

Date .... Catcher name .... Sheet No ....

Searching:	Time started (or resumed) searching	....	....
	*Time whales seen or reported to catcher	....	....
	Whale species	....	....
	Number seen and no. of groups	....	....
	Position found	....	....
	Name of catcher that found whales	....	....
Chasing:	Time started chasing (or confirmed whales)	....	....
	Time whale shot or chasing discontinued	....	....
	Asdic used (Yes/No)	....	....
Handling:	Time whale flagged or alongside for towing	....	....
	Serial No. of catch	....	....
Towing:	:Time started picking up	....	....
	Time finished picking up or started towing	....	....
	Date and time delivered to factory	....	....
Resting:	Time stopped (for drifting or resting)	....	....
	Time finished drifting/resting	....	....
	Time ceased operations	....	....

*Time whales reported to catcher means the time when the catcher is told of the position of a school and starts to move towards it to chase it.

Total searching time	WEATHER CONDITIONS			
Total chasing time	Time	Sea state	Windforce and direction	Visibility
A) with asdic				
B) without asdic	....	....	....	....
Total handling time				
Total towing time	....	....	....	....
Total resting time				
Other time	....	....	....	....
(e.g. bunkering, in port)				

Whales Seen (No. and No. of schools)

Blue .... Bryde's ....
Fin .... Minke ....
Humpback .... Sperm ....
Right .... Others (specify) ....
Sei ....
Signed ....

* Time whales reported to catcher means the time when the catcher is told of the position of a school and starts to move towards it to chase it.

SCHOOLING REPORT TABLE 2

SCHOOLING REPORT TABLE 2

To be completed by pelagic expedition or coastal station for each sperm whale school chased. A separate form to be used each day.

Name of expedition or coastal station ....
Date .... Noon position of factory ship ....

Time School Found ....
Total Number of Whales in School ....
Number of Takeable Whales in School ....
Number of Whales Caught from School by
    each Catcher ....
Name of Catcher ....
Name of Catcher ....
Name of Catcher ....
Name of Catcher ....
Total Number Caught from School ....
Remarks

Explanatory Notes

A. Fill in one column for each school chased with number of whales caught by each catcher taking part in the chase; if catchers chase the school but do not catch from it, enter 0; for catchers in fleet which do not chase that school enter X.

B. A school on this form means a group of whales which are sufficiently close together that a catcher having completed handling one whale can start chasing another whale almost immediately without spending time searching. A solitary whale should be entered as a school of 1 whale.

C. A takeable whale is a whale of a size or kind which the catchers would take if possible. It does not necessarily include all whales above legal size, e.g. if catchers are concentrating on large whales only these would be counted as takeable.

D. Information about catchers from other expeditions or companies operating on the same school should be recorded under Remarks.

Table 1. *Baleen whale stock classification and catch limits* [+] *(excluding Bryde's whales)*

	SEI		MINKE		FIN		BLUE		RIGHT, BOWHEAD, HUMPBACK		PYGMY RIGHT		GRAY	
	Classification	Catch limit	Classification	Catch limit	Classification	Catch limit	Classification	Catch limit	Classification	Catch limit	Classification	Catch limit	Classification	Catch limit
SOUTHERN HEMISPHERE-2002/2003 pelagic season and 2003 coastal season														
Area														
I 120°W-60°W	PS	0	PS	0	PS	0	PS	0	PS	0	PS	0	·	·
II 60°W-0°	PS	0	PS	0	PS	0	PS	0	PS	0	PS	0	·	·
III 0°-70°E	PS	0	PS	0	PS	0	PS	0	PS	0	PS	0	·	·
IV 70°E-130°E	PS	0	PS	0	PS	0	PS	0	PS	0	PS	0	·	·
V 130°E-170°W	PS	0	PS	0	PS	0	PS	0	PS	0	PS	0	·	·
VI 170°W-120°W	PS	0	PS	0	PS	0	PS	0	PS	0	PS	0	·	·
Total catch not to exceed:	·	·	·	·	·	0	·	0	·	0	·	0	·	·
NORTHERN HEMISPHERE-2003 season														
ARCTIC	·	·	·	·	·	·	·	·	PS	·	·	·	·	·
NORTH PACIFIC	·	·	·	·	·	·	·	·	·	·	·	·	·	·
Whole region	PS	0	·	0	PS	0	PS	0	PS	0	·	·	·	·
Okhotsk Sea–West Pacific Stock	·	·	—	·	·	·	·	·	·	·	·	·	·	·
Sea of Japan-Yellow Sea-East China Sea Stock	·	·	PS	0	·	·	·	·	·	·	·	·	·	·
Remainder	·	·	IMS	0	·	·	·	·	·	·	·	·	·	·
Eastern Stock	·	·	·	·	·	·	·	·	·	·	·	·	SMS	[1]
Western Stock	·	·	·	·	·	·	·	·	·	·	·	·	PS	0

NORTH ATLANTIC

Region / Stock												
Whole region	·	·	·	·	·	·	·	·	·	·	·	·
West Greenland Stock	PS	·	·	0	·	·	PS	·	PS	0	PS	0
Newfoundland-Labrador Stock	·	·	·	·	-	19^{2}	·	-	·	·	·	·
Canadian East Coast Stock	-	·	0	·	0	0	·	·	·	·	·	·
Nova Scotia Stock	PS	0	·	PS	·	0	·	·	·	·	·	·
Central Stock	·	·	·	·	SMS	0	·	·	·	·	·	·
East Greenland-Iceland Stock	·	·	·	SMS	·	0	·	·	·	·	·	·
Iceland-Denmark Strait Stock	-	0	·	-	·	0	·	·	·	·	·	·
Spain-Portugal-British Isles Stock	·	·	·	·	·	0	·	·	·	·	·	·
Northeastern Stock	PS*	·	0	·	·	·	·	·	·	·	·	·
West Norway-Faroe Islands Stock	·	·	·	PS	0	·	·	·	·	·	·	·
North Norway Stock	·	·	·	-	·	0	·	·	·	·	·	·
Eastern Stock	-	0	·	·	·	·	·	·	·	·	·	·
NORTHERN INDIAN OCEAN	IMS	0	·	·	·	0	·	PS	0	PS	0	PS	0

[1] Available to be taken by aborigines or a Contracting Government on behalf of aborigines pursuant to paragraph 13(b)2.

[2] Available to be taken by aborigines pursuant to paragraph 13(b)3. Catch limit for each of the years *2003, 2004, 2005, 2006 and 2007.*

+ The catch limits of zero introduced into Table 1 as editorial amendments as a result of the coming into effect of paragraph 10(e) are not binding upon the governments of the countries which lodged and have not withdrawn objections to the said paragraph.

* The Government of Norway presented objection to the classification of the Northeastern Atlantic stock of minke whales as a Protection Stock within the prescribed period. This classification came into force on 30 January 1986 but is not binding on the Government of Norway.

Table 2. *Bryde's whale stock classifications and catch limits*[+]

	Classification	Catch limit
SOUTHERN HEMISPHERE-*2002/2003* pelagic season and *2003* coastal season		
South Atlantic Stock	–	0
Southern Indian Ocean Stock	IMS	0
South African Inshore Stock	–	0
Solomon Islands Stock	IMS	0
Western South Pacific Stock	IMS	0
Eastern South Pacific Stock	IMS	0
Peruvian Stock	–	0
NORTH PACIFIC-*2003* season		
Eastern Stock	IMS	0
Western Stock	IMS	0
East China Sea Stock	PS	0
NORTH ATLANTIC-*2003* season	IMS	0
NORTHERN INDIAN OCEAN-**1999** season	–	0

[+] The catch limits of zero introduced in Table 2 as editorial amendments as a result of the coming into effect of paragraph 10(e) are not binding upon the governments of the countries which lodged and have not withdrawn objections to the said paragraph.

Table 3. *Toothed whale stock classifications and catch limits*[+]

SOUTHERN HEMISPHERE-**2002/2003** pelagic season and **2003** coastal season

Division	Longitudes	SPERM Classification	Catch limit
1	60°W–30°W	–	0
2	30°W–20°E	–	0
3	20°E–60°E	–	0
4	60°E–90°E	–	0
5	90°–130°E	–	0
6	130°E–160°E	–	0
7	160°E–170°W	–	0
8	170°W–100°W	–	0
9	100°W–60°W	–	0
NORTHERN HEMISPHERE-**2003** season			
NORTH PACIFIC			
Western Division		PS	0[1]
Eastern Division		–	0
NORTH ATLANTIC		–	0
NORTHERN INDIAN OCEAN		–	0
		BOTTLENOSE	
NORTH ATLANTIC		PS	0

[+] The catch limits of zero introduced in Table 3 as editorial amendments as a result of the coming into effect of paragraph 10(e) are not binding upon the governments of the countries which lodged and have not withdrawn objections to the said paragraph.

[1] No whales may be taken from this stock until catch limits including any limitations on size and sex are established by the Commission.

Convention on Wetlands of International Importance Especially as Waterfowl Habitat, 2 February 1971

Editorial note

The Convention on Wetlands of International Importance Especially as Waterfowl Habitat, adopted under the auspices of UNESCO, requires Parties to promote the conservation of listed wetlands and the 'wise use' of wetlands in their territory (Article 3(1)). When becoming a Party, each State must nominate at least one suitable wetland to the List of Wetlands of International Importance on the basis of their ecology, botany, zoology, limnology or hydrology, without prejudicing its exclusive sovereign rights over these wetlands (Article 2). Conservation of all wetlands is to be promoted by establishing natural reserves on them with adequate wardening (Article 4(1)). If a Party changes the boundary of a listed wetland in its 'urgent national interest', it should compensate for the loss of wetland resources by creating additional reserves for the protection of an 'adequate' portion of the habitat (Article 4(2)).

Parties are required to consult each other on implementing the Convention with a view to co-ordinating and supporting present and future policies concerning conservation of wetlands and their flora and fauna (Article 5). The Convention also encourages research, exchange of data, training of personnel, and consultation between parties about implementing their obligations (Articles 4(3)). An extraordinary Conference of the Parties held in 1987 amended Articles 6 and 7 (Regina Amendments) establishing a Conference of the Parties which meets regularly to review the implementation of the Convention. The amendments entered into force on 1 May 1994, but have not been ratified by all Parties to the Convention. Bureau duties for the Convention are performed by the International Union for the Conservation of Nature (Article 8).

The text of the Convention reproduced below is the text as amended in 1982 and in 1987 (Paris Protocol and Regina Amendments).

Date of signature: 2 February 1971

Entry into force: 21 December 1975
The *Protocol to Amend the Convention* (Paris, 1982), or 'Paris Protocol', entered into force on 1 October 1986. Since that time, States newly

acceding to the Convention are considered to have acceded to the Paris Protocol as well, unless they have signified their intention not to do so. The *Amendments to Articles 6 and 7 of the Convention* (Regina, 1987), or 'Regina Amendments', entered into force on 1 May 1994.

Depositary: Director General of UNESCO

Contracting Parties
(1971 Ramsar Convention):   Albania, Algeria, Argentina, Armenia, Australia, Austria, Azerbaijan, Bahamas, Bahrain, Bangladesh, Belarus, Belgium, Belize, Benin, Bolivia, Bosnia and Herzegovina, Botswana, Brazil, Bulgaria, Burkina Faso, Burundi, Cambodia, Canada, Chad, Chile, China, Colombia, Congo, Congo (Democratic Republic of), Costa Rica, Cote d'Ivoire, Croatia, Cuba, Cyprus, Czech Republic, Denmark, Djibouti, Dominican Republic, Ecuador, Egypt, El Salvador, Estonia, Finland, France, Gabon, Gambia, Georgia, Germany, Ghana, Greece, Guatemala, Guinea, Guinea-Bissau, Honduras, Hungary, Iceland, India, Indonesia, Iran (Islamic Republic of), Ireland, Israel, Italy, Jamaica, Japan, Jordan, Kenya, Kyrgyzstan, Latvia, Lebanon, Libyan Arab Jamahiriya, Liechtenstein, Lithuania, Luxembourg, Madagascar, Malawi, Malaysia, Mali, Malta, Mauritania, Mauritius, Mexico, Monaco, Mongolia, Morocco, Namibia, Nepal, Netherlands, New Zealand, Nicaragua, Niger, Nigeria, Norway, Pakistan, Palau, Panama, Papua New Guinea, Paraguay, Peru, Philippines, Poland, Portugal, Republic of Korea, Republic of Moldova, Romania, Russian Federation, Saint Lucia, Senegal, Sierra Leone, Slovakia, Slovenia, South Africa, Spain, Sri Lanka, Suriname, Sweden, Switzerland, Syrian Arab Republic, Tajikistan, Tanzania (United Republic of), Thailand, The Former Yugoslav Republic of Macedonia, Togo, Trinidad and Tobago, Tunisia, Turkey, Uganda, Ukraine, United Kingdom,

United States of America, Uruguay, Uzbekistan, Venezuela, Vietnam, Yugoslavia, Zambia.

Website: www.ramsar.org

Convention on Wetlands of International Importance especially as Waterfowl Habitat

The Contracting Parties,

Recognizing the interdependence of Man and his environment;

Considering the fundamental ecological functions of wetlands as regulators of water regimes and as habitats supporting a characteristic flora and fauna, especially waterfowl;

Being convinced that wetlands constitute a resource of great economic, cultural, scientific, and recreational value, the loss of which would be irreparable;

Desiring to stem the progressive encroachment on and loss of wetlands now and in the future;

Recognizing that waterfowl in their seasonal migrations may transcend frontiers and so should be regarded as an international resource;

Being confident that the conservation of wetlands and their flora and fauna can be ensured by combining far-sighted national policies with co-ordinated international action;

Have agreed as follows:

Article 1

1. For the purpose of this Convention wetlands are areas of marsh, fen, peatland or water, whether natural or artificial, permanent or temporary, with water that is static or flowing, fresh, brackish or salt, including areas of marine water the depth of which at low tide does not exceed six metres.

2. For the purpose of this Convention waterfowl are birds ecologically dependent on wetlands.

Article 2

1. Each Contracting Party shall designate suitable wetlands within its territory for inclusion in a List of Wetlands of International Importance, hereinafter referred to as 'the List' which is maintained by the bureau established under Article 8. The boundaries of each wetland shall be precisely described and also delimited on a map and they may incorporate riparian and coastal zones adjacent to the wetlands, and islands or bodies of marine water deeper than six metres at low tide lying within the wetlands, especially where these have importance as waterfowl habitat.

2. Wetlands should be selected for the List on account of their international significance in terms of ecology, botany, zoology, limnology or hydrology. In the first instance wetlands of international importance to waterfowl at any season should be included.

3. The inclusion of a wetland in the List does not prejudice the exclusive sovereign rights of the Contracting Party in whose territory the wetland is situated.

4. Each Contracting Party shall designate at least one wetland to be included in the List when signing this Convention or when depositing its instrument of ratification or accession, as provided in Article 9.

5. Any Contracting Party shall have the right to add to the List further wetlands situated within its territory, to extend the boundaries of those wetlands already included by it in the List, or, because of its urgent national interests, to delete or restrict the boundaries of wetlands already included by it in the List and shall, at the earliest possible time, inform the organization or government responsible for the continuing bureau duties specified in Article 8 of any such changes.

6. Each Contracting Party shall consider its international responsibilities for the conservation, management and wise use of migratory stocks of waterfowl, both when designating entries for the List and when exercising its right to change entries in the List relating to wetlands within its territory.

Article 3

1. The Contracting Parties shall formulate and implement their planning so as to promote the conservation of the wetlands included in the List, and as far as possible the wise use of wetlands in their territory.

2. Each Contracting Party shall arrange to be informed at the earliest possible time if the ecological character of any wetland in its territory and included in the List has changed, is changing or is likely to change as the result of technological developments, pollution or other human interference. Information on such changes shall be passed without delay to the organization or government responsible for the continuing bureau duties specified in Article 8.

Article 4

1. Each Contracting Party shall promote the conservation of wetlands and waterfowl by establishing nature reserves on wetlands, whether they are included in the List or not, and provide adequately for their wardening.

2. Where a Contracting Party in its urgent national interest, deletes or restricts the boundaries of a wetland included in the List, it should as far as possible compensate for any loss of wetland resources, and in particular it should create additional nature reserves for waterfowl and for the protection, either in the same area or elsewhere, of an adequate portion of the original habitat.

3. The Contracting Parties shall encourage research and the exchange of data and publications regarding wetlands and their flora and fauna.

4. The Contracting Parties shall endeavour through management to increase waterfowl populations on appropriate wetlands.

5. The Contracting Parties shall promote the training of personnel competent in the fields of wetland research, management and wardening.

Article 5

The Contracting Parties shall consult with each other about implementing obligations arising from the Convention especially in the case of a wetland extending over the territories of more than one Contracting Party or where a water system is shared by Contracting Parties. They shall at the same time endeavour to coordinate and support present and future policies and regulations concerning the conservation of wetlands and their flora and fauna.

Article 6

1. There shall be established a Conference of the Contracting Parties to review and promote the implementation of this Convention. The Bureau referred to in Article 8, paragraph 1, shall convene ordinary meetings of the Conference of the Contracting Parties at intervals of not more than three years, unless the Conference decides otherwise, and extraordinary meetings at the written requests of at least one third of the Contracting Parties. Each ordinary meeting of the Conference of the Contracting Parties shall determine the time and venue of the next ordinary meeting.

2. The Conference of the Contracting Parties shall be competent:

(a) to discuss the implementation of this Convention;
(b) to discuss additions to and changes in the List;
(c) to consider information regarding changes in the ecological character of wetlands included in the List provided in accordance with paragraph 2 of Article 3;
(d) to make general or specific recommendations to the Contracting Parties regarding the conservation, management and wise use of wetlands and their flora and fauna;
(e) to request relevant international bodies to prepare reports and statistics on matters which are essentially international in character affecting wetlands;
(f) to adopt other recommendations, or resolutions, to promote the functioning of this Convention.

3. The Contracting Parties shall ensure that those responsible at all levels for wetlands management shall be informed of, and take into consideration, recommendations of such Conferences concerning the conservation, management and wise use of wetlands and their flora and fauna.

4. The Conference of the Contracting Parties shall adopt rules of procedure for each of its meetings.

5. The Conference of the Contracting Parties shall establish and keep under review the financial regulations of this Convention. At each of its ordinary meetings, it shall adopt the budget for the next financial period by a two-third majority of Contracting Parties present and voting.

6. Each Contracting Party shall contribute to the budget according to a scale of contributions adopted by unanimity of the Contracting Parties present and voting at a meeting of the ordinary Conference of the Contracting Parties.

Article 7

1. The representatives of the Contracting Parties at such Conferences should include persons who are experts on wetlands or waterfowl by reason of knowledge and experience gained in scientific, administrative or other appropriate capacities.

2. Each of the Contracting Parties represented at a Conference shall have one vote, recommendations, resolutions and decisions being adopted by a simple majority of the Contracting Parties present and voting, unless otherwise provided for in this Convention.

Article 8

1. The International Union for Conservation of Nature and Natural Resources shall perform the continuing bureau duties under this Convention until such time as another organization or government is appointed by a majority of two-thirds of all Contracting Parties.

2. The continuing bureau duties shall be, *inter alia*:

(a) to assist in the convening and organizing of Conferences specified in Article 6;

(b) to maintain the List of Wetlands of International Importance and to be informed by the Contracting Parties of any additions, extensions, deletions or restrictions concerning wetlands included in the List provided in accordance with paragraph 5 of Article 2;

(c) to be informed by the Contracting Parties of any changes in the ecological character of wetlands included in the List provided in accordance with paragraph 2 of Article 3;

(d) to forward notification of any alterations to the List, or changes in character of wetlands included therein, to all Contracting Parties and to arrange for these matters to be discussed at the next Conference;

(e) to make known to the Contracting Party concerned, the recommendations of the Conferences in respect of such alterations to the List or of changes in the character of wetlands included therein.

Article 9

1. This Convention shall remain open for signature indefinitely.

2. Any member of the United Nations or of one of the Specialized Agencies or of the International Atomic Energy Agency or Party to the Statute of the International Court of Justice may become a Party to this Convention by:

(a) signature without reservation as to ratification;
(b) signature subject to ratification followed by ratification;
(c) accession.

3. Ratification or accession shall be effected by the deposit of an instrument of ratification or accession with the Director-General of the United Nations Educational, Scientific and Cultural Organization (hereinafter referred to as 'the Depositary').

Article 10

1. This Convention shall enter into force four months after seven States have become Parties to this Convention in accordance with paragraph 2 of Article 9.

2. Thereafter this Convention shall enter into force for each Contracting Party four months after the day of its signature without reservation as to ratification, or its deposit of an instrument of ratification or accession.

Article 10 bis

1. This Convention may be amended at a meeting of the Contracting Parties convened for that purpose in accordance with this article.

2. Proposals for amendment may be made by any Contracting Party.

3. The text of any proposed amendment and the reasons for it shall be communicated to the organization or government performing the continuing bureau duties under the Convention (hereinafter referred to as 'the Bureau') and shall promptly be communicated by the Bureau to all Contracting Parties. Any comments on the text by the Contracting Parties shall be communicated to the Bureau within three months of the date on which the amendments were communicated to the Contracting Parties by the Bureau. The Bureau shall, immediately after the last day for submission of comments, communicate to the Contracting Parties all comments submitted by that day.

4. A meeting of Contracting Parties to consider an amendment communicated in accordance with paragraph 3 shall be convened by the Bureau upon the written request of one third of the Contracting Parties. The Bureau shall consult the Parties concerning the time and venue of the meeting.

5. Amendments shall be adopted by a two-thirds majority of the Contracting Parties present and voting.

6. An amendment adopted shall enter into force for the Contracting Parties which have accepted it on the first day of the fourth month following the date

on which two thirds of the Contracting Parties have deposited an instrument of acceptance with the Depositary. For each Contracting Party which deposits an instrument of acceptance after the date on which two thirds of the Contracting Parties have deposited an instrument of acceptance, the amendment shall enter into force on the first day of the fourth month following the date of the deposit of its instrument of acceptance.

Article 11

1. This Convention shall continue in force for an indefinite period.

2. Any Contracting Party may denounce this Convention after a period of five years from the date on which it entered into force for that party by giving written notice thereof to the Depositary. Denunciation shall take effect four months after the day on which notice thereof is received by the Depositary.

Article 12

1. The Depositary shall inform all States that have signed and acceded to this Convention as soon as possible of:

(a) signatures to the Convention;
(b) deposits of instruments of ratification of this Convention;
(c) deposits of instruments of accession to this Convention;
(d) the date of entry into force of this Convention;
(e) notifications of denunciation of this Convention.

2. When this Convention has entered into force, the Depositary shall have it registered with the Secretariat of the United Nations in accordance with Article 102 of the Charter.

IN WITNESS WHEREOF, the undersigned, being duly authorized to that effect, have signed this Convention.

DONE at Ramsar this 2nd day of February 1971, in a single original in the English, French, German and Russian languages, all texts being equally authentic* which shall be deposited with the Depositary which shall send true copies thereof to all Contracting Parties.

---

* Pursuant to the Final Act of the Conference to conclude the Protocol, the Depositary provided the second Conference of the Contracting Parties with official versions of the Convention in the Arabic, Chinese and Spanish languages, prepared in consultation with interested Governments and with the assistance of the Bureau.

Convention Concerning the Protection of the World Cultural and Natural Heritage, 16 November 1972

Editorial note

The Convention for the Protection of the World Cultural and Natural Heritage was adopted under the auspices of UNESCO. It applies to 'cultural heritage' and 'natural heritage' which is of 'outstanding universal value' from several points of view (Articles 1 and 2), as defined by reference to, *inter alia*, conservation (Article 2). The Convention places the primary duty upon each State Party to 'do all it can' to identify, protect, present and transmit the natural and cultural heritage to future generations (Article 4). Each Party is required to endeavour to include in its planning the protection of their cultural and natural heritage and to take appropriate measures to protect, conserve and rehabilitate this heritage (Article 5). The Convention further places on the international community as a whole the duty to co-operate in the protection of such heritage, and, accordingly, Parties undertake to provide assistance in the identification, protection, conservation and preservation of cultural and natural heritage when so requested (Article 6).

The Convention establishes a World Heritage Committee within UNESCO, composed of a limited number of experts elected by the Parties meeting in General Assembly (Article 8). On the basis of information submitted by Parties, the definitions of cultural and natural heritage and its own criteria, the Committee is to establish two lists: the World Heritage List and the List of World Heritage in Danger (Article 11). The Committee receives requests for international assistance from Parties for the protection, conservation, presentation or rehabilitation of their cultural and natural heritage, and decides on how the World Heritage Fund is to disburse funds (Article 13).

The World Heritage Fund is composed of compulsory and voluntary contributions from Parties and of other monies collected through fund-raising (Article 15). The compulsory contributions are on a uniform basis as determined by a majority of Parties present and voting at a General Assembly (Article 16(1)). This determination is subject to the rights of Parties to declare, when depositing their instruments of ratification, acceptance or accession, that they are not bound by the provision of the Convention governing compulsory contributions (Article 16(2)), in which case they should still make regular contributions in amounts not less than what their compulsory contribution would have been (Article 16(4)). Non-payment of compulsory or voluntary contributions disqualifies a Party from being a member of the Committee (Article 16(5)).

The Convention sets out the forms of international assistance which the Committee may provide (Article 22) and outlines the conditions and arrangements for such assistance (Part V). Parties shall endeavour to strengthen appreciation and respect of the cultural and natural heritage (Article 27). Parties shall submit reports on the provisions they have adopted in the application of the Convention (Article 29). The Convention may be revised by the General Conference of UNESCO and such revision shall only be binding upon States becoming Parties to the revising Convention (Article 37).

Date of signature:	16 November 1972
Entry into force:	17 December 1975
Depositary:	Director-General of UNESCO
Contracting Parties:	Afghanistan, Albania, Algeria, Andorra, Angola, Antigua and Barbuda, Argentina, Armenia, Australia, Austria, Azerbaijan, Bahrain, Bangladesh, Barbados, Belarus, Belgium, Belize, Benin, Bhutan, Bolivia, Bosnia and Herzegovina, Botswana, Brazil, Bulgaria, Burkina Faso, Burundi, Cambodia, Cameroon, Canada, Cape Verde, Central African Republic, Chad, Chile, China, Colombia, Comoros, Congo, Congo (Democratic Republic of), Costa Rica, Cote d'Ivoire, Croatia, Cuba, Cyprus, Czech Republic, Denmark, Dominica, Dominican Republic, Ecuador, Egypt, El Salvador, Eritrea, Estonia, Ethiopia, Fiji, Finland, France, Gabon, Gambia, Georgia, Germany, Ghana, Greece, Grenada, Guatemala, Guinea, Guyana, Haiti, Holy Sea, Honduras, Hungary, Iceland, India, Indonesia, Iran (Islamic Republic of), Iraq, Ireland, Israel, Italy, Jamaica, Japan, Jordan, Kazakhstan, Kenya, Kiribati, Korea (Democratic People's Republic of), Korea (Republic of), Kuwait, Kyrgyzstan, Lao People's Democratic Republic, Latvia, Lebanon, Liberia, Libyan Arab Jamahiriya, Lithuania, Luxembourg, Madagascar, Malawi, Malaysia, Maldives, Mali, Malta, Marshall Islands, Mauritania, Mauritius, Mexico, Micronesia (Federated States of), Moldova, Monaco, Mongolia, Morocco, Mozambique, Myanmar,

Namibia, Nepal, Netherlands, New Zealand, Nicaragua, Niger, Nigeria, Niue, Norway, Oman, Pakistan, Palau, Panama, Papua New Guinea, Paraguay, Peru, Philippines, Poland, Portugal, Qatar, Romania, Russian Federation, Rwanda, Saint Kitts and Nevis, Saint Lucia, Saint Vincent and the Grenadines, Samoa, San Marino, Saudi Arabia, Senegal, Seychelles, Slovakia, Slovenia, Solomon Islands, South Africa, Spain, Sri Lanka, Sudan, Suriname, Sweden, Switzerland, Syrian Arab Republic, Tajikistan, Tanzania (United Republic of), Thailand, The Former Yugoslav Republic of Macedonia, Togo, Tunisia, Turkey, Turkmenistan, Uganda, Ukraine, United Arab Emirates, United Kingdom, United States of America, Uruguay, Uzbekistan, Vanuatu, Venezuela, Vietnam, Yemen, Yugoslavia, Zambia, Zimbabwe.

Website   http://whc.unesco.org

Convention Concerning the Protection of the World Cultural and Natural Heritage

THE GENERAL CONFERENCE of the United Nations Educational, Scientific and Cultural Organization meeting in Paris from 17 October to 21 November 1972, at its seventeenth session,

Noting that the cultural heritage and the natural heritage are increasingly threatened with destruction not only by the traditional causes of decay, but also by changing social and economic conditions which aggravate the situation with even more formidable phenomena of damage or destruction,

Considering that deterioration or disappearance of any item of the cultural or natural heritage constitutes a harmful impoverishment of the heritage of all the nations of the world,

Considering that protection of this heritage at the national level often remains incomplete because of the scale of the resources which it requires and of the insufficient economic, scientific, and technical resources of the country where the property to be protected is situated,

Recalling that the Constitution of the Organization provides that it will maintain, increase, and diffuse knowledge, by assuring the conservation and protection of the world's heritage, and recommending to the nations concerned the necessary international conventions,

Considering that the existing international conventions, recommendations and resolutions concerning cultural and natural property demonstrate the importance, for all the peoples of the world, of safeguarding this unique and irreplaceable property, to whatever people it may belong,

Considering that parts of the cultural or natural heritage are of outstanding interest and therefore need to be preserved as part of the world heritage of mankind as a whole,

Considering that, in view of the magnitude and gravity of the new dangers threatening them, it is incumbent on the international community as a whole to participate in the protection of the cultural and natural heritage of outstanding universal value, by the granting of collective assistance which, although not taking the place of action by the State concerned, will serve as an efficient complement thereto,

Considering that it is essential for this purpose to adopt new provisions in the form of a convention establishing an effective system of collective protection of the cultural and natural heritage of outstanding universal value, organized on a permanent basis and in accordance with modern scientific methods,

Having decided, at its sixteenth session, that this question should be made the subject of an international convention,

Adopts this sixteenth day of November 1972 this Convention.

I. Definition of the cultural and natural heritage

Article 1

For the purposes of this Convention, the following shall be considered as 'cultural heritage':

monuments: architectural works, works of monumental sculpture and painting, elements or structures of an archaeological nature, inscriptions, cave dwellings and combinations of features, which are of outstanding universal value from the point of view of history, art or science;

groups of buildings: groups of separate or connected buildings which, because of their architecture, their homogeneity or their place in the landscape, are of outstanding universal value from the point of view of history, art or science;

sites: works of man or the combined works of nature and man, and areas including archaeological sites which are of outstanding universal value from the historical, aesthetic, ethnological or anthropological point of view.

Article 2

For the purposes of this Convention, the following shall be considered as 'natural heritage':

natural features consisting of physical and biological formations or groups of such formations, which are of outstanding universal value from the aesthetic or scientific point of view;

geological and physiographical formations and precisely delineated areas which constitute the habitat of threatened species of animals and plants of outstanding universal value from the point of view of science or conservation;

natural sites or precisely delineated natural areas of outstanding universal value from the point of view of science, conservation or natural beauty.

Article 3

It is for each State Party to this Convention to identify and delineate the different properties situated on its territory mentioned in Articles 1 and 2 above.

II. National protection and international protection of the cultural and natural heritage

Article 4

Each State Party to this Convention recognizes that the duty of ensuring the identification, protection, conservation, presentation and transmission to future generations of the cultural and natural heritage referred to in Articles 1 and 2 and situated on its territory, belongs primarily to that State. It will do all it can to this end, to the utmost of its own resources and, where appropriate, with any international assistance and co-operation, in particular, financial, artistic, scientific and technical, which it may be able to obtain.

Article 5

To ensure that effective and active measures are taken for the protection, conservation and presentation of the cultural and natural heritage situated on its territory, each State Party to this Convention shall endeavor, in so far as possible, and as appropriate for each country:

(a) to adopt a general policy which aims to give the cultural and natural heritage a function in the life of the community and to integrate the protection of that heritage into comprehensive planning programmes;
(b) to set up within its territories, where such services do not exist, one or more services for the protection, conservation and presentation of the cultural and natural heritage with an appropriate staff and possessing the means to discharge their functions;

(c) to develop scientific and technical studies and research and to work out such operating methods as will make the State capable of counteracting the dangers that threaten its cultural or natural heritage;

(d) to take the appropriate legal, scientific, technical, administrative and financial measures necessary for the identification, protection, conservation, presentation and rehabilitation of this heritage; and

(e) to foster the establishment or development of national or regional centres for training in the protection, conservation and presentation of the cultural and natural heritage and to encourage scientific research in this field.

Article 6

1. Whilst fully respecting the sovereignty of the States on whose territory the cultural and natural heritage mentioned in Articles 1 and 2 is situated, and without prejudice to property right provided by national legislation, the States Parties to this Convention recognize that such heritage constitutes a world heritage for whose protection it is the duty of the international community as a whole to co-operate.

2. The States Parties undertake, in accordance with the provisions of this Convention, to give their help in the identification, protection, conservation and presentation of the cultural and natural heritage referred to in paragraphs 2 and 4 of Article 11 if the States on whose territory it is situated so request.

3. Each State Party to this Convention undertakes not to take any deliberate measures which might damage directly or indirectly the cultural and natural heritage referred to in Articles 1 and 2 situated on the territory of other States Parties to this Convention.

Article 7

For the purpose of this Convention, international protection of the world cultural and natural heritage shall be understood to mean the establishment of a system of international co-operation and assistance designed to support States Parties to the Convention in their efforts to conserve and identify that heritage.

III. Intergovernmental Committee for the Protection of the World Cultural and Natural Heritage

Article 8

1. An Intergovernmental Committee for the Protection of the Cultural and Natural Heritage of Outstanding Universal Value, called 'the World Heritage Committee', is hereby established within the United Nations Educational, Scientific and Cultural Organization. It shall be composed of 15 States Parties to the Convention, elected by States Parties to the Convention meeting in

general assembly during the ordinary session of the General Conference of the United Nations Educational, Scientific and Cultural Organization. The number of States members of the Committee shall be increased to 21 as from the date of the ordinary session of the General Conference following the entry into force of this Convention for at least 40 States.

2. Election of members of the Committee shall ensure an equitable representation of the different regions and cultures of the world.

3. A representative of the International Centre for the Study of the Preservation and Restoration of Cultural Property (Rome Centre), a representative of the International Council of Monuments and Sites (ICOMOS) and a representative of the International Union for Conservation of Nature and Natural Resources (IUCN), to whom may be added, at the request of States Parties to the Convention meeting in general assembly during the ordinary sessions of the General Conference of the United Nations Educational, Scientific and Cultural Organization, representatives of other intergovernmental or non-governmental organizations, with similar objectives, may attend the meetings of the Committee in an advisory capacity.

Article 9

1. The term of office of States members of the World Heritage Committee shall extend from the end of the ordinary session of the General Conference during which they are elected until the end of its third subsequent ordinary session.

2. The term of office of one-third of the members designated at the time of the first election shall, however, cease at the end of the first ordinary session of the General Conference following that at which they were elected; and the term of office of a further third of the members designated at the same time shall cease at the end of the second ordinary session of the General Conference following that at which they were elected. The names of these members shall be chosen by lot by the President of the General Conference of the United Nations Educational, Scientific and Cultural Organization after the first election.

3. States members of the Committee shall choose as their representatives persons qualified in the field of the cultural or natural heritage.

Article 10

1. The World Heritage Committee shall adopt its Rules of Procedure.

2. The Committee may at any time invite public or private organizations or individuals to participate in its meetings for consultation on particular problems.

3. The Committee may create such consultative bodies as it deems necessary for the performance of its functions.

Article 11

1. Every State Party to this Convention shall, in so far as possible, submit to the World Heritage Committee an inventory of property forming part of the cultural and natural heritage, situated in its territory and suitable for inclusion in the list provided for in paragraph 2 of this Article. This inventory, which shall not be considered exhaustive, shall include documentation about the location of the property in question and its significance.

2. On the basis of the inventories submitted by States in accordance with paragraph 1, the Committee shall establish, keep up to date and publish, under the title of 'World Heritage List,' a list of properties forming part of the cultural heritage and natural heritage, as defined in Articles 1 and 2 of this Convention, which it considers as having outstanding universal value in terms of such criteria as it shall have established. An updated list shall be distributed at least every two years.

3. The inclusion of a property in the World Heritage List requires the consent of the State concerned. The inclusion of a property situated in a territory, sovereignty or jurisdiction over which is claimed by more than one State shall in no way prejudice the rights of the parties to the dispute.

4. The Committee shall establish, keep up to date and publish, whenever circumstances shall so require, under the title of 'List of World Heritage in Danger', a list of the property appearing in the World Heritage List for the conservation of which major operations are necessary and for which assistance has been requested under this Convention. This list shall contain an estimate of the cost of such operations. The list may include only such property forming part of the cultural and natural heritage as is threatened by serious and specific dangers, such as the threat of disappearance caused by accelerated deterioration, large-scale public or private projects or rapid urban or tourist development projects; destruction caused by changes in the use or ownership of the land; major alterations due to unknown causes; abandonment for any reason whatsoever; the outbreak or the threat of an armed conflict; calamities and cataclysms; serious fires, earthquakes, landslides; volcanic eruptions; changes in water level, floods and tidal waves. The Committee may at any time, in case of urgent need, make a new entry in the List of World Heritage in Danger and publicize such entry immediately.

5. The Committee shall define the criteria on the basis of which a property belonging to the cultural or natural heritage may be included in either of the lists mentioned in paragraphs 2 and 4 of this article.

6. Before refusing a request for inclusion in one of the two lists mentioned in paragraphs 2 and 4 of this article, the Committee shall consult the State Party in whose territory the cultural or natural property in question is situated.

7. The Committee shall, with the agreement of the States concerned, co-ordinate and encourage the studies and research needed for the drawing up of the lists referred to in paragraphs 2 and 4 of this article.

Article 12

The fact that a property belonging to the cultural or natural heritage has not been included in either of the two lists mentioned in paragraphs 2 and 4 of Article 11 shall in no way be construed to mean that it does not have an outstanding universal value for purposes other than those resulting from inclusion in these lists.

Article 13

1. The World Heritage Committee shall receive and study requests for international assistance formulated by States Parties to this Convention with respect to property forming part of the cultural or natural heritage, situated in their territories, and included or potentially suitable for inclusion in the lists mentioned referred to in paragraphs 2 and 4 of Article 11. The purpose of such requests may be to secure the protection, conservation, presentation or rehabilitation of such property.

2. Requests for international assistance under paragraph 1 of this article may also be concerned with identification of cultural or natural property defined in Articles 1 and 2, when preliminary investigations have shown that further inquiries would be justified.

3. The Committee shall decide on the action to be taken with regard to these requests, determine where appropriate, the nature and extent of its assistance, and authorize the conclusion, on its behalf, of the necessary arrangements with the government concerned.

4. The Committee shall determine an order of priorities for its operations. It shall in so doing bear in mind the respective importance for the world cultural and natural heritage of the property requiring protection, the need to give international assistance to the property most representative of a natural environment or of the genius and the history of the peoples of the world, the urgency of the work to be done, the resources available to the States on whose territory the threatened property is situated and in particular the extent to which they are able to safeguard such property by their own means.

5. The Committee shall draw up, keep up to date and publicize a list of property for which international assistance has been granted.

6. The Committee shall decide on the use of the resources of the Fund established under Article 15 of this Convention. It shall seek ways of increasing these resources and shall take all useful steps to this end.

7. The Committee shall co-operate with international and national governmental and non-governmental organizations having objectives similar to those of this Convention. For the implementation of its programmes and projects, the Committee may call on such organizations, particularly the International Centre for the Study of the Preservation and Restoration of cultural Property (the Rome Centre), the International Council of Monuments and Sites

(ICOMOS) and the International Union for Conservation of Nature and Natural Resources (IUCN), as well as on public and private bodies and individuals.

8. Decisions of the Committee shall be taken by a majority of two-thirds of its members present and voting. A majority of the members of the Committee shall constitute a quorum.

Article 14

1. The World Heritage Committee shall be assisted by a Secretariat appointed by the Director-General of the United Nations Educational, Scientific and Cultural Organization.

2. The Director-General of the United Nations Educational, Scientific and Cultural Organization, utilizing to the fullest extent possible the services of the International Centre for the Study of the Preservation and the Restoration of Cultural Property (the Rome Centre), the International Council of Monuments and Sites (ICOMOS) and the International Union for Conservation of Nature and Natural Resources (IUCN) in their respective areas of competence and capability, shall prepare the Committee's documentation and the agenda of its meetings and shall have the responsibility for the implementation of its decisions.

IV. Fund for the Protection of the World Cultural and Natural Heritage

Article 15

1. A Fund for the Protection of the World Cultural and Natural Heritage of Outstanding Universal Value, called 'the World Heritage Fund', is hereby established.

2. The Fund shall constitute a trust fund, in conformity with the provisions of the Financial Regulations of the United Nations Educational, Scientific and Cultural Organization.

3. The resources of the Fund shall consist of:

(a) compulsory and voluntary contributions made by States Parties to this Convention,
(b) Contributions, gifts or bequests which may be made by:
   (i) other States;
   (ii) the United Nations Educational, Scientific and Cultural Organization, other organizations of the United Nations system, particularly the United Nations Development Programme or other intergovernmental organizations;
   (iii) public or private bodies or individuals;
(c) any interest due on the resources of the Fund;

(d) funds raised by collections and receipts from events organized for the benefit of the fund; and

(e) all other resources authorized by the Fund's regulations, as drawn up by
the World Heritage Committee.

4. Contributions to the Fund and other forms of assistance made available
to the Committee may be used only for such purposes as the Committee shall
define. The Committee may accept contributions to be used only for a certain
programme or project, provided that the Committee shall have decided on the
implementation of such programme or project. No political conditions may be
attached to contributions made to the Fund.

Article 16

1. Without prejudice to any supplementary voluntary contribution, the
States Parties to this Convention undertake to pay regularly, every two years, to
the World Heritage Fund, contributions, the amount of which, in the form of a
uniform percentage applicable to all States, shall be determined by the General
Assembly of States Parties to the Convention, meeting during the sessions of the
General Conference of the United Nations Educational, Scientific and Cultural
Organization. This decision of the General Assembly requires the majority of
the States Parties present and voting, which have not made the declaration
referred to in paragraph 2 of this Article. In no case shall the compulsory contribution of States Parties to the Convention exceed 1% of the contribution to
the regular budget of the United Nations Educational, Scientific and Cultural
Organization.

2. However, each State referred to in Article 31 or in Article 32 of this
Convention may declare, at the time of the deposit of its instrument of ratification, acceptance or accession, that it shall not be bound by the provisions of
paragraph 1 of this Article.

3. A State Party to the Convention which has made the declaration referred
to in paragraph 2 of this Article may at any time withdraw the said declaration
by notifying the Director-General of the United Nations Educational, Scientific
and Cultural Organization. However, the withdrawal of the declaration shall
not take effect in regard to the compulsory contribution due by the State until
the date of the subsequent General Assembly of States parties to the Convention.

4. In order that the Committee may be able to plan its operations effectively,
the contributions of States Parties to this Convention which have made the
declaration referred to in paragraph 2 of this Article, shall be paid on a regular
basis, at least every two years, and should not be less than the contributions
which they should have paid if they had been bound by the provisions of
paragraph 1 of this Article.

5. Any State Party to the Convention which is in arrears with the payment of
its compulsory or voluntary contribution for the current year and the calendar

year immediately preceding it shall not be eligible as a Member of the World Heritage Committee, although this provision shall not apply to the first election.

The terms of office of any such State which is already a member of the Committee shall terminate at the time of the elections provided for in Article 8, paragraph 1 of this Convention.

Article 17

The States Parties to this Convention shall consider or encourage the establishment of national public and private foundations or associations whose purpose is to invite donations for the protection of the cultural and natural heritage as defined in Articles 1 and 2 of this Convention.

Article 18

The States Parties to this Convention shall give their assistance to international fund-raising campaigns organized for the World Heritage Fund under the auspices of the United Nations Educational, Scientific and Cultural Organization. They shall facilitate collections made by the bodies mentioned in paragraph 3 of Article 15 for this purpose.

V. Conditions and arrangements for international assistance

Article 19

Any State Party to this Convention may request international assistance for property forming part of the cultural or natural heritage of outstanding universal value situated within its territory. It shall submit with its request such information and documentation provided for in Article 21 as it has in its possession and as will enable the Committee to come to a decision.

Article 20

Subject to the provisions of paragraph 2 of Article 13, sub-paragraph (c) of Article 22 and Article 23, international assistance provided for by this Convention may be granted only to property forming part of the cultural and natural heritage which the World Heritage Committee has decided, or may decide, to enter in one of the lists mentioned in paragraphs 2 and 4 of Article 11.

Article 21

1. The World Heritage Committee shall define the procedure by which requests to it for international assistance shall be considered and shall specify the content of the request, which should define the operation contemplated, the work that is necessary, the expected cost thereof, the degree of urgency and the reasons why the resources of the State requesting assistance do not allow it

to meet all the expenses. Such requests must be supported by experts' reports whenever possible.

2. Requests based upon disasters or natural calamities should, by reasons of the urgent work which they may involve, be given immediate, priority consideration by the Committee, which should have a reserve fund at its disposal against such contingencies.

3. Before coming to a decision, the Committee shall carry out such studies and consultations as it deems necessary.

Article 22

Assistance granted by the World Heritage Committee may take the following forms:

(a) studies concerning the artistic, scientific and technical problems raised by the protection, conservation, presentation and rehabilitation of the cultural and natural heritage, as defined in paragraphs 2 and 4 of Article 11 of this Convention;

(b) provisions of experts, technicians and skilled labour to ensure that the approved work is correctly carried out;

(c) training of staff and specialists at all levels in the field of identification, protection, conservation, presentation and rehabilitation of the cultural and natural heritage;

(d) supply of equipment which the State concerned does not possess or is not in a position to acquire;

(e) low-interest or interest-free loans which might be repayable on a long-term basis;

(f) the granting, in exceptional cases and for special reasons, of non-repayable subsidies.

Article 23

The World Heritage Committee may also provide international assistance to national or regional centres for the training of staff and specialists at all levels in the field of identification, protection, conservation, presentation and rehabilitation of the cultural and natural heritage.

Article 24

International assistance on a large scale shall be preceded by detailed scientific, economic and technical studies. These studies shall draw upon the most advanced techniques for the protection, conservation, presentation and rehabilitation of the natural and cultural heritage and shall be consistent with the objectives of this Convention. The studies shall also seek means of making rational use of the resources available in the State concerned.

Article 25

As a general rule, only part of the cost of work necessary shall be borne by the international community. The contribution of the State benefiting from international assistance shall constitute a substantial share of the resources devoted to each programme or project, unless its resources do not permit this.

Article 26

The World Heritage Committee and the recipient State shall define in the agreement they conclude the conditions in which a programme or project for which international assistance under the terms of this Convention is provided, shall be carried out. It shall be the responsibility of the State receiving such international assistance to continue to protect, conserve and present the property so safeguarded, in observance of the conditions laid down by the agreement.

VI. Educational programmes

Article 27

1. The States Parties to this Convention shall endeavor by all appropriate means, and in particular by educational and information programmes, to strengthen appreciation and respect by their peoples of the cultural and natural heritage defined in Articles 1 and 2 of the Convention.

2. They shall undertake to keep the public broadly informed of the dangers threatening this heritage and of the activities carried on in pursuance of this Convention.

Article 28

States Parties to this Convention which receive international assistance under the Convention shall take appropriate measures to make known the importance of the property for which assistance has been received and the role played by such assistance.

VII. Reports

Article 29

1. The States Parties to this Convention shall, in the reports which they submit to the General Conference of the United Nations Educational, Scientific and Cultural Organization on dates and in a manner to be determined by it, give information on the legislative and administrative provisions which they have adopted and other action which they have taken for the application of this Convention, together with details of the experience acquired in this field.

2. These reports shall be brought to the attention of the World Heritage Committee.

3. The Committee shall submit a report on its activities at each of the ordinary sessions of the General Conference of the United Nations Educational, Scientific and Cultural Organization.

VIII. Final clauses

Article 30

This Convention is drawn up in Arabic, English, French, Russian and Spanish, the five texts being equally authoritative.

Article 31

1. This Convention shall be subject to ratification or acceptance by States members of the United Nations Educational, Scientific and Cultural Organization in accordance with their respective constitutional procedures.

2. The instruments of ratification or acceptance shall be deposited with the Director-General of the United Nations Educational, Scientific and Cultural Organization.

Article 32

1. This Convention shall be open to accession by all States not members of the United Nations Educational, Scientific and Cultural Organization which are invited by the General Conference of the Organization to accede to it.

2. Accession shall be effected by the deposit of an instrument of accession with the Director-General of the United Nations Educational, Scientific and Cultural Organization.

Article 33

This Convention shall enter into force three months after the date of the deposit of the twentieth instrument of ratification, acceptance or accession, but only with respect to those States which have deposited their respective instruments of ratification, acceptance or accession on or before that date. It shall enter into force with respect to any other State three months after the deposit of its instrument of ratification, acceptance or accession.

Article 34

The following provisions shall apply to those States Parties to this Convention which have a federal or non-unitary constitutional system:

(a) with regard to the provisions of this Convention, the implementation of which comes under the legal jurisdiction of the federal or central legislative power, the obligations of the federal or central government shall be the same as for those States parties which are not federal States;

(b) with regard to the provisions of this Convention, the implementation of which comes under the legal jurisdiction of individual constituent States, countries, provinces or cantons that are not obliged by the constitutional system of the federation to take legislative measures, the federal government shall inform the competent authorities of such States, countries, provinces or cantons of the said provisions, with its recommendation for their adoption.

Article 35

1. Each State Party to this Convention may denounce the Convention.

2. The denunciation shall be notified by an instrument in writing, deposited with the Director-General of the United Nations Educational, Scientific and Cultural Organization.

3. The denunciation shall take effect twelve months after the receipt of the instrument of denunciation. It shall not affect the financial obligations of the denouncing State until the date on which the withdrawal takes effect.

Article 36

The Director-General of the United Nations Educational, Scientific and Cultural Organization shall inform the States members of the Organization, the States not members of the Organization which are referred to in Article 32, as well as the United Nations, of the deposit of all the instruments of ratification, acceptance, or accession provided for in Articles 31 and 32, and of the denunciations provided for in Article 35.

Article 37

1. This Convention may be revised by the General Conference of the United Nations Educational, Scientific and Cultural Organization. Any such revision shall, however, bind only the States which shall become Parties to the revising convention.

2. If the General Conference should adopt a new convention revising this Convention in whole or in part, then, unless the new convention otherwise provides, this Convention shall cease to be open to ratification, acceptance or accession, as from the date on which the new revising convention enters into force.

Article 38

In conformity with Article 102 of the Charter of the United Nations, this Convention shall be registered with the Secretariat of the United Nations at the request of the Director-General of the United Nations Educational, Scientific and Cultural Organization.

Done in Paris, this twenty-third day of November 1972, in two authentic copies bearing the signature of the President of the seventeenth session of the General Conference and of the Director-General of the United Nations Educational, Scientific and Cultural Organization, which shall be deposited in the archives of the United Nations Educational, Scientific and Cultural Organization, and certified true copies of which shall be delivered to all the States referred to in Articles 31 and 32 as well as to the United Nations.

Convention on International Trade in Endangered Species of Wild Fauna and Flora, 3 March 1973

Editorial note

The Convention to Regulate International Trade in Endangered Species of Wild Fauna and Flora is premised on the view that control or elimination of international markets will contribute to the preservation of endangered species. It classifies species by reference to their endangered status: those in Appendix I are the most endangered and subject to the strictest trade regulation; those in Appendix II are not currently endangered, but are at risk of becoming so if unregulated trade continues; and those in Appendix III are subject to control by national authorities so as to prevent and restrict their exploitation.

Trade in listed species is subject to a system of import and export permits that is linked to input from scientific authorities and is supervised by national management authorities. Trade in species listed in Annex I is highly restricted and will only be permitted if, *inter alia,* (a) the Scientific Authority in the exporting country has determined that the export is not detrimental to the survival of the species and (b) the Management Authority of the importing State is satisfied that the import is not primarily for commercial purposes (Article III). The rules are less strict for trade in species listed in Appendices II and III (Articles IV and V). Trade with non-Parties is permissible so long as documentation comparable to the Convention's requirements is produced (Article X). The Convention's restrictions on trade in listed species do not interfere with a Party's right to take stricter domestic measures, or the right of Parties to comply with international agreements that regulate other aspects of trade (Article XIV).

The Convention establishes a Conference of the Parties to review its implementation (Article XI). A Secretariat arranges the Conferences of the Parties and circulates information relevant to implementing the Convention, and can receive information on the adverse effects of trade in any species lists in Appendices I or II and notify the Party concerned (Article XIII). Upon receipt of such notification, Parties are required to report any relevant facts, propose remedial action, and may request that an inquiry be held on the matter (Article XIII). If negotiations fail to resolve any dispute between Parties, the matter may, by mutual consent, be submitted to binding arbitration, specifically at the

Permanent Court of Arbitration at The Hague (Article XVIII). Amendments to the Appendices are subject to an elaborate procedure depending on which list is affected. A two-thirds majority of those present and voting is required for amendments to Appendices I and II (Article XV), while each Party can unilaterally add or withdraw species to and from Appendix III. As a matter of practice, the Annexes are regularly amended. Amending the Convention itself requires a two-thirds majority vote of those present and voting (Article XVII). To date, the Convention has been amended twice: on 22 June 1979, an amendment (amending Article XI(3)) which allowed the Secretariat to adopt financial provisions was adopted; and on 30 April 1983 provisions (amending Article XXI) allowing regional economic integration organisations to accede to the Convention were adopted. The 1979 amendment has entered into force for the Parties accepting it; the 1983 amendment has not yet entered into force. The Convention only permits specific reservations to amendments of the Appendices, whereupon that Party is treated as a non-party for the purposes of trade in that species (Article XXIII).

Date of signature: 3 March 1973

Entry into force: 1 July 1975

Depositary: Government of the Swiss Confederation

Contracting Parties: Afghanistan, Algeria, Antigua and Barbuda, Argentina, Australia, Austria, Azerbaijan, Bahamas, Bangladesh, Barbados, Belarus, Belgium, Belize, Benin, Bhutan, Bolivia, Botswana, Brazil, Brunei Darussalam, Bulgaria, Burkina Faso, Burundi, Cambodia, Cameroon, Canada, Central African Republic, Chad, Chile, China, Colombia, Comoros, Congo, Congo (Democratic Republic of), Costa Rica, Cote d'Ivoire, Croatia, Cuba, Cyprus, Czech Republic, Denmark, Djibouti, Dominica, Dominican Republic, Ecuador, Egypt, El Salvador, Equatorial Guinea, Eritrea, Estonia, Ethiopia, Fiji, Finland, France, Gabon, Gambia, Georgia, Germany, Ghana, Greece, Grenada, Guatemala, Guinea, Guinea Bissau, Guyana, Honduras, Hungary, Iceland, India, Indonesia, Iran (Islamic Republic of), Ireland, Israel, Italy, Jamaica, Japan, Jordan, Kazakhstan, Kenya, Korea (Republic of), Kuwait, Latvia, Liberia, Libyan Arab Jamahiriya, Liechtenstein, Lithuania, Luxembourg, Madagascar, Malawi, Malaysia, Mali, Malta, Mauritania, Mauritius, Mexico, Moldova, Monaco,

Mongolia, Morocco, Mozambique, Myanmar, Namibia, Nepal, Netherlands, New Zealand, Nicaragua, Niger, Nigeria, Norway, Pakistan, Panama, Papua New Guinea, Paraguay, Peru, Philippines, Poland, Portugal, Qatar, Romania, Russian Federation, Rwanda, Saint Kitts and Nevis, Saint Lucia, Saint Vincent and the Grenadines, São Tomé and Príncipe, Saudi Arabia, Senegal, Serbia and Montenegro, Seychelles, Sierra Leone, Singapore, Slovakia, Slovenia, Somalia, South Africa, Spain, Sri Lanka, Sudan, Suriname, Swaziland, Sweden, Switzerland, Tanzania (United Republic of), Thailand, The Former Yugoslav Republic of Macedonia, Togo, Trinidad and Tobago, Tunisia, Turkey, Uganda, Ukraine, United Arab Emirates, United Kingdom, United States of America, Uruguay, Uzbekistan, Vanuatu, Venezuela, Vietnam, Yemen, Zambia, Zimbabwe.

Website: www.cites.org

Convention on International Trade in Endangered Species of Wild Fauna and Flora

The Contracting States,

Recognizing that wild fauna and flora in their many beautiful and varied forms are an irreplaceable part of the natural systems of the earth which must be protected for this and the generations to come;

Conscious of the ever-growing value of wild fauna and flora from aesthetic, scientific, cultural, recreational and economic points of view;

Recognizing that peoples and States are and should be the best protectors of their own wild fauna and flora;

Recognizing, in addition, that international co-operation is essential for the protection of certain species of wild fauna and flora against over-exploitation through international trade;

Convinced of the urgency of taking appropriate measures to this end;

Have agreed as follows:

Article I
Definitions

For the purpose of the present Convention, unless the context otherwise requires:

(a) 'Species' means any species, subspecies, or geographically separate population thereof;

(b) 'Specimen' means:
  (i) any animal or plant, whether alive or dead;
  (ii) in the case of an animal: for species included in Appendices I and II, any readily recognizable part or derivative thereof; and for species included in Appendix III, any readily recognizable part or derivative thereof specified in Appendix III in relation to the species; and
  (iii) in the case of a plant: for species included in Appendix I, any readily recognizable part or derivative thereof; and for species included in Appendices II and III, any readily recognizable part or derivative thereof specified in Appendices II and III in relation to the species;
(c) 'Trade' means export, re-export, import and introduction from the sea;
(d) 'Re-export' means export of any specimen that has previously been imported;
(e) 'Introduction from the sea' means transportation into a State of specimens of any species which were taken in the marine environment not under the jurisdiction of any State;
(f) 'Scientific Authority' means a national scientific authority designated in accordance with Article IX;
(g) 'Management Authority' means a national management authority designated in accordance with Article IX;
(h) 'Party' means a State for which the present Convention has entered into force.

Article II
Fundamental principles

1. Appendix I shall include all species threatened with extinction which are or may be affected by trade. Trade in specimens of these species must be subject to particularly strict regulation in order not to endanger further their survival and must only be authorized in exceptional circumstances.

2. Appendix II shall include:

(a) all species which although not necessarily now threatened with extinction may become so unless trade in specimens of such species is subject to strict regulation in order to avoid utilization incompatible with their survival; and
(b) other species which must be subject to regulation in order that trade in specimens of certain species referred to in sub-paragraph (a) of this paragraph may be brought under effective control.

3. Appendix III shall include all species which any Party identifies as being subject to regulation within its jurisdiction for the purpose of preventing or restricting exploitation, and as needing the co-operation of other Parties in the control of trade.

4. The Parties shall not allow trade in specimens of species included in Appendices I, II and III except in accordance with the provisions of the present Convention.

Article III
Regulation of trade in specimens of species included in Appendix I

1. All trade in specimens of species included in Appendix I shall be in accordance with the provisions of this Article.

2. The export of any specimen of a species included in Appendix I shall require the prior grant and presentation of an export permit. An export permit shall only be granted when the following conditions have been met:

(a) a Scientific Authority of the State of export has advised that such export will not be detrimental to the survival of that species;

(b) a Management Authority of the State of export is satisfied that the specimen was not obtained in contravention of the laws of that State for the protection of fauna and flora;

(c) a Management Authority of the State of export is satisfied that any living specimen will be so prepared and shipped as to minimize the risk of injury, damage to health or cruel treatment; and

(d) a Management Authority of the State of export is satisfied that an import permit has been granted for the specimen.

3. The import of any specimen of a species included in Appendix I shall require the prior grant and presentation of an import permit and either an export permit or a re-export certificate. An import permit shall only be granted when the following conditions have been met:

(a) a Scientific Authority of the State of import has advised that the import will be for purposes which are not detrimental to the survival of the species involved;

(b) a Scientific Authority of the State of import is satisfied that the proposed recipient of a living specimen is suitably equipped to house and care for it; and

(c) a Management Authority of the State of import is satisfied that the specimen is not to be used for primarily commercial purposes.

4. The re-export of any specimen of a species included in Appendix I shall require the prior grant and presentation of a re-export certificate. A re-export certificate shall only be granted when the following conditions have been met:

(a) a Management Authority of the State of re-export is satisfied that the specimen was imported into that State in accordance with the provisions of the present Convention;

(b) a Management Authority of the State of re-export is satisfied that any living specimen will be so prepared and shipped as to minimize the risk of injury, damage to health or cruel treatment; and

(c) a Management Authority of the State of re-export is satisfied that an import permit has been granted for any living specimen.

5. The introduction from the sea of any specimen of a species included in Appendix I shall require the prior grant of a certificate from a Management Authority of the State of introduction. A certificate shall only be granted when the following conditions have been met:

(a) a Scientific Authority of the State of introduction advises that the introduction will not be detrimental to the survival of the species involved;

(b) a Management Authority of the State of introduction is satisfied that the proposed recipient of a living specimen is suitably equipped to house and care for it; and

(c) a Management Authority of the State of introduction is satisfied that the specimen is not to be used for primarily commercial purposes.

Article IV
Regulation of trade in specimens of species included in Appendix II

1. All trade in specimens of species included in Appendix II shall be in accordance with the provisions of this Article.

2. The export of any specimen of a species included in Appendix II shall require the prior grant and presentation of an export permit. An export permit shall only be granted when the following conditions have been met:

(a) a Scientific Authority of the State of export has advised that such export will not be detrimental to the survival of that species;

(b) a Management Authority of the State of export is satisfied that the specimen was not obtained in contravention of the laws of that State for the protection of fauna and flora; and

(c) a Management Authority of the State of export is satisfied that any living specimen will be so prepared and shipped as to minimize the risk of injury, damage to health or cruel treatment.

3. A Scientific Authority in each Party shall monitor both the export permits granted by that State for specimens of species included in Appendix II and the actual exports of such specimens. Whenever a Scientific Authority determines

that the export of specimens of any such species should be limited in order to maintain that species throughout its range at a level consistent with its role in the ecosystems in which it occurs and well above the level at which that species might become eligible for inclusion in Appendix I, the Scientific Authority shall advise the appropriate Management Authority of suitable measures to be taken to limit the grant of export permits for specimens of that species.

4. The import of any specimen of a species included in Appendix II shall require the prior presentation of either an export permit or a re-export certificate.

5. The re-export of any specimen of a species included in Appendix II shall require the prior grant and presentation of a re-export certificate. A re-export certificate shall only be granted when the following conditions have been met:

(a) a Management Authority of the State of re-export is satisfied that the specimen was imported into that State in accordance with the provisions of the present Convention; and

(b) a Management Authority of the State of re-export is satisfied that any living specimen will be so prepared and shipped as to minimize the risk of injury, damage to health or cruel treatment.

6. The introduction from the sea of any specimen of a species included in Appendix II shall require the prior grant of a certificate from a Management Authority of the State of introduction. A certificate shall only be granted when the following conditions have been met:

(a) a Scientific Authority of the State of introduction advises that the introduction will not be detrimental to the survival of the species involved; and

(b) a Management Authority of the State of introduction is satisfied that any living specimen will be so handled as to minimize the risk of injury, damage to health or cruel treatment.

7. Certificates referred to in paragraph 6 of this Article may be granted on the advice of a Scientific Authority, in consultation with other national scientific authorities or, when appropriate, international scientific authorities, in respect of periods not exceeding one year for total numbers of specimens to be introduced in such periods.

Article V
Regulation of trade in specimens of species included in Appendix III

1. All trade in specimens of species included in Appendix III shall be in accordance with the provisions of this Article.

2. The export of any specimen of a species included in Appendix III from any State which has included that species in Appendix III shall require the prior grant and presentation of an export permit. An export permit shall only be granted when the following conditions have been met:

(a) a Management Authority of the State of export is satisfied that the specimen was not obtained in contravention of the laws of that State for the protection of fauna and flora; and

(b) a Management Authority of the State of export is satisfied that any living specimen will be so prepared and shipped as to minimize the risk of injury, damage to health or cruel treatment.

3. The import of any specimen of a species included in Appendix III shall require, except in circumstances to which paragraph 4 of this Article applies, the prior presentation of a certificate of origin and, where the import is from a State which has included that species in Appendix III, an export permit.

4. In the case of re-export, a certificate granted by the Management Authority of the State of re-export that the specimen was processed in that State or is being re-exported shall be accepted by the State of import as evidence that the provisions of the present Convention have been complied with in respect of the specimen concerned.

Article VI
Permits and certificates

1. Permits and certificates granted under the provisions of Articles III, IV, and V shall be in accordance with the provisions of this Article.

2. An export permit shall contain the information specified in the model set forth in Appendix IV, and may only be used for export within a period of six months from the date on which it was granted.

3. Each permit or certificate shall contain the title of the present Convention, the name and any identifying stamp of the Management Authority granting it and a control number assigned by the Management Authority.

4. Any copies of a permit or certificate issued by a Management Authority shall be clearly marked as copies only and no such copy may be used in place of the original, except to the extent endorsed thereon.

5. A separate permit or certificate shall be required for each consignment of specimens.

6. A Management Authority of the State of import of any specimen shall cancel and retain the export permit or re-export certificate and any corresponding import permit presented in respect of the import of that specimen.

7. Where appropriate and feasible a Management Authority may affix a mark upon any specimen to assist in identifying the specimen. For these purposes 'mark' means any indelible imprint, lead seal or other suitable means of

identifying a specimen, designed in such a way as to render its imitation by unauthorized persons as difficult as possible.

Article VII
Exemptions and other special provisions relating to trade

1. The provisions of Articles III, IV and V shall not apply to the transit or transhipment of specimens through or in the territory of a Party while the specimens remain in Customs control.

2. Where a Management Authority of the State of export or re-export is satisfied that a specimen was acquired before the provisions of the present Convention applied to that specimen, the provisions of Articles III, IV and V shall not apply to that specimen where the Management Authority issues a certificate to that effect.

3. The provisions of Articles III, IV and V shall not apply to specimens that are personal or household effects. This exemption shall not apply where:

(a) in the case of specimens of a species included in Appendix I, they were acquired by the owner outside his State of usual residence, and are being imported into that State; or

(b) in the case of specimens of species included in Appendix II:
   (i) they were acquired by the owner outside his State of usual residence and in a State where removal from the wild occurred;
   (ii) they are being imported into the owner's State of usual residence; and
   (iii) the State where removal from the wild occurred requires the prior grant of export permits before any export of such specimens;

   unless a Management Authority is satisfied that the specimens were acquired before the provisions of the present Convention applied to such specimens.

4. Specimens of an animal species included in Appendix I bred in captivity for commercial purposes, or of a plant species included in Appendix I artificially propagated for commercial purposes, shall be deemed to be specimens of species included in Appendix II.

5. Where a Management Authority of the State of export is satisfied that any specimen of an animal species was bred in captivity or any specimen of a plant species was artificially propagated, or is a part of such an animal or plant or was derived therefrom, a certificate by that Management Authority to that effect shall be accepted in lieu of any of the permits or certificates required under the provisions of Article III, IV or V.

6. The provisions of Articles III, IV and V shall not apply to the non-commercial loan, donation or exchange between scientists or scientific institutions registered by a Management Authority of their State, of herbarium specimens, other preserved, dried or embedded museum specimens, and

live plant material which carry a label issued or approved by a Management Authority.

7. A Management Authority of any State may waive the requirements of Articles III, IV and V and allow the movement without permits or certificates of specimens which form part of a travelling zoo, circus, menagerie, plant exhibition or other travelling exhibition provided that:

(a) the exporter or importer registers full details of such specimens with that Management Authority;
(b) the specimens are in either of the categories specified in paragraph 2 or 5 of this Article; and
(c) the Management Authority is satisfied that any living specimen will be so transported and cared for as to minimize the risk of injury, damage to health or cruel treatment.

Article VIII
Measures to be taken by the Parties

1. The Parties shall take appropriate measures to enforce the provisions of the present Convention and to prohibit trade in specimens in violation thereof. These shall include measures:

(a) to penalize trade in, or possession of, such specimens, or both; and
(b) to provide for the confiscation or return to the State of export of such specimens.

2. In addition to the measures taken under paragraph 1 of this Article, a Party may, when it deems it necessary, provide for any method of internal reimbursement for expenses incurred as a result of the confiscation of a specimen traded in violation of the measures taken in the application of the provisions of the present Convention.

3. As far as possible, the Parties shall ensure that specimens shall pass through any formalities required for trade with a minimum of delay. To facilitate such passage, a Party may designate ports of exit and ports of entry at which specimens must be presented for clearance. The Parties shall ensure further that all living specimens, during any period of transit, holding or shipment, are properly cared for so as to minimize the risk of injury, damage to health or cruel treatment.

4. Where a living specimen is confiscated as a result of measures referred to in paragraph 1 of this Article:

(a) the specimen shall be entrusted to a Management Authority of the State of confiscation;
(b) the Management Authority shall, after consultation with the State of export, return the specimen to that State at the expense of that State, or to a rescue centre or such other place as the Management Authority deems

appropriate and consistent with the purposes of the present Convention; and

(c) the Management Authority may obtain the advice of a Scientific Authority, or may, whenever it considers it desirable, consult the Secretariat in order to facilitate the decision under sub-paragraph (b) of this paragraph, including the choice of a rescue centre or other place.

5. A rescue centre as referred to in paragraph 4 of this Article means an institution designated by a Management Authority to look after the welfare of living specimens, particularly those that have been confiscated.

6. Each Party shall maintain records of trade in specimens of species included in Appendices I, II and III which shall cover:

(a) the names and addresses of exporters and importers; and

(b) the number and type of permits and certificates granted; the States with which such trade occurred; the numbers or quantities and types of specimens, names of species as included in Appendices I, II and III and, where applicable, the size and sex of the specimens in question.

7. Each Party shall prepare periodic reports on its implementation of the present Convention and shall transmit to the Secretariat:

(a) an annual report containing a summary of the information specified in sub-paragraph (b) of paragraph 6 of this Article; and

(b) a biennial report on legislative, regulatory and administrative measures taken to enforce the provisions of the present Convention.

8. The information referred to in paragraph 7 of this Article shall be available to the public where this is not inconsistent with the law of the Party concerned.

Article IX
Management and scientific authorities

1. Each Party shall designate for the purposes of the present Convention:

(a) one or more Management Authorities competent to grant permits or certificates on behalf of that Party; and

(b) one or more Scientific Authorities.

2. A State depositing an instrument of ratification, acceptance, approval or accession shall at that time inform the Depositary Government of the name and address of the Management Authority authorized to communicate with other Parties and with the Secretariat.

3. Any changes in the designations or authorizations under the provisions of this Article shall be communicated by the Party concerned to the Secretariat for transmission to all other Parties.

4. Any Management Authority referred to in paragraph 2 of this Article shall, if so requested by the Secretariat or the Management Authority of another Party, communicate to it impression of stamps, seals or other devices used to authenticate permits or certificates.

Article X
Trade with States not Party to the Convention

Where export or re-export is to, or import is from, a State not a Party to the present Convention, comparable documentation issued by the competent authorities in that State which substantially conforms with the requirements of the present Convention for permits and certificates may be accepted in lieu thereof by any Party.

Article XI
Conference of the Parties

1. The Secretariat shall call a meeting of the Conference of the Parties not later than two years after the entry into force of the present Convention.

2. Thereafter the Secretariat shall convene regular meetings at least once every two years, unless the Conference decides otherwise, and extraordinary meetings at any time on the written request of at least one-third of the Parties.

3. At meetings, whether regular or extraordinary, the Parties shall review the implementation of the present Convention and may:

(a) make such provision as may be necessary to enable the Secretariat to carry out its duties, and adopt financial provisions;

(b) consider and adopt amendments to Appendices I and II in accordance with Article XV;

(c) review the progress made towards the restoration and conservation of the species included in Appendices I, II and III;

(d) receive and consider any reports presented by the Secretariat or by any Party; and

(e) where appropriate, make recommendations for improving the effectiveness of the present Convention.

4. At each regular meeting, the Parties may determine the time and venue of the next regular meeting to be held in accordance with the provisions of paragraph 2 of this Article.

5. At any meeting, the Parties may determine and adopt rules of procedure for the meeting.

6. The United Nations, its Specialized Agencies and the International Atomic Energy Agency, as well as any State not a Party to the present Convention, may be represented at meetings of the Conference by observers, who shall have the right to participate but not to vote.

7. Any body or agency technically qualified in protection, conservation or management of wild fauna and flora, in the following categories, which has informed the Secretariat of its desire to be represented at meetings of the Conference by observers, shall be admitted unless at least one-third of the Parties present object:

(a) international agencies or bodies, either governmental or non-governmental, and national governmental agencies and bodies; and
(b) national non-governmental agencies or bodies which have been approved for this purpose by the State in which they are located. Once admitted, these observers shall have the right to participate but not to vote.

Article XII
The Secretariat

1. Upon entry into force of the present Convention, a Secretariat shall be provided by the Executive Director of the United Nations Environment Programme. To the extent and in the manner he considers appropriate, he may be assisted by suitable inter-governmental or non-governmental international or national agencies and bodies technically qualified in protection, conservation and management of wild fauna and flora.

2. The functions of the Secretariat shall be:

(a) to arrange for and service meetings of the Parties;
(b) to perform the functions entrusted to it under the provisions of Articles XV and XVI of the present Convention;
(c) to undertake scientific and technical studies in accordance with programmes authorized by the Conference of the Parties as will contribute to the implementation of the present Convention, including studies concerning standards for appropriate preparation and shipment of living specimens and the means of identifying specimens;
(d) to study the reports of Parties and to request from Parties such further information with respect thereto as it deems necessary to ensure implementation of the present Convention;
(e) to invite the attention of the Parties to any matter pertaining to the aims of the present Convention;
(f) to publish periodically and distribute to the Parties current editions of Appendices I, II and III together with any information which will facilitate identification of specimens of species included in those Appendices;
(g) to prepare annual reports to the Parties on its work and on the implementation of the present Convention and such other reports as meetings of the Parties may request;

(h) to make recommendations for the implementation of the aims and provisions of the present Convention, including the exchange of information of
a scientific or technical nature;

(i) to perform any other function as may be entrusted to it by the Parties.

Article XIII
International measures

1. When the Secretariat in the light of information received is satisfied that
any species included in Appendix I or II is being affected adversely by trade in
specimens of that species or that the provisions of the present Convention are
not being effectively implemented, it shall communicate such information to
the authorized Management Authority of the Party or Parties concerned.

2. When any Party receives a communication as indicated in paragraph
1 of this Article, it shall, as soon as possible, inform the Secretariat of any
relevant facts insofar as its laws permit and, where appropriate, propose remedial action. Where the Party considers that an inquiry is desirable, such
inquiry may be carried out by one or more persons expressly authorized by the
Party.

3. The information provided by the Party or resulting from any inquiry
as specified in paragraph 2 of this Article shall be reviewed by the next Conference of the Parties which may make whatever recommendations it deems
appropriate.

Article XIV
Effect on domestic legislation and international conventions

1. The provisions of the present Convention shall in no way affect the right
of Parties to adopt:

(a) stricter domestic measures regarding the conditions for trade, taking, possession or transport of specimens of species included in Appendices I, II
and III, or the complete prohibition thereof; or

(b) domestic measures restricting or prohibiting trade, taking, possession or
transport of species not included in Appendix I, II or III.

2. The provisions of the present Convention shall in no way affect the provisions of any domestic measures or the obligations of Parties deriving from
any treaty, convention, or international agreement relating to other aspects of
trade, taking, possession or transport of specimens which is in force or subsequently may enter into force for any Party including any measure pertaining to
the Customs, public health, veterinary or plant quarantine fields.

3. The provisions of the present Convention shall in no way affect the
provisions of, or the obligations deriving from, any treaty, convention or
international agreement concluded or which may be concluded between States
creating a union or regional trade agreement establishing or maintaining a

common external Customs control and removing Customs control between the parties thereto insofar as they relate to trade among the States members of that union or agreement.

4. A State party to the present Convention, which is also a party to any other treaty, convention or international agreement which is in force at the time of the coming into force of the present Convention and under the provisions of which protection is afforded to marine species included in Appendix II, shall be relieved of the obligations imposed on it under the provisions of the present Convention with respect to trade in specimens of species included in Appendix II that are taken by ships registered in that State and in accordance with the provisions of such other treaty, convention or international agreement.

5. Notwithstanding the provisions of Articles III, IV and V, any export of a specimen taken in accordance with paragraph 4 of this Article shall only require a certificate from a Management Authority of the State of introduction to the effect that the specimen was taken in accordance with the provisions of the other treaty, convention or international agreement in question.

6. Nothing in the present Convention shall prejudice the codification and development of the law of the sea by the United Nations Conference on the Law of the Sea convened pursuant to Resolution 2750 C (XXV) of the General Assembly of the United Nations nor the present or future claims and legal views of any State concerning the law of the sea and the nature and extent of coastal and flag State jurisdiction.

Article XV
Amendments to Appendices I and II

1. The following provisions shall apply in relation to amendments to Appendices I and II at meetings of the Conference of the Parties:

(a) Any Party may propose an amendment to Appendix I or II for consideration at the next meeting. The text of the proposed amendment shall be communicated to the Secretariat at least 150 days before the meeting. The Secretariat shall consult the other Parties and interested bodies on the amendment in accordance with the provisions of sub-paragraphs (b) and (c) of paragraph 2 of this Article and shall communicate the response to all Parties not later than 30 days before the meeting.

(b) Amendments shall be adopted by a two-thirds majority of Parties present and voting. For these purposes 'Parties present and voting' means Parties present and casting an affirmative or negative vote. Parties abstaining from voting shall not be counted among the two-thirds required for adopting an amendment.

(c) Amendments adopted at a meeting shall enter into force 90 days after that meeting for all Parties except those which make a reservation in accordance with paragraph 3 of this Article.

2. The following provisions shall apply in relation to amendments to Appendices I and II between meetings of the Conference of the Parties:

(a) Any Party may propose an amendment to Appendix I or II for consideration between meetings by the postal procedures set forth in this paragraph.

(b) For marine species, the Secretariat shall, upon receiving the text of the proposed amendment, immediately communicate it to the Parties. It shall also consult inter-governmental bodies having a function in relation to those species especially with a view to obtaining scientific data these bodies may be able to provide and to ensuring co-ordination with any conservation measures enforced by such bodies. The Secretariat shall communicate the views expressed and data provided by these bodies and its own findings and recommendations to the Parties as soon as possible.

(c) For species other than marine species, the Secretariat shall, upon receiving the text of the proposed amendment, immediately communicate it to the Parties, and, as soon as possible thereafter, its own recommendations.

(d) Any Party may, within 60 days of the date on which the Secretariat communicated its recommendations to the Parties under sub-paragraph (b) or (c) of this paragraph, transmit to the Secretariat any comments on the proposed amendment together with any relevant scientific data and information.

(e) The Secretariat shall communicate the replies received together with its own recommendations to the Parties as soon as possible.

(f) If no objection to the proposed amendment is received by the Secretariat within 30 days of the date the replies and recommendations were communicated under the provisions of sub-paragraph (e) of this paragraph, the amendment shall enter into force 90 days later for all Parties except those which make a reservation in accordance with paragraph 3 of this Article.

(g) If an objection by any Party is received by the Secretariat, the proposed amendment shall be submitted to a postal vote in accordance with the provisions of sub-paragraphs (h), (i) and (j) of this paragraph.

(h) The Secretariat shall notify the Parties that notification of objection has been received.

(i) Unless the Secretariat receives the votes for, against or in abstention from at least one-half of the Parties within 60 days of the date of notification under sub-paragraph (h) of this paragraph, the proposed amendment shall be referred to the next meeting of the Conference for further consideration.

(j) Provided that votes are received from one-half of the Parties, the amendment shall be adopted by a two-thirds majority of Parties casting an affirmative or negative vote.

(k) The Secretariat shall notify all Parties of the result of the vote.

(l) If the proposed amendment is adopted it shall enter into force 90 days after the date of the notification by the Secretariat of its acceptance for all Parties except those which make a reservation in accordance with paragraph 3 of this Article.

3. During the period of 90 days provided for by sub-paragraph (c) of paragraph 1 or sub-paragraph (l) of paragraph 2 of this Article any Party may by notification in writing to the Depositary Government make a reservation with respect to the amendment. Until such reservation is withdrawn the Party shall be treated as a State not a Party to the present Convention with respect to trade in the species concerned.

Article XVI
Appendix III and amendments thereto

1. Any Party may at any time submit to the Secretariat a list of species which it identifies as being subject to regulation within its jurisdiction for the purpose mentioned in paragraph 3 of Article II. Appendix III shall include the names of the Parties submitting the species for inclusion therein, the scientific names of the species so submitted, and any parts or derivatives of the animals or plants concerned that are specified in relation to the species for the purposes of sub-paragraph (b) of Article I.

2. Each list submitted under the provisions of paragraph 1 of this Article shall be communicated to the Parties by the Secretariat as soon as possible after receiving it. The list shall take effect as part of Appendix III 90 days after the date of such communication. At any time after the communication of such list, any Party may by notification in writing to the Depositary Government enter a reservation with respect to any species or any parts or derivatives, and until such reservation is withdrawn, the State shall be treated as a State not a Party to the present Convention with respect to trade in the species or part or derivative concerned.

3. A Party which has submitted a species for inclusion in Appendix III may withdraw it at any time by notification to the Secretariat which shall communicate the withdrawal to all Parties. The withdrawal shall take effect 30 days after the date of such communication.

4. Any Party submitting a list under the provisions of paragraph 1 of this Article shall submit to the Secretariat a copy of all domestic laws and regulations applicable to the protection of such species, together with any interpretations which the Party may deem appropriate or the Secretariat may request. The Party shall, for as long as the species in question is included in Appendix III, submit any amendments of such laws and regulations or any interpretations as they are adopted.

Article XVII
Amendment of the Convention

1. An extraordinary meeting of the Conference of the Parties shall be convened by the Secretariat on the written request of at least one-third of the Parties to consider and adopt amendments to the present Convention. Such amendments shall be adopted by a two-thirds majority of Parties present and voting. For these purposes 'Parties present and voting' means Parties present and casting an affirmative or negative vote. Parties abstaining from voting shall not be counted among the two-thirds required for adopting an amendment.

2. The text of any proposed amendment shall be communicated by the Secretariat to all Parties at least 90 days before the meeting.

3. An amendment shall enter into force for the Parties which have accepted it 60 days after two-thirds of the Parties have deposited an instrument of acceptance of the amendment with the Depositary Government. Thereafter, the amendment shall enter into force for any other Party 60 days after that Party deposits its instrument of acceptance of the amendment.

Article XVIII
Resolution of disputes

1. Any dispute which may arise between two or more Parties with respect to the interpretation or application of the provisions of the present Convention shall be subject to negotiation between the Parties involved in the dispute.

2. If the dispute can not be resolved in accordance with paragraph 1 of this Article, the Parties may, by mutual consent, submit the dispute to arbitration, in particular that of the Permanent Court of Arbitration at The Hague, and the Parties submitting the dispute shall be bound by the arbitral decision.

Article XIX
Signature

The present Convention shall be open for signature at Washington until 30th April 1973 and thereafter at Berne until 31st December 1974.

Article XX
Ratification, acceptance, approval

The present Convention shall be subject to ratification, acceptance or approval. Instruments of ratification, acceptance or approval shall be deposited with the Government of the Swiss Confederation which shall be the Depositary Government.

Article XXI
Accession

The present Convention shall be open indefinitely for accession. Instruments of accession shall be deposited with the Depositary Government.

Article XXII
Entry into force

1. The present Convention shall enter into force 90 days after the date of deposit of the tenth instrument of ratification, acceptance, approval or accession, with the Depositary Government.

2. For each State which ratifies, accepts or approves the present Convention or accedes thereto after the deposit of the tenth instrument of ratification, acceptance, approval or accession, the present Convention shall enter into force 90 days after the deposit by such State of its instrument of ratification, acceptance, approval or accession.

Article XXIII
Reservations

1. The provisions of the present Convention shall not be subject to general reservations. Specific reservations may be entered in accordance with the provisions of this Article and Articles XV and XVI.

2. Any State may, on depositing its instrument of ratification, acceptance, approval or accession, enter a specific reservation with regard to:

(a) any species included in Appendix I, II or III; or
(b) any parts or derivatives specified in relation to a species included in Appendix III.

3. Until a Party withdraws its reservation entered under the provisions of this Article, it shall be treated as a State not a Party to the present Convention with respect to trade in the particular species or parts or derivatives specified in such reservation.

Article XXIV
Denunciation

Any Party may denounce the present Convention by written notification to the Depositary Government at any time. The denunciation shall take effect twelve months after the Depositary Government has received the notification.

Article XXV
Depositary

1. The original of the present Convention, in the Chinese, English, French, Russian and Spanish languages, each version being equally authentic, shall

be deposited with the Depositary Government, which shall transmit certified copies thereof to all States that have signed it or deposited instruments of accession to it.

2. The Depositary Government shall inform all signatory and acceding States and the Secretariat of signatures, deposit of instruments of ratification, acceptance, approval or accession, entry into force of the present Convention, amendments thereto, entry and withdrawal of reservations and notifications of denunciation.

3. As soon as the present Convention enters into force, a certified copy thereof shall be transmitted by the Depositary Government to the Secretariat of the United Nations for registration and publication in accordance with Article 102 of the Charter of the United Nations.

In witness whereof the undersigned Plenipotentiaries, being duly authorized to that effect, have signed the present Convention.

Done at Washington this third day of March, One Thousand Nine Hundred and Seventy-three.

Appendices (*omitted*)

Convention on the Conservation of Migratory Species of Wild Animals, 23 June 1979

Editorial note

The Convention on the Conservation of Migratory Species of Wild Animals applies to all species for which a significant proportion of the population habitually moves across national boundaries (Article I). Obligations of the Parties depend upon the conservation status of the animals for which its territory is a range. For species that are the most endangered (Appendix I), Range States are to 'endeavour' to conserve and restore their habitats, prevent 'as appropriate' activities which adversely affect the species, and prohibit takings except under very limited circumstances (Article III). If the species is not endangered but has an unfavourable conservation status (Appendix II), Range States are encouraged to conclude 'agreements' among themselves on the measures to restore the conservation status of the species (Article IV). The Convention provides guidelines for the content of these 'agreements' (Article V). So far eleven such agreements have been adopted under the Appendix II procedure:

- the 1988 Agreement on the Conservation of Seals in the Wadden Sea Area;
- the 1991 Agreement on Conservation of Bats in Europe;
- the 1992 Agreement on Small Cetaceans in the North Sea and the Baltic;
- the 1994 Memorandum of Understanding concerning Conservation Measures for the Slender-Billed Curlew;
- the 1995 African-Eurasian Migratory Waterbird Agreement;
- the 1996 Agreement on the Conservation of Cetaceans of the Black Sea, Mediterranean Sea and Contiguous Atlantic Area;
- the 1998 Memorandum of Understanding concerning Conservation Measures for the Siberian Crane;
- the 1999 Memorandum of Understanding concerning Conservation Measures for Marine Turtles of the Atlantic Coast of Africa;
- the 2000 Memorandum of Understanding on the Conservation and Management of the Middle-European Population of the Great Bustard;
- the 2001 Memorandum of Understanding on the Conservation and Management of Marine Turtles and their Habitats of the Indian Ocean and South-East Asia; and
- the 2001 Agreement on the Conservation of Albatrosses and Petrels.

Further Agreements are expected to be adopted on waterbirds of the Americas and Asia-Pacific, and for Sahelo-Saharan mammals.

A Conference of the Parties is established by the Convention to take all relevant decisions (Article VII). A Scientific Council is also established to provide advice to the Conference of the Parties (Article VIII). Amendments to the Convention are taken by a two-thirds majority of the Conference of the Parties (Article X). Amendments to the Appendices also require a two-thirds majority, but Parties are permitted to enter reservations to these amendments (Article XI). Dispute settlement is by negotiation or, with the consent of the Parties involved, by binding arbitration (Article XIV). Reservations may only be entered in respect of species listed in the Appendices, for which Parties are considered non-parties with respect to those species (Article XIV).

Date of signature:	23 June 1979
Entry into force:	1 November 1983
Depositary:	Government of the Federal Republic of Germany
Contracting Parties:	Albania, Argentina, Australia, Belgium, Benin, Bolivia, Bulgaria, Burkina Faso, Cameroon, Chad, Chile, Congo, Congo (Democratic Republic of), Croatia, Cyprus, Czech Republic, Denmark, Egypt, European Community, Finland, France, Gambia, Georgia, Germany, Ghana, Greece, Guinea, Guinea Bissau, Hungary, India, Ireland, Israel, Italy, Jordan, Kenya, Latvia, Libyan Arab Jamahiriya, Liechtenstein, Lithuania, Luxembourg, Mali, Malta, Mauritania, Monaco, Mongolia, Morocco, Netherlands, New Zealand, Niger, Nigeria, Norway, Pakistan, Panama, Paraguay, Peru, Philippines, Poland, Portugal, Republic of Moldova, Romania, São Tomé and Príncipe, Saudi Arabia, Senegal, Slovakia, Slovenia, Somalia, South Africa, Spain, Sri Lanka, Sweden, Switzerland, Tajikistan, Tanzania (United Republic of), The Former Yugoslav Republic of Macedonia, Togo, Tunisia, Uganda, Ukraine, United Kingdom, Uruguay.
Website:	www.unep-wcmc.org/cms/

Convention on the Conservation of Migratory Species of Wild Animals

The Contracting Parties,

Recognizing that wild animals in their innumerable forms are an irreplaceable part of the earth's natural system which must be conserved for the good of mankind;

Aware that each generation of man holds the resources of the earth for future generations and has an obligation to ensure that this legacy is conserved and, where utilized, is used wisely;

Conscious of the ever-growing value of wild animals from environmental, ecological, genetic, scientific, aesthetic, recreational, cultural, educational, social and economic points of view;

Concerned particularly with those species of wild animals that migrate across or outside national jurisdictional boundaries;

Recognizing that the States are and must be the protectors of the migratory species of wild animals that live within or pass through their national jurisdictional boundaries;

Convinced that conservation and effective management of migratory species of wild animals require the concerted action of all States within the national jurisdictional boundaries of which such species spend any part of their life cycle;

Recalling Recommendation 32 of the Action Plan adopted by the United Nations Conference on the Human Environment (Stockholm, 1972) and noted with satisfaction at the Twenty-seventh Session of the General Assembly of the United Nations,

Have agreed as follows:

Article I
Interpretation

1. For the purpose of this Convention:

a) 'Migratory species' means the entire population or any geographically separate part of the population of any species or lower taxon of wild animals, a significant proportion of whose members cyclically and predictably cross one or more national jurisdictional boundaries;

b) 'Conservation status of a migratory species' means the sum of the influences acting on the migratory species that may affect its long-term distribution and abundance;

c) 'Conservation status' will be taken as 'favourable' when:

(1) population dynamics data indicate that the migratory species is maintaining itself on a long-term basis as a viable component of its ecosystems;

(2) the range of the migratory species is neither currently being reduced, nor is likely to be reduced, on a long-term basis;

(3) there is, and will be in the foreseeable future sufficient habitat to maintain the population of the migratory species on a long-term basis; and

(4) the distribution and abundance of the migratory species approach historic coverage and levels to the extent that potentially suitable ecosystems exist and to the extent consistent with wise wildlife management;

d) 'Conservation status' will be taken as 'unfavourable' if any of the conditions
set out in sub-paragraph (c) of this paragraph is not met;

e) 'Endangered' in relation to a particular migratory species means that the
migratory species is in danger of extinction throughout all or a significant
portion of its range;

f) 'Range' means all the areas of land or water that a migratory species inhabits,
stays in temporarily, crosses or overflies at any time on its normal migration
route;

g) 'Habitat' means any area in the range of a migratory species which contains
suitable living conditions for that species;

h) 'Range State' in relation to a particular migratory species means any State
(and where appropriate any other Party referred to under subparagraph (k)
of this paragraph) that exercises jurisdiction over any part of the range of
that migratory species, or a State, flag vessels of which are engaged outside
national jurisdictional limits in taking that migratory species;

i) 'Taking' means taking, hunting, fishing, capturing, harassing, deliberate
killing, or attempting to engage in any such conduct;

j) 'Agreement' means an international agreement relating to the conservation
of one or more migratory species as provided for in Articles IV and V of
this Convention; and

k) 'Party' means a State or any regional economic integration organization
constituted by sovereign States which has competence in respect of the negotiation, conclusion and application of international Agreements in matters
covered by this Convention for which this Convention is in force.

2. In matters within their competence, the regional economic integration
organizations which are Parties to this Convention shall in their own name exercise the rights and fulfil the responsibilities which this Convention attributes
to their member States. In such cases the member States of these organizations
shall not be entitled to exercise such rights individually.

3. Where this Convention provides for a decision to be taken by either a two-
thirds majority or a unanimous decision of 'the Parties present and voting' this
shall mean 'the Parties present and casting an affirmative or negative vote'. Those
abstaining from voting shall not be counted amongst 'the Parties present and
voting' in determining the majority.

Article II
Fundamental principles

1. The Parties acknowledge the importance of migratory species being conserved and of Range States agreeing to take action to this end whenever possible

and appropriate, paying special attention to migratory species the conservation status of which is unfavourable, and taking individually or in co-operation appropriate and necessary steps to conserve such species and their habitat.

2. The Parties acknowledge the need to take action to avoid any migratory species becoming endangered.

3. In particular, the Parties:

a) should promote, co-operate in and support research relating to migratory species;
b) shall endeavour to provide immediate protection for migratory species included in Appendix I; and
c) shall endeavour to conclude Agreements covering the conservation and management of migratory species included in Appendix II.

Article III
Endangered migratory species: Appendix I

1. Appendix I shall list migratory species which are endangered.

2. A migratory species may be listed in Appendix I provided that reliable evidence, including the best scientific evidence available, indicates that the species is endangered.

3. A migratory species may be removed from Appendix I when the Conference of the Parties determines that:

a) reliable evidence, including the best scientific evidence available, indicates that the species is no longer endangered, and
b) the species is not likely to become endangered again because of loss of protection due to its removal from Appendix I.

4. Parties that are Range States of a migratory species listed in Appendix I shall endeavour:

a) to conserve and, where feasible and appropriate, restore those habitats of the species which are of importance in removing the species from danger of extinction;
b) to prevent, remove, compensate for or minimize, as appropriate, the adverse effects of activities or obstacles that seriously impede or prevent the migration of the species; and
c) to the extent feasible and appropriate, to prevent, reduce or control factors that are endangering or are likely to further endanger the species, including strictly controlling the introduction of, or controlling or eliminating, already introduced exotic species.

5. Parties that are Range States of a migratory species listed in Appendix I shall prohibit the taking of animals belonging to such species. Exceptions may be made to this prohibition only if:

a) the taking is for scientific purposes;
b) the taking is for the purpose of enhancing the propagation or survival of the affected species;
c) the taking is to accommodate the needs of traditional subsistence users of such species; or
d) extraordinary circumstances so require;
   provided that such exceptions are precise as to content and limited in space and time. Such taking should not operate to the disadvantage of the species.

6. The Conferences of the Parties may recommend to the Parties that are Range States of a migratory species listed in Appendix I that they take further measures considered appropriate to benefit the species.

7. The Parties shall as soon as possible inform the Secretariat of any exceptions made pursuant to paragraph 5 of this Article.

Article IV
Migratory species to be the subject of agreements: Appendix II

1. Appendix II shall list migratory species which have an unfavourable conservation status and which require international agreements for their conservation and management, as well as those which have a conservation status which would significantly benefit from the international cooperation that could be achieved by an international agreement.

2. If the circumstances so warrant, a migratory species may be listed both in Appendix I and Appendix II.

3. Parties that are Range States of migratory species listed in Appendix II shall endeavour to conclude Agreements where these should benefit the species and should give priority to those species in an unfavourable conservation status.

4. Parties are encouraged to take action with a view to concluding agreements for any population or any geographically separate part of the population of any species or lower taxon of wild animals, members of which periodically cross one or more national jurisdiction boundaries.

5. The Secretariat shall be provided with a copy of each Agreement concluded pursuant to the provisions of this Article.

Article V
Guidelines for agreements

1. The object of each Agreement shall be to restore the migratory species concerned to a favourable conservation status or to maintain it in such a status. Each Agreement should deal with those aspects of the conservation and management of the migratory species concerned which serve to achieve that object.

2. Each Agreement should cover the whole of the range of the migratory species concerned and should be open to accession by all Range States of that species, whether or not they are Parties to this Convention.

3. An Agreement should, wherever possible, deal with more than one migratory species.

4. Each Agreement should:

a) identify the migratory species covered;

b) describe the range and migration route of the migratory species;

c) provide for each Party to designate its national authority concerned with the implementation of the Agreement.

d) establish, if necessary, appropriate machinery to assist in carrying out the aims of the Agreement, to monitor its effectiveness, and to prepare reports for the Conference of the Parties;

e) provide for procedures for the settlement of disputes between Parties to the Agreement; and

f) at a minimum, prohibit, in relation to a migratory species of the Order Cetacea, any taking that is not permitted for that migratory species under any other multilateral Agreement and provide for accession to the Agreement by States that are not Range States of that migratory species.

5. Where appropriate and feasible, each Agreement should provide for but not be limited to:

a) periodic review of the conservation status of the migratory species concerned and the identification of the factors which may be harmful to that status;

b) co-ordinated conservation and management plans;

c) research into the ecology and population dynamics of the migratory species concerned, with special regard to migration;

d) the exchange of information on the migratory species concerned, special regard being paid to the exchange of the results of research and of relevant statistics;

e) conservation and, where required and feasible, restoration of the habitats of importance in maintaining a favourable conservation status, and protection of such habitats from disturbances, including strict control of the introduction of, or control of already introduced, exotic species detrimental to the migratory species;

f) maintenance of a network of suitable habitats appropriately disposed in relation to the migration routes;

g) where it appears desirable, the provision of new habitats favourable to the migratory species or reintroduction of the migratory species into favourable habitats;

h) elimination of, to the maximum extent possible, or compensation for activities and obstacles which hinder or impede migration;

i) prevention, reduction or control of the release into the habitat of the migratory species of substances harmful to that migratory species;

j) measures based on sound ecological principles to control and manage the taking of the migratory species;

k) procedures for co-ordinating action to suppress illegal taking;

l) exchange of information on substantial threats to the migratory species;

m) emergency procedures whereby conservation action would be considerably and rapidly strengthened when the conservation status of the migratory species is seriously affected; and

n) making the general public aware of the contents and aims of the Agreement.

Article VI
Range States

1. A list of the Range States of migratory species listed in Appendices I and II shall be kept up to date by the Secretariat using information it has received from the Parties.

2. The Parties shall keep the Secretariat informed in regard to which of the migratory species listed in Appendices I and II they consider themselves to be Range States, including provision of information on their flag vessels engaged outside national jurisdictional limits in taking the migratory species concerned and, where possible, future plans in respect of such taking.

3. The Parties which are Range States for migratory species listed in Appendix I or Appendix II should inform the Conference of the Parties through the Secretariat, at least six months prior to each ordinary meeting of the Conference, on measures that they are taking to implement the provisions of this Convention for these species.

Article VII
The Conference of the Parties

1. The Conference of the Parties shall be the decision-making organ of this Convention.

2. The Secretariat shall call a meeting of the Conference of the Parties not later than two years after the entry into force of this Convention.

3. Thereafter the Secretariat shall convene ordinary meetings of the Conference of the Parties at intervals of not more than three years, unless the Conference decides otherwise, and extraordinary meetings at any time on the written request of at least one-third of the Parties.

4. The Conference of the Parties shall establish and keep under review the financial regulations of this Convention. The Conference of the Parties shall, at each of its ordinary meetings, adopt the budget for the next financial period. Each Party shall contribute to this budget according to a scale to be agreed upon by the Conference. Financial regulations, including the provisions on the budget and the scale of contributions as well as their modifications, shall be adopted by unanimous vote of the Parties present and voting.

5. At each of its meetings the Conference of the Parties shall review the implementation of this Convention and may in particular:

a) review and assess the conservation status of migratory species;
b) review the progress made towards the conservation of migratory species, especially those listed in Appendices I and II;
c) make such provision and provide such guidance as may be necessary to enable the Scientific Council and the Secretariat to carry out their duties;
d) receive and consider any reports presented by the Scientific Council, the Secretariat, any Party or any standing body established pursuant to an Agreement;
e) make recommendations to the Parties for improving the conservation status of migratory species and review the progress being made under Agreements;
f) in those cases where an Agreement has not been concluded, make recommendations for the convening of meetings of the Parties that are Range States of a migratory species or group of migratory species to discuss measures to improve the conservation status of the species;
g) make recommendations to the Parties for improving the effectiveness of this Convention; and
h) decide on any additional measure that should be taken to implement the objectives of this Convention.

6. Each meeting of the Conference of the Parties should determine the time and venue of the next meeting.

7. Any meeting of the Conference of the Parties shall determine and adopt rules of procedure for that meeting. Decisions at a meeting of the Conference of the Parties shall require a two-thirds majority of the Parties present and voting, except where otherwise provided for by this Convention.

8. The United Nations, its Specialized Agencies, the International Atomic Energy Agency, as well as any State not a party to this Convention and, for each Agreement, the body designated by the parties to that Agreement, may be represented by observers at meetings of the Conference of the Parties.

9. Any agency or body technically qualified in protection, conservation and management of migratory species, in the following categories, which has informed the Secretariat of its desire to be represented at meetings of the Conference of the Parties by observers, shall be admitted unless at least one-third of the Parties present object:

a) international agencies or bodies, either governmental or non-governmental, and national governmental agencies and bodies; and
b) national non-governmental agencies or bodies which have been approved for this purpose by the State in which they are located.

Once admitted, these observers shall have the right to participate but not to vote.

Article VIII
The Scientific Council

1. At its first meeting, the Conference of the Parties shall establish a Scientific Council to provide advice on scientific matters.

2. Any Party may appoint a qualified expert as a member of the Scientific Council. In addition, the Scientific Council shall include as members qualified experts selected and appointed by the Conference of the Parties; the number of these experts, the criteria for their selection and the terms of their appointments shall be as determined by the Conference of the Parties.

3. The Scientific Council shall meet at the request of the Secretariat as required by the Conference of the Parties.

4. Subject to the approval of the Conference of the Parties, the Scientific Council shall establish its own rules of procedure.

5. The Conference of the Parties shall determine the functions of the Scientific Council, which may include:

a) providing scientific advice to the Conference of the Parties, to the Secretariat, and, if approved by the Conference of the Parties, to any body set up under this Convention or an Agreement or to any Party;

b) recommending research and the co-ordination of research on migratory species, evaluating the results of such research in order to ascertain the conservation status of migratory species and reporting to the Conference of the Parties on such status and measures for its improvement;

c) making recommendations to the Conference of the Parties as to the migratory species to be included in Appendices I and II, together with an indication of the range of such migratory species;

d) making recommendations to the Conference of the Parties as to specific conservation and management measures to be included in Agreements on migratory species; and

e) recommending to the Conference of the Parties solutions to problems relating to the scientific aspects of the implementation of this Convention, in particular with regard to the habitats of migratory species.

Article IX
The Secretariat

1. For the purposes of this Convention a Secretariat shall be established.

2. Upon entry into force of this Convention, the Secretariat is provided by the Executive Director of the United Nations Environment Programme. To the extent and in the manner he considers appropriate, he may be assisted by suitable intergovernmental or non-governmental, international or national agencies and bodies technically qualified in protection, conservation and management of wild animals.

3. If the United Nations Environment Programme is no longer able to provide the Secretariat, the Conference of the Parties shall make alternative arrangements for the Secretariat.

4. The functions of the Secretariat shall be:

a) to arrange for and service meetings:
  (i) of the Conference of the Parties, and
  (ii) of the Scientific Council;
b) to maintain liaison with and promote liaison between the Parties, the standing bodies set up under Agreements and other international organizations concerned with migratory species;
c) to obtain from any appropriate source reports and other information which will further the objectives and implementation of this Convention and to arrange for the appropriate dissemination of such information;
d) to invite the attention of the Conference of the Parties to any matter pertaining to the objectives of this Convention;
e) to prepare for the Conference of the Parties reports on the work of the Secretariat and on the implementation of this Convention;
f) to maintain and publish a list of Range States of all migratory species included in Appendices I and II;
g) to promote, under the direction of the Conference of the Parties, the conclusion of Agreements;
h) to maintain and make available to the Parties a list of Agreements and, if so required by the Conference of the Parties, to provide any information on such Agreements;
i) to maintain and publish a list of the recommendations made by the Conference of the Parties pursuant to sub-paragraphs (e), (f) and (g) of paragraph 5 of Article VII or of decisions made pursuant to sub-paragraph (h) of that paragraph;
j) to provide for the general public information concerning this Convention and its objectives; and
k) to perform any other function entrusted to it under this Convention or by the Conference of the Parties.

Article X
Amendment of the Convention

1. This Convention may be amended at any ordinary or extraordinary meeting of the Conference of the Parties.

2. Proposals for amendment may be made by any Party.

3. The text of any proposed amendment and the reasons for it shall be communicated to the Secretary at least one hundred and fifty days before the meeting at which it is to be considered and shall promptly be communicated by the Secretary to all Parties. Any comments on the text by the Parties shall be communicated to the Secretariat not less than sixty days before the meeting

begins. The Secretariat shall, immediately after the last day for submission of comments, communicate to the Parties all comments submitted by that day.

4. Amendments shall be adopted by a two-thirds majority of Parties present and voting.

5. An amendment adopted shall enter into force for all Parties which have accepted it on the first day of the third month following the date on which two-thirds of the Parties have deposited an instrument of acceptance with the Depositary. For each Party which deposits an instrument of acceptance after the date on which two-thirds of the Parties have deposited an instrument of acceptance, the amendment shall enter into force for that Party on the first day of the third month following the deposit of its instrument of acceptance.

Article XI
Amendment of the Appendices

1. Appendices I and II may be amended at any ordinary or extraordinary meeting of the Conference of the Parties.

2. Proposals for amendment may be made by any Party.

3. The text of any proposed amendment and the reasons for it, based on the best scientific evidence available, shall be communicated to the Secretariat at least one hundred and fifty days before the meeting and shall promptly be communicated by the Secretariat to all Parties. Any comments on the text by the Parties shall be communicated to the Secretariat not less than sixty days before the meeting begins. The Secretariat shall, immediately after the last day for submission of comments, communicate to the Parties all comments submitted by that day.

4. Amendments shall be adopted by a two-thirds majority of Parties present and voting.

5. An amendment to the Appendices shall enter into force for all Parties ninety days after the meeting of the Conference of the Parties at which it was adopted, except for those Parties which make a reservation in accordance with paragraph 6 of this Article.

6. During the period of ninety days provided for in paragraph 5 of this Article, any Party may by notification in writing to the Depositary make a reservation with respect to the amendment. A reservation to an amendment may be withdrawn by written notification to the Depositary and thereupon the amendment shall enter into force for that Party ninety days after the reservation is withdrawn.

Article XII
Effect on international conventions and other legislation

1. Nothing in this Convention shall prejudice the codification and development of the law of the sea by the United Nations Conference on the Law of the Sea convened pursuant to Resolution 2750 C (XXV) of the General Assembly

of the United Nations nor the present or future claims and legal views of any State concerning the law of the sea and the nature and extent of coastal and flag State jurisdiction.

2. The provisions of this Convention shall in no way affect the rights or obligations of any Party deriving from any existing treaty, convention or Agreement.

3. The provisions of this Convention shall in no way affect the right of Parties to adopt stricter domestic measures concerning the conservation of migratory species listed in Appendices I and II or to adopt domestic measures concerning the conservation of species not listed in Appendices I and II.

Article XIII
Settlement of disputes

1. Any dispute which may arise between two or more Parties with respect to the interpretation or application of the provisions of this Convention shall be subject to negotiation between the Parties involved in the dispute.

2. If the dispute cannot be resolved in accordance with paragraph 1 of this Article, the Parties may, by mutual consent, submit the dispute to arbitration, in particular that of the Permanent Court of Arbitration at The Hague, and the Parties submitting the dispute shall be bound by the arbitral decision.

Article XIV
Reservations

1. The provisions of this Convention shall not be subject to general reservations. Specific reservations may be entered in accordance with the provisions of this Article and Article XI.

2. Any State or regional economic integration organization may, on depositing its instrument of ratification, acceptance, approval or accession, enter a specific reservation with regard to the presence on either Appendix I or Appendix II or both, of any migratory species and shall then not be regarded as a Party in regard to the subject of that reservation until ninety days after the Depositary has transmitted to the Parties notification that such reservation has been withdrawn.

Article XV
Signature

This Convention shall be open for signature at Bonn for all States and any regional economic integration organization until the twenty-second day of June, 1980.

Article XVI
Ratification, acceptance, approval

This Convention shall be subject to ratification, acceptance or approval. Instruments of ratification, acceptance or approval shall be deposited with the Government of the Federal Republic of Germany, which shall be the Depositary.

Article XVII
Accession

After the twenty-second day of June 1980 this Convention shall be open for accession by all non-signatory States and any regional economic integration organization. Instruments of accession shall be deposited with the Depositary.

Article XVIII
Entry into force

1. This Convention shall enter into force on the first day of the third month following the date of deposit of the fifteenth instrument of ratification, acceptance, approval or accession with the Depositary.

2. For each State or each regional economic integration organization which ratifies, accepts or approves this Convention or accedes thereto after the deposit of the fifteenth instrument of ratification, acceptance, approval or accession, this Convention shall enter into force on the first day of the third month following the deposit by such State or such organization of its instrument of ratification, acceptance, approval or accession.

Article XIX
Denunciation

Any Party may denounce this Convention by written notification to the Depositary at any time. The denunciation shall take effect twelve months after the Depositary has received the notification.

Article XX
Depositary

1. The original of this Convention, in the English, French, German, Russian and Spanish languages, each version being equally authentic, shall be deposited with the Depositary. The Depositary shall transmit certified copies of each of these versions to all States and all regional economic integration organizations that have signed the Convention or deposited instruments of accession to it.

2. The Depositary shall, after consultation with the Governments concerned, prepare official versions of the text of this Convention in the Arabic and Chinese languages.

3. The Depositary shall inform all signatory and acceding States and all signatory and acceding regional economic integration organizations and the Secretariat of signatures, deposit of instruments of ratification, acceptance, approval or accession, entry into force of this Convention, amendments thereto, specific reservations and notifications of denunciation.

4. As soon as this Convention enters into force, a certified copy thereof shall be transmitted by the Depositary to the Secretariat of the United Nations for registration and publication in accordance with Article 102 of the Charter of the United Nations.

IN WITNESS WHEREOF the undersigned, being duly authorized to that effect, have signed this Convention.

DONE at Bonn on 23 June 1979.

Appendix I
Interpretation

1. Migratory species included in this Appendix are referred to:

a) by the name of the species or subspecies; or
b) as being all of the migratory species included in a higher taxon or designated part thereof.

2. Other references to taxa higher than species are for the purposes of information or classification only.

3. The abbreviation for *sensu lato* '(s.l.)' is used to denote that the scientific name is used in its extended meaning.

[...]

(The list of species in Appendix I and II is omitted)

Convention on Biological Diversity, 5 June 1992

Editorial note

The Convention on Biological Diversity, adopted under the auspices of UNEP, is designed to protect the earth's biodiversity by promoting 'sustainable use' (defined in Article 2) and by ensuring that its benefits are shared equitably between the developing and developed worlds. The Convention affirms the applicability of Principle 21 of the Stockholm Declaration to this context (Article 3) and provides for the State's responsibility under the Convention for activities under its control both within national jurisdiction and without (Article 4).

The Convention imposes obligations upon States in relation to *in situ* conservation (within a species' natural habitat) and *ex situ* conservation (Articles 8 and 9). The Convention requires Parties to promote the sustainable use of biological resources by, *inter alia,* integrating this objective into national decision-making, providing incentives, undertaking research and training, encouraging public education and requiring environmental impact assessments (Articles 10–14).

The Convention affirms the right of the host State to determine access to its biological resources (Article 15(1)) and creates a presumption rebuttable by the host State that access must be subject to that State's prior informed consent (Article 15(5)). It seeks to channel the benefits derived from the exploitation of biological resources to the State of origin by requiring the extracting Party to share the proceeds and results of research in a 'fair and equitable way', as appropriate, and on mutually agreed terms (Articles 15(7) and 19(2)). The Convention also provides for transfer of technology to developing countries, subject to existing patent and other intellectual property rights (Article 16).

'New and additional' financial resources are to be provided by developed countries to aid developing countries in implementing the objectives of the Convention (Article 20). The Convention does not affect the rights and obligations Parties may have pursuant to other international agreements except where fulfilment of those rights and obligations will cause 'serious damage or threat to biological diversity' (Article 22).

A Conference of the Parties is established by the Convention (Article 23), along with a Secretariat (Article 24) and a subsidiary body to provide scientific, technical and technological advice (Article 25). In addition, the Conference of the Parties set up a financial mechanism for the transfer of funds to developing countries (Article 21). The Global Environmental Facility has been acting as the interim financial mechanism of the Convention. Dispute settlement is by negotiation, mediation and, unless Parties agree otherwise, conciliation (Article 27). On ratification or at any other time, a Party may declare its acceptance of arbitration or the jurisdiction of the ICJ as a means of dispute settlement (Article 27). Amendments to the Convention or any Protocol requires approval of at least a two-thirds majority of the Parties present and voting (Article 29). To date, only one Protocol, the Cartagena Protocol on Biosafety, has been adopted (see below). No reservations to the Convention are permitted (Article 37).

Date of signature: 5 June 1992

Entry into force: 29 December 1993

Depositary: Secretary-General of the United Nations

Contracting Parties: Afghanistan, Albania, Algeria, Angola, Antigua and Barbuda, Argentina, Armenia, Australia, Austria, Azerbaijan, Bahamas, Bahrain, Bangladesh, Barbados, Belarus, Belgium, Belize, Benin, Bhutan, Bolivia, Bosnia and Herzegovina, Botswana, Brazil, Bulgaria, Burkina Faso, Burundi, Cambodia, Cameroon, Canada, Cape Verde, Central African Republic, Chad, Chile, China, Colombia, Comoros, Congo, Congo (Democratic Republic of), Cook Islands, Costa Rica, Cote d'Ivoire, Croatia, Cuba, Cyprus, Czech Republic, Democratic People's Republic of Korea, Denmark, Djibouti, Dominica, Dominican Republic, Ecuador, Egypt, El Salvador, Equatorial Guinea, Eritrea, Estonia, Ethiopia, European Community, Fiji, Finland, France, Gabon, Gambia, Georgia, Germany, Ghana, Greece, Grenada, Guatemala, Guinea, Guinea Bissau, Guyana, Haiti, Honduras, Hungary, Iceland, India, Indonesia, Iran (Islamic Republic of), Ireland, Israel, Italy, Jamaica, Japan, Jordan, Kazakhstan, Kenya, Kiribati, Korea (Republic of), Kuwait, Kyrgyzstan, Lao People's Democratic Republic, Latvia, Lebanon, Lesotho, Liberia, Libyan Arab Jamahiriya, Liechtenstein, Lithuania, Luxembourg, Madagascar, Malawi, Malaysia, Maldives,

Mali, Malta, Marshall Islands, Mauritania, Mauritius, Mexico, Micronesia (Federated States of), Moldova, Monaco, Mongolia, Morocco, Mozambique, Myanmar, Namibia, Nauru, Nepal, Netherlands, New Zealand, Nicaragua, Niger, Nigeria, Niue, Norway, Oman, Pakistan, Palau, Panama, Papua New Guinea, Paraguay, Peru, Philippines, Poland, Portugal, Qatar, Romania, Russian Federation, Rwanda, Saint Kitts and Nevis, Saint Lucia, Saint Vincent and the Grenadines, Samoa, San Marino, São Tomé and Príncipe, Saudi Arabia, Senegal, Seychelles, Sierra Leone, Singapore, Slovakia, Slovenia, Solomon Islands, Somalia, South Africa, Spain, Sri Lanka, Sudan, Suriname, Swaziland, Sweden, Switzerland, Syrian Arab Republic, Tajikistan, Tanzania (United Republic of), The Former Yugoslav Republic of Macedonia, Togo, Tonga, Trinidad and Tobago, Tunisia, Turkmenistan, Tuvalu, Uganda, Ukraine, United Arab Emirates, United Kingdom, Uruguay, Uzbekistan, Vanuatu, Venezuela, Vietnam, Yemen, Yugoslavia, Zambia, Zimbabwe.

Website: www.biodiv.org

Convention on Biological Diversity

Preamble

The Contracting Parties,

Conscious of the intrinsic value of biological diversity and of the ecological, genetic, social, economic, scientific, educational, cultural, recreational and aesthetic values of biological diversity and its components,

Conscious also of the importance of biological diversity for evolution and for maintaining life sustaining systems of the biosphere,

Affirming that the conservation of biological diversity is a common concern of humankind,

Reaffirming that States have sovereign rights over their own biological resources,

Reaffirming also that States are responsible for conserving their biological diversity and for using their biological resources in a sustainable manner,

Concerned that biological diversity is being significantly reduced by certain human activities,

Aware of the general lack of information and knowledge regarding biological diversity and of the urgent need to develop scientific, technical and institutional

capacities to provide the basic understanding upon which to plan and implement appropriate measures,

Noting that it is vital to anticipate, prevent and attack the causes of significant reduction or loss of biological diversity at source,

Noting also that where there is a threat of significant reduction or loss of biological diversity, lack of full scientific certainty should not be used as a reason for postponing measures to avoid or minimize such a threat,

Noting further that the fundamental requirement for the conservation of biological diversity is the *in-situ* conservation of ecosystems and natural habitats and the maintenance and recovery of viable populations of species in their natural surroundings,

Noting further that *ex-situ* measures, preferably in the country of origin, also have an important role to play,

Recognizing the close and traditional dependence of many indigenous and local communities embodying traditional lifestyles on biological resources, and the desirability of sharing equitably benefits arising from the use of traditional knowledge, innovations and practices relevant to the conservation of biological diversity and the sustainable use of its components,

Recognizing also the vital role that women play in the conservation and sustainable use of biological diversity and affirming the need for the full participation of women at all levels of policy-making and implementation for biological diversity conservation,

Stressing the importance of, and the need to promote, international, regional and global cooperation among States and intergovernmental organizations and the non-governmental sector for the conservation of biological diversity and the sustainable use of its components,

Acknowledging that the provision of new and additional financial resources and appropriate access to relevant technologies can be expected to make a substantial difference in the world's ability to address the loss of biological diversity,

Acknowledging further that special provision is required to meet the needs of developing countries, including the provision of new and additional financial resources and appropriate access to relevant technologies,

Noting in this regard the special conditions of the least developed countries and small island States,

Acknowledging that substantial investments are required to conserve biological diversity and that there is the expectation of a broad range of environmental, economic and social benefits from those investments,

Recognizing that economic and social development and poverty eradication are the first and overriding priorities of developing countries,

Aware that conservation and sustainable use of biological diversity is of critical importance for meeting the food, health and other needs of the growing world population, for which purpose access to and sharing of both genetic resources and technologies are essential,

Noting that, ultimately, the conservation and sustainable use of biological diversity will strengthen friendly relations among States and contribute to peace for humankind,

Desiring to enhance and complement existing international arrangements for the conservation of biological diversity and sustainable use of its components, and

Determined to conserve and sustainably use biological diversity for the benefit of present and future generations,

Have agreed as follows:

Article 1
Objectives

The objectives of this Convention, to be pursued in accordance with its relevant provisions, are the conservation of biological diversity, the sustainable use of its components and the fair and equitable sharing of the benefits arising out of the utilization of genetic resources, including by appropriate access to genetic resources and by appropriate transfer of relevant technologies, taking into account all rights over those resources and to technologies, and by appropriate funding.

Article 2
Use of terms

For the purposes of this Convention:

'Biological diversity' means the variability among living organisms from all sources including, *inter alia*, terrestrial, marine and other aquatic ecosystems and the ecological complexes of which they are part; this includes diversity within species, between species and of ecosystems.

'Biological resources' includes genetic resources, organisms or parts thereof, populations, or any other biotic component of ecosystems with actual or potential use or value for humanity.

'Biotechnology' means any technological application that uses biological systems, living organisms, or derivatives thereof, to make or modify products or processes for specific use.

'Country of origin of genetic resources' means the country which possesses those genetic resources in *in-situ* conditions.

'Country providing genetic resources' means the country supplying genetic resources collected from *in-situ* sources, including populations of both wild and domesticated species, or taken from *ex-situ* sources, which may or may not have originated in that country.

'Domesticated or cultivated species' means species in which the evolutionary process has been influenced by humans to meet their needs.

'Ecosystem' means a dynamic complex of plant, animal and micro-organism communities and their non-living environment interacting as a functional unit.

'*Ex-situ* conservation' means the conservation of components of biological diversity outside their natural habitats.

'Genetic material' means any material of plant, animal, microbial or other origin containing functional units of heredity.

'Genetic resources' means genetic material of actual or potential value.

'Habitat' means the place or type of site where an organism or population naturally occurs.

'*In-situ* conditions' means conditions where genetic resources exist within ecosystems and natural habitats, and, in the case of domesticated or cultivated species, in the surroundings where they have developed their distinctive properties.

'*In-situ* conservation' means the conservation of ecosystems and natural habitats and the maintenance and recovery of viable populations of species in their natural surroundings and, in the case of domesticated or cultivated species, in the surroundings where they have developed their distinctive properties.

'Protected area' means a geographically defined area which is designated or regulated and managed to achieve specific conservation objectives.

'Regional economic integration organization' means an organization constituted by sovereign States of a given region, to which its member States have transferred competence in respect of matters governed by this Convention and which has been duly authorized, in accordance with its internal procedures, to sign, ratify, accept, approve or accede to it.

'Sustainable use' means the use of components of biological diversity in a way and at a rate that does not lead to the long-term decline of biological diversity, thereby maintaining its potential to meet the needs and aspirations of present and future generations.

'Technology' includes biotechnology.

Article 3
Principle

States have, in accordance with the Charter of the United Nations and the principles of international law, the sovereign right to exploit their own resources pursuant to their own environmental policies, and the responsibility to ensure that activities within their jurisdiction or control do not cause damage to the environment of other States or of areas beyond the limits of national jurisdiction.

Article 4
Jurisdictional scope

Subject to the rights of other States, and except as otherwise expressly provided in this Convention, the provisions of this Convention apply, in relation to each Contracting Party:

(a) In the case of components of biological diversity, in areas within the limits of its national jurisdiction; and
(b) In the case of processes and activities, regardless of where their effects occur, carried out under its jurisdiction or control, within the area of its national jurisdiction or beyond the limits of national jurisdiction.

Article 5
Cooperation

Each Contracting Party shall, as far as possible and as appropriate, cooperate with other Contracting Parties, directly or, where appropriate, through competent international organizations, in respect of areas beyond national jurisdiction and on other matters of mutual interest, for the conservation and sustainable use of biological diversity.

Article 6
General measures for conservation and sustainable use

Each Contracting Party shall, in accordance with its particular conditions and capabilities:

(a) Develop national strategies, plans or programmes for the conservation and sustainable use of biological diversity or adapt for this purpose existing strategies, plans or programmes which shall reflect, *inter alia*, the measures set out in this Convention relevant to the Contracting Party concerned; and
(b) Integrate, as far as possible and as appropriate, the conservation and sustainable use of biological diversity into relevant sectoral or cross-sectoral plans, programmes and policies.

Article 7
Identification and monitoring

Each Contracting Party shall, as far as possible and as appropriate, in particular for the purposes of Articles 8 to 10:

(a) Identify components of biological diversity important for its conservation and sustainable use having regard to the indicative list of categories set down in Annex I;

(b) Monitor, through sampling and other techniques, the components of biological diversity identified pursuant to subparagraph (a) above, paying particular attention to those requiring urgent conservation measures and those which offer the greatest potential for sustainable use;

(c) Identify processes and categories of activities which have or are likely to have significant adverse impacts on the conservation and sustainable use of biological diversity, and monitor their effects through sampling and other techniques; and

(d) Maintain and organize, by any mechanism data, derived from identification and monitoring activities pursuant to subparagraphs (a), (b) and (c) above.

Article 8
In-situ conservation

Each Contracting Party shall, as far as possible and as appropriate:

(a) Establish a system of protected areas or areas where special measures need to be taken to conserve biological diversity;

(b) Develop, where necessary, guidelines for the selection, establishment and management of protected areas or areas where special measures need to be taken to conserve biological diversity;

(c) Regulate or manage biological resources important for the conservation of biological diversity whether within or outside protected areas, with a view to ensuring their conservation and sustainable use;

(d) Promote the protection of ecosystems, natural habitats and the maintenance of viable populations of species in natural surroundings;

(e) Promote environmentally sound and sustainable development in areas adjacent to protected areas with a view to furthering protection of these areas;

(f) Rehabilitate and restore degraded ecosystems and promote the recovery of threatened species, *inter alia*, through the development and implementation of plans or other management strategies;

(g) Establish or maintain means to regulate, manage or control the risks associated with the use and release of living modified organisms resulting from biotechnology which are likely to have adverse environmental impacts that could affect the conservation and sustainable use of biological diversity, taking also into account the risks to human health;

(h) Prevent the introduction of, control or eradicate those alien species which threaten ecosystems, habitats or species;

(i) Endeavour to provide the conditions needed for compatibility between present uses and the conservation of biological diversity and the sustainable use of its components;

(j) Subject to its national legislation, respect, preserve and maintain knowledge, innovations and practices of indigenous and local communities

embodying traditional lifestyles relevant for the conservation and sustainable use of biological diversity and promote their wider application with
the approval and involvement of the holders of such knowledge, innovations and practices and encourage the equitable sharing of the benefits
arising from the utilization of such knowledge, innovations and practices;

(k) Develop or maintain necessary legislation and/or other regulatory
provisions for the protection of threatened species and populations;

(l) Where a significant adverse effect on biological diversity has been determined pursuant to Article 7, regulate or manage the relevant processes
and categories of activities; and

(m) Cooperate in providing financial and other support for *in-situ* conservation outlined in subparagraphs (a) to (l) above, particularly to developing
countries.

Article 9
Ex-situ conservation

Each Contracting Party shall, as far as possible and as appropriate, and
predominantly for the purpose of complementing *in-situ* measures:

(a) Adopt measures for the ex-situ conservation of components of biological
diversity, preferably in the country of origin of such components;

(b) Establish and maintain facilities for *ex-situ* conservation of and research on
plants, animals and micro-organisms, preferably in the country of origin
of genetic resources;

(c) Adopt measures for the recovery and rehabilitation of threatened species
and for their reintroduction into their natural habitats under appropriate
conditions;

(d) Regulate and manage collection of biological resources from natural habitats for *ex-situ* conservation purposes so as not to threaten ecosystems
and *in-situ* populations of species, except where special temporary *ex-situ*
measures are required under subparagraph (c) above; and

(e) Cooperate in providing financial and other support for *ex-situ* conservation
outlined in subparagraphs (a) to (d) above and in the establishment and
maintenance of *ex-situ* conservation facilities in developing countries.

Article 10
Sustainable use of components of biological diversity

Each Contracting Party shall, as far as possible and as appropriate:

(a) Integrate consideration of the conservation and sustainable use of
biological resources into national decision-making;

(b) Adopt measures relating to the use of biological resources to avoid or
minimize adverse impacts on biological diversity;

(c) Protect and encourage customary use of biological resources in accordance with traditional cultural practices that are compatible with conservation or sustainable use requirements;

(d) Support local populations to develop and implement remedial action in degraded areas where biological diversity has been reduced; and

(e) Encourage cooperation between its governmental authorities and its private sector in developing methods for sustainable use of biological resources.

Article 11
Incentive measures

Each Contracting Party shall, as far as possible and as appropriate, adopt economically and socially sound measures that act as incentives for the conservation and sustainable use of components of biological diversity.

Article 12
Research and training

The Contracting Parties, taking into account the special needs of developing countries, shall:

(a) Establish and maintain programmes for scientific and technical education and training in measures for the identification, conservation and sustainable use of biological diversity and its components and provide support for such education and training for the specific needs of developing countries;

(b) Promote and encourage research which contributes to the conservation and sustainable use of biological diversity, particularly in developing countries, *inter alia*, in accordance with decisions of the Conference of the Parties taken in consequence of recommendations of the Subsidiary Body on Scientific, Technical and Technological Advice; and

(c) In keeping with the provisions of Articles 16, 18 and 20, promote and cooperate in the use of scientific advances in biological diversity research in developing methods for conservation and sustainable use of biological resources.

Article 13
Public education and awareness

The Contracting Parties shall:

(a) Promote and encourage understanding of the importance of, and the measures required for, the conservation of biological diversity, as well as its propagation through media, and the inclusion of these topics in educational programmes; and

(b) Cooperate, as appropriate, with other States and international organizations in developing educational and public awareness programmes, with respect to conservation and sustainable use of biological diversity.

Article 14
Impact assessment and minimizing adverse impacts

1. Each Contracting Party, as far as possible and as appropriate, shall:

(a) Introduce appropriate procedures requiring environmental impact assessment of its proposed projects that are likely to have significant adverse effects on biological diversity with a view to avoiding or minimizing such effects and, where appropriate, allow for public participation in such procedures;

(b) Introduce appropriate arrangements to ensure that the environmental consequences of its programmes and policies that are likely to have significant adverse impacts on biological diversity are duly taken into account;

(c) Promote, on the basis of reciprocity, notification, exchange of information and consultation on activities under their jurisdiction or control which are likely to significantly affect adversely the biological diversity of other States or areas beyond the limits of national jurisdiction, by encouraging the conclusion of bilateral, regional or multilateral arrangements, as appropriate;

(d) In the case of imminent or grave danger or damage, originating under its jurisdiction or control, to biological diversity within the area under jurisdiction of other States or in areas beyond the limits of national jurisdiction, notify immediately the potentially affected States of such danger or damage, as well as initiate action to prevent or minimize such danger or damage; and

(e) Promote national arrangements for emergency responses to activities or events, whether caused naturally or otherwise, which present a grave and imminent danger to biological diversity and encourage international cooperation to supplement such national efforts and, where appropriate and agreed by the States or regional economic integration organizations concerned, to establish joint contingency plans.

2. The Conference of the Parties shall examine, on the basis of studies to be carried out, the issue of liability and redress, including restoration and compensation, for damage to biological diversity, except where such liability is a purely internal matter.

Article 15
Access to genetic resources

1. Recognizing the sovereign rights of States over their natural resources, the authority to determine access to genetic resources rests with the national governments and is subject to national legislation.

2. Each Contracting Party shall endeavour to create conditions to facilitate access to genetic resources for environmentally sound uses by other Contracting Parties and not to impose restrictions that run counter to the objectives of this Convention.

3. For the purpose of this Convention, the genetic resources being provided by a Contracting Party, as referred to in this Article and Articles 16 and 19, are only those that are provided by Contracting Parties that are countries of origin of such resources or by the Parties that have acquired the genetic resources in accordance with this Convention.

4. Access, where granted, shall be on mutually agreed terms and subject to the provisions of this Article.

5. Access to genetic resources shall be subject to prior informed consent of the Contracting Party providing such resources, unless otherwise determined by that Party.

6. Each Contracting Party shall endeavour to develop and carry out scientific research based on genetic resources provided by other Contracting Parties with the full participation of, and where possible in, such Contracting Parties.

7. Each Contracting Party shall take legislative, administrative or policy measures, as appropriate, and in accordance with Articles 16 and 19 and, where necessary, through the financial mechanism established by Articles 20 and 21 with the aim of sharing in a fair and equitable way the results of research and development and the benefits arising from the commercial and other utilization of genetic resources with the Contracting Party providing such resources. Such sharing shall be upon mutually agreed terms.

Article 16
Access to and transfer of technology

1. Each Contracting Party, recognizing that technology includes biotechnology, and that both access to and transfer of technology among Contracting Parties are essential elements for the attainment of the objectives of this Convention, undertakes subject to the provisions of this Article to provide and/or facilitate access for and transfer to other Contracting Parties of technologies that are relevant to the conservation and sustainable use of biological diversity or make use of genetic resources and do not cause significant damage to the environment.

2. Access to and transfer of technology referred to in paragraph 1 above to developing countries shall be provided and/or facilitated under fair and most favourable terms, including on concessional and preferential terms where mutually agreed, and, where necessary, in accordance with the financial mechanism established by Articles 20 and 21. In the case of technology subject to patents and other intellectual property rights, such access and transfer shall be provided on terms which recognize and are consistent with the adequate and effective

protection of intellectual property rights. The application of this paragraph shall be consistent with paragraphs 3, 4 and 5 below.

3. Each Contracting Party shall take legislative, administrative or policy measures, as appropriate, with the aim that Contracting Parties, in particular those that are developing countries, which provide genetic resources are provided access to and transfer of technology which makes use of those resources, on mutually agreed terms, including technology protected by patents and other intellectual property rights, where necessary, through the provisions of Articles 20 and 21 and in accordance with international law and consistent with paragraphs 4 and 5 below.

4. Each Contracting Party shall take legislative, administrative or policy measures, as appropriate, with the aim that the private sector facilitates access to, joint development and transfer of technology referred to in paragraph 1 above for the benefit of both governmental institutions and the private sector of developing countries and in this regard shall abide by the obligations included in paragraphs 1, 2 and 3 above.

5. The Contracting Parties, recognizing that patents and other intellectual property rights may have an influence on the implementation of this Convention, shall cooperate in this regard subject to national legislation and international law in order to ensure that such rights are supportive of and do not run counter to its objectives.

Article 17
Exchange of information

1. The Contracting Parties shall facilitate the exchange of information, from all publicly available sources, relevant to the conservation and sustainable use of biological diversity, taking into account the special needs of developing countries.

2. Such exchange of information shall include exchange of results of technical, scientific and socio-economic research, as well as information on training and surveying programmes, specialized knowledge, indigenous and traditional knowledge as such and in combination with the technologies referred to in Article 16, paragraph 1. It shall also, where feasible, include repatriation of information.

Article 18
Technical and scientific cooperation

1. The Contracting Parties shall promote international technical and scientific cooperation in the field of conservation and sustainable use of biological diversity, where necessary, through the appropriate international and national institutions.

2. Each Contracting Party shall promote technical and scientific cooperation with other Contracting Parties, in particular developing countries,

in implementing this Convention, *inter alia*, through the development and implementation of national policies. In promoting such cooperation, special attention should be given to the development and strengthening of national capabilities, by means of human resources development and institution building.

3. The Conference of the Parties, at its first meeting, shall determine how to establish a clearing-house mechanism to promote and facilitate technical and scientific cooperation.

4. The Contracting Parties shall, in accordance with national legislation and policies, encourage and develop methods of cooperation for the development and use of technologies, including indigenous and traditional technologies, in pursuance of the objectives of this Convention. For this purpose, the Contracting Parties shall also promote cooperation in the training of personnel and exchange of experts.

5. The Contracting Parties shall, subject to mutual agreement, promote the establishment of joint research programmes and joint ventures for the development of technologies relevant to the objectives of this Convention.

Article 19
Handling of biotechnology and distribution of its benefits

1. Each Contracting Party shall take legislative, administrative or policy measures, as appropriate, to provide for the effective participation in biotechnological research activities by those Contracting Parties, especially developing countries, which provide the genetic resources for such research, and where feasible in such Contracting Parties.

2. Each Contracting Party shall take all practicable measures to promote and advance priority access on a fair and equitable basis by Contracting Parties, especially developing countries, to the results and benefits arising from biotechnologies based upon genetic resources provided by those Contracting Parties. Such access shall be on mutually agreed terms.

3. The Parties shall consider the need for and modalities of a protocol setting out appropriate procedures, including, in particular, advance informed agreement, in the field of the safe transfer, handling and use of any living modified organism resulting from biotechnology that may have adverse effect on the conservation and sustainable use of biological diversity.

4. Each Contracting Party shall, directly or by requiring any natural or legal person under its jurisdiction providing the organisms referred to in paragraph 3 above, provide any available information about the use and safety regulations required by that Contracting Party in handling such organisms, as well as any available information on the potential adverse impact of the specific organisms concerned to the Contracting Party into which those organisms are to be introduced.

Article 20
Financial resources

1. Each Contracting Party undertakes to provide, in accordance with its capabilities, financial support and incentives in respect of those national activities which are intended to achieve the objectives of this Convention, in accordance with its national plans, priorities and programmes.

2. The developed country Parties shall provide new and additional financial resources to enable developing country Parties to meet the agreed full incremental costs to them of implementing measures which fulfil the obligations of this Convention and to benefit from its provisions and which costs are agreed between a developing country Party and the institutional structure referred to in Article 21, in accordance with policy, strategy, programme priorities and eligibility criteria and an indicative list of incremental costs established by the Conference of the Parties. Other Parties, including countries undergoing the process of transition to a market economy, may voluntarily assume the obligations of the developed country Parties. For the purpose of this Article, the Conference of the Parties, shall at its first meeting establish a list of developed country Parties and other Parties which voluntarily assume the obligations of the developed country Parties. The Conference of the Parties shall periodically review and if necessary amend the list. Contributions from other countries and sources on a voluntary basis would also be encouraged. The implementation of these commitments shall take into account the need for adequacy, predictability and timely flow of funds and the importance of burden-sharing among the contributing Parties included in the list.

3. The developed country Parties may also provide, and developing country Parties avail themselves of, financial resources related to the implementation of this Convention through bilateral, regional and other multilateral channels.

4. The extent to which developing country Parties will effectively implement their commitments under this Convention will depend on the effective implementation by developed country Parties of their commitments under this Convention related to financial resources and transfer of technology and will take fully into account the fact that economic and social development and eradication of poverty are the first and overriding priorities of the developing country Parties.

5. The Parties shall take full account of the specific needs and special situation of least developed countries in their actions with regard to funding and transfer of technology.

6. The Contracting Parties shall also take into consideration the special conditions resulting from the dependence on, distribution and location of, biological diversity within developing country Parties, in particular small island States.

7. Consideration shall also be given to the special situation of developing countries, including those that are most environmentally vulnerable, such as those with arid and semi-arid zones, coastal and mountainous areas.

Article 21
Financial mechanism

1. There shall be a mechanism for the provision of financial resources to developing country Parties for purposes of this Convention on a grant or concessional basis the essential elements of which are described in this Article. The mechanism shall function under the authority and guidance of, and be accountable to, the Conference of the Parties for purposes of this Convention. The operations of the mechanism shall be carried out by such institutional structure as may be decided upon by the Conference of the Parties at its first meeting. For purposes of this Convention, the Conference of the Parties shall determine the policy, strategy, programme priorities and eligibility criteria relating to the access to and utilization of such resources. The contributions shall be such as to take into account the need for predictability, adequacy and timely flow of funds referred to in Article 20 in accordance with the amount of resources needed to be decided periodically by the Conference of the Parties and the importance of burden-sharing among the contributing Parties included in the list referred to in Article 20, paragraph 2. Voluntary contributions may also be made by the developed country Parties and by other countries and sources. The mechanism shall operate within a democratic and transparent system of governance.

2. Pursuant to the objectives of this Convention, the Conference of the Parties shall at its first meeting determine the policy, strategy and programme priorities, as well as detailed criteria and guidelines for eligibility for access to and utilization of the financial resources including monitoring and evaluation on a regular basis of such utilization. The Conference of the Parties shall decide on the arrangements to give effect to paragraph 1 above after consultation with the institutional structure entrusted with the operation of the financial mechanism.

3. The Conference of the Parties shall review the effectiveness of the mechanism established under this Article, including the criteria and guidelines referred to in paragraph 2 above, not less than two years after the entry into force of this Convention and thereafter on a regular basis. Based on such review, it shall take appropriate action to improve the effectiveness of the mechanism if necessary.

4. The Contracting Parties shall consider strengthening existing financial institutions to provide financial resources for the conservation and sustainable use of biological diversity.

Article 22
Relationship with other international conventions

1. The provisions of this Convention shall not affect the rights and obligations of any Contracting Party deriving from any existing international agreement, except where the exercise of those rights and obligations would cause a serious damage or threat to biological diversity.

2. Contracting Parties shall implement this Convention with respect to the marine environment consistently with the rights and obligations of States under the law of the sea.

Article 23
Conference of the Parties

1. A Conference of the Parties is hereby established. The first meeting of the Conference of the Parties shall be convened by the Executive Director of the United Nations Environment Programme not later than one year after the entry into force of this Convention. Thereafter, ordinary meetings of the Conference of the Parties shall be held at regular intervals to be determined by the Conference at its first meeting.

2. Extraordinary meetings of the Conference of the Parties shall be held at such other times as may be deemed necessary by the Conference, or at the written request of any Party, provided that, within six months of the request being communicated to them by the Secretariat, it is supported by at least one third of the Parties.

3. The Conference of the Parties shall by consensus agree upon and adopt rules of procedure for itself and for any subsidiary body it may establish, as well as financial rules governing the funding of the Secretariat. At each ordinary meeting, it shall adopt a budget for the financial period until the next ordinary meeting.

4. The Conference of the Parties shall keep under review the implementation of this Convention, and, for this purpose, shall:

(a) Establish the form and the intervals for transmitting the information to be submitted in accordance with Article 26 and consider such information as well as reports submitted by any subsidiary body;
(b) Review scientific, technical and technological advice on biological diversity provided in accordance with Article 25;
(c) Consider and adopt, as required, protocols in accordance with Article 28;
(d) Consider and adopt, as required, in accordance with Articles 29 and 30, amendments to this Convention and its annexes;
(e) Consider amendments to any protocol, as well as to any annexes thereto, and, if so decided, recommend their adoption to the parties to the protocol concerned;

(f) Consider and adopt, as required, in accordance with Article 30, additional annexes to this Convention;

(g) Establish such subsidiary bodies, particularly to provide scientific and technical advice, as are deemed necessary for the implementation of this Convention;

(h) Contact, through the Secretariat, the executive bodies of conventions dealing with matters covered by this Convention with a view to establishing appropriate forms of cooperation with them; and

(i) Consider and undertake any additional action that may be required for the achievement of the purposes of this Convention in the light of experience gained in its operation.

5. The United Nations, its specialized agencies and the International Atomic Energy Agency, as well as any State not Party to this Convention, may be represented as observers at meetings of the Conference of the Parties. Any other body or agency, whether governmental or non-governmental, qualified in fields relating to conservation and sustainable use of biological diversity, which has informed the Secretariat of its wish to be represented as an observer at a meeting of the Conference of the Parties, may be admitted unless at least one third of the Parties present object. The admission and participation of observers shall be subject to the rules of procedure adopted by the Conference of the Parties.

Article 24
Secretariat

1. A secretariat is hereby established. Its functions shall be:

(a) To arrange for and service meetings of the Conference of the Parties provided for in Article 23;

(b) To perform the functions assigned to it by any protocol;

(c) To prepare reports on the execution of its functions under this Convention and present them to the Conference of the Parties;

(d) To coordinate with other relevant international bodies and, in particular to enter into such administrative and contractual arrangements as may be required for the effective discharge of its functions; and

(e) To perform such other functions as may be determined by the Conference of the Parties.

2. At its first ordinary meeting, the Conference of the Parties shall designate the secretariat from amongst those existing competent international organizations which have signified their willingness to carry out the secretariat functions under this Convention.

Article 25
Subsidiary Body on Scientific, Technical and Technological Advice

1. A subsidiary body for the provision of scientific, technical and technological advice is hereby established to provide the Conference of the Parties and, as appropriate, its other subsidiary bodies with timely advice relating to the implementation of this Convention. This body shall be open to participation by all Parties and shall be multidisciplinary. It shall comprise government representatives competent in the relevant field of expertise. It shall report regularly to the Conference of the Parties on all aspects of its work.

2. Under the authority of and in accordance with guidelines laid down by the Conference of the Parties, and upon its request, this body shall:

(a) Provide scientific and technical assessments of the status of biological diversity;
(b) Prepare scientific and technical assessments of the effects of types of measures taken in accordance with the provisions of this Convention;
(c) Identify innovative, efficient and state-of-the-art technologies and know-how relating to the conservation and sustainable use of biological diversity and advise on the ways and means of promoting development and/or transferring such technologies;
(d) Provide advice on scientific programmes and international cooperation in research and development related to conservation and sustainable use of biological diversity; and
(e) Respond to scientific, technical, technological and methodological questions that the Conference of the Parties and its subsidiary bodies may put to the body.

3. The functions, terms of reference, organization and operation of this body may be further elaborated by the Conference of the Parties.

Article 26
Reports

Each Contracting Party shall, at intervals to be determined by the Conference of the Parties, present to the Conference of the Parties, reports on measures which it has taken for the implementation of the provisions of this Convention and their effectiveness in meeting the objectives of this Convention.

Article 27
Settlement of disputes

1. In the event of a dispute between Contracting Parties concerning the interpretation or application of this Convention, the parties concerned shall seek solution by negotiation.

2. If the parties concerned cannot reach agreement by negotiation, they may jointly seek the good offices of, or request mediation by, a third party.

3. When ratifying, accepting, approving or acceding to this Convention, or at any time thereafter, a State or regional economic integration organization may declare in writing to the Depositary that for a dispute not resolved in accordance with paragraph 1 or paragraph 2 above, it accepts one or both of the following means of dispute settlement as compulsory:

(a) Arbitration in accordance with the procedure laid down in Part 1 of Annex II;

(b) Submission of the dispute to the International Court of Justice.

4. If the parties to the dispute have not, in accordance with paragaph 3 above, accepted the same or any procedure, the dispute shall be submitted to conciliation in accordance with Part 2 of Annex II unless the parties otherwise agree.

5. The provisions of this Article shall apply with respect to any protocol except as otherwise provided in the protocol concerned.

Article 28
Adoption of protocols

1. The Contracting Parties shall cooperate in the formulation and adoption of protocols to this Convention.

2. Protocols shall be adopted at a meeting of the Conference of the Parties.

3. The text of any proposed protocol shall be communicated to the Contracting Parties by the Secretariat at least six months before such a meeting.

Article 29
Amendment of the Convention or Protocols

1. Amendments to this Convention may be proposed by any Contracting Party. Amendments to any protocol may be proposed by any Party to that protocol.

2. Amendments to this Convention shall be adopted at a meeting of the Conference of the Parties. Amendments to any protocol shall be adopted at a meeting of the Parties to the Protocol in question. The text of any proposed amendment to this Convention or to any protocol, except as may otherwise be provided in such protocol, shall be communicated to the Parties to the instrument in question by the secretariat at least six months before the meeting at which it is proposed for adoption. The secretariat shall also communicate proposed amendments to the signatories to this Convention for information.

3. The Parties shall make every effort to reach agreement on any proposed amendment to this Convention or to any protocol by consensus. If all efforts at consensus have been exhausted, and no agreement reached, the amendment shall as a last resort be adopted by a two-third majority vote of the Parties

to the instrument in question present and voting at the meeting, and shall be submitted by the Depositary to all Parties for ratification, acceptance or approval.

4. Ratification, acceptance or approval of amendments shall be notified to the Depositary in writing. Amendments adopted in accordance with paragraph 3 above shall enter into force among Parties having accepted them on the ninetieth day after the deposit of instruments of ratification, acceptance or approval by at least two thirds of the Contracting Parties to this Convention or of the Parties to the protocol concerned, except as may otherwise be provided in such protocol. Thereafter the amendments shall enter into force for any other Party on the ninetieth day after that Party deposits its instrument of ratification, acceptance or approval of the amendments.

5. For the purposes of this Article, 'Parties present and voting' means Parties present and casting an affirmative or negative vote.

Article 30
Adoption and amendment of Annexes

1. The annexes to this Convention or to any protocol shall form an integral part of the Convention or of such protocol, as the case may be, and, unless expressly provided otherwise, a reference to this Convention or its protocols constitutes at the same time a reference to any annexes thereto. Such annexes shall be restricted to procedural, scientific, technical and administrative matters.

2. Except as may be otherwise provided in any protocol with respect to its annexes, the following procedure shall apply to the proposal, adoption and entry into force of additional annexes to this Convention or of annexes to any protocol:

(a) Annexes to this Convention or to any protocol shall be proposed and adopted according to the procedure laid down in Article 29;

(b) Any Party that is unable to approve an additional annex to this Convention or an annex to any protocol to which it is Party shall so notify the Depositary, in writing, within one year from the date of the communication of the adoption by the Depositary. The Depositary shall without delay notify all Parties of any such notification received. A Party may at any time withdraw a previous declaration of objection and the annexes shall thereupon enter into force for that Party subject to subparagraph (c) below;

(c) On the expiry of one year from the date of the communication of the adoption by the Depositary, the annex shall enter into force for all Parties to this Convention or to any protocol concerned which have not submitted a notification in accordance with the provisions of subparagraph (b) above.

3. The proposal, adoption and entry into force of amendments to annexes to this Convention or to any protocol shall be subject to the same procedure as

for the proposal, adoption and entry into force of annexes to the Convention or annexes to any protocol.

4. If an additional annex or an amendment to an annex is related to an amendment to this Convention or to any protocol, the additional annex or amendment shall not enter into force until such time as the amendment to the Convention or to the protocol concerned enters into force.

Article 31
Right to vote

1. Except as provided for in paragraph 2 below, each Contracting Party to this Convention or to any protocol shall have one vote.

2. Regional economic integration organizations, in matters within their competence, shall exercise their right to vote with a number of votes equal to the number of their member States which are Contracting Parties to this Convention or the relevant protocol. Such organizations shall not exercise their right to vote if their member States exercise theirs, and vice versa.

Article 32
Relationship between this Convention and its Protocols

1. A State or a regional economic integration organization may not become a Party to a protocol unless it is, or becomes at the same time, a Contracting Party to this Convention.

2. Decisions under any protocol shall be taken only by the Parties to the protocol concerned. Any Contracting Party that has not ratified, accepted or approved a protocol may participate as an observer in any meeting of the parties to that protocol.

Article 33
Signature

This Convention shall be open for signature at Rio de Janeiro by all States and any regional economic integration organization from 5 June 1992 until 14 June 1992, and at the United Nations Headquarters in New York from 15 June 1992 to 4 June 1993.

Article 34
Ratification, acceptance or approval

1. This Convention and any protocol shall be subject to ratification, acceptance or approval by States and by regional economic integration organizations. Instruments of ratification, acceptance or approval shall be deposited with the Depositary.

2. Any organization referred to in paragraph 1 above which becomes a Contracting Party to this Convention or any protocol without any of its member States being a Contracting Party shall be bound by all the obligations under

the Convention or the protocol, as the case may be. In the case of such organizations, one or more of whose member States is a Contracting Party to this
Convention or relevant protocol, the organization and its member States shall
decide on their respective responsibilities for the performance of their obligations under the Convention or protocol, as the case may be. In such cases,
the organization and the member States shall not be entitled to exercise rights
under the Convention or relevant protocol concurrently.

3. In their instruments of ratification, acceptance or approval, the organizations referred to in paragraph 1 above shall declare the extent of their
competence with respect to the matters governed by the Convention or the
relevant protocol. These organizations shall also inform the Depositary of any
relevant modification in the extent of their competence.

Article 35
Accession

1. This Convention and any protocol shall be open for accession by States
and by regional economic integration organizations from the date on which the
Convention or the protocol concerned is closed for signature. The instruments
of accession shall be deposited with the Depositary.

2. In their instruments of accession, the organizations referred to in paragraph 1 above shall declare the extent of their competence with respect to the
matters governed by the Convention or the relevant protocol. These organizations shall also inform the Depositary of any relevant modification in the
extent of their competence.

3. The provisions of Article 34, paragraph 2, shall apply to regional economic
integration organizations which accede to this Convention or any protocol.

Article 36
Entry into force

1. This Convention shall enter into force on the ninetieth day after the date
of deposit of the thirtieth instrument of ratification, acceptance, approval or
accession.

2. Any protocol shall enter into force on the ninetieth day after the date of
deposit of the number of instruments of ratification, acceptance, approval or
accession, specified in that protocol, has been deposited.

3. For each Contracting Party which ratifies, accepts or approves this Convention or accedes thereto after the deposit of the thirtieth instrument of ratification, acceptance, approval or accession, it shall enter into force on the ninetieth
day after the date of deposit by such Contracting Party of its instrument of
ratification, acceptance, approval or accession.

4. Any protocol, except as otherwise provided in such protocol, shall enter
into force for a Contracting Party that ratifies, accepts or approves that protocol
or accedes thereto after its entry into force pursuant to paragraph 2 above, on

the ninetieth day after the date on which that Contracting Party deposits its instrument of ratification, acceptance, approval or accession, or on the date on which this Convention enters into force for that Contracting Party, whichever shall be the later.

5. For the purposes of paragraphs 1 and 2 above, any instrument deposited by a regional economic integration organization shall not be counted as additional to those deposited by member States of such organization.

Article 37
Reservations

No reservations may be made to this Convention.

Article 38
Withdrawals

1. At any time after two years from the date on which this Convention has entered into force for a Contracting Party, that Contracting Party may withdraw from the Convention by giving written notification to the Depositary.

2. Any such withdrawal shall take place upon expiry of one year after the date of its receipt by the Depositary, or on such later date as may be specified in the notification of the withdrawal.

3. Any Contracting Party which withdraws from this Convention shall be considered as also having withdrawn from any protocol to which it is party.

Article 39
Financial interim arrangements

Provided that it has been fully restructured in accordance with the require-ments of Article 21, the Global Environment Facility of the United Nations Development Programme, the United Nations Environment Programme and the International Bank for Reconstruction and Development shall be the insti-tutional structure referred to in Article 21 on an interim basis, for the period between the entry into force of this Convention and the first meeting of the Conference of the Parties or until the Conference of the Parties decides which institutional structure will be designated in accordance with Article 21.

Article 40
Secretariat interim arrangements

The secretariat to be provided by the Executive Director of the United Nations Environment Programme shall be the secretariat referred to in Article 24, paragraph 2, on an interim basis for the period between the entry into force of this Convention and the first meeting of the Conference of the Parties.

Article 41
Depositary

The Secretary-General of the United Nations shall assume the functions of Depositary of this Convention and any protocols.

Article 42
Authentic texts

The original of this Convention, of which the Arabic, Chinese, English, French, Russian and Spanish texts are equally authentic, shall be deposited with the Secretary-General of the United Nations.

IN WITNESS WHEREOF the undersigned, being duly authorized to that effect, have signed this Convention.

DONE at Rio de Janeiro on this fifth day of June, one thousand nine hundred and ninety-two.

Annex I
Identification and monitoring

1. Ecosystems and habitats: containing high diversity, large numbers of endemic or threatened species, or wilderness; required by migratory species; of social, economic, cultural or scientific importance; or, which are representative, unique or associated with key evolutionary or other biological processes;

2. Species and communities which are: threatened; wild relatives of domesticated or cultivated species; of medicinal, agricultural or other economic value; or social, scientific or cultural importance; or importance for research into the conservation and sustainable use of biological diversity, such as indicator species; and

3. Described genomes and genes of social, scientific or economic importance.

Annex II

Part 1
Arbitration

Article 1

The claimant party shall notify the secretariat that the parties are referring a dispute to arbitration pursuant to Article 27. The notification shall state the subject-matter of arbitration and include, in particular, the articles of the Convention or the protocol, the interpretation or application of which are at issue. If the parties do not agree on the subject matter of the dispute before the President of the tribunal is designated, the arbitral tribunal shall determine the subject matter. The secretariat shall forward the information thus received to all Contracting Parties to this Convention or to the protocol concerned.

Article 2

1. In disputes between two parties, the arbitral tribunal shall consist of three members. Each of the parties to the dispute shall appoint an arbitrator and the two arbitrators so appointed shall designate by common agreement the third arbitrator who shall be the President of the tribunal. The latter shall not be a national of one of the parties to the dispute, nor have his or her usual place of residence in the territory of one of these parties, nor be employed by any of them, nor have dealt with the case in any other capacity.

2. In disputes between more than two parties, parties in the same interest shall appoint one arbitrator jointly by agreement.

3. Any vacancy shall be filled in the manner prescribed for the initial appointment.

Article 3

1. If the President of the arbitral tribunal has not been designated within two months of the appointment of the second arbitrator, the Secretary-General of the United Nations shall, at the request of a party, designate the President within a further two-month period.

2. If one of the parties to the dispute does not appoint an arbitrator within two months of receipt of the request, the other party may inform the Secretary-General who shall make the designation within a further two-month period.

Article 4

The arbitral tribunal shall render its decisions in accordance with the provisions of this Convention, any protocols concerned, and international law.

Article 5

Unless the parties to the dispute otherwise agree, the arbitral tribunal shall determine its own rules of procedure.

Article 6

The arbitral tribunal may, at the request of one of the parties, recommend essential interim measures of protection.

Article 7

The parties to the dispute shall facilitate the work of the arbitral tribunal and, in particular, using all means at their disposal, shall:

(a) Provide it with all relevant documents, information and facilities; and

(b) Enable it, when necessary, to call witnesses or experts and receive their evidence.

Article 8

The parties and the arbitrators are under an obligation to protect the confidentiality of any information they receive in confidence during the proceedings of the arbitral tribunal.

Article 9

Unless the arbitral tribunal determines otherwise because of the particular circumstances of the case, the costs of the tribunal shall be borne by the parties to the dispute in equal shares. The tribunal shall keep a record of all its costs, and shall furnish a final statement thereof to the parties.

Article 10

Any Contracting Party that has an interest of a legal nature in the subject-matter of the dispute which may be affected by the decision in the case, may intervene in the proceedings with the consent of the tribunal.

Article 11

The tribunal may hear and determine counterclaims arising directly out of the subject-matter of the dispute.

Article 12

Decisions both on procedure and substance of the arbitral tribunal shall be taken by a majority vote of its members.

Article 13

If one of the parties to the dispute does not appear before the arbitral tribunal or fails to defend its case, the other party may request the tribunal to continue the proceedings and to make its award. Absence of a party or a failure of a party to defend its case shall not constitute a bar to the proceedings. Before rendering its final decision, the arbitral tribunal must satisfy itself that the claim is well founded in fact and law.

Article 14

The tribunal shall render its final decision within five months of the date on which it is fully constituted unless it finds it necessary to extend the time-limit for a period which should not exceed five more months.

Article 15

The final decision of the arbitral tribunal shall be confined to the subject-matter of the dispute and shall state the reasons on which it is based. It shall contain the names of the members who have participated and the date of the final decision. Any member of the tribunal may attach a separate or dissenting opinion to the final decision.

Article 16

The award shall be binding on the parties to the dispute. It shall be without appeal unless the parties to the dispute have agreed in advance to an appellate procedure.

Article 17

Any controversy which may arise between the parties to the dispute as regards the interpretation or manner of implementation of the final decision may be submitted by either party for decision to the arbitral tribunal which rendered it.

Annex II

Part 2
Conciliation

Article 1

A conciliation commission shall be created upon the request of one of the parties to the dispute. The commission shall, unless the parties otherwise agree, be composed of five members, two appointed by each Party concerned and a President chosen jointly by those members.

Article 2

In disputes between more than two parties, parties in the same interest shall appoint their members of the commission jointly by agreement. Where two or more parties have separate interests or there is a disagreement as to whether they are of the same interest, they shall appoint their members separately.

Article 3

If any appointments by the parties are not made within two months of the date of the request to create a conciliation commission, the Secretary-General of the United Nations shall, if asked to do so by the party that made the request, make those appointments within a further two-month period.

Article 4

If a President of the conciliation commission has not been chosen within two months of the last of the members of the commission being appointed, the Secretary-General of the United Nations shall, if asked to do so by a party, designate a President within a further two-month period.

Article 5

The conciliation commission shall take its decisions by majority vote of its members. It shall, unless the parties to the dispute otherwise agree, determine its own procedure. It shall render a proposal for resolution of the dispute, which the parties shall consider in good faith.

Article 6

A disagreement as to whether the conciliation commission has competence shall be decided by the commission.

21A

Cartagena Protocol on Biosafety to the Convention on Biological Diversity, 29 January 2000

Editorial note

The Cartagena Protocol on Biosafety was adopted on 29 January 2000. The preamble reaffirms the parties' commitment to the 'precautionary approach' contained in Principle 15 of the Rio Declaration, expresses their awareness of growing public concern over potential adverse effects of transboundary movements of living modified organisms on biological diversity and human health, recognises the 'great potential' of biotechnology and addresses the relationship with trade agreements.

The objective of the Protocol is set forth in Article 1. Parties must ensure that the development, handling, transport, use, transfer and release of any living modified organisms is undertaken in a manner that prevents or reduces the risks to biological diversity, taking also into account risks to human health (Article 2(1) and (2)). They are free to take certain actions that are more protective of biological diversity (Article 2(4)).

The scope of the Protocol is limited to the transboundary movement, transit, handling and use of 'living modified organisms' (LMOs) that may have adverse effects on the conservation and sustainable use of biological diversity, taking also into account risks to human health (Article 4). An LMO is 'any living organism that possesses a novel combination of genetic material obtained through the use of modern biotechnology' (Article 3). LMOs which are pharmaceuticals for humans that are addressed by other relevant international agreements or organisations, or LMOs in transit through a state's territory or destined for contained use, are not subject to the Protocol (Articles 5 and 6).

The principal mechanism for regulating transboundary movement of LMOs for intentional introduction into the environment of the Party of import is the advance informed agreement (AIA) procedure (Article 7). The exporting Party shall notify the Party of import prior to the transboundary movement of the LMO (Article 8) and notification must be acknowledged by the Party of import (Article 9). Article 10 provides that decisions by the Party of import on whether the intentional transboundary movement may proceed shall be taken in accordance with Article 15 (risk assessment). Article 11 outlines the procedure for LMOs intended for direct use as food or feed, or for food processing. Provision is made for review of decisions (Article 12) and for a simplified procedure (Article 13). Parties may enter into bilateral, regional and multilateral agreements or arrangements on intentional transboundary movement of LMOs which are consistent with the objective of the Protocol and do not result in a lower level of protection than that provided for by the Protocol (Article 14). Provisions are made for the identification of risk management measures and strategies to regulate, control and manage risks identified through the risk assessment procedure under Article 15 associated with the use, handling and transboundary movement of LMOs (Article 16). Unintentional transboundary movements of LMOs likely to cause significant adverse effects must be notified to affected or potentially affected States (Article 17). Necessary measures must be taken to ensure that LMOs subject to intentional transboundary movement are handled, packaged and transported under conditions of safety (Article 18). Each Party must designate a national focal point for the application and administration of the activities required by the Protocol (Article 19). The Protocol establishes a Biosafety Clearing-House to, *inter alia*, facilitate exchange of information and assist in the implementation of the Protocol (Article 20). Co-operation for capacity building activities is required by Article 20. Public participation and awareness is to be promoted by the Parties to the Protocol (Article 21). Transboundary movements of LMOs in contravention of the provisions of the Protocol shall be considered illegal (Article 25). Rules and procedures in the field of liability and redress for damage resulting from transboundary movements of LMOs shall be elaborated by the Parties (Article 27).

The Protocol will utilise the institutional arrangements established under the Convention, with the conference of the Parties serving as the meeting of the Parties to the Protocol (Articles 29–31). The meeting of the Parties is to keep the implementation of the Protocol under regular review and may consider and adopt, as required, amendments to the Protocol and its annexes, as well as any additional annexes that are deemed necessary for the implementation of the Protocol (Article 29(4)). Parties must report on implementing measures (Article 33). The meeting of the Parties is directed to establish a non-compliance mechanism, and to evaluate the effectiveness of the Protocol, after five years (Articles 33 and 34). The Protocol will enter into force following the deposit of the fiftieth instrument of ratification (Article 37).

Date of signature:	29 January 2000
Entry into force:	11 September 2003
Depositary:	Secretary-General of the United Nations
Contracting Parties:	Austria, Barbados, Belarus, Bhutan, Bolivia, Botswana, Bulgaria, Cameroon, Colombia, Croatia, Cuba, Czech

Republic, Denmark, Djibouti, Ecuador, European Community, Fiji, France, Ghana, India, Kenya, Lesotho, Liberia, Luxembourg, Maldives, Mali, Marshall Islands, Mauritius, Mexico, Moldova, Mozambique, Nauru, Netherlands, Nicaragua, Niue, Norway, Oman, Palau, Panama, Saint Kitts and Nevis, Samoa, Slovenia, Spain, Sweden, Switzerland, Tanzania, Trinidad and Tobago, Tunisia, Uganda, Ukraine, Venezuela.

Website: www.biodiv.org/biosafety/

Cartagena Protocol on Biosafety to the Convention on Biological Diversity

The Parties to this Protocol,

Being Parties to the Convention on Biological Diversity, hereinafter referred to as 'the Convention',

Recalling Article 19, paragraphs 3 and 4, and Articles 8 (g) and 17 of the Convention,

Recalling also decision II/5 of 17 November 1995 of the Conference of the Parties to the Convention to develop a Protocol on biosafety, specifically focusing on transboundary movement of any living modified organism resulting from modern biotechnology that may have adverse effect on the conservation and sustainable use of biological diversity, setting out for consideration, in particular, appropriate procedures for advance informed agreement,

Reaffirming the precautionary approach contained in Principle 15 of the Rio Declaration on Environment and Development,

Aware of the rapid expansion of modern biotechnology and the growing public concern over its potential adverse effects on biological diversity, taking also into account risks to human health,

Recognizing that modern biotechnology has great potential for human well-being if developed and used with adequate safety measures for the environment and human health,

Recognizing also the crucial importance to humankind of centres of origin and centres of genetic diversity,

Taking into account the limited capabilities of many countries, particularly developing countries, to cope with the nature and scale of known and potential risks associated with living modified organisms,

Recognizing that trade and environment agreements should be mutually supportive with a view to achieving sustainable development,

Emphasizing that this Protocol shall not be interpreted as implying a change in the rights and obligations of a Party under any existing international agreements,

Understanding that the above recital is not intended to subordinate this Protocol to other international agreements,

Have agreed as follows:

Article 1
Objective

In accordance with the precautionary approach contained in Principle 15 of the Rio Declaration on Environment and Development, the objective of this Protocol is to contribute to ensuring an adequate level of protection in the field of the safe transfer, handling and use of living modified organisms resulting from modern biotechnology that may have adverse effects on the conservation and sustainable use of biological diversity, taking also into account risks to human health, and specifically focusing on transboundary movements.

Article 2
General provisions

1. Each Party shall take necessary and appropriate legal, administrative and other measures to implement its obligations under this Protocol.

2. The Parties shall ensure that the development, handling, transport, use, transfer and release of any living modified organisms are undertaken in a manner that prevents or reduces the risks to biological diversity, taking also into account risks to human health.

3. Nothing in this Protocol shall affect in any way the sovereignty of States over their territorial sea established in accordance with international law, and the sovereign rights and the jurisdiction which States have in their exclusive economic zones and their continental shelves in accordance with international law, and the exercise by ships and aircraft of all States of navigational rights and freedoms as provided for in international law and as reflected in relevant international instruments.

4. Nothing in this Protocol shall be interpreted as restricting the right of a Party to take action that is more protective of the conservation and sustainable use of biological diversity than that called for in this Protocol, provided that such action is consistent with the objective and the provisions of this Protocol and is in accordance with that Party's other obligations under international law.

5. The Parties are encouraged to take into account, as appropriate, available expertise, instruments and work undertaken in international forums with competence in the area of risks to human health.

Article 3
Use of terms

For the purposes of this Protocol:

(a) 'Conference of the Parties' means the Conference of the Parties to the Convention;

(b) 'Contained use' means any operation, undertaken within a facility, installation or other physical structure, which involves living modified organisms that are controlled by specific measures that effectively limit their contact with, and their impact on, the external environment;

(c) 'Export' means intentional transboundary movement from one Party to another Party;

(d) 'Exporter' means any legal or natural person, under the jurisdiction of the Party of export, who arranges for a living modified organism to be exported;

(e) 'Import' means intentional transboundary movement into one Party from another Party;

(f) 'Importer' means any legal or natural person, under the jurisdiction of the Party of import, who arranges for a living modified organism to be imported;

(g) 'Living modified organism' means any living organism that possesses a novel combination of genetic material obtained through the use of modern biotechnology;

(h) 'Living organism' means any biological entity capable of transferring or replicating genetic material, including sterile organisms, viruses and viroids;

(i) 'Modern biotechnology' means the application of:
   a. *In vitro* nucleic acid techniques, including recombinant deoxyribonucleic acid (DNA) and direct injection of nucleic acid into cells or organelles, or
   b. Fusion of cells beyond the taxonomic family, that overcome natural physiological reproductive or recombination barriers and that are not techniques used in traditional breeding and selection;

(j) 'Regional economic integration organization' means an organization constituted by sovereign States of a given region, to which its member States have transferred competence in respect of matters governed by this Protocol and which has been duly authorized, in accordance with its internal procedures, to sign, ratify, accept, approve or accede to it;

(k) 'Transboundary movement' means the movement of a living modified organism from one Party to another Party, save that for the purposes of Articles 17 and 24 transboundary movement extends to movement between Parties and non-Parties.

Article 4
Scope

This Protocol shall apply to the transboundary movement, transit, handling and use of all living modified organisms that may have adverse effects on the conservation and sustainable use of biological diversity, taking also into account risks to human health.

Article 5
Pharmaceuticals

Notwithstanding Article 4 and without prejudice to any right of a Party to subject all living modified organisms to risk assessment prior to the making of decisions on import, this Protocol shall not apply to the transboundary movement of living modified organisms which are pharmaceuticals for humans that are addressed by other relevant international agreements or organisations.

Article 6
Transit and contained use

1. Notwithstanding Article 4 and without prejudice to any right of a Party of transit to regulate the transport of living modified organisms through its territory and make available to the Biosafety Clearing-House, any decision of that Party, subject to Article 2, paragraph 3, regarding the transit through its territory of a specific living modified organism, the provisions of this Protocol with respect to the advance informed agreement procedure shall not apply to living modified organisms in transit.

2. Notwithstanding Article 4 and without prejudice to any right of a Party to subject all living modified organisms to risk assessment prior to decisions on import and to set standards for contained use within its jurisdiction, the provisions of this Protocol with respect to the advance informed agreement procedure shall not apply to the transboundary movement of living modified organisms destined for contained use undertaken in accordance with the standards of the Party of import.

Article 7
Application of the advance informed agreement procedure

1. Subject to Articles 5 and 6, the advance informed agreement procedure in Articles 8 to 10 and 12 shall apply prior to the first intentional transboundary movement of living modified organisms for intentional introduction into the environment of the Party of import.

2. 'Intentional introduction into the environment' in paragraph 1 above, does not refer to living modified organisms intended for direct use as food or feed, or for processing.

3. Article 11 shall apply prior to the first transboundary movement of living modified organisms intended for direct use as food or feed, or for processing.

4. The advance informed agreement procedure shall not apply to the intentional transboundary movement of living modified organisms identified in a decision of the Conference of the Parties serving as the meeting of the Parties to this Protocol as being not likely to have adverse effects on the conservation and

sustainable use of biological diversity, taking also into account risks to human health.

Article 8
Notification

1. The Party of export shall notify, or require the exporter to ensure notification to, in writing, the competent national authority of the Party of import prior to the intentional transboundary movement of a living modified organism that falls within the scope of Article 7, paragraph 1. The notification shall contain, at a minimum, the information specified in Annex I.

2. The Party of export shall ensure that there is a legal requirement for the accuracy of information provided by the exporter.

Article 9
Acknowledgement of receipt of notification

1. The Party of import shall acknowledge receipt of the notification, in writing, to the notifier within ninety days of its receipt.

2. The acknowledgement shall state:

(a) The date of receipt of the notification;
(b) Whether the notification, prima facie, contains the information referred to in Article 8;
(c) Whether to proceed according to the domestic regulatory framework of the Party of import or according to the procedure specified in Article 10.

3. The domestic regulatory framework referred to in paragraph 2 (c) above, shall be consistent with this Protocol.

4. A failure by the Party of import to acknowledge receipt of a notification shall not imply its consent to an intentional transboundary movement.

Article 10
Decision procedure

1. Decisions taken by the Party of import shall be in accordance with Article 15.

2. The Party of import shall, within the period of time referred to in Article 9, inform the notifier, in writing, whether the intentional transboundary movement may proceed:

(a) Only after the Party of import has given its written consent; or
(b) After no less than ninety days without a subsequent written consent.

3. Within two hundred and seventy days of the date of receipt of notification, the Party of import shall communicate, in writing, to the notifier and to the Biosafety Clearing-House the decision referred to in paragraph 2 (a) above:

(a) Approving the import, with or without conditions, including how the deci-
    sion will apply to subsequent imports of the same living modified organism;
(b) Prohibiting the import;
(c) Requesting additional relevant information in accordance with its domestic
    regulatory framework or Annex I; in calculating the time within which the
    Party of import is to respond, the number of days it has to wait for additional
    relevant information shall not be taken into account; or
(d) Informing the notifier that the period specified in this paragraph is
    extended by a defined period of time.

4. Except in a case in which consent is unconditional, a decision under
paragraph 3 above, shall set out the reasons on which it is based.

5. A failure by the Party of import to communicate its decision within two
hundred and seventy days of the date of receipt of the notification shall not
imply its consent to an intentional transboundary movement.

6. Lack of scientific certainty due to insufficient relevant scientific information and knowledge regarding the extent of the potential adverse effects of a
living modified organism on the conservation and sustainable use of biological diversity in the Party of import, taking also into account risks to human
health, shall not prevent that Party from taking a decision, as appropriate, with
regard to the import of the living modified organism in question as referred
to in paragraph 3 above, in order to avoid or minimize such potential adverse
effects.

7. The Conference of the Parties serving as the meeting of the Parties shall,
at its first meeting, decide upon appropriate procedures and mechanisms to
facilitate decision-making by Parties of import.

Article 11
Procedure for living modified organisms intended for direct use as food or feed, or for processing

1. A Party that makes a final decision regarding domestic use, including
placing on the market, of a living modified organism that may be subject to
transboundary movement for direct use as food or feed, or for processing
shall, within fifteen days of making that decision, inform the Parties through
the Biosafety Clearing-House. This information shall contain, at a minimum,
the information specified in Annex II. The Party shall provide a copy of the
information, in writing, to the national focal point of each Party that informs the Secretariat in advance that it does not have access to the Biosafety
Clearing-House. This provision shall not apply to decisions regarding field
trials.

2. The Party making a decision under paragraph 1 above, shall ensure that
there is a legal requirement for the accuracy of information provided by the
applicant.

3. Any Party may request additional information from the authority identi-fied in paragraph (b) of Annex II.

4. A Party may take a decision on the import of living modified organisms intended for direct use as food or feed, or for processing, under its domestic regulatory framework that is consistent with the objective of this Protocol.

5. Each Party shall make available to the Biosafety Clearing-House copies of any national laws, regulations and guidelines applicable to the import of living modified organisms intended for direct use as food or feed, or for processing, if available.

6. A developing country Party or a Party with an economy in transition may, in the absence of the domestic regulatory framework referred to in para-graph 4 above, and in exercise of its domestic jurisdiction, declare through the Biosafety Clearing-House that its decision prior to the first import of a living modified organism intended for direct use as food or feed, or for processing, on which information has been provided under paragraph 1 above, will be taken according to the following:

(a) A risk assessment undertaken in accordance with Annex III; and
(b) A decision made within a predictable timeframe, not exceeding two hun-dred and seventy days.

7. Failure by a Party to communicate its decision according to paragraph 6 above, shall not imply its consent or refusal to the import of a living modified organism intended for direct use as food or feed, or for processing, unless otherwise specified by the Party.

8. Lack of scientific certainty due to insufficient relevant scientific informa-tion and knowledge regarding the extent of the potential adverse effects of a living modified organism on the conservation and sustainable use of biological diversity in the Party of import, taking also into account risks to human health, shall not prevent that Party from taking a decision, as appropriate, with regard to the import of that living modified organism intended for direct use as food or feed, or for processing, in order to avoid or minimize such potential adverse effects.

9. A Party may indicate its needs for financial and technical assistance and capacity-building with respect to living modified organisms intended for direct use as food or feed, or for processing. Parties shall cooperate to meet these needs in accordance with Articles 22 and 28.

Article 12
Review of decisions

1. A Party of import may, at any time, in light of new scientific information on potential adverse effects on the conservation and sustainable use of biological diversity, taking also into account the risks to human health, review and change a decision regarding an intentional transboundary movement. In such case, the

Party shall, within thirty days, inform any notifier that has previously notified movements of the living modified organism referred to in such decision, as well as the Biosafety Clearing-House, and shall set out the reasons for its decision.

2. A Party of export or a notifier may request the Party of import to review a decision it has made in respect of it under Article 10 where the Party of export or the notifier considers that:

(a) A change in circumstances has occurred that may influence the outcome of the risk assessment upon which the decision was based; or
(b) Additional relevant scientific or technical information has become available.

3. The Party of import shall respond in writing to such a request within ninety days and set out the reasons for its decision.

4. The Party of import may, at its discretion, require a risk assessment for subsequent imports.

Article 13
Simplified procedure

1. A Party of import may, provided that adequate measures are applied to ensure the safe intentional transboundary movement of living modified organisms in accordance with the objective of this Protocol, specify in advance to the Biosafety Clearing-House:

(a) Cases in which intentional transboundary movement to it may take place at the same time as the movement is notified to the Party of import; and
(b) Imports of living modified organisms to it to be exempted from the advance informed agreement procedure.

Notifications under subparagraph (a) above, may apply to subsequent similar movements to the same Party.

2. The information relating to an intentional transboundary movement that is to be provided in the notifications referred to in paragraph 1 (a) above, shall be the information specified in Annex I.

Article 14
Bilateral, regional and multilateral agreements and arrangements

1. Parties may enter into bilateral, regional and multilateral agreements and arrangements regarding intentional transboundary movements of living modified organisms, consistent with the objective of this Protocol and provided that such agreements and arrangements do not result in a lower level of protection than that provided for by the Protocol.

2. The Parties shall inform each other, through the Biosafety Clearing-House, of any such bilateral, regional and multilateral agreements and arrangements

that they have entered into before or after the date of entry into force of this Protocol.

3. The provisions of this Protocol shall not affect intentional transboundary movements that take place pursuant to such agreements and arrangements as between the parties to those agreements or arrangements.

4. Any Party may determine that its domestic regulations shall apply with respect to specific imports to it and shall notify the Biosafety Clearing-House of its decision.

Article 15
Risk assessment

1. Risk assessments undertaken pursuant to this Protocol shall be carried out in a scientifically sound manner, in accordance with Annex III and taking into account recognized risk assessment techniques. Such risk assessments shall be based, at a minimum, on information provided in accordance with Article 8 and other available scientific evidence in order to identify and evaluate the possible adverse effects of living modified organisms on the conservation and sustainable use of biological diversity, taking also into account risks to human health.

2. The Party of import shall ensure that risk assessments are carried out for decisions taken under Article 10. It may require the exporter to carry out the risk assessment.

3. The cost of risk assessment shall be borne by the notifier if the Party of import so requires.

Article 16
Risk management

1. The Parties shall, taking into account Article 8 (g) of the Convention, establish and maintain appropriate mechanisms, measures and strategies to regulate, manage and control risks identified in the risk assessment provisions of this Protocol associated with the use, handling and transboundary movement of living modified organisms.

2. Measures based on risk assessment shall be imposed to the extent necessary to prevent adverse effects of the living modified organism on the conservation and sustainable use of biological diversity, taking also into account risks to human health, within the territory of the Party of import.

3. Each Party shall take appropriate measures to prevent unintentional transboundary movements of living modified organisms, including such measures as requiring a risk assessment to be carried out prior to the first release of a living modified organism.

4. Without prejudice to paragraph 2 above, each Party shall endeavour to ensure that any living modified organism, whether imported or locally developed, has undergone an appropriate period of observation that is

commensurate with its life-cycle or generation time before it is put to its intended use.

5. Parties shall cooperate with a view to:

(a) Identifying living modified organisms or specific traits of living modified organisms that may have adverse effects on the conservation and sustainable use of biological diversity, taking also into account risks to human health; and
(b) Taking appropriate measures regarding the treatment of such living modified organisms or specific traits.

Article 17
Unintentional transboundary movements and emergency measures

1. Each Party shall take appropriate measures to notify affected or potentially affected States, the Biosafety Clearing-House and, where appropriate, relevant international organizations, when it knows of an occurrence under its jurisdiction resulting in a release that leads, or may lead, to an unintentional transboundary movement of a living modified organism that is likely to have significant adverse effects on the conservation and sustainable use of biological diversity, taking also into account risks to human health in such States. The notification shall be provided as soon as the Party knows of the above situation.

2. Each Party shall, no later than the date of entry into force of this Protocol for it, make available to the Biosafety Clearing-House the relevant details setting out its point of contact for the purposes of receiving notifications under this Article.

3. Any notification arising from paragraph 1 above, should include:

(a) Available relevant information on the estimated quantities and relevant characteristics and/or traits of the living modified organism;
(b) Information on the circumstances and estimated date of the release, and on the use of the living modified organism in the originating Party;
(c) Any available information about the possible adverse effects on the conservation and sustainable use of biological diversity, taking also into account risks to human health, as well as available information about possible risk management measures;
(d) Any other relevant information; and
(e) A point of contact for further information.

4. In order to minimize any significant adverse effects on the conservation and sustainable use of biological diversity, taking also into account risks to human health, each Party, under whose jurisdiction the release of the living modified organism referred to in paragraph 1 above, occurs, shall immediately consult the affected or potentially affected States to enable them to determine

appropriate responses and initiate necessary action, including emergency measures.

Article 18
Handling, transport, packaging and identification

1. In order to avoid adverse effects on the conservation and sustainable use of biological diversity, taking also into account risks to human health, each Party shall take necessary measures to require that living modified organisms that are subject to intentional transboundary movement within the scope of this Protocol are handled, packaged and transported under conditions of safety, taking into consideration relevant international rules and standards.

2. Each Party shall take measures to require that documentation accompanying:

(a) Living modified organisms that are intended for direct use as food or feed, or for processing, clearly identifies that they 'may contain' living modified organisms and are not intended for intentional introduction into the environment, as well as a contact point for further information. The Conference of the Parties serving as the meeting of the Parties to this Protocol shall take a decision on the detailed requirements for this purpose, including specification of their identity and any unique identification, no later than two years after the date of entry into force of this Protocol;

(b) Living modified organisms that are destined for contained use clearly identifies them as living modified organisms; and specifies any requirements for the safe handling, storage, transport and use, the contact point for further information, including the name and address of the individual and institution to whom the living modified organisms are consigned; and

(c) Living modified organisms that are intended for intentional introduction into the environment of the Party of import and any other living modified organisms within the scope of the Protocol, clearly identifies them as living modified organisms; specifies the identity and relevant traits and/or characteristics, any requirements for the safe handling, storage, transport and use, the contact point for further information and, as appropriate, the name and address of the importer and exporter; and contains a declaration that the movement is in conformity with the requirements of this Protocol applicable to the exporter.

3. The Conference of the Parties serving as the meeting of the Parties to this Protocol shall consider the need for and modalities of developing standards with regard to identification, handling, packaging and transport practices, in consultation with other relevant international bodies.

Article 19
Competent national authorities and national focal points

1. Each Party shall designate one national focal point to be responsible on its behalf for liaison with the Secretariat. Each Party shall also designate one or more competent national authorities, which shall be responsible for performing the administrative functions required by this Protocol and which shall be authorized to act on its behalf with respect to those functions. A Party may designate a single entity to fulfil the functions of both focal point and competent national authority.

2. Each Party shall, no later than the date of entry into force of this Protocol for it, notify the Secretariat of the names and addresses of its focal point and its competent national authority or authorities. Where a Party designates more than one competent national authority, it shall convey to the Secretariat, with its notification thereof, relevant information on the respective responsibilities of those authorities. Where applicable, such information shall, at a minimum, specify which competent authority is responsible for which type of living modified organism. Each Party shall forthwith notify the Secretariat of any changes in the designation of its national focal point or in the name and address or responsibilities of its competent national authority or authorities.

3. The Secretariat shall forthwith inform the Parties of the notifications it receives under paragraph 2 above, and shall also make such information available through the Biosafety Clearing-House.

Article 20
Information sharing and the Biosafety Clearing-House

1. A Biosafety Clearing-House is hereby established as part of the clearing-house mechanism under Article 18, paragraph 3, of the Convention, in order to:

(a) Facilitate the exchange of scientific, technical, environmental and legal information on, and experience with, living modified organisms; and
(b) Assist Parties to implement the Protocol, taking into account the special needs of developing country Parties, in particular the least developed and small island developing States among them, and countries with economies in transition as well as countries that are centres of origin and centres of genetic diversity.

2. The Biosafety Clearing-House shall serve as a means through which information is made available for the purposes of paragraph 1 above. It shall provide access to information made available by the Parties relevant to the implementation of the Protocol. It shall also provide access, where possible, to other international biosafety information exchange mechanisms.

3. Without prejudice to the protection of confidential information, each Party shall make available to the Biosafety Clearing-House any information

required to be made available to the Biosafety Clearing-House under this Protocol, and:

(a) Any existing laws, regulations and guidelines for implementation of the Protocol, as well as information required by the Parties for the advance informed agreement procedure;

(b) Any bilateral, regional and multilateral agreements and arrangements;

(c) Summaries of its risk assessments or environmental reviews of living modified organisms generated by its regulatory process, and carried out in accordance with Article 15, including, where appropriate, relevant information regarding products thereof, namely, processed materials that are of living modified organism origin, containing detectable novel combinations of replicable genetic material obtained through the use of modern biotechnology;

(d) Its final decisions regarding the importation or release of living modified organisms; and

(e) Reports submitted by it pursuant to Article 33, including those on implementation of the advance informed agreement procedure.

4. The modalities of the operation of the Biosafety Clearing-House, including reports on its activities, shall be considered and decided upon by the Conference of the Parties serving as the meeting of the Parties to this Protocol at its first meeting, and kept under review thereafter.

Article 21
Confidential information

1. The Party of import shall permit the notifier to identify information submitted under the procedures of this Protocol or required by the Party of import as part of the advance informed agreement procedure of the Protocol that is to be treated as confidential. Justification shall be given in such cases upon request.

2. The Party of import shall consult the notifier if it decides that information identified by the notifier as confidential does not qualify for such treatment and shall, prior to any disclosure, inform the notifier of its decision, providing reasons on request, as well as an opportunity for consultation and for an internal review of the decision prior to disclosure.

3. Each Party shall protect confidential information received under this Protocol, including any confidential information received in the context of the advance informed agreement procedure of the Protocol. Each Party shall ensure that it has procedures to protect such information and shall protect the confidentiality of such information in a manner no less favourable than its treatment of confidential information in connection with domestically produced living modified organisms.

4. The Party of import shall not use such information for a commercial purpose, except with the written consent of the notifier.

5. If a notifier withdraws or has withdrawn a notification, the Party of import shall respect the confidentiality of commercial and industrial information, including research and development information as well as information on which the Party and the notifier disagree as to its confidentiality.

6. Without prejudice to paragraph 5 above, the following information shall not be considered confidential:

(a) The name and address of the notifier;
(b) A general description of the living modified organism or organisms;
(c) A summary of the risk assessment of the effects on the conservation and sustainable use of biological diversity, taking also into account risks to human health; and
(d) Any methods and plans for emergency response.

Article 22
Capacity-building

1. The Parties shall cooperate in the development and/or strengthening of human resources and institutional capacities in biosafety, including biotechnology to the extent that it is required for biosafety, for the purpose of the effective implementation of this Protocol, in developing country Parties, in particular the least developed and small island developing States among them, and in Parties with economies in transition, including through existing global, regional, subregional and national institutions and organizations and, as appropriate, through facilitating private sector involvement.

2. For the purposes of implementing paragraph 1 above, in relation to cooperation, the needs of developing country Parties, in particular the least developed and small island developing States among them, for financial resources and access to and transfer of technology and know-how in accordance with the relevant provisions of the Convention, shall be taken fully into account for capacity-building in biosafety. Cooperation in capacity-building shall, subject to the different situation, capabilities and requirements of each Party, include scientific and technical training in the proper and safe management of biotechnology, and in the use of risk assessment and risk management for biosafety, and the enhancement of technological and institutional capacities in biosafety. The needs of Parties with economies in transition shall also be taken fully into account for such capacity-building in biosafety.

Article 23
Public awareness and participation

1. The Parties shall:

(a) Promote and facilitate public awareness, education and participation concerning the safe transfer, handling and use of living modified organisms in relation to the conservation and sustainable use of biological diversity, taking also into account risks to human health. In doing so, the Parties shall cooperate, as appropriate, with other States and international bodies;

(b) Endeavour to ensure that public awareness and education encompass access to information on living modified organisms identified in accordance with this Protocol that may be imported.

2. The Parties shall, in accordance with their respective laws and regulations, consult the public in the decision-making process regarding living modified organisms and shall make the results of such decisions available to the public, while respecting confidential information in accordance with Article 21.

3. Each Party shall endeavour to inform its public about the means of public access to the Biosafety Clearing-House.

Article 24
Non-parties

1. Transboundary movements of living modified organisms between Parties and non-Parties shall be consistent with the objective of this Protocol. The Parties may enter into bilateral, regional and multilateral agreements and arrangements with non-Parties regarding such transboundary movements.

2. The Parties shall encourage non-Parties to adhere to this Protocol and to contribute appropriate information to the Biosafety Clearing-House on living modified organisms released in, or moved into or out of, areas within their national jurisdictions.

Article 25
Illegal transboundary movements

1. Each Party shall adopt appropriate domestic measures aimed at preventing and, if appropriate, penalizing transboundary movements of living modified organisms carried out in contravention of its domestic measures to implement this Protocol. Such movements shall be deemed illegal transboundary movements.

2. In the case of an illegal transboundary movement, the affected Party may request the Party of origin to dispose, at its own expense, of the living modified organism in question by repatriation or destruction, as appropriate.

3. Each Party shall make available to the Biosafety Clearing-House information concerning cases of illegal transboundary movements pertaining to it.

Article 26
Socio-economic considerations

1. The Parties, in reaching a decision on import under this Protocol or under its domestic measures implementing the Protocol, may take into account,

consistent with their international obligations, socio-economic considerations arising from the impact of living modified organisms on the conservation and sustainable use of biological diversity, especially with regard to the value of biological diversity to indigenous and local communities.

2. The Parties are encouraged to cooperate on research and information exchange on any socio-economic impacts of living modified organisms, especially on indigenous and local communities.

Article 27
Liability and redress

The Conference of the Parties serving as the meeting of the Parties to this Protocol shall, at its first meeting, adopt a process with respect to the appropriate elaboration of international rules and procedures in the field of liability and redress for damage resulting from transboundary movements of living modified organisms, analysing and taking due account of the ongoing processes in international law on these matters, and shall endeavour to complete this process within four years.

Article 28
Financial mechanism and resources

1. In considering financial resources for the implementation of this Protocol, the Parties shall take into account the provisions of Article 20 of the Convention.

2. The financial mechanism established in Article 21 of the Convention shall, through the institutional structure entrusted with its operation, be the financial mechanism for this Protocol.

3. Regarding the capacity-building referred to in Article 22 of this Protocol, the Conference of the Parties serving as the meeting of the Parties to this Protocol, in providing guidance with respect to the financial mechanism referred to in paragraph 2 above, for consideration by the Conference of the Parties, shall take into account the need for financial resources by developing country Parties, in particular the least developed and the small island developing States among them.

4. In the context of paragraph 1 above, the Parties shall also take into account the needs of the developing country Parties, in particular the least developed and the small island developing States among them, and of the Parties with economies in transition, in their efforts to identify and implement their capacity-building requirements for the purposes of the implementation of this Protocol.

5. The guidance to the financial mechanism of the Convention in relevant decisions of the Conference of the Parties, including those agreed before the adoption of this Protocol, shall apply, *mutatis mutandis*, to the provisions of this Article.

6. The developed country Parties may also provide, and the developing country Parties and the Parties with economies in transition avail themselves of,

financial and technological resources for the implementation of the provisions of this Protocol through bilateral, regional and multilateral channels.

Article 29
Conference of the Parties serving as the meeting of the Parties to this Protocol

1. The Conference of the Parties shall serve as the meeting of the Parties to this Protocol.

2. Parties to the Convention that are not Parties to this Protocol may participate as observers in the proceedings of any meeting of the Conference of the Parties serving as the meeting of the Parties to this Protocol. When the Conference of the Parties serves as the meeting of the Parties to this Protocol, decisions under this Protocol shall be taken only by those that are Parties to it.

3. When the Conference of the Parties serves as the meeting of the Parties to this Protocol, any member of the bureau of the Conference of the Parties representing a Party to the Convention but, at that time, not a Party to this Protocol, shall be substituted by a member to be elected by and from among the Parties to this Protocol.

4. The Conference of the Parties serving as the meeting of the Parties to this Protocol shall keep under regular review the implementation of this Protocol and shall make, within its mandate, the decisions necessary to promote its effective implementation. It shall perform the functions assigned to it by this Protocol and shall:

(a) Make recommendations on any matters necessary for the implementation of this Protocol;

(b) Establish such subsidiary bodies as are deemed necessary for the implementation of this Protocol;

(c) Seek and utilize, where appropriate, the services and cooperation of, and information provided by, competent international organizations and intergovernmental and non-governmental bodies;

(d) Establish the form and the intervals for transmitting the information to be submitted in accordance with Article 33 of this Protocol and consider such information as well as reports submitted by any subsidiary body;

(e) Consider and adopt, as required, amendments to this Protocol and its annexes, as well as any additional annexes to this Protocol, that are deemed necessary for the implementation of this Protocol; and

(f) Exercise such other functions as may be required for the implementation of this Protocol.

5. The rules of procedure of the Conference of the Parties and financial rules of the Convention shall be applied, *mutatis mutandis*, under this Protocol, except as may be otherwise decided by consensus by the Conference of the Parties serving as the meeting of the Parties to this Protocol.

6. The first meeting of the Conference of the Parties serving as the meeting of the Parties to this Protocol shall be convened by the Secretariat in conjunction with the first meeting of the Conference of the Parties that is scheduled after the date of the entry into force of this Protocol. Subsequent ordinary meetings of the Conference of the Parties serving as the meeting of the Parties to this Protocol shall be held in conjunction with ordinary meetings of the Conference of the Parties, unless otherwise decided by the Conference of the Parties serving as the meeting of the Parties to this Protocol.

7. Extraordinary meetings of the Conference of the Parties serving as the meeting of the Parties to this Protocol shall be held at such other times as may be deemed necessary by the Conference of the Parties serving as the meeting of the Parties to this Protocol, or at the written request of any Party, provided that, within six months of the request being communicated to the Parties by the Secretariat, it is supported by at least one third of the Parties.

8. The United Nations, its specialized agencies and the International Atomic Energy Agency, as well as any State member thereof or observers thereto not party to the Convention, may be represented as observers at meetings of the Conference of the Parties serving as the meeting of the Parties to this Protocol. Any body or agency, whether national or international, governmental or non-governmental, that is qualified in matters covered by this Protocol and that has informed the Secretariat of its wish to be represented at a meeting of the Conference of the Parties serving as a meeting of the Parties to this Protocol as an observer, may be so admitted, unless at least one third of the Parties present object. Except as otherwise provided in this Article, the admission and participation of observers shall be subject to the rules of procedure, as referred to in paragraph 5 above.

Article 30
Subsidiary bodies

1. Any subsidiary body established by or under the Convention may, upon a decision by the Conference of the Parties serving as the meeting of the Parties to this Protocol, serve the Protocol, in which case the meeting of the Parties shall specify which functions that body shall exercise.

2. Parties to the Convention that are not Parties to this Protocol may participate as observers in the proceedings of any meeting of any such subsidiary bodies. When a subsidiary body of the Convention serves as a subsidiary body to this Protocol, decisions under the Protocol shall be taken only by the Parties to the Protocol.

3. When a subsidiary body of the Convention exercises its functions with regard to matters concerning this Protocol, any member of the bureau of that subsidiary body representing a Party to the Convention but, at that time, not a Party to the Protocol, shall be substituted by a member to be elected by and from among the Parties to the Protocol.

Article 31
Secretariat

1. The Secretariat established by Article 24 of the Convention shall serve as the secretariat to this Protocol.

2. Article 24, paragraph 1, of the Convention on the functions of the Secretariat shall apply, *mutatis mutandis*, to this Protocol.

3. To the extent that they are distinct, the costs of the secretariat services for this Protocol shall be met by the Parties hereto. The Conference of the Parties serving as the meeting of the Parties to this Protocol shall, at its first meeting, decide on the necessary budgetary arrangements to this end.

Article 32
Relationship with the convention

Except as otherwise provided in this Protocol, the provisions of the Convention relating to its protocols shall apply to this Protocol.

Article 33
Monitoring and reporting

Each Party shall monitor the implementation of its obligations under this Protocol, and shall, at intervals to be determined by the Conference of the Parties serving as the meeting of the Parties to this Protocol, report to the Conference of the Parties serving as the meeting of the Parties to this Protocol on measures that it has taken to implement the Protocol.

Article 34
Compliance

The Conference of the Parties serving as the meeting of the Parties to this Protocol shall, at its first meeting, consider and approve cooperative procedures and institutional mechanisms to promote compliance with the provisions of this Protocol and to address cases of non-compliance. These procedures and mechanisms shall include provisions to offer advice or assistance, where appropriate. They shall be separate from, and without prejudice to, the dispute settlement procedures and mechanisms established by Article 27 of the Convention.

Article 35
Assessment and review

The Conference of the Parties serving as the meeting of the Parties to this Protocol shall undertake, five years after the entry into force of this Protocol and at least every five years thereafter, an evaluation of the effectiveness of the Protocol, including an assessment of its procedures and annexes.

Article 36
Signature

This Protocol shall be open for signature at the United Nations Office at Nairobi by States and regional economic integration organizations from 15 to 26 May 2000, and at United Nations Headquarters in New York from 5 June 2000 to 4 June 2001.

Article 37
Entry into force

1. This Protocol shall enter into force on the ninetieth day after the date of deposit of the fiftieth instrument of ratification, acceptance, approval or accession by States or regional economic integration organizations that are Parties to the Convention.

2. This Protocol shall enter into force for a State or regional economic integration organization that ratifies, accepts or approves this Protocol or accedes thereto after its entry into force pursuant to paragraph 1 above, on the ninetieth day after the date on which that State or regional economic integration organization deposits its instrument of ratification, acceptance, approval or accession, or on the date on which the Convention enters into force for that State or regional economic integration organization, whichever shall be the later.

3. For the purposes of paragraphs 1 and 2 above, any instrument deposited by a regional economic integration organization shall not be counted as additional to those deposited by member States of such organization.

Article 38
Reservations

No reservations may be made to this Protocol.

Article 39
Withdrawal

1. At any time after two years from the date on which this Protocol has entered into force for a Party, that Party may withdraw from the Protocol by giving written notification to the Depositary.

2. Any such withdrawal shall take place upon expiry of one year after the date of its receipt by the Depositary, or on such later date as may be specified in the notification of the withdrawal.

Article 40
Authentic texts

The original of this Protocol, of which the Arabic, Chinese, English, French, Russian and Spanish texts are equally authentic, shall be deposited with the Secretary-General of the United Nations.

IN WITNESS WHEREOF the undersigned, being duly authorized to that effect, have signed this Protocol.

DONE at Montreal on this twenty-ninth day of January, two thousand.

Annex I
Information required in notifications under Articles 8, 10 and 13

(a) Name, address and contact details of the exporter.

(b) Name, address and contact details of the importer.

(c) Name and identity of the living modified organism, as well as the domestic classification, if any, of the biosafety level of the living modified organism in the State of export.

(d) Intended date or dates of the transboundary movement, if known.

(e) Taxonomic status, common name, point of collection or acquisition, and characteristics of recipient organism or parental organisms related to biosafety.

(f) Centres of origin and centres of genetic diversity, if known, of the recipient organism and/or the parental organisms and a description of the habitats where the organisms may persist or proliferate.

(g) Taxonomic status, common name, point of collection or acquisition, and characteristics of the donor organism or organisms related to biosafety.

(h) Description of the nucleic acid or the modification introduced, the technique used, and the resulting characteristics of the living modified organism.

(i) Intended use of the living modified organism or products thereof, namely, processed materials that are of living modified organism origin, containing detectable novel combinations of replicable genetic material obtained through the use of modern biotechnology.

(j) Quantity or volume of the living modified organism to be transferred.

(k) A previous and existing risk assessment report consistent with Annex III.

(l) Suggested methods for the safe handling, storage, transport and use, including packaging, labelling, documentation, disposal and contingency procedures, where appropriate.

(m) Regulatory status of the living modified organism within the State of export (for example, whether it is prohibited in the State of export, whether there are other restrictions, or whether it has been approved for general release) and, if the living modified organism is banned in the State of export, the reason or reasons for the ban.

(n) Result and purpose of any notification by the exporter to other States regarding the living modified organism to be transferred.

(o) A declaration that the above-mentioned information is factually correct.

Annex II
Information required concerning living modified organisms intended for direct use as food or feed, or for processing under Article 11

(a) The name and contact details of the applicant for a decision for domestic use.

(b) The name and contact details of the authority responsible for the decision.

(c) Name and identity of the living modified organism.

(d) Description of the gene modification, the technique used, and the resulting characteristics of the living modified organism.

(e) Any unique identification of the living modified organism.

(f) Taxonomic status, common name, point of collection or acquisition, and characteristics of recipient organism or parental organisms related to biosafety.

(g) Centres of origin and centres of genetic diversity, if known, of the recipient organism and/or the parental organisms and a description of the habitats where the organisms may persist or proliferate.

(h) Taxonomic status, common name, point of collection or acquisition, and characteristics of the donor organism or organisms related to biosafety.

(i) Approved uses of the living modified organism.

(j) A risk assessment report consistent with Annex III.

(k) Suggested methods for the safe handling, storage, transport and use, including packaging, labelling, documentation, disposal and contingency procedures, where appropriate.

Annex III
Risk assessment

Objective

1. The objective of risk assessment, under this Protocol, is to identify and evaluate the potential adverse effects of living modified organisms on the conservation and sustainable use of biological diversity in the likely potential receiving environment, taking also into account risks to human health.

Use of risk assessment

2. Risk assessment is, *inter alia*, used by competent authorities to make informed decisions regarding living modified organisms.

General principles

3. Risk assessment should be carried out in a scientifically sound and transparent manner, and can take into account expert advice of, and guidelines developed by, relevant international organizations.

4. Lack of scientific knowledge or scientific consensus should not necessarily be interpreted as indicating a particular level of risk, an absence of risk, or an acceptable risk.

5. Risks associated with living modified organisms or products thereof, namely, processed materials that are of living modified organism origin, containing detectable novel combinations of replicable genetic material obtained through the use of modern biotechnology, should be considered in the context of the risks posed by the non-modified recipients or parental organisms in the likely potential receiving environment.

6. Risk assessment should be carried out on a case-by-case basis. The required information may vary in nature and level of detail from case to case, depending on the living modified organism concerned, its intended use and the likely potential receiving environment.

Methodology

7. The process of risk assessment may on the one hand give rise to a need for further information about specific subjects, which may be identified and requested during the assessment process, while on the other hand information on other subjects may not be relevant in some instances.

8. To fulfil its objective, risk assessment entails, as appropriate, the following steps:

(a) An identification of any novel genotypic and phenotypic characteristics associated with the living modified organism that may have adverse effects on biological diversity in the likely potential receiving environment, taking also into account risks to human health;

(b) An evaluation of the likelihood of these adverse effects being realized, taking into account the level and kind of exposure of the likely potential receiving environment to the living modified organism;

(c) An evaluation of the consequences should these adverse effects be realized;

(d) An estimation of the overall risk posed by the living modified organism based on the evaluation of the likelihood and consequences of the identified adverse effects being realized;

(e) A recommendation as to whether or not the risks are acceptable or manageable, including, where necessary, identification of strategies to manage these risks; and

(f) Where there is uncertainty regarding the level of risk, it may be addressed by requesting further information on the specific issues of concern or by implementing appropriate risk management strategies and/or monitoring the living modified organism in the receiving environment.

Points to consider

9. Depending on the case, risk assessment takes into account the relevant technical and scientific details regarding the characteristics of the following subjects:

(a) *Recipient organism or parental organisms.* The biological characteristics of the recipient organism or parental organisms, including information on taxonomic status, common name, origin, centres of origin and centres of genetic diversity, if known, and a description of the habitat where the organisms may persist or proliferate;

(b) *Donor organism or organisms.* Taxonomic status and common name, source, and the relevant biological characteristics of the donor organisms;

(c) *Vector.* Characteristics of the vector, including its identity, if any, and its source or origin, and its host range;

(d) *Insert or inserts and/or characteristics of modification.* Genetic characteristics of the inserted nucleic acid and the function it specifies, and/or characteristics of the modification introduced;

(e) *Living modified organism.* Identity of the living modified organism, and the differences between the biological characteristics of the living modified organism and those of the recipient organism or parental organisms;

(f) *Detection and identification of the living modified organism.* Suggested detection and identification methods and their specificity, sensitivity and reliability;

(g) *Information relating to the intended use.* Information relating to the intended use of the living modified organism, including new or changed use compared to the recipient organism or parental organisms; and

(h) *Receiving environment.* Information on the location, geographical, climatic and ecological characteristics, including relevant information on biological diversity and centres of origin of the likely potential receiving environment.

22

Non-Legally Binding Authoritative Statement of Principles for a Global Consensus on the Management, Conservation and Sustainable Development of All Types of Forests, 13 June 1992

Editorial note

The Non-Legally Binding Authoritative Statement of Principles for a Global Consensus on the Management, Conservation and Sustainable Development of All Types of Forests, adopted at UNCED and which applies to all forests, aims (i) to relate the subject of forests to the entire range of environmental and developmental issues (Preambular paragraph (a)) and (ii) to have forestry issues examined in a 'balanced manner within the overall context of both the environment and development' (Preambular paragraph (c)). The Principles call for efforts to be undertaken towards 'greening' the world (Principle 8(a)) and towards maintaining and increasing forest cover and productivity in ecologically and economically sound ways (Principle 8(b)).

The Principles affirm that States have the sovereign and inalienable right to utilise, manage and develop their forests in accordance with their development needs and in a manner consistent with 'sustainable development' (Principle 2(a)). They state that 'sustainable' economic, trade and development policies and international aid should be integrated with forest conservation (Principles 3(c), 6(b), 9 and 13(d)). Governments should promote and provide opportunities for the participation of interested parties in the development, implementation and planning of national forest policies (Principle 2(d)). States should, in addition, 'duly support' the culture and rights of indigenous peoples and forest dwellers (Principle 5(a)).

The Principles encourage the promotion of a 'supportive international economic climate conducive to sustained and environmentally sound development of forests in all countries' (Principle 7(a)). The costs of forest conservation and 'sustainable development' should be shared equitably by the international community (Principle 1(b)). In particular, developing countries should receive new and additional financial resources to enable them to 'sustainably' manage, conserve and develop their forest resources (Principle 10). Agreed rules that are non-discriminatory and consistent with international law should govern trade in all forest products (Article 13(a)) and unilateral measures to restrict and/or ban trade in forest products should be removed or avoided (Principle 14).

The Principles deem essential national, international and regional institutional capabilities to the conservation and 'sustainable development' of forests and call for such capabilities to be strengthened (Principle 12(b)).

Non-Legally Binding Authoritative Statement of Principles for a Global Consensus on the Management, Conservation and Sustainable Development of All Types of Forests

Preamble

(a) The subject of forests is related to the entire range of environmental and de-velopment issues and opportunities, including the right to socio-economic development on a sustainable basis.

(b) The guiding objective of these principles is to contribute to the manage-ment, conservation and sustainable development of forests and to provide for their multiple and complementary functions and uses.

(c) Forestry issues and opportunities should be examined in a holistic and bal-anced manner within the overall context of environment and development, taking into consideration the multiple functions and uses of forests, includ-ing traditional uses, and the likely economic and social stress when these uses are constrained or restricted, as well as the potential for development that sustainable forest management can offer.

(d) These principles reflect a first global consensus on forests. In committing themselves to the prompt implementation of these principles, countries also decide to keep them under assessment for their adequacy with regard to further international cooperation on forest issues.

(e) These principles should apply to all types of forests, both natural and planted, in all geographical regions and climatic zones, including austral, boreal, subtemperate, temperate, subtropical and tropical.

(f) All types of forests embody complex and unique ecological processes which are the basis for their present and potential capacity to provide resources to satisfy human needs as well as environmental values, and as such their sound management and conservation is of concern to the Governments of the countries to which they belong and are of value to local communities and to the environment as a whole.

(g) Forests are essential to economic development and the maintenance of all forms of life.

(h) Recognizing that the responsibility for forest management, conservation and sustainable development is in many States allocated among fed-eral/national, state/provincial and local levels of government, each State, in accordance with its constitution and/or national legislation, should pursue these principles at the appropriate level of government.

Principles/elements

1.

(a) 'States have, in accordance with the Charter of the United Nations and the principles of international law, the sovereign right to exploit their own resources pursuant to their own environmental policies and have the responsibility to ensure that activities within their jurisdiction or control do not cause damage to the environment of other States or of areas beyond the limits of national jurisdiction'.

(b) The agreed full incremental cost of achieving benefits associated with forest conservation and sustainable development requires increased international cooperation and should be equitably shared by the international community.

2.

(a) States have the sovereign and inalienable right to utilize, manage and develop their forests in accordance with their development needs and level of socio-economic development and on the basis of national policies consistent with sustainable development and legislation, including the conversion of such areas for other uses within the overall socio-economic development plan and based on rational land-use policies.

(b) Forest resources and forest lands should be sustainably managed to meet the social, economic, ecological, cultural and spiritual human needs of present and future generations. These needs are for forest products and services, such as wood and wood products, water, food, fodder, medicine, fuel, shelter, employment, recreation, habitats for wildlife, landscape diversity, carbon sinks and reservoirs, and for other forest products. Appropriate measures should be taken to protect forests against harmful effects of pollution, including air-borne pollution, fires, pests and diseases, in order to maintain their full multiple value.

(c) The provision of timely, reliable and accurate information on forests and forest ecosystems is essential for public understanding and informed decision-making and should be ensured.

(d) Governments should promote and provide opportunities for the participation of interested parties, including local communities and indigenous people, industries, labour, non-governmental organizations and individuals, forest dwellers and women, in the development, implementation and planning of national forest policies.

3.

(a) National policies and strategies should provide a framework for increased efforts, including the development and strengthening of institutions and

programmes for the management, conservation and sustainable development of forests and forest lands.

(b) International institutional arrangements, building on those organizations
and mechanisms already in existence, as appropriate, should facilitate
international cooperation in the field of forests.

(c) All aspects of environmental protection and social and economic development as they relate to forests and forest lands should be integrated and
comprehensive.

4. The vital role of all types of forests in maintaining the ecological processes
and balance at the local, national, regional and global levels through, *inter alia*,
their role in protecting fragile ecosystems, watersheds and freshwater resources
and as rich storehouses of biodiversity and biological resources and sources of
genetic material for biotechnology products, as well as photosynthesis, should
be recognized.

5.

(a) National forest policies should recognize and duly support the identity,
culture and the rights of indigenous people, their communities and other
communities and forest dwellers. Appropriate conditions should be promoted for these groups to enable them to have an economic stake in forest
use, perform economic activities, and achieve and maintain cultural identity and social organization, as well as adequate levels of livelihood and
well-being, through, *inter alia*, those land tenure arrangements which serve
as incentives for the sustainable management of forests.

(b) The full participation of women in all aspects of the management, conservation and sustainable development of forests should be actively promoted.

6.

(a) All types of forests play an important role in meeting energy requirements
through the provision of a renewable source of bio-energy, particularly in
developing countries, and the demands for fuelwood for household and
industrial needs should be met through sustainable forest management,
afforestation and reforestation. To this end, the potential contribution of
plantations of both indigenous and introduced species for the provision of
both fuel and industrial wood should be recognized.

(b) National policies and programmes should take into account the relationship, where it exists, between the conservation, management and sustainable development of forests and all aspects related to the production,
consumption, recycling and/or final disposal of forest products.

(c) Decisions taken on the management, conservation and sustainable development of forest resources should benefit, to the extent practicable, from
a comprehensive assessment of economic and non-economic values of
forest goods and services and of the environmental costs and benefits. The

development and improvement of methodologies for such evaluations should be promoted.

(d) The role of planted forests and permanent agricultural crops as sustainable and environmentally sound sources of renewable energy and industrial raw material should be recognized, enhanced and promoted. Their contribution to the maintenance of ecological processes, to offsetting pressure on primary/old-growth forest and to providing regional employment and development with the adequate involvement of local inhabitants should be recognized and enhanced.

(e) Natural forests also constitute a source of goods and services, and their conservation, sustainable management and use should be promoted.

7.

(a) Efforts should be made to promote a supportive international economic climate conducive to sustained and environmentally sound development of forests in all countries, which include, *inter alia*, the promotion of sustainable patterns of production and consumption, the eradication of poverty and the promotion of food security.

(b) Specific financial resources should be provided to developing countries with significant forest areas which establish programmes for the conservation of forests including protected natural forest areas. These resources should be directed notably to economic sectors which would stimulate economic and social substitution activities.

8.

(a) Efforts should be undertaken towards the greening of the world. All countries, notably developed countries, should take positive and transparent action towards reforestation, afforestation and forest conservation, as appropriate.

(b) Efforts to maintain and increase forest cover and forest productivity should be undertaken in ecologically, economically and socially sound ways through the rehabilitation, reforestation and re-establishment of trees and forests on unproductive, degraded and deforested lands, as well as through the management of existing forest resources.

(c) The implementation of national policies and programmes aimed at forest management, conservation and sustainable development, particularly in developing countries, should be supported by international financial and technical cooperation, including through the private sector, where appropriate.

(d) Sustainable forest management and use should be carried out in accordance with national development policies and priorities and on the basis of environmentally sound national guidelines. In the formulation of such guidelines, account should be taken, as appropriate and if applicable, of relevant internationally agreed methodologies and criteria.

(e) Forest management should be integrated with management of adjacent areas so as to maintain ecological balance and sustainable productivity.

(f) National policies and/or legislation aimed at management, conservation and sustainable development of forests should include the protection of ecologically viable representative or unique examples of forests, including primary/old-growth forests, cultural, spiritual, historical, religious and other unique and valued forests of national importance.

(g) Access to biological resources, including genetic material, shall be with due regard to the sovereign rights of the countries where the forests are located and to the sharing on mutually agreed terms of technology and profits from biotechnology products that are derived from these resources.

(h) National policies should ensure that environmental impact assessments should be carried out where actions are likely to have significant adverse impacts on important forest resources, and where such actions are subject to a decision of a competent national authority.

9.

(a) The efforts of developing countries to strengthen the management, conservation and sustainable development of their forest resources should be supported by the international community, taking into account the importance of redressing external indebtedness, particularly where aggravated by the net transfer of resources to developed countries, as well as the problem of achieving at least the replacement value of forests through improved market access for forest products, especially processed products. In this respect, special attention should also be given to the countries undergoing the process of transition to market economies.

(b) The problems that hinder efforts to attain the conservation and sustainable use of forest resources and that stem from the lack of alternative options available to local communities, in particular the urban poor and poor rural populations who are economically and socially dependent on forests and forest resources, should be addressed by Governments and the international community.

(c) National policy formulation with respect to all types of forests should take account of the pressures and demands imposed on forest ecosystems and resources from influencing factors outside the forest sector, and intersectoral means of dealing with these pressures and demands should be sought.

10. New and additional financial resources should be provided to developing countries to enable them to sustainably manage, conserve and develop their forest resources, including through afforestation, reforestation and combating deforestation and forest and land degradation.

11. In order to enable, in particular, developing countries to enhance their endogenous capacity and to better manage, conserve and develop their forest resources, the access to and transfer of environmentally sound technologies and corresponding know-how on favourable terms, including on concessional and preferential terms, as mutually agreed, in accordance with the relevant provisions of Agenda 21, should be promoted, facilitated and financed, as appropriate.

12.

(a) Scientific research, forest inventories and assessments carried out by national institutions which take into account, where relevant, biological, physical, social and economic variables, as well as technological development and its application in the field of sustainable forest management, conservation and development, should be strengthened through effective modalities, including international cooperation. In this context, attention should also be given to research and development of sustainably harvested non-wood products.

(b) National and, where appropriate, regional and international institutional capabilities in education, training, science, technology, economics, anthropology and social aspects of forests and forest management are essential to the conservation and sustainable development of forests and should be strengthened.

(c) International exchange of information on the results of forest and forest management research and development should be enhanced and broadened, as appropriate, making full use of education and training institutions, including those in the private sector.

(d) Appropriate indigenous capacity and local knowledge regarding the conservation and sustainable development of forests should, through institutional and financial support and in collaboration with the people in the local communities concerned, be recognized, respected, recorded, developed and, as appropriate, introduced in the implementation of programmes. Benefits arising from the utilization of indigenous knowledge should therefore be equitably shared with such people.

13.

(a) Trade in forest products should be based on non-discriminatory and multilaterally agreed rules and procedures consistent with international trade law and practices. In this context, open and free international trade in forest products should be facilitated.

(b) Reduction or removal of tariff barriers and impediments to the provision of better market access and better prices for higher value-added forest products and their local processing should be encouraged to enable producer countries to better conserve and manage their renewable forest resources.

(c) Incorporation of environmental costs and benefits into market forces and mechanisms, in order to achieve forest conservation and sustainable development, should be encouraged both domestically and internationally.
(d) Forest conservation and sustainable development policies should be integrated with economic, trade and other relevant policies.
(e) Fiscal, trade, industrial, transportation and other policies and practices that may lead to forest degradation should be avoided. Adequate policies, aimed at management, conservation and sustainable development of forests, including, where appropriate, incentives, should be encouraged.

14. Unilateral measures, incompatible with international obligations or agreements, to restrict and/or ban international trade in timber or other forest products should be removed or avoided, in order to attain long-term sustainable forest management.

15. Pollutants, particularly air-borne pollutants, including those responsible for acidic deposition, that are harmful to the health of forest ecosystems at the local, national, regional and global levels should be controlled.

United Nations Convention to Combat Desertification in Countries Experiencing Serious Drought and/or Desertification, Particularly in Africa, 17 June 1994

Editorial note

The United Nations Convention to Combat Desertification in Countries Experiencing Serious Drought and/or Desertification, Particularly in Africa (UNCCD) aims to 'to combat desertification and mitigate the effects of drought in countries experiencing serious drought and/or desertification, particularly in Africa, through effective action at all levels, supported by international cooperation and partnership arrangements, in the framework of an integrated approach which is consistent with Agenda 21, with a view to contributing to the achievement of sustainable development in affected areas' (Article 2).

The Parties shall implement their obligations through existing or prospective arrangements (Article 4(1)). Parties, in pursuing the objectives of the Convention, shall *inter alia* adopt an integrated approach (Article 4(2)(a)), give due attention to the situation of developing countries with regard to trade, marketing arrangements and debt (Article 4(2)(b)) and promote use of financial mechanisms to mobilize resources to affected developing countries (Article 4(2)(h)). Affected country parties (i.e. countries whose lands include, in whole or in part, arid, semi-arid and/or dry sub-humid areas affected or threatened by desertification) are required to develop national action programmes to combat desertification (Article 5). The purpose of the programmes is to identify factors contributing to desertification and practical measures necessary to combat desertification and mitigate the effects of drought such as the establishment of early warning systems, the strengthening of drought contingency plans, the establishment of food security systems and the development of sustainable irrigation programmes. National action programmes must specify the respective roles of government, local communities and land users and the resources available and needed (Article 10(1) and (2)). Development of the national programmes should take a 'bottom-up' approach ensuring the participation of populations and local communities and the creation of an 'enabling environment' at higher levels to facilitate action at national and local levels (Article 3(a)). The programmes should also be integrated with other national policies for sustainable development (Article 5(b)).

Obligations are also placed on developed country parties to provide 'substantial' financial resources and other forms of support to affected developing countries, particularly those in Africa, and to promote and facilitate access by affected country Parties to appropriate technology, knowledge and know-how (Article 6). In implementing the Convention, the Parties must give priority to affected African country Parties, in the light of the particular situation prevailing in that region (Article 7).

The Conference of the Parties reviews the implementation of the Convention, facilitating the exchange of information on implementing measures and adopting amendments to the Convention (Article 22). It is supported by a Permanent Secretariat (Article 23) and a Committee on Science and Technology (Article 24).

Parties are to communicate to the Permanent Secretariat reports on the measures taken to implement the Convention (Article 26). The Conference of the Parties shall consider and adopt procedures for resolution of questions on the implementation of the Convention (Article 27). Disputes shall be settled through negotiation or other peaceful means at the choice of the Parties (Article 28). The Annexes form an integral part of the Convention (Article 29). Procedures for the amendment of the Convention are described in Article 30 and amendments to the Annexes are to follow the procedure described in Article 31. No reservation to the Convention is allowed (Article 37).

Date of signature:	17 June 1994
Entry into force:	26 December 1996
Depositary:	Secretary-General of the United Nations
Contracting Parties:	Afghanistan, Albania, Algeria, Andorra, Angola, Antigua and Barbuda, Argentina, Armenia, Australia, Austria, Azerbaijan, Bahamas, Bahrain, Bangladesh, Barbados, Belarus, Belgium, Belize, Benin, Bolivia, Bosnia and Herzegovina, Botswana, Brazil, Brunei Darussalam, Bulgaria, Burkina Faso, Burundi, Cambodia, Cameroon, Canada, Cape Verde, Central African Republic, Chad, Chile, China, Colombia, Comoros, Congo, Congo (Democratic Republic of), Cook Islands, Costa Rica, Cote d'Ivoire, Croatia, Cuba, Cyprus, Czech Republic, Denmark, Djibouti, Dominica, Dominican Republic, Ecuador, Egypt, El Salvador, Equatorial Guinea, Eritrea, Ethiopia, European Community, Fiji, Finland, France, Gabon, Gambia, Georgia, Germany, Ghana,

Greece, Grenada, Guatemala, Guinea, Guinea Bissau, Guyana, Haiti, Honduras, Hungary, Iceland, India, Indonesia, Iran (Islamic Republic of), Ireland, Israel, Italy, Jamaica, Japan, Jordan, Kazakhstan, Kenya, Kiribati, Korea (Republic of), Kuwait, Kyrgyzstan, Lao People's Democratic Republic, Latvia, Lebanon, Lesotho, Liberia, Libyan Arab Jamahiriya, Liechtenstein, Luxembourg, Madagascar, Malawi, Malaysia, Maldives, Mali, Malta, Marshall Islands, Mauritania, Mauritius, Mexico, Micronesia (Federated States of), Moldova (Republic of), Monaco, Mongolia, Morocco, Mozambique, Myanmar, Namibia, Nauru, Nepal, Netherlands, New Zealand, Nicaragua, Niger, Nigeria, Norway, Oman, Pakistan, Palau, Panama, Papua New Guinea, Paraguay, Peru, Philippines, Poland, Portugal, Qatar, Romania, Rwanda, Saint Kitts and Nevis, Saint Lucia, Saint Vincent and the Grenadines, Samoa, San Marino, São Tomé and Príncipe, Saudi Arabia, Senegal, Seychelles, Sierra Leone, Singapore, Slovakia, Slovenia, Solomon Islands, Somalia, South Africa, Spain, Sri Lanka, Sudan, Suriname, Swaziland, Sweden, Switzerland, Syrian Arab Republic, Tajikistan, Tanzania (United Republic of), Thailand, The Former Yugoslav Republic of Macedonia, Togo, Tonga, Trinidad and Tobago, Tunisia, Turkey, Turkmenistan, Tuvalu, Uganda, Ukraine, United Arab Emirates, United Kingdom, United States of America, Uruguay, Uzbekistan, Vanuatu, Venezuela, Vietnam, Yemen, Zambia, Zimbabwe.

Website: www.unccd.int

United Nations Convention to Combat Desertification in Countries Experiencing Serious Drought and/or Desertification, Particularly in Africa

The Parties to this Convention,

Affirming that human beings in affected or threatened areas are at the centre of concerns to combat desertification and mitigate the effects of drought,

Reflecting the urgent concern of the international community, including States and international organizations, about the adverse impacts of desertification and drought,

Aware that arid, semi-arid and dry sub-humid areas together account for a significant proportion of the Earth's land area and are the habitat and source of livelihood for a large segment of its population,

Acknowledging that desertification and drought are problems of global dimension in that they affect all regions of the world and that joint action of the international community is needed to combat desertification and/or mitigate the effects of drought,

Noting the high concentration of developing countries, notably the least developed countries, among those experiencing serious drought and/or desertification, and the particularly tragic consequences of these phenomena in Africa,

Noting also that desertification is caused by complex interactions among physical, biological, political, social, cultural and economic factors,

Considering the impact of trade and relevant aspects of international economic relations on the ability of affected countries to combat desertification adequately,

Conscious that sustainable economic growth, social development and poverty eradication are priorities of affected developing countries, particularly in Africa, and are essential to meeting sustainability objectives,

Mindful that desertification and drought affect sustainable development through their interrelationships with important social problems such as poverty, poor health and nutrition, lack of food security, and those arising from migration, displacement of persons and demographic dynamics,

Appreciating the significance of the past efforts and experience of States and international organizations in combating desertification and mitigating the effects of drought, particularly in implementing the Plan of Action to Combat Desertification which was adopted at the United Nations Conference on Desertification in 1977,

Realizing that, despite efforts in the past, progress in combating desertification and mitigating the effects of drought has not met expectations and that a new and more effective approach is needed at all levels within the framework of sustainable development,

Recognizing the validity and relevance of decisions adopted at the United Nations Conference on Environment and Development, particularly of Agenda 21 and its chapter 12, which provide a basis for combating desertification,

Reaffirming in this light the commitments of developed countries as contained in paragraph 13 of chapter 33 of Agenda 21,

Recalling General Assembly resolution 47/188, particularly the priority in it prescribed for Africa, and all other relevant United Nations resolutions, decisions and programmes on desertification and drought, as well as relevant declarations by African countries and those from other regions,

Reaffirming the Rio Declaration on Environment and Development which states, in its Principle 2, that States have, in accordance with the Charter of the

United Nations and the principles of international law, the sovereign right to exploit their own resources pursuant to their own environmental and developmental policies, and the responsibility to ensure that activities within their jurisdiction or control do not cause damage to the environment of other States or of areas beyond the limits of national jurisdiction,

Recognizing that national Governments play a critical role in combating desertification and mitigating the effects of drought and that progress in that respect depends on local implementation of action programmes in affected areas,

Recognizing also the importance and necessity of international cooperation and partnership in combating desertification and mitigating the effects of drought,

Recognizing further the importance of the provision to affected developing countries, particularly in Africa, of effective means, *inter alia* substantial financial resources, including new and additional funding, and access to technology, without which it will be difficult for them to implement fully their commitments under this Convention,

Expressing concern over the impact of desertification and drought on affected countries in Central Asia and the Transcaucasus,

Stressing the important role played by women in regions affected by desertification and/or drought, particularly in rural areas of developing countries, and the importance of ensuring the full participation of both men and women at all levels in programmes to combat desertification and mitigate the effects of drought,

Emphasizing the special role of non-governmental organizations and other major groups in programmes to combat desertification and mitigate the effects of drought,

Bearing in mind the relationship between desertification and other environmental problems of global dimension facing the international and national communities,

Bearing also in mind the contribution that combating desertification can make to achieving the objectives of the United Nations Framework Convention on Climate Change, the Convention on Biological Diversity and other related environmental conventions,

Believing that strategies to combat desertification and mitigate the effects of drought will be most effective if they are based on sound systematic observation and rigorous scientific knowledge and if they are continuously re-evaluated,

Recognizing the urgent need to improve the effectiveness and coordination of international cooperation to facilitate the implementation of national plans and priorities,

Determined to take appropriate action in combating desertification and mitigating the effects of drought for the benefit of present and future generations,

Have agreed as follows:

Part I
Introduction

Article 1
Use of terms

For the purposes of this Convention:

(a) 'desertification' means land degradation in arid, semi-arid and dry sub-humid areas resulting from various factors, including climatic variations and human activities;

(b) 'combating desertification' includes activities which are part of the integrated development of land in arid, semi-arid and dry sub-humid areas for sustainable development which are aimed at:
   (i) prevention and/or reduction of land degradation;
   (ii) rehabilitation of partly degraded land; and
   (iii) reclamation of desertified land;

(c) 'drought' means the naturally occurring phenomenon that exists when precipitation has been significantly below normal recorded levels, causing serious hydrological imbalances that adversely affect land resource production systems;

(d) 'mitigating the effects of drought' means activities related to the prediction of drought and intended to reduce the vulnerability of society and natural systems to drought as it relates to combating desertification;

(e) 'land' means the terrestrial bio-productive system that comprises soil, vegetation, other biota, and the ecological and hydrological processes that operate within the system;

(f) 'land degradation' means reduction or loss, in arid, semi-arid and dry sub-humid areas, of the biological or economic productivity and complexity of rainfed cropland, irrigated cropland, or range, pasture, forest and woodlands resulting from land uses or from a process or combination of processes, including processes arising from human activities and habitation patterns, such as:
   (i) soil erosion caused by wind and/or water;
   (ii) deterioration of the physical, chemical and biological or economic properties of soil; and
   (iii) long-term loss of natural vegetation;

(g) 'arid, semi-arid and dry sub-humid areas' means areas, other than polar and sub-polar regions, in which the ratio of annual precipitation to potential evapotranspiration falls within the range from 0.05 to 0.65;

(h) 'affected areas' means arid, semi-arid and/or dry sub-humid areas affected or threatened by desertification;

(i) 'affected countries' means countries whose lands include, in whole or in part, affected areas;

(j) 'regional economic integration organization' means an organization constituted by sovereign States of a given region which has competence in

respect of matters governed by this Convention and has been duly authorized, in accordance with its internal procedures, to sign, ratify, accept,
approve or accede to this Convention;

(k) 'developed country Parties' means developed country Parties and regional
economic integration organizations constituted by developed countries.

Article 2
Objective

1. The objective of this Convention is to combat desertification and mitigate
the effects of drought in countries experiencing serious drought and/or desertification, particularly in Africa, through effective action at all levels, supported
by international cooperation and partnership arrangements, in the framework
of an integrated approach which is consistent with Agenda 21, with a view
to contributing to the achievement of sustainable development in affected
areas.

2. Achieving this objective will involve long-term integrated strategies that
focus simultaneously, in affected areas, on improved productivity of land, and
the rehabilitation, conservation and sustainable management of land and water
resources, leading to improved living conditions, in particular at the community
level.

Article 3
Principles

In order to achieve the objective of this Convention and to implement its
provisions, the Parties shall be guided, *inter alia*, by the following:

(a) the Parties should ensure that decisions on the design and implementation of programmes to combat desertification and/or mitigate the effects
of drought are taken with the participation of populations and local communities and that an enabling environment is created at higher levels to
facilitate action at national and local levels;

(b) the Parties should, in a spirit of international solidarity and partnership,
improve cooperation and coordination at subregional, regional and international levels, and better focus financial, human, organizational and
technical resources where they are needed;

(c) the Parties should develop, in a spirit of partnership, cooperation among all
levels of government, communities, non-governmental organizations and
landholders to establish a better understanding of the nature and value of
land and scarce water resources in affected areas and to work towards their
sustainable use; and

(d) the Parties should take into full consideration the special needs and circumstances of affected developing country Parties, particularly the least
developed among them.

Part II
General provisions

Article 4
General obligations

1. The Parties shall implement their obligations under this Convention, individually or jointly, either through existing or prospective bilateral and multilateral arrangements or a combination thereof, as appropriate, emphasizing the need to coordinate efforts and develop a coherent long-term strategy at all levels.

2. In pursuing the objective of this Convention, the Parties shall:

(a) adopt an integrated approach addressing the physical, biological and socioeconomic aspects of the processes of desertification and drought;
(b) give due attention, within the relevant international and regional bodies, to the situation of affected developing country Parties with regard to international trade, marketing arrangements and debt with a view to establishing an enabling international economic environment conducive to the promotion of sustainable development;
(c) integrate strategies for poverty eradication into efforts to combat desertification and mitigate the effects of drought;
(d) promote cooperation among affected country Parties in the fields of environmental protection and the conservation of land and water resources, as they relate to desertification and drought;
(e) strengthen subregional, regional and international cooperation;
(f) cooperate within relevant intergovernmental organizations;
(g) determine institutional mechanisms, if appropriate, keeping in mind the need to avoid duplication; and
(h) promote the use of existing bilateral and multilateral financial mechanisms and arrangements that mobilize and channel substantial financial resources to affected developing country Parties in combating desertification and mitigating the effects of drought.

3. Affected developing country Parties are eligible for assistance in the implementation of the Convention.

Article 5
Obligations of affected country Parties

In addition to their obligations pursuant to article 4, affected country Parties undertake to:

(a) give due priority to combating desertification and mitigating the effects of drought, and allocate adequate resources in accordance with their circumstances and capabilities;

(b) establish strategies and priorities, within the framework of sustainable development plans and/or policies, to combat desertification and mitigate the effects of drought;

(c) address the underlying causes of desertification and pay special attention to the socio-economic factors contributing to desertification processes;

(d) promote awareness and facilitate the participation of local populations, particularly women and youth, with the support of non-governmental organizations, in efforts to combat desertification and mitigate the effects of drought; and

(e) provide an enabling environment by strengthening, as appropriate, relevant existing legislation and, where they do not exist, enacting new laws and establishing long-term policies and action programmes.

Article 6
Obligations of developed country Parties

In addition to their general obligations pursuant to article 4, developed country Parties undertake to:

(a) actively support, as agreed, individually or jointly, the efforts of affected developing country Parties, particularly those in Africa, and the least developed countries, to combat desertification and mitigate the effects of drought;

(b) provide substantial financial resources and other forms of support to assist affected developing country Parties, particularly those in Africa, effectively to develop and implement their own long-term plans and strategies to combat desertification and mitigate the effects of drought;

(c) promote the mobilization of new and additional funding pursuant to article 20, paragraph 2 (b);

(d) encourage the mobilization of funding from the private sector and other non-governmental sources; and

(e) promote and facilitate access by affected country Parties, particularly affected developing country Parties, to appropriate technology, knowledge and know-how.

Article 7
Priority for Africa

In implementing this Convention, the Parties shall give priority to affected African country Parties, in the light of the particular situation prevailing in that region, while not neglecting affected developing country Parties in other regions.

Article 8
Relationship with other conventions

1. The Parties shall encourage the coordination of activities carried out under this Convention and, if they are Parties to them, under other relevant international agreements, particularly the United Nations Framework Convention on Climate Change and the Convention on Biological Diversity, in order to derive maximum benefit from activities under each agreement while avoiding duplication of effort. The Parties shall encourage the conduct of joint programmes, particularly in the fields of research, training, systematic observation and information collection and exchange, to the extent that such activities may contribute to achieving the objectives of the agreements concerned.

2. The provisions of this Convention shall not affect the rights and obligations of any Party deriving from a bilateral, regional or international agreement into which it has entered prior to the entry into force of this Convention for it.

Part III
Action programmes, scientific and technical co-operation and supporting measures

Section 1
Action programmes

Article 9
Basic approach

1. In carrying out their obligations pursuant to article 5, affected developing country Parties and any other affected country Party in the framework of its regional implementation annex or, otherwise, that has notified the Permanent Secretariat in writing of its intention to prepare a national action programme, shall, as appropriate, prepare, make public and implement national action programmes, utilizing and building, to the extent possible, on existing relevant successful plans and programmes, and subregional and regional action programmes, as the central element of the strategy to combat desertification and mitigate the effects of drought. Such programmes shall be updated through a continuing participatory process on the basis of lessons from field action, as well as the results of research. The preparation of national action programmes shall be closely interlinked with other efforts to formulate national policies for sustainable development.

2. In the provision by developed country Parties of different forms of assistance under the terms of article 6, priority shall be given to supporting, as agreed, national, subregional and regional action programmes of affected developing country Parties, particularly those in Africa, either directly or through relevant multilateral organizations or both.

3. The Parties shall encourage organs, funds and programmes of the United Nations system and other relevant intergovernmental organizations, academic institutions, the scientific community and non-governmental organizations in a position to cooperate, in accordance with their mandates and capabilities, to support the elaboration, implementation and follow-up of action programmes.

Article 10
National action programmes

1. The purpose of national action programmes is to identify the factors contributing to desertification and practical measures necessary to combat desertification and mitigate the effects of drought.

2. National action programmes shall specify the respective roles of government, local communities and land users and the resources available and needed. They shall, *inter alia*:

(a) incorporate long-term strategies to combat desertification and mitigate the effects of drought, emphasize implementation and be integrated with national policies for sustainable development;

(b) allow for modifications to be made in response to changing circumstances and be sufficiently flexible at the local level to cope with different socio-economic, biological and geo-physical conditions;

(c) give particular attention to the implementation of preventive measures for lands that are not yet degraded or which are only slightly degraded;

(d) enhance national climatological, meteorological and hydrological capabilities and the means to provide for drought early warning;

(e) promote policies and strengthen institutional frameworks which develop cooperation and coordination, in a spirit of partnership, between the donor community, governments at all levels, local populations and community groups, and facilitate access by local populations to appropriate information and technology;

(f) provide for effective participation at the local, national and regional levels of non- governmental organizations and local populations, both women and men, particularly resource users, including farmers and pastoralists and their representative organizations, in policy planning, decision-making, and implementation and review of national action programmes; and

(g) require regular review of, and progress reports on, their implementation.

3. National action programmes may include, *inter alia*, some or all of the following measures to prepare for and mitigate the effects of drought:

(a) establishment and/or strengthening, as appropriate, of early warning systems, including local and national facilities and joint systems at the

subregional and regional levels, and mechanisms for assisting environmentally displaced persons;

(b) strengthening of drought preparedness and management, including
drought contingency plans at the local, national, subregional and regional
levels, which take into consideration seasonal to interannual climate predictions;

(c) establishment and/or strengthening, as appropriate, of food security systems, including storage and marketing facilities, particularly in rural areas;

(d) establishment of alternative livelihood projects that could provide incomes
in drought prone areas; and

(e) development of sustainable irrigation programmes for both crops and
livestock.

4. Taking into account the circumstances and requirements specific to each
affected country Party, national action programmes include, as appropriate,
inter alia, measures in some or all of the following priority fields as they relate
to combating desertification and mitigating the effects of drought in affected
areas and to their populations: promotion of alternative livelihoods and improvement of national economic environments with a view to strengthening
programmes aimed at the eradication of poverty and at ensuring food security; demographic dynamics; sustainable management of natural resources;
sustainable agricultural practices; development and efficient use of various energy sources; institutional and legal frameworks; strengthening of capabilities
for assessment and systematic observation, including hydrological and meteorological services, and capacity building, education and public awareness.

Article 11
Subregional and regional action programmes

Affected country Parties shall consult and cooperate to prepare, as appropriate, in accordance with relevant regional implementation annexes, subregional
and/or regional action programmes to harmonize, complement and increase
the efficiency of national programmes. The provisions of article 10 shall apply
mutatis mutandis to subregional and regional programmes. Such cooperation
may include agreed joint programmes for the sustainable management of transboundary natural resources, scientific and technical cooperation, and strengthening of relevant institutions.

Article 12
International cooperation

Affected country Parties, in collaboration with other Parties and the international community, should cooperate to ensure the promotion of an enabling
international environment in the implementation of the Convention. Such cooperation should also cover fields of technology transfer as well as scientific

research and development, information collection and dissemination and financial resources.

Article 13
Support for the elaboration and implementation of action programmes

1. Measures to support action programmes pursuant to article 9 include, *inter alia*:

(a) financial cooperation to provide predictability for action programmes, allowing for necessary long-term planning;

(b) elaboration and use of cooperation mechanisms which better enable support at the local level, including action through non-governmental organizations, in order to promote the replicability of successful pilot programme activities where relevant;

(c) increased flexibility in project design, funding and implementation in keeping with the experimental, iterative approach indicated for participatory action at the local community level; and

(d) as appropriate, administrative and budgetary procedures that increase the efficiency of cooperation and of support programmes.

2. In providing such support to affected developing country Parties, priority shall be given to African country Parties and to least developed country Parties.

Article 14
Coordination in the elaboration and implementation of action programmes

1. The Parties shall work closely together, directly and through relevant intergovernmental organizations, in the elaboration and implementation of action programmes.

2. The Parties shall develop operational mechanisms, particularly at the national and field levels, to ensure the fullest possible coordination among developed country Parties, developing country Parties and relevant intergovernmental and non-governmental organizations, in order to avoid duplication, harmonize interventions and approaches, and maximize the impact of assistance. In affected developing country Parties, priority will be given to coordinating activities related to international cooperation in order to maximize the efficient use of resources, to ensure responsive assistance, and to facilitate the implementation of national action programmes and priorities under this Convention.

Article 15
Regional implementation annexes

Elements for incorporation in action programmes shall be selected and adapted to the socio- economic, geographical and climatic factors applicable to affected country Parties or regions, as well as to their level of development. Guidelines for the preparation of action programmes and their exact focus and content for particular subregions and regions are set out in the regional implementation annexes.

Section 2
Scientific and technical cooperation

Article 16
Information collection, analysis and exchange

The Parties agree, according to their respective capabilities, to integrate and coordinate the collection, analysis and exchange of relevant short term and long term data and information to ensure systematic observation of land degradation in affected areas and to understand better and assess the processes and effects of drought and desertification. This would help accomplish, *inter alia*, early warning and advance planning for periods of adverse climatic variation in a form suited for practical application by users at all levels, including especially local populations. To this end, they shall, as appropriate:

(a) facilitate and strengthen the functioning of the global network of institutions and facilities for the collection, analysis and exchange of information, as well as for systematic observation at all levels, which shall, *inter alia*:
   (i) aim to use compatible standards and systems;
   (ii) encompass relevant data and stations, including in remote areas;
   (iii) use and disseminate modern technology for data collection, transmission and assessment on land degradation; and
   (iv) link national, subregional and regional data and information centres more closely with global information sources;
(b) ensure that the collection, analysis and exchange of information address the needs of local communities and those of decision makers, with a view to resolving specific problems, and that local communities are involved in these activities;
(c) support and further develop bilateral and multilateral programmes and projects aimed at defining, conducting, assessing and financing the collection, analysis and exchange of data and information, including, *inter alia*, integrated sets of physical, biological, social and economic indicators;
(d) make full use of the expertise of competent intergovernmental and non-governmental organizations, particularly to disseminate relevant information and experiences among target groups in different regions;

(e) give full weight to the collection, analysis and exchange of socio-economic data, and their integration with physical and biological data;

(f) exchange and make fully, openly and promptly available information from all publicly available sources relevant to combating desertification and mitigating the effects of drought; and

(g) subject to their respective national legislation and/or policies, exchange information on local and traditional knowledge, ensuring adequate protection for it and providing appropriate return from the benefits derived from it, on an equitable basis and on mutually agreed terms, to the local populations concerned.

Article 17
Research and development

1. The Parties undertake, according to their respective capabilities, to promote technical and scientific cooperation in the fields of combating desertification and mitigating the effects of drought through appropriate national, subregional, regional and international institutions. To this end, they shall support research activities that:

(a) contribute to increased knowledge of the processes leading to desertification and drought and the impact of, and distinction between, causal factors, both natural and human, with a view to combating desertification and mitigating the effects of drought, and achieving improved productivity as well as sustainable use and management of resources;

(b) respond to well defined objectives, address the specific needs of local populations and lead to the identification and implementation of solutions that improve the living standards of people in affected areas;

(c) protect, integrate, enhance and validate traditional and local knowledge, know-how and practices, ensuring, subject to their respective national legislation and/or policies, that the owners of that knowledge will directly benefit on an equitable basis and on mutually agreed terms from any commercial utilization of it or from any technological development derived from that knowledge;

(d) develop and strengthen national, subregional and regional research capabilities in affected developing country Parties, particularly in Africa, including the development of local skills and the strengthening of appropriate capacities, especially in countries with a weak research base, giving particular attention to multidisciplinary and participative socio- economic research;

(e) take into account, where relevant, the relationship between poverty, migration caused by environmental factors, and desertification;

(f) promote the conduct of joint research programmes between national, subregional, regional and international research organizations, in both the

public and private sectors, for the development of improved, affordable
and accessible technologies for sustainable development through effective
participation of local populations and communities; and

(g) enhance the availability of water resources in affected areas, by means of,
inter alia, cloud-seeding.

2. Research priorities for particular regions and subregions, reflecting different local conditions, should be included in action programmes. The Conference
of the Parties shall review research priorities periodically on the advice of the
Committee on Science and Technology.

Article 18
Transfer, acquisition, adaptation and development of technology

1. The Parties undertake, as mutually agreed and in accordance with their
respective national legislation and/or policies, to promote, finance and/or facilitate the financing of the transfer, acquisition, adaptation and development
of environmentally sound, economically viable and socially acceptable technologies relevant to combating desertification and/or mitigating the effects of
drought, with a view to contributing to the achievement of sustainable development in affected areas. Such cooperation shall be conducted bilaterally or
multilaterally, as appropriate, making full use of the expertise of intergovernmental and non-governmental organizations. The Parties shall, in particular:

(a) fully utilize relevant existing national, subregional, regional and international information systems and clearing-houses for the dissemination of
information on available technologies, their sources, their environmental
risks and the broad terms under which they may be acquired;
(b) facilitate access, in particular by affected developing country Parties, on
favourable terms, including on concessional and preferential terms, as mutually agreed, taking into account the need to protect intellectual property
rights, to technologies most suitable to practical application for specific
needs of local populations, paying special attention to the social, cultural,
economic and environmental impact of such technology;
(c) facilitate technology cooperation among affected country Parties through
financial assistance or other appropriate means;
(d) extend technology cooperation with affected developing country Parties,
including, where relevant, joint ventures, especially to sectors which foster
alternative livelihoods; and
(e) take appropriate measures to create domestic market conditions and incentives, fiscal or otherwise, conducive to the development, transfer, acquisition and adaptation of suitable technology, knowledge, know-how and
practices, including measures to ensure adequate and effective protection
of intellectual property rights.

2. The Parties shall, according to their respective capabilities, and subject to their respective national legislation and/or policies, protect, promote and use in particular relevant traditional and local technology, knowledge, know-how and practices and, to that end, they undertake to:

(a) make inventories of such technology, knowledge, know-how and practices and their potential uses with the participation of local populations, and disseminate such information, where appropriate, in cooperation with relevant intergovernmental and non-governmental organizations;

(b) ensure that such technology, knowledge, know-how and practices are adequately protected and that local populations benefit directly, on an equitable basis and as mutually agreed, from any commercial utilization of them or from any technological development derived therefrom;

(c) encourage and actively support the improvement and dissemination of such technology, knowledge, know-how and practices or of the development of new technology based on them; and

(d) facilitate, as appropriate, the adaptation of such technology, knowledge, know-how and practices to wide use and integrate them with modern technology, as appropriate.

Section 3
Supporting measures

Article 19
Capacity building, education and public awareness

1. The Parties recognize the significance of capacity building – that is to say, institution building, training and development of relevant local and national capacities – in efforts to combat desertification and mitigate the effects of drought. They shall promote, as appropriate, capacity- building:

(a) through the full participation at all levels of local people, particularly at the local level, especially women and youth, with the cooperation of non-governmental and local organizations;

(b) by strengthening training and research capacity at the national level in the field of desertification and drought;

(c) by establishing and/or strengthening support and extension services to disseminate relevant technology methods and techniques more effectively, and by training field agents and members of rural organizations in participatory approaches for the conservation and sustainable use of natural resources;

(d) by fostering the use and dissemination of the knowledge, know-how and practices of local people in technical cooperation programmes, wherever possible;

(e) by adapting, where necessary, relevant environmentally sound technology and traditional methods of agriculture and pastoralism to modern socio-economic conditions;

(f) by providing appropriate training and technology in the use of alternative energy sources, particularly renewable energy resources, aimed particularly at reducing dependence on wood for fuel;

(g) through cooperation, as mutually agreed, to strengthen the capacity of affected developing country Parties to develop and implement programmes in the field of collection, analysis and exchange of information pursuant to article 16;

(h) through innovative ways of promoting alternative livelihoods, including training in new skills;

(i) by training of decision makers, managers, and personnel who are responsible for the collection and analysis of data for the dissemination and use of early warning information on drought conditions and for food production;

(j) through more effective operation of existing national institutions and legal frameworks and, where necessary, creation of new ones, along with strengthening of strategic planning and management; and

(k) by means of exchange visitor programmes to enhance capacity building in affected country Parties through a long-term, interactive process of learning and study.

2. Affected developing country Parties shall conduct, in cooperation with other Parties and competent intergovernmental and non-governmental organizations, as appropriate, an interdisciplinary review of available capacity and facilities at the local and national levels, and the potential for strengthening them.

3. The Parties shall cooperate with each other and through competent intergovernmental organizations, as well as with non-governmental organizations, in undertaking and supporting public awareness and educational programmes in both affected and, where relevant, unaffected country Parties to promote understanding of the causes and effects of desertification and drought and of the importance of meeting the objective of this Convention. To that end, they shall:

(a) organize awareness campaigns for the general public;

(b) promote, on a permanent basis, access by the public to relevant information, and wide public participation in education and awareness activities;

(c) encourage the establishment of associations that contribute to public awareness;

(d) develop and exchange educational and public awareness material, where possible in local languages, exchange and second experts to train personnel of affected developing country Parties in carrying out relevant education and awareness programmes, and fully utilize relevant educational material available in competent international bodies;

(e) assess educational needs in affected areas, elaborate appropriate school cur-ricula and expand, as needed, educational and adult literacy programmes and opportunities for all, in particular for girls and women, on the identi-fication, conservation and sustainable use and management of the natural resources of affected areas; and

(f) develop interdisciplinary participatory programmes integrating desertifi-cation and drought awareness into educational systems and in non-formal, adult, distance and practical educational programmes.

4. The Conference of the Parties shall establish and/or strengthen networks of regional education and training centres to combat desertification and mitigate the effects of drought. These networks shall be coordinated by an institution created or designated for that purpose, in order to train scientific, technical and management personnel and to strengthen existing institutions responsi-ble for education and training in affected country Parties, where appropri-ate, with a view to harmonizing programmes and to organizing exchanges of experience among them. These networks shall cooperate closely with relevant intergovernmental and non-governmental organizations to avoid duplication of effort.

Article 20
Financial resources

1. Given the central importance of financing to the achievement of the ob-jective of the Convention, the Parties, taking into account their capabilities, shall make every effort to ensure that adequate financial resources are available for programmes to combat desertification and mitigate the effects of drought.

2. In this connection, developed country Parties, while giving priority to affected African country Parties without neglecting affected developing country Parties in other regions, in accordance with article 7, undertake to:

(a) mobilize substantial financial resources, including grants and concessional loans, in order to support the implementation of programmes to combat desertification and mitigate the effects of drought;

(b) promote the mobilization of adequate, timely and predictable financial resources, including new and additional funding from the Global Environ-ment Facility of the agreed incremental costs of those activities concerning desertification that relate to its four focal areas, in conformity with the rel-evant provisions of the Instrument establishing the Global Environment Facility;

(c) facilitate through international cooperation the transfer of technology, knowledge and know-how; and

(d) explore, in cooperation with affected developing country Parties, innovative methods and incentives for mobilizing and channelling resources,
   including those of foundations, non- governmental organizations and
   other private sector entities, particularly debt swaps and other innovative means which increase financing by reducing the external debt burden
   of affected developing country Parties, particularly those in Africa.

3. Affected developing country Parties, taking into account their capabilities,
undertake to mobilize adequate financial resources for the implementation of
their national action programmes.

4. In mobilizing financial resources, the Parties shall seek full use and continued qualitative improvement of all national, bilateral and multilateral funding sources and mechanisms, using consortia, joint programmes and parallel
financing, and shall seek to involve private sector funding sources and mechanisms, including those of non-governmental organizations. To this end, the
Parties shall fully utilize the operational mechanisms developed pursuant to
article 14.

5. In order to mobilize the financial resources necessary for affected developing country Parties to combat desertification and mitigate the effects of
drought, the Parties shall:

(a) rationalize and strengthen the management of resources already allocated
   for combating desertification and mitigating the effects of drought by using
   them more effectively and efficiently, assessing their successes and shortcomings, removing hindrances to their effective use and, where necessary,
   reorienting programmes in light of the integrated long-term approach
   adopted pursuant to this Convention;
(b) give due priority and attention within the governing bodies of multilateral
   financial institutions, facilities and funds, including regional development
   banks and funds, to supporting affected developing country Parties, particularly those in Africa, in activities which advance implementation of the
   Convention, notably action programmes they undertake in the framework
   of regional implementation annexes; and
(c) examine ways in which regional and subregional cooperation can be
   strengthened to support efforts undertaken at the national level.

6. Other Parties are encouraged to provide, on a voluntary basis, knowledge,
know-how and techniques related to desertification and/or financial resources
to affected developing country Parties.

7. The full implementation by affected developing country Parties, particularly those in Africa, of their obligations under the Convention will be greatly
assisted by the fulfilment by developed country Parties of their obligations under the Convention, including in particular those regarding financial resources
and transfer of technology. In fulfilling their obligations, developed country

Parties should take fully into account that economic and social development and poverty eradication are the first priorities of affected developing country Parties, particularly those in Africa.

Article 21
Financial mechanisms

1. The Conference of the Parties shall promote the availability of financial mechanisms and shall encourage such mechanisms to seek to maximize the availability of funding for affected developing country Parties, particularly those in Africa, to implement the Convention. To this end, the Conference of the Parties shall consider for adoption *inter alia* approaches and policies that:

(a) facilitate the provision of necessary funding at the national, subregional, regional and global levels for activities pursuant to relevant provisions of the Convention;

(b) promote multiple-source funding approaches, mechanisms and arrangements and their assessment, consistent with article 20;

(c) provide on a regular basis, to interested Parties and relevant intergovernmental and non-governmental organizations, information on available sources of funds and on funding patterns in order to facilitate coordination among them;

(d) facilitate the establishment, as appropriate, of mechanisms, such as national desertification funds, including those involving the participation of non-governmental organizations, to channel financial resources rapidly and efficiently to the local level in affected developing country Parties; and

(e) strengthen existing funds and financial mechanisms at the subregional and regional levels, particularly in Africa, to support more effectively the implementation of the Convention.

2. The Conference of the Parties shall also encourage the provision, through various mechanisms within the United Nations system and through multilateral financial institutions, of support at the national, subregional and regional levels to activities that enable developing country Parties to meet their obligations under the Convention.

3. Affected developing country Parties shall utilize, and where necessary, establish and/or strengthen, national coordinating mechanisms, integrated in national development programmes, that would ensure the efficient use of all available financial resources. They shall also utilize participatory processes involving non-governmental organizations, local groups and the private sector, in raising funds, in elaborating as well as implementing programmes and in assuring access to funding by groups at the local level. These actions can be enhanced by improved coordination and flexible programming on the part of those providing assistance.

4. In order to increase the effectiveness and efficiency of existing financial mechanisms, a Global Mechanism to promote actions leading to the mobilization and channelling of substantial financial resources, including for the transfer of technology, on a grant basis, and/or on concessional or other terms, to affected developing country Parties, is hereby established. This Global Mechanism shall function under the authority and guidance of the Conference of the Parties and be accountable to it.

5. The Conference of the Parties shall identify, at its first ordinary session, an organization to house the Global Mechanism. The Conference of the Parties and the organization it has identified shall agree upon modalities for this Global Mechanism to ensure *inter alia* that such Mechanism:

(a) identifies and draws up an inventory of relevant bilateral and multilateral cooperation programmes that are available to implement the Convention;
(b) provides advice, on request, to Parties on innovative methods of financing and sources of financial assistance and on improving the coordination of cooperation activities at the national level;
(c) provides interested Parties and relevant intergovernmental and non-governmental organizations with information on available sources of funds and on funding patterns in order to facilitate coordination among them; and
(d) reports to the Conference of the Parties, beginning at its second ordinary session, on its activities.

6. The Conference of the Parties shall, at its first session, make appropriate arrangements with the organization it has identified to house the Global Mechanism for the administrative operations of such Mechanism, drawing to the extent possible on existing budgetary and human resources.

7. The Conference of the Parties shall, at its third ordinary session, review the policies, operational modalities and activities of the Global Mechanism accountable to it pursuant to paragraph 4, taking into account the provisions of article 7. On the basis of this review, it shall consider and take appropriate action.

Part IV
Institutions

Article 22
Conference of the Parties

1. A Conference of the Parties is hereby established.

2. The Conference of the Parties is the supreme body of the Convention. It shall make, within its mandate, the decisions necessary to promote its effective implementation. In particular, it shall:

(a) regularly review the implementation of the Convention and the functioning of its institutional arrangements in the light of the experience gained at the national, subregional, regional and international levels and on the basis of the evolution of scientific and technological knowledge;

(b) promote and facilitate the exchange of information on measures adopted by the Parties, and determine the form and timetable for transmitting the information to be submitted pursuant to article 26, review the reports and make recommendations on them;

(c) establish such subsidiary bodies as are deemed necessary for the implementation of the Convention;

(d) review reports submitted by its subsidiary bodies and provide guidance to them;

(e) agree upon and adopt, by consensus, rules of procedure and financial rules for itself and any subsidiary bodies;

(f) adopt amendments to the Convention pursuant to articles 30 and 31;

(g) approve a programme and budget for its activities, including those of its subsidiary bodies, and undertake necessary arrangements for their financing;

(h) as appropriate, seek the cooperation of, and utilize the services of and information provided by, competent bodies or agencies, whether national or international, intergovernmental or non-governmental;

(i) promote and strengthen the relationship with other relevant conventions while avoiding duplication of effort; and

(j) exercise such other functions as may be necessary for the achievement of the objective of the Convention.

3. The Conference of the Parties shall, at its first session, adopt its own rules of procedure, by consensus, which shall include decision-making procedures for matters not already covered by decision-making procedures stipulated in the Convention. Such procedures may include specified majorities required for the adoption of particular decisions.

4. The first session of the Conference of the Parties shall be convened by the interim secretariat referred to in article 35 and shall take place not later than one year after the date of entry into force of the Convention. Unless otherwise decided by the Conference of the Parties, the second, third and fourth ordinary sessions shall be held yearly, and thereafter, ordinary sessions shall be held every two years.

5. Extraordinary sessions of the Conference of the Parties shall be held at such other times as may be decided either by the Conference of the Parties in ordinary session or at the written request of any Party, provided that, within three months of the request being communicated to the Parties by the Permanent Secretariat, it is supported by at least one third of the Parties.

6. At each ordinary session, the Conference of the Parties shall elect a Bureau. The structure and functions of the Bureau shall be determined in the rules of procedure. In appointing the Bureau, due regard shall be paid to the need to ensure equitable geographical distribution and adequate representation of affected country Parties, particularly those in Africa.

7. The United Nations, its specialized agencies and any State member thereof or observers thereto not Party to the Convention, may be represented at sessions of the Conference of the Parties as observers. Any body or agency, whether national or international, governmental or non-governmental, which is qualified in matters covered by the Convention, and which has informed the Permanent Secretariat of its wish to be represented at a session of the Conference of the Parties as an observer, may be so admitted unless at least one third of the Parties present object. The admission and participation of observers shall be subject to the rules of procedure adopted by the Conference of the Parties.

8. The Conference of the Parties may request competent national and international organizations which have relevant expertise to provide it with information relevant to article 16, paragraph (g), article 17, paragraph 1 (c) and article 18, paragraph 2(b).

Article 23
Permanent Secretariat

1. A Permanent Secretariat is hereby established.
2. The functions of the Permanent Secretariat shall be:

(a) to make arrangements for sessions of the Conference of the Parties and its subsidiary bodies established under the Convention and to provide them with services as required;
(b) to compile and transmit reports submitted to it;
(c) to facilitate assistance to affected developing country Parties, on request, particularly those in Africa, in the compilation and communication of information required under the Convention;
(d) to coordinate its activities with the secretariats of other relevant international bodies and conventions;
(e) to enter, under the guidance of the Conference of the Parties, into such administrative and contractual arrangements as may be required for the effective discharge of its functions;
(f) to prepare reports on the execution of its functions under this Convention and present them to the Conference of the Parties; and
(g) to perform such other secretariat functions as may be determined by the Conference of the Parties.

3. The Conference of the Parties, at its first session, shall designate a Permanent Secretariat and make arrangements for its functioning.

Article 24
Committee on Science and Technology

1. A Committee on Science and Technology is hereby established as a subsidiary body of the Conference of the Parties to provide it with information and advice on scientific and technological matters relating to combating desertification and mitigating the effects of drought. The Committee shall meet in conjunction with the ordinary sessions of the Conference of the Parties and shall be multidisciplinary and open to the participation of all Parties. It shall be composed of government representatives competent in the relevant fields of expertise. The Conference of the Parties shall decide, at its first session, on the terms of reference of the Committee.

2. The Conference of the Parties shall establish and maintain a roster of independent experts with expertise and experience in the relevant fields. The roster shall be based on nominations received in writing from the Parties, taking into account the need for a multidisciplinary approach and broad geographical representation.

3. The Conference of the Parties may, as necessary, appoint ad hoc panels to provide it, through the Committee, with information and advice on specific issues regarding the state of the art in fields of science and technology relevant to combating desertification and mitigating the effects of drought. These panels shall be composed of experts whose names are taken from the roster, taking into account the need for a multidisciplinary approach and broad geographical representation. These experts shall have scientific backgrounds and field experience and shall be appointed by the Conference of the Parties on the recommendation of the Committee. The Conference of the Parties shall decide on the terms of reference and the modalities of work of these panels.

Article 25
Networking of institutions, agencies and bodies

1. The Committee on Science and Technology shall, under the supervision of the Conference of the Parties, make provision for the undertaking of a survey and evaluation of the relevant existing networks, institutions, agencies and bodies willing to become units of a network. Such a network shall support the implementation of the Convention.

2. On the basis of the results of the survey and evaluation referred to in paragraph 1, the Committee on Science and Technology shall make recommendations to the Conference of the Parties on ways and means to facilitate and strengthen networking of the units at the local, national and other levels,

with a view to ensuring that the thematic needs set out in articles 16 to 19 are addressed.

3. Taking into account these recommendations, the Conference of the Parties shall:

(a) identify those national, subregional, regional and international units that are most appropriate for networking, and recommend operational procedures, and a time frame, for them; and

(b) identify the units best suited to facilitating and strengthening such networking at all levels.

Part V
Procedures

Article 26
Communication of information

1. Each Party shall communicate to the Conference of the Parties for consideration at its ordinary sessions, through the Permanent Secretariat, reports on the measures which it has taken for the implementation of the Convention. The Conference of the Parties shall determine the timetable for submission and the format of such reports.

2. Affected country Parties shall provide a description of the strategies established pursuant to article 5 and of any relevant information on their implementation.

3. Affected country Parties which implement action programmes pursuant to articles 9 to 15 shall provide a detailed description of the programmes and of their implementation.

4. Any group of affected country Parties may make a joint communication on measures taken at the subregional and/or regional levels in the framework of action programmes.

5. Developed country Parties shall report on measures taken to assist in the preparation and implementation of action programmes, including information on the financial resources they have provided, or are providing, under the Convention.

6. Information communicated pursuant to paragraphs 1 to 4 shall be transmitted by the Permanent Secretariat as soon as possible to the Conference of the Parties and to any relevant subsidiary body.

7. The Conference of the Parties shall facilitate the provision to affected developing countries, particularly those in Africa, on request, of technical and financial support in compiling and communicating information in accordance with this article, as well as identifying the technical and financial needs associated with action programmes.

Article 27
Measures to resolve questions on implementation

The Conference of the Parties shall consider and adopt procedures and institutional mechanisms for the resolution of questions that may arise with regard to the implementation of the Convention.

Article 28
Settlement of disputes

1. Parties shall settle any dispute between them concerning the interpretation or application of the Convention through negotiation or other peaceful means of their own choice.

2. When ratifying, accepting, approving, or acceding to the Convention, or at any time thereafter, a Party which is not a regional economic integration organization may declare in a written instrument submitted to the Depositary that, in respect of any dispute concerning the interpretation or application of the Convention, it recognizes one or both of the following means of dispute settlement as compulsory in relation to any Party accepting the same obligation:

(a) arbitration in accordance with procedures adopted by the Conference of the Parties in an annex as soon as practicable;
(b) submission of the dispute to the International Court of Justice.

3. A Party which is a regional economic integration organization may make a declaration with like effect in relation to arbitration in accordance with the procedure referred to in paragraph 2 (a).

4. A declaration made pursuant to paragraph 2 shall remain in force until it expires in accordance with its terms or until three months after written notice of its revocation has been deposited with the Depositary.

5. The expiry of a declaration, a notice of revocation or a new declaration shall not in any way affect proceedings pending before an arbitral tribunal or the International Court of Justice unless the Parties to the dispute otherwise agree.

6. If the Parties to a dispute have not accepted the same or any procedure pursuant to paragraph 2 and if they have not been able to settle their dispute within twelve months following notification by one Party to another that a dispute exists between them, the dispute shall be submitted to conciliation at the request of any Party to the dispute, in accordance with procedures adopted by the Conference of the Parties in an annex as soon as practicable.

Article 29
Status of annexes

1. Annexes form an integral part of the Convention and, unless expressly provided otherwise, a reference to the Convention also constitutes a reference to its annexes.

2. The Parties shall interpret the provisions of the annexes in a manner that is in conformity with their rights and obligations under the articles of this Convention.

Article 30
Amendments to the Convention

1. Any Party may propose amendments to the Convention.

2. Amendments to the Convention shall be adopted at an ordinary session of the Conference of the Parties. The text of any proposed amendment shall be communicated to the Parties by the Permanent Secretariat at least six months before the meeting at which it is proposed for adoption. The Permanent Secretariat shall also communicate proposed amendments to the signatories to the Convention.

3. The Parties shall make every effort to reach agreement on any proposed amendment to the Convention by consensus. If all efforts at consensus have been exhausted and no agreement reached, the amendment shall, as a last resort, be adopted by a two-thirds majority vote of the Parties present and voting at the meeting. The adopted amendment shall be communicated by the Permanent Secretariat to the Depositary, who shall circulate it to all Parties for their ratification, acceptance, approval or accession.

4. Instruments of ratification, acceptance, approval or accession in respect of an amendment shall be deposited with the Depositary. An amendment adopted pursuant to paragraph 3 shall enter into force for those Parties having accepted it on the ninetieth day after the date of receipt by the Depositary of an instrument of ratification, acceptance, approval or accession by at least two thirds of the Parties to the Convention which were Parties at the time of the adoption of the amendment.

5. The amendment shall enter into force for any other Party on the ninetieth day after the date on which that Party deposits with the Depositary its instrument of ratification, acceptance or approval of, or accession to the said amendment.

6. For the purposes of this article and article 31, 'Parties present and voting' means Parties present and casting an affirmative or negative vote.

Article 31
Adoption and amendment of annexes

1. Any additional annex to the Convention and any amendment to an annex shall be proposed and adopted in accordance with the procedure for

amendment of the Convention set forth in article 30, provided that, in adopting an additional regional implementation annex or amendment to any regional implementation annex, the majority provided for in that article shall include a two-thirds majority vote of the Parties of the region concerned present and voting. The adoption or amendment of an annex shall be communicated by the Depositary to all Parties.

2. An annex, other than an additional regional implementation annex, or an amendment to an annex, other than an amendment to any regional implementation annex, that has been adopted in accordance with paragraph 1, shall enter into force for all Parties to the Convention six months after the date of communication by the Depositary to such Parties of the adoption of such annex or amendment, except for those Parties that have notified the Depositary in writing within that period of their non-acceptance of such annex or amendment. Such annex or amendment shall enter into force for Parties which withdraw their notification of non-acceptance on the ninetieth day after the date on which withdrawal of such notification has been received by the Depositary.

3. An additional regional implementation annex or amendment to any regional implementation annex that has been adopted in accordance with paragraph 1, shall enter into force for all Parties to the Convention six months after the date of the communication by the Depositary to such Parties of the adoption of such annex or amendment, except with respect to:

(a) any Party that has notified the Depositary in writing, within such six month period, of its non-acceptance of that additional regional implementation annex or of the amendment to the regional implementation annex, in which case such annex or amendment shall enter into force for Parties which withdraw their notification of non-acceptance on the ninetieth day after the date on which withdrawal of such notification has been received by the Depositary; and

(b) any Party that has made a declaration with respect to additional regional implementation annexes or amendments to regional implementation annexes in accordance with article 34, paragraph 4, in which case any such annex or amendment shall enter into force for such a Party on the ninetieth day after the date of deposit with the Depositary of its instrument of ratification, acceptance, approval or accession with respect to such annex or amendment.

4. If the adoption of an annex or an amendment to an annex involves an amendment to the Convention, that annex or amendment to an annex shall not enter into force until such time as the amendment to the Convention enters into force.

Article 32
Right to vote

1. Except as provided for in paragraph 2, each Party to the Convention shall have one vote.

2. Regional economic integration organizations, in matters within their competence, shall exercise their right to vote with a number of votes equal to the number of their member States that are Parties to the Convention. Such an organization shall not exercise its right to vote if any of its member States exercises its right, and vice versa.

Part VI
Final provisions

Article 33
Signature

This Convention shall be opened for signature at Paris, on 14–15 October 1994, by States Members of the United Nations or any of its specialized agencies or that are Parties to the Statute of the International Court of Justice and by regional economic integration organizations. It shall remain open for signature, thereafter, at the United Nations Headquarters in New York until 13 October 1995.

Article 34
Ratification, acceptance, approval and accession

1. The Convention shall be subject to ratification, acceptance, approval or accession by States and by regional economic integration organizations. It shall be open for accession from the day after the date on which the Convention is closed for signature. Instruments of ratification, acceptance, approval or accession shall be deposited with the Depositary.

2. Any regional economic integration organization which becomes a Party to the Convention without any of its member States being a Party to the Convention shall be bound by all the obligations under the Convention. Where one or more member States of such an organization are also Party to the Convention, the organization and its member States shall decide on their respective responsibilities for the performance of their obligations under the Convention. In such cases, the organization and the member States shall not be entitled to exercise rights under the Convention concurrently.

3. In their instruments of ratification, acceptance, approval or accession, regional economic integration organizations shall declare the extent of their competence with respect to the matters governed by the Convention. They shall also promptly inform the Depositary, who shall in turn inform the Parties, of any substantial modification in the extent of their competence.

4. In its instrument of ratification, acceptance, approval or accession, any Party may declare that, with respect to it, any additional regional implementation annex or any amendment to any regional implementation annex shall enter into force only upon the deposit of its instrument of ratification, acceptance, approval or accession with respect thereto.

Article 35
Interim arrangements

The secretariat functions referred to in article 23 will be carried out on an interim basis by the secretariat established by the General Assembly of the United Nations in its resolution 47/188 of 22 December 1992, until the completion of the first session of the Conference of the Parties.

Article 36
Entry into force

1. The Convention shall enter into force on the ninetieth day after the date of deposit of the fiftieth instrument of ratification, acceptance, approval or accession.

2. For each State or regional economic integration organization ratifying, accepting, approving or acceding to the Convention after the deposit of the fiftieth instrument of ratification, acceptance, approval or accession, the Convention shall enter into force on the ninetieth day after the date of deposit by such State or regional economic integration organization of its instrument of ratification, acceptance, approval or accession.

3. For the purposes of paragraphs 1 and 2, any instrument deposited by a regional economic integration organization shall not be counted as additional to those deposited by States members of the organization.

Article 37
Reservations

No reservations may be made to this Convention.

Article 38
Withdrawal

1. At any time after three years from the date on which the Convention has entered into force for a Party, that Party may withdraw from the Convention by giving written notification to the Depositary.

2. Any such withdrawal shall take effect upon expiry of one year from the date of receipt by the Depositary of the notification of withdrawal, or on such later date as may be specified in the notification of withdrawal.

Article 39
Depositary

The Secretary-General of the United Nations shall be the Depositary of the Convention.

Article 40
Authentic texts

The original of the present Convention, of which the Arabic, Chinese, English, French, Russian and Spanish texts are equally authentic, shall be deposited with the Secretary-General of the United Nations.

IN WITNESS WHEREOF the undersigned, being duly authorized to that effect, have signed the present Convention.

DONE AT Paris, this 17th day of June one thousand nine hundred and ninety-four.

[The text of the Annexes is omitted]

Annex I
Regional implementation Annex for Africa

[. . .]

Annex II
Regional implementation Annex for Asia

[. . .]

Annex III
Regional implementation Annex for Latin America and the Caribbean

[. . .]

Annex IV
Regional implementation Annex for the Northern Mediterranean

[. . .]

Annex V
Regional implementation Annex for Central and Eastern Europe

[. . .]

PART VIA

Hazardous substances and activities: nuclear

Treaty Banning Nuclear Weapon Tests in the Atmosphere, in Outer Space and Under Water, 5 August 1963

Editorial note

In addition to being a step towards general disarmament, the Treaty Banning Nuclear Weapons Tests in the Atmosphere, in Outer Space and Under Water seeks to protect the environment from contamination by radioactive substances. Parties undertake to 'prohibit, prevent or not carry out' any nuclear explosion in their jurisdiction or control that is in the atmosphere, beyond its limits, or under water (Article I(1)(a)). In addition, such tests are banned if they cause radioactive debris to be present outside territorial limits of the State carrying out the test (Article I(1)(b)). Parties further undertake to refrain from 'in any way participating in' any nuclear explosion that would have the effects outlined above (Article I(2)).

Amendments to the Treaty are considered at conferences to which all Parties are invited, convened at the request of at least one-third of the Parties (Article II(1)). Any amendment must have the approval of a majority of all Parties, including that of all original Parties (named in the Preamble) and enters into force for all Parties when ratified by a majority of all Parties including all Original Parties (Article II(2)). Withdrawal from the Treaty is permissible if 'extraordinary events ... have jeopardized the supreme interests of its country' (Article IV).

Date of signature:	5 August 1963
Entry into force:	10 October 1963
Depositary:	Russian Federation, USA and United Kingdom
Contracting Parties:	Afghanistan, Antigua and Barbuda, Argentina, Armenia, Australia, Austria, Bahamas, Bangladesh, Belarus, Belgium, Benin, Bhutan, Bolivia, Botswana, Brazil, Bulgaria, Canada, Cape Verde, Central African Republic, Chad, Chile, Colombia, Congo (Democratic Republic of), Costa Rica, Cote d'Ivoire, Croatia, Cyprus, Czech Republic, Denmark, Dominican Republic, Ecuador,

Egypt, El Salvador, Equatorial Guinea, Fiji, Finland, Gabon, Gambia, Germany, Ghana, Greece, Guatemala, Guinea Bissau, Honduras, Hungary, Iceland, India, Indonesia, Iran (Islamic Republic of), Iraq, Ireland, Israel, Italy, Jamaica, Japan, Jordan, Kenya, Kuwait, Lao People's Democratic Republic, Lebanon, Liberia, Libyan Arab Jamahiriya, Luxembourg, Madagascar, Malawi, Malaysia, Malta, Mauritania, Mauritius, Mexico, Mongolia, Morocco, Myanmar, Nepal, Netherlands, New Zealand, Nicaragua, Niger, Nigeria, Norway, Pakistan, Panama, Papua New Guinea, Peru, Philippines, Poland, Republic of Korea, Romania, Russian Federation, Rwanda, Samoa, San Marino, Senegal, Seychelles, Sierra Leone, Singapore, Slovakia, Slovenia, South Africa, Spain, Sri Lanka, Sudan, Suriname, Swaziland, Sweden, Switzerland, Syrian Arab Republic, Taiwan, Tanzania (United Republic of), Thailand, Togo, Tonga, Trinidad and Tobago, Tunisia, Turkey, Uganda, Ukraine, United Kingdom, United States of America, Uruguay, Venezuela, Zambia.

Treaty Banning Nuclear Weapon Tests in the Atmosphere, in Outer Space and Under Water

The Governments of the United States of America, the United Kingdom of Great Britain and Northern Ireland, and the Union of Soviet Socialist Republics, hereinafter referred to as the 'Original Parties',

Proclaiming as their principal aim the speediest possible achievement of an agreement on general and complete disarmament under strict international control in accordance with the objectives of the United Nations which would put an end to the armaments race and eliminate the incentive to the production and testing of all kinds of weapons, including nuclear weapons,

Seeking to achieve the discontinuance of all test explosions of nuclear weapons for all time, determined to continue negotiations to this end, and desiring to put an end to the contamination of man's environment by radioactive substances,

Have agreed as follows:

Article I

1. Each of the Parties to this Treaty undertakes to prohibit, to prevent, and not to carry out any nuclear weapon test explosion, or any other nuclear explosion, at any place under its jurisdiction or control:

(a) in the atmosphere; beyond its limits, including outer space; or under water, including territorial waters or high seas; or

(b) in any other environment if such explosion causes radioactive debris to be present outside the territorial limits of the State under whose jurisdiction or control such explosion is conducted. It is understood in this connection that the provisions of this subparagraph are without prejudice to the conclusion of a treaty resulting in the permanent banning of all nuclear test explosions, including all such explosions underground, the conclusion of which, as the Parties have stated in the Preamble to this Treaty, they seek to achieve.

2. Each of the Parties to this Treaty undertakes furthermore to refrain from causing, encouraging, or in any way participating in, the carrying out of any nuclear weapon test explosion, or any other nuclear explosion, anywhere which would take place in any of the environments described, or have the effect referred to, in paragraph 1 of this Article.

Article II

1. Any Party may propose amendments to this Treaty. The text of any proposed amendment shall be submitted to the Depositary Governments which shall circulate it to all Parties to this Treaty. Thereafter, if requested to do so by one-third or more of the Parties, the Depositary Governments shall convene a conference, to which they shall invite all the Parties, to consider such amendment.

2. Any amendment to this Treaty must be approved by a majority of the votes of all the Parties to this Treaty, including the votes of all of the Original Parties. The amendment shall enter into force for all Parties upon the deposit of instruments of ratification by a majority of all the Parties, including the instruments of ratification of all of the Original Parties.

Article III

1. This Treaty shall be open to all States for signature. Any State which does not sign this Treaty before its entry into force in accordance with paragraph 3 of this Article may accede to it at any time.

2. This Treaty shall be subject to ratification by signatory States. Instruments of ratification and instruments of accession shall be deposited with the Governments of the Original Parties – the United States of America, the United Kingdom of Great Britain and Northern Ireland, and the Union of Soviet Socialist Republics – which are hereby designated the Depositary Governments.

3. This Treaty shall enter into force after its ratification by all the Original Parties and the deposit of their instruments of ratification.

4. For States whose instruments of ratification or accession are deposited subsequent to the entry into force of this Treaty, it shall enter into force on the date of the deposit of their instruments of ratification or accession.

5. The Depositary Governments shall promptly inform all signatory and acceding States of the date of each signature, the date of deposit of each instrument of ratification of and accession to this Treaty, the date of its entry into force, and the date of receipt of any requests for conferences or other notices.

6. This Treaty shall be registered by the Depositary Governments pursuant to Article 102 of the Charter of the United Nations.

Article IV

This Treaty shall be of unlimited duration.

Each Party shall in exercising its national sovereignty have the right to withdraw from the Treaty if it decides that extraordinary events, related to the subject matter of this Treaty, have jeopardized the supreme interests of its country. It shall give notice of such withdrawal to all other Parties to the Treaty three months in advance.

Article V

This Treaty, of which the English and Russian texts are equally authentic, shall be deposited in the archives of the Depositary Governments. Duly certified copies of this Treaty shall be transmitted by the Depositary Governments to the Governments of the signatory and acceding States.

IN WITNESS WHEREOF the undersigned, duly authorized, have signed this Treaty.

DONE in triplicate at the city of Moscow the fifth day of August, one thousand nine hundred and sixty-three.

Convention on Nuclear Safety, 20 September 1994

Editorial note

The Convention on Nuclear Safety was adopted under the auspices of the International Atomic Energy Agency (IAEA). The Convention has three objectives: to achieve and maintain a high level of nuclear safety worldwide; to establish and maintain effective defences in nuclear installations against potential radiological hazards to protect individuals, society and the environment from harmful effects of ionizing radiation; and to prevent accidents with radiological consequences and to mitigate such consequences should they occur (Article 1). Parties are required to establish a national regulatory body and to establish and maintain a legislative and regulatory framework to govern the safety of nuclear installations, providing *inter alia* for the establishment of applicable national safety requirements and regulations, a system of licensing, a system of regulatory inspection and assessment, and the enforcement of applicable regulations and of the terms of licences, including suspension, modification or revocation (Articles 7 and 8). Parties must give effect to 'general safety considerations' by prioritising safety, and must ensure adequate financial and human resources; implement quality assurance programmes; carry out comprehensive and systematic safety assessment; ensure that radiation exposure to workers and the public is kept as low as reasonably achievable (and that no individual shall be exposed to radiation doses which exceed prescribed national dose limits); and establish on-site and off-site emergency preparedness plans (Articles 10–16). In relation to safety, siting should be evaluated by reference to factors likely to affect safety for the projected lifetime of the installation and for impacts on individuals, society and the environment; design and construction should provide for 'several reliable levels and methods of protection' against the release of radioactive materials, technologies incorporated in the design and construction should be proven by experience or qualified by testing or analysis, and the design should allow for reliable, stable and easily manageable operation; and minimum standards are to be applied with regard to operation, including the principle that the generation of radioactive waste resulting from the operation of a nuclear installation should be kept to the minimum practicable for the process concerned, in activity and in volumes (Articles 17–19). The meeting of the

Contracting Parties is to review reports submitted by the Parties at intervals not exceeding three years (Articles 20 and 21). In the event of disagreements, Parties are to consult with a view to resolving the disagreement (Article 29).

Date of signature: 20 September 1994

Entry into force: 24 October 1996

Depositary: Director-General of the IAEA

Contracting Parties: Argentina, Armenia, Australia, Austria, Bangladesh, Belarus, Belgium, Brazil, Bulgaria, Canada, Chile, China, Croatia, Cyprus, Czech Republic, Denmark, Egypt, Finland, France, Germany, Greece, Hungary, Indonesia, Ireland, Italy, Japan, Korea (Republic of), Latvia, Lebanon, Lithuania, Luxembourg, Mali, Mexico, Moldova (Republic of), Netherlands, Norway, Pakistan, Peru, Poland, Portugal, Romania, Russian Federation, Singapore, Slovakia, Slovenia, South Africa, Spain, Sri Lanka, Sweden, Switzerland, Turkey, Ukraine, United Kingdom, United States of America, EURATOM.

Website: www.iaea.org/worldatom/Documents/Legal/ nukesafety.shtml

Convention on Nuclear Safety

Preamble

The Contracting Parties

   i. *Aware* of the importance to the international community of ensuring that the use of nuclear energy is safe, well regulated and environmentally sound;
  ii. *Reaffirming* the necessity of continuing to promote a high level of nuclear safety worldwide;
 iii. *Reaffirming* that responsibility for nuclear safety rests with the State having jurisdiction over a nuclear installation;
  iv. *Desiring* to promote an effective nuclear safety culture;
   v. *Aware* that accidents at nuclear installations have the potential for trans-boundary impacts;
  vi. *Keeping* in mind the Convention on the Physical Protection of Nuclear Material (1979), the Convention on Early Notification of a Nuclear Accident (1986), and the Convention on Assistance in the Case of a Nuclear Accident or Radiological Emergency (1986);

vii. *Affirming* the importance of international co-operation for the enhancement of nuclear safety through existing bilateral and multilateral mechanisms and the establishment of this incentive Convention;

viii. *Recognizing* that this Convention entails a commitment to the application of fundamental safety principles for nuclear installations rather than of detailed safety standards and that there are internationally formulated safety guidelines which are updated from time to time and so can provide guidance on contemporary means of achieving a high level of safety;

ix. *Affirming* the need to begin promptly the development of an international convention on the safety of radioactive waste management as soon as the ongoing process to develop waste management safety fundamentals has resulted in broad international agreement;

x. *Recognizing* the usefulness of further technical work in connection with the safety of other parts of the nuclear fuel cycle, and that this work may, in time, facilitate the development of current or future international instruments;

Have agreed as follows:

Chapter 1
Objectives, definitions and scope of application

Article 1
Objectives

The objectives of this Convention are:

i. to achieve and maintain a high level of nuclear safety worldwide through the enhancement of national measures and international co-operation including, where appropriate, safety-related technical co-operation;

ii. to establish and maintain effective defences in nuclear installations against potential radiological hazards in order to protect individuals, society and the environment from harmful effects of ionizing radiation from such installations;

iii. to prevent accidents with radiological consequences and to mitigate such consequences should they occur.

Article 2
Definitions

For the purpose of this Convention:

i. 'nuclear installation' means for each Contracting Party any land-based civil nuclear power plant under its jurisdiction including such storage, handling and treatment facilities for radioactive materials as are on the same site and are directly related to the operation of the nuclear power plant. Such a plant ceases to be a nuclear installation when all nuclear fuel elements have been removed permanently from the reactor core and have been stored safely in accordance with approved procedures, and a decommissioning programme has been agreed to by the regulatory body.

ii. 'regulatory body' means for each Contracting Party any body or bodies given the legal authority by that Contracting Party to grant licences and to regulate the siting, design, construction, commissioning, operation or decommissioning of nuclear installations.

iii. 'licence' means any authorization granted by the regulatory body to the applicant to have the responsibility for the siting, design, construction, commissioning, operation or decommissioning of a nuclear installation.

Article 3
Scope of application

This Convention shall apply to the safety of nuclear installations.

Chapter 2
Obligations

a. General provisions

Article 4
Implementing measures

Each Contracting Party shall take, within the framework of its national law, the legislative, regulatory and administrative measures and other steps necessary for implementing its obligations under this Convention.

Article 5
Reporting

Each Contracting Party shall submit for review, prior to each meeting referred to in Article 20, a report on the measures it has taken to implement each of the obligations of this Convention

Article 6
Existing Nuclear Installations

Each Contracting Party shall take the appropriate steps to ensure that the safety of nuclear installations existing at the time the Convention enters into force for that Contracting Party is reviewed as soon as possible. When necessary in the context of this Convention, the Contracting Party shall ensure that all reasonably practicable improvements are made as a matter of urgency to upgrade the safety of the nuclear installation. If such upgrading cannot be achieved, plans should be implemented to shut down the nuclear installation as soon as practically possible. The timing of the shut-down may take into account the whole energy context and possible alternatives as well as the social, environmental and economic impact.

b. Legislation and regulation

Article 7
Legislative and Regulatory Framework

1. Each Contracting Party shall establish and maintain a legislative and regulatory framework to govern the safety of nuclear installations.

2. The legislative and regulatory framework shall provide for:

i. the establishment of applicable national safety requirements and regulations;
ii. a system of licensing with regard to nuclear installations and the prohibition of the operation of a nuclear installation without a licence:
iii. a system of regulatory inspection and assessment of nuclear installations to ascertain compliance with applicable regulations and the terms of licences;
iv. the enforcement of applicable regulations and of the terms of licences, including suspension, modification or revocation.

Article 8
Regulatory body

1. Each Contracting Party shall establish or designate a regulatory body entrusted with the implementation of the legislative and regulatory framework referred to in Article 7, and provided with adequate authority, competence and financial and human resources to fulfil its assigned responsibilities.

2. Each Contracting Party shall take the appropriate steps to ensure an effective separation between the functions of the regulatory body and those of any other body or organization concerned with the promotion or utilization of nuclear energy.

Article 9
Responsibility of the licence holder

Each Contracting Party shall ensure that prime responsibility for the safety of a nuclear installation rests with the holder of the relevant licence and shall take the appropriate steps to ensure that each such licence holder meets its responsibility.

c. General safety considerations

Article 10
Priority to safety

Each Contracting Party shall take the appropriate steps to ensure that all organizations engaged in activities directly related to nuclear installations shall establish policies that give due priority to nuclear safety.

Article 11
Financial and human resources

1. Each Contracting Party shall take the appropriate steps to ensure that adequate financial resources are available to support the safety of each nuclear installation throughout its life.

2. Each Contracting Party shall take the appropriate steps to ensure that sufficient numbers of qualified staff with appropriate education, training and retraining are available for all safety-related activities in or for each nuclear installation, throughout its life.

Article 12
Human factors

Each Contracting Party shall take the appropriate steps to ensure that the capabilities and limitations of human performance are taken into account throughout the life of a nuclear installation.

Article 13
Quality assurance

Each Contracting Party shall take the appropriate steps to ensure that quality assurance programmes are established and implemented with a view to providing confidence that specified requirements for all activities important to nuclear safety are satisfied throughout the life of a nuclear installation.

Article 14
Assessment and verification of safety

Each Contracting Party shall take the appropriate steps to ensure that:

i. comprehensive and systematic safety assessments are carried out before the construction and commissioning of a nuclear installation and throughout its life. Such assessments shall be well documented, subsequently updated in the light of operating experience and significant new safety information, and reviewed under the authority of the regulatory body;

ii. verification by analysis, surveillance, testing and inspection is carried out to ensure that the physical state and the operation of a nuclear installation continue to be in accordance with its design, applicable national safety requirements, and operational limits and conditions.

Article 15
Radiation protection

Each Contracting Party shall take the appropriate steps to ensure that in all operational states the radiation exposure to the workers and the public caused by a nuclear installation shall be kept as low as reasonably achievable and that no individual shall be exposed to radiation doses which exceed prescribed national dose limits.

Article 16
Emergency preparedness

1. Each Contracting Party shall take the appropriate steps to ensure that there are on-site and off-site emergency plans that are routinely tested for nuclear installations and cover the activities to be carried out in the event of an emergency.

For any new nuclear installation, such plans shall be prepared and tested before it commences operation above a low power level agreed by the regulatory body.

2. Each Contracting Party shall take the appropriate steps to ensure that, insofar as they are likely to be affected by a radiological emergency, its own population and the competent authorities of the States in the vicinity of the nuclear installation are provided with appropriate information for emergency planning and response.

3. Contracting Parties which do not have a nuclear installation on their territory, insofar as they are likely to be affected in the event of a radiological emergency at a nuclear installation in the vicinity, shall take the appropriate steps for the preparation and testing of emergency plans for their territory that cover the activities to be carried out in the event of such an emergency.

d. Safety of installations

Article 17
Siting

Each Contracting Party shall take the appropriate steps to ensure that appropriate procedures are established and implemented:

  i. for evaluating all relevant site-related factors likely to affect the safety of a nuclear installation for its projected lifetime;
 ii. for evaluating the likely safety impact of a proposed nuclear installation on individuals, society and the environment;
iii. for re-evaluating as necessary all relevant factors referred to in sub-paragraphs (i) and (ii) so as to ensure the continued safety acceptability of the nuclear installation;
 iv. for consulting Contracting Parties in the vicinity of a proposed nuclear installation, insofar as they are likely to be affected by that installation and, upon request providing the necessary information to such Contracting Parties, in order to enable them to evaluate and make their own assessment of the likely safety impact on their own territory of the nuclear installation.

Article 18
Design and construction

Each Contracting Party shall take the appropriate steps to ensure that:

i. the design and construction of a nuclear installation provides for several reliable levels and methods of protection (defense in depth) against the release of radioactive materials, with a view to preventing the occurrence of accidents and to mitigating their radiological consequences should they occur;

ii. the technologies incorporated in the design and construction of a nuclear installation are proven by experience or qualified by testing or analysis;

iii. the design of a nuclear installation allows for reliable, stable and easily manageable operation, with specific consideration of human factors and the man-machine interface.

Article 19
Operation

Each Contracting Party shall take the appropriate steps to ensure that:

i. the initial authorization to operate a nuclear installation is based upon an appropriate safety analysis and a commissioning programme demonstrating that the installation, as constructed, is consistent with design and safety requirements;

ii. operational limits and conditions derived from the safety analysis, tests and operational experience are defined and revised as necessary for identifying safe boundaries for operation;

iii. operation, maintenance, inspection and testing of a nuclear installation are conducted in accordance with approved procedures;

iv. procedures are established for responding to anticipated operational occurrences and to accidents;

v. necessary engineering and technical support in all safety-related fields is available throughout the lifetime of a nuclear installation;

vi. incidents significant to safety are reported in a timely manner by the holder of the relevant licence to the regulatory body;

vii. programmes to collect and analyse operating experience are established, the results obtained and the conclusions drawn are acted upon and that existing mechanisms are used to share important experience with international bodies and with other operating organizations and regulatory bodies;

viii. the generation of radioactive waste resulting from the operation of a nuclear installation is kept to the minimum practicable for the process concerned, both in activity and in volume, and any necessary treatment and storage of spent fuel and waste directly related to the operation and on the same site as that of the nuclear installation take into consideration conditioning and disposal.

Chapter 3
Meetings of the Contracting Parties

Article 20
Review meetings

1. The Contracting Parties shall hold meetings (hereinafter referred to as 'review meetings') for the purpose of reviewing the reports submitted pursuant to Article 5 in accordance with the procedures adopted under Article 22.

2. Subject to the provisions of Article 24 sub-groups comprised of representatives of Contracting Parties may be established and may function during the review meetings as deemed necessary for the purpose of reviewing specific subjects contained in the reports.

3. Each Contracting Party shall have a reasonable opportunity to discuss the reports submitted by other Contracting Parties and to seek clarification of such reports.

Article 21
Timetable

1. A preparatory meeting of the Contracting Parties shall be held not later than six months after the date of entry into force of this Convention.

2. At this preparatory meeting, the Contracting Parties shall determine the date for the first review meeting. This review meeting shall be held as soon as possible, but not later than thirty months after the date of entry into force of this Convention.

3. At each review meeting, the Contracting Parties shall determine the date for the next such meeting. The interval between review meetings shall not exceed three years.

Article 22
Procedural arrangements

1. At the preparatory meeting held pursuant to Article 21 the Contracting Parties shall prepare and adopt by consensus Rules of Procedure and Financial Rules. The Contracting Parties shall establish in particular and in accordance with the Rules of Procedure:

  i. guidelines regarding the form and structure of the reports to be submitted pursuant to Article 5;
  ii. a date for the submission of such reports;
 iii. the process for reviewing such reports.

2. At review meetings the Contracting Parties may, if necessary, review the arrangements established pursuant to sub-paragraphs (i)-(iii) above, and adopt revisions by consensus unless otherwise provided for in the Rules of Procedure. They may also amend the Rules of Procedure and the Financial Rules, by consensus.

Article 23
Extraordinary meetings

An extraordinary meeting of the Contracting Parties shall be held:

i. if so agreed by a majority of the Contracting Parties present and voting at a meeting, abstentions being considered as voting; or
ii. at the written request of a Contracting Party, within six months of this request having been communicated to the Contracting Parties and notification having been received by the secretariat referred to in Article 28, that the request has been supported by a majority of the Contracting Parties.

Article 24
Attendance

1. Each Contracting Party shall attend meetings of the Contracting Parties and be represented at such meetings by one delegate, and by such alternates, experts and advisers as it deems necessary.

2. The Contracting Parties may invite, by consensus, any intergovernmental organization which is competent in respect of matters governed by this Convention to attend, as an observer, any meeting, or specific sessions thereof. Observers shall be required to accept in writing, and in advance, the provisions of Article 27.

Article 25
Summary reports

The Contracting Parties shall adopt, by consensus, and make available to the public a document addressing issues discussed and conclusions reached during a meeting.

Article 26
Languages

1. The languages of meetings of the Contracting Parties shall be Arabic, Chinese, English, French, Russian and Spanish unless otherwise provided in the Rules of Procedure.

2. Reports submitted pursuant to Article 5 shall be prepared in the national language of the submitting Contracting Party or in a single designated language to be agreed in the Rules of Procedure. Should the report be submitted in a national language other than the designated language, a translation of the report into the designated language shall be provided by the Contracting Party.

3. Notwithstanding the provisions of paragraph 2, if compensated, the secretariat will assume the translation into the designated language of reports submitted in any other language of the meeting.

Article 27
Confidentiality

1. The provisions of this Convention shall not affect the rights and obligations of the Contracting Parties under their law to protect information from disclosure. For the purposes of this Article, 'information' includes, *inter alia*, (i) personal data; (ii) information protected by intellectual property rights or by industrial or commercial confidentiality; and (iii) information relating to national security or to the physical protection of nuclear materials or nuclear installations.

2. When, in the context of this Convention, a Contracting Party provides information identified by it as protected as described in paragraph 1, such information shall be used only for the purposes for which it has been provided and its confidentiality shall be respected.

3. The content of the debates during the reviewing of the reports by the Contracting Parties at each meeting shall be confidential.

Article 28
Secretariat

1. The International Atomic Energy Agency, (hereinafter referred to as the 'Agency') shall provide the secretariat for the meetings of the Contracting Parties.

2. The secretariat shall:

i. convene, prepare and service the meetings of the Contracting Parties;
ii. transmit to the Contracting Parties information received or prepared in accordance with the provisions of this Convention.

The costs incurred by the Agency in carrying out the functions referred to in sub-paragraphs (i) and (ii) above shall be borne by the Agency as part of its regular budget.

3. The Contracting Parties may, by consensus, request the Agency to provide other services in support of meetings of the Contracting Parties. The Agency may provide such services if they can be undertaken within its programme and regular budget. Should this not be possible, the Agency may provide such services if voluntary funding is provided from another source.

Chapter 4
Final clauses and other provisions

Article 29
Resolution of Disagreements

In the event of a disagreement between two or more Contracting Parties concerning the interpretation or application of this Convention, the Contracting

Parties shall consult within the framework of a meeting of the Contracting Parties with a view to resolving the disagreement.

Article 30
Signature, ratification, acceptance, approval, accession

1. This Convention shall be open for signature by all States at the Headquarters of the Agency in Vienna from 20 September 1994 until its entry into force.

2. This Convention is subject to ratification, acceptance or approval by the signatory States.

3. After its entry into force, this Convention shall be open for accession by all States.

4.

i. This Convention shall be open for signature or accession by regional organizations of an integration or other nature, provided that any such organization is constituted by sovereign States and has competence in respect of the negotiation, conclusion and application of international agreements in matters covered by this Convention.

ii. In matters within their competence, such organizations shall, on their own behalf, exercise the rights and fulfil the responsibilities which this Convention attributes to States Parties

iii. When becoming party to this Convention, such an organization shall communicate to the Depositary referred to in Article 34, a declaration indicating which States are members thereof, which articles of this Convention apply to it, and the extent of its competence in the field covered by those articles.

iv. Such an organization shall not hold any vote additional to those of its Member States.

5. Instruments of ratification, acceptance, approval or accession shall be deposited with the Depositary.

Article 31
Entry into force

1. This Convention shall enter into force on the ninetieth day after the date of deposit with the Depositary of the twenty-second instrument of ratification, acceptance or approval, including the instruments of seventeen States, each having at least one nuclear installation which has achieved criticality in a reactor core.

2. For each State or regional organization of an integration of other nature which ratifies, accepts, approves or accedes to this Convention after the date of deposit of the last instrument required to satisfy the conditions set forth in paragraph 1, this Convention shall enter into force on the ninetieth day after

the date of deposit with the Depositary of the appropriate instrument by such a State or organization.

Article 32
Amendments to the Convention

1. Any Contracting party may propose an amendment to this Convention. Proposed amendments shall be considered at a review meeting or an extraordinary meeting.

2. The text of any proposed amendment and the reasons for it shall be provided to the Depositary who shall communicate the proposal to the Contracting Parties promptly and at least ninety days before the meeting for which it is submitted for consideration. Any comments received on such a proposal shall be circulated by the Depositary to the Contracting Parties.

3. The Contracting Parties shall decide after consideration of the proposed amendment whether to adopt it by consensus, or, in the absence of consensus, to submit it to a Diplomatic Conference. A decision to submit a proposed amendment to a Diplomatic Conference shall require a two-thirds majority vote of the Contracting parties present and voting at the meeting, provided that at least one half of the Contracting Parties are present at the time of voting. Abstentions shall be considered as voting.

4. The Diplomatic Conference to consider and adopt amendments to this Convention shall be convened by the Depositary and held no later than one year after the appropriate decision taken in accordance with paragraph 3 of this Article. The Diplomatic Conference shall make every effort to ensure amendments are adopted by consensus. Should this not be possible, amendments shall be adopted with a two-thirds majority of all Contracting Parties.

5. Amendments to this Convention adopted pursuant to paragraphs 3 and 4 above shall be subject to ratification, acceptance, approval, or confirmation by the Contracting Parties and shall enter into force for those Contracting Parties which have ratified, accepted, approved or confirmed them on the ninetieth day after the receipt by the Depositary of the relevant instruments by at least three fourths of the Contracting Parties. For a Contracting Party which subsequently ratifies, accepts, approves or confirms the said amendments, the amendments will enter into force on the ninetieth day after that Contracting Party has deposited its relevant instrument.

Article 33
Denunciation

1. Any Contracting Party may denounce this Convention by written notification to the Depositary.

2. Denunciation shall take effect one year following the date of the receipt of the notification by the Depositary, or on such later date as may be specified in the notification.

Article 34
Depositary

1. The Director General of the Agency shall be the Depositary of this Convention.

2. The Depositary shall inform the Contracting Parties of:

i. the signature of this Convention and of the deposit of instruments of ratification, acceptance, approval or accession, in accordance with Article 30;

ii. the date on which the Convention enters into force, in accordance with Article 31;

iii. the notifications of denunciation of the Convention and the date thereof, made in accordance with Article 33;

iv. the proposed amendments to this Convention submitted by Contracting Parties, the amendments adopted by the relevant Diplomatic Conference or by the meeting of the Contracting Parties, and the date of entry into force of the said amendments, in accordance with Article 32.

Article 35
Authentic texts

The original of this Convention of which the Arabic, Chinese, English, French, Russian and Spanish texts are equally authentic, shall be deposited with the Depositary, who shall send certified copies thereof to the Contracting Parties.

IN WITNESS WHEREOF the undersigned, being duly authorized to that effect, have signed this Convention.

DONE at Vienna on the 20th day of September 1994.

PART VIB

Hazardous substances and activities: pesticides

Convention on the Prior Informed Consent Procedure for Certain Hazardous Chemicals and Pesticides in International Trade, 10 September 1998

Editorial note

The objective of the 1998 Rotterdam Convention on the Prior Informed Consent Procedure for Certain Hazardous Chemicals and Pesticides in International Trade (1998 Chemicals Convention) is 'to promote shared responsibility and cooperative efforts among Parties in the international trade of certain hazardous chemicals in order to protect human health and the environment from potential harm and to contribute to their environmentally sound use, by facilitating information exchange about their characteristics, by providing for a national decision-making process on their import and export and by disseminating these decisions to Parties'(Article 1).

The Convention draws upon the FAO and UNEP voluntary schemes in applying a prior informed consent (PIC) procedure for chemicals listed in Annex III of the Convention, and is applicable to banned or severely restricted chemicals and severely hazardous pesticide formulations (Article 3(1)), subject to certain exceptions (Article 3(2)). Each party is to designate a national authority that shall be authorized to act on its behalf in the performance of the administrative functions required by the Convention (Article 4). With regards to chemicals, a party which has banned or severely restricted a chemical (taken a 'final regulatory action') is to notify the secretariat, which will then forward the information to all parties (Article 5(1) and (2)). With regard to pesticides, any party that is a developing country or a country with an economy in transition and that is experiencing problems caused by a severely hazardous pesticide formulation under conditions of use in its territory may propose to the secretariat the listing in Annex III of the severely hazardous pesticide formulation (Article 6(1)). The secretariat will then forward the proposal to the Chemical Review Committee, which will review the information and recommend to the conference of the parties whether the formulation should be subject to the prior informed consent procedure and, accordingly, listed on Annex III (Article 6(3)–(5)).

The Convention already lists 25 chemicals (or categories of chemicals). It will be for the conference of the parties to add further chemicals to Annex III (chemicals not listed but included in the voluntary PIC procedure shall be included) (Articles 7 and 8). Provisions are also made for the removal of chemicals from the list (Article 9). The criteria for listing (and removing) chemicals and pesticides are set forth in Annexes II and IV. Articles 10 and 11 establish the PIC procedure in respect of imports and exports of chemicals listed in Annex III. The export of banned or severely restricted chemicals which are not so listed is governed by a separate notification procedure (Article 12). The notification must include the information set out in Annex V. Without prejudice to the requirements of the importing party, exported chemicals which are listed on Annex III or which are banned or severely restricted must be labelled to ensure 'adequate availability of information with regard to risks and/or hazards to human health or the environment, taking into account relevant international standards' (Article 13(2)).

The Convention makes provision for general information exchange and technical assistance, as well as implementation of the Convention (Articles 14–16). A conference of the parties is responsible for reviewing and evaluating implementation of the Convention, assisted by a secretariat (FAO and UNEP), and will appoint the Chemical Review Committee and establish a non-compliance mechanism (Articles 17–19). Provision is also made for adoption and amendment of the Convention and its Annexes (Articles 21–22).

The Convention is not expected to enter into force until late 2003 or 2004. In the meantime, the Conference of Plenipotentiaries adopting the Convention decided to change – with immediate effect – the voluntary FAO and UNEP PIC procedures into line with the procedure established by the Convention and operate it as an 'interim PIC procedure'.

Date of signature: 10 September 1998

Entry into force: Not yet in force

Depositary: Secretary-General of the United Nations

Contracting Parties: Austria, Belgium, Bulgaria, Burkina Faso, Cameroon, Canada, Czech Republic, El Salvador, Equatorial Guinea, Ethiopia, European Community, Gambia, Germany, Guinea, Hungary, Italy, Jamaica, Jordan, Kyrgyzstan, Libyan Arab Jamahiriya, Luxembourg, Malaysia, Marshall Islands, Mongolia, Netherlands, Nigeria, Norway, Oman, Panama, Samoa, Saudi Arabia, Senegal, Slovenia, South Africa, Suriname, Switzerland, Tanzania (United Republic of), Thailand, Ukraine, United Arab Emirates.

Website: www.pic.int

Rotterdam Convention on the Prior Informed Consent Procedure for Certain Hazardous Chemicals and Pesticides in International Trade

The Parties to this Convention,

Aware of the harmful impact on human health and the environment from certain hazardous chemicals and pesticides in international trade,

Recalling the pertinent provisions of the Rio Declaration on Environment and Development and chapter 19 of Agenda 21 on 'Environmentally sound management of toxic chemicals, including prevention of illegal international traffic in toxic and dangerous products',

Mindful of the work undertaken by the United Nations Environment Programme (UNEP) and the Food and Agriculture Organization of the United Nations (FAO) in the operation of the voluntary Prior Informed Consent procedure, as set out in the UNEP Amended London Guidelines for the Exchange of Information on Chemicals in International Trade (hereinafter referred to as the 'Amended London Guidelines') and the FAO International Code of Conduct on the Distribution and Use of Pesticides (hereinafter referred to as the 'International Code of Conduct'),

Taking into account the circumstances and particular requirements of developing countries and countries with economies in transition, in particular the need to strengthen national capabilities and capacities for the management of chemicals, including transfer of technology, providing financial and technical assistance and promoting cooperation among the Parties,

Noting the specific needs of some countries for information on transit movements,

Recognizing that good management practices for chemicals should be promoted in all countries, taking into account, *inter alia*, the voluntary standards laid down in the International Code of Conduct and the UNEP Code of Ethics on the International Trade in Chemicals,

Desiring to ensure that hazardous chemicals that are exported from their territory are packaged and labelled in a manner that is adequately protective of human health and the environment, consistent with the principles of the Amended London Guidelines and the International Code of Conduct,

Recognizing that trade and environmental policies should be mutually supportive with a view to achieving sustainable development,

Emphasizing that nothing in this Convention shall be interpreted as implying in any way a change in the rights and obligations of a Party under any existing international agreement applying to chemicals in international trade or to environmental protection,

Understanding that the above recital is not intended to create a hierarchy between this Convention and other international agreements,

Determined to protect human health, including the health of consumers and workers, and the environment against potentially harmful impacts from certain hazardous chemicals and pesticides in international trade,

Have agreed as follows:

Article 1
Objective

The objective of this Convention is to promote shared responsibility and co-operative efforts among Parties in the international trade of certain hazardous chemicals in order to protect human health and the environment from potential harm and to contribute to their environmentally sound use, by facilitating information exchange about their characteristics, by providing for a national decision-making process on their import and export and by disseminating these decisions to Parties.

Article 2
Definitions

For the purposes of this Convention:

(a) 'Chemical' means a substance whether by itself or in a mixture or preparation and whether manufactured or obtained from nature, but does not include any living organism. It consists of the following categories: pesticide (including severely hazardous pesticide formulations) and industrial;

(b) 'Banned chemical' means a chemical all uses of which within one or more categories have been prohibited by final regulatory action, in order to protect human health or the environment. It includes a chemical that has been refused approval for first-time use or has been withdrawn by industry either from the domestic market or from further consideration in the domestic approval process and where there is clear evidence that such action has been taken in order to protect human health or the environment;

(c) 'Severely restricted chemical' means a chemical virtually all use of which within one or more categories has been prohibited by final regulatory action in order to protect human health or the environment, but for which certain specific uses remain allowed. It includes a chemical that has, for virtually all use, been refused for approval or been withdrawn by industry either from the domestic market or from further consideration in the domestic approval process, and where there is clear evidence that such action has been taken in order to protect human health or the environment;

(d) 'Severely hazardous pesticide formulation' means a chemical formulated for pesticidal use that produces severe health or environmental effects observable within a short period of time after single or multiple exposure, under conditions of use;

(e) 'Final regulatory action' means an action taken by a Party, that does not require subsequent regulatory action by that Party, the purpose of which is to ban or severely restrict a chemical;

(f) 'Export' and 'import' mean, in their respective connotations, the movement of a chemical from one Party to another Party, but exclude mere transit operations;

(g) 'Party' means a State or regional economic integration organization that has consented to be bound by this Convention and for which the Convention is in force;

(h) 'Regional economic integration organization' means an organization constituted by sovereign States of a given region to which its member States have transferred competence in respect of matters governed by this Convention and which has been duly authorized, in accordance with its internal procedures, to sign, ratify, accept, approve or accede to this Convention;

(i) 'Chemical Review Committee' means the subsidiary body referred to in paragraph 6 of Article 18.

Article 3
Scope of the Convention

1. This Convention applies to:

(a) Banned or severely restricted chemicals; and
(b) Severely hazardous pesticide formulations.

2. This Convention does not apply to:

(a) Narcotic drugs and psychotropic substances;
(b) Radioactive materials;
(c) Wastes;
(d) Chemical weapons;
(e) Pharmaceuticals, including human and veterinary drugs;
(f) Chemicals used as food additives;
(g) Food;
(h) Chemicals in quantities not likely to affect human health or the environment provided they are imported:
  (i) For the purpose of research or analysis; or
  (ii) By an individual for his or her own personal use in quantities reasonable for such use.

Article 4
Designated national authorities

1. Each Party shall designate one or more national authorities that shall be authorized to act on its behalf in the performance of the administrative functions required by this Convention.

2. Each Party shall seek to ensure that such authority or authorities have sufficient resources to perform their tasks effectively.

3. Each Party shall, no later than the date of the entry into force of this Convention for it, notify the name and address of such authority or authorities to the Secretariat. It shall forthwith notify the Secretariat of any changes in the name and address of such authority or authorities.

4. The Secretariat shall forthwith inform the Parties of the notifications it receives under paragraph 3.

Article 5
Procedures for banned or severely restricted chemicals

1. Each Party that has adopted a final regulatory action shall notify the Secretariat in writing of such action. Such notification shall be made as soon as possible, and in any event no later than ninety days after the date on which the final regulatory action has taken effect, and shall contain the information required by Annex I, where available.

2. Each Party shall, at the date of entry into force of this Convention for it, notify the Secretariat in writing of its final regulatory actions in effect at that time, except that each Party that has submitted notifications of final regulatory actions under the Amended London Guidelines or the International Code of Conduct need not resubmit those notifications.

3. The Secretariat shall, as soon as possible, and in any event no later than six months after receipt of a notification under paragraphs 1 and 2, verify whether the notification contains the information required by Annex I. If the notification contains the information required, the Secretariat shall forthwith forward to all Parties a summary of the information received. If the notification does not contain the information required, it shall inform the notifying Party accordingly.

4. The Secretariat shall every six months communicate to the Parties a synopsis of the information received pursuant to paragraphs 1 and 2, including information regarding those notifications which do not contain all the information required by Annex I.

5. When the Secretariat has received at least one notification from each of two Prior Informed Consent regions regarding a particular chemical that it has verified meet the requirements of Annex I, it shall forward them to the Chemical Review Committee. The composition of the Prior Informed Consent regions shall be defined in a decision to be adopted by consensus at the first meeting of the Conference of the Parties.

6. The Chemical Review Committee shall review the information provided in such notifications and, in accordance with the criteria set out in Annex II, recommend to the Conference of the Parties whether the chemical in question should be made subject to the Prior Informed Consent procedure and, accordingly, be listed in Annex III.

Article 6
Procedures for severely hazardous pesticide formulations

1. Any Party that is a developing country or a country with an economy in transition and that is experiencing problems caused by a severely hazardous pesticide formulation under conditions of use in its territory, may propose to the Secretariat the listing of the severely hazardous pesticide formulation in Annex III. In developing a proposal, the Party may draw upon technical expertise from any relevant source. The proposal shall contain the information required by part 1 of Annex IV.

2. The Secretariat shall, as soon as possible, and in any event no later than six months after receipt of a proposal under paragraph 1, verify whether the proposal contains the information required by part 1 of Annex IV. If the proposal contains the information required, the Secretariat shall forthwith forward to all Parties a summary of the information received. If the proposal does not contain the information required, it shall inform the proposing Party accordingly.

3. The Secretariat shall collect the additional information set out in part 2 of Annex IV regarding the proposal forwarded under paragraph 2.

4. When the requirements of paragraphs 2 and 3 above have been fulfilled with regard to a particular severely hazardous pesticide formulation, the Secretariat shall forward the proposal and the related information to the Chemical Review Committee.

5. The Chemical Review Committee shall review the information provided in the proposal and the additional information collected and, in accordance with the criteria set out in part 3 of Annex IV, recommend to the Conference of the Parties whether the severely hazardous pesticide formulation in question should be made subject to the Prior Informed Consent procedure and, accordingly, be listed in Annex III.

Article 7
Listing of chemicals in Annex III

1. For each chemical that the Chemical Review Committee has decided to recommend for listing in Annex III, it shall prepare a draft decision guidance document. The decision guidance document should, at a minimum, be based on the information specified in Annex I, or, as the case may be, Annex IV, and include information on uses of the chemical in a category other than the category for which the final regulatory action applies.

2. The recommendation referred to in paragraph 1 together with the draft decision guidance document shall be forwarded to the Conference of the Parties. The Conference of the Parties shall decide whether the chemical should be made subject to the Prior Informed Consent procedure and, accordingly, list the chemical in Annex III and approve the draft decision guidance document.

3. When a decision to list a chemical in Annex III has been taken and the related decision guidance document has been approved by the Conference of the Parties, the Secretariat shall forthwith communicate this information to all Parties.

Article 8
Chemicals in the voluntary Prior Informed Consent procedure

For any chemical, other than a chemical listed in Annex III, that has been included in the voluntary Prior Informed Consent procedure before the date of the first meeting of the Conference of the Parties, the Conference of the Parties shall decide at that meeting to list the chemical in Annex III, provided that it is satisfied that all the requirements for listing in that Annex have been fulfilled.

Article 9
Removal of chemicals from Annex III

1. If a Party submits to the Secretariat information that was not available at the time of the decision to list a chemical in Annex III and that information indicates that its listing may no longer be justified in accordance with the relevant criteria in Annex II or, as the case may be, Annex IV, the Secretariat shall forward the information to the Chemical Review Committee.

2. The Chemical Review Committee shall review the information it receives under paragraph 1. For each chemical that the Chemical Review Committee decides, in accordance with the relevant criteria in Annex II or, as the case may be, Annex IV, to recommend for removal from Annex III, it shall prepare a revised draft decision guidance document.

3. A recommendation referred to in paragraph 2 shall be forwarded to the Conference of the Parties and be accompanied by a revised draft decision guidance document. The Conference of the Parties shall decide whether the chemical should be removed from Annex III and whether to approve the revised draft decision guidance document.

4. When a decision to remove a chemical from Annex III has been taken and the revised decision guidance document has been approved by the Conference of the Parties, the Secretariat shall forthwith communicate this information to all Parties.

Article 10
Obligations in relation to imports of chemicals listed in Annex III

1. Each Party shall implement appropriate legislative or administrative measures to ensure timely decisions with respect to the import of chemicals listed in Annex III.

2. Each Party shall transmit to the Secretariat, as soon as possible, and in any event no later than nine months after the date of dispatch of the decision guidance document referred to in paragraph 3 of Article 7, a response concerning

the future import of the chemical concerned. If a Party modifies this response, it shall forthwith submit the revised response to the Secretariat.

3. The Secretariat shall, at the expiration of the time period in paragraph 2, forthwith address to a Party that has not provided such a response, a written request to do so. Should the Party be unable to provide a response, the Secretariat shall, where appropriate, help it to provide a response within the time period specified in the last sentence of paragraph 2 of Article 11.

4. A response under paragraph 2 shall consist of either:

(a) A final decision, pursuant to legislative or administrative measures:
   (i) To consent to import;
   (ii) Not to consent to import; or
   (iii) To consent to import only subject to specified conditions; or
(b) An interim response, which may include:
   (i) An interim decision consenting to import with or without specified conditions, or not consenting to import during the interim period;
   (ii) A statement that a final decision is under active consideration;
   (iii) A request to the Secretariat, or to the Party that notified the final regulatory action, for further information;
   (iv) A request to the Secretariat for assistance in evaluating the chemical.

5. A response under subparagraphs (a) or (b) of paragraph 4 shall relate to the category or categories specified for the chemical in Annex III.

6. A final decision should be accompanied by a description of any legislative or administrative measures upon which it is based.

7. Each Party shall, no later than the date of entry into force of this Convention for it, transmit to the Secretariat responses with respect to each chemical listed in Annex III. A Party that has provided such responses under the Amended London Guidelines or the International Code of Conduct need not resubmit those responses.

8. Each Party shall make its responses under this Article available to those concerned within its jurisdiction, in accordance with its legislative or administrative measures.

9. A Party that, pursuant to paragraphs 2 and 4 above and paragraph 2 of Article 11, takes a decision not to consent to import of a chemical or to consent to its import only under specified conditions shall, if it has not already done so, simultaneously prohibit or make subject to the same conditions:

(a) Import of the chemical from any source; and
(b) Domestic production of the chemical for domestic use.

10. Every six months the Secretariat shall inform all Parties of the responses it has received. Such information shall include a description of the legislative or administrative measures on which the decisions have been based, where

available. The Secretariat shall, in addition, inform the Parties of any cases of failure to transmit a response.

Article 11
Obligations in relation to exports of chemicals listed in Annex III

1. Each exporting Party shall:

(a) Implement appropriate legislative or administrative measures to communicate the responses forwarded by the Secretariat in accordance with paragraph 10 of Article 10 to those concerned within its jurisdiction;

(b) Take appropriate legislative or administrative measures to ensure that exporters within its jurisdiction comply with decisions in each response no later than six months after the date on which the Secretariat first informs the Parties of such response in accordance with paragraph 10 of Article 10;

(c) Advise and assist importing Parties, upon request and as appropriate:
   (i) To obtain further information to help them to take action in accordance with paragraph 4 of Article 10 and paragraph 2 (c) below; and
   (ii) To strengthen their capacities and capabilities to manage chemicals safely during their life-cycle.

2. Each Party shall ensure that a chemical listed in Annex III is not exported from its territory to any importing Party that, in exceptional circumstances, has failed to transmit a response or has transmitted an interim response that does not contain an interim decision, unless:

(a) It is a chemical that, at the time of import, is registered as a chemical in the importing Party; or

(b) It is a chemical for which evidence exists that it has previously been used in, or imported into, the importing Party and in relation to which no regulatory action to prohibit its use has been taken; or

(c) Explicit consent to the import has been sought and received by the exporter through a designated national authority of the importing Party. The importing Party shall respond to such a request within sixty days and shall promptly notify the Secretariat of its decision.

The obligations of exporting Parties under this paragraph shall apply with effect from the expiration of a period of six months from the date on which the Secretariat first informs the Parties, in accordance with paragraph 10 of Article 10, that a Party has failed to transmit a response or has transmitted an interim response that does not contain an interim decision, and shall apply for one year.

Article 12
Export notification

1. Where a chemical that is banned or severely restricted by a Party is exported from its territory, that Party shall provide an export notification to the importing Party. The export notification shall include the information set out in Annex V.

2. The export notification shall be provided for that chemical prior to the first export following adoption of the corresponding final regulatory action. Thereafter, the export notification shall be provided before the first export in any calendar year. The requirement to notify before export may be waived by the designated national authority of the importing Party.

3. An exporting Party shall provide an updated export notification after it has adopted a final regulatory action that results in a major change concerning the ban or severe restriction of that chemical.

4. The importing Party shall acknowledge receipt of the first export notification received after the adoption of the final regulatory action. If the exporting Party does not receive the acknowledgement within thirty days of the dispatch of the export notification, it shall submit a second notification. The exporting Party shall make reasonable efforts to ensure that the importing Party receives the second notification.

5. The obligations of a Party set out in paragraph 1 shall cease when:

(a) The chemical has been listed in Annex III;
(b) The importing Party has provided a response for the chemical to the Secretariat in accordance with paragraph 2 of Article 10; and
(c) The Secretariat has distributed the response to the Parties in accordance with paragraph 10 of Article 10.

Article 13
Information to accompany exported chemicals

1. The Conference of the Parties shall encourage the World Customs Organization to assign specific Harmonized System customs codes to the individual chemicals or groups of chemicals listed in Annex III, as appropriate. Each Party shall require that, whenever a code has been assigned to such a chemical, the shipping document for that chemical bears the code when exported.

2. Without prejudice to any requirements of the importing Party, each Party shall require that both chemicals listed in Annex III and chemicals banned or severely restricted in its territory are, when exported, subject to labelling requirements that ensure adequate availability of information with regard to risks and/or hazards to human health or the environment, taking into account relevant international standards.

3. Without prejudice to any requirements of the importing Party, each Party may require that chemicals subject to environmental or health labelling

requirements in its territory are, when exported, subject to labelling requirements that ensure adequate availability of information with regard to risks and/or hazards to human health or the environment, taking into account relevant international standards.

4. With respect to the chemicals referred to in paragraph 2 that are to be used for occupational purposes, each exporting Party shall require that a safety data sheet that follows an internationally recognized format, setting out the most up-to-date information available, is sent to each importer.

5. The information on the label and on the safety data sheet should, as far as practicable, be given in one or more of the official languages of the importing Party.

Article 14
Information exchange

1. Each Party shall, as appropriate and in accordance with the objective of this Convention, facilitate:

(a) The exchange of scientific, technical, economic and legal information concerning the chemicals within the scope of this Convention, including toxicological, ecotoxicological and safety information;

(b) The provision of publicly available information on domestic regulatory actions relevant to the objectives of this Convention; and

(c) The provision of information to other Parties, directly or through the Secretariat, on domestic regulatory actions that substantially restrict one or more uses of the chemical, as appropriate.

2. Parties that exchange information pursuant to this Convention shall protect any confidential information as mutually agreed.

3. The following information shall not be regarded as confidential for the purposes of this Convention:

(a) The information referred to in Annexes I and IV, submitted pursuant to Articles 5 and 6 respectively;

(b) The information contained in the safety data sheet referred to in paragraph 4 of Article 13;

(c) The expiry date of the chemical;

(d) Information on precautionary measures, including hazard classification, the nature of the risk and the relevant safety advice; and

(e) The summary results of the toxicological and ecotoxicological tests.

4. The production date of the chemical shall generally not be considered confidential for the purposes of this Convention.

5. Any Party requiring information on transit movements through its territory of chemicals listed in Annex III may report its need to the Secretariat, which shall inform all Parties accordingly.

Article 15
Implementation of the Convention

1. Each Party shall take such measures as may be necessary to establish and strengthen its national infrastructures and institutions for the effective implementation of this Convention. These measures may include, as required, the adoption or amendment of national legislative or administrative measures and may also include:

(a) The establishment of national registers and databases including safety information for chemicals;
(b) The encouragement of initiatives by industry to promote chemical safety; and
(c) The promotion of voluntary agreements, taking into consideration the provisions of Article 16.

2. Each Party shall ensure, to the extent practicable, that the public has appropriate access to information on chemical handling and accident management and on alternatives that are safer for human health or the environment than the chemicals listed in Annex III.

3. The Parties agree to cooperate, directly or, where appropriate, through competent international organizations, in the implementation of this Convention at the subregional, regional and global levels.

4. Nothing in this Convention shall be interpreted as restricting the right of the Parties to take action that is more stringently protective of human health and the environment than that called for in this Convention, provided that such action is consistent with the provisions of this Convention and is in accordance with international law.

Article 16
Technical assistance

The Parties shall, taking into account in particular the needs of developing countries and countries with economies in transition, cooperate in promoting technical assistance for the development of the infrastructure and the capacity necessary to manage chemicals to enable implementation of this Convention. Parties with more advanced programmes for regulating chemicals should provide technical assistance, including training, to other Parties in developing their infrastructure and capacity to manage chemicals throughout their life-cycle.

Article 17
Non-compliance

The Conference of the Parties shall, as soon as practicable, develop and approve procedures and institutional mechanisms for determining non-compliance with the provisions of this Convention and for treatment of Parties found to be in non-compliance.

Article 18
Conference of the Parties

1. A Conference of the Parties is hereby established.

2. The first meeting of the Conference of the Parties shall be convened by the Executive Director of UNEP and the Director-General of FAO, acting jointly, no later than one year after the entry into force of this Convention. Thereafter, ordinary meetings of the Conference of the Parties shall be held at regular intervals to be determined by the Conference.

3. Extraordinary meetings of the Conference of the Parties shall be held at such other times as may be deemed necessary by the Conference, or at the written request of any Party provided that it is supported by at least one third of the Parties.

4. The Conference of the Parties shall by consensus agree upon and adopt at its first meeting rules of procedure and financial rules for itself and any subsidiary bodies, as well as financial provisions governing the functioning of the Secretariat.

5. The Conference of the Parties shall keep under continuous review and evaluation the implementation of this Convention. It shall perform the functions assigned to it by the Convention and, to this end, shall:

(a) Establish, further to the requirements of paragraph 6 below, such subsidiary bodies, as it considers necessary for the implementation of the Convention;

(b) Cooperate, where appropriate, with competent international organizations and intergovernmental and non-governmental bodies; and

(c) Consider and undertake any additional action that may be required for the achievement of the objectives of the Convention.

6. The Conference of the Parties shall, at its first meeting, establish a subsidiary body, to be called the Chemical Review Committee, for the purposes of performing the functions assigned to that Committee by this Convention. In this regard:

(a) The members of the Chemical Review Committee shall be appointed by the Conference of the Parties. Membership of the Committee shall consist of a limited number of government-designated experts in chemicals management. The members of the Committee shall be appointed on the basis of equitable geographical distribution, including ensuring a balance between developed and developing Parties;

(b) The Conference of the Parties shall decide on the terms of reference, organization and operation of the Committee;

(c) The Committee shall make every effort to make its recommendations by consensus. If all efforts at consensus have been exhausted, and no consensus reached, such recommendation shall as a last resort be adopted by a two-thirds majority vote of the members present and voting.

7. The United Nations, its specialized agencies and the International Atomic Energy Agency, as well as any State not Party to this Convention, may be represented at meetings of the Conference of the Parties as observers. Any body or agency, whether national or international, governmental or non-governmental, qualified in matters covered by the Convention, and which has informed the Secretariat of its wish to be represented at a meeting of the Conference of the Parties as an observer may be admitted unless at least one third of the Parties present object. The admission and participation of observers shall be subject to the rules of procedure adopted by the Conference of the Parties.

Article 19
Secretariat

1. A Secretariat is hereby established.

2. The functions of the Secretariat shall be:

(a) To make arrangements for meetings of the Conference of the Parties and its subsidiary bodies and to provide them with services as required;

(b) To facilitate assistance to the Parties, particularly developing Parties and Parties with economies in transition, on request, in the implementation of this Convention;

(c) To ensure the necessary coordination with the secretariats of other relevant international bodies;

(d) To enter, under the overall guidance of the Conference of the Parties, into such administrative and contractual arrangements as may be required for the effective discharge of its functions; and

(e) To perform the other secretariat functions specified in this Convention and such other functions as may be determined by the Conference of the Parties.

3. The secretariat functions for this Convention shall be performed jointly by the Executive Director of UNEP and the Director-General of FAO, subject to such arrangements as shall be agreed between them and approved by the Conference of the Parties.

4. The Conference of the Parties may decide, by a three-fourths majority of the Parties present and voting, to entrust the secretariat functions to one or more other competent international organizations, should it find that the Secretariat is not functioning as intended.

Article 20
Settlement of disputes

1. Parties shall settle any dispute between them concerning the interpretation or application of this Convention through negotiation or other peaceful means of their own choice.

2. When ratifying, accepting, approving or acceding to this Convention, or at any time thereafter, a Party that is not a regional economic integration organization may declare in a written instrument submitted to the Depositary that, with respect to any dispute concerning the interpretation or application of the Convention, it recognizes one or both of the following means of dispute settlement as compulsory in relation to any Party accepting the same obligation:

(a) Arbitration in accordance with procedures to be adopted by the Conference of the Parties in an annex as soon as practicable; and

(b) Submission of the dispute to the International Court of Justice.

3. A Party that is a regional economic integration organization may make a declaration with like effect in relation to arbitration in accordance with the procedure referred to in paragraph 2 (a).

4. A declaration made pursuant to paragraph 2 shall remain in force until it expires in accordance with its terms or until three months after written notice of its revocation has been deposited with the Depositary.

5. The expiry of a declaration, a notice of revocation or a new declaration shall not in any way affect proceedings pending before an arbitral tribunal or the International Court of Justice unless the parties to the dispute otherwise agree.

6. If the parties to a dispute have not accepted the same or any procedure pursuant to paragraph 2, and if they have not been able to settle their dispute within twelve months following notification by one party to another that a dispute exists between them, the dispute shall be submitted to a conciliation commission at the request of any party to the dispute. The conciliation commission shall render a report with recommendations. Additional procedures relating to the conciliation commission shall be included in an annex to be adopted by the Conference of the Parties no later than the second meeting of the Conference.

Article 21
Amendments to the Convention

1. Amendments to this Convention may be proposed by any Party.

2. Amendments to this Convention shall be adopted at a meeting of the Conference of the Parties. The text of any proposed amendment shall be communicated to the Parties by the Secretariat at least six months before the meeting at which it is proposed for adoption. The Secretariat shall also communicate

the proposed amendment to the signatories to this Convention and, for information, to the Depositary.

3. The Parties shall make every effort to reach agreement on any proposed amendment to this Convention by consensus. If all efforts at consensus have been exhausted, and no agreement reached, the amendment shall as a last resort be adopted by a three-fourths majority vote of the Parties present and voting at the meeting.

4. The amendment shall be communicated by the Depositary to all Parties for ratification, acceptance or approval.

5. Ratification, acceptance or approval of an amendment shall be notified to the Depositary in writing. An amendment adopted in accordance with paragraph 3 shall enter into force for the Parties having accepted it on the ninetieth day after the date of deposit of instruments of ratification, acceptance or approval by at least three fourths of the Parties. Thereafter, the amendment shall enter into force for any other Party on the ninetieth day after the date on which that Party deposits its instrument of ratification, acceptance or approval of the amendment.

Article 22
Adoption and amendment of annexes

1. Annexes to this Convention shall form an integral part thereof and, unless expressly provided otherwise, a reference to this Convention constitutes at the same time a reference to any annexes thereto.

2. Annexes shall be restricted to procedural, scientific, technical or administrative matters.

3. The following procedure shall apply to the proposal, adoption and entry into force of additional annexes to this Convention:

(a) Additional annexes shall be proposed and adopted according to the procedure laid down in paragraphs 1, 2 and 3 of Article 21;

(b) Any Party that is unable to accept an additional annex shall so notify the Depositary, in writing, within one year from the date of communication of the adoption of the additional annex by the Depositary. The Depositary shall without delay notify all Parties of any such notification received. A Party may at any time withdraw a previous notification of non-acceptance in respect of an additional annex and the annex shall thereupon enter into force for that Party subject to subparagraph (c) below; and

(c) On the expiry of one year from the date of the communication by the Depositary of the adoption of an additional annex, the annex shall enter into force for all Parties that have not submitted a notification in accordance with the provisions of subparagraph (b) above.

4. Except in the case of Annex III, the proposal, adoption and entry into force of amendments to annexes to this Convention shall be subject to the same

procedures as for the proposal, adoption and entry into force of additional annexes to the Convention.

5. The following procedure shall apply to the proposal, adoption and entry into force of amendments to Annex III:

(a) Amendments to Annex III shall be proposed and adopted according to the procedure laid down in Articles 5 to 9 and paragraph 2 of Article 21;

(b) The Conference of the Parties shall take its decisions on adoption by consensus;

(c) A decision to amend Annex III shall forthwith be communicated to the Parties by the Depositary. The amendment shall enter into force for all Parties on a date to be specified in the decision.

6. If an additional annex or an amendment to an annex is related to an amendment to this Convention, the additional annex or amendment shall not enter into force until such time as the amendment to the Convention enters into force.

Article 23
Voting

1. Each Party to this Convention shall have one vote, except as provided for in paragraph 2 below.

2. A regional economic integration organization, on matters within its competence, shall exercise its right to vote with a number of votes equal to the number of its member States that are Parties to this Convention. Such an organization shall not exercise its right to vote if any of its member States exercises its right to vote, and vice versa.

3. For the purposes of this Convention, 'Parties present and voting' means Parties present and casting an affirmative or negative vote.

Article 24
Signature

This Convention shall be open for signature at Rotterdam by all States and regional economic integration organizations on 11 September 1998, and at United Nations Headquarters in New York from 12 September 1998 to 10 September 1999.

Article 25
Ratification, acceptance, approval or accession

1. This Convention shall be subject to ratification, acceptance or approval by States and by regional economic integration organizations. It shall be open for accession by States and by regional economic integration organizations from the day after the date on which the Convention is closed for signature.

Instruments of ratification, acceptance, approval or accession shall be deposited with the Depositary.

2. Any regional economic integration organization that becomes a Party to this Convention without any of its member States being a Party shall be bound by all the obligations under the Convention. In the case of such organizations, one or more of whose member States is a Party to this Convention, the organization and its member States shall decide on their respective responsibilities for the performance of their obligations under the Convention. In such cases, the organization and the member States shall not be entitled to exercise rights under the Convention concurrently.

3. In its instrument of ratification, acceptance, approval or accession, a regional economic integration organization shall declare the extent of its competence in respect of the matters governed by this Convention. Any such organization shall also inform the Depositary, who shall in turn inform the Parties, of any relevant modification in the extent of its competence.

Article 26
Entry into force

1. This Convention shall enter into force on the ninetieth day after the date of deposit of the fiftieth instrument of ratification, acceptance, approval or accession.

2. For each State or regional economic integration organization that ratifies, accepts or approves this Convention or accedes thereto after the deposit of the fiftieth instrument of ratification, acceptance, approval or accession, the Convention shall enter into force on the ninetieth day after the date of deposit by such State or regional economic integration organization of its instrument of ratification, acceptance, approval or accession.

3. For the purpose of paragraphs 1 and 2, any instrument deposited by a regional economic integration organization shall not be counted as additional to those deposited by member States of that organization.

Article 27
Reservations

No reservations may be made to this Convention.

Article 28
Withdrawal

1. At any time after three years from the date on which this Convention has entered into force for a Party, that Party may withdraw from the Convention by giving written notification to the Depositary.

2. Any such withdrawal shall take effect upon expiry of one year from the date of receipt by the Depositary of the notification of withdrawal, or on such later date as may be specified in the notification of withdrawal.

Article 29
Depositary

The Secretary-General of the United Nations shall be the Depositary of this Convention.

Article 30
Authentic texts

The original of this Convention, of which the Arabic, Chinese, English, French, Russian and Spanish texts are equally authentic, shall be deposited with the Secretary-General of the United Nations.

IN WITNESS WHEREOF the undersigned, being duly authorized to that effect, have signed this Convention.

Done at Rotterdam on this tenth day of September, one thousand nine hundred and ninety-eight.

Annex I
Information requirements for notifications made pursuant to Article 5

Notifications shall include:

1. *Properties, identification and uses*
   (a) Common name;
   (b) Chemical name according to an internationally recognized nomenclature (for example, International Union of Pure and Applied Chemistry (IUPAC)), where such nomenclature exists;
   (c) Trade names and names of preparations;
   (d) Code numbers: Chemicals Abstract Service (CAS) number, Harmonized System customs code and other numbers;
   (e) Information on hazard classification, where the chemical is subject to classification requirements;
   (f) Use or uses of the chemical;
   (g) Physico-chemical, toxicological and ecotoxicological properties.
2. *Final regulatory action*
   (a) Information specific to the final regulatory action:
       (i) Summary of the final regulatory action;
       (ii) Reference to the regulatory document;
       (iii) Date of entry into force of the final regulatory action;
       (iv) Indication of whether the final regulatory action was taken on the basis of a risk or hazard evaluation and, if so, information on such evaluation, covering a reference to the relevant documentation;

(v) Reasons for the final regulatory action relevant to human health, including the health of consumers and workers, or the environment;

(vi) Summary of the hazards and risks presented by the chemical to human health, including the health of consumers and workers, or the environment and the expected effect of the final regulatory action;

(b) Category or categories where the final regulatory action has been taken, and for each category:

(i) Use or uses prohibited by the final regulatory action;

(ii) Use or uses that remain allowed;

(iii) Estimation, where available, of quantities of the chemical produced, imported, exported and used;

(c) An indication, to the extent possible, of the likely relevance of the final regulatory action to other States and regions;

(d) Other relevant information that may cover:

(i) Assessment of socio-economic effects of the final regulatory action;

(ii) Information on alternatives and their relative risks, where available, such as:

- Integrated pest management strategies;
- Industrial practices and processes, including cleaner technology.

Annex II
Criteria for listing banned or severely restricted chemicals in Annex III

In reviewing the notifications forwarded by the Secretariat pursuant to paragraph 5 of Article 5, the Chemical Review Committee shall:

(a) Confirm that the final regulatory action has been taken in order to protect human health or the environment;

(b) Establish that the final regulatory action has been taken as a consequence of a risk evaluation. This evaluation shall be based on a review of scientific data in the context of the conditions prevailing in the Party in question. For this purpose, the documentation provided shall demonstrate that:

(i) Data have been generated according to scientifically recognized methods;

(ii) Data reviews have been performed and documented according to generally recognized scientific principles and procedures;

(iii) The final regulatory action was based on a risk evaluation involving prevailing conditions within the Party taking the action;

(c) Consider whether the final regulatory action provides a sufficiently broad basis to merit listing of the chemical in Annex III, by taking into account:

  (i) Whether the final regulatory action led, or would be expected to lead, to a significant decrease in the quantity of the chemical used or the number of its uses;

  (ii) Whether the final regulatory action led to an actual reduction of risk or would be expected to result in a significant reduction of risk for human health or the environment of the Party that submitted the notification;

  (iii) Whether the considerations that led to the final regulatory action being taken are applicable only in a limited geographical area or in other limited circumstances;

  (iv) Whether there is evidence of ongoing international trade in the chemical;

(d) Take into account that intentional misuse is not in itself an adequate reason to list a chemical in Annex III.

Annex III
Chemicals subject to the prior informed consent procedure

Chemical	Relevant CAS number(s)	Category
2,4,5-T	93-76-5	Pesticide
Aldrin	309-00-2	Pesticide
Captafol	2425-06-1	Pesticide
Chlordane	57-74-9	Pesticide
Chlordimeform	6164-98-3	Pesticide
Chlorobenzilate	510-15-6	Pesticide
DDT	50-29-3	Pesticide
Dieldrin	60-57-1	Pesticide
Dinoseb and dinoseb salts	88-85-7	Pesticide
1,2-dibromoethane (EDB)	106-93-4	Pesticide
Fluoroacetamide	640-19-7	Pesticide
HCH (mixed isomers)	608-73-1	Pesticide
Heptachlor	76-44-8	Pesticide
Hexachlorobenzene	118-74-1	Pesticide
Lindane	58-89-9	Pesticide
Mercury compounds, including inorganic mercury compounds, alkyl mercury compounds and alkyloxyalkyl and aryl mercury compounds		Pesticide
Pentachlorophenol	87-86-5	Pesticide

Monocrotophos (Soluble liquid formulations of the substance that exceed 600 g active ingredient/l)	6923-22-4	Severely hazardous pesticide formulation
Methamidophos (Soluble liquid formulations of the substance that exceed 600 g active ingredient/l)	10265-92-6	Severely hazardous pesticide formulation
Phosphamidon (Soluble liquid formulations of the substance that exceed 1000 g active ingredient/l)	13171-21-6 (mixture, (E)&(Z) isomers) 23783-98-4 ((Z)-isomer) 297-99-4 ((E)-isomer)	Severely hazardous pesticide formulation
Methyl-parathion (emulsifiable concentrates (EC) with 19.5%, 40%, 50%, 60% active ingredient and dusts containing 1.5%, 2% and 3% active ingredient)	298-00-0	Severely hazardous pesticide formulation
Parathion (all formulations – aerosols, dustable powder (DP), emulsifiable concentrate (EC), granules (GR) and wettable powders (WP) – of this substance are included, except capsule suspensions (CS))	56-38-2	Severely hazardous pesticide formulation
Crocidolite	12001-28-4	Industrial
Polybrominated biphenyls (PBB)	36355-01-8(hexa-) 27858-07-7 (octa-) 13654-09-6 (deca-)	Industrial
Polychlorinated biphenyls (PCB)	1336-36-3	Industrial
Polychlorinated terphenyls (PCT)	61788-33-8	Industrial
Tris (2,3-dibromopropyl) phosphate	126-72-7	Industrial

Annex IV
Information and criteria for listing severely hazardous pesticide formulations in Annex III

Part 1
Documentation required from a proposing Party

Proposals submitted pursuant to paragraph 1 of Article 6 shall include adequate documentation containing the following information:

(a) Name of the hazardous pesticide formulation;
(b) Name of the active ingredient or ingredients in the formulation;
(c) Relative amount of each active ingredient in the formulation;
(d) Type of formulation;
(e) Trade names and names of the producers, if available;
(f) Common and recognized patterns of use of the formulation within the proposing Party;
(g) A clear description of incidents related to the problem, including the adverse effects and the way in which the formulation was used;
(h) Any regulatory, administrative or other measure taken, or intended to be taken, by the proposing Party in response to such incidents.

Part 2
Information to be collected by the Secretariat

Pursuant to paragraph 3 of Article 6, the Secretariat shall collect relevant information relating to the formulation, including:

(a) The physico-chemical, toxicological and ecotoxicological properties of the formulation;
(b) The existence of handling or applicator restrictions in other States;
(c) Information on incidents related to the formulation in other States;
(d) Information submitted by other Parties, international organizations, non-governmental organizations or other relevant sources, whether national or international;
(e) Risk and/or hazard evaluations, where available;
(f) Indications, if available, of the extent of use of the formulation, such as the number of registrations or production or sales quantity;
(g) Other formulations of the pesticide in question, and incidents, if any, relating to these formulations;
(h) Alternative pest-control practices;
(i) Other information which the Chemical Review Committee may identify as relevant.

Part 3
Criteria for listing severely hazardous pesticide
formulations in Annex III

In reviewing the proposals forwarded by the Secretariat pursuant to paragraph 5 of Article 6, the Chemical Review Committee shall take into account:

(a) The reliability of the evidence indicating that use of the formulation, in accordance with common or recognized practices within the proposing Party, resulted in the reported incidents;
(b) The relevance of such incidents to other States with similar climate, conditions and patterns of use of the formulation;

(c) The existence of handling or applicator restrictions involving technology or techniques that may not be reasonably or widely applied in States lacking the necessary infrastructure;

(d) The significance of reported effects in relation to the quantity of the formulation used;

(e) That intentional misuse is not in itself an adequate reason to list a formulation in Annex III.

Annex V
Information requirements for export notification

1. Export notifications shall contain the following information:

(a) Name and address of the relevant designated national authorities of the exporting Party and the importing Party;

(b) Expected date of export to the importing Party;

(c) Name of the banned or severely restricted chemical and a summary of the information specified in Annex I that is to be provided to the Secretariat in accordance with Article 5. Where more than one such chemical is included in a mixture or preparation, such information shall be provided for each chemical;

(d) A statement indicating, if known, the foreseen category of the chemical and its foreseen use within that category in the importing Party;

(e) Information on precautionary measures to reduce exposure to, and emission of, the chemical;

(f) In the case of a mixture or a preparation, the concentration of the banned or severely restricted chemical or chemicals in question;

(g) Name and address of the importer;

(h) Any additional information that is readily available to the relevant designated national authority of the exporting Party that would be of assistance to the designated national authority of the importing Party.

2. In addition to the information referred to in paragraph 1, the exporting Party shall provide such further information specified in Annex I as may be requested by the importing Party.

Convention on Persistent Organic Pollutants, 22 May 2001

Editorial note

The 2001 Stockholm Convention on Persistent Organic Pollutants (2001 POPs Convention) aims to protect human health and the environment from persistent organic pollutants, and to that end it imposes measures to reduce or eliminate releases from the production and use of certain POPs (Article 1). The Convention is precautionary in approach, and initially targets 12 POPs: Annex A lists those which are targeted for elimination and Annex B lists those which are to be restricted.

Article 3(1) requires parties to eliminate the production and use of all the chemicals listed in Annex A, in accordance with that Annex, and to restrict production and use of chemicals listed in Annex B. Annexes A and B identify 'specific exemptions' in relation to the production and/or use of some but not all of the chemicals, and Annex B additionally identifies certain 'acceptable purposes'. Article 3(2) requires parties to permit imports of chemicals listed in Annex A or Annex B for the purposes of environmentally sound disposal (in accordance with Article 6(1)(d)) or for a use which is permitted for the importing party under Annex A or B (Article 3(2)(a)). It also requires parties to allow exports only for environmentally sound disposal, or to a party which is permitted to use that chemical under Annex A or B, or to a state which is not a party to the Convention but which has provided an annual certification to the exporting party (Article 3(2)(b)). Finally, Article 3(2) also provides that a party may only export an Annex A chemical for which production and use exemptions are no longer in effect for it for the purpose of environmentally sound disposal (Article 3(2)(c)). Parties must take measures to regulate the prevention of production and use of new industrial chemicals which exhibit the characteristics of persistent organic pollutants, taking into account the criteria set forth in Annex D (Article 3(3)). These criteria are also to be taken into account when assessing other pesticides or industrial chemicals already in use but not listed in Annexes A or B (Article 3(4)).

A register for the purpose of identifying Parties that have specific exemptions is established (Article 4). With regard to unintentional production, Article 5 requires parties to take certain measures to reduce releases from anthropogenic sources of the chemicals listed in Annex C, including action plans to identify and address releases, the use of substitutes, and the use of 'best available techniques' and 'best environmental practices'. The Convention also commits parties to develop implementation plans and provides for information exchange, public awareness and information, research and monitoring, and the provision of technical assistance to developing countries and economies in transition (Articles 7, 9–12). Developed countries undertake to provide new and additional financial resources to enable developing countries and economies in transition to meet 'agreed full incremental costs' of implementing measures, and to that end a financial mechanism is 'defined' (Article 13(2) and Article 6). The Global Environmental Facility (GEF) is designated on an interim basis (Article 14). It is recognised that the extent to which developing countries will effectively implement their commitments will depend on the effective implementation by developed country parties of their commitments relating to financial resources, technical assistance and technology transfer (Article 13(4)). The Convention also sets forth reporting requirements and commits the conference of the parties to establish a non-compliance mechanism as soon as practicable (Articles 15 and 17). The conference of the parties is entrusted with implementation of the Convention (and must evaluate the effectiveness of the Convention four years after its entry into force) assisted by a secretariat (UNEP) (Articles 16 and 19–20). Provision is also made for adoption and amendment of the Convention and, in particular, its Annexes (Articles 21 and 22).

Date of signature: 22 May 2001

Entry into force: Not yet in force

Depositary: Secretary-General of the United Nations

Contracting Parties: Austria, Botswana, Canada, Czech Republic, Ethiopia, Fiji, Finland, Iceland, Japan, Korea (Democratic People's Republic of), Lebanon, Lesotho, Liberia, Luxembourg, Marshall Islands, Mexico, Nauru, Netherlands, Norway, Rwanda, Saint Lucia, Samoa, Slovakia, South Africa, Sweden, Trinidad and Tobago, United Arab Emirates, Vietnam.

Website: www.pops.int

Stockholm Convention on Persistent Organic Pollutants

The Parties to this Convention,

   Recognizing that persistent organic pollutants possess toxic properties, resist degradation, bioaccumulate and are transported, through air, water and migratory species, across international boundaries and deposited far from their place of release, where they accumulate in terrestrial and aquatic ecosystems,

Aware of the health concerns, especially in developing countries, resulting from local exposure to persistent organic pollutants, in particular impacts upon women and, through them, upon future generations,

Acknowledging that the Arctic ecosystems and indigenous communities are particularly at risk because of the biomagnification of persistent organic pollutants and that contamination of their traditional foods is a public health issue,

Conscious of the need for global action on persistent organic pollutants,

Mindful of decision 19/13 C of 7 February 1997 of the Governing Council of the United Nations Environment Programme to initiate international action to protect human health and the environment through measures which will reduce and/or eliminate emissions and discharges of persistent organic pollutants,

Recalling the pertinent provisions of the relevant international environmental conventions, especially the Rotterdam Convention on the Prior Informed Consent Procedure for Certain Hazardous Chemicals and Pesticides in International Trade, and the Basel Convention on the Control of Transboundary Movements of Hazardous Wastes and their Disposal including the regional agreements developed within the framework of its Article 11,

Recalling also the pertinent provisions of the Rio Declaration on Environment and Development and Agenda 21,

Acknowledging that precaution underlies the concerns of all the Parties and is embedded within this Convention,

Recognizing that this Convention and other international agreements in the field of trade and the environment are mutually supportive,

Reaffirming that States have, in accordance with the Charter of the United Nations and the principles of international law, the sovereign right to exploit their own resources pursuant to their own environmental and developmental policies, and the responsibility to ensure that activities within their jurisdiction or control do not cause damage to the environment of other States or of areas beyond the limits of national jurisdiction,

Taking into account the circumstances and particular requirements of developing countries, in particular the least developed among them, and countries with economies in transition, especially the need to strengthen their national capabilities for the management of chemicals, including through the transfer of technology, the provision of financial and technical assistance and the promotion of cooperation among the Parties,

Taking full account of the Programme of Action for the Sustainable Development of Small Island Developing States, adopted in Barbados on 6 May 1994,

Noting the respective capabilities of developed and developing countries, as well as the common but differentiated responsibilities of States as set forth in Principle 7 of the Rio Declaration on Environment and Development,

Recognizing the important contribution that the private sector and non-governmental organizations can make to achieving the reduction and/or elimination of emissions and discharges of persistent organic pollutants,

Underlining the importance of manufacturers of persistent organic pollutants taking responsibility for reducing adverse effects caused by their products and for providing information to users, Governments and the public on the hazardous properties of those chemicals,

Conscious of the need to take measures to prevent adverse effects caused by persistent organic pollutants at all stages of their life cycle,

Reaffirming Principle 16 of the Rio Declaration on Environment and Development which states that national authorities should endeavour to promote the internalization of environmental costs and the use of economic instruments, taking into account the approach that the polluter should, in principle, bear the cost of pollution, with due regard to the public interest and without distorting international trade and investment,

Encouraging Parties not having regulatory and assessment schemes for pesticides and industrial chemicals to develop such schemes,

Recognizing the importance of developing and using environmentally sound alternative processes and chemicals,

Determined to protect human health and the environment from the harmful impacts of persistent organic pollutants,

Have agreed as follows:

Article 1
Objective

Mindful of the precautionary approach as set forth in Principle 15 of the Rio Declaration on Environment and Development, the objective of this Convention is to protect human health and the environment from persistent organic pollutants.

Article 2
Definitions

For the purposes of this Convention:

(a) 'Party' means a State or regional economic integration organization that has consented to be bound by this Convention and for which the Convention is in force;

(b) 'Regional economic integration organization' means an organization constituted by sovereign States of a given region to which its member States have transferred competence in respect of matters governed by this Convention and which has been duly authorized, in accordance with its internal procedures, to sign, ratify, accept, approve or accede to this Convention;

(c) 'Parties present and voting' means Parties present and casting an affirmative or negative vote.

Article 3
Measures to reduce or eliminate releases from intentional production and use

1. Each Party shall:

(a) Prohibit and/or take the legal and administrative measures necessary to eliminate:
  (i) Its production and use of the chemicals listed in Annex A subject to the provisions of that Annex; and
  (ii) Its import and export of the chemicals listed in Annex A in accordance with the provisions of paragraph 2; and
(b) Restrict its production and use of the chemicals listed in Annex B in accordance with the provisions of that Annex.

2. Each Party shall take measures to ensure:

(a) That a chemical listed in Annex A or Annex B is imported only:
  (i) For the purpose of environmentally sound disposal as set forth in paragraph 1 (d) of Article 6; or
  (ii) For a use or purpose which is permitted for that Party under Annex A or Annex B;
(b) That a chemical listed in Annex A for which any production or use specific exemption is in effect or a chemical listed in Annex B for which any production or use specific exemption or acceptable purpose is in effect, taking into account any relevant provisions in existing international prior informed consent instruments, is exported only:
  (i) For the purpose of environmentally sound disposal as set forth in paragraph 1 (d) of Article 6;
  (ii) To a Party which is permitted to use that chemical under Annex A or Annex B; or
  (iii) To a State not Party to this Convention which has provided an annual certification to the exporting Party. Such certification shall specify the intended use of the chemical and include a statement that, with respect to that chemical, the importing State is committed to:
    a. Protect human health and the environment by taking the necessary measures to minimize or prevent releases;
    b. Comply with the provisions of paragraph 1 of Article 6; and
    c. Comply, where appropriate, with the provisions of paragraph 2 of Part II of Annex B.

    The certification shall also include any appropriate supporting documentation, such as legislation, regulatory instruments, or administrative or policy guidelines. The exporting Party shall transmit the certification to the Secretariat within sixty days of receipt.

(c) That a chemical listed in Annex A, for which production and use specific exemptions are no longer in effect for any Party, is not exported from it except for the purpose of environmentally sound disposal as set forth in paragraph 1 (d) of Article 6;

(d) For the purposes of this paragraph, the term 'State not Party to this Convention' shall include, with respect to a particular chemical, a State or regional economic integration organization that has not agreed to be bound by the Convention with respect to that chemical.

3. Each Party that has one or more regulatory and assessment schemes for new pesticides or new industrial chemicals shall take measures to regulate with the aim of preventing the production and use of new pesticides or new industrial chemicals which, taking into consideration the criteria in paragraph 1 of Annex D, exhibit the characteristics of persistent organic pollutants.

4. Each Party that has one or more regulatory and assessment schemes for pesticides or industrial chemicals shall, where appropriate, take into consideration within these schemes the criteria in paragraph 1 of Annex D when conducting assessments of pesticides or industrial chemicals currently in use.

5. Except as otherwise provided in this Convention, paragraphs 1 and 2 shall not apply to quantities of a chemical to be used for laboratory-scale research or as a reference standard.

6. Any Party that has a specific exemption in accordance with Annex A or a specific exemption or an acceptable purpose in accordance with Annex B shall take appropriate measures to ensure that any production or use under such exemption or purpose is carried out in a manner that prevents or minimizes human exposure and release into the environment. For exempted uses or acceptable purposes that involve intentional release into the environment under conditions of normal use, such release shall be to the minimum extent necessary, taking into account any applicable standards and guidelines.

Article 4
Register of specific exemptions

1. A Register is hereby established for the purpose of identifying the Parties that have specific exemptions listed in Annex A or Annex B. It shall not identify Parties that make use of the provisions in Annex A or Annex B that may be exercised by all Parties. The Register shall be maintained by the Secretariat and shall be available to the public.

2. The Register shall include:

(a) A list of the types of specific exemptions reproduced from Annex A and Annex B;

(b) A list of the Parties that have a specific exemption listed under Annex A or Annex B; and

(c) A list of the expiry dates for each registered specific exemption.

3. Any State may, on becoming a Party, by means of a notification in writing to the Secretariat, register for one or more types of specific exemptions listed in Annex A or Annex B.

4. Unless an earlier date is indicated in the Register by a Party, or an extension is granted pursuant to paragraph 7, all registrations of specific exemptions shall expire five years after the date of entry into force of this Convention with respect to a particular chemical.

5. At its first meeting, the Conference of the Parties shall decide upon its review process for the entries in the Register.

6. Prior to a review of an entry in the Register, the Party concerned shall submit a report to the Secretariat justifying its continuing need for registration of that exemption. The report shall be circulated by the Secretariat to all Parties. The review of a registration shall be carried out on the basis of all available information. Thereupon, the Conference of the Parties may make such recommendations to the Party concerned as it deems appropriate.

7. The Conference of the Parties may, upon request from the Party concerned, decide to extend the expiry date of a specific exemption for a period of up to five years. In making its decision, the Conference of the Parties shall take due account of the special circumstances of the developing country Parties and Parties with economies in transition.

8. A Party may, at any time, withdraw an entry from the Register for a specific exemption upon written notification to the Secretariat. The withdrawal shall take effect on the date specified in the notification.

9. When there are no longer any Parties registered for a particular type of specific exemption, no new registrations may be made with respect to it.

Article 5
Measures to reduce or eliminate releases from unintentional production

Each Party shall at a minimum take the following measures to reduce the total releases derived from anthropogenic sources of each of the chemicals listed in Annex C, with the goal of their continuing minimization and, where feasible, ultimate elimination:

(a) Develop an action plan or, where appropriate, a regional or subregional action plan within two years of the date of entry into force of this Convention for it, and subsequently implement it as part of its implementation plan specified in Article 7, designed to identify, characterize and address the release of the chemicals listed in Annex C and to facilitate implementation of subparagraphs (b) to (e). The action plan shall include the following elements:

  (i) An evaluation of current and projected releases, including the development and maintenance of source inventories and release estimates, taking into consideration the source categories identified in Annex C;

    (ii) An evaluation of the efficacy of the laws and policies of the Party relating to the management of such releases;

    (iii) Strategies to meet the obligations of this paragraph, taking into account the evaluations in (i) and (ii);

    (iv) Steps to promote education and training with regard to, and awareness of, those strategies;

    (v) A review every five years of those strategies and of their success in meeting the obligations of this paragraph; such reviews shall be included in reports submitted pursuant to Article 15;

    (vi) A schedule for implementation of the action plan, including for the strategies and measures identified therein;

(b) Promote the application of available, feasible and practical measures that can expeditiously achieve a realistic and meaningful level of release reduction or source elimination;

(c) Promote the development and, where it deems appropriate, require the use of substitute or modified materials, products and processes to prevent the formation and release of the chemicals listed in Annex C, taking into consideration the general guidance on prevention and release reduction measures in Annex C and guidelines to be adopted by decision of the Conference of the Parties;

(d) Promote and, in accordance with the implementation schedule of its action plan, require the use of best available techniques for new sources within source categories which a Party has identified as warranting such action in its action plan, with a particular initial focus on source categories identified in Part II of Annex C. In any case, the requirement to use best available techniques for new sources in the categories listed in Part II of that Annex shall be phased in as soon as practicable but no later than four years after the entry into force of the Convention for that Party. For the identified categories, Parties shall promote the use of best environmental practices. When applying best available techniques and best environmental practices, Parties should take into consideration the general guidance on prevention and release reduction measures in that Annex and guidelines on best available techniques and best environmental practices to be adopted by decision of the Conference of the Parties;

(e) Promote, in accordance with its action plan, the use of best available techniques and best environmental practices:

    (i) For existing sources, within the source categories listed in Part II of Annex C and within source categories such as those in Part III of that Annex; and

    (ii) For new sources, within source categories such as those listed in Part III of Annex C which a Party has not addressed under subparagraph (d).

When applying best available techniques and best environmental practices, Parties should take into consideration the general guidance on prevention

and release reduction measures in Annex C and guidelines on best available
techniques and best environmental practices to be adopted by decision of
the Conference of the Parties;

(f) For the purposes of this paragraph and Annex C:

   (i) 'Best available techniques' means the most effective and advanced stage
       in the development of activities and their methods of operation which
       indicate the practical suitability of particular techniques for providing
       in principle the basis for release limitations designed to prevent and,
       where that is not practicable, generally to reduce releases of chemicals
       listed in Part I of Annex C and their impact on the environment as a
       whole. In this regard:

  (ii) 'Techniques' includes both the technology used and the way in which
       the installation is designed, built, maintained, operated and decom-
       missioned;

 (iii) 'Available' techniques means those techniques that are accessible to the
       operator and that are developed on a scale that allows implementation
       in the relevant industrial sector, under economically and technically
       viable conditions, taking into consideration the costs and advantages;
       and

  (iv) 'Best' means most effective in achieving a high general level of protec-
       tion of the environment as a whole;

   (v) 'Best environmental practices' means the application of the most
       appropriate combination of environmental control measures and
       strategies;

  (vi) 'New source' means any source of which the construction or substantial
       modification is commenced at least one year after the date of:
       a. Entry into force of this Convention for the Party concerned; or
       b. Entry into force for the Party concerned of an amendment to
          Annex C where the source becomes subject to the provisions of
          this Convention only by virtue of that amendment.

(g) Release limit values or performance standards may be used by a Party
    to fulfill its commitments for best available techniques under this
    paragraph.

Article 6
Measures to reduce or eliminate releases from stockpiles and wastes

1. In order to ensure that stockpiles consisting of or containing chemicals
listed either in Annex A or Annex B and wastes, including products and articles upon becoming wastes, consisting of, containing or contaminated with
a chemical listed in Annex A, B or C, are managed in a manner protective of
human health and the environment, each Party shall:

(a) Develop appropriate strategies for identifying:
   (i) Stockpiles consisting of or containing chemicals listed either in Annex A or Annex B; and
   (ii) Products and articles in use and wastes consisting of, containing or contaminated with a chemical listed in Annex A, B or C;
(b) Identify, to the extent practicable, stockpiles consisting of or containing chemicals listed either in Annex A or Annex B on the basis of the strategies referred to in subparagraph (a);
(c) Manage stockpiles, as appropriate, in a safe, efficient and environmentally sound manner. Stockpiles of chemicals listed either in Annex A or Annex B, after they are no longer allowed to be used according to any specific exemption specified in Annex A or any specific exemption or acceptable purpose specified in Annex B, except stockpiles which are allowed to be exported according to paragraph 2 of Article 3, shall be deemed to be waste and shall be managed in accordance with subparagraph (d);
(d) Take appropriate measures so that such wastes, including products and articles upon becoming wastes, are:
   (i) Handled, collected, transported and stored in an environmentally sound manner;
   (ii) Disposed of in such a way that the persistent organic pollutant content is destroyed or irreversibly transformed so that they do not exhibit the characteristics of persistent organic pollutants or otherwise disposed of in an environmentally sound manner when destruction or irreversible transformation does not represent the environmentally preferable option or the persistent organic pollutant content is low, taking into account international rules, standards, and guidelines, including those that may be developed pursuant to paragraph 2, and relevant global and regional regimes governing the management of hazardous wastes;
   (iii) Not permitted to be subjected to disposal operations that may lead to recovery, recycling, reclamation, direct reuse or alternative uses of persistent organic pollutants; and
   (iv) Not transported across international boundaries without taking into account relevant international rules, standards and guidelines;
(e) Endeavour to develop appropriate strategies for identifying sites contaminated by chemicals listed in Annex A, B or C; if remediation of those sites is undertaken it shall be performed in an environmentally sound manner.

2. The Conference of the Parties shall cooperate closely with the appropriate bodies of the Basel Convention on the Control of Transboundary Movements of Hazardous Wastes and their Disposal to, *inter alia*:

(a) Establish levels of destruction and irreversible transformation necessary to ensure that the characteristics of persistent organic pollutants as specified in paragraph 1 of Annex D are not exhibited;
(b) Determine what they consider to be the methods that constitute environmentally sound disposal referred to above; and
(c) Work to establish, as appropriate, the concentration levels of the chemicals listed in Annexes A, B and C in order to define the low persistent organic pollutant content referred to in paragraph 1 (d)(ii).

Article 7
Implementation plans

1. Each Party shall:

(a) Develop and endeavour to implement a plan for the implementation of its obligations under this Convention;
(b) Transmit its implementation plan to the Conference of the Parties within two years of the date on which this Convention enters into force for it; and
(c) Review and update, as appropriate, its implementation plan on a periodic basis and in a manner to be specified by a decision of the Conference of the Parties.

2. The Parties shall, where appropriate, cooperate directly or through global, regional and subregional organizations, and consult their national stakeholders, including women's groups and groups involved in the health of children, in order to facilitate the development, implementation and updating of their implementation plans.

3. The Parties shall endeavour to utilize and, where necessary, establish the means to integrate national implementation plans for persistent organic pollutants in their sustainable development strategies where appropriate.

Article 8
Listing of chemicals in Annexes A, B and C

1. A Party may submit a proposal to the Secretariat for listing a chemical in Annexes A, B and/or C. The proposal shall contain the information specified in Annex D. In developing a proposal, a Party may be assisted by other Parties and/or by the Secretariat.

2. The Secretariat shall verify whether the proposal contains the information specified in Annex D. If the Secretariat is satisfied that the proposal contains the information so specified, it shall forward the proposal to the Persistent Organic Pollutants Review Committee.

3. The Committee shall examine the proposal and apply the screening criteria specified in Annex D in a flexible and transparent way, taking all information provided into account in an integrative and balanced manner.

4. If the Committee decides that:

(a) It is satisfied that the screening criteria have been fulfilled, it shall, through the Secretariat, make the proposal and the evaluation of the Committee available to all Parties and observers and invite them to submit the information specified in Annex E; or

(b) It is not satisfied that the screening criteria have been fulfilled, it shall, through the Secretariat, inform all Parties and observers and make the proposal and the evaluation of the Committee available to all Parties and the proposal shall be set aside.

5. Any Party may resubmit a proposal to the Committee that has been set aside by the Committee pursuant to paragraph 4. The resubmission may include any concerns of the Party as well as a justification for additional consideration by the Committee. If, following this procedure, the Committee again sets the proposal aside, the Party may challenge the decision of the Committee and the Conference of the Parties shall consider the matter at its next session. The Conference of the Parties may decide, based on the screening criteria in Annex D and taking into account the evaluation of the Committee and any additional information provided by any Party or observer, that the proposal should proceed.

6. Where the Committee has decided that the screening criteria have been fulfilled, or the Conference of the Parties has decided that the proposal should proceed, the Committee shall further review the proposal, taking into account any relevant additional information received, and shall prepare a draft risk profile in accordance with Annex E. It shall, through the Secretariat, make that draft available to all Parties and observers, collect technical comments from them and, taking those comments into account, complete the risk profile.

7. If, on the basis of the risk profile conducted in accordance with Annex E, the Committee decides:

(a) That the chemical is likely as a result of its long-range environmental transport to lead to significant adverse human health and/or environmental effects such that global action is warranted, the proposal shall proceed. Lack of full scientific certainty shall not prevent the proposal from proceeding. The Committee shall, through the Secretariat, invite information from all Parties and observers relating to the considerations specified in Annex F. It shall then prepare a risk management evaluation that includes an analysis of possible control measures for the chemical in accordance with that Annex; or

(b) That the proposal should not proceed, it shall, through the Secretariat, make the risk profile available to all Parties and observers and set the proposal aside.

8. For any proposal set aside pursuant to paragraph 7 (b), a Party may request the Conference of the Parties to consider instructing the Committee to

invite additional information from the proposing Party and other Parties during a period not to exceed one year. After that period and on the basis of any information received, the Committee shall reconsider the proposal pursuant to paragraph 6 with a priority to be decided by the Conference of the Parties. If, following this procedure, the Committee again sets the proposal aside, the Party may challenge the decision of the Committee and the Conference of the Parties shall consider the matter at its next session. The Conference of the Parties may decide, based on the risk profile prepared in accordance with Annex E and taking into account the evaluation of the Committee and any additional information provided by any Party or observer, that the proposal should proceed. If the Conference of the Parties decides that the proposal shall proceed, the Committee shall then prepare the risk management evaluation.

9. The Committee shall, based on the risk profile referred to in paragraph 6 and the risk management evaluation referred to in paragraph 7 (a) or paragraph 8, recommend whether the chemical should be considered by the Conference of the Parties for listing in Annexes A, B and/or C. The Conference of the Parties, taking due account of the recommendations of the Committee, including any scientific uncertainty, shall decide, in a precautionary manner, whether to list the chemical, and specify its related control measures, in Annexes A, B and/or C.

Article 9
Information exchange

1. Each Party shall facilitate or undertake the exchange of information relevant to:

(a) The reduction or elimination of the production, use and release of persistent organic pollutants; and

(b) Alternatives to persistent organic pollutants, including information relating to their risks as well as to their economic and social costs.

2. The Parties shall exchange the information referred to in paragraph 1 directly or through the Secretariat.

3. Each Party shall designate a national focal point for the exchange of such information.

4. The Secretariat shall serve as a clearing-house mechanism for information on persistent organic pollutants, including information provided by Parties, intergovernmental organizations and nongovernmental organizations.

5. For the purposes of this Convention, information on health and safety of humans and the environment shall not be regarded as confidential. Parties that exchange other information pursuant to this Convention shall protect any confidential information as mutually agreed.

Article 10
Public information, awareness and education

1. Each Party shall, within its capabilities, promote and facilitate:

(a) Awareness among its policy and decision makers with regard to persistent organic pollutants;

(b) Provision to the public of all available information on persistent organic pollutants, taking into account paragraph 5 of Article 9;

(c) Development and implementation, especially for women, children and the least educated, of educational and public awareness programmes on persistent organic pollutants, as well as on their health and environmental effects and on their alternatives;

(d) Public participation in addressing persistent organic pollutants and their health and environmental effects and in developing adequate responses, including opportunities for providing input at the national level regarding implementation of this Convention;

(e) Training of workers, scientists, educators and technical and managerial personnel;

(f) Development and exchange of educational and public awareness materials at the national and international levels; and

(g) Development and implementation of education and training programmes at the national and international levels.

2. Each Party shall, within its capabilities, ensure that the public has access to the public information referred to in paragraph 1 and that the information is kept up-to-date.

3. Each Party shall, within its capabilities, encourage industry and professional users to promote and facilitate the provision of the information referred to in paragraph 1 at the national level and, as appropriate, subregional, regional and global levels.

4. In providing information on persistent organic pollutants and their alternatives, Parties may use safety data sheets, reports, mass media and other means of communication, and may establish information centres at national and regional levels.

5. Each Party shall give sympathetic consideration to developing mechanisms, such as pollutant release and transfer registers, for the collection and dissemination of information on estimates of the annual quantities of the chemicals listed in Annex A, B or C that are released or disposed of.

Article 11
Research, development and monitoring

1. The Parties shall, within their capabilities, at the national and international levels, encourage and/or undertake appropriate research, development,

monitoring and cooperation pertaining to persistent organic pollutants and, where relevant, to their alternatives and to candidate persistent organic pollutants, including on their:

(a) Sources and releases into the environment;
(b) Presence, levels and trends in humans and the environment;
(c) Environmental transport, fate and transformation;
(d) Effects on human health and the environment;
(e) Socio-economic and cultural impacts;
(f) Release reduction and/or elimination; and
(g) Harmonized methodologies for making inventories of generating sources and analytical techniques for the measurement of releases.

2. In undertaking action under paragraph 1, the Parties shall, within their capabilities:

(a) Support and further develop, as appropriate, international programmes, networks and organizations aimed at defining, conducting, assessing and financing research, data collection and monitoring, taking into account the need to minimize duplication of effort;
(b) Support national and international efforts to strengthen national scientific and technical research capabilities, particularly in developing countries and countries with economies in transition, and to promote access to, and the exchange of, data and analyses;
(c) Take into account the concerns and needs, particularly in the field of financial and technical resources, of developing countries and countries with economies in transition and cooperate in improving their capability to participate in the efforts referred to in subparagraphs (a) and (b);
(d) Undertake research work geared towards alleviating the effects of persistent organic pollutants on reproductive health;
(e) Make the results of their research, development and monitoring activities referred to in this paragraph accessible to the public on a timely and regular basis; and
(f) Encourage and/or undertake cooperation with regard to storage and maintenance of information generated from research, development and monitoring.

Article 12
Technical assistance

1. The Parties recognize that rendering of timely and appropriate technical assistance in response to requests from developing country Parties and Parties with economies in transition is essential to the successful implementation of this Convention.

2. The Parties shall cooperate to provide timely and appropriate technical assistance to developing country Parties and Parties with economies in transition, to assist them, taking into account their particular needs, to develop and strengthen their capacity to implement their obligations under this Convention.

3. In this regard, technical assistance to be provided by developed country Parties, and other Parties in accordance with their capabilities, shall include, as appropriate and as mutually agreed, technical assistance for capacity-building relating to implementation of the obligations under this Convention. Further guidance in this regard shall be provided by the Conference of the Parties.

4. The Parties shall establish, as appropriate, arrangements for the purpose of providing technical assistance and promoting the transfer of technology to developing country Parties and Parties with economies in transition relating to the implementation of this Convention. These arrangements shall include regional and subregional centres for capacity-building and transfer of technology to assist developing country Parties and Parties with economies in transition to fulfil their obligations under this Convention. Further guidance in this regard shall be provided by the Conference of the Parties.

5. The Parties shall, in the context of this Article, take full account of the specific needs and special situation of least developed countries and small island developing states in their actions with regard to technical assistance.

Article 13
Financial resources and mechanisms

1. Each Party undertakes to provide, within its capabilities, financial support and incentives in respect of those national activities that are intended to achieve the objective of this Convention in accordance with its national plans, priorities and programmes.

2. The developed country Parties shall provide new and additional financial resources to enable developing country Parties and Parties with economies in transition to meet the agreed full incremental costs of implementing measures which fulfill their obligations under this Convention as agreed between a recipient Party and an entity participating in the mechanism described in paragraph 6. Other Parties may also on a voluntary basis and in accordance with their capabilities provide such financial resources. Contributions from other sources should also be encouraged. The implementation of these commitments shall take into account the need for adequacy, predictability, the timely flow of funds and the importance of burden sharing among the contributing Parties.

3. Developed country Parties, and other Parties in accordance with their capabilities and in accordance with their national plans, priorities and programmes, may also provide and developing country Parties and Parties with economies in transition avail themselves of financial resources to assist in their implementation of this Convention through other bilateral, regional and multilateral sources or channels.

4. The extent to which the developing country Parties will effectively implement their commitments under this Convention will depend on the effective implementation by developed country Parties of their commitments under this Convention relating to financial resources, technical assistance and technology transfer. The fact that sustainable economic and social development and eradication of poverty are the first and overriding priorities of the developing country Parties will be taken fully into account, giving due consideration to the need for the protection of human health and the environment.

5. The Parties shall take full account of the specific needs and special situation of the least developed countries and the small island developing states in their actions with regard to funding.

6. A mechanism for the provision of adequate and sustainable financial resources to developing country Parties and Parties with economies in transition on a grant or concessional basis to assist in their implementation of the Convention is hereby defined. The mechanism shall function under the authority, as appropriate, and guidance of, and be accountable to the Conference of the Parties for the purposes of this Convention. Its operation shall be entrusted to one or more entities, including existing international entities, as may be decided upon by the Conference of the Parties. The mechanism may also include other entities providing multilateral, regional and bilateral financial and technical assistance. Contributions to the mechanism shall be additional to other financial transfers to developing country Parties and Parties with economies in transition as reflected in, and in accordance with, paragraph 2.

7. Pursuant to the objectives of this Convention and paragraph 6, the Conference of the Parties shall at its first meeting adopt appropriate guidance to be provided to the mechanism and shall agree with the entity or entities participating in the financial mechanism upon arrangements to give effect thereto. The guidance shall address, *inter alia*:

(a) The determination of the policy, strategy and programme priorities, as well as clear and detailed criteria and guidelines regarding eligibility for access to and utilization of financial resources including monitoring and evaluation on a regular basis of such utilization;

(b) The provision by the entity or entities of regular reports to the Conference of the Parties on adequacy and sustainability of funding for activities relevant to the implementation of this Convention;

(c) The promotion of multiple-source funding approaches, mechanisms and arrangements;

(d) The modalities for the determination in a predictable and identifiable manner of the amount of funding necessary and available for the implementation of this Convention, keeping in mind that the phasing out of persistent organic pollutants might require sustained funding, and the conditions under which that amount shall be periodically reviewed; and

(e) The modalities for the provision to interested Parties of assistance with needs assessment, information on available sources of funds and on funding patterns in order to facilitate coordination among them.

8. The Conference of the Parties shall review, not later than its second meeting and thereafter on a regular basis, the effectiveness of the mechanism established under this Article, its ability to address the changing needs of the developing country Parties and Parties with economies in transition, the criteria and guidance referred to in paragraph 7, the level of funding as well as the effectiveness of the performance of the institutional entities entrusted to operate the financial mechanism. It shall, based on such review, take appropriate action, if necessary, to improve the effectiveness of the mechanism, including by means of recommendations and guidance on measures to ensure adequate and sustainable funding to meet the needs of the Parties.

Article 14
Interim financial arrangements

The institutional structure of the Global Environment Facility, operated in accordance with the Instrument for the Establishment of the Restructured Global Environment Facility, shall, on an interim basis, be the principal entity entrusted with the operations of the financial mechanism referred to in Article 13, for the period between the date of entry into force of this Convention and the first meeting of the Conference of the Parties, or until such time as the Conference of the Parties decides which institutional structure will be designated in accordance with Article 13. The institutional structure of the Global Environment Facility should fulfill this function through operational measures related specifically to persistent organic pollutants taking into account that new arrangements for this area may be needed.

Article 15
Reporting

1. Each Party shall report to the Conference of the Parties on the measures it has taken to implement the provisions of this Convention and on the effectiveness of such measures in meeting the objectives of the Convention.

2. Each Party shall provide to the Secretariat:

(a) Statistical data on its total quantities of production, import and export of each of the chemicals listed in Annex A and Annex B or a reasonable estimate of such data; and

(b) To the extent practicable, a list of the States from which it has imported each such substance and the States to which it has exported each such substance.

3. Such reporting shall be at periodic intervals and in a format to be decided by the Conference of the Parties at its first meeting.

Article 16
Effectiveness evaluation

1. Commencing four years after the date of entry into force of this Convention, and periodically thereafter at intervals to be decided by the Conference of the Parties, the Conference shall evaluate the effectiveness of this Convention.

2. In order to facilitate such evaluation, the Conference of the Parties shall, at its first meeting, initiate the establishment of arrangements to provide itself with comparable monitoring data on the presence of the chemicals listed in Annexes A, B and C as well as their regional and global environmental transport. These arrangements:

(a) Should be implemented by the Parties on a regional basis when appropriate, in accordance with their technical and financial capabilities, using existing monitoring programmes and mechanisms to the extent possible and promoting harmonization of approaches;
(b) May be supplemented where necessary, taking into account the differences between regions and their capabilities to implement monitoring activities; and
(c) Shall include reports to the Conference of the Parties on the results of the monitoring activities on a regional and global basis at intervals to be specified by the Conference of the Parties.

3. The evaluation described in paragraph 1 shall be conducted on the basis of available scientific, environmental, technical and economic information, including:

(a) Reports and other monitoring information provided pursuant to paragraph 2;
(b) National reports submitted pursuant to Article 15; and
(c) Non-compliance information provided pursuant to the procedures established under Article 17.

Article 17
Non-compliance

The Conference of the Parties shall, as soon as practicable, develop and approve procedures and institutional mechanisms for determining non-compliance with the provisions of this Convention and for the treatment of Parties found to be in non-compliance.

Article 18
Settlement of disputes

1. Parties shall settle any dispute between them concerning the interpretation or application of this Convention through negotiation or other peaceful means of their own choice.

2. When ratifying, accepting, approving or acceding to the Convention, or at any time thereafter, a Party that is not a regional economic integration organization may declare in a written instrument submitted to the depositary that, with respect to any dispute concerning the interpretation or application of the Convention, it recognizes one or both of the following means of dispute settlement as compulsory in relation to any Party accepting the same obligation:

(a) Arbitration in accordance with procedures to be adopted by the Conference of the Parties in an annex as soon as practicable;
(b) Submission of the dispute to the International Court of Justice.

3. A Party that is a regional economic integration organization may make a declaration with like effect in relation to arbitration in accordance with the procedure referred to in paragraph 2(a).

4. A declaration made pursuant to paragraph 2 or paragraph 3 shall remain in force until it expires in accordance with its terms or until three months after written notice of its revocation has been deposited with the depositary.

5. The expiry of a declaration, a notice of revocation or a new declaration shall not in any way affect proceedings pending before an arbitral tribunal or the International Court of Justice unless the parties to the dispute otherwise agree.

6. If the parties to a dispute have not accepted the same or any procedure pursuant to paragraph 2, and if they have not been able to settle their dispute within twelve months following notification by one party to another that a dispute exists between them, the dispute shall be submitted to a conciliation commission at the request of any party to the dispute. The conciliation commission shall render a report with recommendations. Additional procedures relating to the conciliation commission shall be included in an annex to be adopted by the Conference of the Parties no later than at its second meeting.

Article 19
Conference of the Parties

1. A Conference of the Parties is hereby established.

2. The first meeting of the Conference of the Parties shall be convened by the Executive Director of the United Nations Environment Programme no later than one year after the entry into force of this Convention. Thereafter, ordinary meetings of the Conference of the Parties shall be held at regular intervals to be decided by the Conference.

3. Extraordinary meetings of the Conference of the Parties shall be held at such other times as may be deemed necessary by the Conference, or at the written request of any Party provided that it is supported by at least one third of the Parties.

4. The Conference of the Parties shall by consensus agree upon and adopt at its first meeting rules of procedure and financial rules for itself and any

subsidiary bodies, as well as financial provisions governing the functioning of the Secretariat.

5. The Conference of the Parties shall keep under continuous review and evaluation the implementation of this Convention. It shall perform the functions assigned to it by the Convention and, to this end, shall:

(a) Establish, further to the requirements of paragraph 6, such subsidiary bodies as it considers necessary for the implementation of the Convention;

(b) Cooperate, where appropriate, with competent international organizations and intergovernmental and non-governmental bodies; and

(c) Regularly review all information made available to the Parties pursuant to Article 15, including consideration of the effectiveness of paragraph 2(b)(iii) of Article 3;

(d) Consider and undertake any additional action that may be required for the achievement of the objectives of the Convention.

6. The Conference of the Parties shall, at its first meeting, establish a subsidiary body to be called the Persistent Organic Pollutants Review Committee for the purposes of performing the functions assigned to that Committee by this Convention. In this regard:

(a) The members of the Persistent Organic Pollutants Review Committee shall be appointed by the Conference of the Parties. Membership of the Committee shall consist of government-designated experts in chemical assessment or management. The members of the Committee shall be appointed on the basis of equitable geographical distribution;

(b) The Conference of the Parties shall decide on the terms of reference, organization and operation of the Committee; and

(c) The Committee shall make every effort to adopt its recommendations by consensus. If all efforts at consensus have been exhausted, and no consensus reached, such recommendation shall as a last resort be adopted by a two-thirds majority vote of the members present and voting.

7. The Conference of the Parties shall, at its third meeting, evaluate the continued need for the procedure contained in paragraph 2 (b) of Article 3, including consideration of its effectiveness.

8. The United Nations, its specialized agencies and the International Atomic Energy Agency, as well as any State not Party to this Convention, may be represented at meetings of the Conference of the Parties as observers. Any body or agency, whether national or international, governmental or non-governmental, qualified in matters covered by the Convention, and which has informed the Secretariat of its wish to be represented at a meeting of the Conference of the Parties as an observer may be admitted unless at least one third of the Parties present object. The admission and participation of observers shall be subject to the rules of procedure adopted by the Conference of the Parties.

Article 20
Secretariat

1. A Secretariat is hereby established.

2. The functions of the Secretariat shall be:

(a) To make arrangements for meetings of the Conference of the Parties and its subsidiary bodies and to provide them with services as required;

(b) To facilitate assistance to the Parties, particularly developing country Parties and Parties with economies in transition, on request, in the implementation of this Convention;

(c) To ensure the necessary coordination with the secretariats of other relevant international bodies;

(d) To prepare and make available to the Parties periodic reports based on information received pursuant to Article 15 and other available information;

(e) To enter, under the overall guidance of the Conference of the Parties, into such administrative and contractual arrangements as may be required for the effective discharge of its functions; and

(f) To perform the other secretariat functions specified in this Convention and such other functions as may be determined by the Conference of the Parties.

3. The secretariat functions for this Convention shall be performed by the Executive Director of the United Nations Environment Programme, unless the Conference of the Parties decides, by a three-fourths majority of the Parties present and voting, to entrust the secretariat functions to one or more other international organizations.

Article 21
Amendments to the Convention

1. Amendments to this Convention may be proposed by any Party.

2. Amendments to this Convention shall be adopted at a meeting of the Conference of the Parties. The text of any proposed amendment shall be communicated to the Parties by the Secretariat at least six months before the meeting at which it is proposed for adoption. The Secretariat shall also communicate proposed amendments to the signatories to this Convention and, for information, to the depositary.

3. The Parties shall make every effort to reach agreement on any proposed amendment to this Convention by consensus. If all efforts at consensus have been exhausted, and no agreement reached, the amendment shall as a last resort be adopted by a three-fourths majority vote of the Parties present and voting.

4. The amendment shall be communicated by the depositary to all Parties for ratification, acceptance or approval.

5. Ratification, acceptance or approval of an amendment shall be notified to the depositary in writing. An amendment adopted in accordance with paragraph 3 shall enter into force for the Parties having accepted it on the ninetieth day after the date of deposit of instruments of ratification, acceptance or approval by at least three-fourths of the Parties. Thereafter, the amendment shall enter into force for any other Party on the ninetieth day after the date on which that Party deposits its instrument of ratification, acceptance or approval of the amendment.

Article 22
Adoption and amendment of annexes

1. Annexes to this Convention shall form an integral part thereof and, unless expressly provided otherwise, a reference to this Convention constitutes at the same time a reference to any annexes thereto.

2. Any additional annexes shall be restricted to procedural, scientific, technical or administrative matters.

3. The following procedure shall apply to the proposal, adoption and entry into force of additional annexes to this Convention:

(a) Additional annexes shall be proposed and adopted according to the procedure laid down in paragraphs 1, 2 and 3 of Article 21;
(b) Any Party that is unable to accept an additional annex shall so notify the depositary, in writing, within one year from the date of communication by the depositary of the adoption of the additional annex. The depositary shall without delay notify all Parties of any such notification received. A Party may at any time withdraw a previous notification of non-acceptance in respect of any additional annex, and the annex shall thereupon enter into force for that Party subject to subparagraph (c); and
(c) On the expiry of one year from the date of the communication by the depositary of the adoption of an additional annex, the annex shall enter into force for all Parties that have not submitted a notification in accordance with the provisions of subparagraph (b).

4. The proposal, adoption and entry into force of amendments to Annex A, B or C shall be subject to the same procedures as for the proposal, adoption and entry into force of additional annexes to this Convention, except that an amendment to Annex A, B or C shall not enter into force with respect to any Party that has made a declaration with respect to amendment to those Annexes in accordance with paragraph 4 of Article 25, in which case any such amendment shall enter into force for such a Party on the ninetieth day after the date of deposit with the depositary of its instrument of ratification, acceptance, approval or accession with respect to such amendment.

5. The following procedure shall apply to the proposal, adoption and entry into force of an amendment to Annex D, E or F:

(a) Amendments shall be proposed according to the procedure in paragraphs 1 and 2 of Article 21;

(b) The Parties shall take decisions on an amendment to Annex D, E or F by consensus; and

(c) A decision to amend Annex D, E or F shall forthwith be communicated to the Parties by the depositary. The amendment shall enter into force for all Parties on a date to be specified in the decision.

6. If an additional annex or an amendment to an annex is related to an amendment to this Convention, the additional annex or amendment shall not enter into force until such time as the amendment to the Convention enters into force.

Article 23
Right to vote

1. Each Party to this Convention shall have one vote, except as provided for in paragraph 2.

2. A regional economic integration organization, on matters within its competence, shall exercise its right to vote with a number of votes equal to the number of its member States that are Parties to this Convention. Such an organization shall not exercise its right to vote if any of its member States exercises its right to vote, and vice versa.

Article 24
Signature

This Convention shall be open for signature at Stockholm by all States and regional economic integration organizations on 23 May 2001, and at the United Nations Headquarters in New York from 24 May 2001 to 22 May 2002.

Article 25
Ratification, acceptance, approval or accession

1. This Convention shall be subject to ratification, acceptance or approval by States and by regional economic integration organizations. It shall be open for accession by States and by regional economic integration organizations from the day after the date on which the Convention is closed for signature. Instruments of ratification, acceptance, approval or accession shall be deposited with the depositary.

2. Any regional economic integration organization that becomes a Party to this Convention without any of its member States being a Party shall be bound by all the obligations under the Convention. In the case of such organizations,

one or more of whose member States is a Party to this Convention, the organization and its member States shall decide on their respective responsibilities for the performance of their obligations under the Convention. In such cases, the organization and the member States shall not be entitled to exercise rights under the Convention concurrently.

3. In its instrument of ratification, acceptance, approval or accession, a regional economic integration organization shall declare the extent of its competence in respect of the matters governed by this Convention. Any such organization shall also inform the depositary, who shall in turn inform the Parties, of any relevant modification in the extent of its competence.

4. In its instrument of ratification, acceptance, approval or accession, any Party may declare that, with respect to it, any amendment to Annex A, B or C shall enter into force only upon the deposit of its instrument of ratification, acceptance, approval or accession with respect thereto.

Article 26
Entry into force

1. This Convention shall enter into force on the ninetieth day after the date of deposit of the fiftieth instrument of ratification, acceptance, approval or accession.

2. For each State or regional economic integration organization that ratifies, accepts or approves this Convention or accedes thereto after the deposit of the fiftieth instrument of ratification, acceptance, approval or accession, the Convention shall enter into force on the ninetieth day after the date of deposit by such State or regional economic integration organization of its instrument of ratification, acceptance, approval or accession.

3. For the purpose of paragraphs 1 and 2, any instrument deposited by a regional economic integration organization shall not be counted as additional to those deposited by member States of that organization.

Article 27
Reservations

No reservations may be made to this Convention.

Article 28
Withdrawal

1. At any time after three years from the date on which this Convention has entered into force for a Party, that Party may withdraw from the Convention by giving written notification to the depositary.

2. Any such withdrawal shall take effect upon the expiry of one year from the date of receipt by the depositary of the notification of withdrawal, or on such later date as may be specified in the notification of withdrawal.

Article 29
Depositary

The Secretary-General of the United Nations shall be the depositary of this Convention.

Article 30
Authentic texts

The original of this Convention, of which the Arabic, Chinese, English, French, Russian and Spanish texts are equally authentic, shall be deposited with the Secretary-General of the United Nations.

IN WITNESS WHEREOF the undersigned, being duly authorized to that effect, have signed this Convention.

Done at Stockholm on this twenty-second day of May, two thousand and one.

Annex A
Elimination

Part I

Chemical	Activity	Specific exemption
Aldrin* CAS No: 309-00-2	Production	None
	Use	Local ectoparasiticide Insecticide
Chlordane* CAS No: 57-74-9	Production	As allowed for the Parties listed in the Register
	Use	Local ectoparasiticide Insecticide Termiticide Termiticide in buildings and dams Termiticide in roads Additive in plywood adhesives
Dieldrin* CAS No: 60-57-1	Production	None
	Use	In agricultural operations
Endrin* CAS No: 72-20-8	Production	None
	Use	None
Heptachlor* CAS No: 76-44-8	Production	None

(cont.)

Chemical	Activity	Specific exemption
	Use	Termiticide
		Termiticide in structures of houses
		Termiticide (subterranean)
		Wood treatment
		In use in underground cable boxes
Hexachlorobenzene CAS No: 118-74-1	Production	As allowed for the Parties listed in the Register
	Use	Intermediate
		Solvent in pesticide
		Closed system site limited intermediate
Mirex* CAS No: 2385-85-5	Production	As allowed for the Parties listed in the Register
	Use	Termiticide
Toxaphene* CAS No: 8001-35-2	Production	None
	Use	None
Polychlorinated Biphenyls (PCB)*	Production	None
	Use	Articles in use in accordance with the provisions of Part II of this Annex

Notes:

(i) Except as otherwise specified in this Convention, quantities of a chemical occurring as unintentional trace contaminants in products and articles shall not be considered to be listed in this Annex;

(ii) This note shall not be considered as a production and use specific exemption for purposes of paragraph 2 of Article 3. Quantities of a chemical occurring as constituents of articles manufactured or already in use before or on the date of entry into force of the relevant obligation with respect to that chemical, shall not be considered as listed in this Annex, provided that a Party has notified the Secretariat that a particular type of article remains in use within that Party. The Secretariat shall make such notifications publicly available;

(iii) This note, which does not apply to a chemical that has an asterisk following its name in the Chemical column in Part I of this Annex, shall not be considered as a production and use specific exemption for purposes of paragraph 2 of Article 3. Given that no significant quantities of the chemical are expected to reach humans and the environment during the production and use of a closed-system site-limited intermediate, a Party, upon notification to the Secretariat, may allow the production and use of quantities of a chemical listed in this Annex as a closed-system site-limited intermediate that is chemically transformed in the manufacture of other chemicals that, taking into consideration the criteria in paragraph 1 of Annex D, do not exhibit the characteristics of persistent organic pollutants. This notification shall include information on total production and use of such chemical or a reasonable estimate of such information and information regarding the nature of the closed-system site-limited process including the amount of any non-transformed and unintentional trace contamination of the persistent organic pollutant-starting material in the final product. This procedure applies except as otherwise specified in this Annex. The Secretariat shall make such notifications available to the Conference of the Parties and to the public. Such production or use shall not be considered a production or use specific exemption. Such production and use shall cease after a ten-year period, unless the Party concerned submits a new notification to the Secretariat, in which case the period will be extended for an additional ten years unless the Conference of the Parties, after a review of the production and use decides otherwise. The notification procedure can be repeated;

(iv) All the specific exemptions in this Annex may be exercised by Parties that have registered exemptions in respect of them in accordance with Article 4 with the exception of the use of polychlorinated biphenyls in articles in use in accordance with the provisions of Part II of this Annex, which may be exercised by all Parties.

Part II
Polychlorinated biphenyls

Each Party shall:

(a) With regard to the elimination of the use of polychlorinated biphenyls in equipment (e.g. transformers, capacitors or other receptacles containing liquid stocks) by 2025, subject to review by the Conference of the Parties, take action in accordance with the following priorities:

(i) Make determined efforts to identify, label and remove from use equipment containing greater than 10 per cent polychlorinated biphenyls and volumes greater than 5 litres;

    (ii) Make determined efforts to identify, label and remove from use equipment containing greater than 0.05 per cent polychlorinated biphenyls and volumes greater than 5 litres;

    (iii) Endeavour to identify and remove from use equipment containing greater than 0.005 percent polychlorinated biphenyls and volumes greater than 0.05 litres;

(b) Consistent with the priorities in subparagraph (a), promote the following measures to reduce exposures and risk to control the use of polychlorinated biphenyls:

    (i) Use only in intact and non-leaking equipment and only in areas where the risk from environmental release can be minimised and quickly remedied;

    (ii) Not use in equipment in areas associated with the production or processing of food or feed;

    (iii) When used in populated areas, including schools and hospitals, all reasonable measures to protect from electrical failure which could result in a fire, and regular inspection of equipment for leaks;

(c) Notwithstanding paragraph 2 of Article 3, ensure that equipment containing polychlorinated biphenyls, as described in subparagraph (a), shall not be exported or imported except for the purpose of environmentally sound waste management;

(d) Except for maintenance and servicing operations, not allow recovery for the purpose of reuse in other equipment of liquids with polychlorinated biphenyls content above 0.005 per cent;

(e) Make determined efforts designed to lead to environmentally sound waste management of liquids containing polychlorinated biphenyls and equipment contaminated with polychlorinated biphenyls having a polychlorinated biphenyls content above 0.005 per cent, in accordance with paragraph 1 of Article 6, as soon as possible but no later than 2028, subject to review by the Conference of the Parties;

(f) In lieu of note (ii) in Part I of this Annex, endeavour to identify other articles containing more than 0.005 per cent polychlorinated biphenyls (e.g. cable-sheaths, cured caulk and painted objects) and manage them in accordance with paragraph 1 of Article 6;

(g) Provide a report every five years on progress in eliminating polychlorinated biphenyls and submit it to the Conference of the Parties pursuant to Article 15;

(h) The reports described in subparagraph (g) shall, as appropriate, be considered by the Conference of the Parties in its reviews relating to polychlorinated biphenyls. The Conference of the Parties shall review progress towards elimination of polychlorinated biphenyls at five year intervals or other period, as appropriate, taking into account such reports.

Annex B
Restriction

Part I

Chemical	Activity	Acceptable purpose or specific exemption
DDT (1,1,1-trichloro-2, 2-bis(4-chlorophenyl) ethane) CAS No: 50-29-3	Production	Acceptable purpose: Disease vector control use in accordance with Part II of this Annex Specific exemption: Intermediate in production of dicofol Intermediate
	Use	Acceptable purpose: Disease vector control in accordance with Part II of this Annex Specific exemption: Production of dicofol Intermediate

Notes:

(i) Except as otherwise specified in this Convention, quantities of a chemical occurring as unintentional trace contaminants in products and articles shall not be considered to be listed in this Annex;

(ii) This note shall not be considered as a production and use acceptable purpose or specific exemption for purposes of paragraph 2 of Article 3. Quantities of a chemical occurring as constituents of articles manufactured or already in use before or on the date of entry into force of the relevant obligation with respect to that chemical, shall not be considered as listed in this Annex, provided that a Party has notified the Secretariat that a particular type of article remains in use within that Party. The Secretariat shall make such notifications publicly available;

(iii) This note shall not be considered as a production and use specific exemption for purposes of paragraph 2 of Article 3. Given that no significant quantities of the chemical are expected to reach humans and the environment during the production and use of a closed-system site-limited intermediate, a Party, upon notification to the Secretariat, may allow the production and use of quantities of a chemical listed in this Annex as a closed-system site-limited intermediate that is chemically transformed in the manufacture of other chemicals that, taking into consideration the criteria in paragraph 1 of Annex D, do not exhibit the characteristics of persistent organic pollutants. This notification shall include information on total production and use of such chemical or a reasonable estimate of such information and information regarding the nature of the closed-system site-limited process including the amount of any non-transformed and unintentional trace contamination of the persistent organic pollutant-starting material in the final product. This procedure applies except as otherwise specified in this Annex. The Secretariat shall make such notifications available to the Conference of the Parties and to the public. Such production or use shall not be considered a production or use specific exemption. Such production and use shall cease after a ten-year period, unless the Party concerned submits a new notification to the Secretariat, in which case the period will be extended for an additional ten years unless the Conference of the Parties, after a review of the production and use decides otherwise. The notification procedure can be repeated;

(iv) All the specific exemptions in this Annex may be exercised by Parties that have registered in respect of them in accordance with Article 4.

Part II
DDT (1,1,1-trichloro-2,2-bis(4-chlorophenyl)ethane)

1. The production and use of DDT shall be eliminated except for Parties that have notified the Secretariat of their intention to produce and/or use it. A DDT Register is hereby established and shall be available to the public. The Secretariat shall maintain the DDT Register.

2. Each Party that produces and/or uses DDT shall restrict such production and/or use for disease vector control in accordance with the World Health Organization recommendations and guidelines on the use of DDT and when locally safe, effective and affordable alternatives are not available to the Party in question.

3. In the event that a Party not listed in the DDT Register determines that it requires DDT for disease vector control, it shall notify the Secretariat as soon as possible in order to have its name added forthwith to the DDT Register. It shall at the same time notify the World Health Organization.

4. Every three years, each Party that uses DDT shall provide to the Secretariat and the World Health Organization information on the amount used, the conditions of such use and its relevance to that Party's disease management strategy, in a format to be decided by the Conference of the Parties in consultation with the World Health Organization.

5. With the goal of reducing and ultimately eliminating the use of DDT, the Conference of the Parties shall encourage:

(a) Each Party using DDT to develop and implement an action plan as part of the implementation plan specified in Article 7. That action plan shall include:

(i) Development of regulatory and other mechanisms to ensure that DDT use is restricted to disease vector control;

(ii) Implementation of suitable alternative products, methods and strategies, including resistance management strategies to ensure the continuing effectiveness of these alternatives;

(iii) Measures to strengthen health care and to reduce the incidence of the disease.

(b) The Parties, within their capabilities, to promote research and development of safe alternative chemical and non-chemical products, methods and strategies for Parties using DDT, relevant to the conditions of those countries and with the goal of decreasing the human and economic burden of disease. Factors to be promoted when considering alternatives or combinations of alternatives shall include the human health risks and environmental implications of such alternatives. Viable alternatives to DDT shall pose less risk to human health and the environment, be suitable for disease control based on conditions in the Parties in question and be supported with monitoring data.

6. Commencing at its first meeting, and at least every three years thereafter, the Conference of the Parties shall, in consultation with the World Health Organization, evaluate the continued need for DDT for disease vector control on the basis of available scientific, technical, environmental and economic information, including:

(a) The production and use of DDT and the conditions set out in paragraph 2;

(b) The availability, suitability and implementation of the alternatives to DDT; and

(c) Progress in strengthening the capacity of countries to transfer safely to reliance on such alternatives.

7. A Party may, at any time, withdraw its name from the DDT Registry upon written notification to the Secretariat. The withdrawal shall take effect on the date specified in the notification.

Annex C
Unintentional production

Part I
Persistent organic pollutants subject to the requirements of Article 5

This Annex applies to the following persistent organic pollutants when formed and released unintentionally from anthropogenic sources:

Chemical
Polychlorinated dibenzo-p-dioxins and dibenzofurans (PCDD/PCDF)
Hexachlorobenzene (HCB) (CAS No: 118-74-1)
Polychlorinated biphenyls (PCB)

Part II
Source categories

Polychlorinated dibenzo-p-dioxins and dibenzofurans, hexachlorobenzene and polychlorinated biphenyls are unintentionally formed and released from thermal processes involving organic matter and chlorine as a result of incomplete combustion or chemical reactions. The following industrial source categories have the potential for comparatively high formation and release of these chemicals to the environment:

(a) Waste incinerators, including co-incinerators of municipal, hazardous or medical waste or of sewage sludge;
(b) Cement kilns firing hazardous waste;
(c) Production of pulp using elemental chlorine or chemicals generating elemental chlorine for bleaching;
(d) The following thermal processes in the metallurgical industry:
  (i) Secondary copper production;
  (ii) Sinter plants in the iron and steel industry;
  (iii) Secondary aluminium production;
  (iv) Secondary zinc production.

Part III
Source categories

Polychlorinated dibenzo-p-dioxins and dibenzofurans, hexachlorobenzene and polychlorinated biphenyls may also be unintentionally formed and released from the following source categories, including:

(a) Open burning of waste, including burning of landfill sites;
(b) Thermal processes in the metallurgical industry not mentioned in Part II;
(c) Residential combustion sources;
(d) Fossil fuel-fired utility and industrial boilers;
(e) Firing installations for wood and other biomass fuels;
(f) Specific chemical production processes releasing unintentionally formed persistent organic pollutants, especially production of chlorophenols and chloranil;

(g) Crematoria;
(h) Motor vehicles, particularly those burning leaded gasoline;
(i) Destruction of animal carcasses;
(j) Textile and leather dyeing (with chloranil) and finishing (with alkaline extraction);
(k) Shredder plants for the treatment of end of life vehicles;
(l) Smouldering of copper cables;
(m) Waste oil refineries.

Part IV
Definitions

1. For the purposes of this Annex:

(a) 'Polychlorinated biphenyls' means aromatic compounds formed in such a manner that the hydrogen atoms on the biphenyl molecule (two benzene rings bonded together by a single carbon-carbon bond) may be replaced by up to ten chlorine atoms; and
(b) 'Polychlorinated dibenzo-p-dioxins' and 'polychlorinated dibenzofurans' are tricyclic, aromatic compounds formed by two benzene rings connected by two oxygen atoms in polychlorinated dibenzo-p-dioxins and by one oxygen atom and one carbon-carbon bond in polychlorinated dibenzo-furans and the hydrogen atoms of which may be replaced by up to eight chlorine atoms.

2. In this Annex, the toxicity of polychlorinated dibenzo-p-dioxins and dibenzofurans is expressed using the concept of toxic equivalency which measures the relative dioxin-like toxic activity of different congeners of polychlorinated dibenzo-p-dioxins and dibenzofurans and coplanar polychlorinated biphenyls in comparison to 2,3,7,8-tetrachlorodibenzo-p-dioxin. The toxic equivalent factor values to be used for the purposes of this Convention shall be consistent with accepted international standards, commencing with the World Health Organization 1998 mammalian toxic equivalent factor values for polychlorinated dibenzo-p-dioxins and dibenzofurans and coplanar polychlorinated biphenyls. Concentrations are expressed in toxic equivalents.

Part V
General guidance on best available techniques and best environmental practices

This Part provides general guidance to Parties on preventing or reducing releases of the chemicals listed in Part I.

A. General prevention measures relating to both best available techniques and best environmental practices

Priority should be given to the consideration of approaches to prevent the formation and release of the chemicals listed in Part I. Useful measures could include:

(a) The use of low-waste technology;
(b) The use of less hazardous substances;
(c) The promotion of the recovery and recycling of waste and of substances generated and used in a process;
(d) Replacement of feed materials which are persistent organic pollutants or where there is a direct link between the materials and releases of persistent organic pollutants from the source;
(e) Good housekeeping and preventive maintenance programmes;
(f) Improvements in waste management with the aim of the cessation of open and other uncontrolled burning of wastes, including the burning of landfill sites. When considering proposals to construct new waste disposal facilities, consideration should be given to alternatives such as activities to minimize the generation of municipal and medical waste, including resource recovery, reuse, recycling, waste separation and promoting products that generate less waste. Under this approach, public health concerns should be carefully considered;
(g) Minimization of these chemicals as contaminants in products;
(h) Avoiding elemental chlorine or chemicals generating elemental chlorine for bleaching.

B. Best available techniques

The concept of best available techniques is not aimed at the prescription of any specific technique or technology, but at taking into account the technical characteristics of the installation concerned, its geographical location and the local environmental conditions. Appropriate control techniques to reduce releases of the chemicals listed in Part I are in general the same. In determining best available techniques, special consideration should be given, generally or in specific cases, to the following factors, bearing in mind the likely costs and benefits of a measure and consideration of precaution and prevention:

(a) General considerations:
    (i) The nature, effects and mass of the releases concerned: techniques may vary depending on source size;
    (ii) The commissioning dates for new or existing installations;
    (iii) The time needed to introduce the best available technique;

    (iv) The consumption and nature of raw materials used in the process and its energy efficiency;

    (v) The need to prevent or reduce to a minimum the overall impact of the releases to the environment and the risks to it;

    (vi) The need to prevent accidents and to minimize their consequences for the environment;

    (vii) The need to ensure occupational health and safety at workplaces;

    (viii) Comparable processes, facilities or methods of operation which have been tried with success on an industrial scale;

    (ix) Technological advances and changes in scientific knowledge and understanding.

(b) General release reduction measures: When considering proposals to construct new facilities or significantly modify existing facilities using processes that release chemicals listed in this Annex, priority consideration should be given to alternative processes, techniques or practices that have similar usefulness but which avoid the formation and release of such chemicals. In cases where such facilities will be constructed or significantly modified, in addition to the prevention measures outlined in section A of Part V the following reduction measures could also be considered in determining best available techniques:

    (i) Use of improved methods for flue-gas cleaning such as thermal or catalytic oxidation, dust precipitation, or adsorption;

    (ii) Treatment of residuals, wastewater, wastes and sewage sludge by, for example, thermal treatment or rendering them inert or chemical processes that detoxify them;

    (iii) Process changes that lead to the reduction or elimination of releases, such as moving to closed systems;

    (iv) Modification of process designs to improve combustion and prevent formation of the chemicals listed in this Annex, through the control of parameters such as incineration temperature or residence time.

C. Best environmental practices

The Conference of the Parties may develop guidance with regard to best environmental practices.

Annex D
Information requirements and screening criteria

    1. A Party submitting a proposal to list a chemical in Annexes A, B and/or C shall identify the chemical in the manner described in subparagraph (a) and provide the information on the chemical, and its transformation products

where relevant, relating to the screening criteria set out in subparagraphs (b) to (e):

(a) Chemical identity:
    (i) Names, including trade name or names, commercial name or names and synonyms, Chemical Abstracts Service (CAS) Registry number, International Union of Pure and Applied Chemistry (IUPAC) name; and
    (ii) Structure, including specification of isomers, where applicable, and the structure of the chemical class;
(b) Persistence:
    (i) Evidence that the half-life of the chemical in water is greater than two months, or that its half-life in soil is greater than six months, or that its half-life in sediment is greater than six months; or
    (ii) Evidence that the chemical is otherwise sufficiently persistent to justify its consideration within the scope of this Convention;
(c) Bio-accumulation:
    (i) Evidence that the bio-concentration factor or bio-accumulation factor in aquatic species for the chemical is greater than 5,000 or, in the absence of such data, that the log Kow is greater than 5;
    (ii) Evidence that a chemical presents other reasons for concern, such as high bio-accumulation in other species, high toxicity or ecotoxicity; or
    (iii) Monitoring data in biota indicating that the bio-accumulation potential of the chemical is sufficient to justify its consideration within the scope of this Convention;
(d) Potential for long-range environmental transport:
    (i) Measured levels of the chemical in locations distant from the sources of its release that are of potential concern;
    (ii) Monitoring data showing that long-range environmental transport of the chemical, with the potential for transfer to a receiving environment, may have occurred via air, water or migratory species; or
    (iii) Environmental fate properties and/or model results that demonstrate that the chemical has a potential for long-range environmental transport through air, water or migratory species, with the potential for transfer to a receiving environment in locations distant from the sources of its release. For a chemical that migrates significantly through the air, its half-life in air should be greater than two days; and
(e) Adverse effects:
    (i) Evidence of adverse effects to human health or to the environment that justifies consideration of the chemical within the scope of this Convention; or

(ii) Toxicity or ecotoxicity data that indicate the potential for damage to human health or to the environment.

2. The proposing Party shall provide a statement of the reasons for concern including, where possible, a comparison of toxicity or ecotoxicity data with detected or predicted levels of a chemical resulting or anticipated from its long-range environmental transport, and a short statement indicating the need for global control.

3. The proposing Party shall, to the extent possible and taking into account its capabilities, provide additional information to support the review of the proposal referred to in paragraph 6 of Article 8. In developing such a proposal, a Party may draw on technical expertise from any source.

Annex E
Information requirements for the risk profile

The purpose of the review is to evaluate whether the chemical is likely, as a result of its long-range environmental transport, to lead to significant adverse human health and/or environmental effects, such that global action is warranted. For this purpose, a risk profile shall be developed that further elaborates on, and evaluates, the information referred to in Annex D and includes, as far as possible, the following types of information:

(a) Sources, including as appropriate:
  (i) Production data, including quantity and location;
  (ii) Uses; and
  (iii) Releases, such as discharges, losses and emissions;
(b) Hazard assessment for the endpoint or endpoints of concern, including a consideration of toxicological interactions involving multiple chemicals;
(c) Environmental fate, including data and information on the chemical and physical properties of a chemical as well as its persistence and how they are linked to its environmental transport, transfer within and between environmental compartments, degradation and transformation to other chemicals. A determination of the bio-concentration factor or bio-accumulation factor, based on measured values, shall be available, except when monitoring data are judged to meet this need;
(d) Monitoring data;
(e) Exposure in local areas and, in particular, as a result of long-range environmental transport, and including information regarding bio-availability;
(f) National and international risk evaluations, assessments or profiles and labelling information and hazard classifications, as available; and
(g) Status of the chemical under international conventions.

Annex F
Information on socio-economic considerations

An evaluation should be undertaken regarding possible control measures for chemicals under consideration for inclusion in this Convention, encompassing the full range of options, including management and elimination. For this purpose, relevant information should be provided relating to socio-economic considerations associated with possible control measures to enable a decision to be taken by the Conference of the Parties. Such information should reflect due regard for the differing capabilities and conditions among the Parties and should include consideration of the following indicative list of items:

(a) Efficacy and efficiency of possible control measures in meeting risk reduction goals:
    (i) Technical feasibility; and
    (ii) Costs, including environmental and health costs;

(b) Alternatives (products and processes):
    (i) Technical feasibility;
    (ii) Costs, including environmental and health costs;
    (iii) Efficacy;
    (iv) Risk;
    (v) Availability; and
    (vi) Accessibility;

(c) Positive and/or negative impacts on society of implementing possible control measures:
    (i) Health, including public, environmental and occupational health;
    (ii) Agriculture, including aquaculture and forestry;
    (iii) Biota (biodiversity);
    (iv) Economic aspects;
    (v) Movement towards sustainable development; and
    (vi) Social costs;

(d) Waste and disposal implications (in particular, obsolete stocks of pesticides and clean-up of contaminated sites):
    (i) Technical feasibility; and
    (ii) Cost;

(e) Access to information and public education;

(f) Status of control and monitoring capacity; and

(g) Any national or regional control actions taken, including information on alternatives, and other relevant risk management information.

PART VIC

Hazardous substances and activities: waste

Convention on the Control of Transboundary Movements of Hazardous Wastes and Their Disposal, 22 March 1989

Editorial note

The Basel Convention on the Control of Transboundary Movements of Hazardous Wastes and their Disposal regulates the transport and disposal of hazardous and other wastes and seeks to make such transport a matter of public record. The ultimate goal of the Convention is to protect human health and the environment from the dangers of such wastes, in application of the principle that wastes should be disposed of in the State where they were generated. The Convention is premised upon the belief that by requiring the generator to carry out duties regarding transport and disposal of the wastes, the amount of waste generated will be reduced.

The Convention restates the right of every State to ban the entry or disposal of foreign hazardous wastes in its territory (Article 4(1)). For purposes of the Convention wastes are defined as hazardous either by reference to categories set out in Annex I, unless they do not possess the characteristics listed in Annex III, or if so classified by national legislation (Article 1). Many of the Convention's obligations also apply to 'other wastes' listed in Annex II, which encompasses household wastes or residue from incineration from household wastes (Article 1). Excluded from the Convention's ambit are radioactive wastes and wastes discharged from the normal operation of ships so long as they are regulated by other international instruments (Article 1). Parties exercising their right to prohibit the import of hazardous wastes are to inform the other Parties and provide information on any national legislation pertaining to the definition of hazardous waste (Article 3). Each Party must prohibit the export of such wastes to any State which has notified the Party of its import prohibition (Article 4).

Parties are required to take appropriate measures to ensure that the generation of hazardous wastes is reduced to a minimum, to prevent pollution due to such wastes, and to prohibit the import or export of wastes if they have reasons to believe that the wastes will not be managed in an environmentally sound manner (Article 4(2)). Parties must also prohibit the import from or export to States not party to the Convention of hazardous wastes (Article 4(5)), except if done under the authority of an international agreement which does not derogate from the Convention's provisions on 'environmentally sound management of waste' or stipulates provisions which are 'less environmentally sound' (Article 11). In addition, the disposal of hazardous wastes south of 60 degrees latitude is prohibited (Article 4(6)). Any wastes transported or disposed of in contravention of this Convention will be considered illegal traffic in wastes and is to be made a criminal offence (Articles 4(3), 4(4), and 9). Parties are permitted, in accordance with the objectives of the Convention and other rules of international law, to take stricter measures than required by the Convention in order to protect human health and the environment (Article 4(11)).

The Convention sets out the requirements for any transboundary movement of wastes, including notification, packaging, authorisation, and accompanying documentation (Article 4(7)). Movement of wastes will only be permitted if the generating State does not have the technical capacity or suitable sites for disposal or if the importing States requires the wastes as raw material for recycling or recovery industries (Article 4(9)). Before any transboundary movement is permissible, the State of export must notify the State of import and all States of transit (Article 6) and the States of import and of transit must respond in writing consenting to the shipment; conditions may be imposed. All shipments must be covered by insurance as required by the States of import and transit (Article 6) and if a shipment cannot be completed as planned, the State of export has a duty to take back the wastes and ensure their proper disposal (Article 8). The Parties agree to co-operate with each other regarding the exchange of information and technologies, monitoring and research and to assist developing countries in complying with the terms of the Convention (Article 10). Any Party with knowledge of an accident is to inform other States likely to be affected promptly (Article 13). The establishment of a revolving fund is to be considered to assist in the event of an emergency (Article 14). A Protocol developing issues of liability has been adopted under Article 12 (see Document 28B below).

The Convention establishes a Conference of the Parties to review implementation of the Convention and to promote harmonisation of waste management policies (Article 15), and a Secretariat to carry out administrative functions relating to the Convention, including the circulation of information and reports on measures taken by the Parties (Article 16). A Party which believes that another Party is violating the Convention may inform the Secretariat and is required to inform the Party believed to be in breach (Article 19). Dispute settlement is to take place in any peaceful means of the Parties' choice, although the Convention allows Parties to agree to submit their disputes to the International Court of Justice or to the arbitration procedure set out in Annex VI (Article 20). Amendments to the Convention are adopted at the Conference of the Parties by at least a three-fourths majority of those Parties present and voting, and enter into force following acceptance by three-fourths of the Parties (Article 17).

Date of signature: 22 March 1989

Entry into force: 5 May 1992

Depositary: Secretary-General of the United Nations

Contracting Parties: Albania, Algeria, Andorra, Antigua and Barbuda, Argentina, Armenia, Australia, Austria, Azerbaijan, Bahamas, Bahrain, Bangladesh, Barbados, Belarus, Belgium, Belize, Benin, Bhutan, Bolivia, Bosnia and Herzegovina, Botswana, Brazil, Brunei Darussalam, Bulgaria, Burkina Faso, Burundi, Cambodia, Cameroon, Canada, Cape Verde, Chile, China, Colombia, Comoros, Congo (Democratic Republic of), Costa Rica, Cote d'Ivoire, Croatia, Cuba, Cyprus, Czech Republic, Denmark, Djibouti, Dominica, Dominican Republic, Ecuador, Egypt, El Salvador, Estonia, Ethiopia, Finland, France, Gambia, Georgia, Germany, Greece, Guatemala, Guinea, Guyana, Honduras, Hungary, Iceland, India, Indonesia, Iran (Islamic Republic of), Ireland, Israel, Italy, Jamaica, Japan, Jordan, Kenya, Kiribati, Korea (Republic of), Kuwait, Kyrgyzstan, Latvia, Lebanon, Lesotho, Libyan Arab Jamahiriya, Liechtenstein, Lithuania, Luxembourg, Madagascar, Malawi, Malaysia, Maldives, Mali, Malta, Marshall Islands, Mauritania, Mauritius, Mexico, Micronesia (Federated States of), Moldova (Republic of), Monaco, Mongolia, Morocco, Mozambique, Namibia, Nauru, Nepal, Netherlands, New Zealand, Nicaragua, Niger, Nigeria, Norway, Oman, Pakistan, Panama, Papua New Guinea, Paraguay, Peru, Philippines, Poland, Portugal, Qatar, Romania, Russian Federation, Saint Kitts and Nevis, Saint Lucia, Saint Vincent and the Grenadines, Samoa, Saudi Arabia, Senegal, Seychelles, Singapore, Slovakia, Slovenia, South Africa, Spain, Sri Lanka, Sweden, Switzerland, Syrian Arab Republic, Tanzania (United Republic of), Thailand, The Former Yugoslav Republic of Macedonia, Trinidad and Tobago, Tunisia, Turkey, Turkmenistan, Uganda, Ukraine, United Arab Emirates, United Kingdom, Uruguay, Uzbekistan, Venezuela, Vietnam, Yemen, Yugoslavia, Zambia.

Website: www.basel.int

Basel Convention on the Control of Transboundary Movements of Hazardous Wastes and Their Disposal

Preamble

The Parties to this Convention,

Aware of the risk of damage to human health and the environment caused by hazardous wastes and other wastes and the transboundary movement thereof,

Mindful of the growing threat to human health and the environment posed by the increased generation and complexity, and transboundary movement of hazardous wastes and other wastes,

Mindful also that the most effective way of protecting human health and the environment from the dangers posed by such wastes is the reduction of their generation to a minimum in terms of quantity and/or hazard potential,

Convinced that States should take necessary measures to ensure that the management of hazardous wastes and other wastes including their transboundary movement and disposal is consistent with the protection of human health and the environment whatever the place of disposal,

Noting that States should ensure that the generator should carry out duties with regards to the transport and disposal of hazardous wastes and other wastes in a manner that is consistent with the protection of the environment, whatever the place of disposal,

Fully recognizing that any State has the sovereign right to ban the entry or disposal of foreign hazardous wastes and other wastes in its territory,

Recognizing also the increasing desire for the prohibition of transboundary movements of hazardous wastes and their disposal in other States, especially developing countries,

Convinced that hazardous wastes and other wastes should, as far as is compatible with environmentally sound and efficient management, be disposed of in the State where they were generated,

Aware also that transboundary movements of such wastes from the State of their generation to any other State should be permitted only when conducted under conditions which do not endanger human health and the environment, and under conditions in conformity with the provisions of this Convention,

Considering that enhanced control of transboundary movement of hazardous wastes and other wastes will act as an incentive for their environmentally sound management and for the reduction of the volume of such transboundary movement,

Convinced that States should take measures for the proper exchange of information on and control of the transboundary movement of hazardous wastes and other wastes from and to those States,

Noting that a number of international and regional agreements have addressed the issue of protection and preservation of the environment with regard to the transit of dangerous goods,

Taking into account the Declaration of the United Nations Conference on the Human Environment (Stockholm, 1972), the Cairo Guidelines and Principles for the Environmentally Sound Management of Hazardous Wastes adopted by the Governing Council of the United Nations Environment Programme (UNEP) by decision 14/30 of 17 June 1987, the Recommendations of the United Nations Committee of Experts on the Transport of Dangerous Goods (formulated in 1957 and updated biennially), relevant recommendations, declarations, instruments and regulations adopted within the United Nations system and the work and studies done within other international and regional organizations,

Mindful of the spirit, principles, aims and functions of the World Charter for Nature adopted by the General Assembly of the United Nations at its thirty-seventh session (1982) as the rule of ethics in respect of the protection of the human environment and the conservation of natural resources,

Affirming that States are responsible for the fulfilment of their international obligations concerning the protection of human health and protection and preservation of the environment, and are liable in accordance with international law,

Recognizing that in the case of a material breach of the provisions of this Convention or any protocol thereto the relevant international law of treaties shall apply,

Aware of the need to continue the development and implementation of environmentally sound low-waste technologies, recycling options, good housekeeping and management systems with a view to reducing to a minimum the generation of hazardous wastes and other wastes,

Aware also of the growing international concern about the need for stringent control of transboundary movement of hazardous wastes and other wastes, and of the need as far as possible to reduce such movement to a minimum,

Concerned about the problem of illegal transboundary traffic in hazardous wastes and other wastes,

Taking into account also the limited capabilities of the developing countries to manage hazardous wastes and other wastes,

Recognizing the need to promote the transfer of technology for the sound management of hazardous wastes and other wastes produced locally, particularly to the developing countries in accordance with the spirit of the Cairo Guidelines and decision 14/16 of the Governing Council of UNEP on Promotion of the transfer of environmental protection technology,

Recognizing also that hazardous wastes and other wastes should be transported in accordance with relevant international conventions and recommendations,

Convinced also that the transboundary movement of hazardous wastes and other wastes should be permitted only when the transport and the ultimate disposal of such wastes is environmentally sound, and

Determined to protect, by strict control, human health and the environment against the adverse effects which may result from the generation and management of hazardous wastes and other wastes,

Have agreed as follows:

Article 1
Scope of the Convention

1. The following wastes that are subject to transboundary movement shall be 'hazardous wastes' for the purposes of this Convention:

(a) Wastes that belong to any category contained in Annex I, unless they do not possess any of the characteristics contained in Annex III; and

(b) Wastes that are not covered under paragraph (a) but are defined as, or are considered to be, hazardous wastes by the domestic legislation of the Party of export, import or transit.

2. Wastes that belong to any category contained in Annex II that are subject to transboundary movement shall be 'other wastes' for the purposes of this Convention.

3. Wastes which, as a result of being radioactive, are subject to other international control systems, including international instruments, applying specifically to radioactive materials, are excluded from the scope of this Convention.

4. Wastes which derive from the normal operations of a ship, the discharge of which is covered by another international instrument, are excluded from the scope of this Convention.

Article 2
Definitions

For the purposes of this Convention:

1. 'Wastes' are substances or objects which are disposed of or are intended to be disposed of or are required to be disposed of by the provisions of national law;

2. 'Management' means the collection, transport and disposal of hazardous wastes or other wastes, including aftercare of disposal sites;

3. 'Transboundary movement' means any movement of hazardous wastes or other wastes from an area under the national jurisdiction of one State to or through an area under the national jurisdiction of another State or to or through an area not under the national jurisdiction of any State, provided at least two States are involved in the movement;

4. 'Disposal' means any operation specified in Annex IV to this Convention;

5. 'Approved site or facility' means a site or facility for the disposal of hazardous wastes or other wastes which is authorized or permitted to operate

for this purpose by a relevant authority of the State where the site or facility is located;

6. 'Competent authority' means one governmental authority designated by a Party to be responsible, within such geographical areas as the Party may think fit, for receiving the notification of a transboundary movement of hazardous wastes or other wastes, and any information related to it, and for responding to such a notification, as provided in Article 6;

7. 'Focal point' means the entity of a Party referred to in Article 5 responsible for receiving and submitting information as provided for in Articles 13 and 16;

8. 'Environmentally sound management of hazardous wastes or other wastes' means taking all practicable steps to ensure that hazardous wastes or other wastes are managed in a manner which will protect human health and the environment against the adverse effects which may result from such wastes;

9. 'Area under the national jurisdiction of a State' means any land, marine area or air space within which a State exercises administrative and regulatory responsibility in accordance with international law in regard to the protection of human health or the environment;

10. 'State of export' means a Party from which a transboundary movement of hazardous wastes or other wastes is planned to be initiated or is initiated;

11. 'State of import' means a Party to which a transboundary movement of hazardous wastes or other wastes is planned or takes place for the purpose of disposal therein or for the purpose of loading prior to disposal in an area not under the national jurisdiction of any State;

12. 'State of transit' means any State, other than the State of export or import, through which a movement of hazardous wastes or other wastes is planned or takes place;

13. 'States concerned' means Parties which are States of export or import, or transit States, whether or not Parties;

14. 'Person' means any natural or legal person;

15. 'Exporter' means any person under the jurisdiction of the State of export who arranges for hazardous wastes or other wastes to be exported;

16. 'Importer' means any person under the jurisdiction of the State of import who arranges for hazardous wastes or other wastes to be imported;

17. 'Carrier' means any person who carries out the transport of hazardous wastes or other wastes;

18. 'Generator' means any person whose activity produces hazardous wastes or other wastes or, if that person is not known, the person who is in possession and/or control of those wastes;

19. 'Disposer' means any person to whom hazardous wastes or other wastes are shipped and who carries out the disposal of such wastes;

20. 'Political and/or economic integration organization' means an organization constituted by sovereign States to which its member States have transferred

competence in respect of matters governed by this Convention and which has been duly authorized, in accordance with its internal procedures, to sign, ratify, accept, approve, formally confirm or accede to it;

21. 'Illegal traffic' means any transboundary movement of hazardous wastes or other wastes as specified in Article 9.

Article 3
National definitions of hazardous wastes

1. Each Party shall, within six months of becoming a Party to this Convention, inform the Secretariat of the Convention of the wastes, other than those listed in Annexes I and II, considered or defined as hazardous under its national legislation and of any requirements concerning transboundary movement procedures applicable to such wastes.

2. Each Party shall subsequently inform the Secretariat of any significant changes to the information it has provided pursuant to paragraph 1.

3. The Secretariat shall forthwith inform all Parties of the information it has received pursuant to paragraphs 1 and 2.

4. Parties shall be responsible for making the information transmitted to them by the Secretariat under paragraph 3 available to their exporters.

Article 4
General obligations

1.

(a) Parties exercising their right to prohibit the import of hazardous wastes or other wastes for disposal shall inform the other Parties of their decision pursuant to Article 13.

(b) Parties shall prohibit or shall not permit the export of hazardous wastes and other wastes to the Parties which have prohibited the import of such wastes, when notified pursuant to subparagraph (a) above.

(c) Parties shall prohibit or shall not permit the export of hazardous wastes and other wastes if the State of import does not consent in writing to the specific import, in the case where that State of import has not prohibited the import of such wastes.

2. Each Party shall take the appropriate measures to:

(a) Ensure that the generation of hazardous wastes and other wastes within it is reduced to a minimum, taking into account social, technological and economic aspects;

(b) Ensure the availability of adequate disposal facilities, for the environmentally sound management of hazardous wastes and other wastes, that shall be located, to the extent possible, within it, whatever the place of their disposal;

(c) Ensure that persons involved in the management of hazardous wastes or other wastes within it take such steps as are necessary to prevent pollution due to hazardous wastes and other wastes arising from such management and, if such pollution occurs, to minimize the consequences thereof for human health and the environment;

(d) Ensure that the transboundary movement of hazardous wastes and other wastes is reduced to the minimum consistent with the environmentally sound and efficient management of such wastes, and is conducted in a manner which will protect human health and the environment against the adverse effects which may result from such movement;

(e) Not allow the export of hazardous wastes or other wastes to a State or group of States belonging to an economic and/or political integration organization that are Parties, particularly developing countries, which have prohibited by their legislation all imports, or if it has reason to believe that the wastes in question will not be managed in an environmentally sound manner, according to criteria to be decided on by the Parties at their first meeting.

(f) Require that information about a proposed transboundary movement of hazardous wastes and other wastes be provided to the States concerned, according to Annex V A, to state clearly the effects of the proposed movement on human health and the environment;

(g) Prevent the import of hazardous wastes and other wastes if it has reason to believe that the wastes in question will not be managed in an environmentally sound manner;

(h) Co-operate in activities with other Parties and interested organizations, directly and through the Secretariat, including the dissemination of information on the transboundary movement of hazardous wastes and other wastes, in order to improve the environmentally sound management of such wastes and to achieve the prevention of illegal traffic.

3. The Parties consider that illegal traffic in hazardous wastes or other wastes is criminal.

4. Each Party shall take appropriate legal, administrative and other measures to implement and enforce the provisions of this Convention, including measures to prevent and punish conduct in contravention of the Convention.

5. A Party shall not permit hazardous wastes or other wastes to be exported to a non-Party or to be imported from a non-Party.

6. The Parties agree not to allow the export of hazardous wastes or other wastes for disposal within the area south of 60° South latitude, whether or not such wastes are subject to transboundary movement.

888 VIC HAZARDOUS SUBSTANCES AND ACTIVITIES: WASTE

7. Furthermore, each Party shall:

(a) Prohibit all persons under its national jurisdiction from transporting or disposing of hazardous wastes or other wastes unless such persons are authorized or allowed to perform such types of operations;
(b) Require that hazardous wastes and other wastes that are to be the subject of a transboundary movement be packaged, labelled, and transported in conformity with generally accepted and recognized international rules and standards in the field of packaging, labelling, and transport, and that due account is taken of relevant internationally recognized practices;
(c) Require that hazardous wastes and other wastes be accompanied by a movement document from the point at which a transboundary movement commences to the point of disposal.

8. Each Party shall require that hazardous wastes or other wastes, to be exported, are managed in an environmentally sound manner in the State of import or elsewhere. Technical guidelines for the environmentally sound management of wastes subject to this Convention shall be decided by the Parties at their first meeting.

9. Parties shall take the appropriate measures to ensure that the transboundary movement of hazardous wastes and other wastes only be allowed if:

(a) The State of export does not have the technical capacity and the necessary facilities, capacity or suitable disposal sites in order to dispose of the wastes in question in an environmentally sound and efficient manner; or
(b) The wastes in question are required as a raw material for recycling or recovery industries in the State of import; or
(c) The transboundary movement in question is in accordance with other criteria to be decided by the Parties, provided those criteria do not differ from the objectives of this Convention.

10. The obligation under this Convention of States in which hazardous wastes and other wastes are generated to require that those wastes are managed in an environmentally sound manner may not under any circumstances be transferred to the States of import or transit.

11. Nothing in this Convention shall prevent a Party from imposing additional requirements that are consistent with the provisions of this Convention, and are in accordance with the rules of international law, in order better to protect human health and the environment.

12. Nothing in this Convention shall affect in any way the sovereignty of States over their territorial sea established in accordance with international law, and the sovereign rights and the jurisdiction which States have in their exclusive economic zones and their continental shelves in accordance with international law, and the exercise by ships and aircraft of all States of navigational rights

and freedoms as provided for in international law and as reflected in relevant international instruments.

13. Parties shall undertake to review periodically the possibilities for the reduction of the amount and/or the pollution potential of hazardous wastes and other wastes which are exported to other States, in particular to developing countries.

Article 5
Designation of competent authorities and focal point

To facilitate the implementation of this Convention, the Parties shall:

1. Designate or establish one or more competent authorities and one focal point. One competent authority shall be designated to receive the notification in case of a State of transit.
2. Inform the Secretariat, within three months of the date of the entry into force of this Convention for them, which agencies they have designated as their focal point and their competent authorities.
3. Inform the Secretariat, within one month of the date of decision, of any changes regarding the designation made by them under paragraph 2 above.

Article 6
Transboundary movement between Parties

1. The State of export shall notify, or shall require the generator or exporter to notify, in writing, through the channel of the competent authority of the State of export, the competent authority of the States concerned of any proposed transboundary movement of hazardous wastes or other wastes. Such notification shall contain the declarations and information specified in Annex V A, written in a language acceptable to the State of import. Only one notification needs to be sent to each State concerned.

2. The State of import shall respond to the notifier in writing, consenting to the movement with or without conditions, denying permission for the movement, or requesting additional information. A copy of the final response of the State of import shall be sent to the competent authorities of the States concerned which are Parties.

3. The State of export shall not allow the generator or exporter to commence the transboundary movement until it has received written confirmation that:

(a) The notifier has received the written consent of the State of import; and
(b) The notifier has received from the State of import confirmation of the existence of a contract between the exporter and the disposer specifying environmentally sound management of the wastes in question.

4. Each State of transit which is a Party shall promptly acknowledge to the notifier receipt of the notification. It may subsequently respond to the notifier in writing, within 60 days, consenting to the movement with or without conditions, denying permission for the movement, or requesting additional information. The State of export shall not allow the transboundary movement to commence until it has received the written consent of the State of transit. However, if at any time a Party decides not to require prior written consent, either generally or under specific conditions, for transit transboundary movements of hazardous wastes or other wastes, or modifies its requirements in this respect, it shall forthwith inform the other Parties of its decision pursuant to Article 13. In this latter case, if no response is received by the State of export within 60 days of the receipt of a given notification by the State of transit, the State of export may allow the export to proceed through the State of transit.

5. In the case of a transboundary movement of wastes where the wastes are legally defined as or considered to be hazardous wastes only:

(a) By the State of export, the requirements of paragraph 9 of this Article that apply to the importer or disposer and the State of import shall apply *mutatis mutandis* to the exporter and State of export, respectively;

(b) By the State of import, or by the States of import and transit which are Parties, the requirements of paragraphs 1, 3, 4 and 6 of this Article that apply to the exporter and State of export shall apply *mutatis mutandis* to the importer or disposer and State of import, respectively; or

(c) By any State of transit which is a Party, the provisions of paragraph 4 shall apply to such State.

6. The State of export may, subject to the written consent of the States concerned, allow the generator or the exporter to use a general notification where hazardous wastes or other wastes having the same physical and chemical characteristics are shipped regularly to the same disposer via the same customs office of exit of the State of export via the same customs office of entry of the State of import, and, in the case of transit, via the same customs office of entry and exit of the State or States of transit.

7. The States concerned may make their written consent to the use of the general notification referred to in paragraph 6 subject to the supply of certain information, such as the exact quantities or periodical lists of hazardous wastes or other wastes to be shipped.

8. The general notification and written consent referred to in paragraphs 6 and 7 may cover multiple shipments of hazardous wastes or other wastes during a maximum period of 12 months.

9. The Parties shall require that each person who takes charge of a transboundary movement of hazardous wastes or other wastes sign the movement document either upon delivery or receipt of the wastes in question. They shall

also require that the disposer inform both the exporter and the competent authority of the State of export of receipt by the disposer of the wastes in question and, in due course, of the completion of disposal as specified in the notification. If no such information is received within the State of export, the competent authority of the State of export or the exporter shall so notify the State of import.

10. The notification and response required by this Article shall be transmitted to the competent authority of the Parties concerned or to such governmental authority as may be appropriate in the case of non-Parties.

11. Any transboundary movement of hazardous wastes or other wastes shall be covered by insurance, bond or other guarantee as may be required by the State of import or any State of transit which is a Party.

Article 7
Transboundary movement from a Party through States which are not Parties

Paragraph 1 of Article 6 of the Convention shall apply *mutatis mutandis* to transboundary movement of hazardous wastes or other wastes from a Party through a State or States which are not Parties.

Article 8
Duty to re-import

When a transboundary movement of hazardous wastes or other wastes to which the consent of the States concerned has been given, subject to the provisions of this Convention, cannot be completed in accordance with the terms of the contract, the State of export shall ensure that the wastes in question are taken back into the State of export, by the exporter, if alternative arrangements cannot be made for their disposal in an environmentally sound manner, within 90 days from the time that the importing State informed the State of export and the Secretariat, or such other period of time as the States concerned agree. To this end, the State of export and any Party of transit shall not oppose, hinder or prevent the return of those wastes to the State of export.

Article 9
Illegal traffic

1. For the purpose of this Convention, any transboundary movement of hazardous wastes or other wastes:

(a) without notification pursuant to the provisions of this Convention to all States concerned; or
(b) without the consent pursuant to the provisions of this Convention of a State concerned; or

(c) with consent obtained from States concerned through falsification, misrepresentation or fraud; or

(d) that does not conform in a material way with the documents; or

(e) that results in deliberate disposal (e.g. dumping) of hazardous wastes or other wastes in contravention of this Convention and of general principles of international law,

shall be deemed to be illegal traffic.

2. In case of a transboundary movement of hazardous wastes or other wastes deemed to be illegal traffic as the result of conduct on the part of the exporter or generator, the State of export shall ensure that the wastes in question are:

(a) taken back by the exporter or the generator or, if necessary, by itself into the State of export, or, if impracticable,

(b) are otherwise disposed of in accordance with the provisions of this Convention,

within 30 days from the time the State of export has been informed about the illegal traffic or such other period of time as States concerned may agree. To this end the Parties concerned shall not oppose, hinder or prevent the return of those wastes to the State of export.

3. In the case of a transboundary movement of hazardous wastes or other wastes deemed to be illegal traffic as the result of conduct on the part of the importer or disposer, the State of import shall ensure that the wastes in question are disposed of in an environmentally sound manner by the importer or disposer or, if necessary, by itself within 30 days from the time the illegal traffic has come to the attention of the State of import or such other period of time as the States concerned may agree. To this end, the Parties concerned shall co-operate, as necessary, in the disposal of the wastes in an environmentally sound manner.

4. In cases where the responsibility for the illegal traffic cannot be assigned either to the exporter or generator or to the importer or disposer, the Parties concerned or other Parties, as appropriate, shall ensure, through co-operation, that the wastes in question are disposed of as soon as possible in an environmentally sound manner either in the State of export or the State of import or elsewhere as appropriate.

5. Each Party shall introduce appropriate national/domestic legislation to prevent and punish illegal traffic. The Parties shall co-operate with a view to achieving the objects of this Article.

Article 10
International co-operation

1. The Parties shall co-operate with each other in order to improve and achieve environmentally sound management of hazardous wastes and other wastes.

2. To this end, the Parties shall:

(a) Upon request, make available information, whether on a bilateral or multilateral basis, with a view to promoting the environmentally sound management of hazardous wastes and other wastes, including harmonization of technical standards and practices for the adequate management of hazardous wastes and other wastes;

(b) Co-operate in monitoring the effects of the management of hazardous wastes on human health and the environment;

(c) Co-operate, subject to their national laws, regulations and policies, in the development and implementation of new environmentally sound low-waste technologies and the improvement of existing technologies with a view to eliminating, as far as practicable, the generation of hazardous wastes and other wastes and achieving more effective and efficient methods of ensuring their management in an environmentally sound manner, including the study of the economic, social and environmental effects of the adoption of such new or improved technologies;

(d) Co-operate actively, subject to their national laws, regulations and policies, in the transfer of technology and management systems related to the environmentally sound management of hazardous wastes and other wastes. They shall also co-operate in developing the technical capacity among Parties, especially those which may need and request technical assistance in this field;

(e) Co-operate in developing appropriate technical guidelines and/or codes of practice.

3. The Parties shall employ appropriate means to co-operate in order to assist developing countries in the implementation of subparagraphs a, b, c and d of paragraph 2 of Article 4.

4. Taking into account the needs of developing countries, co-operation between Parties and the competent international organizations is encouraged to promote, *inter alia*, public awareness, the development of sound management of hazardous wastes and other wastes and the adoption of new low-waste technologies.

Article 11
Bilateral, multilateral and regional agreements

1. Notwithstanding the provisions of Article 4 paragraph 5, Parties may enter into bilateral, multilateral, or regional agreements or arrangements regarding transboundary movement of hazardous wastes or other wastes with Parties or non-Parties provided that such agreements or arrangements do not derogate from the environmentally sound management of hazardous wastes and other wastes as required by this Convention. These agreements or arrangements shall stipulate provisions which are not less environmentally sound than those

provided for by this Convention in particular taking into account the interests of developing countries.

2. Parties shall notify the Secretariat of any bilateral, multilateral or regional agreements or arrangements referred to in paragraph 1 and those which they have entered into prior to the entry into force of this Convention for them, for the purpose of controlling transboundary movements of hazardous wastes and other wastes which take place entirely among the Parties to such agreements. The provisions of this Convention shall not affect transboundary movements which take place pursuant to such agreements provided that such agreements are compatible with the environmentally sound management of hazardous wastes and other wastes as required by this Convention.

Article 12
Consultations on liability

The Parties shall co-operate with a view to adopting, as soon as practicable, a protocol setting out appropriate rules and procedures in the field of liability and compensation for damage resulting from the transboundary movement and disposal of hazardous wastes and other wastes.

Article 13
Transmission of information

1. The Parties shall, whenever it comes to their knowledge, ensure that, in the case of an accident occurring during the transboundary movement of hazardous wastes or other wastes or their disposal, which are likely to present risks to human health and the environment in other States, those States are immediately informed.

2. The Parties shall inform each other, through the Secretariat, of:

(a) Changes regarding the designation of competent authorities and/or focal points, pursuant to Article 5;
(b) Changes in their national definition of hazardous wastes, pursuant to Article 3;

and, as soon as possible,

(c) Decisions made by them not to consent totally or partially to the import of hazardous wastes or other wastes for disposal within the area under their national jurisdiction;
(d) Decisions taken by them to limit or ban the export of hazardous wastes or other wastes;
(e) Any other information required pursuant to paragraph 4 of this Article.

3. The Parties, consistent with national laws and regulations, shall transmit, through the Secretariat, to the Conference of the Parties established under Article 15, before the end of each calendar year, a report on the previous calendar year, containing the following information:

(a) Competent authorities and focal points that have been designated by them pursuant to Article 5;

(b) Information regarding transboundary movements of hazardous wastes or other wastes in which they have been involved, including:

   (i) The amount of hazardous wastes and other wastes exported, their category, characteristics, destination, any transit country and disposal method as stated on the response to notification;

   (ii) The amount of hazardous wastes and other wastes imported, their category, characteristics, origin, and disposal methods;

   (iii) Disposals which did not proceed as intended;

   (iv) Efforts to achieve a reduction of the amount of hazardous wastes or other wastes subject to transboundary movement;

(c) Information on the measures adopted by them in implementation of this Convention;

(d) Information on available qualified statistics which have been compiled by them on the effects on human health and the environment of the generation, transportation and disposal of hazardous wastes or other wastes;

(e) Information concerning bilateral, multilateral and regional agreements and arrangements entered into pursuant to Article 11 of this Convention;

(f) Information on accidents occurring during the transboundary movement and disposal of hazardous wastes and other wastes and on the measures undertaken to deal with them;

(g) Information on disposal options operated within the area of their national jurisdiction;

(h) Information on measures undertaken for development of technologies for the reduction and/or elimination of production of hazardous wastes and other wastes; and

(i) Such other matters as the Conference of the Parties shall deem relevant.

4. The Parties, consistent with national laws and regulations, shall ensure that copies of each notification concerning any given transboundary movement of hazardous wastes or other wastes, and the response to it, are sent to the Secretariat when a Party considers that its environment may be affected by that transboundary movement has requested that this should be done.

Article 14
Financial aspects

1. The Parties agree that, according to the specific needs of different regions and subregions, regional or subregional centres for training and technology transfers regarding the management of hazardous wastes and other wastes and the minimization of their generation should be established. The Parties shall

decide on the establishment of appropriate funding mechanisms of a voluntary nature.

2. The Parties shall consider the establishment of a revolving fund to assist on an interim basis in case of emergency situations to minimize damage from accidents arising from transboundary movements of hazardous wastes and other wastes or during the disposal of those wastes.

Article 15
Conference of the Parties

1. A Conference of the Parties is hereby established. The first meeting of the Conference of the Parties shall be convened by the Executive Director of UNEP not later than one year after the entry into force of this Convention. Thereafter, ordinary meetings of the Conference of the Parties shall be held at regular intervals to be determined by the Conference at its first meeting.

2. Extraordinary meetings of the Conference of the Parties shall be held at such other times as may be deemed necessary by the Conference, or at the written request of any Party, provided that, within six months of the request being communicated to them by the Secretariat, it is supported by at least one third of the Parties.

3. The Conference of the Parties shall by consensus agree upon and adopt rules of procedure for itself and for any subsidiary body it may establish, as well as financial rules to determine in particular the financial participation of the Parties under this Convention.

4. The Parties at their first meeting shall consider any additional measures needed to assist them in fulfilling their responsibilities with respect to the protection and the preservation of the marine environment in the context of this Convention.

5. The Conference of the Parties shall keep under continuous review and evaluation the effective implementation of this Convention, and, in addition, shall:

(a) Promote the harmonization of appropriate policies, strategies and measures for minimizing harm to human health and the environment by hazardous wastes and other wastes;

(b) Consider and adopt, as required, amendments to this Convention and its annexes, taking into consideration, *inter alia*, available scientific, technical, economic and environmental information;

(c) Consider and undertake any additional action that may be required for the achievement of the purposes of this Convention in the light of experience gained in its operation and in the operation of the agreements and arrangements envisaged in Article 11;

(d) Consider and adopt protocols as required; and

(e) Establish such subsidiary bodies as are deemed necessary for the implementation of this Convention.

6. The United Nations, its specialized agencies, as well as any State not Party to this Convention, may be represented as observers at meetings of the Conference of the Parties. Any other body or agency, whether national or international, governmental or non-governmental, qualified in fields relating to hazardous wastes or other wastes which has informed the Secretariat of its wish to be represented as an observer at a meeting of the Conference of Parties, may be admitted unless at least one third of the Parties present object. The admission and participation of observers shall be subject to the rules of procedure adopted by the Conference of the Parties.

7. The Conference of the Parties shall undertake three years after the entry into force of this Convention, and at least every six years thereafter, an evaluation of its effectiveness and, if deemed necessary, to consider the adoption of a complete or partial ban of transboundary movements of hazardous wastes and other wastes in light of the latest scientific, environmental, technical and economic information.

Article 16
Secretariat

1. The functions of the Secretariat shall be:

(a) To arrange for and service meetings provided for in Articles 15 and 17;
(b) To prepare and transmit reports based upon information received in accordance with Articles 3, 4, 6, 11 and 13 as well as upon information derived from meetings of subsidiary bodies established under Article 15 as well as upon, as appropriate, information provided by relevant intergovernmental and nongovernmental entities;
(c) To prepare reports on its activities carried out in implementation of its functions under this Convention and present them to the Conference of the Parties;
(d) To ensure the necessary coordination with relevant international bodies, and in particular to enter into such administrative and contractual arrangements as may be required for the effective discharge of its functions;
(e) To communicate with Focal Points and Competent Authorities established by the Parties in accordance with Article 5 of this Convention;
(f) To compile information concerning authorized national sites and facilities of Parties available for the disposal of their hazardous wastes and other wastes and to circulate this information among Parties;
(g) To receive and convey information from and to Parties on:
  • sources of technical assistance and training;
  • available technical and scientific know-how;
  • sources of advice and expertise; and

- availability of resources

with a view to assisting them, upon request, in such areas as:

- the handling of the notification system of this Convention;
- the management of hazardous wastes and other wastes;
- environmentally sound technologies relating to hazardous wastes and other wastes; such as low- and non-waste technology;
- the assessment of disposal capabilities and sites;
- the monitoring of hazardous wastes and other wastes; and
- emergency responses;

(h) To provide Parties, upon request, with information on consultants or consulting firms having the necessary technical competence in the field, which can assist them to examine a notification for a transboundary movement, the concurrence of a shipment of hazardous wastes or other wastes with the relevant notification, and/or the fact that the proposed disposal facilities for hazardous wastes or other wastes are environmentally sound, when they have reason to believe that the wastes in question will not be managed in an environmentally sound manner. Any such examination would not be at the expense of the Secretariat;

(i) To assist Parties upon request in their identification of cases of illegal traffic and to circulate immediately to the Parties concerned any information it has received regarding illegal traffic;

(j) To co-operate with Parties and with relevant and competent international organizations and agencies in the provision of experts and equipment for the purpose of rapid assistance to States in the event of an emergency situation; and

(k) To perform such other functions relevant to the purposes of this Convention as may be determined by the Conference of the Parties.

2. The Secretariat functions will be carried out on an interim basis by UNEP until the completion of the first meeting of the Conference of the Parties held pursuant to Article 15.

3. At its first meeting, the Conference of the Parties shall designate the Secretariat from among those existing competent intergovernmental organizations which have signified their willingness to carry out the Secretariat functions under this Convention. At this meeting, the Conference of the Parties shall also evaluate the implementation by the interim Secretariat of the functions assigned to it, in particular under paragraph 1 above, and decide upon the structures appropriate for those functions.

Article 17
Amendment of the Convention

1. Any Party may propose amendments to this Convention and any Party to a protocol may propose amendments to that protocol. Such amendments shall take due account, *inter alia*, of relevant scientific and technical considerations.

2. Amendments to this Convention shall be adopted at a meeting of the Conference of the Parties. Amendments to any protocol shall be adopted at a meeting of the Parties to the protocol in question. The text of any proposed amendment to this Convention or to any protocol, except as may otherwise be provided in such protocol, shall be communicated to the Parties by the Secretariat at least six months before the meeting at which it is proposed for adoption. The Secretariat shall also communicate proposed amendments to the Signatories to this Convention for information.

3. The Parties shall make every effort to reach agreement on any proposed amendment to this Convention by consensus. If all efforts at consensus have been exhausted, and no agreement reached, the amendment shall as a last resort be adopted by a three-fourths majority of the Parties present and voting at the meeting, and shall be submitted by the Depositary to all Parties for ratification, approval, formal confirmation or acceptance.

4. The procedure mentioned in paragraph 3 above shall apply to amendments to any protocol, except that a two thirds majority of the Parties to that protocol present and voting at the meeting shall suffice for their adoption.

5. Instruments of ratification, approval, formal confirmation or acceptance of amendments shall be deposited with the Depositary. Amendments adopted in accordance with paragraphs 3 or 4 above shall enter into force between Parties having accepted them on the ninetieth day after the receipt by the Depositary of their instrument of ratification, approval, formal confirmation or acceptance by at least three-fourths of the Parties who accepted the amendments to the protocol concerned, except as may otherwise be provided in such protocol. The amendments shall enter into force for any other Party on the ninetieth day after that Party deposits its instrument of ratification, approval, formal confirmation or acceptance of the amendments.

6. For the purpose of this Article, 'Parties present and voting' means Parties present and casting an affirmative or negative vote.

Article 18
Adoption and amendment of Annexes

1. The annexes to this Convention or to any protocol shall form an integral part of this Convention or of such protocol, as the case may be and, unless expressly provided otherwise, a reference to this Convention or its protocols constitutes at the same time a reference to any annexes thereto. Such annexes shall be restricted to scientific, technical and administrative matters.

2. Except as may be otherwise provided in any protocol with respect to its annexes, the following procedure shall apply to the proposal, adoption and entry into force of additional annexes to this Convention or of annexes to a protocol:

(a) Annexes to this Convention and its protocols shall be proposed and adopted according to the procedure laid down in Article 17, paragraphs 2, 3 and 4;

(b) Any Party that is unable to accept an additional annex to this Convention or an annex to any protocol to which it is party shall so notify the Depositary, in writing, within six months from the date of the communication of the adoption by the Depositary. The Depositary shall without delay notify all Parties of any such notification received. A Party may at any time substitute an acceptance for a previous declaration of objection and the annexes shall thereupon enter into force for that Party;

(c) On the expiry of six months from the date of the circulation of the communication by the Depositary, the annex shall become effective for all Parties to this Convention or to any protocol concerned, which have not submitted a notification in accordance with the provision of subparagraph (b) above.

3. The proposal, adoption and entry into force of amendments to annexes to this Convention or to any protocol shall be subject to the same procedure as for the proposal, adoption and entry into force of annexes to the Convention or annexes to a protocol. Annexes and amendments thereto shall take due account, *inter alia*, of relevant scientific and technical considerations.

4. If an additional annex or an amendment to an annex involves an amendment to this Convention or to any protocol, the additional annex or amended annex shall not enter into force until such time the amendment to this Convention or to the protocol enters into force.

Article 19
Verification

Any Party which has reason to believe that another Party is acting or has acted in breach of its obligations under this Convention may inform the Secretariat thereof, and in such an event, shall simultaneously and immediately inform, directly or through the Secretariat, the Party against whom the allegations are made. All relevant information should be submitted by the Secretariat to the Parties.

Article 20
Settlement of disputes

1. In case of a dispute between Parties as to the interpretation or application of, or compliance with, this Convention or any protocol thereto, they shall seek a settlement of the dispute through negotiation or any other peaceful means of their own choice.

2. If the Parties concerned cannot settle their dispute through the means mentioned in the preceding paragraph, the dispute, if the Parties to the dispute

agree, shall be submitted to the International Court of Justice or to arbitration under the conditions set out in Annex VI on Arbitration. However, failure to reach common agreement on submission of the dispute to the International Court of Justice or to arbitration shall not absolve the Parties from the responsibility of continuing to seek to resolve it by the means referred to in paragraph 1.

3. When ratifying, accepting, approving, formally confirming or acceding to this Convention, or at any time thereafter, a State or political and/or economic integration organization may declare that it recognizes as compulsory *ipso facto* and without special agreement, in relation to any Party accepting the same obligation:

(a) submission of the dispute to the International Court of Justice; and/or
(b) arbitration in accordance with the procedures set out in Annex VI.

Such declaration shall be notified in writing to the Secretariat which shall communicate it to the Parties.

Article 21
Signature

This Convention shall be open for signature by States, by Namibia, represented by the United Nations Council for Namibia, and by political and/or economic integration organizations, in Basel on 22 March 1989, at the Federal Department of Foreign Affairs of Switzerland in Berne from 23 March 1989 to 30 June 1989 and at United Nations Headquarters in New York from 1 July 1989 to 22 March 1990.

Article 22
Ratification, acceptance, formal confirmation or approval

1. This Convention shall be subject to ratification, acceptance or approval by States and by Namibia, represented by the United Nations Council for Namibia, and to formal confirmation or approval by political and/or economic integration organizations. Instruments of ratification, acceptance, formal confirmation, or approval shall be deposited with the Depositary.

2. Any organization referred to in paragraph 1 above which becomes a Party to this Convention without any of its members States being a Party shall be bound by all the obligations under the Convention. In the case of such organizations, one or more of whose member States is a Party to the Convention, the organization and its member States shall decide on their respective responsibilities for the performance of their obligations under the Convention. In such cases, the organization and the member States shall not be entitled to exercise rights under the Convention concurrently.

3. In their instruments of formal confirmation or approval, the organizations referred to in paragraph 1 above shall declare the extent of their competence with respect to the matters governed by the Convention. These organizations shall also inform the Depositary, who will inform the Parties of any substantial modification in the extent of their competence.

Article 23
Accession

1. This Convention shall be open for accession by States, by Namibia, represented by the United Nations Council for Namibia, and by political and/or economic integration organizations from the day after the date on which the Convention is closed for signature. The instruments of accession shall be deposited with the Depositary.

2. In their instruments of accession, the organizations referred to in paragraph 1 above shall declare the extent of their competence with respect to the matters governed by the Convention. These organizations shall also inform the Depositary of any substantial modification in the extent of their competence.

3. The provisions of Article 22, paragraph 2, shall apply to political and/or economic integration organizations which accede to this Convention.

Article 24
Right to vote

1. Except as provided for in paragraph 2 below, each Contracting Party to this Convention shall have one vote.

2. Political and/or economic integration organizations, in matters within their competence, in accordance with Article 22, paragraph 3, and Article 23, paragraph 2, shall exercise their right to vote with a number of votes equal to the number of their member States which are Parties to the Convention or the relevant protocol. Such organizations shall not exercise their right to vote if their member States exercise theirs, and vice versa.

Article 25
Entry into force

1. This Convention shall enter into force on the ninetieth day after the day of deposit of the twentieth instrument of ratification, acceptance, formal confirmation, approval or accession.

2. For each State or political and/or economic integration organization which ratifies, accepts, approves or formally confirms this Convention or accedes thereto after the date of the deposit of the twentieth instrument of ratification, acceptance, approval, formal confirmation or accession, it shall enter into force on the ninetieth day after the date of deposit by such State or political

and/or economic integration organization of its instrument of ratification, acceptance, approval, formal confirmation or accession.

3. For the purpose of paragraphs 1 and 2 above, any instrument deposited by a political and/or economic integration organization shall not be counted as additional to those deposited by member States of such organization.

Article 26
Reservations and declarations

1. No reservation or exception may be made to this Convention.

2. Paragraph 1 of this Article does not preclude a State or political and/or economic integration organization, when signing, ratifying, accepting, approving, formally confirming or acceding to this Convention, from making declarations or statements, however phrased or named, with a view, *inter alia*, to the harmonization of its laws and regulations with the provisions of this Convention, provided that such declarations or statements do not purport to exclude or to modify the legal effects of the provisions of the Convention in their application to that State.

Article 27
Withdrawal

1. At any time after three years from the date on which this Convention has entered into force for a Party, that Party may withdraw from the Convention by giving written notification to the Depositary.

2. Withdrawal shall be effective one year from receipt of notification by the Depositary, or on such later date as may be specified in the notification.

Article 28
Depositary

The Secretary-General of the United Nations shall be the Depositary of this Convention and of any protocol thereto.

Article 29
Authentic texts

The original Arabic, Chinese, English, French, Russian and Spanish texts of this Convention are equally authentic.

IN WITNESS WHEREOF the undersigned, being duly authorized to that effect, have signed this Convention.

Done at Basle on 22nd day of March 1989.

Annex I
Categories of wastes to be controlled

Waste streams

Y1 Clinical wastes from medical care in hospitals, medical centers and clinics

Y2 Wastes from the production and preparation of pharmaceutical products

Y3 Waste pharmaceuticals, drugs and medicines

Y4 Wastes from the production, formulation and use of biocides and phytopharmaceuticals

Y5 Wastes from the manufacture, formulation and use of wood preserving chemicals

Y6 Wastes from the production, formulation and use of organic solvents

Y7 Wastes from heat treatment and tempering operations containing cyanides

Y8 Waste mineral oils unfit for their originally intended use

Y9 Waste oils/water, hydrocarbons/water mixtures, emulsions

Y10 Waste substances and articles containing or contaminated with polychlorinated biphenyls (PCBs) and/or polychlorinated terphenyls (PCTs) and/or polybrominated biphenyls (PBBs)

Y11 Waste tarry residues arising from refining, distillation and any pyrolytic treatment

Y12 Wastes from production, formulation and use of inks, dyes, pigments, paints, lacquers, varnish

Y13 Wastes from production, formulation and use of resins, latex, plasticizers, glues/adhesives

Y14 Waste chemical substances arising from research and development or teaching activities which are not identified and/or are new and whose effects on man and/or the environment are not known

Y15 Wastes of an explosive nature not subject to other legislation

Y16 Wastes from production, formulation and use of photographic chemicals and processing materials

Y17 Wastes resulting from surface treatment of metals and plastics

Y18 Residues arising from industrial waste disposal operations

Wastes having as constituents

Y19 Metal carbonyls

Y20 Beryllium; beryllium compounds

Y21 Hexavalent chromium compounds

Y22 Copper compounds

Y23 Zinc compounds

Y24 Arsenic; arsenic compounds

Y25 Selenium; selenium compounds

Y26 Cadmium; cadmium compounds

Y27 Antimony; antimony compounds

Y28 Tellurium; tellurium compounds
Y29 Mercury; mercury compounds
Y30 Thallium; thallium compounds
Y31 Lead; lead compounds
Y32 Inorganic fluorine compounds excluding calcium fluoride
Y33 Inorganic cyanides
Y34 Acidic solutions or acids in solid form
Y35 Basic solutions or bases in solid form
Y36 Asbestos (dust and fibres)
Y37 Organic phosphorus compounds
Y38 Organic cyanides
Y39 Phenols; phenol compounds including chlorophenols
Y40 Ethers
Y41 Halogenated organic solvents
Y42 Organic solvents excluding halogenated solvents
Y43 Any congenor of polychlorinated dibenzo-furan
Y44 Any congenor of polychlorinated dibenzo-p-dioxin
Y45 Organohalogen compounds other than substances referred to in this Annex
   (e.g. Y39, Y41, Y42, Y43, Y44)

(a) To facilitate the application of this Convention, and subject to paragraphs
    (b), (c) and (d), wastes listed in Annex VIII are characterized as hazardous
    pursuant to Article 1, paragraph 1 (a), of this Convention, and wastes
    listed in Annex IX are not covered by Article 1, paragraph 1 (a), of this
    Convention.
(b) Designation of a waste on Annex VIII does not preclude, in a particular
    case, the use of Annex III to demonstrate that a waste is not hazardous
    pursuant to Article 1, paragraph 1 (a), of this Convention.
(c) Designation of a waste on Annex IX does not preclude, in a particular
    case, characterization of such a waste as hazardous pursuant to Article 1,
    paragraph 1 (a), of this Convention if it contains Annex I material to an
    extent causing it to exhibit an Annex III characteristic.
(d) Annexes VIII and IX do not affect the application of Article 1, paragraph
    1 (a), of this Convention for the purpose of characterization of wastes.*

* Decision IV/9 adopted by COP4 in 1998 amended the Annex I by adding
these four paragraphs (a, b, c and d) at the end of Annex I, and added two
additional Annexes to the Convention, Annex VIII and Annex IX.

Annex II
Categories of wastes requiring special consideration

Y46 – Wastes collected from households
Y47 – Residues arising from the incineration of household wastes

Annex III
List of hazardous characteristics

UN Class**	Code	Characteristics
1	H1	Explosive An explosive substance or waste is a solid or liquid substance or waste (or mixture of substances or wastes) which is in itself capable by chemical reaction of producing gas at such a temperature and pressure and at such speed as to cause damage to the surroundings.
3	H3	Flammable liquids The word 'flammable' has the same meaning as 'inflammable.' Flammable liquids are liquids, or mixtures of liquids, or liquids containing solids in solution or suspension (for example, paints, varnishes, lacquers, etc., but not including substances or wastes otherwise classified on account of their dangerous characteristics) which give off a flammable vapour at temperatures of not more than 60.5C, closed-cup test, or not more than 65.6C, open-cup test. (Since the results of open-cup tests and of closed-cup tests are not strictly comparable and even individual results by the same test are often variable, regulations varying from the above figures to make allowance for such differences would be within the spirit of this definition)
4.1	H4.1	Flammable solids Solids, or waste solids, other than those classed as explosives, which under conditions encountered in transport are readily combustible, or may cause or contribute to fire through friction.
4.2	H4.2	Substances or wastes liable to spontaneous combustion Substances or wastes which are liable to spontaneous heating under normal conditions encountered in transport, or to heating up on contact with air, and being then liable to catch fire.
4.3	H4.3	Substances or wastes which, in contact with water emit flammable gases Substances or wastes which, by interaction with water, are liable to become spontaneously flammable or to give off flammable gases in dangerous quantities.

(cont.)

UN Class**	Code	Characteristics
5.1	H5.1	Oxidizing Substances or wastes which, while in themselves not necessarily combustible, may, generally by yielding oxygen cause, or contribute to, the combustion of other materials.
5.2	H5.2	Organic Peroxides Organic substances or wastes which contain the bivalent-O-O-structure are thermally unstable substances which may undergo exothermic self-accelerating decomposition.
6.1	H6.1	Poisonous (Acute) Substances or wastes liable either to cause death or serious injury or to harm human health if swallowed or inhaled or by skin contact.
6.2	H6.2	Infectious substances Substances or wastes containing viable micro organisms or their toxins which are known or suspected to cause disease in animals or humans.
8	H8	Corrosives Substances or wastes which, by chemical action, will cause severe damage when in contact with living tissue, or, in the case of leakage, will materially damage, or even destroy, other goods or the means of transport; they may also cause other hazards.
9	H10	Liberation of toxic gases in contact with air or water Substances or wastes which, by interaction with air or water, are liable to give off toxic gases in dangerous quantities.
9	H11	Toxic (Delayed or chronic) Substances or wastes which, if they are inhaled or ingested or if they penetrate the skin, may involve delayed or chronic effects, including carcinogenicity.
9	H12	Ecotoxic Substances or wastes which if released present or may present immediate or delayed adverse impacts to the environment by means of bioaccumulation and/or toxic effects upon biotic systems.
9	H13	Capable, by any means, after disposal, of yielding another material, e.g., leachate, which possesses any of the characteristics listed above.

Tests

The potential hazards posed by certain types of wastes are not yet fully documented; tests to define quantitatively these hazards do not exist. Further research is necessary in order to develop means to characterize potential hazards posed to man and/or the environment by these wastes. Standardized tests have been derived with respect to pure substances and materials. Many countries have developed national tests which can be applied to materials listed in Annex I, in order to decide if these materials exhibit any of the characteristics listed in this Annex.

** Corresponds to the hazard classification system included in the United Nations Recommendations on the Transport of Dangerous Goods (ST/SG/AC.10/1Rev.5, United Nations, New York, 1988)

Annex IV
Disposal operations

A. Operations which do not lead to the possibility of resource recovery, recycling, reclamation, direct re-use or alternative uses

Section A encompasses all such disposal operations which occur in practice.

D1	Deposit into or onto land (e.g., landfill, etc.)
D2	Land treatment (e.g., biodegradation of liquid or sludgy discards in soils, etc.)
D3	Deep injection (e.g., injection of pumpable discards into wells, salt domes of naturally occurring repositories, etc.)
D4	Surface impoundment (e.g., placement of liquid or sludge discards into pits, ponds or l lagoons, etc.)
D5	Specially engineered landfill (e.g. placement into lined discrete cells which are capped and isolated from one another and the environment, etc.)
D6	Release into a water body except seas/oceans
D7	Release into seas/oceans including sea-bed insertion
D8	Biological treatment not specified elsewhere in this Annex which results in final compounds or mixtures which are discarded by means of any of the operations in Section A
D9	Physico chemical treatment not specified elsewhere in this Annex which results in final compounds or mixtures which are discarded by means of any of the operations in Section A (e.g., evaporation, drying, calcination, neutralization, precipitation, etc.)
D10	Incineration on land
D11	Incineration at sea
D12	Permanent storage (e.g., emplacement of containers in a mine, etc.)

(cont.)

D13	Blending or mixing prior to submission to any of the operations in Section A
D14	Repackaging prior to submission to any of the operations in Section A
D15	Storage pending any of the operations in Section A

B. Operations which may lead to resource recovery, recycling reclamation, direct re-use or alternative uses

Section B encompasses all such operations with respect to materials legally defined as or considered to be hazardous wastes and which otherwise would have been destined for operations included in Section A

R1	Use as a fuel (other than in direct incineration) or other means to generate energy
R2	Solvent reclamation/regeneration
R3	Recycling/reclamation of organic substances which are not used as solvents
R4	Recycling/reclamation of metals and metal compounds
R5	Recycling/reclamation of other inorganic materials
R6	Regeneration of acids or bases
R7	Recovery of components used for pollution abatement
R8	Recovery of components from catalysts
R9	Used oil re-refining or other reuses of previously used oil
R10	Land treatment resulting in benefit to agriculture or ecological improvement
R11	Uses of residual materials obtained from any of the operations numbered R1–R10
R12	Exchange of wastes for submission to any of the operations numbered R1–R11
R13	Accumulation of material intended for any operation in Section B

Annex VA
Information to be provided on notification

1. Reason for waste export
2. Exporter of the waste (1)
3. Generator(s) of the waste and site of generation (1)
4. Disposer of the waste and actual site of disposal (1)
5. Intended carrier(s) of the waste or their agents, if known (1)

6. Country of export of the waste
   Competent authority (2)
7. Expected countries of transit
   Competent authority (2)
8. Country of import of the waste
   Competent authority (2)
9. General or single notification
10. Projected date(s) of shipment(s) and period of time over which waste is to be exported and proposed itinerary (including point of entry and exit) (3)
11. Means of transport envisaged (road, rail, sea, air, inland waters)
12. Information relating to insurance (4)
13. Designation and physical description of the waste including Y number and UN number and its composition (5) and information on any special handling requirements including emergency provisions in case of accidents
14. Type of packaging envisaged (e.g. bulk, drummed, tanker)
15. Estimated quantity in weight/volume (6)
16. Process by which the waste is generated (7)
17. For wastes listed in Annex I, classifications from Annex III: hazardous characteristic, H number, and UN class
18. Method of disposal as per Annex IV
19. Declaration by the generator and exporter that the information is correct
20. Information transmitted (including technical description of the plant) to the exporter or generator from the disposer of the waste upon which the latter has based his assessment that there was no reason to believe that the wastes will not be managed in an environmentally sound manner in accordance with the laws and regulations of the country of import
21. Information concerning the contract between the exporter and disposer

Notes

(1) Full name and address, telephone or telefax number and the name, address, telephone, telex or telefax number of the person to be contacted.
(2) Full name and address, telephone, telex or telefax number.
(3) In the case of a general notification covering several shipments, either the expected dates of each shipment or, if this is not known, the expected frequency of the shipments will be required.
(4) Information to be provided on relevant insurance requirements and how they are met by exporter, carrier and disposer.
(5) The nature and the concentration of the most hazardous components, in terms of toxicity and other dangers presented by the waste both in handling and in relation to the proposed disposal method.

(6) In the case of a general notification covering several shipments, both the estimated total quantity and the estimated quantities for each individual shipment will be required.

(7) Insofar as this is necessary to assess the hazard and determine the appropriateness of the proposed disposal operation.

Annex VB
Information to be provided on the movement document

1. Exporter of the waste (1)
2. Generator(s) of the waste and site of generation (1)
3. Disposer of the waste and actual site of disposal (1)
4. Carrier(s) of the waste (1) or his agent(s)
5. Subject of general or single notification
6. The date the transboundary movement started and date(s) and signature on receipt by each person who takes charge of the waste
7. Means of transport (road, rail, inland waterway, sea, air) including countries of export, transit and import, also point of entry and exit where these have been designated
8. General description of the waste (physical state, proper UN shipping name and class, UN number, Y number and H number as applicable)
9. Information on special handling requirements including emergency provision in case of accidents
10. Type and number of packages
11. Quantity in weight/volume
12. Declaration by the generator or exporter that the information is correct
13. Declaration by the generator or exporter indicating no objection from the competent authorities of all States concerned which are Parties
14. Certification by disposer of receipt at designated disposal facility and indication of method of disposal and of the approximate date of disposal

Notes

The information required on the movement document shall where possible be integrated in one document with that required under transport rules. Where this is not possible the information should complement rather than duplicate that required under the transport rules. The movement document shall carry instructions as to who is to provide information and fill-out any form.

(1) Full name and address, telephone or telefax number and the name, address, telephone, telex or telefax number of the person to be contacted in case of emergency.

Annex VI
Arbitration

Article 1

Unless the agreement referred to in Article 20 of the Convention provides otherwise, the arbitration procedure shall be conducted in accordance with Articles 2 to 10 below.

Article 2

The claimant party shall notify the Secretariat that the Parties have agreed to submit the dispute to arbitration pursuant to paragraph 2 or paragraph 3 of Article 20 and include, in particular, the Articles of the Convention the interpretation or application of which are at issue. The Secretariat shall forward the information thus received to all Parties to the Convention.

Article 3

The arbitral tribunal shall consist of three members. Each of the Parties to the dispute shall appoint an arbitrator, and the two arbitrators so appointed shall designate by common agreement the third arbitrator, who shall be the chairman of the tribunal. The latter shall not be a national of one of the Parties to the dispute, nor have his usual place of residence in the territory of one of these Parties, nor be employed by any of them, nor have dealt with the case in any other capacity.

Article 4

1. If the chairman of the arbitral tribunal has not been designated within two months of the appointment of the second arbitrator, the Secretary-General of the United Nations shall, at the request of either Party, designate him within a further two months period.

2. If one of the Parties to the dispute does not appoint an arbitrator within two months of the receipt of the request, the other Party may inform the Secretary-General of the United Nations who shall designate the chairman of the arbitral tribunal within a further two months' period. Upon designation, the chairman of the arbitral tribunal shall request the Party which has not appointed an arbitrator to do so within two months. After such period, he shall inform the Secretary-General of the United Nations, who shall make this appointment within a further two months' period.

Article 5

1. The arbitral tribunal shall render its decision in accordance with international law and in accordance with the provisions of this Convention.

2. Any arbitral tribunal constituted under the provisions of this Annex shall draw up its own rules of procedure.

Article 6

1. The decisions of the arbitral tribunal both on procedure and on substance, shall be taken by majority vote of its members.

2. The tribunal may take all appropriate measures in order to establish the facts. It may, at the request of one of the Parties, recommend essential interim measures of protection.

3. The Parties to the dispute shall provide all facilities necessary for the effective conduct of the proceedings.

4. The absence or default of a Party in the dispute shall not constitute an impediment to the proceedings.

Article 7

The tribunal may hear and determine counter-claims arising directly out of the subject-matter of the dispute.

Article 8

Unless the arbitral tribunal determines otherwise because of the particular circumstances of the case, the expenses of the tribunal, including the remuneration of its members, shall be borne by the Parties to the dispute in equal shares. The tribunal shall keep a record of all its expenses, and shall furnish a final statement thereof to the Parties.

Article 9

Any Party that has an interest of a legal nature in the subject-matter of the dispute which may be affected by the decision in the case, may intervene in the proceedings with the consent of the tribunal.

Article 10

1. The tribunal shall render its award within five months of the date on which it is established unless it finds it necessary to extend the time-limit for a period which should not exceed five months.

2. The award of the arbitral tribunal shall be accompanied by a statement of reasons. It shall be final and binding upon the Parties to the dispute.

3. Any dispute which may arise between the Parties concerning the interpretation or execution of the award may be submitted by either Party to the arbitral tribunal which made the award or, if the latter cannot be seized thereof, to another tribunal constituted for this purpose in the same manner as the first.

Annex VII

[Annex VII is not yet in force. Annex VII is an integral part of the Amendment. It was adopted in 1995 by Decision III/1 which amended the Basel Convention (the so-called Basel Ban, reproduced below as Document 28A).]

Annex VIII
List A

Wastes contained in this Annex are characterized as hazardous under Article 1, paragraph 1 (a), of this Convention, and their designation on this Annex does not preclude the use of Annex III to demonstrate that a waste is not hazardous.

[List omitted]

Annex IX
List B

Wastes contained in the Annex will not be wastes covered by Article 1, paragraph 1 (a), of this Convention unless they contain Annex I material to an extent causing them to exhibit an Annex III characteristic.

[List omitted]

Decision III/1 of the Conference of the Parties (Amendment to the Basel Convention), 22 September 1995 (the 'Basel Ban')

Editorial note

The second conference of the Parties (COP-2) in March 1994 approved an immediate ban on the export from OECD to non-OECD countries of hazardous wastes intended for final disposal and also agreed to ban the export of wastes intended for recovery and recycling by 31 December 1997. The 'Basel Ban', as it became known, was not formally incorporated into the Convention by COP-2 and disputes arose as to whether it was legally binding on the Parties. To resolve the dispute, it was proposed at the third conference of the Parties (COP-3) in September 1995, that the Ban be formally incorporated into the Basel Convention as an amendment. The Basel Ban amendment adopted by COP-3 does not refer to OECD and non-OECD countries, but rather bans hazardous waste exports for final disposal and recycling from 'Annex VII' Parties (members of the EU, OECD and Liechtenstein) to non-Annex VII Parties. The Basel Ban has not yet entered into force as only 35 of the required 62 ratifications have so far been received (Article 17, Basel Convention).

Date of adoption: 22 September 1995

Entry into force: Not yet in force

Depositary: Secretary-General of the United Nations

Contracting Parties: Andorra, Austria, Brunei Darussalam, Bulgaria, China, Cyprus, Czech Republic, Denmark, Ecuador, Estonia, Finland, Gambia, Germany, Luxembourg, Malaysia, Netherlands, Norway, Panama, Paraguay, Poland, Portugal, Qatar, Romania, Saint Lucia, Slovakia, Spain, Sri Lanka, Sweden, Switzerland, Tanzania (United Republic of Tanzania), Trinidad and Tobago, Tunisia, Uruguay, Yugoslavia, United Kingdom.

Website: www.basel.int

Decision Adopted by the Third Conference of the Parties in Geneva, Switzerland, on 22 September 1995 (the 'Basel Ban')

Decision III/1
Amendment to the Basel Convention

The Conference,

Recalling that at the first meeting of the Conference of the Parties to the Basel Convention, a request was made for the prohibition of hazardous waste shipments from industrialized countries to developing countries;

Recalling decision II/12 of the Conference;

Noting that:

- the Technical Working Group is instructed by this Conference to continue its work on hazard characterization of wastes subject to the Basel Convention (decision III/12);
- the Technical Working Group has already commenced its work on the development of lists of wastes which are hazardous and wastes which are not subject to the Convention;
- those lists (document UNEP/CHW.3/Inf.4) already offer useful guidance but are not yet complete or fully accepted;
- the Technical Working Group will develop technical guidelines to assist any Party or State that has sovereign right to conclude agreements or arrangements including those under Article 11 concerning the transboundary movement of hazardous wastes.

1. *Instructs* the Technical Working Group to give full priority to completing the work on hazard characterization and the development of lists and technical guidelines in order to submit them for approval to the fourth meeting of the Conference of the Parties;

2. *Decides* that the Conference of the Parties shall make a decision on a list(s) at its fourth meeting;

3. *Decides* to adopt the following amendment to the Convention:

'Insert new preambular paragraph 7 bis:

> Recognizing that transboundary movements of hazardous wastes, especially to developing countries, have a high risk of not constituting an environmentally sound management of hazardous wastes as required by this Convention;

Insert new Article 4A:

> 1. Each Party listed in Annex VII shall prohibit all transboundary movements of hazardous wastes which are destined for operations according to Annex IV A, to States not listed in Annex VII.

2. Each Party listed in Annex VII shall phase out by 31 December 1997, and prohibit as of that date, all transboundary movements of hazardous wastes under Article 1(i)(a) of the Convention which are destined for operations according to Annex IV B to States not listed in Annex VII. Such transboundary movement shall not be prohibited unless the wastes in question are characterised as hazardous under the Convention.

Annex VII

'Parties and other States which are members of OECD, EC, Liechtenstein.'

Protocol on Liability and Compensation for Damage Resulting from Transboundary Movements of Hazardous Wastes and Their Disposal, 10 December 1999

Editorial note

In 1999, pursuant to Article 12 of the 1989 Basel Convention, parties adopted the Protocol on Liability and Compensation for Damage Resulting from Transboundary Movements of Hazardous Wastes and Their Disposal. The Protocol will establish a comprehensive regime for liability and for adequate and prompt compensation for damage (including damage to persons and property and loss of income deriving from an economic interest in the environment, costs of measures reinstating the impaired environment, and preventive measures (Article 1)). Any person who is in operational control of the wastes must take all reasonable measures to mitigate damage arising from an incident (Article 6).

The Protocol applies to damage due to an incident occurring during a transboundary movement, including illegal traffic and in respect of re-import, 'from the point where the wastes are loaded on the means of transport in an area under the national jurisdiction of the state of export' (Article 3(1) and (4)). Its application is subject to certain other exclusions (Article 3(6)(a) and (b) and (7) and (8)). It covers all damage suffered in an area under the national jurisdiction of a party, but only damage to persons and property and preventive measures in areas beyond national jurisdiction, and provides particular rules where the state of import, but not the state of export, is a party to the Protocol (Article 3(3)(a), (b) and (c)). Special provision is made for damage to states of transit (Article 3(3)(d) and Annex A).

The Basel Protocol generally provides for strict liability, with fault liability where there is a failure to comply with the Convention or damage occurs because of intentional, reckless or negligent acts or omissions (Article 5). The Protocol does not affect the rights and obligations of parties under general international law (Article 16). Under a regime of strict liability, the notifying entity is generally liable for damage until the disposer takes possession of the wastes, at which point liability shifts to the disposer (Article 4(1)), with a special rule governing hazardous wastes within the meaning of Article 1(1)(b) of the 1989 Convention (wastes determined to be hazardous by a party but not included in

Annex I of the Convention) (Article 4(2)). Liability is excluded upon proof of damage arising as a result of certain acts, including armed conflict and insurrection, certain natural phenomenon, and the wrongful conduct of a third party (Article 4(5)).

Liability is limited for non-fault based incidents to amounts determined by domestic law, (Article 12(1) and Annex B(1)) but there are no liability limits for damage from fault-based incidents (Article 12(2)). The Protocol sets minimum liability for damage (Annex B(2)(a)), and liable persons must also have insurance or financial guarantees covering these amounts (Article 14). Claims may be brought in the courts of the party where the damage was suffered, or where the incident occurred, or where the defendant has his habitual residence or principal place of business, and provision is made for the mutual recognition and enforcement of judgments (Articles 17 and 21). Matters not regulated by the Protocol are governed by the law of the competent court (Article 19). Claims under the Protocol are inadmissible unless brought within ten years of the incident and within five years from the date when the claimant knew or ought reasonably to have known of the damage (Article 13).

Date of adoption:	10 December 1999
Entry into force:	Not yet in force.
Depositary:	Secretary-General of the United Nations
Contracting Parties:	No ratifications yet.
Website:	www.basel.int

Protocol on Liability and Compensation for Damage Resulting from Transboundary Movements of Hazardous Wastes and Their Disposal

The Parties to the Protocol,

Having taken into account the relevant provisions of Principle 13 of the 1992 Rio Declaration on Environment and Development, according to which States shall develop international and national legal instruments regarding liability and compensation for the victims of pollution and other environmental damage,

Being Parties to the Basel Convention on the Control of Transboundary Movements of Hazardous Wastes and their Disposal,

Mindful of their obligations under the Convention,

Aware of the risk of damage to human health, property and the environment caused by hazardous wastes and other wastes and the transboundary movement and disposal thereof,

Concerned about the problem of illegal transboundary traffic in hazardous wastes and other wastes,

Committed to Article 12 of the Convention, and emphasizing the need to set out appropriate rules and procedures in the field of liability and compensation for damage resulting from the transboundary movement and disposal of hazardous wastes and other wastes,

Convinced of the need to provide for third party liability and environmental liability in order to ensure that adequate and prompt compensation is available for damage resulting from the transboundary movement and disposal of hazardous wastes and other wastes,

Have agreed as follows:

Article 1
Objective

The objective of the Protocol is to provide for a comprehensive regime for liability and for adequate and prompt compensation for damage resulting from the transboundary movement of hazardous wastes and other wastes and their disposal including illegal traffic in those wastes.

Article 2
Definitions

1. The definitions of terms contained in the Convention apply to the Protocol, unless expressly provided otherwise in the Protocol.

2. For the purposes of the Protocol:

(a) 'The Convention' means the Basel Convention on the Control of Transboundary Movements of Hazardous Wastes and their Disposal;

(b) 'Hazardous wastes and other wastes' means hazardous wastes and other wastes within the meaning of Article 1 of the Convention;

(c) 'Damage' means:
   (i) Loss of life or personal injury;
   (ii) Loss of or damage to property other than property held by the person liable in accordance with the present Protocol;
   (iii) Loss of income directly deriving from an economic interest in any use of the environment, incurred as a result of impairment of the environment, taking into account savings and costs;
   (iv) The costs of measures of reinstatement of the impaired environment, limited to the costs of measures actually taken or to be undertaken; and
   (v) The costs of preventive measures, including any loss or damage caused by such measures, to the extent that the damage arises out of or results from hazardous properties of the wastes involved in the transboundary movement and disposal of hazardous wastes and other wastes subject to the Convention;

(d) 'Measures of reinstatement' means any reasonable measures aiming to assess, reinstate or restore damaged or destroyed components of the environment. Domestic law may indicate who will be entitled to take such measures;

(e) 'Preventive measures' means any reasonable measures taken by any person in response to an incident, to prevent, minimize, or mitigate loss or damage, or to effect environmental clean-up;

(f) 'Contracting Party' means a Party to the Protocol;

(g) 'Protocol' means the present Protocol;

(h) 'Incident' means any occurrence, or series of occurrences having the same origin that causes damage or creates a grave and imminent threat of causing damage;

(i) 'Regional economic integration organization' means an organization constituted by sovereign States to which its member States have transferred competence in respect of matters governed by the Protocol and which has been duly authorized, in accordance with its internal procedures, to sign, ratify, accept, approve, formally confirm or accede to it;

(j) 'Unit of account' means the Special Drawing Right as defined by the International Monetary Fund.

Article 3
Scope of application

1. The Protocol shall apply to damage due to an incident occurring during a transboundary movement of hazardous wastes and other wastes and their disposal, including illegal traffic, from the point where the wastes are loaded on the means of transport in an area under the national jurisdiction of a State of export. Any Contracting Party may by way of notification to the Depositary exclude the application of the Protocol, in respect of all transboundary movements for which it is the State of export, for such incidents which occur in an area under its national jurisdiction, as regards damage in its area of national jurisdiction. The Secretariat shall inform all Contracting Parties of notifications received in accordance with this Article.

2. The Protocol shall apply:

(a) In relation to movements destined for one of the operations specified in Annex IV to the Convention other than D13, D14, D15, R12 or R13, until the time at which the notification of completion of disposal pursuant to Article 6, paragraph 9, of the Convention has occurred, or, where such notification has not been made, completion of disposal has occurred; and

(b) In relation to movements destined for the operations specified in D13, D14, D15, R12 or R13 of Annex IV to the Convention, until completion of the subsequent disposal operation specified in D1 to D12 and R1 to R11 of Annex IV to the Convention.

3.

(a) The Protocol shall apply only to damage suffered in an area under the national jurisdiction of a Contracting Party arising from an incident as referred to in paragraph 1;

(b) When the State of import, but not the State of export, is a Contracting Party, the Protocol shall apply only with respect to damage arising from an incident as referred to in paragraph 1 which takes place after the moment at which the disposer has taken possession of the hazardous wastes and other wastes. When the State of export, but not the State of import, is a Contracting Party, the Protocol shall apply only with respect to damage arising from an incident as referred to in paragraph 1 which takes place prior to the moment at which the disposer takes possession of the hazardous wastes and other wastes. When neither the State of export nor the State of import is a Contracting Party, the Protocol shall not apply;

(c) Notwithstanding subparagraph (a), the Protocol shall also apply to the damages specified in Article 2, subparagraphs 2 (c) (i), (ii) and (v), of the Protocol occurring in areas beyond any national jurisdiction;

(d) Notwithstanding subparagraph (a), the Protocol shall, in relation to rights under the Protocol, also apply to damages suffered in an area under the national jurisdiction of a State of transit which is not a Contracting Party provided that such State appears in Annex A and has acceded to a multilateral or regional agreement concerning transboundary movements of hazardous waste which is in force.
Subparagraph (b) will apply *mutatis mutandis.*

4. Notwithstanding paragraph 1, in case of re-importation under Article 8 or Article 9, subparagraph 2 (a), and Article 9, paragraph 4, of the Convention, the provisions of the Protocol shall apply until the hazardous wastes and other wastes reach the original State of export.

5. Nothing in the Protocol shall affect in any way the sovereignty of States over their territorial seas and their jurisdiction and the right in their respective exclusive economic zones and continental shelves in accordance with international law.

6. Notwithstanding paragraph 1 and subject to paragraph 2 of this Article:

(a) The Protocol shall not apply to damage that has arisen from a transboundary movement of hazardous wastes and other wastes that has commenced before the entry into force of the Protocol for the Contracting Party concerned;

(b) The Protocol shall apply to damage resulting from an incident occurring during a transboundary movement of wastes falling under Article 1, subparagraph 1 (b), of the Convention only if those wastes have been notified in accordance with Article 3 of the Convention by the State of export or

import, or both, and the damage arises in an area under the national jurisdiction of a State, including a State of transit, that has defined or considers
those wastes as hazardous provided that the requirements of Article 3 of the
Convention have been met. In this case strict liability shall be channelled
in accordance with Article 4 of the Protocol.

7.

(a) The Protocol shall not apply to damage due to an incident occurring during
   a transboundary movement of hazardous wastes and other wastes and
   their disposal pursuant to a bilateral, multilateral or regional agreement or
   arrangement concluded and notified in accordance with Article 11 of the
   Convention if:
   (i) The damage occurred in an area under the national jurisdiction of any
       of the Parties to the agreement or arrangement;
   (ii) There exists a liability and compensation regime, which is in force
       and is applicable to the damage resulting from such a transboundary
       movement or disposal provided it fully meets, or exceeds the objective
       of the Protocol by providing a high level of protection to persons who
       have suffered damage;
   (iii) The Party to the Article 11 agreement or arrangement in which the
       damage has occurred has previously notified the Depositary of the
       non-application of the Protocol to any damage occurring in an area
       under its national jurisdiction due to an incident resulting from move-
       ments or disposals referred to in this subparagraph; and
   (iv) The Parties to the Article 11 agreement or arrangement have not de-
       clared that the Protocol shall be applicable;
(b) In order to promote transparency, a Contracting Party that has notified
   the Depositary of the non-application of the Protocol shall notify the
   Secretariat of the applicable liability and compensation regime referred
   to in subparagraph (a) (ii) and include a description of the regime. The
   Secretariat shall submit to the Meeting of the Parties, on a regular basis,
   summary reports on the notifications received;
(c) After a notification pursuant to subparagraph (a) (iii) is made, actions for
   compensation for damage to which subparagraph (a) (i) applies may not
   be made under the Protocol.

8. The exclusion set out in paragraph 7 of this Article shall neither affect any
of the rights or obligations under the Protocol of a Contracting Party which is
not party to the agreement or arrangement mentioned above, nor shall it affect
rights of States of transit which are not Contracting Parties.

9. Article 3, paragraph 2, shall not affect the application of Article 16 to all
Contracting Parties.

Article 4
Strict liability

1. The person who notifies in accordance with Article 6 of the Convention, shall be liable for damage until the disposer has taken possession of the hazardous wastes and other wastes. Thereafter the disposer shall be liable for damage. If the State of export is the notifier or if no notification has taken place, the exporter shall be liable for damage until the disposer has taken possession of the hazardous wastes and other wastes. With respect to Article 3, subparagraph 6 (b), of the Protocol, Article 6, paragraph 5, of the Convention shall apply *mutatis mutandis.* Thereafter the disposer shall be liable for damage.

2. Without prejudice to paragraph 1, with respect to wastes under Article 1, subparagraph 1 (b), of the Convention that have been notified as hazardous by the State of import in accordance with Article 3 of the Convention but not by the State of export, the importer shall be liable until the disposer has taken possession of the wastes, if the State of import is the notifier or if no notification has taken place. Thereafter the disposer shall be liable for damage.

3. Should the hazardous wastes and other wastes be re-imported in accordance with Article 8 of the Convention, the person who notified shall be liable for damage from the time the hazardous wastes leave the disposal site, until the wastes are taken into possession by the exporter, if applicable, or by the alternate disposer.

4. Should the hazardous wastes and other wastes be re-imported under Article 9, subparagraph 2 (a), or Article 9, paragraph 4, of the Convention, subject to Article 3 of the Protocol, the person who re-imports shall be held liable for damage until the wastes are taken into possession by the exporter if applicable, or by the alternate disposer.

5. No liability in accordance with this Article shall attach to the person referred to in paragraphs 1 and 2 of this Article, if that person proves that the damage was:

(a) The result of an act of armed conflict, hostilities, civil war or insurrection;
(b) The result of a natural phenomenon of exceptional, inevitable, unforeseeable and irresistible character;
(c) Wholly the result of compliance with a compulsory measure of a public authority of the State where the damage occurred; or
(d) Wholly the result of the wrongful intentional conduct of a third party, including the person who suffered the damage.

6. If two or more persons are liable according to this Article, the claimant shall have the right to seek full compensation for the damage from any or all of the persons liable.

Article 5
Fault-based liability

Without prejudice to Article 4, any person shall be liable for damage caused or contributed to by his lack of compliance with the provisions implementing the Convention or by his wrongful intentional, reckless or negligent acts or omissions. This Article shall not affect the domestic law of the Contracting Parties governing liability of servants and agents.

Article 6
Preventive measures

1. Subject to any requirement of domestic law any person in operational control of hazardous wastes and other wastes at the time of an incident shall take all reasonable measures to mitigate damage arising therefrom.

2. Notwithstanding any other provision in the Protocol, any person in possession and/or control of hazardous wastes and other wastes for the sole purpose of taking preventive measures, provided that this person acted reasonably and in accordance with any domestic law regarding preventive measures, is not thereby subject to liability under the Protocol.

Article 7
Combined cause of the damage

1. Where damage is caused by wastes covered by the Protocol and wastes not covered by the Protocol, a person otherwise liable shall only be liable according to the Protocol in proportion to the contribution made by the wastes covered by the Protocol to the damage.

2. The proportion of the contribution to the damage of the wastes referred to in paragraph 1 shall be determined with regard to the volume and properties of the wastes involved, and the type of damage occurring.

3. In respect of damage where it is not possible to distinguish between the contribution made by wastes covered by the Protocol and wastes not covered by the Protocol, all damage shall be considered to be covered by the Protocol.

Article 8
Right of recourse

1. Any person liable under the Protocol shall be entitled to a right of recourse in accordance with the rules of procedure of the competent court:

(a) Against any other person also liable under the Protocol; and
(b) As expressly provided for in contractual arrangements.

2. Nothing in the Protocol shall prejudice any rights of recourse to which the person liable might be entitled pursuant to the law of the competent court.

Article 9
Contributory fault

Compensation may be reduced or disallowed if the person who suffered the damage, or a person for whom he is responsible under the domestic law, by his own fault, has caused or contributed to the damage having regard to all circumstances.

Article 10
Implementation

1. The Contracting Parties shall adopt the legislative, regulatory and administrative measures necessary to implement the Protocol.

2. In order to promote transparency, Contracting Parties shall inform the Secretariat of measures to implement the Protocol, including any limits of liability established pursuant to paragraph 1 of Annex B.

3. The provisions of the Protocol shall be applied without discrimination based on nationality, domicile or residence.

Article 11
Conflicts with other liability and compensation agreements

Whenever the provisions of the Protocol and the provisions of a bilateral, multilateral or regional agreement apply to liability and compensation for damage caused by an incident arising during the same portion of a transboundary movement, the Protocol shall not apply provided the other agreement is in force for the Party or Parties concerned and had been opened for signature when the Protocol was opened for signature, even if the agreement was amended afterwards.

Article 12
Financial limits

1. Financial limits for the liability under Article 4 of the Protocol are specified in Annex B to the Protocol. Such limits shall not include any interest or costs awarded by the competent court.

2. There shall be no financial limit on liability under Article 5.

Article 13
Time limit of liability

1. Claims for compensation under the Protocol shall not be admissible unless they are brought within ten years from the date of the incident.

2. Claims for compensation under the Protocol shall not be admissible unless they are brought within five years from the date the claimant knew or ought reasonably to have known of the damage provided that the time limits established pursuant to paragraph 1 of this Article are not exceeded.

3. Where the incident consists of a series of occurrences having the same-origin, time limits established pursuant to this Article shall run from the date of the last of such occurrences. Where the incident consists of a continuous occurrence, such time limits shall run from the end of that continuous occurrence.

Article 14
Insurance and other financial guarantees

1. The persons liable under Article 4 shall establish and maintain during the period of the time limit of liability, insurance, bonds or other financial guarantees covering their liability under Article 4 of the Protocol for amounts not less than the minimum limits specified in paragraph 2 of Annex B. States may fulfil their obligation under this paragraph by a declaration of self-insurance. Nothing in this paragraph shall prevent the use of deductibles or co-payments as between the insurer and the insured, but the failure of the insured to pay any deductible or co-payment shall not be a defence against the person who has suffered the damage.

2. With regard to the liability of the notifier, or exporter under Article 4, paragraph 1, or of the importer under Article 4, paragraph 2, insurance, bonds or other financial guarantees referred to in paragraph 1 of this Article shall only be drawn upon in order to provide compensation for damage covered by Article 2 of the Protocol.

3. A document reflecting the coverage of the liability of the notifier or exporter under Article 4, paragraph 1, or of the importer under Article 4, paragraph 2, of the Protocol shall accompany the notification referred to in Article 6 of the Convention. Proof of coverage of the liability of the disposer shall be delivered to the competent authorities of the State of import.

4. Any claim under the Protocol may be asserted directly against any person providing insurance, bonds or other financial guarantees. The insurer or the person providing the financial guarantee shall have the right to require the person liable under Article 4 to be joined in the proceedings. Insurers and persons providing financial guarantees may invoke the defences which the person liable under Article 4 would be entitled to invoke.

5. Notwithstanding paragraph 4, a Contracting Party shall, by notification to the Depositary at the time of signature, ratification, or approval of, or accession to the Protocol, indicate if it does not provide for a right to bring a direct action pursuant to paragraph 4. The Secretariat shall maintain a record of the Contracting Parties who have given notification pursuant to this paragraph.

Article 15
Financial mechanism

1. Where compensation under the Protocol does not cover the costs of damage, additional and supplementary measures aimed at ensuring adequate and prompt compensation may be taken using existing mechanisms.

2. The Meeting of the Parties shall keep under review the need for and possibility of improving existing mechanisms or establishing a new mechanism.

Article 16
State responsibility

The Protocol shall not affect the rights and obligations of the Contracting Parties under the rules of general international law with respect to State responsibility.

Procedures

Article 17
Competent courts

1. Claims for compensation under the Protocol may be brought in the courts of a Contracting Party only where either:

(a) The damage was suffered; or
(b) The incident occurred; or
(c) The defendant has his habitual residence, or has his principal place of business.

2. Each Contracting Party shall ensure that its courts possess the necessary competence to entertain such claims for compensation.

Article 18
Related actions

1. Where related actions are brought in the courts of different Parties, any court other than the court first seized may, while the actions are pending at first instance, stay its proceedings.

2. A court may, on the application of one of the Parties, decline jurisdiction if the law of that court permits the consolidation of related actions and another court has jurisdiction over both actions.

3. For the purpose of this Article, actions are deemed to be related where they are so closely connected that it is expedient to hear and determine them together to avoid the risk of irreconcilable judgements resulting from separate proceedings.

Article 19
Applicable law

All matters of substance or procedure regarding claims before the competent court which are not specifically regulated in the Protocol shall be governed by the law of that court including any rules of such law relating to conflict of laws.

Article 20
Relation between the Protocol and the law of the competent court

1. Subject to paragraph 2, nothing in the Protocol shall be construed as limiting or derogating from any rights of persons who have suffered damage, or as limiting the protection or reinstatement of the environment which may be provided under domestic law.

2. No claims for compensation for damage based on the strict liability of the notifier or the exporter liable under Article 4, paragraph 1, or the importer liable under Article 4, paragraph 2, of the Protocol, shall be made otherwise than in accordance with the Protocol.

Article 21
Mutual recognition and enforcement of judgements

1. Any judgement of a court having jurisdiction in accordance with Article 17 of the Protocol, which is enforceable in the State of origin and is no longer subject to ordinary forms of review, shall be recognized in any Contracting Party as soon as the formalities required in that Party have been completed, except:

(a) Where the judgement was obtained by fraud;
(b) Where the defendant was not given reasonable notice and a fair opportunity to present his case;
(c) Where the judgement is irreconcilable with an earlier judgement validly pronounced in another Contracting Party with regard to the same cause of action and the same parties; or
(d) Where the judgement is contrary to the public policy of the Contracting Party in which its recognition is sought.

2. A judgement recognized under paragraph 1 of this Article shall be enforceable in each Contracting Party as soon as the formalities required in that Party have been completed. The formalities shall not permit the merits of the case to be re-opened.

3. The provisions of paragraphs 1 and 2 of this Article shall not apply between Contracting Parties that are Parties to an agreement or arrangement in force on mutual recognition and enforcement of judgements under which the judgement would be recognizable and enforceable.

Article 22
Relationship of the Protocol with the Basel Convention

Except as otherwise provided in the Protocol, the provisions of the Convention relating to its Protocols shall apply to the Protocol.

Article 23
Amendment of Annex B

1. At its sixth meeting, the Conference of the Parties to the Basel Convention may amend paragraph 2 of Annex B following the procedure set out in Article 18 of the Basel Convention.

2. Such an amendment may be made before the Protocol enters into force.

Final clauses

Article 24
Meeting of the Parties

1. A Meeting of the Parties is hereby established. The Secretariat shall convene the first Meeting of the Parties in conjunction with the first meeting of the Conference of the Parties to the Convention after entry into force of the Protocol.

2. Subsequent ordinary Meetings of the Parties shall be held in conjunction with meetings of the Conference of the Parties to the Convention unless the Meeting of the Parties decides otherwise. Extraordinary Meetings of the Parties shall be held at such other times as may be deemed necessary by a Meeting of the Parties, or at the written request of any Contracting Party, provided that within six months of such a request being communicated to them by the Secretariat, it is supported by at least one third of the Contracting Parties.

3. The Contracting Parties, at their first meeting, shall adopt by consensus rules of procedure for their meetings as well as financial rules.

4. The functions of the Meeting of the Parties shall be:

(a) To review the implementation of and compliance with the Protocol;
(b) To provide for reporting and establish guidelines and procedures for such reporting where necessary;
(c) To consider and adopt, where necessary, proposals for amendment of the Protocol or any annexes and for any new annexes; and
(d) To consider and undertake any additional action that may be required for the purposes of the Protocol.

Article 25
Secretariat

1. For the purposes of the Protocol, the Secretariat shall:

(a) Arrange for and service Meetings of the Parties as provided for in Article 24;
(b) Prepare reports, including financial data, on its activities carried out in implementation of its functions under the Protocol and present them to the Meeting of the Parties;

(c) Ensure the necessary coordination with relevant international bodies, and in particular enter into such administrative and contractual arrangements as may be required for the effective discharge of its functions;

(d) Compile information concerning the national laws and administrative provisions of Contracting Parties implementing the Protocol;

(e) Cooperate with Contracting Parties and with relevant and competent international organisations and agencies in the provision of experts and equipment for the purpose of rapid assistance to States in the event of an emergency situation;

(f) Encourage non-Parties to attend the Meetings of the Parties as observers and to act in accordance with the provisions of the Protocol; and

(g) Perform such other functions for the achievement of the purposes of this Protocol as may be assigned to it by the Meetings of the Parties.

2. The secretariat functions shall be carried out by the Secretariat of the Basel Convention.

Article 26
Signature

The Protocol shall be open for signature by States and by regional economic integration organizations Parties to the Basel Convention in Berne at the Federal Department of Foreign Affairs of Switzerland from 6 to 17 March 2000 and at United Nations Headquarters in New York from 1 April 2000 to 10 December 2000.

Article 27
Ratification, acceptance, formal confirmation or approval

1. The Protocol shall be subject to ratification, acceptance or approval by States and to formal confirmation or approval by regional economic integration organizations. Instruments of ratification, acceptance, formal confirmation, or approval shall be deposited with the Depositary.

2. Any organization referred to in paragraph 1 of this Article which becomes a Contracting Party without any of its member States being a Contracting Party shall be bound by all the obligations under the Protocol. In the case of such organizations, one or more of whose member States is a Contracting Party, the organization and its member States shall decide on their respective responsibilities for the performance of their obligations under the Protocol. In such cases, the organization and the member States shall not be entitled to exercise rights under the Protocol concurrently.

3. In their instruments of formal confirmation or approval, the organizations referred to in paragraph 1 of this Article shall declare the extent of their competence with respect to the matters governed by the Protocol. These

organizations shall also inform the Depositary, who will inform the Contracting Parties, of any substantial modification in the extent of their competence.

Article 28
Accession

1. The Protocol shall be open for accession by any States and by any regional economic integration organization Party to the Basel Convention which has not signed the Protocol. The instruments of accession shall be deposited with the Depositary.

2. In their instruments of accession, the organizations referred to in paragraph 1 of this Article shall declare the extent of their competence with respect to the matters governed by the Protocol. These organizations shall also inform the Depositary of any substantial modification in the extent of their competence.

3. The provisions of Article 27, paragraph 2, shall apply to regional economic integration organizations which accede to the Protocol.

Article 29
Entry into force

1. The Protocol shall enter into force on the ninetieth day after the date of deposit of the twentieth instrument of ratification, acceptance, formal confirmation, approval or accession.

2. For each State or regional economic integration organization which ratifies, accepts, approves or formally confirms the Protocol or accedes thereto after the date of the deposit of the twentieth instrument of ratification, acceptance, approval, formal confirmation or accession, it shall enter into force on the ninetieth day after the date of deposit by such State or regional economic integration organization of its instrument of ratification, acceptance, approval, formal confirmation or accession.

3. For the purpose of paragraphs 1 and 2 of this Article, any instrument deposited by a regional economic integration organization shall not be counted as additional to those deposited by member States of such organization.

Article 30
Reservations and declarations

1. No reservation or exception may be made to the Protocol. For the purposes of the Protocol, notifications according to Article 3, paragraph 1, Article 3, paragraph 6, or Article 14, paragraph 5, shall not be regarded as reservations or exceptions.

2. Paragraph 1 of this Article does not preclude a State or a regional economic integration organization, when signing, ratifying, accepting, approving, formally confirming or acceding to the Protocol, from making declarations or statements, however phrased or named, with a view, *inter alia*, to the

harmonization of its laws and regulations with the provisions of the Protocol, provided that such declarations or statements do not purport to exclude or to modify the legal effects of the provisions of the Protocol in their application to that State or that organization.

Article 31
Withdrawal

1. At any time after three years from the date on which the Protocol has entered into force for a Contracting Party, that Contracting Party may withdraw from the Protocol by giving written notification to the Depositary.

2. Withdrawal shall be effective one year from receipt of notification by the Depositary, or on such later date as may be specified in the notification.

Article 32
Depositary

The Secretary-General of the United Nations shall be the Depositary of the Protocol.

Article 33
Authentic texts

The original Arabic, Chinese, English, French, Russian and Spanish texts of the Protocol are equally authentic.

Annex A
List of States of transit as referred to in Article 3, subparagraph 3 (d)

1. Antigua and Barbuda
2. Bahamas
3. Bahrain
4. Barbados
5. Cape Verde
6. Comoros
7. Cook Islands
8. Cuba
9. Cyprus
10. Dominica
11. Dominican Republic
12. Fiji
13. Grenada
14. Haiti
15. Jamaica
16. Kiribati

17. Maldives
18. Malta
19. Marshall Islands
20. Mauritius
21. Micronesia (Federated States of)
22. Nauru
23. Netherlands (on behalf of Aruba and the Netherlands Antilles)
24. New Zealand (on behalf of Tokelau)
25. Niue
26. Palau
27. Papua New Guinea
28. Samoa
29. São Tomé and Príncipe
30. Seychelles
31. Singapore
32. Solomon Islands
33. St. Lucia
34. St. Kitts and Nevis
35. St. Vincent and the Grenadines
36. Tonga
37. Trinidad and Tobago
38. Tuvalu
39. Vanuatu

Annex B
Financial limits

1. Financial limits for the liability under Article 4 of the Protocol shall be determined by domestic law.
2. The limits of liability shall:

(a) For the notifier, exporter or importer, for any one incident, be not less than:
   (i)   1 million units of account for shipments up to and including 5 tonnes;
   (ii) 2 million units of account for shipments exceeding 5 tonnes, up to and including 25 tonnes;
   (iii) 4 million units of account for shipments exceeding 25 tonnes, up to and including 50 tonnes;
   (iv) 6 million units of account for shipments exceeding 50 tonnes, up to and including to 1,000 tonnes;
   (v)   10 million units of account for shipments exceeding 1,000 tonnes, up to and including 10,000 tonnes;
   (vi) Plus an additional 1,000 units of account for each additional tonne up to a maximum of 30 million units of account;

(b) For the disposer, for any one incident, be not less than 2 million units of account for any one incident.

3. The amounts referred to in paragraph 2 shall be reviewed by the Contracting Parties on a regular basis taking into account, *inter alia*, the potential risks posed to the environment by the movement of hazardous wastes and other wastes and their disposal, recycling, and the nature, quantity and hazardous properties of the wastes.

Convention on the Ban of the Import into Africa and the Control of Transboundary Movement and Management of Hazardous Wastes within Africa, 29 January 1991

Editorial note

The Bamako Convention on the Ban of the Import into Africa and the Control of Transboundary Movement and Management of Hazardous Wastes within Africa, adopted under the auspices of the OAU, is a regional agreement which prohibits the importation of hazardous wastes into Africa but permits its regulated movement within Africa. The ban on importation of hazardous wastes is absolute and any violation of it is considered a criminal act (Article 4(1)). The dumping of hazardous wastes at sea is also prohibited (Article 4(2)). Hazardous wastes is defined by the Convention by reference to category and characteristics outlined in the Annexes to the Convention (Article 2(1)). Wastes will also be hazardous if they are so defined by domestic legislation of a Party of export, import or transit, and will be deemed to be hazardous if they are banned or not registered with governmental authorities in the manufacturing country for human health or environmental reasons (Article 2(1)). The Convention applies to radioactive wastes (Article 2(2)), but not those discharged through the normal operation of ships which are regulated by other international instruments (Article 2(3)).

The 'preventive, precautionary' approach to pollution problems is to guide the Parties and they are required to co-operate to implement the 'precautionary principle' by applying clean production techniques (Article 4(3)(f)). Parties are further required to promote clean production methods that apply to a product's entire life cycle (Article 4(3)(g)).

In regulating intra-African traffic in hazardous wastes, the Convention adopts many of the provisions of the 1989 Basel Convention. Specifically, it imposes duties on States including: (a) the obligation to prevent the export of hazardous wastes to States which have prohibited its import or where it is suspected that waste management will not occur in an 'environmentally sound manner' (defined in Articles 1(10) and 4(3)(i)); and (b) the obligation to allow transboundary movement of wastes only if the exporting State lacks the capacity to dispose of the wastes in an 'environmentally sound and efficient manner' or if it is in accordance with other criteria decided by the Parties (Article 4(3)(n)). The Parties undertake to enforce the obligations of the Convention in accordance with national and international law (Article 4(4)(a)). Nothing in the Convention prevents the imposition of additional requirements to protect human life and the environment, so long as they are consistent with the Convention and international law (Article 4(4)(b)). The Convention provides for a similar notification and consent procedure between States of export, import and transit to that found in the Basel Convention (Article 6). Exporting States must reimport wastes whose transboundary movement cannot be completed in accordance with its contractual terms or they must provide, within ninety days, an 'environmentally sound' alternative arrangement for disposal (Article 8). In addition to being required to punish offenders (Article 9(2)), exporting States must take back any wastes that are transferred illegally (Article 9(3)). Parties are permitted to enter into agreements with non-Parties to move hazardous wastes within Africa, but these agreements may not derogate from the Convention's requirements of 'environmentally sound management' (Article 11(1)).

The Convention establishes a Conference of the Parties to review and evaluate the implementation of the Convention (Article 15). A Secretariat arranges meetings of the Conference of the Parties, receives and transmits information, and assists in the identification of cases of illegal traffic in hazardous wastes (Article 16). Dispute settlement is by negotiation or any other means selected by the Parties involved, but in the event of failure of these means, the dispute must go before the ICJ or arbitration (Article 20). Amendments to the Convention and its Protocols require a two-thirds majority of those present and voting (Article 17). Reservations are not permitted to the Convention but declarations are (Article 26).

Date of adoption:	29 January 1991
Entry into force:	22 April 1998
Depositary:	Secretary-General of the African Union
Contracting Parties:	Benin, Burkina Faso, Burundi, Cameroon, Central African Republic, Chad, Cote d'Ivoire, Djibouti, Egypt, Guinea, Guinea-Bissau, Lesotho, Libyan Arab Jamahiriya, Mali, Mauritius, Niger, Rwanda, Senegal, Somalia, Swaziland, Tanzania, Togo, Tunisia, Zimbabwe.
Website:	www.africa-union.org

Convention on the Ban of the Import into Africa and the Control of Transboundary Movement and Management of Hazardous Wastes within Africa

Preamble

The Parties to this Convention,

1. *Mindful* of the growing threat to human health and the environment posed by the increased generation and the complexity of hazardous wastes,

2. *Further mindful* that the most effective way of protecting human health and the environment from the dangers posed by such wastes is the reduction of their generation to a minimum in terms of quantity and/or hazard potential,

3. *Aware* of the risk of damage to human health and the environment caused by transboundary movements of hazardous wastes,

4. *Reiterating* that States should ensure that the generator should carry out his responsibilities with regard to the transport and disposal of hazardous wastes in a manner that is consistent with the protection of human health and environment, whatever the place of disposal,

5. *Recalling* relevant chapters of the Charter of the Organisation of African Unity (OAU) on environmental protection, the African Charter for Human and Peoples' Rights, Chapter IX of the Lagos Plan of Action and other Recommendations adopted by the Organisation of African Unity on the environment,

6. *Further recognizing* the sovereignty of States to ban the importation into, and the transit through, their territory, of hazardous wastes and substances for environmental and human health reasons,

7. *Recognizing also* the increasing mobilisation in Africa for the prohibition of transboundary movements of hazardous wastes and their disposal in African countries,

8. *Convinced* that hazardous wastes should, as far as is compatible with environmentally sound and efficient management, be disposed in the State where they were generated,

9. *Convinced* that the effective control and minimisation of transboundary movements of hazardous wastes will act as an incentive, in Africa and elsewhere, for the reduction of the volume of the generation of such wastes,

10. *Noting* that a number of international and regional agreements deal with the problem of the protection and preservation of the environment with regard to the transit of dangerous goods,

11. *Taking into account* the Declaration of the United Nations Conference on the Human Environment (Stockholm, 1972), the Cairo Guidelines and Principles for the Environmentally Sound Management of Hazardous Wastes adopted by the Governing Council of the United Nations Environment Programme (UNEP) by Decision 14/30 of 17 June 1987, the Recommendations of the United Nations Committee of Experts on the Transport of Dangerous Goods (formulated in 1957 and updated biennially), the Charter of Human

Rights, relevant recommendations, declarations, instruments and regulations adopted within the United Nations System, the relevant articles of the 1989 Basel Convention on the Control of Transboundary Movements of Hazardous Wastes and their Disposal which allow for the establishment of regional agreements which may be equal to or stronger than its own provisions, Article 39 of the Lomé IV Convention relating to the international movement of hazardous wastes and radioactive wastes, African intergovernmental organisations and the work and studies done within other international and regional organisations,

12. *Mindful* of the spirit, principles, aims and functions of the African Convention on the Conservation of Nature and Natural Resources adopted by the African Heads of State and Government in Algiers (1968) and the World Charter for Nature adopted by the General Assembly of the United Nations at its Thirty-seventh Session (1982) as the rule of ethics in respect of the protection of the human environment and the conservation of natural resources,

13. *Concerned* by the problem of transboundary traffic in hazardous wastes,

14. *Recognizing* the need to promote the development of clean production methods, including clean technologies, for the sound management of hazardous wastes produced in Africa, in particular, to avoid, minimize and eliminate the generation of such wastes,

15. *Recognizing also* that where necessary hazardous wastes should be transported in accordance with relevant international conventions and recommendations,

16. *Determined* to protect, by strict control, the human health of the African population and the environment against the adverse effects which may result from the generation of hazardous wastes,

17. *Affirming* a commitment also to responsibly address the problem of hazardous wastes originating within the Continent of Africa,
Have agreed as follows:

Article 1
Definitions

For the purpose of this Convention:

1. 'Wastes' are substances or materials which are disposed of, or are intended to be disposed of, or are required to be disposed of by the provisions of national law;
2. 'Hazardous wastes' means wastes as specified in Article 2 of this Convention;
3. 'Management' means the prevention and reduction of hazardous wastes and the collection, transport, storage, and treatment either for the reuse or disposal, of hazardous wastes including after-care of disposal sites;

4. 'Transboundary movement' means any movement of hazardous wastes from an area under the national jurisdiction of any State to or through an area under the national jurisdiction of another State, or to or through an area not under the national jurisdiction of another State, provided at least two States are involved in the movement;

5. 'Clean production methods' means production or industrial systems which avoid, or eliminate the generation of hazardous wastes and hazardous products in conformity with Article 4, section 3 (f) and (g) of this Convention;

6. 'Disposal' means any operation specified in Annex III to this Convention;

7. 'Approved site or facility' means a site or facility for the disposal of hazardous wastes which is authorized or permitted to operate for this purpose by a relevant authority of the State where the site or facility is located;

8. 'Competent authority' means one governmental authority designated by a Party to be responsible, within such geographical areas as the Party may think fit, for receiving the notification of a transboundary movement of hazardous wastes and any information related to it, and for responding to such a notification, as provided in Article 6 of this Convention;

9. 'Focal point' means the entity of a Party referred to in Article 5 of this Convention responsible for receiving and submitting information as provided for in Articles 13 and 16;

10. 'Environmentally sound management of hazardous wastes' means taking all practicable steps to ensure that hazardous wastes are managed in a manner which will protect human health and the environment against the adverse effects which may result from such wastes;

11. 'Area under the national jurisdiction of a State' means any land, marine area or airspace within which a State exercises administrative and regulatory responsibility in accordance with international law in regard to the protection of human health or the environment;

12. 'State of export' means a Party from which a transboundary movement of hazardous wastes is planned to be initiated or is initiated;

13. 'State of import' means a State to which a transboundary movement is planned or takes place for the purpose of disposal therein or for the purpose of loading prior to disposal in an area not under the national jurisdiction of any State;

14. 'State of transit' means any State, other than the State of export or import, through which a movement of hazardous wastes is planned or takes place;

15. 'States concerned' means States of export or import, or transit states, whether or not Parties;

16. 'Person' means any natural or legal person;

17. 'Exporter' means any person under the jurisdiction of the State of export who arranges for hazardous wastes to be exported;

18. 'Importer' means any person under the jurisdiction of the State of import who arranges for hazardous wastes to be imported;
19. 'Carrier' means any person who carries out the transport of hazardous wastes;
20. 'Generator' means any person whose activity produces hazardous wastes, or, if that person is not known, the person who is in possession and/or control of those wastes;
21. 'Disposer' means any person to whom hazardous wastes are shipped and who carries out the disposal of such wastes;
22. 'Illegal traffic' means any transboundary movement of hazardous wastes as specified in Article 9 of this Convention;
23. 'Dumping at sea' means the deliberate disposal of hazardous wastes at sea from vessels, aircraft, platforms or other man-made structures at sea, and includes ocean incineration and disposal into the seabed and sub-seabed.

Article 2
Scope of the Convention

1. The following substances shall be 'hazardous wastes' for the purposes of this convention:

(a) Wastes that belong to any category contained in Annex I of this Convention;
(b) Wastes that are not covered under paragraph (a) above but are defined as, or are considered to be, hazardous wastes by the domestic legislation of the Party of export, import or transit;
(c) Wastes which possess any of the characteristics contained in Annex II of this Convention;
(d) Hazardous substances which have been banned, cancelled or refused registration by government regulatory action, or voluntarily withdrawn from registration in the country of manufacture, for human health or environmental reasons.

2. Wastes which, as a result of being radioactive, are subject to any international control systems, including international instruments, applying specifically to radioactive materials, are included in the scope of this Convention.

3. Wastes which derive from the normal operations of a ship, the discharge of which is covered by another international instrument, shall not fall within the scope of this convention.

Article 3
National definitions of hazardous wastes

1. Each State shall, within six months of becoming a Party to this Convention, inform the Secretariat of the Convention of the wastes, other than those listed in Annex I of this Convention, considered or defined as hazardous under its

national legislation and of any requirements concerning transboundary movement procedures applicable to such wastes.

2. Each Party shall subsequently inform the Secretariat of any significant changes to the information it has provided pursuant to Paragraph 1 of this Article.

3. The Secretariat shall forthwith inform all Parties of the information it has received pursuant to paragraphs 1 and 2 of this Article.

4. Parties shall be responsible for making the information transmitted to them by the Secretariat under Paragraph 3 of this Article available to their exporters and other appropriate bodies.

Article 4
General obligations

1. *Hazardous Waste Import Ban*

All Parties shall take appropriate legal, administrative and other measures within the area under their jurisdiction to prohibit the import of all hazardous wastes, for any reason, into Africa from non-Contracting Parties. Such import shall be deemed illegal and a criminal act. All Parties shall:

(a) Forward as soon as possible, all information relating to such illegal hazardous waste import activity to the Secretariat who shall distribute the information to all Contracting Parties;

(b) Co-operate to ensure that no imports of hazardous wastes from a non-Party enter a Party to this Convention. To this end, the Parties shall, at the Conference of the Contracting Parties to this Convention, consider other enforcement mechanisms.

2. *Ban on Dumping of Hazardous Wastes at Sea and Internal Waters*

(a) Parties in conformity with related international conventions and instruments shall, in the exercise of their jurisdiction within their internal waters, waterways, territorial seas, exclusive economic zones and continental shelf, adopt legal, administrative and other appropriate measures to control all carriers from non-Parties, and prohibit the dumping at sea of hazardous wastes, including their incineration at sea and their disposal in the seabed and sub-seabed;

Any dumping of hazardous wastes at sea, including incineration at sea as well as seabed and sub-seabed disposal, by Contracting Parties, whether in internal waters, waterways, territorial seas, exclusive economic zones or high seas shall be deemed to be illegal;

(b) Parties shall forward, as soon as possible, all information relating to dumping of hazardous wastes to the Secretariat which shall distribute the information to all Contracting Parties.

3. *Waste Generation in Africa*

Each Party shall:

(a) Ensure that hazardous waste generators submit to the Secretariat reports regarding the wastes that they generate in order to enable the Secretariat of the Convention to produce a complete hazardous waste audit;

(b) Impose strict, unlimited liability as well as joint and several liability on hazardous waste generators;

(c) Ensure that the generation of hazardous wastes within the area under its jurisdiction is reduced to a minimum taking into account social, technological and economic aspects;

(d) Ensure the availability of adequate treatment and disposal facilities, for the environmentally sound management of hazardous wastes which shall be located, to the extent possible, within its jurisdiction;

(e) Ensure that persons involved in the management of hazardous wastes within its jurisdiction take such steps as are necessary to prevent pollution arising from such wastes and, if such pollution occurs, to minimize the consequence thereof for human health and the environment;

The adoption of precautionary measures:

(f) Each Party shall strive to adopt and implement the preventive, precautionary approach to pollution problems which entails, *inter alia*, preventing the release into the environment of substances which may cause harm to humans or the environment without waiting for scientific proof regarding such harm. The Parties shall co-operate with each other in taking the appropriate measures to implement the precautionary principle to pollution prevention through the application of clean production methods, rather than the pursuit of a permissible emissions approach based on assimilative capacity assumptions;

(g) In this respect Parties shall promote clean production methods applicable to entire product life cycles including:
   - raw material selection, extraction and processing;
   - product conceptualisation, design, manufacture and assemblage;
   - materials transport during all phases;
   - industrial and household usage;
   - reintroduction of the product into industrial systems or nature when it no longer serves a useful function;

   Clean production shall not include 'end-of-pipe' pollution controls such as filters and scrubbers, or chemical, physical or biological treatment. Measures which reduce the volume of waste by incineration or concentration, mask the hazard by dilution, or transfer pollutants from one environmental medium to another, are also excluded;

(h) The issue of preventing the transfer to Africa of polluting technologies shall be kept under systematic review by the Secretariat of the Conference and periodic reports shall be made to the Conference of the Parties;

Obligations in the transport and transboundary movement of hazardous wastes from Contracting Parties:

(i) Each Party shall prevent the export of hazardous wastes to States which have prohibited by their legislation or international agreement all such imports, or if it has reason to believe that the wastes in question will not be managed in an environmentally sound manner, according to criteria to be decided on by the Parties at their first meeting;

(j) A Party shall not permit hazardous wastes to be exported to a State which does not have the facilities for treating or disposing of them in an environmentally sound manner;

(k) Each Party shall ensure that hazardous wastes to be exported are managed in an environmentally sound manner in the State of import and transit. Technical guidelines for the environmentally sound management of wastes subject to this Convention shall be decided by the Parties at their first meeting;

(l) The Parties agree not to allow the export of hazardous wastes for disposal within the area South of 60 degrees South Latitude, whether or not such wastes are subject to transboundary movement;

(m) Furthermore, each Party shall:

(i) Prohibit all persons under its national jurisdiction from transporting, storing or disposing of hazardous wastes unless such persons are authorized or allowed to perform such operations;

(ii) Ensure that hazardous wastes that are to be the subject of a transboundary movement are packaged, labelled, and transported in conformity with generally accepted and recognized international rules and standards in the field of packaging, labelling, and transport, and that due account is taken of relevant internationally recognized practices;

(iii) Ensure that hazardous wastes be accompanied by a movement document, containing information specified in Annex IV B, from the point at which a transboundary movement commences to the point of disposal;

(n) Parties shall take the appropriate measures to ensure that the transboundary movements of hazardous wastes only are allowed if:

(i) The State of export does not have the technical capacity and the necessary facilities, capacity or suitable disposal sites in order to dispose of the wastes in question in an environmentally sound and efficient manner; or

(ii) The transboundary movement in question is in accordance with other criteria to be decided by the Parties, provided those criteria do not differ from the objectives of this Convention;

(o) Under this Convention, the obligation of States in which hazardous wastes are generated, requiring that those wastes are managed in an environmentally sound manner, may not under any circumstances be transferred to the States of import or transit;

(p) Parties shall undertake to review periodically the possibilities for the reduction of the amount and/or the pollution potential of hazardous wastes which are exported to other States;

(q) Parties exercising their right to prohibit the import of hazardous wastes for disposal shall inform the other Parties of their decision pursuant to Article 13 of this Convention;

(r) Parties shall prohibit or shall not permit the export of hazardous wastes to States which have prohibited the import of such wastes, when notified by the secretariat or any competent authority pursuant to sub-paragraph (q) above;

(s) Parties shall prohibit or shall not permit the export of hazardous wastes if the State of import does not consent in writing to the specific import, in the case where that State of import has not prohibited the import of such wastes;

(t) Parties shall ensure that the transboundary movement of hazardous wastes is reduced to the minimum consistent with the environmentally sound and efficient management of such wastes, and is conducted in a manner which will protect human health and the environment against the adverse effects which may result from such movement;

(u) Parties shall require that information about a proposed transboundary movement of hazardous wastes be provided to the States concerned, according to Annex IV A of this Convention, and clearly state the potential dangers of the wastes on human health and the environment.

4. *Furthermore*

(a) Parties shall undertake to enforce the obligations of this Convention against offenders and infringements according to relevant national laws and/or international law;

(b) Nothing in this Convention shall prevent a Party from imposing additional requirements that are consistent with the provisions of this Convention, and are in accordance with the rules of international law, in order to better protect human health and the environment;

(c) This Convention recognizes the sovereignty of States over their territorial sea, waterways, and air space established in accordance with international law, and jurisdiction which States have in their exclusive economic zone and their continental shelves in accordance with international law, and the exercise by ships and aircraft of all States of navigation rights and freedoms as provided for in international law and as reflected in relevant international instruments.

Article 5
Designation of competent authorities, focal point and Dumpwatch

To facilitate the implementation of this Convention, the Parties shall:

1. Designate or establish one or more competent authorities and one focal point. One competent authority shall be designated to receive the notification in case of a State of transit.
2. Inform the Secretariat, within three months of the date of the entry into force of this Convention for them, which agencies they have designated as their focal point and their competent authorities.
3. Inform the Secretariat, within one month of the date of decision, of any changes regarding the designations made by them under paragraph 2 above.
4. Appoint a national body to act as a Dumpwatch. In such capacity as a Dumpwatch, the designated national body only will be required to co-ordinate with the concerned governmental and non-governmental bodies.

Article 6
Transboundary movement and notification procedures

1. The State of export shall notify, or shall require the generator or exporter to notify, in writing, through the channel of the competent authority of the State of export, the competent authority of the States concerned of any proposed transboundary movement of hazardous wastes. Such notification shall contain the declarations and information specified in Annex IV A of this Convention, written in a language acceptable to the State of import. Only one notification needs to be sent to each State concerned.

2. The Party of import shall respond to the notifier in writing consenting to the movement with or without conditions, denying permission for the movement, or requesting additional information. A copy of the final response of the State of import shall be sent to the competent authorities of the States concerned.

3. The State of export shall not allow the transboundary movement until it has received:

(a) written consent of the State of import; and
(b) from the State of import, written confirmation of the existence of a contract between the exporter and the disposer specifying environmentally sound management of the wastes in question.

4. Each State of transit which is a Party shall promptly acknowledge to the notifier receipt of the notification. It may subsequently respond to the

notifier in writing, within 60 days, consenting to the movement with or without conditions, denying permission for the movement, or requesting additional information. The State of export shall not allow the transboundary movement to commence until it has received the written consent of the State of transit.

5. In the case of a transboundary movement of hazardous wastes where the wastes are legally defined as or considered to be hazardous wastes only:

(a) By the State of export, the requirements of paragraph 8 of this Article that apply to the importer or disposer and the State of import shall apply *mutatis mutandis* to the exporter and State of export, respectively;
(b) By the Party of import, or by the States of import and transit which are Parties, the requirements of paragraphs 1, 3, 4 and 6 of this Article that apply to the exporter and State of export shall apply *mutatis mutandis* to the importer or disposer and Party of import, respectively; or
(c) By any State of transit which is a Party to this Convention, the provisions of paragraph 4 of this Article shall apply to such State.

6. The State of export shall use a shipment specific notification even where hazardous wastes having the same physical and chemical characteristics are shipped regularly to the same disposer via the same customs office of entry of the State of import, and in the case of transit, via the same customs office of entry and exit of the State or States of transit; specific notification of each and every shipment shall be required and contain the information in Annex IV A of this Convention.

7. Each Party to this Convention shall limit their points or ports of entry and notify the Secretariat to this effect for distribution to all Contracting Parties. Such points and ports shall be the only ones permitted for the transboundary movement of hazardous wastes.

8. The Parties to this Convention shall require that each person who takes charge of a transboundary movement of hazardous wastes sign the movement document either upon delivery or receipt of the wastes in question. They shall also require that the disposer inform both the exporter and the competent authority of the State of export of receipt by the disposer of the wastes in question and, in due course, of the completion of disposal as specified in the notification. If no such information is received within the State of export, the competent authority of the State of export or the exporter shall so notify the State of import.

9. The notification and response required by this Article shall be transmitted to the competent authority of the States concerned or to such governmental authority as may be appropriate in the case of non-Parties.

10. Any transboundary movement of hazardous wastes shall be covered by insurance, bond or other guarantee as may be required by the State of import or any State of transit.

Article 7
Transboundary movement from a Party through States which are not Parties

Paragraph 2 and 4 of Article 6 of this Convention shall apply *mutatis mutandis* to transboundary movements of hazardous wastes from a Party through a State or States which are not Parties.

Article 8
Duty to re-import

When a transboundary movement of hazardous wastes to which the consent of the States concerned has been given, subject to the provisions of this Convention, cannot be completed in accordance with the terms of the contract, the State of export shall ensure that the wastes in question are taken back into the State of export, by the exporter, if alternative arrangements cannot be made for their disposal in an environmentally sound manner within a maximum of 90 days from the time that the importing State informed the State of export and the Secretariat. To this end, the State of export and any Party of transit shall not oppose, hinder or prevent the return of those wastes to the State of export.

Article 9
Illegal traffic

1. For the purpose of this Convention, any transboundary movement of hazardous wastes under the following situations shall be deemed to be illegal traffic:

(a) if carried out without notification, pursuant to the provisions of this Convention, to all States concerned; or
(b) if carried out without the consent, pursuant to the provisions of this Convention, of a State concerned; or
(c) if consent is obtained from States concerned through falsification, misrepresentation or fraud; or
(d) if it does not conform in a material way with the documents; or
(e) if it results in deliberate disposal of hazardous wastes in contravention of this Convention and of general principles of international law.

2. Each Party shall introduce appropriate national legislation for imposing criminal penalties on all persons who have planned, committed, or assisted in such illegal imports. Such penalties shall be sufficiently high to both punish and deter such conduct.

3. In case of a transboundary movement of hazardous wastes deemed to be illegal traffic as the result of conduct on the part of the exporter or generator, the State of export shall ensure that the wastes in question are taken back by the

exporter or generator or if necessary by itself into the State of export, within 30 days from the time the State of export has been informed about the illegal traffic. To this end the Parties concerned shall not oppose, hinder or prevent the return of those wastes to the State of export and appropriate legal action shall be taken against the contravenor(s).

4. In the case of a transboundary movement of hazardous wastes deemed to be illegal traffic as the result of conduct on the part of the importer or disposer, the Party of import shall ensure that the wastes in question are returned to the exporter by the importer and that legal proceedings according to the provisions of this Convention are taken against the contravenor(s).

Article 10
Intra-African co-operation

1. The Parties to this Convention shall co-operate with one another and with relevant African organisations, to improve and achieve the environmentally sound management of hazardous wastes.

2. To this end, the Parties shall:

(a) Make available information, whether on a bilateral or multilateral basis, with a view to promoting clean production methods and the environmentally sound management of hazardous wastes, including harmonisation of technical standards and practices for the adequate management of hazardous wastes;

(b) Co-operate in monitoring the effects of the management of hazardous wastes on human health and the environment;

(c) Co-operate, subject to their national laws, regulations and policies, in the development and implementation of new environmentally sound clean production technologies and the improvement of existing technologies with a view to eliminating, as far as practicable, the generation of hazardous wastes and achieving more effective and efficient methods of ensuring their management in an environmentally sound manner, including the study of the economic, social and environmental effects of the adoption of such new and improved technologies;

(d) Co-operate actively, subject to their national laws, regulations and policies, in the transfer of technology and management systems related to the environmentally sound management of hazardous wastes. They shall also co-operate in developing the technical capacity among Parties, especially those which may need and request technical assistance in this field;

(e) Co-operate in developing appropriate technical guidelines and/or codes of practice;

(f) Co-operate in the exchange and dissemination of information on the movement of hazardous wastes in conformity with Article 13 of this Convention.

Article 11
International co-operation, bilateral, multilateral and regional agreements

1. Parties to this Convention may enter into bilateral, multilateral, or regional agreements or arrangements regarding the transboundary movement and management of hazardous wastes generated in Africa with Parties or non-Parties provided that such agreements or arrangements do not derogate from the environmentally sound management of hazardous wastes as required by this Convention. These agreements or arrangements shall stipulate provisions which are no less environmentally sound than those provided for by this Convention.

2. Parties shall notify the Secretariat of any bilateral, multilateral or regional agreements or arrangements referred to in paragraph 1 of this Article and those which they have entered into prior to the entry into force of this Convention for them, for the purpose of controlling transboundary movements of hazardous wastes which take place entirely among the Parties to such agreements. The provisions of this Convention shall not affect transboundary movements of hazardous wastes generated in Africa which take place pursuant to such agreements provided that such agreements are compatible with the environmentally sound management of hazardous wastes as required by this Convention.

3. Each Contracting Party shall prohibit vessels flying its flag or aircraft registered in its territory from carrying out activities in contravention of this Convention.

4. Parties shall use appropriate measures to promote South-South co-operation in the implementation of this Convention.

5. Taking into account the needs of developing countries, co-operation between international organisations is encouraged in order to promote, among other things, public awareness, the development of rational management of hazardous waste, and the adoption of new and non/less polluting technologies.

Article 12
Liabilities and compensation

The Conference of Parties shall set up an *Ad Hoc* expert organ to prepare a draft Protocol setting out appropriate rules and procedures in the field of liabilities and compensation for damage resulting from the transboundary movement of hazardous wastes.

Article 13
Transmission of information

1. The Parties shall ensure that in the case of an accident occurring during the transboundary movement of hazardous wastes or their disposal which is

likely to present risks to human health and the environment in other States, those States are immediately informed.

2. The States shall inform each other, through the Secretariat, of:

(a) Changes regarding the designation of competent authorities and/or focal points, pursuant to Article 5 of this Convention;
(b) Changes in their national definition of hazardous wastes, pursuant to Article 3 of this Convention;
(c) Decisions made by them to limit or ban the import of hazardous wastes;
(d) Any other information required pursuant to paragraph 4 of this Article.

3. The Parties, consistent with national laws and regulations, shall set up information collection and dissemination mechanisms on hazardous wastes. They shall transmit such information through the Secretariat, to the Conference of the Parties established under Article 15 of this Convention, before the end of each calendar year, in a report on the previous calendar year, containing the following information:

(a) Competent authorities, Dumpwatch, and focal points that have been designated by them pursuant to Article 5 of this Convention;
(b) Information regarding transboundary movements of hazardous wastes in which they have been involved, including:
  (i) The quantity of hazardous wastes exported, their category, characteristics, destination, any transit country and disposal method as stated on the notification;
  (ii) The amount of hazardous wastes imported, their category, characteristics, origin, and disposal methods;
  (iii) Disposals which did not proceed as intended;
  (iv) Efforts to achieve a reduction of the amount of hazardous wastes subject to transboundary movement;
(c) Information on the measures adopted by them in the implementation of this Convention;
(d) Information on available qualified statistics – which have been compiled by them on the effects on human health and the environment of the generation, transportation, and disposal of hazardous wastes – as part of the information required in conformity with Article 4 Section 3 (a) of this Convention;
(e) Information concerning bilateral, multilateral and regional agreements and arrangements entered into pursuant to Article 11 of this Convention;
(f) Information on accidents occurring during the transboundary movements, treatment and disposal of hazardous wastes and on the measures undertaken to deal with them;
(g) Information on treatment and disposal options operated within the area under their national jurisdiction;

(h) Information on measures undertaken for the development of clean production methods, including clean production technologies, for the reduction and/or elimination of the production of hazardous wastes; and

(i) Such other matters as the Conference of the Parties shall deem relevant.

4. The Parties, consistent with national laws and regulations, shall ensure that copies of each notification concerning any given transboundary movement of hazardous wastes, and the response to it, are sent to the Secretariat.

Article 14
Financial aspects

1. The regular budget of the Conference of Parties, as required in Articles 15 and 16 of this Convention, shall be prepared by the Secretariat and approved by the Conference.

2. Parties shall, at the first meeting of the Conference of the Parties, agree on a scale of contributions to the recurrent budget of the Secretariat.

3. The Parties shall also consider the establishment of a revolving fund to assist on an interim basis in case of emergency situations to minimize damage from disasters or accidents arising from transboundary movements of hazardous wastes or during the disposal of such wastes.

4. The Parties agree that, according to the specific needs of different regions and sub-regions, regional or sub-regional centres for training and technology transfers regarding the management of hazardous wastes and the minimisation of their generation should be established, as well as appropriate funding mechanisms of a voluntary nature.

Article 15
Conference of the Parties

1. A Conference of the Parties is hereby established. The first meeting of the Conference of the Parties shall be convened by the Secretary-General of the OAU not later than one year after the entry into force of this Convention. Thereafter, ordinary meetings of the Conference of the Parties shall be held at regular intervals to be determined by the Conference at its first meeting.

2. The Conference of the Parties shall adopt Rules of Procedure for itself and for any subsidiary body it may establish, as well as financial rules to determine in particular the financial participation of the Parties to this Convention.

3. The Parties at their first meeting shall consider any additional measures needed to assist them in fulfilling their responsibilities with respect to the protection and the preservation of the marine and inland waters environments in the context of this Convention.

4. The Conference of the Parties shall keep under continuous review and evaluation the effective implementation of this Convention, and in addition, shall:

(a) promote the harmonisation of appropriate policies, strategies and measures for minimizing harm to human health and the environment by hazardous wastes;

(b) consider and adopt, as required, amendments to this Convention and its annexes, taking into consideration, *inter alia*, available scientific, technical, economic and environmental information;

(c) consider and undertake any additional action that may be required for the achievement of the purpose of this Convention in the light of experience gained in its operation and in the operation of the agreements and arrangements envisaged in Article 11 of this Convention;

(d) consider and adopt protocols as required;

(e) establish such subsidiary bodies as are deemed necessary for the implementation of this Convention; and

(f) make decisions for the peaceful settlement of disputes arising from the transboundary movement of hazardous wastes, if need be, according to international law.

5. Organisations may be represented as observers at meetings of the Conference of the Parties. Any body or agency, whether national or international, governmental or non-governmental, qualified in fields relating to hazardous wastes which has informed the Secretariat, may be represented as an observer at a meeting of the Conference of the Parties. The admission and participation of observers shall be subject to the rules of procedure adopted by the Conference of the Parties.

Article 16
Secretariat

1. The functions of the Secretariat shall be:

(a) To arrange for, and service, meetings provided for in Article 15 and 17 of this Convention;

(b) To prepare and transmit reports based upon information received in accordance with Articles 3, 4, 6, 11, and 13 of this Convention as well as upon information derived from meetings of subsidiary bodies established under Article 15 of this Convention as well as upon, as appropriate, information provided by relevant inter-governmental and non-governmental entities;

(c) To prepare reports on its activities carried out in the implementation of its functions under this Convention and present them to the Conference of the Parties;

(d) To ensure the necessary co-ordination with relevant international bodies, and in particular to enter into such administrative and contractual arrangements as may be required for the effective discharge of its functions;

(e) To communicate with focal points, competent authorities and Dumpwatch established by the Parties in accordance with Article 5 of this Convention as well as appropriate inter-governmental and non-governmental organisations which may provide assistance in the implementation of this Convention;

(f) To compile information concerning approved national sites and facilities of Parties available for the disposal of their hazardous wastes and to circulate this information;

(g) To receive and convey information from and to Parties on:
   • sources of technical assistance and training;
   • available technical and scientific know-how;
   • sources of advice and expertise; and
   • availability of resources;

   With a view to assisting them in such areas as:
   • the handling of the notification system of this Convention;
   • the management of hazardous wastes;
   • environmentally sound clean production methods relating to hazardous wastes, such as clean production technologies;
   • the assessment of disposal capabilities and sites;
   • the monitoring of hazardous wastes; and
   • emergency responses;

(h) To provide Parties to this Convention with information on consultants or consulting firms having the necessary technical competence in the field, which can assist them with examining a notification for a transboundary movement, the concurrence of a shipment of hazardous wastes with the relevant notification, and/or whether the proposed disposal facilities for hazardous wastes are environmentally sound, when they have reason to believe that the wastes in question will not be managed in an environmentally sound manner. Any such examinations would not be at the expense of the Secretariat;

(i) To assist Parties to this Convention in their identification of cases of illegal traffic and to circulate immediately to the Parties concerned any information it has received regarding illegal traffic;

(j) To co-operate with Parties to this Convention and with relevant and competent international organisations and agencies in the provision of experts and equipment for the purpose of rapid assistance to States in the event of an emergency situation; and

(k) To perform such other functions relevant to the purposes of this Convention as may be determined by the Conference of the Parties.

2. The Secretariat's functions will be carried out on an interim basis by the OAU jointly with the United Nations Economic Commission for Africa (ECA) until the completion of the first meeting of the Conference of the Parties held pursuant to Article 15 of this Convention. At this meeting, the Conference of the Parties shall also evaluate the implementation by the interim Secretariat of

the functions assigned to it, in particular under paragraph 1 above, and decide upon the structures appropriate for those functions.

Article 17
Amendment of the Convention and of Protocols

1. Any Party may propose amendments to this Convention and any Party to a Protocol may propose amendments to that Protocol. Such amendments shall take due account, *inter alia,* of relevant scientific, technical, environmental and social considerations.

2. Amendments to this Convention shall be adopted at a meeting of the Conference of the Parties. Amendments to any Protocol shall be adopted at a meeting of the Parties to the Protocol in question. The text of any proposed amendment to this Convention or to any Protocol, except as may otherwise be provided in such Protocol, shall be communicated to the Parties by the Secretariat at least six months before the meeting at which it is proposed for adoption. The Secretariat shall also communicate proposed amendments to the Signatories to this Convention for their information.

3. The Parties shall make every effort to reach agreement on any proposed amendment to this Convention by consensus. If all efforts at consensus have been exhausted, and no agreement reached, the amendment shall, as a last resort, be adopted by a two-thirds majority vote of the Parties present and voting at the meeting, and shall be submitted by the Depositary to all Parties for ratification, approval, formal confirmation or acceptance.

Amendment of Protocols to this Convention

4. The procedure specified in paragraph 3 above shall apply to amendments to any protocol, except that a two-thirds majority of the Parties to that Protocol present and voting at the meeting shall suffice for their adoption.

General Provisions

5. Instruments of ratification, approval, formal confirmation or acceptance of amendments shall be deposited with the Depositary. Amendments adopted in accordance with paragraph 3 or 4 above shall enter into force between Parties having accepted them, on the ninetieth day after the receipt by the Depositary of the instrument of ratification, approval, formal confirmation or acceptance by at least two-thirds of the Parties who accepted the amendments to the Protocol concerned, except as may otherwise be provided in such Protocol. The amendments shall enter into force for any other Party on the ninetieth day after that Party deposits its instrument of ratification, approval, formal confirmation or acceptance of the amendments.

6. For the purpose of this Article, 'Parties present and voting' means Parties present and casting an affirmative or negative vote.

Article 18
Adoption and amendment of Annexes

1. The annexes to this Convention or to any Protocol shall form an integral part of this Convention or of such Protocol, as the case may be and, unless expressly provided otherwise, a reference to this Convention or its Protocols constitutes at the same time a reference to any annexes thereto. Such annexes shall be restricted to scientific, technical and administrative matters.

2. Except as may be otherwise provided in any Protocol with respect to its annexes, the following procedures shall apply to the proposal, adoption and entry into force of additional annexes to this Convention or of annexes to a protocol:

(a) Annexes to this Convention and its Protocols shall be proposed and adopted according to the procedure laid down in Article 17, paragraphs 1, 2, 3, and 4 of this Convention;

(b) Any Party that is unable to accept an additional annex to this Convention or an annex to any Protocol to which it is Party shall so notify the Depositary, in writing, within six months from the date of the communication of the adoption by the Depositary. The Depositary shall without delay notify all Parties of any such notification received. A Party may at any time substitute an acceptance for a previous declaration of objection and the annexes shall thereupon enter into force for that Party;

(c) Upon the expiration of six months from the date of the circulation of the communication by the Depositary, the annex shall become effective for all Parties to this Convention or to any Protocol concerned, which have not submitted a notification in accordance with the provision of sub-paragraph (b) above.

3. The proposal, adoption and entry into force of amendments to annexes to this Convention or to any Protocol shall be subject to the same procedure as for the proposal, adoption and entry into force of annexes to the Convention or annexes to a Protocol. Annexes and amendments thereto shall take due account, *inter alia*, of relevant scientific and technical considerations.

4. If an additional annex or an amendment to an annex involves an amendment to this Convention or to any Protocol, the additional annex or amended annex shall not enter into force until such time as the amendment to this Convention or to the Protocol enters into force.

Article 19
Verification

Any Party which has reason to believe that another Party is acting or has acted in breach of its obligations under this Convention must inform the Secretariat thereof, and in such an event, shall simultaneously and immediately inform, directly or through the Secretariat, the Party against whom the allegations are made. The Secretariat shall carry out a verification of the substance of the allegation and submit a report thereof to all the Parties to this Convention.

Article 20
Settlement of disputes

1. In case of dispute between Parties as to the interpretation or application of, or compliance with, this Convention or any Protocol thereto, the Parties shall seek a settlement of the dispute through negotiations or any other peaceful means of their own choice.

2. If the Parties concerned cannot settle their dispute as provided in paragraph 1 of this Article, the dispute shall be submitted either to an *Ad Hoc* organ set up by the Conference for this purpose, or to the International Court of Justice.

3. The conduct of arbitration of disputes between Parties by the *Ad Hoc* organ provided for in paragraph 2 of this Article shall be as provided in Annex V of this Convention.

Article 21
Signature

This Convention shall be open for signature by Member States of the OAU for a period of six months from 30 January 1991 to 30 July 1991.

Article 22
Ratification, acceptance, formal confirmation or approval

1. This Convention shall be subject to ratification, acceptance, formal confirmation, or approval by Member States of the OAU. Instruments of ratification, acceptance, formal confirmation, or approval shall be deposited with the Depository.

2. Parties shall be bound by all obligations of this Convention.

Article 23
Accession

This Convention shall be open for accession by Member States of the OAU from the day after the date on which the Convention is closed for signature. The instruments of accession shall be deposited with the Depositary.

Article 24
Right to vote

Each Contracting Party to this Convention shall have one vote.

Article 25
Entry into force

1. This Convention shall enter into force on the ninetieth day after the date of deposit of the tenth instrument of ratification from Parties signatory to this Convention.

2. For each State which ratifies this Convention or accedes thereto after the date of the deposit of the tenth instrument of ratification, it shall enter into force on the ninetieth day after the date of deposit by such State of its instrument of accession or ratification.

Article 26
Reservations and declarations

1. No reservations or exception may be made to this Convention.

2. Paragraph 1 of this Article does not preclude a State when signing, ratifying, or acceding to this Convention, from making declarations or statements, however phrased or named, with a view, *inter alia*, to the harmonisation of its laws and regulations with the provisions of this Convention, provided that such declarations or statements do not purport to exclude or to modify the legal effects of the provisions of the Convention in their application to that State.

Article 27
Withdrawal

1. At any time after three years from the date on which this Convention has entered into force for a Party, that Party may withdraw from the Convention by giving written notification to the Depositary.

2. Withdrawal shall be effective one year after receipt of notification by the Depository, or on such later date as may be specified in the notification.

3. Withdrawal shall not exempt the withdrawing Party from fulfilling any obligations it might have incurred under this Convention.

Article 28
Depositary

The Secretary-General of the Organisation of African Unity shall be the Depositary for this Convention and of any Protocol thereto.

Article 29
Registration

This Convention, as soon as it enters into force, shall be registered with the Secretary-General of the United Nations (UN) in conformity with Article 102 of the Charter of the UN.

Article 30
Authentic texts

The Arabic, English, French and Portuguese texts of this Convention are equally authentic.

IN WITNESS WHEREOF the undersigned, being duly authorized to that effect, have signed this Convention.

Adopted in Bamako, Mali, on 29 January 1991.

Annex I
Categories of wastes which are hazardous wastes

Waste streams

Y0 All wastes containing or contaminated by radionuclides, the concentration or properties of which result from human activity

Y1 Clinical wastes from medical care in hospitals, medical centers and clinics

Y2 Wastes from the production and preparation of pharmaceutical products

Y3 Waste pharmaceuticals, drugs and medicines

Y4 Wastes from the production, formulation and use of biocides and phytopharmaceuticals

Y5 Wastes from the manufacture, formulation and use of wood preserving chemicals

Y6 Wastes from the production, formulation and use of organic solvents

Y7 Wastes from heat treatment and tempering operations containing cyanides

Y8 Waste mineral oils unfit for their originally intended use

Y9 Waste oils/water, hydrocarbons/water mixtures, emulsions

Y10 Waste substances and articles containing or contaminated with polychlorinated biphenyls (PCBs) and/or polychlorinated terphenyls (PCTs) and/or polybrominated biphenyls (PBBs)

Y11 Waste tarry residues arising from refining, distillation and anypyrolytic treatment

Y12 Wastes from production, formulation and use of inks, dyes, pigments, paints, lacquers, varnish

Y13 Wastes from production, formulation and use of resins, latex, plasticizers, glues/adhesives

Y14 Waste chemical substances arising from research and development or teaching activities which are not identified and/or are new and whose effects on man and/or the environment are not known

Y15 Wastes of an explosive nature not subject to other legislation

Y16 Wastes from production, formulation and use of photographic chemicals and processing materials

Y17 Wastes resulting from surface treatment of metals and plastics

Y18 residues arising from industrial waste disposal operations

Y46 Wastes collected from households, including sewage and sewage sludges

Y47 Residues arising from the incineration of household wastes

Wastes having as constituents

Y19 Metal carbonyls
Y20 Beryllium; beryllium compounds
Y21 Hexavalent chromium compounds
Y22 Copper compounds
Y23 Zinc compounds
Y24 Arsenic; arsenic compounds
Y25 Selenium; selenium compounds
Y26 Cadmium; cadmium compounds
Y27 Antimony; antimony compounds
Y28 Tellurium; tellurium compounds
Y29 Mercury; mercury compounds
Y30 Thallium; thallium compounds
Y31 Lead; lead compounds
Y32 Inorganic fluorine compounds excluding calcium fluoride
Y33 Inorganic cyanides
Y34 Acidic solutions or acids in solid form
Y35 Basic solutions or bases in solid form
Y36 Asbestos (dust and fibres)
Y37 Organic phosphorous compounds
Y38 Organic cyanides
Y39 Phenols; phenolcompounds including chlorophenols
Y40 Ethers
Y41 Halogenated organic solvents
Y42 Organic solvents excluding halogenated solvents
Y43 Any congener of polychlorinated dibenzo-furan
Y44 Any congener of polychlorinated dibenzo-p-dioxin
Y45 Organohalogen compounds other than substances referred to in this Annex (e.g., Y39, Y41, Y42, Y43, Y44).

Annex II
List of hazardous characteristics

UN Class*	Code	Characteristics
1	H1	Explosive An explosive substance or waste is a solid or liquid substance or waste (or mixture of substances or wastes) which is in itself capable by chemical reaction or producing gas at such a temperature and pressure and at such a speed as to cause damage to the surroundings.

(*cont.*)

UN Class*	Code	Characteristics
3	H3	Flammable liquids The word 'flammable' has the same meaning as 'inflammable'. Flammable liquids are liquids, or mixtures of liquids, or liquids containing solids in solution or suspension (for example paints, varnishes, lacquers, etc., but not including substances or wastes otherwise classified on account of their dangerous characteristics) which give off a flammable vapour at temperatures of not more than 60.5 degrees C, closed-cup test, or not more than 65.6 degrees C, open-cup test. (Since the results of open-cup tests and of closed-cup tests are not strictly comparable and even individual results by the same test are often variable, regulations varying from the above figures to make allowance for such difference would be within the spirit of this definition).
4.1	H4.1	Flammable solids Solids, or waste solids, other than those classed as explosives, which under conditions encountered in transport are readily combustible, or may cause or contribute to fire through friction.
4.2	H4.2	Substances or wastes liable to spontaneous combustion Substances or wastes which are liable to spontaneous heating under normal conditions encountered in transport, or to heating up on contact with air, and being then liable to catch fire.
4.3	H4.3	Substances or wastes which, in contact with water emit flammable gases Substances or wastes which, by interaction with water, are liable to become spontaneously flammable or to give off flammable gases in dangerous quantities.
5.1	H5.1	Oxidizing Substances or wastes which, while in themselves not necessarily combustible, may, generally by yielding oxygen, cause or contribute to the combustion of other materials.
5.2	H5.2	Organic peroxides Organic substances or wastes which contain the bivalent-O-O-structure are thermally unstable substances which may undergo exothermic self- accelerating decomposition.

(cont.)

UN Class*	Code	Characteristics
6.1	H6.1	Poisonous (Acute) Substances or wastes liable either to cause death or serious injury or to harm human health if swallowed or inhaled or by skin contact.
6.2	H6.2	Infectious substances Substances or wastes containing viable micro organisms or their toxins which are known or suspected to cause disease in animals or humans.
8	H8	Corrosives Substances or wastes which, by chemical action, will cause severe damage when in contact with living tissue, or in the case of leakage, will materially damage, or even destroy, other goods or the means of transport; they may also cause other hazards.
9	H10	Liberation of toxic gases in contact with air or water Substances or wastes which, by interaction with air or water, are liable to give off toxic gases in dangerous quantities.
9	H11	Toxic (Delayed or chronic) Substances or wastes which, if they are inhaled or ingested or if they penetrate the skin, may involve delayed or chronic effects, including carcinogenicity.
9	H12	Ecotoxic Substances or wastes which if released present or may present immediate or delayed adverse impacts to the environment by means of bioaccumulation and/or toxic effects upon biotic systems.
9	H13	Capable, by any means, after disposal, of yielding another material, e.g., leachate, which possesses any of the characteristics listed above.

*Corresponds to the hazardous classification system included in the United Nations Recommendations on the transport of Dangerous Goods (ST/SG/AC.10/1/Rev.5, United Nations, New York, 1988).

Annex III
Disposal operations

D1 Deposit into or onto land (e.g., landfill, etc.)

D2 Land treatment (e.g., biodegradation of liquid or sludgy discards in soils, etc.)

D3 Deep injection (e.g., injection of pumpable discards into wells, salt domes or naturally occurring repositories, etc.)

D4 Surface impoundment (e.g. placement of liquid or sludge discards into pits, ponds, or lagoons, etc.)

D5 Specially engineered landfill (e.g., placement into lined discrete cells which are capped and isolated from one another and the environment, etc.)

D6 Release into a water body except seas/oceans

D7 Release into seas/oceans including sea-bed insertion

D8 Biological treatment not specified elsewhere in this Annex which results in final compounds or mixtures which are discarded by means of any of the operations in Annex III

D9 Physico-chemical treatment not specified elsewhere in this Annex which results in final compounds or mixtures which are discarded by means of any of the operations in Annex III (e.g., evaporation, drying, calcination, neutralisation precipitation, etc.)

D10 Incineration on land

D11 Incineration at sea

D12 Permanent storage (e.g., emplacement of containers in a mine, etc.)

D13 Blending or mixing prior to submission to any of the operations in Annex III

D14 Repackaging prior to submission to any of the operations in Annex III

D15 Storage pending any of the operations in Annex III

D16 Use as a fuel (other than in direct incineration) or other means to generate energy

D17 Solvent reclamation/regeneration

D18 Recycling/reclamation of organic substances which are not used as solvents

D19 Recycling/reclamation of metals and metal compounds

D20 Recycling/reclamation of other inorganic materials

D21 Regeneration of acids and bases

D22 Recovery of components used for pollution abatement

D23 Recovery of components from catalysts

D24 Used oil re-refining or other reuses of previously used oil

D25 Land treatment resulting in benefit to agriculture or ecological improvement

D26 Uses of residual materials obtained from any of the operations numbered D1–D25

D27 Exchange of wastes for submission to any of the operations numbered D1–D26

D28 Accumulation of material intended for any operation in Annex III

Annex IV A
Information to be provided on notification

1. Reason for waste export
2. Exporter of the waste (1)
3. Generator(s) of the waste and site of generation (1)
4. Importer and Disposer of the waste and actual site of disposal (1)
5. Intended carrier(s) of the waste or their agents, if known (1)
6. Country of export of the waste
   Competent authority (2)
7. Countries of transit
   Competent authority (2)
8. Country of import of the waste
   Competent authority (2)
9. Projected date of shipment and period of time over which waste is to be exported and proposed itinerary (including point of entry and exit)
10. Means of transport envisaged (road, rail, sea, air, inland waters)
11. Information relating to insurance (3)
12. Designation and physical description of the waste including Y number and UN number and its composition (4) and information on any special handling requirements including emergency provisions in case of accidents.
13. Type of packaging envisaged (e.g., bulk, drummer, tanker)
14. Estimated quantity in weight/volume
15. Process by which the waste is generated (5)
16. Waste classifications from Annex II of this Convention: Hazardous characteristics, H number, and UN class
17. Method of disposal as per Annex III of this Convention
18. Declaration by the generator and exporter that the information is correct.
19. Information transmitted (including technical description of the plant) to the exporter or generator from the disposer of the waste upon which the latter has based his assessment that there was no reason to believe that the wastes will not be managed in an environmentally sound manner in accordance with the laws and regulations of the country of import
20. Information concerning the contract between the exporter and disposer

Notes

(1) Full name and address, telephone, telex or telefax number and the name, address, telephone, telex, or telefax number of the person to be contacted.
(2) Full name and address, telephone, telex or telefax number.

(3) Information to be provided on relevant insurance requirements and how they are met by exporter, carrier, and disposer.
(4) The nature and the concentration of the most hazardous components, in terms of toxicity and other dangers presented by the waste both in handling and in relation to the proposed disposal method.
(5) Insofar as this is necessary to assess the hazard and determine the appropriateness of the proposed disposal operation.

Annex IV B
Information to be provided on the movement document

1. Exporter of the waste (1)
2. Generator(s) of the waste and site of generation (1)
3. Disposer of the waste and actual site of disposal (1)
4. Carrier(s) of the waste (1) or his agent(s)
5. The date the transboundary movement started and date(s) and signature on receipt by each person who takes charge of the waste
6. Means of transport (road, rail, inland waterway, sea, air) including countries of export, transit and import, also point of entry and exit where these have been designated
7. General description of the waste (physical state, proper UN shipping name and class, UN number, Y number and H number as applicable)
8. Information on special handling requirements including emergency provisions in case of accidents
9. Type and number of packages
10. Quantity in weight/volume
11. Declaration by the generator or exporter that the information is correct
12. Declaration by the generator or exporter indicating no objection from the competent authorities of all States concerned
13. Certification by disposer of receipt at designated disposal facility and indication of method of disposal and of the appropriate date of disposal

Notes

The information required on the movement document shall where possible be integrated into one document with that required under transport rules. Where this is not possible, the information should complement rather than duplicate that required under the transport rules. The movement document shall carry instructions as to who is to provide information and fill-out any form.

1. Full name and address, telephone, telex or telefax number and the name, address, telephone, telex or telefax number of the person to be contacted in case of emergency.

Annex V
Arbitration

Article 1

Unless the agreement referred to in Article 20 of the Convention provides otherwise, the arbitration procedure shall be conducted in accordance with Articles 2 to 10 below.

Article 2

The claimant Party shall notify the Secretariat that the Parties have agreed to submit the dispute to arbitration pursuant to paragraph 1 or paragraph 2 of Article 20 of this Convention and include, in particular, the Articles of the Convention, and the interpretation or application of which are at issue. The Secretariat shall forward the information thus received to all Parties to the Convention.

Article 3

The arbitral tribunal shall consist of three members. Each of the Parties to the dispute shall appoint an arbitrator, and the two arbitrators so appointed shall designate by common agreement the third arbitrator, who shall be the chairman of the tribunal. The latter shall not be a national of one of the parties to the dispute, nor have his usual place of residence in one of the Parties, nor be employed by any of them, nor have dealt with the case in any other capacity.

Article 4

1. If the chairman of the arbitral tribunal has not been designated within two months of the appointment of the second arbitrator, the Secretary-General of the OAU shall, at the request of either Party, designate him within a further two months period.

2. If one of the Parties to the dispute does not appoint an arbitrator within two months of the receipt of the request, the other Party may inform the Secretary-General of the OAU who shall designate the chairman of the arbitral tribunal within a further two months period. Upon designation, the chairman of the arbitral tribunal shall request the Party which has not appointed an arbitrator to do so within two months. After such period, he shall inform the Secretary-General of the OAU who shall make this appointment within a further two month's period.

Article 5

1. The arbitral tribunal shall render its decision in accordance with international law and in accordance with the provisions of this Convention.

2. Any arbitral tribunal constituted under the provisions of this Annex shall draw up its own rules of procedure.

Article 6

1. The decisions of the arbitral tribunal both on procedure and on substance, shall be taken by majority vote of its members.

2. The tribunal may take all appropriate measures in order to establish the facts. It may, at the request of one of the Parties, recommend essential interim measures of protection.

3. The Parties to the dispute shall provide all facilities necessary for the effective conduct of the proceedings.

4. The absence or default of a Party in the dispute shall not constitute an impediment to the proceedings.

Article 7

The tribunal may hear and determine counter-claims arising directly out of the subject-matter of the dispute.

Article 8

Unless the arbitral tribunal determines otherwise because of the particular circumstances of the case, the expenses of the tribunal, including the remuneration of its members, shall be borne by the Parties to the dispute in equal shares. The tribunal shall keep a record of all its expenses, and shall furnish a final statement thereof to the Parties.

Article 9

Any Party that has an interest of a legal nature in the subject-matter of the dispute which may be affected by the decision in the case, may intervene in the proceedings with the consent of the tribunal.

Article 10

1. The tribunal shall render its award within five months of the date on which it is established unless it finds it necessary to extend the time-limit for a period which should not exceed five months.

2. The award of the arbitral tribunal shall be accompanied by a statement of reasons. It shall be final and binding upon the Parties to the dispute.

3. Any dispute which may arise between the Parties concerning the interpretation or execution of the award may be submitted by either Party to the arbitral tribunal which made the award or, if the latter cannot be seized thereof, to another tribunal constituted for this purpose in the same manner as the first.

Code of Practice on the International Transboundary Movement of Radioactive Waste, 21 September 1990

Editorial note

The IAEA Code of Practice on the International Transboundary Movement of Radioactive Waste arose in part out of public reaction to unauthorised transboundary movement of radioactive waste to developing countries and concerns over how such wastes were managed and disposed of. The basic principles of the Code are that each State should minimise the amount of radioactive waste it produces (paragraph 2) and that any radioactive waste under its jurisdiction or control should be 'safely managed and disposed of' so as to protect human health and the environment (paragraph 1).

Against this background, the Code affirms the sovereign right of every State to prohibit the movement of radioactive waste on its territory (paragraph 3). If a State does choose to involve itself in the transboundary movement of such waste, it should ensure that this takes place according to 'international safety standard' (paragraph 4) and, subject to the relevant rules of international law, after the sending, receiving and transit States have all been notified of such movement and given their consent (paragraph 5). States should establish an authority to regulate the transboundary movement of radioactive waste (paragraph 6) and should not permit the receipt of such waste unless it can manage and dispose of it in accordance with 'international safety standards' (paragraph 7). A corresponding duty is placed on the sending State who should be satisfied, prior to shipment and on the basis of the receiving State's consent, that the receiving State can manage and dispose of the waste according to 'international safety standards' (paragraph 7). If the transfer is not completed in accordance with the Code, the sending State should either readmit the waste or arrange a safe alternative for it (paragraph 10). States should enact provisions of national law covering liability and compensation for damage caused by the transboundary movement of radioactive waste (paragraph 8) and non-compliance with the Code (paragraph 9).

Date of adoption: 21 September 1990

Website: www.iaea.org

IAEA Code of Practice on the International Transboundary Movement of Radioactive Waste

The Group of Experts,*

(i) Taking note that nuclear power generation and the utilization of radioisotopes involve the generation of radioactive waste,

(ii) Aware of the potential hazards for human health and the environment that could result from the improper management or disposal of radioactive waste,

(iii) Aware of public concern about any unauthorized international transboundary movement of radioactive waste, particularly to the territory of developing countries, and the danger of improper management and disposal of such waste,

(iv) Aware of the need to continue to promote high standards of radiation protection worldwide and to strengthen international co-operation, both multilateral and bilateral, in the field of nuclear safety and radioactive waste management,

(v) Emphasizing that such co-operation should take into account the needs of developing countries and may include the exchange of information, the transfer of technology and the provision of assistance,

(vi) Taking into account the IAEA's safety principles, which require, *inter alia*, that 'policies and criteria for radiation protection of populations outside national borders from releases of radioactive substances should not be less stringent than those for the population within the country of release',[1]

(vii) Taking into account the IAEA safety standards and guidelines relevant to the international transboundary movement of radioactive waste, including standards and guidelines for radiological protection, the safe transport of radioactive material, the safe management and disposal of radioactive waste, the safety of nuclear facilities, and the physical protection of nuclear materials,

(viii) Recalling the Convention on Early Notification of a Nuclear Accident and the Convention on Assistance in the Case of a Nuclear Accident or Radiological Emergency,

(ix) Mindful of the relevant principles and norms of international law,

---

* The Code of Practice was elaborated by a Group of Experts established pursuant to resolution GC(XXXII)/RES/490, 'Dumping of Nuclear Waste', adopted by the General Conference in 1988. The Code was adopted on 21 September 1990, by the General Conference, by resolution GC(XXXIV)/RES/530, and requested the Director General – *inter alia* – to take all necessary steps to ensure wide dissemination of the Code of Practice at both the national and the international level.

[1] Safety Principles and Technical Criteria for the Underground Disposal of High-level Radioactive Wastes, Safety Series 99, 1989.

(x) Taking into account the provisions of the Basel Convention on the Control of Transboundary Movements of Hazardous Wastes and their Disposal and other relevant international instruments, and

(xi) Recognizing the global role of the IAEA in the area of nuclear safety, radiation protection and radioactive waste management and disposal;

Decides that the following Code of Practice should serve as guidelines to States for, *inter alia*, the development and harmonization of policies and laws on the international transboundary movement of radioactive waste.

1. Scope

This Code applies to the international transboundary movement of radioactive waste.

It relies on international standards for the safe transport of radioactive material and the physical protection of nuclear material, as well as the standards for basic nuclear safety and radiation protection and radioactive waste management; it does not establish separate guidance in these areas. Furthermore, this Code, which is advisory, does not affect in any way existing and future arrangements among States which relate to matters covered by it and are compatible with its objectives.[2]

2. Definitions

For the purpose of this Code:

'*radioactive waste*' is any material that contains or is contaminated with radionuclides at concentrations or radioactivity levels greater than the 'exempt quantities'[3] established by the competent authorities and for which no use is foreseen.[4]

'*disposal*' means the emplacement of waste in a repository, or at a given location, without the intention of retrieval.

---

[2] Nothing in this Code prejudices or affects in any way the exercise by ships and aircraft of all States of maritime and air navigation rights and freedoms under customary international law, as reflected in the 1982 United Nations Convention on the Law of the Sea, and under other relevant international legal instruments.

[3] 'Exempt quantities', in relation to radioactive waste, are levels of radionuclide concentration, surface contamination, radiation and/or total activity below which the competent authority decides to exempt from regulatory requirements because the individual and collective effective dose equivalents received from them are so low that such levels are not significant for purposes of radiation protection. Such exempt quantities should be agreed by the competent authorities in the countries concerned with the international transboundary radioactive waste movement.

[4] Spent fuel which is not intended for disposal is not considered to be radioactive waste.

'*management*' means all activities, administrative and operational, that are involved in the handling, treatment, conditioning, transportation and storage of waste.

'*competent authority*' means an authority designated or otherwise recognized by a government for specific purposes in connection with radiation protection and/or nuclear safety.

3. Basic principles

General

1. Every State should take the appropriate steps necessary to ensure that radioactive waste within its territory, or under its jurisdiction or control is safely managed and disposed of, to ensure the protection of human health and the environment.

2. Every State should take the appropriate steps necessary to minimize the amount of radioactive waste, taking into account social, environmental, technological and economic considerations.

International transboundary movement

3. It is the sovereign right of every State to prohibit the movement of radioactive waste into from or through its territory.

4. Every State involved in the international transboundary movement of radioactive waste should take the appropriate steps necessary to ensure that such movement is undertaken in a manner consistent with international safety standards.

5. Every State should take the appropriate steps necessary to ensure that, subject to the relevant norms of international law, the international transboundary movement of radioactive waste takes place only with the prior notification and consent of the sending, receiving and transit States in accordance with their respective laws and regulations.

6. Every State involved in the international transboundary movement of radioactive waste should have a relevant regulatory authority and adopt appropriate procedures as necessary for the regulation of such movement.

7. No receiving State should permit the receipt of radioactive waste for management or disposal unless it has the administrative and technical capacity and regulatory structure to manage and dispose of such waste in a manner consistent with international safety standards. The sending State should satisfy itself in accordance with the receiving State's consent that the above requirement is met prior to the international transboundary movement of radioactive waste.

8. Every State should take the appropriate steps to introduce into its national laws and regulations relevant provisions as necessary for liability,

compensation or other remedies for damage that could arise from the international transboundary movement of radioactive waste.

9. Every State should take the appropriate steps necessary, including the adoption of laws and regulations, to ensure that the international transboundary movement of radioactive waste is carried out in accordance with this Code.

International co-operation

10. The sending State should take the appropriate steps necessary to permit readmission into its territory of any radioactive waste previously transferred from its territory if such transfer is not or cannot be completed in conformity with this Code, unless an alternative safe arrangement can be made.[5]

11. States should co-operate at the bilateral, regional and international levels for the purpose of preventing any international transboundary movement of radioactive waste that is not in conformity with this Code.

4. Role of the IAEA

The IAEA should continue to collect and disseminate information on the laws, regulations and technical standards pertaining to radioactive waste management and disposal, develop relevant technical standards and provide advice and assistance on all aspects of radioactive waste management and disposal, having particular regard to the needs of developing countries.

The IAEA should review this Code as appropriate, taking into account experience gained and technological developments.

---

[5] The above would not apply to waste which is associated with, or results from, a service provided by the sending State to the receiving State and which is subject to a contractual arrangement between them that such waste be returned to the receiving State.

PART VII

Human rights and the environment

Introduction

Editorial note

As it has developed, international environmental law raises many issues familiar to international human rights lawyers. In the environmental context, questions related to the existence and application of minimum international standards and the proper role of individuals and other non-governmental organisations in the international legal process have raised analogous issues to those arising in international human rights law. The development of international human rights law predates international environmental law and provides a rich source of experience. Since the 1960s the two subjects have developed in parallel, intersecting with increasing frequency. The extent to which international environmental law should adopt an anthropocentric approach, based on the view that environmental protection is primarily justified as a means of protecting humans rather than as an end in itself, was an important issue at UNCED. The Rio Declaration supports an anthropocentric approach: the first Principle states that 'Human beings are at the centre of concerns for sustainable development. They are entitled to a healthy and productive life in harmony with nature.' Legal developments in other fora and contexts, however, reflect a greater environmental consciousness and suggest that the protection of the environment is increasingly an objective justified in its own terms, and not simply a means of protecting humans.

Only two regional human rights treaties expressly recognise environmental rights, the African Charter and the San Salvador Protocol to the 1969 ACHR. The relationship between environmental protection and economic and social rights is recognised in other treaties, for example in the 1989 Convention on the Rights of the Child, which requires education for '[t]he development of respect for the natural environment' (Article 29(e)).

An alternative approach has emerged, in the absence of rights being granted in relation to the environment, whereby victims bring claims on the basis that personal or property rights have been violated. A series of judgments by the European Court of Human Rights illustrates how such a claim might now be made, although it is apparent that each case must be taken on its own merits. The European Court of Human Rights has shown itself to be more open to environmental claims, particularly in cases involving Article 8 claims to the effect that a correct balance has not been struck between individual and community interests, with the leading decision being *Lopez-Ostra* v *Spain (judgment of 9 December 1994).*

Reproduced below are the texts of the relevant provisions of selected human right treaties exemplifying the two above-mentioned approaches.

European Convention on Human Rights and Fundamental Freedoms, 4 November 1950 (extract)

Article 8
Right to respect for private and family life

1. Everyone has the right to respect for his private and family life, his home and his correspondence.

2. There shall be no interference by a public authority with the exercise of this right except such as is in accordance with the law and is necessary in a democratic society in the interests of national security, public safety or the economic well-being of the country, for the prevention of disorder or crime, for the protection of health or morals, or for the protection of the rights and freedoms of others.

African Charter on Human and Peoples' Rights, 27 June 1981 (extract)

Article 24

All peoples shall have the right to a general satisfactory environment favorable to their development.

Additional Protocol to the American Convention on Human Rights in the Area of Economic, Social and Cultural Rights (the 'Protocol of San Salvador'), 17 November 1988 (extract)

Article 11

1. Everyone shall have the right to live in a healthy environment and to have access to basic public services.

2. The state parties shall promote the protection, preservation and improvement of the environment.

[...]

PART VIII

War and the environment

Convention on the Prohibition of Military or Any Other Hostile Use of Environmental Modification Techniques, 18 May 1977

Editorial note

The Convention on the Prohibition of Military or Any Other Hostile Use of Environmental Modification Techniques, adopted under the auspices of the Conference of the Committee of Disarmament, is designed to prevent the environment from being manipulated for military purposes. The fundamental obligation placed on Parties is to prevent the use of 'environmental modification techniques' for hostile purposes in a manner that causes 'widespread, long-lasting or severe effects' to another Party (Article I(1)). 'Environmental modification techniques' are defined as techniques which change, by 'deliberate manipulation of natural processes', the Earth's 'dynamics, composition or structure' (Article II). The Convention, however, permits the use of 'environmental modification techniques' for peaceful purposes, subject to other applicable rules of international law (Article III(1)).

The Convention creates two institutions. To assist in the co-operative implementation of the Convention, a Party may request that a Consultative Committee of Experts be convened for the purposes of gathering facts and making recommendations (Articles V(1) and V(2)). A Conference of the Parties is also established which reviews the operation and effectiveness of the Convention (Article VII(2)). In the event that a Party suspects another Party of breaching its obligations under the Convention, a complaint can be lodged with the Security Council of the United Nations, which shall investigate the matter (Articles V(3) and V(4)). If the Security Council finds that a violation of the Convention has harmed or is likely to harm a Party, other Parties are required to provide assistance to that Party should that Party so request (Article V(5)). Amendments enter into force for those accepting them following acceptance by a majority of Parties (Article VI(2)).

Date of signature: 18 May 1977

Entry into force: 5 October 1978

Depositary: Secretary-General of the United Nations

Contracting Parties: Afghanistan, Algeria, Antigua and Barbuda, Argentina, Australia, Austria, Bangladesh, Belgium, Benin, Brazil, Brunei Darussalam, Bulgaria, Canada, Cape Verde, Chile, Cuba, Cyprus, Czech Republic, Denmark, Dominica, Egypt, Finland, Germany, Ghana, Greece, Guatemala, Hungary, India, Ireland, Italy, Japan, Korea (Democratic People's Republic of), Korea (Republic of), Kuwait, Laos, Lebanon, Liberia, Luxembourg, Malawi, Mauritius, Mongolia, Netherlands, New Zealand, Niger, Norway, Pakistan, Papua New Guinea, Poland, Romania, Russian Federation, St. Kitts and Nevis, St. Lucia, St. Vincent and the Grenadines, São Tomé and Príncipe, Solomon Islands, Spain, Sri Lanka, Sweden, Switzerland, Tunisia, Ukraine, United Kingdom, United States of America, Uruguay, Vietnam, Yemen.

Convention on the Prohibition of Military or Any Other Hostile Use of Environmental Modification Techniques

The States Parties to this Convention,

Guided by the interest of consolidating peace, and wishing to contribute to the cause of halting the arms race, and of bringing about general and complete disarmament under strict and effective international control, and of saving mankind from the danger of using new means of warfare,

Determined to continue negotiations with a view to achieving effective progress towards further measures in the field of disarmament,

Recognizing that scientific and technical advances may open new possibilities with respect to modification of the environment,

Recalling the Declaration of the United Nations Conference on the Human Environment adopted at Stockholm on 16 June 1972,

Realizing that the use of environmental modification techniques for peaceful purposes could improve the interrelationship of man and nature and contribute to the preservation and improvement of the environment for the benefit of present and future generations,

Recognizing, however, that military or any other hostile use of such techniques could have effects extremely harmful to human welfare,

Desiring to prohibit effectively military or any other hostile use of environmental modification techniques in order to eliminate the dangers to mankind from such use, and affirming their willingness to work towards the achievement of this objective,

Desiring also to contribute to the strengthening of trust among nations and to the further improvement of the international situation in accordance with the purposes and principles of the Charter of the United Nations,

Have agreed as follows:

Article I

1. Each State Party to this Convention undertakes not to engage in military or any other hostile use of environmental modification techniques having widespread, long-lasting or severe effects as the means of destruction, damage or injury to any other State Party.

2. Each State Party to this Convention undertakes not to assist, encourage or induce any State, group of States or international organization to engage in activities contrary to the provisions of paragraph 1 of this article.

Article II

As used in Article I, the term 'environmental modification techniques' refers to any technique for changing – through the deliberate manipulation of natural processes – the dynamics, composition or structure of the Earth, including its biota, lithosphere, hydrosphere and atmosphere, or of outer space.

Article III

1. The provisions of this Convention shall not hinder the use of environmental modification techniques for peaceful purposes and shall be without prejudice to the generally recognized principles and applicable rules of international law concerning such use.

2. The States Parties to this Convention undertake to facilitate, and have the right to participate in, the fullest possible exchange of scientific and technological information on the use of environmental modification techniques for peaceful purposes. States Parties in a position to do so shall contribute, alone or together with other States or international organizations, to international economic and scientific co-operation in the preservation, improvement, and peaceful utilization of the environment, with due consideration for the needs of the developing areas of the world.

Article IV

Each State Party to this Convention undertakes to take any measures it considers necessary in accordance with its constitutional processes to prohibit and prevent any activity in violation of the provisions of the Convention anywhere under its jurisdiction or control.

Article V

1. The States Parties to this Convention undertake to consult one another and to cooperate in solving any problems which may arise in relation to the objectives of, or in the application of the provisions of, the Convention. Consultation and cooperation pursuant to this article may also be undertaken through appropriate international procedures within the framework of the United

Nations and in accordance with its Charter. These international procedures may include the services of appropriate international organizations, as well as of a Consultative Committee of Experts as provided for in paragraph 2 of this article.

2. For the purposes set forth in paragraph 1 of this article, the Depositary shall, within one month of the receipt of a request from any State Party to this Convention, convene a Consultative Committee of Experts. Any State Party may appoint an expert to the Committee whose functions and rules of procedure are set out in the annex, which constitutes an integral part of this Convention. The Committee shall transmit to the Depositary a summary of its findings of fact, incorporating all views and information presented to the Committee during its proceedings. The Depositary shall distribute the summary to all States Parties.

3. Any State Party to this Convention which has reason to believe that any other State Party is acting in breach of obligations deriving from the provisions of the Convention may lodge a complaint with the Security Council of the United Nations. Such a complaint should include all relevant information as well as all possible evidence supporting its validity.

4. Each State Party to this Convention undertakes to cooperate in carrying out any investigation which the Security Council may initiate, in accordance with the provisions of the Charter of the United Nations, on the basis of the complaint received by the Council. The Security Council shall inform the States Parties of the results of the investigation.

5. Each State Party to this Convention undertakes to provide or support assistance, in accordance with the provisions of the Charter of the United Nations, to any State Party which so requests, if the Security Council decides that such Party has been harmed or is likely to be harmed as a result of violation of the Convention.

Article VI

1. Any State Party to this Convention may propose amendments to the Convention. The text of any proposed amendment shall be submitted to the Depositary who shall promptly circulate it to all States Parties.

2. An amendment shall enter into force for all States Parties to this Convention which have accepted it, upon the deposit with the Depositary of instruments of acceptance by a majority of States Parties. Thereafter it shall enter into force for any remaining State Party on the date of deposit of its instrument of acceptance.

Article VII

This Convention shall be of unlimited duration.

Article VIII

1. Five years after the entry into force of this Convention, a conference of the States Parties to the Convention shall be convened by the Depositary at Geneva, Switzerland. The conference shall review the operation of the Convention with a view to ensuring that its purposes and provisions are being realized, and shall in particular examine the effectiveness of the provisions of paragraph 1 of Article I in eliminating the dangers of military or any other hostile use of environmental modification techniques.

2. At intervals of not less than five years thereafter, a majority of the States Parties to the Convention may obtain, by submitting a proposal to this effect to the Depositary, the convening of a conference with the same objectives.

3. If no conference has been convened pursuant to paragraph 2 of this article within ten years following the conclusion of a previous conference, the Depositary shall solicit the views of all States Parties to the Convention, concerning the convening of such a conference. If one third or ten of the States Parties, whichever number is less, respond affirmatively, the Depositary shall take immediate steps to convene the conference.

Article IX

1. This Convention shall be open to all States for signature. Any State which does not sign the Convention before its entry into force in accordance with paragraph 3 of this article may accede to it at any time.

2. This Convention shall be subject to ratification by signatory States. Instruments of ratification or accession shall be deposited with the Secretary-General of the United Nations.

3. This Convention shall enter into force upon the deposit of instruments of ratification by twenty Governments in accordance with paragraph 2 of this article.

4. For those States whose instruments of ratification or accession are deposited after the entry into force of this Convention, it shall enter into force on the date of the deposit of their instruments of ratification or accession.

5. The Depositary shall promptly inform all signatory and acceding States of the date of each signature, the date of deposit of each instrument of ratification or accession and the date of the entry into force of this Convention and of any amendments thereto, as well as of the receipt of other notices.

6. This Convention shall be registered by the Depositary in accordance with Article 102 of the Charter of the United Nations.

Article X

This Convention, of which the English, Arabic, Chinese, French, Russian, and Spanish texts are equally authentic, shall be deposited with the

Secretary-General of the United Nations, who shall send certified copies thereof to the Governments of the signatory and acceding States.

IN WITNESS WHEREOF, the undersigned, being duly authorized thereto by their respective governments, have signed this Convention, opened for signature at Geneva on the eighteenth day of May, one thousand nine hundred and seventy-seven.

[Annex omitted]

Protocol I Additional to the Geneva Convention of 12 August 1949, and Relating to the Protection of Victims of International Armed Conflicts, 8 June 1977 (extracts)

Editorial note

The Geneva Protocol I Additional to the Geneva Convention of 12 August 1949, Relating to the Protection of Victims of Armed Conflicts seeks to protect the environment by two techniques: (a) by setting standards and thresholds for permissible harm and (b) by establishing rules on targetry.

The Protocol expressly prohibits intentional harm to the environment and the utilisation of means and methods of warfare which 'may be expected' to cause such harm (Articles 35(3) and 55(1)). The threshold above which harm to the environment is proscribed is when it becomes 'widespread, long-term and severe' (Article 35(3)) and the population is threatened (Article 55(1)). All weapons, means and methods of warfare are required to be evaluated before use to determine their compliance with the Protocol and other international law (Article 36). Parties are required to take precautionary measures as attackers to minimise attacks on civilian objects (Article 57) and as defenders to protect civilian objects from the effects of military operations (Article 58).

In addition, the environment is protected by the prohibition on attacks on certain objects (Article 52). The Protocol prohibits attacks on objects deemed indispensable to civilian life, including foodstuffs, agricultural areas, crops, livestock and drinking water supplies (Article 54(2)). This immunity from attack is partially lifted if these objects provide sustenance or direct support of military forces (Article 54(3)) and derogations are permitted in defence of an invasion on a Party's own territory (Article 54(5)). The Protocol also protects dams, dykes and nuclear electrical generating stations from attack, subject to those objects not providing support for military operations (Article 56). The Protocol allows for the establishment of non-defended localities which may not be the object of attack (Article 59) and demilitarised zones to which military operations may not be extended unless otherwise agreed by the belligerents (Article 60).

Date of adoption:	8 June 1977
Entry into force:	7 December 1979
Depositary:	Swiss Government
Contracting Parties:	Albania, Algeria, Angola, Antigua and Barbuda, Argentina, Armenia, Australia, Austria, Bahamas, Bahrain, Bangladesh, Barbados, Belarus, Belgium, Belize, Benin, Bolivia, Bosnia and Herzegovina, Botswana, Brazil, Brunei Darussalam, Bulgaria, Burkina Faso, Burundi, Cambodia, Cameroon, Canada, Cape Verde, Central African Republic, Chad, Chile, China, Colombia, Comoros, Congo, Congo (Democratic Republic of), Cook Islands, Costa Rica, Cote d'Ivoire, Croatia, Cuba, Cyprus, Czech Republic, Denmark, Djibouti, Dominica, Dominican Republic, Ecuador, Egypt, El Salvador, Equatorial Guinea, Estonia, Ethiopia, Finland, France, Gabon, Gambia, Georgia, Germany, Ghana, Greece, Grenada, Guatemala, Guinea, Guinea Bissau, Guyana, Holy Sea, Honduras, Hungary, Iceland, Ireland, Italy, Jamaica, Jordan, Kazakhstan, Kenya, Korea (Democratic People's Republic of), Korea (Republic of), Kuwait, Kyrgyzstan, Lao People's Democratic Republic, Latvia, Lebanon, Lesotho, Liberia, Libyan Arab Jamahiriya, Liechtenstein, Lithuania, Luxembourg, Madagascar, Malawi, Maldives, Mali, Malta, Mauritania, Mauritius, Mexico, Micronesia (Federated States of), Moldova (Republic of), Monaco, Mongolia, Mozambique, Namibia, Netherlands, New Zealand, Nicaragua, Niger, Nigeria, Norway, Oman, Palau, Panama, Paraguay, Peru, Poland, Portugal, Qatar, Romania, Russian Federation, Rwanda, Saint Kitts and Nevis, Saint Lucia, Saint Vincent and the Grenadines, Samoa, San Marino, São Tomé and Príncipe, Saudi Arabia, Senegal, Seychelles, Sierra Leone, Slovakia, Slovenia, Solomon Islands, South Africa, Spain, Suriname, Swaziland, Sweden, Switzerland, Syrian Arab Republic, Tajikistan, Tanzania (United Republic of), The Former Yugoslav Republic of Macedonia, Togo, Tonga, Trinidad and Tobago, Tunisia, Turkmenistan, Uganda, Ukraine, United Arab Emirates, United Kingdom, Uruguay, Uzbekistan, Vanuatu, Venezuela, Vietnam, Yemen, Yugoslavia, Zambia, Zimbabwe.

**Protocol I Additional to the Geneva Convention of
12 August 1949, and Relating to the Protection of Victims
of International Armed Conflicts**

[...]

Part III
Methods and means of warfare combatant and prisoner-of-war status

Section I
Methods and means of warfare

Article 35
Basic rules

1. In any armed conflict, the right of the Parties to the conflict to choose methods or means of warfare is not unlimited.

2. It is prohibited to employ weapons, projectiles and material and methods of warfare of a nature to cause superfluous injury or unnecessary suffering.

3. It is prohibited to employ methods or means of warfare which are intended, or may be expected, to cause widespread, long-term and severe damage to the natural environment.

Article 36
New weapons

In the study, development, acquisition or adoption of a new weapon, means or method of warfare, a High Contracting Party is under an obligation to determine whether its employment would, in some or all circumstances, be prohibited by this Protocol or by any other rule of international law applicable to the High Contracting Party.

[...]

Chapter III
Civilian objects

Article 52
General protection of civilian objects

1. Civilian objects shall not be the object of attack or of reprisals. Civilian objects are all objects which are not military objectives as defined in paragraph 2.

2. Attacks shall be limited strictly to military objectives. In so far as objects are concerned, military objectives are limited to those objects which by their nature, location, purpose or use make an effective contribution to military

action and whose total or partial destruction, capture or neutralization, in the circumstances ruling at the time, offers a definite military advantage.

3. In case of doubt whether an object which is normally dedicated to civilian purposes, such as a place of worship, a house or other dwelling or a school, is being used to make an effective contribution to military action, it shall be presumed not to be so used.

Article 53
Protection of cultural objects and of places of worship

Without prejudice to the provisions of the Hague Convention for the Protection of Cultural Property in the Event of Armed Conflict of 14 May 1954, and of other relevant international instruments, it is prohibited:

(a) To commit any acts of hostility directed against the historic monuments, works of art or places of worship which constitute the cultural or spiritual heritage of peoples;
(b) To use such objects in support of the military effort;
(c) To make such objects the object of reprisals.

Article 54
Protection of objects indispensable to the survival of the civilian population

1. Starvation of civilians as a method of warfare is prohibited.

2. It is prohibited to attack, destroy, remove or render useless objects indispensable to the survival of the civilian population, such as foodstuffs, agricultural areas for the production of foodstuffs, crops, livestock, drinking water installations and supplies and irrigation works, for the specific purpose of denying them for their sustenance value to the civilian population or to the adverse Party, whatever the motive, whether in order to starve out civilians, to cause them to move away, or for any other motive.

3. The prohibitions in paragraph 2 shall not apply to such of the objects covered by it as are used by an adverse Party:

(a) As sustenance solely for the members of its armed forces; or
(b) If not as sustenance, then in direct support of military action, provided, however, that in no event shall actions against these objects be taken which may be expected to leave the civilian population with such inadequate food or water as to cause its starvation or force its movement.

4. These objects shall not be made the object of reprisals.

5. In recognition of the vital requirements of any Party to the conflict in the defence of its national territory against invasion, derogation from the prohibitions contained in paragraph 2 may be made by a Party to the conflict within

such territory under its own control where required by imperative military necessity.

Article 55
Protection of the natural environment

1. Care shall be taken in warfare to protect the natural environment against widespread, long-term and severe damage. This protection includes a prohibition of the use of methods or means of warfare which are intended or may be expected to cause such damage to the natural environment and thereby to prejudice the health or survival of the population.

2. Attacks against the natural environment by way of reprisals are prohibited.

Article 56
Protection of works and installations containing dangerous forces

1. Works or installations containing dangerous forces, namely dams, dykes and nuclear electrical generating stations, shall not be made the object of attack, even where these objects are military objectives, if such attack may cause the release of dangerous forces and consequent severe losses among the civilian population. Other military objectives located at or in the vicinity of these works or installations shall not be made the object of attack if such attack may cause the release of dangerous forces from the works or installations and consequent severe losses among the civilian population.

2. The special protection against attack provided by paragraph 1 shall cease:

(a) For a dam or a dyke only if it is used for other than its normal function and in regular, significant and direct support of military operations and if such attack is the only feasible way to terminate such support;
(b) For a nuclear electrical generating station only if it provides electric power in regular, significant and direct support of military operations and if such attack is the only feasible way to terminate such support;
(c) For other military objectives located at or in the vicinity of these works or installations only if they are used in regular, significant and direct support of military operations and if such attack is the only feasible way to terminate such support.

3. In all cases, the civilian population and individual civilians shall remain entitled to all the protection accorded them by international law, including the protection of the precautionary measures provided for in Article 57. If the protection ceases and any of the works, installations or military objectives mentioned in paragraph I is attacked, all practical precautions shall be taken to avoid the release of the dangerous forces.

4. It is prohibited to make any of the works, installations or military objectives mentioned in paragraph 1 the object of reprisals.

5. The Parties to the conflict shall endeavour to avoid locating any military objectives in the vicinity of the works or installations mentioned in paragraph 1. Nevertheless, installations erected for the sole purpose of defending the protected works or installations from attack are permissible and shall not themselves be made the object of attack, provided that they are not used in hostilities except for defensive actions necessary to respond to attacks against the protected works or installations and that their armament is limited to weapons capable only of repelling hostile action against the protected works or installations.

6. The High Contracting Parties and the Parties to the conflict are urged to conclude further agreements among themselves to provide additional protection for objects containing dangerous forces.

7. In order to facilitate the identification of the objects protected by this article, the Parties to the conflict may mark them with a special sign consisting of a group of three bright orange circles placed on the same axis, as specified in Article 16 of Annex I to this Protocol. The absence of such marking in no way relieves any Party to the conflict of its obligations under this Article.

Chapter IV
Precautionary measures

Article 57
Precautions in attack

1. In the conduct of military operations, constant care shall be taken to spare the civilian population, civilians and civilian objects.

2. With respect to attacks, the following precautions shall be taken:

(a) Those who plan or decide upon an attack shall:
  (i) Do everything feasible to verify that the objectives to be attacked are neither civilians nor civilian objects and are not subject to special protection but are military objectives within the meaning of paragraph 2 of Article 52 and that it is not prohibited by the provisions of this Protocol to attack them;
  (ii) Take all feasible precautions in the choice of means and methods of attack with a view to avoiding, and in any event to minimizing, incidental loss of civilian life, injury to civilians and damage to civilian objects;
  (iii) Refrain from deciding to launch any attack which may be expected to cause incidental loss of civilian life, injury to civilians, damage to civilian objects, or a combination thereof, which would be excessive in relation to the concrete and direct military advantage anticipated;
(b) An attack shall be cancelled or suspended if it becomes apparent that the objective is not a military one or is subject to special protection or that the attack may be expected to cause incidental loss of civilian life, injury

to civilians, damage to civilian objects, or a combination thereof, which would be excessive in relation to the concrete and direct military advantage anticipated;

(c) Effective advance warning shall be given of attacks which may affect the civilian population, unless circumstances do not permit.

3. When a choice is possible between several military objectives for obtaining a similar military advantage, the objective to be selected shall be that the attack on which may be expected to cause the least danger to civilian lives and to civilian objects.

4. In the conduct of military operations at sea or in the air, each Party to the conflict shall, in conformity with its rights and duties under the rules of international law applicable in armed conflict, take all reasonable precautions to avoid losses of civilian lives and damage to civilian objects.

5. No provision of this Article may be construed as authorizing any attacks against the civilian population, civilians or civilian objects.

Article 58
Precautions against the effects of attacks

The Parties to the conflict shall, to the maximum extent feasible:

(a) Without prejudice to Article 49 of the Fourth Convention, endeavour to remove the civilian population, individual civilians and civilian objects under their control from the vicinity of military objectives;

(b) Avoid locating military objectives within or near densely populated areas;

(c) Take the other necessary precautions to protect the civilian population, individual civilians and civilian objects under their control against the dangers resulting from military operations.

Chapter V
Localities and zones under special protection

Article 59
Non-defended localities

1. It is prohibited for the Parties to the conflict to attack, by any means whatsoever, non-defended localities.

2. The appropriate authorities of a Party to the conflict may declare as a non-defended locality any inhabited place near or in a zone where armed forces are in contact which is open for occupation by an adverse Party. Such a locality shall fulfil the following conditions:

(a) All combatants, as well as mobile weapons and mobile military equipment must have been evacuated;

(b) No hostile use shall be made of fixed military installations or establishments;

(c) No acts of hostility shall be committed by the authorities or by the population; and

(d) No activities in support of military operations shall be undertaken.

3. The presence, in this locality, of persons specially protected under the Conventions and this Protocol, and of police forces retained for the sole purpose of maintaining law and order, is not contrary to the conditions laid down in paragraph 2.

4. The declaration made under paragraph 2 shall be addressed to the adverse Party and shall define and describe, as precisely as possible, the limits of the non-defended locality. The Party to the conflict to which the declaration is addressed shall acknowledge its receipt and shall treat the locality as a non-defended locality unless the conditions laid down in paragraph 2 are not in fact fulfilled, in which event it shall immediately so inform the Party making the declaration. Even if the conditions laid down in paragraph 2 are not fulfilled, the locality shall continue to enjoy the protection provided by the other provisions of this Protocol and the other rules of international law applicable in armed conflict.

5. The Parties to the conflict may agree on the establishment of non-defended localities even if such localities do not fulfil the conditions laid down in paragraph 2. The agreement should define and describe, as precisely as possible, the limits of the non-defended locality; if necessary, it may lay down the methods of supervision.

6. The Party which is in control of a locality governed by such an agreement shall mark it, so far as possible, by such signs as may be agreed upon with the other Party, which shall be displayed where they are clearly visible, especially on its perimeter and limits and on highways.

7. A locality loses its status as a non-defended locality when it ceases to fulfil the conditions laid down in paragraph 2 or in the agreement referred to in paragraph 5. In such an eventuality, the locality shall continue to enjoy the protection provided by the other provisions of this Protocol and the other rules of international law applicable in armed conflict.

Article 60
Demilitarized zones

1. It is prohibited for the Parties to the conflict to extend their military operations to zones on which they have conferred by agreement the status of demilitarized zone, if such extension is contrary to the terms of this agreement.

2. The agreement shall be an express agreement, may be concluded verbally or in writing, either directly or through a Protecting Power or any impartial humanitarian organization, and may consist of reciprocal and concordant

declarations. The agreement may be concluded in peacetime, as well as after the outbreak of hostilities, and should define and describe, as precisely as possible, the limits of the demilitarized zone and, if necessary, lay down the methods of supervision.

3. The subject of such an agreement shall normally be any zone which fulfils the following conditions:

(a) All combatants, as well as mobile weapons and mobile military equipment, must have been evacuated;
(b) No hostile use shall be made of fixed military installations or establishments;
(c) No acts of hostility shall be committed by the authorities or by the population; and
(d) Any activity linked to the military effort must have ceased.

The Parties to the conflict shall agree upon the interpretation to be given to the condition laid down in sub-paragraph (d) and upon persons to be admitted to the demilitarized zone other than those mentioned in paragraph 4.

4. The presence, in this zone, of persons specially protected under the Conventions and this Protocol, and of police forces retained for the sole purpose of maintaining law and order, is not contrary to the conditions laid down in paragraph 3.

5. The Party which is in control of such a zone shall mark it, so far as possible, by such signs as may be agreed upon with the other Party, which shall be displayed where they are clearly visible, especially on its perimeter and limits and on highways.

6. If the fighting draws near to a demilitarized zone, and if the Parties to the conflict have so agreed, none of them may use the zone for purposes related to the conduct of military operations or unilaterally revoke its status.

7. If one of the Parties to the conflict commits a material breach of the provisions of paragraphs 3 or 6, the other Party shall be released from its obligations under the agreement conferring upon the zone the status of demilitarized zone. In such an eventuality, the zone loses its status but shall continue to enjoy the protection provided by the other provisions of this Protocol and the other rules of international law applicable in armed conflict.

[. . .]

United Nations Security Council Resolution 687, 3 April 1991 (extract)

Editorial note

UN Security Council Resolution 687 (1991), adopted in the aftermath of the 1991 Gulf War, assigns responsibility and liability to Iraq for, *inter alia*, environmental damage and depletion of natural resources resulting from its invasion and occupation of Kuwait. The Resolution creates a Claims Commission to determine the amount of liability which Iraq has incurred.

Text reprinted from: UN Doc. S/RES/687(1991)

UN Security Council Resolution 687

The Security Council:

[...]

16. *Reaffirms* that Iraq, without prejudice to the debts and obligations of Iraq arising prior to 2 August 1990, which will be addressed through the normal mechanisms, is liable under international law for any direct loss, damage, including environmental damage and the depletion of natural resources, or injury to foreign Governments, nationals and corporations, as a result of Iraq's unlawful invasion and occupation of Kuwait.
[...]

PART IX

Trade and the environment

Agreement Establishing the World Trade Organization, 15 April 1994 (extracts)

Editorial note

The General Agreement on Tariffs and Trade was originally adopted in 1947 as the main international arrangement to encourage trade between states. The GATT was drafted in response to the protectionist policies of the 1920s and 1930s, which were perceived as major causes of the Great Depression. In December 1993, after seven years of negotiation, the Trade Negotiations Committee of the Uruguay Round adopted by consensus the Final Act. The Final Act includes the Agreement establishing the World Trade Organisation (WTO) and annexed agreements on, *inter alia:* the General Agreement on Tariffs and Trade 1994 (GATT 1994), the General Agreement on Trade in Services (GATS), the Agreement on Trade-Related Aspects of Intellectual Property Rights (TRIPS), and the Understanding on Rules and Procedures Governing the Settlement of Disputes (DSU). These and related agreements were opened for signature at Marrakesh on 15 April 1994 and entered into force on 1 January 1995. By joining the WTO Parties become legally bound by the annexed agreements (with the exclusion of the Plurilateral Agreements, Annex IV to the Agreements Establishing the WTO, which are optional).

The entire package established a permanent organisation, the WTO, which has become an important forum for addressing issues related to trade and environment. The WTO replaces the former GATT Council as 'the common institutional framework for the conduct of trade relations among its Members in matters related to the agreements and associated legal instruments included in the Annexes' to the WTO Agreement.

Although it does not have express environmental objectives, the Preamble recognises that the WTO must allow 'the optimal use of the world's resources in accordance with the objective of sustainable development' and seek 'both to protect and preserve the environment and enhance the means for doing so in a manner consistent with' the respective needs and concerns of the parties at different levels of economic development. The WTO's tasks are to implement the WTO Agreement and the Multilateral Trade Agreements; to provide the framework for the implementation of the Plurilateral Trade Agreements; to administer the DSU and the Trade Policy Review Mechanism; to provide a forum for the negotiations among Members; and to co-operate with the World Bank and the IMF.

Despite the new institutional overlay, the GATT 1994 remains the central substantive agreement under the WTO umbrella, which is designed to encourage trade between WTO members by reducing tariffs and preventing trade barriers.

The core of the GATT is reflected in two policies: (a) unconditional 'most favoured nation' treatment should be conferred to all Parties so that any 'advantage, favour, privilege or immunity' granted in respect of a product from one Party should apply in respect of all other Parties (Article I); and (b) non-discrimination should apply in respect of laws, regulations, and requirements for 'like products' as between domestic and imported products (Article III). The GATT further prohibits, subject to specific exceptions, the imposition of quantitative restrictions on the import of goods and export of any products (Article XI). General exceptions to the GATT's requirements are permitted, so long as they are neither discriminatory nor disguised restrictions on trade, if they are, *inter alia*, necessary to protect human, animal or plant life or health (Article XX(b)) or relate to the conservation of exhaustible natural resources (Article XX(g)).

Among the other agreements, of particular relevance for trade and the environment are the Agreement on Technical Barriers to Trade (TBT Agreement) and the Agreement on the Application of Sanitary and Phytosanitary Measures (SPS Agreement). The two agreements deal with national regulatory standards: the SPS Agreement deals with measures designed to protect human, animal and plant life or health, and the TBT Agreement covers other technical standards not regulated by the SPS Agreement. The main objective of the TBT Agreement is to ensure that technical regulations and standards, including packaging, labelling and marking requirements and methods of certifying conformity with technical regulations and standards, are not adopted or applied so as to create unnecessary obstacles to trade. Environmental regulations may be technical barriers to trade. The TBT Agreement adopts the principles of national treatment and non-discrimination by stating that, in relation to such technical regulations or standards, imported products are not to receive less favourable treatment 'than that accorded to like products of national origin and to like products originating in any other country' (Article 2(1)). WTO Members must also ensure that technical regulations 'are not prepared, adopted or applied with a view to or with the effect of creating unnecessary obstacles to international trade'. Accordingly, technical regulations must not be 'more trade-restrictive than necessary to fulfil a legitimate objective, taking account of the risks non-fulfilment would create' (Article 2(2)). The list of 'legitimate objectives' in Article 2(2) includes 'the protection of human health or safety, animal or plant life or health, or the environment'. In assessing the risks to health or the environment, the relevant factors for consideration include 'available scientific and technical information, related processing technology or intended end-uses of products' (Article 2(2)).

The SPS Agreement lays down the conditions governing sanitary and phytosanitary (SPS) measures enacted by Members, amplifying Article XX(b) and confirming that measures consistent with the Agreement are deemed to meet the requirements of that Article (Article 2(4)).

The SPS Agreement affirms the right of each WTO Member to take SPS measures necessary for the protection of human, animal and plant life or health, subject to the provisions of the Agreement, in particular their trade restrictiveness and the need for scientific justification (Article 2(1)). Members must observe national treatment and non-discrimination principles in the design of their measures, must accept the SPS measures of other Members as equivalent if the exporting Member objectively demonstrates equivalency and must not apply SPS measures in a manner that would constitute a disguised restriction on international trade (Article 2(3) and (4)). Members must also ensure that their SPS measures are applied only to the extent necessary, are based on scientific principles and are not maintained without sufficient scientific evidence (Article 2(2)).

SPS measures that 'conform to' international standards are deemed necessary to protect human, animal and plant life or health and are presumed to be consistent with the SPS Agreement (Article 3(2)). Members are not prevented from introducing or maintaining SPS measures which are stricter than those reflected in international standards 'if there is a scientific justification, or as a consequence of the level of sanitary or phytosanitary protection a Member determines to be appropriate in accordance with the relevant provisions of paragraphs 1 through 8 of Article 5'(Article 3(3)). Article 5 provides that Members are to ensure their SPS measures are based on a risk assessment. Where relevant scientific evidence is insufficient to allow a full risk assessment, Article 5(7) allows the adoption of provisional SPS measures by a Member 'on the basis of available pertinent information' and subject to undertaking a subsequent risk assessment within a 'reasonable' period of time.

One of the most controversial WTO agreements is the Agreement on Trade Related Aspects of Intellectual Property Rights (TRIPS Agreement). The TRIPS Agreement establishes a regime requiring WTO Members to make patents available for any inventions, whether products or processes, in all fields of technology without discrimination, subject to the normal tests of novelty, inventiveness and industrial applicability. It also requires that patents be available and patent rights enjoyable without discrimination as to the place of invention and whether products are imported or locally produced. The TRIPS Agreement allows exceptions to the general rule on patentability, of which two are environmentally relevant. The first is that patents should not be granted to inventions which are contrary to *ordre public* or morality (including inventions dangerous to human, animal or plant life or health or seriously prejudicial to the environment)

(Article 27(2)). The second exception is that members may exclude plants and animals other than micro-organisms and essentially biological processes for the production of plants or animals other than non-biological and microbiological processes (Article 27(3)(b)).

Extracts from the Agreement Establishing the WTO, the GATT, the TBT Agreement, the SPS Agreement and the TRIPS Agreement are reproduced below.

Date of adoption:	15 April 1994
Entry into force:	1 January 1995
Depositary:	Director-General of the World Trade Organization
Contracting Parties:	Albania, Angola, Antigua and Barbuda, Argentina, Armenia, Australia, Austria, Bahrain, Bangladesh, Barbados, Belgium, Belize, Benin, Bolivia, Botswana, Brazil, Brunei Darussalam, Bulgaria, Burkina Faso, Burundi, Cameroon, Canada, Central African Republic, Chad, Chile, China, Colombia, Congo, Costa Rica, Côte d'Ivoire, Croatia, Cuba, Cyprus, Czech Republic, Democratic Republic of the Congo, Denmark, Djibouti, Dominica, Dominican Republic, Ecuador, Egypt, El Salvador, Estonia, European Communities, Fiji, Finland, France, Gabon, The Gambia, Georgia, Germany, Ghana, Greece, Grenada, Guatemala Guinea, Guinea Bissau Guyana, Haiti, Honduras, Hong Kong, China, Hungary, Iceland, India, Indonesia, Ireland, Israel, Italy, Jamaica, Japan, Jordan, Kenya, Korea, Republic of Kuwait Kyrgyz Republic, Latvia, Lesotho, Liechtenstein, Lithuania, Luxembourg, Macao, China, Madagascar, Malawi, Malaysia, Maldives, Mali, Malta, Mauritania, Mauritius, Mexico, Moldova, Mongolia, Morocco, Mozambique, Myanmar, Namibia, Netherlands, New Zealand, Nicaragua, Niger, Nigeria, Norway, Oman, Pakistan, Panama, Papua New Guinea, Paraguay, Peru, Philippines, Poland, Portugal, Qatar, Romania, Rwanda, Saint Kitts and Nevis, Saint Lucia, Saint Vincent & the Grenadines, Senegal, Separate Customs Territory of Taiwan, Penghu, Kinmen and Matsu, Sierra Leone, Singapore, Slovak Republic, Slovenia, Solomon Islands, South Africa, Spain, Sri Lanka, Suriname, Swaziland, Sweden, Switzerland, Tanzania, Thailand, Togo, Trinidad and Tobago, Tunisia,

Turkey, Uganda, United Arab Emirates, United Kingdom, United States of America, Uruguay, Venezuela, Zambia, Zimbabwe

Website: www.wto.org

Agreement Establishing the World Trade Organization

Preamble

The *Parties* to this Agreement,

Recognizing that their relations in the field of trade and economic endeavour should be conducted with a view to raising standards of living, ensuring full employment and a large and steadily growing volume of real income and effective demand, and expanding the production of and trade in goods and services, while allowing for the optimal use of the world's resources in accordance with the objective of sustainable development, seeking both to protect and preserve the environment and to enhance the means for doing so in a manner consistent with their respective needs and concerns at different levels of economic development, . . .

[. . .]

General Agreement on Tariffs and Trade, 1947/1994 (extracts)

[...]

Article I
General most-favoured-nation treatment

1. With respect to customs duties and charges of any kind imposed on or in connection with importation or exportation or imposed on the international transfer of payments for imports or exports, and with respect to the method of levying such duties and charges, and with respect to all rules and formalities in connection with importation and exportation, and with respect to all matters referred to in paragraphs 2 and 4 of Article III, any advantage, favour, privilege or immunity granted by any contracting party to any product originating in or destined for any other country shall be accorded immediately and unconditionally to the like product originating in or destined for the territories of all other contracting parties.

2. The provisions of paragraph 1 of this Article shall not require the elimination of any preferences in respect of import duties or charges which do not exceed the levels provided for in paragraph 4 of this Article and which fall within the following descriptions:

(a) Preferences in force exclusively between two or more of the territories listed in Annex A, subject to the conditions set forth therein;
(b) Preferences in force exclusively between two or more territories which on July 1, 1939, were connected by common sovereignty or relations of protection or suzerainty and which are listed in Annexes B, C and D, subject to the conditions set forth therein;
(c) Preferences in force exclusively between the United States of America and the Republic of Cuba;
(d) Preferences in force exclusively between neighbouring countries listed in Annexes E and F.

3. The provisions of paragraph 1 shall not apply to preferences between the countries formerly a part of the Ottoman Empire and detached from it on July 24, 1923, provided such preferences are approved under paragraph 5[1], of

---

[1] The authentic text erroneously reads 'sub-paragraph 5(a)'.

Article XXV which shall be applied in this respect in the light of paragraph 1 of Article XXIX.

4. The margin of preference on any product in respect of which a preference is permitted under paragraph 2 of this Article but is not specifically set forth as a maximum margin of preference in the appropriate Schedule annexed to this Agreement shall not exceed:

(a) in respect of duties or charges on any product described in such Schedule, the difference between the most-favoured-nation and preferential rates provided for therein; if no preferential rate is provided for, the preferential rate shall for the purposes of this paragraph be taken to be that in force on April 10, 1947, and, if no most-favoured-nation rate is provided for, the margin shall not exceed the difference between the most-favoured-nation and preferential rates existing on April 10, 1947;

(b) in respect of duties or charges on any product not described in the appropriate Schedule, the difference between the most-favoured-nation and preferential rates existing on April 10, 1947.

In the case of the contracting parties named in Annex G, the date of April 10, 1947, referred to in subparagraph (a) and (b) of this paragraph shall be replaced by the respective dates set forth in that Annex.

[…]

Article III
National treatment on internal taxation and regulation

1. The contracting parties recognize that internal taxes and other internal charges, and laws, regulations and requirements affecting the internal sale, offering for sale, purchase, transportation, distribution or use of products, and internal quantitative regulations requiring the mixture, processing or use of products in specified amounts or proportions, should not be applied to imported or domestic products so as to afford protection to domestic production.

2. The products of the territory of any contracting party imported into the territory of any other contracting party shall not be subject, directly or indirectly, to internal taxes or other internal charges of any kind in excess of those applied, directly or indirectly, to like domestic products. Moreover, no contracting party shall otherwise apply internal taxes or other internal charges to imported or domestic products in a manner contrary to the principles set forth in paragraph 1.

3. With respect to any existing internal tax which is inconsistent with the provisions of paragraph 2, but which is specifically authorized under a trade agreement, in force on April 10, 1947, in which the import duty on the taxed product is bound against increase, the contracting party imposing the tax shall be free to postpone the application of the provisions of paragraph 2 to such

tax until such time as it can obtain release from the obligations of such trade agreement in order to permit the increase of such duty to the extent necessary to compensate for the elimination of the protective element of the tax.

4. The products of the territory of any contracting party imported into the territory of any other contracting party shall be accorded treatment no less favourable than that accorded to like products of national origin in respect of all laws, regulations and requirements affecting their internal sale, offering for sale, purchase, transportation, distribution or use. The provisions of this paragraph shall not prevent the application of differential internal transportation charges which are based exclusively on the economic operation of the means of transport and not on the nationality of the product.

5. No contracting party shall establish or maintain any internal quantitative regulation relating to the mixture, processing or use of products in specified amounts or proportions which requires, directly or indirectly, that any specified amount or proportion of any product which is the subject of the regulation must be supplied from domestic sources. Moreover, no contracting party shall otherwise apply internal quantitative regulations in a manner contrary to the principles set forth in paragraph 1.

6. The provisions of paragraph 5 shall not apply to any internal quantitative regulation in force in the territory of any contracting party on July 1, 1939, April 10, 1947, or March 24, 1948, at the option of that contracting party; *Provided* that any such regulation which is contrary to the provisions of paragraph 5 shall not be modified to the detriment of imports and shall be treated as a customs duty for the purpose of negotiation.

7. No internal quantitative regulation relating to the mixture, processing or use of products in specified amounts or proportions shall be applied in such a manner as to allocate any such amount or proportion among external sources of supply.

8.

(a) The provisions of this Article shall not apply to laws, regulations or requirements governing the procurement by governmental agencies of products purchased for governmental purposes and not with a view to commercial resale or with a view to use in the production of goods for commercial sale.

(b) The provisions of this Article shall not prevent the payment of subsidies exclusively to domestic producers, including payments to domestic producers derived from the proceeds of internal taxes or charges applied consistently with the provisions of this Article and subsidies effected through governmental purchases of domestic products.

9. The contracting parties recognize that internal maximum price control measures, even though conforming to the other provisions of this Article, can have effects prejudicial to the interests of contracting parties supplying imported products. Accordingly, contracting parties applying such measures

shall take account of the interests of exporting contracting parties with a view to avoiding to the fullest practicable extent such prejudicial effects.

10. The provisions of this Article shall not prevent any contracting party from establishing or maintaining internal quantitative regulations relating to exposed cinematograph films and meeting the requirements of Article IV.

[...]

Article XI
General elimination of quantitative restrictions

1. No prohibitions or restrictions other than duties, taxes or other charges, whether made effective through quotas, import or export licences or other measures, shall be instituted or maintained by any contracting party on the importation of any product of the territory of any other contracting party or on the exportation or sale for export of any product destined for the territory of any other contracting party.

2. The provisions of paragraph 1 of this Article shall not extend to the following:

(a) Export prohibitions or restrictions temporarily applied to prevent or relieve critical shortages of foodstuffs or other products essential to the exporting contracting party;

(b) Import and export prohibitions or restrictions necessary to the application of standards or regulations for the classification, grading or marketing of commodities in international trade;

(c) Import restrictions on any agricultural or fisheries product, imported in any form, necessary to the enforcement of governmental measures which operate:

  (i) to restrict the quantities of the like domestic product permitted to be marketed or produced, or, if there is no substantial domestic production of the like product, of a domestic product for which the imported product can be directly substituted; or

  (ii) to remove a temporary surplus of the like domestic product, or, if there is no substantial domestic production of the like product, of a domestic product for which the imported product can be directly substituted, by making the surplus available to certain groups of domestic consumers free of charge or at prices below the current market level; or

  (iii) to restrict the quantities permitted to be produced of any animal product the production of which is directly dependent, wholly or mainly, on the imported commodity, if the domestic production of that commodity is relatively negligible.

Any contracting party applying restrictions on the importation of any product pursuant to subparagraph (c) of this paragraph shall give public notice of the total quantity or value of the product permitted to be imported during a specified future period and of any change in such quantity or value. Moreover, any restrictions applied under (i) above shall not be such as will reduce the total of imports relative to the total of domestic production, as compared with the proportion which might reasonably be expected to rule between the two in the absence of restrictions. In determining this proportion, the contracting party shall pay due regard to the proportion prevailing during a previous representative period and to any special factors which may have affected or may be affecting the trade in the product concerned.

[...]

Article XX
General exceptions

Subject to the requirement that such measures are not applied in a manner which would constitute a means of arbitrary or unjustifiable discrimination between countries where the same conditions prevail, or a disguised restriction on international trade, nothing in this Agreement shall be construed to prevent the adoption or enforcement by any contracting party of measures:

(a) necessary to protect public morals;
(b) necessary to protect human, animal or plant life or health;
(c) relating to the importations or exportations of gold or silver;
(d) necessary to secure compliance with laws or regulations which are not inconsistent with the provisions of this Agreement, including those relating to customs enforcement, the enforcement of monopolies operated under paragraph 4 of Article II and Article XVII, the protection of patents, trade marks and copyrights, and the prevention of deceptive practices;
(e) relating to the products of prison labour;
(f) imposed for the protection of national treasures of artistic, historic or archaeological value;
(g) relating to the conservation of exhaustible natural resources if such measures are made effective in conjunction with restrictions on domestic production or consumption;
(h) undertaken in pursuance of obligations under any intergovernmental commodity agreement which conforms to criteria submitted to the CONTRACTING PARTIES and not disapproved by them or which is itself so submitted and not so disapproved;
(i) involving restrictions on exports of domestic materials necessary to ensure essential quantities of such materials to a domestic processing industry during periods when the domestic price of such materials is held below the world price as part of a governmental stabilization plan; *Provided* that such restrictions shall not operate to increase the exports of or the protection

afforded to such domestic industry, and shall not depart from the provisions of this Agreement relating to non-discrimination;

(j) essential to the acquisition or distribution of products in general or local short supply; *Provided* that any such measures shall be consistent with the principle that all contracting parties are entitled to an equitable share of the international supply of such products, and that any such measures, which are inconsistent with the other provisions of the Agreement shall be discontinued as soon as the conditions giving rise to them have ceased to exist. The CONTRACTING PARTIES shall review the need for this sub-paragraph not later than 30 June 1960.

[...]

Agreement on Technical Barriers to Trade (extracts)

Preamble

Members,

[...]

Recognizing that no country should be prevented from taking measures necessary to ensure the quality of its exports, or for the protection of human, animal or plant life or health, of the environment, or for the prevention of deceptive practices, at the levels it considers appropriate, subject to the requirement that they are not applied in a manner which would constitute a means of arbitrary or unjustifiable discrimination between countries where the same conditions prevail or a disguised restriction on international trade, ...

[...]

Article 2
Preparation, adoption and application of technical regulations by central government bodies

With respect to their central government bodies:

2.1 Members shall ensure that in respect of technical regulations, products imported from the territory of any Member shall be accorded treatment no less favourable than that accorded to like products of national origin and to like products originating in any other country.

2.2 Members shall ensure that technical regulations are not prepared, adopted or applied with a view to or with the effect of creating unnecessary obstacles to international trade. For this purpose, technical regulations shall not be more trade-restrictive than necessary to fulfil a legitimate objective, taking account of the risks non-fulfilment would create. Such legitimate objectives are, *inter alia:* national security requirements; the prevention of deceptive practices; protection of human health or safety, animal or plant life or health, or the environment. In assessing such risks, relevant elements of consideration are, *inter alia:* available scientific and technical information, related processing technology or intended end-uses of products.

2.3 Technical regulations shall not be maintained if the circumstances or objectives giving rise to their adoption no longer exist or if the changed
circumstances or objectives can be addressed in a less trade-restrictive
manner.

2.4 Where technical regulations are required and relevant international standards exist or their completion is imminent, Members shall use them, or
the relevant parts of them, as a basis for their technical regulations except
when such international standards or relevant parts would be an ineffec-
tive or inappropriate means for the fulfilment of the legitimate objectives
pursued, for instance because of fundamental climatic or geographical
factors or fundamental technological problems.

2.5 A Member preparing, adopting or applying a technical regulation which
may have a significant effect on trade of other Members shall, upon the
request of another Member, explain the justification for that technical
regulation in terms of the provisions of paragraphs 2 to 4. Whenever a
technical regulation is prepared, adopted or applied for one of the legitimate objectives explicitly mentioned in paragraph 2, and is in accordance
with relevant international standards, it shall be rebuttably presumed not
to create an unnecessary obstacle to international trade.

2.6 With a view to harmonizing technical regulations on as wide a basis as
possible, Members shall play a full part, within the limits of their resources,
in the preparation by appropriate international standardizing bodies of
international standards for products for which they either have adopted,
or expect to adopt, technical regulations.

2.7 Members shall give positive consideration to accepting as equivalent technical regulations of other Members, even if these regulations differ from
their own, provided they are satisfied that these regulations adequately
fulfil the objectives of their own regulations.

2.8 Wherever appropriate, Members shall specify technical regulations based
on product requirements in terms of performance rather than design or
descriptive characteristics.

2.9 Whenever a relevant international standard does not exist or the technical
content of a proposed technical regulation is not in accordance with the
technical content of relevant international standards, and if the technical regulation may have a significant effect on trade of other Members,
Members shall:

2.9.1 publish a notice in a publication at an early appropriate stage, in
such a manner as to enable interested parties in other Members to
become acquainted with it, that they propose to introduce a particular technical regulation;

2.9.2 notify other Members through the Secretariat of the products to be
covered by the proposed technical regulation, together with a brief
indication of its objective and rationale. Such notifications shall take

place at an early appropriate stage, when amendments can still be introduced and comments taken into account;

    2.9.3 upon request, provide to other Members particulars or copies of the proposed technical regulation and, whenever possible, identify the parts which in substance deviate from relevant international standards;

    2.9.4 without discrimination, allow reasonable time for other Members to make comments in writing, discuss these comments upon request, and take these written comments and the results of these discussions into account.

2.10 Subject to the provisions in the lead-in to paragraph 9, where urgent problems of safety, health, environmental protection or national security arise or threaten to arise for a Member, that Member may omit such of the steps enumerated in paragraph 9 as it finds necessary, provided that the Member, upon adoption of a technical regulation, shall:

    2.10.1 notify immediately other Members through the Secretariat of the particular technical regulation and the products covered, with a brief indication of the objective and the rationale of the technical regulation, including the nature of the urgent problems;

    2.10.2 upon request, provide other Members with copies of the technical regulation;

    2.10.3 without discrimination, allow other Members to present their comments in writing, discuss these comments upon request, and take these written comments and the results of these discussions into account.

2.11 Members shall ensure that all technical regulations which have been adopted are published promptly or otherwise made available in such a manner as to enable interested parties in other Members to become acquainted with them.

2.12 Except in those urgent circumstances referred to in paragraph 10, Members shall allow a reasonable interval between the publication of technical regulations and their entry into force in order to allow time for producers in exporting Members, and particularly in developing country Members, to adapt their products or methods of production to the requirements of the importing Member.

[...]

Agreement on the Application of Sanitary and Phytosanitary Measures (extracts)

Members,

Reaffirming that no Member should be prevented from adopting or enforcing measures necessary to protect human, animal or plant life or health, subject to the requirement that these measures are not applied in a manner which would constitute a means of arbitrary or unjustifiable discrimination between Members where the same conditions prevail or a disguised restriction on international trade;

[...]

Article 1
General provisions

1. This Agreement applies to all sanitary and phytosanitary measures which may, directly or indirectly, affect international trade. Such measures shall be developed and applied in accordance with the provisions of this Agreement.

2. For the purposes of this Agreement, the definitions provided in Annex A shall apply.

3. The annexes are an integral part of this Agreement.

4. Nothing in this Agreement shall affect the rights of Members under the Agreement on Technical Barriers to Trade with respect to measures not within the scope of this Agreement.

Article 2
Basic rights and obligations

1. Members have the right to take sanitary and phytosanitary measures necessary for the protection of human, animal or plant life or health, provided that such measures are not inconsistent with the provisions of this Agreement.

2. Members shall ensure that any sanitary or phytosanitary measure is applied only to the extent necessary to protect human, animal or plant life or health, is based on scientific principles and is not maintained without sufficient scientific evidence, except as provided for in paragraph 7 of Article 5.

3. Members shall ensure that their sanitary and phytosanitary measures do not arbitrarily or unjustifiably discriminate between Members where identical

or similar conditions prevail, including between their own territory and that of other Members. Sanitary and phytosanitary measures shall not be applied in a manner which would constitute a disguised restriction on international trade.

4. Sanitary or phytosanitary measures which conform to the relevant provisions of this Agreement shall be presumed to be in accordance with the obligations of the Members under the provisions of GATT 1994 which relate to the use of sanitary or phytosanitary measures, in particular the provisions of Article XX(b).

Article 3
Harmonization

1. To harmonize sanitary and phytosanitary measures on as wide a basis as possible, Members shall base their sanitary or phytosanitary measures on international standards, guidelines or recommendations, where they exist, except as otherwise provided for in this Agreement, and in particular in paragraph 3.

2. Sanitary or phytosanitary measures which conform to international standards, guidelines or recommendations shall be deemed to be necessary to protect human, animal or plant life or health, and presumed to be consistent with the relevant provisions of this Agreement and of GATT 1994.

3. Members may introduce or maintain sanitary or phytosanitary measures which result in a higher level of sanitary or phytosanitary protection than would be achieved by measures based on the relevant international standards, guidelines or recommendations, if there is a scientific justification, or as a consequence of the level of sanitary or phytosanitary protection a Member determines to be appropriate in accordance with the relevant provisions of paragraphs 1 through 8 of Article 5.[1] Notwithstanding the above, all measures which result in a level of sanitary or phytosanitary protection different from that which would be achieved by measures based on international standards, guidelines or recommendations shall not be inconsistent with any other provision of this Agreement.

4. Members shall play a full part, within the limits of their resources, in the relevant international organizations and their subsidiary bodies, in particular the Codex Alimentarius Commission, the International Office of Epizootics, and the international and regional organizations operating within the framework of the International Plant Protection Convention, to promote within these organizations the development and periodic review of standards, guidelines and recommendations with respect to all aspects of sanitary and phytosanitary measures.

---

[1] For the purposes of paragraph 3 of Article 3, there is a scientific justification if, on the basis of an examination and evaluation of available scientific information in conformity with the relevant provisions of this Agreement, a Member determines that the relevant international standards, guidelines or recommendations are not sufficient to achieve its appropriate level of sanitary or phytosanitary protection.

5. The Committee on Sanitary and Phytosanitary Measures provided for in paragraphs 1 and 4 of Article 12 (referred to in this Agreement as the 'Committee') shall develop a procedure to monitor the process of international harmonization and coordinate efforts in this regard with the relevant international organizations.

[...]

Article 5
Assessment of risk and determination of the appropriate level of sanitary or phytosanitary protection

1. Members shall ensure that their sanitary or phytosanitary measures are based on an assessment, as appropriate to the circumstances, of the risks to human, animal or plant life or health, taking into account risk assessment techniques developed by the relevant international organizations.

2. In the assessment of risks, Members shall take into account available scientific evidence; relevant processes and production methods; relevant inspection, sampling and testing methods; prevalence of specific diseases or pests; existence of pest- or disease-free areas; relevant ecological and environmental conditions; and quarantine or other treatment.

3. In assessing the risk to animal or plant life or health and determining the measure to be applied for achieving the appropriate level of sanitary or phytosanitary protection from such risk, Members shall take into account as relevant economic factors: the potential damage in terms of loss of production or sales in the event of the entry, establishment or spread of a pest or disease; the costs of control or eradication in the territory of the importing Member; and the relative cost-effectiveness of alternative approaches to limiting risks.

4. Members should, when determining the appropriate level of sanitary or phytosanitary protection, take into account the objective of minimizing negative trade effects.

5. With the objective of achieving consistency in the application of the concept of appropriate level of sanitary or phytosanitary protection against risks to human life or health, or to animal and plant life or health, each Member shall avoid arbitrary or unjustifiable distinctions in the levels it considers to be appropriate in different situations, if such distinctions result in discrimination or a disguised restriction on international trade. Members shall cooperate in the Committee, in accordance with paragraphs 1, 2 and 3 of Article 12, to develop guidelines to further the practical implementation of this provision. In developing the guidelines, the Committee shall take into account all relevant factors, including the exceptional character of human health risks to which people voluntarily expose themselves.

6. Without prejudice to paragraph 2 of Article 3, when establishing or maintaining sanitary or phytosanitary measures to achieve the appropriate level of

sanitary or phytosanitary protection, Members shall ensure that such measures are not more trade-restrictive than required to achieve their appropriate level of sanitary or phytosanitary protection, taking into account technical and economic feasibility. [3]

7. In cases where relevant scientific evidence is insufficient, a Member may provisionally adopt sanitary or phytosanitary measures on the basis of available pertinent information, including that from the relevant international organizations as well as from sanitary or phytosanitary measures applied by other Members. In such circumstances, Members shall seek to obtain the additional information necessary for a more objective assessment of risk and review the sanitary or phytosanitary measure accordingly within a reasonable period of time.

8. When a Member has reason to believe that a specific sanitary or phytosanitary measure introduced or maintained by another Member is constraining, or has the potential to constrain, its exports and the measure is not based on the relevant international standards, guidelines or recommendations, or such standards, guidelines or recommendations do not exist, an explanation of the reasons for such sanitary or phytosanitary measure may be requested and shall be provided by the Member maintaining the measure.

[...]

Annex A
Definitions [4]

1. *Sanitary or phytosanitary measure* – Any measure applied:

(a) to protect animal or plant life or health within the territory of the Member from risks arising from the entry, establishment or spread of pests, diseases, disease-carrying organisms or disease-causing organisms;

(b) to protect human or animal life or health within the territory of the Member from risks arising from additives, contaminants, toxins or disease-causing organisms in foods, beverages or feedstuffs;

(c) to protect human life or health within the territory of the Member from risks arising from diseases carried by animals, plants or products thereof, or from the entry, establishment or spread of pests; or

(d) to prevent or limit other damage within the territory of the Member from the entry, establishment or spread of pests.

---

[3] For purposes of paragraph 6 of Article 5, a measure is not more trade-restrictive than required unless there is another measure, reasonably available taking into account technical and economic feasibility, that achieves the appropriate level of sanitary or phytosanitary protection and is significantly less restrictive to trade.

[4] For the purpose of these definitions, 'animal' includes fish and wild fauna; 'plant' includes forests and wild flora; 'pests' include weeds; and 'contaminants' include pesticide and veterinary drug residues and extraneous matter.

Sanitary or phytosanitary measures include all relevant laws, decrees, regulations, requirements and procedures including, *inter alia*, end product criteria; processes and production methods; testing, inspection, certification and approval procedures; quarantine treatments including relevant requirements associated with the transport of animals or plants, or with the materials necessary for their survival during transport; provisions on relevant statistical methods, sampling procedures and methods of risk assessment; and packaging and labelling requirements directly related to food safety.

[...]

Agreement on Trade Related Aspects of Intellectual Property Rights (extracts)

[...]

Article 27
Patentable subject matter

1. Subject to the provisions of paragraphs 2 and 3, patents shall be available for any inventions, whether products or processes, in all fields of technology, provided that they are new, involve an inventive step and are capable of industrial application.[5] Subject to paragraph 4 of Article 65, paragraph 8 of Article 70 and paragraph 3 of this Article, patents shall be available and patent rights enjoyable without discrimination as to the place of invention, the field of technology and whether products are imported or locally produced.

2. Members may exclude from patentability inventions, the prevention within their territory of the commercial exploitation of which is necessary to protect *ordre public* or morality, including to protect human, animal or plant life or health or to avoid serious prejudice to the environment, provided that such exclusion is not made merely because the exploitation is prohibited by their law.

3. Members may also exclude from patentability:

(a) diagnostic, therapeutic and surgical methods for the treatment of humans or animals;

(b) plants and animals other than micro-organisms, and essentially biological processes for the production of plants or animals other than non-biological and microbiological processes. However, Members shall provide for the protection of plant varieties either by patents or by an effective *sui generis* system or by any combination thereof. The provisions of this subparagraph shall be reviewed four years after the date of entry into force of the WTO Agreement.

[...]

---

[5] For the purposes of this Article, the terms 'inventive step' and 'capable of industrial application' may be deemed by a Member to be synonymous with the terms 'non-obvious' and 'useful' respectively.

PART X

Environmental impact assessment and access to information

Convention on Environmental Impact Assessment in a Transboundary Context, 25 February 1991

Editorial note

The Convention on Environmental Impact Assessment in a Transboundary Context, which was adopted under the auspices of the UNECE, is designed to promote co-operation between States whose environmental, cultural or socio-economic conditions are likely to be affected (referred to as 'transboundary impact' in Article 1(viii)) by another State's activities.

The Convention requires States to carry out an environmental impact assessment procedure for all activities listed in Appendix I that are likely to have a 'significant adverse transboundary impact' (Article 2(2)). That procedure is to allow for public participation and must result in production of the environmental impact assessment documentation set out in Appendix II (Article 2(2)). Environmental impact assessments as described in the Convention are required for all activities listed in Appendix I which are likely to cause 'significant adverse transboundary impact' (Article 2(3)). Parties may decide, by mutual consent, to extend the Convention's application to activities not listed in Appendix I but which are likely none the less to cause a 'significant adverse transboundary impact' (Articles 2(5) and 3(7)). Criteria for determining 'significant adverse impact' are set out in Appendix III of the Convention (Article 2(5)). States planning an activity likely to cause a 'significant transboundary environmental impact' are required to notify other States likely to be affected of the proposed project (Articles 2(4) and 3(1)) and allow the public of affected States to participate in the environmental impact assessment procedure in the same manner as its own public (Article 2(6)). The Convention does not affect the rights of Parties to protect information covered by industrial or commercial secrecy or national security (Article 2(8)) or to enact more stringent measures than provided for by the Convention (Article 2(9)). The Convention also does not affect any obligations Parties may have under international law regarding transboundary impacts (Article 2(10)).

Once a Party is notified of a project likely to have a 'significant adverse transboundary impact' on it, it must decide whether it wishes to participate in the environmental assessment procedure (Article 3(3)). If it does choose to participate, an information exchange on the likely impacts must take place between the concerned States (Article 3(5) and (6)). In the event that a Party believes that it may be affected by a 'significant adverse transboundary impact' and has not been notified, the concerned Parties shall exchange information and hold discussions on whether that impact will likely take place (Article 3(7)). The Convention establishes a procedure for determining this issue in the event of a dispute between Parties (Appendix IV). Parties are to ensure that 'due account' is taken of the results of any environmental impact assessment in reaching a final decision on the proposed activity (Article 6(1)).

The Convention requires the Parties to meet as necessary to review the implementation of the Convention (Article 11). Dispute settlement can take place by any means chosen by the Parties involved, although the Convention allows for disputes to be submitted to the ICJ or to binding arbitration in accordance with Appendix VII (Article 15). Amendments require a three-fourths majority of those Parties present and voting and become binding on those Parties accepting them following ratification, approval or acceptance by three-fourths of the Parties (Article 14).

Date of signature: 25 February 1991

Entry into force: 10 September 1997

Depositary: Secretary-General of the United Nations

Contracting Parties: Albania, Armenia, Austria, Azerbaijan, Belgium, Bulgaria, Canada, Croatia, Cyprus, Czech Republic, Denmark, Estonia, European Community, Finland, France, Germany, Greece, Hungary, Ireland, Italy, Kazakhstan, Kyrgyzstan, Latvia, Liechtenstein, Lithuania, Luxembourg, Moldova (Republic of), Netherlands, Norway, Poland, Portugal, Romania, Slovakia, Slovenia, Spain, Sweden, Switzerland, The Former Yugoslav Republic of Macedonia, Ukraine, United Kingdom.

Website: www.unece.org/env/eia/

Convention on Environmental Impact Assessment in a Transboundary Context

The Parties to this Convention,

  Aware of the interrelationship between economic activities and their environmental consequences,

  Affirming the need to ensure environmentally sound and sustainable development,

Determined to enhance international co-operation in assessing environmental impact in particular in a transboundary context,

Mindful of the need and importance to develop anticipatory policies and of preventing, mitigating and monitoring significant adverse environmental impact in general and more specifically in a transboundary context,

Recalling the relevant provisions of the Charter of the United Nations, the Declaration of the Stockholm Conference on the Human Environment, the Final Act of the Conference on Security and Co-operation in Europe (CSCE) and the Concluding Documents of the Madrid and Vienna Meetings of Representatives of the Participating States of the CSCE,

Commending the ongoing activities of States to ensure that, through their national legal and administrative provisions and their national policies, environmental impact assessment is carried out,

Conscious of the need to give explicit consideration to environmental factors at an early stage in the decision-making process by applying environmental impact assessment, at all appropriate administrative levels, as a necessary tool to improve the quality of information presented to decision makers so that environmentally sound decisions can be made paying careful attention to minimizing significant adverse impact, particularly in a transboundary context,

Mindful of the efforts of international organizations to promote the use of environmental impact assessment both at the national and international levels, and taking into account work on environmental impact assessment carried out under the auspices of the United Nations Economic Commission for Europe, in particular results achieved by the Seminar on Environmental Impact Assessment (September 1987, Warsaw, Poland) as well as noting the Goals and Principles on environmental impact assessment adopted by the Governing Council of the United Nations Environment Programme, and the Ministerial Declaration on Sustainable Development (May 1990, Bergen, Norway),

Have agreed as follows:

Article 1
Definitions

For the purposes of this Convention,

(i) 'Parties' means, unless the text otherwise indicates, the Contracting Parties to this Convention;

(ii) 'Party of origin' means the Contracting Party or Parties to this Convention under whose jurisdiction a proposed activity is envisaged to take place;

(iii) 'Affected Party' means the Contracting Party or Parties to this Convention likely to be affected by the transboundary impact of a proposed activity;

(iv) 'Concerned Parties' means the Party of origin and the affected Party of an environmental impact assessment pursuant to this Convention;

(v) 'Proposed activity' means any activity or any major change to an activity subject to a decision of a competent authority in accordance with an applicable national procedure;

(vi) 'Environmental impact assessment' means a national procedure for evaluating the likely impact of a proposed activity on the environment;

(vii) 'Impact' means any effect caused by a proposed activity on the environment including human health and safety, flora, fauna, soil, air, water, climate, landscape and historical monuments or other physical structures or the interaction among these factors; it also includes effects on cultural heritage or socio-economic conditions resulting from alterations to those factors;

(viii) 'Transboundary impact' means any impact, not exclusively of a global nature, within an area under the jurisdiction of a Party caused by a proposed activity the physical origin of which is situated wholly or in part within the area under the jurisdiction of another Party;

(ix) 'Competent authority' means the national authority or authorities designated by a Party as responsible for performing the tasks covered by this Convention and/or the authority or authorities entrusted by a Party with decision-making powers regarding a proposed activity;

(x) 'The Public' means one or more natural or legal persons.

Article 2
General provisions

1. The Parties shall, either individually or jointly, take all appropriate and effective measures to prevent, reduce and control significant adverse transboundary environmental impact from proposed activities.

2. Each Party shall take the necessary legal, administrative or other measures to implement the provisions of this Convention, including, with respect to proposed activities listed in Appendix I that are likely to cause significant adverse transboundary impact, the establishment of an environmental impact assessment procedure that permits public participation and preparation of the environmental impact assessment documentation described in Appendix II.

3. The Party of origin shall ensure that in accordance with the provisions of this Convention an environmental impact assessment is undertaken prior to a decision to authorize or undertake a proposed activity listed in Appendix I that is likely to cause a significant adverse transboundary impact.

4. The Party of origin shall, consistent with the provisions of this Convention, ensure that affected Parties are notified of a proposed activity listed in Appendix I that is likely to cause a significant adverse transboundary impact.

5. Concerned Parties shall, at the initiative of any such Party, enter into discussions on whether one or more proposed activities not listed in Appendix I is or are likely to cause a significant adverse transboundary impact and thus

should be treated as if it or they were so listed. Where those Parties so agree, the activity or activities shall be thus treated. General guidance for identifying criteria to determine significant adverse impact is set forth in Appendix III.

6. The Party of origin shall provide, in accordance with the provisions of this Convention, an opportunity to the public in the areas likely to be affected to participate in relevant environmental impact assessment procedures regarding proposed activities and shall ensure that the opportunity provided to the public of the affected Party is equivalent to that provided to the public of the Party of origin.

7. Environmental impact assessments as required by this Convention shall, as a minimum requirement, be undertaken at the project level of the proposed activity. To the extent appropriate, the Parties shall endeavour to apply the principles of environmental impact assessment to policies, plans and programmes.

8. The provisions of this Convention shall not affect the right of Parties to implement national laws, regulations, administrative provisions or accepted legal practices protecting information the supply of which would be prejudicial to industrial and commercial secrecy or national security.

9. The provisions of this Convention shall not affect the right of particular Parties to implement, by bilateral or multilateral agreement where appropriate, more stringent measures than those of this Convention.

10. The provisions of this Convention shall not prejudice any obligations of the Parties under international law with regard to activities having or likely to have a transboundary impact.

Article 3
Notification

1. For a proposed activity listed in Appendix I that is likely to cause a significant adverse transboundary impact, the Party of origin shall, for the purposes of ensuring adequate and effective consultations under Article 5, notify any Party which it considers may be an affected Party as early as possible and no later than when informing its own public about that proposed activity.

2. This notification shall contain, *inter alia*:

(a) Information on the proposed activity, including any available information on its possible transboundary impact;
(b) The nature of the possible decision; and
(c) An indication of a reasonable time within which a response under paragraph 3 of this Article is required, taking into account the nature of the proposed activity; and may include the information set out in paragraph 5 of this Article.

3. The affected Party shall respond to the Party of origin within the time specified in the notification, acknowledging receipt of the notification, and

shall indicate whether it intends to participate in the environmental impact assessment procedure.

4. If the affected Party indicates that it does not intend to participate in the environmental impact assessment procedure, or if it does not respond within the time specified in the notification, the provisions in paragraphs 5, 6, 7 and 8 of this Article and in Articles 4 to 7 will not apply. In such circumstances the right of a Party of origin to determine whether to carry out an environmental impact assessment on the basis of its national law and practice is not prejudiced.

5. Upon receipt of a response from the affected Party indicating its desire to participate in the environmental impact assessment procedure, the Party of origin shall, if it has not already done so, provide to the affected Party:

(a) Relevant information regarding the environmental impact assessment procedure, including an indication of the time schedule for transmittal of comments; and

(b) Relevant information on the proposed activity and its possible significant adverse transboundary impact.

6. An affected Party shall, at the request of the Party of origin, provide the latter with reasonably obtainable information relating to the potentially affected environment under the jurisdiction of the affected Party, where such information is necessary for the preparation of the environmental impact assessment documentation. The information shall be furnished promptly and, as appropriate, through a joint body where one exists.

7. When a Party considers that it would be affected by a significant adverse transboundary impact of a proposed activity listed in Appendix I, and when no notification has taken place in accordance with paragraph 1 of this Article, the concerned Parties shall, at the request of the affected Party, exchange sufficient information for the purposes of holding discussions on whether there is likely to be a significant adverse transboundary impact. If those Parties agree that there is likely to be a significant adverse transboundary impact, the provisions of this Convention shall apply accordingly. If those Parties cannot agree whether there is likely to be a significant adverse transboundary impact, any such Party may submit that question to an inquiry commission in accordance with the provisions of Appendix IV to advise on the likelihood of significant adverse transboundary impact, unless they agree on another method of settling this question.

8. The concerned Parties shall ensure that the public of the affected Party in the areas likely to be affected be informed of, and be provided with possibilities for making comments or objections on, the proposed activity, and for the transmittal of these comments or objections to the competent authority of the Party of origin, either directly to this authority or, where appropriate, through the Party of origin.

Article 4
Preparation of the environmental impact assessment documentation

1. The environmental impact assessment documentation to be submitted to the competent authority of the Party of origin shall contain, as a minimum, the information described in Appendix II.

2. The Party of origin shall furnish the affected Party, as appropriate through a joint body where one exists, with the environmental impact assessment documentation. The concerned Parties shall arrange for distribution of the documentation to the authorities and the public of the affected Party in the areas likely to be affected and for the submission of comments to the competent authority of the Party of origin, either directly to this authority or, where appropriate, through the Party of origin within a reasonable time before the final decision is taken on the proposed activity.

Article 5
Consultations on the basis of the environmental
impact assessment documentation

The Party of origin shall, after completion of the environmental impact assessment documentation, without undue delay enter into consultations with the affected Party concerning, *inter alia*, the potential transboundary impact of the proposed activity and measures to reduce or eliminate its impact. Consultations may relate to:

(a) Possible alternatives to the proposed activity, including the no-action alternative and possible measures to mitigate significant adverse transboundary impact and to monitor the effects of such measures at the expense of the Party of origin;

(b) Other forms of possible mutual assistance in reducing any significant adverse transboundary impact of the proposed activity; and

(c) Any other appropriate matters relating to the proposed activity.

The Parties shall agree, at the commencement of such consultations, on a reasonable time-frame for the duration of the consultation period. Any such consultations may be conducted through an appropriate joint body, where one exists.

Article 6
Final decision

1. The Parties shall ensure that, in the final decision on the proposed activity, due account is taken of the outcome of the environmental impact assessment, including the environmental impact assessment documentation, as well as the comments thereon received pursuant to Article 3, paragraph 8 and Article 4, paragraph 2, and the outcome of the consultations as referred to in Article 5.

2. The Party of origin shall provide to the affected Party the final decision on the proposed activity along with the reasons and considerations on which it was based.

3. If additional information on the significant transboundary impact of a proposed activity, which was not available at the time a decision was made with respect to that activity and which could have materially affected the decision, becomes available to a concerned Party before work on that activity commences, that Party shall immediately inform the other concerned Party or Parties. If one of the concerned Parties so requests, consultations shall be held as to whether the decision needs to be revised.

Article 7
Post-project analysis

1. The concerned Parties, at the request of any such Party, shall determine whether, and if so to what extent, a post-project analysis shall be carried out, taking into account the likely significant adverse transboundary impact of the activity for which an environmental impact assessment has been undertaken pursuant to this Convention. Any post-project analysis undertaken shall include, in particular, the surveillance of the activity and the determination of any adverse transboundary impact. Such surveillance and determination may be undertaken with a view to achieving the objectives listed in Appendix V.

2. When, as a result of post-project analysis, the Party of origin or the affected Party has reasonable grounds for concluding that there is a significant adverse transboundary impact or factors have been discovered which may result in such an impact, it shall immediately inform the other Party. The concerned Parties shall then consult on necessary measures to reduce or eliminate the impact.

Article 8
Bilateral and multilateral co-operation

The Parties may continue existing or enter into new bilateral or multilateral agreements or other arrangements in order to implement their obligations under this Convention. Such agreements or other arrangements may be based on the elements listed in Appendix VI.

Article 9
Research programmes

The Parties shall give special consideration to the setting up, or intensification of, specific research programmes aimed at:

(a) Improving existing qualitative and quantitative methods for assessing the impacts of proposed activities;
(b) Achieving a better understanding of cause-effect relationships and their role in integrated environmental management;

(c) Analysing and monitoring the efficient implementation of decisions on proposed activities with the intention of minimizing or preventing impacts;

(d) Developing methods to stimulate creative approaches in the search for environmentally sound alternatives to proposed activities, production and consumption patterns;

(e) Developing methodologies for the application of the principles of environmental impact assessment at the macro-economic level.

The results of the programmes listed above shall be exchanged by the Parties.

Article 10
Status of the Appendices

The Appendices attached to this Convention form an integral part of the Convention.

Article 11
Meeting of Parties

1. The Parties shall meet, so far as possible, in connection with the annual sessions of the Senior Advisers to ECE Governments on Environmental and Water Problems. The first meeting of the Parties shall be convened not later than one year after the date of the entry into force of this Convention. Thereafter, meetings of the Parties shall be held at such other times as may be deemed necessary by a meeting of the Parties, or at the written request of any Party, provided that, within six months of the request being communicated to them by the secretariat, it is supported by at least one third of the Parties.

2. The Parties shall keep under continuous review the implementation of this Convention, and, with this purpose in mind, shall:

(a) Review the policies and methodological approaches to environmental impact assessment by the Parties with a view to further improving environmental impact assessment procedures in a transboundary context;

(b) Exchange information regarding experience gained in concluding and implementing bilateral and multilateral agreements or other arrangements regarding the use of environmental impact assessment in a transboundary context to which one or more of the Parties are party;

(c) Seek, where appropriate, the services of competent international bodies and scientific committees in methodological and technical aspects pertinent to the achievement of the purposes of this Convention;

(d) At their first meeting, consider and by consensus adopt rules of procedure for their meetings;

(e) Consider and, where necessary, adopt proposals for amendments to this Convention;

(f) Consider and undertake any additional action that may be required for the achievement of the purposes of this Convention.

Article 12
Right to vote

1. Each Party to this Convention shall have one vote.

2. Except as provided for in paragraph 1 of this Article, regional economic integration organizations, in matters within their competence, shall exercise their right to vote with a number of votes equal to the number of their member States which are Parties to this Convention. Such organizations shall not exercise their right to vote if their member States exercise theirs, and vice versa.

Article 13
Secretariat

The Executive Secretary of the Economic Commission for Europe shall carry out the following secretariat functions:

(a) The convening and preparing of meetings of the Parties;
(b) The transmission of reports and other information received in accordance with the provisions of this Convention to the Parties; and
(c) The performance of other functions as may be provided for in this Convention or as may be determined by the Parties.

Article 14
Amendments to the Convention

1. Any Party may propose amendments to this Convention.

2. Proposed amendments shall be submitted in writing to the secretariat, which shall communicate them to all Parties. The proposed amendments shall be discussed at the next meeting of the Parties, provided these proposals have been circulated by the secretariat to the Parties at least ninety days in advance.

3. The Parties shall make every effort to reach agreement on any proposed amendment to this Convention by consensus. If all efforts at consensus have been exhausted, and no agreement reached, the amendment shall as a last resort be adopted by a three-fourths majority vote of the Parties present and voting at the meeting.

4. Amendments to this Convention adopted in accordance with paragraph 3 of this Article shall be submitted by the Depositary to all Parties for ratification, approval or acceptance. They shall enter into force for Parties having ratified, approved or accepted them on the ninetieth day after the receipt by the Depositary of notification of their ratification, approval or acceptance by at least three fourths of these Parties. Thereafter they shall enter into force for any other Party on the ninetieth day after that Party deposits its instrument of ratification, approval or acceptance of the amendments.

5. For the purpose of this Article, 'Parties present and voting' means Parties present and casting an affirmative or negative vote.

6. The voting procedure set forth in paragraph 3 of this Article is not intended to constitute a precedent for future agreements negotiated within the Economic Commission for Europe.

Article 15
Settlement of disputes

1. If a dispute arises between two or more Parties about the interpretation or application of this Convention, they shall seek a solution by negotiation or by any other method of dispute settlement acceptable to the parties to the dispute.

2. When signing, ratifying, accepting, approving or acceding to this Convention, or at any time thereafter, a Party may declare in writing to the Depositary that for a dispute not resolved in accordance with paragraph 1 of this Article, it accepts one or both of the following means of dispute settlement as compulsory in relation to any Party accepting the same obligation:

(a) Submission of the dispute to the International Court of Justice;
(b) Arbitration in accordance with the procedure set out in Appendix VII.

3. If the parties to the dispute have accepted both means of dispute settlement referred to in paragraph 2 of this Article, the dispute may be submitted only to the International Court of Justice, unless the parties agree otherwise.

Article 16
Signature

This Convention shall be open for signature at Espoo (Finland) from 25 February to 1 March 1991 and thereafter at United Nations Headquarters in New York until 2 September 1991 by States members of the Economic Commission for Europe as well as States having consultative status with the Economic Commission for Europe pursuant to paragraph 8 of the Economic and Social Council resolution 36 (IV) of 28 March 1947, and by regional economic integration organizations constituted by sovereign States members of the Economic Commission for Europe to which their member States have transferred competence in respect of matters governed by this Convention, including the competence to enter into treaties in respect of these matters.

Article 17
Ratification, acceptance, approval and accession

1. This Convention shall be subject to ratification, acceptance or approval by signatory States and regional economic integration organizations.

2. This Convention shall be open for accession as from 3 September 1991 by the States and organizations referred to in Article 16.

3. The instruments of ratification, acceptance, approval or accession shall be deposited with the Secretary-General of the United Nations, who shall perform the functions of Depositary.

4. Any organization referred to in Article 16 which becomes a Party to this Convention without any of its member States being a Party shall be bound by all the obligations under this Convention. In the case of such organizations, one or more of whose member States is a Party to this Convention, the organization and its member States shall decide on their respective responsibilities for the performance of their obligations under this Convention. In such cases, the organization and the member States shall not be entitled to exercise rights under this Convention concurrently.

5. In their instruments of ratification, acceptance, approval or accession, the regional economic integration organizations referred to in Article 16 shall declare the extent of their competence with respect to the matters governed by this Convention. These organizations shall also inform the Depositary of any relevant modification to the extent of their competence.

Article 18
Entry into force

1. This Convention shall enter into force on the ninetieth day after the date of deposit of the sixteenth instrument of ratification, acceptance, approval or accession.

2. For the purposes of paragraph 1 of this Article, any instrument deposited by a regional economic integration organization shall not be counted as additional to those deposited by States members of such an organization.

3. For each State or organization referred to in Article 16 which ratifies, accepts or approves this Convention or accedes thereto after the deposit of the sixteenth instrument of ratification, acceptance, approval or accession, this Convention shall enter into force on the ninetieth day after the date of deposit by such State or organization of its instrument of ratification, acceptance, approval or accession.

Article 19
Withdrawal

At any time after four years from the date on which this Convention has come into force with respect to a Party, that Party may withdraw from this Convention by giving written notification to the Depositary. Any such withdrawal shall take effect on the ninetieth day after the date of its receipt by the Depositary. Any such withdrawal shall not affect the application of Articles 3 to 6 of this Convention to a proposed activity in respect of which a notification has been made pursuant to Article 3, paragraph 1, or a request has been made pursuant to Article 3, paragraph 7, before such withdrawal took effect.

Article 20
Authentic texts

The original of this Convention, of which the English, French and Russian texts are equally authentic, shall be deposited with the Secretary-General of the United Nations.

IN WITNESS WHEREOF the undersigned, being duly authorized thereto, have signed this Convention.

DONE at Espoo (Finland), this twenty-fifth day of February one thousand nine hundred and ninety-one.

Appendix I
List of activities

1. Crude oil refineries (excluding undertakings manufacturing only lubricants from crude oil) and installations for the gasification and liquefaction of 500 tonnes or more of coal or bituminous shale per day.
2. Thermal power stations and other combustion installations with a heat output of 300 megawatts or more and nuclear power stations and other nuclear reactors (except research installations for the production and conversion of fissionable and fertile materials, whose maximum power does not exceed 1 kilowatt continuous thermal load).
3. Installations solely designed for the production or enrichment of nuclear fuels, for the reprocessing of irradiated nuclear fuels or for the storage, disposal and processing of radioactive waste.
4. Major installations for the initial smelting of cast-iron and steel and for the production of non-ferrous metals.
5. Installations for the extraction of asbestos and for the processing and transformation of asbestos and products containing asbestos: for asbestos-cement products, with an annual production of more than 20,000 tonnes finished product; for friction material, with an annual production of more than 50 tonnes finished product; and for other asbestos utilization of more than 200 tonnes per year.
6. Integrated chemical installations.
7. Construction of motorways, express roads* and lines for long-distance railway traffic and of airports with a basic runway length of 2,100 metres or more.
8. Large-diameter oil and gas pipelines.
9. Trading ports and also inland waterways and ports for inland-waterway traffic which permit the passage of vessels of over 1,350 tonnes.

---

* For the purposes of this Convention:
  - 'Motorway' means a road specially designed and built for motor traffic, which does not serve properties bordering on it, and which:
    (a) Is provided, except at special points or temporarily, with separate carriageways for the two directions of traffic, separated from each other by a dividing strip not intended for traffic or, exceptionally, by other means;
    (b) Does not cross at level with any road, railway or tramway track, or footpath; and
    (c) Is specially sign-posted as a motorway.
  - 'Express road' means a road reserved for motor traffic accessible only from interchanges or controlled junctions and on which, in particular, stopping and parking are prohibited on the running carriageway(s).

10. Waste-disposal installations for the incineration, chemical treatment or landfill of toxic and dangerous wastes.
11. Large dams and reservoirs.
12. Groundwater abstraction activities in cases where the annual volume of water to be abstracted amounts to 10 million cubic metres or more.
13. Pulp and paper manufacturing of 200 air-dried metric tonnes or more per day.
14. Major mining, on-site extraction and processing of metal ores or coal.
15. Offshore hydrocarbon production.
16. Major storage facilities for petroleum, petrochemical and chemical products.
17. Deforestation of large areas.

Appendix II
Content of the environmental impact assessment documentation

Information to be included in the environmental impact assessment documentation shall, as a minimum, contain, in accordance with Article 4:

(a) A description of the proposed activity and its purpose;
(b) A description, where appropriate, of reasonable alternatives (for example, locational or technological) to the proposed activity and also the no-action alternative;
(c) A description of the environment likely to be significantly affected by the proposed activity and its alternatives;
(d) A description of the potential environmental impact of the proposed activity and its alternatives and an estimation of its significance;
(e) A description of mitigation measures to keep adverse environmental impact to a minimum;
(f) An explicit indication of predictive methods and underlying assumptions as well as the relevant environmental data used;
(g) An identification of gaps in knowledge and uncertainties encountered in compiling the required information;
(h) Where appropriate, an outline for monitoring and management programmes and any plans for post-project analysis; and
(i) A non-technical summary including a visual presentation as appropriate (maps, graphs, etc.).

Appendix III
General criteria to assist in the determination of the environmental significance of activities not listed in Appendix I

1. In considering proposed activities to which Article 2, paragraph 5, applies, the concerned Parties may consider whether the activity is likely to have a

significant adverse transboundary impact in particular by virtue of one or more of the following criteria:

(a) Size: proposed activities which are large for the type of the activity;
(b) Location: proposed activities which are located in or close to an area of special environmental sensitivity or importance (such as wetlands designated under the Ramsar Convention, national parks, nature reserves, sites of special scientific interest, or sites of archaeological, cultural or historical importance); also, proposed activities in locations where the characteristics of proposed development would be likely to have significant effects on the population;
(c) Effects: proposed activities with particularly complex and potentially adverse effects, including those giving rise to serious effects on humans or on valued species or organisms, those which threaten the existing or potential use of an affected area and those causing additional loading which cannot be sustained by the carrying capacity of the environment.

2. The concerned Parties shall consider for this purpose proposed activities which are located close to an international frontier as well as more remote proposed activities which could give rise to significant transboundary effects far removed from the site of development.

Appendix IV
Inquiry procedure

1. The requesting Party or Parties shall notify the secretariat that it or they submit(s) the question of whether a proposed activity listed in Appendix I is likely to have a significant adverse transboundary impact to an inquiry commission established in accordance with the provisions of this Appendix. This notification shall state the subject-matter of the inquiry. The secretariat shall notify immediately all Parties to this Convention of this submission.

2. The inquiry commission shall consist of three members. Both the requesting party and the other party to the inquiry procedure shall appoint a scientific or technical expert, and the two experts so appointed shall designate by common agreement the third expert, who shall be the president of the inquiry commission. The latter shall not be a national of one of the parties to the inquiry procedure, nor have his or her usual place of residence in the territory of one of these parties, nor be employed by any of them, nor have dealt with the matter in any other capacity.

3. If the president of the inquiry commission has not been designated within two months of the appointment of the second expert, the Executive Secretary of the Economic Commission for Europe shall, at the request of either party, designate the president within a further two-month period.

4. If one of the parties to the inquiry procedure does not appoint an expert within one month of its receipt of the notification by the secretariat, the other

party may inform the Executive Secretary of the Economic Commission for Europe, who shall designate the president of the inquiry commission within a further two-month period. Upon designation, the president of the inquiry commission shall request the party which has not appointed an expert to do so within one month. After such a period, the president shall inform the Executive Secretary of the Economic Commission for Europe, who shall make this appointment within a further two-month period.

5. The inquiry commission shall adopt its own rules of procedure.

6. The inquiry commission may take all appropriate measures in order to carry out its functions.

7. The parties to the inquiry procedure shall facilitate the work of the inquiry commission and, in particular, using all means at their disposal, shall:

(a) Provide it with all relevant documents, facilities and information; and
(b) Enable it, where necessary, to call witnesses or experts and receive their evidence.

8. The parties and the experts shall protect the confidentiality of any information they receive in confidence during the work of the inquiry commission.

9. If one of the parties to the inquiry procedure does not appear before the inquiry commission or fails to present its case, the other party may request the inquiry commission to continue the proceedings and to complete its work. Absence of a party or failure of a party to present its case shall not constitute a bar to the continuation and completion of the work of the inquiry commission.

10. Unless the inquiry commission determines otherwise because of the particular circumstances of the matter, the expenses of the inquiry commission, including the remuneration of its members, shall be borne by the parties to the inquiry procedure in equal shares. The inquiry commission shall keep a record of all its expenses, and shall furnish a final statement thereof to the parties.

11. Any Party having an interest of a factual nature in the subject-matter of the inquiry procedure, and which may be affected by an opinion in the matter, may intervene in the proceedings with the consent of the inquiry commission.

12. The decisions of the inquiry commission on matters of procedure shall be taken by majority vote of its members. The final opinion of the inquiry commission shall reflect the view of the majority of its members and shall include any dissenting view.

13. The inquiry commission shall present its final opinion within two months of the date on which it was established unless it finds it necessary to extend this time limit for a period which should not exceed two months.

14. The final opinion of the inquiry commission shall be based on accepted scientific principles. The final opinion shall be transmitted by the inquiry commission to the parties to the inquiry procedure and to the secretariat.

Appendix V
Post-project analysis

Objectives include:

(a) Monitoring compliance with the conditions as set out in the authorization or approval of the activity and the effectiveness of mitigation measures;

(b) Review of an impact for proper management and in order to cope with uncertainties;

(c) Verification of past predictions in order to transfer experience to future activities of the same type.

Appendix VI
Elements for bilateral and multilateral co-operation

1. Concerned Parties may set up, where appropriate, institutional arrangements or enlarge the mandate of existing institutional arrangements within the framework of bilateral and multilateral agreements in order to give full effect to this Convention.

2. Bilateral and multilateral agreements or other arrangements may include:

(a) Any additional requirements for the implementation of this Convention, taking into account the specific conditions of the subregion concerned;

(b) Institutional, administrative and other arrangements, to be made on a reciprocal and equivalent basis;

(c) Harmonization of their policies and measures for the protection of the environment in order to attain the greatest possible similarity in standards and methods related to the implementation of environmental impact assessment;

(d) Developing, improving, and/or harmonizing methods for the identification, measurement, prediction and assessment of impacts, and for post-project analysis;

(e) Developing and/or improving methods and programmes for the collection, analysis, storage and timely dissemination of comparable data regarding environmental quality in order to provide input into environmental impact assessment;

(f) The establishment of threshold levels and more specified criteria for defining the significance of transboundary impacts related to the location, nature or size of proposed activities, for which environmental impact assessment in accordance with the provisions of this Convention shall be applied; and the establishment of critical loads of transboundary pollution;

(g) Undertaking, where appropriate, joint environmental impact assessment, development of joint monitoring programmes, intercalibration of monitoring devices and harmonization of methodologies with a view to rendering the data and information obtained compatible.

Appendix VII
Arbitration

1. The claimant Party or Parties shall notify the secretariat that the Parties have agreed to submit the dispute to arbitration pursuant to Article 15, paragraph 2, of this Convention. The notification shall state the subject-matter of arbitration and include, in particular, the Articles of this Convention, the interpretation or application of which are at issue. The secretariat shall forward the information received to all Parties to this Convention.

2. The arbitral tribunal shall consist of three members. Both the claimant Party or Parties and the other Party or Parties to the dispute shall appoint an arbitrator, and the two arbitrators so appointed shall designate by common agreement the third arbitrator, who shall be the president of the arbitral tribunal. The latter shall not be a national of one of the parties to the dispute, nor have his or her usual place of residence in the territory of one of these parties, nor be employed by any of them, nor have dealt with the case in any other capacity.

3. If the president of the arbitral tribunal has not been designated within two months of the appointment of the second arbitrator, the Executive Secretary of the Economic Commission for Europe shall, at the request of either party to the dispute, designate the president within a further two-month period.

4. If one of the parties to the dispute does not appoint an arbitrator within two months of the receipt of the request, the other party may inform the Executive Secretary of the Economic Commission for Europe, who shall designate the president of the arbitral tribunal within a further two-month period. Upon designation, the president of the arbitral tribunal shall request the party which has not appointed an arbitrator to do so within two months. After such a period, the president shall inform the Executive Secretary of the Economic Commission for Europe, who shall make this appointment within a further two-month period.

5. The arbitral tribunal shall render its decision in accordance with international law and in accordance with the provisions of this Convention.

6. Any arbitral tribunal constituted under the provisions set out herein shall draw up its own rules of procedure.

7. The decisions of the arbitral tribunal, both on procedure and on substance, shall be taken by majority vote of its members.

8. The tribunal may take all appropriate measures in order to establish the facts.

9. The parties to the dispute shall facilitate the work of the arbitral tribunal and, in particular, using all means at their disposal, shall:

(a) Provide it with all relevant documents, facilities and information; and
(b) Enable it, where necessary, to call witnesses or experts and receive their evidence.

10. The parties and the arbitrators shall protect the confidentiality of any information they receive in confidence during the proceedings of the arbitral tribunal.

11. The arbitral tribunal may, at the request of one of the parties, recommend interim measures of protection.

12. If one of the parties to the dispute does not appear before the arbitral tribunal or fails to defend its case, the other party may request the tribunal to continue the proceedings and to render its final decision. Absence of a party or failure of a party to defend its case shall not constitute a bar to the proceedings. Before rendering its final decision, the arbitral tribunal must satisfy itself that the claim is well founded in fact and law.

13. The arbitral tribunal may hear and determine counter-claims arising directly out of the subject-matter of the dispute.

14. Unless the arbitral tribunal determines otherwise because of the particular circumstances of the case, the expenses of the tribunal, including the remuneration of its members, shall be borne by the parties to the dispute in equal shares. The tribunal shall keep a record of all its expenses, and shall furnish a final statement thereof to the parties.

15. Any Party to this Convention having an interest of a legal nature in the subject-matter of the dispute, and which may be affected by a decision in the case, may intervene in the proceedings with the consent of the tribunal.

16. The arbitral tribunal shall render its award within five months of the date on which it is established unless it finds it necessary to extend the time limit for a period which should not exceed five months.

17. The award of the arbitral tribunal shall be accompanied by a statement of reasons. It shall be final and binding upon all parties to the dispute. The award will be transmitted by the arbitral tribunal to the parties to the dispute and to the secretariat. The secretariat will forward the information received to all Parties to this Convention.

18. Any dispute which may arise between the parties concerning the interpretation or execution of the award may be submitted by either party to the arbitral tribunal which made the award or, if the latter cannot be seized thereof, to another tribunal constituted for this purpose in the same manner as the first.

Protocol on Strategic Environmental Assessment, 21 May 2003

Editorial note

The Protocol on Strategic Environmental Assessment (SEA) was adopted at an Extraordinary meeting of the Parties to the EIA Convention during the Ministerial 'Environment for Europe' Conference (21–23 May 2003, Kiev, Ukraine) to ensure that environmental, including health, considerations are taken into account in the development of plans and programmes, policies and legislation (Article 1 (a) and (b)). The Protocol's objective is to establish clear, transparent and effective procedures for SEA, providing for public participation and to further sustainable development (Article 1(c) (d) and (e)). The Protocol defines plans and programmes (Article 2(5)), SEA (Article 2(6)), environmental, including health, effects (Article 2(7)) and the public (Article 2(8)).

Each Party must take the necessary legislative and administrative measures to implement the Protocol and must ensure that its officials assist and provide guidance to the public in the matters covered by the Protocol (Article 3 (1) and (2)). Persons exercising their rights in conformity with the Protocol must not be penalised or harassed in any way and the public should be able to exercise the rights conferred by the Protocol without discrimination as to citizenship, nationality or domicile and, in the case of companies, without discrimination as to where they are registered or effectively carry out their activities (Article 3(6) and (7)).

Parties shall ensure that 'plans and programmes' undergo a SEA when they are likely to have significant environmental, including health, effects (Article 4(1)). SEAs shall be carried out for plans and programmes which are prepared for agriculture, forestry, fisheries, energy, industry including mining, transport, regional development, waste management, water management, telecommunications, tourism, town and country planning or land use, and which set the framework for future development consent for projects listed in Annex I and any other project listed in Annex II that requires an environmental impact assessment under national legislation (Article 4(2)). Parties may determine that plans and programmes other than those mentioned in Article 4(2) require SEA (Article 4(3)), according to the provisions laid out in Article 5(1). Plans and programmes whose sole purpose is to serve national defence or civil emergencies and financial or budget plans and programmes are excluded from the application of the Protocol (Article 4(5)).

Parties shall ensure that an environmental report is prepared for plans and programmes subject to SEA (Article 7(1)). The environmental report shall identify, describe and evaluate the likely significant environmental, including health, effects of implementing the plan or programme and its reasonable alternatives (Article 7(2)). The report shall contain the information specified in Annex IV to the Protocol (Article 7(2)). Parties shall establish arrangements for the determination of the relevant information to be included in the environmental report in accordance with Article 7(2) (Article 6).

Parties shall ensure early, timely and effective opportunities for public participation (Article 8) and shall designate the environmental and health authorities which are to be consulted in an early, timely and effective manner (Article 9). When the plan or programme is likely to have significant transboundary effects, the Party of origin must notify the affected Party as early as possible before the adoption of the plan or programme (Article 10).

Parties shall ensure that when a plan or programme is adopted due account is taken of the conclusions of the environmental report, the measures to prevent, reduce or mitigate the adverse effects identified in the environmental report and the comments received by the public, by the relevant environmental and health authorities and through transboundary consultation (Article 11(1)). The adopted plan or programme, with a summarising statement, is to be made available to the public, the authorities and the other Parties consulted under Article 10 (Article 11). The Protocol also requires monitoring (Article 12). Parties shall endeavour to ensure that environmental, including health, concerns are considered and integrated to the extent appropriate in the preparation of its proposals for policies and legislation that are likely to have significant effects on the environment, including health (Article 13).

The meeting of the Parties to the Protocol is held with the meeting of the Parties of the Convention on Environmental Impact Assessment in a Transboundary Context (Article 14). The Protocol shall enter into force on the ninetieth day after the deposit of the sixteenth instrument of ratification, acceptance, approval or accession (Article 24).

Date of signature: 21 May 2003

Entry into force: Not yet in force

Depositary: Secretary-General of the United Nations

Contracting Parties: None at present

Website: www.unece.org/env/eia/

Protocol on Strategic Environmental Assessment

The Parties to this Protocol,

Recognizing the importance of integrating environmental, including health, considerations into the preparation and adoption of plans and programmes and, to the extent appropriate, policies and legislation,

Committing themselves to promoting sustainable development and therefore basing themselves on the conclusions of the United Nations Conference on Environment and Development (Rio de Janeiro, Brazil, 1992), in particular principles 4 and 10 of the Rio Declaration on Environment and Development and Agenda 21, as well as the outcome of the third Ministerial Conference on Environment and Health (London, 1999) and the World Summit on Sustainable Development (Johannesburg, South Africa, 2002),

Bearing in mind the Convention on Environmental Impact Assessment in a Transboundary Context, done at Espoo, Finland, on 25 February 1991, and decision II/9 of its Parties at Sofia on 26 and 27 February 2001, in which it was decided to prepare a legally binding protocol on strategic environmental assessment,

Recognizing that strategic environmental assessment should have an important role in the preparation and adoption of plans, programmes, and, to the extent appropriate, policies and legislation, and that the wider application of the principles of environmental impact assessment to plans, programmes, policies and legislation will further strengthen the systematic analysis of their significant environmental effects,

Acknowledging the Convention on Access to Information, Public Participation in Decision-making and Access to Justice in Environmental Matters, done at Aarhus, Denmark, on 25 June 1998, and taking note of the relevant paragraphs of the Lucca Declaration, adopted at the first meeting of its Parties,

Conscious, therefore, of the importance of providing for public participation in strategic environmental assessment,

Acknowledging the benefits to the health and well-being of present and future generations that will follow if the need to protect and improve people's health is taken into account as an integral part of strategic environmental assessment, and recognizing the work led by the World Health Organization in this respect,

Mindful of the need for and importance of enhancing international cooperation in assessing the transboundary environmental, including health, effects of proposed plans and programmes, and, to the extent appropriate, policies and legislation,

Have agreed as follows:

Article 1
Objective

The objective of this Protocol is to provide for a high level of protection of the environment, including health, by:

(a) Ensuring that environmental, including health, considerations are thoroughly taken into account in the development of plans and programmes;

(b) Contributing to the consideration of environmental, including health, concerns in the preparation of policies and legislation;

(c) Establishing clear, transparent and effective procedures for strategic environmental assessment;

(d) Providing for public participation in strategic environmental assessment; and

(e) Integrating by these means environmental, including health, concerns into measures and instruments designed to further sustainable development.

Article 2
Definitions

For the purposes of this Protocol,

1. 'Convention' means the Convention on Environmental Impact Assessment in a Transboundary Context;

2. 'Party' means, unless the text indicates otherwise, a Contracting Party to this Protocol;

3. 'Party of origin' means a Party or Parties to this Protocol within whose jurisdiction the preparation of a plan or programme is envisaged;

4. 'Affected Party' means a Party or Parties to this Protocol likely to be affected by the transboundary environmental, including health, effects of a plan or programme;

5. 'Plans and programmes' means plans and programmes and any modifications to them that are:
   (a) Required by legislative, regulatory or administrative provisions; and
   (b) Subject to preparation and/or adoption by an authority or prepared by an authority for adoption, through a formal procedure, by a parliament or a government;

6. 'Strategic environmental assessment' means the evaluation of the likely environmental, including health, effects, which comprises the determination of the scope of an environmental report and its preparation, the carrying-out of public participation and consultations, and the taking into account of the environmental report and the results of the public participation and consultations in a plan or programme;

7. 'Environmental, including health, effect' means any effect on the environment, including human health, flora, fauna, biodiversity, soil, climate, air, water, landscape, natural sites, material assets, cultural heritage and the interaction among these factors;

8. 'The public' means one or more natural or legal persons and, in accordance with national legislation or practice, their associations, organizations or groups.

Article 3
General provisions

1. Each Party shall take the necessary legislative, regulatory and other appropriate measures to implement the provisions of this Protocol within a clear, transparent framework.

2. Each Party shall endeavour to ensure that officials and authorities assist and provide guidance to the public in matters covered by this Protocol.

3. Each Party shall provide for appropriate recognition of and support to associations, organizations or groups promoting environmental, including health, protection in the context of this Protocol.

4. The provisions of this Protocol shall not affect the right of a Party to maintain or introduce additional measures in relation to issues covered by this Protocol.

5. Each Party shall promote the objectives of this Protocol in relevant international decision-making processes and within the framework of relevant international organizations.

6. Each Party shall ensure that persons exercising their rights in conformity with the provisions of this Protocol shall not be penalized, persecuted or harassed in any way for their involvement. This provision shall not affect the powers of national courts to award reasonable costs in judicial proceedings.

7. Within the scope of the relevant provisions of this Protocol, the public shall be able to exercise its rights without discrimination as to citizenship, nationality or domicile and, in the case of a legal person, without discrimination as to where it has its registered seat or an effective centre of its activities.

Article 4
Field of application concerning plans and programmes

1. Each Party shall ensure that a strategic environmental assessment is carried out for plans and programmes referred to in paragraphs 2, 3 and 4 which are likely to have significant environmental, including health, effects.

2. A strategic environmental assessment shall be carried out for plans and programmes which are prepared for agriculture, forestry, fisheries, energy, industry including mining, transport, regional development, waste management, water management, telecommunications, tourism, town and country planning or land use, and which set the framework for future development consent for projects listed in annex I and any other project listed in annex II that requires an environmental impact assessment under national legislation.

3. For plans and programmes other than those subject to paragraph 2 which set the framework for future development consent of projects, a strategic environmental assessment shall be carried out where a Party so determines according to article 5, paragraph 1.

4. For plans and programmes referred to in paragraph 2 which determine the use of small areas at local level and for minor modifications to plans and programmes referred to in paragraph 2, a strategic environmental assessment

shall be carried out only where a Party so determines according to article 5, paragraph 1.

5. The following plans and programmes are not subject to this Protocol:

(a) Plans and programmes whose sole purpose is to serve national defence or civil emergencies;

(b) Financial or budget plans and programmes.

Article 5
Screening

1. Each Party shall determine whether plans and programmes referred to in article 4, paragraphs 3 and 4, are likely to have significant environmental, including health, effects either through a case-by-case examination or by specifying types of plans and programmes or by combining both approaches. For this purpose each Party shall in all cases take into account the criteria set out in annex III.

2. Each Party shall ensure that the environmental and health authorities referred to in article 9, paragraph 1, are consulted when applying the procedures referred to in paragraph 1 above.

3. To the extent appropriate, each Party shall endeavour to provide opportunities for the participation of the public concerned in the screening of plans and programmes under this article.

4. Each Party shall ensure timely public availability of the conclusions pursuant to paragraph 1, including the reasons for not requiring a strategic environmental assessment, whether by public notices or by other appropriate means, such as electronic media.

Article 6
Scoping

1. Each Party shall establish arrangements for the determination of the relevant information to be included in the environmental report in accordance with article 7, paragraph 2.

2. Each Party shall ensure that the environmental and health authorities referred to in article 9, paragraph 1, are consulted when determining the relevant information to be included in the environmental report.

3. To the extent appropriate, each Party shall endeavour to provide opportunities for the participation of the public concerned when determining the relevant information to be included in the environmental report.

Article 7
Environmental report

1. For plans and programmes subject to strategic environmental assessment, each Party shall ensure that an environmental report is prepared.

2. The environmental report shall, in accordance with the determination under article 6, identify, describe and evaluate the likely significant environmental, including health, effects of implementing the plan or programme and its reasonable alternatives. The report shall contain such information specified in annex IV as may reasonably be required, taking into account:

(a) Current knowledge and methods of assessment;
(b) The contents and the level of detail of the plan or programme and its stage in the decision-making process;
(c) The interests of the public; and
(d) The information needs of the decision-making body.

3. Each Party shall ensure that environmental reports are of sufficient quality to meet the requirements of this Protocol.

Article 8
Public participation

1. Each Party shall ensure early, timely and effective opportunities for public participation, when all options are open, in the strategic environmental assessment of plans and programmes.

2. Each Party, using electronic media or other appropriate means, shall ensure the timely public availability of the draft plan or programme and the environmental report.

3. Each Party shall ensure that the public concerned, including relevant non-governmental organizations, is identified for the purposes of paragraphs 1 and 4.

4. Each Party shall ensure that the public referred to in paragraph 3 has the opportunity to express its opinion on the draft plan or programme and the environmental report within a reasonable time frame.

5. Each Party shall ensure that the detailed arrangements for informing the public and consulting the public concerned are determined and made publicly available. For this purpose, each Party shall take into account to the extent appropriate the elements listed in annex V.

Article 9
Consultation with environmental and health authorities

1. Each Party shall designate the authorities to be consulted which, by reason of their specific environmental or health responsibilities, are likely to be concerned by the environmental, including health, effects of the implementation of the plan or programme.

2. The draft plan or programme and the environmental report shall be made available to the authorities referred to in paragraph 1.

3. Each Party shall ensure that the authorities referred to in paragraph 1 are given, in an early, timely and effective manner, the opportunity to express their opinion on the draft plan or programme and the environmental report.

4. Each Party shall determine the detailed arrangements for informing and consulting the environmental and health authorities referred to in paragraph 1.

Article 10
Transboundary consultations

1. Where a Party of origin considers that the implementation of a plan or programme is likely to have significant transboundary environmental, including health, effects or where a Party likely to be significantly affected so requests, the Party of origin shall as early as possible before the adoption of the plan or programme notify the affected Party.

2. This notification shall contain, *inter alia*:

(a) The draft plan or programme and the environmental report including information on its possible transboundary environmental, including health, effects; and
(b) Information regarding the decision-making procedure, including an indication of a reasonable time schedule for the transmission of comments.

3. The affected Party shall, within the time specified in the notification, indicate to the Party of origin whether it wishes to enter into consultations before the adoption of the plan or programme and, if it so indicates, the Parties concerned shall enter into consultations concerning the likely transboundary environmental, including health, effects of implementing the plan or programme and the measures envisaged to prevent, reduce or mitigate adverse effects.

4. Where such consultations take place, the Parties concerned shall agree on detailed arrangements to ensure that the public concerned and the authorities referred to in article 9, paragraph 1, in the affected Party are informed and given an opportunity to forward their opinion on the draft plan or programme and the environmental report within a reasonable time frame.

Article 11
Decision

1. Each Party shall ensure that when a plan or programme is adopted due account is taken of:

(a) The conclusions of the environmental report;
(b) The measures to prevent, reduce or mitigate the adverse effects identified in the environmental report; and
(c) The comments received in accordance with articles 8 to 10.

2. Each Party shall ensure that, when a plan or programme is adopted, the public, the authorities referred to in article 9, paragraph 1, and the Parties consulted according to article 10 are informed, and that the plan or programme is made available to them together with a statement summarizing how the environmental, including health, considerations have been integrated into it, how the comments received in accordance with articles 8 to 10 have been taken into account and the reasons for adopting it in the light of the reasonable alternatives considered.

Article 12
Monitoring

1. Each Party shall monitor the significant environmental, including health, effects of the implementation of the plans and programmes, adopted under article 11 in order, *inter alia*, to identify, at an early stage, unforeseen adverse effects and to be able to undertake appropriate remedial action.

2. The results of the monitoring undertaken shall be made available, in accordance with national legislation, to the authorities referred to in article 9, paragraph 1, and to the public.

Article 13
Policies and legislation

1. Each Party shall endeavour to ensure that environmental, including health, concerns are considered and integrated to the extent appropriate in the preparation of its proposals for policies and legislation that are likely to have significant effects on the environment, including health.

2. In applying paragraph 1, each Party shall consider the appropriate principles and elements of this Protocol.

3. Each Party shall determine, where appropriate, the practical arrangements for the consideration and integration of environmental, including health, concerns in accordance with paragraph 1, taking into account the need for transparency in decision-making.

4. Each Party shall report to the Meeting of the Parties to the Convention serving as the Meeting of the Parties to this Protocol on its application of this article.

Article 14
The Meeting of the Parties to the Convention serving as the Meeting of the Parties to the Protocol

1. The Meeting of the Parties to the Convention shall serve as the Meeting of the Parties to this Protocol. The first meeting of the Parties to the Convention serving as the Meeting of the Parties to this Protocol shall be convened not later than one year after the date of entry into force of this Protocol, and in

conjunction with a meeting of the Parties to the Convention, if a meeting of the latter is scheduled within that period. Subsequent meetings of the Parties to the Convention serving as the Meeting of the Parties to this Protocol shall be held in conjunction with meetings of the Parties to the Convention, unless otherwise decided by the Meeting of the Parties to the Convention serving as the Meeting of the Parties to this Protocol.

2. Parties to the Convention which are not Parties to this Protocol may participate as observers in the proceedings of any session of the Meeting of the Parties to the Convention serving as the Meeting of the Parties to this Protocol. When the Meeting of the Parties to the Convention serves as the Meeting of the Parties to this Protocol, decisions under this Protocol shall be taken only by the Parties to this Protocol.

3. When the Meeting of the Parties to the Convention serves as the Meeting of the Parties to this Protocol, any member of the Bureau of the Meeting of the Parties representing a Party to the Convention that is not, at that time, a Party to this Protocol shall be replaced by another member to be elected by and from amongst the Parties to this Protocol.

4. The Meeting of the Parties to the Convention serving as the Meeting of the Parties to this Protocol shall keep under regular review the implementation of this Protocol and, for this purpose, shall:

(a) Review policies for and methodological approaches to strategic environmental assessment with a view to further improving the procedures provided for under this Protocol;

(b) Exchange information regarding experience gained in strategic environmental assessment and in the implementation of this Protocol;

(c) Seek, where appropriate, the services and cooperation of competent bodies having expertise pertinent to the achievement of the purposes of this Protocol;

(d) Establish such subsidiary bodies as it considers necessary for the implementation of this Protocol;

(e) Where necessary, consider and adopt proposals for amendments to this Protocol; and

(f) Consider and undertake any additional action, including action to be carried out jointly under this Protocol and the Convention, that may be required for the achievement of the purposes of this Protocol.

5. The rules of procedure of the Meeting of the Parties to the Convention shall be applied *mutatis mutandis* under this Protocol, except as may otherwise be decided by consensus by the Meeting of the Parties serving as the Meeting of the Parties to this Protocol.

6. At its first meeting, the Meeting of the Parties to the Convention serving as the Meeting of the Parties to this Protocol shall consider and adopt the

modalities for applying the procedure for the review of compliance with the Convention to this Protocol.

7. Each Party shall, at intervals to be determined by the Meeting of the Parties to the Convention serving as the Meeting of the Parties to this Protocol, report to the Meeting of the Parties to the Convention serving as the Meeting of the Parties to the Protocol on measures that it has taken to implement the Protocol.

Article 15
Relationship to other international agreements

The relevant provisions of this Protocol shall apply without prejudice to the UNECE Conventions on Environmental Impact Assessment in a Transboundary Context and on Access to Information, Public Participation in Decision-making and Access to Justice in Environmental Matters.

Article 16
Right to vote

1. Except as provided for in paragraph 2 below, each Party to this Protocol shall have one vote.

2. Regional economic integration organizations, in matters within their competence, shall exercise their right to vote with a number of votes equal to the number of their member States which are Parties to this Protocol. Such organizations shall not exercise their right to vote if their member States exercise theirs, and vice versa.

Article 17
Secretariat

The secretariat established by article 13 of the Convention shall serve as the secretariat of this Protocol and article 13, paragraphs (a) to (c), of the Convention on the functions of the secretariat shall apply *mutatis mutandis* to this Protocol.

Article 18
Annexes

The annexes to this Protocol shall constitute an integral part thereof.

Article 19
Amendments to the Protocol

1. Any Party may propose amendments to this Protocol.

2. Subject to paragraph 3, the procedure for proposing, adopting and the entry into force of amendments to the Convention laid down in paragraphs 2 to

5 of article 14 of the Convention shall apply, *mutatis mutandis*, to amendments to this Protocol.

3. For the purpose of this Protocol, the three fourths of the Parties required for an amendment to enter into force for Parties having ratified, approved or accepted it, shall be calculated on the basis of the number of Parties at the time of the adoption of the amendment.

Article 20
Settlement of disputes

The provisions on the settlement of disputes of article 15 of the Convention shall apply *mutatis mutandis* to this Protocol.

Article 21
Signature

This Protocol shall be open for signature at Kiev (Ukraine) from 21 to 23 May 2003 and thereafter at United Nations Headquarters in New York until 31 December 2003, by States members of the Economic Commission for Europe as well as States having consultative status with the Economic Commission for Europe pursuant to paragraphs 8 and 11 of Economic and Social Council resolution 36 (IV) of 28 March 1947, and by regional economic integration organizations constituted by sovereign States members of the Economic Commission for Europe to which their member States have transferred competence over matters governed by this Protocol, including the competence to enter into treaties in respect of these matters.

Article 22
Depositary

The Secretary-General of the United Nations shall act as the Depositary of this Protocol.

Article 23
Ratification, acceptance, approval and accession

1. This Protocol shall be subject to ratification, acceptance or approval by signatory States and regional economic integration organizations referred to in article 21.

2. This Protocol shall be open for accession as from 1 January 2004 by the States and regional economic integration organizations referred to in article 21.

3. Any other State, not referred to in paragraph 2 above, that is a Member of the United Nations may accede to the Protocol upon approval by the Meeting of the Parties to the Convention serving as the Meeting of the Parties to the Protocol.

4. Any regional economic integration organization referred to in article 21 which becomes a Party to this Protocol without any of its member States being a Party shall be bound by all the obligations under this Protocol. If one or more of such an organization's member States is a Party to this Protocol, the organization and its member States shall decide on their respective responsibilities for the performance of their obligations under this Protocol. In such cases, the organization and its member States shall not be entitled to exercise rights under this Protocol concurrently.

5. In their instruments of ratification, acceptance, approval or accession, the regional economic integration organizations referred to in article 21 shall declare the extent of their competence with respect to the matters governed by this Protocol. These organizations shall also inform the Depositary of any relevant modification to the extent of their competence.

Article 24
Entry into force

1. This Protocol shall enter into force on the ninetieth day after the date of deposit of the sixteenth instrument of ratification, acceptance, approval or accession.

2. For the purposes of paragraph 1 above, any instrument deposited by a regional economic integration organization referred to in article 21 shall not be counted as additional to those deposited by States members of such an organization.

3. For each State or regional economic integration organization referred to in article 21 which ratifies, accepts or approves this Protocol or accedes thereto after the deposit of the sixteenth instrument of ratification, acceptance, approval or accession, the Protocol shall enter into force on the ninetieth day after the date of deposit by such State or organization of its instrument of ratification, acceptance, approval or accession.

4. This Protocol shall apply to plans, programmes, policies and legislation for which the first formal preparatory act is subsequent to the date on which this Protocol enters into force. Where the Party under whose jurisdiction the preparation of a plan, programme, policy or legislation is envisaged is one for which paragraph 3 applies, this Protocol shall apply to plans, programmes, policies and legislation for which the first formal preparatory act is subsequent to the date on which this Protocol comes into force for that Party.

Article 25
Withdrawal

At any time after four years from the date on which this Protocol has come into force with respect to a Party, that Party may withdraw from the Protocol by giving written notification to the Depositary. Any such withdrawal shall take effect on the ninetieth day after the date of its receipt by the Depositary. Any such withdrawal shall not affect the application of articles 5 to 9, 11 and 13 with respect to a strategic environmental assessment under this Protocol which has already been started, or the application of article 10 with respect to a notification or request which has already been made, before such withdrawal takes effect.

Article 26
Authentic texts

The original of this Protocol, of which the English, French and Russian texts are equally authentic, shall be deposited with the Secretary-General of the United Nations.

In witness whereof the undersigned, being duly authorized thereto, have signed this Protocol.

Done at Kiev (Ukraine), this twenty-first day of May, two thousand and three.

Annex I
List of projects as referred to in Article 4, paragraph 2

1. Crude oil refineries (excluding undertakings manufacturing only lubricants from crude oil) and installations for the gasification and liquefaction of 500 metric tons or more of coal or bituminous shale per day.
2. Thermal power stations and other combustion installations with a heat output of 300 megawatts or more and nuclear power stations and other nuclear reactors (except research installations for the production and conversion of fissionable and fertile materials, whose maximum power does not exceed 1 kilowatt continuous thermal load).
3. Installations solely designed for the production or enrichment of nuclear fuels, for the reprocessing of irradiated nuclear fuels or for the storage, disposal and processing of radioactive waste.
4. Major installations for the initial smelting of cast-iron and steel and for the production of non-ferrous metals.
5. Installations for the extraction of asbestos and for the processing and transformation of asbestos and products containing asbestos: for asbestos-cement products, with an annual production of more than 20,000 metric tons of finished product; for friction material, with an annual production of more than 50 metric tons of finished product; and for other asbestos utilization of more than 200 metric tons per year.
6. Integrated chemical installations.

7. Construction of motorways, express roads* and lines for long-distance railway traffic and of airports** with a basic runway length of 2,100 metres or more.
8. Large-diameter oil and gas pipelines.
9. Trading ports and also inland waterways and ports for inland-waterway traffic which permit the passage of vessels of over 1,350 metric tons.
10. Waste-disposal installations for the incineration, chemical treatment or landfill of toxic and dangerous wastes.
11. Large dams and reservoirs.
12. Groundwater abstraction activities in cases where the annual volume of water to be abstracted amounts to 10 million cubic metres or more.
13. Pulp and paper manufacturing of 200 air-dried metric tons or more per day.
14. Major mining, on-site extraction and processing of metal ores or coal.
15. Offshore hydrocarbon production.
16. Major storage facilities for petroleum, petrochemical and chemical products.
17. Deforestation of large areas.

Annex II
Any other projects referred to in Article 4, paragraph 2

1. Projects for the restructuring of rural land holdings.
2. Projects for the use of uncultivated land or semi-natural areas for intensive agricultural purposes.
3. Water management projects for agriculture, including irrigation and land drainage projects.
4. Intensive livestock installations (including poultry).
5. Initial afforestation and deforestation for the purposes of conversion to another type of land use.

* For the purposes of this Protocol:
  - 'Motorway' means a road specially designed and built for motor traffic, which does not serve properties bordering on it, and which:
    (a) Is provided, except at special points or temporarily, with separate carriageways for the two directions of traffic, separated from each other by a dividing strip not intended for traffic or, exceptionally, by other means;
    (b) Does not cross at level with any road, railway or tramway track, or footpath; and
    (c) Is specially sign-posted as a motorway.
  - 'Express road' means a road reserved for motor traffic accessible only from interchanges or controlled junctions and on which, in particular, stopping and parking are prohibited on the running carriageway(s).

** For the purposes of this Protocol, 'airport' means an airport which complies with the definition in the 1944 Chicago Convention setting up the International Civil Aviation Organization (annex 14).

6. Intensive fish farming.
7. Nuclear power stations and other nuclear reactors* including the dismantling or decommissioning of such power stations or reactors (except research installations for the production and conversion of fissionable and fertile materials whose maximum power does not exceed 1 kilowatt continuous thermal load), as far as not included in annex I.
8. Construction of overhead electrical power lines with a voltage of 220 kilovolts or more and a length of 15 kilometres or more and other projects for the transmission of electrical energy by overhead cables.
9. Industrial installations for the production of electricity, steam and hot water.
10. Industrial installations for carrying gas, steam and hot water.
11. Surface storage of fossil fuels and natural gas.
12. Underground storage of combustible gases.
13. Industrial briquetting of coal and lignite.
14. Installations for hydroelectric energy production.
15. Installations for the harnessing of wind power for energy production (wind farms).
16. Installations, as far as not included in annex I, designed:
    – For the production or enrichment of nuclear fuel;
    – For the processing of irradiated nuclear fuel;
    – For the final disposal of irradiated nuclear fuel;
    – Solely for the final disposal of radioactive waste;
    – Solely for the storage (planned for more than 10 years) of irradiated nuclear fuels in a different site than the production site; or
    – For the processing and storage of radioactive waste.
17. Quarries, open cast mining and peat extraction, as far as not included in annex I.
18. Underground mining, as far as not included in annex I.
19. Extraction of minerals by marine or fluvial dredging.
20. Deep drillings (in particular geothermal drilling, drilling for the storage of nuclear waste material, drilling for water supplies), with the exception of drillings for investigating the stability of the soil.
21. Surface industrial installations for the extraction of coal, petroleum, natural gas and ores, as well as bituminous shale.
22. Integrated works for the initial smelting of cast iron and steel, as far as not included in annex I.
23. Installations for the production of pig iron or steel (primary or secondary fusion) including continuous casting.

---

* For the purposes of this Protocol, nuclear power stations and other nuclear reactors cease to be such an installation when all nuclear fuel and other radioactively contaminated elements have been removed permanently from the installation site.

24. Installations for the processing of ferrous metals (hot-rolling mills, smitheries with hammers, application of protective fused metal coats).
25. Ferrous metal foundries.
26. Installations for the production of non-ferrous crude metals from ore, concentrates or secondary raw materials by metallurgical, chemical or electrolytic processes, as far as not included in annex I.
27. Installations for the smelting, including the alloyage, of non-ferrous metals excluding precious metals, including recovered products (refining, foundry casting, etc.), as far as not included in annex I.
28. Installations for surface treatment of metals and plastic materials using an electrolytic or chemical process.
29. Manufacture and assembly of motor vehicles and manufacture of motor-vehicle engines.
30. Shipyards.
31. Installations for the construction and repair of aircraft.
32. Manufacture of railway equipment.
33. Swaging by explosives.
34. Installations for the roasting and sintering of metallic ores.
35. Coke ovens (dry coal distillation).
36. Installations for the manufacture of cement.
37. Installations for the manufacture of glass including glass fibre.
38. Installations for smelting mineral substances including the production of mineral fibres.
39. Manufacture of ceramic products by burning, in particular roofing tiles, bricks, refractory bricks, tiles, stoneware or porcelain.
40. Installations for the production of chemicals or treatment of intermediate products, as far as not included in annex I.
41. Production of pesticides and pharmaceutical products, paint and varnishes, elastomers and peroxides.
42. Installations for the storage of petroleum, petrochemical, or chemical products, as far as not included in annex I.
43. Manufacture of vegetable and animal oils and fats.
44. Packing and canning of animal and vegetable products.
45. Manufacture of dairy products.
46. Brewing and malting.
47. Confectionery and syrup manufacture.
48. Installations for the slaughter of animals.
49. Industrial starch manufacturing installations.
50. Fish meal and fish-oil factories.
51. Sugar factories.
52. Industrial plants for the production of pulp, paper and board, as far as not included in annex I.

53. Plants for the pre treatment or dyeing of fibres or textiles.
54. Plants for the tanning of hides and skins.
55. Cellulose-processing and production installations.
56. Manufacture and treatment of elastomer-based products.
57. Installations for the manufacture of artificial mineral fibres.
58. Installations for the recovery or destruction of explosive substances.
59. Installations for the production of asbestos and the manufacture of asbestos products, as far as not included in annex I.
60. Knackers' yards.
61. Test benches for engines, turbines or reactors.
62. Permanent racing and test tracks for motorized vehicles.
63. Pipelines for transport of gas or oil, as far as not included in annex I.
64. Pipelines for transport of chemicals with a diameter of more than 800 mm and a length of more than 40 km.
65. Construction of railways and intermodal transshipment facilities, and of intermodal terminals, as far as not included in annex I.
66. Construction of tramways, elevated and underground railways, suspended lines or similar lines of a particular type used exclusively or mainly for passenger transport.
67. Construction of roads, including realignment and/or widening of any existing road, as far as not included in annex I.
68. Construction of harbours and port installations, including fishing harbours, as far as not included in annex I.
69. Construction of inland waterways and ports for inland-waterway traffic, as far as not included in annex I.
70. Trading ports, piers for loading and unloading connected to land and outside ports, as far as not included in annex I.
71. Canalization and flood-relief works.
72. Construction of airports** and airfields, as far as not included in annex I.
73. Waste-disposal installations (including landfill), as far as not included in annex I.
74. Installations for the incineration or chemical treatment of non-hazardous waste.
75. Storage of scrap iron, including scrap vehicles.
76. Sludge deposition sites.
77. Groundwater abstraction or artificial groundwater recharge, as far as not included in annex I.
78. Works for the transfer of water resources between river basins.

** For the purposes of this Protocol, 'airport' means an airport which complies with the definition in the 1944 Chicago Convention setting up the International Civil Aviation Organization (annex 14).

79. Waste-water treatment plants.
80. Dams and other installations designed for the holding-back or for the long-term or permanent storage of water, as far as not included in annex I.
81. Coastal work to combat erosion and maritime works capable of altering the coast through the construction, for example, of dykes, moles, jetties and other sea defence works, excluding the maintenance and reconstruction of such works.
82. Installations of long-distance aqueducts.
83. Ski runs, ski lifts and cable cars and associated developments.
84. Marinas.
85. Holiday villages and hotel complexes outside urban areas and associated developments.
86. Permanent campsites and caravan sites.
87. Theme parks.
88. Industrial estate development projects.
89. Urban development projects, including the construction of shopping centres and car parks.
90. Reclamation of land from the sea.

Annex III
Criteria for determining of the likely significant environmental, including health, effects referred to in Article 5, paragraph 1

1. The relevance of the plan or programme to the integration of environmental, including health, considerations in particular with a view to promoting sustainable development.
2. The degree to which the plan or programme sets a framework for projects and other activities, either with regard to location, nature, size and operating conditions or by allocating resources.
3. The degree to which the plan or programme influences other plans and programmes including those in a hierarchy.
4. Environmental, including health, problems relevant to the plan or programme.
5. The nature of the environmental, including health, effects such as probability, duration, frequency, reversibility, magnitude and extent (such as geographical area or size of population likely to be affected).
6. The risks to the environment, including health.
7. The transboundary nature of effects.
8. The degree to which the plan or programme will affect valuable or vulnerable areas including landscapes with a recognized national or international protection status.

Annex IV
Information referred to in Article 7, paragraph 2

1. The contents and the main objectives of the plan or programme and its link with other plans or programmes.
2. The relevant aspects of the current state of the environment, including health, and the likely evolution thereof should the plan or programme not be implemented.
3. The characteristics of the environment, including health, in areas likely to be significantly affected.
4. The environmental, including health, problems which are relevant to the plan or programme.
5. The environmental, including health, objectives established at international, national and other levels which are relevant to the plan or programme, and the ways in which these objectives and other environmental, including health, considerations have been taken into account during its preparation.
6. The likely significant environmental, including health, effects* as defined in article 2, paragraph 7.
7. Measures to prevent, reduce or mitigate any significant adverse effects on the environment, including health, which may result from the implementation of the plan or programme.
8. An outline of the reasons for selecting the alternatives dealt with and a description of how the assessment was undertaken including difficulties encountered in providing the information to be included such as technical deficiencies or lack of knowledge.
9. Measures envisaged for monitoring environmental, including health, effects of the implementation of the plan or programme.
10. The likely significant transboundary environmental, including health, effects.
11. A non-technical summary of the information provided.

Annex V
Information referred to in Article 8, paragraph 5

1. The proposed plan or programme and its nature.
2. The authority responsible for its adoption.
3. The envisaged procedure, including:
   (a) The commencement of the procedure;
   (b) The opportunities for the public to participate;

---

* These effects should include secondary, cumulative, synergistic, short-, medium- and long-term, permanent and temporary, positive and negative effects.

    (c) The time and venue of any envisaged public hearing;

    (d) The authority from which relevant information can be obtained and where the relevant information has been deposited for examination by the public;

    (e) The authority to which comments or questions can be submitted and the time schedule for the transmittal of comments or questions; and

    (f) What environmental, including health, information relevant to the proposed plan or programme is available.

4. Whether the plan or programme is likely to be subject to a transboundary assessment procedure.

Convention on the Transboundary Effects of Industrial Accidents, 17 March 1992

Editorial note

The Convention on the Transboundary Effects of Industrial Accidents, adopted under the auspices of the UNECE, is intended to regulate State and other actions relating to 'industrial accidents' capable of causing transboundary harm (Article 1). Not all 'industrial accidents' are covered by the Convention: nuclear accidents, accidents at military installations, dam failures and others are excluded (Article 2(2)).

The Convention requires each Party to identify all 'hazardous activities' (defined in Article 1(b) as activities where a hazardous substance in quantities equal or greater to that specified in Annex I is present and capable of causing transboundary effects) within its jurisdiction and to notify other Parties which may be affected by it (Article 4(1)). Compulsory consultation between concerned Parties is provided for at the request of any such Party to determine whether an activity is hazardous and capable of causing transboundary effects (Article 4(2)). In the event of disagreement on this issue, Parties may resort to the inquiry procedure set out in Annex II (Article 4(2)). Similarly, Parties can agree to treat any other activity not covered by Annex I as a 'hazardous activity', whereupon the relevant obligations of the Convention apply (Article 4(5)). Parties are further required to take 'appropriate measures' to prevent industrial accidents and Annex IV provides guidance for such measures (Article 6(1)). Siting decisions for hazardous activities must be taken with a view towards minimising transboundary adverse effects (Article 7). The Convention also requires Parties to take 'appropriate measures' for emergency preparedness and implement on- and off-site contingency plans (Article 8). Parties are required to ensure that the public in areas likely to be affected are provided with 'adequate information' in accordance with Annex VIII (Article 9(1)). Parties are to grant non-discriminatory access, in accordance with their domestic legal systems, to any relevant judicial or administrative proceedings (Article 9(3)).

Parties are required to establish and operate effective industrial accidents notification systems, to notify other affected Parties in the event of an industrial accident, and activate contingency measures (Article 10). If an industrial accident occurs, a Party may request assistance from other Parties, and the Convention requires co-operation by Parties in the provision of any assistance they agree to render (Article 12). The Convention requires Parties to support international efforts to develop the law on responsibility and liability (Article 13). Certain limitations on the supply of information and protection of confidentiality are provided for (Article 22). Parties' rights to enact more stringent measures than provided by the Convention are unaffected (Article 24).

The Convention establishes a Conference of the Parties which is to meet regularly to review the implementation of the Convention, carry out advisory functions, and consider matters related to the Convention's implementation and development (Article 20). Dispute settlement is to occur by any means chosen by the Parties involved and the Convention allows disputes to be submitted to arbitration in accordance with procedures outlined in Annex XIII or to the jurisdiction of the ICJ (Article 21). The Convention can be amended if an amendment is adopted by a consensus of the Parties, except in respect of Annex I where amendments can be passed by a nine-tenths majority vote of all parties present and voting (Article 26). Amendments enter into force for those accepting them following acceptance by sixteen Parties (Article 26), with the exception of amendments to Annex I which ultimately enter into force for all Parties save in the event that sixteen Parties indicate that they are unable to accept them (Article 27).

A Protocol on civil liability for transboundary damage caused by hazardous activities was adopted in May 2003 by the Parties to the Convention jointly with the Parties to the Convention on the Protection and Use of Transboundary Watercourses and International Lakes.

Date of signature: 22 March 1985

Entry into force: 19 April 2000

Depositary: Secretary-General of the United Nations

Contracting Parties: Albania, Armenia, Austria, Bulgaria, Croatia, Czech Republic, Denmark, Estonia, European Community, Finland, Germany, Greece, Hungary, Italy, Kazakhstan, Lithuania, Luxembourg, Moldova (Republic of), Monaco, Norway, Russian Federation, Slovenia, Spain, Sweden, Switzerland, United Kingdom.

Website: www.unece.org/env/teia/

Convention on the Transboundary Effects of Industrial Accidents

Preamble

The Parties to this Convention,

Mindful of the special importance, in the interest of present and future generations, of protecting human beings and the environment against the effects of industrial accidents,

Recognizing the importance and urgency of preventing serious adverse effects of industrial accidents on human beings and the environment, and of promoting all measures that stimulate the rational, economic and efficient use of preventive, preparedness and response measures to enable environmentally sound and sustainable economic development,

Taking into account the fact that the effects of industrial accidents may make themselves felt across borders, and require cooperation among States,

Affirming the need to promote active international cooperation among the States concerned before, during and after an accident, to enhance appropriate policies and to reinforce and coordinate action at all appropriate levels for promoting the prevention of, preparedness for and response to the transboundary effects of industrial accidents,

Noting the importance and usefulness of bilateral and multilateral arrangements for the prevention of, preparedness for and response to the effects of industrial accidents,

Conscious of the role played in this respect by the United Nations Economic Commission for Europe (ECE) and recalling, *inter alia*, the ECE Code of Conduct on Accidental Pollution of Transboundary Inland Waters and the Convention on Environmental Impact Assessment in a Transboundary Context,

Having regard to the relevant provisions of the Final Act of the Conference on Security and Cooperation in Europe (CSCE), the Concluding Document of the Vienna Meeting of Representatives of the Participating States of the CSCE, and the outcome of the Sofia Meeting on the Protection of the Environment of the CSCE, as well as to pertinent activities and mechanisms in the United Nations Environment Programme (UNEP), in particular the APELL programme, in the International Labour Organisation (ILO), in particular the Code of Practice on the Prevention of Major Industrial Accidents, and in other relevant international organizations,

Considering the pertinent provisions of the Declaration of the United Nations Conference on the Human Environment, and in particular principle 21, according to which States have, in accordance with the Charter of the United Nations and the principles of international law, the sovereign right to exploit their own resources pursuant to their own environmental policies, and the responsibility to ensure that activities within their jurisdiction or control do not cause damage to the environment of other States or of areas beyond the limits of national jurisdiction,

Taking account of the polluter-pays principle as a general principle of international environmental law,

Underlining the principles of international law and custom, in particular the principles of good-neighbourliness, reciprocity, non-discrimination and good faith,

Have agreed as follows:

Article 1
Definitions

For the purposes of this Convention,

(a) 'Industrial accident' means an event resulting from an uncontrolled development in the course of any activity involving hazardous substances either:
  (i) In an installation, for example during manufacture, use, storage, handling, or disposal; or
  (ii) During transportation in so far as it is covered by paragraph 2(d) of Article 2;

(b) 'Hazardous activity' means any activity in which one or more hazardous substances are present or may be present in quantities at or in excess of the threshold quantities listed in Annex I hereto, and which is capable of causing transboundary effects;

(c) 'Effects' means any direct or indirect, immediate or delayed adverse consequences caused by an industrial accident on, *inter alia*:
  (i) Human beings, flora and fauna;
  (ii) Soil, water, air and landscape;
  (iii) The interaction between the factors in (i) and (ii);
  (iv) Material assets and cultural heritage, including historical monuments;

(d) 'Transboundary effects' means serious effects within the jurisdiction of a Party as a result of an industrial accident occurring within the jurisdiction of another Party;

(e) 'Operator' means any natural or legal person, including public authorities, in charge of an activity, e.g. supervising, planning to carry out or carrying out an activity;

(f) 'Party' means, unless the text otherwise indicates, a Contracting Party to this Convention;

(g) 'Party of origin' means any Party or Parties under whose jurisdiction an industrial accident occurs or is capable of occurring;

(h) 'Affected Party' means any Party or Parties affected or capable of being affected by transboundary effects of an industrial accident;

(i) 'Parties concerned' means any Party of origin and any affected Party;

(j) 'The public' means one or more natural or legal persons.

Article 2
Scope

1. This Convention shall apply to the prevention of, preparedness for and response to industrial accidents capable of causing transboundary effects, including the effects of such accidents caused by natural disasters, and to international cooperation concerning mutual assistance, research and development, exchange of information and exchange of technology in the area of prevention of, preparedness for and response to industrial accidents.

2. This Convention shall not apply to:

(a) Nuclear accidents or radiological emergencies;

(b) Accidents at military installations;

(c) Dam failures, with the exception of the effects of industrial accidents caused by such failures;

(d) Land-based transport accidents with the exception of:
   (i) Emergency response to such accidents;
   (ii) Transportation on the site of the hazardous activity;

(e) Accidental release of genetically modified organisms;

(f) Accidents caused by activities in the marine environment, including seabed exploration or exploitation;

(g) Spills of oil or other harmful substances at sea.

Article 3
General provisions

1. The Parties shall, taking into account efforts already made at national and international levels, take appropriate measures and cooperate within the framework of this Convention, to protect human beings and the environment against industrial accidents by preventing such accidents as far as possible, by reducing their frequency and severity and by mitigating their effects. To this end, preventive, preparedness and response measures, including restoration measures, shall be applied.

2. The Parties shall, by means of exchange of information, consultation and other cooperative measures and without undue delay, develop and implement policies and strategies for reducing the risks of industrial accidents and improving preventive, preparedness and response measures, including restoration measures, taking into account, in order to avoid unnecessary duplication, efforts already made at national and international levels.

3. The Parties shall ensure that the operator is obliged to take all measures necessary for the safe performance of the hazardous activity and for the prevention of industrial accidents.

4. To implement the provisions of this Convention, the Parties shall take appropriate legislative, regulatory, administrative and financial measures for the prevention of, preparedness for and response to industrial accidents.

5. The provisions of this Convention shall not prejudice any obligations of the Parties under international law with regard to industrial accidents and hazardous activities.

Article 4
Identification, consultation and advice

1. For the purpose of undertaking preventive measures and setting up preparedness measures, the Party of origin shall take measures, as appropriate, to identify hazardous activities within its jurisdiction and to ensure that affected Parties are notified of any such proposed or existing activity.

2. Parties concerned shall, at the initiative of any such Party, enter into discussions on the identification of those hazardous activities that are, reasonably, capable of causing transboundary effects. If the Parties concerned do not agree on whether an activity is such a hazardous activity, any such Party may, unless the Parties concerned agree on another method of resolving the question, submit that question to an inquiry commission in accordance with the provisions of Annex II hereto for advice.

3. The Parties shall, with respect to proposed or existing hazardous activities, apply the procedures set out in Annex III hereto.

4. When a hazardous activity is subject to an environmental impact assessment in accordance with the Convention on Environmental Impact Assessment in a Transboundary Context and that assessment includes an evaluation of the transboundary effects of industrial accidents from the hazardous activity which is performed in conformity with the terms of this Convention, the final decision taken for the purposes of the Convention on Environmental Impact Assessment in a Transboundary Context shall fulfil the relevant requirements of this Convention.

Article 5
Voluntary extension

Parties concerned should, at the initiative of any of them, enter into discussions on whether to treat an activity not covered by Annex I as a hazardous activity. Upon mutual agreement, they may use an advisory mechanism of their choice, or an inquiry commission in accordance with Annex II, to advise them. Where the Parties concerned so agree, this Convention, or any part thereof, shall apply to the activity in question as if it were a hazardous activity.

Article 6
Prevention

1. The Parties shall take appropriate measures for the prevention of industrial accidents, including measures to induce action by operators to reduce the risk

of industrial accidents. Such measures may include, but are not limited to those referred to in Annex IV hereto.

2. With regard to any hazardous activity, the Party of origin shall require the operator to demonstrate the safe performance of the hazardous activity by the provision of information such as basic details of the process, including but not limited to, analysis and evaluation as detailed in Annex V hereto.

Article 7
Decision-making on siting

Within the framework of its legal system, the Party of origin shall, with the objective of minimizing the risk to the population and the environment of all affected Parties, seek the establishment of policies on the siting of new hazardous activities and on significant modifications to existing hazardous activities. Within the framework of their legal systems, the affected Parties shall seek the establishment of policies on significant developments in areas which could be affected by transboundary effects of an industrial accident arising out of a hazardous activity so as to minimize the risks involved. In elaborating and establishing these policies, the Parties should consider the matters set out in Annex V, paragraph 2, subparagraphs (1) to (8), and Annex VI hereto.

Article 8
Emergency preparedness

1. The Parties shall take appropriate measures to establish and maintain adequate emergency preparedness to respond to industrial accidents. The Parties shall ensure that preparedness measures are taken to mitigate transboundary effects of such accidents, on-site duties being undertaken by operators. These measures may include, but are not limited to those referred to in Annex VII hereto. In particular, the Parties concerned shall inform each other of their contingency plans.

2. The Party of origin shall ensure for hazardous activities the preparation and implementation of on-site contingency plans, including suitable measures for response and other measures to prevent and minimize transboundary effects. The Party of origin shall provide to the other Parties concerned the elements it has for the elaboration of contingency plans.

3. Each Party shall ensure for hazardous activities the preparation and implementation of off-site contingency plans covering measures to be taken within its territory to prevent and minimize transboundary effects. In preparing these plans, account shall be taken of the conclusions of analysis and evaluation, in particular the matters set out in Annex V, paragraph 2, subparagraphs (1) to (5). Parties concerned shall endeavour to make such plans compatible. Where appropriate, joint off-site contingency plans shall be drawn up in order to facilitate the adoption of adequate response measures.

4. Contingency plans should be reviewed regularly, or when circumstances so require, taking into account the experience gained in dealing with actual emergencies.

Article 9
Information to, and participation of the public

1. The Parties shall ensure that adequate information is given to the public in the areas capable of being affected by an industrial accident arising out of a hazardous activity. This information shall be transmitted through such channels as the Parties deem appropriate, shall include the elements contained in Annex VIII hereto and should take into account matters set out in Annex V, paragraph 2, subparagraphs (1) to (4) and (9).

2. The Party of origin shall, in accordance with the provisions of this Convention and whenever possible and appropriate, give the public in the areas capable of being affected an opportunity to participate in relevant procedures with the aim of making known its views and concerns on prevention and preparedness measures, and shall ensure that the opportunity given to the public of the affected Party is equivalent to that given to the public of the Party of origin.

3. The Parties shall, in accordance with their legal systems and, if desired, on a reciprocal basis provide natural or legal persons who are being or are capable of being adversely affected by the transboundary effects of an industrial accident in the territory of a Party, with access to, and treatment in the relevant administrative and judicial proceedings, including the possibilities of starting a legal action and appealing a decision affecting their rights, equivalent to those available to persons within their own jurisdiction.

Article 10
Industrial accident notification systems

1. The Parties shall, with the aim of obtaining and transmitting industrial accident notifications containing information needed to counteract transboundary effects, provide for the establishment and operation of compatible and efficient industrial accident notification systems at appropriate levels.

2. In the event of an industrial accident, or imminent threat thereof, which causes or is capable of causing transboundary effects, the Party of origin shall ensure that affected Parties are, without delay, notified at appropriate levels through the industrial accident notification systems. Such notification shall include the elements contained in Annex IX hereto.

3. The Parties concerned shall ensure that, in the event of an industrial accident or imminent threat thereof, the contingency plans prepared in accordance with Article 8 are activated as soon as possible and to the extent appropriate to the circumstances.

Article 11
Response

1. The Parties shall ensure that, in the event of an industrial accident, or imminent threat thereof, adequate response measures are taken, as soon as possible and using the most efficient practices, to contain and minimize effects.

2. In the event of an industrial accident, or imminent threat thereof, which causes or is capable of causing transboundary effects, the Parties concerned shall ensure that the effects are assessed – where appropriate, jointly for the purpose of taking adequate response measures. The Parties concerned shall endeavour to coordinate their response measures.

Article 12
Mutual assistance

1. If a Party needs assistance in the event of an industrial accident, it may ask for assistance from other Parties, indicating the scope and type of assistance required. A Party to whom a request for assistance is directed shall promptly decide and inform the requesting Party whether it is in a position to render the assistance required and indicate the scope and terms of the assistance that might be rendered.

2. The Parties concerned shall cooperate to facilitate the prompt provision of assistance agreed to under paragraph 1 of this Article, including, where appropriate, action to minimize the consequences and effects of the industrial accident, and to provide general assistance. Where Parties do not have bilateral or multilateral agreements which cover their arrangements for providing mutual assistance, the assistance shall be rendered in accordance with Annex X hereto, unless the Parties agree otherwise.

Article 13
Responsibility and liability

The Parties shall support appropriate international efforts to elaborate rules, criteria and procedures in the field of responsibility and liability.

Article 14
Research and development

The Parties shall, as appropriate, initiate and cooperate in the conduct of research into, and in the development of methods and technologies for the prevention of, preparedness for and response to industrial accidents. For these purposes, the Parties shall encourage and actively promote scientific and technological cooperation, including research into less hazardous processes aimed at limiting accident hazards and preventing and limiting the consequences of industrial accidents.

Article 15
Exchange of information

The Parties shall, at the multilateral or bilateral level, exchange reasonably obtainable information, including the elements contained in Annex XI hereto.

Article 16
Exchange of technology

1. The Parties shall, consistent with their laws, regulations and practices, facilitate the exchange of technology for the prevention of, preparedness for and response to the effects of industrial accidents, particularly through the promotion of:

(a) Exchange of available technology on various financial bases;
(b) Direct industrial contacts and cooperation;
(c) Exchange of information and experience;
(d) Provision of technical assistance.

2. In promoting the activities specified in paragraph 1, subpararagraphs (a) to (d) of this Article, the Parties shall create favourable conditions by facilitating contacts and cooperation among appropriate organizations and individuals in both the private and the public sectors that are capable of providing technology, design and engineering services, equipment or finance.

Article 17
Competent authorities and points of contact

1. Each Party shall designate or establish one or more competent authorities for the purposes of this Convention.

2. Without prejudice to other arrangements at the bilateral or multilateral level, each Party shall designate or establish one point of contact for the purpose of industrial accident notifications pursuant to Article 10, and one point of contact for the purpose of mutual assistance pursuant to Article 12. These points of contact should preferably be the same.

3. Each Party shall, within three months of the date of entry into force of this Convention for that Party, inform the other Parties, through the secretariat referred to in Article 20, which body or bodies it has designated as its point(s) of contact and as its competent authority or authorities.

4. Each Party shall, within one month of the date of decision, inform the other Parties, through the secretariat, of any changes regarding the designation(s) it has made under paragraph 3 of this Article.

5. Each Party shall keep its point of contact and industrial accident notification systems pursuant to Article 10 operational at all times.

6. Each Party shall keep its point of contact and the authorities responsible for making and receiving requests for, and accepting offers of assistance pursuant to Article 12 operational at all times.

Article 18
Conference of the Parties

1. The representatives of the Parties shall constitute the Conference of the Parties of this Convention and hold their meetings on a regular basis. The first meeting of the Conference of the Parties shall be convened not later than one year after the date of the entry into force of this Convention. Thereafter, a meeting of the Conference of the Parties shall be held at least once a year or at the written request of any Party, provided that, within six months of the request being communicated to them by the secretariat, it is supported by at least one third of the Parties.

2. The Conference of the Parties shall:

(a) Review the implementation of this Convention;

(b) Carry out advisory functions aimed at strengthening the ability of Parties to prevent, prepare for and respond to the transboundary effects of industrial accidents, and at facilitating the provision of technical assistance and advice at the request of Parties faced with industrial accidents;

(c) Establish, as appropriate, working groups and other appropriate mechanisms to consider matters related to the implementation and development of this Convention and, to this end, to prepare appropriate studies and other documentation and submit recommendations for consideration by the Conference of the Parties;

(d) Fulfil such other functions as may be appropriate under the provisions of this Convention;

(e) At its first meeting, consider and, by consensus, adopt rules of procedure for its meetings.

3. The Conference of the Parties, in discharging its functions, shall, when it deems appropriate, also cooperate with other relevant international organizations.

4. The Conference of the Parties shall, at its first meeting, establish a programme of work, in particular with regard to the items contained in Annex XII hereto. The Conference of the Parties shall also decide on the method of work, including the use of national centres and cooperation with relevant international organizations and the establishment of a system with a view to facilitating the implementation of this Convention, in particular for mutual assistance in the event of an industrial accident, and building upon pertinent existing activities within relevant international organizations. As part of the programme of work, the Conference of the Parties shall review existing national, regional and international centres, and other bodies and programmes aimed at coordinating

information and efforts in the prevention of, preparedness for and response to industrial accidents, with a view to determining what additional international institutions or centres may be needed to carry out the tasks listed in Annex XII.

5. The Conference of the Parties shall, at its first meeting, commence consideration of procedures to create more favourable conditions for the exchange of technology for the prevention of, preparedness for and response to the effects of industrial accidents.

6. The Conference of the Parties shall adopt guidelines and criteria to facilitate the identification of hazardous activities for the purposes of this Convention.

Article 19
Right to vote

1. Except as provided for in paragraph 2 of this Article, each Party to this Convention shall have one vote.

2. Regional economic integration organizations as defined in Article 27 shall, in matters within their competence, exercise their right to vote with a number of votes equal to the number of their member States which are Parties to this Convention. Such organizations shall not exercise their right to vote if their member States exercise theirs, and vice versa.

Article 20
Secretariat

The Executive Secretary of the Economic Commission for Europe shall carry out the following secretariat functions:

(a) Convene and prepare meetings of the Parties;
(b) Transmit to the Parties reports and other information received in accordance with the provisions of this Convention;
(c) Such other functions as may be determined by the Parties.

Article 21
Settlement of disputes

1. If a dispute arises between two or more Parties about the interpretation or application of this Convention, they shall seek a solution by negotiation or by any other method of dispute settlement acceptable to the parties to the dispute.

2. When signing, ratifying, accepting, approving or acceding to this Convention, or at any time thereafter, a Party may declare in writing to the Depositary that, for a dispute not resolved in accordance with paragraph 1 of this Article, it accepts one or both of the following means of dispute settlement as compulsory in relation to any Party accepting the same obligation:

(a) Submission of the dispute to the International Court of Justice;
(b) Arbitration in accordance with the procedure set out in Annex XIII hereto.

3. If the parties to the dispute have accepted both means of dispute settlement referred to in paragraph 2 of this Article, the dispute may be submitted only to the International Court of Justice, unless the parties to the dispute agree otherwise.

Article 22
Limitations on the supply of information

1. The provisions of this Convention shall not affect the rights or the obligations of Parties in accordance with their national laws, regulations, administrative provisions or accepted legal practices and applicable international regulations to protect information related to personal data, industrial and commercial secrecy, including intellectual property, or national security.

2. If a Party nevertheless decides to supply such protected information to another Party, the Party receiving such protected information shall respect the confidentiality of the information received and the conditions under which it is supplied, and shall only use that information for the purposes for which it was supplied.

Article 23
Implementation

The Parties shall report periodically on the implementation of this Convention.

Article 24
Bilateral and multilateral agreements

1. The Parties may, in order to implement their obligations under this Convention, continue existing or enter into new bilateral or multilateral agreements or other arrangements.

2. The provisions of this Convention shall not affect the right of Parties to take, by bilateral or multilateral agreement where appropriate, more stringent measures than those required by this Convention.

Article 25
Status of Annexes

The Annexes to this Convention form an integral part of the Convention.

Article 26
Amendments to the Convention

1. Any Party may propose amendments to this Convention.

2. The text of any proposed amendment to this Convention shall be submitted in writing to the Executive Secretary of the Economic Commission for Europe, who shall circulate it to all Parties. The Conference of the Parties shall discuss proposed amendments at its next annual meeting, provided that such

proposals have been circulated to the Parties by the Executive Secretary of the Economic Commission for Europe at least ninety days in advance.

3. For amendments to this Convention - other than those to Annex I, for which the procedure is described in paragraph 4 of this Article:

(a) Amendments shall be adopted by consensus of the Parties present at the meeting and shall be submitted by the Depositary to all Parties for ratification, acceptance or approval;

(b) Instruments of ratification, acceptance or approval of amendments shall be deposited with the Depositary. Amendments adopted in accordance with this Article shall enter into force for Parties that have accepted them on the ninetieth day following the day of receipt by the Depositary of the sixteenth instrument of ratification, acceptance or approval;

(c) Thereafter, amendments shall enter into force for any other Party on the ninetieth day after that Party deposits its instruments of ratification, acceptance or approval of the amendments.

4. For amendments to Annex I:

(a) The Parties shall make every effort to reach agreement by consensus. If all efforts at consensus have been exhausted and no agreement reached, the amendments shall, as a last resort, be adopted by a nine-tenths majority vote of the Parties present and voting at the meeting. If adopted by the Conference of the Parties, the amendments shall be communicated to the Parties and recommended for approval;

(b) On the expiry of twelve months from the date of their communication by the Executive Secretary of the Economic Commission for Europe, the amendments to Annex I shall become effective for those Parties to this Convention which have not submitted a notification in accordance with the provisions of paragraph 4(c) of this Article, provided that at least sixteen Parties have not submitted such a notification;

(c) Any Party that is unable to approve an amendment to Annex I of this Convention shall so notify the Executive Secretary of the Economic Commission for Europe in writing within twelve months from the date of the communication of the adoption. The Executive Secretary shall without delay notify all Parties of any such notification received. A Party may at any time substitute an acceptance for its previous notification and the amendment to Annex I shall thereupon enter into force for that Party.

(d) For the purpose of this paragraph 'Parties present and voting' means Parties present and casting an affirmative or negative vote.

Article 27
Signature

This Convention shall be open for signature at Helsinki from 17 to 18 March 1992 inclusive, and thereafter at United Nations Headquarters in New York until 18 September 1992, by States members of the Economic Commission for Europe, as well as States having consultative status with the Economic Commission for Europe pursuant to paragraph 8 of Economic and Social Council resolution 36 (IV) of 28 March 1947, and by regional economic integration organizations constituted by sovereign States members of the Economic Commission for Europe to which their member States have transferred competence in respect of matters governed by this Convention, including the competence to enter into treaties in respect of these matters.

Article 28
Depositary

The Secretary-General of the United Nations shall act as the Depositary of this Convention.

Article 29
Ratification, acceptance, approval and accession

1. This Convention shall be subject to ratification, acceptance or approval by the signatory States and regional economic integration organizations referred to in Article 27.

2. This Convention shall be open for accession by the States and organizations referred to in Article 27.

3. Any organization referred to in Article 27 which becomes Party to this Convention without any of its member States being a Party shall be bound by all the obligations under this Convention. In the case of such organizations, one or more of whose member States is a Party to this Convention, the organization and its member States shall decide on their respective responsibilities for the performance of their obligations under this Convention. In such cases, the organization and the member States shall not be entitled to exercise rights under this Convention concurrently.

4. In their instruments of ratification, acceptance, approval or accession, the regional economic integration organizations referred to in Article 27 shall declare the extent of their competence with respect to the matters governed by this Convention. These organizations shall also inform the Depositary of any substantial modification to the extent of their competence.

Article 30
Entry into force

1. This Convention shall enter into force on the ninetieth day after the date of deposit of the sixteenth instrument of ratification, acceptance, approval or accession.

2. For the purposes of paragraph 1 of this Article, any instrument deposited by an organization referred to in Article 27 shall not be counted as additional to those deposited by States members of such an organization.

3. For each State or organization referred to in Article 27 which ratifies, accepts or approves this Convention or accedes thereto after the deposit of the sixteenth instrument of ratification, acceptance, approval or accession, this Convention shall enter into force on the ninetieth day after the date of deposit by such State or organization of its instrument of ratification, acceptance, approval or accession.

Article 31
Withdrawal

1. At any time after three years from the date on which this Convention has come into force with respect to a Party, that Party may withdraw from this Convention by giving written notification to the Depositary. Any such withdrawal shall take effect on the ninetieth day after the date of the receipt of the notification by the Depositary.

2. Any such withdrawal shall not affect the application of Article 4 to an activity in respect of which a notification has been made pursuant to Article 4, paragraph 1, or a request for discussions has been made pursuant to Article 4, paragraph 2.

Article 32
Authentic texts

The original of this Convention, of which the English, French and Russian texts are equally authentic, shall be deposited with the Secretary-General of the United Nations.

IN WITNESS WHEREOF the undersigned, being duly authorized thereto, have signed this Convention.

DONE at Helsinki, this seventeenth day of March one thousand nine hundred and ninety-two.

Annex I
Hazardous substances for the purposes of defining hazardous activities

The quantities set out below relate to each activity or group of activities. Where a range of quantities is given in Part I, the threshold quantities are the maximum quantities given in each range. Five years after the entry into force of this Convention, the lowest quantity given in each range shall become the threshold quantity, unless amended.

Where a substance or preparation named in Part II also falls within a category in Part I, the threshold quantity set out in Part II shall be used.

For the identification of hazardous activities, Parties shall take into consideration the foreseeable possibility of aggravation of the hazards involved and the quantities of the hazardous substances and their proximity, whether under the charge of one or more operators.

Part I
Categories of substances and preparations not specifically named in Part II

Category	Threshold quantity (tonnes)
1. Flammable gases (1a) including LPG	200
2. Highly flammable liquids (1b)	50,000
3. Very toxic (1c)	20
4. Toxic (1d)	500–200
5. Oxidizing (1e)	500–200
6. Explosive (1f)	200–50
7. Flammable liquids (1g) (handled under special conditions of pressure and temperature)	200
8. Dangerous for the environment (1h)	200

Part II
Named substances

Substance	Threshold quantity (tonnes)
1. Ammonia	500
2a. Ammonium nitrate (2)	2,500
2b. Ammonium nitrate in the form of fertilizers (3)	10,000
3. Acrylonitrile	200
4. Chlorine	25
5. Ethylene oxide	50
6. Hydrogen cyanide	20
7. Hydrogen fluoride	50
8. Hydrogen sulphide	50
9. Sulphur dioxide	250
10. Sulphur trioxide	75
11. Lead alkyls	50
12. Phosgene	0.75
13. Methyl isocyanate	0.15

Notes

1. *Indicative criteria.* In the absence of other appropriate criteria, Parties may use the following criteria when classifying substances or preparations for the purposes of Part I of this Annex.

(a) FLAMMABLE GASES: substances which in the gaseous state at normal pressure and mixed with air become flammable and the boiling point of which at normal pressure is 20°C or below;

(b) HIGHLY FLAMMABLE LIQUIDS: substances which have a flash point lower than 21°C and the boiling point of which at normal pressure is above 20°C;

(c) VERY TOXIC: substances with properties corresponding to those in table 1 or table 2 below, and which, owing to their physical and chemical properties, are capable of creating industrial accident hazards.

Table 1

$LD_{50}(oral)(1)$ mg/kg body weight $LD_{50}<=25$	$LD_{50}(dermal)(2)$ mg/kg body weight $LD_{50}<=50$	$LC_{50}(3)$ mg/l(inhalation) $LC_{50}<=0.5$

(1) LD_{50} oral in rats
(2) LD_{50} dermal in rats or rabbits
(3) LC_{50} by inhalation (four hours) in
   rats

Table 2

Discriminating dose mg/kg body weight	<5

where the acute oral toxicity in animals of the substance has been determined using the fixed-dose procedure.

(d) TOXIC: substances with properties corresponding to those in table 3 or 4 and having physical and chemical properties capable of creating industrial accident hazards.

Table 3

$LD_{50}(oral)(1)$ mg/kg body weight $25 < LD_{50}<=200$	$LD_{50}(dermal)(2)$ mg/kg body weight $50 < LD_{50}<=400$	$LC_{50}(3)$ mg/l(inhalation) $0.5 < LC_{50} <=2$

(1) LD_{50} oral in rats
(2) LD_{50} dermal in rats or rabbits
(3) LC_{50} by inhalation (four hours) in
   rats

Table 4

Discriminating dose mg/kg body weight	=5

where the acute oral toxicity in animals of the substance has been determined using the fixed-dose procedure.

(e) OXIDIZING: substances which give rise to highly exothermic reaction when in contact with other substances, particularly flammable substances.
(f) EXPLOSIVE: substances which may explode under the effect of flame or which are more sensitive to shocks or friction than dinitrobenzene.
(g) FLAMMABLE LIQUIDS: substances which have a flash point lower than 55°C and which remain liquid under pressure, where particular processing conditions, such as high pressure and high temperature, may create industrial accident hazards.
(h) DANGEROUS FOR THE ENVIRONMENT: substances showing the values for acute toxicity to the aquatic environment corresponding to table 5.

Table 5

$LC_{50}(1)$ mg/l $LC_{50} <= 10$	$EC_{50}(2)$ mg/l $EC_{50} <= 10$	$IC_{50}(3)$ mg/l $IC_{50} <= 10$

(1) LC_{50} fish (96 hours)
(2) EC_{50} daphnia (48 hours)
(3) IC_{50} algae (72 hours)
where the substance is not readily degradable, or the log Pow > 3.0 (unless the experimentally determined BCF < 100).

(i) LD - lethal dose
(j) LC – lethal concentration
(k) EC – effective concentration
(l) IC – inhibiting concentration
(m) Pow – partition coefficient octanol/water
(n) BCF – bioconcentration factor

2. This applies to ammonium nitrate and mixtures of ammonium nitrate where the nitrogen content derived from the ammonium nitrate is > 28% by weight, and to aqueous solutions of ammonium nitrate where the concentration of ammonium nitrate is > 90% by weight.

3. This applies to straight ammonium nitrate fertilizers and to compound fertilizers where the nitrogen content derived from the ammonium nitrate is > 28% by weight (a compound fertilizer contains ammonium nitrate together with phosphate and/or potash).

4. Mixtures and preparations containing such substances shall be treated in the same way as the pure substance unless they no longer exhibit equivalent properties and are not capable of producing transboundary effects.

Annex II
Inquiry commission procedure pursuant to Articles 4 and 5

1. The requesting Party or Parties shall notify the secretariat that it or they is (are) submitting question(s) to an inquiry commission established in accordance with the provisions of this Annex. The notification shall state the subject-matter of the inquiry. The secretariat shall immediately inform all Parties to the Convention of this submission.

2. The inquiry commission shall consist of three members. Both the requesting party and the other party to the inquiry procedure shall appoint a scientific or technical expert and the two experts so appointed shall designate by common agreement a third expert, who shall be the president of the inquiry commission. The latter shall not be a national of one of the parties to the inquiry procedure, nor have his or her usual place of residence in the territory of one of these parties, nor be employed by any of them, nor have dealt with the case in any other capacity.

3. If the president of the inquiry commission has not been designated within two months of the appointment of the second expert, the Executive Secretary of the Economic Commission for Europe shall, at the request of either party, designate the president within a further two-month period.

4. If one of the parties to the inquiry procedure does not appoint an expert within one month of its receipt of the notification by the secretariat, the other party may inform the Executive Secretary of the Economic Commission for Europe, who shall designate the president of the inquiry commission within a further two-month period. Upon designation, the president of the inquiry commission shall request the party which has not appointed an expert to do so within one month. If it fails to do so within that period, the president shall inform the Executive Secretary of the Economic Commission for Europe who shall make this appointment within a further two-month period.

5. The inquiry commission shall adopt its own rules of procedure.

6. The inquiry commission may take all appropriate measures in order to carry out its functions.

7. The parties to the inquiry procedure shall facilitate the work of the inquiry commission and in particular shall, using all means at their disposal:

(a) Provide the inquiry commission with all relevant documents, facilities and information;

(b) Enable the inquiry commission, where necessary, to call witnesses or experts and receive their evidence.

8. The parties and the experts shall protect the confidentiality of any information they receive in confidence during the work of the inquiry commission.

9. If one of the parties to the inquiry procedure does not appear before the inquiry commission or fails to present its case, the other party may request the inquiry commission to continue the proceedings and to complete its work. Absence of a party or failure of a party to present its case shall not constitute a bar to the continuation and completion of the work of the inquiry commission.

10. Unless the inquiry commission determines otherwise because of the particular circumstances of the matter, the expenses of the inquiry commission, including the remuneration of its members, shall be borne equally by the parties to the inquiry procedure. The inquiry commission shall keep a record of all its expenses and shall furnish a final statement thereof to the parties.

11. Any Party which has an interest of a factual nature in the subject-matter of the inquiry procedure and which may be affected by an opinion in the matter may intervene in the proceedings with the consent of the inquiry commission.

12. The decisions of the inquiry commission on matters of the procedure shall be taken by majority vote of its members. The final opinion of the inquiry commission shall reflect the view of the majority of its members and shall include any dissenting view.

13. The inquiry commission shall present its final opinion within two months of the date on which it was established, unless it finds it necessary to extend this time-limit for a period which should not exceed two months.

14. The final opinion of the inquiry commission shall be based on accepted scientific principles. The final opinion shall be transmitted by the inquiry commission to the parties to the inquiry procedure and to the secretariat.

Annex III
Procedures pursuant to Article 4

1. A Party of origin may request consultations with another Party, in accordance with paragraphs 2 to 5 of this Annex, in order to determine whether that Party is an affected Party.

2. For a proposed or existing hazardous activity, the Party of origin shall, for the purposes of ensuring adequate and effective consultations, provide for the notification at appropriate levels of any Party that it considers may be an affected Party as early as possible and no later than when informing its own public about that proposed or existing activity. For existing hazardous activities such notification shall be provided no later than two years after the entry into force of this Convention for a Party of origin.

3. The notification shall contain, *inter alia*:

(a) Information on the hazardous activity, including any available information or report, such as information produced in accordance with Article 6, on its possible transboundary effects in the event of an industrial accident;

(b) An indication of a reasonable time within which a response under paragraph 4 of this Annex is required, taking into account the nature of the activity;

and may include the information set out in paragraph 6 of this Annex.

4. The notified Parties shall respond to the Party of origin within the time specified in the notification, acknowledging receipt of the notification and indicating whether they intend to enter into consultation.

5. If a notified Party indicates that it does not intend to enter into consultation, or if it does not respond within the time specified in the notification, the provisions set down in the following paragraphs of this Annex shall not apply. In such circumstances, the right of a Party of origin to determine whether to carry out an assessment and analysis on the basis of its national law and practice is not prejudiced.

6. Upon receipt of a response from a notified Party indicating its desire to enter into consultation, the Party of origin shall, if it has not already done so, provide to the notified Party:

(a) Relevant information regarding the time schedule for analysis, including an indication of the time schedule for the transmittal of comments;

(b) Relevant information on the hazardous activity and its transboundary effects in the event of an industrial accident;

(c) The opportunity to participate in evaluations of the information or any report demonstrating possible transboundary effects.

7. An affected Party shall, at the request of the Party of origin, provide the latter with reasonably obtainable information relating to the area under the jurisdiction of the affected Party capable of being affected, where such information is necessary for the preparation of the assessment and analysis and measures. The information shall be furnished promptly and, as appropriate, through a joint body where one exists.

8. The Party of origin shall furnish the affected Party directly, as appropriate, or, where one exists, through a joint body with the analysis and evaluation documentation as described in Annex V, paragraphs 1 and 2.

9. The Parties concerned shall inform the public in areas reasonably capable of being affected by the hazardous activity and shall arrange for the distribution of the analysis and evaluation documentation to it and to authorities in the relevant areas. The Parties shall ensure them an opportunity for making comments on, or objections to, the hazardous activity and shall arrange for their views to be submitted to the competent authority of the Party of origin,

either directly to that authority or, where appropriate, through the Party of origin, within a reasonable time.

10. The Party of origin shall, after completion of the analysis and evaluation documentation, enter without undue delay into consultations with the affected Party concerning, *inter alia*, the transboundary effects of the hazardous activity in the event of an industrial accident, and measures to reduce or eliminate its effects. The consultations may relate to:

(a) Possible alternatives to the hazardous activity, including the no-action alternative, and possible measures to mitigate transboundary effects at the expense of the Party of origin;

(b) Other forms of possible mutual assistance for reducing any transboundary effects:

(c) Any other appropriate matters.

The Parties concerned shall, on the commencement of such consultations, agree on a reasonable time-frame for the duration of the consultation period. Any such consultations may be conducted through an appropriate joint body, where one exists.

11. The Parties concerned shall ensure that due account is taken of the analysis and evaluation, as well as of the comments received pursuant to paragraph 9 of this Annex and of the outcome of the consultations referred to in paragraph 10 of this Annex.

12. The Party of origin shall notify the affected Parties of any decision on the activity, along with the reasons and considerations on which it was based.

13. If, after additional and relevant information concerning the transboundary effects of a hazardous activity and which was not available at the time consultations were held with respect to that activity, becomes available to a Party concerned, that Party shall immediately inform the other Party or Parties concerned. If one of the Parties concerned so requests, renewed consultations shall be held.

Annex IV
Preventive measures pursuant to Article 6

The following measures may be carried out, depending on national laws and practices, by Parties, competent authorities, operators, or by joint efforts:

1. The setting of general or specific safety objectives;
2. The adoption of legislative provisions or guidelines concerning safety measures and safety standards;
3. The identification of those hazardous activities which require special preventive measures, which may include a licensing or authorization system;
4. The evaluation of risk analyses or of safety studies for hazardous activities and an action plan for the implementation of necessary measures;

5. The provision to the competent authorities of the information needed to assess risks;
6. The application of the most appropriate technology in order to prevent industrial accidents and protect human beings and the environment;
7. The undertaking, in order to prevent industrial accidents, of the appropriate education and training of all persons engaged in hazardous activities on-site under both normal and abnormal conditions;
8. The establishment of internal managerial structures and practices designed to implement and maintain safety regulations effectively;
9. The monitoring and auditing of hazardous activities and the carrying out of inspections.

Annex V
Analysis and evaluation

1. The analysis and evaluation of the hazardous activity should be performed with a scope and to a depth which vary depending on the purpose for which they are carried out.

2. The following table illustrates, for the purposes of the related Articles, matters which should be considered in the analysis and evaluation, for the purposes listed:

Purpose of analysis	Matters to be considered
Emergency planning under Article 8	(1) The quantities and properties of hazardous substances on the site; (2) Brief descriptive scenarios of a representative sample of industrial accidents possibly arising from the hazardous activity, including an indication of the likelihood of each; (3) For each scenario: (a) The approximate quantity of a release; (b) The extent and severity of the resulting consequences both for people and for the non-human environment in favourable and unfavourable conditions, including the extent of resulting hazard zones; (c) The time-scale within which the industrial accident could develop from the initiating event; (d) Any action which could be taken to minimize the likelihood of escalation.

(*cont.*)

(cont.)

Purpose of analysis	Matters to be considered
	(4) The size and distribution of the population in the vicinity, including any large concentrations of people potentially in the hazard zone;
	(5) The age, mobility and susceptibility of that population.
	In addition to items (1) to (5) above:
Decision-making on siting under Article 7	(6) The severity of the harm inflicted on people and the environment, depending on the nature and circumstances of the release;
	(7) The distance from the location of the hazardous activity at which harmful effects on people and the environment may reasonably occur in the event of an industrial accident;
	(8) The same information not only for the present situation but also for planned or reasonably foreseeable future developments.
Information to the public under Article 9	In addition to items (1) to (4) above:
	(9) The people who may be affected by an industrial accident.
Preventive measures under Article 6	In addition to items (4) to (9) above, more detailed versions of the descriptions and assessments set out in items (1) to (3) will be needed for preventive measures. In addition to those descriptions and assessments, the following matters should also be covered:
	(10) The conditions and quantities in which hazardous materials are handled;
	(11) A list of the scenarios for the types of industrial accidents with serious effects, to include examples covering the full range of incident size and the possibility of effects from adjacent activities;
	(12) For each scenario, a description of the events which could initiate an industrial accident and the steps whereby it could escalate;
	(13) An assessment, at least in general terms, of the likelihood of each step occurring, taking into account the arrangements in (14);
	(14) A description of the preventive measures in terms of both equipment and procedures designed to minimize the likelihood of each step occurring;

(cont.)

(*cont.*)

Purpose of analysis	Matters to be considered
	(15) An assessment of the effects that deviations from normal operating conditions could have, and the consequent arrangements for safe shut-down of the hazardous activity or any part thereof in an emergency, and of the need for staff training to ensure that potentially serious deviations are recognized at an early stage and appropriate action taken;
	(16) An assessment of the extent to which modifications, repair work and maintenance work on the hazardous activity could place the control measures at risk, and the consequent arrangements to ensure that control is maintained.

Annex VI
Decision-making on siting pursuant to Article 7

The following illustrates the matters which should be considered pursuant to Article 7:

1. The results of risk analysis and evaluation, including an evaluation pursuant to Annex V of the physical characteristics of the area in which the hazardous activity is being planned;
2. The results of consultations and public participation processes;
3. An analysis of the increase or decrease of the risk caused by any development in the territory of the affected Party in relation to an existing hazardous activity in the territory of the Party of origin;
4. The evaluation of the environmental risks, including any transboundary effects;
5. An evaluation of the new hazardous activities which could be a source of risk;
6. A consideration of the siting of new, and significant modifications to existing hazardous activities at a safe distance from existing centres of population, as well as the establishment of a safety area around hazardous activities; within such areas, developments which would increase the populations at risk, or otherwise increase the severity of the risk, should be closely examined.

Annex VII
Emergency preparedness measures pursuant to Article 8

1. All contingency plans, both on- and off-site, should be coordinated to provide a comprehensive and effective response to industrial accidents.

2. The contingency plans should include the actions necessary to localize emergencies and to prevent or minimize their transboundary effects. They should also include arrangements for warning people and, where appropriate, arrangements for their evacuation, other protective or rescue actions and health services.

3. Contingency plans should give on-site personnel, people who might be affected off site and rescue forces, details of technical and organizational procedures which are appropriate for response in the event of an industrial accident capable of having transboundary effects and to prevent and minimize effects on people and the environment, both on and off site.

4. Examples of matters which could be covered by on-site contingency plans include:

(a) Organizational roles and responsibilities on site for dealing with an emergency;
(b) A description of the action which should be taken in the event of an industrial accident, or an imminent threat thereof, in order to control the condition or event, or details of where such a description can be found;
(c) A description of the equipment and resources available;
(d) Arrangements for providing early warning of industrial accidents to the public authority responsible for the off-site emergency response, including the type of information which should be included in an initial warning and the arrangements for providing more detailed information as it becomes available;
(e) Arrangements for training personnel in the duties they will be expected to perform.

5. Examples of matters which could be covered by off-site contingency plans include:

(a) Organizational roles and responsibilities off-site for dealing with an emergency, including how integration with on-site plans is to be achieved;
(b) Methods and procedures to be followed by emergency and medical personnel;
(c) Methods for rapidly determining the affected area;
(d) Arrangements for ensuring that prompt industrial accident notification is made to affected or potentially affected Parties and that that liaison is maintained subsequently;

(e) Identification of resources necessary to implement the plan and the arrangements for coordination;

(f) Arrangements for providing information to the public including, where appropriate, the arrangements for reinforcing and repeating the information provided to the public pursuant to article 9;

(g) Arrangements for training and exercises.

6. Contingency plans could include the measures for: treatment; collection; clean-up; storage; removal and safe disposal of hazardous substances and contaminated material; and restoration.

Annex VIII
Information to the public pursuant to Article 9

1. The name of the company, address of the hazardous activity and identification by position held of the person giving the information;

2. An explanation in simple terms of the hazardous activity, including the risks;

3. The common names or the generic names or the general danger classification of the substances and preparations which are involved in the hazardous activity, with an indication of their principal dangerous characteristics;

4. General information resulting from an environmental impact assessment, if available and relevant;

5. The general information relating to the nature of an industrial accident that could possibly occur in the hazardous activity, including its potential effects on the population and the environment;

6. Adequate information on how the affected population will be warned and kept informed in the event of an industrial accident;

7. Adequate information on the actions the affected population should take and on the behaviour they should adopt in the event of an industrial accident;

8. Adequate information on arrangements made regarding the hazardous activity, including liaison with the emergency services, to deal with industrial accidents, to reduce the severity of the industrial accidents and to mitigate their effects;

9. General information on the emergency services' off-site contingency plan, drawn up to cope with any off-site effects, including the transboundary effects of an industrial accident;

10. General information on special requirements and conditions to which the hazardous activity is subject according to the relevant national regulations and/or administrative provisions, including licensing or authorization systems;

11. Details of where further relevant information can be obtained.

Annex IX
Industrial accident notification systems pursuant to Article 10

1. The industrial accident notification systems shall enable the speediest possible transmission of data and forecasts according to previously determined codes using compatible data-transmission and data-treatment systems for emergency warning and response, and for measures to minimize and contain the consequences of transboundary effects, taking account of different needs at different levels.

2. The industrial accident notification shall include the following:

(a) The type and magnitude of the industrial accident, the hazardous substances involved (if known), and the severity of its possible effects;
(b) The time of occurrence and exact location of the accident;
(c) Such other available information as necessary for an efficient response to the industrial accident.

3. The industrial accident notification shall be supplemented at appropriate intervals, or whenever required, by further relevant information on the development of the situation concerning transboundary effects.

4. Regular tests and reviews of the effectiveness of the industrial accident notification systems shall be undertaken, including the regular training of the personnel involved. Where appropriate, such tests, reviews and training shall be performed jointly.

Annex X
Mutual assistance pursuant to Article 12

1. The overall direction, control, coordination and supervision of the assistance is the responsibility of the requesting Party. The personnel involved in the assisting operation shall act in accordance with the relevant laws of the requesting Party. The appropriate authorities of the requesting Party shall cooperate with the authority designated by the assisting Party, pursuant to Article 17, as being in charge of the immediate operational supervision of the personnel and the equipment provided by the assisting Party.

2. The requesting Party shall, to the extent of its capabilities, provide local facilities and services for the proper and effective administration of the assistance, and shall ensure the protection of personnel, equipment and materials brought into its territory by, or on behalf of, the assisting Party for such a purpose.

3. Unless otherwise agreed by the Parties concerned, assistance shall be provided at the expense of the requesting Party. The assisting Party may at any time waive wholly or partly the reimbursement of costs.

4. The requesting Party shall use its best efforts to afford to the assisting Party and persons acting on its behalf the privileges, immunities or facilities necessary for the expeditious performance of their assistance functions. The requesting Party shall not be required to apply this provision to its own nationals or permanent residents or to afford them the privileges and immunities referred to above.

5. A Party shall, at the request of the requesting or assisting Party, endeavour to facilitate the transit through its territory of duly notified personnel, equipment and property involved in the assistance to and from the requesting Party.

6. The requesting Party shall facilitate the entry into, stay in and departure from its national territory of duly notified personnel and of equipment and property involved in the assistance.

7. With regard to acts resulting directly from the assistance provided, the requesting Party shall, in respect of the death of or injury to persons, damage to or loss of property, or damage to the environment caused within its territory in the course of the provision of the assistance requested, hold harmless and indemnify the assisting Party or persons acting on its behalf and compensate them for death or injury suffered by them and for loss of or damage to equipment or other property involved in the assistance. The requesting Party shall be responsible for dealing with claims brought by third parties against the assisting Party or persons acting on its behalf.

8. The Parties concerned shall cooperate closely in order to facilitate the settlement of legal proceedings and claims which could result from assistance operations.

9. Any Party may request assistance relating to the medical treatment or the temporary relocation in the territory of another Party of persons involved in an accident.

10. The affected or requesting Party may at any time, after appropriate consultations and by notification, request the termination of assistance received or provided under this Convention. Once such a request has been made, the Parties concerned shall consult one another with a view to making arrangements for the proper termination of the assistance.

Annex XI
Exchange of information pursuant to Article 15

Information shall include the following elements, which can also be the subject of multilateral and bilateral cooperation:

(a) Legislative and administrative measures, policies, objectives and priorities for prevention, preparedness and response, scientific activities and

technical measures to reduce the risk of industrial accidents from hazardous activities, including the mitigation of transboundary effects;

(b) Measures and contingency plans at the appropriate level affecting other
Parties;

(c) Programmes for monitoring, planning, research and development, including their implementation and surveillance;

(d) Measures taken regarding prevention of, preparedness for and response to
industrial accidents;

(e) Experience with industrial accidents and cooperation in response to industrial accidents with transboundary effects;

(f) The development and application of the best available technologies for
improved environmental protection and safety;

(g) Emergency preparedness and response;

(h) Methods used for the prediction of risks, including criteria for the monitoring and assessment of transboundary effects.

Annex XII
Tasks for mutual assistance pursuant to Article 18, paragraph 4

1. Information and data collection and dissemination

(a) Establishment and operation of an industrial accident notification system that can provide information on industrial accidents and on experts,
in order to involve the experts as rapidly as possible in providing assistance;

(b) Establishment and operation of a data bank for the reception, processing
and distribution of necessary information on industrial accidents, including their effects, and also on measures applied and their effectiveness;

(c) Elaboration and maintenance of a list of hazardous substances, including
their relevant characteristics, and of information on how to deal with those
in the event of an industrial accident;

(d) Establishment and maintenance of a register of experts to provide consultative and other kinds of assistance regarding preventive, preparedness and
response measures, including restoration measures;

(e) Maintenance of a list of hazardous activities;

(f) Production and maintenance of a list of hazardous substances covered by
the provisions of Annex I, Part I.

2. Research, training and methodologies

(a) Development and provision of models based on experience from industrial accidents, and scenarios for preventive, preparedness and response
measures;

(b) Promotion of education and training, organization of international symposia and promotion of cooperation in research and development.

3. Technical assistance

(a) Fulfillment of advisory functions aimed at strengthening the ability to apply preventive, preparedness and response measures;
(b) Undertaking, at the request of a Party, of inspections of its hazardous activities and the provision of assistance in organizing its national inspections according to the requirements of this Convention.

4. Assistance in the case of an emergency
Provision, at the request of a Party, of assistance by, *inter alia*, sending experts to the site of an industrial accident to provide consultative and other kinds of assistance in response to the industrial accident.

Annex XIII
Arbitration

1. The claimant Party or Parties shall notify the secretariat that the Parties have agreed to submit the dispute to arbitration pursuant to Article 21, paragraph 2 of this Convention. The notification shall state the subject-matter of arbitration and include, in particular, the Articles of this Convention, the interpretation or application of which is at issue. The secretariat shall forward the information received to all Parties to this Convention.

2. The arbitral tribunal shall consist of three members. Both the claimant Party or Parties and the other Party or Parties to the dispute shall appoint an arbitrator, and the two arbitrators so appointed shall designate by common agreement the third arbitrator, who shall be the president of the arbitral tribunal. The latter shall not be a national of one of the parties to the dispute, nor have his or her usual place of residence in the territory of one of these parties, nor be employed by any of them, nor have dealt with the case in any other capacity.

3. If the president of the arbitral tribunal has not been designated within two months of the appointment of the second arbitrator, the Executive Secretary of the Economic Commission for Europe shall, at the request of either party to the dispute, designate the president within a further two-month period.

4. If one of the parties to the dispute does not appoint an arbitrator within two months of the receipt of the request, the other party may so inform the Executive Secretary of the Economic Commission for Europe, who shall designate the president of the arbitral tribunal within a further two-month period. Upon designation, the president of the arbitral tribunal shall request the party which has not appointed an arbitrator to do so within two months. If it fails to do

so within that period, the president shall inform the Executive Secretary of the Economic Commission for Europe, who shall make this appointment within a further two-month period.

5. The arbitral tribunal shall render its decision in accordance with international law and in accordance with the provisions of this Convention.

6. Any arbitral tribunal constituted under the provisions set out herein shall draw up its own rules of procedure.

7. The decisions of the arbitral tribunal, both on procedure and on substance, shall be taken by majority vote of its members.

8. The tribunal may take all appropriate measures to establish the facts.

9. The parties to the dispute shall facilitate the work of the arbitral tribunal and, in particular shall, using all means at their disposal:

(a) Provide the tribunal with all relevant documents, facilities and information;
(b) Enable the tribunal, where necessary, to call witnesses or experts and receive their evidence.

10. The parties to the dispute and the arbitrators shall protect the confidentiality of any information they receive in confidence during the proceedings of the arbitral tribunal.

11. The arbitral tribunal may, at the request of one of the parties, recommend interim measures of protection.

12. If one of the parties to the dispute does not appear before the arbitral tribunal or fails to defend its case, the other party may request the tribunal to continue the proceedings and to render its final decision. Absence of a party or failure of a party to defend its case shall not constitute a bar to the proceedings.

13. The arbitral tribunal may hear and determine counter-claims arising directly out of the subject-matter of the dispute.

14. Unless the arbitral tribunal determines otherwise because of the particular circumstances of the case, the expenses of the tribunal, including the remuneration of its members, shall be borne equally by the parties to the dispute. The tribunal shall keep a record of all its expenses and shall furnish a final statement thereof to the parties to the dispute.

15. Any Party to this Convention which has an interest of a legal nature in the subject-matter of the dispute and which may be affected by a decision in the case, may intervene in the proceedings with the consent of the tribunal.

16. The arbitral tribunal shall render its award within five months of the date on which it is established unless it finds it necessary to extend the time-limit for a period which should not exceed five months.

17. The award of the arbitral tribunal shall be accompanied by a statement of reasons. It shall be final and binding upon all parties to the dispute. The award will be transmitted by the arbitral tribunal to the parties to the dispute

and to the secretariat. The secretariat will forward the information received to all Parties to this Convention.

18. Any dispute which may arise between the parties concerning the interpretation or execution of the award may be submitted by either party to the arbitral tribunal which made the award or, if the latter cannot be seized thereof, to another tribunal constituted for this purpose in the same manner as the first.

World Bank Operational Policy 4.01 on Environmental Assessment, January 1999

Editorial note

The World Bank first adopted Operational Directive 4.01 on Environmental Assessment in 1989, its objective being to ensure that the development options adopted were sound and enduring from an environmental perspective and that environmental consequences were recognised at an early stage in the project cycle and included in the project scheme. The Directive was the subject of significant criticism, including the failure to provide for a 'no-action alternative' whereby the project may be stopped because the environmental risks are too great to allow the project to proceed at all, and its silence as to mandatory requirements concerning the provision of information to local populations and their right to participate in the environmental impact assessment process. In 1999 the policy was converted into a new format, now reflected in Operation Policy (OP) 4.01 and Bank Procedures (BP) 4.01, which has sought to address these and other issues. The Bank Procedures explain how the Bank staff shall implement the Bank's policies.

By OP 4.01 the World Bank requires environmental assessment (EA) of projects proposed for Bank financing to help ensure that they are environmentally sound and sustainable, and thus to improve decision-making (paragraph 1). EA is described as a process, which evaluates a project's potential environmental risks and impacts in its area of influence; examines project alternatives; identifies ways of improving project selection, siting, planning, design, and implementation; and includes the process of mitigating and managing adverse environmental impacts throughout project implementation. It is premised on the Bank preference for 'preventive measures over mitigatory or compensatory measures, whenever feasible' (paragraph 2). The borrower is responsible for carrying out the EA, which may comprise one or more of an environmental impact assessment (EIA), a regional or sectoral EA, an environmental audit, a hazard or risk assessment, and an environmental management plan (EMP) (Annex C to OP 4.01 describes the EMP). The Bank is responsible for environmental screening of each proposed project to determine the appropriate extent and type of EA, and classifies the proposed project into one of four categories. A proposed project is Category A if it is 'likely to have significant adverse environmental impacts that are sensitive, diverse, or unprecedented', and will normally require an EIA (or a comprehensive regional or sectoral EA). OP 4.01 Annex B describes the content of a Category A environmental assessment report (to include executive summary; policy, legal, and administrative framework; project description; baseline data; environmental impacts; analysis of alternatives; environmental management plan (EMP)). A proposed project is classified as Category B if its potential adverse environmental impacts are site-specific, if few of them are irreversible, and if mitigatory measures can be designed more readily than for Category A projects. The scope of EA for a Category B project will be narrower. A proposed project is classified as Category C if it is likely to have minimal or no adverse environmental impacts. A proposed project is classified as Category FI if it involves investment of Bank funds through a financial intermediary, in subprojects that may result in adverse environmental impacts. Environmental assessments are also required for special project types. Category A and B projects must be subject to public consultation (paragraph 15).

Date of adoption: January 1999

Website: www.worldbank.org/environmentalassessment

World Bank Operational Policy 4.01 on Environmental Assessment

1. The Bank[1] requires environmental assessment (EA) of projects proposed for Bank financing to help ensure that they are environmentally sound and sustainable, and thus to improve decision making.

2. EA is a process whose breadth, depth, and type of analysis depend on the nature, scale, and potential environmental impact of the proposed project. EA evaluates a project's potential environmental risks and impacts in its area of influence; examines project alternatives; identifies ways of improving project selection, siting, planning, design, and implementation by preventing, minimizing, mitigating, or compensating for adverse environmental impacts and

---

[1] 'Bank' includes IDA; 'EA' refers to the entire process set out in OP/BP 4.01; 'loans' includes credits; 'borrower' includes, for guarantee operations, a private or public project sponsor receiving from another financial institution a loan guaranteed by the Bank; and 'project' covers all operations financed by Bank loans or guarantees except structural adjustment loans (for which the environmental provisions are set out in OP/BP 8.60, *Adjustment Lending*, forthcoming) and debt and debt service operations, and also includes projects under adaptable lending – adaptable program loans (APLs) and learning and innovation loans (LILs) – and projects and components funded under the Global Environment Facility. The project is described in Schedule 2 to the Loan/Credit Agreement. This policy applies to all components of the project, regardless of the source of financing. [*Other footnotes omitted.*]

enhancing positive impacts; and includes the process of mitigating and managing adverse environmental impacts throughout project implementation. The Bank favors preventive measures over mitigatory or compensatory measures, whenever feasible.

3. EA takes into account the natural environment (air, water, and land); human health and safety; social aspects (involuntary resettlement, indigenous peoples, and cultural property); and transboundary and global environmental aspects. EA considers natural and social aspects in an integrated way. It also takes into account the variations in project and country conditions; the findings of country environmental studies; national environmental action plans; the country's overall policy framework, national legislation, and institutional capabilities related to the environment and social aspects; and obligations of the country, pertaining to project activities, under relevant international environmental treaties and agreements. The Bank does not finance project activities that would contravene such country obligations, as identified during the EA. EA is initiated as early as possible in project processing and is integrated closely with the economic, financial, institutional, social, and technical analyses of a proposed project.

4. The borrower is responsible for carrying out the EA. For Category A projects, the borrower retains independent EA experts not affiliated with the project to carry out the EA. For Category A projects that are highly risky or contentious or that involve serious and multidimensional environmental concerns, the borrower should normally also engage an advisory panel of independent, internationally recognized environmental specialists to advise on all aspects of the project relevant to the EA. The role of the advisory panel depends on the degree to which project preparation has progressed, and on the extent and quality of any EA work completed, at the time the Bank begins to consider the project.

5. The Bank advises the borrower on the Bank's EA requirements. The Bank reviews the findings and recommendations of the EA to determine whether they provide an adequate basis for processing the project for Bank financing. When the borrower has completed or partially completed EA work prior to the Bank's involvement in a project, the Bank reviews the EA to ensure its consistency with this policy. The Bank may, if appropriate, require additional EA work, including public consultation and disclosure.

6. The *Pollution Prevention and Abatement Handbook* describes pollution prevention and abatement measures and emission levels that are normally acceptable to the Bank. However, taking into account borrower country legislation and local conditions, the EA may recommend alternative emission levels and approaches to pollution prevention and abatement for the project. The EA report must provide full and detailed justification for the levels and approaches chosen for the particular project or site.

EA instruments

7. Depending on the project, a range of instruments can be used to satisfy the Bank's EA requirement: environmental impact assessment (EIA), regional or sectoral EA, environmental audit, hazard or risk assessment, and environmental management plan (EMP). EA applies one or more of these instruments, or elements of them, as appropriate. When the project is likely to have sectoral or regional impacts, sectoral or regional EA is required.

Environmental screening

8. The Bank undertakes environmental screening of each proposed project to determine the appropriate extent and type of EA. The Bank classifies the proposed project into one of four categories, depending on the type, location, sensitivity, and scale of the project and the nature and magnitude of its potential environmental impacts.

(a) *Category A*: A proposed project is classified as Category A if it is likely to have significant adverse environmental impacts that are sensitive, diverse, or unprecedented. These impacts may affect an area broader than the sites or facilities subject to physical works. EA for a Category A project examines the project's potential negative and positive environmental impacts, compares them with those of feasible alternatives (including the 'without project' situation), and recommends any measures needed to prevent, minimize, mitigate, or compensate for adverse impacts and improve environmental performance. For a Category A project, the borrower is responsible for preparing a report, normally an EIA (or a suitably comprehensive regional or sectoral EA) that includes, as necessary, elements of the other instruments referred to in para. 7.

(b) *Category B*: A proposed project is classified as Category B if its potential adverse environmental impacts on human populations or environmentally important areas – including wetlands, forests, grasslands, and other natural habitats – are less adverse than those of Category A projects. These impacts are site-specific; few if any of them are irreversible; and in most cases mitigatory measures can be designed more readily than for Category A projects. The scope of EA for a Category B project may vary from project to project, but it is narrower than that of Category A EA. Like Category A EA, it examines the project's potential negative and positive environmental impacts and recommends any measures needed to prevent, minimize, mitigate, or compensate for adverse impacts and improve environmental performance. The findings and results of Category B EA are described in the project documentation (Project Appraisal Document and Project Information Document).

(c) *Category C*: A proposed project is classified as Category C if it is likely to have minimal or no adverse environmental impacts. Beyond screening, no further EA action is required for a Category C project.

(d) *CategoryFI*: A proposed project is classified as Category FI if it involves investment of Bank funds through a financial intermediary, in subprojects that may result in adverse environmental impacts.

EA for special project types

Sector investment lending

9. For sector investment loans (SILs), during the preparation of each proposed subproject, the project coordinating entity or implementing institution carries out appropriate EA according to country requirements and the requirements of this policy. The Bank appraises and, if necessary, includes in the SIL components to strengthen, the capabilities of the coordinating entity or the implementing institution to (a) screen subprojects, (b) obtain the necessary expertise to carry out EA, (c) review all findings and results of EA for individual subprojects, (d) ensure implementation of mitigation measures (including, where applicable, an EMP), and (e) monitor environmental conditions during project implementation. If the Bank is not satisfied that adequate capacity exists for carrying out EA, all Category A subprojects and, as appropriate, Category B subprojects – including any EA reports – are subject to prior review and approval by the Bank.

Sector adjustment lending

10. Sector adjustment loans (SECALs) are subject to the requirements of this policy. EA for a SECAL assesses the potential environmental impacts of planned policy, institutional, and regulatory actions under the loan.

Financial intermediary lending

11. For a financial intermediary (FI) operation, the Bank requires that each FI screen proposed subprojects and ensure that subborrowers carry out appropriate EA for each subproject. Before approving a subproject, the FI verifies (through its own staff, outside experts, or existing environmental institutions) that the subproject meets the environmental requirements of appropriate national and local authorities and is consistent with this OP and other applicable environmental policies of the Bank.

12. In appraising a proposed FI operation, the Bank reviews the adequacy of country environmental requirements relevant to the project and the proposed EA arrangements for subprojects, including the mechanisms and responsibilities for environmental screening and review of EA results. When necessary, the

Bank ensures that the project includes components to strengthen such EA arrangements. For FI operations expected to have Category A subprojects, prior to the Bank's appraisal each identified participating FI provides to the Bank a written assessment of the institutional mechanisms (including, as necessary, identification of measures to strengthen capacity) for its subproject EA work. If the Bank is not satisfied that adequate capacity exists for carrying out EA, all Category A subprojects and, as appropriate, Category B subprojects – including EA reports – are subject to prior review and approval by the Bank.

Emergency recovery projects

13. The policy set out in OP 4.01 normally applies to emergency recovery projects processed under OP 8.50, *Emergency Recovery Assistance.* However, when compliance with any requirement of this policy would prevent the effective and timely achievement of the objectives of an emergency recovery project, the Bank may exempt the project from such a requirement. The justification for any such exemption is recorded in the loan documents. In all cases, however, the Bank requires at a minimum that (a) the extent to which the emergency was precipitated or exacerbated by inappropriate environmental practices be determined as part of the preparation of such projects, and (b) any necessary corrective measures be built into either the emergency project or a future lending operation.

Institutional capacity

14. When the borrower has inadequate legal or technical capacity to carry out key EA-related functions (such as review of EA, environmental monitoring, inspections, or management of mitigatory measures) for a proposed project, the project includes components to strengthen that capacity.

Public consultation

15. For all Category A and B projects proposed for IBRD or IDA financing, during the EA process, the borrower consults project-affected groups and local nongovernmental organizations (NGOs) about the project's environmental aspects and takes their views into account. The borrower initiates such consultations as early as possible. For Category A projects, the borrower consults these groups at least twice: (a) shortly after environmental screening and before the terms of reference for the EA are finalized; and (b) once a draft EA report is prepared. In addition, the borrower consults with such groups throughout project implementation as necessary to address EA-related issues that affect them.

Disclosure

16. For meaningful consultations between the borrower and project-affected groups and local NGOs on all Category A and B projects proposed for IBRD or IDA financing, the borrower provides relevant material in a timely manner

prior to consultation and in a form and language that are understandable and accessible to the groups being consulted.

17. For a Category A project, the borrower provides for the initial consultation a summary of the proposed project's objectives, description, and potential impacts; for consultation after the draft EA report is prepared, the borrower provides a summary of the EA's conclusions. In addition, for a Category A project, the borrower makes the draft EA report available at a public place accessible to project-affected groups and local NGOs. For SILs and FI operations, the borrower/FI ensures that EA reports for Category A subprojects are made available in a public place accessible to affected groups and local NGOs.

18. Any separate Category B report for a project proposed for IDA financing is made available to project-affected groups and local NGOs. Public availability in the borrowing country and official receipt by the Bank of Category A reports for projects proposed for IBRD or IDA financing, and of any Category B EA report for projects proposed for IDA funding, are prerequisites to Bank appraisal of these projects.

19. Once the borrower officially transmits the Category A EA report to the Bank, the Bank distributes the summary (in English) to the executive directors (EDs) and makes the report available through its InfoShop. Once the borrower officially transmits any separate Category B EA report to the Bank, the Bank makes it available through its InfoShop. If the borrower objects to the Bank's releasing an EA report through the World Bank InfoShop, Bank staff (a) do not continue processing an IDA project, or (b) for an IBRD project, submit the issue of further processing to the EDs.

Implementation

20. During project implementation, the borrower reports on (a) compliance with measures agreed with the Bank on the basis of the findings and results of the EA, including implementation of any EMP, as set out in the project documents; (b) the status of mitigatory measures; and (c) the findings of monitoring programs. The Bank bases supervision of the project's environmental aspects on the findings and recommendations of the EA, including measures set out in the legal agreements, any EMP, and other project documents.

[*Footnotes omitted*]

Annex A
Definitions

1. *Environmental audit:* An instrument to determine the nature and extent of all environmental areas of concern at an existing facility. The audit identifies and justifies appropriate measures to mitigate the areas of concern, estimates the cost of the measures, and recommends a schedule for implementing them. For certain projects, the EA report may consist of an environmental audit alone; in other cases, the audit is part of the EA documentation.

2. *Environmental impact assessment (EIA)*: An instrument to identify and assess the potential environmental impacts of a proposed project, evaluate alternatives, and design appropriate mitigation, management, and monitoring measures. Projects and subprojects need EIA to address important issues not covered by any applicable regional or sectoral EA.

3. *Environmental management plan (EMP)*: An instrument that details (a) the measures to be taken during the implementation and operation of a project to eliminate or offset adverse environmental impacts, or to reduce them to acceptable levels; and (b) the actions needed to implement these measures. The EMP is an integral part of Category A EAs (irrespective of other instruments used). EAs for Category B projects may also result in an EMP.

4. *Hazard assessment*: An instrument for identifying, analyzing, and controlling hazards associated with the presence of dangerous materials and conditions at a project site. The Bank requires a hazard assessment for projects involving certain inflammable, explosive, reactive, and toxic materials when they are present at a site in quantities above a specified threshold level. For certain projects, the EA report may consist of the hazard assessment alone; in other cases, the hazard assessment is part of the EA documentation.

5. *Project area of influence*: The area likely to be affected by the project, including all its ancillary aspects, such as power transmission corridors, pipelines, canals, tunnels, relocation and access roads, borrow and disposal areas, and construction camps, as well as unplanned developments induced by the project (e.g., spontaneous settlement, logging, or shifting agriculture along access roads). The area of influence may include, for example, (a) the watershed within which the project is located; (b) any affected estuary and coastal zone; (c) off-site areas required for resettlement or compensatory tracts; (d) the airshed (e.g., where airborne pollution such as smoke or dust may enter or leave the area of influence); (e) migratory routes of humans, wildlife, or fish, particularly where they relate to public health, economic activities, or environmental conservation; and (f) areas used for livelihood activities (hunting, fishing, grazing, gathering, agriculture, etc.) or religious or ceremonial purposes of a customary nature.

6. *Regional EA*: An instrument that examines environmental issues and impacts associated with a particular strategy, policy, plan, or program, or with a series of projects for a particular region (e.g., an urban area, a watershed, or a coastal zone); evaluates and compares the impacts against those of alternative options; assesses legal and institutional aspects relevant to the issues and impacts; and recommends broad measures to strengthen environmental management in the region. Regional EA pays particular attention to potential cumulative impacts of multiple activities.

7. *Risk assessment*: An instrument for estimating the probability of harm occurring from the presence of dangerous conditions or materials at a project site. Risk represents the likelihood and significance of a potential hazard being

realized; therefore, a hazard assessment often precedes a risk assessment, or the two are conducted as one exercise. Risk assessment is a flexible method of analysis, a systematic approach to organizing and analyzing scientific information about potentially hazardous activities or about substances that might pose risks under specified conditions. The Bank routinely requires risk assessment for projects involving handling, storage, or disposal of hazardous materials and waste, the construction of dams, or major construction works in locations vulnerable to seismic activity or other potentially damaging natural events. For certain projects, the EA report may consist of the risk assessment alone; in other cases, the risk assessment is part of the EA documentation.

8. *Sectoral EA:* An instrument that examines environmental issues and impacts associated with a particular strategy, policy, plan, or program, or with a series of projects for a specific sector (e.g., power, transport, or agriculture); evaluates and compares the impacts against those of alternative options; assesses legal and institutional aspects relevant to the issues and impacts; and recommends broad measures to strengthen environmental management in the sector. Sectoral EA pays particular attention to potential cumulative impacts of multiple activities.

Annex B
Content of an environmental assessment report for a Category A project

1. An environmental assessment (EA) report for a Category A project focuses on the significant environmental issues of a project. The report's scope and level of detail should be commensurate with the project's potential impacts. The report submitted to the Bank is prepared in English, French, or Spanish, and the executive summary in English.

2. The EA report should include the following items (not necessarily in the order shown):

(a) *Executive summary.* Concisely discusses significant findings and recommended actions.

(b) *Policy, legal, and administrative framework.* Discusses the policy, legal, and administrative framework within which the EA is carried out. Explains the environmental requirements of any cofinanciers. Identifies relevant international environmental agreements to which the country is a party.

(c) *Project description.* Concisely describes the proposed project and its geographic, ecological, social, and temporal context, including any offsite investments that may be required (e.g., dedicated pipelines, access roads, power plants, water supply, housing, and raw material and product storage facilities). Indicates the need for any resettlement plan or indigenous peoples development plan (see also subpara. (h)(v) below). Normally includes a map showing the project site and the project's area of influence.

(d) *Baseline data.* Assesses the dimensions of the study area and describes relevant physical, biological, and socioeconomic conditions, including any changes anticipated before the project commences. Also takes into account current and proposed development activities within the project area but not directly connected to the project. Data should be relevant to decisions about project location, design, operation, or mitigatory measures. The section indicates the accuracy, reliability, and sources of the data.

(e) *Environmental impacts.* Predicts and assesses the project's likely positive and negative impacts, in quantitative terms to the extent possible. Identifies mitigation measures and any residual negative impacts that cannot be mitigated. Explores opportunities for environmental enhancement. Identifies and estimates the extent and quality of available data, key data gaps, and uncertainties associated with predictions, and specifies topics that do not require further attention.

(f) *Analysis of alternatives.* Systematically compares feasible alternatives to the proposed project site, technology, design, and operation – including the 'without project' situation – in terms of their potential environmental impacts; the feasibility of mitigating these impacts; their capital and recurrent costs; their suitability under local conditions; and their institutional, training, and monitoring requirements. For each of the alternatives, quantifies the environmental impacts to the extent possible, and attaches economic values where feasible. States the basis for selecting the particular project design proposed and justifies recommended emission levels and approaches to pollution prevention and abatement.

(g) *Environmental management plan (EMP).* Covers mitigation measures, monitoring, and institutional strengthening; see outline in OP 4.01, Annex C.

(h) *Appendixes*
   (i) List of EA report preparers – individuals and organizations.
  (ii) References – written materials both published and unpublished, used in study preparation.
 (iii) Record of interagency and consultation meetings, including consultations for obtaining the informed views of the affected people and local nongovernmental organizations (NGOs). The record specifies any means other than consultations (e.g., surveys) that were used to obtain the views of affected groups and local NGOs.
 (iv) Tables presenting the relevant data referred to or summarized in the main text.
  (v) List of associated reports (e.g., resettlement plan or indigenous peoples development plan).

[Footnotes omitted]

Annex C
Environmental management plan

1. A project's environmental management plan (EMP) consists of the set of mitigation, monitoring, and institutional measures to be taken during implementation and operation to eliminate adverse environmental and social impacts, offset them, or reduce them to acceptable levels. The plan also includes the actions needed to implement these measures. Management plans are essential elements of EA reports for Category A projects; for many Category B projects, the EA may result in a management plan only. To prepare a management plan, the borrower and its EA design team (a) identify the set of responses to potentially adverse impacts; (b) determine requirements for ensuring that those responses are made effectively and in a timely manner; and (c) describe the means for meeting those requirements. More specifically, the EMP includes the following components.

Mitigation

2. The EMP identifies feasible and cost-effective measures that may reduce potentially significant adverse environmental impacts to acceptable levels. The plan includes compensatory measures if mitigation measures are not feasible, cost-effective, or sufficient. Specifically, the EMP

(a) identifies and summarizes all anticipated significant adverse environmental impacts (including those involving indigenous people or involuntary resettlement);
(b) describes – with technical details – each mitigation measure, including the type of impact to which it relates and the conditions under which it is required (e.g., continuously or in the event of contingencies), together with designs, equipment descriptions, and operating procedures, as appropriate;
(c) estimates any potential environmental impacts of these measures; and
(d) provides linkage with any other mitigation plans (e.g., for involuntary resettlement, indigenous peoples, or cultural property) required for the project.

Monitoring

3. Environmental monitoring during project implementation provides information about key environmental aspects of the project, particularly the environmental impacts of the project and the effectiveness of mitigation measures. Such information enables the borrower and the Bank to evaluate the success of mitigation as part of project supervision, and allows corrective action to be taken when needed. Therefore, the EMP identifies monitoring objectives and specifies the type of monitoring, with linkages to the impacts assessed in the EA report and the mitigation measures described in the EMP. Specifically, the monitoring section of the EMP provides

(a) a specific description, and technical details, of monitoring measures, including the parameters to be measured, methods to be used, sampling locations, frequency of measurements, detection limits (where appropriate), and definition of thresholds that will signal the need for corrective actions; and

(b) monitoring and reporting procedures to (i) ensure early detection of conditions that necessitate particular mitigation measures, and (ii) furnish information on the progress and results of mitigation.

Capacity development and training

4. To support timely and effective implementation of environmental project components and mitigation measures, the EMP draws on the EA's assessment of the existence, role, and capability of environmental units on site or at the agency and ministry level. If necessary, the EMP recommends the establishment or expansion of such units, and the training of staff, to allow implementation of EA recommendations. Specifically, the EMP provides a specific description of institutional arrangements – who is responsible for carrying out the mitigatory and monitoring measures (e.g., for operation, supervision, enforcement, monitoring of implementation, remedial action, financing, reporting, and staff training). To strengthen environmental management capability in the agencies responsible for implementation, most EMPs cover one or more of the following additional topics: (a) technical assistance programs, (b) procurement of equipment and supplies, and (c) organizational changes.

Implementation schedule and cost estimates

5. For all three aspects (mitigation, monitoring, and capacity development), the EMP provides (a) an implementation schedule for measures that must be carried out as part of the project, showing phasing and coordination with overall project implementation plans; and (b) the capital and recurrent cost estimates and sources of funds for implementing the EMP. These figures are also integrated into the total project cost tables.

Integration of EMP with project

6. The borrower's decision to proceed with a project, and the Bank's decision to support it, are predicated in part on the expectation that the EMP will be executed effectively. Consequently, the Bank expects the plan to be specific in its description of the individual mitigation and monitoring measures and its assignment of institutional responsibilities, and it must be integrated into the project's overall planning, design, budget, and implementation. Such integration is achieved by establishing the EMP within the project so that the plan will receive funding and supervision along with the other components.

[Footnotes omitted]

Convention on Access to Information, Public Participation in Decision-Making and Access to Justice in Environmental Matters, 25 June 1998

Editorial note

The 1998 Aarhus Convention is built on three pillars: access to information, public participation in environmental decision-making, and access to justice in environmental matters. The Convention obliges parties to ensure that public authorities make available to the public 'environmental information' without any interest having to be stated, generally in the form requested, and without an unreasonable charge being made (Articles 4(1) and 9). The definition of environmental information is broader than earlier instruments, making express reference, for example, to factors of biodiversity such as genetically modified organisms, and a broad range of measures (such as environmental agreements, policies, plans and programmes and cost-benefit and other economic analyses and assumptions used in environmental decision-making) (Article 2(3)). Requests are to be responded to within one month and the exceptions are to be interpreted restrictively (Article 4(2), (3) and (4)). A refusal to disclose information is to be subject to review (Articles 4(7) and 9). The Convention also imposes a positive obligation on a public authority which does not hold the information to inform the applicant where it might be applied for, and makes provision for the separation of information which would be exempted from disclosure so that the remainder may be disclosed (Article 4(5) and (6)).

Article 5 of the Convention imposes a range of positive obligations on parties, beginning with the requirement that public authorities 'possess and update' environmental information relevant to their functions and to establish mandatory systems to ensure adequate flow of information to public authorities about activities which may significantly affect the environment (Article 5(1)(a) and (b)). In the event of any imminent threat to human health or the environment (from any source), public authorities must immediately disseminate all information which could enable the public to take measures to prevent or mitigate the harm arising from the threat (Article 5(1)(c)). Parties are also required to ensure that public authorities make environmental information available to the public in transparent and accessible ways, to ensure that such information progressively becomes available in electronic databases, to publish (at least every four years) a national report on the state of the environment, and to take measures to disseminate national and international legislation and measures, including treaties (Article 5(2)–(4)). The private sector is also targeted, although via the state: parties 'shall encourage operators whose activities have a significant impact on the environment to inform the public regularly of the environmental impact of their activities and products, where appropriate within the framework of voluntary eco-labelling or eco-auditing schemes or by other means' (Article 5(6)). Each party must take steps to establish progressively a 'coherent, nationwide system of pollution inventories or registers on a structured, computerized and publicly accessible database' (Article 5(9)).

The public concerned by proposed activities listed in Annex I to the Convention and certain other activities shall be informed, either by public notice or individually as appropriate (Article 6(1) and (2)). Public participation procedures must include reasonable time-frames to allow sufficient time for informing the public (Article 6(3)). Public participation shall be provided when all options are open and effective participation can take place (Article 6(4)). The public is to have access for examination to all relevant information (Article 6(5)). Parties shall ensure that in the decision due account is taken of the outcome of public participation (Article 6(8)) and make appropriate provisions for public participation concerning plans, programmes and policies relating to the environment (Article 7). Parties shall strive to promote effective public participation during the preparation of executive regulations and/or generally applicable legally binding normative instruments (Article 8).

Any person who considers that his or her request for information has been ignored or wrongly refused is to have access to a review procedure before a court of law or another independent body (Article 9(1)). Members of the public concerned are to have access to a review procedure before a court of law or other independent body to challenge the substantive and procedural legality of any decision, act or omission subject to the public consultation procedure (Article 9(2)) and to administrative or judicial procedures to challenge acts and omissions by private persons and public authorities which contravene provisions of national law relating to the environment (Article 9(3)).

The Convention provides for a meeting of the Parties responsible for, *inter alia*, reviewing its implementation (Article 10).

Article 15 required Parties to establish a non-confrontational, non-judicial and consultative procedure to review compliance with the Convention. A Compliance Committee and a procedure for the review of the Convention were adopted at the first meeting of the Parties (Lucca, Italy, 21–23 October 2002). The procedure is the first compliance procedure in an environmental treaty that provides that communications may be brought before the Committee by one or more members of the public concerning that Party's compliance with the Convention.

The meeting of the Parties, at an extraordinary meeting held in Kiev in 2003, adopted a Protocol on Pollutant Release and Transfer Registers (see below Document 41A).

Date of signature: 25 June 1998

Entry into force: 30 October 2001

Depositary: Secretary-General of the United Nations

Contracting Parties: Albania, Armenia, Azerbaijan, Belarus, Belgium, Denmark, Estonia, France, Georgia, Hungary, Italy, Kazakhstan, Kyrgyzstan, Latvia, Lithuania, Malta, Moldova (Republic of), Poland, Romania, Tajikistan, The Former Yugoslav Republic of Macedonia, Turkmenistan, Ukraine.

Website: www.unece.org/env/pp/

Convention on Access to Information, Public Participation in Decision-Making and Access to Justice in Environmental Matters

The Parties to this Convention,

Recalling principle l of the Stockholm Declaration on the Human Environment,

Recalling also principle 10 of the Rio Declaration on Environment and Development,

Recalling further General Assembly resolutions 37/7 of 28 October 1982 on the World Charter for Nature and 45/94 of 14 December 1990 on the need to ensure a healthy environment for the well-being of individuals,

Recalling the European Charter on Environment and Health adopted at the First European Conference on Environment and Health of the World Health Organization in Frankfurt-am-Main, Germany, on 8 December 1989,

Affirming the need to protect, preserve and improve the state of the environment and to ensure sustainable and environmentally sound development,

Recognizing that adequate protection of the environment is essential to human well-being and the enjoyment of basic human rights, including the right to life itself,

Recognizing also that every person has the right to live in an environment adequate to his or her health and well-being, and the duty, both individually and in association with others, to protect and improve the environment for the benefit of present and future generations,

Considering that, to be able to assert this right and observe this duty, citizens must have access to information, be entitled to participate in decision-making and have access to justice in environmental matters, and acknowledging in this regard that citizens may need assistance in order to exercise their rights,

Recognizing that, in the field of the environment, improved access to information and public participation in decision-making enhance the quality and the implementation of decisions, contribute to public awareness of environmental issues, give the public the opportunity to express its concerns and enable public authorities to take due account of such concerns,

Aiming thereby to further the accountability of and transparency in decision-making and to strengthen public support for decisions on the environment,

Recognizing the desirability of transparency in all branches of government and inviting legislative bodies to implement the principles of this Convention in their proceedings,

Recognizing also that the public needs to be aware of the procedures for participation in environmental decision-making, have free access to them and know how to use them,

Recognizing further the importance of the respective roles that individual citizens, non-governmental organizations and the private sector can play in environmental protection,

Desiring to promote environmental education to further the understanding of the environment and sustainable development and to encourage widespread public awareness of, and participation in, decisions affecting the environment and sustainable development,

Noting, in this context, the importance of making use of the media and of electronic or other, future forms of communication,

Recognizing the importance of fully integrating environmental considerations in governmental decision-making and the consequent need for public authorities to be in possession of accurate, comprehensive and up-to-date environmental information,

Acknowledging that public authorities hold environmental information in the public interest,

Concerned that effective judicial mechanisms should be accessible to the public, including organizations, so that its legitimate interests are protected and the law is enforced,

Noting the importance of adequate product information being provided to consumers to enable them to make informed environmental choices,

Recognizing the concern of the public about the deliberate release of genetically modified organisms into the environment and the need for increased transparency and greater public participation in decision-making in this field,

Convinced that the implementation of this Convention will contribute to strengthening democracy in the region of the United Nations Economic Commission for Europe (ECE),

Conscious of the role played in this respect by ECE and recalling, *inter alia*, the ECE Guidelines on Access to Environmental Information and Public Participation in Environmental Decision-making endorsed in the Ministerial

Declaration adopted at the Third Ministerial Conference 'Environment for Europe' in Sofia, Bulgaria, on 25 October 1995,

Bearing in mind the relevant provisions in the Convention on Environmental Impact Assessment in a Transboundary Context, done at Espoo, Finland, on 25 February 1991, and the Convention on the Transboundary Effects of Industrial Accidents and the Convention on the Protection and Use of Transboundary Watercourses and International Lakes, both done at Helsinki on 17 March 1992, and other regional conventions,

Conscious that the adoption of this Convention will have contributed to the further strengthening of the 'Environment for Europe' process and to the results of the Fourth Ministerial Conference in Aarhus, Denmark, in June 1998,

Have agreed as follows:

Article 1
Objective

In order to contribute to the protection of the right of every person of present and future generations to live in an environment adequate to his or her health and well-being, each Party shall guarantee the rights of access to information, public participation in decision-making, and access to justice in environmental matters in accordance with the provisions of this Convention.

Article 2
Definitions

For the purposes of this Convention,

1. 'Party' means, unless the text otherwise indicates, a Contracting Party to this Convention;
2. 'Public authority' means:
   (a) Government at national, regional and other level;
   (b) Natural or legal persons performing public administrative functions under national law, including specific duties, activities or services in relation to the environment;
   (c) Any other natural or legal persons having public responsibilities or functions, or providing public services, in relation to the environment, under the control of a body or person falling within subparagraphs (a) or (b) above;
   (d) The institutions of any regional economic integration organization referred to in article 17 which is a Party to this Convention. This definition does not include bodies or institutions acting in a judicial or legislative capacity;
3. 'Environmental information' means any information in written, visual, aural, electronic or any other material form on:

(a) The state of elements of the environment, such as air and atmosphere, water, soil, land, landscape and natural sites, biological diversity and its components, including genetically modified organisms, and the interaction among these elements;

(b) Factors, such as substances, energy, noise and radiation, and activities or measures, including administrative measures, environmental agreements, policies, legislation, plans and programmes, affecting or likely to affect the elements of the environment within the scope of subparagraph (a) above, and cost-benefit and other economic analyses and assumptions used in environmental decision-making;

(c) The state of human health and safety, conditions of human life, cultural sites and built structures, inasmuch as they are or may be affected by the state of the elements of the environment or, through these elements, by the factors, activities or measures referred to in subparagraph (b) above;

4. 'The public' means one or more natural or legal persons, and, in accordance with national legislation or practice, their associations, organizations or groups;

5. 'The public concerned' means the public affected or likely to be affected by, or having an interest in, the environmental decision-making; for the purposes of this definition, non-governmental organizations promoting environmental protection and meeting any requirements under national law shall be deemed to have an interest.

Article 3
General provisions

1. Each Party shall take the necessary legislative, regulatory and other measures, including measures to achieve compatibility between the provisions implementing the information, public participation and access-to-justice provisions in this Convention, as well as proper enforcement measures, to establish and maintain a clear, transparent and consistent framework to implement the provisions of this Convention.

2. Each Party shall endeavour to ensure that officials and authorities assist and provide guidance to the public in seeking access to information, in facilitating participation in decision-making and in seeking access to justice in environmental matters.

3. Each Party shall promote environmental education and environmental awareness among the public, especially on how to obtain access to information, to participate in decision-making and to obtain access to justice in environmental matters.

4. Each Party shall provide for appropriate recognition of and support to associations, organizations or groups promoting environmental protection and ensure that its national legal system is consistent with this obligation.

5. The provisions of this Convention shall not affect the right of a Party to maintain or introduce measures providing for broader access to information, more extensive public participation in decision-making and wider access to justice in environmental matters than required by this Convention.

6. This Convention shall not require any derogation from existing rights of access to information, public participation in decision-making and access to justice in environmental matters.

7. Each Party shall promote the application of the principles of this Convention in international environmental decision-making processes and within the framework of international organizations in matters relating to the environment.

8. Each Party shall ensure that persons exercising their rights in conformity with the provisions of this Convention shall not be penalized, persecuted or harassed in any way for their involvement. This provision shall not affect the powers of national courts to award reasonable costs in judicial proceedings.

9. Within the scope of the relevant provisions of this Convention, the public shall have access to information, have the possibility to participate in decision-making and have access to justice in environmental matters without discrimination as to citizenship, nationality or domicile and, in the case of a legal person, without discrimination as to where it has its registered seat or an effective centre of its activities.

Article 4
Access to environmental information

1. Each Party shall ensure that, subject to the following paragraphs of this article, public authorities, in response to a request for environmental information, make such information available to the public, within the framework of national legislation, including, where requested and subject to subparagraph (b) below, copies of the actual documentation containing or comprising such information:

(a) Without an interest having to be stated;
(b) In the form requested unless:
    (i) It is reasonable for the public authority to make it available in another form, in which case reasons shall be given for making it available in that form; or
    (ii) The information is already publicly available in another form.

2. The environmental information referred to in paragraph 1 above shall be made available as soon as possible and at the latest within one month after the request has been submitted, unless the volume and the complexity of the information justify an extension of this period up to two months after the request. The applicant shall be informed of any extension and of the reasons justifying it.

3. A request for environmental information may be refused if:

(a) The public authority to which the request is addressed does not hold the environmental information requested;
(b) The request is manifestly unreasonable or formulated in too general a manner; or
(c) The request concerns material in the course of completion or concerns internal communications of public authorities where such an exemption is provided for in national law or customary practice, taking into account the public interest served by disclosure.

4. A request for environmental information may be refused if the disclosure would adversely affect:

(a) The confidentiality of the proceedings of public authorities, where such confidentiality is provided for under national law;
(b) International relations, national defence or public security;
(c) The course of justice, the ability of a person to receive a fair trial or the ability of a public authority to conduct an enquiry of a criminal or disciplinary nature;
(d) The confidentiality of commercial and industrial information, where such confidentiality is protected by law in order to protect a legitimate economic interest. Within this framework, information on emissions which is relevant for the protection of the environment shall be disclosed;
(e) Intellectual property rights;
(f) The confidentiality of personal data and/or files relating to a natural person where that person has not consented to the disclosure of the information to the public, where such confidentiality is provided for in national law;
(g) The interests of a third party which has supplied the information requested without that party being under or capable of being put under a legal obligation to do so, and where that party does not consent to the release of the material; or
(h) The environment to which the information relates, such as the breeding sites of rare species.

The aforementioned grounds for refusal shall be interpreted in a restrictive way, taking into account the public interest served by disclosure and taking into account whether the information requested relates to emissions into the environment.

5. Where a public authority does not hold the environmental information requested, this public authority shall, as promptly as possible, inform the applicant of the public authority to which it believes it is possible to apply for the information requested or transfer the request to that authority and inform the applicant accordingly.

6. Each Party shall ensure that, if information exempted from disclosure under paragraphs 3 (c) and 4 above can be separated out without prejudice to the

confidentiality of the information exempted, public authorities make available the remainder of the environmental information that has been requested.

7. A refusal of a request shall be in writing if the request was in writing or the applicant so requests. A refusal shall state the reasons for the refusal and give information on access to the review procedure provided for in accordance with article 9. The refusal shall be made as soon as possible and at the latest within one month, unless the complexity of the information justifies an extension of this period up to two months after the request. The applicant shall be informed of any extension and of the reasons justifying it.

8. Each Party may allow its public authorities to make a charge for supplying information, but such charge shall not exceed a reasonable amount. Public authorities intending to make such a charge for supplying information shall make available to applicants a schedule of charges which may be levied, indicating the circumstances in which they may be levied or waived and when the supply of information is conditional on the advance payment of such a charge.

Article 5
Collection and dissemination of environmental information

1. Each Party shall ensure that:

(a) Public authorities possess and update environmental information which is relevant to their functions;
(b) Mandatory systems are established so that there is an adequate flow of information to public authorities about proposed and existing activities which may significantly affect the environment;
(c) In the event of any imminent threat to human health or the environment, whether caused by human activities or due to natural causes, all information which could enable the public to take measures to prevent or mitigate harm arising from the threat and is held by a public authority is disseminated immediately and without delay to members of the public who may be affected.

2. Each Party shall ensure that, within the framework of national legislation, the way in which public authorities make environmental information available to the public is transparent and that environmental information is effectively accessible, *inter alia*, by:

(a) Providing sufficient information to the public about the type and scope of environmental information held by the relevant public authorities, the basic terms and conditions under which such information is made available and accessible, and the process by which it can be obtained;
(b) Establishing and maintaining practical arrangements, such as:
    (i) Publicly accessible lists, registers or files;

(ii) Requiring officials to support the public in seeking access to information under this Convention; and

(iii) The identification of points of contact; and

(c) Providing access to the environmental information contained in lists, registers or files as referred to in subparagraph (b) (i) above free of charge.

3. Each Party shall ensure that environmental information progressively becomes available in electronic databases which are easily accessible to the public through public telecommunications networks. Information accessible in this form should include:

(a) Reports on the state of the environment, as referred to in paragraph 4 below;

(b) Texts of legislation on or relating to the environment;

(c) As appropriate, policies, plans and programmes on or relating to the environment, and environmental agreements; and

(d) Other information, to the extent that the availability of such information in this form would facilitate the application of national law implementing this Convention, provided that such information is already available in electronic form.

4. Each Party shall, at regular intervals not exceeding three or four years, publish and disseminate a national report on the state of the environment, including information on the quality of the environment and information on pressures on the environment.

5. Each Party shall take measures within the framework of its legislation for the purpose of disseminating, *inter alia*:

(a) Legislation and policy documents such as documents on strategies, policies, programmes and action plans relating to the environment, and progress reports on their implementation, prepared at various levels of government;

(b) International treaties, conventions and agreements on environmental issues; and

(c) Other significant international documents on environmental issues, as appropriate.

6. Each Party shall encourage operators whose activities have a significant impact on the environment to inform the public regularly of the environmental impact of their activities and products, where appropriate within the framework of voluntary eco-labelling or eco-auditing schemes or by other means.

7. Each Party shall:

(a) Publish the facts and analyses of facts which it considers relevant and important in framing major environmental policy proposals;

(b) Publish, or otherwise make accessible, available explanatory material on its dealings with the public in matters falling within the scope of this Convention; and

(c) Provide in an appropriate form information on the performance of public functions or the provision of public services relating to the environment by government at all levels.

8. Each Party shall develop mechanisms with a view to ensuring that sufficient product information is made available to the public in a manner which enables consumers to make informed environmental choices.

9. Each Party shall take steps to establish progressively, taking into account international processes where appropriate, a coherent, nationwide system of pollution inventories or registers on a structured, computerized and publicly accessible database compiled through standardized reporting. Such a system may include inputs, releases and transfers of a specified range of substances and products, including water, energy and resource use, from a specified range of activities to environmental media and to on-site and offsite treatment and disposal sites.

10. Nothing in this article may prejudice the right of Parties to refuse to disclose certain environmental information in accordance with article 4, paragraphs 3 and 4.

Article 6
Public participation in decisions on specific activities

1. Each Party:

(a) Shall apply the provisions of this article with respect to decisions on whether to permit proposed activities listed in annex I;

(b) Shall, in accordance with its national law, also apply the provisions of this article to decisions on proposed activities not listed in annex I which may have a significant effect on the environment. To this end, Parties shall determine whether such a proposed activity is subject to these provisions; and

(c) May decide, on a case-by-case basis if so provided under national law, not to apply the provisions of this article to proposed activities serving national defence purposes, if that Party deems that such application would have an adverse effect on these purposes.

2. The public concerned shall be informed, either by public notice or individually as appropriate, early in an environmental decision-making procedure, and in an adequate, timely and effective manner, *inter alia*, of:

(a) The proposed activity and the application on which a decision will be taken;
(b) The nature of possible decisions or the draft decision;
(c) The public authority responsible for making the decision;

(d) The envisaged procedure, including, as and when this information can be provided:
  (i) The commencement of the procedure;
  (ii) The opportunities for the public to participate;
  (iii) The time and venue of any envisaged public hearing;
  (iv) An indication of the public authority from which relevant information can be obtained and where the relevant information has been deposited for examination by the public;
  (v) An indication of the relevant public authority or any other official body to which comments or questions can be submitted and of the time schedule for transmittal of comments or questions; and
  (vi) An indication of what environmental information relevant to the proposed activity is available; and
(e) The fact that the activity is subject to a national or transboundary environmental impact assessment procedure.

3. The public participation procedures shall include reasonable time-frames for the different phases, allowing sufficient time for informing the public in accordance with paragraph 2 above and for the public to prepare and participate effectively during the environmental decision-making.

4. Each Party shall provide for early public participation, when all options are open and effective public participation can take place.

5. Each Party should, where appropriate, encourage prospective applicants to identify the public concerned, to enter into discussions, and to provide information regarding the objectives of their application before applying for a permit.

6. Each Party shall require the competent public authorities to give the public concerned access for examination, upon request where so required under national law, free of charge and as soon as it becomes available, to all information relevant to the decision-making referred to in this article that is available at the time of the public participation procedure, without prejudice to the right of Parties to refuse to disclose certain information in accordance with article 4, paragraphs 3 and 4. The relevant information shall include at least, and without prejudice to the provisions of article 4:

(a) A description of the site and the physical and technical characteristics of the proposed activity, including an estimate of the expected residues and emissions;
(b) A description of the significant effects of the proposed activity on the environment;
(c) A description of the measures envisaged to prevent and/or reduce the effects, including emissions;
(d) A non-technical summary of the above;
(e) An outline of the main alternatives studied by the applicant; and

(f) In accordance with national legislation, the main reports and advice issued to the public authority at the time when the public concerned shall be informed in accordance with paragraph 2 above.

7. Procedures for public participation shall allow the public to submit, in writing or, as appropriate, at a public hearing or inquiry with the applicant, any comments, information, analyses or opinions that it considers relevant to the proposed activity.

8. Each Party shall ensure that in the decision due account is taken of the outcome of the public participation.

9. Each Party shall ensure that, when the decision has been taken by the public authority, the public is promptly informed of the decision in accordance with the appropriate procedures. Each Party shall make accessible to the public the text of the decision along with the reasons and considerations on which the decision is based.

10. Each Party shall ensure that, when a public authority reconsiders or updates the operating conditions for an activity referred to in paragraph 1, the provisions of paragraphs 2 to 9 of this article are applied *mutatis mutandis*, and where appropriate.

11. Each Party shall, within the framework of its national law, apply, to the extent feasible and appropriate, provisions of this article to decisions on whether to permit the deliberate release of genetically modified organisms into the environment.

Article 7
Public participation concerning plans, programmes and policies relating to the environment

Each Party shall make appropriate practical and/or other provisions for the public to participate during the preparation of plans and programmes relating to the environment, within a transparent and fair framework, having provided the necessary information to the public. Within this framework, article 6, paragraphs 3, 4 and 8, shall be applied. The public which may participate shall be identified by the relevant public authority, taking into account the objectives of this Convention. To the extent appropriate, each Party shall endeavour to provide opportunities for public participation in the preparation of policies relating to the environment.

Article 8
Public participation during the preparation of executive regulations and/or generally applicable legally binding normative instruments

Each Party shall strive to promote effective public participation at an appropriate stage, and while options are still open, during the preparation by public

authorities of executive regulations and other generally applicable legally binding rules that may have a significant effect on the environment. To this end, the
following steps should be taken:

(a) Time-frames sufficient for effective participation should be fixed;
(b) Draft rules should be published or otherwise made publicly available; and
(c) The public should be given the opportunity to comment, directly or
    through representative consultative bodies.

The result of the public participation shall be taken into account as far as
possible.

Article 9
Access to justice

1. Each Party shall, within the framework of its national legislation, ensure
that any person who considers that his or her request for information under
article 4 has been ignored, wrongfully refused, whether in part or in full, inadequately answered, or otherwise not dealt with in accordance with the provisions
of that article, has access to a review procedure before a court of law or another
independent and impartial body established by law. In the circumstances where
a Party provides for such a review by a court of law, it shall ensure that such
a person also has access to an expeditious procedure established by law that
is free of charge or inexpensive for reconsideration by a public authority or
review by an independent and impartial body other than a court of law.

Final decisions under this paragraph 1 shall be binding on the public authority holding the information. Reasons shall be stated in writing, at least where
access to information is refused under this paragraph.

2. Each Party shall, within the framework of its national legislation, ensure
that members of the public concerned

(a) Having a sufficient interest or, alternatively,
(b) Maintaining impairment of a right, where the administrative procedural
    law of a Party requires this as a precondition,

have access to a review procedure before a court of law and/or another independent and impartial body established by law, to challenge the substantive and
procedural legality of any decision, act or omission subject to the provisions of
article 6 and, where so provided for under national law and without prejudice
to paragraph 3 below, of other relevant provisions of this Convention.

What constitutes a sufficient interest and impairment of a right shall be determined in accordance with the requirements of national law and consistently
with the objective of giving the public concerned wide access to justice within
the scope of this Convention. To this end, the interest of any non-governmental
organization meeting the requirements referred to in article 2, paragraph 5,
shall be deemed sufficient for the purpose of subparagraph (a) above. Such

organizations shall also be deemed to have rights capable of being impaired for the purpose of subparagraph (b) above.

The provisions of this paragraph 2 shall not exclude the possibility of a preliminary review procedure before an administrative authority and shall not affect the requirement of exhaustion of administrative review procedures prior to recourse to judicial review procedures, where such a requirement exists under national law.

3. In addition and without prejudice to the review procedures referred to in paragraphs 1 and 2 above, each Party shall ensure that, where they meet the criteria, if any, laid down in its national law, members of the public have access to administrative or judicial procedures to challenge acts and omissions by private persons and public authorities which contravene provisions of its national law relating to the environment.

4. In addition and without prejudice to paragraph 1 above, the procedures referred to in paragraphs 1, 2 and 3 above shall provide adequate and effective remedies, including injunctive relief as appropriate, and be fair, equitable, timely and not prohibitively expensive. Decisions under this article shall be given or recorded in writing. Decisions of courts, and whenever possible of other bodies, shall be publicly accessible.

5. In order to further the effectiveness of the provisions of this article, each Party shall ensure that information is provided to the public on access to administrative and judicial review procedures and shall consider the establishment of appropriate assistance mechanisms to remove or reduce financial and other barriers to access to justice.

Article 10
Meeting of the Parties

1. The first meeting of the Parties shall be convened no later than one year after the date of the entry into force of this Convention. Thereafter, an ordinary meeting of the Parties shall be held at least once every two years, unless otherwise decided by the Parties, or at the written request of any Party, provided that, within six months of the request being communicated to all Parties by the Executive Secretary of the Economic Commission for Europe, the said request is supported by at least one third of the Parties.

2. At their meetings, the Parties shall keep under continuous review the implementation of this Convention on the basis of regular reporting by the Parties, and, with this purpose in mind, shall:

(a) Review the policies for and legal and methodological approaches to access to information, public participation in decision-making and access to justice in environmental matters, with a view to further improving them;

(b) Exchange information regarding experience gained in concluding and implementing bilateral and multilateral agreements or other arrangements having relevance to the purposes of this Convention and to which one or more of the Parties are a party;

(c) Seek, where appropriate, the services of relevant ECE bodies and other competent international bodies and specific committees in all aspects pertinent to the achievement of the purposes of this Convention;

(d) Establish any subsidiary bodies as they deem necessary;

(e) Prepare, where appropriate, protocols to this Convention;

(f) Consider and adopt proposals for amendments to this Convention in accordance with the provisions of article 14;

(g) Consider and undertake any additional action that may be required for the achievement of the purposes of this Convention;

(h) At their first meeting, consider and by consensus adopt rules of procedure for their meetings and the meetings of subsidiary bodies;

(i) At their first meeting, review their experience in implementing the provisions of article 5, paragraph 9, and consider what steps are necessary to develop further the system referred to in that paragraph, taking into account international processes and developments, including the elaboration of an appropriate instrument concerning pollution release and transfer registers or inventories which could be annexed to this Convention.

3. The Meeting of the Parties may, as necessary, consider establishing financial arrangements on a consensus basis.

4. The United Nations, its specialized agencies and the International Atomic Energy Agency, as well as any State or regional economic integration organization entitled under article 17 to sign this Convention but which is not a Party to this Convention, and any intergovernmental organization qualified in the fields to which this Convention relates, shall be entitled to participate as observers in the meetings of the Parties.

5. Any non-governmental organization, qualified in the fields to which this Convention relates, which has informed the Executive Secretary of the Economic Commission for Europe of its wish to be represented at a meeting of the Parties shall be entitled to participate as an observer unless at least one third of the Parties present in the meeting raise objections.

6. For the purposes of paragraphs 4 and 5 above, the rules of procedure referred to in paragraph 2 (h) above shall provide for practical arrangements for the admittance procedure and other relevant terms.

Article 11
Right to vote

1. Except as provided for in paragraph 2 below, each Party to this Convention shall have one vote.

2. Regional economic integration organizations, in matters within their competence, shall exercise their right to vote with a number of votes equal to the

number of their member States which are Parties to this Convention. Such organizations shall not exercise their right to vote if their member States exercise theirs, and vice versa.

Article 12
Secretariat

The Executive Secretary of the Economic Commission for Europe shall carry out the following secretariat functions:

(a) The convening and preparing of meetings of the Parties;
(b) The transmission to the Parties of reports and other information received in accordance with the provisions of this Convention; and
(c) Such other functions as may be determined by the Parties.

Article 13
Annexes

The annexes to this Convention shall constitute an integral part thereof.

Article 14
Amendments to the Convention

1. Any Party may propose amendments to this Convention.

2. The text of any proposed amendment to this Convention shall be submitted in writing to the Executive Secretary of the Economic Commission for Europe, who shall communicate it to all Parties at least ninety days before the meeting of the Parties at which it is proposed for adoption.

3. The Parties shall make every effort to reach agreement on any proposed amendment to this Convention by consensus. If all efforts at consensus have been exhausted, and no agreement reached, the amendment shall as a last resort be adopted by a three-fourths majority vote of the Parties present and voting at the meeting.

4. Amendments to this Convention adopted in accordance with paragraph 3 above shall be communicated by the Depositary to all Parties for ratification, approval or acceptance. Amendments to this Convention other than those to an annex shall enter into force for Parties having ratified, approved or accepted them on the ninetieth day after the receipt by the Depositary of notification of their ratification, approval or acceptance by at least three fourths of these Parties. Thereafter they shall enter into force for any other Party on the ninetieth day after that Party deposits its instrument of ratification, approval or acceptance of the amendments.

5. Any Party that is unable to approve an amendment to an annex to this Convention shall so notify the Depositary in writing within twelve months from the date of the communication of the adoption. The Depositary shall without delay notify all Parties of any such notification received. A Party may at any

time substitute an acceptance for its previous notification and, upon deposit of an instrument of acceptance with the Depositary, the amendments to such an annex shall become effective for that Party.

6. On the expiry of twelve months from the date of its communication by the Depositary as provided for in paragraph 4 above an amendment to an annex shall become effective for those Parties which have not submitted a notification to the Depositary in accordance with the provisions of paragraph 5 above, provided that not more than one third of the Parties have submitted such a notification.

7. For the purposes of this article, 'Parties present and voting' means Parties present and casting an affirmative or negative vote.

Article 15
Review of compliance

The Meeting of the Parties shall establish, on a consensus basis, optional arrangements of a non-confrontational, non-judicial and consultative nature for reviewing compliance with the provisions of this Convention. These arrangements shall allow for appropriate public involvement and may include the option of considering communications from members of the public on matters related to this Convention.

Article 16
Settlement of disputes

1. If a dispute arises between two or more Parties about the interpretation or application of this Convention, they shall seek a solution by negotiation or by any other means of dispute settlement acceptable to the parties to the dispute.

2. When signing, ratifying, accepting, approving or acceding to this Convention, or at any time thereafter, a Party may declare in writing to the Depositary that, for a dispute not resolved in accordance with paragraph 1 above, it accepts one or both of the following means of dispute settlement as compulsory in relation to any Party accepting the same obligation:

(a) Submission of the dispute to the International Court of Justice;
(b) Arbitration in accordance with the procedure set out in annex II.

3. If the parties to the dispute have accepted both means of dispute settlement referred to in paragraph 2 above, the dispute may be submitted only to the International Court of Justice, unless the parties agree otherwise.

Article 17
Signature

This Convention shall be open for signature at Aarhus (Denmark) on 25 June 1998, and thereafter at United Nations Headquarters in New York until 21 December 1998, by States members of the Economic Commission for Europe as well as States having consultative status with the Economic Commission for Europe pursuant to paragraphs 8 and 11 of Economic and Social Council resolution 36 (IV) of 28 March 1947, and by regional economic integration organizations constituted by sovereign States members of the Economic Commission for Europe to which their member States have transferred competence over matters governed by this Convention, including the competence to enter into treaties in respect of these matters.

Article 18
Depositary

The Secretary-General of the United Nations shall act as the Depositary of this Convention.

Article 19
Ratification, acceptance, approval and accession

1. This Convention shall be subject to ratification, acceptance or approval by signatory States and regional economic integration organizations.

2. This Convention shall be open for accession as from 22 December 1998 by the States and regional economic integration organizations referred to in article 17.

3. Any other State, not referred to in paragraph 2 above, that is a Member of the United Nations may accede to the Convention upon approval by the Meeting of the Parties.

4. Any organization referred to in article 17 which becomes a Party to this Convention without any of its member States being a Party shall be bound by all the obligations under this Convention. If one or more of such an organization's member States is a Party to this Convention, the organization and its member States shall decide on their respective responsibilities for the performance of their obligations under this Convention. In such cases, the organization and the member States shall not be entitled to exercise rights under this Convention concurrently.

5. In their instruments of ratification, acceptance, approval or accession, the regional economic integration organizations referred to in article 17 shall declare the extent of their competence with respect to the matters governed by this Convention. These organizations shall also inform the Depositary of any substantial modification to the extent of their competence.

Article 20
Entry into force

1. This Convention shall enter into force on the ninetieth day after the date of deposit of the sixteenth instrument of ratification, acceptance, approval or accession.

2. For the purposes of paragraph 1 above, any instrument deposited by a regional economic integration organization shall not be counted as additional to those deposited by States members of such an organization.

3. For each State or organization referred to in article 17 which ratifies, accepts or approves this Convention or accedes thereto after the deposit of the sixteenth instrument of ratification, acceptance, approval or accession, the Convention shall enter into force on the ninetieth day after the date of deposit by such State or organization of its instrument of ratification, acceptance, approval or accession.

Article 21
Withdrawal

At any time after three years from the date on which this Convention has come into force with respect to a Party, that Party may withdraw from the Convention by giving written notification to the Depositary. Any such withdrawal shall take effect on the ninetieth day after the date of its receipt by the Depositary.

Article 22
Authentic texts

The original of this Convention, of which the English, French and Russian texts are equally authentic, shall be deposited with the Secretary-General of the United Nations.

IN WITNESS WHEREOF the undersigned, being duly authorized thereto, have signed this Convention.

DONE at Aarhus (Denmark), this twenty-fifth day of June, one thousand nine hundred and ninety-eight.

Annex I
List of activities referred to in Article 6, paragraph 1(a)

1. Energy sector:

- Mineral oil and gas refineries;
- Installations for gasification and liquefaction;
- Thermal power stations and other combustion installations with a heat input of 50 megawatts (MW) or more;
- Coke ovens;
- Nuclear power stations and other nuclear reactors including the dismantling or decommissioning of such power stations or reactors (1) (except research installations for the production and conversion of fissionable and fertile materials whose maximum power does not exceed 1 kW continuous thermal load);

- Installations for the reprocessing of irradiated nuclear fuel;
- Installations designed:
  - For the production or enrichment of nuclear fuel;
  - For the processing of irradiated nuclear fuel or high-level radioactive waste;
  - For the final disposal of irradiated nuclear fuel;
  - Solely for the final disposal of radioactive waste;
  - Solely for the storage (planned for more than 10 years) of irradiated nuclear fuels or radioactive waste in a different site than the production site.

2. Production and processing of metals:

- Metal ore (including sulphide ore) roasting or sintering installations;
- Installations for the production of pig-iron or steel (primary or secondary fusion) including continuous casting, with a capacity exceeding 2.5 tons per hour;
- Installations for the processing of ferrous metals:
  - (i) Hot-rolling mills with a capacity exceeding 20 tons of crude steel per hour;
  - (ii) Smitheries with hammers the energy of which exceeds 50 kilojoules per hammer, where the calorific power used exceeds 20 MW;
  - (iii) Application of protective fused metal coats with an input exceeding 2 tons of crude steel per hour;
- Ferrous metal foundries with a production capacity exceeding 20 tons per day;
- Installations:
  - (i) For the production of non-ferrous crude metals from ore, concentrates or secondary raw materials by metallurgical, chemical or electrolytic processes;
  - (ii) For the smelting, including the alloying, of non-ferrous metals, including recovered products (refining, foundry casting, etc.), with a melting capacity exceeding 4 tons per day for lead and cadmium or 20 tons per day for all other metals;
- Installations for surface treatment of metals and plastic materials using an electrolytic or chemical process where the volume of the treatment vats exceeds 30 m^3.

3. Mineral industry:

- Installations for the production of cement clinker in rotary kilns with a production capacity exceeding 500 tons per day or lime in rotary kilns with a production capacity exceeding 50 tons per day or in other furnaces with a production capacity exceeding 50 tons per day;
- Installations for the production of asbestos and the manufacture of asbestos-based products;

- Installations for the manufacture of glass including glass fibre with a melting capacity exceeding 20 tons per day;
- Installations for melting mineral substances including the production of mineral fibres with a melting capacity exceeding 20 tons per day;
- Installations for the manufacture of ceramic products by firing, in particular roofing tiles, bricks, refractory bricks, tiles, stoneware or porcelain, with a production capacity exceeding 75 tons per day, and/or with a kiln capacity exceeding 4 m^3 and with a setting density per kiln exceeding 300 kg/m^3.

4. Chemical industry: Production within the meaning of the categories of activities contained in this paragraph means the production on an industrial scale by chemical processing of substances or groups of substances listed in subparagraphs (a) to (g):

(a) Chemical installations for the production of basic organic chemicals, such as:
   (i) Simple hydrocarbons (linear or cyclic, saturated or unsaturated, aliphatic or aromatic);
   (ii) Oxygen-containing hydrocarbons such as alcohols, aldehydes, ketones, carboxylic acids, esters, acetates, ethers, peroxides, epoxy resins;
   (iii) Sulphurous hydrocarbons;
   (iv) Nitrogenous hydrocarbons such as amines, amides, nitrous compounds, nitro compounds or nitrate compounds, nitriles, cyanates, isocyanates;
   (v) Phosphorus-containing hydrocarbons;
   (vi) Halogenic hydrocarbons;
   (vii) Organometallic compounds;
   (viii) Basic plastic materials (polymers, synthetic fibres and cellulose-based fibres);
   (ix) Synthetic rubbers;
   (x) Dyes and pigments;
   (xi) Surface-active agents and surfactants;
(b) Chemical installations for the production of basic inorganic chemicals, such as:
   (i) Gases, such as ammonia, chlorine or hydrogen chloride, fluorine or hydrogen fluoride, carbon oxides, sulphur compounds, nitrogen oxides, hydrogen, sulphur dioxide, carbonyl chloride;
   (ii) Acids, such as chromic acid, hydrofluoric acid, phosphoric acid, nitric acid, hydrochloric acid, sulphuric acid, oleum, sulphurous acids;
   (iii) Bases, such as ammonium hydroxide, potassium hydroxide, sodium hydroxide;
   (iv) Salts, such as ammonium chloride, potassium chlorate, potassium carbonate, sodium carbonate, perborate, silver nitrate;

   (v) Non-metals, metal oxides or other inorganic compounds such as cal-
       cium carbide, silicon, silicon carbide;
(c) Chemical installations for the production of phosphorous-, nitrogen- or
    potassium-based fertilizers (simple or compound fertilizers);
(d) Chemical installations for the production of basic plant health products
    and of biocides;
(e) Installations using a chemical or biological process for the production of
    basic pharmaceutical products;
(f) Chemical installations for the production of explosives;
(g) Chemical installations in which chemical or biological processing is used
    for the production of protein feed additives, ferments and other protein
    substances.

   5. Waste management:

• Installations for the incineration, recovery, chemical treatment or landfill of
  hazardous waste;
• Installations for the incineration of municipal waste with a capacity exceeding
  3 tons per hour;
• Installations for the disposal of non-hazardous waste with a capacity exceeding 50 tons per day;
• Landfills receiving more than 10 tons per day or with a total capacity exceeding
  25 000 tons, excluding landfills of inert waste.

   6. Waste-water treatment plants with a capacity exceeding 150 000 population equivalent.
   7. Industrial plants for the:

(a) Production of pulp from timber or similar fibrous materials;
(b) Production of paper and board with a production capacity exceeding
    20 tons per day.

   8.

(a) Construction of lines for long-distance railway traffic and of airports (2)
    with a basic runway length of 2 100 m or more;
(b) Construction of motorways and express roads; (3)
(c) Construction of a new road of four or more lanes, or realignment and/or
    widening of an existing road of two lanes or less so as to provide four or
    more lanes, where such new road, or realigned and/or widened section of
    road, would be 10 km or more in a continuous length.

   9.

(a) Inland waterways and ports for inland-waterway traffic which permit the
    passage of vessels of over 1 350 tons;

(b) Trading ports, piers for loading and unloading connected to land and outside ports (excluding ferry piers) which can take vessels of over 1 350 tons.

10. Groundwater abstraction or artificial groundwater recharge schemes where the annual volume of water abstracted or recharged is equivalent to or exceeds 10 million cubic metres.

11.

(a) Works for the transfer of water resources between river basins where this transfer aims at preventing possible shortages of water and where the amount of water transferred exceeds 100 million cubic metres/year;
(b) In all other cases, works for the transfer of water resources between river basins where the multiannual average flow of the basin of abstraction exceeds 2 000 million cubic metres/year and where the amount of water transferred exceeds 5% of this flow.

In both cases transfers of piped drinking water are excluded.

12. Extraction of petroleum and natural gas for commercial purposes where the amount extracted exceeds 500 tons/day in the case of petroleum and 500,000 cubic metres/day in the case of gas.

13. Dams and other installations designed for the holding back or permanent storage of water, where a new or additional amount of water held back or stored exceeds 10 million cubic metres.

14. Pipelines for the transport of gas, oil or chemicals with a diameter of more than 800 mm and a length of more than 40 km.

15. Installations for the intensive rearing of poultry or pigs with more than:

(a) 40 000 places for poultry;
(b) 2 000 places for production pigs (over 30 kg); or
(c) 750 places for sows.

16. Quarries and opencast mining where the surface of the site exceeds 25 hectares, or peat extraction, where the surface of the site exceeds 150 hectares.

17. Construction of overhead electrical power lines with a voltage of 220 kV or more and a length of more than 15 km.

18. Installations for the storage of petroleum, petrochemical, or chemical products with a capacity of 200 000 tons or more.

19. Other activities:

• Plants for the pretreatment (operations such as washing, bleaching, mercerization) or dyeing of fibres or textiles where the treatment capacity exceeds 10 tons per day;
• Plants for the tanning of hides and skins where the treatment capacity exceeds 12 tons of finished products per day;

(a) Slaughterhouses with a carcass production capacity greater than 50 tons per day;

(b) Treatment and processing intended for the production of food products from:

(i) Animal raw materials (other than milk) with a finished product production capacity greater than 75 tons per day;

(ii) Vegetable raw materials with a finished product production capacity greater than 300 tons per day (average value on a quarterly basis);

(c) Treatment and processing of milk, the quantity of milk received being greater than 200 tons per day (average value on an annual basis);

- Installations for the disposal or recycling of animal carcasses and animal waste with a treatment capacity exceeding 10 tons per day;
- Installations for the surface treatment of substances, objects or products using organic solvents, in particular for dressing, printing, coating, degreasing, waterproofing, sizing, painting, cleaning or impregnating, with a consumption capacity of more than 150 kg per hour or more than 200 tons per year;
- Installations for the production of carbon (hard-burnt coal) or electro-graphite by means of incineration or graphitization.

20. Any activity not covered by paragraphs 1–19 above where public participation is provided for under an environmental impact assessment procedure in accordance with national legislation.

21. The provision of article 6, paragraph 1 (a) of this Convention, does not apply to any of the above projects undertaken exclusively or mainly for research, development and testing of new methods or products for less than two years unless they would be likely to cause a significant adverse effect on environment or health.

22. Any change to or extension of activities, where such a change or extension in itself meets the criteria/thresholds set out in this annex, shall be subject to article 6, paragraph 1 (a) of this Convention. Any other change or extension of activities shall be subject to article 6, paragraph 1 (b) of this Convention.

Notes

1. Nuclear power stations and other nuclear reactors cease to be such an installation when all nuclear fuel and other radioactively contaminated elements have been removed permanently from the installation site.

2. For the purposes of this Convention, 'airport' means an airport which complies with the definition in the 1944 Chicago Convention setting up the International Civil Aviation Organization (Annex 14).

3. For the purposes of this Convention, 'express road' means a road which complies with the definition in the European Agreement on Main International Traffic Arteries of 15 November 1975.

Annex II
Arbitration

1. In the event of a dispute being submitted for arbitration pursuant to article 16, paragraph 2, of this Convention, a party or parties shall notify the secretariat of the subject matter of arbitration and indicate, in particular, the articles of this Convention whose interpretation or application is at issue. The secretariat shall forward the information received to all Parties to this Convention.

2. The arbitral tribunal shall consist of three members. Both the claimant party or parties and the other party or parties to the dispute shall appoint an arbitrator, and the two arbitrators so appointed shall designate by common agreement the third arbitrator, who shall be the president of the arbitral tribunal. The latter shall not be a national of one of the parties to the dispute, nor have his or her usual place of residence in the territory of one of these parties, nor be employed by any of them, nor have dealt with the case in any other capacity.

3. If the president of the arbitral tribunal has not been designated within two months of the appointment of the second arbitrator, the Executive Secretary of the Economic Commission for Europe shall, at the request of either party to the dispute, designate the president within a further two-month period.

4. If one of the parties to the dispute does not appoint an arbitrator within two months of the receipt of the request, the other party may so inform the Executive Secretary of the Economic Commission for Europe, who shall designate the president of the arbitral tribunal within a further two-month period. Upon designation, the president of the arbitral tribunal shall request the party which has not appointed an arbitrator to do so within two months. If it fails to do so within that period, the president shall so inform the Executive Secretary of the Economic Commission for Europe, who shall make this appointment within a further two-month period.

5. The arbitral tribunal shall render its decision in accordance with international law and the provisions of this Convention.

6. Any arbitral tribunal constituted under the provisions set out in this annex shall draw up its own rules of procedure.

7. The decisions of the arbitral tribunal, both on procedure and on substance, shall be taken by majority vote of its members.

8. The tribunal may take all appropriate measures to establish the facts.

9. The parties to the dispute shall facilitate the work of the arbitral tribunal and, in particular, using all means at their disposal, shall:

(a) Provide it with all relevant documents, facilities and information;
(b) Enable it, where necessary, to call witnesses or experts and receive their evidence.

10. The parties and the arbitrators shall protect the confidentiality of any information that they receive in confidence during the proceedings of the arbitral tribunal.

11. The arbitral tribunal may, at the request of one of the parties, recommend interim measures of protection.

12. If one of the parties to the dispute does not appear before the arbitral tribunal or fails to defend its case, the other party may request the tribunal to continue the proceedings and to render its final decision. Absence of a party or failure of a party to defend its case shall not constitute a bar to the proceedings.

13. The arbitral tribunal may hear and determine counter-claims arising directly out of the subject matter of the dispute.

14. Unless the arbitral tribunal determines otherwise because of the particular circumstances of the case, the expenses of the tribunal, including the remuneration of its members, shall be borne by the parties to the dispute in equal shares. The tribunal shall keep a record of all its expenses, and shall furnish a final statement thereof to the parties.

15. Any Party to this Convention which has an interest of a legal nature in the subject matter of the dispute, and which may be affected by a decision in the case, may intervene in the proceedings with the consent of the tribunal.

16. The arbitral tribunal shall render its award within five months of the date on which it is established, unless it finds it necessary to extend the time limit for a period which should not exceed five months.

17. The award of the arbitral tribunal shall be accompanied by a statement of reasons. It shall be final and binding upon all parties to the dispute. The award will be transmitted by the arbitral tribunal to the parties to the dispute and to the secretariat. The secretariat will forward the information received to all Parties to this Convention.

18. Any dispute which may arise between the parties concerning the interpretation or execution of the award may be submitted by either party to the arbitral tribunal which made the award or, if the latter cannot be seized thereof, to another tribunal constituted for this purpose in the same manner as the first.

Compliance Committee and Procedures for the Review of Compliance[1]

The Meeting,

Determined to promote and improve compliance with the Convention on Access to Information, Public Participation in Decision-making and Access to Justice in Environmental Matters and recalling its article 15,

Recognizing the necessity for rigorous reporting by the Parties on their compliance with the Convention,

Establishes the Compliance Committee for the review of compliance by the Parties with their obligations under the Convention, and

Decides that the structure and functions of the Compliance Committee and the procedures for the review of compliance shall be those set out in the annex to this decision.

Annex

Structure and functions of the Compliance Committee and procedures for the review of compliance

I. Structure

1. The Committee shall consist of eight members, who shall serve in their personal capacity.

2. The Committee shall be composed of nationals of the Parties and Signatories to the Convention who shall be persons of high moral character and recognized competence in the fields to which the Convention relates, including persons having legal experience.

3. The Committee may not include more than one national of the same State.

4. Candidates meeting the requirements of paragraph 2 shall be nominated by Parties, Signatories and non-governmental organizations falling within the scope of article 10, paragraph 5, of the Convention and promoting environmental protection, for election pursuant to paragraph 7.

---

[1] DECISION I/7, First Meeting of the Parties to the Convention on Access to Information, Public Participation in Decision-making and Access to Justice in Environmental Matters, Lucca, Italy, 21–23 October 2002.

5. Unless the Meeting of the Parties, in a particular instance, decides otherwise, the procedure for the nomination of candidates for the Committee shall be the following:

(a) Nominations shall be sent to the secretariat in at least one of the official languages of the Convention not later than 12 weeks before the opening of the meeting of the Parties during which the election is to take place;

(b) Each nomination shall be accompanied by a curriculum vitae (CV) of the candidate not exceeding 600 words and may include supporting material;

(c) The secretariat shall distribute the nominations and the CVs, together with any supporting material, in accordance with rule 10 of the Rules of Procedure.

6. Committee members shall be elected on the basis of nominations in accordance with paragraphs 4 and 5. The Meeting of the Parties shall give due consideration to all nominations.

7. The Meeting of the Parties shall elect the members of the Committee by consensus or, failing consensus, by secret ballot.

8. In the election of the Committee, consideration should be given to the geographical distribution of membership and diversity of experience.

9. The Meeting of the Parties shall, as soon as practicable, elect four members to the Committee to serve until the end of the next ordinary meeting and four members to serve a full term of office. At each ordinary meeting thereafter, the Meeting of the Parties shall elect four members for a full term of office. Outgoing members may be re-elected once for a further full term of office, unless in a given case the Meeting of the Parties decides otherwise. A full term of office commences at the end of an ordinary meeting of the Parties and runs until the second ordinary meeting of the Parties thereafter. The Committee shall elect its own Chairperson and Vice-Chairperson.

10. If a member of the Committee can no longer perform his or her duties as member of the Committee for any reason, the Bureau of the Meeting of the Parties shall appoint another member fulfilling the criteria in this chapter to serve the remainder of the term, subject to the approval of the Committee.

11. Every member serving on the Committee shall, before taking up his or her duties, make a solemn declaration in a meeting of the Committee that he or she will perform his or her functions impartially and conscientiously.

II. Meetings

12. The Committee shall, unless it decides otherwise, meet at least once a year. The secretariat shall arrange for and service the meetings of the Committee.

III. Functions of the Committee

13. The Committee shall:

(a) Consider any submission, referral or communication made in accordance with paragraphs 15 to 24 below;
(b) Prepare, at the request of the Meeting of the Parties, a report on compliance with or implementation of the provisions of the Convention; and
(c) Monitor, assess and facilitate the implementation of and compliance with the reporting requirements under article 10, paragraph 2, of the Convention;

and act pursuant to paragraphs 36 and 37.

14. The Committee may examine compliance issues and make recommendations if and as appropriate.

IV. Submission by Parties

15. A submission may be brought before the Committee by one or more Parties that have reservations about another Party's compliance with its obligations under the Convention. Such a submission shall be addressed in writing to the secretariat and supported by corroborating information. The secretariat shall, within two weeks of receiving a submission, send a copy of it to the Party whose compliance is at issue. Any reply and supporting information shall be submitted to the secretariat and to the Parties involved within three months or such longer period as the circumstances of a particular case may require but in no case later than six months. The secretariat shall transmit the submission and the reply, as well as all corroborating and supporting information, to the Committee, which shall consider the matter as soon as practicable.

16. A submission may be brought before the Committee by a Party that concludes that, despite its best endeavours, it is or will be unable to comply fully with its obligations under the Convention. Such a submission shall be addressed in writing to the secretariat and explain, in particular, the specific circumstances that the Party considers to be the cause of its non-compliance. The secretariat shall transmit the submission to the Committee, which shall consider the matter as soon as practicable.

V. Referrals by the Secretariat

17. Where the secretariat, in particular upon considering the reports submitted in accordance with the Convention's reporting requirements, becomes aware of possible non-compliance by a Party with its obligations under the Convention, it may request the Party concerned to furnish necessary information about the matter. If there is no response or the matter is not resolved within three months, or such longer period as the circumstances of the matter

may require but in no case later than six months, the secretariat shall bring the matter to the attention of the Committee, which shall consider the matter as soon as practicable.

VI. Communications from the public

18. On the expiry of twelve months from either the date of adoption of this decision or from the date of the entry into force of the Convention with respect to a Party, whichever is the later, communications may be brought before the Committee by one or more members of the public concerning that Party's compliance with the Convention, unless that Party has notified the Depositary in writing by the end of the applicable period that it is unable to accept, for a period of not more than four years, the consideration of such communications by the Committee. The Depositary shall without delay notify all Parties of any such notification received. During the four-year period mentioned above, the Party may revoke its notification thereby accepting that, from that date, communications may be brought before the Committee by one or more members of the public concerning that Party's compliance with the Convention.

19. The communications referred to in paragraph 18 shall be addressed to the Committee through the secretariat in writing and may be in electronic form. The communications shall be supported by corroborating information.

20. The Committee shall consider any such communication unless it determines that the communication is:

(a) Anonymous;
(b) An abuse of the right to make such communications;
(c) Manifestly unreasonable;
(d) Incompatible with the provisions of this decision or with the Convention.

21. The Committee should at all relevant stages take into account any available domestic remedy unless the application of the remedy is unreasonably prolonged or obviously does not provide an effective and sufficient means of redress.

22. Subject to the provisions of paragraph 20, the Committee shall as soon as possible bring any communications submitted to it under paragraph 18 to the attention of the Party alleged to be in non-compliance.

23. A Party shall, as soon as possible but not later than five months after any communication is brought to its attention by the Committee, submit to the Committee written explanations or statements clarifying the matter and describing any response that it may have made.

24. The Committee shall, as soon as practicable, further consider communications submitted to it pursuant to this chapter and take into account all relevant written information made available to it, and may hold hearings.

VII. Information gathering

25. To assist the performance of its functions, the Committee may:

(a) Request further information on matters under its consideration;
(b) Undertake, with the consent of any Party concerned, information gathering in the territory of that Party;
(c) Consider any relevant information submitted to it; and
(d) Seek the services of experts and advisers as appropriate.

VIII. Confidentiality

26. Save as otherwise provided for in this chapter, no information held by the Committee shall be kept confidential.

27. The Committee and any person involved in its work shall ensure the confidentiality of any information that falls within the scope of the exceptions provided for in article 4, paragraphs 3 (c) and 4, of the Convention and that has been provided in confidence.

28. The Committee and any person involved in its work shall ensure the confidentiality of information that has been provided to it in confidence by a Party when making a submission in respect of its own compliance in accordance with paragraph 16 above.

29. Information submitted to the Committee, including all information relating to the identity of the member of the public submitting the information, shall be kept confidential if submitted by a person who asks that it be kept confidential because of a concern that he or she may be penalized, persecuted or harassed.

30. If necessary to ensure the confidentiality of information in any of the above cases, the Committee shall hold closed meetings.

31. Committee reports shall not contain any information that the Committee must keep confidential under paragraphs 27 to 29 above. Information that the Committee must keep confidential under paragraph 29 shall not be made available to any Party. All other information that the Committee receives in confidence and that is related to any recommendations by the Committee to the Meeting of the Parties shall be made available to any Party upon its request; that Party shall ensure the confidentiality of the information that it has received in confidence.

IX. Entitlement to participate

32. A Party in respect of which a submission, referral or communication is made or which makes a submission, as well as the member of the public

making a communication, shall be entitled to participate in the discussions of the Committee with respect to that submission, referral or communication.

33. The Party and the member of the public shall not take part in the preparation and adoption of any findings, any measures or any recommendations of the Committee.

34. The Committee shall send a copy of its draft findings, draft measures and any draft recommendations to the Parties concerned and the member of the public who submitted the communication if applicable, and shall take into account any comments made by them in the finalization of those findings, measures and recommendations.

X. Committee reports to the Meeting of the Parties

35. The Committee shall report on its activities at each ordinary meeting of the Parties and make such recommendations, as it considers appropriate. Each report shall be finalized by the Committee not later than twelve weeks in advance of the meeting of the Parties at which it is to be considered. Every effort shall be made to adopt the report by consensus. Where this is not possible, the report shall reflect the views of all the Committee members. Committee reports shall be available to the public.

XI. Consideration by the Compliance Committee

36. Pending consideration by the Meeting of the Parties, with a view to addressing compliance issues without delay, the Compliance Committee may:

(a) In consultation with the Party concerned, take the measures listed in paragraph 37 (a);
(b) Subject to agreement with the Party concerned, take the measures listed in paragraph 37 (b), (c) and (d).

XII. Consideration by the Meeting of the Parties

37. The Meeting of the Parties may, upon consideration of a report and any recommendations of the Committee, decide upon appropriate measures to bring about full compliance with the Convention. The Meeting of the Parties may, depending on the particular question before it and taking into account the cause, degree and frequency of the non-compliance, decide upon one or more of the following measures:

(a) Provide advice and facilitate assistance to individual Parties regarding the implementation of the Convention;
(b) Make recommendations to the Party concerned;
(c) Request the Party concerned to submit a strategy, including a time schedule, to the Compliance Committee regarding the achievement of compliance with the Convention and to report on the implementation of this strategy;

(d) In cases of communications from the public, make recommendations to the Party concerned on specific measures to address the matter raised by the member of the public;

(e) Issue declarations of non-compliance;

(f) Issue cautions;

(g) Suspend, in accordance with the applicable rules of international law concerning the suspension of the operation of a treaty, the special rights and privileges accorded to the Party concerned under the Convention;

(h) Take such other non-confrontational, non-judicial and consultative measures as may be appropriate.

XIII. Relationship between settlement of disputes and the compliance procedure

38. The present compliance procedure shall be without prejudice to article 16 of the Convention on the settlement of disputes.

XIV. Enhancement of synergies

39. In order to enhance synergies between this compliance procedure and compliance procedures under other agreements, the Meeting of the Parties may request the Compliance Committee to communicate as appropriate with the relevant bodies of those agreements and report back to it, including with recommendations as appropriate. The Compliance Committee may also submit a report to the Meeting of the Parties on relevant developments between the sessions of the Meeting of the Parties.

Protocol on Pollutant Release and Transfer Registers, 21 May 2003

Editorial note

The objective of the Protocol on Pollutant Release and Transfer Registers is to enhance public access to information through the establishment of coherent, integrated, nationwide pollutant release and transfer registers (PRTRs) which could facilitate public participation in environmental decision-making and contribute to pollution prevention and reduction (Article 1). Parties shall be guided by the precautionary approach in implementing the Protocol (Article 3(4)). Each Party shall establish and maintain public accessible national PRTRs (Article 4). Parties shall ensure that data held in PRTRs is presented in both aggregated and non-aggregated forms (Article 5). The registers shall include information on releases of pollutants, off-site transfers and releases of pollutants from diffuse-sources (Article 6). Article 7 contains provisions on reporting requirements which are imposed upon the owners or the operators of facilities undertaking activities specified in annexes to the Protocol or operators or owners of facilities whose activities are above specified thresholds (Article 7(1)). The owners or operators of facilities required to report shall submit the information on pollutant release and transfer specified by Article 7(5)(a) to (f). Owners and operators are required to collect data and keep records (Article 9). Owners and operators shall assure the quality of the information that they report (Article 10). Parties shall ensure public access to information contained in PRTRs without an interest having to be stated (Article 11). Confidential information may be withheld from the public (Article 12). Parties shall ensure appropriate opportunities for public participation in the development of national PRTRs (Article 13). Parties shall ensure that any person that considers that his or her request for information has been ignored or wrongly denied or inadequately answered has access to a review procedure before a court of law or other independent body (Article 14). Parties shall promote public awareness of their PRTRs and shall ensure assistance and guidance for accessing and understanding the registers (Article 15). Parties shall co-operate, as appropriate, in the implementation of the Protocol and share information (Article 16). The meeting of the Parties of the Aarhus Convention shall be held with the meeting of the Parties to the Protocol (Article 17). The

Protocol shall enter into force on the ninetieth day after the day of deposit of the sixteenth instrument of ratification, acceptance, approval or accession (Article 27).

Date of signature: 21 May 2003

Entry into force: Not yet in force

Depositary: Secretary-General of the United Nations

Contracting Parties: None at present

Website: www.unece.org/env/pp/

Protocol on Pollutant Release and Transfer Registers

The Parties to this Protocol,

Recalling article 5, paragraph 9, and article 10, paragraph 2, of the 1998 Convention on Access to Information, Public Participation in Decision-making and Access to Justice in Environmental Matters (the Aarhus Convention),

Recognizing that pollutant release and transfer registers provide an important mechanism to increase corporate accountability, reduce pollution and promote sustainable development, as stated in the Lucca Declaration adopted at the first meeting of the Parties to the Aarhus Convention,

Having regard to principle 10 of the 1992 Rio Declaration on Environment and Development,

Having regard also to the principles and commitments agreed to at the 1992 United Nations Conference on Environment and Development, in particular the provisions in chapter 19 of Agenda 21,

Taking note of the Programme for the Further Implementation of Agenda 21, adopted by the General Assembly of the United Nations at its nineteenth special session, 1997, in which it called for, *inter alia,* enhanced national capacities and capabilities for information collection, processing and dissemination, to facilitate public access to information on global environmental issues through appropriate means,

Having regard to the Plan of Implementation of the 2002 World Summit on Sustainable Development, which encourages the development of coherent, integrated information on chemicals, such as through national pollutant release and transfer registers,

Taking into account the work of the Intergovernmental Forum on Chemical Safety, in particular the 2000 Bahia Declaration on Chemical Safety, the Priorities for Action Beyond 2000 and the Pollutant Release and Transfer Register/Emission Inventory Action Plan,

Taking into account also the activities undertaken within the framework of the Inter-Organization Programme for the Sound Management of Chemicals,

Taking into account furthermore the work of the Organisation for Economic Co-operation and Development, in particular its Council Recommendation on Implementing Pollutant Release and Transfer Registers, in which the Council calls upon member countries to establish and make publicly available national pollutant release and transfer registers,

Wishing to provide a mechanism contributing to the ability of every person of present and future generations to live in an environment adequate to his or her health and well-being, by ensuring the development of publicly accessible environmental information systems,

Wishing also to ensure that the development of such systems takes into account principles contributing to sustainable development such as the precautionary approach set forth in principle 15 of the 1992 Rio Declaration on Environment and Development,

Recognizing the link between adequate environmental information systems and the exercise of the rights contained in the Aarhus Convention,

Noting the need for cooperation with other international initiatives concerning pollutants and waste, including the 2001 Stockholm Convention on Persistent Organic Pollutants and the 1989 Basel Convention on the Control of Transboundary Movements of Hazardous Wastes and their Disposal,

Recognizing that the objectives of an integrated approach to minimizing pollution and the amount of waste resulting from the operation of industrial installations and other sources are to achieve a high level of protection for the environment as a whole, to move towards sustainable and environmentally sound development and to protect the health of present and future generations,

Convinced of the value of pollutant release and transfer registers as a cost-effective tool for encouraging improvements in environmental performance, for providing public access to information on pollutants released into and transferred in and through communities, and for use by Governments in tracking trends, demonstrating progress in pollution reduction, monitoring compliance with certain international agreements, setting priorities and evaluating progress achieved through environmental policies and programmes,

Believing that pollutant release and transfer registers can bring tangible benefits to industry through the improved management of pollutants,

Noting the opportunities for using data from pollutant release and transfer registers, combined with health, environmental, demographic, economic or other types of relevant information, for the purpose of gaining a better understanding of potential problems, identifying 'hot spots', taking preventive and mitigating measures, and setting environmental management priorities,

Recognizing the importance of protecting the privacy of identified or identifiable natural persons in the processing of information reported to pollutant release and transfer registers in accordance with applicable international standards relating to data protection,

Recognizing also the importance of developing internationally compatible national pollutant release and transfer register systems to increase the comparability of data,

Noting that many member States of the United Nations Economic Commission for Europe, the European Community and the Parties to the North American Free Trade Agreement are acting to collect data on pollutant releases and transfers from various sources and to make these data publicly accessible, and recognizing especially in this area the long and valuable experience in certain countries,

Taking into account the different approaches in existing emission registers and the need to avoid duplication, and recognizing therefore that a certain degree of flexibility is needed,

Urging the progressive development of national pollutant release and transfer registers,

Urging also the establishment of links between national pollutant release and transfer registers and information systems on other releases of public concern,

Have agreed as follows:

Article 1
Objective

The objective of this Protocol is to enhance public access to information through the establishment of coherent, integrated, nationwide pollutant release and transfer registers (PRTRs) in accordance with the provisions of this Protocol, which could facilitate public participation in environmental decision-making as well as contribute to the prevention and reduction of pollution of the environment.

Article 2
Definitions

For the purposes of this Protocol,

1. 'Party' means, unless the text indicates otherwise, a State or a regional economic integration organization referred to in article 24 which has consented to be bound by this Protocol and for which the Protocol is in force;

2. 'Convention' means the Convention on Access to Information, Public Participation in Decision-making and Access to Justice in Environmental Matters, done at Aarhus, Denmark, on 25 June 1998;

3. 'The public' means one or more natural or legal persons, and, in accordance with national legislation or practice, their associations, organizations or groups;

4. 'Facility' means one or more installations on the same site, or on adjoining sites, that are owned or operated by the same natural or legal person;

5. 'Competent authority' means the national authority or authorities, or any other competent body or bodies, designated by a Party to manage a national pollutant release and transfer register system;

6. 'Pollutant' means a substance or a group of substances that may be harmful to the environment or to human health on account of its properties and of its introduction into the environment;

7. 'Release' means any introduction of pollutants into the environment as a result of any human activity, whether deliberate or accidental, routine or non-routine, including spilling, emitting, discharging, injecting, disposing or dumping, or through sewer systems without final waste-water treatment;

8. 'Off-site transfer' means the movement beyond the boundaries of the facility of either pollutants or waste destined for disposal or recovery and of pollutants in waste water destined for waste-water treatment;

9. 'Diffuse sources' means the many smaller or scattered sources from which pollutants may be released to land, air or water, whose combined impact on those media may be significant and for which it is impractical to collect reports from each individual source;

10. The terms 'national' and 'nationwide' shall, with respect to the obligations under the Protocol on Parties that are regional economic integration organizations, be construed as applying to the region in question unless otherwise indicated;

11. 'Waste' means substances or objects which are:

(a) Disposed of or recovered;
(b) Intended to be disposed of or recovered; or
(c) Required by the provisions of national law to be disposed of or recovered;

12. 'Hazardous waste' means waste that is defined as hazardous by the provisions of national law;

13. 'Other waste' means waste that is not hazardous waste;

14. 'Waste water' means used water containing substances or objects that is subject to regulation by national law.

Article 3
General provisions

1. Each Party shall take the necessary legislative, regulatory and other measures, and appropriate enforcement measures, to implement the provisions of this Protocol.

2. The provisions of this Protocol shall not affect the right of a Party to maintain or introduce a more extensive or more publicly accessible pollutant release and transfer register than required by this Protocol.

3. Each Party shall take the necessary measures to require that employees of a facility and members of the public who report a violation by a facility of national laws implementing this Protocol to public authorities are not penalized,

persecuted or harassed by that facility or public authorities for their actions in reporting the violation.

4. In the implementation of this Protocol, each Party shall be guided by the precautionary approach as set forth in principle 15 of the 1992 Rio Declaration on Environment and Development.

5. To reduce duplicative reporting, pollutant release and transfer register systems may be integrated to the degree practicable with existing information sources such as reporting mechanisms under licences or operating permits.

6. Parties shall strive to achieve convergence among national pollutant release and transfer registers.

Article 4
Core elements of a pollutant release and transfer register system

In accordance with this Protocol, each Party shall establish and maintain a publicly accessible national pollutant release and transfer register that:

(a) Is facility-specific with respect to reporting on point sources;
(b) Accommodates reporting on diffuse sources;
(c) Is pollutant-specific or waste-specific, as appropriate;
(d) Is multimedia, distinguishing among releases to air, land and water;
(e) Includes information on transfers;
(f) Is based on mandatory reporting on a periodic basis;
(g) Includes standardized and timely data, a limited number of standardized reporting thresholds and limited provisions, if any, for confidentiality;
(h) Is coherent and designed to be user-friendly and publicly accessible, including in electronic form;
(i) Allows for public participation in its development and modification; and
(j) Is a structured, computerized database or several linked databases maintained by the competent authority.

Article 5
Design and structure

1. Each Party shall ensure that the data held on the register referred to in article 4 are presented in both aggregated and non-aggregated forms, so that releases and transfers can be searched and identified according to:

(a) Facility and its geographical location;
(b) Activity;
(c) Owner or operator, and, as appropriate, company;
(d) Pollutant or waste, as appropriate;
(e) Each of the environmental media into which the pollutant is released; and
(f) As specified in article 7, paragraph 5, the destination of the transfer and, where appropriate, the disposal or recovery operation for waste.

2. Each Party shall also ensure that the data can be searched and identified according to those diffuse sources which have been included in the register.

3. Each Party shall design its register taking into account the possibility of its future expansion and ensuring that the reporting data from at least the ten previous reporting years are publicly accessible.

4. The register shall be designed for maximum ease of public access through electronic means, such as the Internet. The design shall allow that, under normal operating conditions, the information on the register is continuously and immediately available through electronic means.

5. Each Party should provide links in its register to its relevant existing, publicly accessible databases on subject matters related to environmental protection.

6. Each Party shall provide links in its register to the pollutant release and transfer registers of other Parties to the Protocol and, where feasible, to those of other countries.

Article 6
Scope of the register

1. Each Party shall ensure that its register includes the information on:

(a) Releases of pollutants required to be reported under article 7, paragraph 2;
(b) Off-site transfers required to be reported under article 7, paragraph 2; and
(c) Releases of pollutants from diffuse sources required under article 7, paragraph 4.

2. Having assessed the experience gained from the development of national pollutant release and transfer registers and the implementation of this Protocol, and taking into account relevant international processes, the Meeting of the Parties shall review the reporting requirements under this Protocol and shall consider the following issues in its further development:

(a) Revision of the activities specified in annex I;
(b) Revision of the pollutants specified in annex II;
(c) Revision of the thresholds in annexes I and II; and
(d) Inclusion of other relevant aspects such as information on on-site transfers, storage, the specification of reporting requirements for diffuse sources or the development of criteria for including pollutants under this Protocol.

Article 7
Reporting requirements

1. Each Party shall either:

(a) Require the owner or the operator of each individual facility within its jurisdiction that undertakes one or more of the activities specified in annex I above the applicable capacity threshold specified in annex I, column 1, and:

   (i) Releases any pollutant specified in annex II in quantities exceeding the applicable thresholds specified in annex II, column 1;

   (ii) Transfers off-site any pollutant specified in annex II in quantities exceeding the applicable threshold specified in annex II, column 2, where the Party has opted for pollutant-specific reporting of transfers pursuant to paragraph 5 (d);

   (iii) Transfers off-site hazardous waste exceeding 2 tons per year or other waste exceeding 2,000 tons per year, where the Party has opted for waste-specific reporting of transfers pursuant to paragraph 5 (d); or

   (iv) Transfers off-site any pollutant specified in annex II in waste water destined for waste-water treatment in quantities exceeding the applicable threshold specified in annex II, column 1b;

to undertake the obligation imposed on that owner or operator pursuant to paragraph 2; or

(b) Require the owner or the operator of each individual facility within its jurisdiction that undertakes one or more of the activities specified in annex I at or above the employee threshold specified in annex I, column 2, and manufactures, processes or uses any pollutant specified in annex II in quantities exceeding the applicable threshold specified in annex II, column 3, to undertake the obligation imposed on that owner or operator pursuant to paragraph 2.

2. Each Party shall require the owner or operator of a facility referred to in paragraph 1 to submit the information specified in paragraphs 5 and 6, and in accordance with the requirements therein, with respect to those pollutants and wastes for which thresholds were exceeded.

3. In order to achieve the objective of this Protocol, a Party may decide with respect to a particular pollutant to apply either a release threshold or a manufacture, process or use threshold, provided that this increases the relevant information on releases or transfers available in its register.

4. Each Party shall ensure that its competent authority collects, or shall designate one or more public authorities or competent bodies to collect, the information on releases of pollutants from diffuse sources specified in paragraphs 7 and 8, for inclusion in its register.

5. Each Party shall require the owners or operators of the facilities required to report under paragraph 2 to complete and submit to its competent authority, the following information on a facility-specific basis:

(a) The name, street address, geographical location and the activity or activities of the reporting facility, and the name of the owner or operator, and, as appropriate, company;

(b) The name and numerical identifier of each pollutant required to be reported pursuant to paragraph 2;

(c) The amount of each pollutant required to be reported pursuant to paragraph 2 released from the facility to the environment in the reporting year, both in aggregate and according to whether the release is to air, to water or to land, including by underground injection;

(d) Either:

    (i) The amount of each pollutant required to be reported pursuant to paragraph 2 that is transferred off-site in the reporting year, distinguishing between the amounts transferred for disposal and for recovery, and the name and address of the facility receiving the transfer; or

    (ii) The amount of waste required to be reported pursuant to paragraph 2 transferred off-site in the reporting year, distinguishing between hazardous waste and other waste, for any operations of recovery or disposal, indicating respectively with 'R' or 'D' whether the waste is destined for recovery or disposal pursuant to annex III and, for transboundary movements of hazardous waste, the name and address of the recoverer or disposer of the waste and the actual recovery or disposal site receiving the transfer;

(e) The amount of each pollutant in waste water required to be reported pursuant to paragraph 2 transferred off-site in the reporting year; and

(f) The type of methodology used to derive the information referred to in subparagraphs (c) to (e), according to article 9, paragraph 2, indicating whether the information is based on measurement, calculation or estimation.

6. The information referred to in paragraph 5 (c) to (e) shall include information on releases and transfers resulting from routine activities and from extraordinary events.

7. Each Party shall present on its register, in an adequate spatial disaggregation, the information on releases of pollutants from diffuse sources for which that Party determines that data are being collected by the relevant authorities and can be practicably included. Where the Party determines that no such data exist, it shall take measures to initiate reporting on releases of relevant pollutants from one or more diffuse sources in accordance with its national priorities.

8. The information referred to in paragraph 7 shall include information on the type of methodology used to derive the information.

Article 8
Reporting cycle

1. Each Party shall ensure that the information required to be incorporated in its register is publicly available, compiled and presented on the register by

calendar year. The reporting year is the calendar year to which that information relates. For each Party, the first reporting year is the calendar year after the Protocol enters into force for that Party. The reporting required under article 7 shall be annual. However, the second reporting year may be the second calendar year following the first reporting year.

2. Each Party that is not a regional economic integration organization shall ensure that the information is incorporated into its register within fifteen months from the end of each reporting year. However, the information for the first reporting year shall be incorporated into its register within two years from the end of that reporting year.

3. Each Party that is a regional economic integration organization shall ensure that the information for a particular reporting year is incorporated into its register six months after the Parties that are not regional economic integration organizations are required to do so.

Article 9
Data collection and record-keeping

1. Each Party shall require the owners or operators of the facilities subject to the reporting requirements of article 7 to collect the data needed to determine, in accordance with paragraph 2 below and with appropriate frequency, the facility's releases and off-site transfers subject to reporting under article 7 and to keep available for the competent authorities the records of the data from which the reported information was derived for a period of five years, starting from the end of the reporting year concerned. These records shall also describe the methodology used for data gathering.

2. Each Party shall require the owners or operators of the facilities subject to reporting under article 7 to use the best available information, which may include monitoring data, emission factors, mass balance equations, indirect monitoring or other calculations, engineering judgments and other methods. Where appropriate, this should be done in accordance with internationally approved methodologies.

Article 10
Quality assessment

1. Each Party shall require the owners or operators of the facilities subject to the reporting requirements of article 7, paragraph 1, to assure the quality of the information that they report.

2. Each Party shall ensure that the data contained in its register are subject to quality assessment by the competent authority, in particular as to their completeness, consistency and credibility, taking into account any guidelines that may be developed by the Meeting of the Parties.

Article 11
Public access to information

1. Each Party shall ensure public access to information contained in its pollutant release and transfer register, without an interest having to be stated, and according to the provisions of this Protocol, primarily by ensuring that its register provides for direct electronic access through public telecommunications networks.

2. Where the information contained in its register is not easily publicly accessible by direct electronic means, each Party shall ensure that its competent authority upon request provides that information by any other effective means, as soon as possible and at the latest within one month after the request has been submitted.

3. Subject to paragraph 4, each Party shall ensure that access to information contained in its register is free of charge.

4. Each Party may allow its competent authority to make a charge for reproducing and mailing the specific information referred to in paragraph 2, but such charge shall not exceed a reasonable amount.

5. Where the information contained in its register is not easily publicly accessible by direct electronic means, each Party shall facilitate electronic access to its register in publicly accessible locations, for example in public libraries, offices of local authorities or other appropriate places.

Article 12
Confidentiality

1. Each Party may authorize the competent authority to keep information held on the register confidential where public disclosure of that information would adversely affect:

(a) International relations, national defence or public security;
(b) The course of justice, the ability of a person to receive a fair trial or the ability of a public authority to conduct an enquiry of a criminal or disciplinary nature;
(c) The confidentiality of commercial and industrial information, where such confidentiality is protected by law in order to protect a legitimate economic interest;
(d) Intellectual property rights; or
(e) The confidentiality of personal data and/or files relating to a natural person if that person has not consented to the disclosure of the information to the public, where such confidentiality is provided for in national law.

The aforementioned grounds for confidentiality shall be interpreted in a restrictive way, taking into account the public interest served by disclosure and whether the information relates to releases into the environment.

2. Within the framework of paragraph 1 (c), any information on releases which is relevant for the protection of the environment shall be considered for disclosure according to national law.

3. Whenever information is kept confidential according to paragraph 1, the register shall indicate what type of information has been withheld, through, for example, providing generic chemical information if possible, and for what reason it has been withheld.

Article 13
Public participation in the development of national pollutant release and transfer registers

1. Each Party shall ensure appropriate opportunities for public participation in the development of its national pollutant release and transfer register, within the framework of its national law.

2. For the purpose of paragraph 1, each Party shall provide the opportunity for free public access to the information on the proposed measures concerning the development of its national pollutant release and transfer register and for the submission of any comments, information, analyses or opinions that are relevant to the decision-making process, and the relevant authority shall take due account of such public input.

3. Each Party shall ensure that, when a decision to establish or significantly change its register has been taken, information on the decision and the considerations on which it is based are made publicly available in a timely manner.

Article 14
Access to justice

1. Each Party shall, within the framework of its national legislation, ensure that any person who considers that his or her request for information under article 11, paragraph 2, has been ignored, wrongfully refused, whether in part or in full, inadequately answered, or otherwise not dealt with in accordance with the provisions of that paragraph has access to a review procedure before a court of law or another independent and impartial body established by law.

2. The requirements in paragraph 1 are without prejudice to the respective rights and obligations of Parties under existing treaties applicable between them dealing with the subject matter of this article.

Article 15
Capacity-building

1. Each Party shall promote public awareness of its pollutant release and transfer register, and shall ensure that assistance and guidance are provided in accessing its register and in understanding and using the information contained in it.

2. Each Party should provide adequate capacity-building for and guidance to the responsible authorities and bodies to assist them in carrying out their duties under this Protocol.

Article 16
International cooperation

1. The Parties shall, as appropriate, cooperate and assist each other:

(a) In international actions in support of the objectives of this Protocol;
(b) On the basis of mutual agreement between the Parties concerned, in implementing national systems in pursuance of this Protocol;
(c) In sharing information under this Protocol on releases and transfers within border areas; and
(d) In sharing information under this Protocol concerning transfers among Parties.

2. The Parties shall encourage cooperation among each other and with relevant international organizations, as appropriate, to promote:

(a) Public awareness at the international level;
(b) The transfer of technology; and
(c) The provision of technical assistance to Parties that are developing countries and Parties with economies in transition in matters relating to this Protocol.

Article 17
Meeting of the Parties

1. A Meeting of the Parties is hereby established. Its first session shall be convened no later than two years after the entry into force of this Protocol. Thereafter, ordinary sessions of the Meeting of the Parties shall be held sequentially with or parallel to ordinary meetings of the Parties to the Convention, unless otherwise decided by the Parties to this Protocol. The Meeting of the Parties shall hold an extraordinary session if it so decides in the course of an ordinary session or at the written request of any Party provided that, within six months of it being communicated by the Executive Secretary of the Economic Commission for Europe to all Parties, the said request is supported by at least one third of these Parties.

2. The Meeting of the Parties shall keep under continuous review the implementation and development of this Protocol on the basis of regular reporting by the Parties and, with this purpose in mind, shall:

(a) Review the development of pollutant release and transfer registers, and promote their progressive strengthening and convergence;
(b) Establish guidelines facilitating reporting by the Parties to it, bearing in mind the need to avoid duplication of effort in this regard;
(c) Establish a programme of work;

(d) Consider and, where appropriate, adopt measures to strengthen international cooperation in accordance with article 16;

(e) Establish such subsidiary bodies as it deems necessary;

(f) Consider and adopt proposals for such amendments to this Protocol and its annexes as are deemed necessary for the purposes of this Protocol, in accordance with the provisions of article 20;

(g) At its first session, consider and by consensus adopt rules of procedure for its sessions and those of its subsidiary bodies, taking into account any rules of procedure adopted by the Meeting of the Parties to the Convention;

(h) Consider establishing financial arrangements by consensus and technical assistance mechanisms to facilitate the implementation of this Protocol;

(i) Seek, where appropriate, the services of other relevant international bodies in the achievement of the objectives of this Protocol; and

(j) Consider and take any additional action that may be required to further the objectives of this Protocol, such as the adoption of guidelines and recommendations which promote its implementation.

3. The Meeting of the Parties shall facilitate the exchange of information on the experience gained in reporting transfers using the pollutant-specific and waste-specific approaches, and shall review that experience in order to investigate the possibility of convergence between the two approaches, taking into account the public interest in information in accordance with article 1 and the overall effectiveness of national pollutant release and transfer registers.

4. The United Nations, its specialized agencies and the International Atomic Energy Agency, as well as any State or regional economic integration organization entitled under article 24 to sign this Protocol but which is not a Party to it, and any intergovernmental organization qualified in the fields to which the Protocol relates, shall be entitled to participate as observers in the sessions of the Meeting of the Parties. Their admission and participation shall be subject to the rules of procedure adopted by the Meeting of the Parties.

5. Any non-governmental organization qualified in the fields to which this Protocol relates which has informed the Executive Secretary of the Economic Commission for Europe of its wish to be represented at a session of the Meeting of the Parties shall be entitled to participate as an observer unless one third of the Parties present at the session raise objections. Their admission and participation shall be subject to the rules of procedure adopted by the Meeting of the Parties.

Article 18
Right to vote

1. Except as provided for in paragraph 2, each Party to this Protocol shall have one vote.

2. Regional economic integration organizations, in matters within their competence, shall exercise their right to vote with a number of votes equal to the

number of their member States which are Parties. Such organizations shall not exercise their right to vote if their member States exercise theirs, and vice versa.

Article 19
Annexes

Annexes to this Protocol shall form an integral part thereof and, unless expressly provided otherwise, a reference to this Protocol constitutes at the same time a reference to any annexes thereto.

Article 20
Amendments

1. Any Party may propose amendments to this Protocol.

2. Proposals for amendments to this Protocol shall be considered at a session of the Meeting of the Parties.

3. Any proposed amendment to this Protocol shall be submitted in writing to the secretariat, which shall communicate it at least six months before the session at which it is proposed for adoption to all Parties, to other States and regional economic integration organizations that have consented to be bound by the Protocol and for which it has not yet entered into force and to Signatories.

4. The Parties shall make every effort to reach agreement on any proposed amendment to this Protocol by consensus. If all efforts at consensus have been exhausted, and no agreement reached, the amendment shall as a last resort be adopted by a three-fourths majority vote of the Parties present and voting at the session.

5. For the purposes of this article, 'Parties present and voting' means Parties present and casting an affirmative or negative vote.

6. Any amendment to this Protocol adopted in accordance with paragraph 4 shall be communicated by the secretariat to the Depositary, who shall circulate it to all Parties, to other States and regional economic integration organizations that have consented to be bound by the Protocol and for which it has not yet entered into force and to Signatories.

7. An amendment, other than one to an annex, shall enter into force for those Parties having ratified, accepted or approved it on the ninetieth day after the date of receipt by the Depositary of the instruments of ratification, acceptance or approval by at least three fourths of those which were Parties at the time of its adoption. Thereafter it shall enter into force for any other Party on the ninetieth day after that Party deposits its instrument of ratification, acceptance or approval of the amendment.

8. In the case of an amendment to an annex, a Party that does not accept such an amendment shall so notify the Depositary in writing within twelve months from the date of its circulation by the Depositary. The Depositary shall without delay inform all Parties of any such notification received. A Party may

at any time withdraw a previous notification of non-acceptance, whereupon the amendment to an annex shall enter into force for that Party.

9. On the expiry of twelve months from the date of its circulation by the Depositary as provided for in paragraph 6, an amendment to an annex shall enter into force for those Parties which have not submitted a notification to the Depositary in accordance with paragraph 8, provided that, at that time, not more than one third of those which were Parties at the time of the adoption of the amendment have submitted such a notification.

10. If an amendment to an annex is directly related to an amendment to this Protocol, it shall not enter into force until such time as the amendment to this Protocol enters into force.

Article 21
Secretariat

The Executive Secretary of the Economic Commission for Europe shall carry out the following secretariat functions for this Protocol:

(a) The preparation and servicing of the sessions of the Meeting of the Parties;
(b) The transmission to the Parties of reports and other information received in accordance with the provisions of this Protocol;
(c) The reporting to the Meeting of the Parties on the activities of the secretariat; and
(d) Such other functions as may be determined by the Meeting of the Parties on the basis of available resources.

Article 22
Review of compliance

At its first session, the Meeting of the Parties shall by consensus establish co-operative procedures and institutional arrangements of a non-judicial, non-adversarial and consultative nature to assess and promote compliance with the provisions of this Protocol and to address cases of non-compliance. In establishing these procedures and arrangements, the Meeting of the Parties shall consider, *inter alia*, whether to allow for information to be received from members of the public on matters related to this Protocol.

Article 23
Settlement of disputes

1. If a dispute arises between two or more Parties about the interpretation or application of this Protocol, they shall seek a solution by negotiation or by any other peaceful means of dispute settlement acceptable to the parties to the dispute.

2. When signing, ratifying, accepting, approving or acceding to this Protocol, or at any time thereafter, a State may declare in writing to the Depositary that, for a dispute not resolved in accordance with paragraph 1, it accepts one or

both of the following means of dispute settlement as compulsory in relation to any Party accepting the same obligation:

(a) Submission of the dispute to the International Court of Justice;
(b) Arbitration in accordance with the procedure set out in annex IV.

A regional economic integration organization may make a declaration with like effect in relation to arbitration in accordance with the procedures referred to in subparagraph (b).

3. If the parties to the dispute have accepted both means of dispute settlement referred to in paragraph 2, the dispute may be submitted only to the International Court of Justice, unless the parties to the dispute agree otherwise.

Article 24
Signature

This Protocol shall be open for signature at Kiev (Ukraine) from 21 to 23 May 2003 on the occasion of the fifth Ministerial Conference 'Environment for Europe,' and thereafter at United Nations Headquarters in New York until 31 December 2003, by all States which are members of the United Nations and by regional economic integration organizations constituted by sovereign States members of the United Nations to which their member States have transferred competence over matters governed by this Protocol, including the competence to enter into treaties in respect of these matters.

Article 25
Depositary

The Secretary-General of the United Nations shall act as the Depositary of this Protocol.

Article 26
Ratification, acceptance, approval and accession

1. This Protocol shall be subject to ratification, acceptance or approval by signatory States and regional economic integration organizations referred to in article 24.

2. This Protocol shall be open for accession as from 1 January 2004 by the States and regional economic integration organizations referred to in article 24.

3. Any regional economic integration organization referred to in article 24 which becomes a Party without any of its member States being a Party shall be bound by all the obligations under this Protocol. If one or more member States of such an organization is a Party, the organization and its member States shall decide on their respective responsibilities for the performance of their obligations under this Protocol. In such cases, the organization and the member States shall not be entitled to exercise rights under this Protocol concurrently.

4. In their instruments of ratification, acceptance, approval or accession, the regional economic integration organizations referred to in article 24 shall declare the extent of their competence with respect to the matters governed by this Protocol. These organizations shall also inform the Depositary of any substantial modifications to the extent of their competence.

Article 27
Entry into force

1. This Protocol shall enter into force on the ninetieth day after the date of deposit of the sixteenth instrument of ratification, acceptance, approval or accession.

2. For the purposes of paragraph 1, any instrument deposited by a regional economic integration organization shall not be counted as additional to those deposited by the States members of such an organization.

3. For each State or regional economic integration organization which ratifies, accepts or approves this Protocol or accedes thereto after the deposit of the sixteenth instrument of ratification, acceptance, approval or accession, the Protocol shall enter into force on the ninetieth day after the date of deposit by such State or organization of its instrument of ratification, acceptance, approval or accession.

Article 28
Reservations

No reservations may be made to this Protocol.

Article 29
Withdrawal

At any time after three years from the date on which this Protocol has come into force with respect to a Party, that Party may withdraw from the Protocol by giving written notification to the Depositary. Any such withdrawal shall take effect on the ninetieth day after the date of its receipt by the Depositary.

Article 30
Authentic texts

The original of this Protocol, of which the English, French and Russian texts are equally authentic, shall be deposited with the Secretary-General of the United Nations.

IN WITNESS WHEREOF the undersigned, being duly authorized thereto, have signed this Protocol.

DONE at Kiev, this twenty-first day of May, two thousand and three.

Annex I
Activities

No.	Activity	Capacity threshold (column 1)	Employee threshold (column 2)
1.	**Energy sector**		
(a)	Mineral oil and gas refineries	*	
(b)	Installations for gasification and liquefaction	*	
(c)	Thermal power stations and other combustion installations	With a heat input of 50 megawatts (MW)	10 employees
(d)	Coke ovens	*	
(e)	Coal rolling mills	With a capacity of 1 ton per hour	
(f)	Installations for the manufacture of coal products and solid smokeless fuel	*	
2.	**Production and processing of metals**		
(a)	Metal ore (including sulphide ore) roasting or sintering installations	*	
(b)	Installations for the production of pig iron or steel (primary or secondary melting) including continuous casting	With a capacity of 2.5 tons per hour	
(c)	Installations for the processing of ferrous metals:		
	(i) Hot-rolling mills	With a capacity of 20 tons of crude steel per hour	10 employees
	(ii) Smitheries with hammers	With an energy of 50 kilojoules per hammer, where the calorific power used exceeds 20 MW	
	(iii) Application of protective fused metal coats	With an input of 2 tons of crude steel per hour	
(d)	Ferrous metal foundries	With a production capacity of 20 tons per day	

(*cont.*)

(cont.)

No. Activity	Capacity threshold (column 1)	Employee threshold (column 2)
(e) Installations: (i) For the production of non-ferrous crude metals from ore, concentrates or secondary raw materials by metallurgical, chemical or electrolytic processes	*	
(ii) For the smelting, including the alloying, of non-ferrous metals, including recovered products (refining, foundry casting, etc.)	With a melting capacity of 4 tons per day for lead and cadmium or 20 tons per day for all other metals	10 employees
(f) Installations for surface treatment of metals and plastic materials using an electrolytic or chemical process	Where the volume of the treatment vats equals 30 m^3	
3. Mineral industry (a) Underground mining and related operations	*	
(b) Opencast mining	Where the surface of the area being mined equals 25 hectares	
(c) Installations for the production of: (i) Cement clinker in rotary kilns	With a production capacity of 500 tons per day	10 employees
(ii) Lime in rotary kilns	With a production capacity exceeding 50 tons per day	
(iii) Cement clinker or lime in other furnaces	With a production capacity of 50 tons per day	
(d) Installations for the production of asbestos and the manufacture of asbestos-based products	*	

(cont.)

(cont.)

No.	Activity	Capacity threshold (column 1)	Employee threshold (column 2)
(e)	Installations for the manufacture of glass, including glass fibre	With a melting capacity of 20 tons per day	
(f)	Installations for melting mineral substances, including the production of mineral fibres	With a melting capacity of 20 tons per day	
(g)	Installations for the manufacture of ceramic products by firing, in particular roofing tiles, bricks, refractory bricks, tiles, stoneware or porcelain	With a production capacity of 75 tons per day, or with a kiln capacity of 4 m^3 and with a setting density per kiln of 300 kg/m^3	
4.	**Chemical industry**		
(a)	Chemical installations for the production on an industrial scale of basic organic chemicals, such as:		
	(i) Simple hydrocarbons (linear or cyclic, saturated or unsaturated, aliphatic or aromatic)		
	(ii) Oxygen-containing hydrocarbons such as alcohols, aldehydes, ketones, carboxylic acids, esters, acetates, ethers, peroxides, epoxy resins		
	(iii) Sulphurous hydrocarbons	*	10 employees
	(iv) Nitrogenous hydrocarbons such as amines, amides, nitrous compounds, nitro compounds or nitrate compounds, nitriles, cyanates, isocyanates		
	(v) Phosphorus-containing hydrocarbons		
	(vi) Halogenic hydrocarbons		
	(vii) Organometallic compounds		
	(viii) Basic plastic materials (polymers, synthetic fibres and cellulose-based fibres)		

(cont.)

(cont.)

No.	Activity	Capacity threshold (column 1)	Employee threshold (column 2)
	(ix) Synthetic rubbers (x) Dyes and pigments (xi) Surface-active agents and surfactants		
(b)	Chemical installations for the production on an industrial scale of basic inorganic chemicals, such as: (i) Gases, such as ammonia, chlorine or hydrogen chloride, fluorine or hydrogen fluoride, carbonoxides, sulphur compounds, nitrogen oxides, hydrogen, sulphur dioxide, carbonyl chloride (ii) Acids, such as chromic acid, hydrofluoric acid, phosphoric acid, nitric acid, hydrochloric acid, sulphuric acid, oleum, sulphurous acids (iii) Bases, such as ammonium hydroxide, potassium hydroxide, sodium hydroxide (iv) Salts, such as ammonium chloride, potassium chlorate, potassium carbonate, sodium carbonate, perborate, silver nitrate (v) Non-metals, metal oxides or other inorganic compounds such as calcium carbide, silicon, silicon carbide	*	10 employees
(c)	Chemical installations for the production on an industrial scale of phosphorous-, nitrogen- or potassium-based fertilizers (simple or compound fertilizers)	*	
(d)	Chemical installations for the production on an industrial scale of basic plant health products and of biocides	*	

(cont.)

(cont.)

No.	Activity	Capacity threshold (column 1)	Employee threshold (column 2)
(e)	Installations using a chemical or biological process for the production on an industrial scale of basic pharmaceutical products	*	10 employees
(f)	Installations for the production on an industrial scale of explosives and pyrotechnic products	*	
5.	**Waste and waste-water management**		
(a)	Installations for the incineration, pyrolysis, recovery, chemical treatment or landfilling of hazardous waste	Receiving 10 tons per day	
(b)	Installations for the incineration of municipal waste	With a capacity of 3 tons per hour	
(c)	Installations for the disposal of non-hazardous waste	With a capacity of 50 tons per day	
(d)	Landfills (excluding landfills of inert waste)	Receiving 10 tons per day or with a total capacity of 25,000 tons	10 employees
(e)	Installations for the disposal or recycling of animal carcasses and animal waste	With a treatment capacity of 10 tons per day	
(f)	Municipal waste-water treatment plants	With a capacity of 100,000 population equivalents	
(g)	Independently operated industrial waste-water treatment plants which serve one or more activities of this annex	With a capacity of 10,000 m^3 per day	
6.	**Paper and wood production and processing**		
(a)	Industrial plants for the production of pulp from timber or similar fibrous materials	*	10 employees

(cont.)

(cont.)

No.	Activity	Capacity threshold (column 1)	Employee threshold (column 2)
(b)	Industrial plants for the production of paper and board and other primary wood products (such as chipboard, fibreboard and plywood)	With a production capacity of 20 tons per day	
(c)	Industrial plants for the preservation of wood and wood products with chemicals	With a production capacity of 50 m^3 per day	
7.	**Intensive livestock production and aquaculture**		
(a)	Installations for the intensive rearing of poultry or pigs	(i) With 40,000 places for poultry (ii) With 2,000 places for production pigs (over 30 kg) (iii) With 750 places for sows	10 employees
(b)	Intensive aquaculture	1,000 tons of fish and shellfish per year	
8.	**Animal and vegetable products from the food and beverage sector**		
(a)	Slaughterhouses	With a carcass production capacity of 50 tons per day	
(b)	Treatment and processing intended for the production of food and beverage products from:		10 employees
	(i) Animal raw materials (other than milk)	With a finished product production capacity of 75 tons per day	
	(ii) Vegetable raw materials	With a finished product production capacity of 300 tons per day (average value on a quarterly basis)	

(cont.)

(cont.)

No. Activity	Capacity threshold (column 1)	Employee threshold (column 2)
(c) Treatment and processing of milk	With a capacity to receive 200 tons of milk per day (average value on an annual basis)	
9. Other activities		
(a) Plants for the pretreatment (operations such as washing, bleaching, mercerization) or dyeing of fibres or textiles	With a treatment capacity of 10 tons per day	
(b) Plants for the tanning of hides and skins	With a treatment capacity of 12 tons of finished product per day	
(c) Installations for the surface treatment of substances, objects or products using organic solvents, in particular for dressing, printing, coating, degreasing, waterproofing, sizing, painting, cleaning or impregnating	With a consumption capacity of 150 kg per hour or 200 tons per year	10 employees
(d) Installations for the production of carbon (hard-burnt coal) or electrographite by means of incineration or graphitization	*	
(e) Installations for the building of, and painting or removal of paint from ships	With a capacity for ships 100 m long	

Explanatory notes:

Column 1 contains the capacity thresholds referred to in article 7, paragraph 1 (a).

An asterisk (*) indicates that no capacity threshold is applicable (all facilities are subject to reporting).

Column 2 contains the employee threshold referred to in article 7, paragraph 1 (b).

'10 employees' means the equivalent of 10 full-time employees.

Annex II
Pollutants

| No. | CAS number | Pollutant | Threshold for releases (column 1) | | | Threshold for off-site transfers of pollutants (column 2) kg/year | Manufacture, process or use threshold (column 3) kg/year |
			To air (column 1a) kg/year	to water (column 1b) kg/year	to land (column 1c) kg/year		
1	74-82-8	Methane (CH_4)	100 000	-	-	-	*
2	630-08-0	Carbon monoxide (CO)	500 000	-	-	-	*
3	124-38-9	Carbon dioxide (CO_2)	100 million	-	-	-	*
4		Hydro-fluorocarbons (HFCs)	100	-	-	-	*
5	10024-97-2	Nitrous oxide (N_2O)	10 000	-	-	-	*
6	7664-41-7	Ammonia (NH_3)	10 000	-	-	-	10 000
7		Non-methane volatile organic compounds (NMVOC)	100 000	-	-	-	*
8		Nitrogen oxides (NO_x/NO_2)	100 000	-	-	-	*
9		Perfluorocarbons (PFCs)	100	-	-	-	*
10	2551-62-4	Sulphur hexafluoride (SF_6)	50	-	-	-	*
11		Sulphur oxides (SO_x/SO_2)	150 000	-	-	-	*

No.	CAS number	Substance					
12		Total nitrogen	-	50 000	50 000	10 000	10 000
13		Total phosphorus	-	5 000	5 000	10 000	10 000
14		Hydrochlorofluorocarbons (HCFCs)	1	-	-	100	10 000
15		Chlorofluorocarbons (CFCs)	1	-	-	100	10 000
16		Halons	1	-	-	100	10 000
17	7440-38-2	Arsenic and compounds (as As)	20	5	5	50	50
18	7440-43-9	Cadmium and compounds (as Cd)	10	5	5	5	5
19	7440-47-3	Chromium and compounds (as Cr)	100	50	50	200	10 000
20	7440-50-8	Copper and compounds (as Cu)	100	50	50	500	10 000
21	7439-97-6	Mercury and compounds (as Hg)	10	1	1	5	5
22	7440-02-0	Nickel and compounds (as Ni)	50	20	20	500	10 000
23	7439-92-1	Lead and compounds (as Pb)	200	20	20	50	50
24	7440-66-6	Zinc and compounds (as Zn)	200	100	100	1 000	10 000
25	15972-60-8	Alachlor	-	1	1	5	10 000
26	309-00-2	Aldrin	1	1	1	1	1

(cont.)

(cont.)

| No. | CAS number | Pollutant | Threshold for releases (column 1) | | | Threshold for off-site transfers of pollutants (column 2) kg/year | Manufacture, process or use threshold (column 3) kg/year |
			To air (column 1a) kg/year	to water (column 1b) kg/year	to land (column 1c) kg/year		
27	1912-24-9	Atrazine	-	1	1	5	10 000
28	57-74-9	Chlordane	1	1	1	1	1
29	143-50-0	Chlordecone	1	1	1	1	1
30	470-90-6	Chlorfenvinphos	-	1	1	5	10 000
31	85535-84-8	Chloro-alkanes, C_{10}-C_{13}	-	1	1	10	10 000
32	2921-88-2	Chlorpyrifos	-	1	1	5	10 000
33	50-29-3	DDT	1	1	1	1	1
34	107-06-2	1,2-dichloroethane (EDC)	1 000	10	10	100	10 000
35	75-09-2	Dichloromethane (DCM)	1 000	10	10	100	10 000
36	60-57-1	Dieldrin	1	1	1	1	1
37	330-54-1	Diuron	-	1	1	5	10 000
38	115-29-7	Endosulphan	-	1	1	5	10 000
39	72-20-8	Endrin	1	1	1	1	1
40		Halogenated organic compounds (as AOX)	-	1 000	1 000	1 000	10 000
41	76-44-8	Heptachlor	1	1	1	1	1
42	118-74-1	Hexachlorobenzene (HCB)	10	1	1	1	5

No.	CAS	Substance					
43	87-68-3	Hexachlorobutadiene (HCBD)	-	1	1	5	10 000
44	608-73-1	1,2,3,4,5,6-hexachlorocyclohexane (HCH)	10	1	1	1	10
45	58-89-9	Lindane	1	1	1	1	1
46	2385-85-5	Mirex	1	1	1	1	1
47		PCDD + PCDF (dioxins + furans) (as Teq)	0.001	0.001	0.001	0.001	0.001
48	608-93-5	Pentachlorobenzene	1	1	1	5	50
49	87-86-5	Pentachlorophenol (PCP)	10	1	1	5	10 000
50	1336-36-3	Polychlorinated biphenyls (PCBs)	0.1	0.1	0.1	1	50
51	122-34-9	Simazine	-	1	1	5	10 000
52	127-18-4	Tetrachloroethylene (PER)	2 000	-	-	1 000	10 000
53	56-23-5	Tetrachloromethane (TCM)	100	-	-	1 000	10 000
54	12002-48-1	Trichlorobenzenes (TCBs)	10	-	-	1 000	10 000
55	71-55-6	1,1,1-trichloroethane	100	-	-	1 000	10 000
56	79-34-5	1,1,2,2-tetrachloroethane	50	-	-	1 000	10 000
57	79-01-6	Trichloroethylene	2 000	-	-	1 000	10 000
58	67-66-3	Trichloromethane	500	-	-	1 000	10 000
59	8001-35-2	Toxaphene	1	1	1	1	1

(cont.)

(cont.)

No.	CAS number	Pollutant	Threshold for releases (column 1)			Threshold for off-site transfers of pollutants (column 2) kg/year	Manufacture, process or use threshold (column 3) kg/year
			To air (column 1a) kg/year	to water (column 1b) kg/year	to land (column 1c) kg/year		
60	75-01-4	Vinyl chloride	1 000	10	10	100	10 000
61	120-12-7	Anthracene	50	1	1	50	50
62	71-43-2	Benzene	1 000	200 (as BTEX)[a]	200 (as BTEX)[a]	2 000 (as BTEX)[a]	10 000
63		Brominated diphenylethers (PBDE)	-	1	1	5	10 000
64		Nonylphenol ethoxylates (NP/NPEs) and related substances	-	1	1	5	10 000
65	100-41-4	Ethyl benzene	-	200 (as BTEX)[a]	200 (as BTEX)[a]	2 000 (as BTEX)[a]	10 000
66	75-21-8	Ethylene oxide	1 000	10	10	100	10 000
67	34123-59-6	Isoproturon	-	1	1	5	10 000
68	91-20-3	Naphthalene	100	10	10	100	10 000
69		Organotin compounds (as total Sn)	-	50	50	50	10 000
70	117-81-7	Di-(2-ethyl hexyl) phthalate (DEHP)	10	1	1	100	10 000
71	108-95-2	Phenols (as total C)	-	20	20	200	10 000
72		Polycyclic aromatic hydrocarbons (PAHs)[b]	50	5	5	50	50

No.	CAS number	Pollutant					
73	108-88-3	Toluene	-	200 (as BTEX)[a]	200 (as BTEX)[a]	2 000 (as BTEX)[a]	10 000
74		Tributyltin and compounds	-	1	1	5	10 000
75		Triphenyltin and compounds	-	1	1	5	10 000
76		Total organic carbon (TOC) (as total C or COD/3)	-	50 000	-	-	**
77	1582-09-8	Trifluralin	-	1	1	5	10 000
78	1330-20-7	Xylenes	-	200 (as BTEX)[a]	200 (as BTEX)[a]	2 000 (as BTEX)[a]	10 000
79		Chlorides (as total Cl)	-	2 million	2 million	2 million	10 000[c]
80		Chlorine and inorganic compounds (as HCl)	10 000	-	-	-	10 000
81	1332-21-4	Asbestos	1	1	1	10	10 000
82		Cyanides (as total CN)	-	50	50	500	10 000
83		Fluorides (as total F)	-	2 000	2 000	10 000	10 000[c]
84		Fluorine and inorganic compounds (as HF)	5 000	-	-	-	10 000
85	74-90-8	Hydrogen cyanide (HCN)	200	-	-	-	10 000
86		Particulate matter (PM10)	50 000	-	-	-	*

[a] Single pollutants are to be reported if the threshold for BTEX (the sum parameter of benzene, toluene, ethyl benzene, xylene) is exceeded.

[b] Polycyclic aromatic hydrocarbons (PAHs) are to be measured as benzo(a)pyrene (50-32-8), benzo(b)fluoranthene (205-99-2), benzo(k)fluoranthene (207-08-9), indeno(1,2,3-cd)pyrene (193-39-5) (derived from the Protocol on Persistent Organic Pollutants to the Convention on Long-range Transboundary Air Pollution).

[c] As inorganic compounds.

Explanatory notes:

The CAS number of the pollutant means the precise identifier in Chemical Abstracts Service.

Column 1 contains the thresholds referred to in article 7, paragraph 1 (a)(i) and (iv). If the threshold in a given sub-column (air, water or land) is exceeded, reporting of releases or, for pollutants in waste water destined for waste-water treatment, transfers to the environmental medium referred to in that sub-column is required with respect to the facility in question, for those Parties which have opted for a system of reporting pursuant to article 7, paragraph 1 (a).

Column 2 contains the thresholds referred to in article 7, paragraph 1 (a)(ii). If the threshold in this column is exceeded for a given pollutant, reporting of the off-site transfer of that pollutant is required with respect to the facility in question, for those Parties which have opted for a system of reporting pursuant to article 7, paragraph 1 (a)(ii).

Column 3 contains the thresholds referred to in article 7, paragraph (1)(b). If the threshold in this column is exceeded for a given pollutant, reporting of the releases and off-site transfers of that pollutant is required with respect to the facility in question, for those Parties which have opted for a system of reporting pursuant to article 7, paragraph 1 (b).

A hyphen (-) indicates that the parameter in question does not trigger a reporting requirement.

An asterisk (*) indicates that, for this pollutant, the release threshold in column (1)(a) is to be used rather than a manufacture, process or use threshold.

A double asterisk (**) indicates that, for this pollutant, the release threshold in column (1)(b) is to be used rather than a manufacture, process or use threshold.

Annex III

Part A
Disposal operations ('D')

- Deposit into or onto land (e.g. landfill)
- Land treatment (e.g. biodegradation of liquid or sludgy discards in soils)
- Deep injection (e.g. injection of pumpable discards into wells, salt domes of naturally occurring repositories)
- Surface impoundment (e.g. placement of liquid or sludge discards into pits, ponds or lagoons)
- Specially engineered landfill (e.g. placement into lined discrete cells which are capped and isolated from one another and the environment)
- Release into a water body except seas/oceans
- Release into seas/oceans including sea-bed insertion

- Biological treatment not specified elsewhere in this annex which results in final compounds or mixtures which are discarded by means of any of the operations specified in this part
- Physico-chemical treatment not specified elsewhere in this annex which results in final compounds or mixtures which are discarded by means of any of the operations specified in this part (e.g. evaporation, drying, calcination, neutralization, precipitation)
- Incineration on land
- Incineration at sea
- Permanent storage (e.g. emplacement of containers in a mine)
- Blending or mixing prior to submission to any of the operations specified in this part
- Repackaging prior to submission to any of the operations specified in this part
- Storage pending any of the operations specified in this part

Part B
Recovery operations ('R')

- Use as a fuel (other than in direct incineration) or other means to generate energy
- Solvent reclamation/regeneration
- Recycling/reclamation of organic substances which are not used as solvents
- Recycling/reclamation of metals and metal compounds
- Recycling/reclamation of other inorganic materials
- Regeneration of acids or bases
- Recovery of components used for pollution abatement
- Recovery of components from catalysts
- Used oil re-refining or other reuses of previously used oil
- Land treatment resulting in benefit to agriculture or ecological improvement
- Uses of residual materials obtained from any of the recovery operations specified above in this part
- Exchange of wastes for submission to any of the recovery operations specified above in this part
- Accumulation of material intended for any operation specified in this part

Annex IV
Arbitration

1. In the event of a dispute being submitted for arbitration pursuant to article 23, paragraph 2, of this Protocol, a party or parties shall notify the other party or parties to the dispute by diplomatic means as well as the secretariat of the subject matter of arbitration and indicate, in particular, the articles of this

Protocol whose interpretation or application is at issue. The secretariat shall forward the information received to all Parties to this Protocol.

2. The arbitral tribunal shall consist of three members. Both the claimant party or parties and the other party or parties to the dispute shall appoint an arbitrator, and the two arbitrators so appointed shall designate by common agreement the third arbitrator, who shall be the president of the arbitral tribunal. The latter shall not be a national of one of the parties to the dispute, nor have his or her usual place of residence in the territory of one of these parties, nor be employed by any of them, nor have dealt with the case in any other capacity.

3. If the president of the arbitral tribunal has not been designated within two months of the appointment of the second arbitrator, the Executive Secretary of the Economic Commission for Europe shall, at the request of either party to the dispute, designate the president within a further two-month period.

4. If one of the parties to the dispute does not appoint an arbitrator within two months of the notification referred to in paragraph 1, the other party may so inform the Executive Secretary of the Economic Commission for Europe, who shall designate the president of the arbitral tribunal within a further two-month period. Upon designation, the president of the arbitral tribunal shall request the party which has not appointed an arbitrator to do so within two months. If it fails to do so within that period, the president shall so inform the Executive Secretary of the Economic Commission for Europe, who shall make this appointment within a further two-month period.

5. The arbitral tribunal shall render its decision in accordance with international law and the provisions of this Protocol.

6. Any arbitral tribunal constituted under the provisions set out in this annex shall draw up its own rules of procedure.

7. The decisions of the arbitral tribunal, both on procedure and on substance, shall be taken by majority vote of its members.

8. The arbitral tribunal may take all appropriate measures to establish the facts.

9. The parties to the dispute shall facilitate the work of the arbitral tribunal and, in particular, using all means at their disposal, shall:

(a) Provide it with all relevant documents, facilities and information;
(b) Enable it, where necessary, to call witnesses or experts and receive their evidence.

10. The parties and the arbitrators shall protect the confidentiality of any information that they receive in confidence during the proceedings of the arbitral tribunal.

11. The arbitral tribunal may, at the request of one of the parties, recommend interim measures of protection.

12. If one of the parties to the dispute does not appear before the arbitral tribunal or fails to defend its case, the other party may request the tribunal to continue the proceedings and to render its final decision. Absence of a party or failure of a party to defend its case shall not constitute a bar to the proceedings. Before rendering its final decision, the arbitral tribunal must satisfy itself that the claim is well founded in fact and law.

13. The arbitral tribunal may hear and determine counterclaims arising directly out of the subject matter of the dispute.

14. Unless the arbitral tribunal determines otherwise because of the particular circumstances of the case, the expenses of the tribunal, including the remuneration of its members, shall be borne by the parties to the dispute in equal shares. The tribunal shall keep a record of all its expenses, and shall furnish a final statement thereof to the parties.

15. Any Party to this Protocol which has an interest of a legal nature in the subject matter of the dispute, and which may be affected by a decision in the case, may intervene in the proceedings with the consent of the tribunal.

16. The arbitral tribunal shall render its award within five months of the date on which it is established, unless it finds it necessary to extend the time limit for a period which should not exceed five months.

17. The award of the arbitral tribunal shall be accompanied by a statement of reasons. It shall be final and binding upon all parties to the dispute. The award will be transmitted by the arbitral tribunal to the parties to the dispute and to the secretariat. The secretariat will forward the information received to all Parties to this Protocol.

18. Any dispute which may arise between the parties concerning the interpretation or execution of the award may be submitted by either party to the arbitral tribunal which made the award or, if the latter cannot be seized thereof, to another tribunal constituted for this purpose in the same manner as the first.

PART XI

Liability for environmental damage and
breaches of environmental obligations

International Convention on Civil Liability for Oil Pollution Damage, 27 November 1992

Editorial note

The international regime on civil liability for oil pollution damage was originally found in the 1969 Convention on Civil Liability for Oil Pollution Damage. The 1969 Convention was the subject of three amending Protocols, most recently by the 1992 Liability Protocol. With the entry into force of the 1992 Protocol the 1969 Convention is known as the 1992 International Convention on Civil Liability for Oil Pollution Damage.

The Convention establishes the liability of the owner of a ship for pollution damage caused by oil escaping from the ship as a result of an incident on the territory of a party (including its territorial sea), and covers preventive measures to minimise such damage (Articles II and III(1)). 'Pollution damage' is defined as 'loss or damage caused outside the ship by contamination resulting from the escape or discharge of oil from the ship, wherever such escape or discharge may occur, provided that compensation for impairment of the environment other than loss of profit from such impairment shall be limited to costs of reasonable measures of reinstatement actually undertaken or to be undertaken' (Article I(6)(a)) and 'the costs of preventative measures and further loss or damage caused by preventative measures' (Article I(6)(b)).

The Convention establishes joint and several liability for damage which is not 'reasonably separable', and allows a limited number of exceptions, including war and hostilities, intentional acts, governmental negligence and contributory negligence, and it extinguishes all other claims for compensation (Articles III(2) and (3) and IV). The owner can limit liability to 3 million units of account for a ship not exceeding 5,000 units of tonnage and 420 SDR for each additional unit of tonnage to a maximum of 59.7 million SDR (Article V(1)), but may not avail itself of the limit if the incident is the result of the owner's personal fault act or omission (Article V(2). The IMO's Legal Committee increased the compensation limits by 'tacitly amending' the Convention to 4.51 million SDR for ships not exceeding 5,000 units of gross tonnage and 631 SDR for each additional unit of tonnage to a maximum, at 140,000 units of tonnage, of 89.77 million SDR. The amendment will enter into force on 1 November 2003.

The owner must maintain insurance or other financial security to cover its liability and, to limit its liability, establish a fund for the total sum of liability with the court in which action is brought (Articles V(3), VI and VII). Claims may be brought before the courts of any party or parties in which the pollution damage has occurred or the preventive measures have been taken, and judgments are generally recognisable and enforceable in the courts of all parties (Articles IX(1) and X). The court in which a fund is established is exclusively competent to apportion and distribute the fund (Article IX(3)).

Article XIIbis of the Convention establishes a hierarchical relationship between the 1992 Liability Convention and the 1992 Fund Convention by providing for the prior application of the latter. The Convention does not apply to warships or other ships owned or operated by a state and being used at the time of the incident for non-commercial purposes (Article XI(1)).

Date of signature:	27 November 1992
Entry into force:	30 May 1996
Depositary:	Secretary-General of the IMO
Contracting Parties:	Algeria, Angola, Antigua and Barbuda, Argentina, Australia, Bahamas, Barbados, Belgium, Belize, Brunei Darussalam, Cambodia, Cameroon, Canada, Chile, China, Colombia, Comoros, Congo, Croatia, Cyprus, Denmark, Djibouti, Dominica, Dominican Republic, Egypt, El Salvador, Fiji, Finland, France, Gabon, Georgia, Greece, Grenada, Guinea, Iceland, India, Indonesia, Ireland, Italy, Jamaica, Japan, Kenya, Latvia, Liberia, Lithuania, Madagascar, Malta, Marshall Islands, Mauritius, Mexico, Monaco, Morocco, Mozambique, Namibia, Netherlands, New Zealand, Nigeria, Norway, Oman, Panama, Papua New Guinea, Philippines, Poland, Portugal, Qatar, Republic of Korea, Romania, Russian Federation, Saint Vincent and the Grenadines, Samoa, Seychelles, Sierra Leone, Singapore, Slovenia, Spain, Sri Lanka, Sweden, Switzerland, Tanzania (United Republic of), Tonga, Trinidad and Tobago, Tunisia, Turkey, United Arab Emirates, United Kingdom, Uruguay, Vanuatu, Venezuela, Hong Kong-China (Associate Member).
Website:	www.imo.org

International Convention on Civil Liability for Oil Pollution Damage

The States Parties to the present Convention,

Conscious of the dangers of pollution posed by the worldwide maritime carriage of oil in bulk,

Convinced of the need to ensure that adequate compensation is available to persons who suffer damage caused by pollution resulting from the escape or discharge of oil from ships,

Desiring to adopt uniform international rules and procedures for determining questions of liability and providing adequate compensation in such cases,

Have agreed as follows:

Article I

For the purposes of this Convention:

1. 'Ship' means any sea-going vessel and seaborne craft of any type whatsoever constructed or adapted for the carriage of oil in bulk as cargo, provided that a ship capable of carrying oil and other cargoes shall be regarded as a ship only when it is actually carrying oil in bulk as cargo and during any voyage following such carriage unless it is proved that it has no residues of such carriage of oil in bulk aboard.

2. 'Person' means any individual or partnership or any public or private body, whether corporate or not, including a State or any of its constituent subdivisions.

3. 'Owner' means the person or persons registered as the owner of the ship or, in the absence of registration, the person or persons owning the ship. However in the case of a ship owned by a State and operated by a company which in that State is registered as the ship's operator, 'owner' shall mean such company.

4. 'State of the ship's registry' means in relation to registered ships the State of registration of the ship, and in relation to unregistered ships the State whose flag the ship is flying.

5. 'Oil' means any persistent hydrocarbon mineral oil such as crude oil, fuel oil, heavy diesel oil and lubricating oil, whether carried on board a ship as cargo or in the bunkers of such a ship.

6. 'Pollution damage' means:
   (a) loss or damage caused outside the ship by contamination resulting from the escape or discharge of oil from the ship, wherever such escape or discharge may occur, provided that compensation for impairment of the environment other than loss of profit from such impairment shall be limited to costs of reasonable measures of reinstatement actually undertaken or to be undertaken;

(b) the costs of preventive measures and further loss or damage caused by preventive measures.

7. 'Preventive measures' means any reasonable measures taken by any person after an incident has occurred to prevent or minimize pollution damage.

8. 'Incident' means any occurrence, or series of occurrences having the same origin, which causes pollution damage or creates a grave and imminent threat of causing such damage.

9. 'Organization' means the International Maritime Organization.

10. '1969 Liability Convention' means the International Convention on Civil Liability for Oil Pollution Damage, 1969. For States Parties to the Protocol of 1976 to that Convention, the term shall be deemed to include the 1969 Liability Convention as amended by that Protocol.

Article II

This Convention shall apply exclusively:

(a) to pollution damage caused:
  (i) in the territory, including the territorial sea, of a Contracting State, and
  (ii) in the exclusive economic zone of a Contracting State, established in accordance with international law, or, if a Contracting State has not established such a zone, in an area beyond and adjacent to the territorial sea of that State determined by that State in accordance with international law and extending not more than 200 nautical miles from the baselines from which the breadth of its territorial sea is measured;

(b) to preventive measures, wherever taken, to prevent or minimize such damage.

Article III

1. Except as provided in paragraphs 2 and 3 of this Article, the owner of a ship at the time of an incident, or, where the incident consists of a series of occurrences, at the time of the first such occurrence, shall be liable for any pollution damage caused by the ship as a result of the incident.

2. No liability for pollution damage shall attach to the owner if he proves that the damage:

(a) resulted from an act of war, hostilities, civil war, insurrection or a natural phenomenon of an exceptional, inevitable and irresistible character, or

(b) was wholly caused by an act or omission done with intent to cause damage by a third party, or

(c) was wholly caused by the negligence or other wrongful act of any Government or other authority responsible for the maintenance of lights or other navigational aids in the exercise of that function.

3. If the owner proves that the pollution damage resulted wholly or partially either from an act or omission done with intent to cause damage by the person who suffered the damage or from the negligence of that person, the owner may be exonerated wholly or partially from his liability to such person.

4. No claim for compensation for pollution damage may be made against the owner otherwise than in accordance with this Convention. Subject to paragraph 5 of this Article, no claim for compensation for pollution damage under this Convention or otherwise may be made against:

(a) the servants or agents of the owner or the members of the crew;
(b) the pilot or any other person who, without being a member of the crew, performs services for the ship;
(c) any charterer (howsoever described, including a bareboat charterer), manager or operator of the ship;
(d) any person performing salvage operations with the consent of the owner or on the instructions of a competent public authority;
(e) any person taking preventive measures;
(f) all servants or agents of persons mentioned in subparagraphs (c), (d) and (e);

unless the damage resulted from their personal act or omission, committed with the intent to cause such damage, or recklessly and with knowledge that such damage would probably result.

5. Nothing in this Convention shall prejudice any right of recourse of the owner against third parties.

Article IV

When an incident involving two or more ships occurs and pollution damage results therefrom, the owners of all the ships concerned, unless exonerated under Article III, shall be jointly and severally liable for all such damage which is not reasonably separable.

Article V

1. The owner of a ship shall be entitled to limit his liability under this Convention in respect of any one incident to an aggregate amount calculated as follows:

(a) 3 million units of account for a ship not exceeding 5,000 units of tonnage;
(b) for a ship with a tonnage in excess thereof, for each additional unit of tonnage, 420 units of account in addition to the amount mentioned in sub-paragraph (a);

provided, however, that this aggregate amount shall not in any event exceed 59.7 million units of account.[1]

---

[1] The reference to '3 million units of account' shall read '4,510,000 units of account'; the reference to '420 units of account' shall read '631 units of account'; and the reference to '59.7 million units of account' shall read '89,770,000 units of account' after the

2. The owner shall not be entitled to limit his liability under this Convention if it is proved that the pollution damage resulted from his personal act or omission, committed with the intent to cause such damage, or recklessly and with knowledge that such damage would probably result.

3. For the purpose of availing himself of the benefit of limitation provided for in paragraph 1 of this Article the owner shall constitute a fund for the total sum representing the limit of his liability with the Court or other competent authority of any one of the Contracting States in which action is brought under Article IX or, if no action is brought, with any Court or other competent authority in any one of the Contracting States in which an action can be brought under Article IX. The fund can be constituted either by depositing the sum or by producing a bank guarantee or other guarantee, acceptable under the legislation of the Contracting State where the fund is constituted, and considered to be adequate by the Court or other competent authority.

4. The fund shall be distributed among the claimants in proportion to the amounts of their established claims.

5. If before the fund is distributed the owner or any of his servants or agents or any person providing him insurance or other financial security has as a result of the incident in question, paid compensation for pollution damage, such person shall, up to the amount he has paid, acquire by subrogation the rights which the person so compensated would have enjoyed under this Convention.

6. The right of subrogation provided for in paragraph 5 of this Article may also be exercised by a person other than those mentioned therein in respect of any amount of compensation for pollution damage which he may have paid but only to the extent that such subrogation is permitted under the applicable national law.

7. Where the owner or any other person establishes that he may be compelled to pay at a later date in whole or in part any such amount of compensation, with regard to which such person would have enjoyed a right of subrogation under paragraphs 5 or 6 of this Article, had the compensation been paid before the fund was distributed, the Court or other competent authority of the State where the fund has been constituted may order that a sufficient sum shall be provisionally set aside to enable such person at such later date to enforce his claim against the fund.

8. Claims in respect of expenses reasonably incurred or sacrifices reasonably made by the owner voluntarily to prevent or minimize pollution damage shall rank equally with other claims against the fund.

9.

(a) The 'unit of account' referred to in paragraph 1 of this Article is the Special Drawing Right as defined by the International Monetary Fund. The amounts mentioned in paragraph 1 shall be converted into national

amendments approved by the Legal Committee of the International Maritime Organization on 18 October 2000.

currency on the basis of the value of that currency by reference to the Special Drawing Right on the date of the constitution of the fund referred to in paragraph 3. The value of the national currency, in terms of the Special Drawing Right, of a Contracting State which is a member of the International Monetary Fund shall be calculated in accordance with the method of valuation applied by the International Monetary Fund in effect on the date in question for its operations and transactions. The value of the national currency, in terms of the Special Drawing Right, of a Contracting State which is not a member of the International Monetary Fund shall be calculated in a manner determined by that State.

(b) Nevertheless, a Contracting State which is not a member of the International Monetary Fund and whose law does not permit the application of the provisions of paragraph 9(a) may, at the time of ratification, acceptance, approval of or accession to this Convention or at any time thereafter, declare that the unit of account referred to in paragraph 9(a) shall be equal to 15 gold francs. The gold franc referred to in this paragraph corresponds to sixty-five and a half milligrammes of gold of millesimal fineness nine hundred. The conversion of the gold franc into the national currency shall be made according to the law of the State concerned.

(c) The calculation mentioned in the last sentence of paragraph 9(a) and the conversion mentioned in paragraph 9(b) shall be made in such manner as to express in the national currency of the Contracting State as far as possible the same real value for the amounts in paragraph 1 as would result from the application of the first three sentences of paragraph 9(a). Contracting States shall communicate to the depositary the manner of calculation pursuant to paragraph 9(a), or the result of the conversion in paragraph 9(b) as the case may be, when depositing an instrument of ratification, acceptance, approval of or accession to this Convention and whenever there is a change in either.

10. For the purpose of this Article the ship's tonnage shall be the gross tonnage calculated in accordance with the tonnage measurement regulations contained in Annex I of the International Convention on Tonnage Measurement of Ships, 1969.

11. The insurer or other person providing financial security shall be entitled to constitute a fund in accordance with this Article on the same conditions and having the same effect as if it were constituted by the owner. Such a fund may be constituted even if, under the provisions of paragraph 2, the owner is not entitled to limit his liability, but its constitution shall in that case not prejudice the rights of any claimant against the owner.

Article VI

1. Where the owner, after an incident, has constituted a fund in accordance with Article V, and is entitled to limit his liability,

(a) no person having a claim for pollution damage arising out of that incident shall be entitled to exercise any right against any other assets of the owner in respect of such claim;

(b) the Court or other competent authority of any Contracting State shall order the release of any ship or other property belonging to the owner which has been arrested in respect of a claim for pollution damage arising out of that incident, and shall similarly release any bail or other security furnished to avoid such arrest.

2. The foregoing shall, however, only apply if the claimant has access to the Court administering the fund and the fund is actually available in respect of his claim.

Article VII

1. The owner of a ship registered in a Contracting State and carrying more than 2,000 tons of oil in bulk as cargo shall be required to maintain insurance or other financial security, such as the guarantee of a bank or a certificate delivered by an international compensation fund in the sums fixed by applying the limits of liability prescribed in Article V, paragraph 1 to cover his liability for pollution damage under this Convention.

2. A certificate attesting that insurance or other financial security is in force in accordance with the provisions of this Convention shall be issued to each ship after the appropriate authority of a Contracting State has determined that the requirements of paragraph 1 have been complied with. With respect to a ship registered in a Contracting State such certificate shall be issued or certified by the appropriate authority of the State of the ship's registry; with respect to a ship not registered in a Contracting State it may be issued or certified by the appropriate authority of any Contracting State. This certificate shall be in the form of the annexed model and shall contain the following particulars:

(a) name of ship and port of registration;
(b) name and principal place of business of owner;
(c) type of security;
(d) name and principal place of business of insurer or other person giving security and, where appropriate, place of business where the insurance or security is established;
(e) period of validity of certificate which shall not be longer than the period of validity of the insurance or other security.

3. The certificate shall be in the official language or languages of the issuing State. If the language used is neither English nor French, the text shall include a translation into one of these languages.

4. The certificate shall be carried on board the ship and a copy shall be deposited with the authorities who keep the record of the ship's registry or, if

the ship is not registered in a Contracting State, with the authorities of the State issuing or certifying the certificate.

5. An insurance or other financial security shall not satisfy the requirements of this Article if it can cease, for reasons other than the expiry of the period of validity of the insurance or security specified in the certificate under paragraph 2 of this Article, before three months have elapsed from the date on which notice of its termination is given to the authorities referred to in paragraph 4 of this Article, unless the certificate has been surrendered to these authorities or a new certificate has been issued within the said period. The foregoing provisions shall similarly apply to any modification which results in the insurance or security no longer satisfying the requirements of this Article.

6. The State of registry shall, subject to the provisions of this Article, determine the conditions of issue and validity of the certificate.

7. Certificates issued or certified under the authority of a Contracting State in accordance with paragraph 2 shall be accepted by other Contracting States for the purposes of this Convention and shall be regarded by other Contracting States as having the same force as certificates issued or certified by them even if issued or certified in respect of a ship not registered in a Contracting State. A Contracting State may at any time request consultation with the issuing or certifying State should it believe that the insurer or guarantor named in the certificate is not financially capable of meeting the obligations imposed by this Convention.

8. Any claim for compensation for pollution damage may be brought directly against the insurer or other person providing financial security for the owner's liability for pollution damage. In such case the defendant may, even if the owner is not entitled to limit his liability according to Article V, paragraph 2, avail himself of the limits of liability prescribed in Article V, paragraph 1. He may further avail himself of the defences (other than the bankruptcy or winding up of the owner) which the owner himself would have been entitled to invoke. Furthermore, the defendant may avail himself of the defence that the pollution damage resulted from the wilful misconduct of the owner himself, but the defendant shall not avail himself of any other defence which he might have been entitled to invoke in proceedings brought by the owner against him. The defendant shall in any event have the right to require the owner to be joined in the proceedings.

9. Any sums provided by insurance or by other financial security maintained in accordance with paragraph 1 of this Article shall be available exclusively for the satisfaction of claims under this Convention.

10. A Contracting State shall not permit a ship under its flag to which this Article applies to trade unless a certificate has been issued under paragraph 2 or 12 of this Article.

11. Subject to the provisions of this Article, each Contracting State shall ensure, under its national legislation, that insurance or other security to the

extent specified in paragraph 1 of this Article is in force in respect of any ship, wherever registered, entering or leaving a port in its territory, or arriving at or leaving an off-shore terminal in its territorial sea, if the ship actually carries more than 2,000 tons of oil in bulk as cargo.

12. If insurance or other financial security is not maintained in respect of a ship owned by a Contracting State, the provisions of this Article relating thereto shall not be applicable to such ship, but the ship shall carry a certificate issued by the appropriate authorities of the State or the ships registry stating that the ship is owned by that State and that the ship's liability is covered within the limits prescribed by Article V, paragraph 1. Such a certificate shall follow as closely as practicable the model prescribed by paragraph 2 of this Article.

Article VIII

Rights of compensation under this Convention shall be extinguished unless an action is brought thereunder within three years from the date when the damage occurred. However, in no case shall an action be brought after six years from the date of the incident which caused the damage. Where this incident consists of a series of occurrences, the six years' period shall run from the date at the first such occurrence.

Article IX

1. Where an incident has caused pollution damage in the territory, including the territorial sea or an area referred to in Article II, of one or more Contracting States or preventive measures have been taken to prevent or minimize pollution damage in such territory including the territorial sea or area, actions for compensation may only be brought in the Courts of any such Contracting State or States. Reasonable notice of any such action shall be given to the defendant.

2. Each Contracting State shall ensure that its Courts possess the necessary jurisdiction to entertain such actions for compensation.

3. After the fund has been constituted in accordance with Article V the Courts of the State in which the fund is constituted shall be exclusively competent to determine all matters relating to the apportionment and distribution of the fund.

Article X

1. Any judgment given by a Court with jurisdiction in accordance with Article IX which is enforceable in the State of origin where it is no longer subject to ordinary forms of review, shall be recognized in any Contracting State, except:

(a) where the judgment was obtained by fraud; or
(b) where the defendant was not given reasonable notice and a fair opportunity to present his case.

2. A judgment recognized under paragraph 1 of this Article shall be enforceable in each Contracting State as soon as the formalities required in that State have been complied with. The formalities shall not permit the merits of the case to be re-opened.

Article XI

1. The provisions of this Convention shall not apply to warships or other ships owned or operated by a State and used, for the time being, only on government non-commercial service.

2. With respect to ships owned by a Contracting State and used for commercial purposes, each State shall be subject to suit in the jurisdictions set forth in Article IX and shall waive all defences based on its status as a sovereign State.

Article XII

This Convention shall supersede any International Conventions in force or open for signature, ratification or accession at the date on which the Convention is opened for signature, but only to the extent that such Conventions would be in conflict with it; however, nothing in this Article shall affect the obligations of Contracting States to non-Contracting States arising under such International Conventions.

Article XII bis
Transitional provisions

The following transitional provisions shall apply in the case of a State which at the time of an incident is a Party both to this Convention and to the 1969 Liability Convention:

(a) where an incident has caused pollution damage within the scope of this Convention, liability under this Convention shall be deemed to be discharged if, and to the extent that, it also arises under the 1969 Liability Convention;

(b) where an incident has caused pollution damage within the scope of this Convention, and the State is a Party both to this Convention and to the International Convention on the Establishment of an International Fund for Compensation for Oil Pollution Damage, 1971, liability remaining to be discharged after the application of sub-paragraph (a) of this Article shall arise under this Convention only to the extent that pollution damage remains uncompensated after application of the said 1971 Convention;

(c) in the application of Article III, paragraph 4, of this Convention the expression 'this Convention' shall be interpreted as referring to this Convention or the 1969 Liability Convention, as appropriate;

(d) in the application of Article V, paragraph 3, of this Convention the total sum of the fund to be constituted shall be reduced by the amount by which liability has been deemed to be discharged in accordance with sub-paragraph (a) of this Article.

Article XII ter
Final clauses

The final clauses of this Convention shall be Articles 12 to 18 of the Protocol of 1992 to amend the 1969 Liability Convention. References in this Convention to Contracting States shall be taken to mean references to the Contracting States of that Protocol.

Final clauses of the Protocol of 1992 to amend the 1969
Civil Liability Convention

Article 12
Signature, ratification, acceptance, approval and accession

1. This Protocol shall be open for signature at London from 15 January 1993 to 14 January 1994 by all States.

2. Subject to paragraph 4, any State may become a Party to this Protocol by:

(a) signature subject to ratification, acceptance or approval followed by ratification, acceptance or approval; or
(b) accession.

3. Ratification, acceptance, approval or accession shall be effected by the deposit of a formal instrument to that effect with the Secretary-General of the Organization.

4. Any Contracting State to the International Convention on the Establishment of an International Fund for Compensation for Oil Pollution Damage, 1971, hereinafter referred to as the 1971 Fund Convention, may ratify, accept, approve or accede to this Protocol only if it ratifies, accepts, approves or accedes to the Protocol of 1992 to amend that Convention at the same time, unless it denounces the 1971 Fund Convention to take effect on the date when this Protocol enters into force for that State.

5. A State which is a Party to this Protocol but not a Party to the 1969 Liability Convention shall be bound by the provisions of the 1969 Liability Convention as amended by this Protocol in relation to other States Parties hereto, but shall not be bound by the provisions of the 1969 Liability Convention in relation to States Parties thereto.

6. Any instrument of ratification, acceptance, approval or accession deposited after the entry into force of an amendment to the 1969 Liability Convention as amended by this Protocol shall be deemed to apply to the Convention so amended, as modified by such amendment.

Article 13
Entry into force

1. This Protocol shall enter into force twelve months following the date on which ten States including four States each with not less than one million units of gross tanker tonnage have deposited instruments of ratification, acceptance, approval or accession with the Secretary-General of the Organization.

2. However, any Contracting State to the 1971 Fund Convention may, at the time of the deposit of its instrument of ratification, acceptance, approval or accession in respect of this Protocol, declare that such instrument shall be deemed not to be effective for the purposes of this Article until the end of the six-month period in Article 31 of the Protocol of 1992 to amend the 1971 Fund Convention. A State which is not a Contracting State to the 1971 Fund Convention but which deposits an instrument of ratification, acceptance, approval or accession in respect of the Protocol of 1992 to amend the 1971 Fund Convention may also make a declaration in accordance with this paragraph at the same time.

3. Any State which has made a declaration in accordance with the preceding paragraph may withdraw it at any time by means of a notification addressed to the Secretary-General of the Organization. Any such withdrawal shall take effect on the date the notification is received, provided that such State shall be deemed to have deposited its instrument of ratification, acceptance, approval or accession in respect of this Protocol on that date.

4. For any State which ratifies, accepts, approves or accedes to it after the conditions in paragraph 1 for entry into force have been met, this Protocol shall enter into force twelve months following the date of deposit by such State of the appropriate instrument.

Article 14
Revision and amendment

1. A Conference for the purpose of revising or amending the 1992 Liability Convention may be convened by the Organization.

2. The Organization shall convene a Conference of Contracting States for the purpose of revising or amending the 1992 Liability Convention at the request of not less than one third of the Contracting States.

Article 15
Amendments of limitation amounts

1. Upon the request of at least one quarter of the Contracting States any proposal to amend the limits of liability laid down in Article V, paragraph 1, of the 1969 Liability Convention as amended by this Protocol shall be circulated by the Secretary-General to all Members of the Organization and to all Contracting States.

2. Any amendment proposed and circulated as above shall be submitted to the Legal Committee of the Organization for consideration at a date at least six months after the date of its circulation.

3. All Contracting States to the 1969 Liability Convention as amended by this Protocol, whether or not Members of the Organization, shall be entitled to participate in the proceedings of the Legal Committee for the consideration and adoption of amendments.

4. Amendments shall be adopted by a two-thirds majority of the Contracting States present and voting in the Legal Committee, expanded as provided for in paragraph 3, on condition that at least one half of the Contracting States shall be present at the time of voting.

5. When acting on a proposal to amend the limits, the Legal Committee shall take into account the experience of incidents and in particular the amount of damage resulting therefrom, changes in the monetary values and the effect of the proposed amendment on the cost of insurance. It shall also take into account the relationship between the limits in Article V, paragraph 1, of the 1969 Liability Convention as amended by this Protocol and those in Article 4, paragraph 4, of the International Convention on the Establishment of an International Fund for Compensation for Oil Pollution Damage, 1992.

6.

(a) No amendment of the limits of liability under this Article may be considered before 15 January 1998 nor less than five years from the date of entry into force of a previous amendment under this Article. No amendment under this Article shall be considered before this Protocol has entered into force.

(b) No limit may be increased so as to exceed an amount which corresponds to the limit laid down in the 1969 Liability Convention as amended by this Protocol increased by 6 per cent per year calculated on a compound basis from 15 January 1993.

(c) No limit may be increased so as to exceed an amount which corresponds to the limit laid down in the 1969 Liability Convention as amended by this Protocol multiplied by 3.

7. Any amendment adopted in accordance with paragraph 4 shall be notified by the Organization to all Contracting States. The amendment shall be deemed to have been accepted at the end of a period of eighteen months after the date of notification, unless within that period not less than one quarter of the States that were Contracting States at the time of the adoption of the amendment by the Legal Committee have communicated to the Organization that they do not accept the amendment in which case the amendment is rejected and shall have no effect.

8. An amendment deemed to have been accepted in accordance with paragraph 7 shall enter into force eighteen months after its acceptance.

9. All Contracting States shall be bound by the amendment, unless they denounce this Protocol in accordance with Article 16, paragraphs 1 and 2, at least six months before the amendment enters into force. Such denunciation shall take effect when the amendment enters into force.

10. When an amendment has been adopted by the Legal Committee but the eighteen-month period for its acceptance has not yet expired, a State which becomes a Contracting State during that period shall be bound by the amendment if it enters into force. A State which becomes a Contracting State after that period shall be bound by an amendment which has been accepted in accordance with paragraph 7. In the cases referred to in this paragraph, a State becomes bound by an amendment when that amendment enters into force, or when this Protocol enters into force for that Stare, if later.

Article 16
Denunciation

1. This Protocol may be denounced by any Party at any rime after the date on which it enters into force for that Party.

2. Denunciation shall be effected by the deposit of an instrument with the Secretary-General of the Organization.

3. A denunciation shall take effect twelve months, or such longer period as may be specified in the instrument of denunciation, after its deposit with the Secretary-General of the Organization.

4. As between the Parties to this Protocol, denunciation by any of them of the 1969 Liability Convention in accordance with Article XVI thereof shall not be construed in any way as a denunciation of the 1969 Liability Convention as amended by this Protocol.

5. Denunciation of the Protocol of 1992 to amend the 1971 Fund Convention by a State which remains a Parry to the 1971 Fund Convention shall be deemed to be a denunciation of this Protocol. Such denunciation shall take effect on the date on which denunciation of the Protocol of 1992 to amend the 1971 Fund Convention takes effect according to Article 34 of that Protocol.

Article 17
Depositary

1. This Protocol and any amendments accepted under Article 15 shall be deposited with the Secretary-General of the Organization.

2. The Secretary-General of the Organization shall:

(a) inform all States which have signed or acceded to this Protocol of:

   (i) each new signature or deposit of an instrument together with the date thereof;

  (ii) each declaration and notification under Article 13 and each declaration and communication under Article V, paragraph 9, of the 1992 Liability Convention;

 (iii) the date of entry into force of this Protocol;

 (iv) any proposal to amend limits of liability which has been made in accordance with Article 15, paragraph 1;

  (v) any amendment which has been adopted in accordance with Article 15, paragraph 4;

 (vi) any amendment deemed to have been accepted under Article 15, paragraph 7, together with the date on which that amendment shall enter into force in accordance with paragraphs 8 and 9 of that Article;

(vii) the deposit of any instrument of denunciation of this Protocol together with the date of the deposit and the date on which it takes effect;

(viii) any denunciation deemed to have been made under Article 16, paragraph 5;

 (ix) any communication called for by any Article of this Protocol;

(b) transmit certified true copies of this Protocol to all Signatory States and to all States which accede to this Protocol.

3. As soon as this Protocol enters into force, the text shall be transmitted by the Secretary-General of the Organization to the Secretariat of the United Nations for registration and publication in accordance with Article 102 of the Charter of the United Nations.

Article 18
Languages

This Protocol is established in a single original in the Arabic, Chinese, English, French, Russian and Spanish languages, each text being equally authentic.

Annex
Certificate of insurance or other financial security in respect of civil liability for oil pollution damage

Issued in accordance with the provisions of Article VII of the International Convention on Civil Liability for Oil Pollution Damage, 1992.

Name of ship	Distinctive number of letters	Port of registry	Name and address of owner

This is to certify that there is in force in respect of the above-named ship a policy of insurance or other financial security satisfying the requirements of Article VII of the International Convention on Civil Liability for Oil Pollution Damage, 1992.

Type of Security ....

....

Duration of Security ....

....

Name and Address of the Insurer(s) and/or Guarantor(s) ....

Name ....

Address ....

This certificate is valid until..

Issued or certified by the Government of..

....

(Full designation of the State)

At .... On ....

(Place)   (Date)

....
(Signature and Title of issuing or certifying official)

Explanatory Notes:

1. If desired, the designation of the State may include a reference to the competent public authority of the country where the certificate is issued.
2. If the total amount of security has been furnished by more than one source, the amount of each of them should be indicated.
3. If security is furnished in several forms, these should be enumerated.
4. The entry "Duration of Security" must stipulate the date on which such security takes effect.

International Convention on the Establishment of an International Fund for Compensation for Oil Pollution Damage, 27 November 1992

Editorial note

The 1992 (originally 1971) Fund Convention was adopted under the auspices of an International Legal Conference on Marine Pollution Damage to provide additional compensation for victims of oil pollution and to transfer some of the economic consequences to the owners of the oil cargo, as well as the ship owner subject to the original 1969 Convention on Liability and Compensation for Oil Pollution Damage. The original 1971 Convention was amended by three Protocols, most recently by the 1992 Fund Protocol. With the entry into force of the 1992 Protocol, the 1971 Fund Convention is known as the International Convention on the Establishment of an International Fund For Oil Pollution Damage, 1992 (1992 Fund Convention). The 1971 Fund Convention has ceased to be in force on 24 November 2002, when the number of 1971 Fund Member States fell below 25.

The 1992 Fund Convention adopts the same definitions as the 1992 Convention on Liability and Compensation for Oil Pollution Damage (1992 CLC) (Article 1). The 1992 Convention, which establishes an International Oil Pollution Compensation Fund (IOPC Fund), has as its objective to provide compensation for pollution damage which is inadequately compensated by the 1992 CLC (Article 2(1)).

To fulfil its objective, the Fund pays compensation to any person suffering pollution damage if that person has been unable to obtain 'full and adequate' compensation under the 1992 CLC because no liability arises under that Convention, or the owner cannot meet obligations under that Convention, or the liability exceeds the limit established by the Convention (Article 4(1)). The 1992 Fund Convention limits the obligation of the Fund in certain situations, including war, lack of evidence that the damage resulted from an incident involving one or more ships, damage by warships or state operated non-commercial ships, and contributory negligence (Article 4(2) and (3)). The 1992 Fund Convention provides that the total amount of compensation paid by the Fund shall in respect of any one incident be limited to 135 million SDR per incident or for certain natural damage, and to 200 million SDR for any period when there are three parties to the Convention where the combined

1198

relevant quantities of contributing oil received by persons in the territories of those parties equalled or exceeded 600 million tons in the preceding year (Article 4(4)). Such limits have been increased by a resolution adopted by the Legal Committee of the International Maritime Organization on 18 October 2000.

The 1992 Fund Convention limits periods for the bringing of claims, and requires any action against the Fund for compensation to be brought only before a court competent under Article IX of the 1992 CLC (Articles 6 and 7(1)). Where an action has been brought before a court against an owner under the 1992 CLC that court has exclusive competence over any action against the Fund under Article 4 of the 1992 Fund Convention in respect of the same damage (Article 7(3)). Where that court is in a state which is not a party to the 1992 Fund Convention, the claimant may bring the case before the court where the Fund is headquartered (London) or any court of a party to the 1992 Fund Convention competent under Article IX of the 1992 CLC (Article 7(3)). The 1992 Fund Convention also sets forth rules concerning the effect of judgments on the Fund, the recognition and enforcement of judgments, and rights of recourse and subrogation (Articles 7(6), 8 and 9).

Annual contributions to the Fund are made, in respect of each party, by any person (including associated persons) who has received a total of more than 150,000 tons of contributing oil in the ports or terminals in the territory of that party contributing oil carried by sea, and contributing oil first received in any installations situated in the territory of that party which has first been carried by sea and discharged in a port or terminal of a non-party (Articles 10(1) and (2) and 12). The assessment of each person's annual contribution which may be needed to balance the budget comprises a proportion of the total amount of contributions required by the Fund to fulfil its estimated annual expenditure (Article 12(2) and (3)).

The IOPC Fund, which has legal personality under the laws of each party (Article 2(2)), comprises an Assembly, a Secretariat and an Executive Committee (Articles 16 to 30). The Assembly, in which all parties to the Convention are members, has overall responsibility for the administration of the Fund and proper execution of the Convention, and its functions include approving the settlement of claims, taking decisions in respect of distributions under Article 4(5) and provisional payments, and electing the Executive Committee (Articles 17 and 18). There are fifteen members of the Executive Committee, elected on the basis of equitable geographic distribution, including parties particularly exposed to the risks of oil pollution and having large tanker fleets, and approximately one half from those parties in whose territory the largest quantities of oil were received (Article 22). The functions of the Executive Committee include approving the settlement of claims and giving instructions to the Director (Article 26).

Date of signature: 27 November 1992

Entry into force: 30 May 1996

Depositary: Secretary-General of the IMO

Contracting Parties: Algeria, Angola, Antigua and Barbuda, Argentina, Australia, Bahamas, Barbados, Belgium, Belize, Brunei Darussalam, Cambodia, Cameroon, Canada, Colombia, Comoros, Congo, Croatia, Cyprus, Denmark, Djibouti, Dominica, Dominican Republic, Fiji, Finland, France, Gabon, Georgia, Greece, Grenada, Guinea, Iceland, India, Ireland, Italy, Jamaica, Japan, Kenya, Latvia, Liberia, Lithuania, Madagascar, Malta, Marshall Islands, Mauritius, Mexico, Monaco, Morocco, Mozambique, Namibia, Netherlands, New Zealand, Nigeria, Norway, Oman, Panama, Papua New Guinea, Philippines, Poland, Portugal, Qatar, Republic of Korea, Russian Federation, Saint Vincent and the Grenadines, Samoa, Seychelles, Sierra Leone, Singapore, Slovenia, Spain, Sri Lanka, Sweden, Tanzania (United Republic of), Tonga, Trinidad and Tobago, Tunisia, Turkey, United Arab Emirates, United Kingdom, Uruguay, Vanuatu, Venezuela, Hong Kong-China (Associate Member).

Website: www.iopcfund.org

International Convention on the Establishment of an International Fund for Compensation for Oil Pollution Damage

The States Parties to the present Convention,

Being Parties to the International Convention on Civil Liability for Oil Pollution Damage, adopted at Brussels on 29 November 1969,

Conscious of the dangers of pollution posed by the world-wide maritime carriage of oil in bulk,

Convinced of the need to ensure that adequate compensation is available to persons who suffer damage caused by pollution resulting from the escape or discharge of oil from ships,

Considering that the International Convention of 29 November 1969, on Civil Liability for Oil Pollution Damage, by providing a regime for compensation for pollution damage in Contracting States and for the costs of measures, wherever taken, to prevent or minimize such damage, represents a considerable progress towards the achievement of this aim,

Considering however that this regime does not afford full compensation for victims of oil pollution damage in all cases while it imposes an additional financial burden on shipowners,

Considering further that the economic consequences of oil pollution damage resulting from the escape or discharge of oil carried in bulk at sea by ships should not exclusively be borne by the shipping industry but should in part be borne by the oil cargo interests,

Convinced of the need to elaborate a compensation and indemnification system supplementary to the International Convention on Civil Liability for Oil Pollution Damage with a view to ensuring that full compensation will be available to victims of oil pollution incidents and that the shipowners are at the same time given relief in respect of the additional financial burdens imposed on them by the said Convention,

Taking note of the Resolution on the Establishment of an International Compensation Fund for Oil Pollution Damage which was adopted on 29 November 1969 by the International Legal Conference on Marine Pollution Damage,

Have agreed as follows:

General Provisions

Article 1

For the purposes of this Convention:

(1) '1992 Liability Convention' means the International Convention on Civil Liability for Oil Pollution Damage, 1992.

(1bis) '1971 Fund Convention' means the International Convention on the Establishment of an International Fund for Compensation for Oil Pollution Damage, 1971. For States Parties to the Protocol of 1976 to that Convention, the term shall be deemed to include the 1971 Fund Convention as amended by that Protocol.

(2) 'Ship', 'Person', 'Owner', 'Oil', 'Pollution Damage', 'Preventive Measures', 'Incident', and 'Organization' have the same meaning as in Article I of the 1992 Liability Convention.

(3) 'Contributing Oil' means crude oil and fuel oil as defined in subparagraphs (a) and (b) below:

  (a) 'Crude Oil' means any liquid hydrocarbon mixture occurring naturally in the earth whether or not treated to render it suitable for transportation. It also includes crude oils from which certain distillate fractions have been removed (sometimes referred to as 'topped crudes') or to which certain distillate fractions have been added (sometimes referred to as 'spiked' or 'reconstituted' crudes).

  (b) 'Fuel Oil' means heavy distillates or residues from crude oil or blends of such materials intended for use as a fuel for the production of heat or power of a quality equivalent to the 'American Society for Testing and Materials' Specification for Number Four Fuel Oil (Designation D 396–69)', or heavier.

(4) 'Unit of account' has the same meaning as in Article V, paragraph 9, of the 1992 Liability Convention.

(5) 'Ship's tonnage' has the same meaning as in Article V, paragraph 10, of the 1992 Liability Convention.

(6) 'Ton', in relation to oil, means a metric ton.

(7) 'Guarantor' means any person providing insurance or other financial security to cover an owner's liability in pursuance of Article VII, paragraph 1, of the 1992 Liability Convention.

(8) 'Terminal installation' means any site for the storage of oil in bulk which is capable of receiving oil from waterborne transportation, including any facility situated off-shore and linked to such site.

(9) Where an incident consists of a series of occurrences, it shall be treated as having occurred on the date of the first such occurrence.

Article 2

1. An International Fund for compensation for pollution damage, to be named 'The International Oil Pollution Compensation Fund 1992' and hereinafter referred to as 'the Fund', is hereby established with the following aims:

(a) to provide compensation for pollution damage to the extent that the protection afforded by the 1992 Liability Convention is inadequate;

(b) to give effect to the related purposes set out in this Convention.

2. The Fund shall in each Contracting State be recognized as a legal person capable under the laws of that State of assuming rights and obligations and of being a party in legal proceedings before the courts of that State. Each Contracting State shall recognize the Director of the Fund (hereinafter referred to as 'The Director') as the legal representative of the Fund.

Article 3

This Convention shall apply exclusively:

(a) to pollution damage caused:
   (i) in the territory, including the territorial sea, of a Contracting State, and
   (ii) in the exclusive economic zone of a Contracting State, established in accordance with international law, or, if a Contracting State has not established such a zone, in an area beyond and adjacent to the territorial sea of that State determined by that State in accordance with international law and extending not more than 200 nautical miles from the baselines from which the breadth of its territorial sea is measured;
(b) to preventive measures, wherever taken, to prevent or minimize such damage.

Compensation

Article 4

1. For the purpose of fulfilling its function under Article 2, paragraph 1 (a), the Fund shall pay compensation to any person suffering pollution damage if such person has been unable to obtain full and adequate compensation for the damage under the terms of the 1992 Liability Convention,

(a) because no liability for the damage arises under the 1992 Liability Convention;

(b) because the owner liable for the damage under the 1992 Liability Convention is financially incapable of meeting his obligations in full and any financial security that may be provided under Article VII of that Convention does not cover or is insufficient to satisfy the claims for compensation for the damage; an owner being treated as financially incapable of meeting his obligations and a financial security being treated as insufficient if the person suffering the damage has been unable to obtain full satisfaction of the amount of compensation due under the 1992 Liability Convention after having taken all reasonable steps to pursue the legal remedies available to him;

(c) because the damage exceeds the owners liability under the 1992 Liability Convention as limited pursuant to Article V, paragraph 1, of that Convention or under the terms of any other international Convention in force or open for signature, ratification or accession at the date of this Convention.

Expenses reasonably incurred or sacrifices reasonably made by the owner voluntarily to prevent or minimize pollution damage shall be treated as pollution damage for the purposes of this Article.

2. The Fund shall incur no obligation under the preceding paragraph if:

(a) it proves that the pollution damage resulted from an act of war, hostilities, civil war or insurrection or was caused by oil which has escaped or been discharged from a warship or other ship owned or operated by a State and used, at the time of the incident, only on Government non-commercial service; or

(b) the claimant cannot prove that the damage resulted from an incident involving one or more ships.

3. If the Fund proves that the pollution damage resulted wholly or partially either from an act or omission done with the intent to cause damage by the person who suffered the damage or from the negligence of that person, the Fund may be exonerated wholly or partially from its obligation to pay compensation to such person. The Fund shall in any event be exonerated to the extent that the shipowner may have been exonerated under Article III, paragraph 3, of the

1992 Liability Convention. However, there shall be no such exoneration of the Fund with regard to preventive measures.

4.

(a) Except as otherwise provided in sub-paragraphs (b) and (c) of this para-graph, the aggregate amount of compensation payable by the Fund under this Article shall in respect of any one incident be limited, so that the total sum of that amount and the amount of compensation actually paid under the 1992 Liability Convention for pollution damage within the scope of application of this Convention as defined in Article 3 shall not exceed 135 million units of account.[1]

(b) Except as otherwise provided in sub-paragraph (c), the aggregate amount of compensation payable by the Fund under this Article for pollution damage resulting from a natural phenomenon of an exceptional, inevitable and irresistible character shall not exceed 135 million units of account.[1]

(c) The maximum amount of compensation referred to in sub-paragraphs (a) and (b) shall be 200 million units of account[1] with respect to any incident occurring during any period when there are three Parties to this Convention in respect of which the combined relevant quantity of contributing oil received by persons in the territories of such Parties, during the preceding calendar year, equalled or exceeded 600 million tons.

(d) Interest accrued on a fund constituted in accordance with Article V, para-graph 3, of the 1992 Liability Convention, if any, shall not be taken into account for the computation of the maximum compensation payable by the Fund under this Article.

(e) The amounts mentioned in this Article shall be converted into national currency on the basis of the value of that currency by reference to the Special Drawing Right on the date of the decision of the Assembly of the Fund as to the first date of payment of compensation.

5. Where the amount of established claims against the Fund exceeds the aggregate amount of compensation payable under paragraph 4, the amount available shall be distributed in such a manner that the proportion between any established claim and the amount of compensation actually recovered by the claimant under this Convention shall be the same for all claimants.

6. The Assembly of the Fund may decide that, in exceptional cases, com-pensation in accordance with this Convention can be paid even if the owner of the ship has not constituted a fund in accordance with Article V, paragraph 3,

---

[1] The reference in paragraph (a) to '135 million units of account' shall read '203,000,000 units of account'; the reference in paragraph (b) to '135 million units of account' shall read '203,000,000 units of account'; and the reference in paragraph (c) to '200 millions million units of account' shall read '300,740,000 units of account' after the amendments approved by the Legal Committee of the International Maritime Organization on 18 October 2000.

of the 1992 Liability Convention. In such case paragraph 4(e) of this Article applies accordingly.

7. The Fund shall, at the request of a Contracting State, use its good offices as necessary to assist that State to secure promptly such personnel, material and services as are necessary to enable the State to take measures to prevent or mitigate pollution damage arising from an incident in respect of which the Fund may be called upon to pay compensation under this Convention.

8. The Fund may on conditions to be laid down in the Internal Regulations provide credit facilities with a view to the taking of preventive measures against pollution damage arising from a particular incident in respect of which the Fund may be called upon to pay compensation under this Convention.

Article 5

[*deleted*]

Article 6

Rights to compensation under Article 4 shall be extinguished unless an action is brought thereunder or a notification has been made pursuant to Article 7, paragraph 6, within three years from the date when the damage occurred. However, in no case shall an action be brought after six years from the date of the incident which caused the damage.

Article 7

1. Subject to the subsequent provisions of this Article, any action against the Fund for compensation under Article 4 of this Convention shall be brought only before a court competent under Article IX of the 1992 Liability Convention in respect of actions against the owner who is or who would, but for the provisions of Article III, paragraph 2, of that Convention, have been liable for pollution damage caused by the relevant incident.

2. Each Contracting State shall ensure that its courts possess the necessary jurisdiction to entertain such actions against the Fund as are referred to in paragraph 1.

3. Where an action for compensation for pollution damage has been brought before a court competent under Article IX of the 1992 Liability Convention against the owner of a ship or his guarantor, such court shall have exclusive jurisdictional competence over any action against the Fund for compensation under the provisions of Article 4 of this Convention in respect of the same damage. However, where an action for compensation for pollution damage under the 1992 Liability Convention has been brought before a court in a State Party to the 1992 Liability Convention but not to this Convention, any action against the Fund under Article 4 of this Convention shall at the option of the claimant be brought either before a court of the State where the Fund has its

headquarters or before any court of a State Party to this Convention competent under Article IX of the 1992 Liability Convention.

4. Each Contracting Party shall ensure that the Fund shall have the right to intervene as a party to any legal proceedings in accordance with Article IX of the 1992 Liability Convention before a competent court of the State against the owner of a ship or his guarantor.

5. Except as otherwise provided in paragraph 6, the Fund shall not be bound by any judgment or decision in proceedings to which it has not been a party or by any settlement to which is not a party.

6. Without prejudice to the provisions of paragraph 4, where an action under the 1992 Liability Convention for compensation for pollution damage has been brought against the owner or his guarantor before a competent court in a Contracting State, each party to the proceedings shall be entitled under the national law of that State to notify the Fund of the proceedings. Where such notification has been made in accordance with the formalities required by the law of the court seized and in such time and in such a manner that the Fund has in fact been in a position effectively to intervene as a party to the proceedings, any judgment rendered by the court in such proceedings shall, after it has become final and enforceable in the State where the judgment was given, become binding upon the Fund in the sense that the facts and findings in that judgment may not be disputed by the Fund even if the Fund has not actually intervened in the proceedings.

Article 8

Subject to any decision concerning the distribution referred to in Article 4, paragraph 5, any judgment given against the Fund by a court having jurisdiction in accordance with Article 7, paragraphs 1 and 3, shall, when it has become enforceable in the State of origin and is in that State no longer subject to ordinary forms of review, be recognized and enforceable in each Contracting State on the same conditions as are prescribed in Article X of the 1992 Liability Convention.

Article 9

1. The Fund shall, in respect of any amount of compensation for pollution damage paid by the Fund in accordance with Article 4, paragraph 1, of this Convention, acquire by subrogation the rights that the person so compensated may enjoy under the 1992 Liability Convention against the owner or his guarantor.

2. Nothing in this Convention shall prejudice any right of recourse or subrogation of the Fund against persons other than those referred to in the preceding paragraph. In any event the right of the Fund to subrogation against such person shall not be less favourable than that of an insurer of the person to whom compensation has been paid.

3. Without prejudice to any other rights of subrogation or recourse against the Fund which may exist, a Contracting State or agency thereof which has paid compensation for pollution damage in accordance with provisions of national law shall acquire by subrogation the rights which the person so compensated would have enjoyed under this Convention.

Contributions

Article 10

1. Annual contributions to the Fund shall be made in respect of each Contracting State by any person who, in the calendar year referred to in Article 12, paragraph 2(a) or (b), has received in total quantities exceeding 150,000 tons:

(a) in the ports or terminal installations in the territory of that State contributing oil carried by sea to such ports or terminal installations; and

(b) in any installations situated in the territory of that Contracting State contributing oil which has been carried by sea and discharged in a port or terminal installation of a non-Contracting State, provided that contributing oil shall only be taken into account by virtue of this sub-paragraph on first receipt in a Contracting State after its discharge in that non-Contracting State.

2.

(a) For the purposes of paragraph 1, where the quantity of contributing oil received in the territory of a Contracting State by any person in a calendar year when aggregated with the quantity of contributing oil received in the same Contracting State in that year by any associated person or persons exceeds 150,000 tons, such person shall pay contributions in respect of the actual quantity received by him notwithstanding that that quantity did not exceed 150,000 tons.

(b) 'Associated person' means any subsidiary or commonly controlled entity. The question whether a person comes within this definition shall be determined by the national law of the State concerned.

Article 11

[*deleted*]

Article 12

1. With a view to assessing the amount of annual contributions due, if any, and taking account of the necessity to maintain sufficient liquid funds, the Assembly shall for each calendar year make an estimate in the form of a budget of:

(i) Expenditure

(a) costs and expenses of the administration of the Fund in the relevant year and any deficit from operations in preceding years;
(b) payments to be made by the Fund in the relevant year for the satisfaction of claims against the Fund due under Article 4, including repayment on loans previously taken by the Fund for the satisfaction of such claims, to the extent that the aggregate amount of such claims in respect of any one incident does not exceed four million units of account;
(c) payments to be made by the Fund in the relevant year for the satisfaction of claims against the Fund due under Article 4, including repayments on loans previously taken by the Fund for the satisfaction of such claims, to the extent that the aggregate amount of such claims in respect of any one incident is in excess of four million units of account;

(ii) Income
(a) surplus funds from operations in preceding years, including any interest;
(b) annual contributions, if required to balance the budget;
(c) any other income.

2. The Assembly shall decide the total amount of contributions to be levied. On the basis of that decision, the Director shall, in respect of each Contracting State, calculate for each person referred to in Article 10 the amount of his annual contribution:

(a) in so far as the contribution is for the satisfaction of payments referred to in paragraph 1(i)(a) and (b) on the basis of a fixed sum for each ton of contributing oil received in the relevant State by such persons during the preceding calendar year; and
(b) in so far as the contribution is for the satisfaction of payments referred to in paragraph 1(i)(c) of this Article on the basis of a fixed sum for each ton of contributing oil received by such person during the calendar year preceding that in which the incident in question occurred, provided that State was a Party to this Convention at the date of the incident.

3. The sums referred to in paragraph 2 above shall be arrived at by dividing the relevant total amount of contributions required by the total amount of contributing oil received in all Contracting States in the relevant year.
4. The annual contribution shall be due on the date to be laid down in the Internal Regulations of the Fund. The Assembly may decide on a different date of payment.
5. The Assembly may decide, under conditions to be laid down in the Financial Regulations of the Fund, to make transfers between funds received

in accordance with Article 12(2)(a) and funds received in accordance with Article 12(2)(b).

Article 13

1. The amount of any contribution due under Article 12 and which is in arrears shall bear interest at a rate which shall be determined in accordance with the Internal Regulations of the Fund, provided that different rates may be fixed for different circumstances.

2. Each Contracting State shall ensure that any obligation to contribute to the Fund arising under this Convention in respect of oil received within the territory of that State is fulfilled and shall take any appropriate measures under its law, including the imposing of such sanctions as it may deem necessary, with a view to the effective execution of any such obligation; provided, however, that such measures shall only be directed against those persons who are under an obligation to contribute to the Fund.

3. Where a person who is liable in accordance with the provisions of Articles 10 and 12 to make contributions to the Fund does not fulfil his obligations in respect of any such contribution or any part thereof and is in arrear, the Director shall take all appropriate action against such person on behalf of the Fund with a view to the recovery of the amount due. However, where the defaulting contributor is manifestly insolvent or the circumstances otherwise so warrant the Assembly may, upon recommendation of the Director, decide that no action shall be taken or continued against the contributor.

Article 14

1. Each Contracting State may at the time when it deposits its instrument of ratification or accession or at any time thereafter declare that it assumes itself obligations that are incumbent under this Convention on any person who is liable to contribute to the Fund in accordance with Article 10, paragraph 1, in respect of oil received within the territory of that State. Such declaration shall be made in writing and shall specify which obligations are assumed.

2. Where a declaration under paragraph 1 is made prior to the entry into force of this Convention in accordance with Article 40, it shall be deposited with the Secretary-General of the Organization who shall after the entry into force of the Convention communicate the declaration to the Director.

3. A declaration under paragraph 1 which is made after the entry into force of this Convention shall be deposited with the Director.

4. A declaration made in accordance with this Article may be withdrawn by the relevant State giving notice thereof in writing to the Director. Such notification shall take effect three months after the Director's receipt thereof.

5. Any State which is bound by a declaration made under this Article shall, in any proceedings brought against it before a competent court in respect of

any obligation specified in the declaration, waive any immunity that it would otherwise be entitled to invoke.

Article 15

1. Each Contracting State shall ensure that any person who receives contributing oil within its territory in such quantities that he is liable to contribute to the Fund appears on a list to be established and kept up to date by the Director in accordance with the subsequent provisions of this Article.

2. For the purposes set out in paragraph 1, each Contracting State shall communicate, at a time and in the manner to be prescribed in the Internal Regulations, to the Director the name and address of any person who in respect of that State is liable to contribute to the Fund pursuant to Article 10, as well as data on the relevant quantities of contributing oil received by any such person during the preceding calendar year.

3. For the purposes of ascertaining who are, at any given time, the persons liable to contribute to the Fund in accordance with Article 10, paragraph 1, and of establishing, where applicable, the quantities of oil to be taken into account for any such person when determining the amount of his contribution, the list shall be *prima facie* evidence of the facts stated therein.

4. Where a Contracting State does not fulfil its obligations to submit to the Director the communication referred to in paragraph 2 and this results in a financial loss for the Fund, that Contracting State shall be liable to compensate the Fund for such loss. The Assembly shall, on the recommendation of the Director, decide whether such compensation shall be payable by that Contracting State.

Organization and administration

Article 16

The Fund shall have an Assembly and a Secretariat headed by a Director.

Assembly

Article 17

The Assembly shall consist of all Contracting States to this Convention.

Article 18

The functions of the Assembly shall be:

1. to elect at each regular session its Chairman and two Vice-Chairmen who shall hold office until the next regular session;
2. to determine its own rules of procedure, subject to the provisions of this Convention;

3. to adopt Internal Regulations necessary for the proper functioning of the Fund;

4. to appoint the Director and make provisions for the appointment of such other personnel as may be necessary and determine the terms and conditions of service of the Director and other personnel;

5. to adopt the annual budget and fix the annual contributions;

6. to appoint auditors and approve the accounts of the Fund;

7. to approve settlements of claims against the Fund, to take decisions in respect of the distribution among claimants of the available amount of compensation in accordance with Article 4, paragraph 5, and to determine the terms and conditions according to which provisional payments in respect of claims shall be made with a view to ensuring that victims of pollution damage are compensated as promptly as possible;

8. [*deleted*];

9. to establish any temporary or permanent subsidiary body it may consider to be necessary, to define its terms of reference and to give it the authority needed to perform the functions entrusted to it; when appointing the members of such body, the Assembly shall endeavour to secure an equitable geographical distribution of members and to ensure that the Contracting States, in respect of which the largest quantities of contributing oil are being received, are appropriately represented; the Rules of Procedure of the Assembly may be applied, *mutatis mutandis*, for the work of such subsidiary body;

10. to determine which non-Contracting States and which inter-governmental and international non-governmental organizations shall be admitted to take part, without voting rights, in meetings of the Assembly and subsidiary bodies;

11. to give instructions concerning the administration of the Fund to the Director and subsidiary bodies;

12. [*deleted*];

13. to supervise the proper execution of the Convention and of its own decisions;

14. to perform such other functions as are allocated to it under the Convention or are otherwise necessary for the proper operation of the Fund.

Article 19

1. Regular sessions of the Assembly shall take place once every calendar year upon convocation by the Director.

2. Extraordinary sessions of the Assembly shall be convened by the Director at the request of at least one third of the members of the Assembly and may be convened on the Director's own initiative after consultation with the Chairman of the Assembly. The Director shall give members at least thirty days' notice of such sessions.

Article 20

A majority of the members of the Assembly shall constitute a quorum for its meetings.

[*heading deleted*]

Articles 21–27

[*deleted*]

Secretariat

Article 28

1. The Secretariat shall comprise the Director and such staff as the administration of the Fund may require.
2. The Director shall be the legal representative of the Fund.

Article 29

1. The Director shall be the chief administrative officer of the Fund. Subject to the instructions given to him by the Assembly, he shall perform those functions which are assigned to him by this Convention, the Internal Regulations of the Fund and the Assembly.
2. The Director shall in particular:

(a) appoint the personnel required for the administration of the Fund;
(b) take all appropriate measures with a view to the proper administration of the Fund's assets;
(c) collect the contributions due under this Convention while observing in particular the provisions of Article 13, paragraph 3;
(d) to the extent necessary to deal with claims against the Fund and carry out the other functions of the Fund, employ the services of legal, financial and other experts;
(e) take all appropriate measures for dealing with claims against the Fund within the limits and on conditions to be laid down in the Internal Regulations, including the final settlement of claims without the prior approval of the Assembly where these Regulations so provide;
(f) prepare and submit to the Assembly the financial statements and budget estimates for each calendar year;
(g) prepare, in consultation with the Chairman of the Assembly, and publish a report of the activities of the Fund during the previous calendar year;
(h) prepare, collect and circulate the papers, documents, agenda, minutes and information that may be required for the work of the Assembly and subsidiary bodies.

Article 30

In the performance of their duties the Director and the staff and experts appointed by him shall not seek or receive instructions from any Government or from any authority external to the Fund. They shall refrain from any action which might reflect on their position as international officials. Each Contracting State on its part undertakes to respect the exclusively international character of the responsibilities of the Director and the staff and experts appointed by him, and not to seek to influence them in the discharge of their duties.

Finances

Article 31

1. Each Contracting State shall bear the salary, travel and other expenses of its own delegation to the Assembly and of its representatives on subsidiary bodies.

2. Any other expenses incurred in the operation of the Fund shall be borne by the Fund.

Voting

Article 32

The following provisions shall apply to voting in the Assembly:

(a) each member shall have one vote;

(b) except as otherwise provided in Article 33, decisions of the Assembly shall be by a majority vote of the members present and voting;

(c) decisions where a three-fourths or a two-thirds majority is required shall be by a three-fourths or two-thirds majority vote, as the case may be, of those present;

(d) for the purpose of this Article the phrase 'members present' means 'members present at the meeting at the time of the vote', and the phrase 'members present and voting' means 'members present and casting an affirmative or negative vote'. Members who abstain from voting shall be considered as not voting.

Article 33

The following decisions of the Assembly shall require a two-thirds majority:

(a) a decision under Article 13, paragraph 3, not to take or continue action against a contributor;

(b) the appointment of the Director under Article 18, paragraph 4;

(c) the establishment of subsidiary bodies, under Article 18, paragraph 9, and matters relating to such establishment.

Article 34

1. The Fund, its assets, income, including contributions, and other property shall enjoy in all Contracting States exemption from all direct taxation.

2. When the Fund makes substantial purchases of movable or immovable property, or has important work carried out which is necessary for the exercise of its official activities and the cost of which includes indirect taxes or sales taxes, the Governments of Member States shall take, whenever possible, appropriate measures for the remission or refund of the amount of such duties and taxes.

3. No exemption shall be accorded in the case of duties, taxes or dues which merely constitute payment for public utility services.

4. The Fund shall enjoy exemption from all customs duties, taxes and other related taxes on articles imported or exported by it or on its behalf for its official use. Articles thus imported shall not be transferred either for consideration or gratis on the territory of the country into which they have been imported except on conditions agreed by the Government of that country.

5. Persons contributing to the Fund and victims and owners of ships receiving compensation from the Fund shall be subject to the fiscal legislation of the Stare where they are taxable, no special exemption or other benefit being conferred on them in this respect.

6. Information relating to individual contributors supplied for the purpose of this Convention shall not be divulged outside the Fund except in so far as it may be strictly necessary to enable the Fund to carry out its functions including the bringing and defending of legal proceedings.

7. Independently of existing or future regulations concerning currency or transfers, Contracting States shall authorize the transfer and payment of any contribution to the Fund and of any compensation paid by the Fund without any restriction.

Transitional Provisions

Article 35

Claims for compensation under Article 4 arising from incidents occurring after the date of entry into force of this Convention may not be brought against the Fund earlier than the one hundred and twentieth day after that date.

Article 36

The Secretary-General of the Organization shall convene the first session of the Assembly. This session shall take place as soon as possible after entry into force of this Convention and, in any case, not more than thirty days after such entry into force.

Article 36 bis

The following transitional provisions shall apply in the period, hereinafter referred to as the transitional period, commencing with the date of entry into
force of this Convention and ending with the date on which the denunciations provided for in Article 31 of the 1992 Protocol to amend the 1971 Fund
Convention take effect:

(a) In the application of paragraph l(a) of Article 2 of this Convention, the
reference to the 1992 Liability Convention shall include reference to the
International Convention on Civil Liability for Oil Pollution Damage, 1969,
either in its original version or as amended by the Protocol thereto of 1976
(referred to in this Article as 'the 1969 Liability Convention'), and also the
1971 Fund Convention.

(b) Where an incident has caused pollution damage within the scope of this
Convention, the Fund shall pay compensation to any person suffering pollution damage only if, and to the extent that, such person has been unable
to obtain full and adequate compensation for the damage under the terms
of the 1969 Liability Convention, the 1971 Fund Convention and the 1992
Liability Convention, provided that, in respect of pollution damage within
the scope of this Convention in respect of a Party to this Convention but not
a Party to the 1971 Fund Convention, the Fund shall pay compensation to
any person suffering pollution damage only if, and to the extent that, such
person would have been unable to obtain full and adequate compensation
had that State been party to each of the above-mentioned Conventions.

(c) In the application of Article 4 of this Convention, the amount to be taken
into account in determining the aggregate amount of compensation payable
by the Fund shall also include the amount of compensation actually paid
under the 1969 Liability Convention, if any, and the amount of compensation actually paid or deemed to have been paid under the 1971 Fund
Convention.

(d) Paragraph 1 of Article 9 of this Convention shall also apply to the rights
enjoyed under the 1969 Liability Convention.

Article 36 ter

1. Subject to paragraph 4 of this Article, the aggregate amount of the annual contributions payable in respect of contributing oil received in a single
Contracting State during a calendar year shall not exceed 27.5% of the total
amount of annual contributions pursuant to the 1992 Protocol to amend the
1971 Fund Convention, in respect of that calendar year.

2. If the application of the provisions in paragraphs 2 and 3 of Article 12
would result in the aggregate amount of the contributions payable by contributors in a single Contracting State in respect of a given calendar year exceeding 27.5% of the total annual contributions, the contributions payable by all

contributors in that State shall be reduced *pro rata* so that their aggregate contributions equal 27.5% of the total annual contributions to the Fund in respect of that year.

3. If the contributions payable by persons in a given Contracting State shall be reduced pursuant to paragraph 2 of this Article, the contributions payable by persons in all other Contracting States shall be increased *pro rata* so as to ensure that the total amount of contributions payable by all persons liable to contribute to the Fund in respect of the calendar year in question will reach the total amount of contributions decided by the Assembly.

4. The provisions in paragraphs 1 to 3 of this Article shall operate until the total quantity of contributing oil received in all Contracting States in a calendar year has reached 750 million tons or until a period of 5 years after the date of entry into force of the said 1992 Protocol has elapsed, whichever occurs earlier.

Article 36 quater

Notwithstanding the provisions of this Convention, the following provisions shall apply to the administration of the Fund during the period in which both the 1971 Fund Convention and this Convention are in force:

(a) The Secretariat of the Fund, established by the 1971 Fund Convention (hereinafter referred to as 'the 1971 Fund'), headed by the Director, may also function as the Secretariat and the Director of the Fund.

(b) If, in accordance with sub-paragraph (a), the Secretariat and the Director of the 1971 Fund also perform the function of Secretariat and Director of the Fund, the Fund shall be represented, in cases of conflict of interests between the 1971 Fund and the Fund, by the Chairman of the Assembly of the Fund.

(c) The Director and the staff and experts appointed by him, performing their duties under this Convention and the 1971 Fund Convention, shall not be regarded as contravening the provisions of Article 30 of this Convention in so far as they discharge their duties in accordance with this Article.

(d) The Assembly of the Fund shall endeavour not to take decisions which are incompatible with decisions taken by the Assembly of the 1971 Fund. If differences of opinion with respect to common administrative issues arise, the Assembly of the Fund shall try to reach a consensus with the Assembly of the 1971 Fund, in a spirit of mutual co-operation and with the common aims of both organizations in mind.

(e) The Fund may succeed to the rights, obligations and assets of the 1971 Fund if the Assembly of the 1971 Fund so decides, in accordance with Article 44, paragraph 2, of the 1971 Fund Convention.

(f) The Fund shall reimburse to the 1971 Fund all costs and expenses arising from administrative services performed by the 1971 Fund on behalf of the Fund.

Article 36 quinquies
Final clauses

The final clauses of this Convention shall be Articles 28 to 39 of the Protocol of 1992 to amend the 1971 Fund Convention. References in this Convention to Contracting States shall be taken to mean references to the Contracting States of that Protocol.

Final clauses of the Protocol of 1992 to amend the 1971 Fund Convention

Article 28
Signature, ratification, acceptance, approval and accession

1. This Protocol shall be open for signature at London from 15 January 1993 to 14 January 1994 by any State which has signed the 1992 Liability Convention.

2. Subject to paragraph 4, this Protocol shall be ratified, accepted or approved by States which have signed it.

3. Subject to paragraph 4, this Protocol is open for accession by States which did not sign it.

4. This Protocol may be ratified, accepted, approved or acceded to only by States which have ratified, accepted, approved or acceded to the 1992 Liability Convention.

5. Ratification, acceptance, approval or accession shall be effected by the deposit of a formal instrument to that effect with the Secretary-General of the Organization.

6. A State which is a Party to this Protocol but is not a Party to the 1971 Fund Convention shall be bound by the provisions of the 1971 Fund Convention as amended by this Protocol in relation to other Parties hereto, but shall not be bound by the provisions of the 1971 Fund Convention in relation to Parties thereto.

7. Any instrument of ratification, acceptance, approval or accession deposited after the entry into force of an amendment to the 1971 Fund Convention as amended by this Protocol shall be deemed to apply to the Convention so amended, as modified by such amendment.

Article 29
Information on contributing oil

1. Before this Protocol comes into force for a State, that State shall, when depositing an instrument referred to in Article 28, paragraph 5, and annually thereafter at a date to be determined by the Secretary-General of the Organization, communicate to him the name and address of any person who in respect of that State would be liable to contribute to the Fund pursuant to Article 10 of the 1971 Fund Convention as amended by this Protocol as well as data on

the relevant quantities of contributing oil received by any such person in the territory of that State during the preceding calendar year.

2. During the transitional period, the Director shall, for Parties, communicate annually to the Secretary-General of the Organization data on quantities of contributing oil received by persons liable to contribute to the Fund pursuant to Article 10 of the 1971 Fund Convention as amended by this Protocol.

Article 30
Entry into force

1. This Protocol shall enter into force twelve months following the date on which the following requirements are fulfilled:

(a) at least eight States have deposited instruments of ratification, acceptance, approval or accession with the Secretary-General of the Organization; and

(b) the Secretary-General of the Organization has received information in accordance with Article 29 that those persons who would be liable to contribute pursuant to Article 10 of the 1971 Fund Convention as amended by this Protocol have received during the preceding calendar year a total quantity of at least 450 million tons of contributing oil.

2. However, this Protocol shall not enter into force before the 1992 Liability Convention has entered into force.

3. For each State which ratifies, accepts, approves or accedes to this Protocol after the conditions in paragraph 1 for entry into force have been met, the Protocol shall enter into force twelve months following the date of the deposit by such State of the appropriate instrument.

4. Any State may, at the time of the deposit of its instrument of ratification, acceptance, approval or accession in respect of this Protocol declare that such instrument shall not take effect for the purpose of this Article until the end of the six-month period in Article 31.

5. Any State which has made a declaration in accordance with the preceding paragraph may withdraw it at any time by means of a notification addressed to the Secretary-General of the Organization. Any such withdrawal shall take effect on the date the notification is received, and any State making such a withdrawal shall be deemed to have deposited its instrument of ratification, acceptance, approval or accession in respect of this Protocol on that date.

6. Any State which has made a declaration under Article 13, paragraph 2, of the Protocol of 1992 to amend the 1969 Liability Convention shall be deemed to have also made a declaration under paragraph 4 of this Article. Withdrawal of a declaration under the said Article 13, paragraph 2, shall be deemed to constitute withdrawal also under paragraph 5 of this Article.

Article 31
Denunciation of the 1969 and 1971 Conventions

Subject to Article 30, within six months following the date on which the following requirements are fulfilled:

(a) at least eight States have become Parties to this Protocol or have deposited instruments of ratification, acceptance, approval or accession with the Secretary-General of the Organization, whether or not subject to Article 30, paragraph 4, and

(b) the Secretary-General of the Organization has received information in accordance with Article 29 that those persons who are or would be liable to contribute pursuant to Article 10 of the 1971 Fund Convention as amended by this Protocol have received during the preceding calendar year a total quantity of at least 750 million tons of contributing oil;

each Party to this Protocol and each State which has deposited an instrument of ratification, acceptance, approval or accession, whether or not subject to Article 30, paragraph 4, shall, if party thereto, denounce the 1971 Fund Convention and the 1969 Liability Convention with effect twelve months after the expiry of the above-mentioned six-month period.

Article 32
Revision and amendment

1. A conference for the purpose of revising or amending the 1992 Fund Convention may be convened by the Organization.

2. The Organization shall convene a Conference of Contracting States for the purpose of revising or amending the 1992 Fund Convention at the request of not less than one third of all Contracting States.

Article 33
Amendment of compensation limits

1. Upon the request of at least one quarter of the Contracting States, any proposal to amend the limits of amounts of compensation laid down in Article 4, paragraph 4, of the 1971 Fund Convention as amended by this Protocol shall be circulated by the Secretary-General to all Members of the Organization and to all Contracting States.

2. Any amendment proposed and circulated as above shall be submitted to the Legal Committee of the Organization for consideration at a date at least six months after the date of its circulation.

3. All Contracting States to the 1971 Fund Convention as amended by this Protocol, whether or not Members of the Organization, shall be entitled to participate in the proceedings of the Legal Committee for the consideration and adoption of amendments.

4. Amendments shall be adopted by a two-thirds majority of the Contracting States present and voting in the Legal Committee, expanded as provided for in paragraph 3, on condition that at least one half of the Contracting States shall be present at the time of voting.

5. When acting on a proposal to amend the limits, the Legal Committee shall take into account the experience of incidents and in particular the amount of damage resulting therefrom and changes in the monetary values. It shall also take into account the relationship between the limits in Article 4, paragraph 4, of the 1971 Fund Convention as amended by this Protocol and those in Article V, paragraph 1 of the International Convention on Civil Liability for Oil Pollution Damage, 1992.

6.

(a) No amendment of the limits under this Article may be considered before 15 January 1998 nor less than five years from the date of entry into force of a previous amendment under this Article. No amendment under this Article shall be considered before this Protocol has entered into force.

(b) No limit may be increased so as to exceed an amount which corresponds to the limit laid down in the 1971 Fund Convention as amended by this Protocol increased by six per cent per year calculated on a compound basis from 15 January 1993.

(c) No limit may be increased so as to exceed an amount which corresponds to the limit laid down in the 1971 Fund Convention as amended by this Protocol multiplied by three.

7. Any amendment adopted in accordance with paragraph 4 shall be notified by the Organization to all Contracting States. The amendment shall be deemed to have been accepted at the end of a period of eighteen months after the date of notification unless within that period not less than one quarter of the States that were Contracting States at the time of the adoption of the amendment by the Legal Committee have communicated to the Organization that they do not accept the amendment in which case the amendment is rejected and shall have no effect.

8. An amendment deemed to have been accepted in accordance with paragraph 7 shall enter into force eighteen months after its acceptance.

9. All Contracting States shall be bound by the amendment, unless they denounce this Protocol in accordance with Article 34, paragraphs 1 and 2, at least six months before the amendment enters into force. Such denunciation shall take effect when the amendment enters into force.

10. When an amendment has been adopted by the Legal Committee but the eighteen-month period for its acceptance has not yet expired, a State which becomes a Contracting State during that period shall be bound by the amendment if it enters into force. A State which becomes a Contracting State after that period shall be bound by an amendment which has been accepted in

accordance with paragraph 7. In the cases referred to in this paragraph, a State becomes bound by an amendment when that amendment enters into force, or when this Protocol enters into force for that State, if later.

Article 34
Denunciation

1. This Protocol may be denounced by any Party at any time after the date on which it enters into force for that Party.

2. Denunciation shall be effected by the deposit of an instrument with the Secretary-General of the Organization.

3. A denunciation shall take effect twelve months, or such longer period as may be specified in the instrument of denunciation, after its deposit with the Secretary-General of the Organization.

4. Denunciation of the 1992 Liability Convention shall be deemed to be a denunciation of this Protocol. Such denunciation shall take effect on the date on which denunciation of the Protocol of 1992 to amend the 1969 Liability Convention takes effect according to Article 16 of that Protocol.

5. Any Contracting State to this Protocol which has not denounced the 1971 Fund Convention and the 1969 Liability Convention as required by Article 31 shall be deemed to have denounced this Protocol with effect twelve months after the expiry of the six-month period mentioned in that Article. As from the date on which the denunciations provided for in Article 31 take effect, any Party to this Protocol which deposits an instrument of ratification, acceptance, approval or accession to the 1969 Liability Convention shall be deemed to have denounced this Protocol with effect from the date on which such instrument takes effect.

6. As between the Parties to this Protocol, denunciation by any of them of the 1971 Fund Convention in accordance with Article 41 thereof shall not be construed in any way as a denunciation of the 1971 Fund Convention as amended by this Protocol.

7. Notwithstanding a denunciation of this Protocol by a Party pursuant to this Article, any provisions of this Protocol relating to the obligations to make contributions under Article 10 of the 1971 Fund Convention as amended by this Protocol with respect to an incident referred to in Article 12, paragraph 2(b), of that amended Convention and occurring before the denunciation takes effect shall continue to apply.

Article 35
Extraordinary sessions of the Assembly

1. Any Contracting State may, within ninety days after the deposit of an instrument of denunciation the result of which it considers will significantly increase the level of contributions for the remaining Contracting States, request the Director to convene an extraordinary session of the Assembly. The Director

shall convene the Assembly to meet not later than sixty days after receipt of the request.

2. The Director may convene, on his own initiative, an extraordinary session of the Assembly to meet within sixty days after the deposit of any instrument of denunciation, if he considers that such denunciation will result in a significant increase in the level of contributions of the remaining Contracting States.

3. If the Assembly at an extraordinary session convened in accordance with paragraph 1 or 2 decides that the denunciation will result in a significant increase in the level of contributions for the remaining Contracting States, any such State may, not later than one hundred and twenty days before the date on which the denunciation takes effect, denounce this Protocol with effect from the same date.

Article 36
Termination

1. This Protocol shall cease to be in force on the date when the number of Contracting States falls below three.

2. States which are bound by this Protocol on the day before the date it ceases to be in force shall enable the Fund to exercise its functions as described under Article 37 of this Protocol and shall, for that purpose only, remain bound by this Protocol.

Article 37
Winding up of the Fund

1. If this Protocol ceases to be in force, the Fund shall nevertheless:

(a) meet its obligations in respect of any incident occurring before the Protocol ceased to be in force;

(b) be entitled to exercise its rights to contributions to the extent that these contributions are necessary to meet the obligations under sub-paragraph (a), including expenses for the administration of the Fund necessary for this purpose.

2. The Assembly shall take all appropriate measures to complete the winding up of the Fund including the distribution in an equitable manner of any remaining assets among those persons who have contributed to the Fund.

3. For the purposes of this Article the Fund shall remain a legal person.

Article 38
Depositary

1. This Protocol and any amendments accepted under Article 33 shall be deposited with the Secretary-General of the Organization.

2. The Secretary-General of the Organization shall:

(a) inform all States which have signed or acceded to this Protocol of:
- (i)   each new signature or deposit of an instrument together with the date thereof;
- (ii) each declaration and notification under Article 30 including declarations and withdrawals deemed to have been made in accordance with that Article;
- (iii) the date of entry into force of this Protocol;
- (iv) the date by which denunciations provided for in Article 31 are required to be made;
- (v) any proposal to amend limits of amounts of compensation which has been made in accordance with Article 33, paragraph 1;
- (vi) any amendment which has been adopted in accordance with Article 33, paragraph 4;
- (vii) any amendment deemed to have been accepted under Article 33, paragraph 7, together with the date on which that amendment shall enter into force in accordance with paragraph 8 and 9 of that Article;
- (viii) the deposit of an instrument of denunciation of this Protocol together with the date of the deposit and the date on which it takes effect;
- (ix) any denunciation deemed to have been made under Article 34, paragraph 5;
- (x) any communication called for by any Article in this Protocol;

(b) transmit certified true copies of this Protocol to all Signatory States and to all States which accede to the Protocol.

3. As soon as this Protocol enters into force, the text shall be transmitted by the Secretary-General of the Organization to the Secretariat of the United Nations for registration and publication in accordance with Article 102 of the Charter of the United Nations.

Article 39
Languages

This Protocol is established in a single original in the Arabic, Chinese, English, French, Russian and Spanish languages, each text being equally authentic.

DONE at London this twenty-seventh day of November one thousand nine hundred and ninety-two.

IN WITNESS WHEREOF the undersigned being duly authorized for that purpose have signed this Protocol.

Articles on the Responsibility of States for Internationally Wrongful Acts, adopted by the International Law Commission at its fifty-third session, 2001

Editorial note

The ILC's Articles on State Responsibility are an attempt to codify the basic principles of international law governing wrongful acts and their consequences. The ILC divided its task in four parts. Part One is on the internationally wrongful act of a State. Part Two defines the content of the international responsibility of a State. Part Three deals with the implementation of the international responsibility of a State. Part Four contains general provisions. The Articles were adopted by the International Commission at its fifty-third session in 2001.

The central proposition of Part I is that State responsibility is triggered by 'every internationally wrongful act of a State' (Article 1), which is defined as an act of State when conduct consisting of an action or omission is attributable to the State under international law and constitutes a breach of an international obligation (Article 2). The characterization of a wrongful act is governed by international law, regardless of the characterization of the same act as lawful by internal law (Article 3). Chapter II, Part One, outlines the rules governing the attribution of acts to a State (Articles 4–11), while Chapter III elaborates on breaches of international obligations (Articles 12–15). Chapter IV outlines the rules governing the responsibility of a State in connection with the act of another State (Articles 16–19). Chapter IV identifies several defences available to a State which preclude wrongfulness, including consent by another State (Article 20), self-defence (Article 21), countermeasures in respect of an internationally wrongful act (Article 22), *force majeure* (Article 23), distress (Article 24) and necessity (Article 25). No defence precludes the wrongfulness of any act of State not in conformity with peremptory norms of general international law (Article 26).

Part Two of the Articles outlines the content of the international responsibility of States. Chapter I outlines the general principles and specifies that the international responsibility of a State for internationally wrongfully acts involves legal consequences as set out in the Draft Articles (Article 28). The State responsible for a wrongful act has a continued duty to perform the obligation breached (Article 29). The State responsible for the internationally wrongful act must cease the act and offer guarantees of non-repetition (Article 30). The responsible State has an obligation to make reparation for the injury caused, including any damage, material or moral (Article 31). States may not rely on their national legislation to justify failure to comply with their obligations under Part Two (Article 32). The obligations of the responsible State may be owed to another State, to several States or to the international community as a whole, depending on the character and content of the international obligation and the circumstances of the breach (Article 33). Chapter II elaborates on the forms of reparation for the injury caused by the internationally wrongful act (Articles 34–39). Full reparation for the injury caused shall take the form of restitution, compensation and satisfaction, singly or in combination (Article 34). Chapter III specifies the rules applicable to serious breaches of obligations under peremptory norms of general international law (Articles 40 and 41). A breach of such obligations is serious if it involves a gross or systematic failure by the responsible State to fulfil the obligations in question (Article 40(2)). States are required to co-operate to bring to an end by lawful means any serious breach of such obligations and no State shall recognize as lawful a situation created by the serious breach (Article 41).

Part Three of the Articles outlines the rules for the implementation of the international responsibility of a State. Chapter I spells out the rules on the invocation of the responsibility of a State (Articles 42–48). Article 42 provides for the invocation of the responsibility by an injured State, Article 46 by a plurality of injured States and Article 48 by a State other than an injured State. Chapter II specifies the object and limits of countermeasures (Articles 49–54). Countermeasures shall not affect the obligation to refrain from the threat or use of force, obligations for the protection of fundamental human rights, obligations of a humanitarian character prohibiting reprisals, or other obligations under peremptory norms of general international law (Article 50).

Part Four contains general provisions. Article 55 specifies that the Articles do not apply when wrongful acts are governed by special rules of international law. The Articles are without prejudice to any question of the responsibility under international law of an international organization (Article 57) and of individual responsibility under international law of any person acting on behalf of a State (Article 58). Finally, the Articles are without prejudice to the Charter of the United Nations (Article 59).

Websites: www.un.org/law/ilc/index.htm
           www.un.org/law/ilc/texts/State_responsibility/
              responsibilityfra.htm

ILC Articles on Responsibility of States for Internationally Wrongful Acts

Part One
The internationally wrongful act of a State

Chapter I
General principles

Article 1
Responsibility of a State for its internationally wrongful acts

Every internationally wrongful act of a State entails the international responsibility of that State.

Article 2
Elements of an internationally wrongful act of a State

There is an internationally wrongful act of a State when conduct consisting of an action or omission:

(a) Is attributable to the State under international law; and
(b) Constitutes a breach of an international obligation of the State.

Article 3
Characterization of an act of a State as internationally wrongful

The characterization of an act of a State as internationally wrongful is governed by international law. Such characterization is not affected by the characterization of the same act as lawful by internal law.

Chapter II
Attribution of conduct to a State

Article 4
Conduct of organs of a State

1. The conduct of any State organ shall be considered an act of that State under international law, whether the organ exercises legislative, executive, judicial or any other functions, whatever position it holds in the organization of the State, and whatever its character as an organ of the central government or of a territorial unit of the State.

2. An organ includes any person or entity which has that status in accordance with the internal law of the State.

Article 5
Conduct of persons or entities exercising elements of governmental authority

The conduct of a person or entity which is not an organ of the State under article 4 but which is empowered by the law of that State to exercise elements of the governmental authority shall be considered an act of the State under international law, provided the person or entity is acting in that capacity in the particular instance.

Article 6
Conduct of organs placed at the disposal of a State by another State

The conduct of an organ placed at the disposal of a State by another State shall be considered an act of the former State under international law if the organ is acting in the exercise of elements of the governmental authority of the State at whose disposal it is placed.

Article 7
Excess of authority or contravention of instructions

The conduct of an organ of a State or of a person or entity empowered to exercise elements of the governmental authority shall be considered an act of the State under international law if the organ, person or entity acts in that capacity, even if it exceeds its authority or contravenes instructions.

Article 8
Conduct directed or controlled by a State

The conduct of a person or group of persons shall be considered an act of a State under international law if the person or group of persons is in fact acting on the instructions of, or under the direction or control of, that State in carrying out the conduct.

Article 9
Conduct carried out in the absence or default of the official authorities

The conduct of a person or group of persons shall be considered an act of a State under international law if the person or group of persons is in fact exercising elements of the governmental authority in the absence or default of the official authorities and in circumstances such as to call for the exercise of those elements of authority.

Article 10
Conduct of an insurrectional or other movement

1. The conduct of an insurrectional movement which becomes the new government of a State shall be considered an act of that State under international law.

2. The conduct of a movement, insurrectional or other, which succeeds in establishing a new State in part of the territory of a pre-existing State or in a territory under its administration shall be considered an act of the new State under international law.

3. This article is without prejudice to the attribution to a State of any conduct, however related to that of the movement concerned, which is to be considered an act of that State by virtue of articles 4 to 9.

Article 11
Conduct acknowledged and adopted by a State as its own

Conduct which is not attributable to a State under the preceding articles shall nevertheless be considered an act of that State under international law if and to the extent that the State acknowledges and adopts the conduct in question as its own.

Chapter III
Breach of an international obligation

Article 12
Existence of a breach of an international obligation

There is a breach of an international obligation by a State when an act of that State is not in conformity with what is required of it by that obligation, regardless of its origin or character.

Article 13
International obligation in force for a State

An act of a State does not constitute a breach of an international obligation unless the State is bound by the obligation in question at the time the act occurs.

Article 14
Extension in time of the breach of an international obligation

1. The breach of an international obligation by an act of a State not having a continuing character occurs at the moment when the act is performed, even if its effects continue.

2. The breach of an international obligation by an act of a State having a continuing character extends over the entire period during which the act continues and remains not in conformity with the international obligation.

3. The breach of an international obligation requiring a State to prevent a given event occurs when the event occurs and extends over the entire period during which the event continues and remains not in conformity with that obligation.

Article 15
Breach consisting of a composite act

1. The breach of an international obligation by a State through a series of actions or omissions defined in aggregate as wrongful, occurs when the action or omission occurs which, taken with the other actions or omissions, is sufficient to constitute the wrongful act.

2. In such a case, the breach extends over the entire period starting with the first of the actions or omissions of the series and lasts for as long as these actions or omissions are repeated and remain not in conformity with the international obligation.

Chapter IV
Responsibility of a State in connection with the act of another State

Article 16
Aid or assistance in the commission of an internationally wrongful act

A State which aids or assists another State in the commission of an internationally wrongful act by the latter is internationally responsible for doing so if:

(a) That State does so with knowledge of the circumstances of the internationally wrongful act; and
(b) The act would be internationally wrongful if committed by that State.

Article 17
Direction and control exercised over the commission of an internationally wrongful act

A State which directs and controls another State in the commission of an internationally wrongful act by the latter is internationally responsible for that act if:

(a) That State does so with knowledge of the circumstances of the internationally wrongful act; and
(b) The act would be internationally wrongful if committed by that State.

Article 18
Coercion of another State

A State which coerces another State to commit an act is internationally responsible for that act if:

(a) The act would, but for the coercion, be an internationally wrongful act of the coerced State; and

(b) The coercing State does so with knowledge of the circumstances of the act.

Article 19
Effect of this chapter

This chapter is without prejudice to the international responsibility, under other provisions of these articles, of the State which commits the act in question, or of any other State.

Chapter V
Circumstances precluding wrongfulness

Article 20
Consent

Valid consent by a State to the commission of a given act by another State precludes the wrongfulness of that act in relation to the former State to the extent that the act remains within the limits of that consent.

Article 21
Self-defence

The wrongfulness of an act of a State is precluded if the act constitutes a lawful measure of self-defence taken in conformity with the Charter of the United Nations.

Article 22
Countermeasures in respect of an internationally wrongful act

The wrongfulness of an act of a State not in conformity with an international obligation towards another State is precluded if and to the extent that the act constitutes a countermeasure taken against the latter State in accordance with chapter II of Part Three.

Article 23
Force majeure

1. The wrongfulness of an act of a State not in conformity with an international obligation of that State is precluded if the act is due to *force majeure*, that is the occurrence of an irresistible force or of an unforeseen event, beyond the

control of the State, making it materially impossible in the circumstances to
perform the obligation.

2. Paragraph 1 does not apply if:

(a) The situation of *force majeure* is due, either alone or in combination with
     other factors, to the conduct of the State invoking it; or
(b) The State has assumed the risk of that situation occurring.

Article 24
Distress

1. The wrongfulness of an act of a State not in conformity with an international obligation of that State is precluded if the author of the act in question
has no other reasonable way, in a situation of distress, of saving the author's
life or the lives of other persons entrusted to the author's care.

2. Paragraph 1 does not apply if:

(a) The situation of distress is due, either alone or in combination with other
     factors, to the conduct of the State invoking it; or
(b) The act in question is likely to create a comparable or greater peril.

Article 25
Necessity

1. Necessity may not be invoked by a State as a ground for precluding the
wrongfulness of an act not in conformity with an international obligation of
that State unless the act:

(a) Is the only way for the State to safeguard an essential interest against a grave
     and imminent peril; and
(b) Does not seriously impair an essential interest of the State or States towards
     which the obligation exists, or of the international community as a whole.

2. In any case, necessity may not be invoked by a State as a ground for
precluding wrongfulness if:

(a) The international obligation in question excludes the possibility of invoking
     necessity; or
(b) The State has contributed to the situation of necessity.

Article 26
Compliance with peremptory norms

Nothing in this chapter precludes the wrongfulness of any act of a State which
is not in conformity with an obligation arising under a peremptory norm of
general international law.

Article 27
Consequences of invoking a circumstance precluding wrongfulness

The invocation of a circumstance precluding wrongfulness in accordance with this chapter is without prejudice to:

(a) Compliance with the obligation in question, if and to the extent that the circumstance precluding wrongfulness no longer exists;
(b) The question of compensation for any material loss caused by the act in question.

Part Two
Content of the international responsibility of a State

Chapter I
General principles

Article 28
Legal consequences of an internationally wrongful act

The international responsibility of a State which is entailed by an internationally wrongful act in accordance with the provisions of Part One involves legal consequences as set out in this Part.

Article 29
Continued duty of performance

The legal consequences of an internationally wrongful act under this Part do not affect the continued duty of the responsible State to perform the obligation breached.

Article 30
Cessation and non-repetition

The State responsible for the internationally wrongful act is under an obligation:

(a) To cease that act, if it is continuing;
(b) To offer appropriate assurances and guarantees of non-repetition, if circumstances so require.

Article 31
Reparation

1. The responsible State is under an obligation to make full reparation for the injury caused by the internationally wrongful act.

2. Injury includes any damage, whether material or moral, caused by the internationally wrongful act of a State.

Article 32
Irrelevance of internal law

The responsible State may not rely on the provisions of its internal law as justification for failure to comply with its obligations under this Part.

Article 33
Scope of international obligations set out in this Part

1. The obligations of the responsible State set out in this Part may be owed to another State, to several States, or to the international community as a whole, depending in particular on the character and content of the international obligation and on the circumstances of the breach.

2. This Part is without prejudice to any right, arising from the international responsibility of a State, which may accrue directly to any person or entity other than a State.

Chapter II
Reparation for injury

Article 34
Forms of reparation

Full reparation for the injury caused by the internationally wrongful act shall take the form of restitution, compensation and satisfaction, either singly or in combination, in accordance with the provisions of this chapter.

Article 35
Restitution

A State responsible for an internationally wrongful act is under an obligation to make restitution, that is, to re-establish the situation which existed before the wrongful act was committed, provided and to the extent that restitution:

(a) Is not materially impossible;
(b) Does not involve a burden out of all proportion to the benefit deriving from restitution instead of compensation.

Article 36
Compensation

1. The State responsible for an internationally wrongful act is under an obligation to compensate for the damage caused thereby, insofar as such damage is not made good by restitution.

2. The compensation shall cover any financially assessable damage including loss of profits insofar as it is established.

Article 37
Satisfaction

1. The State responsible for an internationally wrongful act is under an obligation to give satisfaction for the injury caused by that act insofar as it cannot be made good by restitution or compensation.

2. Satisfaction may consist in an acknowledgement of the breach, an expression of regret, a formal apology or another appropriate modality.

3. Satisfaction shall not be out of proportion to the injury and may not take a form humiliating to the responsible State.

Article 38
Interest

1. Interest on any principal sum due under this chapter shall be payable when necessary in order to ensure full reparation. The interest rate and mode of calculation shall be set so as to achieve that result.

2. Interest runs from the date when the principal sum should have been paid until the date the obligation to pay is fulfilled.

Article 39
Contribution to the injury

In the determination of reparation, account shall be taken of the contribution to the injury by wilful or negligent action or omission of the injured State or any person or entity in relation to whom reparation is sought.

Chapter III
Serious breaches of obligations under peremptory norms of general international law

Article 40
Application of this chapter

1. This chapter applies to the international responsibility which is entailed by a serious breach by a State of an obligation arising under a peremptory norm of general international law.

2. A breach of such an obligation is serious if it involves a gross or systematic failure by the responsible State to fulfil the obligation.

Article 41
Particular consequences of a serious breach of an obligation under this chapter

1. States shall cooperate to bring to an end through lawful means any serious breach within the meaning of article 40.

2. No State shall recognize as lawful a situation created by a serious breach within the meaning of article 40, nor render aid or assistance in maintaining that situation.

3. This article is without prejudice to the other consequences referred to in this Part and to such further consequences that a breach to which this chapter applies may entail under international law.

Part Three
The implementation of the international responsibility of a State

Chapter I
Invocation of the responsibility of a State

Article 42
Invocation of responsibility by an injured State

A State is entitled as an injured State to invoke the responsibility of another State if the obligation breached is owed to:

(a) That State individually; or
(b) A group of States including that State, or the international community as a whole, and the breach of the obligation:
  (i) Specially affects that State; or
  (ii) Is of such a character as radically to change the position of all the other States to which the obligation is owed with respect to the further performance of the obligation.

Article 43
Notice of claim by an injured State

1. An injured State which invokes the responsibility of another State shall give notice of its claim to that State.

2. The injured State may specify in particular:

(a) The conduct that the responsible State should take in order to cease the wrongful act, if it is continuing;
(b) What form reparation should take in accordance with the provisions of Part Two.

Article 44
Admissibility of claims

The responsibility of a State may not be invoked if:

(a) The claim is not brought in accordance with any applicable rule relating to the nationality of claims;
(b) The claim is one to which the rule of exhaustion of local remedies applies and any available and effective local remedy has not been exhausted.

Article 45
Loss of the right to invoke responsibility

The responsibility of a State may not be invoked if:

(a) The injured State has validly waived the claim;
(b) The injured State is to be considered as having, by reason of its conduct, validly acquiesced in the lapse of the claim.

Article 46
Plurality of injured States

Where several States are injured by the same internationally wrongful act, each injured State may separately invoke the responsibility of the State which has committed the internationally wrongful act.

Article 47
Plurality of responsible States

1. Where several States are responsible for the same internationally wrongful act, the responsibility of each State may be invoked in relation to that act.

2. Paragraph 1:

(a) Does not permit any injured State to recover, by way of compensation, more than the damage it has suffered;
(b) Is without prejudice to any right of recourse against the other responsible States.

Article 48
Invocation of responsibility by a State other than an injured State

1. Any State other than an injured State is entitled to invoke the responsibility of another State in accordance with paragraph 2 if:

(a) The obligation breached is owed to a group of States including that State, and is established for the protection of a collective interest of the group; or
(b) The obligation breached is owed to the international community as a whole.

2. Any State entitled to invoke responsibility under paragraph 1 may claim from the responsible State:

(a) Cessation of the internationally wrongful act, and assurances and guarantees of non-repetition in accordance with article 30; and
(b) Performance of the obligation of reparation in accordance with the preceding articles, in the interest of the injured State or of the beneficiaries of the obligation breached.

3. The requirements for the invocation of responsibility by an injured State under articles 43, 44 and 45 apply to an invocation of responsibility by a State entitled to do so under paragraph 1.

Chapter II
Countermeasures

Article 49
Object and limits of countermeasures

1. An injured State may only take countermeasures against a State which is responsible for an internationally wrongful act in order to induce that State to comply with its obligations under Part Two.

2. Countermeasures are limited to the non-performance for the time being of international obligations of the State taking the measures towards the responsible State.

3. Countermeasures shall, as far as possible, be taken in such a way as to permit the resumption of performance of the obligations in question.

Article 50
Obligations not affected by countermeasures

1. Countermeasures shall not affect:

(a) The obligation to refrain from the threat or use of force as embodied in the Charter of the United Nations;
(b) Obligations for the protection of fundamental human rights;
(c) Obligations of a humanitarian character prohibiting reprisals;
(d) Other obligations under peremptory norms of general international law.

2. A State taking countermeasures is not relieved from fulfilling its obligations:

(a) Under any dispute settlement procedure applicable between it and the responsible State;
(b) To respect the inviolability of diplomatic or consular agents, premises, archives and documents.

Article 51
Proportionality

Countermeasures must be commensurate with the injury suffered, taking into account the gravity of the internationally wrongful act and the rights in question.

Article 52
Conditions relating to resort to countermeasures

1. Before taking countermeasures, an injured State shall:

(a) Call on the responsible State, in accordance with article 43, to fulfil its obligations under Part Two;
(b) Notify the responsible State of any decision to take countermeasures and offer to negotiate with that State.

2. Notwithstanding paragraph 1 (b), the injured State may take such urgent countermeasures as are necessary to preserve its rights.

3. Countermeasures may not be taken, and if already taken must be suspended without undue delay if:

(a) The internationally wrongful act has ceased; and
(b) The dispute is pending before a court or tribunal which has the authority to make decisions binding on the parties.

4. Paragraph 3 does not apply if the responsible State fails to implement the dispute settlement procedures in good faith.

Article 53
Termination of countermeasures

Countermeasures shall be terminated as soon as the responsible State has complied with its obligations under Part Two in relation to the internationally wrongful act.

Article 54
Measures taken by States other than an injured State

This chapter does not prejudice the right of any State, entitled under article 48, paragraph 1 to invoke the responsibility of another State, to take lawful measures against that State to ensure cessation of the breach and reparation in the interest of the injured State or of the beneficiaries of the obligation breached.

Part Four
General provisions

Article 55
Lex specialis

These articles do not apply where and to the extent that the conditions for the existence of an internationally wrongful act or the content or implementation of the international responsibility of a State are governed by special rules of international law.

Article 56
Questions of State responsibility not regulated by these articles

The applicable rules of international law continue to govern questions concerning the responsibility of a State for an internationally wrongful act to the extent that they are not regulated by these articles.

Article 57
Responsibility of an international organization

These articles are without prejudice to any question of the responsibility under international law of an international organization, or of any State for the conduct of an international organization.

Article 58
Individual responsibility

These articles are without prejudice to any question of the individual responsibility under international law of any person acting on behalf of a State.

Article 59
Charter of the United Nations

These articles are without prejudice to the Charter of the United Nations.

Convention on Civil Liability for Damage Resulting from Activities Dangerous to the Environment, 21 June 1993

Editorial note

The Convention on Civil Liability for Damage Resulting from Activities Dangerous to the Environment, negotiated under the auspices of the Council of Europe, has as its object the assurance of 'adequate' compensation as well as prevention and reinstatement (Article 1). The Convention applies to all incidents causing damage or grave or imminent threat of damage (defined extensively so as to include injury to life, property and the environment (Article 2(7)) within the territory or jurisdiction of a Party (Article 3)). The Convention does not apply to damage arising from carriage, from nuclear substances regulated by the Paris or Vienna Convention or at least as favourable internal law (Article 4(1) and 4(2)). It also does not apply to the extent that the Convention is inconsistent with worker's compensation or social security laws (Article 4(3)).

The Convention's central provision deems an operator of an installation strictly liable for damage caused by engaging in a dangerous activity (Article 4(1)). If an incident is a continuous or series of occurrences having the same origin, or damage is the result of incidents occurring in several installations or sites where dangerous activities are conducted, all operators controlling the dangerous activity during any of the occurrences are jointly and severally liable except to the extent that an operator can show that it caused only a part of the damage (Articles 4(2), 4(3) and 11). In addition, operators of waste deposits are strictly liable where that waste causes damage (Article 7(1)). The Convention expressly does not preclude an operator's recourse against third parties (Articles 6(5) and 7(4)). In determining the causal link between an incident and damage, courts are required to take account of the inherent danger in the activity that such damage will occur (Article 10). The Convention creates several exemptions to liability, the onus of proof being on the operator, if the damage was caused by: armed conflict or extraordinary natural phenomena; the intentional act of a third party; compliance with measure taken by a public authority; pollution 'at tolerable levels under local relevant circumstances'; or activity 'taken lawfully in the interests of the person suffering the damage' where it was 'reasonable' to expose him or her to that risk (Article 8). If the damage was caused due to the fault of the person suffering, compensation owing may be reduced or disallowed (Article 9). Parties are required to ensure, where appropriate, that operators either participate in a financial security scheme or have a financial guarantee to cover their liability under the Convention (Article 12). The Convention establishes a limitation period for bringing actions for compensation of three years from when the claimant knew or ought reasonably to have known about the damage and the identity of the operator, with an absolute limitation period of thirty years from the date of the incident (Article 17).

Subject to instances of confidentiality, public security, or relating to matters under investigation or *sub judice*, the Convention provides that individuals are to be entitled to access to information relating to the environment held by public authorities or bodies with public responsibilities for the environment (Articles 14 and 15). Individuals and operators may, at the discretion of the court, be provided with information to establish claims for compensation under the Convention (Article 16).

The Convention permits environmental organisations to request at any time, subject to internal law, for the prohibition of dangerous activities or an order requiring that the operator take measures to prevent an incident or damage, take measures to prevent damage after an incident, or take measures of reinstatement (Article 18). Actions for compensation may only be brought within a Party where the damage was suffered, the dangerous activity was conducted or where the defendant habitually resides (Article 19(1)). Requests by environmental organisations referred to above may only occur, where prohibition is sought, in the place the dangerous activity occurs, while in all other cases where the dangerous activity occurs or where the measures are to be taken (Article 19). The Convention requires judgments to be recognised and enforced in any Party, except where, *inter alia*, it is contrary to the public policy in that Party or the decision is irreconcilable with an earlier decision in a dispute between the same Parties either in that Party or in other States (Article 23). The rules for the jurisdiction, recognition and enforcement of judgments are superseded by any treaty to which two or more Parties are bound (Article 24).

A Standing Committee is established (Article 26) to keep under review problems relating to the Convention (Article 27). The Convention provides a detailed procedure for its amendment, including allowing tacit amendments to Annex I on the initiative of the EEC (Articles 29–31). Reservations are permitted in respect of the following: to limit, on the basis of reciprocity, the scope of the Convention to apply to damage suffered in the territory of non-Parties; to provide in internal law an exemption from liability in certain circumstances where the operator can prove that the state of scientific knowledge at the time of incident was such that it did not enable the dangerous properties of the substance or the risk involved in the operation to be discovered; or not to entitle environmental organisations to make the requests provided for above

(Article 35). The Convention will enter into force following the expression of consent to be bound by it by three States two of which must be members of the Council of Europe (Article 32).

Date of signature   21 June 1993

Entry into force: Not yet in force.

Depositary: Secretary-General of the Council of Europe

Contracting Parties: No ratifications yet.

Websites: www.coe.int
                         http://conventions.coe.int/Treaty/EN/
                         CadreListeTraites.htm

Convention on Civil Liability for Damage Resulting from Activities Dangerous to the Environment

The member States of the Council of Europe, the other States and the European Economic Community signatory hereto,

Considering that the aim of the Council of Europe is to achieve a greater unity between its members;

Noting that one of the objectives of the Council of Europe is to contribute to the quality of life of human beings, in particular by promoting a natural, healthy and agreeable environment;

Considering the wish of the Council of Europe to co-operate with other States in the field of nature conservation and protection of the environment;

Realising that man, the environment and property are exposed to specific dangers caused by certain activities;

Considering that emissions released in one country may cause damage in another country and that, therefore, the problems of adequate compensation for such damage are also of an international nature;

Having regard to the desirability of providing for strict liability in this field taking into account the 'Polluter Pays' Principle;

Mindful of the work which has already been carried out at an international level, in particular to prevent damage and to deal with damage caused by nuclear substances and the carriage of dangerous goods;

Having noted Principle 13 of the 1992 Rio Declaration on Environment and Development, according to which 'States shall develop national law regarding liability and compensation for the victims of pollution and other environmental damage; they shall also co-operate in an expeditious and more determined manner to develop further international law regarding liability and compensation for adverse effects of environmental damage caused by activities within their jurisdiction or control to areas beyond their jurisdiction';

Recognising the need to adopt further measures to deal with grave and imminent threats of damage from dangerous activities and to facilitate the burden of proof for persons requesting compensation for such damage,

Have agreed as follows:

Chapter I
General provisions

Article 1
Object and purpose

This Convention aims at ensuring adequate compensation for damage resulting from activities dangerous to the environment and also provides for means of prevention and reinstatement.

Article 2
Definitions

For the purpose of this Convention:

1. 'Dangerous activity' means one or more of the following activities provided that it is performed professionally, including activities conducted by public authorities:
   a. the production, handling, storage, use or discharge of one or more dangerous substances or any operation of a similar nature dealing with such substances;
   b. the production, culturing, handling, storage, use, destruction, disposal, release or any other operation dealing with one or more:
      • genetically modified organisms which as a result of the properties of the organism, the genetic modification and the conditions under which the operation is exercised, pose a significant risk for man, the environment or property;
      • micro-organisms which as a result of their properties and the conditions under which the operation is exercised pose a significant risk for man, the environment or property, such as those micro-organisms which are pathogenic or which produce toxins;
   c. the operation of an installation or site for the incineration, treatment, handling or recycling of waste, such as those installations or sites specified in Annex II, provided that the quantities involved pose a significant risk for man, the environment or property;
   d. the operation of a site for the permanent deposit of waste.
2. 'Dangerous substance' means:

    a. substances or preparations which have properties which constitute a significant risk for man, the environment or property. A substance or preparation which is explosive, oxidizing, extremely flammable, highly flammable, flammable, very toxic, toxic, harmful, corrosive, irritant, sensitizing, carcinogenic, mutagenic, toxic for reproduction or dangerous for the environment within the meaning of Annex I, Part A to this Convention shall in any event be deemed to constitute such a risk;

    b. substances specified in Annex I, Part B to this Convention. Without prejudice to the application of sub-paragraph a above, Annex I, Part B may restrict the specification of dangerous substances to certain quantities or concentrations, certain risks or certain situations.

3. 'Genetically modified organism' means any organism in which the genetic material has been altered in a way which does not occur naturally by mating and/or natural recombination.

However, the following genetically modified organisms are not covered by the Convention:

- organisms obtained by mutagenesis on condition that the genetic modification does not involve the use of genetically modified organisms as recipient organisms; and
- plants obtained by cell fusion (including protoplast fusion) if the resulting plant can also be produced by traditional breeding methods and on condition that the genetic modification does not involve the use of genetically modified organisms as parental organisms.

'Organism' refers to any biological entity capable of replication or of transferring genetic material.

4. 'Micro-organism' means any microbiological entity, cellular or non-cellular, capable of replication or of transferring genetic material.

5. 'Operator' means the person who exercises the control of a dangerous activity.

6. 'Person' means any individual or partnership or any body governed by public or private law, whether corporate or not, including a State or any of its constituent subdivisions.

7. 'Damage' means:

    (a) loss of life or personal injury;

    (b) loss of or damage to property other than to the installation itself or property held under the control of the operator, at the site of the dangerous activity;

    (c) loss or damage by impairment of the environment in so far as this is not considered to be damage within the meaning of sub-paragraphs a or b above provided that compensation for impairment of the environment, other than for loss of profit from such impairment, shall be limited to the costs of measures of reinstatement actually undertaken or to be undertaken;

(d) the costs of preventive measures and any loss or damage caused by preventive measures,

to the extent that the loss or damage referred to in sub-paragraphs a to c of this paragraph arises out of or results from the hazardous properties of the dangerous substances, genetically modified organisms or micro-organisms or arises or results from waste.

8. 'Measures of reinstatement' means any reasonable measures aiming to re-instate or restore damaged or destroyed components of the environment, or to introduce, where reasonable, the equivalent of these components into the environment. Internal law may indicate who will be entitled to take such measures.

9. 'Preventive measures' means any reasonable measures taken by any person, after an incident has occurred to prevent or minimise loss or damage as referred to in paragraph 7, sub-paragraphs a to c of this article.

10. 'Environment' includes:
    • natural resources both abiotic and biotic, such as air, water, soil, fauna and flora and the interaction between the same factors;
    • property which forms part of the cultural heritage; and
    • the characteristic aspects of the landscape.

11. 'Incident' means any sudden occurrence or continuous occurrence or any series of occurrences having the same origin, which causes damage or creates a grave and imminent threat of causing damage.

Article 3
Geographical scope

Without prejudice to the provisions of Chapter III, this Convention shall apply:

a. when the incident occurs in the territory of a Party, as determined in accordance with Article 34, regardless of where the damage is suffered;

b. when the incident occurs outside the territory referred to in sub-paragraph a above and the conflict of laws rules lead to the application of the law in force for the territory referred to in sub-paragraph a above.

Article 4
Exceptions

1. This Convention shall not apply to damage arising from carriage; carriage includes the period from the beginning of the process of loading until the end of the process of unloading. However, the Convention shall apply to carriage by pipeline, as well as to carriage performed entirely in an installation or on a site unaccessible to the public where it is accessory to other activities and is an integral part thereof.

2. This Convention shall not apply to damage caused by a nuclear substance:

a. arising from a nuclear incident the liability of which is regulated either by the Paris Convention of 29 July 1960 on third party liability in the field of nuclear energy, and its Additional Protocol of 28 January 1964, or the Vienna Convention of 21 May 1963 on civil liability for nuclear damage; or

b. if liability for such damage is regulated by a specific internal law, provided that such law is as favourable, with regard to compensation for damage, as any of the instruments referred to under sub-paragraph a above.

3. This Convention shall not apply to the extent that it is incompatible with the rules of the applicable law relating to workmen's compensation or social security schemes.

Chapter II
Liability

Article 5
Transitional provisions

1. The provisions of this chapter shall apply to incidents occurring after the entry into force of the Convention in respect of a Party. When the incident consists of a continuous occurrence or a series of occurrences having the same origin and part of these occurrences took place before the entry into force of this Convention, this chapter shall only apply to damage caused by occurrences or part of a continuous occurrence taking place after the entry into force.

2. In respect of damage caused by waste deposited at a site for the permanent deposit of waste the provisions of this chapter shall apply to damage which becomes known after the entry into force of the Convention in respect of the Party on the territory of which the site is situated. However this chapter shall not apply if:

a. the site was closed in accordance with the provisions of internal law before the entry into force of the Convention;

b. the operator proves, in the case where the operation of the site continues after that entry into force of the Convention, that the damage was caused solely by waste deposited there before that entry into force.

Article 6
Liability in respect of substances, organisms and certain waste installations or sites

1. The operator in respect of a dangerous activity mentioned under Article 2, paragraph 1, sub-paragraphs a to c shall be liable for the damage caused by the activity as a result of incidents at the time or during the period when he was exercising the control of that activity.

2. If an incident consists of a continuous occurrence, all operators successively exercising the control of the dangerous activity during that occurrence shall be jointly and severally liable. However, the operator who proves that the occurrence during the period when he was exercising the control of the dangerous activity caused only a part of the damage shall be liable for that part of the damage only.

3. If an incident consists of a series of occurrences having the same origin, the operators at the time of any such occurrence shall be jointly and severally liable. However, the operator who proves that the occurrence at the time when he was exercising the control of the dangerous activity caused only a part of the damage shall be liable for that part of the damage only.

4. If the damage resulting from a dangerous activity becomes known after all such dangerous activity in the installation or on the site has ceased, the last operator of this activity shall be liable for that damage unless he or the person who suffered damage proves that all or part of the damage resulted from an incident which occurred at a time before he became the operator. If it is so proved, the provisions of paragraphs 1 to 3 of this article shall apply.

5. Nothing in this Convention shall prejudice any right of recourse of the operator against any third party.

Article 7
Liability in respect of sites for the permanent deposit of waste

1. The operator of a site for the permanent deposit of waste at the time when damage caused by waste deposited at that site becomes known, shall be liable for this damage. Should the damage caused by waste deposited before the closure of such a site become known after that closure, the last operator shall be liable.

2. Liability under this article shall apply to the exclusion of any liability of the operator under Article 6, irrespective of the nature of the waste.

3. Liability under this article shall apply to the exclusion of any liability of the operator under Article 6 if the same operator conducts another dangerous activity on the site for the permanent deposit of waste.

However, if this operator or the person who has suffered damage proves that only a part of the damage was caused by the activity concerning the permanent deposit of waste, this article shall only apply to that part of the damage.

4. Nothing in this Convention shall prejudice any right of recourse of the operator against any third party.

Article 8
Exemptions

The operator shall not be liable under this Convention for damage which he proves:

a. was caused by an act of war, hostilities, civil war, insurrection or a natural phenomenon of an exceptional, inevitable and irresistible character;
b. was caused by an act done with the intent to cause damage by a third party, despite safety measures appropriate to the type of dangerous activity in question;
c. resulted necessarily from compliance with a specific order or compulsory measure of a public authority;
d. was caused by pollution at tolerable levels under local relevant circumstances; or
e. was caused by a dangerous activity taken lawfully in the interests of the person who suffered the damage, whereby it was reasonable towards this person to expose him to the risks of the dangerous activity.

Article 9
Fault of the person who suffered the damage

If the person who suffered the damage or a person for whom he is responsible under internal law, has, by his own fault, contributed to the damage, the compensation may be reduced or disallowed having regard to all the circumstances.

Article 10
Causality

When considering evidence of the causal link between the incident and the damage or, in the context of a dangerous activity as defined in Article 2, paragraph 1, sub-paragraph d, between the activity and the damage, the court shall take due account of the increased danger of causing such damage inherent in the dangerous activity.

Article 11
Plurality of installations or sites

When damage results from incidents which have occurred in several installations or on several sites where dangerous activities are conducted or from dangerous activities under Article 2, paragraph 1, sub-paragraph d, the operators of the installations or sites concerned shall be jointly and severally liable for all such damage. However, the operator who proves that only part of the damage was caused by an incident in the installation or on the site where he conducts the dangerous activity or by a dangerous activity under Article 2, paragraph 1, sub-paragraph d, shall be liable for that part of the damage only.

Article 12
Compulsory financial security scheme

Each Party shall ensure that where appropriate, taking due account of the risks of the activity, operators conducting a dangerous activity on its territory be required to participate in a financial security scheme or to have and maintain a financial guarantee up to a certain limit, of such type and terms as specified by internal law, to cover the liability under this Convention.

Chapter III
Access to information

Article 13
Definition of public authorities

For the purpose of this chapter 'public authorities' means any public administration of a Party at national, regional or local level with responsibilities, and possessing information relating to the environment, with the exception of bodies acting in a judicial or legislative capacity.

Article 14
Access to information held by public authorities

1. Any person shall, at his request and without his having to prove an interest, have access to information relating to the environment held by public authorities. The Parties shall define the practical arrangements under which such information is effectively made available.

2. The right of access may be restricted under internal law where it affects:

- the confidentiality of the proceedings of public authorities, international relations and national defence;
- public security;
- matters which are or have been *sub judice*, or under enquiry (including disciplinary enquiries), or which are the subject of preliminary investigation proceedings;
- commercial and industrial confidentiality, including intellectual property;
- the confidentiality of personal data and/or files;
- material supplied by a third party without that party being under a legal obligation to do so; or
- material, the disclosure of which would make it more likely that the environment to which that material related would be damaged.

Information held by public authorities shall be supplied in part where it is possible to separate out information on items concerning the interests referred to above.

3. A request for information may be refused where it would involve the supply of unfinished documents or data or internal communications, or where the request is manifestly unreasonable or formulated in too general a manner.

4. A public authority shall respond to a person requesting information as soon as possible and at the latest within two months. The reasons for a refusal to provide the information requested must be given.

5. A person who considers that his request for information has been unreasonably refused or ignored, or has been inadequately answered by a public authority, may seek a judicial or administrative review of the decision, in accordance with the relevant internal legal system.

6. The Parties may make a charge for supplying the information, but such a charge may not exceed a reasonable cost.

Article 15
Access to information held by bodies with public responsibilities for the environment

On the same terms and conditions as those set out in Article 14 any person shall have access to information relating to the environment held by bodies with public responsibilities for the environment and under the control of a public authority. Access shall be given via the competent public administration or directly by the bodies themselves.

Article 16
Access to specific information held by operators

1. The person who suffered the damage may, at any time, request the court to order an operator to provide him with specific information, in so far as this is necessary to establish the existence of a claim for compensation under this Convention.

2. Where, under this Convention, a claim for compensation is made to an operator, whether or not in the framework of judicial proceedings, this operator may request the court to order another operator to provide him with specific information, in so far as this is necessary to establish the extent of his possible obligation to compensate the person who has suffered the damage, or of his own right to compensation from the other operator.

3. The operator shall be required to provide information under paragraphs 1 and 2 of this article concerning the elements which are available to him and dealing essentially with the particulars of the equipment, the machinery used, the kind and concentration of the dangerous substances or waste as well as the nature of genetically modified organisms or micro-organisms.

4. These measures shall not affect measures of investigation which may legally be ordered under internal law.

5. The court may refuse a request which places a disproportionate burden on the operator, taking into account all the interests involved.

6. In addition to the restrictions under Article 14, paragraph 2 of this Convention, which shall apply *mutatis mutandis*, the operator may refuse to provide information where such information would incriminate him.

7. Any reasonable charge shall be paid by the person requesting the information. The operator may require an appropriate guarantee for such payment. However a court, when allowing a claim for compensation, may establish that

this charge shall be borne by the operator, except to the extent that the request resulted in unnecessary costs.

Chapter IV
Actions for compensation and other claims

Article 17
Limitation periods

1. Actions for compensation under this Convention shall be subject to a limitation period of three years from the date on which the claimant knew or ought reasonably to have known of the damage and of the identity of the operator. The laws of the Parties regulating suspension or interruption of limitation periods shall apply to the limitation period prescribed in this paragraph.

2. However, in no case shall actions be brought after thirty years from the date of the incident which caused the damage. Where the incident consists of a continuous occurrence the thirty years' period shall run from the end of that occurrence. Where the incident consists of a series of occurrences having the same origin the thirty years' period shall run from the date of the last of such occurrences. In respect of a site for the permanent deposit of waste the thirty years' period shall at the latest run from the date on which the site was closed in accordance with the provisions of internal law.

Article 18
Requests by organizations

1. Any association or foundation which according to its statutes aims at the protection of the environment and which complies with any further conditions of internal law of the Party where the request is submitted may, at any time, request:

a. the prohibition of a dangerous activity which is unlawful and poses a grave threat of damage to the environment;
b. that the operator be ordered to take measures to prevent an incident or damage;
c. that the operator be ordered to take measures, after an incident, to prevent damage; or
d. that the operator be ordered to take measures of reinstatement.

2. Internal law may stipulate cases where the request is inadmissible.

3. Internal law may specify the body, whether administrative or judicial, before which the request referred to in paragraph 1 above should be made. In all cases provision shall be made for a right of review.

4. Before deciding upon a request mentioned under paragraph 1 above the requested body may, in view of the general interests involved, hear the competent public authorities.

5. When the internal law of a Party requires that the association or foundation has its registered seat or the effective centre of its activities in its territory, the Party may declare at any time, by means of a notification addressed to the Secretary General of the Council of Europe, that, on the basis of reciprocity, an association or foundation having its seat or centre of activities in the territory of another Party and complying in that other Party with the other conditions mentioned in paragraph 1 above shall have the right to submit requests in accordance with paragraphs 1 to 3 above. The declaration will become effective on the first day of the month following the expiration of a period of three months after the date of its reception by the Secretary General.

Article 19
Jurisdiction

1. Actions for compensation under this Convention may only be brought within a Party at the court of the place:

a. where the damage was suffered;
b. where the dangerous activity was conducted; or
c. where the defendant has his habitual residence.

2. Requests for access to specific information held by operators under Article 16, paragraphs 1 and 2 may only be submitted within a Party at the court of the place:

a. where the dangerous activity is conducted; or
b. where the operator who may be required to provide the information has his habitual residence.

3. Requests by organisations under Article 18, paragraph 1, sub-paragraph a may only be submitted within a Party at the court or, if internal law so provides, at a competent administrative authority of the place where the dangerous activity is or will be conducted.

4. Requests by organisations under Article 18, paragraph 1, sub-paragraphs b, c and d may only be submitted within a Party at the court or, if internal law so provides, at a competent administrative authority:

a. of the place where the dangerous activity is or will be conducted; or
b. of the place where the measures are to be taken.

Article 20
Notification

The court shall stay the proceedings so long as it is not shown that the defendant has been able to receive the document instituting the proceedings or an equivalent document in sufficient time to enable him to arrange for his defence, or that all necessary steps have been taken to this end.

Article 21
Lis pendens

1. Where proceedings involving the same cause of action and between the same parties are brought in the courts of different Parties, any court other than the court first seised shall of its own motion stay its proceedings until such time as the jurisdiction of the court first seised is established.

2. Where the jurisdiction of the court first seised is established, any court other than the court first seised shall decline jurisdiction in favour of that court.

Article 22
Related actions

1. Where related actions are brought in the courts of different Parties, any court other than the court first seised may, while the actions are pending at first instance, stay its proceedings.

2. A court other than the court first seised may also, on the application of one of the parties, decline jurisdiction if the law of that court permits the consolidation of related actions and the court first seised has jurisdiction over both actions.

3. For the purposes of this article, actions are deemed to be related where they are so closely connected that it is expedient to hear and determine them together to avoid the risk of irreconcilable judgments resulting from separate proceedings.

Article 23
Recognition and enforcement

1. Any decision given by a court with jurisdiction in accordance with Article 19 above where it is no longer subject to ordinary forms of review, shall be recognised in any Party, unless:

a. such recognition is contrary to public policy in the Party in which recognition is sought;

b. it was given in default of appearance and the defendant was not duly served with the document which instituted the proceedings or with an equivalent document in sufficient time to enable him to arrange for his defence;

c. the decision is irreconcilable with a decision given in a dispute between the same parties in the Party in which recognition is sought; or

d. the decision is irreconcilable with an earlier decision given in another State involving the same cause of action and between the same parties, provided that this latter decision fulfils the conditions necessary for its recognition in the Party addressed.

2. A decision recognised under paragraph 1 above which is enforceable in the Party of origin shall be enforceable in each Party as soon as the formalities required by that Party have been completed. The formalities shall not permit the merits of the case to be re-opened.

Article 24
Other treaties relating to jurisdiction, recognition and enforcement

Whenever two or more Parties are bound by a treaty establishing rules of jurisdiction or providing for recognition and enforcement in a Party of decisions given in another Party, the provisions of that treaty shall replace the corresponding provisions of Articles 19 to 23.

Chapter V
Relation between this Convention and other provisions

Article 25
Relation between this Convention and other provisions

1. Nothing in this Convention shall be construed as limiting or derogating from any of the rights of the persons who have suffered the damage or as limiting the provisions concerning the protection or reinstatement of the environment which may be provided under the laws of any Party or under any other treaty to which it is a Party.

2. In their mutual relations, Parties which are members of the European Economic Community shall apply Community rules and shall therefore not apply the rules arising from this Convention except in so far as there is no Community rule governing the particular subject concerned.

Chapter VI
The Standing Committee

Article 26
The Standing Committee

1. For the purposes of this Convention, a Standing Committee is hereby set up.

2. Each Party may be represented on the Standing Committee by one or more delegates.

3. Each delegation shall have one vote. However, within the areas of its competence the European Economic Community shall exercise its right to vote

in the Standing Committee with a number of votes equal to the number of its member States which are Parties to this Convention. It shall not exercise its right to vote in cases where the member States exercise theirs and conversely. As long as no member State of the European Economic Community is a Party, the Community as a Party shall have one vote.

4. Any State referred to in Article 32 or invited to accede to the Convention in accordance with the provisions of Article 33 which is not a Party to this Convention may be represented on the Standing Committee by an observer. If the European Economic Community is not a Party it may be represented on the Standing Committee by an observer.

5. Unless, at least one month before the meeting, a Party has informed the Secretary General of its objection, the Standing Committee may invite the following to attend as observers at all its meetings or one or part of a meeting:

- any State not referred to in paragraph 4 above;
- any international or national, governmental or non-governmental body technically qualified in the fields covered by this Convention.

6. The Standing Committee may seek the advice of experts in order to discharge its functions.

7. The Standing Committee shall be convened by the Secretary General of the Council of Europe. It shall meet whenever one-third of the Parties or the Committee of Ministers of the Council of Europe so request.

8. One-third of the Parties shall constitute a quorum for holding a meeting of the Standing Committee.

9. Decisions may only be taken in the Standing Committee if at least one-half of the Parties are present.

10. Subject to Articles 27 and 29 to 31 the decisions of the Standing Committee shall be taken by a majority of the members present.

11. Subject to the provisions of this Convention the Standing Committee shall draw up its own rules of procedure.

Article 27
Functions of the Standing Committee

The Standing Committee shall keep under review problems relating to this Convention. It may, in particular:

a. consider any question of a general nature referred to it concerning interpretation or implementation of the Convention. The Standing Committee's conclusions concerning implementation of the Convention may take the form of a recommendation; recommendations shall be adopted by a three quarters majority of the votes cast;
b. propose any necessary amendments to the Convention including its annexes and examine those proposed in accordance with Articles 29 to 31.

Article 28
Reports of the Standing Committee

After each meeting, the Standing Committee shall forward to the Parties and the Committee of Ministers of the Council of Europe a report on its discussions and any decisions taken.

Chapter VII
Amendments to the Convention

Article 29
Amendments to the Articles

1. Any amendment to the articles of this Convention proposed by a Party or the Standing Committee shall be communicated to the Secretary General of the Council of Europe and forwarded by him at least two months before the meeting of the Standing Committee to the member States of the Council of Europe, to the European Economic Community, to any Signatory, to any Party, to any State invited to sign this Convention in accordance with the provisions of Article 32 and to any State invited to accede to it in accordance with the provisions of Article 33.

2. Any amendment proposed in accordance with the provisions of the preceding paragraph shall be examined by the Standing Committee which:

a. for amendments to Articles 1 to 25 shall submit the text adopted by a three-quarters majority of the votes cast to the Parties for acceptance;
b. for amendments to Articles 26 to 37 shall submit the text adopted by a three-quarters majority of the votes cast to the Committee of Ministers for approval. After its approval, this text shall be forwarded to the Parties for acceptance.

3. Any amendment to Articles 1 to 25 shall enter into force, in respect of those Parties which have accepted it, on the first day of the month following the expiration of a period of one month after the date on which three Parties, including at least two member States of the Council of Europe, have informed the Secretary General that they have accepted it. In respect of any Party which subsequently accepts it, the amendment shall enter into force on the first day of the month following the expiration of a period of one month after the date on which that Party has informed the Secretary General of its acceptance.

4. Any amendment to Articles 26 to 37 shall enter into force on the first day of the month following the expiration of a period of one month after the date on which all Parties have informed the Secretary General that they have accepted it.

Article 30
Amendments to the annexes

1. Any amendment to the annexes of this Convention proposed by a Party or the Standing Committee shall be communicated to the Secretary General of the Council of Europe and forwarded by him at least two months before the meeting of the Standing Committee to the member States of the Council of Europe, to the European Economic Community, to any Signatory, to any Party, to any State invited to sign this Convention in accordance with the provisions of Article 32 and to any State invited to accede to it in accordance with the provisions of Article 33.

2. Any amendment proposed in accordance with the provisions of the preceding paragraph or, where appropriate, of Article 31 shall be examined by the Standing Committee, which may adopt it by a three-quarters majority of the votes cast. The text adopted shall be forwarded to the Parties.

3. On the first day of the month following the expiration of a period of eighteen months after its adoption by the Standing Committee, unless more than one-third of the Parties have notified objections, any amendment shall enter into force for those Parties which have not notified objections.

Article 31
Tacit amendments to Annex I, Parts A and B

1. Whenever the European Economic Community adopts an amendment to one of the annexes to the directives referred to in Annex I, Parts A and B of this Convention, the Secretary General shall communicate it to all the Parties not later than four months after its publication in the Official Journal of the European Communities.

2. Within a time limit of six months after this communication, any Party may request that the amendment be submitted to the Standing Committee, in which case the procedure under Article 30, paragraphs 2 and 3, shall be followed. If no Party requests the submission of the amendment to the Standing Committee, the provisions of paragraph 3 below shall apply.

3. On the first day of the month following the expiration of a period of eighteen months after the communication of the amendment to all Parties, and unless more than one-third of the Parties have notified objections, the amendment shall enter into force for those Parties which have not notified objections.

However, the entry into force of the amendment shall be postponed to the date fixed for the member States of the European Economic Community for the compliance of their domestic law with the directive, if this date is later than that resulting from the time limit stated in the first part of this paragraph.

Chapter VIII
Final clauses

Article 32
Signature, ratification and entry into force

1. This Convention shall be open for signature by the member States of the Council of Europe, the non-member States which have participated in its elaboration and by the European Economic Community.

2. This Convention is subject to ratification, acceptance or approval. Instruments of ratification, acceptance or approval shall be deposited with the Secretary General of the Council of Europe.

3. This Convention shall enter into force on the first day of the month following the expiration of a period of three months after the date on which three States, including at least two member States of the Council of Europe, have expressed their consent to be bound by the Convention in accordance with the provisions of paragraph 2 of the present article.

4. In respect of any Signatory which subsequently expresses its consent to be bound by it, the Convention shall enter into force on the first day of the month following the expiration of a period of three months after the date of the deposit of its instrument of ratification, acceptance or approval.

Article 33
Non-member States

1. After the entry into force of this Convention, the Committee of Ministers of the Council of Europe may, on its own initiative or following a proposal from the Standing Committee and after consultation of the Parties, invite any non-member State of the Council of Europe to accede to this Convention by a decision taken by the majority provided for in Article 20, sub-paragraph d of the Statute of the Council of Europe, and by the unanimous vote of the representatives of the Contracting States entitled to sit on the Committee of Ministers.

2. In respect of any acceding State, the Convention shall enter into force on the first day of the month following the expiration of a period of three months after the date of deposit of the instrument of accession with the Secretary General of the Council of Europe.

Article 34
Territories

1. Any Signatory may, at the time of signature or when depositing its instrument of ratification, acceptance or approval, specify the territory or territories to which this Convention shall apply. Any other State may formulate the same declaration when depositing its instrument of accession.

2. Any Party may, at any later date, by a declaration addressed to the Secretary General of the Council of Europe, extend the application of this Convention to any other territory specified in the declaration and for whose international relations it is responsible or on whose behalf it is authorised to give undertakings. In respect of such territory the Convention shall enter into force on the first day of the month following the expiration of a period of three months after the date of receipt of such declaration by the Secretary General.

3. Any declaration made under the two preceding paragraphs may, in respect of any territory specified in such declaration, be withdrawn by a notification addressed to the Secretary General. The withdrawal shall become effective on the first day of the month following the expiration of a period of three months after the date of receipt of such notification by the Secretary General.

Article 35
Reservations

1. Any Signatory may declare, at the time of signature or when depositing its instrument of ratification, acceptance or approval, that it reserves the right:

a. to apply Article 3, sub-paragraph a, to damage suffered in the territory of the States which are not Parties to this Convention only on the basis of reciprocity;
b. to provide in its internal law that, without prejudice to Article 8, the operator shall not be liable if he proves that in the case of damage caused by a dangerous activity mentioned under Article 2, paragraph 1, sub-paragraphs a and b, the state of scientific and technical knowledge at the time of the incident was not such as to enable the existence of the dangerous properties of the substance or the significant risk involved in the operation dealing with the organism to be discovered;
c. not to apply Article 18.

Any other State may formulate the same reservations when depositing its instrument of accession.

2. Any Signatory or any other State which makes use of a reservation shall notify the Secretary General of the Council of Europe of the relevant contents of its internal law.

3. Any Party which extends the application of this Convention to a territory mentioned in the declaration referred to in Article 34, paragraph 2, may, in respect of the territory concerned, make a reservation in accordance with the provisions of the preceding paragraphs.

4. No reservation shall be made to the provisions of this Convention, except those mentioned in this article.

5. Any Party which has made one of the reservations mentioned in this article may withdraw it by means of a declaration addressed to the Secretary General of the Council of Europe. The withdrawal shall become effective on the first day of the month following the expiration of a period of one month after the date of its receipt by the Secretary General.

Article 36
Denunciation

1. Any Party may at any time denounce this Convention by means of a notification addressed to the Secretary General of the Council of Europe.

2. Such denunciation shall become effective on the first day of the month following the expiration of a period of three months after the date of receipt of notification by the Secretary General.

Article 37
Notifications

The Secretary General of the Council of Europe shall notify the member States of the Council, any Signatory, any Party and any other State which has been invited to accede to this Convention of:

a. any signature;
b. the deposit of any instrument of ratification, acceptance, approval or accession;
c. any date of entry into force of this Convention in accordance with Articles 32 or 33;
d. any amendment adopted in accordance with Articles 29, 30 or 31, and the date on which such an amendment enters into force;
e. any declaration made under the provisions of Articles 18 or 34;
f. any reservation and withdrawal of reservation made in pursuance of the provisions of Article 35;
g. any other act, notification or communication relating to this Convention.

IN WITNESS WHEREOF the undersigned, being duly authorised thereto, have signed this Convention.

DONE at Lugano, this 21st day of June 1993, in English and French, both texts being equally authentic, in a single copy which shall be deposited in the archives of the Council of Europe. The Secretary General of the Council of Europe shall transmit certified copies to each member State of the Council of Europe, to the non-member States which have participated in the elaboration of this Convention, to the European Economic Community and to any State invited to accede to this Convention.

Annex I
Dangerous substances

A. *Criteria and methods to be applied to catagories of dangerous substances* (Article 2, paragraph 2, sub-paragraph a)

The properties referred to in Article 2, paragraph 2, sub-paragraph a, shall be determined by the criteria and methods referred to in or annexed to:

- the Council Directive of the European Communities 67/548/EEC of 27 June 1967 (OJEC No. L196/1) on the approximation of the laws, regulations and administrative provisions relating to the classification, packaging and labelling of dangerous substances
- as amended, for the seventh time, in the Council Directive of the European Communities 92/32/EEC of 30 April 1992 (OJEC No. L154/1), and
- as adapted to technical progress, for the sixteenth time, by Commission Directive of the European Communities 92/37/EEC of 30 April 1992 (OJEC No. L154/30),
- the Council Directive of the European Communities 88/379/EEC of 7 June 1988 (OJEC No. L187/14) on the approximation of the laws, regulations and administrative provisions of the member States relating to the classification, packaging and labelling of dangerous preparations as adapted to technical progress by the Directive of the Commission of the European Communities 90/492/EEC of 5 October 1990 (OJEC No. L275/35).

B. *List of dangerous substances* (Article 2, paragraph 2, sub-paragraph b)

The substances referred to in Article 2, paragraph 2, sub-paragraph b, shall be those listed in Annex I of the Council Directive of the European Communities 67/548/EEC of 27 June 1967 (OJEC No. L196/1), on the approximation of the laws regulations and administrative provisions relating to the classification, packaging and labelling of dangerous substances as adapted to technical progress, for the sixteenth time, by Commission Directive of the European Communities 92/37/EEC of 30 April 1992 (OJEC No. L154/30).

Annex II

Installations or sites for the incineration, treatment, handling or recycling of waste (See Article 2, paragraph 1, sub-paragraph c)

1. Installations or sites for the partial or complete disposal of solid, liquid or gaseous wastes by incineration on land or at sea.
2. Installations or sites for thermal degradation of solid, gaseous or liquid wastes under reduced oxygen supply.

3. Installations or sites for high temperature degradation or thermal degasification of solid, gaseous or liquid wastes.
4. Installations or sites for thermal recovery of compounds from solid or liquid wastes.
5. Installations or sites for chemical, physical or biological treatment of wastes for recycling or disposal.
6. Installations or sites for blending or mix prior to submission to the operation of a site for permanent deposit.
7. Installations or sites for repacking prior to submission to the operation of a site for permanent deposit.
8. Installations or sites for handling and treatment of solid, liquid or gaseous wastes for re-use or recycling such as:
   - solvent reclamation/regeneration;
   - recycling/reclamation of organic substances (not used as solvents) and inorganic materials;
   - regeneration of acid and bases;
   - recovery of components used for pollution abatement;
   - recovery of components from catalysts;
   - waste oil re-refining or other re-uses of waste oil;
   - recovery of components from discarded cars.
9. Installations or sites for storage of materials intended for submission to any operation in this annex or to the operation of a site for the permanent deposit of waste, temporary storage excluded, pending collection, on the site where it is produced.

International Convention on Liability and Compensation for Damage in Connection with the Carriage of Hazardous and Noxious Substances by Sea, 3 May 1996

Editorial note

The IMO's 1996 International Convention on Liability and Compensation for Damage in Connection with the Carriage of Hazardous Substances and Noxious Substances by Sea (1996 HNS Convention) aims at regulating liability and compensation to persons who suffer damage caused by incidents during the carriage by sea of hazardous and noxious substances. The Convention provides a two-tiered system of liability and compensation similar to the 1992 International Convention on Civil Liability for Oil Pollution Damage and the 1992 International Convention on the Establishment of an International Fund for Compensation for Oil Pollution Damage.

Damage is defined in Article 1(6) and includes 'loss or damage by contamination of the environment caused by the hazardous and noxious substances, provided that compensation for impairment of the environment other than loss of profit from such impairment shall be limited to costs of reasonable measures of reinstatement actually undertaken or to be undertaken' (Article 1(6)(c)).

The approach of the HNS Convention follows the 1992 CLC. Chapter II establishes a regime of strict liability for ship owners and a list of defences to liability, rules for joint and several liability for damage that is not reasonably separable by ship owner (Articles 7 and 8). Article 9(1) limits the ship owner's liability to specified amounts; Article 9(2), however, imposes no limit to liability if the ship owner intended to cause damage or acted recklessly with knowledge that damage would result. Ship owners are required to maintain a compulsory insurance or other financial security (Article 12). Chapter III establishes the HNS Fund which, like the 1992 Fund Convention for oil pollution, will compensate any person who suffers damage under Chapter II but is unable to obtain compensation because the ship owner is not liable, the ship owner is incapable of meeting all its financial obligations, or the damages exceed the ship owner's liability under Chapter II (Articles 13–24). The Convention also establishes an Assembly of its Contracting Parties (Article 25) and a Secretariat for the administration of the HNS Fund (Article 29). Actions for compensation can be brought within three years from the date when the person suffering damage knew or ought reasonably to have known of the damage and identity of the owner and in no case later than ten years from the dates of the incident which caused the damage (Article 37). Articles 38 and 39 respectively deal with the jurisdictional competence for such actions against the owner of the ship and against the HNS Fund or for action taken by the HNS Fund. Article 40 provides for the recognition and enforcement of judgments given by courts exercising jurisdiction under the provisions of the Convention. The Convention will enter into force in accordance with its Article 46.

Date of signature: 3 May 1996

Entry into force: Not yet in force.

Depositary: Secretary-General of the IMO

Contracting Parties: Angola, Russian Federation

Website: www.imo.org

International Convention on Liability and Compensation for Damage in Connection with the Carriage of Hazardous and Noxious Substances by Sea

Preamble

The States Parties to the present Convention,

Conscious of the dangers posed by the worldwide carriage by sea of hazardous and noxious substances,

Convinced of the need to ensure that adequate, prompt and effective compensation is available to persons who suffer damage caused by incidents in connection with the carriage by sea of such substances,

Desiring to adopt uniform international rules and procedures for determining questions of liability and compensation in respect of such damage,

Considering that the economic consequences of damage caused by the carriage by sea of hazardous and noxious substances should be shared by the shipping industry and the cargo interests involved,

Have agreed as follows:

Chapter I
General provisions

Definitions

Article 1

For the purposes of this Convention:

1. 'Ship' means any seagoing vessel and seaborne craft, of any type whatsoever.
2. 'Person' means any individual or partnership or any public or private body, whether corporate or not, including a State or any of its constituent subdivisions.
3. 'Owner' means the person or persons registered as the owner of the ship or, in the absence of registration, the person or persons owning the ship. However, in the case of a ship owned by a State and operated by a company which in that State is registered as the ship's operator, 'owner' shall mean such company.
4. 'Receiver' means either:
   (a) the person who physically receives contributing cargo discharged in the ports and terminals of a State Party; provided that if at the time of receipt the person who physically receives the cargo acts as an agent for another who is subject to the jurisdiction of any State Party, then the principal shall be deemed to be the receiver, if the agent discloses the principal to the HNS Fund; or
   (b) the person in the State Party who in accordance with the national law of that State Party is deemed to be the receiver of contributing cargo discharged in the ports and terminals of a State Party, provided that the total contributing cargo received according to such national law is substantially the same as that which would have been received under (a).
5. 'Hazardous and noxious substances' (HNS) means:
   (a) any substances, materials and articles carried on board a ship as cargo, referred to in (i) to (vii) below:
      (i) oils carried in bulk listed in appendix I of Annex I to the International Convention for the Prevention of Pollution from Ships, 1973, as modified by the Protocol of 1978 relating thereto, as amended;
      (ii) noxious liquid substances carried in bulk referred to in appendix II of Annex II to the International Convention for the Prevention of Pollution from Ships, 1973, as modified by the Protocol of 1978 relating thereto, as amended, and those substances and mixtures provisionally categorized as falling in pollution category A, B, C or D in accordance with regulation 3(4) of the said Annex II;
      (iii) dangerous liquid substances carried in bulk listed in chapter 17 of the International Code for the Construction and Equipment of Ships Carrying Dangerous Chemicals in Bulk, 1983, as amended,

and the dangerous products for which the preliminary suitable conditions for the carriage have been prescribed by the Administration and port administrations involved in accordance with paragraph 1.1.3 of the Code;

(iv) dangerous, hazardous and harmful substances, materials and articles in packaged form covered by the International Maritime Dangerous Goods Code, as amended;

(v) liquefied gases as listed in chapter 19 of the International Code for the Construction and Equipment of Ships Carrying Liquefied Gases in Bulk, 1983, as amended, and the products for which preliminary suitable conditions for the carriage have been prescribed by the Administration and port administrations involved in accordance with paragraph 1.1.6 of the Code;

(vi) liquid substances carried in bulk with a flashpoint not exceeding 60°C (measured by a closed cup test);

(vii) solid bulk materials possessing chemical hazards covered by appendix B of the Code of Safe Practice for Solid Bulk Cargoes, as amended, to the extent that these substances are also subject to the provisions of the International Maritime Dangerous Goods Code when carried in packaged form; and (b) residues from the previous carriage in bulk of substances referred to in (a)(i) to (iii) and (v) to (vii) above.

6. 'Damage' means:

(a) loss of life or personal injury on board or outside the ship carrying the hazardous and noxious substances caused by those substances;

(b) loss of or damage to property outside the ship carrying the hazardous and noxious substances caused by those substances;

(c) loss or damage by contamination of the environment caused by the hazardous and noxious substances, provided that compensation for impairment of the environment other than loss of profit from such impairment shall be limited to costs of reasonable measures of reinstatement actually undertaken or to be undertaken; and

(d) the costs of preventive measures and further loss or damage caused by preventive measures.

Where it is not reasonably possible to separate damage caused by the hazardous and noxious substances from that caused by other factors, all such damage shall be deemed to be caused by the hazardous and noxious substances except if, and to the extent that, the damage caused by other factors is damage of a type referred to in article 4, paragraph 3.

In this paragraph, 'caused by those substances' means caused by the hazardous or noxious nature of the substances.

7. 'Preventive measures' means any reasonable measures taken by any person after an incident has occurred to prevent or minimize damage.

8. 'Incident' means any occurrence or series of occurrences having the same origin, which causes damage or creates a grave and imminent threat of causing damage.

9. 'Carriage by sea' means the period from the time when the hazardous and noxious substances enter any part of the ship's equipment, on loading, to the time they cease to be present in any part of the ship's equipment, on discharge. If no ship's equipment is used, the period begins and ends respectively when the hazardous and noxious substances cross the ship's rail.

10. 'Contributing cargo' means any hazardous and noxious substances which are carried by sea as cargo to a port or terminal in the territory of a State Party and discharged in that State. Cargo in transit which is transferred directly, or through a port or terminal, from one ship to another, either wholly or in part, in the course of carriage from the port or terminal of original loading to the port or terminal of final destination shall be considered as contributing cargo only in respect of receipt at the final destination.

11. The 'HNS Fund' means the International Hazardous and Noxious Substances Fund established under article 13.

12. 'Unit of account' means the Special Drawing Right as defined by the International Monetary Fund.

13. 'State of the ship's registry' means in relation to a registered ship the State of registration of the ship, and in relation to an unregistered ship the State whose flag the ship is entitled to fly.

14. 'Terminal' means any site for the storage of hazardous and noxious substances received from waterborne transportation, including any facility situated offshore and linked by pipeline or otherwise to such site.

15. 'Director' means the Director of the HNS Fund.

16. 'Organization' means the International Maritime Organization.

17. 'Secretary-General' means the Secretary-General of the Organization.

Annexes

Article 2

The Annexes to this Convention shall constitute an integral part of this Convention.

Scope of application

Article 3

This Convention shall apply exclusively:

(a) to any damage caused in the territory, including the territorial sea, of a State Party;

(b) to damage by contamination of the environment caused in the exclusive economic zone of a State Party, established in accordance with international law, or, if a State Party has not established such a zone, in an area beyond and adjacent to the territorial sea of that State determined by that State in accordance with international law and extending not more than 200 nautical miles from the baselines from which the breadth of its territorial sea is measured;

(c) to damage, other than damage by contamination of the environment, caused outside the territory, including the territorial sea, of any State, if this damage has been caused by a substance carried on board a ship registered in a State Party or, in the case of an unregistered ship, on board a ship entitled to fly the flag of a State Party; and

(d) to preventive measures, wherever taken.

Article 4

1. This Convention shall apply to claims, other than claims arising out of any contract for the carriage of goods and passengers, for damage arising from the carriage of hazardous and noxious substances by sea.

2. This Convention shall not apply to the extent that its provisions are incompatible with those of the applicable law relating to workers' compensation or social security schemes.

3. This Convention shall not apply:

(a) to pollution damage as defined in the International Convention on Civil Liability for Oil Pollution Damage, 1969, as amended, whether or not compensation is payable in respect of it under that Convention; and

(b) to damage caused by a radioactive material of class 7 either in the International Maritime Dangerous Goods Code, as amended, or in appendix B of the Code of Safe Practice for Solid Bulk Cargoes, as amended.

4. Except as provided in paragraph 5, the provisions of this Convention shall not apply to warships, naval auxiliary or other ships owned or operated by a State and used, for the time being, only on Government non commercial service.

5. A State Party may decide to apply this Convention to its warships or other vessels described in paragraph 4, in which case it shall notify the Secretary-General thereof specifying the terms and conditions of such application.

6. With respect to ships owned by a State Party and used for commercial purposes, each State shall be subject to suit in the jurisdictions set forth in article 38 and shall waive all defences based on its status as a sovereign State.

Article 5

1. A State may, at the time of ratification, acceptance, approval of, or accession to, this Convention, or any time thereafter, declare that this Convention does not apply to ships:

(a) which do not exceed 200 gross tonnage; and
(b) which carry hazardous and noxious substances only in packaged form; and
(c) while they are engaged on voyages between ports or facilities of that State.

2. Where two neighbouring States agree that this Convention does not apply also to ships which are covered by paragraph 1(a) and (b) while engaged on voyages between ports or facilities of those States, the States concerned may declare that the exclusion from the application of this Convention declared under paragraph 1 covers also ships referred to in this paragraph.

3. Any State which has made the declaration under paragraph 1 or 2 may withdraw such declaration at any time.

4. A declaration made under paragraph 1 or 2, and the withdrawal of the declaration made under paragraph 3, shall be deposited with the Secretary-General who shall, after the entry into force of this Convention, communicate it to the Director.

5. Where a State has made a declaration under paragraph 1 or 2 and has not withdrawn it, hazardous and noxious substances carried on board ships covered by that paragraph shall not be considered to be contributing cargo for the purpose of application of articles 18, 20, article 21, paragraph 5 and article 43.

6. The HNS Fund is not liable to pay compensation for damage caused by substances carried by a ship to which the Convention does not apply pursuant to a declaration made under paragraph 1 or 2, to the extent that:

(a) the damage as defined in article 1, paragraph 6(a), (b) or (c) was caused in:
   (i) the territory, including the territorial sea, of the State which has made the declaration, or in the case of neighbouring States which have made a declaration under paragraph 2, of either of them; or
   (ii) the exclusive economic zone, or area mentioned in article 3(b), of the State or States referred to in (i);
(b) the damage includes measures taken to prevent or minimize such damage.

Duties of State Parties

Article 6

Each State Party shall ensure that any obligation arising under this Convention is fulfilled and shall take appropriate measures under its law including the imposing of sanctions as it may deem necessary, with a view to the effective execution of any such obligation.

Chapter II
Liability

Liability of the owner

Article 7

1. Except as provided in paragraphs 2 and 3, the owner at the time of an incident shall be liable for damage caused by any hazardous and noxious substances in connection with their carriage by sea on board the ship, provided that if an incident consists of a series of occurrences having the same origin the liability shall attach to the owner at the time of the first of such occurrences.

2. No liability shall attach to the owner if the owner proves that:

(a) the damage resulted from an act of war, hostilities, civil war, insurrection or a natural phenomenon of an exceptional, inevitable and irresistible character; or
(b) the damage was wholly caused by an act or omission done with the intent to cause damage by a third party; or
(c) the damage was wholly caused by the negligence or other wrongful act of any Government or other authority responsible for the maintenance of lights or other navigational aids in the exercise of that function; or
(d) the failure of the shipper or any other person to furnish information concerning the hazardous and noxious nature of the substances shipped either
  (i) has caused the damage, wholly or partly; or
  (ii) has led the owner not to obtain insurance in accordance with article 12;

provided that neither the owner nor its servants or agents knew or ought reasonably to have known of the hazardous and noxious nature of the substances shipped.

3. If the owner proves that the damage resulted wholly or partly either from an act or omission done with intent to cause damage by the person who suffered the damage or from the negligence of that person, the owner may be exonerated wholly or partially from liability to such person.

4. No claim for compensation for damage shall be made against the owner otherwise than in accordance with this Convention.

5. Subject to paragraph 6, no claim for compensation for damage under this Convention or otherwise may be made against:

(a) the servants or agents of the owner or the members of the crew;
(b) the pilot or any other person who, without being a member of the crew, performs services for the ship;

(c) any charterer (howsoever described, including a bareboat charterer), manager or operator of the ship;
(d) any person performing salvage operations with the consent of the owner
or on the instructions of a competent public authority;
(e) any person taking preventive measures; and
(f) the servants or agents of persons mentioned in (c), (d) and (e);

unless the damage resulted from their personal act or omission, committed
with the intent to cause such damage, or recklessly and with knowledge that
such damage would probably result.

6. Nothing in this Convention shall prejudice any existing right of recourse
of the owner against any third party, including, but not limited to, the shipper
or the receiver of the substance causing the damage, or the persons indicated
in paragraph 5.

Incidents involving two or more ships

Article 8

1. Whenever damage has resulted from an incident involving two or more
ships each of which is carrying hazardous and noxious substances, each owner,
unless exonerated under article 7, shall be liable for the damage.

The owners shall be jointly and severally liable for all such damage which is
not reasonably separable.

2. However, owners shall be entitled to the limits of liability applicable to
each of them under article 9.

3. Nothing in this article shall prejudice any right of recourse of an owner
against any other owner.

Limitation of liability

Article 9

1. The owner of a ship shall be entitled to limit liability under this Convention
in respect of any one incident to an aggregate amount calculated as follows:

(a) 10 million units of account for a ship not exceeding 2,000 units of tonnage;
and
(b) for a ship with a tonnage in excess thereof, the following amount in addition
to that mentioned in (a):
– for each unit of tonnage from 2,001 to 50,000 units of tonnage, 1,500
units of account
– for each unit of tonnage in excess of 50,000 units of tonnage, 360 units
of account
provided, however, that this aggregate amount shall not in any event exceed
100 million units of account.

2. The owner shall not be entitled to limit liability under this Convention if it is proved that the damage resulted from the personal act or omission of the owner, committed with the intent to cause such damage, or recklessly and with knowledge that such damage would probably result.

3. The owner shall, for the purpose of benefiting from the limitation provided for in paragraph 1, constitute a fund for the total sum representing the limit of liability established in accordance with paragraph 1 with the court or other competent authority of any one of the States Parties in which action is brought under article 38 or, if no action is brought, with any court or other competent authority in any one of the States Parties in which an action can be brought under article 38. The fund can be constituted either by depositing the sum or by producing a bank guarantee or other guarantee, acceptable under the law of the State Party where the fund is constituted, and considered to be adequate by the court or other competent authority.

4. Subject to the provisions of article 11, the fund shall be distributed among the claimants in proportion to the amounts of their established claims.

5. If before the fund is distributed the owner or any of the servants or agents of the owner or any person providing to the owner insurance or other financial security has as a result of the incident in question, paid compensation for damage, such person shall, up to the amount that person has paid, acquire by subrogation the rights which the person so compensated would have enjoyed under this Convention.

6. The right of subrogation provided for in paragraph 5 may also be exercised by a person other than those mentioned therein in respect of any amount of compensation for damage which such person may have paid but only to the extent that such subrogation is permitted under the applicable national law.

7. Where owners or other persons establish that they may be compelled to pay at a later date in whole or in part any such amount of compensation, with regard to which the right of subrogation would have been enjoyed under paragraphs 5 or 6 had the compensation been paid before the fund was distributed, the court or other competent authority of the State where the fund has been constituted may order that a sufficient sum shall be provisionally set aside to enable such person at such later date to enforce the claim against the fund.

8. Claims in respect of expenses reasonably incurred or sacrifices reasonably made by the owner voluntarily to prevent or minimize damage shall rank equally with other claims against the fund.

9.

(a) The amounts mentioned in paragraph 1 shall be converted into national currency on the basis of the value of that currency by reference to the Special Drawing Right on the date of the constitution of the fund referred to in paragraph 3. The value of the national currency, in terms of the Special Drawing Right, of a State Party which is a member of the International

Monetary Fund, shall be calculated in accordance with the method of valuation applied by the International Monetary Fund in effect on the date in question for its operations and transactions. The value of the national currency, in terms of the Special Drawing Right, of a State Party which is not a member of the International Monetary Fund, shall be calculated in a manner determined by that State.

(b) Nevertheless, a State Party which is not a member of the International Monetary Fund and whose law does not permit the application of the provisions of paragraph 9(a) may, at the time of ratification, acceptance, approval of or accession to this Convention or at any time thereafter, declare that the unit of account referred to in paragraph 9(a) shall be equal to 15 gold francs. The gold franc referred to in this paragraph corresponds to sixty-five-and-a-half milligrammes of gold of millesimal fineness nine hundred. The conversion of the gold franc into the national currency shall be made according to the law of the State concerned.

(c) The calculation mentioned in the last sentence of paragraph 9(a) and the conversion mentioned in paragraph 9(b) shall be made in such manner as to express in the national currency of the State Party as far as possible the same real value for the amounts in paragraph 1 as would result from the application of the first two sentences of paragraph 9(a). States Parties shall communicate to the Secretary-General the manner of calculation pursuant to paragraph 9(a), or the result of the conversion in paragraph 9(b) as the case may be, when depositing an instrument of ratification, acceptance, approval of or accession to this Convention and whenever there is a change in either.

10. For the purpose of this article the ship's tonnage shall be the gross tonnage calculated in accordance with the tonnage measurement regulations contained in Annex I of the International Convention on Tonnage Measurement of Ships, 1969.

11. The insurer or other person providing financial security shall be entitled to constitute a fund in accordance with this article on the same conditions and having the same effect as if it were constituted by the owner. Such a fund may be constituted even if, under the provisions of paragraph 2, the owner is not entitled to limitation of liability, but its constitution shall in that case not prejudice the rights of any claimant against the owner.

Article 10

1. Where the owner, after an incident, has constituted a fund in accordance with article 9 and is entitled to limit liability:

(a) no person having a claim for damage arising out of that incident shall be entitled to exercise any right against any other assets of the owner in respect of such claim; and

(b) the court or other competent authority of any State Party shall order the release of any ship or other property belonging to the owner which has been arrested in respect of a claim for damage arising out of that incident, and shall similarly release any bail or other security furnished to avoid such arrest.

2. The foregoing shall, however, only apply if the claimant has access to the court administering the fund and the fund is actually available in respect of the claim.

Death and injury

Article 11

Claims in respect of death or personal injury have priority over other claims save to the extent that the aggregate of such claims exceeds two-thirds of the total amount established in accordance with article 9, paragraph 1.

Compulsory insurance of the owner

Article 12

1. The owner of a ship registered in a State Party and actually carrying hazardous and noxious substances shall be required to maintain insurance or other financial security, such as the guarantee of a bank or similar financial institution, in the sums fixed by applying the limits of liability prescribed in article 9, paragraph 1, to cover liability for damage under this Convention.

2. A compulsory insurance certificate attesting that insurance or other financial security is in force in accordance with the provisions of this Convention shall be issued to each ship after the appropriate authority of a State Party has determined that the requirements of paragraph 1 have been complied with. With respect to a ship registered in a State Party such compulsory insurance certificate shall be issued or certified by the appropriate authority of the State of the ship's registry; with respect to a ship not registered in a State Party it may be issued or certified by the appropriate authority of any State Party. This compulsory insurance certificate shall be in the form of the model set out in Annex I and shall contain the following particulars:

(a) name of the ship, distinctive number or letters and port of registry;
(b) name and principal place of business of the owner;
(c) IMO ship identification number;
(d) type and duration of security;
(e) name and principal place of business of insurer or other person giving security and, where appropriate, place of business where the insurance or security is established; and

(f) period of validity of certificate, which shall not be longer than the period of validity of the insurance or other security.

3. The compulsory insurance certificate shall be in the official language or languages of the issuing State. If the language used is neither English, nor French nor Spanish, the text shall include a translation into one of these languages.

4. The compulsory insurance certificate shall be carried on board the ship and a copy shall be deposited with the authorities who keep the record of the ship's registry or, if the ship is not registered in a State Party, with the authority of the State issuing or certifying the certificate.

5. An insurance or other financial security shall not satisfy the requirements of this article if it can cease, for reasons other than the expiry of the period of validity of the insurance or security specified in the certificate under paragraph 2, before three months have elapsed from the date on which notice of its termination is given to the authorities referred to in paragraph 4, unless the compulsory insurance certificate has been [surrendered to these authorities or a new certificate has been]* issued within the said period. The foregoing provisions shall similarly apply to any modification which results in the insurance or security no longer satisfying the requirements of this article.

6. The State of the ship's registry shall, subject to the provisions of this article, determine the conditions of issue and validity of the compulsory insurance certificate.

7. Compulsory insurance certificates issued or certified under the authority of a State Party in accordance with paragraph 2 shall be accepted by other States Parties for the purposes of this Convention and shall be regarded by other States Parties as having the same force as compulsory insurance certificates issued or certified by them even if issued or certified in respect of a ship not registered in a State Party. A State Party may at any time request consultation with the issuing or certifying State should it believe that the insurer or guarantor named in the compulsory insurance certificate is not financially capable of meeting the obligations imposed by this Convention.

8. Any claim for compensation for damage may be brought directly against the insurer or other person providing financial security for the owner's liability for damage. In such case the defendant may, even if the owner is not entitled to limitation of liability, benefit from the limit of liability prescribed in accordance with paragraph 1. The defendant may further invoke the defences (other than the bankruptcy or winding up of the owner) which the owner would have been entitled to invoke. Furthermore, the defendant may invoke the defence that the damage resulted from the wilful misconduct of the owner, but the defendant

---

* The words in square brackets have probably been omitted in the authentic text by error.

shall not invoke any other defence which the defendant might have been entitled to invoke in proceedings brought by the owner against the defendant. The defendant shall in any event have the right to require the owner to be joined in the proceedings.

9. Any sums provided by insurance or by other financial security maintained in accordance with paragraph 1 shall be available exclusively for the satisfaction of claims under this Convention.

10. A State Party shall not permit a ship under its flag to which this article applies to trade unless a certificate has been issued under paragraph 2 or 12.

11. Subject to the provisions of this article, each State Party shall ensure, under its national law, that insurance or other security in the sums specified in paragraph 1 is in force in respect of any ship, wherever registered, entering or leaving a port in its territory, or arriving at or leaving an offshore facility in its territorial sea.

12. If insurance or other financial security is not maintained in respect of a ship owned by a State Party, the provisions of this article relating thereto shall not be applicable to such ship, but the ship shall carry a compulsory insurance certificate issued by the appropriate authorities of the State of the ship's registry stating that the ship is owned by that State and that the ship's liability is covered within the limit prescribed in accordance with paragraph 1. Such a compulsory insurance certificate shall follow as closely as possible the model prescribed by paragraph 2.

Chapter III
Compensation by the International Hazardous and Noxious Substances Fund (HNS Fund)

Establishment of the HNS Fund

Article 13

1. The International Hazardous and Noxious Substances Fund (HNS Fund) is hereby established with the following aims:

(a) to provide compensation for damage in connection with the carriage of hazardous and noxious substances by sea, to the extent that the protection afforded by chapter II is inadequate or not available; and
(b) to give effect to the related tasks set out in article 15.

2. The HNS Fund shall in each State Party be recognized as a legal person capable under the laws of that State of assuming rights and obligations and of being a party in legal proceedings before the courts of that State. Each State Party shall recognize the Director as the legal representative of the HNS Fund.

Compensation

Article 14

1. For the purpose of fulfilling its function under article 13, paragraph 1(a), the HNS Fund shall pay compensation to any person suffering damage if such person has been unable to obtain full and adequate compensation for the damage under the terms of chapter II:

(a) because no liability for the damage arises under chapter II;

(b) because the owner liable for the damage under chapter II is financially incapable of meeting the obligations under this Convention in full and any financial security that may be provided under chapter II does not cover or is insufficient to satisfy the claims for compensation for damage; an owner being treated as financially incapable of meeting these obligations and a financial security being treated as insufficient if the person suffering the damage has been unable to obtain full satisfaction of the amount of compensation due under chapter II after having taken all reasonable steps to pursue the available legal remedies;

(c) because the damage exceeds the owner's liability under the terms of chapter II.

2. Expenses reasonably incurred or sacrifices reasonably made by the owner voluntarily to prevent or minimize damage shall be treated as damage for the purposes of this article.

3. The HNS Fund shall incur no obligation under the preceding paragraphs if:

(a) it proves that the damage resulted from an act of war, hostilities, civil war or insurrection or was caused by hazardous and noxious substances which had escaped or been discharged from a warship or other ship owned or operated by a State and used, at the time of the incident, only on Government non-commercial service; or

(b) the claimant cannot prove that there is a reasonable probability that the damage resulted from an incident involving one or more ships.

4. If the HNS Fund proves that the damage resulted wholly or partly either from an act or omission done with intent to cause damage by the person who suffered the damage or from the negligence of that person, the HNS Fund may be exonerated wholly or partially from its obligation to pay compensation to such person. The HNS Fund shall in any event be exonerated to the extent that the owner may have been exonerated under article 7, paragraph 3. However, there shall be no such exoneration of the HNS Fund with regard to preventive measures.

5.

(a) Except as otherwise provided in subparagraph (b), the aggregate amount of compensation payable by the HNS Fund under this article shall in respect of any one incident be limited, so that the total sum of that amount and any amount of compensation actually paid under chapter II for damage within the scope of application of this Convention as defined in article 3 shall not exceed 250 million units of account.

(b) The aggregate amount of compensation payable by the HNS Fund under this article for damage resulting from a natural phenomenon of an exceptional, inevitable and irresistible character shall not exceed 250 million units of account.

(c) Interest accrued on a fund constituted in accordance with article 9, paragraph 3, if any, shall not be taken into account for the computation of the maximum compensation payable by the HNS Fund under this article.

(d) The amounts mentioned in this article shall be converted into national currency on the basis of the value of that currency with reference to the Special Drawing Right on the date of the decision of the Assembly of the HNS Fund as to the first date of payment of compensation.

6. Where the amount of established claims against the HNS Fund exceeds the aggregate amount of compensation payable under paragraph 5, the amount available shall be distributed in such a manner that the proportion between any established claim and the amount of compensation actually recovered by the claimant under this Convention shall be the same for all claimants. Claims in respect of death or personal injury shall have priority over other claims, however, save to the extent that the aggregate of such claims exceeds two-thirds of the total amount established in accordance with paragraph 5.

7. The Assembly of the HNS Fund may decide that, in exceptional cases, compensation in accordance with this Convention can be paid even if the owner has not constituted a fund in accordance with chapter II. In such cases paragraph 5(d) applies accordingly.

Related tasks of the HNS Fund

Article 15

For the purpose of fulfilling its function under article 13, paragraph 1(a), the HNS Fund shall have the following tasks:

(a) to consider claims made against the HNS Fund;

(b) to prepare an estimate in the form of a budget for each calendar year of:
   Expenditure:
   (i) costs and expenses of the administration of the HNS Fund in the relevant year and any deficit from operations in the preceding years; and
   (ii) payments to be made by the HNS Fund in the relevant year;

Income:

(iii) surplus funds from operations in preceding years, including any interest;

(iv) initial contributions to be paid in the course of the year;

 (v) annual contributions if required to balance the budget; and

(vi) any other income;

(c) to use at the request of a State Party its good offices as necessary to assist that State to secure promptly such personnel, material and services as are necessary to enable the State to take measures to prevent or mitigate damage arising from an incident in respect of which the HNS Fund may be called upon to pay compensation under this Convention; and

(d) to provide, on conditions laid down in the internal regulations, credit facilities with a view to the taking of preventive measures against damage arising from a particular incident in respect of which the HNS Fund may be called upon to pay compensation under this Convention.

General provisions on contributions

Article 16

1. The HNS Fund shall have a general account, which shall be divided into sectors.

2. The HNS Fund shall, subject to article 19, paragraphs 3 and 4, also have separate accounts in respect of:

(a) oil as defined in article 1, paragraph 5(a)(i) (oil account);

(b) liquefied natural gases of light hydrocarbons with methane as the main constituent (LNG) (LNG account); and

(c) liquefied petroleum gases of light hydrocarbons with propane and butane as the main constituents (LPG) (LPG account).

3. There shall be initial contributions and, as required, annual contributions to the HNS Fund.

4. Contributions to the HNS Fund shall be made into the general account in accordance with article 18, to separate accounts in accordance with article 19 and to either the general account or separate accounts in accordance with article 20 or article 21, paragraph 5. Subject to article 19, paragraph 6, the general account shall be available to compensate damage caused by hazardous and noxious substances covered by that account, and a separate account shall be available to compensate damage caused by a hazardous and noxious substance covered by that account.

5. For the purposes of article 18, article 19, paragraph 1(a)(i), paragraph 1(a)(ii) and paragraph 1(c), article 20 and article 21, paragraph 5, where the quantity of a given type of contributing cargo received in the territory of a State

Party by any person in a calendar year when aggregated with the quantities of the same type of cargo received in the same State Party in that year by any associated person or persons exceeds the limit specified in the respective subparagraphs, such a person shall pay contributions in respect of the actual quantity received by that person notwithstanding that that quantity did not exceed the respective limit.

6. 'Associated person' means any subsidiary or commonly controlled entity. The question whether a person comes within this definition shall be determined by the national law of the State concerned.

General provisions on annual contributions

Article 17

1. Annual contributions to the general account and to each separate account shall be levied only as required to make payments by the account in question.

2. Annual contributions payable pursuant to articles 18, 19 and article 21, paragraph 5 shall be determined by the Assembly and shall be calculated in accordance with those articles on the basis of the units of contributing cargo received or, in respect of cargoes referred to in article 19, paragraph 1(b), discharged during the preceding calendar year or such other year as the Assembly may decide.

3. The Assembly shall decide the total amount of annual contributions to be levied to the general account and to each separate account. Following that decision the Director shall, in respect of each State Party, calculate for each person liable to pay contributions in accordance with article 18, article 19, paragraph 1 and article 21, paragraph 5, the amount of that person's annual contribution to each account, on the basis of a fixed sum for each unit of contributing cargo reported in respect of the person during the preceding calendar year or such other year as the Assembly may decide. For the general account, the abovementioned fixed sum per unit of contributing cargo for each sector shall be calculated pursuant to the regulations contained in Annex II to this Convention. For each separate account, the fixed sum per unit of contributing cargo referred to above shall be calculated by dividing the total annual contribution to be levied to that account by the total quantity of cargo contributing to that account.

4. The Assembly may also levy annual contributions for administrative costs and decide on the distribution of such costs between the sectors of the general account and the separate accounts.

5. The Assembly shall also decide on the distribution between the relevant accounts and sectors of amounts paid in compensation for damage caused by two or more substances which fall within different accounts or sectors, on the

basis of an estimate of the extent to which each of the substances involved contributed to the damage.

Annual contributions to the general account

Article 18

1. Subject to article 16, paragraph 5, annual contributions to the general account shall be made in respect of each State Party by any person who was the receiver in that State in the preceding calendar year, or such other year as the Assembly may decide, of aggregate quantities exceeding 20,000 tonnes of contributing cargo, other than substances referred to in article 19, paragraph 1, which fall within the following sectors:

(a) solid bulk materials referred to in article 1, paragraph 5(a)(vii);
(b) substances referred to in paragraph 2; and
(c) other substances.

2. Annual contributions shall also be payable to the general account by persons who would have been liable to pay contributions to a separate account in accordance with article 19, paragraph 1 had its operation not been postponed or suspended in accordance with article 19. Each separate account the operation of which has been postponed or suspended under article 19 shall form a separate sector within the general account.

Annual contributions to separate accounts

Article 19

1. Subject to article 16, paragraph 5, annual contributions to separate accounts shall be made in respect of each State Party:

(a) in the case of the oil account,
   (i) by any person who has received in that State in the preceding calendar year, or such other year as the Assembly may decide, total quantities exceeding 150,000 tonnes of contributing oil as defined in article 1, paragraph 3 of the International Convention on the Establishment of an International Fund for Compensation for Oil Pollution Damage, 1971, as amended, and who is or would be liable to pay contributions to the International Oil Pollution Compensation Fund in accordance with article 10 of that Convention; and
  (ii) by any person who was the receiver in that State in the preceding calendar year, or such other year as the Assembly may decide, of total quantities exceeding 20,000 tonnes of other oils carried in bulk listed in appendix I of Annex I to the International Convention for the

Prevention of Pollution from Ships, 1973, as modified by the Protocol of 1978 relating thereto, as amended;

(b) in the case of the LNG account, by any person who in the preceding calendar year, or such other year as the Assembly may decide, immediately prior to its discharge, held title to an LNG cargo discharged in a port or terminal of that State;

(c) in the case of the LPG account, by any person who in the preceding calendar year, or such other year as the Assembly may decide, was the receiver in that State of total quantities exceeding 20,000 tonnes of LPG.

2. Subject to paragraph 3, the separate accounts referred to in paragraph 1 above shall become effective at the same time as the general account.

3. The initial operation of a separate account referred to in article 16, paragraph 2 shall be postponed until such time as the quantities of contributing cargo in respect of that account during the preceding calendar year, or such other year as the Assembly may decide, exceed the following levels:

(a) 350 million tonnes of contributing cargo in respect of the oil account;

(b) 20 million tonnes of contributing cargo in respect of the LNG account; and

(c) 15 million tonnes of contributing cargo in respect of the LPG account.

4. The Assembly may suspend the operation of a separate account if:

(a) the quantities of contributing cargo in respect of that account during the preceding calendar year fall below the respective level specified in paragraph 3; or

(b) when six months have elapsed from the date when the contributions were due, the total unpaid contributions to that account exceed ten per cent of the most recent levy to that account in accordance with paragraph 1.

5. The Assembly may reinstate the operation of a separate account which has been suspended in accordance with paragraph 4.

6. Any person who would be liable to pay contributions to a separate account the operation of which has been postponed in accordance with paragraph 3 or suspended in accordance with paragraph 4, shall pay into the general account the contributions due by that person in respect of that separate account. For the purpose of calculating future contributions, the postponed or suspended separate account shall form a new sector in the general account and shall be subject to the HNS points system defined in Annex II.

Initial contributions

Article 20

1. In respect of each State Party, initial contributions shall be made of an amount which shall for each person liable to pay contributions in accordance

with article 16, paragraph 5, articles 18, 19 and article 21, paragraph 5 be calculated on the basis of a fixed sum, equal for the general account and each separate account, for each unit of contributing cargo received or, in the case of LNG, discharged in that State, during the calendar year preceding that in which this Convention enters into force for that State.

2. The fixed sum and the units for the different sectors within the general account as well as for each separate account referred to in paragraph 1 shall be determined by the Assembly.

3. Initial contributions shall be paid within three months following the date on which the HNS Fund issues invoices in respect of each State Party to persons liable to pay contributions in accordance with paragraph 1.

Reports

Article 21

1. Each State Party shall ensure that any person liable to pay contributions in accordance with articles 18, 19 or paragraph 5 of this article appears on a list to be established and kept up to date by the Director in accordance with the provisions of this article.

2. For the purposes set out in paragraph 1, each State Party shall communicate to the Director, at a time and in the manner to be prescribed in the internal regulations of the HNS Fund, the name and address of any person who in respect of the State is liable to pay contributions in accordance with articles 18, 19 or paragraph 5 of this article, as well as data on the relevant quantities of contributing cargo for which such a person is liable to contribute in respect of the preceding calendar year.

3. For the purposes of ascertaining who are, at any given time, the persons liable to pay contributions in accordance with articles 18, 19 or paragraph 5 of this article and of establishing, where applicable, the quantities of cargo to be taken into account for any such person when determining the amount of the contribution, the list shall be *prima facie* evidence of the facts stated therein.

4. Where a State Party does not fulfil its obligations to communicate to the Director the information referred to in paragraph 2 and this results in a financial loss for the HNS Fund, that State Party shall be liable to compensate the HNS Fund for such loss. The Assembly shall, on the recommendation of the Director, decide whether such compensation shall be payable by a State Party.

5. In respect of contributing cargo carried from one port or terminal of a State Party to another port or terminal located in the same State and discharged there, States Parties shall have the option of submitting to the HNS Fund a report with an annual aggregate quantity for each account covering all receipts of contributing cargo, including any quantities in respect of which contributions are payable pursuant to article 16, paragraph 5. The State Party shall, at the time of reporting, either:

(a) notify the HNS Fund that that State will pay the aggregate amount for each account in respect of the relevant year in one lump sum to the HNS Fund; or

(b) instruct the HNS Fund to levy the aggregate amount for each account by invoicing individual receivers or, in the case of LNG, the title holder who discharges within the jurisdiction of that State Party, for the amount payable by each of them. These persons shall be identified in accordance with the national law of the State concerned.

Non-payment of contributions

Article 22

1. The amount of any contribution due under articles 18, 19, 20 or article 21, paragraph 5 and which is in arrears shall bear interest at a rate which shall be determined in accordance with the internal regulations of the HNS Fund, provided that different rates may be fixed for different circumstances.

2. Where a person who is liable to pay contributions in accordance with articles 18, 19, 20 or article 21, paragraph 5 does not fulfil the obligations in respect of any such contribution or any part thereof and is in arrears, the Director shall take all appropriate action, including court action, against such a person on behalf of the HNS Fund with a view to the recovery of the amount due. However, where the defaulting contributor is manifestly insolvent or the circumstances otherwise so warrant, the Assembly may, upon recommendation of the Director, decide that no action shall be taken or continued against the contributor.

Optional liability of States Parties for the payment of contributions

Article 23

1. Without prejudice to article 21, paragraph 5, a State Party may at the time when it deposits its instrument of ratification, acceptance, approval or accession or at any time thereafter declare that it assumes responsibility for obligations imposed by this Convention on any person liable to pay contributions in accordance with articles 18, 19, 20 or article 21, paragraph 5 in respect of hazardous and noxious substances received or discharged in the territory of that State. Such a declaration shall be made in writing and shall specify which obligations are assumed.

2. Where a declaration under paragraph 1 is made prior to the entry into force of this Convention in accordance with article 46, it shall be deposited with the Secretary-General who shall after the entry into force of this Convention communicate the declaration to the Director.

3. A declaration under paragraph 1 which is made after the entry into force of this Convention shall be deposited with the Director.

4. A declaration made in accordance with this article may be withdrawn by the relevant State giving notice thereof in writing to the Director. Such a notification shall take effect three months after the Director's receipt thereof.

5. Any State which is bound by a declaration made under this article shall, in any proceedings brought against it before a competent court in respect of any obligation specified in the declaration, waive any immunity that it would otherwise be entitled to invoke.

Organization and administration
Article 24
The HNS Fund shall have an Assembly and a Secretariat headed by the Director.

Assembly
Article 25
The Assembly shall consist of all States Parties to this Convention.

Article 26
The functions of the Assembly shall be:

(a) to elect at each regular session its President and two Vice-Presidents who shall hold office until the next regular session;
(b) to determine its own rules of procedure, subject to the provisions of this Convention;
(c) to develop, apply and keep under review internal and financial regulations relating to the aim of the HNS Fund as described in article 13, paragraph 1(a), and the related tasks of the HNS Fund listed in article 15;
(d) to appoint the Director and make provisions for the appointment of such other personnel as may be necessary and determine the terms and conditions of service of the Director and other personnel;
(e) to adopt the annual budget prepared in accordance with article 15(b);
(f) to consider and approve as necessary any recommendation of the Director regarding the scope of definition of contributing cargo;
(g) to appoint auditors and approve the accounts of the HNS Fund;
(h) to approve settlements of claims against the HNS Fund, to take decisions in respect of the distribution among claimants of the available amount of compensation in accordance with article 14 and to determine the terms and conditions according to which provisional payments in respect of claims shall be made with a view to ensuring that victims of damage are compensated as promptly as possible;

(i) to establish a Committee on Claims for Compensation with at least 7 and not more than 15 members and any temporary or permanent subsidiary body it may consider to be necessary, to define its terms of reference and to give it the authority needed to perform the functions entrusted to it; when appointing the members of such body, the Assembly shall endeavour to secure an equitable geographical distribution of members and to ensure that the States Parties are appropriately represented; the Rules of Procedure of the Assembly may be applied, *mutatis mutandis*, for the work of such subsidiary body;

(j) to determine which States not party to this Convention, which Associate Members of the Organization and which intergovernmental and international non-governmental organizations shall be admitted to take part, without voting rights, in meetings of the Assembly and subsidiary bodies;

(k) to give instructions concerning the administration of the HNS Fund to the Director and subsidiary bodies;

(l) to supervise the proper execution of this Convention and of its own decisions;

(m) to review every five years the implementation of this Convention with particular reference to the performance of the system for the calculation of levies and the contribution mechanism for domestic trade; and

(n) to perform such other functions as are allocated to it under this Convention or are otherwise necessary for the proper operation of the HNS Fund.

Article 27

1. Regular sessions of the Assembly shall take place once every calendar year upon convocation by the Director.

2. Extraordinary sessions of the Assembly shall be convened by the Director at the request of at least one-third of the members of the Assembly and may be convened on the Director's own initiative after consultation with the President of the Assembly. The Director shall give members at least thirty days' notice of such sessions.

Article 28

A majority of the members of the Assembly shall constitute a quorum for its meetings.

Secretariat

Article 29

1. The Secretariat shall comprise the Director and such staff as the administration of the HNS Fund may require.

2. The Director shall be the legal representative of the HNS Fund.

Article 30

1. The Director shall be the chief administrative officer of the HNS Fund. Subject to the instructions given by the Assembly, the Director shall perform those functions which are assigned to the Director by this Convention, the internal regulations of the HNS Fund and the Assembly.

2. The Director shall in particular:

(a) appoint the personnel required for the administration of the HNS Fund;
(b) take all appropriate measures with a view to the proper administration of the assets of the HNS Fund;
(c) collect the contributions due under this Convention while observing in particular the provisions of article 22, paragraph 2;
(d) to the extent necessary to deal with claims against the HNS Fund and to carry out the other functions of the HNS Fund, employ the services of legal, financial and other experts;
(e) take all appropriate measures for dealing with claims against the HNS Fund, within the limits and on conditions to be laid down in the internal regulations of the HNS Fund, including the final settlement of claims without the prior approval of the Assembly where these regulations so provide;
(f) prepare and submit to the Assembly the financial statements and budget estimates for each calendar year;
(g) prepare, in consultation with the President of the Assembly, and publish a report on the activities of the HNS Fund during the previous calendar year; and
(h) prepare, collect and circulate the documents and information which may be required for the work of the Assembly and subsidiary bodies.

Article 31

In the performance of their duties the Director and the staff and experts appointed by the Director shall not seek or receive instructions from any Government or from any authority external to the HNS Fund. They shall refrain from any action which might adversely reflect on their position as international officials. Each State Party on its part undertakes to respect the exclusively international character of the responsibilities of the Director and the staff and experts appointed by the Director, and not to seek to influence them in the discharge of their duties.

Finances

Article 32

1. Each State Party shall bear the salary, travel and other expenses of its own delegation to the Assembly and of its representatives on subsidiary bodies.

2. Any other expenses incurred in the operation of the HNS Fund shall be borne by the HNS Fund.

Voting

Article 33

The following provisions shall apply to voting in the Assembly:

(a) each member shall have one vote;
(b) except as otherwise provided in article 34, decisions of the Assembly shall be made by a majority vote of the members present and voting;
(c) decisions where a two-thirds majority is required shall be a two-thirds majority vote of members present; and
(d) for the purpose of this article the phrase 'members present' means 'members present at the meeting at the time of the vote', and the phrase 'members present and voting' means 'members present and casting an affirmative or negative vote'. Members who abstain from voting shall be considered as not voting.

Article 34

The following decisions of the Assembly shall require a two-thirds majority:

(a) a decision under article 19, paragraphs 4 or 5 to suspend or reinstate the operation of a separate account;
(b) a decision under article 22, paragraph 2, not to take or continue action against a contributor;
(c) the appointment of the Director under article 26(d);
(d) the establishment of subsidiary bodies, under article 26(i), and matters relating to such establishment; and
(e) a decision under article 51, paragraph 1, that this Convention shall continue to be in force.

Tax exemptions and currency regulations

Article 35

1. The HNS Fund, its assets, income, including contributions, and other property necessary for the exercise of its functions as described in article 13, paragraph 1, shall enjoy in all States Parties exemption from all direct taxation.

2. When the HNS Fund makes substantial purchases of movable or immovable property, or of services which are necessary for the exercise of its official activities in order to achieve its aims as set out in article 13, paragraph 1, the cost of which include indirect taxes or sales taxes, the Governments of the States Parties shall take, whenever possible, appropriate measures for the remission or refund of the amount of such duties and taxes. Goods thus acquired shall not be sold against payment or given away free of charge unless it is done according to conditions approved by the Government of the State having granted or supported the remission or refund.

3. No exemption shall be accorded in the case of duties, taxes or dues which merely constitute payment for public utility services.

4. The HNS Fund shall enjoy exemption from all customs duties, taxes and other related taxes on articles imported or exported by it or on its behalf for its official use. Articles thus imported shall not be transferred either for consideration or gratis on the territory of the country into which they have been imported except on conditions agreed by the Government of that country.

5. Persons contributing to the HNS Fund as well as victims and owners receiving compensation from the HNS Fund shall be subject to the fiscal legislation of the State where they are taxable, no special exemption or other benefit being conferred on them in this respect.

6. Notwithstanding existing or future regulations concerning currency or transfers, States Parties shall authorize the transfer and payment of any contribution to the HNS Fund and of any compensation paid by the HNS Fund without any restriction.

Confidentiality of information

Article 36

Information relating to individual contributors supplied for the purpose of this Convention shall not be divulged outside the HNS Fund except in so far as it may be strictly necessary to enable the HNS Fund to carry out its functions including the bringing and defending of legal proceedings.

Chapter IV
Claims and actions

Limitation of actions

Article 37

1. Rights to compensation under chapter II shall be extinguished unless an action is brought thereunder within three years from the date when the person suffering the damage knew or ought reasonably to have known of the damage and of the identity of the owner.

2. Rights to compensation under chapter III shall be extinguished unless an action is brought thereunder or a notification has been made pursuant to article 39, paragraph 7, within three years from the date when the person suffering the damage knew or ought reasonably to have known of the damage.

3. In no case, however, shall an action be brought later than ten years from the date of the incident which caused the damage.

4. Where the incident consists of a series of occurrences, the ten-year period mentioned in paragraph 3 shall run from the date of the last of such occurrences.

Jurisdiction in respect of action against the owner

Article 38

1. Where an incident has caused damage in the territory, including the territorial sea or in an area referred to in article 3(b), of one or more States Parties, or preventive measures have been taken to prevent or minimize damage in such territory including the territorial sea or in such area, actions for compensation may be brought against the owner or other person providing financial security for the owner's liability only in the courts of any such States Parties.

2. Where an incident has caused damage exclusively outside the territory, including the territorial sea, of any State and either the conditions for application of this Convention set out in article 3(c) have been fulfilled or preventive measures to prevent or minimize such damage have been taken, actions for compensation may be brought against the owner or other person providing financial security for the owner's liability only in the courts of:

(a) the State Party where the ship is registered or, in the case of an unregistered ship, the State Party whose flag the ship is entitled to fly; or

(b) the State Party where the owner has habitual residence or where the principal place of business of the owner is established; or

(c) the State Party where a fund has been constituted in accordance with article 9, paragraph 3.

3. Reasonable notice of any action taken under paragraph 1 or 2 shall be given to the defendant.

4. Each State Party shall ensure that its courts have jurisdiction to entertain actions for compensation under this Convention.

5. After a fund under article 9 has been constituted by the owner or by the insurer or other person providing financial security in accordance with article 12, the courts of the State in which such fund is constituted shall have exclusive jurisdiction to determine all matters relating to the apportionment and distribution of the fund.

Jurisdiction in respect of action against the HNS Fund or taken by the HNS Fund

Article 39

1. Subject to the subsequent provisions of this article, any action against the HNS Fund for compensation under article 14 shall be brought only before a court having jurisdiction under article 38 in respect of actions against the owner who is liable for damage caused by the relevant incident or before a court in a State Party which would have been competent if an owner had been liable.

2. In the event that the ship carrying the hazardous or noxious substances which caused the damage has not been identified, the provisions of article 38, paragraph 1, shall apply *mutatis mutandis* to actions against the HNS Fund.

3. Each State Party shall ensure that its courts have jurisdiction to entertain such actions against the HNS Fund as are referred to in paragraph 1.

4. Where an action for compensation for damage has been brought before a court against the owner or the owner's guarantor, such court shall have exclusive jurisdiction over any action against the HNS Fund for compensation under the provisions of article 14 in respect of the same damage.

5. Each State Party shall ensure that the HNS Fund shall have the right to intervene as a party to any legal proceedings instituted in accordance with this Convention before a competent court of that State against the owner or the owner's guarantor.

6. Except as otherwise provided in paragraph 7, the HNS Fund shall not be bound by any judgement or decision in proceedings to which it has not been a party or by any settlement to which it is not a party.

7. Without prejudice to the provisions of paragraph 5, where an action under this Convention for compensation for damage has been brought against an owner or the owner's guarantor before a competent court in a State Party, each party to the proceedings shall be entitled under the national law of that State to notify the HNS Fund of the proceedings. Where such notification has been made in accordance with the formalities required by the law of the court seized and in such time and in such a manner that the HNS Fund has in fact been in a position effectively to intervene as a party to the proceedings, any judgement rendered by the court in such proceedings shall, after it has become final and enforceable in the State where the judgement was given, become binding upon the HNS Fund in the sense that the facts and findings in that judgement may not be disputed by the HNS Fund even if the HNS Fund has not actually intervened in the proceedings.

Recognition and enforcement

Article 40

1. Any judgement given by a court with jurisdiction in accordance with article 38, which is enforceable in the State of origin where it is no longer subject to ordinary forms of review, shall be recognized in any State Party, except:

(a) where the judgement was obtained by fraud; or
(b) where the defendant was not given reasonable notice and a fair opportunity to present the case.

2. A judgement recognized under paragraph 1 shall be enforceable in each State Party as soon as the formalities required in that State have been complied with. The formalities shall not permit the merits of the case to be re-opened.

3. Subject to any decision concerning the distribution referred to in article 14, paragraph 6, any judgement given against the HNS Fund by a court having

jurisdiction in accordance with article 39, paragraphs 1 and 3 shall, when it has become enforceable in the State of origin and is in that State no longer subject to ordinary forms of review, be recognized and enforceable in each State Party.

Subrogation and recourse

Article 41

1. The HNS Fund shall, in respect of any amount of compensation for damage paid by the HNS Fund in accordance with article 14, paragraph 1, acquire by subrogation the rights that the person so compensated may enjoy against the owner or the owner's guarantor.

2. Nothing in this Convention shall prejudice any rights of recourse or subrogation of the HNS Fund against any person, including persons referred to in article 7, paragraph 2(d), other than those referred to in the previous paragraph, in so far as they can limit their liability. In any event the right of the HNS Fund to subrogation against such persons shall not be less favourable than that of an insurer of the person to whom compensation has been paid.

3. Without prejudice to any other rights of subrogation or recourse against the HNS Fund which may exist, a State Party or agency thereof which has paid compensation for damage in accordance with provisions of national law shall acquire by subrogation the rights which the person so compensated would have enjoyed under this Convention.

Supersession clause

Article 42

This Convention shall supersede any convention in force or open for signature, ratification or accession at the date on which this Convention is opened for signature, but only to the extent that such convention would be in conflict with it; however, nothing in this article shall affect the obligations of States Parties to States not party to this Convention arising under such convention.

Chapter V
Transitional provisions

Information on contributing cargo

Article 43

When depositing an instrument referred to in article 45, paragraph 3, and annually thereafter until this Convention enters into force for a State, that State shall submit to the Secretary-General data on the relevant quantities of contributing cargo received or, in the case of LNG, discharged in that State during the preceding calendar year in respect of the general account and each separate account.

First session of the Assembly

Article 44

The Secretary-General shall convene the first session of the Assembly. This session shall take place as soon as possible after the entry into force of this Convention and, in any case, not more than thirty days after such entry into force.

Chapter VI
Final clauses

Signature, ratification, acceptance, approval and accession

Article 45

1. This Convention shall be open for signature at the Headquarters of the Organization from 1 October 1996 to 30 September 1997 and shall thereafter remain open for accession.

2. States may express their consent to be bound by this Convention by:

(a) signature without reservation as to ratification, acceptance or approval; or
(b) signature subject to ratification, acceptance or approval, followed by ratification, acceptance or approval; or
(c) accession.

3. Ratification, acceptance, approval or accession shall be effected by the deposit of an instrument to that effect with the Secretary-General.

Entry into force

Article 46

1. This Convention shall enter into force eighteen months after the date on which the following conditions are fulfilled:

(a) at least twelve States, including four States each with not less than 2 million units of gross tonnage, have expressed their consent to be bound by it, and
(b) the Secretary-General has received information in accordance with article 43 that those persons in such States who would be liable to contribute pursuant to article 18, paragraphs 1(a) and (c) have received during the preceding calendar year a total quantity of at least 40 million tonnes of cargo contributing to the general account.

2. For a State which expresses its consent to be bound by this Convention after the conditions for entry into force have been met, such consent shall take effect three months after the date of expression of such consent, or on the date on which this Convention enters into force in accordance with paragraph 1, whichever is the later.

Revision and amendment

Article 47

1. A conference for the purpose of revising or amending this Convention may be convened by the Organization.

2. The Secretary-General shall convene a conference of the States Parties to this Convention for revising or amending the Convention, at the request of six States Parties or one-third of the States Parties, whichever is the higher figure.

3. Any consent to be bound by this Convention expressed after the date of entry into force of an amendment to this Convention shall be deemed to apply to the Convention as amended.

Amendment of limits

Article 48

1. Without prejudice to the provisions of article 47, the special procedure in this article shall apply solely for the purposes of amending the limits set out in article 9, paragraph 1 and article 14, paragraph 5.

2. Upon the request of at least one half, but in no case less than six, of the States Parties, any proposal to amend the limits specified in article 9, paragraph 1, and article 14, paragraph 5, shall be circulated by the Secretary-General to all Members of the Organization and to all Contracting States.

3. Any amendment proposed and circulated as above shall be submitted to the Legal Committee of the Organization (the Legal Committee) for consideration at a date at least six months after the date of its circulation.

4. All Contracting States, whether or not Members of the Organization, shall be entitled to participate in the proceedings of the Legal Committee for the consideration and adoption of amendments.

5. Amendments shall be adopted by a two-thirds majority of the Contracting States present and voting in the Legal Committee, expanded as provided in paragraph 4, on condition that at least one half of the Contracting States shall be present at the time of voting.

6. When acting on a proposal to amend the limits, the Legal Committee shall take into account the experience of incidents and, in particular, the amount of damage resulting therefrom, changes in the monetary values and the effect of the proposed amendment on the cost of insurance. It shall also take into

account the relationship between the limits established in article 9, paragraph 1, and those in article 14, paragraph 5.

7.

(a) No amendment of the limits under this article may be considered less than five years from the date this Convention was opened for signature nor less than five years from the date of entry into force of a previous amendment under this article.

(b) No limit may be increased so as to exceed an amount which corresponds to a limit laid down in this Convention increased by six per cent per year calculated on a compound basis from the date on which this Convention was opened for signature.

(c) No limit may be increased so as to exceed an amount which corresponds to a limit laid down in this Convention multiplied by three.

8. Any amendment adopted in accordance with paragraph 5 shall be notified by the Organization to all Contracting States. The amendment shall be deemed to have been accepted at the end of a period of eighteen months after the date of notification, unless within that period no less than one-fourth of the States which were Contracting States at the time of the adoption of the amendment have communicated to the Secretary-General that they do not accept the amendment, in which case the amendment is rejected and shall have no effect.

9. An amendment deemed to have been accepted in accordance with paragraph 8 shall enter into force eighteen months after its acceptance.

10. All Contracting States shall be bound by the amendment, unless they denounce this Convention in accordance with article 49, paragraphs 1 and 2, at least six months before the amendment enters into force. Such denunciation shall take effect when the amendment enters into force.

11. When an amendment has been adopted but the eighteen month period for its acceptance has not yet expired, a State which becomes a Contracting State during that period shall be bound by the amendment if it enters into force. A State which becomes a Contracting State after that period shall be bound by an amendment which has been accepted in accordance with paragraph 8. In the cases referred to in this paragraph, a State becomes bound by an amendment when that amendment enters into force, or when this Convention enters into force for that State, if later.

Denunciation

Article 49

1. This Convention may be denounced by any State Party at any time after the date on which it enters into force for that State Party.

2. Denunciation shall be effected by the deposit of an instrument of denunciation with the Secretary-General.

3. Denunciation shall take effect twelve months, or such longer period as may be specified in the instrument of denunciation, after its deposit with the Secretary-General.

4. Notwithstanding a denunciation by a State Party pursuant to this article, any provisions of this Convention relating to obligations to make contributions under articles 18, 19 or article 21, paragraph 5 in respect of such payments of compensation as the Assembly may decide relating to an incident which occurs before the denunciation takes effect shall continue to apply.

Extraordinary sessions of the Assembly

Article 50

1. Any State Party may, within ninety days after the deposit of an instrument of denunciation the result of which it considers will significantly increase the level of contributions from the remaining States Parties, request the Director to convene an extraordinary session of the Assembly. The Director shall convene the Assembly to meet not less than sixty days after receipt of the request.

2. The Director may take the initiative to convene an extraordinary session of the Assembly to meet within sixty days after the deposit of any instrument of denunciation, if the Director considers that such denunciation will result in a significant increase in the level of contributions from the remaining States Parties.

3. If the Assembly, at an extraordinary session, convened in accordance with paragraph 1 or 2 decides that the denunciation will result in a significant increase in the level of contributions from the remaining States Parties, any such State may, not later than one hundred and twenty days before the date on which the denunciation takes effect, denounce this Convention with effect from the same date.

Cessation

Article 51

1. This Convention shall cease to be in force:

(a) on the date when the number of States Parties falls below 6; or
(b) twelve months after the date on which data concerning a previous calendar year were to be communicated to the Director in accordance with article 21, if the data shows that the total quantity of contributing cargo to the general account in accordance with article 18, paragraphs 1(a) and (c) received in the States Parties in that preceding calendar year was less than 30 million tonnes.

Notwithstanding (b), if the total quantity of contributing cargo to the general account in accordance with article 18, paragraphs 1(a) and (c) received in the

States Parties in the preceding calendar year was less than 30 million tonnes but more than 25 million tonnes, the Assembly may, if it considers that this was due to exceptional circumstances and is not likely to be repeated, decide before the expiry of the above-mentioned twelve month period that the Convention shall continue to be in force. The Assembly may not, however, take such a decision in more than two subsequent years.

2. States which are bound by this Convention on the day before the date it ceases to be in force shall enable the HNS Fund to exercise its functions as described under article 52 and shall, for that purpose only, remain bound by this Convention.

Winding up of the HNS Fund

Article 52

1. If this Convention ceases to be in force, the HNS Fund shall nevertheless:

(a) meet its obligations in respect of any incident occurring before this Convention ceased to be in force; and

(b) be entitled to exercise its rights to contributions to the extent that these contributions are necessary to meet the obligations under (a), including expenses for the administration of the HNS Fund necessary for this purpose.

2. The Assembly shall take all appropriate measures to complete the winding up of the HNS Fund including the distribution in an equitable manner of any remaining assets among those persons who have contributed to the HNS Fund.

3. For the purposes of this article the HNS Fund shall remain a legal person.

Depositary

Article 53

1. This Convention and any amendment adopted under article 48 shall be deposited with the Secretary-General.

2. The Secretary-General shall:

(a) inform all States which have signed this Convention or acceded thereto, and all Members of the Organization, of:

   (i) each new signature or deposit of an instrument of ratification, acceptance, approval or accession together with the date thereof;

  (ii) the date of entry into force of this Convention;

 (iii) any proposal to amend the limits on the amounts of compensation which has been made in accordance with article 48, paragraph 2;

 (iv) any amendment which has been adopted in accordance with article 48, paragraph 5;

(v) any amendment deemed to have been accepted under article 48, paragraph 8, together with the date on which that amendment shall enter into force in accordance with paragraphs 9 and 10 of that article;

(vi) the deposit of any instrument of denunciation of this Convention together with the date on which it is received and the date on which the denunciation takes effect; and

(vii) any communication called for by any article in this Convention; and

(b) transmit certified true copies of this Convention to all States which have signed this Convention or acceded thereto.

3. As soon as this Convention enters into force, a certified true copy thereof shall be transmitted by the depositary to the Secretary-General of the United Nations for registration and publication in accordance with Article 102 of the Charter of the United Nations.

Languages

Article 54

This Convention is established in a single original in the Arabic, Chinese, English, French, Russian and Spanish languages, each text being equally authentic.

DONE AT LONDON this third day of May one thousand nine hundred and ninetysix.

IN WITNESS WHEREOF the undersigned, being duly authorized by their respective Governments for that purpose, have signed this Convention.

Annexes

Annex I
Certificate of insurance or other financial security in respect of liability for damage caused by hazardous and noxious substances (HNS)

Issued in accordance with the provisions of Article 12 of the International Convention on Liability and Compensation for Damage in Connection with the Carriage of Hazardous and Noxious Substances by Sea, 1996

Name of ship ....

Distinctive number or letters ....

IMO ship identification number Port of registry ....

Name and full address of the principal place of business of the owner ....

....

This is to certify that there is in force in respect of the above named ship a policy of insurance or other financial security satisfying the requirements of Article 12 of the International Convention on Liability and Compensation for Damage in Connection with the Carriage of Hazardous and Noxious Substances by Sea, 1996.

Type of security ....

Duration of security ....

Name and address of the insurer(s) and/or guarantor(s) ....

....

Name ....

Address ....

This certificate is valid until ....

Issued or certified by the Government of (Full designation of the State) ....

....

At (Place) ....

On (Date) ....

(Signature and Title of issuing or certifying official) ....

Explanatory Notes:

1. If desired, the designation of the State may include a reference to the competent public authority of the country where the certificate is issued.
2. If the total amount of security has been furnished by more than one source, the amount of each of them should be indicated.
3. If security is furnished in several forms, these should be enumerated.
4. The entry 'Duration of the Security' must stipulate the date on which such security takes effect.
5. The entry 'Address' of the insurer(s) and/or guarantor(s) must indicate the principal place of business of the insurer(s) and/or guarantor(s). If appropriate, the place of business where the insurance or other security is established shall be indicated.

Annex II
Regulations for the calculation of annual contributions to the general account

Regulation 1

1. The fixed sum referred to in article 17, paragraph 3 shall be determined for each sector in accordance with these regulations.

2. When it is necessary to calculate contributions for more than one sector of the general account, a separate fixed sum per unit of contributing cargo shall be calculated for each of the following sectors as may be required:

(a) solid bulk materials referred to in article 1, paragraph 5(a)(vii);
(b) oil, if the operation of the oil account is postponed or suspended;
(c) LNG, if the operation of the LNG account is postponed or suspended;
(d) LPG, if the operation of the LPG account is postponed or suspended;
(e) other substances.

Regulation 2

1. For each sector, the fixed sum per unit of contributing cargo shall be the product of the levy per HNS point and the sector factor for that sector.

2. The levy per HNS point shall be the total annual contributions to be levied to the general account divided by the total HNS points for all sectors.

3. The total HNS points for each sector shall be the product of the total volume, measured in metric tonnes, of contributing cargo for that sector and the corresponding sector factor.

4. A sector factor shall be calculated as the weighted arithmetic average of the claims/volume ratio for that sector for the relevant year and the previous nine years, according to this regulation.

5. Except as provided in paragraph 6, the claims/volume ratio for each of these years shall be calculated as follows:

(a) established claims, measured in units of account converted from the claim currency using the rate applicable on the date of the incident in question, for damage caused by substances in respect of which contributions to the HNS Fund are due for the relevant year; divided by
(b) the volume of contributing cargo corresponding to the relevant year.

6. In cases where the information required in paragraphs 5(a) and (b) is not available, the following values shall be used for the claims/volume ratio for each of the missing years:

(a) solid bulk materials referred to in article 1, paragraph 5 (a)(vii) 0
(b) oil, if the operation of the oil account is postponed 0
(c) LNG, if the operation of the LNG account is postponed 0
(d) LPG, if the operation of the LPG account is postponed 0
(e) other substances 0.0001

7. The arithmetic average of the ten years shall be weighted on a decreasing linear scale, so that the ratio of the relevant year shall have a weight of 10,

the year prior to the relevant year shall have a weight of 9, the next preceding year shall have a weight of 8, and so on, until the tenth year has a weight of 1.

8. If the operation of a separate account has been suspended, the relevant sector factor shall be calculated in accordance with those provisions of this regulation which the Assembly shall consider appropriate.

PART XII

The Antarctic

Antarctic Treaty, 1 December 1959

Editorial note

The primary objective of the Antarctic Treaty is to ensure that only activities for peaceful purposes take place in the Antarctic (Article I). In addition, the Treaty seeks to promote scientific research and co-operation among the Parties (Articles II and III). The Treaty does not confirm or deny the claims by several States to territorial sovereignty and other rights in the Antarctic (Article IV) and does not affect the rights under international law of States in respect of the high seas within the Antarctica region (Article VI). Nuclear explosions and the disposal of radioactive waste in the Antarctic are prohibited, subject to the conclusion of an international agreement on nuclear energy by the Consultative Parties (Article V). The Consultative Parties are those who are either named in the Preamble or who become so designated by conducting 'substantial scientific research' in the region (Article IX).

An inspection system is established (Article VII). The Treaty requires representatives of the Consultative Parties to meet at 'suitable intervals' to consult on matters relating to the Antarctic, including the preservation and conservation of living resources (Article IX(1)). The Treaty provides for the submission on consent of any dispute to the ICJ, but failure to agree on a reference to the ICJ does not relieve Parties of their obligations to settle the dispute by other peaceful means (Article XI). Amendments require the unanimous agreement of the Consultative Parties and enter into force when all have ratified them (Article XII(1)(a)). Other Parties are bound by these amendments once they ratify them, but if no notice of ratification is received by the depositary from those other Parties within two years of the amendment's entry into force for the Consultative Parties, those Parties are deemed to have withdrawn from the Treaty (Article XII(1)(b)).

Date of signature: 1 December 1959

Entry into force: 23 June 1961

Depositary: Government of the United States of America

Contracting Parties: Consultative Parties: Argentina, Australia, Belgium, Brazil, Bulgaria, Chile, China, Ecuador, Finland, France, Germany, India, Italy, Japan, Korea (Republic of), Netherlands, New Zealand, Norway, Peru, Poland, Russian Federation, South Africa, Spain, Sweden, United Kingdom, United States of America, Uruguay
Acceding States: Austria, Canada, Colombia, Cuba, Czech Republic, Democratic People's Republic of Korea, Denmark, Greece, Guatemala, Hungary, Papua New Guinea, Romania, Slovakia, Switzerland, Turkey, Ukraine, Venezuela.

Antarctic Treaty

The Governments of Argentina, Australia, Belgium, Chile, the French Republic, Japan, New Zealand, Norway, the Union of South Africa, the Union of Soviet Socialist Republics, the United Kingdom of Great Britain and Northern Ireland, and the United States of America,

Recognizing that it is in the interest of all mankind that Antarctica shall continue for ever to be used exclusively for peaceful purposes and shall not become the scene or object of international discord;

Acknowledging the substantial contributions to scientific knowledge resulting from international cooperation in scientific investigation in Antarctica;

Convinced that the establishment of a firm foundation for the continuation and development of such cooperation on the basis of freedom of scientific investigation in Antarctica as applied during the International Geophysical Year accords with the interests of science and the progress of all mankind;

Convinced also that a treaty ensuring the use of Antarctica for peaceful purposes only and the continuance of international harmony in Antarctica will further the purposes and principles embodied in the Charter of the United Nations;

Have agreed as follows:

Article I

1. Antarctica shall be used for peaceful purposes only. There shall be prohibited, *inter alia*, any measure of a military nature, such as the establishment of military bases and fortifications, the carrying out of military manoeuvres, as well as the testing of any type of weapon.

2. The present Treaty shall not prevent the use of military personnel or equipment for scientific research or for any other peaceful purpose.

Article II

Freedom of scientific investigation in Antarctica and cooperation toward that end, as applied during the International Geophysical Year, shall continue, subject to the provisions of the present Treaty.

Article III

1. In order to promote international cooperation in scientific investigation in Antarctica, as provided for in Article II of the present Treaty, the Contracting Parties agree that, to the greatest extent feasible and practicable:

a. information regarding plans for scientific programs in Antarctica shall be exchanged to permit maximum economy of and efficiency of operations;
b. scientific personnel shall be exchanged in Antarctica between expeditions and stations;
c. scientific observations and results from Antarctica shall be exchanged and made freely available.

2. In implementing this Article, every encouragement shall be given to the establishment of cooperative working relations with those Specialized Agencies of the United Nations and other international organizations having a scientific or technical interest in Antarctica.

Article IV

1. Nothing contained in the present Treaty shall be interpreted as:

a. a renunciation by any Contracting Party of previously asserted rights of or claims to territorial sovereignty in Antarctica;
b. a renunciation or diminution by any Contracting Party of any basis of claim to territorial sovereignty in Antarctica which it may have whether as a result of its activities or those of its nationals in Antarctica, or otherwise;
c. prejudicing the position of any Contracting Party as regards its recognition or non-recognition of any other State's rights of or claim or basis of claim to territorial sovereignty in Antarctica.

2. No acts or activities taking place while the present Treaty is in force shall constitute a basis for asserting, supporting or denying a claim to territorial sovereignty in Antarctica or create any rights of sovereignty in Antarctica. No new claim, or enlargement of an existing claim, to territorial sovereignty in Antarctica shall be asserted while the present Treaty is in force.

Article V

1. Any nuclear explosions in Antarctica and the disposal there of radioactive waste material shall be prohibited.

2. In the event of the conclusion of international agreements concerning the use of nuclear energy, including nuclear explosions and the disposal of radioactive waste material, to which all of the Contracting Parties whose representatives are entitled to participate in the meetings provided for under Article IX are parties, the rules established under such agreements shall apply in Antarctica.

Article VI

The provisions of the present Treaty shall apply to the area south of 60° South Latitude, including all ice shelves, but nothing in the present Treaty shall prejudice or in any way affect the rights, or the exercise of the rights, of any State under international law with regard to the high seas within that area.

Article VII

1. In order to promote the objectives and ensure the observance of the provisions of the present Treaty, each Contracting Party whose representatives are entitled to participate in the meetings referred to in Article IX of the Treaty shall have the right to designate observers to carry out any inspection provided for by the present Article. Observers shall be nationals of the Contracting Parties which designate them. The names of observers shall be communicated to every other Contracting Party having the right to designate observers, and like notice shall be given of the termination of their appointment.

2. Each observer designated in accordance with the provisions of paragraph 1 of this Article shall have complete freedom of access at any time to any or all areas of Antarctica.

3. All areas of Antarctica, including all stations, installations and equipment within those areas, and all ships and aircraft at points of discharging or embarking cargoes or personnel in Antarctica, shall be open at all times to inspection by any observers designated in accordance with paragraph 1 of this Article.

4. Aerial observation may be carried out at any time over any or all areas of Antarctica by any of the Contracting Parties having the right to designate observers.

5. Each Contracting Party shall, at the time when the present Treaty enters into force for it, inform the other Contracting Parties, and thereafter shall give them notice in advance, of

a. all expeditions to and within Antarctica, on the part of its ships or nationals, and all expeditions to Antarctica organized in or proceeding from its territory;
b. all stations in Antarctica occupied by its nationals; and
c. any military personnel or equipment intended to be introduced by it into Antarctica subject to the conditions prescribed in paragraph 2 of Article I of the present Treaty.

Article VIII

1. In order to facilitate the exercise of their functions under the present Treaty, and without prejudice to the respective positions of the Contracting Parties relating to jurisdiction over all other persons in Antarctica, observers designated under paragraph 1 of Article VII and scientific personnel exchanged under sub-paragraph 1(b) of Article III of the Treaty, and members of the staffs accompanying any such persons, shall be subject only to the jurisdiction of the Contracting Party of which they are nationals in respect of all acts or omissions occurring while they are in Antarctica for the purpose of exercising their functions.

2. Without prejudice to the provisions of paragraph 1 of this Article, and pending the adoption of measures in pursuance of subparagraph 1(e) of Article IX, the Contracting Parties concerned in any case of dispute with regard to the exercise of jurisdiction in Antarctica shall immediately consult together with a view to reaching a mutually acceptable solution.

Article IX

1. Representatives of the Contracting Parties named in the preamble to the present Treaty shall meet at the City of Canberra within two months after the date of entry into force of the Treaty, and thereafter at suitable intervals and places, for the purpose of exchanging information, consulting together on matters of common interest pertaining to Antarctica, and formulating and considering, and recommending to their Governments, measures in furtherance of the principles and objectives of the Treaty, including measures regarding:

a. use of Antarctica for peaceful purposes only;
b. facilitation of scientific research in Antarctica;
c. facilitation of international scientific cooperation in Antarctica;
d. facilitation of the exercise of the rights of inspection provided for in Article VII of the Treaty;
e. questions relating to the exercise of jurisdiction in Antarctica;
f. preservation and conservation of living resources in Antarctica.

2. Each Contracting Party which has become a party to the present Treaty by accession under Article XIII shall be entitled to appoint representatives to participate in the meetings referred to in paragraph 1 of the present Article, during such times as that Contracting Party demonstrates its interest in Antarctica by conducting substantial research activity there, such as the establishment of a scientific station or the despatch of a scientific expedition.

3. Reports from the observers referred to in Article VII of the present Treaty shall be transmitted to the representatives of the Contracting Parties participating in the meetings referred to in paragraph 1 of the present Article.

4. The measures referred to in paragraph 1 of this Article shall become effective when approved by all the Contracting Parties whose representatives were entitled to participate in the meetings held to consider those measures.

5. Any or all of the rights established in the present Treaty may be exercised as from the date of entry into force of the Treaty whether or not any measures facilitating the exercise of such rights have been proposed, considered or approved as provided in this Article.

Article X

Each of the Contracting Parties undertakes to exert appropriate efforts, consistent with the Charter of the United Nations, to the end that no one engages in any activity in Antarctica contrary to the principles or purposes of the present Treaty.

Article XI

1. If any dispute arises between two or more of the Contracting Parties concerning the interpretation or application of the present Treaty, those Contracting Parties shall consult among themselves with a view to having the dispute resolved by negotiation, inquiry, mediation, conciliation, arbitration, judicial settlement or other peaceful means of their own choice.

2. Any dispute of this character not so resolved shall, with the consent, in each case, of all parties to the dispute, be referred to the International Court of Justice for settlement; but failure to reach agreement on reference to the International Court shall not absolve parties to the dispute from the responsibility of continuing to seek to resolve it by any of the various peaceful means referred to in paragraph 1 of this Article.

Article XII

1a. The present Treaty may be modified or amended at any time by unanimous agreement of the Contracting Parties whose representatives are entitled to participate in the meetings provided for under Article IX. Any such modification or amendment shall enter into force when the depositary Government has received notice from all such Contracting Parties that they have ratified it.

b. Such modification or amendment shall thereafter enter into force as to any other Contracting Party when notice of ratification by it has been received by the depositary Government. Any such Contracting Party from which no notice of ratification is received within a period of two years from the date of entry into force of the modification or amendment in accordance with the provision of subparagraph 1(a) of this Article shall be deemed to have withdrawn from the present Treaty on the date of the expiration of such period.

2a. If after the expiration of thirty years from the date of entry into force of the present Treaty, any of the Contracting Parties whose representatives are entitled to participate in the meetings provided for under Article IX so requests by a communication addressed to the depositary Government, a Conference of all the Contracting Parties shall be held as soon as practicable to review the operation of the Treaty.

b. Any modification or amendment to the present Treaty which is approved at such a Conference by a majority of the Contracting Parties there represented, including a majority of those whose representatives are entitled to participate in the meetings provided for under Article IX, shall be communicated by the depositary Government to all Contracting Parties immediately after the termination of the Conference and shall enter into force in accordance with the provisions of paragraph 1 of the present Article.

c. If any such modification or amendment has not entered into force in accordance with the provisions of subparagraph 1(a) of this Article within a period of two years after the date of its communication to all the Contracting Parties, any Contracting Party may at any time after the expiration of that period give notice to the depositary Government of its withdrawal from the present Treaty; and such withdrawal shall take effect two years after the receipt of the notice by the depositary Government.

Article XIII

1. The present Treaty shall be subject to ratification by the signatory States. It shall be open for accession by any State which is a Member of the United Nations, or by any other State which may be invited to accede to the Treaty with the consent of all the Contracting Parties whose representatives are entitled to participate in the meetings provided for under Article IX of the Treaty.

2. Ratification of or accession to the present Treaty shall be effected by each State in accordance with its constitutional processes.

3. Instruments of ratification and instruments of accession shall be deposited with the Government of the United States of America, hereby designated as the depositary Government.

4. The depositary Government shall inform all signatory and acceding States of the date of each deposit of an instrument of ratification or accession, and the date of entry into force of the Treaty and of any modification or amendment thereto.

5. Upon the deposit of instruments of ratification by all the signatory States, the present Treaty shall enter into force for those States and for States which have deposited instruments of accession. Thereafter the Treaty shall enter into force for any acceding State upon the deposit of its instruments of accession.

6. The present Treaty shall be registered by the depositary Government pursuant to Article 102 of the Charter of the United Nations.

Article XIV

The present Treaty, done in the English, French, Russian and Spanish languages, each version being equally authentic, shall be deposited in the archives of the Government of the United States of America, which shall transmit duly certified copies thereof to the Governments of the signatory and acceding States.

IN WITNESS WHEREOF, the undersigned Plenipotentiaries, duly authorized, have signed the present Treaty.

DONE at Washington this first day of December, one thousand nine hundred and fifty-nine.

Protocol on Environmental Protection to the Antarctic Treaty, 4 October 1991

Editorial note

The object of the Protocol on Environmental Protection to the Antarctic Treaty is to create comprehensive protection of Antarctica's environment and dependent and associated ecosystems (Article 2). To achieve this end, the Protocol requires this protection to be considered 'fundamental' in the planning and conduct of all activities in the region (Article 3(1)). The Protocol further requires Parties to plan their activities on the basis of information sufficient to make prior assessments and informed judgements in respect of their impact on the Antarctic environment (Article 3(2)(c)). In particular, the environmental impact assessment procedures set forth in Annex I to the Protocol are to be followed for any activities related to scientific research, tourism or which require advance notice pursuant to the Antarctic Treaty (Article 8). Attached to the Protocol are four other Annexes which create specific environmental obligations: Annex II is on conservation of fauna and flora; Annex III covers waste disposal and management; Annex IV regulates the marine environment; Annex V provides for the creation of specially protected areas. In addition, the Protocol prohibits any activities connected to mineral resources other than scientific research (Article 7) and requires Parties to establish contingency response plans for environmental emergencies (Article 15).

Each Party is required to take appropriate measures to ensure compliance with the Protocol, notify other Parties of the measures it has taken, and notify other Parties of any activity which affects the implementation of the Protocol (Article 13). The Protocol provides for the inspections set out in the Antarctic Treaty to also examine compliance with the Protocol (Article 14). Parties are required to prepare annual reports on the implementation of the Protocol which are to be circulated to all Parties and made available to the public (Article 17).

The Antarctic Treaty Consultative Meetings are to set the general policy for achieving the comprehensive protection of the Antarctic environment and adopt measures in accordance with the Antarctic Treaty to implement the Protocol (Article 10(1)). The Protocol further establishes the Committee for

Environmental Protection (Article 11) to provide advice and recommendations to the Parties on the implementation of the Protocol (Article 12). Parties are permitted at any time to declare that the International Court of Justice and/or the Arbitral Tribunal provided for in the Schedule to the Protocol shall resolve any dispute regarding those provisions which pertain to mineral resources mining, environmental impact assessment, emergency response procedures, or the Annexes, to the extent that this is not in conflict with the particular Annex concerned (Article 19). If the means for resolving such a dispute is not agreed upon within twelve months of the initial request for consultations on it (Article 18), the dispute shall go, at the request of any involved Party, either to the Arbitral Tribunal or to the ICJ, unless the Parties involved otherwise agree (Article 20). Amendments to the Protocol are to occur in accordance with the procedures set forth in the Antarctic Treaty (Article 25(1)). Amendments to the Annexes are also to take place in accordance with the Antarctic Treaty, except as provided for in the Annexes themselves (Article 9). After fifty years of the date of entry into force, a Review Conference shall be held at the request of any Antarctic Treaty Consultative Party which may adopt amendments (Article 25(2)). Such amendments must be adopted by a majority of Parties, including a three-fourths majority of the Antarctic Treaty Consultative Parties (Article 19(3)) and enter into force upon ratification by three-fourths of the Antarctic Treaty Consultative Parties, including all such Parties at the time of the Protocol's adoption (Article 25(4)). Any amendment to the prohibition on resource mining must include a binding regime to determine whether and under what circumstances such activities take place and which safeguards the interests of the States listed in Article IV of the Antarctic Treaty (Article 25(5)). Reservations are not permitted to the Protocol (Article 24). The Protocol has entered into force on 14 January 1998.

Date of signature: 4 October 1991

Entry into force: 14 January 1998

Depositary: Government of the United States of America

Contracting Parties: Argentina, Australia, Austria, Belgium, Brazil, Canada, Chile, China, Colombia, Czech Republic, Denmark, Ecuador, Finland, France, Greece, Hungary, India, Italy, Japan, Netherlands, New Zealand, Norway, Peru, Poland, Korea (Democratic People's Republic of), Korea (Republic of), Romania, Russian Federation, Slovakia, South Africa, Spain, Sweden, Switzerland, United Kingdom, United States of America, Uruguay.

Protocol on Environmental Protection to the Antarctic Treaty

Preamble

The States Parties to this Protocol to the Antarctic Treaty, hereinafter referred to as the Parties,

Convinced of the need to enhance the protection of the Antarctic environment and dependent and associated ecosystems;

Convinced of the need to strengthen the Antarctic Treaty system so as to ensure that Antarctica shall continue forever to be used exclusively for peaceful purposes and shall not become the scene or object of international discord;

Bearing in mind the special legal and political status of Antarctica and the special responsibility of the Antarctic Treaty Consultative Parties to ensure that all activities in Antarctica are consistent with the purposes and principles of the Antarctic Treaty;

Recalling the designation of Antarctica as a Special Conservation Area and other measures adopted under the Antarctic Treaty system to protect the Antarctic environment and dependent and associated ecosystems;

Acknowledging further the unique opportunities Antarctica offers for scientific monitoring of and research on processes of global as well as regional importance;

Reaffirming the conservation principles of the Convention on the Conservation of Antarctic Marine Living Resources;

Convinced that the development of a comprehensive regime for the protection of the Antarctic environment and dependent and associated ecosystems is in the interest of mankind as a whole;

Desiring to supplement the Antarctic Treaty to this end;

Have agreed as follows:

Article 1
Definitions

For the purposes of this Protocol:

(a) 'The Antarctic Treaty' means the Antarctic Treaty done at Washington on 1 December 1959;

(b) 'Antarctic Treaty area' means the area to which the provisions of the Antarctic Treaty apply in accordance with Article VI of that Treaty;

(c) 'Antarctic Treaty Consultative Meetings' means the meetings referred to in Article IX of the Antarctic Treaty;

(d) 'Antarctic Treaty Consultative Parties' means the Contracting Parties to the Antarctic Treaty entitled to appoint representatives to participate in the meetings referred to in Article IX of that Treaty;

(e) 'Antarctic Treaty system' means the Antarctic Treaty, the measures in effect under that Treaty, its associated separate international instruments in force and the measures in effect under those instruments;

(f) 'Arbitral Tribunal' means the Arbitral Tribunal established in accordance
   with the Schedule to this Protocol, which forms an integral part thereof;
(g) 'Committee' means the Committee for Environmental Protection established in accordance with Article 11.

Article 2
Objective and designation

The Parties commit themselves to the comprehensive protection of the Antarctic environment and dependent and associated ecosystems and hereby designate
Antarctica as a natural reserve, devoted to peace and science.

Article 3
Environmental principles

1. The protection of the Antarctic environment and dependent and associated ecosystems and the intrinsic value of Antarctica, including its wilderness
and aesthetic values and its value as an area for the conduct of scientific research,
in particular research essential to understanding the global environment, shall
be fundamental considerations in the planning and conduct of all activities in
the Antarctic Treaty area.

2. To this end:

(a) activities in the Antarctic Treaty area shall be planned and conducted so as
   to limit adverse impacts on the Antarctic environment and dependent and
   associated ecosystems;
(b) activities in the Antarctic Treaty area shall be planned and conducted so as
   to avoid:
   (i) adverse effects on climate or weather patterns;
   (ii) significant adverse effects on air or water quality;
   (iii) significant changes in the atmospheric, terrestrial (including aquatic),
      glacial or marine environments;
   (iv) detrimental changes in the distribution, abundance or productivity
      of species or populations of species of fauna and flora;
   (v) further jeopardy to endangered or threatened species or populations
      of such species; or
   (vi) degradation of, or substantial risk to, areas of biological, scientific,
      historic, aesthetic or wilderness significance;
(c) activities in the Antarctic Treaty area shall be planned and conducted on the
   basis of information sufficient to allow prior assessments of, and informed
   judgments about, their possible impacts on the Antarctic environment and
   dependent and associated ecosystems and on the value of Antarctica for the
   conduct of scientific research; such judgments shall take full account of:
   (i) the scope of the activity, including its area, duration and intensity;
   (ii) the cumulative impacts of the activity, both by itself and in combina-
      tion with other activities in the Antarctic Treaty area;

    (iii) whether the activity will detrimentally affect any other activity in the Antarctic Treaty area;

    (iv) whether technology and procedures are available to provide for environmentally safe operations;

    (v) whether there exists the capacity to monitor key environmental parameters and ecosystem components so as to identify and provide early warning of any adverse effects of the activity and to provide for such modification of operating procedures as may be necessary in the light of the results of monitoring or increased knowledge of the Antarctic environment and dependent and associated ecosystems; and

    (vi) whether there exists the capacity to respond promptly and effectively to accidents, particularly those with potential environmental effects;

(d) regular and effective monitoring shall take place to allow assessment of the impacts of ongoing activities, including the verification of predicted impacts;

(e) regular and effective monitoring shall take place to facilitate early detection of the possible unforeseen effects of activities carried on both within and outside the Antarctic Treaty area on the Antarctic environment and dependent and associated ecosystems.

3. Activities shall be planned and conducted in the Antarctic Treaty area so as to accord priority to scientific research and to preserve the value of Antarctica as an area for the conduct of such research, including research essential to understanding the global environment.

4. Activities undertaken in the Antarctic Treaty area pursuant to scientific research programmes, tourism and all other governmental and non-governmental activities in the Antarctic Treaty area for which advance notice is required in accordance with Article VII (5) of the Antarctic Treaty, including associated logistic support activities, shall:

(a) take place in a manner consistent with the principles in this Article; and

(b) be modified, suspended or cancelled if they result in or threaten to result in impacts upon the Antarctic environment or dependent or associated ecosystems inconsistent with those principles.

Article 4
Relationship with the other components of the Antarctic Treaty system

1. This Protocol shall supplement the Antarctic Treaty and shall neither modify nor amend that Treaty.

2. Nothing in this Protocol shall derogate from the rights and obligations of the Parties to this Protocol under the other international instruments in force within the Antarctic Treaty system.

Article 5
Consistency with the other components of the Antarctic Treaty system

The Parties shall consult and co-operate with the Contracting Parties to the other international instruments in force within the Antarctic Treaty system and their respective institutions with a view to ensuring the achievement of the objectives and principles of this Protocol and avoiding any interference with the achievement of the objectives and principles of those instruments or any inconsistency between the implementation of those instruments and of this Protocol.

Article 6
Co-operation

1. The Parties shall co-operate in the planning and conduct of activities in the Antarctic Treaty area. To this end, each Party shall endeavour to:

(a) promote co-operative programmes of scientific, technical and educational value, concerning the protection of the Antarctic environment and dependent and associated ecosystems;

(b) provide appropriate assistance to other Parties in the preparation of environmental impact assessments;

(c) provide to other Parties upon request information relevant to any potential environmental risk and assistance to minimize the effects of accidents which may damage the Antarctic environment or dependent and associated ecosystems;

(d) consult with other Parties with regard to the choice of sites for prospective stations and other facilities so as to avoid the cumulative impacts caused by their excessive concentration in any location;

(e) where appropriate, undertake joint expeditions and share the use of stations and other facilities; and

(f) carry out such steps as may be agreed upon at Antarctic Treaty Consultative Meetings.

2. Each Party undertakes, to the extent possible, to share information that may be helpful to other Parties in planning and conducting their activities in the Antarctic Treaty area, with a view to the protection of the Antarctic environment and dependent and associated ecosystems.

3. The Parties shall co-operate with those Parties which may exercise jurisdiction in areas adjacent to the Antarctic Treaty area with a view to ensuring

that activities in the Antarctic Treaty area do not have adverse environmental impacts on those areas.

Article 7
Prohibition of mineral resource activities

Any activity relating to mineral resources, other than scientific research, shall be prohibited.

Article 8
Environmental impact assessment

1. Proposed activities referred to in paragraph 2 below shall be subject to the procedures set out in Annex I for prior assessment of the impacts of those activities on the Antarctic environment or on dependent or associated ecosystems according to whether those activities are identified as having:

(a) less than a minor or transitory impact;
(b) a minor or transitory impact; or
(c) more than a minor or transitory impact.

2. Each Party shall ensure that the assessment procedures set out in Annex I are applied in the planning processes leading to decisions about any activities undertaken in the Antarctic Treaty area pursuant to scientific research programmes, tourism and all other governmental and non-governmental activities in the Antarctic Treaty area for which advance notice is required under Article VII (5) of the Antarctic Treaty, including associated logistic support activities.

3. The assessment procedures set out in Annex I shall apply to any change in an activity whether the change arises from an increase or decrease in the intensity of an existing activity, from the addition of an activity, the decommissioning of a facility, or otherwise.

4. Where activities are planned jointly by more than one Party, the Parties involved shall nominate one of their number to coordinate the implementation of the environmental impact assessment procedures set out in Annex I.

Article 9
Annexes

1. The Annexes to this Protocol shall form an integral part thereof.
2. Annexes, additional to Annexes I–IV, may be adopted and become effective in accordance with Article IX of the Antarctic Treaty.
3. Amendments and modifications to Annexes may be adopted and become effective in accordance with Article IX of the Antarctic Treaty, provided that

any Annex may itself make provision for amendments and modifications to become effective on an accelerated basis.

4. Annexes and any amendments and modifications thereto which have become effective in accordance with paragraphs 2 and 3 above shall, unless an Annex itself provides otherwise in respect of the entry into effect of any amendment or modification thereto, become effective for a Contracting Party to the Antarctic Treaty which is not an Antarctic Treaty Consultative Party, or which was not an Antarctic Treaty Consultative Party at the time of the adoption, when notice of approval of that Contracting Party has been received by the Depositary.

5. Annexes shall, except to the extent that an Annex provides otherwise, be subject to the procedures for dispute settlement set out in Articles 18 to 20.

Article 10
Antarctic Treaty Consultative Meetings

1. Antarctic Treaty Consultative Meetings shall, drawing upon the best scientific and technical advice available:

(a) define, in accordance with the provisions of this Protocol, the general policy for the comprehensive protection of the Antarctic environment and dependent and associated ecosystems; and

(b) adopt measures under Article IX of the Antarctic Treaty for the implementation of this Protocol.

2. Antarctic Treaty Consultative Meetings shall review the work of the Committee and shall draw fully upon its advice and recommendations in carrying out the tasks referred to in paragraph 1 above, as well as upon the advice of the Scientific Committee on Antarctic Research.

Article 11
Committee for Environmental Protection

1. There is hereby established the Committee for Environmental Protection.

2. Each Party shall be entitled to be a member of the Committee and to appoint a representative who may be accompanied by experts and advisers.

3. Observer status in the Committee shall be open to any Contracting Party to the Antarctic Treaty which is not a Party to this Protocol.

4. The Committee shall invite the President of the Scientific Committee on Antarctic Research and the Chairman of the Scientific Committee for the Conservation of Antarctic Marine Living Resources to participate as observers at its sessions. The Committee may also, with the approval of the Antarctic Treaty Consultative Meeting, invite such other relevant scientific, environmental

and technical organisations which can contribute to its work to participate as observers at its sessions.

5. The Committee shall present a report on each of its sessions to the Antarctic Treaty Consultative Meeting. The report shall cover all matters considered at the session and shall reflect the views expressed. The report shall be circulated to the Parties and to observers attending the session, and shall thereupon be made publicly available.

6. The Committee shall adopt its rules of procedure which shall be subject to approval by the Antarctic Treaty Consultative Meeting.

Article 12
Functions of the Committee

1. The functions of the Committee shall be to provide advice and formulate recommendations to the Parties in connection with the implementation of this Protocol, including the operation of its Annexes, for consideration at Antarctic Treaty Consultative Meetings, and to perform such other functions as may be referred to it by the Antarctic Treaty Consultative Meetings. In particular, it shall provide advice on:

(a) the effectiveness of measures taken pursuant to this Protocol;

(b) the need to update, strengthen or otherwise improve such measures;

(c) the need for additional measures, including the need for additional Annexes, where appropriate;

(d) the application and implementation of the environmental impact assessment procedures set out in Article 8 and Annex I;

(e) means of minimising or mitigating environmental impacts of activities in the Antarctic Treaty area;

(f) procedures for situations requiring urgent action, including response action in environmental emergencies;

(g) the operation and further elaboration of the Antarctic Protected Area system;

(h) inspection procedures, including formats for inspection reports and check-lists for the conduct of inspections;

(i) the collection, archiving, exchange and evaluation of information related to environmental protection;

(j) the state of the Antarctic environment; and

(k) the need for scientific research, including environmental monitoring, related to the implementation of this Protocol.

2. In carrying out its functions, the Committee shall, as appropriate, consult with the Scientific Committee on Antarctic Research, the Scientific Committee for the Conservation of Antarctic Marine Living Resources and other relevant scientific, environmental and technical organizations.

Article 13
Compliance with this Protocol

1. Each Party shall take appropriate measures within its competence, including the adoption of laws and regulations, administrative actions and enforcement measures, to ensure compliance with this Protocol.

2. Each Party shall exert appropriate efforts, consistent with the Charter of the United Nations, to the end that no one engages in any activity contrary to this Protocol.

3. Each Party shall notify all other Parties of the measures it takes pursuant to paragraphs 1 and 2 above.

4. Each Party shall draw the attention of all other Parties to any activity which in its opinion affects the implementation of the objectives and principles of this Protocol.

5. The Antarctic Treaty Consultative Meetings shall draw the attention of any State which is not a Party to this Protocol to any activity undertaken by that State, its agencies, instrumentalities, natural or juridical persons, ships, aircraft or other means of transport which affects the implementation of the objectives and principles of this Protocol.

Article 14
Inspection

1. In order to promote the protection of the Antarctic environment and dependent and associated ecosystems, and to ensure compliance with this Protocol, the Antarctic Treaty Consultative Parties shall arrange, individually or collectively, for inspections by observers to be made in accordance with Article VII of the Antarctic Treaty.

2. Observers are:

(a) observers designated by any Antarctic Treaty Consultative Party who shall be nationals of that Party; and

(b) any observers designated at Antarctic Treaty Consultative Meetings to carry out inspections under procedures to be established by an Antarctic Treaty Consultative Meeting.

3. Parties shall co-operate fully with observers undertaking inspections, and shall ensure that during inspections, observers are given access to all parts of stations, installations, equipment, ships and aircraft open to inspection under Article VII (3) of the Antarctic Treaty, as well as to all records maintained thereon which are called for pursuant to this Protocol.

4. Reports of inspections shall be sent to the Parties whose stations, installations, equipment, ships or aircraft are covered by the reports. After those Parties have been given the opportunity to comment, the reports and any comments thereon shall be circulated to all the Parties and to the Committee, considered

at the next Antarctic Treaty Consultative Meeting, and thereafter made publicly available.

Article 15
Emergency response action

1. In order to respond to environmental emergencies in the Antarctic Treaty area, each Party agrees to:

(a) provide for prompt and effective response action to such emergencies which might arise in the performance of scientific research programmes, tourism and all other governmental and nongovernmental activities in the Antarctic Treaty area for which advance notice is required under Article VII (5) of the Antarctic Treaty, including associated logistic support activities; and

(b) establish contingency plans for response to incidents with potential adverse effects on the Antarctic environment or dependent and associated ecosystems.

2. To this end, the Parties shall:

(a) co-operate in the formulation and implementation of such contingency plans; and

(b) establish procedures for immediate notification of, and co-operative response to, environmental emergencies.

3. In the implementation of this Article, the Parties shall draw upon the advice of the appropriate international organisations.

Article 16
Liability

Consistent with the objectives of this Protocol for the comprehensive protection of the Antarctic environment and dependent and associated ecosystems, the Parties undertake to elaborate rules and procedures relating to liability for damage arising from activities taking place in the Antarctic Treaty area and covered by this Protocol. Those rules and procedures shall be included in one or more Annexes to be adopted in accordance with Article 9 (2).

Article 17
Annual report by Parties

1. Each Party shall report annually on the steps taken to implement this Protocol. Such reports shall include notifications made in accordance with Article 13 (3), contingency plans established in accordance with Article 15 and any other notifications and information called for pursuant to this Protocol for which there is no other provision concerning the circulation and exchange of information.

2. Reports made in accordance with paragraph 1 above shall be circulated to all Parties and to the Committee, considered at the next Antarctic Treaty Consultative Meeting, and made publicly available.

Article 18
Dispute settlement

If a dispute arises concerning the interpretation or application of this Protocol, the parties to the dispute shall, at the request of any one of them, consult among themselves as soon as possible with a view to having the dispute resolved by negotiation, inquiry, mediation, conciliation arbitration, judicial settlement or other peaceful means to which the parties to the dispute agree.

Article 19
Choice of dispute settlement procedure

1. Each Party, when signing, ratifying, accepting, approving or acceding to this Protocol, or at any time thereafter, may choose, by written declaration, one or both of the following means for the settlement of disputes concerning the interpretation or application of Articles 7, 8 and 15 and, except to the extent that an Annex provides otherwise, the provisions of any Annex and, insofar as it relates to these Articles and provisions, Article 13:

(a) the International Court of Justice;
(b) the Arbitral Tribunal.

2. A declaration made under paragraph 1 above shall not affect the operation of Article 18 and Article 20 (2).

3. A Party which has not made a declaration under paragraph 1 above or in respect of which a declaration is no longer in force shall be deemed to have accepted the competence of the Arbitral Tribunal.

4. If the parties to a dispute have accepted the same means for the settlement of a dispute, the dispute may be submitted only to that procedure, unless the parties otherwise agree.

5. If the parties to a dispute have not accepted the same means for the settlement of a dispute, or if they have both accepted both means, the dispute may be submitted only to the Arbitral Tribunal, unless the parties otherwise agree.

6. A declaration made under paragraph 1 above shall remain in force until it expires in accordance with its terms or until three months after written notice of revocation has been deposited with the Depositary.

7. A new declaration, a notice of revocation or the expiry of a declaration shall not in any way affect proceedings pending before the International Court of Justice or the Arbitral Tribunal, unless the parties to the dispute otherwise agree.

8. Declarations and notices referred to in this Article shall be deposited with the Depositary who shall transmit copies thereof to all Parties.

Article 20
Dispute settlement procedure

1. If the parties to a dispute concerning the interpretation or application of Articles 7, 8 or 15 or, except to the extent that an Annex provides otherwise, the provisions of any Annex or, insofar as it relates to these Articles and provisions, Article 13, have not agreed on a means for resolving it within 12 months of the request for consultation pursuant to Article 18, the dispute shall be referred, at the request of any party to the dispute, for settlement in accordance with the procedure determined by Article 19 (4) and (5).

2. The Arbitral Tribunal shall not be competent to decide or rule upon any matter within the scope of Article IV of the Antarctic Treaty. In addition, nothing in this Protocol shall be interpreted as conferring competence or jurisdiction on the International Court of Justice or any other tribunal established for the purpose of settling disputes between Parties to decide or otherwise rule upon any matter within the scope of Article IV of the Antarctic Treaty.

Article 21
Signature

This Protocol shall be open for signature at Madrid on the 4th of October 1991 and thereafter at Washington until the 3rd of October 1992 by any State which is a Contracting Party to the Antarctic Treaty.

Article 22
Ratification, acceptance, approval or accession

1. This Protocol is subject to ratification, acceptance or approval by signatory States.

2. After the 3rd of October 1992 this Protocol shall be open for accession by any State which is a Contracting Party to the Antarctic Treaty.

3. Instruments of ratification, acceptance, approval or accession shall be deposited with the Government of the United States of America, hereby designated as the Depositary.

4. After the date on which this Protocol has entered into force, the Antarctic Treaty Consultative Parties shall not act upon a notification regarding the entitlement of a Contracting Party to the Antarctic Treaty to appoint representatives to participate in Antarctic Treaty Consultative Meetings in accordance with Article IX (2) of the Antarctic Treaty unless that Contracting Party has first ratified, accepted, approved or acceded to this Protocol.

Article 23
Entry into force

1. This Protocol shall enter into force on the thirtieth day following the date of deposit of instruments of ratification, acceptance, approval or accession by

all States which are Antarctic Treaty Consultative Parties at the date on which this Protocol is adopted.

2. For each Contracting Party to the Antarctic Treaty which, subsequent to the date of entry into force of this Protocol, deposits an instrument of ratification, acceptance, approval or accession, this Protocol shall enter into force on the thirtieth day following such deposit.

Article 24
Reservations

Reservations to this Protocol shall not be permitted.

Article 25
Modification or amendment

1. Without prejudice to the provisions of Article 9, this Protocol may be modified or amended at any time in accordance with the procedures set forth in Article XII (1) (a) and (b) of the Antarctic Treaty.

2. If, after the expiration of 50 years from the date of entry into force of this Protocol, any of the Antarctic Treaty Consultative Parties so requests by a communication addressed to the Depositary, a conference shall be held as soon as practicable to review the operation of this Protocol.

3. A modification or amendment proposed at any Review Conference called pursuant to paragraph 2 above shall be adopted by a majority of the Parties, including 3/4 of the States which are Antarctic Treaty Consultative Parties at the time of adoption of this Protocol.

4. A modification or amendment adopted pursuant to paragraph 3 above shall enter into force upon ratification, acceptance, approval or accession by 3/4 of the Antarctic Treaty Consultative Parties, including ratification, acceptance, approval or accession by all States which are Antarctic Treaty Consultative Parties at the time of adoption of this Protocol.

5.

(a) With respect to Article 7, the prohibition on Antarctic mineral resource activities contained therein shall continue unless there is in force a binding legal regime on Antarctic mineral resource activities that includes an agreed means for determining whether, and, if so, under which conditions, any such activities would be acceptable. This regime shall fully safeguard the interests of all States referred to in Article IV of the Antarctic Treaty and apply the principles thereof. Therefore, if a modification or amendment to Article 7 is proposed at a Review Conference referred to in paragraph 2 above, it shall include such a binding legal regime.

(b) If any such modification or amendment has not entered into force within 3 years of the date of its adoption, any Party may at any time thereafter notify to the Depositary of its withdrawal from this Protocol, and such withdrawal shall take effect 2 years after receipt of the notification by the Depositary.

Article 26
Notifications by the Depositary

The Depositary shall notify all Contracting Parties to the Antarctic Treaty of the following:

(a) signatures of this Protocol and the deposit of instruments of ratification, acceptance, approval or accession;
(b) the date of entry into force of this Protocol and any additional Annex thereto;
(c) the date of entry into force of any amendment or modification to this Protocol;
(d) the deposit of declarations and notices pursuant to Article 19; and
(e) any notification received pursuant to Article 25 (5) (b).

Article 27
Authentic texts and registration with the United Nations

1. This Protocol, done in the English, French, Russian and Spanish languages, each version being equally authentic, shall be deposited in the archives of the Government of the United States of America, which shall transmit duly certified copies thereof to all Contracting Parties to the Antarctic Treaty.

2. This Protocol shall be registered by the Depositary pursuant to Article 102 of the Charter of the United Nations.

Schedule
Arbitration

Article 1

1. The Arbitral Tribunal shall be constituted and shall function in accordance with the Protocol, including this Schedule.

2. The Secretary referred to in this Schedule is the Secretary General of the Permanent Court of Arbitration.

Article 2

1. Each Party shall be entitled to designate up to three Arbitrators, at least one of whom shall be designated within three months of the entry into force of the Protocol for that Party. Each Arbitrator shall be experienced in Antarctic affairs, have thorough knowledge of international law and enjoy the highest reputation for fairness, competence and integrity. The names of the persons so designated shall constitute the list of Arbitrators. Each Party shall at all times maintain the name of at least one Arbitrator on the list.

2. Subject to paragraph 3 below, an Arbitrator designated by a Party shall remain on the list for a period of five years and shall be eligible for redesignation by that Party for additional five year periods.

3. A Party which designated an Arbitrator may withdraw the name of that Arbitrator from the list. If an Arbitrator dies or if a Party for any reason withdraws from the list the name of an Arbitrator designated by it, the Party which designated the Arbitrator in question shall notify the Secretary promptly. An Arbitrator whose name is withdrawn from the list shall continue to serve on any Arbitral Tribunal to which that Arbitrator has been appointed until the completion of proceedings before the Arbitral Tribunal.

4. The Secretary shall ensure that an up-to-date list is maintained of the Arbitrators designated pursuant to this Article.

Article 3

1. The Arbitral Tribunal shall be composed of three Arbitrators who shall be appointed as follows:

(a) The party to the dispute commencing the proceedings shall appoint one Arbitrator, who may be its national, from the list referred to in Article 2. This appointment shall be included in the notification referred to in Article 4.

(b) Within 40 days of the receipt of that notification, the other party to the dispute shall appoint the second Arbitrator, who may be its national, from the list referred to in Article 2.

(c) Within 60 days of the appointment of the second Arbitrator, the parties to the dispute shall appoint by agreement the third Arbitrator from the list referred to in Article 2.
   The third Arbitrator shall not be either a national of a party to the dispute, or a person designated for the list referred to in Article 2 by a party to the dispute, or of the same nationality as either of the first two Arbitrators. The third Arbitrator shall be the Chairperson of the Arbitral Tribunal.

(d) If the second Arbitrator has not been appointed within the prescribed period, or if the parties to the dispute have not reached agreement within the prescribed period on the appointment of the third Arbitrator, the Arbitrator or Arbitrators shall be appointed, at the request of any party to the dispute and within 30 days of the receipt of such request, by the President of the International Court of Justice from the list referred to in Article 2 and subject to the conditions prescribed in subparagraphs (b) and (c) above. In performing the functions accorded him or her in this subparagraph, the President of the Court shall consult the parties to the dispute.

(e) If the President of the International Court of Justice is unable to perform the functions accorded him or her in subparagraph (d) above or is a national of a party to the dispute, the functions shall be performed by the Vice-President of the Court, except that if the Vice-President is unable to perform the functions or is a national of a party to the dispute the functions shall be performed by the next most senior member of the Court who is available and is not a national of a party to the dispute.

2. Any vacancy shall be filled in the manner prescribed for the initial appointment.

3. In any dispute involving more than two Parties, those Parties having the same interest shall appoint one Arbitrator by agreement within the period specified in paragraph 1 (b) above.

Article 4

The party to the dispute commencing proceedings shall so notify the other party or parties to the dispute and the Secretary in writing. Such notification shall include a statement of the claim and the grounds on which it is based. The notification shall be transmitted by the Secretary to all Parties.

Article 5

1. Unless the parties to the dispute agree otherwise, arbitration shall take place at The Hague, where the records of the Arbitral Tribunal shall be kept. The Arbitral Tribunal shall adopt its own rules of procedure. Such rules shall ensure that each party to the dispute has a full opportunity to be heard and to present its case and shall also ensure that the proceedings are conducted expeditiously.

2. The Arbitral Tribunal may hear and decide counterclaims arising out of the dispute.

Article 6

1. The Arbitral Tribunal, where it considers that prima facie it has jurisdiction under the Protocol, may:

(a) at the request of any party to a dispute, indicate such provisional measures as it considers necessary to preserve the respective rights of the parties to the dispute;
(b) prescribe any provisional measures which it considers appropriate under the circumstances to prevent serious harm to the Antarctic environment or dependent or associated ecosystems.

2. The parties to the dispute shall comply promptly with any provisional measures prescribed under paragraph 1 (b) above pending an award under Article 10.

3. Notwithstanding the time period in Article 20 of the Protocol, a party to a dispute may at any time, by notification to the other party or parties to the dispute and to the Secretary in accordance with Article 4, request that the Arbitral Tribunal be constituted as a matter of exceptional urgency to indicate

or prescribe emergency provisional measures in accordance with this Article. In such case, the Arbitral Tribunal shall be constituted as soon as possible in accordance with Article 3, except that the time periods in Article 3 (1) (b), (c) and (d) shall be reduced to 14 days in each case. The Arbitral Tribunal shall decide upon the request for emergency provisional measures within two months of the appointment of its Chairperson.

4. Following a decision by the Arbitral Tribunal upon a request for emergency provisional measures in accordance with paragraph 3 above, settlement of the dispute shall proceed in accordance with Articles 18, 19 and 20 of the Protocol.

Article 7

Any Party which believes it has a legal interest, whether general or individual, which may be substantially affected by the award of an Arbitral Tribunal, may, unless the Arbitral Tribunal decides otherwise, intervene in the proceedings.

Article 8

The parties to the dispute shall facilitate the work of the Arbitral Tribunal and, in particular, in accordance with their law and using all means at their disposal, shall provide it with all relevant documents and information, and enable it, when necessary, to call witnesses or experts and receive their evidence.

Article 9

If one of the parties to the dispute does not appear before the Arbitral Tribunal or fails to defend its case, any other party to the dispute may request the Arbitral Tribunal to continue the proceedings and make its award.

Article 10

1. The Arbitral Tribunal shall, on the basis of the provisions of the Protocol and other applicable rules and principles of international law that are not incompatible with such provisions, decide such disputes as are submitted to it.

2. The Arbitral Tribunal may decide, *ex aequo et bono*, a dispute submitted to it, if the parties to the dispute so agree.

Article 11

1. Before making its award, the Arbitral Tribunal shall satisfy itself that it has competence in respect of the dispute and that the claim or counterclaim is well founded in fact and law.

2. The award shall be accompanied by a statement of reasons for the decision and shall be communicated to the Secretary who shall transmit it to all Parties.

3. The award shall be final and binding on the parties to the dispute and on any Party which intervened in the proceedings and shall be complied with without delay. The Arbitral Tribunal shall interpret the award at the request of a party to the dispute or of any intervening Party.

4. The award shall have no binding force except in respect of that particular case.

5. Unless the Arbitral Tribunal decides otherwise, the expenses of the Arbitral Tribunal, including the remuneration of the Arbitrators, shall be borne by the parties to the dispute in equal shares.

Article 12

All decisions of the Arbitral Tribunal, including those referred to in Articles 5, 6 and 11, shall be made by a majority of the Arbitrators who may not abstain from voting.

Article 13

1. This Schedule may be amended or modified by a measure adopted in accordance with Article IX (1) of the Antarctic Treaty. Unless the measure specifies otherwise, the amendment or modification shall be deemed to have been approved, and shall become effective, one year after the close of the Antarctic Treaty Consultative Meeting at which it was adopted, unless one or more of the Antarctic Treaty Consultative Parties notifies the Depositary, within that time period, that it wishes an extension of that period or that it is unable to approve the measure.

2. Any amendment or modification of this Schedule which becomes effective in accordance with paragraph 1 above shall thereafter become effective as to any other Party when notice of approval by it has been received by the Depositary.

Annex I
Environmental impact assessment

Article 1
Preliminary stage

1. The environmental impacts of proposed activities referred to in Article 8 of the Protocol shall, before their commencement, be considered in accordance with appropriate national procedures.

2. If an activity is determined as having less than a minor or transitory impact, the activity may proceed forthwith.

Article 2
Initial environmental evaluation

1. Unless it has been determined that an activity will have less than a minor or transitory impact, or unless a Comprehensive Environmental Evaluation is being prepared in accordance with Article 3, an Initial Environmental Evaluation shall be prepared. It shall contain sufficient detail to assess whether

a proposed activity may have more than a minor or transitory impact and shall include:

(a) a description of the proposed activity, including its purpose, location, duration, and intensity; and
(b) consideration of alternatives to the proposed activity and any impacts that the activity may have, including consideration of cumulative impacts in the light of existing and known planned activities.

2. If an Initial Environmental Evaluation indicates that a proposed activity is likely to have no more than a minor or transitory impact, the activity may proceed, provided that appropriate procedures, which may include monitoring, are put in place to assess and verify the impact of the activity.

Article 3
Comprehensive environmental evaluation

1. If an Initial Environmental Evaluation indicates or if it is otherwise determined that a proposed activity is likely to have more than a minor or transitory impact, a Comprehensive Environmental Evaluation shall be prepared.
2. A Comprehensive Environmental Evaluation shall include:

(a) a description of the proposed activity including its purpose, location, duration and intensity, and possible alternatives to the activity, including the alternative of not proceeding, and the consequences of those alternatives;
(b) a description of the initial environmental reference state with which predicted changes are to be compared and a prediction of the future environmental reference state in the absence of the proposed activity;
(c) a description of the methods and data used to forecast the impacts of the proposed activity;
(d) estimation of the nature, extent, duration, and intensity of the likely direct impacts of the proposed activity;
(e) consideration of possible indirect or second order impacts of the proposed activity;
(f) consideration of cumulative impacts of the proposed activity in the light of existing activities and other known planned activities;
(g) identification of measures, including monitoring programmes, that could be taken to minimise or mitigate impacts of the proposed activity and to detect unforeseen impacts and that could provide early warning of any adverse effects of the activity as well as to deal promptly and effectively with accidents;
(h) identification of unavoidable impacts of the proposed activity;
(i) consideration of the effects of the proposed activity on the conduct of scientific research and on other existing uses and values;

(j) an identification of gaps in knowledge and uncertainties encountered in compiling the information required under this paragraph;
(k) a non-technical summary of the information provided under this paragraph; and
(l) the name and address of the person or organization which prepared the Comprehensive Environmental Evaluation and the address to which comments thereon should be directed.

3. The draft Comprehensive Environmental Evaluation shall be made publicly available and shall be circulated to all Parties, which shall also make it publicly available, for comment. A period of 90 days shall be allowed for the receipt of comments.

4. The draft Comprehensive Environmental Evaluation shall be forwarded to the Committee at the same time as it is circulated to the Parties, and at least 120 days before the next Antarctic Treaty Consultative Meeting, for consideration as appropriate.

5. No final decision shall be taken to proceed with the proposed activity in the Antarctic Treaty area unless there has been an opportunity for consideration of the draft Comprehensive Environmental Evaluation by the Antarctic Treaty Consultative Meeting on the advice of the Committee, provided that no decision to proceed with a proposed activity shall be delayed through the operation of this paragraph for longer than 15 months from the date of circulation of the draft Comprehensive Environmental Evaluation.

6. A final Comprehensive Environmental Evaluation shall address and shall include or summarise comments received on the draft Comprehensive Environmental Evaluation. The final Comprehensive Environmental Evaluation, notice of any decisions relating thereto, and any evaluation of the significance of the predicted impacts in relation to the advantages of the proposed activity, shall be circulated to all Parties, which shall also make them publicly available, at least 60 days before the commencement of the proposed activity in the Antarctic Treaty area.

Article 4
Decisions to be based on comprehensive environmental evaluations

Any decision on whether a proposed activity, to which Article 3 applies, should proceed, and, if so, whether in its original or in a modified form, shall be based on the Comprehensive Environmental Evaluation as well as other relevant considerations.

Article 5
Monitoring

1. Procedures shall be put in place, including appropriate monitoring of key environmental indicators, to assess and verify the impact of any activity

that proceeds following the completion of a Comprehensive Environmental Evaluation.

2. The procedures referred to in paragraph 1 above and in Article 2 (2) shall be designed to provide a regular and verifiable record of the impacts of the activity in order, *inter alia*, to:

(a) enable assessments to be made of the extent to which such impacts are consistent with the Protocol; and

(b) provide information useful for minimising or mitigating impacts, and, where appropriate, information on the need for suspension, cancellation or modification of the activity.

Article 6
Circulation of information

1. The following information shall be circulated to the Parties, forwarded to the Committee and made publicly available:

(a) a description of the procedures referred to in Article 1;

(b) an annual list of any Initial Environmental Evaluations prepared in accordance with Article 2 and any decisions taken in consequence thereof;

(c) significant information obtained, and any action taken in consequence thereof, from procedures put in place in accordance with Articles 2(2) and 5; and

(d) information referred to in Article 3 (6).

2. Any Initial Environmental Evaluation prepared in accordance with Article 2 shall be made available on request.

Article 7
Cases of emergency

1. This Annex shall not apply in cases of emergency relating to the safety of human life or of ships, aircraft or equipment and facilities of high value, or the protection of the environment, which require an activity to be undertaken without completion of the procedures set out in this Annex.

2. Notice of activities undertaken in cases of emergency, which would otherwise have required preparation of a Comprehensive Environmental Evaluation, shall be circulated immediately to all Parties and to the Committee and a full explanation of the activities carried out shall be provided within 90 days of those activities.

Article 8
Amendment or modification

1. This Annex may be amended or modified by a measure adopted in accordance with Article IX (1) of the Antarctic Treaty. Unless the measure specifies otherwise, the amendment or modification shall be deemed to have been

approved, and shall become effective, one year after the close of the Antarctic Treaty Consultative Meeting at which it was adopted, unless one or more of the Antarctic Treaty Consultative Parties notifies the Depositary, within that period, that it wishes an extension of that period or that it is unable to approve the measure.

2. Any amendment or modification of this Annex which becomes effective in accordance with paragraph 1 above shall thereafter become effective as to any other Party when notice of approval by it has been received by the Depositary.

Annex II
Conservation of Antarctic fauna and flora

Article 1
Definitions

For the purposes of this Annex:

(a) 'native mammal' means any member of any species belonging to the Class Mammalia, indigenous to the Antarctic Treaty area or occurring there seasonally through natural migrations;

(b) 'native bird' means any member, at any stage of its life cycle (including eggs), of any species of the Class Aves indigenous to the Antarctic Treaty area or occurring there seasonally through natural migrations;

(c) 'native plant' means any terrestrial or freshwater vegetation, including bryophytes, lichens, fungi and algae, at any stage of its life cycle (including seeds, and other propagules), indigenous to the Antarctic Treaty area;

(d) 'native invertebrate' means any terrestrial or freshwater invertebrate, at any stage of its life cycle, indigenous to the Antarctic Treaty area;

(e) 'appropriate authority' means any person or agency authorized by a Party to issue permits under this Annex;

(f) 'permit' means a formal permission in writing issued by an appropriate authority;

(g) 'take' or 'taking' means to kill, injure, capture, handle or molest, a native mammal or bird, or to remove or damage such quantities of native plants that their local distribution or abundance would be significantly affected;

(h) 'harmful interference' means:

  (i) flying or landing helicopters or other aircraft in a manner that disturbs concentrations of birds and seals;

  (ii) using vehicles or vessels, including hovercraft and small boats, in a manner that disturbs concentrations of birds and seals;

  (iii) using explosives or firearms in a manner that disturbs concentrations of birds and seals;

  (iv) wilfully disturbing breeding or moulting birds or concentrations of birds and seals by persons on foot;

(v) significantly damaging concentrations of native terrestrial plants by landing aircraft, driving vehicles, or walking on them, or by other means; and

(vi) any activity that results in the significant adverse modification of habitats of any species or population of native mammal, bird, plant or invertebrate.

(i) 'International Convention for the Regulation of Whaling' means the Convention done at Washington on 2 December 1946.

Article 2
Cases of emergency

1. This Annex shall not apply in cases of emergency relating to the safety of human life or of ships, aircraft, or equipment and facilities of high value, or the protection of the environment.

2. Notice of activities undertaken in cases of emergency shall be circulated immediately to all Parties and to the Committee.

Article 3
Protection of native fauna and flora

1. Taking or harmful interference shall be prohibited, except in accordance with a permit.

2. Such permits shall specify the authorized activity, including when, where and by whom it is to be conducted and shall be issued only in the following circumstances:

(a) to provide specimens for scientific study or scientific information;

(b) to provide specimens for museums, herbaria, zoological and botanical gardens, or other educational or cultural institutions or uses; and

(c) to provide for unavoidable consequences of scientific activities not otherwise authorized under sub-paragraphs (a) or (b) above, or of the construction and operation of scientific support facilities.

3. The issue of such permits shall be limited so as to ensure that:

(a) no more native mammals, birds, or plants are taken than are strictly necessary to meet the purposes set forth in paragraph 2 above;

(b) only small numbers of native mammals or birds are killed and in no case more native mammals or birds are killed from local populations than can, in combination with other permitted takings, normally be replaced by natural reproduction in the following season; and

(c) the diversity of species, as well as the habitats essential to their existence, and the balance of the ecological systems existing within the Antarctic Treaty area are maintained.

4. Any species of native mammals, birds and plants listed in Appendix A to this Annex shall be designated 'Specially Protected Species', and shall be accorded special protection by the Parties.

5. A permit shall not be issued to take a Specially Protected Species unless the taking:

(a) is for a compelling scientific purpose;
(b) will not jeopardize the survival or recovery of that species or local population; and
(c) uses non-lethal techniques where appropriate.

6. All taking of native mammals and birds shall be done in the manner that involves the least degree of pain and suffering practicable.

Article 4
Introduction of non-native species, parasites and diseases

1. No species of animal or plant not native to the Antarctic Treaty area shall be introduced onto land or ice shelves, or into water in the Antarctic Treaty area except in accordance with a permit.

2. Dogs shall not be introduced onto land or ice shelves and dogs currently in those areas shall be removed by April 1, 1994.

3. Permits under paragraph 1 above shall be issued to allow the importation only of the animals and plants listed in Appendix B to this Annex and shall specify the species, numbers and, if appropriate, age and sex and precautions to be taken to prevent escape or contact with native fauna and flora.

4. Any plant or animal for which a permit has been issued in accordance with paragraphs 1 and 3 above, shall, prior to expiration of the permit, be removed from the Antarctic Treaty area or be disposed of by incineration or equally effective means that eliminates risk to native fauna or flora. The permit shall specify this obligation. Any other plant or animal introduced into the Antarctic Treaty area not native to that area, including any progeny, shall be removed or disposed of, by incineration or by equally effective means, so as to be rendered sterile, unless it is determined that they pose no risk to native flora or fauna.

5. Nothing in this Article shall apply to the importation of food into the Antarctic Treaty area provided that no live animals are imported for this purpose and all plants and animal parts and products are kept under carefully controlled conditions and disposed of in accordance with Annex III to the Protocol and Appendix C to this Annex.

6. Each Party shall require that precautions, including those listed in Appendix C to this Annex, be taken to prevent the introduction of micro-organisms (e.g., viruses, bacteria, parasites, yeasts, fungi) not present in the native fauna and flora.

Article 5
Information

Each Party shall prepare and make available information setting forth, in particular, prohibited activities and providing lists of Specially Protected Species and relevant Protected Areas to all those persons present in or intending to enter the Antarctic Treaty area with a view to ensuring that such persons understand and observe the provisions of this Annex.

Article 6
Exchange of information

1. The Parties shall make arrangements for:

(a) collecting and exchanging records (including records of permits) and statistics concerning the numbers or quantities of each species of native mammal, bird or plant taken annually in the Antarctic Treaty area;
(b) obtaining and exchanging information as to the status of native mammals, birds, plants, and invertebrates in the Antarctic Treaty area, and the extent to which any species or population needs protection;
(c) establishing a common form in which this information shall be submitted by Parties in accordance with paragraph 2 below.

2. Each Party shall inform the other Parties as well as the Committee before the end of November of each year of any step taken pursuant to paragraph 1 above and of the number and nature of permits issued under this Annex in the preceding period of 1st July to 30th June.

Article 7
Relationship with other agreements outside the Antarctic Treaty system

Nothing in this Annex shall derogate from the rights and obligations of Parties under the International Convention for the Regulation of Whaling.

Article 8
Review

The Parties shall keep under continuing review measures for the conservation of Antarctic fauna and flora, taking into account any recommendations from the Committee.

Article 9
Amendment or modification

1. This Annex may be amended or modified by a measure adopted in accordance with Article IX (1) of the Antarctic Treaty. Unless the measure specifies otherwise, the amendment or modification shall be deemed to have been

approved, and shall become effective, one year after the close of the Antarctic Treaty Consultative Meeting at which it was adopted, unless one or more of the Antarctic Treaty Consultative Parties notifies the Depositary, within that time period, that it wishes an extension of that period or that it is unable to approve the measure.

2. Any amendment or modification of this Annex which becomes effective in accordance with paragraph 1 above shall thereafter become effective as to any other Party when notice of approval by it has been received by the Depositary.

Appendices to the Annex

Appendix A
Specially protected species

All species of the genus *Arctocephalus*, Fur Seals. *Ommatophoca rossii*, Ross Seal.

Appendix B
Importation of animals and plants

The following animals and plants may be imported into the Antarctic Treaty area in accordance with permits issued under Article 4 of this Annex:

(a) domestic plants; and
(b) laboratory animals and plants including viruses, bacteria, yeasts and fungi.

Appendix C
Precautions to prevent introduction of micro-organisms

1. Poultry. No live poultry or other living birds shall be brought into the Antarctic Treaty area. Before dressed poultry is packaged for shipment to the Antarctic Treaty area, it shall be inspected for evidence of disease, such as Newcastle's Disease, tuberculosis, and yeast infection. Any poultry or parts not consumed shall be removed from the Antarctic Treaty area or disposed of by incineration or equivalent means that eliminates risks to native flora and fauna.

2. The importation of non-sterile soil shall be avoided to the maximum extent practicable.

Annex III
Waste disposal and waste management

Article 1
General obligations

1. This Annex shall apply to activities undertaken in the Antarctic Treaty area pursuant to scientific research programmes, tourism and all other governmental and nongovernmental activities in the Antarctic Treaty area for

which advance notice is required under Article VII (5) of the Antarctic Treaty, including associated logistic support activities.

2. The amount of wastes produced or disposed of in the Antarctic Treaty area shall be reduced as far as practicable so as to minimise impact on the Antarctic environment and to minimise interference with the natural values of Antarctica, with scientific research and with other uses of Antarctica which are consistent with the Antarctic Treaty.

3. Waste storage, disposal and removal from the Antarctic Treaty area, as well as recycling and source reduction, shall be essential considerations in the planning and conduct of activities in the Antarctic Treaty area.

4. Wastes removed from the Antarctic Treaty area shall, to the maximum extent practicable, be returned to the country from which the activities generating the waste were organized or to any other country in which arrangements have been made for the disposal of such wastes in accordance with relevant international agreements.

5. Past and present waste disposal sites on land and abandoned work sites of Antarctic activities shall be cleaned up by the generator of such wastes and the user of such sites. This obligation shall not be interpreted as requiring:

(a) the removal of any structure designated as a historic site or monument; or
(b) the removal of any structure or waste material in circumstances where the removal by any practical option would result in greater adverse environmental impact than leaving the structure or waste material in its existing location.

Article 2
Waste disposal by removal from the Antarctic Treaty area

1. The following wastes, if generated after entry into force of this Annex, shall be removed from the Antarctic Treaty area by the generator of such wastes:

(a) radio-active materials;
(b) electrical batteries;
(c) fuel, both liquid and solid;
(d) wastes containing harmful levels of heavy metals or acutely toxic or harmful persistent compounds;
(e) poly-vinyl chloride (PVC), polyurethane foam, polystyrene foam, rubber and lubricating oils, treated timbers and other products which contain additives that could produce harmful emissions if incinerated;
(f) all other plastic wastes, except low density polyethylene containers (such as bags for storing wastes), provided that such containers shall be incinerated in accordance with Article 3(1);
(g) fuel drums; and
(h) other solid, non-combustible wastes;

provided that the obligation to remove drums and solid non-combustible wastes contained in subparagraphs (g) and (h) above shall not apply in circumstances where the removal of such wastes by any practical option would result in greater adverse environmental impact than leaving them in their existing locations.

2. Liquid wastes which are not covered by paragraph 1 above and sewage and domestic liquid wastes, shall, to the maximum extent practicable, be removed from the Antarctic Treaty area by the generator of such wastes.

3. The following wastes shall be removed from the Antarctic Treaty area by the generator of such wastes, unless incinerated, autoclaved or otherwise treated to be made sterile:

(a) residues of carcasses of imported animals;
(b) laboratory culture of micro-organisms and plant pathogens; and
(c) introduced avian products.

Article 3
Waste disposal by incineration

1. Subject to paragraph 2 below, combustible wastes, other than those referred to in Article 2 (1), which are not removed from the Antarctic Treaty area shall be burnt in incinerators which to the maximum extent practicable reduce harmful emissions. Any emission standards and equipment guidelines which may be recommended by, *inter alia*, the Committee and the Scientific Committee on Antarctic Research shall be taken into account. The solid residue of such incineration shall be removed from the Antarctic Treaty area.

2. All open burning of wastes shall be phased out as soon as practicable, but no later than the end of the 1998/1999 season. Pending the completion of such phase-out, when it is necessary to dispose of wastes by open burning, allowance shall be made for the wind direction and speed and the type of wastes to be burnt to limit particulate deposition and to avoid such deposition over areas of special biological, scientific, historic, aesthetic or wilderness significance including, in particular, areas accorded protection under the Antarctic Treaty.

Article 4
Other waste disposal on land

1. Wastes not removed or disposed of in accordance with Articles 2 and 3 shall not be disposed of onto ice-free areas or into fresh water systems.

2. Sewage, domestic liquid wastes and other liquid wastes not removed from the Antarctic Treaty area in accordance with Article 2, shall, to the maximum extent practicable, not be disposed of onto sea ice, ice shelves or the grounded ice-sheet, provided that such wastes which are generated by stations located inland on ice shelves or on the grounded ice-sheet may be disposed of in deep ice pits where such disposal is the only practicable option. Such pits shall not

be located on known ice-flow lines which terminate at ice-free areas or in areas of high ablation.

3. Wastes generated at field camps shall, to the maximum extent practicable, be removed by the generator of such wastes to supporting stations or ships for disposal in accordance with this Annex.

Article 5
Disposal of waste in the sea

1. Sewage and domestic liquid wastes may be discharged directly into the sea, taking into account the assimilative capacity of the receiving marine environment and provided that:

(a) such discharge is located, wherever practicable, where conditions exist for initial dilution and rapid dispersal; and

(b) large quantities of such wastes (generated in a station where the average weekly occupancy over the austral summer is approximately 30 individuals or more) shall be treated at least by maceration.

2. The by-product of sewage treatment by the Rotary Biological Contacter process or similar processes may be disposed of into the sea provided that such disposal does not adversely affect the local environment, and provided also that any such disposal at sea shall be in accordance with Annex IV to the Protocol.

Article 6
Storage of waste

All wastes to be removed from the Antarctic Treaty area, or otherwise disposed of, shall be stored in such a way as to prevent their dispersal into the environment.

Article 7
Prohibited products

No polychlorinated biphenyls (PCBs), non-sterile soil, polystyrene beads, chips or similar forms of packaging, or pesticides (other than those required for scientific, medical or hygiene purposes) shall be introduced onto land or ice shelves or into water in the Antarctic Treaty area.

Article 8
Waste management planning

1. Each Party which itself conducts activities in the Antarctic Treaty area shall, in respect of those activities, establish a waste disposal classification system as a basis for recording wastes and to facilitate studies aimed at evaluating the environmental impacts of scientific activity and associated logistic support. To that end, wastes produced shall be classified as:

(a) sewage and domestic liquid wastes (Group 1);
(b) other liquid wastes and chemicals, including fuels and lubricants (Group 2);
(c) solids to be combusted (Group 3);
(d) other solid wastes (Group 4); and
(e) radioactive material (Group 5).

2. In order to reduce further the impact of waste on the Antarctic environment, each such Party shall prepare and annually review and update its waste management plans (including waste reduction, storage and disposal), specifying for each fixed site, for field camps generally, and for each ship (other than small boats that are part of the operations of fixed sites or of ships and taking into account existing management plans for ships):

(a) programmes for cleaning up existing waste disposal sites and abandoned work sites;
(b) current and planned waste management arrangements, including final disposal;
(c) current and planned arrangements for analysing the environmental effects of waste and waste management; and
(d) other efforts to minimise any environmental effects of wastes and waste management.

3. Each such Party shall, as far as is practicable, also prepare an inventory of locations of past activities (such as traverses, fuel depots, field bases, crashed aircraft) before the information is lost, so that such locations can be taken into account in planning future scientific programmes (such as snow chemistry, pollutants in lichens or ice core drilling).

Article 9
Circulation and review of waste management plans

1. The waste management plans prepared in accordance with Article 8, reports on their implementation, and the inventories referred to in Article 8(3), shall be included in the annual exchanges of information in accordance with Articles III and VII of the Antarctic Treaty and related Recommendations under Article IX of the Antarctic Treaty.

2. Each Party shall send copies of its waste management plans, and reports on their implementation and review, to the Committee.

3. The Committee may review waste management plans and reports thereon and may offer comments, including suggestions for minimising impacts and modifications and improvement to the plans, for the consideration of the Parties.

4. The Parties may exchange information and provide advice on, *inter alia*, available low waste technologies, reconversion of existing installations, special requirements for effluents, and appropriate disposal and discharge methods.

Article 10
Management practices

Each Party shall:

(a) designate a waste management official to develop and monitor waste management plans; in the field, this responsibility shall be delegated to an appropriate person at each site;

(b) ensure that members of its expeditions receive training designed to limit the impact of its operations on the Antarctic environment and to inform them of requirements of this Annex; and

(c) discourage the use of poly-vinyl chloride (PVC) products and ensure that its expeditions to the Antarctic Treaty area are advised of any PVC products they may introduce into that area in order that these products may be removed subsequently in accordance with this Annex.

Article 11
Review

This Annex shall be subject to regular review in order to ensure that it is updated to reflect improvement in waste disposal technology and procedures and to ensure thereby maximum protection of the Antarctic environment.

Article 12
Cases of emergency

1. This Annex shall not apply in cases of emergency relating to the safety of human life or of ships, aircraft or equipment and facilities of high value or the protection of the environment.

2. Notice of activities undertaken in cases of emergency shall be circulated immediately to all Parties and to the Committee.

Article 13
Amendment or modification

1. This Annex may be amended or modified by a measure adopted in accordance with Article IX (1) of the Antarctic Treaty. Unless the measure specifies otherwise, the amendment or modification shall be deemed to have been approved, and shall become effective, one year after the close of the Antarctic Treaty Consultative Meeting at which it was adopted, unless one or more of the Antarctic Treaty Consultative Parties notifies the Depositary, within that time period, that it wishes an extension of that period or that it is unable to approve the amendment.

2. Any amendment or modification of this Annex which becomes effective in accordance with paragraph 1 above shall thereafter become effective as to any other Party when notice of approval by it has been received by the Depositary.

Annex IV
Prevention of marine pollution

Article 1
Definitions

For the purposes of this Annex:

(a) 'discharge' means any release howsoever caused from a ship and includes any escape, disposal, spilling, leaking, pumping, emitting or emptying;

(b) 'garbage' means all kinds of victual, domestic and operational waste excluding fresh fish and parts thereof, generated during the normal operation of the ship, except those substances which are covered by Articles 3 and 4;

(c) 'MARPOL 73/78' means the International Convention for the Prevention of Pollution from Ships, 1973, as amended by the Protocol of 1978 relating thereto and by any other amendment in force thereafter;

(d) 'noxious liquid substance' means any noxious liquid substance as defined in Annex II of MARPOL 73/78;

(e) 'oil' means petroleum in any form including crude oil, fuel oil, sludge, oil refuse and refined oil products (other than petrochemicals which are subject to the provisions of Article 4);

(f) 'oily mixture' means a mixture with any oil content; and

(g) 'ship' means a vessel of any type whatsoever operating in the marine environment and includes hydrofoil boats, air-cushion vehicles, submersibles, floating craft and fixed or floating platforms.

Article 2
Application

This Annex applies, with respect to each Party, to ships entitled to fly its flag and to any other ship engaged in or supporting its Antarctic operations, while operating in the Antarctic Treaty area.

Article 3
Discharge of oil

1. Any discharge into the sea of oil or oily mixture shall be prohibited, except in cases permitted under Annex I of MARPOL 73/78.
While operating in the Antarctic Treaty area, ships shall retain on board all sludge, dirty ballast, tank washing waters and other oily residues and mixtures which may not be discharged into the sea. Ships shall discharge these residues only outside the Antarctic Treaty area, at reception facilities or as otherwise permitted under Annex I of MARPOL 73/78.

2. This Article shall not apply to:

(a) the discharge into the sea of oil or oily mixture resulting from damage to a ship or its equipment:
   (i) provided that all reasonable precautions have been taken after the occurrence of the damage or discovery of the discharge for the purpose of preventing or minimising the discharge; and
   (ii) except if the owner or the Master acted either with intent to cause damage, or recklessly and with the knowledge that damage would probably result; or
(b) the discharge into the sea of substances containing oil which are being used for the purpose of combating specific pollution incidents in order to minimise the damage from pollution.

Article 4
Discharge of noxious liquid substances

The discharge into the sea of any noxious liquid substance, and any other chemical or other substances, in quantities or concentrations that are harmful to the marine environment, shall be prohibited.

Article 5
Disposal of garbage

1. The disposal into the sea of all plastics, including but not limited to synthetic ropes, synthetic fishing nets, and plastic garbage bags, shall be prohibited.

2. The disposal into the sea of all other garbage, including paper products, rags, glass, metal, bottles, crockery, incineration ash, dunnage, lining and packing materials, shall be prohibited.

3. The disposal into the sea of food wastes may be permitted when they have been passed through a comminuter or grinder, provided that such disposal shall, except in cases permitted under Annex V of MARPOL 73/78, be made as far as practicable from land and ice shelves but in any case not less than 12 nautical miles from the nearest land or ice shelf. Such comminuted or ground food wastes shall be capable of passing through a screen with openings no greater than 25 millimeters.

4. When a substance or material covered by this article is mixed with other such substance or material for discharge or disposal, having different disposal or discharge requirements, the most stringent disposal or discharge requirements shall apply.

5. The provisions of paragraphs 1 and 2 above shall not apply to:

(a) the escape of garbage resulting from damage to a ship or its equipment provided all reasonable precautions have been taken, before and after the occurrence of the damage, for the purpose of preventing or minimising the escape; or

(b) the accidental loss of synthetic fishing nets, provided all reasonable precautions have been taken to prevent such loss.

6. The Parties shall, where appropriate, require the use of garbage record books.

Article 6
Discharge of sewage

1. Except where it would unduly impair Antarctic operations:

(a) each Party shall eliminate all discharge into the sea of untreated sewage ('sewage' being defined in Annex IV of MARPOL 73/78) within 12 nautical miles of land or ice shelves;
(b) beyond such distance, sewage stored in a holding tank shall not be discharged instantaneously but at a moderate rate and, where practicable, while the ship is en route at a speed of no less than 4 knots. This paragraph does not apply to ships certified to carry not more than 10 persons.

2. The Parties shall, where appropriate, require the use of sewage record books.

Article 7
Cases of emergency

1. Articles 3, 4, 5 and 6 of this Annex shall not apply in cases of emergency relating to the safety of a ship and those on board or saving life at sea.
2. Notice of activities undertaken in cases of emergency shall be circulated immediately to all Parties and to the Committee.

Article 8
Effect on dependent and associated ecosystems

In implementing the provisions of this Annex, due consideration shall be given to the need to avoid detrimental effects on dependent and associated ecosystems, outside the Antarctic Treaty area.

Article 9
Ship retention capacity and reception facilities

1. Each Party shall undertake to ensure that all ships entitled to fly its flag and any other ship engaged in or supporting its Antarctic operations, before entering the Antarctic Treaty area, are fitted with a tank or tanks of sufficient capacity on board for the retention of all sludge, dirty ballast, tank washing water and other oily residues and mixtures, and have sufficient capacity on board for the retention of garbage, while operating in the Antarctic Treaty area and have concluded arrangements to discharge such oily residues and garbage

at a reception facility after leaving that area. Ships shall also have sufficient capacity on board for the retention of noxious liquid substances.

2. Each Party at whose ports ships depart en route to or arrive from the Antarctic Treaty area undertakes to ensure that as soon as practicable adequate facilities are provided for the reception of all sludge, dirty ballast, tank washing water, other oily residues and mixtures, and garbage from ships, without causing undue delay, and according to the needs of the ships using them.

3. Parties operating ships which depart to or arrive from the Antarctic Treaty area at ports of other Parties shall consult with those Parties with a view to ensuring that the establishment of port reception facilities does not place an inequitable burden on Parties adjacent to the Antarctic Treaty area.

Article 10
Design, construction, manning and equipment of ships

In the design, construction, manning and equipment of ships engaged in or supporting Antarctic operations, each Party shall take into account the objectives of this Annex.

Article 11
Sovereign immunity

1. This Annex shall not apply to any warship, naval auxiliary or other ship owned or operated by a State and used, for the time being, only on government non-commercial service. However, each Party shall ensure by the adoption of appropriate measures not impairing the operations or operational capabilities of such ships owned or operated by it, that such ships act in a manner consistent, so far as is reasonable and practicable, with this Annex.

2. In applying paragraph 1 above, each Party shall take into account the importance of protecting the Antarctic environment.

3. Each Party shall inform the other Parties of how it implements this provision.

4. The dispute settlement procedure set out in Articles 18 to 20 of the Protocol shall not apply to this Article.

Article 12
Preventive measures and emergency preparedness and response

1. In order to respond more effectively to marine pollution emergencies or the threat thereof in the Antarctic Treaty area, the Parties, in accordance with Article 15 of the Protocol, shall develop contingency plans for marine pollution response in the Antarctic Treaty area, including contingency plans for ships (other than small boats that are part of the operations of fixed sites or of ships) operating in the Antarctic Treaty area, particularly ships carrying oil as cargo, and for oil spills, originating from coastal installations, which enter into the marine environment. To this end they shall:

(a) co-operate in the formulation and implementation of such plans; and

(b) draw on the advice of the Committee, the International Maritime Organization and other international organizations.

2. The Parties shall also establish procedures for co-operative response to pollution emergencies and shall take appropriate response actions in accordance with such procedures.

Article 13
Review

The Parties shall keep under continuous review the provisions of this Annex and other measures to prevent, reduce and respond to pollution of the Antarctic marine environment, including any amendments and new regulations adopted under MARPOL 73/78, with a view to achieving the objectives of this Annex.

Article 14
Relationship with MARPOL 73/78

With respect to those Parties which are also Parties to MARPOL 73/78, nothing in this Annex shall derogate from the specific rights and obligations thereunder.

Article 15
Amendment or modification

1. This Annex may be amended or modified by a measure adopted in accordance with Article IX (1) of the Antarctic Treaty. Unless the measure specifies otherwise, the amendment or modification shall be deemed to have been approved, and shall become effective, one year after the close of the Antarctic Treaty Consultative Meeting at which it was adopted, unless one or more of the Antarctic Treaty Consultative Parties notifies the Depositary, within that time period, that it wishes an extension of that period or that it is unable to approve the measure.

2. Any amendment or modification of this Annex which becomes effective in accordance with paragraph 1 above shall thereafter become effective as to any other Party when notice of approval by it has been received by the Depositary.

Annex V
Area protection and management
Article 1
Definitions

For the purposes of this Annex:

(a) 'appropriate authority' means any person or agency authorised by a Party to issue permits under this Annex;

(b) 'permit' means a formal permission in writing issued by an appropriate authority;

(c) 'Management Plan' means a plan to manage the activities and protect the special value or values in an Antarctic Specially Protected Area or an Antarctic Specially Managed Area.

Article 2
Objectives

For the purposes set out in this Annex, any area, including any marine area, may be designated as an Antarctic Specially Protected Area or an Antarctic Specially Managed Area. Activities in those Areas shall be prohibited, restricted or managed in accordance with Management Plans adopted under the provisions of this Annex.

Article 3
Antarctic Specially Protected Areas

1. Any area, including any marine area, may be designated as an Antarctic Specially Protected Area to protect outstanding environmental, scientific, historic, aesthetic or wilderness values, any combination of those values, or ongoing or planned scientific research.

2. Parties shall seek to identify, within a systematic environmental-geographical framework, and to include in the series of Antarctic Specially Protected Areas:

(a) areas kept inviolate from human interference so that future comparisons may be possible with localities that have been affected by human activities;

(b) representative examples of major terrestrial, including glacial and aquatic, ecosystems and marine ecosystems;

(c) areas with important or unusual assemblages of species, including major colonies of breeding native birds or mammals;

(d) the type locality or only known habitat of any species;

(e) areas of particular interest to on-going or planned scientific research;

(f) examples of outstanding geological, glaciological or geomorphological features;

(g) areas of outstanding aesthetic and wilderness value;

(h) sites or monuments or recognised historic value; and

(i) such other areas as may be appropriate to protect the values set out in paragraph 1 above.

3. Specially Protected Areas and Sites of Special Scientific Interest designated as such by past Antarctic Treaty Consultative Meetings are hereby designated as Antarctic Specially Protected Areas and shall be renamed and renumbered accordingly.

4. Entry into an Antarctic Specially Protected Area shall be prohibited except in accordance with a permit issued under Article 7.

Article 4
Antarctic Specially Managed Areas

1. Any area, including any marine area, where activities are being conducted or may in the future be conducted, may be designated as an Antarctic Specially Managed Area to assist in the planning and co-ordination of activities, avoid possible conflicts, improve co-operation between Parties or minimise environmental impacts.

2. Antarctic Specially Managed Areas may include:

(a) areas where activities pose risks of mutual interference or cumulative environmental impacts; and
(b) sites or monuments of recognised historic value.

3. Entry into an Antarctic Specially Managed Area shall not require a permit.

4. Notwithstanding paragraph 3 above, an Antarctic Specially Managed Area may contain one or more Antarctic Specially Protected Areas, entry into which shall be prohibited except in accordance with a permit issued under Article 7.

Article 5
Management Plans

1. Any Party, the Committee, the Scientific Committee for Antarctic Research or the Commission for the Conservation of Antarctic Marine Living Resources may propose an area for designation as an Antarctic Specially Protected Area or an Antarctic Specially Managed Area by submitting a proposed Management Plan to the Antarctic Treaty Consultative Meeting.

2. The area proposed for designation shall be of sufficient size to protect the values for which the special protection or management is required.

3. Proposed Management Plans shall include, as appropriate:

(a) a description of the value or values for which special protection or management is required;
(b) a statement of the aims and objectives of the Management Plan for the protection or management of those values;
(c) management activities which are to be undertaken to protect the values for which special protection or management is required;
(d) a period of designation, if any;
(e) a description of the area, including:
  (i) the geographical co-ordinates, boundary markers and natural features that delineate the area;

(ii) access to the area by land, sea or air including marine approaches and anchorages, pedestrian and vehicular routes within the area, and aircraft routes and landing areas;

(iii) the location of structures, including scientific stations, research or refuge facilities, both within the area and near to it; and

(iv) the location in or near the area of other Antarctic Specially Protected Areas or Antarctic Specially Managed Areas designated under this Annex, or other protected areas designated in accordance with measures adopted under other components of the Antarctic Treaty System;

(f) the identification of zones within the area, in which activities are to be prohibited, restricted or managed for the purpose of achieving the aims and objectives referred to in subparagraph b. above;

(g) maps and photographs that show clearly the boundary of the area in relation to surrounding features and key features within the area;

(h) supporting documentation;

(i) in respect of an area proposed for designation as an Antarctic Specially Protected Area, a clear description of the conditions under which permits may be granted by the appropriate authority regarding:

(i) access to and movement within or over the area;

(ii) activities which are or may be conducted within the area, including restrictions on time and place;

(iii) the installation, modification, or removal of structures;

(iv) the location of field camps;

(v) restrictions on materials and organisms which may be brought into the area;

(vi) the taking of or harmful interference with native flora and fauna;

(vii) the collection or removal of anything not brought into the area by the permit holder;

(viii) the disposal of waste;

(ix) measures that may be necessary to ensure that the aims and objectives of the Management Plan can continue to be met; and

(x) requirements for reports to be made to the appropriate authority regarding visits to the area;

(j) in respect of an area proposed for designation as an Antarctic Specially Managed Area, a code of conduct regarding:

(i) access to and movement within or over the area;

(ii) activities which are or may be conducted within the area, including restrictions on time and place;

(iii) the installation, modification, or removal of structures;

(iv) the location of field camps;

(v) the taking of or harmful interference with native flora and fauna;

(vi) the collection or removal of anything not brought into the area by the visitor;

(vii) the disposal of waste; and

(viii) any requirements for reports to be made to the appropriate authority regarding visits to the area; and

(k) provisions relating to the circumstances in which Parties should seek to exchange information in advance of activities which they propose to conduct.

Article 6
Designation procedures

1. Proposed Management Plans shall be forwarded to the Committee, the Scientific Committee on Antarctic Research and, as appropriate, to the Commission for the Conservation of Antarctic Marine Living Resources. In formulating its advice to the Antarctic Treaty Consultative Meeting, the Committee shall take into account any comments provided by the Scientific Committee on Antarctic Research and, as appropriate, by the Commission for the Conservation of Antarctic Marine Living Resources. Thereafter, Management Plans may be approved by the Antarctic Treaty Consultative Parties by a measure adopted at an Antarctic Treaty Consultative Meeting in accordance with Article IX(1) of the Antarctic Treaty. Unless the measure specifies otherwise, the Plan shall be deemed to have been approved 90 days after the close of the Antarctic Treaty Consultative Meeting at which it was adopted, unless one or more of the Consultative Parties notifies the Depositary, within that time period, that it wishes an extension of that period or is unable to approve the measure.

2. Having regard to the provisions of Articles 4 and 5 of the Protocol, no marine area shall be designated as an Antarctic Specially Protected Area or an Antarctic Specially Managed Area without the prior approval of the Commission for the Conservation of Antarctic Marine Living Resources.

3. Designation of an Antarctic Specially Protected Area or an Antarctic Specially Managed Area shall be for an indefinite period unless the Management Plan provides otherwise. A review of a Management Plan shall be initiated at least every five years. The Plan shall be updated as necessary.

4. Management Plans may be amended or revoked in accordance with paragraph 1 above.

5. Upon approval Management Plans shall be circulated promptly by the Depositary to all Parties. The Depositary shall maintain a record of all currently approved Management Plans.

Article 7
Permits

1. Each Party shall appoint an appropriate authority to issue permits to enter and engage in activities within an Antarctic Specially Protected Area in accordance with the requirements of the Management Plan relating to that Area. The permit shall be accompanied by the relevant sections of the Management Plan and shall specify the extent and location of the Area, the authorised

activities and when, where and by whom the activities are authorised and any other conditions imposed by the Management Plan.

2. In the case of a Specially Protected Area designated as such by past Antarctic Treaty Consultative Meetings which does not have a Management Plan, the appropriate authority may issue a permit for a compelling scientific purpose which cannot be served elsewhere and which will not jeopardise the natural ecological system in that Area.

3. Each Party shall require a permit-holder to carry a copy of the permit while in the Antarctic Specially Protected Area concerned.

Article 8
Historic sites and monuments

1. Sites or monuments of recognised historic value which have been designated as Antarctic Specially Protected Areas or Antarctic Specially Managed Areas, or which are located within such Areas, shall be listed as Historic Sites and Monuments.

2. Any Party may propose a site or monument of recognised historic value which has not been designated as an Antarctic Specially Protected Area or an Antarctic Specially Managed Area, or which is not located within such an Area, for listing as a Historic Site or Monument. The proposal for listing may be approved by the Antarctic Treaty Consultative Parties by a measure adopted at an Antarctic Treaty Consultative Meeting in accordance with Article IX(1) of the Antarctic Treaty. Unless the measure specifies otherwise, the proposal shall be deemed to have been approved 90 days after the close of the Antarctic Treaty Consultative Meeting at which it was adopted, unless one or more of the Consultative Parties notifies the Depositary, within that time period, that it wishes an extension of that period or is unable to approve the measure.

3. Existing Historic Sites and Monuments which have been listed as such by previous Antarctic Treaty Consultative Meetings shall be included in the list of Historic Sites and Monuments under this Article.

4. Listed Historic Sites and Monuments shall not be damaged, removed or destroyed.

5. The list of Historic Sites and Monuments may be amended in accordance with paragraph 2 above. The Depositary shall maintain a list of current Historic Sites and Monuments.

Article 9
Information and publicity

1. With a view to ensuring that all persons visiting or proposing to visit Antarctica understand and observe the provisions of this Annex, each Party shall make available information setting forth, in particular:

(a) the location of Antarctic Specially Protected Areas and Antarctic Specially Managed Areas;
(b) listing and maps of those Areas;
(c) the Management Plans, including listings of prohibitions relevant to each Area;
(d) the location of Historic Sites and Monuments and any relevant prohibition or restriction.

2. Each Party shall ensure that the location and, if possible, the limits of Antarctic Specially Protected Areas, Antarctic Specially Managed Areas and Historic Sites and Monuments are shown on its topographic maps, hydrographic charts and in other relevant publications.

3. Parties shall co-operate to ensure that, where appropriate, the boundaries of Antarctic Specially Protected Areas, Antarctic Specially Managed Areas and Historic Sites and Monuments are suitably marked on the site.

Article 10
Exchange of information

1. The Parties shall make arrangements for:

(a) collecting and exchanging records, including records of permits and reports of visits, including inspection visits, to Antarctic Specially Protected Areas and reports of inspection visits to Antarctic Specially Managed Areas;
(b) obtaining and exchanging information on any significant change or damage to any Antarctic Specially Managed Area, Antarctic Specially Protected Area or Historic Site or Monument; and
(c) establishing common forms in which records and information shall be submitted by Parties in accordance with paragraph 2 below.

2. Each Party shall inform the other Parties and the Committee before the end of November of each year of the number and nature of permits issued under this Annex in the preceding period of 1st July to 30th June.

3. Each Party conducting, funding or authorising research or other activities in Antarctic Specially Protected Areas or Antarctic Specially Managed Areas shall maintain a record of such activities and in the annual exchange of information in accordance with the Antarctic Treaty shall provide summary descriptions of the activities conducted by persons subject to its jurisdiction in such areas in the preceding year.

4. Each Party shall inform the other Parties and the Committee before the end of November each year of measures it has taken to implement this Annex, including any site inspections and any steps it has taken to address instances of activities in contravention of the provisions of the approved Management

Plan for an Antarctic Specially Protected Area or Antarctic Specially Managed
Area.

Article 11
Cases of emergency

1. The restrictions laid down and authorised by this Annex shall not apply
in cases of emergency involving safety of human life or of ships, aircraft, or
equipment and facilities of high value or the protection of the environment.

2. Notice of activities undertaken in cases of emergency shall be circulated
immediately to all Parties and to the Committee.

Article 12
Amendment or modification

1. This Annex may be amended or modified by a measure adopted in accordance with Article IX (1) of the Antarctic Treaty. Unless the measure specifies
otherwise, the amendment or modification shall be deemed to have been approved, and shall become effective, one year after the close of the Antarctic
Treaty Consultative Meeting at which it was adopted, unless one or more of the
Antarctic Treaty Consultative Parties notifies the Depositary, within that time
period, that it wishes an extension of that period or that it is unable to approve
the measure.

2. Any amendment or modification of this Annex which becomes effective in
accordance with paragraph 1 above shall thereafter become effective as to any
other Party when notice of approval by it has been received by the Depositary.

Convention for the Conservation of Antarctic Seals, 1 June 1972

Editorial note

The Convention for the Conservation of Antarctic Seals prohibits the capturing or killing of enumerate species of seal in the area south of 60° South Latitude, except as provided in the Convention (Article 2). In addition to the Annex which specifies particular measures that Parties adopt to promote the 'conservation, scientific study and rational and humane use of seal resources' (Article 3). The Convention provides for the grant of permits to kill or capture 'limited quantities' of seals not in accordance with the Convention, if to do so will provide: 'indispensable' food to men and dogs; or for scientific research; or for museums, educational or cultural institutions (Article 4(1)).

The Scientific Committee on Antarctic Research of the International Council of Scientific Unions (SCAR) is to provide scientific advice to the Parties and act as a medium for information exchange (Article 5). The Convention requires Parties to follow the findings of SCAR on when the permissible catch limits are likely to be exceeded and to cease killing and capturing seals accordingly (Article 5(5)). Once commercial sealing begins in the Antarctic, the Convention requires Parties to enter into consultations with each other with a view to establishing: an 'effective system of control, including inspection' over the Convention's implementation; a Commission; and a Scientific Advisory Committee (Article 6(1)). Such consultations must take place at the request of a Party if SCAR reports that a particular harvest is having a 'significantly harmful effect' on the total stock or on the ecological system (Article 6(3)). The Convention requires the Parties to meet every five years to review the operation of the Convention (Article 7). An amendment to the Convention enters into force when it is ratified or accepted by all Parties (Article 8(3)). An amendment to the Annex enters into force for those Parties approving it after two-thirds of the Parties have notified the Depository of their approval of it, although a special procedure is provided in the event that a Party lodges an objection (Article 9). The Convention limits the States which may become signatories (Article 10) and allows the accession of other States only with the consent of the Parties (Article 12) (Article 9(3)).

Date of signature: 1 June 1972

Entry into force: 11 March 1978

Depositary: Government of the United Kingdom

Contracting Parties: Argentina, Australia, Belgium, Brazil, Canada, Chile, France, Germany, Italy, Japan, Norway, Poland, Russian Federation, South Africa, United Kingdom, United States of America.

Convention for the Conservation of Antarctic Seals

The Contracting Parties,

Recalling the Agreed Measures for the Conservation of Antarctic Fauna and Flora adopted under the Antarctic Treaty signed at Washington on 1 December 1959;

Recognizing the general concern about the vulnerability of Antarctic seals to commercial exploitation and the consequent need for effective conservation measures;

Recognizing that the stocks of Antarctic seals are an important living resource in the marine environment which requires an international agreement for its effective conservation;

Recognizing that this resource should not be depleted by over-exploitation, and hence that any harvesting should be regulated so as not to exceed the levels of the optimum sustainable yield;

Recognizing that in order to improve scientific knowledge and so place exploitation on a rational basis, every effort should be made both to encourage biological and other research on Antarctic seal populations and to gain information from such research and from the statistics of future sealing operations, so that further suitable regulations may be formulated;

Noting that the Scientific Committee on Antarctic Research of the International Council of Scientific Unions (SCAR) is willing to carry out the tasks requested of it in this Convention;

Desiring to promote and achieve the objectives of protection, scientific study and rational use of Antarctic seals, and to maintain a satisfactory balance within the ecological system;

Have agreed as follows:

Article 1
Scope

1. This Convention applies to the seas south of 60° South Latitude, in respect of which the Contracting Parties affirm the provisions of Article IV of the Antarctic Treaty.

2. This Convention may be applicable to any or all of the following species:

Southern elephant seal *Mirounga leonina,*
Leopard seal *Hydrurga leptonyx,*
Weddell seal *Leptonychotes weddelli,*
Crabeater seal *Lobodon carcinophagus,*
Ross seal *Ommatophoca rossi,*
Southern fur seals *Arctocephalus* sp.

3. The Annex to this Convention forms an integral part thereof.

Article 2
Implementation

1. The Contracting Parties agree that the species of seals enumerated in Article 1 shall not be killed or captured within the Convention area by their nationals or vessels under their respective flags except in accordance with the provisions of this Convention.

2. Each Contracting Party shall adopt for its nationals and for vessels under its flag such laws, regulations and other measures, including a permit system as appropriate, as may be necessary to implement this Convention.

Article 3
Annexed measures

1. This Convention includes an Annex specifying measures which the Contracting Parties hereby adopt. Contracting Parties may from time to time in the future adopt other measures with respect to the conservation, scientific study and rational and humane use of seal resources, prescribing *inter alia*:

a) permissible catch;
b) protected and unprotected species;
c) open and closed seasons;
d) open and closed areas, including the designation of reserves;
e) the designation of special areas where there shall be no disturbance of seals;
f) limits relating to sex, size, or age for each species;
g) restrictions relating to time of day and duration, limitations of effort and methods of sealing;
h) types and specifications of gear and apparatus and appliances which may be used;
i) catch returns and other statistical and biological records;
j) procedures for facilitating the review and assessment of scientific information;
k) other regulatory measures including an effective system of inspection.

2. The measures adopted under paragraph (1) of this Article shall be based upon the best scientific and technical evidence available.

3. The Annex may from time to time be amended in accordance with the procedures provided for in Article 9.

Article 4
Special permits

1. Notwithstanding the provisions of this Convention, any Contracting Party may issue permits to kill or capture seals in limited quantities and in conformity with the objectives and principles of this Convention for the following purposes:

a) to provide indispensable food for men or dogs;
b) to provide for scientific research; or
c) to provide specimens for museums, educational or cultural institutions.

2. Each Contracting Party shall, as soon as possible, inform the other Contracting Parties and SCAR of the purpose and content of all permits issued under paragraph (1) of this Article and subsequently of the numbers of seals killed or captured under these permits.

Article 5
Exchange of information and scientific advice

1. Each Contracting Party shall provide to the other Contracting Parties and to SCAR the information specified in the Annex within the period indicated therein.

2. Each Contracting Party shall also provide to the other Contracting Parties and to SCAR before 31 October each year information on any steps it has taken in accordance with Article 2 of this Convention during the preceding period of 1 July to 30 June.

3. Contracting Parties which have no information report under the two preceding paragraphs shall indicate this formally before 31 October each year.

4. SCAR is invited:

a) to assess information received pursuant to this Article; encourage exchange of scientific data and information among the Contracting Parties; recommend programmes for scientific research; recommend statistical and biological data to be collected by sealing expeditions within the Convention area; and suggest amendments to the Annex; and
b) to report on the basis of the statistical, biological and other evidence available when the harvest of any species of seal in the Convention area is having a significantly harmful effect on the total stocks of such species or on the ecological system in any particular locality.

5. SCAR is invited to notify the Depositary which shall report to the Contracting Parties when SCAR estimates in any sealing season that the permissible catch limits for any species are likely to be exceeded and, in that case,

to provide an estimate of the date upon which the permissible catch limits will be reached. Each Contracting party shall then take appropriate measures to prevent its nationals and vessels under its flag from killing or capturing seals of that species after the estimated date until the Contracting Parties decide otherwise.

6. SCAR may if necessary seek the technical assistance of the Food and Agriculture Organization of the United Nations in making its assessments.

7. Notwithstanding the provisions of paragraph (1) of Article 1 the Contracting Parties shall, in accordance with their internal law, report to each other and to SCAR, for consideration, statistics relating to the Antarctic seals listed in paragraph (2) of Article 1 which have been killed or captured by their nationals and vessels under their respective flags in the area of floating sea ice north of 60° South latitude.

Article 6
Consultations between Contracting Parties

1. At any time after commercial sealing has begun a Contracting Party may propose through the Depositary that a meeting of Contracting Parties be convened with a view to:

a) establishing by a two-thirds majority of the Contracting Parties, including the concurring votes of all States signatory to this Convention present at the meeting, an effective system of control, including inspection, over the implementation of the provisions of this Convention;
b) establishing a commission to perform such functions under this Convention as the Contracting Parties may deem necessary; or
c) considering other proposals, including:
   (i) the provision of independent scientific advice;
   (ii) the establishment, by a two-thirds majority, of a scientific advisory committee which may be assigned some or all of the functions requested of SCAR under this Convention, if commercial sealing reaches significant proportions;
   (iii) the carrying out of scientific programmes with the participation of the Contracting Parties; and
   (iv) the provision of further regulatory measures, including moratoria.

2. if one-third of the Contracting Parties indicate agreement the Depositary shall convene such a meeting, as soon as possible.

3. A meeting shall be held at the request of any Contracting Party, if SCAR reports that the harvest of any species of Antarctic seal in the area to which this Convention applies is having a significantly harmful effect on the total stocks or the ecological system in any particular locality.

Article 7
Review of operations

The Contracting Parties shall meet within five years after the entry into force of this Convention and at least every five years thereafter to review the operation of the Convention.

Article 8
Amendments to the Convention

1. This Convention may be amended at any time. The text of any amendment proposed by a Contracting Party shall be submitted to the Depositary, which shall transmit it to all the Contracting Parties.

2. If one-third of the Contracting Parties request a meeting to discuss the proposed amendment the Depositary shall call such a meeting.

3. An amendment shall enter into force when the Depositary has received instruments of ratification or acceptance thereof from all the Contracting Parties.

Article 9
Amendments to the Annex

1. Any Contracting Party may propose amendments to the Annex to this Convention. The text of any such proposed amendment shall be submitted to the Depositary which shall transmit it to all Contracting Parties.

2. Each such proposed amendment shall become effective for all Contracting Parties six months after the date appearing on the notification from the Depositary to the Contracting Parties, if within 120 days of the notification date, no objection has been received and two-thirds of the Contracting Parties have notified the Depositary in writing of their approval.

3. If an objection is received from any Contracting Party within 120 days of the notification date, the matter shall be considered by the Contracting Parties at their next meeting. If unanimity on the matter is not reached at the meeting, the Contracting Parties shall notify the Depositary within 120 days from the date of the closure of the meeting of their approval or rejection of the original amendment or of any new amendment proposed by the meeting. If, by the end of this period, two-thirds of the Contracting Parties have approved such amendment, it shall become effective six months from the date of the closure of the meeting for those Contracting Parties which have by then notified their approval.

4. Any Contracting Party which has objected to a proposed amendment may at any time withdraw that objection, and the proposed amendment shall become effective with respect to such Party immediately if the amendment is already in effect, or at such time as it becomes effective under the terms of this Article.

5. The Depositary shall notify each Contracting Party immediately upon receipt of each approval or objection, of each withdrawal of objection, and of the entry into force of any amendment.

6. Any State which becomes a party to this Convention after an amendment to the Annex has entered into force shall be bound by the Annex as so amended. Any State which becomes a Party to this Convention during the period when a proposed amendment is pending may approve or object to such an amendment within the time limits applicable to other Contracting Parties.

Article 10
Signature

This Convention shall be open for signature at London from 1 June to 31 December 1972 by States participating in the Conference on the Conservation of Antarctic Seals held at London from 3 to 11 February 1972.

Article 11
Ratification

This Convention is subject to ratification or acceptance. Instruments of ratification or acceptance shall be deposited with the Government of the United Kingdom of Great Britain and Northern Ireland, hereby designated as the Depositary.

Article 12
Accession

This Convention shall be open for accession by any State which may be invited to accede to this Convention with the consent of all the Contracting Parties.

Article 13
Entry into force

1. This Convention shall enter into force on the thirtieth day following the date of deposit of the seventh instrument of ratification or acceptance.

2. Thereafter this Convention shall enter into force for each ratifying, accepting or acceding State on the thirtieth day after deposit by such State of its instrument of ratification, acceptance or accession.

Article 14
Withdrawal

Any Contracting Party may withdraw from this Convention on 30 June of any year by giving notice on or before 1 January of the same year to the Depositary, which upon receipt of such a notice shall at once communicate it to the other Contracting Parties. Any other Contracting Party may, in like manner, within one month of the receipt of a copy of such a notice from the Depositary, give notice of withdrawal, so that the Convention shall cease to be in force on 30 June of the same year with respect to the Contracting Party giving such notice.

Article l5
Notification by the Depositary

The Depositary shall notify all signatory and acceding States of the following:

a) signatures of this Convention, the deposit of instruments of ratification, acceptance or accession and notices of withdrawal;
b) the date of entry into force of this Convention and of any amendments to it or its Annex.

Article 16
Certified copies and registration

1. This Convention, done in the English, French, Russian and Spanish languages, each version being equally authentic, shall be deposited in the archives of the Government of the United Kingdom of Great Britain and Northern Ireland, which shall transmit duly certified copies thereof to all signatory and acceding States.

2. This Convention shall be registered by the Depositary pursuant to Article 102 of the Charter of the United Nations.

IN WITNESS WHEREOF, the undersigned, duly authorized, have signed this Convention.

DONE at London, this 1st day of June 1972.

[Annex omitted]

Convention on the Conservation of Antarctic Marine Living Resources, 20 May 1980

Editorial note

The Convention on the Conservation of Antarctic Marine Living Resources was concluded to develop and implement conservation measures aimed at protecting Antarctic marine resources from over-harvesting. The following conservation principles must be complied with when engaging in harvesting or other related activities: prevention of decreases in harvested populations to levels below which stable recruitment cannot be ensured; maintenance of ecological relationship with dependent and related species; and prevention of changes to the marine ecosystem which are not reversible over two or three decades (Article II). Parties agree to abide by the principles and purposes of the Antarctic Treaty and comply with the recommendations on environmental protection of the Antarctic Treaty Consultative Parties, regardless of whether they are Parties to that Treaty (Articles III–V).

The Convention establishes the Commission on the Conservation of Antarctic Marine Living Resources composed of representatives of those Parties which participated in the meeting at which the Convention was adopted and of those Parties acceding to the Convention which engage in research or harvesting in relation to marine living resources (Article VII). Each member of the Commission must contribute to its budget, with Members giving equally for the first five years and thereafter contributing proportionally based on the amount of resources harvested (Article XIX). The Commission is to facilitate scientific research; compile, analyse, disseminate and publish information on harvested and dependent species; formulate conservation measures and implement a system of observation and inspection on board ships engaged in harvesting or scientific research (Article IX(1)). The conservation measures developed may include designating the quantities of any species which may be harvested or designating regions which necessitate special protection (Article IX(2)). The Commission is to consider measures recommended by existing fisheries commissions when developing these conservation measures (Article IX(5)). The Commission is also to consider the recommendations of the Scientific Committee for the Conservation of Antarctic Marine Living Resources (established under Article XIV), which is a forum for consultation and co-operation in the collection, study and exchange of scientific information assessing the trends of populations of Antarctic marine living resources (Article XV). The Commission is to notify each Contracting Party of the conservation measures it has adopted which become binding on each Party unless a Party notifies the Commission within ninety days that it is unable to accept them (Article IX(6)). Commission decisions on matters of substance are taken by consensus (Article XII). Disputes must be settled amicably among the Parties involved, and may be submitted on consent to the ICJ or to arbitration in accordance with the Annex to the Convention (Article XXV). The Convention limits the States which may become signatories (Article XXVI), but permits the accession of any State interested in research or harvesting activities to which the Convention applies (Article XXIX).

Date of signature:	20 May 1980
Entry into force:	7 April 1982
Depositary:	Government of Australia
Contracting Parties:	Argentina, Australia, Belgium, Brazil, Bulgaria, Canada, Chile, European Community, Finland, France, Germany, Greece, India, Italy, Japan, Korea (Republic of), Namibia, Netherlands, New Zealand, Norway, Peru, Poland, Russian Federation, South Africa, Spain, Sweden, Ukraine, United Kingdom, United States of America, Uruguay, Vanuatu.
Website:	http://www.ccamlr.org

Convention on the Conservation of Antarctic Marine Living Resources

The Contracting Parties,

Recognising the importance of safeguarding the environment and protecting the integrity of the ecosystem of the seas surrounding Antarctica;

Noting the concentration of marine living resources found in Antarctic waters and the increased interest in the possibilities offered by the utilization of these resources as a source of protein;

Conscious of the urgency of ensuring the conservation of Antarctic marine living resources;

Considering that it is essential to increase knowledge of the Antarctic marine ecosystem and its components so as to be able to base decisions on harvesting on sound scientific information;

Believing that the conservation of Antarctic marine living resources calls for international cooperation with due regard for the provisions of the Antarctic Treaty and with the active involvement of all States engaged in research or harvesting activities in Antarctic waters;

Recognising the prime responsibilities of the Antarctic Treaty Consultative Parties for the protection and preservation of the Antarctic environment and, in particular, their responsibilities under Article IX, paragraph 1(f) of the Antarctic Treaty in respect of the preservation and conservation of living resources in Antarctica;

Recalling the action already taken by the Antarctic Treaty Consultative Parties including in particular the Agreed Measures for the Conservation of Antarctic Fauna and Flora, as well as the provisions of the Convention for the Conservation of Antarctic Seals;

Bearing in mind the concern regarding the conservation of Antarctic marine living resources expressed by the Consultative Parties at the Ninth Consultative Meeting of the Antarctic Treaty and the importance of the provisions of Recommendation IX-2 which led to the establishment of the present Convention;

Believing that it is in the interest of all mankind to preserve the waters surrounding the Antarctic continent for peaceful purposes only and to prevent their becoming the scene or object of international discord;

Recognising, in the light of the foregoing, that it is desirable to establish suitable machinery for recommending, promoting, deciding upon and coordinating the measures and scientific studies needed to ensure the conservation of Antarctic marine living organisms;

Have agreed as follows:

Article I

1. This Convention applies to the Antarctic marine living resources of the area south of 60° South latitude and to the Antarctic marine living resources of the area between that latitude and the Antarctic Convergence which form part of the Antarctic marine ecosystem.

2. Antarctic marine living resources means the populations of fin fish, molluscs, crustaceans and all other species of living organisms, including birds, found south of the Antarctic Convergence.

3. The Antarctic marine ecosystem means the complex of relationships of Antarctic marine living resources with each other and with their physical environment.

4. The Antarctic Convergence shall be deemed to be a line joining the following points along parallels of latitude and meridians of longitude: 50° S, 0°; 50° S, 30° E; 45° S, 30° E; 45° S, 80° E; 55° S, 80° E, 55° S, 150° E; 60° S, 150° E; 60° S, 50° W; 50° S, 50° W; 50° S, 0°.

Article II

1. The objective of this Convention is the conservation of Antarctic marine living resources.

2. For the purposes of this Convention, the term 'conservation' includes rational use.

3. Any harvesting and associated activities in the area to which this Convention applies shall be conducted in accordance with the provisions of this Convention and with the following principles of conservation:

(a) prevention of decrease in the size of any harvested population to levels below those which ensure its stable recruitment. For this purpose its size should not be allowed to fall below a level close to that which ensures the greatest net annual increment;

(b) maintenance of the ecological relationships between harvested, dependent and related populations of Antarctic marine living resources and the restoration of depleted populations to the levels defined in sub-paragraph (a) above; and

(c) prevention of changes or minimization of the risk of changes in the marine ecosystem which are not potentially reversible over two or three decades, taking into account the state of available knowledge of the direct and indirect impact of harvesting, the effect of the introduction of alien species, the effects of associated activities on the marine ecosystem and of the effects of environmental changes, with the aim of making possible the sustained conservation of Antarctic marine living resources.

Article III

The Contracting Parties, whether or not they are Parties to the Antarctic Treaty, agree that they will not engage in any activities in the Antarctic Treaty area contrary to the principles and purposes of that Treaty and that, in their relations with each other, they are bound by the obligations contained in Articles I and V of the Antarctic Treaty.

Article IV

1. With respect to the Antarctic Treaty area, all Contracting Parties, whether or not they are Parties to the Antarctic Treaty, are bound by Articles IV and VI of the Antarctic Treaty in their relations with each other.

2. Nothing in this Convention and no acts or activities taking place while the present Convention is in force shall:

(a) constitute a basis for asserting, supporting or denying a claim to territorial sovereignty in the Antarctic Treaty area or create any rights of sovereignty in the Antarctic Treaty area;

(b) be interpreted as a renunciation or diminution by any Contracting Party of, or as prejudicing, any right or claim or basis of claim to exercise coastal State jurisdiction under international law within the area to which this Convention applies;

(c) be interpreted as prejudicing the position of any Contracting Party as regards its recognition or non-recognition of any such right, claim or basis of claim;

(d) affect the provision of Article IV, paragraph 2, of the Antarctic Treaty that no new claim, or enlargement of an existing claim, to territorial sovereignty in Antarctica shall be asserted while the Antarctic Treaty is in force.

Article V

1. The Contracting Parties which are not Parties to the Antarctic Treaty acknowledge the special obligations and responsibilities of the Antarctic Treaty Consultative Parties for the protection and preservation of the environment of the Antarctic Treaty area.

2. The Contracting Parties which are not Parties to the Antarctic Treaty agree that, in their activities in the Antarctic Treaty area, they will observe as and when appropriate the Agreed Measures for the Conservation of Antarctic Fauna and Flora and such other measures as have been recommended by the Antarctic Treaty Consultative Parties in fulfilment of their responsibility for the protection of the Antarctic environment from all forms of harmful human interference.

3. For the purposes of this Convention, 'Antarctic Treaty Consultative Parties' means the Contracting Parties to the Antarctic Treaty whose Representatives participate in meetings under Article IX of the Antarctic Treaty.

Article VI

Nothing in this Convention shall derogate from the rights and obligations of Contracting Parties under the International Convention for the Regulation of Whaling and the Convention for the Conservation of Antarctic Seals.

Article VII

1. The Contracting Parties hereby establish and agree to maintain the Commission for the Conservation of Antarctic Marine Living Resources (hereinafter referred to as 'the Commission').

2. Membership in the Commission shall be as follows:

(a) each Contracting Party which participated in the meeting at which this Convention was adopted shall be a Member of the Commission;

(b) each State Party which has acceded to this Convention pursuant to Article XXIX shall be entitled to be a Member of the Commission during such

time as that acceding party is engaged in research or harvesting activities
in relation to the marine living resources to which this Convention applies;

(c) each regional economic integration organization which has acceded to this
Convention pursuant to Article XXIX shall be entitled to be a Member of
the Commission during such time as its States members are so entitled;

(d) a Contracting Party seeking to participate in the work of the Commission
pursuant to sub-paragraphs (b) and (c) above shall notify the Depositary of
the basis upon which it seeks to become a Member of the Commission and
of its willingness to accept conservation measures in force. The Depositary
shall communicate to each Member of the Commission such notification
and accompanying information. Within two months of receipt of such
communication from the Depositary, any Member of the Commission
may request that a special meeting of the Commission be held to consider
the matter. Upon receipt of such request, the Depositary shall call such a
meeting. If there is no request for a meeting, the Contracting Party submitting the notification shall be deemed to have satisfied the requirements
for Commission Membership.

3. Each Member of the Commission shall be represented by one representative who may be accompanied by alternate representatives and advisers.

Article VIII

The Commission shall have legal personality and shall enjoy in the territory of
each of the States Parties such legal capacity as may be necessary to perform
its function and achieve the purposes of this Convention. The privileges and
immunities to be enjoyed by the Commission and its staff in the territory of
a State Party shall be determined by agreement between the Commission and
the State Party concerned.

Article IX

1. The function of the Commission shall be to give effect to the objective
and principles set out in Article II of this Convention. To this end, it shall:

(a) facilitate research into and comprehensive studies of Antarctic marine
living resources and of the Antarctic marine ecosystem;

(b) compile data on the status of and changes in population of Antarctic marine living resources and on factors affecting the distribution, abundance
and productivity of harvested species and dependent or related species or
populations;

(c) ensure the acquisition of catch and effort statistics on harvested populations;

(d) analyse, disseminate and publish the information referred to in sub-
paragraphs (b) and (c) above and the reports of the Scientific Committee;

(e) identify conservation needs and analyse the effectiveness of conservation measures;

(f) formulate, adopt and revise conservation measures on the basis of the best scientific evidence available, subject to the provisions of paragraph 5 of this Article;

(g) implement the system of observation and inspection established under Article XXIV of this Convention;

(h) carry out such other activities as are necessary to fulfil the objective of this Convention.

2. The conservation measures referred to in paragraph 1(f) above include the following:

(a) the designation of the quantity of any species which may be harvested in the area to which this Convention applies;

(b) the designation of regions and sub-regions based on the distribution of populations of Antarctic marine living resources;

(c) the designation of the quantity which may be harvested from the populations of regions and sub-regions;

(d) the designation of protected species;

(e) the designation of the size, age and, as appropriate, sex of species which may be harvested;

(f) the designation of open and closed seasons for harvesting;

(g) the designation of the opening and closing of areas, regions or sub-regions for purposes of scientific study or conservation, including special areas for protection and scientific study;

(h) regulation of the effort employed and methods of harvesting, including fishing gear, with a view, *inter alia*, to avoiding undue concentration of harvesting in any region or sub-region;

(i) the taking of such other conservation measures as the Commission considers necessary for the fulfilment of the objective of this Convention, including measures concerning the effects of harvesting and associated activities on components of the marine ecosystem other than the harvested populations.

3. The Commission shall publish and maintain a record of all conservation measures in force.

4. In exercising its functions under paragraph 1 above, the Commission shall take full account of the recommendations and advice of the Scientific Committee.

5. The Commission shall take full account of any relevant measures or regulations established or recommended by the Consultative Meetings pursuant to Article IX of the Antarctic Treaty or by existing fisheries commissions responsible for species which may enter the area to which this Convention applies, in

order that there shall be no inconsistency between the rights and obligations of a Contracting Party under such regulations or measures and conservation measures which may be adopted by the Commission.

6. Conservation measures adopted by the Commission in accordance with this Convention shall be implemented by Members of the Commission in the following manner:

(a) the Commission shall notify conservation measures to all Members of the Commission;

(b) conservation measures shall become binding upon all Members of the Commission 180 days after such notification, except as provided in subparagraphs (c) and (d) below;

(c) if a Member of the Commission, within ninety days following the notification specified in subparagraph (a), notifies the Commission that it is unable to accept the conservation measure, in whole or in part, the measure shall not, to the extent stated, be binding upon that Member of the Commission;

(d) in the event that any Member of the Commission invokes the procedure set forth in subparagraph (c) above, the Commission shall meet at the request of any Member of the Commission to review the conservation measure. At the time of such meeting and within thirty days following the meeting, any Member of the Commission shall have the right to declare that it is no longer able to accept the conservation measure, in which case the Member shall no longer be bound by such measure.

Article X

1. The Commission shall draw the attention of any State which is not a Party to this Convention to any activity undertaken by its nationals or vessels which, in the opinion of the Commission, affects the implementation of the objective of this Convention.

2. The Commission shall draw the attention of all Contracting Parties to any activity which, in the opinion of the Commission, affects the implementation by a Contracting Party of the objective of this Convention or the compliance by that Contracting Party with its obligations under this Convention.

Article XI

The Commission shall seek to co-operate with Contracting Parties which may exercise jurisdiction in marine areas adjacent to the area to which this Convention applies in respect of the conservation of any stock or stocks of associated species which occur both within those areas and the area to which this Convention applies, with a view to harmonizing the conservation measures adopted in respect of such stocks.

Article XII

1. Decisions of the Commission on matters of substance shall be taken by consensus. The question of whether a matter is one of substance shall be treated as a matter of substance.

2. Decisions on matters other than those referred to in paragraph 1 above shall be taken by a simple majority of the Members of the Commission present and voting.

3. In Commission consideration of any item requiring a decision, it shall be made clear whether a regional economic integration organization will participate in the taking of the decision and, if so, whether any of its member States will also participate. The number of Contracting Parties so participating shall not exceed the number of member States of the regional economic integration organization which are Members of the Commission.

4. In the taking of decisions pursuant to this Article, a regional economic integration organization shall have only one vote.

Article XIII

1. The headquarters of the Commission shall be established at Hobart, Tasmania, Australia.

2. The Commission shall hold a regular annual meeting. Other meetings shall also be held at the request of one-third of its members and as otherwise provided in this Convention. The first meeting of the Commission shall be held within three months of the entry into force of this Convention, provided that among the Contracting Parties there are at least two States conducting harvesting activities within the area to which this Convention applies. The first meeting shall, in any event, be held within one year of the entry into force of this Convention. The Depositary shall consult with the signatory States regarding the first Commission meeting, taking into account that a broad representation of such States is necessary for the effective operation of the Commission.

3. The Depositary shall convene the first meeting of the Commission at the headquarters of the Commission. Thereafter, meetings of the Commission shall be held at its headquarters, unless it decides otherwise.

4. The Commission shall elect from among its members a Chairman and Vice-Chairman, each of whom shall serve for a term of two years and shall be eligible for re-election for one additional term. The first Chairman shall, however, be elected for an initial term of three years. The Chairman and Vice-Chairman shall not be representatives of the same Contracting Party.

5. The Commission shall adopt and amend as necessary the rules of procedure for the conduct of its meetings, except with respect to the matters dealt with in Article XII of this Convention.

6. The Commission may establish such subsidiary bodies as are necessary for the performance of its functions.

Article XIV

1. The Contracting Parties hereby establish the Scientific Committee for the Conservation of Antarctic Marine Living Resources (hereinafter referred to as the 'Scientific Committee') which shall be a consultative body to the Commission. The Scientific Committee shall normally meet at the headquarters of the Commission unless the Scientific Committee decides otherwise.

2. Each Member of the Commission shall be a member of the Scientific Committee and shall appoint a representative with suitable scientific qualifications who may be accompanied by other experts and advisers.

3. The Scientific Committee may seek the advice of other scientists and experts as may be required on an *ad hoc* basis.

Article XV

1. The Scientific Committee shall provide a forum for consultation and co-operation concerning the collection, study and exchange of information with respect to the marine living resources to which this Convention applies. It shall encourage and promote co-operation in the field of scientific research in order to extend knowledge of the marine living resources of the Antarctic marine ecosystem.

2. The Scientific Committee shall conduct such activities as the Commission may direct in pursuance of the objective of this Convention and shall:

(a) establish criteria and methods to be used for determinations concerning the conservation measures referred to in Article IX of this Convention;
(b) regularly assess the status and trends of the populations of Antarctic marine living resources;
(c) analyse data concerning the direct and indirect effects of harvesting on the populations of Antarctic marine living resources;
(d) assess the effects of proposed changes in the methods or levels of harvesting and proposed conservation measures;
(e) transmit assessments, analyses, reports and recommendations to the Commission as requested or on its own initiative regarding measures and research to implement the objective of this Convention;
(f) formulate proposals for the conduct of international and national programs of research into Antarctic marine living resources.

3. In carrying out its functions, the Scientific Committee shall have regard to the work of other relevant technical and scientific organizations and to the scientific activities conducted within the framework of the Antarctic Treaty.

Article XVI

1. The first meeting of the Scientific Committee shall be held within three months of the first meeting of the Commission. The Scientific Committee shall meet thereafter as often as may be necessary to fulfil its functions.

2. The Scientific Committee shall adopt and amend as necessary its rules of procedure. The rules and any amendments thereto shall be approved by the Commission. The rules shall include procedures for the presentation of minority reports.

3. The Scientific Committee may establish, with the approval of the Commission, such subsidiary bodies as are necessary for the performance of its functions.

Article XVII

1. The Commission shall appoint an Executive Secretary to serve the Commission and Scientific Committee according to such procedures and on such terms and conditions as the Commission may determine. His term of office shall be for four years and he shall be eligible for reappointment.

2. The Commission shall authorize such staff establishment for the Secretariat as may be necessary and the Executive Secretary shall appoint, direct and supervise such staff according to such rules and procedures and on such terms and conditions as the Commission may determine.

3. The Executive Secretary and Secretariat shall perform the functions entrusted to them by the Commission.

Article XVIII

The official languages of the Commission and of the Scientific Committee shall be English, French, Russian and Spanish.

Article XIX

1. At each annual meeting, the Commission shall adopt by consensus its budget and the budget of the Scientific Committee.

2. A draft budget for the Commission and the Scientific Committee and any subsidiary bodies shall be prepared by the Executive Secretary and submitted to the Members of the Commission at least sixty days before the annual meeting of the Commission.

3. Each Member of the Commission shall contribute to the budget. Until the expiration of five years after the entry into force of this Convention, the contribution of each Member of the Commission shall be equal. Thereafter the contribution shall be determined in accordance with two criteria: the amount harvested and an equal sharing among all Members of the Commission. The Commission shall determine by consensus the proportion in which these two criteria shall apply.

4. The financial activities of the Commission and Scientific Committee shall be conducted in accordance with financial regulations adopted by the Commission and shall be subject to an annual audit by external auditors selected by the Commission.

5. Each Member of the Commission shall meet its own expenses arising from attendance at meetings of the Commission and of the Scientific Committee.

6. A Member of the Commission that fails to pay its contributions for two consecutive years shall not, during the period of its default, have the right to participate in the taking of decisions in the Commission.

Article XX

1. The Members of the Commission shall, to the greatest extent possible, provide annually to the Commission and to the Scientific Committee such statistical, biological and other data and information as the Commission and Scientific Committee may require in the exercise of their functions.

2. The Members of the Commission shall provide, in the manner and at such intervals as may be prescribed, information about their harvesting activities, including fishing areas and vessels, so as to enable reliable catch and effort statistics to be compiled.

3. The Members of the Commission shall provide to the Commission at such intervals as may be prescribed information on steps taken to implement the conservation measures adopted by the Commission.

4. The Members of the Commission agree that in any of their harvesting activities, advantage shall be taken of opportunities to collect data needed to assess the impact of harvesting.

Article XXI

1. Each Contracting Party shall take appropriate measures within its competence to ensure compliance with the provisions of this Convention and with conservation measures adopted by the Commission to which the Party is bound in accordance with Article IX of this Convention.

2. Each Contracting Party shall transmit to the Commission information on measures taken pursuant to paragraph 1 above, including the imposition of sanctions for any violation.

Article XXII

1. Each Contracting Party undertakes to exert appropriate efforts, consistent with the Charter of the United Nations, to the end that no one engages in any activity contrary to the objective of this Convention.

2. Each Contracting Party shall notify the Commission of any such activity which comes to its attention.

Article XXIII

1. The Commission and the Scientific Committee shall co-operate with the Antarctic Treaty Consultative Parties on matters falling within the competence of the latter.

2. The Commission and the Scientific Committee shall co-operate, as appropriate, with the Food and Agriculture Organization of the United Nations and with other Specialised Agencies.

3. The Commission and the Scientific Committee shall seek to develop co-operative working relationships, as appropriate, with inter-governmental and non-governmental organizations which could contribute to their work, including the Scientific Committee on Antarctic Research, the Scientific Committee on Oceanic Research and the International Whaling Commission.

4. The Commission may enter into agreements with the organizations referred to in this Article and with other organizations as may be appropriate. The Commission and the Scientific Committee may invite such organizations to send observers to their meetings and to meetings of their subsidiary bodies.

Article XXIV

1. In order to promote the objective and ensure observance of the provisions of this Convention, the Contracting Parties agree that a system of observation and inspection shall be established.

2. The system of observation and inspection shall be elaborated by the Commission on the basis of the following principles:

(a) Contracting Parties shall co-operate with each other to ensure the effective implementation of the system of observation and inspection, taking account of the existing international practice. This system shall include, *inter alia*, procedures for boarding and inspection by observers and inspectors designated by the Members of the Commission and procedures for flag State prosecution and sanctions on the basis of evidence resulting from such boarding and inspections. A report of such prosecutions and sanctions imposed shall be included in the information referred to in Article XXI of this Convention;

(b) in order to verify compliance with measures adopted under this Convention, observation and inspection shall be carried out on board vessels engaged in scientific research or harvesting of marine living resources in the area to which this Convention applies, through observers and inspectors designated by the Members of the Commission and operating under terms and conditions to be established by the Commission;

(c) designated observers and inspectors shall remain subject to the jurisdiction of the Contracting Party of which they are nationals. They shall report to the Member of the Commission by which they have been designated which in turn shall report to the Commission.

3. Pending the establishment of the system of observation and inspection, the Members of the Commission shall seek to establish interim arrangements to designate observers and inspectors and such designated observers and inspectors shall be entitled to carry out inspections in accordance with the principles set out in paragraph 2 above.

Article XXV

1. If any dispute arises between two or more of the Contracting Parties concerning the interpretation or application of this Convention, those Contracting Parties shall consult among themselves with a view to having the dispute resolved by negotiation, inquiry, mediation, conciliation, arbitration, judicial settlement or other peaceful means of their own choice.

2. Any dispute of this character not so resolved shall, with the consent in each case of all Parties to the dispute, be referred for settlement to the International Court of Justice or to arbitration; but failure to reach agreement on reference to the International Court or to arbitration shall not absolve Parties to the dispute from the responsibility of continuing to seek to resolve it by any of the various peaceful means referred to in paragraph 1 above.

3. In cases where the dispute is referred to arbitration, the arbitral tribunal shall be constituted as provided in the Annex to this Convention.

Article XXVI

1. This Convention shall be open for signature at Canberra from 1 August to 31 December 1980 by the States participating in the Conference on the Conservation of Antarctic Marine Living Resources held at Canberra from 7 to 20 May 1980.

2. The States which so sign will be the original signatory States of the Convention.

Article XXVII

1. This Convention is subject to ratification, acceptance or approval by signatory States.

2. Instruments of ratification, acceptance or approval shall be deposited with the Government of Australia, hereby designated as the Depositary.

Article XXVIII

1. This Convention shall enter into force on the thirtieth day following the date of deposit of the eighth instrument of ratification, acceptance or approval by States referred to in paragraph 1 of Article XXVI of this Convention.

2. With respect to each State or regional economic integration organization which subsequent to the date of entry into force of this Convention deposits an instrument of ratification, acceptance, approval or accession, the Convention shall enter into force on the thirtieth day following such deposit.

Article XXIX

1. This Convention shall be open for accession by any State interested in research or harvesting activities in relation to the marine living resources to which this Convention applies.

2. This Convention shall be open for accession by regional economic integration organizations constituted by sovereign States which include among their members one or more States Members of the Commission and to which the States members of the organization have transferred, in whole or in part, competences with regard to the matters covered by this Convention. The accession of such regional economic integration organizations shall be the subject of consultations among Members of the Commission.

Article XXX

1. This Convention may be amended at any time.

2. If one-third of the Members of the Commission request a meeting to discuss a proposed amendment the Depositary shall call such a meeting.

3. An amendment shall enter into force when the Depositary has received instruments of ratification, acceptance or approval thereof from all the Members of the Commission.

4. Such amendment shall thereafter enter into force as to any other Contracting Party when notice of ratification, acceptance or approval by it has been received by the Depositary. Any such Contracting Party from which no such notice has been received within a period of one year from the date of entry into force of the amendment in accordance with paragraph 3 above shall be deemed to have withdrawn from this Convention.

Article XXXI

1. Any Contracting Party may withdraw from this Convention on 30 June of any year, by giving written notice not later than 1 January of the same year to the Depositary, which, upon receipt of such a notice, shall communicate it forthwith to the other Contracting Parties.

2. Any other Contracting Party may, within sixty days of the receipt of a copy of such a notice from the Depositary, give written notice of withdrawal to the Depositary in which case the Convention shall cease to be in force on 30 June of the same year with respect to the Contracting Party giving such notice.

3. Withdrawal from this Convention by any Member of the Commission shall not affect its financial obligations under this Convention.

Article XXXII

The Depositary shall notify all Contracting Parties of the following:

(a) signatures of this Convention and the deposit of instruments of ratification, acceptance, approval or accession;
(b) the date of entry into force of this Convention and of any amendment thereto.

Article XXXIII

1. This Convention, of which the English, French, Russian and Spanish texts are equally authentic, shall be deposited with the Government of Australia which shall transmit duly certified copies thereof to all signatory and acceding Parties.

2. This Convention shall be registered by the Depositary pursuant to Article 102 of the Charter of the United Nations.

DRAWN UP at Canberra this twentieth day of May 1980.

IN WITNESS WHEREOF the undersigned, being duly authorized have signed this Convention.

Annex for an arbitral tribunal

The arbitral tribunal referred to in paragraph 3 of Article XXV shall be composed of three arbitrators who shall be appointed as follows:

The Party commencing proceedings shall communicate the name of an arbitrator to the other Party which, in turn, within a period of forty days following such notification, shall communicate the name of the second arbitrator. The Parties shall, within a period of sixty days following the appointment of the second arbitrator, appoint the third arbitrator, who shall not be a national of either Party and shall not be of the same nationality as either of the first two arbitrators. The third arbitrator shall preside over the tribunal.

If the second arbitrator has not been appointed within the prescribed period, or if the Parties have not reached agreement within the prescribed period on the appointment of the third arbitrator, that arbitrator shall be appointed, at the request of either Party, by the Secretary-General of the Permanent Court of Arbitration, from among persons of international standing not having the nationality of a State which is a Party to this Convention.

The arbitral tribunal shall decide where its headquarters will be located and shall adopt its own rules of procedure.

The award of the arbitral tribunal shall be made by a majority of its members, who may not abstain from voting.

Any Contracting Party which is not a Party to the dispute may intervene in the proceedings with the consent of the arbitral tribunal.

The award of the arbitral tribunal shall be final and binding on all Parties to the dispute and on any Party which intervenes in the proceedings and shall be complied with without delay. The arbitral tribunal shall interpret the award at the request of one of the Parties to the dispute or of any intervening Party.

Unless the arbitral tribunal determines otherwise because of the particular circumstances of the case, the expenses of the tribunal, including the remuneration of its members, shall be borne by the Parties to the dispute in equal shares.